CONSTITUTIONAL LAW FOR A CHANGING AMERICA

A SHORT COURSE

FOURTH EDITION

LEE EPSTEIN
Northwestern University School of Law

THOMAS G. WALKER
Emory University

CQ PRESS

A DIVISION OF SAGE
WASHINGTON, D.C.

CQ Press
2300 N Street, NW, Suite 800
Washington, DC 20037

Phone, 202-729-1900; toll-free, 1-866-4CQ-PRESS (1-866-427-7737)

Web: www.cqpress.com

Cover Design: TGD Communications, Alexandria, Virginia
Composition: BMWW, Baltimore, Maryland

∞ The paper used in this publication exceeds the requirements of the American National Standard for Information Sciences—Permanence of Paper for Printed Library Materials, ANSI Z39.48-1992.

Printed and bound in the United States of America

12   11   10   09   08   1   2   3   4   5

Library of Congress Cataloging-in-Publication Data

Epstein, Lee
    Constitutional law for a changing America : a short course / Lee Epstein, Thomas G. Walker. — 4th ed.
        p. cm.
    Includes bibliographical references and index.
    ISBN 978-0-87289-605-5 (alk. paper)
        1. Constitutional law—United States.   2. Civil rights—United States.
3. Judicial process—United States.   I. Walker, Thomas G.   II. Title.

    KF4749.E668 2008
    342.73—dc22

                                                          2008041166

To my niece and nephews
Alexandra, Brian, Jason, and Zach—L. E.

To Nicole—T. G. W.

CONTENTS

TABLES, FIGURES, AND BOXES

PREFACE

Over the past two decades or so, constitutional law texts for political science courses have experienced a radical change. At one time, relatively short volumes, containing either excerpts from landmark cases or narratives of them, dominated the market. Now, large, almost mammoth books abound—some in a single volume, others in two volumes, but all designed for a two-semester sequence.

This trend, while fitting compatibly with the needs of many instructors, bypassed others, including those who teach institutional powers, civil liberties, rights, and justice in a single academic term and those who prefer a shorter core text. *Constitutional Law for a Changing America: A Short Course* was designed as an alternative text for these instructors. The first edition appeared in 1996. Its positive reception encouraged us to prepare the second and third editions, and now the fourth.

Like its predecessors, this edition of *A Short Course* seeks to combine the best features of the traditional, concise volumes—it interweaves excerpts of the Court's most important decisions and narratives of major developments in the law. For example, our discussion of the right to counsel offers not only the landmark decision *Gideon v. Wainwright* (1963), but also an account of the critical cases preceding *Gideon,* such as *Powell v. Alabama* (1932), and those following it, such as *Scott v. Illinois* (1979).

At the same time, we thought it important to move beyond the traditional texts and write a book that reflects the exciting nature of constitutional law. In doing so, we were not without guidance. For nearly two decades we have been producing *Constitutional Law for a Changing America,* now in its sixth edition. This two-volume book, we believe, provides an accessible yet sophisticated and contemporary take on the subject.

A Short Course, then, although presenting cases and other materials in ways quite distinct from our two-volume book, maintains some of its most desirable features. First, we approach constitutional law, as we do in *Constitutional Law for a Changing America,* from a political science perspective, demonstrating how political and social forces—not just legal factors—influence the development of the law. The justices carry out their duties in the context of the political, economic, and social environment that surrounds them. Accordingly, throughout *A Short Course,* we highlight how relevant political events, personnel changes on the Court, interest groups, and even public opinion may have affected the judicial decision-making process.

Second, just as our two-volume set seeks to animate the subject, so too does *A Short Course.* To us and, we suspect, most instructors, constitutional law is an exciting subject, but we realize that some students may not (at least initially) share our enthusiasm. To whet their appetites, we develop the human side of landmark litigation. Where possible, we include photographs of litigants and places that figured prominently in cases. For each excerpted case, we provide a detailed description, in accessible prose, of the dispute that gave rise to the suit. Students are spared the task of digging out facts from Court opinions and can plunge ahead to the ruling with the contours of the dispute firmly in mind. We also present information about the political environment surrounding various cases in tables, figures, and boxes that supplement the narrative and case excerpts.

Third, because many adopters of *Constitutional Law for a Changing America* have commented favorably on the supporting material we provide in those volumes, we maintain that feature in *A Short Course.* Along these lines, chapter 2, "Understanding the Supreme Court," reviews not only the procedures the Court uses to decide cases but also the various legal and extralegal approaches scholars have invoked to understand and explain why the Court rules as it does. The back of the book contains a wealth of reference material, including texts of the U.S. Constitution and *Federalist Paper*, No. 78; descriptions of the Court's history and the justices who have served on it; and even an example of how to brief a case.

Fourth, this edition of *A Short Course* takes advantage of the expanding resources available to students of constitutional law that can be found on the Internet. With each excerpted opinion we provide locations on the Internet where students may read the full, unabridged decision. We also alert students whenever the oral arguments for a case have been made available on the Internet by the Oyez Project.

With each edition we attempt to enhance the coverage and accessibility of the material in ways that go beyond the standard updating of information. In the previous edition we introduced two innovative features and have retained them here. The first is a series of "Aftermath" boxes sprinkled throughout the text. These boxes are a response to our own experiences in the classroom when confronted with questions such as: "Whatever happened to Ernesto Miranda?" The Aftermath boxes discuss what occurred after the Supreme Court handed down its decision. In addition to providing human interest material, they lead to interesting discussions about the Court's impact on the lives of ordinary Americans. We hope these materials demonstrate to students that Supreme Court cases are more than merely legal names and citations; they involve real people involved in real disputes.

A second major change was our effort to respond to an inevitable question facing any author of a constitutional law text: Which Supreme Court cases should be included? Other than classic decisions such as *Marbury v. Madison*, instructors have differing ideas of which cases best illustrate the various points of constitutional law. Each has his or her list of personal favorites; however, given the page limitations of a printed book, not every instructor's preferences can be satisfied.

We have attempted to overcome this problem by creating an electronic archive of more than three hundred supplemental Supreme Court decisions. These cases are excerpted using the same format as the case excerpts that appear in this printed volume. The archive allows instructors to use additional cases or to substitute favorite cases for those that appear in the printed text. The archive also provides an efficient source of material for students who want to read more deeply into the law and for instructors who wish to direct their students to an easily accessible information source for paper assignments. The cases included in the archive are identified in the text in bold italic type and are listed in Appendix 10. The archive can be accessed on the Internet at: http://clca.cqpress.com.

We keep the electronic archive current between printed editions. Instructors and students no longer must wait until the next edition is published to have ready access to recent rulings presented in a format designed for classroom use.

Finally, instructors who have used *A Short Course* in the past will notice a new chapter in this edition. For decades the Supreme Court avoided cases that presented occasions to interpret the Second Amendment, even as the lower courts occasionally reached contradictory conclusions on its meaning. In *District of Columbia v. Heller* (2008) the justices ended their silence, holding that the Constitution guarantees an individual right to keep and bear arms. The new chapter includes an excerpt of *Heller* and provides students with its historical context and thoughts on possible future developments.

ACKNOWLEDGMENTS

The roots of this fourth edition of *A Short Course* extend back to our two-volume book. As a consequence, those who influenced the development of the original version of *Constitutional Law for a Changing America* influenced this project as well. We are particularly grateful to Joanne Daniels, Brenda Carter, and Charisse Kiino. Joanne, a former editor at CQ Press, conceived of a constitutional law book that would be accessible, sophisticated, and contemporary. She brought the concept to our attention and helped us develop it. Brenda guided us through the completion of the project and its subsequent editions and urged us to go forward with *A Short Course*. Her support for our projects has been constant and strong, and her advice always wise. Charisse, our current editor, brought new enthusiasm and ideas to this book.

Her responsiveness to our needs and requests has been extraordinary. Working with her has been a joy.

Other members of the CQ Press team also deserve our thanks and praise. Neither of us is quite sure what we would do without Carolyn Goldinger. To say she has copyedited nearly every edition of the volumes in the *Constitutional Law for a Changing America* series is true enough. But she has done so much more than perfect our writing and check our facts. On each edition she edits, Carolyn contributes many ideas for presentation and content. There is not a better copy editor in this business. Period. We are especially grateful for the efforts of Talia Greenberg for shepherding this edition through production. Allie McKay, Dwain Smith, and Jerry Orvedahl deserve thanks for their work on the case archive and the ancillaries created by Timothy Johnson. Finally, other members of the CQ Press family, too numerous to mention, brought ideas, enthusiasm, and efficiency to the project.

Over the years, we have also benefited from the suggestions of numerous scholars who read our manuscripts, offered suggestions, provided data, or shared their thoughts about constitutional law. We are especially grateful to Judith A. Baer, Ralph Baker, Lawrence Baum, Robert W. Bennett, John Brigham, Steven G. Calabresi, Gregory A. Caldeira, Bradley C. Canon, Robert A. Carp, Phillip J. Cooper, Sue Davis, John Fliter, John B. Gates, Leslie Goldstein, Edward V. Heck, Jack Knight, Joseph F. Kobylka, John A. Maltese, John O. McGinnis, Kevin McGuire, Wayne McIntosh, Susan Mezey, Richard L. Pacelle Jr., Martin H. Redish, C. K. Rowland, Jeffrey A. Segal, Donald Songer, Harold Spaeth, and Harry P. Stumpf. We would like to thank John Brigham of the University of Massachusetts, Paula A. Franzese of Barnard College, Lori Cox Han of Austin College, and Gordon P. Henderson of Widener University for their suggestions on previous editions. We are also grateful to those instructors and students who have used *Constitutional Law for a Changing America* and sent us comments and suggestions, especially Akiba J. Covitz, Alec C. Ewald, and Neil Snortland.

Finally, we acknowledge the encouragement of our friends and families. We are forever grateful to our former professors for instilling in us their genuine interest in and curiosity about things judicial and legal and to our home institutions for providing substantial support of our efforts.

Any errors of omission or commission, of course, remain our sole responsibility. We encourage students and instructors alike to comment on the book and to inform us of any errors. Contact us at: *lee-epstein@northwestern .edu* or *polstw@emory.edu.*

PART I
THE U.S. CONSTITUTION

According to President Franklin D. Roosevelt, "Like the Bible, it ought to be read again and again."[1] Henry Clay said it was "made not merely for the generation that then existed, but for posterity—unlimited, undefined, endless, perpetual posterity."[2] Justice Hugo Black carried one with him virtually all the time. The object of all this admiration? The United States Constitution. To be sure, the Constitution has its flaws and its share of detractors, but most Americans take great pride in their charter. And why not? It is, after all, the world's oldest written constitution.

In what follows, we provide a brief introduction to the document—in particular, the circumstances under which it was written, the basic principles underlying it, and some controversies surrounding it. This material may not be new to you, but, as the balance of this book is devoted to the Supreme Court's interpretation of the Constitution and its amendments, we think it is worth reviewing.

THE ROAD TO THE U.S. CONSTITUTION

While the fledgling United States was fighting for its independence from England, it was being run (and the war conducted) by the Continental Congress. Although this body had no formal authority, it met in session from 1774 through the end of the war in 1781, establishing itself as a "de facto" government. But it may have been something more than that. About a year into the Revolutionary War, Congress took steps toward nationhood. On July 2, 1776, it passed a resolution declaring the "United Colonies free and independent states." Two days later, on July 4, it formalized this proclamation in the Declaration of Independence, in which the nation's founders used the term *United States of America* for the first time.[3] But even before the adoption of the Declaration of Independence, the Continental Congress had selected a group of delegates to make recommendations for the formation of a national government. Composed of representatives of each of the thirteen colonies, this committee labored for several months to produce a proposal for a national charter, the Articles of Confederation.[4] Congress passed the proposal and submitted it to the states for ratification in November 1777. Ratification was achieved in March 1781, when Maryland—a two-year holdout—gave its approval.

The Articles of Confederation represented the nation's first written charter, but the document changed the way the government operated very little; it merely institutionalized practices that had emerged prior to 1774. For example, rather than provide for a compact between the people and the government, the 1781 charter institutionalized "a league of friendship" among the states, one that rested on strong notions of state sovereignty. This is

1. Quoted in Michael Kammen, ed., *The Origins of the American Constitution* (New York: Penguin Books, 1986), vii.
2. Speech to the Senate, January 29, 1850.
3. A full text of the Declaration of Independence may be found on the Internet at: http://www.constitution.org/usdeclar.htm.
4. The full text of the Articles of Confederation may be found on the Internet at: http://www.yale.edu/lawweb/avalon/artconf.htm.

FIGURE I-1 The Structure and Powers of Government under the Articles of Confederation

The States		

Congress

Had the Power to	Lacked the Power to
Declare war and make peace	Provide for effective treaty-making
Enter into treaties and alliances	power and control of foreign relations;
Establish and control armed forces	it could not compel states to respect
Requisition men and money from states	treaties
Regulate coinage	Compel states to meet military quotas;
Borrow money and issue bills of credit	it could not draft soldiers
Fix uniform standards of weight and	Regulate interstate and foreign commerce;
measurement	it left each state free to set up its own tariff
Create admiralty courts	system
Create a postal system	Collect taxes directly from the people; it had
Regulate Indian affairs	to rely on states to collect and forward
Guarantee citizens of each state the rights	taxes
and privileges of citizens in the several	Compel states to pay their share of govern-
states when in another state	ment costs
Adjudicate disputes between states upon	Provide and maintain a sound monetary
state petition	system or issue paper money; this was
	left up to the states, and monies in
	circulation differed tremendously in value

Committee of the States

(Composed of representatives of all
the states to act in the name of
Congress between sessions)

Officers

(Congress appointed officers to do some of
the executive work)

SOURCE: Adopted from Steffein W. Schmidt, Mack C. Shelley II,
and Barbara A. Bardes, *American Government and Politics Today*
(St. Paul: West, 1989), 34–35.

not to suggest that the articles failed to provide for a central government. As we can see in Figure I-1, which depicts the structure and powers of government, the articles created a national governing apparatus, however simple and weak. There was a one-house legislature, but no formal federal executive or judiciary. And while the legislature had some power, most notably in the area of foreign affairs, it derived its authority from the states that had created it, not from the people.

The condition of the United States under the Articles of Confederation was not entirely satisfactory. Because it allowed Congress only to "requisition" funds and not to tax, the federal government was virtually broke. Between 1781 and 1783 the national legislature requested $10 million from the states and received only $1.5 million. Given the foreign debts the United States had accumulated during the war, this problem was particularly troublesome.

• Because Congress lacked a concrete way to regulate foreign commerce, treaties between other countries and the Confederation were of limited value. Some European nations (England and Spain, for example) took advantage by imposing restrictions on trade that made it difficult for America to export goods.

• Because the government lacked coercive power over the states, mutual cooperation among them quickly dissipated. They engaged in trading practices that hurt one another economically. In short, the states acted more like thirteen separate countries than a union or even a confederation.

• Because the exercise of most national authority required the approval of nine states and the passage of amendments required unanimity, the articles stymied Congress. Indeed, the divisions among the states at the time made the approval of nine states for any action of substance rare, and the required unanimity for amendment nonexistent.

Despite these obstacles, the government accomplished many notable goals during the years the articles were in effect: It brought the Revolutionary War to a successful end and paved the way for the 1783 Treaty of Paris, which helped make the United States a presence on the international scene. Moreover, the charter served an important purpose. It prevented the states from going their separate ways until a better system could be put in place.

Still, the shortcomings of the Articles of Confederation were becoming more and more apparent, and by the mid-1780s several dissidents, including James Madison of Virginia and Alexander Hamilton of New York, had held a series of meetings to arouse interest in revising the system of government. At one, in Annapolis in September 1786, they urged the states to send delegations to another meeting scheduled for the following May in Philadelphia. Their plea could not have come at a more opportune time. Just the month before, a former Revolutionary War captain, Daniel Shays, had led disgruntled and armed farmers to rebellion in Massachusetts. They were protesting the poor state of the economy, especially as it affected farmers.

Shays's Rebellion was suppressed by state forces, but it was seen as yet another sign that the articles needed amending. In February 1787 Congress issued a call for a convention to reevaluate the current national system. It was clear, however, that Congress did not want a whole new charter; in fact, the resolution stated that the delegates were to meet "for the sole and express purpose of revising the Articles of Confederation."

But the fifty-five delegates who gathered in Philadelphia quickly realized that they would be doing more than "revising" the articles. They would be framing a new charter. We can attribute this change in purpose, at least in part, to the Virginia delegation. When it arrived in Philadelphia on May 14, 1787, the day the convention was supposed to start, only the Pennsylvania delegation was already there. Although lacking a quorum, the Virginia contingent used the eleven-day delay to its advantage, crafting a series of proposals. The Virginians called for a wholly new government structure, composed of a strong three-branch national government empowered to lead the nation.

Known as the Virginia Plan, these proposals were formally introduced to the delegates on May 29, just four days after the convention began. And, although it was the target of a counterproposal submitted by the New Jersey delegation, the Virginia Plan set the tone for the convention. It served as the basis for many of the ensuing debates and, as we shall see, for the Constitution itself *(see Table 1-1)*.

The delegates had much to accomplish during the four-month convention period. Arguments between large and small states over the structure of the new government and its relationship to the states threatened to deadlock the meeting. Indeed, it is almost a miracle that the delegates were able to frame a new constitution, which they did in just a few months. One can speculate that the founders succeeded in part because they were able to close their meetings to the public, a feat almost inconceivable today. A contemporary convention of the states would be a media circus. Moreover, it is hard to imagine that delegates from fifty states could even agree to frame a new charter, much less do it in four months.

The difficulties facing such an enterprise raise an important issue. A modern constitutional convention would be hard pressed to reach consensus because the delegates would bring with them diverse interests and aims. What about back in 1787? Who were the framers and what were their motives? If, as had been recorded, they were such a fractious bunch, how could they have reached accord so rapidly?

These questions have been the subject of lively debates among scholars. Many agree with historian Melvin I. Urofsky, who wrote of the Constitutional Convention, "Few gatherings in the history of this or any other country could boast such a concentration of talent." And, "despite [the framers'] average age of forty-two [they] had

TABLE 1-1   The Virginia Plan, the New Jersey Plan, and the Constitution

Item	Virginia Plan	New Jersey Plan	Constitution
Legislature	Two houses	One house	Two houses
Legislative representation	Both houses based on population	Equal for each state	One house based on population; one house with two votes from each state
Legislative power	Veto authority over state legislation	Authority to levy taxes and regulate commerce	Authority to levy tariffs and regulate commerce; authority to compel state compliance with national policies
Executive	Single; elected by legislature for a single term	Plural; removable by majority of state legislatures	Single; chosen by Electoral College; removal by national legislature
Courts	National judiciary elected by legislature	No provision	Supreme Court appointed by executive, confirmed by Senate

SOURCE: Paul Johnson et al., *American Government* (Boston: Houghton Mifflin, 1990), 47.

extensive experience in government and were fully conversant with political theories of the Enlightenment."[5]

The framers, to be sure, were an impressive group. Thirty-three of them had served in the Revolutionary War, forty-two had attended the Continental Congress, and two had signed the Declaration of Independence; two would go on to serve as U.S. presidents, sixteen as governors, and two as chief justices of the United States.

Nevertheless, some would take issue with Urofsky's statement. Because the framers were a relatively homogeneous lot—all white men, many of whom had been educated at the country's best schools—it has been suggested that the document they produced was biased in various ways. In 1987 Justice Thurgood Marshall said that the Constitution was "defective from the start," that its first words—"We the People"—excluded "the majority of American citizens," because it left out blacks and women. He further alleged that the framers "could not have imagined, nor would they have accepted, that the document they were drafting would one day be construed by a Supreme Court to which had been appointed a woman and the descendant of an African slave."[6] Along the same lines is the point of view expressed by historian Charles Beard in his controversial work, *An Economic Interpretation of the Constitution of the United States*, which depicts the framers as self-serving. Beard says the Constitution was an "economic document" devised to protect the "property interests" of those who wrote it.

Various scholars have refuted these allegations; Beard's work, in particular, has been largely negated by other studies.[7] Still, *by today's standards* it is impossible to deny that the original Constitution was a racist and sexist document or that the framers wrote it in a way that benefited them.

Given these charges, how has the Constitution survived for so long, particularly as the U.S. population has become increasingly diverse. The answer lies in part with the Supreme Court, which generally has analyzed the document in light of its contemporary context. That is, some justices have viewed the Constitution as a living document and have sought to adapt it to the times. In addition, the founders provided for an amending process to keep the document alive. That we can alter the Constitution to fit changing needs and expectations is obvi-

5. Melvin I. Urofsky and Paul Finkelman, *A March of Liberty*, 2nd ed. (New York: Oxford University Press, 2002), 95.

6. Quoted in the *Washington Post*, May 7, 1987.

7. See, for example, Robert E. Brown's *Charles Beard and the Constitution* (Princeton: Princeton University Press, 1956), 198. Brown concludes, "We would be doing a grave injustice to the political sagacity of the Founding Fathers if we assumed that property or personal gain was their only motive."

ously important. The original document held a slave, who had no rights of citizenship at all, to be three-fifths of a person for the purposes of representation. In the aftermath of the Civil War, the country recognized the outrageousness of such a provision and added three amendments to alter the status of blacks and provide full equality under law.

This is not to suggest that controversies surrounding the Constitution no longer exist. To the contrary, charges abound that the document has retained an elitist or otherwise biased flavor. Some argue that the amending process is too cumbersome, that it is too slanted toward majority will. Others point to the Supreme Court as the culprit. Critics have variously asserted that at certain times the Court has reinforced the biases of the framers and at other times it has strayed from the wisdom of the nation's founding.

Throughout this volume, you will have many opportunities to evaluate these controversies. For now, however, we turn our attention to some of the basic features of that controversial document, the U.S. Constitution.

UNDERLYING PRINCIPLES OF THE CONSTITUTION

Table 1-1 sets forth the basic proposals considered at the convention and how they got translated into the Constitution. What it does not show are the fundamental principles underlying, though not necessarily explicit in, the Constitution. Three are particularly important: the separation of powers/checks and balances doctrine, which governs relations among the branches of government; federalism, which governs relations between the federal government and the states; and individual rights, which governs relations between the government and the people.

Separation of Powers/Checks and Balances

One of the fundamental weaknesses of the Articles of Confederation was the charter's failure to establish a strong and authoritative federal government. It created a national legislature, but that body had few powers, and those it did have were kept in check by the states. The new constitution overcame this deficiency by creating a national government with three branches—the legislature, the executive, and the judiciary—and by providing each with significant power and authority over its sphere. Moreover, the three newly devised institutions were constitutionally and politically independent from one another (see Figure 1-2).

The specific powers that each branch was given are spelled out in Articles I, II, and III of the Constitution. Section 8 of Article I is especially explicit, empowering Congress to lay and collect taxes, to regulate commerce, and so forth. Nevertheless, many questions have arisen over the scope of these powers as they are wielded by the three institutions. Consider a few examples:

Article I gives Congress the power to raise and support armies and to provide and maintain a navy. But Article I does not specifically empower Congress to initiate and operate a draft. Does that omission mean that Congress may not do so?

Article II provides the president with the power to "nominate, and by and with the Advice and Consent of the Senate, [to] appoint . . . Officers of the United States," but it does not specifically empower the president to fire such officers. May the president independently dismiss appointees, or is the "advice and consent" of the Senate also necessary?

Article III provides the federal courts with the authority to hear cases involving federal laws. But it does not specifically empower these courts to strike down such laws if they are incompatible with the Constitution. Does that mean federal courts lack the power of judicial review?

These examples illustrate just a handful of the questions involving institutional powers the U.S. Supreme Court has addressed.

But institutional powers are only one side of the coin. The other side—constraints on those powers—is also worthy of consideration. The framers not only gave each branch distinct power and authority within its own sphere, but provided explicit checks on the exercise of those powers such that each branch can impose limits on the primary functions of the others. They also made the institutions responsible to different sets of constituencies. They took these steps—creating an intricate system

FIGURE I-2   The Separation of Powers/Checks and Balances

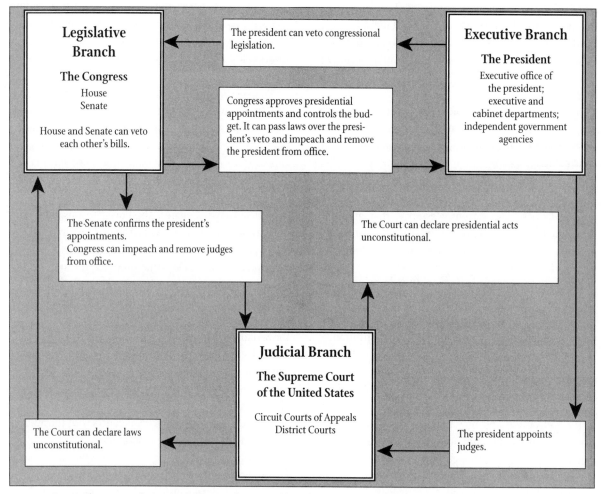

SOURCE: Janet A. Flammang et al., *American Politics in a Changing World* (Pacific Grove, Calif.: Brooks/Cole, 1990), 41.

of checks and balances—because they feared the concentration of powers in a single branch.

Although this system has worked successfully, it too has produced numerous constitutional questions, many of which become apparent when we have a politically divided government, such as a Democratic president and a Republican Congress, and one or the other is seeking to assert its authority. What is truly interesting about such cases is the fact that they continue to appear at the Court's doorstep; despite the passage of more than two hundred years, the justices have yet to resolve all the "big" constitutional questions.

By reading the cases and narrative that follow, you will develop an understanding of how the Court has addressed questions relating to the separation of powers/checks and balances system.

Federalism

Another weakness of the Articles of Confederation was how they envisioned the relationship between the federal government and the states. As already noted, state control of the national legislature made Congress a weak and dependent institution. The states had set up the Articles of Confederation; therefore, they empowered Congress.

The U.S. Constitution overcame this liability in two ways. First, it created three branches of government, all with significant authority. Second, it set out a plan of operation for the exercise of state and federal power. Called federalism, it works today under the following constitutional guidelines:

• The Constitution grants certain legislative, executive, and judicial powers to the national government. Those not granted to the national government are reserved to the states.

• The Constitution makes the national government supreme. The Constitution, all laws passed in pursuance thereof, and treaties are the supreme law of the land. American citizens, most of whom are also state citizens, owe their primary allegiance to the national government; officers of the state governments owe the same allegiance.

• The Constitution denies some powers to both national and state governments, some only to the national government, and still others only to the state governments.

By making the national government supreme in its spheres of authority, the Constitution corrected a flaw in the Articles of Confederation. But, in spite of the best efforts of the framers to spell out the nature of federal-state relations, the Constitution left open many questions. For example, the Constitution authorizes Congress to lay and collect taxes but does not specify whether the states may exercise powers that are reserved to the federal government. States are not expressly prohibited from collecting taxes. Therefore, may Congress and the states both operate taxing systems?

As you know, the answer to this question is yes, but why that is so is not explicitly answered by the Constitution. As a result, it has been left largely to elected government bodies through legislation and to the courts through interpretation to define the specifics of state-federal relations. The Supreme Court, in particular, by defining the boundaries of federal and state power, has helped shape the contours of American federalism.

Individual Rights and Liberties

For many of the framers, the most important purpose of the new Constitution was to safeguard individual rights and liberties. That is why they created a limited government that would wield only those powers delegated to it and would be checked by its own component parts—the states and the people. The majority of the founders felt it unnecessary to load the Constitution with specific individual rights, such as those later spelled out in the Bill of Rights. As Alexander Hamilton put it, "The Constitution is itself . . . a Bill of Rights." Under it, the government could exercise only those functions specifically bestowed upon it; all other rights remained with the people. Hamilton and others felt that adding a list of rights might even be dangerous because it inevitably would leave some out.

For this reason and possibly others—for example, some argue that the framers were too exhausted to continue—the Constitution was sent to the states without a bill of rights. That omission became the source of major controversy and served as the vehicle by which states exacted a compromise over the Constitution's ratification.

In the next chapter we describe that compromise, which took the form of the first ten amendments to the Constitution—the Bill of Rights. It is enough to note for now that the eventual ratification of the Bill of Rights, on December 15, 1791, quieted those who had voiced objections. But the guarantees it contains continue to serve as fodder for debate and, most relevant here, for Supreme Court litigation. Many of these debates involve the construct of specific guarantees, such as free speech and free exercise of religion, under which individuals seek relief when governments allegedly infringe upon their rights. They also involve clashes between the authority of the government to protect the safety, health, morals, and general welfare of citizens and the right of individuals not to be deprived of their liberty without due process of law.

CHAPTER 1

THE LIVING CONSTITUTION

In May 1787 the founders of the United States met in Philadelphia for the sole and express purpose of revising the Articles of Confederation, but within a month they had dramatically altered their mission. Viewing the articles as unworkable, they decided to start afresh. What emerged just four months later, on September 17, was an entirely new government scheme embodied in the U.S. Constitution.

The framers were quite pleased with their handiwork; when they had finished, they "adjourned to City Tavern, dined together and took cordial leave of each other."[1] After the long, hot summer in Philadelphia, most of the delegates left for home, confident that the new document would receive speedy passage by the states. At first, it appeared as if their optimism was justified. As Table 1-1 depicts, before the year was out, four states had ratified the Constitution—three by unanimous votes. But after January 1788, the pace began to slow. By this time, a movement opposed to ratification was growing and marshaling arguments to deter state convention delegates. What these opponents, the Anti-Federalists, feared most was the Constitution's new balance of power. They believed that strong state governments provided the best defense against the concentration of too much power in the national government, and that the Constitution tipped the scales in favor of federal power. These fears were countered by the Federalists, who favored ratification.

Although their arguments and writings took many forms, among the most important was a series of eighty-five articles published in New York newspapers under the pen name "Publius." Written by John Jay, James Madison, and Alexander Hamilton, *The Federalist Papers* continue to provide insight into the objectives and intent of the founders.[2]

Debates between the Federalists and their opponents often were highly philosophical in tone, with emphasis on the appropriate roles and powers of national institutions. In the states, however, ratification drives were full of the stuff of ordinary politics—deal making. Massachusetts provides a case in point. After three weeks of debate among the delegates, Federalist leaders realized that they would never achieve victory without the support of Gov. John Hancock. They went to his house and proposed that he endorse ratification on the condition that a series of amendments be tacked on for consideration by Congress. The governor agreed, but in return he wanted to become president of the United States if Virginia failed to ratify or if George Washington refused to serve. Or he would accept the vice presidency. With the deal cut, Hancock went to the state convention to propose the compromise—the ratification of the Constitution with amendments. The delegates agreed, making Massachusetts the sixth state to ratify.[3]

---

1. *1787*, compiled by historians of the Independence National Historical Park (New York: Exeter Books, 1987), 191.

2. *The Federalist Papers* are available on the Internet at: http://thomas.loc.gov/home/histdox/fedpapers.html.

3. J. T. Keenan, *The Constitution of the United States: An Unfolding Story,* 2nd ed. (Chicago: Dorsey Press, 1988).

TABLE 1-1 The Ratification of the Constitution

State	Date of Action	Decision	Margin
Delaware	December 7, 1787	ratified	30–0
Pennsylvania	December 12, 1787	ratified	46–23
New Jersey	December 18, 1787	ratified	38–0
Georgia	December 31, 1787	ratified	26–0
Connecticut	January 8, 1788	ratified	128–40
Massachusetts	February 6, 1788	ratified with amendments	187–168
Maryland	April 26, 1788	ratified	63–11
South Carolina	May 23, 1788	ratified with amendments	149–73
New Hampshire	June 21, 1788	ratified with amendments	57–47
Virginia	June 25, 1788	ratified with amendments	89–79
New York	July 26, 1788	ratified with amendments	30–27
North Carolina	August 2, 1788	rejected	184–84
	November 21, 1789	ratified with amendments	194–77
Rhode Island	May 29, 1790	ratified with amendments	34–32

SOURCES: Ratifying documents in the Avalon Project at Yale Law School (http://www.yale.edu/lawweb/avalon/constpap.htm); Ralph Mitchell, *CQ's Guide to the U.S. Constitution,* 2nd ed. Washington, D.C., Congressional Quarterly, 1994), 28–30.

This compromise, the call for a bill of rights, caught on, and the Federalists used it wherever close votes were likely. As it turned out, they needed to do so quite often. As Table 1-1 indicates, of the nine states ratifying after January 1788, seven recommended that the new Congress consider amendments. Indeed, New York and Virginia probably would not have agreed to the Constitution without such an addition; Virginia actually called for a second constitutional convention for that purpose. Other states began devising their own wish lists—enumerations of specific rights they wanted put into the document.

Why were states so reluctant to ratify the Constitution without a bill of rights? Some viewed the proposed document with downright suspicion because of the extensive powers it would grant to the national government. But more tended to agree with Thomas Jefferson, who in a letter to James Madison argued that "a bill of rights is what the people are entitled to against every government on earth, general and particular, and what no just government should refuse, or rest on inference."

What Jefferson's remark suggests is that many thought well of the new system of government but were troubled by the lack of a declaration of rights. Remember that at the time Americans clearly understood concepts of *fundamental* and *inalienable* rights, those that inherently belonged to them and that no government could deny. Even England, the country they fought against to gain their freedom, had such guarantees. The Magna Carta of 1215 and the Bill of Rights of 1689 gave Britons the right to a jury trial, to protection against cruel and unusual punishment, and so forth. Moreover, after the Revolution, virtually every state constitution included a philosophical statement about the relationship between citizens and their government or a listing of fifteen to twenty inalienable rights such as religious freedom and electoral independence. Small wonder that the call for such a statement or enumeration of rights became a battle cry. If it was so widespread, why had the framers failed to include it in the original document. Did they not anticipate the reaction?

Records of the 1787 constitutional debates indicate that, in fact, the delegates considered specific individual guarantees on at least four separate occasions.[4] On Au-

---

4. The following discussion comes from Daniel A. Farber and Suzanna Sherry, *A History of the American Constitution,* 2nd ed. (St. Paul: Thomson/West, 2005), 316–317. This book reprints verbatim debates over the Constitution and Bill of Rights.

gust 20 Charles Pinckney submitted a proposal that included several guarantees, such as freedom of the press and the eradication of religious affiliation requirements for holding public office, but the various committees never considered his plan. On September 12, 14, and 16, just before the close of the convention, some tried, again without success, to persuade the delegates to enumerate specific guarantees. At one point, George Mason said that a bill of rights "would give great quiet to the people; and with the aid of the state delegations, a bill might be prepared in a few hours." This motion was unanimously defeated by those remaining in attendance. On the convention's last day, Edmund Randolph made a desperate plea that the delegates allow the states to submit amendments and then convene a second convention. To this, Pinckney responded, "Conventions are serious things, and ought not to be repeated."

Why the majority of delegates showed no enthusiasm for these suggestions is a matter of scholarly debate. Some claim that the pleas came too late, that the framers wanted to complete their mission by September 15 and were simply unwilling to stay in Philadelphia even one day longer. Others disagree, arguing that the framers were more concerned with the structure of government than with individual rights, and that the plan they devised—one based on enumerated, not unlimited, powers—would foreclose the need for a bill of rights. Hamilton wrote, "The Constitution is itself . . . a Bill of Rights."[5] Under it the government could exercise only those functions specifically bestowed upon it; all remaining rights lay with the people. He also asserted that "independent of those which relate to the structure of government," the Constitution did, in fact, contain some of the more necessary specific guarantees. For example, Article I, Section 9, prohibits bills of attainder, ex post facto laws, and the suspension of writs of habeas corpus. Hamilton and others further argued that no list of rights could be complete.

Despite these misgivings, the reality of the political environment caused many Federalists to change their views on including a bill of rights. They realized that if they did not accede to state demands, either the Consti-

tution would not be ratified or a new convention would be necessary. Since neither alternative was particularly attractive, they agreed to amend the Constitution as soon as the new government came into power.

In May 1789, one month after the start of the new Congress, Madison announced to the House of Representatives that he would draft a bill of rights and submit it within the coming month. As it turned out, the task proved a bit more difficult than he thought; the state conventions had submitted nearly two hundred amendments, some of which would have decreased significantly the power of the national government. After sifting through these lists, Madison at first thought it might be best to incorporate the amendments into the Constitution's text, but he soon changed his mind. Instead, he presented the House with the following statement, echoing the views expressed in the Declaration of Independence: "That there be prefixed to the Constitution a declaration, that all power is originally vested in, and consequently derived from, the people."[6]

The legislators rejected this proposal, preferring a listing of rights to a philosophical statement. Madison returned to his task, eventually fashioning a list of seventeen amendments. When he took it back to the House, however, the list was greeted with suspicion and opposition. Some members of Congress, even those who had argued for a bill of rights, now did not want to be bothered with the proposals, insisting that they had more important business to settle. One suggested that other nations would not see the United States "as a serious trading partner as long as it was still tinkering with its constitution instead of organizing its government."[7]

Finally, in July 1789, after Madison had prodded and even begged, the House considered his proposals. A special committee scrutinized them and reported a few days later, and the House adopted, with some modification, Madison's seventeen amendments. The Senate approved some and rejected others, so that by the time the Bill of

---

5. *The Federalist Papers*, No. 84.

6. The full text of Madison's statement is available in Neil H. Cogan, *Contexts of the Constitution: A Documentary Collection on Principles of American Constitutional Law* (New York: Foundation Press, 1999), 813–815.

7. Farber and Sherry, *A History of the American Constitution*, 330.

Rights was submitted to the states on October 2, 1789, only twelve remained.[8]

The states ended up ratifying ten of the twelve. The amendments that did not receive approval were the original Articles I and II. Article I dealt with the number of representatives:

After the first enumeration required by the first article of the Constitution, there shall be one Representative for every thirty thousand, until the number shall amount to one hundred, after which the proportion shall be so regulated by Congress, that there shall be not less than one hundred Representatives, nor less than one Representative for every forty thousand persons, until the number of Representatives shall amount to two hundred; after which the proportion shall be so regulated by Congress, that there shall not be less than two hundred Representatives, nor more than one Representative for every fifty thousand persons.

Article II contained the following provision:

No law varying the compensation for the services of the Senators and Representatives shall take effect, until an election of Representatives shall have intervened.

This article also failed to garner sufficient support from the states in the 1790s and did not become a part of the Bill of Rights. Unlike the original Article I, however, the legislative compensation provision eventually took its place in the Constitution. In 1992, more than two hundred years after the amendment was first proposed, it was ratified by the states and became the Twenty-seventh Amendment to the U.S. Constitution.

Why the states originally refused to pass this amendment, along with the original Article I, is something of a mystery, for few records of state ratification proceedings exist. What we do know is that when Virginia ratified on December 15, 1791, the Bill of Rights became part of the U.S. Constitution.

THE AMENDMENT PROCESS

It is truly remarkable that Congress proposed and the states ratified the first ten amendments to the Constitution in three years; since then only seventeen others

have been added! Undoubtedly, this reticence would have pleased the writers of the Constitution. They wanted to create a government that would have some permanence, even though they recognized the need for flexibility. One of the major flaws in the Articles of Confederation, some thought, was the amending process because changing that document required the approval of all thirteen states. The framers imagined an amending procedure that would be "bendable but not trendable, tough but not insurmountable, responsive to genuine waves of popular desire, yet impervious to self-serving campaigns of factional groups."[9]

In Article V the framers established a two-step process for altering the Constitution (see Table 1-2). Proposing a constitutional amendment is the first step. This may be done either by a two-thirds vote of both houses of Congress or by two-thirds of the states petitioning for a constitutional convention. To date, all proposed constitutional amendments have been the product of congressional action. A second constitutional convention has never been called.[10] This method has been avoided because it raises serious questions. Would the delegates to such a convention deliberate only the amendments under consideration, or would they be able to take up any or all parts of the Constitution? Remember that the 1787 Philadelphia delegates met solely to amend the Articles of Confederation, but they ended up reframing the entire system of government.

The second step is ratification. Here, too, the framers allowed two options. Proposed amendments may be ratified by three-fourths of the state legislatures or by three-fourths of special state ratifying conventions. Historically, only the Twenty-first Amendment, which repealed Prohibition, was ratified by state conventions. The others were all ratified by the required number of state legislatures.

---

9. Keenan, *The Constitution of the United States*, 41.

10. This is not to say that attempts to call a constitutional convention have never been made. Perhaps the most widely reported was Sen. Everett Dirksen's effort to get the states to request a national convention for the purpose of overturning *Reynolds v. Sims*, the Supreme Court's 1964 reapportionment decision. He failed, by one state, to do so. A later attempt by the states to initiate constitutional change was a proposed amendment to require a balanced federal budget. This effort stalled with just two additional states required to call a convention.

---

8. Among those rejected was the one Madison prized above all others: that the states would have to abide by many of the enumerated guarantees.

TABLE 1-2 Methods of Amending the Constitution

Proposed By	Ratified By	Used For
Two-thirds vote in both houses of Congress	State legislatures in three-fourths of the states	26 amendments
Two-thirds vote in both houses of Congress	Ratifying conventions in three-fourths of the states	21st Amendment
Constitutional convention (called at the request of two-thirds of the states)	State legislatures in three-fourths of the states	Never used
Constitutional convention (called at the request of two-thirds of the states)	Ratifying conventions in three-fourths of the states	Never used

By mid-2008 Congress had considered more than ten thousand amendments and sent only thirty-three to the states for ratification. Among the six that did not receive the approval of a sufficient number of states were the Child Labor Amendment (proposed in 1924) that would have placed restraints on "the labor of persons under 18 years of age" and the equal rights amendment (proposed in 1972) that stated "equality of rights under law shall not be denied or abridged by the United States or any State on account of sex." Suggestions for new constitutional amendments continue to be advanced. In 2006, for example, the House of Representatives voted on the federal marriage amendment, which defines marriage as "the union of a man and a woman." The amendment failed to obtain the necessary two-thirds vote.

THE SUPREME COURT AND THE LIVING CONSTITUTION

So far, our discussion of the amendment process has not mentioned the president or the Supreme Court. The reason is that neither has any formal constitutional role in it. We do not want to suggest, however, that these institutions have nothing to do with the process; both have significant, albeit informal, functions. Presidents often instigate and support proposals for constitutional amendments. Indeed, virtually every chief executive has wanted some alteration to the Constitution. In his first inaugural address, George Washington urged adoption of a bill of rights; during his presidency, George W. Bush, in response to state court rulings allowing same-sex marriages, endorsed the proposed marriage amendment.

The Court also has played at least three important roles in the process: instigator, interpreter, and nationalizer.

The Court as an Instigator of Constitutional Amendments

Of the seventeen additions to the Constitution after the Bill of Rights, Congress proposed four specifically to overturn Supreme Court decisions *(see Box 1-1)*. Many consider one of these—the Fourteenth—the single most important addition since 1791.

Many of the proposals considered by Congress were aimed at similar objectives, among them the failed child labor and equal rights amendments, both of which emanated, at least in part, from Supreme Court rulings rejecting their premises. These two ultimately were passed by Congress, but not ratified by the states. More recently, Congress has considered the following amendments, all of which were aimed at overturning Court decisions: a human life amendment that would make abortion illegal (in response to *Roe v. Wade*, 1973); a school prayer amendment that would allow public school children to engage in prayer (in response to *Engel v. Vitale*, 1962, and *School District of Abington Township v. Schempp*, 1963); and a flag desecration amendment that would prohibit mutilation of the American flag (in response to *Texas v. Johnson*, 1989).

The Court as an Interpreter of the Amendment Process

The Court has been asked to interpret Article V, which deals with the amendment process, but it has been hesitant to do so. Consider *Coleman v. Miller* (1939),

BOX 1-1 FOUR AMENDMENTS THAT OVERTURNED SUPREME COURT DECISIONS

THE ELEVENTH

When Chisholm sued Georgia in 1793 and the Supreme Court dropped a bombshell on states-righters by agreeing to hear the case, Anti-Federalists were outraged. Congress responded swiftly by proposing the Eleventh Amendment, which was ratified by the requisite three-fourths of the states within a year, though not declared ratified until 1798. The amendment protects states against suits by citizens of another state or of another country.

THE FOURTEENTH

Congress and the High Court tangled again after the *Dred Scott v. Sandford* (sometimes spelled Dread Scott by abolitionists) case of 1857. Nine separate decisions were rendered on this case, but Chief Justice Roger B. Taney spoke for the "majority" in declaring that slaves could not be citizens and that Congress had exceeded its purview in prohibiting slavery in the territories. A Civil War and a few years of Reconstruction intervened before the Fourteenth Amendment, which conferred citizenship on all persons born or naturalized in the United States, could correct the *Scott* ruling.

THE SIXTEENTH

Congress next "got around the Supreme Court" through the passage of the Sixteenth Amendment, which legalized the income tax. In 1895 the Court turned down a federal income tax law on grounds that the Constitution requires taxes to be apportioned among the states proportionately according to population. But, in a spirit of cooperation, the Court invited Congress to overthrow the objection by means of an amendment. Congress proposed the Sixteenth Amendment in 1909, and the states ratified it in 1913.

THE TWENTY-SIXTH

President Richard Nixon, although signing a change in the Voting Rights Act that allowed eighteen-year-olds to vote in federal, state, and local elections, expressed doubt that the law was constitutional. Suit was speedily arranged, and the Court confirmed the president's misgivings in a 5–4 rejection that said, in effect: "The Congress does not have jurisdiction over state and local elections."

At a time when eighteen-year-olds were losing their lives in Vietnam, the Twenty-sixth Amendment had wide popular approval. In record time it was proposed by Congress in March 1971 and ratified in June, giving eighteen-year-olds the right to vote in national, state, and local elections.

SOURCE: From *The Constitution of the United States: An Unfolding Story*, 2nd ed., by J. T. Keenan, 42–43. Copyright © 1988 by The Dorsey Press. Reprinted by permission of the publisher, Brooks/Cole, Pacific Grove, Calif.

---

which involved the actions of the Kansas legislature over the child labor amendment.[11] Proposed by Congress in 1924, the amendment stated: "The Congress shall have power to limit, regulate, and prohibit the labor of persons under eighteen years of age." In January 1925 Kansas legislators rejected the child labor amendment. The issue arose again, however, when the state senate reconsidered the amendment in January 1937. At that time, the legislative body split 20–20, with the lieutenant governor casting the decisive vote in favor of the amendment. Members of the Kansas legislature (mostly those who opposed the amendment) challenged the 1937 vote on two grounds: They questioned the ability of the lieutenant governor to break the tie and, more generally, they opposed the reconsideration of an amendment that previously had been rejected. The legislators asserted that the amendment had "lost its vitality" because "of that rejection and the failure of ratification within a reasonable time limit." Writing for the Court, Chief Justice Charles Evans Hughes refused to address this point. Rather, he asserted that the suit raised questions, particularly those pertaining to recision, that were political and, therefore, nonjusticiable. In his words, "the ultimate authority" over the amendment process was Congress, not the Court.

---

11. Boldface type indicates that the opinions in the case can be found in the online archive. For a complete list, see Appendix 10, pages 766–768.

Over the years, the Court has followed the *Coleman* approach, leaving questions regarding the interpretation of Article V to Congress. Consider how it treated its most recent Article V case, ***NOW v. Idaho*** (1982). At issue was a 1978 act of Congress that extended the original deadline for state ratification of the equal rights amendment from 1979 to 1982 and rejected a clause that would have permitted state legislatures to rescind their prior approval. In the wake of a strong anti-ERA movement, Idaho, which had passed the amendment in the early 1970s, decided to ignore federal law and retract its original vote.[12] The National Organization for Women challenged the state's action, and in 1982 the Court docketed the case for argument. But, upon the request of the U.S. solicitor general, it dismissed the suit as moot: The congressionally extended time period for ratification had run out, and the controversy was no longer viable.

The Court as a Nationalizer of the Bill of Rights

In 1789, as we have noted, James Madison submitted to the First Congress a list of seventeen suggested amendments, mostly aimed at safeguarding personal freedoms against tyranny by the federal government. In a speech to the House, he suggested that "in revising the Constitution, we may throw into that section, which interdicts the abuse of certain powers of the State legislatures, some other provisions of equal, if not greater importance than those already made." To that end, Madison's fourteenth amendment proposal said that "no State shall violate the equal right of conscience, freedom of the press, or trial by jury in criminal cases."[13] This article failed to garner congressional approval and was never considered by the states.

Although scholars now agree that Madison viewed his fourteenth amendment as the most significant among the seventeen he proposed, Congress's refusal to adopt it may have meant that the founders never intended for the Bill of Rights to be applied to the states or their local governments. The language of the amendments lends some support to this interpretation. Consider the First Amendment to the U.S. Constitution: "Congress shall make no law . . . abridging the freedom of speech." Note that the wording specifically and exclusively limits the powers of Congress, reflecting the fact that the Bill of Rights was added to the Constitution because of fear that the *federal* government might become too powerful and encroach upon individual rights.

Does this language mean that state legislatures *may* enact laws curtailing their citizens' free speech? For more than one hundred years it did. The U.S. Supreme Court, following historical interpretations and emphasizing the intention of the framers of the Constitution, refused to nationalize the Bill of Rights by making its protections as binding on the state governments as they are on the federal government. Not being restricted by the federal Bill of Rights, the states were free to recognize those freedoms they deemed important and to develop their own guarantees against state violations of those rights.

Through a doctrine called selective incorporation, however, this interpretation is no longer valid. Under this doctrine, the Court uses the Fourteenth Amendment's due process clause ("Nor shall any State deprive any person of life, liberty, or property, without due process of law") to apply certain rights to the states. That is, through incorporation the Supreme Court has informed state governments that they too must abide by most guarantees contained in the first eight amendments of the federal Constitution. But, as Table 1-3 shows, the process by which Americans obtained these rights was long; in fact, early litigants who clamored for incorporation (in the major cases) actually lost many of their disputes.

That is no longer the case: We can now take for granted that the states in which we live must not infringe on our right to exercise our religion freely, to feel safe in our homes against unwarranted government intrusions, and so forth. Seen in this way, Madison may have lost the battle to see his Fourteenth Article become a part of the Constitution, but he won the larger war. For all practical purposes and with only a few exceptions *(see the note in Table 1-3)*, a present reading of the Constitution now ensures that the basic civil liberties of the citizens of the

12. Three other states—Kentucky, Nebraska, and Tennessee—also rescinded.

13. James Madison, Speech before the House of Representatives, June 7, 1789.

TABLE 1-3 Cases Incorporating Provisions of the Bill of Rights into the Due Process Clause of the Fourteenth Amendment

Constitutional Provision	Case	Year
First Amendment		
Freedom of speech and press	*Gitlow v. New York*	1925
Freedom of assembly	*DeJonge v. Oregon*	1937
Freedom of petition	*Hague v. CIO*	1939
Free exercise of religion	*Cantwell v. Connecticut*	1940
Establishment of religion	*Everson v. Board of Education*	1947
Fourth Amendment		
Unreasonable search and seizure	*Wolf v. Colorado*	1949
Exclusionary rule	*Mapp v. Ohio*	1961
Fifth Amendment		
Payment of compensation for the taking of private property	*Chicago, Burlington and Quincy R. Co. v. Chicago*	1897
Self-incrimination	*Malloy v. Hogan*	1964
Double jeopardy	*Benton v. Maryland*	1969
When jeopardy attaches	*Crist v. Bretz*	1978
Sixth Amendment		
Public trial	*In re Oliver*	1948
Due notice	*Cole v. Arkansas*	1948
Right to counsel (felonies)	*Gideon v. Wainwright*	1963
Confrontation and cross-examination of adverse witnesses	*Pointer v. Texas*	1965
Speedy trial	*Klopfer v. North Carolina*	1967
Compulsory process to obtain witnesses	*Washington v. Texas*	1967
Jury trial	*Duncan v. Louisiana*	1968
Right to counsel (misdemeanor when jail is possible)	*Argersinger v. Hamlin*	1972
Eighth Amendment		
Cruel and unusual punishment	*Louisiana ex rel. Francis v. Resweber*	1947
Ninth Amendment		
Privacy[a]	*Griswold v. Connecticut*	1965

NOTE: Provisions the Court has not incorporated: Second Amendment right to keep and bear arms; Third Amendment right against quartering soldiers; Fifth Amendment right to a grand jury hearing; Seventh Amendment right to a jury trial in civil cases; and Eighth Amendment right against excessive bail and fines.

a. The word *privacy* does not appear in the Ninth Amendment (nor anywhere in the text of the Constitution). In *Griswold* several members of the Court viewed the Ninth Amendment as guaranteeing (and incorporating) that right.

United States are uniformly protected against infringement by any government entity—federal, state, or local.

READINGS

Alderman, Ellen, and Caroline Kennedy. *In Our Defense: The Bill of Rights in Action.* New York: William Morrow, 1991.

Bach, Stanley. *The Amending Process in Congress.* Hauppauge, N.Y.: Novinka Books, 2003.

Cortner, Richard C. *The Supreme Court and the Second Bill of Rights.* Madison: University of Wisconsin Press, 1981.

Farber, Daniel A., and Suzanna Sherry. *A History of the American Constitution,* 2nd ed. St. Paul: Thomson/West, 2005.

Glasser, Ira. *Visions of Liberty.* New York: Arcade, 1991.

Hickok, Eugene W., Jr., ed. *The Bill of Rights: Original Meaning and Current Understanding.* Charlottesville: University Press of Virginia, 1991.

Kyvig, David E. *Explicit and Authentic Acts: Amending the U.S. Constitution, 1776–1995.* Lawrence: University Press of Kansas, 1996.

Maltz, Earl M. *The Fourteenth Amendment and the Law of the Constitution.* Durham: Carolina Academic Press, 2003.

Rutland, Robert A. *The Birth of the Bill of Rights, 1776–1791.* Chapel Hill: University of North Carolina Press, 1955.

Vose, Clement E. *Constitutional Change.* Lexington, Mass: Lexington Books, 1972.

CHAPTER 2

UNDERSTANDING THE SUPREME COURT

This book is devoted to narrative and opinion excerpts that show how the U.S. Supreme Court has interpreted the Constitution. As a student approaching constitutional law, perhaps for the first time, you may think it is odd that the subject requires so many pages of text. After all, in length, the Constitution and its amendments could fit easily into many Court decisions. Moreover, the document itself—its language—seems so clear.

First impressions, however, can be deceiving. Even apparently clear constitutional scriptures do not necessarily lend themselves to clear constitutional interpretation. For example, according to Article II, Section 2, the president "shall be Commander in Chief of the Army and Navy of the United States." Sounds simple enough, but could you, based on those words, answer the following questions, all of which have been posed to the Court?

• May a president, during times of war, order a blockage of certain American ports?

• May Congress delegate to the president the power to order an arms embargo against nations at war?

• May the president, during times of war, order that "traitors" be tried by military tribunals, rather than by civilian courts?

• May the president, during times of international crisis, authorize the creation of military camps to intern potential "traitors" to prevent sabotage?

What these and other questions arising from the different sections of the Constitution illustrate is that a gap

sometimes exists between the document's words and reality. Although the language seems explicit, its meaning can be elusive and difficult to follow. Accordingly, justices have developed various approaches to resolving disputes.

But, as Figure 2-1 shows, a great deal happens before the justices actually decide cases. We begin our discussion with a brief overview of the steps depicted in this figure. Next, we consider explanations for the choices justices make in the final and most important stage of the decision-making process, the resolution of disputes. Finally, we provide information on how to find Supreme Court decisions and, more generally, to conduct legal research.

PROCESSING SUPREME COURT CASES

During the 2006–2007 term more than 8,800 new cases arrived at the Supreme Court's doorstep. Yet the justices decided, with a written opinion, only 74.[1] The disparity between the number of parties that want the Court to resolve their disputes and the number the Court agrees to resolve raises some questions: How do the justices decide which cases to hear? What happens to the cases it rejects? What happens to those it agrees to resolve? We address these and other questions by describing how the Court processes its cases.

Deciding to Decide: The Supreme Court's Caseload

As the figures on the 2006–2007 term indicate, the Court heard and decided less than 1 percent of the cases

---

1. Data courtesy of the clerk of the U.S. Supreme Court.

FIGURE 2-1 The Processing of Cases

OCCURS THROUGHOUT TERM

Court Receives Requests for Review (8,500–9,000)
- appeals (e.g., suits under the Voting Rights Acts)
- certification (requests by lower courts for answers to legal questions)
- petitions for writ of certiorari (most common request for review)
- requests for original review

OCCURS THROUGHOUT TERM

Cases Are Docketed
- original docket (cases coming under its original jurisdiction)
- appellate docket (all other cases)

OCCURS THROUGHOUT TERM

Justices Review Docketed Cases
- chief justice prepares discuss lists (approximately 20–30 percent of docketed cases)
- chief justice circulates discuss lists prior to conferences; the associate justices can add but not substract cases

THURSDAYS

Conferences
- selection of cases for review, for denial of review
- Rule of Four: Four or more justices must agree to review most cases

BEGINS MONDAYS AFTER CONFERENCE

Announcement of Action on Cases

Clerk Sets Date for Oral Argument
- usually not less than three months after the Court has granted review

Attorneys File Briefs
- appellant must file within forty-five days from when Court granted review
- appellee must file within thirty days of receipt of appellant's brief

SEVEN TWO-WEEK SESSIONS, FROM OCTOBER THROUGH APRIL ON MONDAYS, TUESDAYS, WEDNESDAYS

Oral Arguments
- Court typically hears two cases per day, with each case receiving one hour of Court's time

FRIDAYS

Conferences
- discussion of cases
- tentative votes

Assignment of Majority Opinion

Drafting and Circulation of Opinions

Issuing and Announcing of Opinions

Reporting of Opinions
- *U.S. Reports* (U.S.) (official reporter system)
- *Lawyers' Edition* (L.Ed.)
- *Supreme Court Reporter* (S.Ct.)
- *U.S. Law Week* (U.S.L.W.)
- electronic reporter systems (WESTLAW, LEXIS)
- Supreme Court Web site (http://www.supreme courtus.gov/)

SOURCE: Compiled by authors.

it received. Although this percentage is low even by contemporary standards, it follows a more general trend in Supreme Court decision making: The number of requests for Supreme Court review has increased dramatically over the last century, but the number of cases the Court formally decides each year has slightly declined. In 1930, for example, the Court accepted for review 159 of the 726 requests it received. Six decades later, in 1990, the number of cases granted review fell to 141, but the number of cases brought to the Court reached 6,302—nearly nine times the 1930 figure.[2]

How do cases get to the Supreme Court? How does the Court decide which cases will get a formal review and which will be rejected? Why does the Court make the choices that it does? Each of these questions is fundamental to an understanding of judicial decision making.

How Cases Get to the Court: Jurisdiction and the Routes of Appeal. Cases come to the Supreme Court in one of four ways: by requests for review under the Court's original jurisdiction or by one of three appellate routes—appeals, certification, and petitions for writs of certiorari (*see Figure 2-1*).

Original cases are those that have not been heard by any other court. Article III of the Constitution authorizes such suits in cases involving ambassadors from foreign countries and those to which a state is a party. But because congressional legislation permits lower courts to exercise concurrent authority over most cases meeting the Article III requirements, the Court does not have exclusive jurisdiction over them. Consequently, the Court normally accepts, on its original jurisdiction, only those cases in which one state is suing another (usually over a disputed boundary) and sends the rest back to the lower courts for an initial ruling. That is why, in recent years, original jurisdiction cases make up only a small fraction of the cases coming into the Court—typically fewer than five cases per term.

Most cases reach the Court under its appellate jurisdiction, meaning that a lower federal or state court has

2. Data are from Lee Epstein, Jeffrey A. Segal, Harold J. Spaeth, and Thomas G. Walker, *The Supreme Court Compendium: Data, Decisions, and Developments*, 4th ed. (Washington, D.C.: CQ Press, 2007), Tables 2-5 and 2-6.

already rendered a decision and one of the parties is asking the Supreme Court to review that decision. As Figure 2-2 shows, such cases typically come from one of the nation's federal courts of appeals or state supreme courts. The U.S. Supreme Court, the nation's highest tribunal, is the court of last resort.

To invoke the Court's appellate jurisdiction, litigants can take one of three routes, depending on the nature of their dispute: appeal as a matter of right, certification, and certiorari. Cases falling into the first category (normally called "on appeal") present issues that Congress has determined are so important that a ruling by the Supreme Court is necessary. Prior to 1988 these included cases in which a lower court declared a state or federal law unconstitutional or in which a state court upheld a state statute challenged as being in violation of the U.S. Constitution. Although the justices were supposed to decide such appeals, they often found ways to deal with them more expediently—by either finding technical reasons not to consider them or issuing summary decisions (shorthand rulings). At the Court's urging, in 1988 Congress virtually eliminated "mandatory" appeals. Today the Court is legally obliged to hear only those few cases (typically involving the Voting Rights Act) appealed from special three-judge district courts. When the Court agrees to hear such cases, it issues an order noting its "probable jurisdiction."

A second, rarely used route to the Court is certification. Under the Court's appellate jurisdiction and by an act of Congress, lower appellate courts can file writs of certification, asking the justices to respond to questions aimed at clarifying federal law. Because only judges may use this route, very few cases come to the Court this way. Moreover, the justices may accept a question certified to them or dismiss it.

That leaves the third and most common path, a request for a writ of certiorari (from the Latin, meaning "to be informed"). In a petition for a writ of certiorari, the litigants desiring Supreme Court review ask the Court, literally, to become "informed" about their cases by requesting the lower court to send up the record. Most of the nine thousand or so cases that arrive each year come as requests for certiorari. The Court, exercising its ability to choose the cases to review, grants certiorari to about 1

FIGURE 2-2   The American Court System

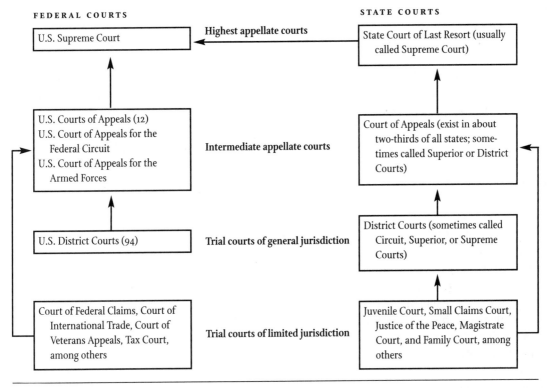

SOURCE: Compiled by authors.

percent of these petitions. Granting certiorari means that the justices have decided to give the case full review; denying certiorari means that the decision of the lower court remains in force.

How the Court Decides: The Case Selection Process. "Deciding to decide" presents something of mixed benefit to the justices. On the one hand, winnowing out the approximately eighty to ninety cases to review from thousands of requests is an arduous task. It requires the justices or their law clerks to look over hundreds of thousands of pages of briefs and other memoranda. On the other hand, the ability to exercise discretion frees the Court from one of the major constraints on judicial bodies: the lack of agenda control. The justices may not be able to reach out and propose cases for review, in the way that members of Congress can propose legislation, but

the enormous number of petitions ensures that they can resolve at least some issues important to them.

Many scholars have tried to determine what makes a case "certworthy," that is, worthy of review by the Supreme Court. Before we review some of their findings, let us consider the case selection process itself.

Each year the original pool of petitions faces several checkpoints along the way *(see Figure 2-1, page 21)*, which significantly reduce the amount of time the Court, acting as a collegial body, spends on deciding what to decide. The staff members in the office of the Supreme Court clerk act as the first gatekeepers. When a petition for certiorari arrives, the clerk's office examines it to make sure it is in reasonably proper form, that it conforms to precise Court rules. Briefs must be "prepared in a 6⅛- by 9¼-inch booklet . . . typeset in a Century family 12-point type with 2-point or more leading between lines." The rules governing petitions from indigent parties, called "in forma pauperis" petitions, are much looser. The Court's primary concern is that the petition be legible.[3]

The clerk's office gives all acceptable petitions an identification number, called a docket number, and forwards copies to the chambers of the individual justices. Each justice reviews the petitions, making independent decisions about which cases she or he feels are worthy of a full hearing. Some have their clerks read and summarize all the petitions.[4] Most justices use the "certiorari pool system" in which clerks from different chambers collaborate in reading and then writing memoranda on the petitions. Either way, the justices use their clerks' reports as a basis to make case selection decisions.

During this process, the chief justice plays a special role, serving as yet another checkpoint on petitions. Before the full Court meets to make case selection decisions, the chief circulates a "discuss list," containing those cases he feels worthy of full Court consideration; any justice may add cases to (but not subtract from) this list. About 20 percent of the cases that come to the Court make it onto the list and are actually discussed by the justices in conference—the rest are automatically denied review.[5]

This much we know. Because the Court's conferences are attended only by the justices and held in private, we cannot say precisely what transpires in them; we can offer only a rough picture based on scholarly assessments, the comments of justices, and our own examination of the private papers of a few who retired from the bench. These sources tell us that the discussion of each petition begins with the chief justice presenting a short summary of the facts and, typically, stating his vote. The associate justices, who sit at a rectangular table in order of seniority, then comment on each petition, with the most senior justice speaking first and the newest member last. The

associates also usually provide some indication of how they will vote on certiorari—indeed, as Figure 2-3 shows, the justices record certiorari (and merits votes) in their docket books. But, given the large number of petitions, the justices apparently discuss few cases in detail.

By tradition, the Court adheres to the so-called Rule of Four: It grants certiorari to those cases receiving the affirmative vote of at least four justices. The Court identifies the cases accepted and rejected on a "certified orders list," which is released to the public. For cases granted certiorari or in which probable jurisdiction is noted, the clerk informs participating attorneys, who then have specified time limits in which to turn in their written legal arguments ("briefs"), and the case is scheduled for oral argument.

Considerations Affecting Case Selection Decisions. Scholars have identified two sets of factors that affect the Court's decision to accept or reject a certiorari petition: legal and political considerations.[6] Legal considerations are listed in Rule 10, which the Court has established to govern the certiorari decision-making process:

Review on a writ of certiorari is not a matter of right, but of judicial discretion. A petition for a writ of certiorari will be granted only for compelling reasons. The following, although neither controlling nor fully measuring the Court's discretion, indicate the character of the reasons the Court considers:

(a) a United States court of appeals has entered a decision in conflict with the decision of another United States court of appeals on the same important matter; has decided an important federal question in a way that conflicts with a decision by a state court of last resort; or has so far departed from the accepted and usual course of judicial proceedings, or sanctioned such a departure by a lower court, as to call for an exercise of this Court's supervisory power;

3. See Rules 33 and 39 of the Rules of the Supreme Court of the United States, adopted July 17, 2007; effective October 1, 2007. The Court's rules can be found on the Internet at: http://www.supremecourtus.gov/ctrules/2007rulesofthecourt.pdf.

4. Supreme Court justices are authorized to hire four law clerks each. Typically, these clerks are outstanding recent graduates of the nation's better law schools.

5. For information on the importance of the discuss list, see Gregory A. Caldeira and John R. Wright, "The Discuss List: Agenda Building in the Supreme Court," *Law and Society Review* 24 (1990): 807–836.

6. Some scholars have noted a third set, procedural considerations. These emanate from Article III, which—under the Court's interpretation—places constraints on the ability of federal tribunals to hear and decide cases. In Chapter 3, we review these constraints in some detail. Here we note two that are particularly important for the review decision: the case must be appropriate for judicial resolution in that it presents a real "case" and "controversy" (justiciability), and the appropriate person must bring the case (standing). Unless these procedural criteria are met, the Court—at least theoretically—will deny review. It is worth noting, however, that because most petitions meet these criteria, they are not especially useful in helping the justices make their case selection decisions.

FIGURE 2-3 A Page from Justice Blackmun's Docket Books

	HOLD FOR	DEFER		CERT.			JURISDICTIONAL STATEMENT				MERITS		MOTION		
		RELIST	CVSG	G	D	G & R	N	POST	DIS	AFF	REV	AFF	G	D	
Rehnquist, Ch. J.				✓							✓				
White, J.				3							✓				
Blackmun, J.				✓							✓				
Stevens, J.				✓							✓				
O'Connor, J.				3								✓			
Scalia, J.					✓							✓			
Kennedy, J.				✓							✓				
Souter, J.				✓								✓			
Thomas, J.					✓							✓			

SOURCE: Dockets of Harry A. Blackmun, Manuscript Division, Library of Congress, Washington, D.C.

NOTE: As the docket sheet shows, the justices have a number of options when they meet to vote on cert. They can grant (G) the petition or deny (D) it. They also can cast a "Join 3" (3) vote. Justices may have different interpretations of a Join 3 but, at the very least, it tells the others that the justice agrees to supply a vote in favor of cert if three other justices support granting review. In the MERITS column, REV=reverse the decision of the Court below; AFF=affirm the decision of the court below.

(b) a state court of last resort has decided an important federal question in a way that conflicts with the decision of another state court of last resort or of a United States court of appeals;

(c) a state court or a United States court of appeals has decided an important question of federal law that has not been, but should be, settled by this Court, or has decided an important federal question in a way that conflicts with relevant decisions of this Court.

A petition for a writ of certiorari is rarely granted when the asserted error consists of erroneous factual findings or the misapplication of a properly stated rule of law.

To what extent do the considerations outlined in Rule 10 affect the Court? The answer is mixed. On the one hand, the Court seems to follow its dictates. The presence of actual conflict among federal courts or between federal courts (a concern of Rule 10) substantially increases the likelihood of review. If actual conflict is present in a case, a 33 percent chance exists that the Court will grant review—as compared with the usual certiorari rate of less than 5 percent.[7] On the other hand, Rule 10 is not all that helpful in understanding how the justices respond to certiorari petitions. The Court may use the existence of actual conflict as a threshold (cases that do not present conflict may be rejected), but it does not accept all cases with conflict because there are too many.[8]

The legal considerations encapsulated in Rule 10, then, may act as constraints on the justices' behavior, but they do not necessarily further our understanding of what occurs in cases that meet the criteria. That is why scholars have looked elsewhere—to political factors that may influence the Court's case selection process. Three of these are particularly important. The first centers on the U.S. solicitor general (SG), the attorney who represents the U.S. government before the Supreme Court. Simply stated, when the SG files a petition for certiorari, the Court is very likely to grant it. In fact, the Court accepts about 70 percent to 80 percent of the cases in which the federal government is the petitioning party.

Scholars posit a number of reasons for the solicitor general's success as a petitioner. One is that the Court is cognizant of the SG's special role. A presidential appointee whose decisions often reflect the administration's philosophy, the SG also represents the interests of the United States. As the nation's highest court, the Supreme

7. See Gregory A. Caldeira and John R. Wright, "Organized Interests and Agenda Setting in the U.S. Supreme Court," *American Political Science Review* 82 (1988): 1109–27.

8. In fact, during any given term, the Court rejects hundreds of cases in which real conflicts exist. See Lawrence Baum, *The Supreme Court*, 9th ed. (Washington, D.C.: CQ Press, 2006), 96–97.

Court cannot ignore these interests. Another reason is that the justices rely on the solicitor general to act as a filter; that is, they expect the SG to examine carefully the cases to which the government is a party and to bring only the most important to their attention. Finally, because solicitors general are involved in so much Supreme Court litigation, they acquire a great deal of knowledge about the Court that other litigants do not. They are repeat players, who know the rules of the game and can use them to their advantage. For example, they know how to structure their petitions to attract the attention and interest of the justices.

The second political factor is the amicus curiae (friend of the court) brief. These briefs may be filed by interest groups at the certiorari stage (see Box 2-1). Research by Gregory A. Caldeira and John R. Wright shows that amicus briefs significantly increase a case's chance to be heard, and multiple briefs have a greater effect.[9] Another interesting finding of their study is that even when groups file in opposition to granting certiorari, they increase—rather than decrease—the probability that the Court will hear the case.

What can we make of these findings? Most important is this: The justices may not be strongly influenced by the arguments contained in these briefs (if they were, why would briefs in opposition to certiorari have the opposite effect?), but they seem to use them as cues. In other words, because amicus curiae briefs filed at the certiorari stage are somewhat uncommon (about 8 percent of all petitions are accompanied by amicus briefs), they serve to single out a case, to draw the justices' attention. If major organizations are sufficiently interested in an appeal to file briefs in support of (or against) Court review, then the petition for certiorari is probably worth the justices' serious consideration.

In addition, we have strong reasons to suspect that a third political factor—the ideology of the justices—affects actions on certiorari petitions. Researchers tell us that the justices of the liberal Warren Court (1953–1969) were more likely to grant review to cases in which the lower court reached a conservative decision so that they could reverse it, while those of the moderately conservative Burger Court (1969–1986) took liberal cases to reverse. It is reasonable to believe that the current justices are just as likely as their predecessors to vote on the basis of their ideology. Scholarly studies also suggest that justices engage in strategic voting behavior at the certiorari stage. In other words, justices are forward thinking; they consider the implications of their certiorari vote for the later merits stage, asking themselves: If I vote to grant a particular petition, what are the odds of my position winning down the road? As one justice explained his calculations: "I might think the Nebraska Supreme Court made a horrible decision, but I wouldn't want to take the case, for if we take the case and affirm it, then it would become precedent."[10]

The Role of Attorneys

Once the Supreme Court agrees to decide a case, the clerk of the Court informs the parties. Their attorneys have two methods of presenting their side of the dispute to the justices: written and oral arguments.

Written Arguments. Briefs (written legal arguments) are the major vehicles by which parties to Supreme Court cases document their positions. Under the Court's rules, the appealing party (known as the appellant or petitioner) must submit its briefs within forty-five days of the time the Court grants certiorari; the opposing party (known as the appellee or respondent) has thirty days after receipt of the appellant's brief to respond with arguments urging affirmance of the lower court ruling.

The Court has specific rules covering the presentation and format of the briefs. For example, the briefs of both parties must be submitted in forty copies and not exceed fifty pages in length. Rule 24 outlines the material that briefs must contain, such as a declaration of the questions presented for review, a statement of the Court's jurisdiction over the case, a list of relevant legal authorities, and a detailed argument for affirmance or reversal.

The clerk sends the briefs to the justices, who normally study them before oral argument. Written briefs are im-

9. Caldeira and Wright, "Organized Interests and Agenda Setting in the U.S. Supreme Court."

10. Quoted in H. W. Perry Jr., *Deciding to Decide* (Cambridge: Harvard University Press, 1991), 200.

BOX 2-1   AMICUS CURIAE PARTICIPATION

The amicus curiae practice probably originates in Roman law. A judge would often appoint a *consilium* (officer of the court) to advise him on points where the judge was in doubt. That may be why the term *amicus curiae* translates from the Latin as "friend of the court." But today it is the rare amicus who is a friend of the court. Instead, contemporary briefs almost always are a friend of a party, supporting one side over the other at the certiorari and merits stages. Consider the brief filed in *United States v. Virginia* (1996), the cover of which is reprinted here. In that case, the National Women's Law Center and other organizations supported the federal government's request to have the Court hear the case. They, along with the United States, believed that the court below erred when it allowed Virginia to maintain a single-sex admissions policy at Virginia Military Institute. These groups were anything but neutral participants.

How does an organization become an amicus curiae participant in the Supreme Court of the United States? Under the Court's rules, groups wishing to file an amicus brief at the cert or merits stage must obtain the written consent of the parties to the litigation (the federal and state governments are exempt from this requirement). If the parties refuse to give their consent, the group can file a motion with the Court asking for its permission. The Court today almost always grants these motions.

IN THE
Supreme Court of the United States
OCTOBER TERM, 1994
JUNE 26, 1995
NO. 94-1941

————— • —————

UNITED STATES OF AMERICA, *Petitioner*

—V.—

COMMONWEALTH OF VIRGINIA, et al., *Respondents.*

ON PETITION FOR A WRIT OF CERTIORARI TO THE UNITED STATES
COURT OF APPEALS FOR THE FOURTH CIRCUIT

BRIEF OF AMICI CURIAE NATIONAL WOMEN'S LAW CENTER, AMERICAN CIVIL LIBERTIES UNION, THE AMERICAN ASSOCIATION OF UNIVERSITY WOMEN, B'NAI B'RITH WOMEN, CENTER FOR ADVANCEMENT OF PUBLIC POLICY, CENTER FOR WOMEN POLICY STUDIES, COALITION OF LABOR UNION WOMEN, CONNECTICUT WOMEN'S EDUCATION AND LEGAL FUND, EQUAL RIGHTS ADVOCATES, FEDERALLY EMPLOYED WOMEN, INC., NATIONAL COUNCIL OF JEWISH WOMEN, INC., NATIONAL COUNCIL OF NEGRO WOMEN, NATIONAL EDUCATION ASSOCIATION, THE NATIONAL GAY AND LESBIAN TASK FORCE, NATIONAL ORGANIZATION FOR WOMEN, THE NATIONAL WOMAN'S PARTY, NATIONAL WOMEN'S CONFERENCE COMMITTEE, NATIONAL WOMEN'S POLITICAL CAUCUS, NOW LEGAL DEFENSE AND EDUCATION FUND, TRIAL LAWYERS FOR PUBLIC JUSTICE, WOMEN EMPLOYED, WOMEN'S LAW PROJECT, AND THE WOMEN'S LEGAL DEFENSE FUND IN SUPPORT OF THE PETITION

MARCIA D. GREENBERGER, DEBORAH L. BRAKE
National Women's Law Center, 11 Dupont Circle, Suite 800,
Washington, D.C. 20036

SARA L. MANDELBAUM, STEVEN R. SHAPIRO, JANET GALLAGHER
American Civil Liberties Union, 132 W. 43rd Street, New York, NY 10036

ROBERT N. WEINER, *Counsel for Record*, WALTER J. ROCKLER,
PETER G. NEIMAN, MARK ECKENWILER, ARNOLD & PORTER
555 12th Street, N.W., Washington, D.C. 20004
(202) 942-5000
Counsel for Amici Curiae

portant because the justices may use them to formulate the questions they ask the attorneys representing the parties. The briefs also serve as a permanent record of the positions of the parties, available to the justices for consultation after oral arguments when they decide the case outcome. A well-crafted brief can place into the hands of the justices arguments, legal references, and suggested remedies that later may be incorporated into the opinion.

The Court rules also allow interested persons, organizations, and government units to participate as amici curiae on the merits—just as they are permitted to file such briefs at the review stage. Those wishing to submit friend of the court briefs must obtain the written permission of the parties or of the Court. Only the federal government and state governments are exempt from this requirement.

Oral Argument. Attorneys also have the opportunity to present their cases orally before the justices. Each side has thirty minutes to convince the Court of the merits of its position and to field questions from the justices. The justices are allowed to interrupt the attorneys at any time with comments and questions, as an exchange between Justice Byron White and Sarah Weddington, the attorney representing Jane Roe in *Roe v. Wade* (1973), indicates. White got the ball rolling when he asked Weddington to respond to an issue her brief had not addressed: whether abortions should be performed during all stages of pregnancy or should somehow be limited. The following discussion ensued:

White: And the statute doesn't make any distinction based upon at what period of pregnancy the abortion is performed?

Weddington: No, Your Honor. There is no time limit or indication of time, whatsoever. So I think—

White: What is your constitutional position there?

Weddington: As to a time limit—

White: What about whatever clause of the Constitution you rest on—Ninth Amendment, due process . . . —that takes you right up to the time of birth?

Weddington: It is our position that the freedom involved is that of a woman to determine whether or not to continue a pregnancy. Obviously I have a much more difficult time saying that the State has no interest in late pregnancy.

White: Why? Why is that?

Weddington: I think that's more the emotional response to a late pregnancy, rather than it is any constitutional—

White: Emotional response by whom?

Weddington: I guess by persons considering the issue outside the legal context, I think, as far as the State—

White: Well, do you or don't you say that the constitutional—

Weddington: I would say constitutional—

White: —right you insist on reaches up to the time of birth, or—

Weddington: The Constitution, as I read it . . . attaches protection to the person at the time of birth.

In the Court's early years, there was little doubt about the importance of such exchanges, of oral arguments in general. Because attorneys did not always prepare written briefs, the justices relied on oral presentations to provide them with information about the cases and to help them formulate their arguments. Oral arguments were considered important public events, opportunities to see the most prominent attorneys of the day at work. Arguments often went on for days: *Gibbons v. Ogden* (1824), the landmark commerce clause case, was argued for five days, and *McCulloch v. Maryland* (1819), the litigation challenging the constitutionality of the national bank, took nine days to argue.

Scholars, lawyers, and judges have questioned the effectiveness of oral argument and its role in decision making. Chief Justice Earl Warren maintained that they made little difference to the outcome. Once the justices have read the briefs and studied related cases, most have relatively firm views on how the case should be decided, and oral arguments change few minds. Justice William J. Brennan, however, maintained that they are extremely important, as they help justices to clarify core arguments. Oral arguments may or may not be good predictors of the Court's final votes, but at the least they provide some indication of what the justices believe to be the central issues of the case. In addition, we should not forget the symbolic importance of the oral argument stage, as it is the only part of the Court's decision-making process that occurs in public.

It is unlikely that this debate will ever be resolved, but now you have an opportunity to form your own opinion.

Through the efforts of Jerry Goldman, a political scientist, oral arguments in many cases are now available on the World Wide Web (http://www.oyez.org).

The Supreme Court Decides

After the Court hears oral argument, it meets in a private conference to discuss the case and to take a preliminary vote. Following is a description of the Court's conference procedures and of two events that come after the conference: the assignment of the opinion of the Court and the opinion circulation period.

The Conference. In these days of "government in the sunshine" the Court stands alone in its insistence that its decisions take place in a private conference, with no one in attendance except the justices. Congress has agreed by exempting the federal courts from open-government and freedom-of-information legislation. There are two basic reasons. First, the Supreme Court—which, unlike Congress, lacks an electoral connection—is supposed to base its decisions on factors other than public opinion. Opening up deliberations to press scrutiny, for example, might encourage the justices to take notice of popular sentiment, which is not supposed to influence them. Or so the argument goes. Second, although in conference the Court reaches tentative decisions on cases, the opinions explaining the decisions remain to be written. This process can take many weeks or even months, and the decision is not final until the opinions have been written, circulated, and approved. Because the decisions can have a major impact on politics and the economy, any party having advance knowledge of case outcomes could use that information for unfair business and political advantage.

The system works so well that with only a few exceptions the justices have not experienced information leaks. It is therefore impossible to know precisely what occurs in the deliberation of any particular case. We can, however, piece together the procedures and the general nature of the Court's discussions from the papers of retired justices and the comments of others.

We know that the chief justice presides over the deliberations. He calls up the case for discussion and then presents his views on the issues and how the case should be decided. The remaining justices state their views and votes in order of seniority.

The level and intensity of discussion, as Justice Brennan's notes from conference deliberations reveal, differ from case to case. In some, it appears that the justices have very little to say. The chief presents his views and the rest note their agreement. In others, every Court member has something to add. It is unclear to what extent conferences affect the final decisions. It would be unusual for a justice to enter the conference room without having reached a tentative position on the cases to be discussed; after all, he or she has read the briefs and listened to oral arguments. But the conference is the first opportunity the justices have to review cases as a group and to size up the positions of their colleagues. This sort of information, as we shall see, may be important as the justices begin the process of crafting and circulating opinions.

Opinion Assignment. The conference typically leads to a tentative outcome and vote. What happens at this point is critical because it determines who assigns the opinion of the Court, and the opinion of the Court is its only authoritative policy statement, the only one that establishes precedent. Under Court norms, the chief justice assigns the writing of the opinion when the chief votes with the majority. The chief may decide to write the opinion or assign it to one of the other justices who voted with the majority. When the chief justice votes with the minority, the assignment task falls to the most senior member of the Court who voted with the majority.

In making these assignments, the chief justice (or the senior associate in the majority) takes many factors into account. Forrest Maltzman and Paul J. Wahlbeck examined the opinion assignments of Chief Justice William Rehnquist.[11] These scholars discovered that the chief justice tried to equalize the distribution of the Court's workload. Rehnquist's management made sense: The Court will not run efficiently, given the burdensome nature of opinion writing, if some justices are given many more as-

---

11. "May It Please the Chief? Opinion Assignments in the Rehnquist Court," *American Journal of Political Science* 40 (1996): 421–443.

signments than others. The research also suggests that Rehnquist took into account the justices' particular areas of expertise. He recognized that some of his colleagues have more knowledge of particular areas of the law than others, and he tended to assign accordingly. By encouraging specialization, Rehnquist may have been trying to increase the quality of opinions and reduce the time to write them. Maltzman and Wahlbeck noted that when a case was decided by a one-vote margin, Rehnquist assigned the opinion to a moderate member of the majority rather than to an extreme member. His reasoning seems clear: If the writer in a close case drafts an opinion with which other members of the majority are uncomfortable, the majority may become a minority because the opinion may drive justices to the other side. Rehnquist tried to minimize this risk by asking justices squarely in the middle of the majority coalition to write the opinion.

Opinion Circulation. Regardless of the factors the chief considers in making assignments, one thing is clear: The opinion writer is a critical actor in the opinion circulation phase, which eventually leads to the final decision of the Court. After drafting an opinion with the help of law clerks, the writer begins the process by circulating it to the others.

Once the justices receive the first draft of the opinion, they have many options. First, they can join the opinion, meaning that they agree with it and want no changes. Second, they can ask the opinion writer to make changes; that is, they can bargain with the writer over the content of and even the disposition—to reverse or affirm the lower court ruling—offered in the draft. The following memo, sent from Brennan to White, is a good example: "I've mentioned to you that I favor your approach to this case and want if possible to join your opinion. If you find the following suggestions . . . acceptable, I can join you."[12]

Third, they can tell the opinion writer that they plan to circulate a dissenting or concurring opinion. A dissenting opinion means that the writer disagrees with the disposition the majority opinion reaches and with the rationale it invokes; a concurring opinion generally agrees

with the disposition but not with the rationale. Finally, justices can tell the opinion writer that they await further writings, meaning that they want to study various dissents or concurrences before they decide what to do.

As justices circulate their opinions and revise them—the average majority opinion undergoes three to four revisions in response to colleagues' comments—several different opinions on the same case, at various stages of development, will be floating around the Court over the course of several months. Because this same process is replicated for each case the Court decides with a formal written opinion, it is possible that at any one time scores of different opinions may be working their way from chamber to chamber.

Eventually, the final version of the opinion is reached, and each justice expresses a position in writing or signs an opinion of another justice. This is how the final vote is taken. When all of the justices have declared themselves, the only remaining step is for the Court to announce its decision to the public.

SUPREME COURT DECISION MAKING: THE ROLE OF LAW AND LEGAL PRINCIPLES

So far, we have examined the processes the justices follow to reach decisions on the disputes brought before them. We have answered basic questions about the institutional procedures the Court uses to carry out its responsibilities. The questions we have not addressed are why the justices reach particular decisions and what forces play a role in determining their choices.

As you might imagine, the responses to these questions are many, but they can be categorized into two groups. One focuses on the role of law, broadly defined, in determining how justices interpret the Constitution, emphasizing, among other things, the importance of its words, the intent of the framers, and precedent (previously decided constitutional rulings). The other emphasizes the role of politics, stressing, among other factors, the particular ideological views of the justices, the mood of the public, and the political preferences of the executive and legislative branches.

Commentators often define these two sides as "should" versus "do." That is, they say the justices *should*

12. Memorandum from Justice Brennan to Justice White, December 9, 1976, re: 75-104, *United Jewish Organizations v. Carey.*

interpret the Constitution in line with, say, the language of the text of the document or in accord with precedent. They reason that justices are supposed to shed all of their personal biases, preferences, and partisan attachments when they take their seats on the bench. But, it is argued, justices *do not* shed these biases, preferences, and attachments; rather, their decisions often reflect the justices' own politics or the political views of those around them.

To the extent that approaches grounded in law originated to answer the question of how justices *should* decide pending disputes, we understand why the difference between the two groups is often cast in terms of "should" versus "do." But, for several reasons, we ask you to think about whether the justices actually use these "should" approaches to reach decisions and not merely to camouflage their politics. One reason is that the justices themselves often say they look to the intent of the framers, the words of the Constitution, previously decided cases, and other "law" approaches to resolve disputes because they consider them appropriate criteria for reaching decisions. Another is that some scholars express agreement with the justices, arguing that Court members cannot follow their own personal preferences, the whims of the public, or other nonlegally relevant factors "if they are to have the continued respect of their colleagues, the wider [legal] community, citizens, and leaders." Rather, they "must be principled in their decision-making process." [13]

Whether they are principled in their decision making is for you to determine as you read the cases to come. First, however, it is necessary to have some sense of approaches grounded in law—or what some call modes of constitutional interpretation—that the justices frequently say they employ. In what follows, we consider some of the more important approaches and describe the philosophies that support their use.

Original Intent

It was more than two hundred years ago that the Supreme Court first invoked the term *the intention of the framers*. In *Hylton v. United States* (1796) Justice William

Paterson wrote: "It was . . . obviously the intention of the framers of the Constitution, that Congress should possess full power over every species of taxable property, except exports." Nearly two centuries later, in *Hustler Magazine v. Falwell* (1988) the Court used the same grounds to find that cartoon parodies, however obnoxious, constitute expression protected by the First Amendment.

Undoubtedly, over the long history of the Supreme Court its justices have looked to the intent of the framers of the Constitution and its amendments to reach conclusions about disputes before them. But why? What possible relevance could eighteenth-century intentions have for today's controversies? Advocates of this approach offer several answers. First, they assert that the framers acted in a calculated manner. The delegates to the Constitutional Convention debated at length not only basic principles but also the specific words that were to be included in the new Constitution. The convention agreed upon language that meant something. The intentions of the framers, as reflected in the words they used, should be respected and applied by contemporary justices.

Second, if they scrutinize the intent of the framers, justices can deduce "constitutional truths," which they can apply to cases. Doing so, proponents argue, would produce neutral principles of law and eliminate value-laden decisions.[14]

Finally, supporters of this mode of analysis argue that it fosters stability in law. They assert that the law today is far too fluid, that it changes with the ideological whims of the justices, creating havoc for those who must interpret and implement Court decisions. Lower court judges, lawyers, and even ordinary citizens do not know if today's rights will be rights tomorrow. Following a jurisprudence of original intent would eliminate such confusion because it provides a principle that justices would consistently follow.

Many Supreme Court opinions contemplate the original intent of the framers (or its variants, which we describe below), and at least one justice on the current Court—Clarence Thomas—regularly invokes originalism to answer a wide range of questions, from limits on

13. Ronald Kahn, "Institutional Norms and Supreme Court Decision Making: The Rehnquist Court on Privacy and Religion," in *Supreme Court Decision Making: New Institutionalist Approaches*, ed. Cornell W. Clayton and Howard Gillman (Chicago: University of Chicago Press, 1999), 176.

14. See, for example, Robert Bork, "Neutral Principles and Some First Amendment Problems," *Indiana Law Journal* 47 (1971): 1–35.

campaign spending to the appropriate balance of power between the states and the federal government.[15]

Such a jurisprudential course would have angered Thomas's predecessor, Thurgood Marshall, who did not believe that the Constitution was "forever 'fixed' at the Philadelphia Convention." Nor did Marshall find "the wisdom, foresight, and sense of justice exhibited by the framers"—in light of the 1787 Convention's treatment of women and blacks—"particularly profound."[16]

Brennan raised similar objections when he argued in 1985 that if the justices employed only this approach the Constitution would lose its applicability and be rendered useless:

We current Justices read the Constitution in the only way that we can: as Twentieth Century Americans. We look to the history of the time of the framing and to the intervening history of interpretation. But the ultimate question must be, what do the words of the text mean in our time? For the genius of the Constitution rests not in any static meaning it might have had in a world that is dead and gone, but in the adaptability of its great principles to cope with current problems and current needs. What the constitutional fundamentals meant to the wisdom of other times cannot be their measure to the vision of our time. Similarly, what those fundamentals mean for us, our descendants will learn, cannot be the measure to the vision of their time.[17]

Another criticism is that the Constitution embodies not one intent but many. Political scientists Jeffrey A. Segal and Harold J. Spaeth pose some interesting questions: "Who were the Framers? All fifty-five of the delegates who showed up at one time or another in Philadelphia during the summer of 1787? Some came and went. . . . Some probably had not read [the Constitution]. Assuredly, they were not all of a single mind."[18]

Finally, from which sources should justices divine the original intentions of the framers? They could look at the records of the constitutional debates and at the founders' journals and papers, but those documents often fail to provide a single clear message. Justice Robert H. Jackson made this point when he wrote:

Just what our forefathers did envision, or would have envisioned had they foreseen modern conditions, must be divined from materials almost as enigmatic as the dreams Joseph was called upon to interpret for Pharaoh. A century and a half of partisan debate and scholarly specification yields no net result but only supplies more or less apt quotations from respected sources on each side of any question. They largely cancel each other.[19]

Textualism I: Literalism

On the surface, the literal brand of textualism resembles the doctrine of original intent: It puts a premium on the Constitution. But this is where the similarity ends. In an effort to prevent the infusion of new meanings from sources outside the text of the Constitution, adherents of original intent seek to deduce constitutional truths by examining the intended meanings behind the words. Literalists consider only the plain meaning of the words in the Constitution (their literal meaning) and apply them to disputes. Justice Antonin Scalia (see Box 2-2) explained the differences between the approaches in a 1996 speech:

I belong to a school, a small but hardy school, called "textualists" or "originalists." That used to be "constitutional orthodoxy" in the United States. The theory of originalism treats a constitution like a statute, and gives it the meaning that its words were understood to bear at the time they were promulgated. You will sometimes hear it described as the theory of original intent. You will never hear me refer to original intent, because as I say I am first of all a textualist, and secondly an originalist. If you are a textualist, you don't care about the intent, and I don't care if the framers of the Constitution had some secret meaning in mind when they adopted its words. I take the words as they were promulgated to the people of the United States, and what is the fairly understood meaning of those words.[20]

15. Many scholars also advocate originalism. For a particularly intelligent defense, see Keith E. Whittington, *Constitutional Interpretation: Textual Meaning, Original Intent, and Judicial Review* (Lawrence: University Press of Kansas, 1999).

16. Thurgood Marshall, "Reflections on the Bicentennial of the United States Constitution," *Harvard Law Review* 101 (1987): 1.

17. William J. Brennan Jr., Address to the Text and Teaching Symposium, Georgetown University, October 12, 1985, Washington, D.C.

18. Jeffrey A. Segal and Harold J. Spaeth, *The Supreme Court and the Attitudinal Model* (Cambridge: Cambridge University Press, 1993), 39.

19. *Youngstown Sheet & Tube Co. v. Sawyer* (1952).

20. Antonin Scalia, "A Theory of Constitutional Interpretation," Remarks at the Catholic University of America, Washington, D.C., October 18, 1996.

BOX 2-2   ANTONIN SCALIA (1986–)

Antonin Scalia was the first person of Italian ancestry to be appointed to the Supreme Court and the first Roman Catholic since William J. Brennan Jr. was named in 1956. He was born March 11, 1936, in Trenton, New Jersey, to Eugene Scalia, a professor of Romance languages who had emigrated from Italy, and Catherine Panaro Scalia, a schoolteacher whose parents also had emigrated from Italy. Scalia grew up in Queens, where he attended Jesuit schools.

Scalia graduated from Georgetown University and Harvard Law School. The year he graduated from law school, he married Maureen McCarthy. Scalia spent seven years in private practice in Cleveland, Ohio, with the law firm of Jones, Day, Reavis, and Pogue, but left practice to teach at the University of Virginia School of Law in the late 1960s. Early in his career, he developed a strong individual style marked by a keen legal intellect and a certain whimsicality. He made playful use of language, would sometimes sing at public appearances, and liked to entertain friends with his piano playing.

Scalia was drawn to government service during the Nixon administration, which he joined in 1971 as general counsel of the White House Office of Telecommunications Policy. From that post, he became chairman of the Administrative Conference of the United States, and in 1974 he joined the Justice Department as assistant attorney general in charge of the Office of Legal Counsel, the same post William H. Rehnquist held from 1969 to 1971.

Scalia remained in that position through the Nixon and Ford administrations. He returned to teaching and held posts at Georgetown University Law School, the University of Chicago Law School, and Stanford University Law School. He was then named by President Reagan to the U.S. Court of Appeals for the District of Columbia Circuit in 1982.

Scalia developed a reputation as an outspoken conservative with very definite views of the law. He believed the power of the courts was limited. He also took a strong interest in the interpretation of statutes, arguing that the only legitimate guide for judges is the actual text of a statute and its related provisions. In 1986 Reagan promoted him to the U.S. Supreme Court.

True to his pattern on the appeals court, Scalia has established himself as one of the most conservative members of the Supreme Court. He is not willing to acknowledge any individual right not clearly set forth in the language of the Constitution. In *Webster v. Reproductive Health Services* (1989) and *Cruzan v. Director, Missouri Department of Health* (1990), to cite two examples, Scalia rejected any constitutional basis for the right to an abortion or the right to refuse life-sustaining treatment. In 1996 he wrote an angry dissent in *Romer v. Evans,* arguing that Colorado voters had the right to amend their state constitution to ban any local ordinances attempting to protect homosexuals. Seven years later, his equally angry dissent in *Lawrence v. Texas* accused the justices of bending to the whims of a "law-profession culture that has largely signed on to the so-called homosexual agenda."

SOURCE: Adapted from David Savage, *Guide to the U.S. Supreme Court,* 4th ed. (Washington, D.C.: CQ Press, 2004), 1017–1018.

Under Scalia's brand of textualism it is fair game for justices to go beyond the literal meaning of the words and consider what they would have originally meant to the people of that time—a type of textual analysis to which we will return presently. To other textualists, whom we might call pure textualists or *literalists,* it is only the words in the constitutional text, and the words alone, that justices ought to consider.

Although strains of literalism run through the opinions of many justices, Hugo L. Black is most closely associated with this view. During his thirty-four-year tenure on the Court, Black reiterated the literalist philosophy.

His own words best describe his position. Consider his approach to interpreting the First Amendment:

My view is, without deviation, without exception, without any ifs, buts, or whereases, that freedom of speech means that government shall not do anything to people . . . either for the views they have or the views they express or the words they speak or write. Some people would have you believe that this is a very radical position, and maybe it is. But all I am doing is following what to me is the clear wording of the First Amendment. . . . As I have said innumerable times before I simply believe that "Congress shall make no law" means Congress shall make no law. . . . Thus we have the absolute command of the First Amendment that no law shall be passed by Congress abridging freedom of speech or the press.[21]

Why did Black advocate literalism? Like original intent adherents, he viewed his own approach as a value-neutral form of jurisprudence. If justices looked only at the words of the Constitution, their decisions would reflect not their own ideological or political values, but rather those of the document. Black's opinions provide good illustrations. Although he almost always supported claims of free *speech* against government challenges, he refused to extend constitutional protection to *expression* that took forms other than pure speech. He asserted that activities such as flag burning and the wearing of armbands, even if designed to express political views, fell outside of the speech protected by the First Amendment.

Despite the high regard scholars have for Black, many have actively attacked his jurisprudence. Some assert that it led him to take some rather odd positions, particularly in cases involving the First Amendment. Most analysts and justices—even those considered liberal—agree that obscene materials fall outside of the First Amendment's protection of freedom of the press and that states can prohibit their dissemination. But, in opinion after opinion, Black clung to the view that no publication could be banned on the ground that it was obscene.

Segal and Spaeth raise another problem with literalism: It supposes a precision in the English language that does not exist. Not only may words, including those used by the framers, have multiple meanings, but also the meanings themselves may be quite contrary. For example, the common legal word *sanction*, as Segal and Spaeth note, means both to punish and to approve.[22] How, then, would a literalist construe the word in deciding a case in which its meaning was important? As Oliver Wendell Holmes Jr. once put it: "A word is not a crystal, transparent and unchanged, it is the skin of a living thought and may vary greatly in color and content according to the circumstances and the time in which it is used."[23]

Textualism II: Meaning of the Words

Advocates of textual approaches suggest that justices need look no further than the words of the Constitution to reach decisions. But, as we previously suggested, adherents do not necessarily approach the task of interpreting the "words" in the same way. Black claimed that he was loath to go beyond the literal meaning of the words, but Scalia is not so reticent. Indeed, under his "meaning of the words" or "original understanding" brand of textualism, it is appropriate for justices to ask what the words would have ordinarily meant to the people at the time they were written.[24]

The merits of this approach are similar to those of literalism and originalism. By focusing on how the framers defined their own words and then applying their definitions to disputes over constitutional provisions, this approach seeks to generate value-neutral and ideology-free jurisprudence. Indeed, one of the most important developers of this approach, William W. Crosskey, specifically embraced it to counter "sophistries" of the "living-document" view of the Constitution.[25]

Chief Justice Rehnquist's opinion in *Nixon v. United States* (1993) provides a particularly good illustration of the value of the meaning-of-the-words approach. Here, the Court considered a challenge to the procedures the

21. Hugo L. Black, *A Constitutional Faith* (New York: Knopf, 1969), 45–46.

22. Jeffrey A. Segal and Harold J. Spaeth, *The Supreme Court and the Attitudinal Model Revisited* (Cambridge: Cambridge University Press, 2002), 54.

23. *Towne v. Eisner* (1918).

24. See his "Originalism: The Lesser Evil," *University of Cincinnati Law Review* 57 (1989): 849–866.

25. W. W. Crosskey, *Politics and the Constitution in the History of the United States* (Chicago: University of Chicago Press, 1953), 1172–73.

Senate used to impeach a federal judge, Walter L. Nixon Jr. Rather than having the entire Senate try the case, a special twelve-member committee heard it and reported to the full body. Nixon argued that this procedure violated Article I of the Constitution, which states, "The Senate shall have the sole power to try all Impeachments." But before he addressed Nixon's claim, Rehnquist sought to determine whether courts had any business resolving such disputes. He used a meaning-of-the-words approach to consider the word *try* in Article I:

Petitioner argues that the word "try" in the first sentence imposes by implication an additional requirement on the Senate in that the proceedings must be in the nature of a judicial trial. . . . There are several difficulties with this position which lead us ultimately to reject it. The word "try," both in 1787 and later, has considerably broader meanings than those to which petitioner would limit it. Older dictionaries define try as "[t]o examine" or "[t]o examine as a judge." See S. Johnson, A Dictionary of the English Language (1785). In more modern usage the term has various meanings. For example, try can mean "to examine or investigate judicially," "to conduct the trial of," or "to put to the test by experiment, investigation. . . ." Webster's Third New International Dictionary (1971).

Like the other modes we have examined, the meaning-of-the-words approach is not without its critics. One objection is similar to that leveled at originalism: It is too static. Political scientist C. Herman Pritchett noted that like originalism, it can "make a nation the prisoner of its past, and reject any constitutional development save constitutional amendment." [26]

Another criticism is that it may be just as difficult for justices to establish the meaning of words as it is to establish the original intent behind them. Attempting to understand what the framers meant by each word can be a far more daunting task in the run-of-the-mill case than it was for Rehnquist in *Nixon*. It might even require the development of a specialized dictionary, which could take years of research to compile and still not have any value—determinate or otherwise. Besides, scholars argue, even if we could create a dictionary that would help shed light on the meaning of particular words at the times they

were written, it would tell us little about the significance of such constitutional phrases as "due process of law" or "cruel and unusual punishment."

Logical Reasoning

Unlike originalism or the meaning-of-the-words approach, logical reasoning is not necessarily dependent on historical interpretations of particular constitutional provisions. Rather, it suggests that judges should engage in logical analysis. Such an analysis often takes the form of a syllogism—a type of logic in which justices draw a conclusion from two assumed premises, a major and a minor one.

John Marshall's opinion in *Marbury v. Madison* (1803) provides an often-cited example of logical reasoning in action:

MAJOR PREMISE: A law repugnant to the Constitution is void.

MINOR PREMISE: This law is repugnant to the Constitution.

CONCLUSION: Therefore, this law is void.

The beauty of logical analysis, as this example illustrates, is that the resulting decision takes on an objective, perhaps even a scientific, aura. In other words, Marshall's syllogism suggests that anybody with a logical mind would reach the same conclusion. But is this necessarily so?

Consider another syllogism:

MAJOR PREMISE: Sweden has many storks.
MINOR PREMISE: Storks deliver babies.
CONCLUSION: Therefore, Sweden has many babies.

We know that storks do not deliver babies, and therein lies the major problem with logical reasoning: Because it can be undertaken in the absence of any factual analysis, almost any conclusion can result. To see this, compare the two syllogisms. If we assume that the major premises of both are accurate, then the soundness of their conclusions rests with the factual accuracy of their minor premises. Obviously, storks do not deliver babies, but is Marshall's minor premise any more believable or, more to the point, logically driven? Put another

26. C. Herman Pritchett, *Constitutional Law of the Federal System* (Englewood Cliffs, N.J.: Prentice-Hall, 1984), 37.

way, can logic reveal whether a particular law is repugnant to the Constitution?

To many the answer is no. As Justice Holmes put it:

The life of the law has not been logic: it has been experience. The felt necessities of the time, the prevalent moral and political theories, intuitions of public policy, avowed or unconscious, even the prejudices which judges share with their fellow-men, have had a good deal more to do than the syllogism in determining the rules by which men should be governed.[27]

Stare Decisis

Translated from Latin, *stare decisis* means "let the decision stand." What the term suggests is that, as a general rule, jurists should decide cases on the basis of previously established precedent. In shorthand terms, judicial tribunals should honor prior rulings.

The benefits of this approach are fairly evident. If justices rely on past cases to resolve current cases, some scholars argue, the law the Court generates becomes predictable and stable. Justice Harlan F. Stone acknowledged the value of precedent in a somewhat more ironic way: "The rule of stare decisis embodies a wise policy because it is often more important that a rule of law be settled than that it be settled right."[28] The message, however, is the same: If the Court adheres to past decisions, it provides some direction to all who labor in the legal enterprise. Lower court judges know how they should and should not decide cases; lawyers can frame their arguments in accord with the lessons of past cases; legislators understand what they can and cannot enact or regulate; and so forth.

Precedent, then, can be an important and useful factor in Supreme Court decision making. Along these lines, it is interesting to note that the Court rarely reverses itself; it has done so fewer than three hundred times over its entire history. Even modern-day Courts, as Table 2-1 shows, have been loath to overrule precedents. In the more than fifty years covered in the table, the Court has overturned only 138 precedents, or about 2.6 per term.

TABLE 2-1   Precedents Overruled, 1953–2006 Terms

Court Era (Terms)	Number of Terms	Number of Overruled Precedents	Average Number of Overrulings Per Term
Warren Court (1953–1968)	16	43	2.7
Burger Court (1969–1985)	17	47	2.8
Rehnquist Court (1986–2004)	19	44	2.3
Roberts Court (2005–2006)	2	4	2

SOURCE: Supreme Court Database, with orally argued citation as the unit of analysis. The table includes cases in which the majority opinion formally altered precedent, as well as those in which the Court claimed that a precedent was no longer good law. For more details on the data, see Harold J. Spaeth's documentation to the U.S. Supreme Court Judicial Database, available at: *http://www.polisci.msu.edu/pljp/databases.html.*

What is more, the justices almost always cite previous rulings in their decisions; indeed, it is the rare Court opinion that does not mention other cases.[29] Finally, several scholars have verified that precedent helps to explain Court decisions in some areas of the law. In one study, analysts found that the Court reacted quite consistently to legal doctrine presented in more than fifteen years of death penalty litigation. Put differently, using precedent from past cases, the researchers could correctly categorize the outcomes (for or against the death penalty) in 75 percent of sixty-four cases decided since 1972.[30] Scholarly work considering precedent in search and seizure litigation had similar success.[31]

Despite these data, we should not conclude that the justices necessarily follow this approach. Many claim that judicial appeal to precedent often is mere window dress-

27. *The Common Law,* quoted by Max Lerner in *The Mind and Faith of Justice Holmes* (New York: Modern Library, 1943), 51–52.

28. *United States v. Underwriters Association* (1944).

29. See Jack Knight and Lee Epstein, "The Norm of Stare Decisis," *American Journal of Political Science* 40 (1996): 1018–35.

30. Tracey E. George and Lee Epstein, "On the Nature of Supreme Court Decision Making," *American Political Science Review* 86 (1992): 323–337.

31. Jeffrey A. Segal, "Predicting Supreme Court Cases Probabilistically: The Search and Seizure Cases, 1962–1984," *American Political Science Review* (1984): 891–900.

ing, used to hide ideologies and values, rather than a substantive form of analysis. There are several reasons for this allegation.

First, the Supreme Court has generated so much precedent that it is usually possible to find support for any conclusion. By way of proof, turn to any page of any opinion in this book and you probably will find the writers—both for the majority and the dissenters—citing precedent.

Second, it may be difficult to locate the rule of law emerging in a majority opinion. To identify what qualifies as precedent, one must strip away the nonessentials of an opinion and expose the basic reasons for the Supreme Court's decision. This process is generally referred to as "establishing the principle of the case," or the *ratio decidendi*. Other points made in a given opinion—those unnecessary to the decision reached in the case or that relate to a factual situation other than the one actually before the Court—are called *obiter dicta*. Such expressions carry no legal weight and judges are not bound by them. It is up to courts to separate the *ratio decidendi* from *dicta*. This task can be difficult, but it provides a way for justices to skirt precedent with which they do not agree. All they need to do is declare parts of the precedent to be *dicta*. Or justices can brush aside even the *ratio decidendi* when it suits their interests.

A scholarly study of the role of precedent in Supreme Court decision making analyzes a third reason. Two political scientists hypothesized that if precedent matters, it ought to affect the subsequent decisions of members of the Court. If a justice dissented from a decision establishing a particular precedent, the same justice would not dissent from a subsequent application of the precedent. But that was not the case. Of the eighteen justices included in the study, only two occasionally subjugated their preferences to precedent.[32]

Finally, and most interesting, many justices recognize the limits of stare decisis in cases involving constitutional interpretation. Justices often say that when constitutional issues are involved, stare decisis is a less rigid rule than it

might normally be. This view strikes many as prudent. The Constitution is difficult to amend. When the justices realize they have made a mistake or come to see issues differently, an alteration in precedent may be the only practical way to correct the situation. Justice Black may have said it best:

Ordinarily it is sound policy to adhere to prior decisions but this practice has quite properly never been a blind, inflexible rule. Courts are not omniscient. Like every other human agency, they too can profit from trial and error, from experience and reflection. As others have demonstrated, the principle commonly referred to as stare decisis has never been thought to extend so far as to prevent the courts from correcting their own errors. . . . Indeed, the Court has a special responsibility where questions of constitutional law are involved to review its decisions from time to time and where compelling reasons present themselves to refuse to follow erroneous precedents; otherwise mistakes in interpreting the Constitution are extremely difficult to alleviate and needlessly so.[33]

In fact, of the 138 precedents overruled between the 1953 and 2006 terms *(see Table 2-1)*, about two-thirds involved constitutional issues.

Another form of decision making based on precedent occurs when the justices consult the practices and rulings of other jurisdictions. Although not binding by the rule of stare decisis, the experiences of other courts can be quite helpful. Often the justices will look to rulings of early English courts for meaning of Anglo-American legal traditions. The Court may also survey the rulings of state supreme courts to arrive at an understanding of generally accepted legal principles. In addition, contemporary justices turn to the experiences of the courts of other nations whose judges often confront issues relevant to disputes the U.S. Supreme Court must settle.

Balancing Approaches

So far we have examined five modes of analysis that are not case specific, meaning that conclusions reached by literalists and original intent advocates on points of law would not waiver with the facts of a given case. In a free speech case, a literalist would always hold that Congress may never regulate pure speech. Supporters of a

---

32. Jeffrey A. Segal and Harold J. Spaeth, "The Influence of Stare Decisis on the Votes of U.S. Supreme Court Justices," *American Journal of Political Science* 40 (1996): 971–1003.

33. *Green v. United States* (1958).

balancing approach take a position that is more case specific than philosophical; that is, in each case they balance the interests of the individual against those of the government. Their decisions can vary because at times an individual's right to engage in an activity outweighs the government's interest in prohibiting it, while at other times the reverse holds true.

The balancing approach, however, is not monolithic. Some justices take a strict view of balancing, giving the interests of individuals and governments equal weight. They justify doing so on constitutional and philosophical grounds, saying, for example, that while the First Amendment protects individual speech, the text of the Constitution gives legislatures the power to enact laws that may sometimes interfere with speech. The Court, according to this view, should initially give equal weight to both and then balance them to determine which should fall.

Justice John Marshall Harlan's opinion in *Barenblatt v. United States* (1959) demonstrates this theory in practice. Among the issues raised was whether a congressional committee could question an individual about his political beliefs and associations. Lloyd Barenblatt alleged that he could refuse to answer such questions because they infringed on his First Amendment rights. Harlan wrote: "Where First Amendment rights are asserted to bar governmental interrogation, resolution of the issue always involves a balancing by the courts of the competing private and public interests at stake in the particular circumstances shown." He held that, in this instance, the scale favored the government over Barenblatt.

Not all applications of the balancing approach value the competing interests equally. In accordance with a philosophy of judicial restraint, Justice Felix Frankfurter often balanced government interests versus individual interests but with a finger on the scale, giving preference to the state over the individual. He did so in the belief that a body made up of unelected judges should not lightly overturn laws passed by legislatures composed of representatives elected by the populace. In his view,

the framers of the Constitution denied . . . legislative powers to the federal judiciary. They chose instead to insulate the judiciary from the legislative function. They did not grant to this Court supervision over legislation. . . . The removal of unwise

laws from the statute books . . . lies not to the court but to the ballot and to the processes of democratic government.[34]

In contrast to Frankfurter's perspective is the preferred freedoms position, which also balances interests, but tips the scale to favor the individual's rights and liberties. It holds that the liberties included in the First Amendment occupy a preferred position in the hierarchy of constitutional values. When laws restricting these rights are challenged, the normal presumption of constitutionality is waived and the government bears a heavy burden of proof in attempting to justify its actions.

Still another variant of balancing is cost-benefit analysis. Justices often appraise alternative rulings by forecasting their consequences. In doing so they weigh the advantages likely to flow from a particular ruling against the adverse consequences of the decision, and their estimates can influence choices among plausible constitutional interpretations.

One of the recurring issues the Supreme Court confronted during much of the twentieth century was the application of the exclusionary rule, which forbids use in criminal proceedings of evidence gathered by means of an unconstitutional search and seizure. Claims that the rule hampers the conviction of criminals have affected judicial attitudes, as Justice Byron White admitted in *United States v. Leon* (1984): "The substantial social costs exacted by the exclusionary rule for the vindication of Fourth Amendment rights have long been a source of concern." In *Leon* a majority of the justices applied a "cost-benefit" calculus to justify a "good faith" seizure by police on an invalid search warrant.

When you encounter cases that engage in this sort of analysis, you might ask questions raised by some critics of the approach: By what account of values should judges weigh costs and benefits? How do they take into account the different people whom a decision may simultaneously reward and punish?

SUPREME COURT DECISION MAKING: THE ROLE OF POLITICS

So far in our discussion we have not mentioned the justices' ideologies, their political party affiliations, or

34. *West Virginia v. Barnette* (1943).

their personal views on various public policy issues. The reason is that legal approaches to Supreme Court decision making do not admit that these factors figure into the way the Court arrives at its decisions. Instead, they suggest that justices divorce themselves from their personal and political biases and settle disputes based upon the law. The approaches we now consider posit a quite different vision of Supreme Court decision making. They argue that the forces that drive the justices are anything but legal in composition and that it is unrealistic to expect justices to shed all their preferences and values and to ignore public opinion when they put on their black robes. Rather, the justices are people who—like all of us—have strong and pervasive political biases and partisan attachments.

Because justices usually do not admit that they are swayed by the public or that they vote according to their ideologies, our discussion of the role politics plays in Supreme Court decision making is distinct from that of the law. Here you will find little in the way of supporting statements from Court members, for it is an unusual justice indeed who admits to following anything but legally relevant criteria in deciding cases. Instead, we have included the results of decades of research by scholars who think that political and other extralegal forces shape judicial decisions. We organize these approaches into three categories: preference-based, strategic, and external forces. See if you think these scholarly accounts are persuasive.

Preference-Based Approaches

Preference-based approaches argue that justices are rational decision makers who hold certain values they would like to see reflected in the outcomes of Court cases. The two most prevalent preference-based approaches stress the importance of judicial attitudes and roles.

Judicial Attitudes. Attitudinal approaches emphasize the importance of the justices' ideologies. Typically, scholars examining the ideologies of the justices discuss the degree to which a justice is conservative or liberal—as in "Justice X has conservative views on issues of criminal law," or "Justice Y has liberal views on free speech." This school of thought holds that when a case comes before

the Court each justice evaluates the facts of the dispute and arrives at a decision consistent with his or her personal ideology.

One of the first scholars to study systematically the importance of the personal attitudes of the justices was C. Herman Pritchett.[35] Examining the Court during the 1930s and 1940s, the New Deal period, Pritchett was not satisfied with traditional legal explanations, such as precedent, of judicial decisions. If precedent drove Court rulings, why did various justices consistently reach different conclusions in interpreting the same legal provisions? Pritchett concluded that the law alone was insufficient to explain votes. He found that personal attitudes have a strong influence on judicial decisions. Justices with liberal ideologies consistently voted for liberal outcomes, and those with conservative ideologies systematically voted for conservative outcomes. Based on their voting patterns, Pritchett was able to place the justices of that era on a left-right continuum.

Pritchett's findings touched off an explosion of research on the influence of attitudes on Supreme Court decision making.[36] Much of this scholarship describes how liberal or conservative the various justices were and attempts to predict their voting behavior based on their attitudinal preferences. To understand some of these differences, consider the material in Figure 2-4, which presents the voting records of the present chief justice, John Roberts, and his three immediate predecessors, Earl Warren, Warren Burger, and William Rehnquist. The data report the percentage of times each voted in the liberal direction in two different issue areas: civil liberties and economics.

The data show dramatic differences among these four jurists, especially with regard to civil liberties. Cases in this category include disputes over issues such as the First

35. C. Herman Pritchett, *The Roosevelt Court* (New York: Macmillan, 1948); and Pritchett, "Divisions of Opinion Among Justices of the U.S. Supreme Court, 1939–1941," *American Political Science Review* 35 (1941): 890–898.

36. The classic works in this area are Pritchett, *The Roosevelt Court;* Glendon Schubert, *The Judicial Mind* (Evanston, Ill.: Northwestern University Press, 1965); and David W. Rohde and Harold J. Spaeth, *Supreme Court Decision Making.* For a lucid, modern-day treatment, see Segal and Spaeth, *The Supreme Court and the Attitudinal Model Revisited.*

FIGURE 2-4   Liberal Voting of the Chief Justices, 1953–2006 Terms

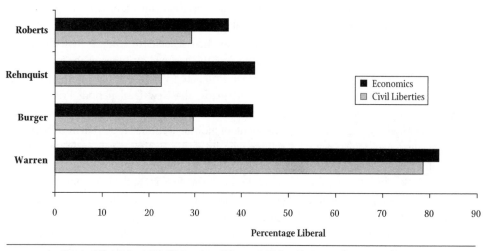

SOURCE: Lee Epstein, Jeffrey A. Segal, Harold J. Spaeth, and Thomas G. Walker, *The Supreme Court Compendium: Data, Decisions, and Developments,* 4th ed. (Washington, D.C.: CQ Press, 2007), Table 6-4.
    NOTE: The data in this figure are based on decisions reached during the following tenures: Earl Warren, 1953–1968; Warren Burger, 1969–1985; William Rehnquist, 1972–2005; John Roberts, 2005–2006.

Amendment freedoms of religion, speech, and press; the right to privacy; the rights of the criminally accused; and illegal discrimination. The liberal position is a vote in favor of the individual who is claiming a denial of these basic rights. Warren supported the liberal side almost 80 percent of the time, but Burger, Rehnquist, and Roberts did so in less than 30 percent.

Economics cases involve challenges to the government's authority to regulate the economy. The liberal position supports an active role by the government in controlling business and economic activity. Here, too, the four chiefs show different ideological positions. Warren is the most liberal of the four, ruling in favor of government regulatory activity in better than 80 percent of the cases, while Burger, Rehnquist, and Roberts support such government activity in less than half. These data are typical of the findings of most such studies. Within given issue areas, individual justices tend to show consistent ideological predispositions.

Moreover, we often hear that a particular Court is ideologically predisposed toward one side or the other. Sometimes an entire Court era is described in terms of its political preferences, such as the "liberal" Warren Court or the "conservative" Rehnquist Court. Figure 2-5 con-

firms that these labels have some basis in fact. Looking at the two lines from left to right, from the 1953 through 2006, note the downward trend, indicating the increased conservatism of the Court in economics and civil liberties cases.

How valuable are the ideological terms used to describe particular justices or Courts in helping us understand judicial decision making? On the one hand, knowledge of justices' ideologies can lead to fairly accurate predictions about their voting behavior. Suppose that the Roberts Court hands down a decision dealing with the death penalty and that the vote in the case is 7–2 in favor of the criminal defendant. The most conservative members of the Court (at least on death penalty cases) are Justices Antonin Scalia and Clarence Thomas—they almost always vote against the defendant. If we predicted that it was Scalia and Thomas who cast the two dissenting votes in our hypothetical death penalty case, we would almost certainly be right.[37]

On the other hand, preference-based approaches are not foolproof. First, how do we know if a particular justice

37. We adopt this example from Segal and Spaeth, *The Supreme Court and the Attitudinal Model,* 223.

FIGURE 2-5   Court Decisions on Economics and Civil Liberties, 1953–2006 Terms

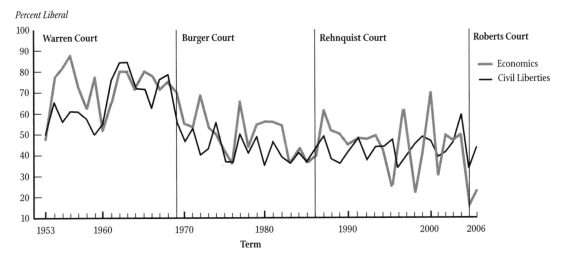

Percent Liberal

SOURCE: Lee Epstein, Jeffrey A. Segal, Harold J. Spaeth, and Thomas G. Walker, *The Supreme Court Compendium: Data, Decisions, and Developments,* 4th ed. (Washington, D.C.: CQ Press, 2007), Table 3-8.

is liberal or conservative? The answer typically is that we know a justice is liberal or conservative because he or she casts liberal or conservative votes. Scalia favors conservative positions on the Court because he is a conservative; we know he is a conservative because he favors conservative positions in the cases he decides. This is circular reasoning indeed. Second, knowing that a justice is liberal or conservative or that the Court decided a case in a liberal or conservative way does not tell us much about the Court's (or the country's) policy positions. To say that *Roe v. Wade* (1973) is a liberal decision is to say little about the policies governing abortion in the United States. If it did, this book would be nothing more than a list of cases labeled liberal or conservative. But such labels would give us no sense of two hundred years of constitutional interpretation.

Finally, we must understand that ideological labels are occasionally time-dependent, that they are bound to particular historical eras. In *Muller v. Oregon* (1908) the Supreme Court upheld a state law that set a maximum number on the hours women (but not men) could work. How would you, as a twenty-first-century student, view such an opinion? You probably would classify it as conservative because it seems to patronize and protect women. But in the context of the early 1900s most con-

sidered *Muller* to be a liberal ruling because it allowed the government to regulate business.

A related problem is that some decisions do not fall neatly on a single conservative-liberal dimension. In *Wisconsin v. Mitchell* (1993) the Court upheld a state law that increased the sentence for crimes if the defendant "intentionally selects the person against whom the crime is committed" on the basis of race, religion, national origin, sexual orientation, and other similar criteria. Is this ruling liberal or conservative? If you view the law as penalizing racial or ethnic hatred, you would likely see it as a liberal decision, but if you see the law as treating criminal defendants more harshly and penalizing a person because of what he or she believes or says, the ruling is conservative.

Judicial Role. Another concept within the preference-based category is the judicial role, which scholars have defined as a set of norms that constrain the behavior of jurists.[38] In other words, some students of the Court argue that each justice has a view of his or her role, one that

38. See James L. Gibson, "Judges' Role Orientations, Attitudes, and Decisions: An Interactive Model," *American Political Science Review* 72 (1978): 911–924.

is based upon fundamental beliefs of what a good judge should do or what the proper role of the Court should be. The belief is that jurists vote in accordance with these role conceptions.

Analysts typically discuss judicial roles in terms of activism and restraint. An activist justice believes that the proper role of the Court is to assert independent positions in deciding cases, to review the actions of the other branches vigorously, to be willing to strike down unconstitutional acts, and to impose far-reaching remedies for legal wrongs whenever necessary. Restraint-oriented justices take the opposite position. Courts should not become involved in the operations of the other branches unless absolutely necessary. The benefit of the doubt should be given to actions taken by elected officials. Courts should impose remedies that are narrowly tailored to correct a specific legal wrong.

Based on these definitions, we might expect to find activist justices more willing than their opposites to strike down legislation. Therefore, a natural question to ask is this: To what extent have specific jurists practiced judicial activism or restraint? The data in Table 2-2 address this question by reporting the votes of justices on the current Court in cases in which the majority declared federal, state, or local legislation unconstitutional. Note the wide variation among the justices, even for those who sat together and therefore heard many of the same cases. Compare Justice Anthony Kennedy's rate of 94.4 percent (meaning that he almost always voted with the majority to strike down laws) with Justice Scalia's 76.9 percent—a difference of nearly eighteen percentage points, despite the fact that Kennedy's and Scalia's service on the Court has overlapped for two decades.

Even more interesting may be the behavior of Justice Frankfurter, who served on the Court between 1939 and 1962. In many Supreme Court opinions, Frankfurter declared his adherence to the doctrine of judicial restraint. But relevant data suggest otherwise. During his last nine years on the bench, Frankfurter voted with the majority to overturn state and federal laws in 76.6 percent of the sixty-four cases in which he participated.

The Frankfurter example should make clear that what justices say they do and what they actually do may be two

TABLE 2-2 Votes in Support of and Opposition to Decisions Declaring Legislation Unconstitutional: The Current Court

Justice	All Laws	%	Federal Laws Only	%
Alito	4/0	100	1/0	100
Breyer	49/21	70	17/15	53.1
Ginsburg	53/25	67.9	16/16	50
Kennedy	114/9	92.7	34/2	94.4
Roberts	4/0	100	1/0	100
Scalia	93/44	67.9	30/9	76.9
Souter	78/19	80.4	20/12	62.5
Stevens	207/52	79.9	26/22	54.2
Thomas	63/28	69.2	26/6	81.3

SOURCE: Lee Epstein, Jeffrey A. Segal, Harold J. Spaeth, and Thomas G. Walker, *The Supreme Court Compendium: Data, Decisions, and Developments,* 4th ed. (Washington, D.C.: CQ Press, 2007), Table 6-10.

NOTE: Figures to the left of the slash indicate the number of votes cast in favor of striking down legislation; figures to the right indicate the number of votes in favor of upholding the legislation. Percentages indicate the percentage of cases in which the justice voted with the majority to declare legislation unconstitutional.

different things. It also illustrates a less obvious point: Judicial activism and restraint do not necessarily equal judicial liberalism and conservatism. An activist judge need not be liberal, and a judge who practices restraint need not be conservative. As for Frankfurter, scholars argue that in his voting behavior he was "a staunch economic conservative" who was willing to strike down laws that impinged on his policy preferences.[39] Among the twenty-seven justices who served on the Court between 1953 and 1996, only three—Harlan, Charles E. Whittaker, and Thomas—supported liberal outcomes in economic cases at a rate lower than Frankfurter's 39 percent. In other words, in some areas of the law, Frankfurter was a conservative activist.

It is also true that so-called liberal Courts are no more likely to strike down legislation than are conservative Courts. For example, the Court registered high rates of declaring statutes unconstitutional in the 1920s, 1970s, and 1980s—all periods of relative conservatism. Such activism calls into question the existence of a strong relationship between ideology and judicial role.

39. See Segal and Spaeth, *The Supreme Court and the Attitudinal Model,* 236–237.

We have shown that one can use measures, such as the number of laws struck down, to assess the extent to which justices practice judicial activism or restraint. But does such information help us understand Supreme Court decision making? This question is difficult to answer because few scholars have studied the relationship between roles and voting in a systematic way.

The paucity of scholarly work on judicial roles leads to one criticism of the approach: It is virtually impossible to separate roles from attitudes. When Justice Frankfurter voted to uphold an economically conservative law, can we necessarily conclude that he was practicing restraint? The answer, quite clearly, is no. It may have been his conservative attitude toward economic cases—not restraint—that led him to uphold the law. Another criticism of role approaches is similar to that leveled at attitudinal factors—they tell us very little about the resulting policy in a case. Again, to say that *Roe v. Wade* was an activist decision because it struck down abortion laws nationwide is to say nothing about the policy content of the opinion.

Strategic Approaches

Strategic accounts of judicial decisions rest on a few simple propositions: Justices may be primarily seekers of legal policy (as the attitudinal adherents claim), or they may be motivated by jurisprudential principles (as the approaches grounded on law suggest)—but they are not unconstrained actors who make decisions based solely on their own ideological attitudes or jurisprudential desires. Rather, justices are strategic actors who realize that their ability to achieve their goals—whatever those goals might be—depends on a consideration of the preferences of other relevant actors (such as their colleagues on the Court and members of other political institutions), the choices they expect others to make, and the institutional context in which they act. Scholars term this approach "strategic" because the ideas it contains are derived from the rational choice paradigm, on which strategic analysis is based and as it has largely been used by economists and political scientists. Accordingly, we can restate the strategic argument this way: The choices of justices can best be explained as strategic behavior and not merely as a response to ideological or jurisprudential values.[40]

Such approaches to Supreme Court decision making seem to be sensible because a justice can do very little alone. It takes a majority vote to decide a case and a majority agreeing on a single opinion to set precedent. Under such conditions, human interaction is important and case outcomes—not to mention the rationale of decisions—can be influenced by the nature of relations among the members of the group.

Although scholars have not considered strategic approaches to the degree that they have studied judicial attitudes, a number of influential works point to their importance. Research that began in the 1960s and continues today into the private papers of former justices consistently has shown that through intellectual persuasion, effective bargaining over opinion writing, informal lobbying, and so forth, justices have influenced the actions of their colleagues.[41]

How does strategic behavior manifest itself? One possibility is through vote changes. During the deliberations that take place after oral arguments, the justices discuss the case and vote on it. These votes do not become final until the opinions are completed and the decision is made public (*see Figure 2-1, page 21*). Research has shown that between the initial vote on the merits of cases and the official announcement of the decision at least one vote switch occurs more than 50 percent of the time.[42] This figure indicates that justices change their minds—a phenomenon that seems inexplicable if we believe that justices are simply liberals or conservatives and always vote in accord with their preferences.

40. For more details on this approach, see Lee Epstein and Jack Knight, *The Choices Justices Make* (Washington, D.C.: CQ Press, 1998).

41. Walter F. Murphy, *Elements of Judicial Strategy* (Chicago: University of Chicago Press, 1964); David J. Danelski, "The Influence of the Chief Justice in the Decisional Process of the Supreme Court," in *The Federal Judicial System*, ed. Thomas P. Jahnige and Sheldon Goldman (New York: Holt, Rinehart, and Winston, 1968); J. Woodford Howard, "On the Fluidity of Judicial Choice," *American Political Science Review* 62 (1968): 43–56.

42. Saul Brenner, "Fluidity on the Supreme Court, 1956–1967," *American Journal of Political Science* 26 (1982): 388–390; Brenner, "Fluidity on the United States Supreme Court: A Re-examination," *American Journal of Political Science* 24 (1980): 526–535; Forest Maltzman and Paul J. Wahlbeck, "Strategic Considerations as Vote Fluidity on the Burger Court," *American Political Science Review* 90 (1996): 581–592.

Vote shifts are just one manifestation of the interdependence of the Court's decision-making process. Another is the revision of opinions that occurs in almost every Court case. As opinion writers try to accommodate their colleagues' wishes, their drafts may undergo five, ten, even fifteen revisions. Bargaining over the content of an opinion is important because it can significantly alter the policy ultimately expressed. *Griswold v. Connecticut* (1965), in which the Court considered the constitutionality of a state law that prohibited the dissemination of birth control devices and information, even to married couples, provides a clear example. In his initial draft of the majority opinion, Justice Douglas struck down the law on the grounds that it interfered with the First Amendment's right to association. A memorandum from Justice Brennan persuaded Douglas to alter his rationale and to establish the foundation for a right to privacy. If Douglas's initial draft had been approved by the majority, *Griswold* would have become a precedent supporting freedom of association rather than a landmark decision on the right to privacy.

One problem with the strategic approach is that we do not know enough about it. To date, scholarly treatments have been few in number. We do not know the extent to which a case like *Griswold* represents the rule or the anomaly. Until analysts begin to study interdependent decision making more systematically, which manuscript collections such as Powell's, Marshall's, and Brennan's make possible, the general value of this approach will remain unknown.

External Factors

In addition to internal bargaining, strategic approaches (as well as others) take account of political pressures that come from outside the Court. We consider three sources of such influence: public opinion, partisan politics, and interest groups. While reading about these sources of influence, keep in mind that one of the fundamental differences between the Supreme Court and the political branches is that there is no direct electoral connection between the justices and the public. Once appointed, justices may serve for life. They are not accountable to the public and are not required to undergo any periodic reevaluation of their decisions. So why would

they let the stuff of ordinary politics, such as public opinion and interest groups, influence their opinions?

Public Opinion. We know that the president and members of Congress are always trying to find out what the people are thinking. Conducting and analyzing public opinion polls are never-ending tasks. There is good reason for these activities. The political branches are supposed to represent the people, and the incumbents' reelection prospects can be jeopardized by straying too far from what the public wants. But federal judges—including Supreme Court justices—are not dependent upon pleasing the public to stay in office, and they do not serve in the same kind of representative capacity that legislators do.

Does that mean that the justices are unaffected by public opinion? Some scholars claim that the answer, for at least three reasons, is no. First, because justices are political appointees, nominated and approved by popularly elected officials, it is logical that they reflect, however subtly, the views of the majority. It is probably true that an individual radically out of step with either the president or the Senate would not be nominated, much less confirmed. Second, the Court, at least occasionally, views public opinion as a legitimate guide for decisions. It has even gone so far as to incorporate that dimension into some of its jurisprudential standards. For example, in evaluating whether certain kinds of punishments violate the Eighth Amendment's prohibition against cruel and unusual punishment, the Court proclaimed that it would look toward "evolving standards of decency," as defined by public sentiment.[43] The third reason relates to the Court as an institution. Put simply, the justices have no mechanism for enforcing their decisions. Instead, they depend on other political officials to support their positions and on general public compliance, especially when controversial Court opinions have ramifications beyond the particular concerns of the parties to the suit.

Certainly, we can think of particular cases that lend support to these claims—cases in which the Court seems to have embraced public opinion, especially under conditions of extreme national stress. One example occurred during World War II. In *Korematsu v. United States* (1944)

43. *Trop v. Dulles* (1958).

the justices endorsed the government's program to remove all Japanese Americans from the Pacific Coast states and relocate them to inland detention centers. It seems clear that the justices were swept up in the same wartime apprehensions as the rest of the nation. But it is equally easy to summon examples of the Court handing down rulings that fly in the face of what the public wants. The most obvious example occurred after Franklin D. Roosevelt's 1932 election to the presidency. By choosing Roosevelt and electing many Democrats to Congress, the voters sent a clear signal that they wanted the government to take vigorous action to end the Great Depression. The president and Congress responded with many laws—the so-called New Deal legislation—but the Court remained unmoved by the public's endorsement of Roosevelt and his legislation. In case after case, at least until 1937, the justices struck down many of the laws and administrative programs designed to get the nation's economy moving again.

Systematic research scrutinizing the correspondence between various measures of public opinion and trends in Court decisions has yielded equally mixed results.[44] At the end of the day, the question of whether public opinion affects Supreme Court decision making (and if so, to what degree and through what mechanism) remains an open one.

Partisan Politics. Public opinion is not the only political factor that influences the justices, according to some scholars. As Jonathan Casper wrote, we cannot overestimate "the importance of the political context in which the Court does its work." In his view, the statement that the Court follows the election returns "recognizes that the choices the Court makes are related to developments in the broader political system."[45] In other words, the po-

litical environment has an effect on Court behavior. In fact, many assert that the Court is responsive to the influence of partisan politics, both internally and externally.

On the inner workings of the Court, social scientists long have argued that political creatures inhabit the Court, that justices are not simply neutral arbiters of the law. Since 1789, the beginning of constitutional government in the United States, those who have ascended to the bench have come from the political institutions of government or, at the very least, have been affiliated with a particular political party. Judicial scholars recognize that justices bring with them the philosophies of those partisan attachments. Just as the members of the present Court tend to reflect the views of the Republican Party or Democratic Party, so too did the justices who came from the ranks of the Federalists and Jeffersonians. As one might expect, justices who affiliate with the Democratic Party tend to be more liberal in their decision making than those who are Republicans. Some commentators say that *Bush v. Gore* (2000), in which the Supreme Court issued a ruling that virtually ensured that George W. Bush would become president, provides an example. In that case, five of the seven Republicans on the Court "voted" for Bush, while the Court's two Democrats "voted" for Gore.

Political pressures from the outside can also affect the Court. Although the justices have no electoral connection or mandate of responsiveness, the other institutions of government have some influence on judicial behavior; naturally, the direction of that influence reflects the partisan composition of those branches. The Court has always had a complex relationship with the president, a relationship that provides the president with several possible ways to influence judicial decisions. The president has some direct links with the Court, including (1) the president's power to nominate justices and shape the Court; (2) personal relationships with sitting justices, including Franklin Roosevelt's with James Byrnes, Lyndon Johnson's with Abe Fortas, and Richard Nixon's with Warren Burger; and (3) the notion that the president, having been elected within the previous four years, may carry a popular mandate, reflecting the preferences of the people, which would affect the environment within which the Court operates.

44. Thomas Marshall, *Public Opinion and the Supreme Court* (New York: Unwin Hyman, 1989); William Mishler and Reginald S. Sheehan, "The Supreme Court as a Counter-Majoritarian Institution? The Impact of Public Opinion on Supreme Court Decisions," *American Political Science Review* 87 (1993): 89–101; Helmut Norpoth and Jeffrey A. Segal, "Popular Influence in Supreme Court Decisions," *American Political Science Review* 88 (1994): 711–716; James A. Stimson, Michael B. MacKuen, and Robert S. Erikson, "Dynamic Representation," *American Political Science Review* 89 (1995): 556.

45. Jonathan Casper, *The Politics of Civil Liberties* (New York: Harper and Row, 1972), 293.

A less direct source of influence is the executive branch, which operates under the president's command. The bureaucracy can assist the Court in implementing its policies, or it can hinder the Court by refusing to do so, a fact of which the justices are well aware. As a judicial body, the Supreme Court cannot implement or execute its own decisions. The Court often must depend on the executive branch to give its decisions legitimacy through action. The Court, therefore, may act strategically, anticipating the wishes of the executive branch and responding accordingly to avoid a confrontation that could threaten its legitimacy. *Marbury v. Madison* (1803), in which the Court enunciated the doctrine of judicial review, is the classic example *(see chapter 3 for an excerpt)*. Some scholars suggest that the justices knew if they ruled in a certain direction, the administration would not carry out their orders. Because the Court felt that such a failure would threaten the legitimacy of judicial institutions, it crafted its opinion in a way that would not force the administration to take action, but would send a message about its displeasure with the administration's politics.

Another indirect source of presidential influence is the U.S. solicitor general. We have already discussed the SG's success as a petitioning party, and the office can have an equally pronounced effect at the merits stage. In fact, data indicate that, whether acting as an amicus curiae or as a party to a suit, the SG's office is generally able to persuade the justices to adopt its preferred positions.[46]

Presidential influence is also demonstrated in the kinds of arguments a solicitor general brings into the Court. That is, solicitors general representing Democratic administrations tend to present more liberal arguments; those from the ranks of the Republican Party, more conservative arguments.

Congress, too—or so some argue—can influence Supreme Court decision making. Like the president, the legislature has many powers over the Court the justices cannot ignore.[47] Some of these resemble presidential powers—the Senate's role in confirmation proceedings,

the implementation of judicial decisions—but there are others. Congress can restrict the Court's jurisdiction to hear cases, enact legislation or propose constitutional amendments to recast Court decisions, and hold judicial salaries constant. To forestall a congressional attack, the Court might accede to legislative wishes. Often-cited examples include the Court's willingness to defer to the Republican Congress after the Civil War and to approve New Deal legislation after Roosevelt proposed his Court-packing plan in 1937.

Some argue that these examples represent anomalies, not the rule. The Court, they say, has no reason to respond strategically to Congress because it is so rare that the legislature threatens, much less takes action, against the judiciary. Only infrequently has Congress removed the jurisdiction of the federal courts to hear particular kinds of cases, most prominently just after the Civil War and more recently in the wake of the war on terrorism. This argument needs to be kept in mind as you read the cases that pit the Court against Congress and the president.

Interest Groups. Few observers would doubt that the Supreme Court is involved in the political process. We see manifestations of politics in virtually every aspect of the Court's work, from the nomination and confirmation of justices to the factors that influence their decisions. But perhaps the most striking example of this politicization is the incursion of organized interests into the judicial process.

Naturally, interest groups may not attempt to persuade the Supreme Court the same way lobbyists deal with Congress. It would be grossly improper for the representatives of an interest group to approach a Supreme Court justice directly. Instead, interest groups try to influence Court decisions by submitting amicus curiae briefs. Presenting a written legal argument to the Court allows interest groups to make their views known to the justices, even when the group is not a direct party to the litigation.

These days, it is a rare case before the U.S. Supreme Court that does not attract such submissions. On average, organized interests filed at least one amicus brief in well over 90 percent of all cases decided by full opinion between 1986 and 2006. In addition to participating as

46. See Epstein, Segal, Spaeth, and Walker, *The Supreme Court Compendium*, Tables 7-14 and 7-15.
47. See William N. Eskridge Jr., "Overriding Supreme Court Statutory Interpretation Decisions," *Yale Law Journal* 101 (1991): 331–455.

amici, groups are sponsoring cases—that is, providing litigants with attorneys and the money necessary to pursue their cases—in record numbers.

The explosion of interest group participation in Supreme Court litigation raises two questions. First, why do groups go to the Court? The answer is obvious: They want to influence the Court's decisions. But groups also go to the Supreme Court to achieve other, more subtle ends. One is the setting of institutional agendas; by filing amicus curiae briefs at the case-selection stage or by bringing cases to the Court's attention, organizations seek to influence the justices' decisions on which disputes to hear. Group participation also may serve as a counterbalance to other interests that have competing goals. So, if Planned Parenthood, a pro-choice group, observes the Life Legal Defense Fund, a pro-life group, filing an amicus curiae brief in an abortion case—or vice versa—it too may enter the dispute to ensure that its side is represented in the proceedings. Finally, groups go to the Court to publicize their causes and their organizations.

The second question is this: Can groups influence the outcomes of Supreme Court decisions? This question has no simple answer. When interest groups participate on both sides, it is reasonable to speculate that one or more exerted some intellectual influence or at least that the intervention of groups on the winning side neutralized the arguments of those who lost. But measuring the degree of influence is difficult. When a justice votes in favor of an interest group's position, we do not know if the group's participation caused the justice to alter his or her opinion, or whether the group's efforts only reinforced a conclusion the justice had already reached.

We can be more certain that many cases would not get into any court, much less the U.S. Supreme Court, without the help of an interest group. Therefore, we can say that because judges have to wait for cases to come before them, groups help set the judicial agenda. It may be that many judges, especially judges on appellate courts, look on interest groups as sources of important information that otherwise would not come to their attention. In addition, interest groups, especially those that regularly participate in litigation, have legal staffs that are not only expert in presenting arguments to the Court but that also

are adept at cooperating with other interest groups in coordinated efforts to achieve mutual legal goals.

On the other hand, there is equally compelling evidence to suggest that groups are no more successful than other interests. One study paired similar cases decided by the same district court judge, the same year, with the only major difference being that one case was sponsored by a group, the other by a nongroup. The study found no major differences between the two.[48] Research by Donald Songer and Reginald Sheehan reached almost the same conclusion about the effectiveness of amicus curiae briefs in Supreme Court litigation.[49] These scholars found that briefs other than those filed by the United States had little impact on Supreme Court decisions.

In short, the debate over the influence of interest groups continues. And it is one that you will be able to enter, for within the case excerpts we often provide information on the arguments of amici and attorneys. This will provide you with an opportunity to compare arguments with the opinions of the justices.

CONDUCTING RESEARCH ON THE SUPREME COURT

As you can see, considerable disagreement exists in the scholarly and legal communities over why justices decide cases as they do, and various approaches show up in many of the Court's opinions discussed in this book. Keep in mind, however, that the opinions here are excerpts, designed to highlight the most important points of the various majority, dissenting, and concurring opinions. Occasionally, you may want to read the decisions in their entirety. Following is an explanation of how to locate opinions and other kinds of information on the Court and its members.

Locating Supreme Court Decisions

U.S. Supreme Court decisions are published by various reporters. The four major reporters are *United States*

48. Lee Epstein and C. K. Rowland, "Debunking the Myth of Interest Group Invincibility in the Court," *American Political Science Review* 85 (1991): 205–217.

49. Donald R. Songer and Reginald S. Sheehan, "Interest Group Success in the Courts: Amicus Participation in the Supreme Court," *Political Research Quarterly* 46 (1993): 339–354.

TABLE 2-3 Reporting Systems

Reporter/Publisher	Form of Citation (terms)	Description
United States Reports Government Printing Office	Dall. 1–4 (1790–1800) Cr. 1–15 (1801–1815) Wheat. 1–12 (1816–1827) Pet. 1–16 (1828–1843) How. 1–24 (1843–1861) Bl. 1–2 (1861–1862) Wall. 1–23 (1863–1875) U.S. 91– (1875–)	Contains official text of opinions of the Court. Includes tables of cases reported, cases and statutes cited, miscellaneous materials, and subject index. Includes most of the Court's decisions. Court opinions prior to 1875 are cited by the name of the reporter of the Court. For example, Dall. stands for Alexander J. Dallas, the first reporter.

United States Supreme Court Reports,
Lawyers' Edition
    Lawyers' Cooperative
    Publishing Company
	L. Ed.
	L. Ed. 2d
		Contains official reports of opinions of the Court. Additionally, provides per curiam and other decisions not found elsewhere. Summarizes individual majority and dissenting opinions and counsel briefs.

Supreme Court Reporter West Publishing Company	S. Ct.	Contains official reports of opinions of the Court. Contains annotated reports and indexes of case names. Includes opinions of justices in chambers. Appears semi-monthly.
United States Law Week Bureau of National Affairs	U.S.L.W.	Weekly periodical service that contains full text of Court decisions. Includes four indexes: topical, table of cases, docket number table, and proceedings section. Contains summary of cases filed recently, journal of proceedings, summary of orders, arguments before the Court, argued cases awaiting decisions, review of Court's work, and review of Court's docket.

SOURCES: Lee Epstein, Jeffrey A. Segal, Harold J. Spaeth, and Thomas G. Walker, *The Supreme Court Compendium: Data, Decisions, and Developments*, 4th ed. (Washington, D.C.: CQ Press, 2007), Table 2-9. Dates of reporters are from David Savage, *Guide to the U.S. Supreme Court*, 4th ed. (Washington, D.C.: CQ Press, 2004).

Reports; United States Supreme Court Reports, Lawyers' Edition; Supreme Court Reporter; and *U.S. Law Week.* All contain the opinions of the Court, but they vary in the kinds of ancillary material they provide. For example, as shown in Table 2-3, the *Lawyers' Edition* contains excerpts of the briefs of attorneys submitted in orally argued cases; *U.S. Law Week* provides a topical index of cases on the Court's docket; and so forth.

Locating cases within these reporters is easy if you know the case citation. Case citations, as the table shows, take different forms, but they all work in roughly the same way. To see how, turn to page 431 to find an excerpt of *Texas v. Johnson* (1989). Directly under the case name is a citation: 491 U.S. 397, which means that the case of *Texas v. Johnson* appears in volume 491, page 397,

of *U.S. Reports.*[50] The first set of numbers is the volume number; the *U.S.* is the form of citation for the *U.S. Reports;* and the second set of numbers is the starting page of the case.

Texas v. Johnson also can be located in the three other reporters. The citations are as follows:

Lawyers' Edition: 105 L. Ed. 2d 342 (1989)
Supreme Court Reporter: 109 S. Ct. 2533 (1989)
U.S. Law Week: 57 U.S.L.W. 4770 (1989)

50. In this book, we list only the *U.S. Reports* citation because it is the official record of Supreme Court decisions. It is the only reporter published by the federal government; the three others are privately printed. Almost every law library has *U.S. Reports.* If your college does not have a law school, check with your librarians. If they have any Court reporter, it is probably *U.S. Reports.*

Note that the initials vary by reporter but they parallel the *U.S. Reports* in that the first set of numbers is the volume number and the second set, the starting page number.

If you do not know the citation for a particular case, try to find out the year it was decided. With this information, you can check the index of the appropriate volume of the *U.S. Reports* or of other reporters. If you know the approximate date of the decision, try the Supreme Court's Case Citation Finder, http://www.supremecourt us.gov/opinions/casefinder.html.

Supreme Court opinions are also available in various electronic forms. First, several companies maintain databases of the decisions of federal and state courts, along with a wealth of other information. In many colleges and universities these services—LEXIS-NEXIS and Westlaw— may be available only to law school students. But you should check with your librarians to see if your school allows access to other students, perhaps via Academic Universe (a subset of the LEXIS-NEXIS service). Second, the Legal Information Institute (LII) at Cornell Law School (www.law.cornell.edu/), Findlaw (www.find law.com/casecode/supreme.html), and FedWorld (www. fedworld.gov/supcourt/index.htm)—to name three—contain Supreme Court opinions and offer an array of indexes and search capabilities. You can read the opinions online, have them e-mailed to you, or download them immediately. If a case we have excerpted in this volume is located in one of these electronic archives, we have noted the URL after the case citation.

Locating Other Information on the Supreme Court and Its Members

As you might imagine, there is no shortage of reference material on the Court. Three good (print) starting points are the following:

1. *The Supreme Court Compendium: Data, Decisions, and Developments,* fourth edition, contains information on the following aspects of Court activity: the Court's development, review process, opinions and decisions, judicial background, voting patterns, and impact.[51] You will find data as varied as the number of cases the Court decided during a particular term, the votes in the Senate on Supreme Court nominees, and the law schools the justices attended.

2. *Guide to the U.S. Supreme Court,* fourth edition, provides a fairly detailed history of the Court. It also summarizes the holdings in landmark cases and provides brief biographies of the justices.[52]

3. *The Oxford Companion to the Supreme Court of the United States* is an encyclopedia, containing entries on the justices, important cases, the amendments to the Constitution, and so forth.[53]

The U.S. Supreme Court also gets a great deal of attention on the Web. The Legal Information Institute (http://www.law.cornell.edu/) is particularly useful. In addition to opinions, the LII contains links to various documents, such as the U.S. Code and state statutes, and to a vast array of legal indexes and libraries. If you are unable to find the material you are looking for here, you may locate it by clicking on one of the links.

Another worthwhile site is "On the Docket," a project of the Medill School of Journalism at Northwestern University (http://docket.medill. northwestern.edu/). Housed here are extensive summaries of pending Court cases, as well as links to briefs filed by the parties and amici.

As already mentioned, you can listen to selected oral arguments of the Court at the Oyez Project site (http://www.oyez.org). Oyez contains audio files of Supreme Court oral arguments for selected constitutional cases decided since the 1950s. For those cases included in the archive, we provide the URLs.

These are just a few of the many sites—perhaps hundreds—that contain information on the federal courts. But there is at least one other important electronic source of information on the Court worthy of mention—Harold J. Spaeth's computer-dependent U.S. Supreme Court Judicial Databases. They provide a wealth of data beginning with the Vinson Court (1946 term) to the present. Among

---

51. Epstein, Segal, Spaeth, and Walker, *The Supreme Court Compendium.*

52. David Savage, *Guide to the U.S. Supreme Court,* 4th ed. (Washington, D.C.: CQ Press, 2004).

53. Kermit Hall, ed., *The Oxford Companion to the Supreme Court of the United States*, 2nd ed. (New York: Oxford University Press, 2005).

the many attributes of Court decisions coded by Spaeth are the names of the courts making the original decision, the identities of the parties to the cases, the policy context of a case, and the votes of each justice. Indeed, we deployed one of Spaeth's databases to create many of the charts and tables you have just read. You can obtain all the databases and accompanying documentation, free of charge at *http://www.as.uky.edu/polisci/ulmerproject/sct data.htm*.

In this chapter, we have examined Supreme Court procedures and attempted to shed some light on how and why justices make the choices they do. Our consideration of preference-based factors, for example, highlighted the role ideology plays in Court decision making, and our discussion of political explanations emphasized public opinion and interest groups. After reading this chapter, you may have concluded that the justices are relatively free to go about their business as they please. But, as we shall see in the next chapter, that is not necessarily so. Although Court members have a good deal of power and the freedom to exercise it, they also face considerable institutional obstacles. It is to the subjects of judicial power and constraints that we now turn.

READINGS

Ackerman, Bruce. *We the People.* Cambridge: Harvard University Press, 1991.

Amar, Akhil Reed. *The Bill of Rights: Creation and Reconstruction.* New Haven: Yale University Press, 1998.

Baum, Lawrence. *The Supreme Court,* 9th ed. Washington, D.C.: CQ Press, 2006.

Bickel, Alexander. *The Least Dangerous Branch of Government.* Indianapolis: Bobbs-Merrill, 1962.

Bork, Robert. "Neutral Principles and Some First Amendment Problems." *Indiana Law Journal* 47 (1971): 1–35.

Brenner, Saul, and Harold J. Spaeth. *Stare Indecisis: The Alteration of Precedent on the Supreme Court, 1946–1992.* New York: Cambridge University Press, 1995.

Carter, Lief H. *Contemporary Constitutional Lawmaking.* New York: Pergamon Press, 1985.

Clayton, Cornell W., and Howard Gillman, eds. *Supreme Court Decision Making: New Institutionalist Approaches.* Chicago: University of Chicago Press, 1999.

Crosskey, W. W., and William Jeffrey Jr. *Politics and the Constitution in the History of the United States.* Chicago: University of Chicago Press, 1980.

Epstein, Lee, and Jack Knight. *The Choices Justices Make.* Washington, D.C.: CQ Press, 1998.

Epstein, Lee, Jeffrey A. Segal, Harold J. Spaeth, and Thomas G. Walker. *The Supreme Court Compendium: Data, Decisions, and Developments,* 4th ed. Washington, D.C.: CQ Press, 2007.

Farber, Daniel A., and Suzanna Sherry. *Desperately Seeking Certainty.* Chicago: University of Chicago Press, 2002.

Goldstein, Leslie Friedman. *In Defense of the Text.* Savage, Md.: Rowman and Littlefield, 1991.

Levinson, Sanford V. *Constitutional Faith.* Princeton: Princeton University Press, 1988.

Levy, Leonard W. *Origins of the Bill of Rights.* New Haven: Yale University Press, 1999.

Lynch, Joseph M. *Negotiating the Constitution: The Earliest Debates over Original Intent.* Ithaca: Cornell University Press, 1999.

Maltzman, Forrest, Paul J. Wahlbeck, and James Spriggs. *Crafting Law on the Supreme Court: The Collegial Game.* New York: Cambridge University Press, 2000.

Marshall, Thomas. *Public Opinion and the Supreme Court.* New York: Unwin Hyman, 1989.

Murphy, Walter F. *Elements of Judicial Strategy.* Chicago: University of Chicago Press, 1964.

Pacelle, Richard L., Jr. *The Transformation of the Supreme Court's Agenda.* Boulder: Westview Press, 1991.

Perry, H. W., Jr. *Deciding to Decide: Agenda Setting in the United States Supreme Court.* Cambridge: Harvard University Press, 1991.

Posner, Richard. *The Problems of Jurisprudence.* Cambridge: Harvard University Press, 1990.

Pritchett, C. Herman. *The Roosevelt Court.* New York: Macmillan, 1948.

Segal, Jeffrey A., and Harold J. Spaeth. *The Supreme Court and the Attitudinal Model Revisited.* Cambridge: Cambridge University Press, 2002.

Spaeth, Harold J., and Jeffrey A. Segal. *Majority Rule or Minority Will.* New York: Cambridge University Press, 1999.

van Geel, T. R. *Understanding Supreme Court Opinions.* New York: Longman, 1991.

Wechsler, Herbert. "Toward Neutral Principles of Constitutional Law." *Harvard Law Review* 43 (1959): 1–35.

PART II
INSTITUTIONAL AUTHORITY

STRUCTURING THE FEDERAL SYSTEM

One of the first things anyone learns in an American government course is that two concepts undergird our constitutional system. The first is the separation of powers doctrine, under which each of the branches has a distinct function: The legislature makes the laws, the executive implements those laws, and the judiciary interprets them. The second is the notion of checks and balances. Each branch of government imposes limits on the primary functions of the others. For example, the Supreme Court may interpret laws and even strike them down as being in violation of the Constitution. But Congress can attempt to pass legislation to override the Court's decision. If Congress succeeds, the president has the option of vetoing the law, in which case, Congress must decide whether to override the president's veto. Seen in this way, the rule of checks and balances inherent in the system of separation of powers suggests that policy in the United States emanates not from the separate actions of the branches of government but from the interaction among them.

To move beyond the basics of the powers and constraints of institutions requires a consideration of two important subjects. First, we must understand the separation of powers doctrine and why the framers of the Constitution adopted it, a subject we take up in the following pages. Second, because of the unique role played by the judiciary in the American government system, we must grasp the importance of the Supreme Court's decisions relating to the authority of the three branches of government as well as the constitutional constraints placed upon those institutions. We consider these matters in the next three chapters.

ORIGINS OF THE SEPARATION OF POWERS/CHECKS AND BALANCES SYSTEM

Even a casual comparison of the Articles of Confederation with the Constitution reveals major differences in the way the two documents structured the national government (*see Figure 1-1, page 4*). Under the articles, the powers of government were concentrated in the legislature, a unicameral Congress, with the states having equal voting powers. There was no executive or judicial branch separate and independent from the legislature. Issues of separation of powers and checks and balances were not particularly relevant to the articles, largely because the national government had little power that might be abused. The states were capable of checking anything the central government proposed and provided whatever restraints the newly independent nation needed.

The government under the articles failed for the most part because it lacked sufficient power and authority to cope with the problems of the day. The requirements for amending the document were so restrictive that fundamental change within the articles proved impossible. When the Constitutional Convention met in Philadelphia in 1787, the delegates soon concluded that the articles had to be scrapped and replaced with a charter that would provide more effective power for the national government. The framers had experienced conditions of economic decline, crippling taxation policies, interstate barriers to commerce, and isolated but alarming insurrections among the lower economic classes. They saw a newly structured national government as the only method of dealing with the problems besetting the nation in the aftermath of the Revolution.

But allocating significant power to the national government was not without its risks. Many of the framers feared the creation of a federal power capable of dominating the states and abusing individual liberties. It was apparent to all that the new government would have to be structured in a way that the potential for abuse and excess would be minimized. The concept of the separation of powers and its twin, the idea of checks and balances, appealed to the framers as the best way to accomplish these necessary restraints.

The theory of separation of powers was not new to the framers. They were introduced to it by the political philosophy of the day and by their own political experiences. The theories of James Harrington (1611–1677) and Charles de Montesquieu (1689–1755) were particularly influential in this respect. Harrington was an English political philosopher whose emphasis on the importance of property found a sympathetic audience among the former colonists. Harrington's primary work, *Oceana*, published in 1656, was a widely read description of a model government. Incorporated into Harrington's ideal state was the notion that government powers ought to be divided into three parts. A senate made up of the intellectual elite would propose laws; the people, guided by the senate's wisdom, would enact the laws; and a magistrate would execute the laws. This system, Harrington argued, would impose an important balance that would maintain a stable government and protect rights to property.

Harrington's concept of a separation of powers was less well developed than that later proposed by Montesquieu, a French political theorist. Many scholars consider his *Spirit of the Laws* (1748), widely circulated during the second half of the eighteenth century, to be the classic treatise on the separation of powers philosophy. Montesquieu was concerned about government abuse of liberty. In his estimation, liberty could not long prevail if too much power accrued to a single ruler or a single branch of government. He flatly warned, "When the legislative and executive powers are united in the same person, or the same body of magistrates, there can be no liberty. . . . Again, there is no liberty if the judicial power be not separated from the legislative and executive." Although Montesquieu's message was directed at the citizens of his own country, he found a more receptive audience in the United States.

The influence of these political thinkers was reinforced by the political experiences of the framers. The settlers came to the New World largely to escape the abuses of the European governments. The treatment of the colonies by George III taught them that executives were not to be trusted with too much power. They also feared an independent and powerful judiciary, especially if it were not answerable to the people. The framers undoubtedly had the most confidence in the legislature, but they also knew it too had the potential of exceeding proper bounds. The English experience during the reign of Oliver Cromwell was lesson enough that muting the power of the king did not necessarily lead to the elimination of government abuse. What the framers sought was balance, a system in which each branch of government would be strong enough to stop excessive power from flowing into the hands of any other single branch. This necessary balance, as John Adams pointed out in his *Defense of the Constitutions of Government of the United States of America*, would also have the advantage of being able to keep the power-hungry aristocracy in check and prevent the majority from taking the rights away from the minority.

SEPARATION OF POWERS AND THE CONSTITUTION

The debates at the Constitutional Convention and the various plans that were presented for the delegates' consideration all focused on the issue of dividing government power among the three branches as well as between the national government and the states. A general fear of a concentration of power permeated all the discussions. James Madison noted, "The truth is, all men having power ought to be distrusted to a certain degree." The framers' solution to the exceedingly difficult problem of expanding government power, while at the same time reducing the probability of abuse, was found in their proposed new Constitution of the United States.

Although the term *separation of powers* is nowhere to be found in the document, the Constitution plainly adopts the central tenets of the theory. A reading of the first lines of each of the first three articles makes this point clearly.

All legislative Powers herein granted shall be vested in a Congress of the United States, which shall consist of a Senate and House of Representatives. (Article I)

The executive Power shall be vested in a President of the United States of America. (Article II)

The judicial Power of the United States, shall be vested in one supreme Court, and in such inferior Courts as the Congress may from time to time ordain and establish. (Article III)

In the scheme of government incorporated into the Constitution, the legislative, executive, and judicial powers each resided in a separate branch of government. Unless otherwise specified in the document, each branch was limited to the political function granted to it, and that function could not be exercised by either of the other two branches.

In addition to the separation concept, the framers placed into the Constitution a number of mixed powers. Although the document reserves certain functions for specific branches, it also provides explicit checks on the exercise of those powers. As a consequence, each branch of government imposes limits on the primary functions of the others. A few examples illustrate this point.

Congress has the right to pass legislation, but the president may veto those bills.

The president may veto bills passed by Congress, but the legislature may override that veto.

The president may make treaties with foreign powers, but the Senate must ratify those treaties.

The president is commander in chief of the army and navy, but Congress must pass legislation to raise armies, regulate the military, and declare war.

The president may nominate federal judges, but the Senate must confirm them.

The judiciary may interpret the law and even strike down laws as violating the Constitution, but Congress may pass new legislation or propose constitutional amendments.

Congress may pass laws, but the executive must enforce them.

In addition to providing for these offsetting powers, the framers structured each branch so that the criteria and procedures for selecting the officials of each institution differed, as did their tenures. Consequently, each branch has a slightly different source of political power. In the original scheme these differences were even more pronounced than they are today.

In the original version of the Constitution the two houses of Congress were politically dependent upon different selection processes. Members of the House were, as they are today, directly elected by the people, and the seats were apportioned among the states on the basis of population. With terms of only two years, the representatives were required to go back to the people for review on a frequent and regular basis. Senators, on the other hand, were, and still are, representatives of whole states, with each state having two members in the upper chamber. But senators originally were selected by the state legislatures, a system that was not changed until the Seventeenth Amendment, which imposed popular election of senators, was ratified in 1913. The six-year, staggered terms of senators were intended to make the upper house less immediately responsive to the volatile nature of public opinion.

The Constitution dictated that the president be selected by the Electoral College, a group of political elites selected by the people or their representatives who would exercise judgment in casting their ballots among presidential candidates. Although the electors over time have ceased to perform any truly independent selection function, presidential selection remains a step away from direct popular election. The president's four-year term places the office squarely between the tenures conferred on representatives and senators. The original Constitution placed no limits on the number of terms a president could serve, but a traditional two-term limit was observed until 1940 and then imposed by constitutional amendment in 1951.

Differing altogether from the other two branches is the judiciary, which was assigned the least democratic selection system. The people have no direct role in the selection or retention of federal judges. Instead, the president nominates individuals for the federal bench, and the Senate confirms them. Once in office, federal judges serve for terms of good behavior, removable against their will only through impeachment. The framers intended to make the judiciary independent. To do so they created a system in which judges would not depend on the mood of the masses or on a single appointing power. Furthermore, judges would be accountable only to their own philosophies and consciences, with no periodic review or reassessment required.

Through a division of powers, an imposition of checks, and a variation in selection and tenure requirements, the framers hoped to achieve the balanced government they desired. This structure, they thought, would be the greatest protection against abuses of power and government violations of personal liberties and property rights. Many delegates to the Constitutional Convention considered this system of separation of powers a much more effective method of protecting civil liberties than the formal pronouncements of a bill of rights.

Most political observers would conclude that the framers' invention has worked remarkably well. As the government has evolved through the years, the relative strengths of the branches have changed back and forth. At certain times, the judiciary was exceptionally weak, such as during the pre-Marshall era and the years surrounding the Civil War. At other times, the judiciary has been criticized as being too powerful, such as when it repeatedly blocked New Deal legislation in the 1930s or expanded civil liberties during the Warren Court era. The executive also has led the other branches in political power. Beginning with the tenure of Franklin Roosevelt, and extending into the 1970s, one often heard references to the "imperial presidency." But when one branch gains too much power and abuses occur, as in the case of Richard Nixon and the Watergate crisis of the 1970s, the system tends to reimpose the balance the framers intended.

As you read the next three chapters, consider the Supreme Court's decisions against the framers' original understandings of the separation of powers. What powers does each branch have? What are the sources of those powers? How do the powers of one branch offset those of the other two? How has the balance of power among the branches evolved since the Constitution was drafted in 1787?

In addition to assessing their powers, look for areas of conflict among the branches. American political history has been marked with interbranch disputes. The resolution of those disputes, often through Supreme Court decisions, has determined how political power is allocated and exercised. Undoubtedly, the ongoing and inevitable tensions among the branches will continue to spawn constitutional controversies. To the Supreme Court will be left the task of settling such disputes in a manner that is both true to the principles of the founders and responsive to the needs of our times.

CHAPTER 3
THE JUDICIARY

Concerned about the growth of child pornography, especially on the Internet, Congress passed the Child Pornography Prevention Act of 1996. The law prohibited "any visual depiction, including any photograph, film, video, picture, or computer or computer generated image or picture" that "is or appears to be of a minor engaging in sexually explicit conduct."

In *Ashcroft v. Free Speech Coalition* (2002) the U.S. Supreme Court struck down the law for violating the First Amendment's freedom of expression guarantees. The justices found that the law went beyond a valid regulation of obscenity. Not only did the statute fail to conform to the standards set by the Court in previous obscenity decisions, but also its overbroad provisions prohibited legitimate accounts of the sexual behavior of minors.

In many ways, the Court's action was less than startling. For nearly two centuries federal courts have exerted the power of judicial review, the power to review acts of government to determine their compatibility with the U.S. Constitution. And, even though the Constitution does not explicitly give them such power, the courts' authority to do so has been challenged only occasionally. Today we take for granted the notion that federal courts may review government actions and strike them down if they violate constitutional mandates.

Nevertheless, when courts exert this power, as the U.S. Supreme Court did in *Ashcroft v. Free Speech Coalition*, they provoke controversy. Look at it from this perspective: Congress, composed of *elected* officials, passed the Child Pornography Prevention Act, which was then rendered invalid by a Supreme Court of nine *unelected* judges. Such an occurrence strikes some people as quite odd, perhaps even antidemocratic. Why should Americans allow a branch of government over which there is no electoral control to review and nullify the actions of elected government officials? This chapter attempts to answer that question and further our understanding of the federal judiciary and its powers.

We first explore the circumstances leading to the adoption of Article III of the Constitution, which outlines the contours of judicial power. Next, we turn to the development of judicial review in the United States. Judicial review is the primary check that federal courts have on the other branches of government. Because this power can be awesome in scope, many tend to emphasize it but overlook the factors that constrain its use, as well as other checks on the power of the Court. Therefore, in the final section of this chapter, we explore the limits on judicial power.

ESTABLISHMENT OF THE FEDERAL JUDICIARY

The federal judicial system is built on a foundation created by two major statements of the 1780s: Article III of the U.S. Constitution and the Judiciary Act of 1789. In this section we consider both, with an emphasis on their content and the debate they provoked. Note, in particular, the degree to which the major controversies reflect more general concerns about federalism. Designing and fine-tuning the U.S. system of government required many compromises over the balance of power between the federal government and the states, and Article III and the Judiciary Act are no exceptions.

Article III

The framers of the Constitution spent days upon days debating the contents of Article I (dealing with the legislature) and Article II (centering on the executive), but they had comparatively little trouble drafting Article III. Indeed, it caused the least controversy of any major constitutional provision. Why? One reason is that the states and Great Britain had well-established court systems, and the founders had firsthand knowledge about the workings of courts—knowledge they lacked about the other political institutions they were creating. Also, thirty-four of the fifty-five delegates to the Constitutional Convention were lawyers or at least had some training in the law. They held a common vision of the general role courts should play in the new polity.[1]

That vision was expressed by Alexander Hamilton in Federalist No. 78. Hamilton specifically referred to the judiciary as the "least dangerous branch" of government; he (and virtually all of the founders) saw the courts as legal, not political, bodies. He wrote, "If judges should be disposed to exercise *will* instead of *judgment,* the consequences would equally be the substitution of their pleasure to that of the legislative body." To ensure that judges did not become legislators, the framers agreed on the need for judicial independence. They sought to accomplish this goal by giving jurists life tenure rather than subjecting them to periodic public checks through the electoral process. Furthermore, they placed a provision in Article III prohibiting the reduction of judicial salaries during terms of continuous service, thereby barring economic retaliation by legislators upset with court decisions.

That the framers shared a fundamental view of the role of the federal judiciary does not mean that they agreed on all the specifics. They had many debates over the structure of the American legal system. They agreed

that there would be at least one federal court, the Supreme Court of the United States, but disagreed over the establishment of federal tribunals inferior to the Supreme Court. The Virginia Plan, which served as the basis for many of the proposals debated at the convention, suggested that Congress should establish lower federal courts. Delegates who favored a strong national government agreed with this plan, and some of them wanted to use Article III to create such courts.

But delegates who favored states' rights over those of the national government vehemently objected to the creation of any federal tribunals, other than the U.S. Supreme Court. As one delegate, Pierce Butler of South Carolina, put it, "The people will not bear such innovations. The states will revolt at such encroachments."[2] Instead of creating new federal courts, states' rights delegates proposed that the existing state courts should hear cases in the first instance, with an allowance for appeals to the U.S. Supreme Court. In the end, the issue was unresolved and the delegates left the matter of the lower courts for Congress to determine. In other words, Article III does not create lower federal courts; rather, it gives Congress the option of doing so. In the words of Article III, Section 1, "The judicial Power of the United States, shall be vested in one supreme Court, and in such inferior Courts as the Congress may from time to time ordain and establish."

The First Congress (with its Federalist majority) took full advantage of Section 1 by immediately passing the Judiciary Act of 1789, which established lower federal courts. That Congress would take such an action was not a surprise: The majority of the founders anticipated the law because much of Article III—specifically Section 2, the longest part—defines the jurisdiction of these federal courts that did not yet exist. By spelling out their jurisdiction, the framers provided the courts with the authority to hear cases involving certain subjects or brought by certain parties. The framers also defined the jurisdiction of the U.S. Supreme Court, the one judicial body they did create. Its jurisdiction was defined in terms of original and appellate authority (see Box 3-1).

---

1. See Daniel A. Farber and Suzanna Sherry, *A History of the American Constitution,* 2nd ed. (St. Paul: Thomson/West, 2005), 65.

2. Quoted in ibid., 71.

Jurisdiction of the Lower Federal Courts

Subjects Falling under Their Authority

- Cases involving the U.S. Constitution, federal laws, and treaties
- Cases affecting ambassadors, public ministers, and consuls
- Cases of admiralty and maritime jurisdiction

Parties Falling under Their Authority

- United States
- Controversies between two or more states
- Controversies between a state and citizens of another state[a]
- Controversies between citizens of different states
- Controversies between citizens of the same state claiming lands under grants of different states
- Controversies between a state, or the citizens thereof, and foreign states, citizens, or subjects

Jurisdiction of the Supreme Court

Original Jurisdiction

- Cases affecting ambassadors, public ministers, and consuls
- Cases to which a state is a party

Appellate Jurisdiction

- Cases falling under the jurisdiction of the lower federal courts, "with such Exceptions, and under such Regulations as the Congress shall make."

a. In 1795 this was modified by the Eleventh Amendment, which removed from federal jurisdiction those cases in which a state is sued by the citizens of another state.

ginia Plan, while others suggested that appointments be left to the Senate. In the end, the delegates decided that the appointment power should be given to the president, with the "advice and consent" of the Senate. Accordingly, the power to appoint federal judges is located in Article II, the section describing the executive power, rather than Article III. Since 1789 the Senate's "advice and consent" role has been read to mean that it must approve presidential nominees by a majority vote. And the Senate has taken this role quite seriously, rejecting outright 12 of the 158 Supreme Court nominees since 1795—a greater number (proportionately speaking) than for any other category of presidential appointees requiring Senate approval.

Another source of debate was the proposal by James Madison for the creation of a council of revision, which would be composed of Supreme Court justices and the president of the United States and have the power to veto legislative acts. But, as Daniel A. Farber and Suzanna Sherry write, "Madison or one of his fellow nationalists proposed this Council of Revision four separate times, and each time it was soundly defeated."[3] In *Marbury v. Madison* (1803) Chief Justice John Marshall in essence articulated such veto power for the Court. Those who take a dim view of Marshall's decision occasionally point to the delegates' rejection of a council of revision as proof that Marshall skirted the founders' intent.

The Judiciary Act of 1789

It fell to the First Congress to give life to the court system outlined in Article III of the Constitution. The Judiciary Act of 1789 is a long and relatively complex law that, at its core, had two purposes. First, it established a federal court structure by providing for a Supreme Court, circuit courts, and district courts. Under the law, the Supreme Court was to have one chief justice and five associate justices. That the Court initially had only six members illustrates an important point: Congress, not the U.S. Constitution, determines the number of justices on the Supreme Court. Since 1869 that number has been fixed at nine.

A second area of contention at the 1787 convention was the appointment of federal judges. Again, the Virginia Plan's suggestion—that Congress appoint these judges—served as the focus of debate. Some of the delegates wanted the language of Article III to reflect the Vir-

3. Farber and Sherry, *A History of the American Constitution*, 88.

FIGURE 3-1 The Federal Court System under the Judiciary Act of 1789

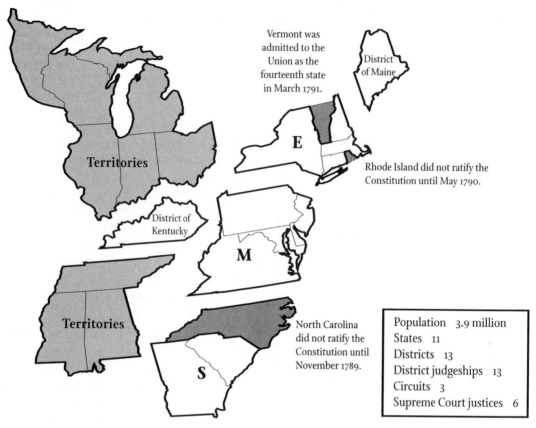

Vermont was admitted to the Union as the fourteenth state in March 1791.

District of Maine

E

Rhode Island did not ratify the Constitution until May 1790.

Territories

District of Kentucky

M

Territories

North Carolina did not ratify the Constitution until November 1789.

S

Population	3.9 million
States	11
Districts	13
District judgeships	13
Circuits	3
Supreme Court justices	6

SOURCE: Russell R. Wheeler and Cynthia Harrison, *Creating the Federal Judicial System,* 2nd ed. (Washington, D.C.: Federal Judicial Center, 1994), 5.

NOTE: The First Judiciary Act created thirteen districts and placed eleven of them in three circuits: the Eastern, Middle, and Southern. Each district had a district court, a trial court with a single district judge and primarily admiralty jurisdiction. A circuit court also met in each district of the circuit and was composed of the district judge and two Supreme Court justices. The circuit courts exercised primarily diversity and criminal jurisdiction and heard appeals from the district courts in some cases. The districts of Maine and Kentucky (parts of the states of Massachusetts and Virginia, respectively) were part of no circuit; their district courts exercised both district and circuit court jurisdiction.

As Figure 3-1 shows, the act also created thirteen district courts. Each of the eleven states that had ratified the Constitution received a court, with separate tribunals created for Maine and Kentucky, which were then parts of Massachusetts and Virginia, respectively. District courts, then as now, were presided over by one judge. But the three newly established circuit courts were quite extraordinary in composition. Congress grouped the district courts—except Kentucky and Maine—geographically into the eastern, middle, or southern circuits and put one district court judge and two Supreme Court justices in

charge of each. In other words, three judges would hear cases in the circuits. Today, the circuit courts of appeals continue to hear cases in panels of three, but district or Supreme Court judges normally do not sit on these panels. Instead, the president appoints judges specifically to the circuit courts of appeals.

A second goal of the Judiciary Act was to specify the jurisdiction of the federal courts. Section 2 of Article III speaks broadly about the authority of federal courts, giving them jurisdiction over cases involving particular parties or subjects or, in the case of the Supreme Court, original and appellate jurisdiction *(see Box 3-1)*. The Judiciary Act provided more specific information, defining the parameters of authority for each of the newly established courts and for the U.S. Supreme Court. The district courts were to serve as trial courts, hearing cases involving admiralty issues, forfeitures and penalties, petty federal crimes, and minor U.S. civil cases. Congress recognized that some of these courts would be busier than others and fixed judicial salaries accordingly. For example, Delaware judges received only $800 for their services, while their counterparts in South Carolina, a coastal state that would generate many admiralty disputes, earned $1,800.[4]

Unlike today's courts, the original circuit courts were trial courts with jurisdiction over cases involving citizens from different states and over major federal criminal and civil cases. Congress also gave these courts limited appellate authority to hear major civil and admiralty disputes coming out of the district courts.

Finally, the 1789 act contained several important provisions concerning the jurisdiction of the U.S. Supreme Court. Section 13 reiterated the Court's authority over suits in the first instance (its original jurisdiction) and gave the justices appellate jurisdiction over major civil disputes, those involving more than $2,000—a good deal of money back then. Section 13 also spoke about the Court's authority to issue writs of mandamus, judicial orders that command a public official to carry out a particular act or duty: "The Supreme Court . . . shall have the power to issue . . . writs of mandamus, in cases warranted by the principles and usages of law, to any courts appointed, or persons holding office, under the authority of the United States." This matter may seem trivial, but, as we shall see, the Court's interpretation of this particular provision formed the centerpiece for *Marbury v. Madison*.

Another part of the act—Section 25—expanded the Court's appellate authority under Article III, enabling it to review certain kinds of cases coming out of the states. Specifically, the Supreme Court could now hear appeals from the highest state courts if those tribunals upheld a state law against claims that the law violated the U.S. Constitution or denied some claim based on the Constitution, federal laws, or treaties.

At first glance, the components of the 1789 act—its establishment of a federal court system and of rules governing that system—appear to favor the Federalists' position. Recall that Anti-Federalist delegates at the Constitutional Convention did not want the document even to mention lower federal tribunals, much less to give Congress the authority to establish them. The 1789 act does that and more: It goes so far as to give the Supreme Court the power to review state supreme court cases—surely an Anti-Federalist's worst nightmare! But it would be a mistake to believe that the act did not take into account the position taken by states' rights advocates. For example, the 1789 act used state lines as the boundaries for the district and circuit courts. Tying federal judicial districts to state boundaries may have been a concession to the Anti-Federalists who wanted the judges of the federal courts to feel a part of the state's legal and political culture.

Whichever side won or lost, it is true that passage of the 1789 Judiciary Act was a defining moment in American legal history. It established the first federal court system, one that is strikingly similar to today's system. And, as the following pages reveal, it paved the way for landmark constitutional cases—*Marbury v. Madison*, **Martin v. Hunter's Lessee**, and **Cohens v. Virginia**—all of which centered on judicial review, the major power of the federal judiciary.

JUDICIAL REVIEW

Even though judicial review is a powerful tool of federal courts and there is some evidence that the framers intended courts to have it, it is not mentioned in the Constitution. Early in U.S. history, federal courts claimed it for themselves. In **Hylton v. United States** (1796), Daniel Hylton challenged the constitutionality of a 1793 federal tax on carriages. According to Hylton, the act violated the constitutional mandate that direct taxes must be apportioned on the basis of population. With only three justices participating, the Court upheld the act. But even by considering the matter, the Court in effect used its authority to review acts of Congress.

---

4. Russell R. Wheeler and Cynthia Harrison, *Creating the Federal Judicial System* (Washington, D.C.: Federal Judicial Center, 1989), 6.

Not until 1803, however, did the Court invoke judicial review to strike down legislation deemed incompatible with the U.S. Constitution. That decision came in the landmark case *Marbury v. Madison.* How does Chief Justice Marshall justify the Court's power to strike down legislation in light of the failure of the newly framed Constitution to confer on it judicial review?

Marbury v. Madison

1 Cr. (5 U.S.) 137 (1803)
http://laws.findlaw.com/US/5/137.html
Vote: 4 (Chase, Marshall, Paterson, Washington)
      0

Opinion of the Court: Marshall
Not participating: Cushing, Moore

When voting in the presidential election of 1800 was over, it was apparent that Federalist president John Adams had lost after a long and bitter campaign, but it was not known who had won. The voting resulted in a tie between Republican candidate Thomas Jefferson and his running mate, Aaron Burr, and the election had to be settled in the House of Representatives. In February 1801 the House elected Jefferson. Because the Federalists had lost both the presidential election and their majority in Congress, they took steps before they left office to maintain control of the third branch of government, the judiciary. The lame-duck Congress enacted the Circuit Court Act of 1801, which created six new circuit courts and several district courts to accommodate the new states of Kentucky, Tennessee, and Vermont. These new courts needed judges and support staff such as attorneys, marshals, and clerks. As a result, during the last six months of his term in office, Adams made more than two hundred nominations, with sixteen judgeships (called the "midnight appointments" because of the rush to complete them before Adams's term expired) approved by the Senate during his last two weeks in office.

An even more important opportunity arose in December 1800, when the third chief justice of the United States, Federalist Oliver Ellsworth, resigned so that Adams—not Jefferson—could name his replacement. Adams first of-

President John Adams, who signed judicial commissions, the so-called "midnight appointments," on his last night in office. Several appointees, including William Marbury, did not receive their commissions. The Jefferson administration's refusal to deliver them led to the famous case of *Marbury v. Madison* (1803) in which the Supreme Court clearly asserted its power of judicial review.

fered the post to John Jay, who had served as the first chief justice before leaving to take the more prestigious office of governor of New York. When Jay refused, Adams turned to his secretary of state, John Marshall, an ardent Federalist. The Senate confirmed Marshall in January 1801, but he also continued as secretary of state.

In addition, the Federalist Congress passed the Organic Act, which authorized Adams to appoint forty-two justices of the peace for the District of Columbia. It was this seemingly innocuous law that set the stage for the dramatic case of *Marbury v. Madison.* In the confusion of the Adams administration's last days in office, Marshall, the outgoing secretary of state, failed to deliver some of these commissions. When the new administration came into office, James Madison, the new secretary of state, acting under orders from Jefferson, refused to deliver at least five commissions.[5] Indeed, some years later, Jefferson explained the situation in this way:

I found the commissions on the table of the Department of State, on my entrance into office, and I forbade their delivery. Whatever is in the Executive offices is certainly deemed to be in the hands of the President, and in this case, was actually in my hands, because when I countermanded them, there was as yet no Secretary of State.[6]

As a result, in 1801 William Marbury and three others who were denied their commissions went directly to the Supreme Court and asked it to issue a writ of mandamus, ordering Madison to deliver the commissions. Marbury could take his case directly to the Court because Section 13 of the 1789 Judiciary Act gave the Court the power to issue writs of mandamus to anyone holding federal office.

In this volatile political climate, Marshall, now serving as chief justice, was perhaps in the most tenuous position of all. On the one hand, he had been a supporter of the Federalist Party, which now looked to him to "scold" the Jefferson administration. On the other, Marshall wanted to avoid a confrontation between the Jefferson administration and the Supreme Court, which not only seemed imminent but also could end in disaster for the struggling nation. Note the year in which the Court handed down the decision in *Marbury*. The case was not decided until two years after Marbury filed suit because Congress and the Jefferson administration had abolished the 1802 term of the Court.

The following opinion of the court was delivered by the CHIEF JUSTICE.

Opinion of the Court.

The peculiar delicacy of this case, the novelty of some of its circumstances, and the real difficulty attending the points which occur in it, require a complete exposition of the principles, on which the opinion to be given by the court, is founded. . . .

In the order in which the court has viewed this subject, the following questions have been considered and decided.

1st. Has the applicant a right to the commission he demands?

2dly. If he has a right, and that right has been violated, do the laws of his country afford him a remedy?

3dly. If they do afford him a remedy, is it a *mandamus* issuing from this court?

The first object of enquiry is,

1st. Has the applicant a right to the commission he demands. . . .

In order to determine whether he is entitled to this commission, it becomes necessary to enquire whether he has been appointed to the office. For if he has been appointed, the law continues him in office for five years, and he is entitled to the possession of those evidences of office, which, being completed, became his property. . . .

It is . . . decidedly the opinion of the court, that when a commission has been signed by the President, the appointment is made; and that the commission is complete, when the seal of the United States has been affixed to it by the secretary of state. . . .

Mr. Marbury, then, since his commission was signed by the President, and sealed by the secretary of state, was appointed; and as the law creating the office, gave the officer a right to hold for five years, independent of the executive, the appointment was not revocable; but vested in the officer legal rights, which are protected by the laws of his country.

To withhold his commission, therefore, is an act deemed by the court not warranted by law, but violative of a vested legal right.

This brings us to the second enquiry; which is,

2dly. If he has a right, and that right has been violated, do the laws of his country afford him a remedy?

The very essence of civil liberty certainly consists in the right of every individual to claim the protection of the laws, whenever he receives an injury. One of the first duties of government is to afford that protection. . . .

The government of the United States has been emphatically termed a government of laws, and not of men. It will certainly cease to deserve this high appellation, if the laws furnish no remedy for the violation of a vested legal right. . . .

It is then the opinion of the court,

---

5. Historical accounts differ, but it seems that Jefferson decreased the number of Adams's appointments to justice of the peace positions to thirty from forty-two. Twenty-five of the thirty appointees received their commissions, but five—including William Marbury—did not. See Francis N. Stites, *John Marshall* (Boston: Little, Brown, 1981), 84.

6. Quoted in Charles Warren, *The Supreme Court in United States History*, Vol. 1 (Boston: Little, Brown, 1922), 244.

BOX 3-2 JOHN MARSHALL (1801–1835)

THE ELDEST of fifteen children, John Marshall was born September 24, 1755, in a log cabin on the Virginia frontier near Germantown. His father, descended from Welsh immigrants, was an assistant surveyor to George Washington and member of the Virginia House of Burgesses. His mother was the daughter of an educated Scottish clergyman.

As a youth, Marshall was tutored by two clergymen, but his primary teacher was his father, who introduced him to the study of English literature and Blackstone's *Commentaries on the Laws of England.*

During the Revolutionary War, young Marshall participated in the siege of Norfolk as a member of the Culpeper Minute Men and was present at Brandywine, Monmouth, Stony Point, and Valley Forge as a member of the third Virginia Regiment. In 1779 he returned home to await another assignment but was never recalled. He left the Continental Army with the rank of captain in 1781.

Marshall was self-taught in the law; his only formal instruction came in 1780 when he attended George Wythe's course of law lectures at the College of William and Mary. He was admitted to the bar that same year and gradually developed a lucrative practice, specializing in defending Virginians against their pre–Revolutionary War British creditors.

On January 3, 1783, Marshall married Mary Willis Ambler, daughter of the Virginia state treasurer, and established a home in Richmond. The couple had ten children, only six of whom survived to maturity. Marshall spent many years attending to the needs of his wife, who suffered from a chronic illness. She died December 25, 1831.

From 1796 until about 1806, Marshall's life was dominated by the pressures of meeting debts incurred by a land investment he had made in the northern neck of Virginia. It has been speculated that his need for money motivated him to write *The Life of George Washington,* which appeared in five volumes from 1804 to 1807. He later condensed the work into a schoolbook, but it proved not to be the answer to his financial difficulties.

1st. That by signing the commission of Mr. Marbury, the president of the United States appointed him a justice of peace, for the county of Washington in the district of Columbia; and that the seal of the United States, affixed thereto by the secretary of state, is conclusive testimony of the verity of the signature, and of the completion of the appointment; and that the appointment conferred on him a legal right to the office for the space of five years.

2dly. That, having this legal title to the office, he has a consequent right to the commission; a refusal to deliver which, is a plain violation of that right, for which the laws of his country afford him a remedy.

It remains to be enquired whether,

3dly. He is entitled to the remedy for which he applies. . . .

The act to establish the judicial courts of the United States authorizes the supreme court "to issue writs of mandamus, in cases warranted by the principles and usages of law, to any courts appointed, or persons holding office, under the authority of the United States."

The secretary of state, being a person holding an office under the authority of the United States, is precisely within the letter of the description; and if this court is not authorized to issue a writ of mandamus to such an officer, it must be because the law is unconstitutional, and therefore absolutely incapable of conferring the authority, and assigning the duties which its words purport to confer and assign.

Marshall was elected to the Virginia House of Delegates from Fauquier County in 1782 and 1784. He reentered the House in 1787 and was instrumental in Virginia's ratification of the new U.S. Constitution. At the state ratifying convention his primary attention was directed to the need for judicial review. By 1789 Marshall was considered to be a leading Federalist in the state.

Marshall refused many appointments in the Federalist administrations of George Washington and John Adams, including U.S. attorney general in 1795, associate justice of the Supreme Court in 1798, and secretary of war in 1800. In 1796 he refused an appointment by President Adams as minister to France, but the following year he agreed to serve as one of three special envoys sent to smooth relations with that country. This mission, known as the "XYZ Affair," failed when French diplomats demanded a bribe as a condition for negotiation. Congress, however, was greatly impressed by the stubborn resistance of the American emissaries, and Marshall received a generous grant as a reward for his participation.

In 1799 Washington persuaded Marshall to run for the U.S. House of Representatives as a Federalist from Richmond. His career in the House was brief, however, for in 1800 he became secretary of state under Adams. When Adams retired to his home in Massachusetts for a few months that year, Marshall served as the effective head of government.

Chief Justice Oliver Ellsworth resigned in 1800, and Adams offered the position to John Jay, who had been the Court's first chief justice. Jay declined, and the Federalists urged Adams to elevate Associate Justice William Paterson. But on January 20, 1801, Adams nominated Marshall instead. The Senate confirmed Marshall on January 27 by a voice vote.

As the primary founder of the American system of constitutional law, including the doctrine of judicial review, Marshall participated in more than 1,000 Supreme Court decisions, writing more than 500 of them himself. In 1807 he presided over the treason trial of Aaron Burr in the Richmond circuit court, locking horns with Thomas Jefferson, who sought an absolute conviction. Burr was acquitted.

In 1831, at age seventy-six, Marshall underwent successful surgery in Philadelphia for the removal of kidney stones. Three years later, he developed an enlarged liver, and his health declined rapidly. Marshall died in Philadelphia on July 6, 1835, three months short of his eightieth birthday. Legend has it that the Liberty Bell cracked as it tolled in mourning.

SOURCE: Adapted from David Savage, *Guide to the U.S. Supreme Court*, 4th ed. (Washington, D.C.: CQ Press, 2004), 929–930.

The constitution vests the whole judicial power of the United States in one supreme court, and such inferior courts as congress shall, from time to time, ordain and establish. This power is expressly extended to all cases arising under the laws of the United States; and consequently, in some form, may be exercised over the present case; because the right claimed is given by a law of the United States.

In the distribution of this power it is declared that "the supreme court shall have original jurisdiction in all cases affecting ambassadors, other public ministers and consuls, and those in which a state shall be a party. In all other cases, the supreme court shall have appellate jurisdiction."

It has been insisted, at the bar, that as the original grant of jurisdiction, to the supreme and inferior courts, is general, and the clause, assigning original jurisdiction to the supreme court, contains no negative or restrictive words; the power remains to the legislature, to assign original jurisdiction to that court in other cases than those specified in the article which has been recited; provided those cases belong to the judicial power of the United States.

If it had been intended to leave it in the discretion of the legislature to apportion the judicial power between the supreme and inferior courts according to the will of that body, it would certainly have been useless to have proceeded further than to have defined the judicial power, and the tri-

William Marbury, whose suit against James Madison led to a landmark decision in 1803. John Marshall's opinion in *Marbury v. Madison* established the Court's authority to review the constitutionality of acts of Congress.

bunals in which it should be vested. The subsequent part of the section is mere surplussage, is entirely without meaning, if such is to be the construction. If congress remains at liberty to give this court appellate jurisdiction, where the constitution has declared their jurisdiction shall be original; and original jurisdiction where the constitution has declared it shall be appellate; the distribution of jurisdiction, made in the constitution, is form without substance.

Affirmative words are often, in their operation, negative of other objects than those affirmed; and in this case, a negative or exclusive sense must be given to them or they have no operation at all.

It cannot be presumed that any clause in the constitution is intended to be without effect; and therefore such a construction is inadmissible, unless the words require it.

If the solicitude of the convention, respecting our peace with foreign powers, induced a provision that the supreme court should take original jurisdiction in cases which might be supposed to affect them; yet the clause would have proceeded no further than to provide for such cases, if no further restriction on the powers of congress had been intended. That they should have appellate jurisdiction in all other cases, with such exceptions as congress might make, is no restriction; unless the words be deemed exclusive of original jurisdiction.

When an instrument organizing fundamentally a judicial system, divides it into one supreme, and so many inferior courts as the legislature may ordain and establish; then enumerates its powers, and proceeds so far to distribute them, as to define the jurisdiction of the supreme court by declaring the cases in which it shall take original jurisdiction, and that in others it shall take appellate jurisdiction; the plain import of the words seems to be, that in one class of cases its jurisdiction is original, and not appellate; in the other it is appellate, and not original. If any other construction would render the clause inoperative, that is an additional reason for rejecting such other construction, and for adhering to their obvious meaning.

To enable this court then to issue a mandamus, it must be shewn to be an exercise of appellate jurisdiction, or to be necessary to enable them to exercise appellate jurisdiction.

It has been stated at the bar that the appellate jurisdiction may be exercised in a variety of forms, and that if it be the will of the legislature that a mandamus should be used for that purpose, that will must be obeyed. This is true, yet the jurisdiction must be appellate, not original.

It is the essential criterion of appellate jurisdiction, that it revises and corrects the proceedings in a cause already instituted, and does not create that cause. Although, therefore, a mandamus may be directed to courts, yet to issue such a writ to an officer for the delivery of a paper, is in effect the same as to sustain an original action for that paper, and therefore seems not to belong to appellate, but to original jurisdiction. Neither is it necessary in such a case as this, to enable the court to exercise its appellate jurisdiction.

The authority, therefore, given to the supreme court, by the act establishing the judicial courts of the United States, to issue writs of mandamus to public officers, appears not to be warranted by the constitution; and it becomes necessary to enquire whether a jurisdiction, so conferred, can be exercised.

The question, whether an act, repugnant to the constitution, can become the law of the land, is a question deeply interesting to the United States; but, happily, not of an intricacy proportioned to its interest. It seems only necessary to recognise certain principles, supposed to have been long and well established, to decide it.

That the people have an original right to establish, for their future government, such principles as, in their opinion, shall most conduce to their own happiness, is the basis, on which the whole American fabric has been erected. The exercise of this original right is a very great exertion; nor can it, nor ought it to be frequently repeated. The principles, therefore, so established, are deemed fundamental. And as the authority, from which they proceed, is supreme, and can seldom act, they are designed to be permanent.

This original and supreme will organizes the government, and assigns, to different departments, their respective powers. It may either stop here; or establish certain limits not to be transcended by those departments.

The government of the United States is of the latter description. The powers of the legislature are defined, and limited; and that those limits may not be mistaken, or forgotten, the constitution is written. To what purpose are powers limited, and to what purpose is that limitation committed to writing, if these limits may, at any time, be passed by those intended to be restrained? The distinction, between a government with limited and unlimited powers, is abolished, if those limits do not confine the persons on whom they are imposed, and if acts prohibited and acts allowed, are of equal obligation. It is a proposition too plain to be contested, that the constitution controls any legislative act repugnant to it; or, that the legislature may alter the constitution by an ordinary act.

Between these alternatives there is no middle ground. The constitution is either a superior, paramount law, unchangeable by ordinary means, or it is on a level with ordinary legislative acts, and like other acts, is alterable when the legislature shall please to alter it.

If the former part of the alternative be true, then a legislative act contrary to the constitution is not law: if the latter part be true, then written constitutions are absurd attempts, on the part of the people, to limit a power, in its own nature illimitable.

Certainly all those who have framed written constitutions contemplate them as forming the fundamental and paramount law of the nation, and consequently the theory of every such government must be, that an act of the legislature, repugnant to the constitution, is void.

This theory is essentially attached to a written constitution, and is consequently to be considered, by this court, as one of the fundamental principles of our society. It is not therefore to be lost sight of in the further consideration of this subject.

If an act of the legislature, repugnant to the constitution, is void, does it, notwithstanding its invalidity, bind the courts, and oblige them to give it effect? Or, in other words, though it be not law, does it constitute a rule as operative as if it was a law? This would be to overthrow in fact what was established in theory; and would seem, at first view, an absurdity too gross to be insisted on. It shall, however, receive a more attentive consideration.

It is emphatically the province and duty of the judicial department to say what the law is. Those who apply the rule to particular cases, must of necessity expound and interpret that rule. If two laws conflict with each other, the courts must decide on the operation of each.

So if a law be in opposition to the constitution; if both the law and the constitution apply to a particular case, so that the court must either decide that case conformably to the law, disregarding the constitution; or conformably to the constitution, disregarding the law; the court must determine which of these conflicting rules governs the case. This is of the very essence of judicial duty.

If then the courts are to regard the constitution; and the constitution is superior to any ordinary act of the legislature; the constitution, and not such ordinary act, must govern the case to which they both apply.

Those then who controvert the principle that the constitution is to be considered, in court, as a paramount law, are reduced to the necessity of maintaining that courts must close their eyes on the constitution, and see only the law.

This doctrine would subvert the very foundation of all written constitutions. It would declare that an act, which, according to the principles and theory of our government, is entirely void; is yet, in practice, completely obligatory. It would declare, that if the legislature shall do what is expressly forbidden, such act, notwithstanding the express prohibition, is in reality effectual. It would be giving to the legislature a practical and real omnipotence, with the same breath which professes to restrict their powers within narrow limits. It is prescribing limits, and declaring that those limits may be passed at pleasure.

That it thus reduces to nothing what we have deemed the greatest improvement on political institutions—a written constitution—would of itself be sufficient, in America, where written constitutions have been viewed with so much reverence, for rejecting the construction. But the peculiar expressions of the constitution of the United States furnish additional arguments in favour of its rejection.

The judicial power of the United States is extended to all cases arising under the constitution.

Could it be the intention of those who gave this power, to say that, in using it, the constitution should not be looked into? That a case arising under the constitution should be decided without examining the instrument under which it arises?

This is too extravagant to be maintained.

In some cases then, the constitution must be looked into by the judges. And if they can open it at all, what part of it are they forbidden to read, or to obey?

There are many other parts of the constitution which serve to illustrate this subject.

It is declared that "no tax or duty shall be laid on articles exported from any state." Suppose a duty on the export of cotton, of tobacco, or of flour; and a suit instituted to recover it. Ought judgment to be rendered in such a case? ought the judges to close their eyes on the constitution, and only see the law?

The constitution declares that "no bill of attainder or *ex post facto* law shall be passed."

If, however, such a bill should be passed and a person should be prosecuted under it; must the court condemn to death those victims whom the constitution endeavours to preserve?

"No person," says the constitution, "shall be convicted of treason unless on the testimony of two witnesses to the same overt act, or on confession in open court."

Here the language of the constitution is addressed especially to the courts. It prescribes, directly for them, a rule of evidence not to be departed from. If the legislature should change that rule, and declare *one* witness, or a confession *out* of court, sufficient for conviction, must the constitutional principle yield to the legislative act?

From these, and many other selections which might be made, it is apparent, that the Framers of the constitution contemplated that instrument, as a rule for the government of *courts,* as well as of the legislature.

Why otherwise does it direct the judges to take an oath to support it? This oath certainly applies, in an especial manner, to their conduct in their official character. How immoral to impose it on them, if they were to be used as the instruments, and the knowing instruments, for violating what they swear to support!

The oath of office, too, imposed by the legislature, is completely demonstrative of the legislative opinion on this subject. It is in these words, "I do solemnly swear that I will administer justice without respect to persons, and do equal right to the poor and to the rich; and that I will faithfully and impartially discharge all the duties incumbent on me as according to the best of my abilities and understanding, agreeably to *the constitution,* and laws of the United States."

Why does a judge swear to discharge his duties agreeably to the constitution of the United States, if that constitution forms no rule for his government? if it is closed upon him, and cannot be inspected by him?

If such be the real state of things, this is worse than solemn mockery. To prescribe, or to take this oath, becomes equally a crime.

It is also not entirely unworthy of observation, that in declaring what shall be the *supreme law* of the land, the *constitution* itself is first mentioned; and not the laws of the United States generally, but those only which shall be made in *pursuance* of the constitution, have that rank.

Thus, the particular phraseology of the constitution of the United States confirms and strengthens the principle, supposed to be essential to all written constitutions, that a law repugnant to the constitution is void; and that *courts,* as well as other departments, are bound by that instrument.

The rule must be discharged.

Scholars differ about Marshall's opinion in *Marbury,* but even his critics acknowledge his shrewdness. Think about the way the chief justice dealt with a most delicate political situation. By ruling against Marbury, who never did receive his commission *(see Box 3-3),* Marshall avoided a potentially devastating clash with the new president; but, by exerting the power of judicial review, he sent a clear signal to Jefferson that the Court was going to be an important part of the American government.

BOX 3-3 AFTERMATH . . .
MARBURY V. MADISON

FROM meager beginnings, William Marbury gained political and economic influence in his home state of Maryland and became a strong supporter of John Adams and the Federalist Party. Unlike others of his day who rose in wealth through agriculture or trade, Marbury made his way to prominence through banking and finance. At age thirty-eight, he saw his appointment to be a justice of the peace as a public validation of his rising economic status and social prestige. Marbury never received his judicial position; instead, he returned to his financial activities, ultimately becoming the president of a bank in Georgetown. He died in 1835, the same year as Chief Justice John Marshall.

Other participants in the famous decision played major roles in the early history of our nation. Thomas Jefferson, who refused to honor Marbury's appointment, served two terms as chief executive, leaving office in 1809 as one of the nation's most revered presidents. James Madison, the secretary of state who carried out Jefferson's order depriving Marbury of his judgeship, became the nation's fourth president, serving from 1809 to 1817. Following the *Marbury* decision, Chief Justice Marshall led the Court for an additional thirty-two years. His tenure was marked with fundamental rulings expanding the power of the judiciary and enhancing the position of the federal government relative to the states. He is rightfully regarded as history's most influential chief justice.

Although the *Marbury* decision established the power of judicial review, it is ironic that the Marshall Court never again used its authority to strike down a piece of congressional legislation. In fact, it was not until *Scott v. Sandford* (1857), more than two decades after Marshall's death, that the Court once again invalidated a congressional statute.

SOURCES: John A. Garraty, "The Case of the Missing Commissions," in John A. Garraty, *Quarrels That Have Shaped the Constitution* (New York: Harper and Row, 1962); David F. Forte, "Marbury's Travail: Federalist Politics and William Marbury's Appointment as Justice of the Peace," *Catholic University Law Review* 45 (1996): 349–402.

The decision helped to establish John Marshall's reputation as perhaps the greatest justice in Supreme Court history. *Marbury* was just the first in what would be a long line of seminal Marshall decisions. But most important here, *Marbury* fully established the Court's authority to review and strike down government actions that were incompatible with the Constitution. In Marshall's view, such authority, while not explicit in the Constitution, was clearly intended by the framers of that document.

Note that in *Marbury* the Court addressed only the power to review acts of the federal government. Could the Court exert judicial review over the states? According to Section 25 of the 1789 Judiciary Act, indeed, it could. Recall from our discussion of the act that Congress expanded the Supreme Court's appellate jurisdiction to encompass appeals from the highest state courts, if those tribunals upheld a state law against challenges of unconstitutionality or denied some claim based on the U.S. Constitution, federal laws, or treaties. But the mere existence of this statute did not necessarily mean that either state courts or the Supreme Court would follow it. Because Section 25 expanded the Supreme Court's jurisdiction, it was always possible that the justices might question Congress's authority to do so, even though the section involved appellate, not original, jurisdiction.

More important was the potentially hostile reaction from the states, which in the 1780s and 1790s zealously guarded their power from federal encroachment. Even if the Court were to take advantage of its ability to review state court decisions, it was more than likely that state courts would disregard its rulings. Still, threats from the states did not deter the Court. In two cases coming from Virginia, *Martin v. Hunter's Lessee* (1816) and *Cohens v. Virginia* (1821), the justices asserted their power to review state court decisions by upholding Section 25 of the Judiciary Act. In so doing, they took the opportunity to refute claims that allowing the Court to review state court decisions would destroy the independence of state court judges. As Justice Joseph Story wrote in *Martin*:

[S]uch a right [cannot be] deemed to impair the independence of state judges. It is assuming the very ground in controversy to assert that they possess an absolute independence of the United States. In respect to the powers granted to the United States, they are not independent; they are expressly bound to obedience by the letter of the constitution; and if they should unintentionally transcend their authority, or misconstrue the constitution, there is no more reason for giving their judgments an absolute and irresistible force, than for giving it to the acts of the other coordinate departments of state sovereignty.

Story also offered a "motive of another kind" for the Court's ruling—a motive he called "perfectly compatible with the most sincere respect for state tribunals":

That motive is the importance, and even necessity of *uniformity* of decisions throughout the whole United States, upon all subjects within the purview of the constitution. Judges of equal learning and integrity, in different states, might differently interpret a statute, or a treaty of the United States, or even the constitution itself: If there were no revising authority to control these jarring and discordant judgments, and harmonize them into uniformity, the laws, the treaties, and the constitution of the United States would be different in different states, and might, perhaps, never have precisely the same construction, obligation, or efficacy, in any two states. The public mischiefs that would attend such a state of things would be truly deplorable; and it cannot be believed that they could have escaped the enlightened convention which formed the constitution. What, indeed, might then have been only prophecy, has now become fact; and the appellate jurisdiction must continue to be the only adequate remedy for such evils.

Marbury, Martin, and *Cohens* firmly established the power of federal courts to exert judicial review over national and state actions. What they did not do, and perhaps could not do, was put an end to the controversies surrounding judicial review.

Some of the complaints with the Court's decisions were heard while Marshall was still on the bench. Jefferson griped about *Marbury* until his last days. In an 1823 letter, he wrote:

This practice of Judge Marshall, of travelling out of his case to prescribe what the law would be in a moot case not before the court, is very irregular and very censurable. . . . [In *Marbury v. Madison*] the Court determined at once, that being an original process, they had no cognizance of it; and therefore the question before them was ended. But the Chief Justice went on to lay down what the law would be, had they jurisdiction of the case, to wit: that they should command the delivery. The object was clearly to instruct any other court having the jurisdiction, what they should do if *Marbury* should apply to them. Besides the impropriety of this gratuitous interference, could anything

exceed the perversion of law? . . . *Yet this case of* Marbury *and* Madison *is continually cited by bench and bar, as if it were settled law, without any animadversion on its being merely an obiter dissertation of the Chief Justice.* (Emphasis added.)[7]

Strong words from one of our nation's most revered presidents!

But Jefferson was not the last to complain about Marshall's opinion. Some critics pick apart specific aspects of the ruling. Jefferson's comment also falls into this category. He argued that once Marshall ruled that the Court did not have jurisdiction to hear the case, he should have dismissed it. Another criticism of Marshall's opinion is that Section 13 of the 1789 Judiciary Act—which *Marbury* held unconstitutional—did not "even remotely suggest an expansion of the Supreme Court's original jurisdiction." If this is so, then Marshall "had nothing to declare unconstitutional"![8]

More contemporary criticisms of judicial review center on the fact that it is essentially an antidemocratic institution. Nonelected judges, opponents argue, should routinely defer to the elected legislative and executive branches. Activist judges who nullify policies that are popularly supported thwart democratic goals. Often cited is the Court's use of judicial review during the 1930s, when the justices struck down economic policies designed to end the Great Depression—policies that the American people overwhelmingly endorsed.

Supporters argue that the power of judicial review is necessary to keep the federal government and the states within proper constitutional bounds and to protect minority rights from infringement by political majorities. They claim, for example, that the exercise of judicial review was instrumental in ending racial segregation, protecting the rights of the criminally accused, and establishing a right to privacy.

In spite of these debates, there is little doubt that judicial review has become an accepted power, and one that

7. Quoted in Andrew A. Lipscomb, *The Writings of Thomas Jefferson,* Vol. 15 (Washington, D.C.: Thomas Jefferson Memorial Association, 1905), 447–448.

8. Jeffrey A. Segal and Harold J. Spaeth, *The Supreme Court and the Attitudinal Model Revisited* (Cambridge: Cambridge University Press, 2002), 24. A counter to this argument is that people of the day must have considered Section 13 as expanding the Court's original jurisdiction, or else why did Marbury bring his suit directly to the Supreme Court?

is exercised not infrequently. Between 1986 and 2006 the Court handed down more than thirty decisions striking down all or parts of federal statutes and nearly one hundred rulings invalidating state or local laws.[9]

CONSTRAINTS ON JUDICIAL POWER

Given all the attention paid to judicial review, it is easy to forget that the power of courts to exercise it and their judicial authority, more generally, have substantial limits. Article III—or the Court's interpretation of it—places three major constraints on the ability of federal tribunals to hear and decide cases: The court must have authority to hear a case (jurisdiction); the case must be appropriate for judicial resolution (justiciability); and the appropriate party must bring the case (standing). In what follows, we review doctrine surrounding these constraints. As you read this discussion, consider not only the Court's interpretation of its own limits but also the justifications it offers. Note, in particular, how fluid these can be: At times the Court tends to construe the rules loosely, while at other times the justices are anxious to enforce them. What factors might explain these different tendencies? Or, to put it another way, to what extent do these constraints limit the Court's authority?

Jurisdiction

According to Chief Justice Salmon P. Chase, "Without jurisdiction the court cannot proceed at all in any cause. Jurisdiction is power to declare the law, and when it ceases to exist, the only function remaining to the court is that of announcing the fact and dismissing the cause."[10] In other words, a court cannot hear a case unless it has the authority—the jurisdiction—to do so.

Article III, Section 2, defines the jurisdiction of U.S. federal courts. Lower courts have the authority to hear cases and controversies involving particular parties and subject matter. The U.S. Supreme Court's jurisdiction is divided into original and appellate: The former are classes of cases that originate in the Court; the latter are those it hears after a lower court has ruled.

To what extent does jurisdiction actually constrain the federal courts? *Marbury v. Madison* provides some answers, although contradictory, to this question. Chief Justice Marshall informed Congress that it could not alter the original jurisdiction of the Court. Having reached this conclusion, perhaps Marshall should have simply dismissed the case on the ground that the Court lacked authority to hear it, but that is not what he did.

Marbury remains an authoritative ruling on original jurisdiction. The issue of appellate jurisdiction is a bit more complex. Article III explicitly states that for those cases over which the Court does not have original jurisdiction, it "shall have appellate Jurisdiction . . . with such Exceptions, and under such Regulations as the Congress shall make." In other words, the exceptions clause seems to give Congress authority to alter the Court's appellate jurisdiction.

In *Martin v. Hunter's Lessee* and *Cohens v. Virginia* the Supreme Court agreed that Congress has the power to expand the Court's appellate jurisdiction; in those cases, the Court upheld the additions made to its appellate jurisdiction under Section 25 of the Judiciary Act. The question the Court addresses in *Ex parte McCardle* is a bit different. Here the justices must determine if Congress can use its power under the exceptions clause to *remove* the Court's appellate jurisdiction over a particular category of cases.

Ex parte McCardle

7 Wall. (74 U.S.) 506 (1869)

http://laws.findlaw.com/US/74/506.html

Vote: 8 (Chase, Clifford, Davis, Field, Grier, Miller, Nelson, Swayne)

0

Opinion of the Court: Chase

After the Civil War the Radical Republicans in Congress imposed a series of restrictions on the South.[11]

9. Lee Epstein, Jeffrey A. Segal, Harold J. Spaeth, and Thomas G. Walker, *The Supreme Court Compendium: Data, Decisions, and Developments*, 4th ed. (Washington, D.C.: CQ Press, 2007), Tables 2-15 and 2-16.

10. *Ex parte McCardle* (1869).

11. For more information on *McCardle*, see Lee Epstein and Thomas G. Walker, "The Role of the Supreme Court in American Society: Playing the Reconstruction Game," in *Contemplating Courts*, ed. Lee Epstein (Washington, D.C.: CQ Press, 1995), 315–346.

Known as the Reconstruction laws, they in effect placed the region under military rule. Journalist William McCardle opposed these measures and wrote editorials urging resistance to them. As a result, he was arrested for publishing allegedly "incendiary and libelous articles" and held for a trial before a military tribunal, established under Reconstruction.

Because he was a civilian, not a member of any militia, McCardle alleged that he was being illegally held. He petitioned for a writ of habeas corpus—an order issued to determine if a person held in custody is being unlawfully detained or imprisoned—under an 1867 act, which gave federal judges power to grant habeas corpus to any person restrained in violation of the U.S. Constitution. When this effort failed, McCardle appealed to the U.S. Supreme Court.

In early March 1868 the *McCardle* case "was very thoroughly and ably [presented] upon the merits" to the U.S. Supreme Court. It was clear to most observers that "no Justice was still making up his mind": The Court's sympathies, as was widely known, lay with McCardle.[12] But before the justices could issue their decision, Congress, on March 27, 1868, enacted a law repealing the 1867 Habeas Corpus Act and removing the Supreme Court's authority to hear appeals emanating from it. This move was meant either to punish the Court or send it a strong message. Two years before *McCardle*, in 1866, the Court had invalidated President Abraham Lincoln's use of military tribunals in certain areas, and Congress did not want to see the Court take similar action in this dispute.[13] The legislature felt so strongly on this issue that after President Andrew Johnson vetoed the 1868 repealer act, Congress overrode the veto.

The Court responded by redocketing the case for oral arguments in March 1869. During the arguments and in its briefs, the government made its position clear: When the jurisdiction of a court to determine a case or a class of cases depends upon a statute and that statute is repealed, the jurisdiction ceases absolutely. In short, the government contended that the Court no longer had authority to hear the case and should dismiss it.

The CHIEF JUSTICE delivered the opinion of the Court.

It is unnecessary to consider whether, if Congress had made no exceptions and no regulations, this court might not have exercised general appellate jurisdiction under rules prescribed by itself. From among the earliest Acts of the first Congress, at its first session, was the Act of September 24th, 1789, to establish the judicial courts of the United States. That Act provided for the organization of this court, and prescribed regulations for the exercise of its jurisdiction. . . .

The exception to appellate jurisdiction in the case before us . . . is not an inference from the affirmation of other appellate jurisdiction. It is made in terms. The provision of the Act of 1867, affirming the appellate jurisdiction of this court in cases of habeas corpus, is expressly repealed. It is hardly possible to imagine a plainer instance of positive exception.

We are not at liberty to inquire into the motives of the Legislature. We can only examine into its power under the Constitution; and the power to make exceptions to the appellate jurisdiction of this court is given by express words.

What, then, is the effect of the repealing Act upon the case before us? We cannot doubt as to this. Without jurisdiction the court cannot proceed at all in any cause. Jurisdiction is power to declare the law, and when it ceases to exist, the only function remaining to the court is that of announcing the fact and dismissing the cause. And this is not less clear upon authority than upon principle. . . .

It is quite clear, therefore, that this . . . court cannot proceed to pronounce judgment in this case, for it has no longer jurisdiction of the appeal; and judicial duty is not less fitly performed by declining ungranted jurisdiction than in exercising firmly that which the Constitution and the laws confer. . . .

The appeal of the petitioner in this case must be dismissed for want of jurisdiction.

As we can see, the Court acceded and declined to hear the case. *McCardle* suggests that Congress has the authority to remove the Court's appellate jurisdiction as it deems necessary. Since *McCardle*, however, Congress has rarely enacted laws aimed directly at limiting the Court's appellate jurisdiction, even though it often threatens to

---

12. Charles Fairman, *History of the Supreme Court of the United States,* Vol. 7: *Reconstruction and Reunion* (New York: Macmillan, 1971), 456.

13. That action came in *Ex parte Milligan* (1866), discussed in chapter 5.

TABLE 3-1 A Sample of Congressional Proposals Aimed at Eliminating the U.S. Supreme Court's Appellate Jurisdiction

Issue	Supreme Court Decision Provoking Proposal	Proposal
Communist infiltration/ Security programs	*Schware v. Board of Bar Examiners* (1957) in which the Supreme Court refused to allow states to use "inferences regarding moral character" (i.e., past association with a subversive cause) to exclude applicants for admission to the bar.	1958 proposal that would have eliminated the Court's appellate jurisdiction over any "regulation pertaining to the admission of persons to the practice of law."
Criminal confessions	*Miranda v. Arizona* (1966) in which the Court required police to read those under arrest a series of rights.	1968 proposal that removed the Court's jurisdiction to hear state cases involving the admissibility of confessions.
School busing	*Swann v. Charlotte-Mecklenburg County* (1971) in which the Court permitted district courts to fashion their own school desegregation plans, which may include the busing of students to other schools.	During the 1970s and 1980s many proposals were offered to curb the Court's authority to hear busing cases and to limit the authority of courts to order busing.
School prayer	*Engel v. Vitale* (1962) and *Abington School District v. Schempp* (1963), which eliminated voluntary and mandatory prayer in school.	Several proposals, with a major effort coming in 1979, that would have eliminated the Supreme Court's as well as all other federal courts' ability to hear any cases involving voluntary school prayer.
Abortion	*Roe v. Wade* (1973) in which the Supreme Court struck down state laws criminalizing abortion. *Roe* legalized abortion during the first two trimesters of pregnancy.	During the 1970s and 1980s several proposals were offered to remove the Court's authority to hear abortion cases.

SOURCE: Adapted from Kathleen M. Sullivan and Gerald Gunther, *Constitutional Law*, 15th ed. (New York: Foundation Press, 2004), 83–85.

do so and sometimes proposes such legislation. Table 3-1 lists some of the proposals members of Congress have offered. Most involve controversial issues—abortion, prayer in school, busing—leading to the conclusion that modern Congresses are no different from the one that passed the 1868 repealer act: They would like to use the exceptions clause as a political tool, as a way to restrain the Court, but they have yet to do so successfully.

In spite of *McCardle*, there are several reasons to believe that the Court might not uphold the sorts of proposals depicted in Table 3-1. After all, *McCardle* was something of an odd case. According to many scholars, the Court had no choice but to acquiesce to Congress if it wanted to retain its legitimacy in post–Civil War America. The pressures of the day, rather than the Constitution or the beliefs of the justices, may have led to the decision. Then there is the argument that taken to its extreme, ju-

risdiction stripping could render the Court virtually powerless. Would the framers have created an institution only to allow Congress to destroy it? Many scholars say no.

More modern justices have expressed different opinions on the power of Congress to alter the justices' authority to hear cases appealed from the lower courts. In 1949 Justice Felix Frankfurter wrote, "Congress need not give this Court any appellate power; it may withdraw appellate jurisdiction once conferred and it may do so even while a case is *sub judice* [before a judge]."[14] Thirteen years later, Justice William O. Douglas remarked, "There is a serious question whether the *McCardle* case could command a majority view today."[15]

---

14. *National Mutual Insurance Co. v. Tidewater Transfer Co.* (1949).
15. *Glidden Co. v. Zdanok* (1962).

Just how far the Court would allow Congress to use the exceptions clause remains an open question until such litigation occurs. Until then, Chief Justice Chase perhaps summed up the situation best when he noted after *McCardle* had been decided that use of the exceptions clause was "unusual and hardly to be justified except upon some imperious public exigency."[16]

Justiciability

According to Article III, the federal courts' judicial power is restricted to "cases" and "controversies." Taken together, these words mean that a lawsuit must be justiciable—appropriate or suitable for a federal tribunal to hear or to solve. As Chief Justice Earl Warren asserted, cases and controversies

are two complementary but somewhat different limitations. In part those words limit the business of federal courts to questions presented in an adversary context and in a form historically viewed as capable of resolution through the judicial process. And in part those words define the role assigned to the judiciary in a tripartite allocation of power to assure that the federal courts will not intrude into areas committed to the other branches of government. Justiciability is the term of art employed to give expression to this dual limitation placed upon federal courts by the case-and-controversy doctrine.[17]

Although Warren also suggested that "justiciability is itself a concept of uncertain meaning and scope," he elucidated several characteristics of litigation that would render it nonjusticiable. In this section, we treat five: advisory opinions, collusion, mootness, ripeness, and political questions.

Advisory Opinions. A few states and some foreign countries require judges of the highest court to advise the executive or legislature, when so requested, as to their views on the constitutionality of a proposed policy. Since the time of Chief Justice John Jay, however, federal judges in the United States have refused to issue advisory opinions. They do not render such advice because hypothetical questions present no real controversy. The language of the Constitution does not explicitly prohibit advisory opinions as opinions, but the framers rejected a proposal

that would have permitted the other branches of government to request judicial rulings "upon important questions of law, and upon solemn occasions." Madison was critical of this proposal on the ground that the judiciary should have jurisdiction only over "cases of a Judiciary Nature."[18]

The Supreme Court agreed. In July 1793 Secretary of State Jefferson asked the justices if they would be willing to address questions concerning the appropriate role America should play in the ongoing British-French war. Jefferson wrote that President George Washington "would be much relieved if he found himself free to refer questions [involving the war] to the opinions of the judges of the Supreme Court in the United States, whose knowledge . . . would secure us against errors dangerous to the peace of the United States."[19] Less than a month later the justices denied Jefferson's request with a reply written directly to the president:

We have considered [the] letter written by your direction to us by the Secretary of State [regarding] the lines of separation drawn by the Constitution between the three departments of government. These being in certain respects checks upon each other, and our being judges of a court in the last resort, are considerations which afford strong arguments against the propriety of our extra-judicially deciding the questions alluded to, especially as the power given by the Constitution to the President, of calling on the heads of departments for opinions, seems to have been *purposely* as well as expressly united to the *executive* departments.[20]

With these words, the justices sounded the death knell for advisory opinions: They would violate the separation of powers principle embedded in the Constitution. The subject has resurfaced only a few times in U.S. history; in the 1930s, for example, President Franklin Roosevelt considered a proposal that would require the Court to issue advisory opinions on the constitutionality of federal laws. But Roosevelt quickly gave up on the idea at least in part because of its dubious constitutionality.

16. *Ex parte Yerger* (1869).
17. *Flast v. Cohen* (1968).

18. Quoted by Farber and Sherry in *A History of the American Constitution,* 87.
19. The full text of Jefferson's letter is in Henry M. Hart Jr. and Albert M. Sacks, *The Legal Process,* ed. William N. Eskridge Jr. and Philip P. Frickey (Westbury, N.Y.: Foundation Press, 1994), 630–632.
20. Quoted in ibid., 637.

Nevertheless, scholars still debate the Court's 1793 letter to Washington. Some agree with the justices' logic. Others assert that more institutional factors were at work; perhaps the Court—out of concern for its institutional legitimacy—did not want to become embroiled in "political" disputes at this early phase in its development. Whatever the reason, all subsequent Courts have followed that 1793 precedent: requests for advisory opinions to the *U.S. Supreme Court* present nonjusticiable disputes.[21]

Collusive Suits. Justiciability also precludes collusive lawsuits. The Court will not decide cases in which the litigants (1) want the same outcome, (2) evince no real adversity between them, or (3) are merely testing the law. Why the Court deems collusive suits nonjusticiable is well illustrated in *Muskrat v. United States* (1911). At issue here were several federal laws involving land distribution and appropriations to Native Americans. To determine whether these laws were constitutional, Congress enacted a statute authorizing David Muskrat and other Native Americans to challenge the land distribution law in court. This legislation also ordered the courts to give priority to Muskrat's suit and allowed the attorney general to defend his claim. Furthermore, Congress agreed to pay Muskrat's legal fees if his suit was successful. When the dispute reached the U.S. Supreme Court, the panel dismissed it. Justice William Day wrote:

[T]here is neither more nor less in this [litigation] than an attempt to provide for a judicial determination, final in this court, of the constitutional validity of an act of Congress. Is such a determination within the judicial power conferred by the Constitution, as the same has been interpreted and defined in the authoritative decisions to which we have referred? We think it is not. That judicial power, as we have seen, is the right to determine actual controversies arising between adverse litigants, duly instituted in courts of proper jurisdiction. The right to declare a law unconstitutional arises because an act of Congress relied upon by one or the other of such parties in determining their rights is in conflict with the fundamental law. The exercise of this, the most important and delicate duty of this court, is not given to it as a body with revisory power over the action of Congress, but because the rights of the litigants in justiciable controversies require the court to choose between the

fundamental law and a law purporting to be enacted within constitutional authority, but in fact beyond the power delegated to the legislative branch of the Government. This attempt to obtain a judicial declaration of the validity of the act of Congress is not presented in a "case" or "controversy," to which, under the Constitution of the United States, the judicial power alone extends.

The Court, however, has not always followed the *Muskrat* precedent. Indeed, several collusive suits resulted in landmark decisions, including *Pollock v. Farmers' Loan and Trust Co.* (1895), in which the Court declared the federal income tax unconstitutional. The litigants in this dispute, a bank and a stockholder in the bank, both wanted the same outcome—the demise of the tax. *Carter v. Carter Coal Co.* (1936) is also exemplary. Here the Court agreed to resolve a dispute over a major piece of New Deal legislation despite the fact that the litigants, a company and its president, both wanted the legislation to be declared unconstitutional.

Why did the Court resolve these disputes evincing collusion but dismiss *Muskrat*? One answer is that the Court might overlook some element of collusion if the suit presents a real controversy or the potential for one. But some analysts see it differently. The temptation to set "good" public policy (or strike down "bad" public policy), they say, is sometimes too strong for the justices to follow their own rules.

Mootness. In general, the Court will not decide cases in which the controversy is no longer live by the time the case reaches its doorstep. *DeFunis v. Odegaard* (1974) provides one example. Rejected for admission to the University of Washington Law School, Marco DeFunis Jr. brought suit against the school, alleging that it had engaged in reverse discrimination, that it had denied him a place while accepting statistically less qualified minority students. In 1971 a trial court found merit in his claim and ordered that the university admit him. While DeFunis was in his second year of legal education at the University of Washington, the state's high court reversed the trial judge's ruling. DeFunis then appealed to the U.S. Supreme Court. By that time, DeFunis had registered for his final quarter in school. In a *per curiam* opinion, the Court refused to rule on the merits of DeFunis's claim, asserting that it was moot:

21. We emphasize the Supreme Court because some state courts do, in fact, issue advisory opinions.

Because [DeFunis] will complete his law school studies at the end of the term for which he has now registered regardless of any decision this Court might reach on the merits of this litigation, we conclude that the Court cannot, consistently with the limitations of Art. III of the Constitution, consider the substantive constitutional issues tendered by the parties.

Still, the rules governing mootness are a bit fuzzier than the *DeFunis* opinion characterized them. In *Roe v. Wade* (1973) the Court legalized abortions performed during the first two trimesters of pregnancy. Norma McCorvey, also known as Jane Roe, was pregnant when she filed suit in 1970, and by the time the Court handed down the decision in 1973, she had long since given birth and put her baby up for adoption. But the justices did not declare this case moot. Why not? What made *Roe* different from *DeFunis*?

The justices provided two legal justifications. First, DeFunis brought the litigation in his own behalf, but *Roe* was a class action—a lawsuit brought by one or more persons who represent themselves and all others similarly situated. Second, DeFunis had been admitted to law school, and he would "never again be required to run the gauntlet." Roe could become pregnant again; that is, pregnancy is a situation capable of repetition or recurrence. Are these reasonable points? Or is it possible, as some suspect, that the Court developed them to avoid particular legal issues? In either case, it is clear that mootness may be a rather slippery concept, open to interpretation by different justices and Courts.

Ripeness. Related to the concepts of advisory opinions and mootness is that of ripeness. Under existing Court interpretation a case is nonjusticiable if the controversy is premature—has insufficiently gelled—for review. *International Longshoreman's Union v. Boyd* (1954) provides an illustration. In 1952 Congress passed a law mandating that all aliens seeking admission into the United States from Alaska be "examined" as if they were entering from a foreign country. Believing that the law might affect seasonal laborers working in Alaska temporarily, a union challenged the law. Writing for the Court, Justice Frankfurter dismissed the suit. In his view,

Appellants in effect asked [the Court] to rule that a statute the sanctions of which had not been set in motion against individuals on whose behalf relief was sought, because an occasion for doing so had not arisen, would not be applied to them if in the future such a contingency should arise. That is not a lawsuit to enforce a right; it is an endeavor to obtain a court's assurance that a statute does not govern hypothetical situations that may or may not make the challenged statute applicable. Determination of the . . . constitutionality of the legislation in advance of its immediate adverse effect in the context of a concrete case involves too remote and abstract an inquiry for the proper exercise of the judicial function.

In addition, the ripeness requirement mandates that a party exhaust all available administrative and lower court remedies before seeking review by the Supreme Court. Until lower court review opportunities have been fully explored the case is not ready for the justices to hear.

Political Questions. Another type of nonjusticiable suit involves a political question. Chief Justice Marshall stated in *Marbury v. Madison:*

The province of the court is, solely, to decide on the rights of individuals, not to inquire how the executive, or executive officers, perform duties in which they have a discretion. Questions in their nature political, or which are, by the constitution and laws, submitted to the executive, can never be made in this court.

In other words, there is a class of disputes, often presenting claims that cannot be settled by an interpretation of the law, that is best left to the political branches.

But what exactly constitutes a political question? The Supreme Court first attempted an answer in **Luther v. Borden** (1849). *Luther* involved a dispute between the existing government of Rhode Island and an opposition group—the "Dorrites"—that was trying to institute a new government and a constitution (which Rhode Island did not have, as it was still operating under its royal charter). Believing that the Dorrites' activities amounted to insurrection, the state government sought to suppress the rebels through arrests made, in some instances, by police who entered homes without search warrants. Martin Luther, one of the arrested Dorrites, sued state officials for trespass. He argued that the royal charter denied citizens a republican form of government, as mandated by the guarantee clause of Article IV: "The United States shall guarantee to every State in this Union a Republican Form of Government, and shall protect each of them against Invasion; and on Application of the Legislature, or the Executive (when the Legislature cannot be convened) against domestic Violence."

But the Supreme Court refused to go along with Luther. Writing for the majority, Chief Justice Roger B. Taney held that the Court should avoid deciding any question arising out of the guarantee clause because such questions are inherently "political." He based the opinion largely on the words of Article IV, which he believed governed relations between the states and the federal government, not governments and courts.

For the next hundred years or so, the Court maintained Taney's position: Any case involving the guarantee clause constituted a nonjusticiable dispute. An example is *Colegrove v. Green* (1946). At issue in *Colegrove* was legislative malapportionment. The national census determines how many members of the U.S. House of Representatives each state is assigned, but the state legislatures are responsible for drawing the boundaries for the congressional districts. In 1900 most states had districts of relatively equal numbers of constituents, but many failed to keep pace with the great migration of people from the rural areas to the cities that occurred in the subsequent decades. The result was malapportionment, with some congressional districts having many times the number of residents as other districts. With the population shift to the cities, the number of representatives from urban areas should have increased, but state legislatures, dominated by rural interests, refused to give political power to the cities by properly redrawing district lines to keep the population of districts equal. *Colegrove* challenged the malapportioned congressional districts in Illinois as being in violation of the guarantee clause.

Writing for the Court, Justice Frankfurter dismissed *Colegrove*. He invoked the logic of *Luther* to hold that the question of legislative reapportionment within states was left open by the Constitution. If the Court intervened in this matter, it would be acting in a way "hostile to a democratic system." Put in different terms, reapportionment constituted a "political thicket" into which "courts ought not enter."

As a result of the Court's decision in *Colegrove*, disparities between the voting power of urban and rural citizens continued to grow. Naturally, many citizens and organizations wanted to force legislatures to reapportion, but

under *Colegrove* they could not do so using the guarantee clause.

Finally, in *Baker v. Carr* (1962) the Supreme Court changed its position on reapportionment. Here, malapportioned state legislative districts in Tennessee were challenged not for violating the guarantee clause but as inconsistent with the demands of the Fourteenth Amendment's equal protection clause, which says that no state shall "deny to any person within its jurisdiction the equal protection of the laws." The state urged the Supreme Court to apply the *Colegrove* precedent and dismiss the case, but the justices did not. In a landmark opinion for the majority in *Baker*, Justice William J. Brennan Jr. set out a definition of a political question:

Prominent on the surface of any case held to involve a political question is found a textually demonstrable constitutional commitment of the issue to a coordinate political department; or a lack of judicially discoverable and manageable standards for resolving it; or the impossibility of deciding without an initial policy determination of a kind clearly for nonjudicial discretion; or the impossibility of a court's undertaking independent resolution without expressing lack of the respect due coordinate branches of government; or an unusual need for unquestioning adherence to a political decision already made; or the potentiality of embarrassment from multifarious pronouncements by various departments on one question.

Applying this definition to Baker's suit challenging Tennessee's districting system, Brennan concluded that the case should not be dismissed on political question grounds:

The question here is the consistency of state action with the Federal Constitution. We have no question decided, or to be decided, by a political branch of government coequal with this Court. Nor do we risk embarrassment of our government abroad, or grave disturbance at home if we take issue with Tennessee as to the constitutionality of her action here challenged. Nor need the appellants, in order to succeed in this action, ask the Court to enter upon policy determinations for which judicially manageable standards are lacking. Judicial standards under the Equal Protection Clause are well developed and familiar, and it has been open to courts since the enactment of the Fourteenth Amendment to determine, if on the particular facts they must, that a discrimination reflects no policy, but simply arbitrary and capricious action.

To put it another way, had the case been brought under the guarantee clause, "it could not have succeeded." But, as Brennan argued, "the nonjusticiability of claims resting on the Guaranty Clause which arises from their embodiment of questions that were thought 'political,' can have no bearing upon the justiciability of the equal protection claim presented in this case."

Baker is important for a number of reasons. One is that it opened the window for judicial resolution of reapportionment cases. Another, and more relevant here, is that it established a clear doctrinal base for determining political questions. Note that Brennan's opinion did not lead to the demise of the political questions doctrine. Over the years, the Court has used it to dismiss a range of substantive disputes. Indeed, as recently as 1993 in the case of *Nixon v. United States,* the Court relied heavily on *Baker v. Carr* to rule that the procedures used by Congress to handle impeachments involved political questions not subject to judicial review.

Standing to Sue

Another constraint on federal judicial power is the requirement that the party bringing a lawsuit have "standing to sue." Not everyone is entitled to the use of the federal courts to challenge the constitutionality of a law or government action. A party must have standing to qualify as an appropriate litigant. According to the Court's interpretation of Article III, standing requires that (1) the party must have suffered a concrete injury or be in imminent danger of suffering such a loss; (2) the injury must be "fairly traceable" to the challenged action of the defendant (usually the government in constitutional cases); and (3) the party must show that a favorable court decision is likely to provide redress.[22] In general these three elements are designed, as Justice Brennan noted in *Baker,* "to assure . . . concrete adverseness which sharpens the presentation of issues upon which the Court so largely depends for illumination of difficult constitutional questions."

In many disputes, the litigants have little difficulty meeting the standing requirements mandated by Article III. A citizen who has been denied the right to vote on the basis of race, a criminal defendant sentenced to death, and a church member jailed for religious proselytizing would have sufficient standing to challenge the federal or state laws that may have deprived them of their rights. But what about parties who wish to challenge some government action on the ground that they are taxpayers? Such claims raise an important question: Does the mere fact that one pays taxes provide a sufficient basis for standing?

In general, the answer is no. In addition to the three constitutionally derived requirements, the Court has articulated several prudential considerations to govern standing. Among the most prominent are those that limit generalized grievance suits—mostly those brought by parties whose only injury is as a taxpayer who wants to prevent the government from spending money. Consider *Frothingham v. Mellon* (1923), a lawsuit filed by Harriet Frothingham to challenge the constitutionality of the Sheppard-Towner Maternity Act. The statute provided federal aid to the states to fund programs designed to reduce infant mortality rates—to which Frothingham was opposed on the ground that the law was an unconstitutional intrusion into the rights of the states. She did not want her federal tax dollars to fund it, and her attorneys argued that as a taxpayer she had sufficient grounds to bring suit.

The Court refused to adopt this position, holding that Frothingham lacked standing to bring the litigation. Justice George Sutherland wrote for the majority:

If one taxpayer may champion and litigate such a cause, then every other taxpayer may do the same, not only in respect of the statute here under review but also in respect of every other appropriation act and statute whose administration requires the outlay of public money, and whose validity may be questioned. The bare suggestion of such a result, with its attendant inconveniences, goes far to sustain the conclusion which we have reached, that a suit of this character cannot be maintained.

He also outlined an approach to standing:

The party . . . must be able to show not only that the statute is invalid but that he has sustained or is immediately in danger of

---

22. See *Lujan v. Defenders of Wildlife,* 504 U.S. 555 (1992), which lays out these three elements.

sustaining some direct injury as the result of its enforcement, and not merely that he suffers in some indefinite way in common with people generally.

For the next forty years, *Frothingham* served as a major bar to taxpayer suits. Unless litigants could demonstrate that a government program injured them or threatened to do so—beyond the mere expenditure of tax dollars—they could not bring suit. In *Flast v. Cohen* (1968), however, the Court carved out an exception to the rule. *Flast* involved seven taxpayers who sought to challenge federal expenditures made under the Elementary and Secondary Education Act of 1965. Under this law, states could apply to the federal government for grants to assist in the education of children from low-income families. They could obtain funds for the acquisition of textbooks, school library materials, and so forth. The taxpayers alleged that some of the funds disbursed under this act were used to finance "instruction in reading, arithmetic, and other subjects and for guidance in religious and sectarian schools." Such expenditures, they argued, violated the First Amendment's prohibition on religious establishment: "Congress shall make no law respecting an establishment of religion."

A three-judge district court dismissed their complaint. It reasoned that because the plaintiffs had suffered no real injury and because their only claim of standing rested "solely on their status as federal taxpayers," they failed to meet the criteria established in *Frothingham*.

Writing for the Court, Chief Justice Warren disagreed. And, in so doing, he completely revamped the *Frothingham* standard. To determine whether a taxpayer has the requisite "personal stake" to bring suit, Warren wrote:

[I]t is both appropriate and necessary to look to the substantive issues for another purpose, namely, to determine whether there is a logical nexus between the status asserted and the claim sought to be adjudicated. . . . The nexus demanded of federal taxpayers has two aspects to it. First, the taxpayer must establish a logical link between that status and the type of legislative enactment attacked. Thus, a taxpayer will be a proper party to allege the unconstitutionality only of exercises of congressional power under the taxing and spending clause of Art. I, §8, of the Constitution. It will not be sufficient to allege an incidental expenditure of tax funds in the administration of an essentially regulatory statute. . . . Secondly, the taxpayer must establish a

nexus between that status and the precise nature of the constitutional infringement alleged. Under this requirement, the taxpayer must show that the challenged enactment exceeds specific constitutional limitations imposed upon the exercise of the congressional taxing and spending power and not simply that the enactment is generally beyond the powers delegated to Congress by Art. I, §8. When both nexuses are established, the litigant will have shown a taxpayer's stake in the outcome of the controversy and will be a proper and appropriate party to invoke a federal court's jurisdiction.

Applying this standard to the dispute at hand, Warren found that the *Flast* taxpayers had standing.

Their constitutional challenge is made to an exercise by Congress of its power under Art. I, §8, to spend for the general welfare, and the challenged program involves a substantial expenditure of federal tax funds. In addition, appellants have alleged that the challenged expenditures violate the Establishment and Free Exercise Clauses of the First Amendment.

Would Harriet Frothingham have met this new, more relaxed standard? To this question, Warren answered no:

The allegations of the taxpayer in *Frothingham v. Mellon* were quite different from those made in this case, and the result in *Frothingham* is consistent with the test of taxpayer standing announced today. The taxpayer in *Frothingham* attacked a federal spending program and she, therefore, established the first nexus required. However, she lacked standing because her constitutional attack was not based on an allegation that Congress, in enacting the Maternity Act of 1921, had breached a specific limitation upon its taxing and spending power. . . . In essence, Mrs. Frothingham was attempting to assert the States' interest in their legislative prerogatives and not a federal taxpayer's interest in being free of taxing and spending in contravention of specific constitutional limitations imposed upon Congress' taxing and spending power.

In the end, *Flast* did not overrule *Frothingham;* in fact, as the above quote indicates, the Court was careful to indicate that had the 1968 ruling been applied to *Frothingham,* the plaintiff still would have been unable to attain standing. Still, some thought that *Flast* substantially revised the 1923 precedent. It seemed that if taxpayers could indicate a logical link between their status and the legislation, and one between their status and a specific constitutional infringement, then they might have standing.

In the years since *Flast,* however, the Court has indicated that unless the suit is a virtual carbon-copy of

BOX 3-4 JUSTICE BRANDEIS, CONCURRING IN
ASHWANDER V. TENNESSEE VALLEY AUTHORITY

In 1936 Justice Louis D. Brandeis delineated, in a concurring opinion in *Ashwander v. Tennessee Valley Authority*, a set of Court-formulated rules useful in avoiding constitutional decisions. A portion of his opinion setting forth those rules, minus case citations and footnotes, follows:

The Court developed, for its own governance in the cases confessedly within its jurisdiction, a series of rules under which it has avoided passing upon a large part of all the constitutional questions pressed upon it for decision. They are:

1. The Court will not pass upon the constitutionality of legislation in a friendly, non-adversary, proceeding, declining because to decide such questions "is legitimate only in the last resort, and as a necessity in the determination of real, earnest and vital controversy between individuals. It never was the thought that, by means of a friendly suit, a party beaten in the legislature could transfer to the courts an inquiry as to the constitutionality of the legislative act."

2. The Court will not "anticipate a question of constitutional law in advance of the necessity of deciding it." "It is not the habit of the Court to decide questions of a constitutional nature unless absolutely necessary to a decision of the case."

3. The Court will not "formulate a rule of constitutional law broader than is required by the precise facts to which it is to be applied."

4. The Court will not pass upon a constitutional question although properly presented by the record, if there is also present some other ground upon which the case may be disposed of. This rule has found most varied application. Thus, if a case can be decided on either of two grounds, one involving a constitutional question, the other a question of statutory construction or general law, the Court will decide only the latter. Appeals from the highest court of a state challenging its decision of a question under the Federal Constitution are frequently dismissed because the judgment can be sustained on an independent state ground.

5. The Court will not pass upon the validity of a statute upon complaint of one who fails to show that he is injured by its operation. Among the many applications of this rule, none is more striking than the denial of the right of challenge to one who lacks a personal or property right. Thus, the challenge by a public official interested only in the performance of his official duty will not be entertained. . . .

6. "The Court will not pass upon the constitutionality of a statute at the instance of one who has availed himself of its benefits."

7. "When the validity of an act of the Congress is drawn in question, and even if a serious doubt of constitutionality is raised, it is a cardinal principle that this Court will first ascertain whether a construction of the statute is fairly possible by which the question may be avoided."

that case, it will maintain its general ban against general grievance suits. *Hein v. Freedom from Religion Foundation* (2007) supplies an example. The foundation brought this establishment clause suit to challenge activities associated with President George W. Bush's White House Office of Faith-Based and Community Initiatives. It claimed it had standing because its individual members were federal taxpayers opposed to executive branch use of congressional appropriations for activities that allegedly promoted religious community groups over secular ones. The Supreme Court disagreed. Because these were executive branch programs, they did not meet the *Flast* standard. More broadly, in his judgment of the Court, Justice Samuel Alito noted that "the payment of taxes is generally not enough to establish standing to challenge an action taken by the Federal Government." *Flast*, he wrote, was a "narrow exception."

Constraints on Judicial Power and the Separation of Powers System

The jurisdiction, justiciability, and standing requirements place considerable constraints on the exercise of judicial power. Yet it is important to note that these doctrines largely come from the Court's own interpretation of Article III and its view of the proper role of the judiciary—the constraints are largely self-imposed. In *Ash-*

wander v. Tennessee Valley Authority (1936) Justice Louis Brandeis took the opportunity in a concurring opinion to provide a summary of the principles of judicial self-restraint as they pertain to constitutional interpretation *(see Box 3-4)*. These "Ashwander Principles" serve as perhaps the best single statement of how the Court limits its own powers—and especially its exercise of judicial review.

It would be a mistake, however, to conclude that the use of judicial power is limited only by self-imposed constraints. Rather, members of the executive and legislative branches also have expectations concerning the appropriate limits of judicial authority. If the justices are perceived as exceeding their role by failing to restrain the use of their own powers, a reaction from the political branches may occur. Congress could pass statutes or propose constitutional amendments to counteract decisions of the Court. The legislature might also alter the Court's appellate jurisdiction or fail to provide the Court with its requested levels of funding. The political branches might react by being slow to implement and enforce Court rulings. And the president and Senate could use their powers in the judicial selection process to fill Court vacancies with new justices whose views on judicial power are more consistent with their own.

The justices are fully aware that the president and Congress have the ability to impose such checks, and on occasion they may exercise their powers with at least some consideration of how other government actors may respond. Therefore, constraints on judicial power not only emanate from Article III and the Court's interpretation of it but also from the constitutional separation of powers—a system giving each governmental branch a role in keeping the other branches within their legitimate bounds.

READINGS

Adamany, David. "The Supreme Court," in *The American Courts: A Critical Assessment.* John B. Gates and Charles A. Johnson, eds. Washington, D.C.: CQ Press, 1991.

Barkow, Rachel E. "More Supreme than Court? The Fall of the Political Question Doctrine and the Rise of Judicial Supremacy." *Columbia Law Review* 102 (2002): 237–334.

Bickel, Alexander M. *The Least Dangerous Branch.* New York: Bobbs-Merrill, 1962.

Burbank, Stephen B., and Barry Friedman, eds. *Judicial Independence at the Crossroads: An Interdisciplinary Approach.* Thousand Oaks, Calif.: Sage Publications, 2002.

Caldeira, Gregory A. "Courts and Public Opinion," in *The American Courts: A Critical Assessment.* John B. Gates and Charles A. Johnson, eds. Washington, D.C.: CQ Press, 1991.

Canon, Bradley C. "Defining the Dimensions of Judicial Activism." *Judicature* 66 (1983): 236–247.

Casper, Jonathan D. "The Supreme Court and National Policy Making." *American Political Science Review* 70 (1976): 50–63.

Choper, Jesse H. *Judicial Review and the National Political Process.* Chicago: University of Chicago Press, 1980.

Clinton, Robert Lowry. *Marbury v. Madison and Judicial Review.* Lawrence: University Press of Kansas, 1989.

Dahl, Robert. "Decision Making in a Democracy: The Supreme Court as a National Policy-Maker." *Journal of Public Law* 6 (1957): 279–295.

Devins, Neal, and Keith E. Whittington, eds. *Congress and the Constitution.* Durham: Duke University Press, 2005.

Ely, John Hart. *Democracy and Distrust.* Cambridge: Harvard University Press, 1980.

Epstein, Lee, Jack Knight, and Andrew Martin. "The Supreme Court as a *Strategic* National Policy Maker." *Emory Law Journal* 50 (2001): 583–612.

Fisher, Louis. *Constitutional Dialogues.* Princeton: Princeton University Press, 1988.

Franck, Thomas M. *Political Questions/Judicial Answers: Does the Rule of Law Apply to Foreign Affairs?* Princeton: Princeton University Press, 1992.

Gettleman, Marvin E. *The Dorr Rebellion: A Study in American Radicalism, 1833–1849.* New York: Random House, 1973.

Grofman, Bernard, ed. *Political Gerrymandering and the Courts.* New York: Agathon Press, 1990.

Henkin, Louis. "Is There a 'Political Question' Doctrine?" *Yale Law Journal* 85 (1976): 597–625.

Kramer, Larry D. *The People Themselves: Popular Constitutionalism and Judicial Review.* New York: Oxford University Press, 2004.

Langer, Laura. *Judicial Review in State Supreme Courts: A Comparative Study.* Albany: State University of New York Press, 2002.

Lasser, William. *The Limits of Judicial Power.* Chapel Hill: University of North Carolina Press, 1988.

Marcus, Maeva, ed. *Origins of the Federal Judiciary: Essays on the Judiciary Act of 1789.* New York: Oxford University Press, 1992.

Meernik, James, and Joseph Ignagni. "Judicial Review and Coordinate Construction of the Constitution." *American Journal of Political Science* 41 (1997): 447–467.

Murphy, Walter F. *Congress and the Court.* Chicago: University of Chicago Press, 1962.

Nelson, William E. *Marbury v. Madison: The Origins and Legacy of Judicial Review.* Lawrence: University Press of Kansas, 2000.

Orren, Karen. "Standing to Sue: Interest Group Conflict in the Federal Courts." *American Political Science Review* 70 (1976): 723–741.

Peretti, Terri Jennings. *In Defense of a Political Court.* Princeton: Princeton University Press, 1999.

Radcliffe, James E. *The Case-or-Controversy Provision.* University Park: Pennsylvania State University Press, 1978.

Rosenberg, Gerald N. *The Hollow Hope.* 2nd ed. Chicago: University of Chicago Press, 2008.

Sunstein, Cass R. *One Case at a Time: Judicial Minimalism on the Supreme Court.* Cambridge: Harvard University Press, 1999.

Strum, Philippa. *Judicial Activism.* Pacific Grove, Calif.: Brooks/Cole, 1991.

———. *The Supreme Court and Political Questions.* Tuscaloosa: University of Alabama Press, 1974.

Wolfe, Christopher. *The Rise of Modern Judicial Review.* New York: Basic Books, 1986.

CHAPTER 4
THE LEGISLATURE

A rticle I of the U.S. Constitution is its longest and most explicit. The founders established Congress's authority to make laws and spelled out in great detail the powers Congress did and did not have over its own operations. Reading through Article I, we might assume that this part of the Constitution would not have been the source of much litigation. After all, given its specificity, how much room for interpretation could there be?

For cases involving Congress's authority over its internal affairs, this assumption would be accurate. The Supreme Court has heard relatively few cases touching upon the first seven sections of Article I, which deal with the various qualifications for membership in Congress, the ability of the chambers to punish members, and certain privileges enjoyed by the members. When the Court has ruled, it generally, but not always, has given the legislature great latitude over its own business.

That assumption is, however, incorrect when we consider cases that deal directly with Congress's most basic power, the enactment of laws, and with its role in American government. Article I, Section 8, enumerates specifically the substantive areas in which Congress may legislate. But is it too specific, failing to foresee how congressional powers might need to be exercised in areas it does not cover? Some examples: Section 8 provides Congress with the power to borrow and coin money, but not with the authority to print paper money for the payment of debts. Since 1792 congressional committees have held investigations and hearings, but no clause in Section 8 authorizes them to do so. In general, the Supreme Court

has had to determine whether legislative action that is not explicitly covered in Article I falls within Congress's authority, and that is why the Court so often has examined statutes passed by Congress.

There is another reason. As we saw earlier, and as we shall see throughout this book, basic (and purposeful) tensions were built into the design of the government. Sometimes disputes occur between the branches of the federal government; in other instances, between the federal government and the states; and often, between government and individuals. Emanating from the basic principles underlying the structure of government—federalism, the separation of powers, and checks and balances—these conflicts have provided the stuff of myriad legal disputes, and the Court has been right in the middle of many of them.

ARTICLE I: HISTORICAL OVERVIEW

The problems Congress and the nation faced under the Articles of Confederation made it clear to the delegates attending the Constitutional Convention of 1787 that a very different kind of legislature was necessary if the United States was to endure. But what form would that legislature take? And what powers would it have? These questions produced a great deal of discussion during the convention; indeed, debates over the structure and powers of Congress occupied more than half of the framers' time.[1]

---

1. Michael Malbin, "Framing a Congress to Channel Ambition," in *This Constitution: Our Enduring Legacy*, ed. American Political Science Association and American Historical Association (Washington, D.C.: Congressional Quarterly, 1986), 55.

Structure and Composition of Congress

The Virginia Plan set the tone for the Constitutional Convention and became the backbone for Article I. Essentially, the plan called for a bicameral legislature, with the number of representatives in each house apportioned on the basis of state population. Under this scheme, the lower house (now the House of Representatives) would be elected by the people, and the upper house (the Senate) would be chosen by the lower based on recommendations from state legislatures.

The framers dealt with two aspects of the Virginia Plan with relative ease. Almost all agreed on the need for a bicameral legislature. Accord on this point was not surprising; by 1787 only four states had a one-house legislature. The plan for selecting the upper house provoked more discussion. Some thought that having the lower house elect the upper would make the Senate subservient to the House and upset the delicate checks and balances system. Instead, the delegates agreed that the Senate should be selected by state legislatures. (The Seventeenth Amendment to the Constitution, ratified in 1913, changed this method of selection. Senators, like representatives, are now elected by the people.)

The third aspect of the Virginia Plan—the composition of the houses of Congress—generated some of the most acrimonious debates of the convention. As historians Alfred Kelly, Winfred Harbison, and Herman Belz put it: "Would the constituent units be the states, represented equally by delegates chosen by state legislatures, as the small-state group desired? Or would the constituent element be the people of the United States . . . with representation in both chambers apportioned according to population, as the large-state group wished?"[2] On one level, the answer to this question involved the straightforward motivation of self-interest. Naturally, the large states wanted both chambers to be based on population; they would send more representatives to the new Congress. The smaller states thought all states should have equal representation in the houses; they regarded their plan as the only way to avoid tyranny by a majority. On

2. *The American Constitution: Its Origins and Development,* 7th ed. (New York: W. W. Norton, 1991), 90.

another level, the issue of composition went to the core of the Philadelphia enterprise. The approach advocated by the small states would signify the importance of the states in the new system of government, while that put forth in the Virginia Plan would suggest that the federal government received its power directly from the people rather than from the states.

It is no wonder, then, that the delegates had so much trouble resolving this issue: It defined the basic character of the new government. In the end they took the course of action that characterized many of their decisions—they agreed to disagree. Specifically, the delegates reached a compromise under which the House of Representatives would be constituted on the basis of population, and the Senate would have two delegates from each state.

Reaching this compromise was crucial to the success of the convention. Without it, the delegates might have left without framing a constitution. But because the founders split the difference between the demands of the small and large states, they never fully dealt with the critical underlying issue: Do the people or do the states empower the federal government? The impact of this lingering question on the development of the country is addressed in chapter 6. Here, we note that not only has this question been at the center of many disputes brought to the Supreme Court, but also that it was a leading cause of the Civil War.

Powers of Congress

Americans today rarely debate issues concerning the structure and composition of Congress: Most of us simply accept the arrangements outlined in the Constitution. Instead, we tend to concern ourselves with what Congress does or does not do, with its ability to change our lives—sometimes dramatically—through the exercise of its lawmaking powers. Should Congress increase taxes? Pass health care reform? Provide aid for the homeless? Authorize military action? Such policy questions—not structural issues—generate heated debate among Americans.

In 1787 the situation was reversed. The framers fiercely debated issues involving the makeup of the legislature, but they generally agreed about what particular

BOX 4-1 THE POWERS OF CONGRESS

Article I, Section 8, of the Constitution grants Congress the following specific powers:

To lay and collect taxes, duties, imposts, and excises

To pay the debts and provide for the common defence and general welfare of the United States

To borrow money

To regulate commerce with foreign nations, among the states, and with the Indian tribes

To establish uniform rules for naturalization and bankruptcies

To coin money, regulate its value, and fix a standard for weights and measures

To provide for the punishment of counterfeiting

To establish a post office

To establish copyright and patent laws

To create lower courts

To define crimes on the high seas

To declare war

To raise and support armies

To establish and maintain a navy

To create rules regulating the land and naval forces

To call forth the militia to enforce the laws, suppress insurrections, and repel invasions

To organize, arm, and discipline the militia

To pass all legislation over the district that becomes the seat of government

To make all laws necessary and proper to the execution of the foregoing powers

---

powers it would have. This consensus probably reflected their experience under the Articles of Confederation: severe economic problems due in no small part, as the framers knew, to "congressional impotence." [3]

To correct these problems, Article I, Section 8, which lists nineteen powers given to Congress by the delegates *(see Box 4-1)*, contains many provisions relating to the economy. Consider the problem of raising money. Under the Articles of Confederation the legislature could not

3. Daniel A. Farber and Suzanna Sherry, *A History of the American Constitution*, 2nd ed. (St. Paul: Thomson/West, 2005), 189.

collect taxes from the people, but had to rely on the less-than-dependable states to collect and forward taxes (between 1781 and 1783, the legislature requested $10 million from the states but received only $1.5 million). In response, the first power given to Congress in the newly minted Constitution was to "lay and collect taxes."

Although the framers agreed on these powers, two others provoked heated discussions. The first concerned a proposal in the Virginia Plan to give Congress veto authority over state legislation. This idea had the strong support of James Madison, who argued that the states would put their own particular concerns above the general interest. Madison and others who supported this veto proposal were once again reacting to the problems produced by the Articles of Confederation. Because the federal government lacked any coercive power over the states, mutual cooperation among them was virtually nonexistent. They engaged in practices that hurt one another economically and, in general, acted more like thirteen separate countries than a union or even a confederation. But the majority of delegates thought that the states would oppose a congressional veto and jeopardize ratification. Accordingly, they compromised with Article VI, the supremacy clause, which made the Constitution, U.S. laws, and treaties "the supreme law of the land," binding all judges in all the states to follow them.

The second source of controversy was this question: Would Congress be able to exercise powers that were not listed in Article I, Section 8, or was Congress limited to those explicitly named? Some analysts would argue that the last clause of Article I, Section 8, the necessary and proper clause, addressed this question by granting Congress the power "To make all Laws which shall be necessary and proper for carrying into Execution the foregoing Powers." But is that interpretation correct? Even after they agreed on the wording of that clause (with little discussion), the delegates continued to raise the issue in various debates. Delegate James McHenry wrote about a conversation that occurred on September 6: "Spoke to Gov. Morris Fitzsimmons . . . to insert a power . . . enabling the legislature to erect piers for protection of shipping in winter. . . . Mr. Gov.: thinks it may be done under the words of the 1 clause 1 sect 7 art. amended—'and provide for the common defense and general welfare.' "[4] In other words, Fitzsimmons was arguing that one of Congress's enumerated powers (to provide for the common defense and general welfare) implied the power to erect piers. Under this argument, then, Congress could assert powers beyond its enumerated powers.

A majority of the founders may have agreed with Fitzsimmons. Because the question of congressional power is central to understanding the role Congress plays in American society, we shall return to it. At this point, however, we consider the Court's interpretation of the first parts of Article I, which lay out the structure of Congress and its authority over its internal affairs.

MEMBERS OF CONGRESS: QUALIFICATIONS, IMMUNITY, AND DISCIPLINE

While the framers were debating Congress's structure and composition, they were also thinking about what qualifications legislators should have, how members could be punished if they failed to behave in accord with congressional norms, and how they might safeguard the independence and integrity of the institution. Each of these matters was addressed in Article I, but the Supreme Court occasionally has been called upon to resolve questions the framers did not anticipate.

Membership in Congress: Seating and Discipline

In addition to specifying the structure and composition of Congress, Article I contains the requirements that must be met by all prospective members of the institution:

- A senator must be at least thirty years old and have been a citizen of the United States not less than nine years (Section 3, Clause 3).
- A representative must be at least twenty-five years old and have been a citizen not less than seven years (Section 2, Clause 2).
- Every member of Congress must be, when elected, an inhabitant of the state that he or she is to represent (Section 2, Clause 2, and Section 3, Clause 3).

4. Ibid., 199.

- No one may be a member of Congress who holds any other "Office under the United States" (Section 6, Clause 2).

Finally, Section 3 of the Fourteenth Amendment states that no person may be a senator or a representative who, having previously taken an oath as a member of Congress to support the Constitution, has engaged in rebellion against the United States or given aid or comfort to its enemies, unless Congress has removed such disability by a two-thirds vote of both houses.

With only a few exceptions, these standards in themselves have not caused much controversy or litigation. Some legal questions, however, have arisen with respect to their relationship to Article I, Section 5, which reads: "Each House shall be the Judge of the Elections, Returns and Qualifications of its own Members." Several interpretations are possible. One is that this clause ought to be read in conjunction with the Article I requirements for members; that is, Congress cannot deny a duly elected person a seat in the institution unless that person fails to meet the specified criteria. Another interpretation is that Congress is free to develop additional qualifications, independent of those specified elsewhere.

For most of the nation's history, the Supreme Court stayed away from such disputes, even though Congress occasionally acted as if it could add qualifications or ignore them when they were not met. During the Civil War, Congress enacted the Test Oath Law (1862), which required incoming members to "swear . . . that they had never voluntarily borne arms against the United States." Moreover, as shown in Table 4-1, both the House and the Senate have refused to seat properly elected individuals, sometimes on extraconstitutional grounds. The Senate excluded Phillip Thomas on loyalty grounds when it was discovered that he had given $100 to his son when the son entered Confederate military service. And the House refused to seat Brigham H. Roberts because he had been convicted of violating an antipolygamy law.

Investigating the Roberts case, a congressional committee concluded that the Constitution did not prohibit Congress from imposing qualifications for membership in addition to those specified in Article I. As shown in

TABLE 4-1 Duly Elected Members of Congress Excluded

Chamber (Year)	Member-elect (Party-State)	Grounds for Exclusion
Senate (1793)	Albert Gallatin (D-Pa.)	Citizenship
House (1823)	John Bailey (Ind.-Mass.)	Residence
House (1867)	John Y. Brown (D-Ky.)	Loyalty
House (1867)	John D. Young (D-Ky.)	Loyalty
House (1867)	John A. Wimpy (Ind.-Ga.)	Loyalty
House (1867)	W. D. Simpson (Ind.-S.C.)	Loyalty
Senate (1867)	Phillip F. Thomas (D-Md.)	Loyalty
House (1870)	Benjamin F. Whittemore (R-S.C.)	Malfeasance
House (1900)	Brigham H. Roberts (D-Utah)	Polygamy
House (1919)	Victor L. Berger (Socialist-Wis.)	Sedition
House (1920)	Victor L. Berger (Socialist-Wis.)	Sedition
House (1967)	Adam C. Powell Jr. (D-N.Y.)	Misconduct

SOURCE: *Guide to Congress*, 6th ed. (Washington, D.C.: CQ Press, 2007), 1079, 1081.

Table 4-1, the House and Senate both subscribed to this theory. The question of whether the Supreme Court would follow suit remained largely unaddressed until 1969, when the Court decided *Powell v. McCormack*, a case in which it squarely responded to Congress's traditional approach to seating qualifications.

Rep. Adam Clayton Powell Jr. was one of the most interesting and controversial figures ever to serve in Congress. As pastor of the Abyssinian Baptist Church in Harlem, one of the nation's largest congregations, Powell had been a force within that New York City community since the 1930s. This influence only increased when he was elected to the House in 1944 (he received nominations from both the Democratic and Republican Parties) and continued to be reelected by wide margins for the next twenty-five years.

Powell never had problems with his constituents; but his relations with his colleagues were another matter. By the early 1960s he had acquired enough seniority to chair the House Committee on Education and Labor, but he had become unpopular. Other House members disliked his opulent, unconventional lifestyle, his unpredictable leadership, and his use of the media to suit his political ends. Moreover, by that time, Powell had become entangled in various legal controversies; for example, he refused to pay damages assessed against him in a defamation of character suit and actively sought to avert efforts to compel him to pay.

The 89th Congress (1965–1966) launched an inquiry into Powell's activities. This investigation yielded two major violations of House rules: Powell had used federal monies to fly a woman staff member with him on trips to his vacation home in the Bahamas and to pay his former wife a salary of $20,000, even though she did not work in his district or Washington office, in accordance with law. Even though Powell was reelected in November 1966, the House refused to seat him pending further investigation.

In March 1967 the new investigation reached two conclusions: (1) from a constitutional standpoint, Powell met the requirements for office: He was older than twenty-five, had been a citizen of the United States for seven years, and he lived in New York; and (2) Powell had sought to evade the fine associated with the defamation of character offense, had misused public funds, and filed false expenditure reports. The committee recommended "that Powell be sworn and seated as a member of . . . Congress but that he be censured by the House, fined $40,000 and be deprived of his seniority." The House, however, rejected that recommendation and instead adopted by a vote of 307–116 a resolution that excluded Powell from the House

Rep. Adam Clayton Powell Jr. gives an impromptu news conference January 9, 1967. That was the year the House of Representatives voted to exclude him from its chambers, even though he had been duly elected to office. In *Powell v. McCormack* (1969) the Court held that because Powell met the constitutional standards for membership, the House could not refuse to seat him.

and directed House Speaker John McCormack to notify the governor of New York that the seat was vacant.

Powell was not one to accept such a decision lying down. He and thirteen constituents filed a lawsuit against McCormack and other members of Congress, claiming that Congress's refusal to seat him violated the letter of the Constitution. In other words, because Powell met the requirements for office and was properly elected, the House had no choice but to seat him. In his view, Article I, Section 5—"Each House shall be the judge of the Elections, Returns and Qualifications of its own Members"—

gave Congress no authority to exclude members who met the constitutional standards for office. McCormack's attorneys thought otherwise. In their opinion and in accord with institutional tradition, the Court should read the qualifications clause and Section 5 separately. They argued that the House has the authority to exclude members, even if they meet constitutional standards.

The justices held for Powell. In his opinion for the majority, Chief Justice Earl Warren relied heavily on the records of the constitutional debates to conclude that the framers intended to "deny either branch of Congress the authority to add or to otherwise vary the membership qualifications expressly set forth in the Constitution." Warren also asserted that even if the intent of the framers had been less clear, the Court would "nevertheless have been compelled to resolve any ambiguity in favor of a narrow construction of the scope of Congress' power to exclude members-elect." Why? Warren put it this way:

A fundamental principle of our representative democracy is, in Hamilton's words, "that the people should choose whom they please to govern them." As Madison pointed out at the Convention, this principle is undermined as much by limiting whom the people can select as by limiting the franchise itself. In apparent agreement with this basic philosophy, the Convention adopted his suggestion limiting the power to expel. To allow essentially that same power to be exercised under the guise of judging qualifications, would be to ignore Madison's warning, against "vesting an improper & dangerous power in the Legislature." . . . Unquestionably, Congress has an interest in preserving its institutional integrity, but in most cases that interest can be sufficiently safeguarded by the exercise of its power to punish its members for disorderly behavior and, in extreme cases, to expel a member with the concurrence of two-thirds. In short, both the intention of the Framers, to the extent it can be determined, and an examination of the basic principles of our democratic system persuade us that the Constitution does not vest in the Congress a discretionary power to deny membership by a majority vote.

Chief Justice Warren's holding in *Powell* was clear: Because Powell was duly elected and because he met the constitutional standards for membership, the House could not refuse to seat him. Or, as Warren emphatically noted, "Congress is limited to the standing qualifications prescribed in the Constitution."

An important question to ask yourself about *Powell* concerns its relevance to one of the more interesting recent debates about Article I: Does the U.S. Constitution give states the power to enact term limits for members of the U.S. Congress? In *U.S. Term Limits v. Thornton* (1995), the Court addressed this question. As you read the majority opinion, compare it with Chief Justice Warren's position in *Powell v. McCormack:* Does the rationale used by the majority in *Thornton* square with the reasoning in *Powell?* Also pay close attention to the way that both the majority and dissenting opinions deal with various approaches designed to unearth the intent of the framers or the original understanding of the founding generation. Is *Thornton* yet another example of the difficulty of applying these modes of analysis to actual cases?

U.S. Term Limits v. Thornton

514 U.S. 779 (1995)
http://laws.findlaw.com/US/514/779.html
Oral arguments may be found at: http://www.oyez.org
Vote: 5 (Breyer, Ginsburg, Kennedy, Souter, Stevens)
   4 (O'Connor, Rehnquist, Scalia, Thomas)
Opinion of the Court: Stevens
Concurring opinion: Kennedy
Dissenting opinion: Thomas

Between 1990 and 1995 twenty-three states passed statutes imposing term limits on their federal representatives. *Thornton* involved one of those initiatives—Amendment 73 to the Arkansas Constitution, which prohibited from the ballot anyone seeking reelection who previously had served two terms in the U.S. Senate or three terms in the U.S. House of Representatives. It permitted anyone to be elected as a write-in candidate, presumably as a way of allowing for the reelection of a popular incumbent.

Arkansas voters approved the amendment in 1992, and it was to apply to all persons seeking reelection after January 1, 1993. But about two months before that date, various citizens of Arkansas, including Rep. Ray Thornton, and the League of Women Voters filed suit asking a state court to declare the amendment unconstitutional as

a violation of Article I of the U.S. Constitution. In particular, looking back to *Powell v. McCormack* (1969), they claimed that the federal Constitution establishes the sole qualifications for federal office, and the states may not alter them. The state and U.S. Term Limits, an organization supporting the amendment, responded with a number of arguments. First, they pointed to Section 4 of Article I, which says: "The Times, Places and Manner of holding Elections for Senators and Representatives, shall be prescribed in each State by the Legislature thereof." In their view, this section, not the qualifications clauses, is applicable because term limits seek to regulate access to the ballot, not qualifications for office. Second, they suggested that *Powell* spoke only about the ability of the U.S. House of Representatives, not of the states, to set qualifications. Finally, because the Constitution does not explicitly prohibit the states from setting qualifications for office, it is a power reserved to them under the Tenth Amendment.

The Arkansas courts disagreed. The lower court struck down the amendment as a violation of Article I of the U.S. Constitution, and in 1994 the Arkansas Supreme Court affirmed. According to the justices: "The qualifications clauses fix the sole requirement for congressional service. This is not a power left to the states." With this defeat in hand, amendment proponents appealed to the U.S. Supreme Court, which agreed to hear the case.

JUSTICE STEVENS delivered the opinion of the Court.

Today's cases present a challenge to an amendment to the Arkansas State Constitution that prohibits the name of an otherwise-eligible candidate for Congress from appearing on the general election ballot if that candidate has already served three terms in the House of Representatives or two terms in the Senate. The Arkansas Supreme Court held that the amendment violates the Federal Constitution. We agree with that holding. Such a state-imposed restriction is contrary to the "fundamental principle of our representative democracy," embodied in the Constitution, that "the people should choose whom they please to govern them." *Powell v. McCormack* (1969). Allowing individual States to adopt their own qualifications for congressional service would be inconsistent with the Framers' vision of a uniform National Legislature representing the people of the United

States. If the qualifications set forth in the text of the Constitution are to be changed, that text must be amended.

As the opinions of the Arkansas Supreme Court suggest, the constitutionality of Amendment 73 depends critically on the resolution of two distinct issues. The first is whether the Constitution forbids States from adding to or altering the qualifications specifically enumerated in the Constitution. The second is, if the Constitution does so forbid, whether the fact that Amendment 73 is formulated as a ballot access restriction rather than as an outright disqualification is of constitutional significance. Our resolution of these issues draws upon our prior resolution of a related but distinct issue: whether Congress has the power to add to or alter the qualifications of its Members.

Twenty-six years ago, in *Powell v. McCormack*, we reviewed the history and text of the Qualifications Clauses in a case involving an attempted exclusion of a duly elected Member of Congress. The principal issue was whether the power granted to each House in Art. I, §5, to judge the "Qualifications of its own Members" includes the power to impose qualifications other than those set forth in the text of the Constitution. In an opinion by Chief Justice Warren for eight Members of the Court, we held that it does not. Because of the obvious importance of the issue, the Court's review of the history and meaning of the relevant constitutional text was especially thorough. We therefore begin our analysis today with a . . . statement of what we decided in that case. . . .

Powell . . . establishes two important propositions: first, that the "relevant historical materials" compel the conclusion that, at least with respect to qualifications imposed by Congress, the Framers intended the qualifications listed in the Constitution to be exclusive; and second, that that conclusion is equally compelled by an understanding of the "fundamental principle of our representative democracy . . . 'that the people should choose whom they please to govern them.' " . . .

Unsurprisingly, the state courts and lower federal courts have similarly concluded that *Powell* conclusively resolved the issue whether Congress has the power to impose additional qualifications.

In sum, after examining *Powell*'s historical analysis and its articulation of the "basic principles of our democratic system," we reaffirm that the qualifications for service in Congress set forth in the text of the Constitution are "fixed," at least in the sense that they may not be supplemented by Congress.

Our reaffirmation of *Powell*, does not necessarily resolve the specific questions presented in these cases. For petitioners argue that whatever the constitutionality of additional qualifications for membership imposed by Congress, the historical and textual materials discussed in *Powell* do not support the conclusion that the Constitution prohibits additional qualifications imposed by States. In the absence of such a constitutional prohibition, petitioners argue, the Tenth Amendment and the principle of reserved powers require that States be allowed to add such qualifications.

Before addressing these arguments, we find it appropriate to take note of the striking unanimity among the courts that have considered the issue. None of the overwhelming array of briefs submitted by the parties and amici has called to our attention even a single case in which a state court or federal court has approved of a State's addition of qualifications for a member of Congress. To the contrary, an impressive number of courts have determined that States lack the authority to add qualifications. . . . This impressive and uniform body of judicial decisions . . . indicates that the obstacles confronting petitioners are formidable indeed.

Petitioners argue that the Constitution contains no express prohibition against state-added qualifications, and that Amendment 73 is therefore an appropriate exercise of a State's reserved power to place additional restrictions on the choices that its own voters may make. We disagree for two independent reasons. First, we conclude that the power to add qualifications is not within the "original powers" of the States, and thus is not reserved to the States by the Tenth Amendment. Second, even if States possessed some original power in this area, we conclude that the Framers intended the Constitution to be the exclusive source of qualifications for members of Congress, and that the Framers thereby "divested" States of any power to add qualifications. . . .

Contrary to petitioners' assertions, the power to add qualifications is not part of the original powers of sovereignty that the Tenth Amendment reserved to the States. Petitioners' Tenth Amendment argument misconceives the nature of the right at issue because that Amendment could only "reserve" that which existed before. As Justice Joseph Story recognized, "the states can exercise no powers whatsoever, which exclusively spring out of the existence of the national government, which the constitution does not delegate to them. . . . No state can say, that it has reserved, what it never possessed." . . .

With respect to setting qualifications for service in Congress, no such right existed before the Constitution was ratified. The contrary argument overlooks the revolutionary character of the government that the Framers conceived. Prior to the adoption of the Constitution, the States joined together under the Articles of Confederation. In that system, "the States retained most of their sovereignty, like independent nations bound together only by treaties." After the Constitutional Convention convened, the Framers were presented with, and eventually adopted a variation of, "a plan not merely to amend the Articles of Confederation but to create an entirely new government with a National Executive, National Judiciary, and a National Legislature." In adopting that plan, the Framers envisioned a uniform national system, rejecting the notion that the Nation was a collection of States, and instead creating a direct link between the National Government and the people of the United States. In that National Government, representatives owe primary allegiance not to the people of a State but to the people of a Nation. . . .

In short, as the Framers recognized, electing representatives to the National Legislature was a new right, arising from the Constitution itself. The Tenth Amendment thus provides no basis for concluding that the States possess reserved power to add qualifications to those that are fixed in the Constitution. Instead, any state power to set the qualifications for membership in Congress must derive not from the reserved powers of state sovereignty, but rather from the delegated powers of national sovereignty. In the absence of any constitutional delegation to the States of power to add qualifications to those enumerated in the Constitution, such a power does not exist.

Even if we believed that States possessed as part of their original powers some control over congressional qualifications, the text and structure of the Constitution, the relevant historical materials, and, most importantly, the "basic principles of our democratic system" all demonstrate that the Qualifications Clauses were intended to preclude the States from exercising any such power and to fix as exclusive the qualifications in the Constitution. . . .

The available affirmative evidence indicates the Framers' intent that States have no role in the setting of qualifications. In Federalist Paper No. 52, dealing with the House of Representatives, Madison addressed the "qualifications of the electors and the elected." . . .

"A representative of the United States must be of the age of twenty-five years; must have been seven years a citizen of the United States; must, at the time of his election be an inhabitant of the State he is to represent; and, during the time of his service must be in no office under the United States. Under these reasonable limitations, the door of this part of the federal government is open to merit of every description, whether native or adoptive, whether young or old, and without regard to poverty or wealth, or to any particular profession of religious faith." . . .

We also find compelling the complete absence in the ratification debates of any assertion that States had the power to add qualifications. In those debates, the question whether to require term limits, or "rotation," was a major source of controversy. The draft of the Constitution that was submitted for ratification contained no provision for rotation. In arguments that echo in the preamble to Arkansas' Amendment 73, opponents of ratification condemned the absence of a rotation requirement, noting that "there is no doubt that senators will hold their office perpetually; and in this situation, they must of necessity lose their dependence, and their attachments to the people." . . . At several ratification conventions, participants proposed amendments that would have required rotation.

The Federalists' responses to those criticisms and proposals addressed the merits of the issue, arguing that rotation was incompatible with the people's right to choose. . . . Hamilton argued that the representatives' need for reelection rather than mandatory rotation was the more effective way to keep representatives responsive to the people, because "when a man knows he must quit his station, let his merit be what it may, he will turn his attention chiefly to his own emolument."

Regardless of which side has the better of the debate over rotation, it is most striking that nowhere in the extensive ratification debates have we found any statement by either a proponent or an opponent of rotation that the draft constitution would permit States to require rotation for the representatives of their own citizens. . . .

Our conclusion that States lack the power to impose qualifications vindicates the same "fundamental principle of our representative democracy" that we recognized in *Powell*, namely that "the people should choose whom they please to govern them."

. . . [T]he *Powell* Court recognized that an egalitarian ideal—that election to the National Legislature should be open to all people of merit—provided a critical foundation for the Constitutional structure. This egalitarian theme echoes throughout the constitutional debates. In The Federalist No. 57, for example, Madison wrote: "Who are to be the objects of popular choice? Every citizen whose merit may recommend him to the esteem and confidence of his country. No qualification of wealth, of birth, of religious faith, or of civil profession is permitted to fetter the judgment or disappoint the inclination of the people." . . .

Similarly, we believe that state-imposed qualifications, as much as congressionally imposed qualifications, would undermine the second critical idea recognized in *Powell*: that an aspect of sovereignty is the right of the people to vote for whom they wish. Again, the source of the qualification is of little moment in assessing the qualification's restrictive impact.

Finally, state-imposed restrictions, unlike the congressionally imposed restrictions at issue in *Powell*, violate a third idea central to this basic principle: that the right to choose representatives belongs not to the States, but to the people. . . .

The Framers deemed this principle critical when they discussed qualifications. For example, during the debates on residency requirements, Morris noted that in the House, "the people at large, not the States, are represented." Similarly, George Read noted that the Framers "were forming a National Government and such a regulation would correspond little with the idea that we were one people." James Wilson "enforced the same consideration." . . .

Petitioners attempt to overcome this formidable array of evidence against the States' power to impose qualifications by arguing that the practice of the States immediately after the adoption of the Constitution demonstrates their understanding that they possessed such power. One may properly question the extent to which the States' own practice is a reliable indicator of the contours of restrictions that the Constitution imposed on States, especially when no court has ever upheld a state-imposed qualification of any sort. . . . But petitioners' argument is unpersuasive even on its own terms. At the time of the Convention, "almost all the State Constitutions required members of their Legislatures to pos-

sess considerable property." Despite this near uniformity, only one State, Virginia, placed similar restrictions on members of Congress, requiring that a representative be, inter alia, a "freeholder." Just 15 years after imposing a property qualification, Virginia replaced that requirement with a provision requiring that representatives be only "qualified according to the constitution of the United States." . . .

In sum, the available historical and textual evidence, read in light of the basic principles of democracy underlying the Constitution and recognized by this Court in *Powell*, reveal the Framers' intent that neither Congress nor the States should possess the power to supplement the exclusive qualifications set forth in the text of the Constitution.

Petitioners argue that, even if States may not add qualifications, Amendment 73 is constitutional because it is not such a qualification, and because Amendment 73 is a permissible exercise of state power to regulate the "Times, Places and Manner of Holding Elections." We reject these contentions.

Unlike §§1 and 2 of Amendment 73, which create absolute bars to service for long-term incumbents running for state office, §3 merely provides that certain Senators and Representatives shall not be certified as candidates and shall not have their names appear on the ballot. They may run as write-in candidates and, if elected, they may serve. Petitioners contend that only a legal bar to service creates an impermissible qualification, and that Amendment 73 is therefore consistent with the Constitution. . . .

We need not decide whether petitioners' narrow understanding of qualifications is correct because, even if it is, Amendment 73 may not stand. As we have often noted, " 'constitutional rights would be of little value if they could be . . . indirectly denied.' " The Constitution "nullifies sophisticated as well as simple-minded modes" of infringing on Constitutional protections.

In our view, Amendment 73 is an indirect attempt to accomplish what the Constitution prohibits Arkansas from accomplishing directly. As the plurality opinion of the Arkansas Supreme Court recognized, Amendment 73 is an "effort to dress eligibility to stand for Congress in ballot access clothing," because the "intent and the effect of Amendment 73 are to disqualify congressional incumbents from further service." We must, of course, accept the State Court's view of the purpose of its own law: we are thus authoritatively informed that the sole purpose of §3 of Amendment 73 was to attempt to achieve a result that is forbidden by the Federal Constitution. Indeed, it cannot be seriously contended that the intent behind Amendment 73 is other than to prevent the election of incumbents. The preamble of Amendment 73 states explicitly: "The people of Arkansas . . . herein limit the terms of elected officials." Sections 1 and 2 create absolute limits on the number of terms that may be served. There is no hint that §3 was intended to have any other purpose. Petitioners do, however, contest the Arkansas Supreme Court's conclusion that the Amendment has the same practical effect as an absolute bar. They argue that the possibility of a write-in campaign creates a real possibility for victory, especially for an entrenched incumbent. One may reasonably question the merits of that contention. Indeed, we are advised by the state court that there is nothing more than a faint glimmer of possibility that the excluded candidate will win. Our prior cases, too, have suggested that write-in candidates have only a slight chance of victory. But even if petitioners are correct that incumbents may occasionally win reelection as write-in candidates, there is no denying that the ballot restrictions will make it significantly more difficult for the barred candidate to win the election. In our view, an amendment with the avowed purpose and obvious effect of evading the requirements of the Qualifications Clauses by handicapping a class of candidates cannot stand. . . .

Petitioners make the related argument that Amendment 73 merely regulates the "Manner" of elections, and that the Amendment is therefore a permissible exercise of state power under Article I, §4, cl. 1 (the Elections Clause) to regulate the "Times, Places and Manner" of elections. We cannot agree. A necessary consequence of petitioners' argument is that Congress itself would have the power to "make or alter" a measure such as Amendment 73. That the Framers would have approved of such a result is unfathomable. As our decision in *Powell* and our discussion above make clear, the Framers were particularly concerned that a grant to Congress of the authority to set its own qualifications would lead inevitably to congressional self-aggrandizement and the upsetting of the delicate constitutional balance. Petitioners would have us believe, however, that even as the Framers carefully circumscribed congressional power to set qualifications, they intended to allow Congress to achieve the same result by simply formulating the regulation as a ballot access restriction under the Elections Clause. We refuse to adopt an interpretation of the Elections Clause that would so cavalierly disregard what the Framers intended to be a fundamental constitutional safeguard. . . .

The merits of term limits, or "rotation," have been the subject of debate since the formation of our Constitution, when the Framers unanimously rejected a proposal to add such limits to the Constitution. The cogent arguments on both sides of the question that were articulated during the process of ratification largely retain their force today. Over half the States have adopted measures that impose such limits on some offices either directly or indirectly, and the Nation as a whole, notably by constitutional amendment, has imposed a limit on the number of terms that the President may serve. Term limits, like any other qualification for office, unquestionably restrict the ability of voters to vote for whom they wish. On the other hand, such limits may provide for the infusion of fresh ideas and new perspectives, and may decrease the likelihood that representatives will lose touch with their constituents. It is not our province to resolve this longstanding debate.

We are, however, firmly convinced that allowing the several States to adopt term limits for congressional service would effect a fundamental change in the constitutional framework. Any such change must come not by legislation adopted either by Congress or by an individual State, but rather—as have other important changes in the electoral process—through the Amendment procedures set forth in Article V. The Framers decided that the qualifications for service in the Congress of the United States be fixed in the Constitution and be uniform throughout the Nation. That decision reflects the Framers' understanding that Members of Congress are chosen by separate constituencies, but that they become, when elected, servants of the people of the United States. They are not merely delegates appointed by separate, sovereign States; they occupy offices that are integral and essential components of a single National Government. In the absence of a properly passed constitutional amendment, allowing individual States to craft their own qualifications for Congress would thus erode the structure envisioned by the Framers, a structure that was designed, in the words of the Preamble to our Constitution, to form a "more perfect Union."

The judgment is affirmed.
It is so ordered.

JUSTICE THOMAS, with whom THE CHIEF JUSTICE, JUSTICE O'CONNOR, and JUSTICE SCALIA join, dissenting.

It is ironic that the Court bases today's decision on the right of the people to "choose whom they please to govern them." Under our Constitution, there is only one State whose people have the right to "choose whom they please" to represent Arkansas in Congress. The Court holds, however, that neither the elected legislature of that State nor the people themselves (acting by ballot initiative) may prescribe any qualifications for those representatives. The majority therefore defends the right of the people of Arkansas to "choose whom they please to govern them" by invalidating a provision that won nearly 60% of the votes cast in a direct election and that carried every congressional district in the State.

I dissent. Nothing in the Constitution deprives the people of each State of the power to prescribe eligibility requirements for the candidates who seek to represent them in Congress. The Constitution is simply silent on this question. And where the Constitution is silent, it raises no bar to action by the States or the people.

Because the majority fundamentally misunderstands the notion of "reserved" powers, I start with some first principles. Contrary to the majority's suggestion, the people of the States need not point to any affirmative grant of power in the Constitution in order to prescribe qualifications for their representatives in Congress, or to authorize their elected state legislators to do so.

Our system of government rests on one overriding principle: all power stems from the consent of the people. To phrase the principle in this way, however, is to be imprecise about something important to the notion of "reserved" powers. The ultimate source of the Constitution's authority is the consent of the people of each individual State, not the consent of the undifferentiated people of the Nation as a whole. . . .

When they adopted the Federal Constitution, of course, the people of each State surrendered some of their authority to the United States (and hence to entities accountable to the people of other States as well as to themselves). They affirmatively deprived their States of certain powers and they affirmatively conferred certain powers upon the Federal Government. Because the people of the several States are the only true source of power, however, the Federal Government enjoys no authority beyond what the Constitution confers: the Federal Government's powers are limited and enumerated. In the words of Justice Black, "the United States is entirely a creature of the Constitution. Its power and authority have no other source."

In each State, the remainder of the people's powers—"the powers not delegated to the United States by the Constitution, nor prohibited by it to the States,"—are either delegated to the state government or retained by the people. The Federal Constitution does not specify which of these two possibilities obtains; it is up to the various state constitutions to declare which powers the people of each State have delegated to their state government. As far as the Federal Constitution is concerned, then, the States can exercise all powers that the Constitution does not withhold from them. The Federal Government and the States thus face different default rules: where the Constitution is silent about the exercise of a particular power—that is, where the Constitution does not speak either expressly or by necessary implication—the Federal Government lacks that power and the States enjoy it.

These basic principles are enshrined in the Tenth Amendment, which declares that all powers neither delegated to the Federal Government nor prohibited to the States "are reserved to the States respectively, or to the people." With this careful last phrase, the Amendment avoids taking any position on the division of power between the state governments and the people of the States: it is up to the people of each State to determine which "reserved" powers their state government may exercise. . . .

The majority begins by announcing an enormous and untenable limitation on the principle expressed by the Tenth Amendment. According to the majority, the States possess only those powers that the Constitution affirmatively grants to them or that they enjoyed before the Constitution was adopted; the Tenth Amendment "could only 'reserve' that which existed before." From the fact that the States had not previously enjoyed any powers over the particular institutions of the Federal Government established by the Constitution, the majority derives a rule precisely opposite to the one that the Amendment actually prescribes: "'The states can exercise no powers whatsoever, which exclusively spring out of the existence of the national government, which the constitution does not delegate to them.'"

. . . Given the fundamental principle that all governmental powers stem from the people of the States, it would simply be incoherent to assert that the people of the States could not reserve any powers that they had not previously controlled.

The Tenth Amendment's use of the word "reserved" does not help the majority's position. If someone says that the power to use a particular facility is reserved to some group, he is not saying anything about whether that group has previously used the facility. He is merely saying that the people who control the facility have designated that group as the entity with authority to use it. The Tenth Amendment is similar: the people of the States, from whom all governmental powers stem, have specified that all powers not prohibited to the States by the Federal Constitution are reserved "to the States respectively, or to the people."

The majority is therefore quite wrong to conclude that the people of the States cannot authorize their state governments to exercise any powers that were unknown to the States when the Federal Constitution was drafted. Indeed, the majority's position frustrates the apparent purpose of the Amendment's final phrase. The Amendment does not pre-empt any limitations on state power found in the state constitutions, as it might have done if it simply had said that the powers not delegated to the Federal Government are reserved to the States. But the Amendment also does not prevent the people of the States from amending their state constitutions to remove limitations that were in effect when the Federal Constitution and the Bill of Rights were ratified. . . .

I take it to be established, then, that the people of Arkansas do enjoy "reserved" powers over the selection of their representatives in Congress. . . . Whatever one might think of the wisdom of this arrangement, we may not override the decision of the people of Arkansas unless something in the Federal Constitution deprives them of the power to enact such measures.

The majority settles on "the Qualifications Clauses" as the constitutional provisions that Amendment 73 violates. . . . [T]he Qualifications Clauses are merely straightforward recitations of the minimum eligibility requirements that the Framers thought it essential for every Member of Congress to meet. They restrict state power only in that they prevent the States from abolishing all eligibility requirements for membership in Congress. . . .

To the extent that they bear on this case, the records of the Philadelphia Convention affirmatively support my unwillingness to find hidden meaning in the Qualifications Clauses, while the surviving records from the ratification debates help neither side. As for the postratification period, five States supplemented the constitutional disqualifications in their very first election laws. The historical evidence thus refutes any notion that the Qualifications Clauses were generally understood to be exclusive. Yet the majority must establish just such an understanding in order to justify its position that the Clauses impose unstated prohibitions on the States and the people. In my view, the historical evidence is simply inadequate to warrant the majority's conclusion that the Qualifications Clauses mean anything more than what they say.

The decision in *U.S. Term Limits v. Thornton*, coupled with the *Powell* ruling, authoritatively settles the issue of qualifications for congressional office. The Constitution's age, residency, and citizenship requirements are a complete statement of congressional eligibility standards. Without a constitutional amendment granting such authority, neither Congress nor the states may add to or delete from those requirements.

The Speech or Debate Clause

The Constitution provides mechanisms for Congress to discipline its members, but it also contains a safeguard against harassment or intimidation. Article I, Section 6, specifies:

The Senators and Representatives . . . shall in all Cases, except Treason, Felony, and Breach of the Peace, be privileged from Arrest during their Attendance at the Session of their respective Houses, and in going to and returning from the same; and for any Speech or Debate in either House, they shall not be questioned in any other Place.

Called the speech or debate clause, this privilege of membership emanates from British practice. The English Parliament, during its struggles with the Crown, asserted that its members were immune from arrest during its sessions, and the English Bill of Rights embodies this guarantee. The importance of the speech or debate clause's protection is undeniable: Without it, a president could order the arrest of, or otherwise intimidate, members of Congress who disagreed with the administration. The framers thought the protection was necessary "to protect the integrity of the legislative process by insuring the independence of individual legislators."[5]

The language of the speech or debate clause has generated two kinds of constitutional questions: What is protected? Who is protected? The reach of the clause was first addressed by the Court in **Kilbourn v. Thompson** (1881). In *Kilbourn* the Court dealt primarily with the scope of congressional investigations, but it also noted that the clause extends to

written reports presented . . . by its committees, to resolutions offered, which, though in writing, must be reproduced in speech, and to the act of voting, whether it is done vocally or by passing between the tellers. In short, to things generally done in a session [of Congress] by one of its members in relation to the business before it.

With only some minor modifications, *Kilbourn* remained the Court's most significant statement on the speech or debate clause until 1972, when **Gravel v. United States** was decided. This case had important implications for both dimensions of Section 6.

Gravel began on June 29, 1971, when Sen. Mike Gravel, D-Alaska, held a public meeting of the Subcommittee on Buildings and Grounds, of which he was the chair. Before the hearing began, Gravel made a statement about the Vietnam War, noting that it was "relevant to his subcommittee . . . because of its effects upon the domestic economy and . . . the lack of federal funds to provide for adequate public facilities." He then read portions of a classified government document, now known as the Pentagon Papers, which provided details of U.S. involvement in the war. After he finished, Gravel introduced the forty-seven-volume document into the committee's record and later arranged for its publication by Beacon Press, a publishing division of the Unitarian Universalist Association.

The Justice Department began an investigation to determine how the classified Pentagon Papers were released. It requested a district court judge to convene a grand jury, which in turn subpoenaed, among others, Senator Gravel's aide, Dr. Leonard Rodberg. Gravel and

Rodberg asked the court to quash the subpoena, claiming protection under the speech or debate clause.

When it reached the Supreme Court, *Gravel* presented the justices with the two classic questions: Who is covered and what is covered under the speech or debate clause? The government argued that the clause applied only to Senator Gravel and not his aide. Gravel countered with the argument that the job of a contemporary legislator demanded a more expanded view of protection if the spirit and goals of the speech or debate clause were to be realized. In effect, forcing Rodberg to testify would be tantamount to requiring Gravel to do so.

As for who was protected, Justice Byron R. White, who wrote the majority opinion, held that the clause gave similar protection to both the senator and his aide. For

it is literally impossible, in view of the complexities of the modern legislative process, . . . for Members of Congress to perform their legislative tasks without the help of aides and assistants; the day-to-day work of such aides is so critical to the Members' performance that they must be treated as the latter's alter egos; and that if they are not so recognized, the central role of the Speech or Debate Clause—to prevent intimidation of legislators by the Executive and accountability before a possibly hostile judiciary—will inevitably be diminished and frustrated.

At the same time, however, White asserted that speech or debate clause protection was not absolute. Both the senator and the aide could be questioned for activities that had no direct connection to or "impinged upon" the legislative process. Because "private publication by Senator Gravel through the cooperation of Beacon Press was in no way essential to the deliberations of the Senate," the speech or debate clause did not provide immunity to Rodberg from testifying before the grand jury about the publishing arrangement between Gravel and Beacon Press "or about his own participation, if any, in the alleged transaction, so long as legislative acts of the Senator are not impugned."

Despite the specificity of the Court's ruling in *Gravel*, it did not put an end to controversies under the speech or debate clause. Indeed, as illustrated in Table 4-2, in the 1970s the Court decided several important issues that were left open by *Gravel*. For the most part, these decisions supported congressional immunity. For example, in *United States v. Helstoski* (1979) the justices refused to al-

5. *United States v. Brewster* (1972).

TABLE 4-2 Speech or Debate Clause Cases after *Gravel v. United States*

Case	Legal Question	Court's Response
United States v. Brewster (1972)	Does the speech or debate clause protect members of Congress from prosecution for alleged bribery to perform a legislative act?	The clause protects members from inquiry into legislative acts; it does not protect all conduct relating to the legislative process.
Doe v. McMillan (1973)	Does the speech or debate clause protect members (and their staff) and other persons who were involved in creating and distributing a report on the D.C. school system that identified, by name, specific children and did so in a negative way?	The clause offers absolute immunity to members and staff, but not to individuals who, acting under congressional authority, distributed the materials.
Eastland v. U.S. Servicemen's Fund (1975)	Does the speech or debate clause protect members against a suit brought by an organization to stop the implementation of a subpoena ordering a bank to produce certain records?	The clause offers absolute protection because the activities fall within the "legitimate legislative" sphere.
Davis v. Passman (1979)	Does the speech or debate clause protect a member against charges of sex discrimination?	The Court decided the case on Fifth Amendment grounds and reached no result on the member's claim that he was protected by the speech or debate clause.
United States v. Helstoski (1979)	Does the speech or debate clause protect a member against prosecution (for accepting bribes), when evidence introduced in that action hinges on past legislative acts?	The clause does not permit the introduction of evidence involving past legislative acts.
Hutchinson v. Proxmire (1979)	Does the speech or debate clause protect a member from a civil suit in response to negative statements made to the press and in newsletters about a government grant awardee's research?	The clause does not protect a member from a libel judgment when information is disseminated to the press and the public through newsletters.

low prosecutors to introduce evidence into a court proceeding against a former member of Congress involving legislative activities. *Hutchinson v. Proxmire* (1979), however, was a defeat for congressional authority. Here the Court examined a dispute arising when Sen. William Proxmire, D-Wis., on the floor of the Senate and later in a newsletter and on television, labeled Ronald R. Hutchinson's federally funded research virtually worthless and a waste of taxpayers' money. Hutchinson brought a libel suit against Proxmire. When the case reached the Court, the justices addressed the issue of whether the speech or debate clause immunized the senator from a libel proceeding on the ground that he had first made the remarks on the chamber's floor. The Court held that it did not:

A speech by Proxmire in the Senate would be wholly immune and would be available to other Members of Congress and the public in the Congressional Record. But neither the newsletters nor the press release was "essential to the deliberations of the Senate," and neither was part of the deliberative process.

Although speech or debate clause cases no longer occupy much of the justices' attention, exceptions occasionally arise. In 2008 the Justice Department asked the Court to review a decision by the U.S. Court of Appeals for the District of Columbia, holding that the speech or debate clause gave members of Congress some protection against searches—with warrants—of their congressional offices. The Justice Department was investigating Rep. William Jefferson, D-La., for taking bribes and claimed that the D.C. court's ruling would impede its ability to enforce federal law against Jefferson and other lawmakers. The Supreme Court refused to hear the case, *United States v. Rayburn House Office Building, Room 2113.*

THE SOURCES AND SCOPE OF LEGISLATIVE POWERS

As noted above, Article I, Section 8, contains a virtual laundry list of Congress's powers. These enumerated powers, covered in seventeen clauses, establish congressional authority to regulate commerce, to lay and collect taxes, to establish post offices, and so forth. The enumerated powers pose few constitutional problems: Those that the Constitution names, Congress clearly has.

But questions have arisen over other aspects of congressional power. First, does the legislative branch have powers beyond those specified by the Constitution? Despite the fact that the framers left this question unaddressed, as noted in Table 4-3, the Court has not hesitated to answer it affirmatively, suggesting that Congress has implied and inherent powers in addition to those listed in Article I. In this section, we examine the cases in which the Court located those sources. We also focus on a second, more complex, question: What constraints are there on Congress's ability to exercise these powers?

As you read the next cases, keep in mind not only the sources of legislative power but also the scope of that power. How has the Court sought to constrain Congress and, more important, why? What pressures have been brought to bear on the justices in making their decisions?

Enumerated and Implied Powers

The Constitution's specific list of congressional powers leaves no doubt that Congress has these powers. Where debate has occurred is over the question of whether Congress has more powers, or was intended to have more powers, than those specifically granted. And if so, how broad should they be? Those who look to the plain language of the Constitution or to the intent of the framers would find few concrete answers, although both camps would point to the same clause. Article I, Section 8, Clause 18, provides that Congress shall have the power

to make all Laws which shall be necessary and proper for carrying into Execution the foregoing Powers, and all other Powers vested by this Constitution in the Government of the United States, or in any Department or Officer thereof.

TABLE 4-3 Sources of Congressional Power

Power[a]	Defined	Example
Enumerated powers	Those that the Constitution expressly grants	Article I, Section 8. Includes the power to borrow money, raise armies, regulate commerce.
Implied powers	Those that may be inferred from power expressly granted	Article I, Section 8, Clauses 2–17, in conjunction with Clause 18, the necessary and proper clause. For example, the enumerated power of raising and supporting armies leads to the implied power of operating a draft.
Inherent powers	Those powers that do not depend on constitutional grants but grow out of the very existence of the national government	Foreign affairs. Foreign affairs powers are those that the national government would have even if the Constitution were silent, because they are powers that all nations have under international law. For example, the federal government can issue orders prohibiting U.S. businesses from selling arms to particular nations.
Amendment-enforcing powers	Those powers contained in some constitutional amendments that provide Congress with the ability to enforce them	Amendments 13, 14, and 15, for example, state that Congress shall have the power to enforce the article by "appropriate legislation."

SOURCE: Adopted from J. W. Peltason, *Understanding the Constitution,* 14th ed. (Fort Worth, Texas: Harcourt Brace, 1997), 20–21.
   a. Some analysts suggest that Congress also possesses resulting powers (those that result when several enumerated powers are added together) and inherited powers (those that Congress inherited from the British Parliament).

John Marshall and the Implied Powers Doctrine. Called by various names—the necessary and proper clause, the elastic clause, or the sweeping clause—this provision was the subject of heated debate early in the nation's history. Many affiliated with the Federalist Party, which favored a strong national government, argued for a loose construction of the clause. In their view, the framers inserted it into the Constitution to provide Congress with some "flexibility"; in other words, Congress could exercise powers beyond those listed in the Constitution, those that were "necessary and proper" for implementing legislative activity. In contrast, the Jeffersonians asserted the need for a strict interpretation of the clause; in their view, it constricted congressional powers, rather than expanded them. In other words, congressional exercise of power under the necessary and proper clause could be only that power necessary to carry out its enumerated functions.

Which view would the Supreme Court adopt? Would it interpret the necessary and proper clause strictly or loosely? This was one of two major questions at the core of *McCulloch v. Maryland* (1819), which many consider the Court's most important explication of congressional powers.[6] Indeed, some suggest that this opinion was Chief Justice John Marshall's finest. As you read this case, consider not only the Court's holding, but also the language and logic of *McCulloch.* Why is it such an extraordinary statement?

McCulloch v. Maryland

4 Wheat. (17 U.S.) 316 (1819)
http://law.findlaw.com/US/17/316.html
Vote: 6 (Duvall, Johnson, Livingston, Marshall, Story,
    Washington)
    0
Opinion of the Court: Marshall
Not participating: Todd

Although we take for granted the ability of the federal government to operate a banking system—today called the Federal Reserve System—in the eighteenth and into the nineteenth century this topic was a political battle-

ground. The first sign of controversy came as early as 1790, when George Washington's secretary of the Treasury, Alexander Hamilton, asked Congress to adopt a series of proposals amounting to a comprehensive economic plan for the new nation. Among Hamilton's proposals was the creation of a Bank of the United States, which would receive deposits, disburse funds, and make loans; and Congress enacted a bill authorizing the founding of the first federal bank.

When the bill arrived at President Washington's desk, however, he did not sign it immediately. He wanted to ascertain whether in fact Congress could create a bank, since it lacked explicit constitutional authority to do so. To this end he asked Hamilton, Secretary of State Thomas Jefferson, and Attorney General Edmund Randolph for their opinions on the bank's constitutionality.

Box 4-2 provides excerpts of Hamilton's and Jefferson's responses. We offer them not only because they reached different conclusions—Hamilton argued that it was constitutional, Jefferson that it was not—but also because they represent the classic competing theories of congressional power. Moreover, they illustrate the limits of interpreting the Constitution by looking at the intent of the framers. Does it seem odd that just four years after the founding of the country, two of its foremost leaders could have such different views? In his argument, Hamilton, in fact, noted that there was a "conflicting recollection" of a convention debate highly relevant to the bank issue.[7] In the end, the president was persuaded by Hamilton and signed the bill. Congress then created the First Bank of the United States in 1791, chartering it for a twenty-year period.

Nevertheless, the bank controversy did not disappear. Among other factors, the bank became a symbol of the loose-construction, nationally oriented Federalist Party, which had lost considerable power from its heyday in the 1790s. Indeed, by the turn of the century, a strict-construction approach to congressional power was among

---

6. The other question involved federalism. See chapter 6.

7. One scholar notes that the framers rejected a proposal that would have allowed Congress to establish corporations; in fact, they did so in part because of the possibility that Congress would create banks. See Jethro Lieberman, *Milestones!* (St. Paul: West, 1976), 118. Still, Hamilton argued that debate was unclear.

BOX 4-2   JEFFERSON AND HAMILTON ON THE BANK OF THE UNITED STATES

OPINION ON THE CONSTITUTIONALITY OF A NATIONAL BANK (1791)

Thomas Jefferson

To take a single step beyond the boundaries . . . specially drawn around the powers of Congress, is to take possession of a boundless field of power, no longer susceptible of any definition.

The incorporation of a bank, and other powers assumed by this bill have not, in my opinion, been delegated to the U.S. by the Constitution.

I. They are not among the powers specially enumerated, for these are

1. A power to *lay taxes* for the purpose of paying the debts of the U.S. But no debt is paid by this bill, nor any tax laid. . . .

2. "to borrow money." But this bill neither borrows money, nor ensures the borrowing of it. . . .

3. "to regulate commerce with foreign nations, and among the states, and with the Indian tribes." To erect a bank, and to regulate commerce, are very different acts. . . .

II. Nor are they within either of the general phrases, which are the two following.

1. "To lay taxes to provide for the general welfare of the U.S." that is to say "to lay taxes *for the purpose* of providing for the general welfare." For the laying of taxes is the *power* and the general welfare the *purpose* for which the power is to be exercised. They are not to lay taxes ad libitum *for any purpose they please; but only to pay the debts or provide for the welfare of the Union.* In like manner they are not *to do anything they please* to provide for the general welfare, but only *to lay taxes* for that purpose. To consider the latter

phrase, not as describing the purpose of the first, but as giving a distinct and independent power to do any act they please, which might be for the good of the Union, would render all the preceding and subsequent enumerations of power completely useless. It would reduce the whole instrument to a single phrase, that of instituting a Congress with power to do whatever would be for the good of the U.S. and as they would be the sole judges of the good or evil, it would be also a power to do whatever evil they pleased. . . . Certainly no such universal power was meant to be given them. It was intended to lace them up straitly within the enumerated powers, and those without which, as means, these powers could not be carried into effect. It is known that the very power now proposed *as a means*, was rejected *as an end*, by the Convention which formed the constitution. . . .

2. The second general phrase is "to make all laws *necessary* and proper for carrying into execution the enumerated powers." But they can all be carried into execution without a bank. A bank therefore is not *necessary*, and consequently not authorised by this phrase.

It has been much urged that a bank will give great facility, or convenience in the collection of taxes. Suppose this were true: yet the constitution allows only the means which are "necessary" not those which are merely "convenient" for effecting the enumerated powers. If such a latitude of construction be allowed to this phrase as to give any non-enumerated power, it will go to every one, for there is no one which ingenuity may not torture into a *convenience, in some way or other,* to *some one* of so long a list of enumerated powers. It would swallow up all the delegated powers, and reduce the whole to one phrase as before observed. Therefore it was that the constitution restrained them to the *necessary* means,

---

the primary ideas endorsed by the Federalists' competitors, the Jeffersonian Republicans. To no one's surprise, and despite the fact the bank had done an able job, the Republican Congress refused to renew its charter in 1811.

After the War of 1812, it became apparent even to the Republicans that Congress should recharter the bank. During the war, the lack of a national bank for purposes

of borrowing money and transferring funds became a source of embarrassment to the administration. Moreover, with the absence of a federal bank, state-chartered institutions flooded the market with worthless notes, contributing to economic problems throughout the country. Amid renewed controversy and cries for strict constructionism, Congress in 1816 created the second Bank of that is to say, to those means without which the grant of the power would be nugatory.

OPINION AS TO THE CONSTITUTIONALITY OF THE BANK OF THE UNITED STATES (1791)

Alexander Hamilton

Now it appears to the Secretary of the Treasury that this *general principle* is *inherent* in the very *definition* of government, and *essential* to every step of the progress to be made by that of the United States, namely: That every power vested in a government is in its nature *sovereign,* and includes, by *force* of the *term,* a right to employ all the *means* requisite and fairly applicable to the attainment of the *ends* of such power, and which are not precluded by restrictions and exceptions specified in the Constitution, or not immoral, or not contrary to the *essential ends* of political society.

This principle, in its application to government in general, would be admitted as an axiom; and it will be incumbent upon those who may incline to deny it, to prove a distinction, and to show that a rule which, in the general system of things, is essential to the preservation of the social order, is inapplicable to the United States. . . .

This general and indisputable principle puts at once an end to the *abstract* question, whether the United States have power to erect a corporation; that is to say, to give a *legal* or *artificial capacity* to one or more persons, distinct from the *natural.* For it is unquestionably incident to *sovereign power* to erect corporations, and consequently to *that* of the United States, in *relation* to the *objects* intrusted to the management of the government. . . .

Another argument made use of by the Secretary of State is, the rejection of a proposition by the Convention to empower Congress to make corporations, either generally, or for some special purpose.

What was the precise nature or extent of this proposition, or what the reasons for refusing it, is not ascertained by any authentic document, or even by accurate recollection. . . .

But whatever may have been the nature of the proposition, or the reasons for rejecting it, it includes nothing in respect to the real merits of the question. The Secretary of State will not deny that, whatever may have been the intention of the framers of a constitution or of a law, that intention is to be sought for in the instrument itself, according to the usual and established rules of construction. Nothing is more common than for laws to *express* and *effect* more or less than was intended. If, then, a power to erect a corporation in any case be deducible, by fair inference, from the whole or any part of the numerous provisions of the Constitution of the United States, arguments drawn from extrinsic circumstances, regarding the intention of the Convention, must be rejected. . . .

To establish such a right, it remains to show the relation of such an institution to one or more of the specified powers of the government. Accordingly it is affirmed that it has a relation, more or less direct, to the power of collecting taxes, to that of borrowing money, to that of regulating trade between the States, and to those of raising and maintaining fleets and armies. To the two former the relation may be said to be immediate; and in the last place it will be argued, that it is clearly within the provision which authorizes the making of all *needful rules and regulations* concerning the *property* of the United States, as the same has been practised upon the government.

A bank relates to the collection of taxes in two ways—*indirectly,* by increasing the quantity of circulating medium and quickening circulation, which facilitates the means of paying directly, by creating a *convenient species* of medium in which they are to be paid. . . .

SOURCE: Melvin I. Urofsky, ed., *Documents of American Constitutional and Legal History,* Vol. I (New York: Knopf, 1989), 132–139.

the United States, granting it a twenty-year charter and $35 million in capital.

Some scholars have suggested that a challenge to the new bank was inevitable, primarily because the Supreme Court had never decided whether the first bank was constitutional. It is possible, however, that litigation would not have materialized had the second bank performed its

function as well as its predecessor did, but it did not. It flourished during the postwar economic boom, mainly because it was fiscally aggressive and encouraged speculative investing. These practices caught up to bank officials when, in 1818, in anticipation of a recession, they began calling in the bank's outstanding loans. As a result, they brought down banks throughout the South and West, which had overextended themselves. To make matters worse, accusations of fraud and embezzlement were rampant within several of the bank's eighteen branches, particularly those in Maryland, Pennsylvania, and Virginia. Among those most seriously implicated was James McCulloch, the cashier of the Baltimore branch bank and its main lobbyist in Washington. According to some accounts, his illegal financial schemes had cost the branch more than $1 million.

As a result of these allegations, Congress began to hold hearings on the bank. In addition, some states reacted by attempting to regulate branches located within their borders. Maryland mandated that branches of the bank in the state pay either a 2 percent tax on all bank notes or a fee of $15,000. When a state official came to collect from the Baltimore branch, McCulloch refused to pay and, by refusing, set the stage for a monumental confrontation between the United States and Maryland on two major issues. The first involved the bank itself: Did Congress, in the absence of an explicit constitutional authorization, have the power to charter the bank? Second, did the state exceed its powers by seeking to tax a federal entity?

By the time the case reached the Supreme Court, it was clear that something significant was going to happen. The Court reporter noted that *McCulloch* involved "a constitutional question of great importance." The justices waived their rule that permitted only two attorneys per side and allowed three each.[8] Oral arguments took nine days.

Both sides were ably represented. Some commentators praise Daniel Webster's oratory for the federal government's side as extraordinary, but it was former attorney general and Maryland senator William Pinkney with whom the Court was most taken. Justice Joseph Story said later, "I never, in my whole life, heard a greater speech."[9] The gist of his arguments (and those of his colleagues) was familiar stuff; Pinkney largely reiterated Hamilton's original defense of the bank, particularly his interpretation of the necessary and proper clause.

Maryland's legal representation may have appeared less astute. According to one account, "it has been rumored" that one of the state's lawyers, Attorney General Luther Martin, "was drunk when he made his two-day-long argument. If he was, it apparently did not affect his acuity." For his side, he reiterated parts of Jefferson's argument against the bank, added some on the subject of states' rights, and "closed his argument by reading from John Marshall's own speeches in the Virginia convention."[10]

CHIEF JUSTICE MARSHALL delivered the opinion of the Court.

The constitution of our country, in its most interesting and vital parts, is to be considered; the conflicting powers of the government of the Union and of its members, as marked in that constitution, are to be discussed; and an opinion given, which may essentially influence the great operations of the government. No tribunal can approach such a question without a deep sense of its importance, and of the awful responsibility involved in its decision. But it must be decided peacefully, or remain a source of hostile legislation, perhaps of hostility of a still more serious nature; and if it is to be so decided, by this tribunal alone can the decision be made. On the Supreme Court of the United States has the constitution of our country devolved this important duty.

The first question . . . is, has Congress power to incorporate a bank? . . .

This government is acknowledged by all to be one of enumerated powers. The principle, that it can exercise only the powers granted to it, would seem too apparent to have required to be enforced by all those arguments which its enlightened friends, while it was depending before the people, found it necessary to urge. That principle is now universally admitted. But the question respecting the extent of the powers actually granted, is perpetually arising, and will probably continue to arise, as long as our system shall exist. . . .

Among the enumerated powers, we do not find that of establishing a bank or creating a corporation. But there is no phrase in the instrument which, like the articles of confederation, excludes incidental or implied powers; and which requires that everything granted shall be expressly

8. Fred W. Friendly and Martha J. H. Elliot, *The Constitution—That Delicate Balance* (New York: Random House, 1984), 256.

9. Quoted in Lieberman, *Milestones!* 122.

10. Farber and Sherry, *A History of the American Constitution*, 357.

and minutely described. Even the 10th amendment, which was framed for the purpose of quieting the excessive jealousies which had been excited, omits the word "expressly," and declares only that the powers "not delegated to the United States, nor prohibited to the states, are reserved to the states or to the people;" thus leaving the question, whether the particular power which may become the subject of contest has been delegated to the one government, or prohibited to the other, to depend on a fair construction of the whole instrument. . . . A constitution, to contain an accurate detail of all the subdivisions of which its great powers will admit, and of all the means by which they may be carried into execution, would partake of a prolixity of a legal code, and could scarcely be embraced by the human mind. It would probably never be understood by the public. Its nature, therefore, requires, that only its great outlines should be marked, its important objects designated, and the minor ingredients which compose those objects be deduced from the nature of the objects themselves. That this idea was entertained by the framers of the American constitution, is not only to be inferred from the nature of the instrument, but from the language. Why else were some of the limitations, found in the ninth section of the 1st article, introduced? It is also, in some degree, warranted by their having omitted to use any restrictive term which might prevent its receiving a fair and just interpretation. In considering this question, then, we must never forget that it is a constitution we are expounding.

Although, among the enumerated powers of government, we do not find the word "bank" or "incorporation," we find the great powers to lay and collect taxes; to borrow money; to regulate commerce; to declare and conduct a war; and to raise and support armies and navies. The sword and the purse, all the external relations, and no inconsiderable portion of the industry of the nation, are entrusted to its government. It can never be pretended that these vast powers draw after them others of inferior importance, merely because they are inferior. Such an idea can never be advanced. But it may with great reason be contended, that a government, entrusted with such ample powers, on the due execution of which the happiness and prosperity of the nation so vitally depends, must also be entrusted with ample means for their execution. The power being given, it is the interest of the nation to facilitate its execution. It can never be their interest, and cannot be presumed to have been their intention, to clog and embarrass its execution by withholding the most appropriate means. . . .

The government which has a right to do an act, and has imposed on it the duty of performing that act, must, according to the dictates of reason, be allowed to select the means; and those who contend that it may not select any appropriate means, that one particular mode of effecting the object is excepted, take upon themselves the burden of establishing that exception. . . .

But the constitution of the United States has not left the right of Congress to employ the necessary means for the execution of the powers conferred on the government to general reasoning. To its enumeration of powers is added that of making "all laws which shall be necessary and proper, for carrying into execution the foregoing powers, and all other powers vested by this constitution, in the government of the United States, or in any department thereof."

The counsel for the State of Maryland have urged various arguments, to prove that this clause, though in terms a grant of power, is not so in effect; but is really restrictive of the general right, which might otherwise be implied, of selecting means for executing the enumerated powers. . . .

The word "necessary" is considered as controlling the whole sentence, and as limiting the right to pass laws for the execution of the granted powers, to such as are indispensable, and without which the power would be nugatory. That it excludes the choice of means, and leaves to Congress, in each case, that only which is most direct and simple.

Is it true that this is the sense in which the word "necessary" is always used? Does it always import an absolute physical necessity, so strong that one thing, to which another may be termed necessary, cannot exist without that other? We think it does not. If reference be had to its use, in the common affairs of the world, or in approved authors, we find that it frequently imports no more than that one thing is convenient, or useful, or essential to another. To employ the means necessary to an end, is generally understood as employing any means calculated to produce the end, and not as being confined to those single means, without which the end would be entirely unattainable. . . . This word, . . . like others, is used in various senses; and, in its construction, the subject, the context, the intention of the person using them, are all to be taken into view.

Let this be done in the case under consideration. The subject is the execution of those great powers on which the welfare of a nation essentially depends. It must have been the intention of those who gave these powers, to insure, as far as human prudence could insure, their beneficial execution. This could not be done by confiding the choice of means to such narrow limits as not to leave it in the power of Congress to adopt any which might be appropriate, and which were conducive to the end. This provision is made in a constitution intended to endure for ages to come, and, consequently, to be adapted to the various crises of human affairs. To have prescribed the means by which government should, in all future time, execute its powers, would have been to change, entirely, the character of the instrument, and give it the properties of a legal code. It would have been an unwise attempt to provide, by immutable rules, for exigencies which, if foreseen at all, must have been seen dimly, and which can be best provided for as they occur. To have declared that the best means shall not be used, but those alone without which the power given would be nugatory, would have been to deprive the legislature of the capacity to avail itself of experience, to exercise its reason, and to accommodate its legislation to circumstances. . . .

The baneful influence of this narrow construction on all the operations of the government, and the absolute impracticability of maintaining it without rendering the government incompetent to its great objects, might be illustrated by numerous examples drawn from the constitution, and from our laws. . . .

In ascertaining the sense in which the word "necessary" is used in this clause of the constitution, we may derive some aid from that with which it is associated. Congress shall have power "to make all laws which shall be necessary and proper to carry into execution" the powers of the government. If the word "necessary" was used in that strict and rigorous sense for which the counsel for the state of Maryland contend, it would be an extraordinary departure from the usual course of the human mind, as exhibited in composition, to add a word, the only possible effect of which is to qualify that strict and rigorous meaning; to present to the mind the idea of some choice of means of legislation not straightened and compressed within the narrow limits for which gentlemen contend.

But the argument which most conclusively demonstrates the error of the construction contended for by the counsel for the state of Maryland, is founded on the intention of the convention, as manifested in the whole clause. To waste time

and argument in proving that without it Congress might carry its powers into execution, would be not much less idle than to hold a lighted taper to the sun. As little can it be required to prove, that in the absence of this clause, Congress would have some choice of means. That it might employ those which, in its judgment, would most advantageously effect the object to be accomplished. That any means adapted to the end, any means which tended directly to the execution of the constitutional powers of the government, were in themselves constitutional. This clause, as construed by the state of Maryland, would abridge, and almost annihilate this useful and necessary right of the legislature to select its means. That this could not be intended, is, we should think, had it not been already controverted, too apparent for controversy. We think so for the following reasons:

1st. The clause is placed among the powers of Congress, not among the limitations on those powers.

2d. Its terms purport to enlarge, not to diminish the powers vested in the government. . . .

We admit, as all must admit, that the powers of the government are limited, and that its limits are not to be transcended. But we think the sound construction of the constitution must allow to the national legislature that discretion, with respect to the means by which the powers it confers are to be carried into execution, which will enable that body to perform the high duties assigned to it, in the manner most beneficial to the people. Let the end be legitimate, let it be within the scope of the constitution, and all means which are appropriate, which are plainly adapted to that end, which are not prohibited, but consist with the letter and spirit of the constitution, are constitutional.

That a corporation must be considered as a means not less usual, not of higher dignity, not more requiring a particular specification than other means, has been sufficiently proved. If we look to the origin of corporations, to the manner in which they have been framed in that government from which we have derived most of our legal principles and ideas, or to the uses to which they have been applied, we find no reason to suppose that a constitution, omitting, and wisely omitting, to enumerate all the means for carrying into execution the great powers vested in government, ought to have specified this. Had it been intended to grant this power as one which should be distinct and independent, to be exercised in any case whatever, it would have found a place among the enumerated powers of the government. But being considered merely as a means, to be employed only for the purpose of carrying into execution the given powers, there could be no motive for particularly mentioning it. . . .

If a corporation may be employed indiscriminately with other means to carry into execution the powers of the government, no particular reason can be assigned for excluding the use of a bank, if required for its fiscal operations. To use one, must be within the discretion of Congress, if it be an appropriate mode of executing the powers of government. That it is a convenient, a useful, and essential instrument in the prosecution of its fiscal operations, is not now a subject of controversy. All those who have been concerned in the administration of our finances, have concurred in representing the importance and necessity; and so strongly have they been felt, that statesmen of the first class, whose previous opinions against it had been confirmed by every circumstance which can fix the human judgment, have yielded those opinions to the exigencies of the nation. Under the confederation, Congress, justifying the measure by its necessity, transcended perhaps its powers to obtain the advantage of a bank; and our own legislation attests the universal conviction of the utility of this measure. The time has passed away when it can be necessary to enter into any discussion in order to prove the importance of this instrument, as a means to effect the legitimate objects of the government.

But, were its necessity less apparent, none can deny its being an appropriate measure; and if it is, the degree of its necessity, as has been very justly observed, is to be discussed in another place. Should Congress, in the execution of its powers, adopt measures which are prohibited by the constitution; or should Congress, under the pretext of executing its powers, pass laws for the accomplishment of objects not entrusted to the government, it would become the painful duty of this tribunal, should a case requiring such a decision come before it, to say that such an act was not the law of the land. But where the law is not prohibited, and is really calculated to effect any of the objects entrusted to the government, to undertake here to inquire into the degree of its necessity, would be to pass the line which circumscribes the judicial department, and to tread on legislative ground. This court disclaims all pretensions to such a power. . . .

After the most deliberate consideration, it is the unanimous and decided opinion of this court that the act to incorporate the bank of the United States is a law made in pursuance of the constitution, and is a part of the supreme law of the land.

As we can see, Marshall fully adopted Hamilton's reasoning and the government's claims. Some even felt his opinion was a virtual transcript of the oral arguments presented by the federal attorneys.[11] Given that Marshall issued *McCulloch* just three days after the case had been presented, it is more likely, as others suspect, that he had written the opinion the previous summer.

Either way, *McCulloch* stands as a landmark decision. By holding that Congress has powers beyond those enumerated, that it has implied powers, Marshall set into law a largely Hamiltonian version of congressional authority:

Let the end be legitimate, let it be within the scope of the constitution, and all means which are appropriate, which are plainly adapted to that end, which are not prohibited, but consist with the letter and spirit of the constitution, are constitutional.

And in so doing, he might very well have accomplished his stated objective: to allow the Constitution "to endure for ages to come."

The immediate reaction to Marshall's opinion was interesting in that it focused less on the portion we have dealt with here—congressional powers—and more on the federalism dimension, which we take up in chapter 6. Nevertheless, the long-term effect of his interpretation of the necessary and proper clause has been significant: Congress now exercises many powers not named in the Constitution but implied from it.

Power to Investigate. Of all the implied powers now asserted by Congress, the power to investigate merits close examination. Many think it is one of the most important congressional powers. As Woodrow Wilson noted: "The informing function of Congress should be preferred even to its legislative function." Another president, Harry Truman, concurred: "The power of investigation is one of the most important powers of Congress. The manner in which that power is exercised will largely determine the position and prestige of the Congress in the future."[12] In

---

11. Friendly and Elliot, *The Constitution*, 259.
12. Quoted in *Guide to Congress*, 3rd ed. (Washington, D.C.: Congressional Quarterly, 1982), 161.

addition, the scope of congressional authority in this area has been the subject of some rather interesting, perhaps conflicting, and most definitely controversial Supreme Court opinions.

What has never been controversial, however, is Congress's ability to conduct investigations. After all, to legislate effectively requires the gathering of information to determine if new laws are necessary and, if so, how best to construct them. Although this power is not an enumerated power, there is little question that legislatures can hold inquiries. Some analysts refer to it as an incidental power that legislatures have by virtue of being legislatures. Others call it an inherited power that the British Parliament willed to Congress or, alternatively, an implied power. Congress took advantage of this privilege virtually from the beginning, holding its first investigation in 1792. Since then no period of American history has been without investigations.

If the power of Congress to investigate is so well entrenched, what is controversial about the practice? We can point to several areas of dispute. One is the scope of the power—into what subjects may Congress inquire? Another is subpoena power: May Congress summon witnesses and punish, by holding in contempt, those who do not cooperate with the investigating body? And, if so, what sorts of rights, if any, do witnesses have? Some argue that the power to call and punish witnesses may be implied from the inherent nature of legislative authority. Congress is, by definition, *the* lawmaking institution, and an inherent quality of such an institution is the power to investigate. To function, Congress must have the authority to summon witnesses and punish those who do not comply, and both chambers have always availed themselves of this authority. As early as 1795 Congress jailed for contempt a man who had tried to bribe a member of Congress. The Supreme Court theoretically approved of the contempt practice as early as 1821.[13] But it was not until *Kilbourn v. Thompson* (1881) that the justices attempted to provide firm answers to questions about Congress's power to summon and punish witnesses and on the scope of congressional investigations.

Kilbourn involved a House investigation into a private banking firm. An important witness, Hallett Kilbourn, refused to produce documents demanded by the inquiring committee. By a House order, Kilbourn was held in contempt and jailed. When he was released, he sued various officials and representatives for false arrest. In his view, the investigation was not legitimate because it concerned private, not public, matters and, as such, he would resist "the naked, arbitrary power of the House to investigate private businesses in which nobody but me and my customers have concern."[14]

The Supreme Court agreed. In what some have called a rather narrow ruling on legislative powers, the justices said that Congress could punish witnesses only if the inquiry itself was within the "legitimate cognizance" of the institution. With this ruling, the Court seemed to establish several limits on the scope of investigations. Inquiries (1) must not "invade areas constitutionally reserved to the courts or the executive"; (2) must deal "with subjects on which Congress could validly legislate"; and (3) must suggest, in the resolutions authorizing the investigation, a "congressional interest in legislating on that subject."[15] In general, then, *Kilbourn* said that Congress could hold inquiries only into subjects that are specifically grounded within its constitutional purview and, in particular, that the "private affairs of individuals," where the inquiry could result in "no valid legislation," did not fall into that category.

Forty-six years later, in **McGrain v. Daugherty** (1927), the Court was once again called on to examine the scope of congressional investigative authority. In 1922 Congress began an investigation of a huge scandal known as Teapot Dome. It involved the alleged bribery of public officials by private companies to obtain leasing rights to government-held oil reserves, including the Teapot Dome reserves in Wyoming. Although initial inquiries centered on employees of the Department of the Interior, Congress soon turned its attention to the Justice Department. It was thought that Attorney General Harry M. Daugh-

13. *Anderson v. Dunn* (1821).

14. Quoted in *Guide to Congress*, 4th ed. (Washington, D.C.: Congressional Quarterly, 1991), 224.

15. C. Herman Pritchett, *Constitutional Law of the Federal System* (Englewood Cliffs, N.J.: Prentice Hall, 1984), 191.

Attorney General Harry M. Daugherty, whose brother Mally S. Daugherty refused to appear before the Senate to answer questions concerning the Teapot Dome Scandal, in which both were implicated. In *McGrain v. Daugherty* the Court affirmed congressional power to investigate, even without an explicitly stated legislative purpose.

erty was involved in fraudulent activities because he failed to prosecute wrongdoers. As part of that inquiry, a Senate committee ordered the attorney general's brother, Mally S. Daugherty, to appear before it and to produce documents. Mally was a bank president, and the committee suspected that he was involved in the scandal.

This suspicion grew stronger with the resignation of the attorney general and the subsequent refusal of his brother to appear before the committee. The Senate had Mally Daugherty arrested. He, in turn, challenged the committee's authority to compel him—through arrest—to testify against his brother. Picking up on one of the limits of investigation emanating from *Kilbourn*, Mally's lawyer argued that "the arrest of Mr. Daugherty is the result of an attempt of the Senate to vest its committee with judicial power." The U.S. government's brief also used *Kilbourn* to frame its arguments: "The investigation

ordered by the Senate, in the course of which the testimony of the Appellee [Daugherty] and the production of books and records of the bank of which he is President were required, was legislative in its character."

The Court agreed with the government. Writing for the majority, Justice Willis Van Devanter held that "the power of inquiry—with process to enforce it—is an essential and appropriate auxiliary to the legislative function." In other words, he firmly established Congress's power to inquire and to enforce that power with the ability to punish as an implied power. This was an important affirmation of a long-standing practice. Since 1795 congressional committees had often invoked their power to punish, issuing more than 380 contempt citations over the years. If a committee does so and the parent chamber approves the action by a simple majority, the case is forwarded to a U.S. attorney for possible prosecution. Still, in *McGrain* the justices were unwilling to allow a virtually limitless use of that power. Although they ruled for the government and backed away from the rigid stance of *Kilbourn*, they continued to assert that Congress could not inquire, generally speaking, into private affairs. In this case, however, "the object of the investigation and of the effort to secure the witness's testimony was to obtain information for legislative purposes."

In addition to shedding light on Congress's ability to "inquire," *McGrain* provides some insight into a controversial area of congressional inquiries: the rights of witnesses. Even as it ruled against Daugherty, the Court held that witnesses may refuse to answer "where the bounds of the power are exceeded or the questions are not pertinent to the matter under inquiry."

This window of opportunity for witnesses to refuse to testify became quite important during World War II and in the postwar period when, out of fear of an influx of foreign ideologies into the United States, Congress embarked on a new type of investigation: the "inquisitorial panel." In short, the overriding purpose of the antisubversive hearings was "exposure," not necessarily "information."

The investigations carried on in the Senate by Joseph McCarthy and by the House Un-American Activities Committee (HUAC) in the 1940s and 1950s produced intense controversy and criticism. At that time, the fear of

Members of the House Un-American Activities Committee Richard Nixon, R-Calif. *(left)*, and J. Parnell Thomas, R-N.J. *(right)*, review testimony with committee investigator Robert Stripling following a 1948 espionage hearing.

communism was so pervasive that even being called to testify before McCarthy or HUAC created such suspicion that individuals lost their jobs, were placed on blacklists, and so forth. Moreover, many witnesses were sufficiently scared of being branded Communist sympathizers or supporters that they refused to testify or asserted constitutional protections against so doing, which resulted in an unusually high number of contempt citations. Between 1792 and 1942 Congress issued 108 citations; from 1945 to 1957, fourteen committees presented 226 contempt citations to their respective chambers. HUAC alone held 144 "uncooperative" witnesses in contempt.

In the late 1950s the Supreme Court decided two major cases involving the rights of witnesses to refuse to answer questions. In the first, *Watkins v. United States* (1957), the justices considered HUAC's efforts to secure information from John T. Watkins, a labor union organizer. In response to committee questions probing his knowledge of Communist activities, Watkins agreed to talk about his own relationship with the Communist Party as well as the activities of those he knew still to be active in the party. But Watkins refused to answer ques-

tions about people whom he knew to have separated themselves from the party. He claimed that these individuals were not relevant to the committee's legislative purpose. After he was convicted for contempt, Watkins appealed. The justices ruled in his favor, concluding that the committee's questions that had been challenged were not pertinent to its legislative function. Instead, the Court described the actions of the committee to be nothing more than exposure for the sake of exposure.

Two years later, the Court issued its ruling in *Barenblatt v. United States* (1959), which seemingly ran counter to the *Watkins* precedent. A HUAC subcommittee subpoenaed Lloyd Barenblatt to appear before it. An earlier witness had implicated Barenblatt in Communist activities while he was a graduate student at the University of Michigan several years before. The legislators asked Barenblatt a series of questions about his current or past involvement in the Communist Party or Communist-oriented groups. When he refused to answer these questions, Barenblatt was found in contempt of Congress. On appeal, the Supreme Court ruled in favor of the congressional committee. The majority decided that the purpose

The Supreme Court upheld the conviction of Lloyd Barenblatt
(left) for contempt of Congress. Barenblatt had refused to testify
about his beliefs and his membership in a university club.
Shown at a rally November 5, 1959, with Willard Uphaus, another defendant, Barenblatt thanked the ACLU and other organizations that helped him fight his case.

of the inquiry was more clearly defined than had been
the case in the questioning of Watkins and that Barenblatt's personal activities were relevant to the committee's legislative purpose.

The different results in *Watkins* and *Barenblatt* have
led scholars to ask whether the Court had acted consistently. The majority in *Barenblatt* went to great lengths to
indicate that it did—indeed, that *Barenblatt* amounted to
nothing more or less than a "clarification" of *Watkins.*
But many legal analysts, along with Justice Hugo Black,
who wrote a dissenting opinion in *Barenblatt,* suggest
that at minimum the justices backed away from *Watkins,*
and others say that *Barenblatt* signaled a sort of reversal
of the earlier ruling.

If *Barenblatt* was a reversal, how can we explain the
shift, which occurred within a two-year period? There are
two possibilities. The first is that *Barenblatt* constituted "a
strategic withdrawal" because at the time the Court was
under "pressure of Congress and some sectors of public
opinion."[16] In particular, *Watkins* and other "liberal" deci-

sions on subversive activity and on discrimination such
as *Brown v. Board of Education* (1954) made the Court the
target of numerous congressional proposals. A few even
sought to remove the Court's jurisdiction to hear cases involving subversive activities. According to some observers, the justices felt the heat and acceded to congressional
pressure. Another explanation is that personnel changes
produced a more conservative Court, that *Barenblatt* represented a move "back toward a more conservative position" ushered in by President Dwight Eisenhower's appointments of Charles Whittaker and Potter Stewart.

Either way, the explanations indicate the susceptibil-
ity of the Court to political influences outside and inside its chambers. As the dangers associated with the
cold war began to ebb, the justices again had a change of
heart on the rights of witnesses. In case after case in the
1960s, they reversed the convictions of many whom Congress had cited for contempt. In so doing, the Court has
sought to strike a balance between the rights of individuals and those of legislatures, no easy task because of the
substantive nature of the power to investigate.

Inherent Powers

As we have seen, Congress has enumerated powers as
well as powers that can be implied or inferred from, or
are incidental to, its role as the lawmaking institution. In
addition, many analysts argue that Congress has certain
inherent powers that are neither explicit nor even implied by the Constitution, but which somehow attach
themselves to sovereign states *(see Table 4-3, page 98).*

As Justice Story defined them, inherent powers are
those that result "from the whole mass of the powers of
the National Government, and from the nature of political society, [not as] a consequence or incident of the powers specifically enumerated."[17]

Although theorists had long espoused this concept, it
found its way into constitutional law in *United States v.
Curtiss-Wright Export Corp.* (1936). As you read this case,
pay particular attention to Justice George Sutherland's explication of inherent powers. How does he define them?

16. C. Herman Pritchett, *Congress Versus the Supreme Court* (Minneapolis: University of Minnesota Press, 1961), 12.

17. *Commentaries on the Constitution,* Vol. 3 (New York: Da Capo Press;
reprint of 1833 edition, 1970), 124.

More important, how does he square the existence of inherent powers with the idea of a government based on enumeration?

United States v. Curtiss-Wright Export Corp.

299 U.S. 304 (1936)
http://laws.findlaw.com/US/299/304.html
*Vote: 7 (Brandeis, Butler, Cardozo, Hughes, Roberts,
        Sutherland, Van Devanter)
    1 (McReynolds)*
Opinion of the Court: Sutherland
Not participating: Stone

After Charles Lindbergh's 1927 transatlantic flight, the aviation industry began to boom. Americans were convinced that air travel would take its place as the new mode of transportation.[18] Many new companies formed to build aircraft, and among them was Curtiss-Wright.

Although it started off on a strong footing, Curtiss-Wright soon fell prey to the Great Depression and lost $13 million between 1930 and 1931. To avoid going bankrupt, it looked beyond the United States into the foreign market, where money still could be made. Curtiss-Wright, however, was selling its wares not to other private companies but to foreign governments involved in military conflicts and in need of warplanes.

The company found a ready buyer in Bolivia, which since 1932 had been at war with Paraguay over the Chaco, a region east of Bolivia. Landlocked Bolivia was determined to take control of the Chaco to gain access to the Atlantic Ocean. Bolivia became an excellent customer of Curtiss-Wright's, buying thirty-four planes in the early 1930s. The Chaco war, in turn, enabled the company to survive the Depression.

Things began to turn sour in 1934. Books and articles appeared attacking companies like Curtiss-Wright as "merchants of death." More important, the League of Nations wanted to put an end to the Chaco war and asked

---

18. We adopt what follows from Robert A. Divine, "The Case of the Smuggled Bombers," in *Quarrels That Have Shaped the Constitution*, ed. John A. Garraty (New York: Harper and Row, 1987).

---

the United States to help. In response, President Franklin D. Roosevelt asked Congress to pass a resolution enabling him to prohibit the sale of arms to the warring countries. It did so on May 28, 1934.

[I]f the President finds that the prohibition of the sale of arms and munitions of war in the United States to those countries now engaged in armed conflict in the Chaco may contribute to the reestablishment of peace between those countries, and if after consultation with the governments of other American Republics and with their cooperation, as well as that of such other governments as he may deem necessary, he makes proclamation to that effect, it shall be unlawful to sell, except under such limitations and exceptions as the President prescribes, any arms or munitions of war in any place in the United States to the countries now engaged in that armed conflict, or to any person, company, or association acting in the interest of either country, until otherwise ordered by the President or by Congress.

Whoever sells any arms or munitions of war . . . shall . . . be punished by a fine not exceeding $10,000 or by imprisonment not exceeding two years, or both.

Shortly after the resolution was enacted, Roosevelt issued an order embargoing weapon sales to Bolivia and Paraguay. Curtiss-Wright refused to comply with the order and tried to get around it by disguising bombers as passenger planes. Eventually, the company got caught and was charged with violating the order.

Curtiss-Wright challenged the government's action. Among its arguments when the case reached the Court, the most pertinent was the contention that the 1934 resolution was invalid because it gave "uncontrolled" lawmaking "discretion" to the president. On this score, the company's reasoning appeared strong: In *Panama Refining Company v. Ryan* (1935) the Court had struck down a congressional act on the ground that the legislature had delegated lawmaking authority to the president without sufficient guidelines. In Curtiss-Wright's view, the 1934 resolution was no different from the law struck down in *Panama Refining*.

The U.S. government tried to distinguish the facts in this case from those in the 1935 decision, saying that the congressional delegation of power in *Panama Refining* involved domestic, not international, affairs. This distinction was important, in the government's argument, because "from the beginning of the government, in the conduct of foreign affairs, Congress has followed the practice of conferring upon the President power similar to that conferred by the present resolution." By way of example, U.S. attorneys indicated that as early as 1794, Congress had given the president the "duty of determining" when embargoes should be laid "upon vessels in ports of the United States bound for foreign ports."

MR. JUSTICE SUTHERLAND delivered the opinion of the Court.

It is contended that by the Joint Resolution, the going into effect and continued operation of the resolution was conditioned (a) upon the President's judgment as to its beneficial effect upon the reestablishment of peace between the countries engaged in armed conflict in the Chaco; (b) upon the making of a proclamation, which was left to his unfettered discretion, thus constituting an attempted substitution of the President's will for that of Congress; (c) upon the making of a proclamation putting an end to the operation of the resolution, which again was left to the President's unfettered discretion; and (d) further, that the extent of its operation in particular cases was subject to limitation and exception by the President, controlled by no standard. In each of these particulars, appellees urge that Congress abdicated its essential functions and delegated them to the Executive.

Whether, if the Joint Resolution had related solely to internal affairs it would be open to the challenge that it constituted an unlawful delegation of legislative power to the Executive, we find it unnecessary to determine. The whole aim of the resolution is to affect a situation entirely external to the United States, and falling within the category of foreign affairs. The determination which we are called to make, therefore, is whether the Joint Resolution, as applied to that situation, is vulnerable to attack under the rule that forbids a delegation of the law-making power. In other words, assuming (but not deciding) that the challenged delegation, if it were confined to internal affairs, would be invalid, may it nevertheless be sustained on the ground that its exclusive aim is to afford a remedy for a hurtful condition within foreign territory?

It will contribute to the elucidation of the question if we first consider the differences between the powers of the Federal government in respect of foreign or external affairs and those in respect of domestic or internal affairs. That there are differences between them, and that these differences are fundamental, may not be doubted.

The two classes of powers are different, both in respect of their origin and their nature. The broad statement that the Federal government can exercise no powers except those specifically enumerated in the Constitution, and such implied powers as are necessary and proper to carry into effect the enumerated powers, is categorically true only in respect of our internal affairs. In that field, the primary purpose of the Constitution was to carve from the general mass of legislative powers *then possessed by the states* such portions as it was thought desirable to vest in the Federal government, leaving those not included in the enumeration still in the states. That this doctrine applies only to powers which the states had, is self-evident. And since the states severally never possessed international powers, such powers could not have been carved from the mass of state powers but obviously were transmitted to the United States from some other source. During the colonial period, those powers were possessed exclusively by and were entirely under the control of the Crown. By the Declaration of Independence, "the Representatives of the United States of America" declared the United [not the several] Colonies to be free and independent states, and as such to have "full Power to levy War, conclude Peace, contract Alliances, establish Commerce and to do all other Acts and Things which Independent States may of right do."

As a result of the separation from Great Britain by the colonies, acting as a unit, the powers of external sovereignty passed from the Crown not to the colonies severally, but to the colonies in their collective and corporate capacity as the United States of America. Even before the Declaration, the colonies were a unit in foreign affairs, acting through a common agency—namely the Continental Congress, composed of delegates from the thirteen colonies. That agency exercised the powers of war and peace, raised an army, created a navy, and finally adopted the Declaration of Independence. Rulers come and go; governments end and forms of government change; but sovereignty survives. A political society cannot endure without a supreme will somewhere. Sovereignty is never held in suspense. When, therefore, the external sovereignty of Great Britain in respect of the colonies ceased, it immediately passed to the Union. . . .

The Union existed before the Constitution, which was ordained and established among other things to form "a more perfect Union." Prior to that event, it is clear that the Union, declared by the Articles of Confederation to be "perpetual," was the sole possessor of external sovereignty, and in the Union it remained without change save in so far as the Constitution in express terms qualified its exercise. The Framers' Convention was called and exerted its powers upon the irrefutable postulate that though the states were several their people in respect of foreign affairs were one. . . .

It results that the investment of the Federal government with the powers of external sovereignty did not depend upon the affirmative grants of the Constitution. The powers to declare and wage war, to conclude peace, to make treaties, to maintain diplomatic relations with other sovereignties, if they had never been mentioned in the Constitution, would have vested in the Federal government as necessary concomitants of nationality. Neither the Constitution nor the laws passed in pursuance of it have any force in foreign territory unless in respect of our own citizens . . . and operations of the nation in such territory must be governed by treaties, international understandings and compacts, and the principles of international law. As a member of the family of nations, the right and power of the United States in that field are equal to the right and power of the other members of the international family. Otherwise, the United States is not completely sovereign. . . .

Practically every volume of the United States Statutes contains one or more acts or joint resolutions of Congress authorizing action by the President in respect of subjects affecting foreign relations, which either leave the exercise of the power to his unrestricted judgment, or provide a standard far more general than that which has always been considered requisite with regard to domestic affairs. . . .

The result of holding that the joint resolution here under attack is void and unenforceable as constituting an unlawful delegation of legislative power would be to stamp this multitude of comparable acts and resolutions as likewise invalid. And while this court may not, and should not, hesitate to declare acts of Congress, however many times repeated, to be unconstitutional if beyond all rational doubt it finds them to be so, an impressive array of legislation such as we have just set forth, enacted by nearly every Congress from the beginning of our national existence to the present day, must be given unusual weight in the process of reaching a correct determination of the problem. A legislative practice such as we have here, evidenced not by only occasional instances, but marked by the movement of a steady stream for a century and a half of time, goes a long way in the direction of proving the presence of unassailable ground for the constitutionality of the practice, to be found in the origin and history of the power involved, or in its nature, or in both combined. . . .

The uniform, long-continued and undisputed legislative practice just disclosed rests upon an admissible view of the Constitution which, even if the practice found far less support in principle than we think it does, we should not feel at liberty at this late day to disturb.

We deem it unnecessary to consider, seriatim, the several clauses which are said to evidence the unconstitutionality of the Joint Resolution as involving an unlawful delegation of legislative power. It is enough to summarize by saying that, both upon principle and in accordance with precedent, we conclude there is sufficient warrant for the broad discretion vested in the President to determine whether the enforcement of the statute will have a beneficial effect upon the reestablishment of peace in the affected countries; whether he shall make proclamation to bring the resolution into operation; whether and when the resolution shall cease to operate and to make proclamation accordingly; and to prescribe limitations and exceptions to which the enforcement of the resolution shall be subject.

Curtiss-Wright was an important ruling. As we shall see later in this chapter, the decision ran directly counter to what the Court was doing in other areas of the law. At the same time it was striking down many segments of Roosevelt's New Deal, in part on the ground that the laws were unconstitutional delegations of power, here the Court upheld congressional authority to delegate power. Why it did so brings us to another important, and for present purposes more relevant, aspect of the decision: the distinction between foreign and domestic affairs. Sutherland justified the delegation of power on the ground that it involved external affairs, whereas the Court's rulings on the New Deal programs involved domestic programs.

In this dichotomy the majority found the concept of inherent powers. In its view, the U.S. Constitution transferred some domestic powers from the states to the federal government, leaving some with the states or the people. That is why Congress cannot exercise authority over internal affairs beyond that which is explicitly enumerated or can be implied from that document. In contrast, no such transfer occurred or could have occurred for authority over foreign affairs. Because the states never had such power to begin with, they could not have bestowed it on the federal government. Rather, "authority over foreign affairs is an inherent power, which attaches automatically to the federal government as a sovereign entity, and derives from the Constitution only as the Constitution is the creator of that sovereign entity."[19] It is not Congress specifically but the federal government that enjoys complete authority over foreign relations, which is an inherent power of sovereign nations, one that is derived not from their charters but from their status. As constitutional law scholar Louis Henkin summarized:

Foreign affairs are national affairs. The United States is a single nation-state, and it is the United States (not the States of the Union, singly or together) that has relations with other nations, and the United States Government that conducts these relations and makes foreign policy.[20]

Although it has not escaped criticism, Sutherland's opinion remains authoritative doctrine. Its conceptualization of the federal government's inherent power over foreign affairs provides that entity with considerable leeway. And it is a doctrine to which the Court continues, generally speaking, to subscribe.

Amendment-Enforcing Power

Many discussions of congressional powers end with those inherent to sovereign nations. But it is important to understand, especially today, another source of legislative authority—amendment-enforcing power—because Congress makes frequent use of it as a basis for legislation. Seven constitutional amendments contain some variant of the following language: Congress shall have the power to enforce, by appropriate legislation, the provisions of this article *(see Table 4-3, page 98)*. For example, the first section of the Fifteenth Amendment says, "The right of citizens of the United States to vote shall not be denied . . . on account of race," and this statement is followed by an enforcement provision. Presumably, the writers of this Reconstruction amendment intended, at the very least, to implement its mandate by allowing Congress to pass legislation forbidding states to deny blacks the right to vote. One result of this amendment-enforcing power was passage of the Voting Rights Act of 1965, the nation's most far-reaching and effective regulation of the electoral process. These amendment-enforcing provisions give Congress power to act in areas not previously authorized. The Voting Rights Act may never have come into being had the Fifteenth Amendment not expanded the federal government's power to regulate elections. For the most part, the Supreme Court has given Congress wide latitude to legislate on the basis of these amendment-enforcing powers.[21] But it has not abdicated its role altogether. In accordance with the language of the enforcement provision, the Court must determine whether the congressional law is "appropriate."

CONGRESS AND THE SEPARATION OF POWERS

In our discussion so far, you may have noted a pattern in the Court's decisions dealing with the sources and scope of congressional power. On the whole, with a few scattered exceptions, the Court has allowed Congress a good deal of leeway in exercising enumerated and extra-constitutional power, especially in disputes involving that body's power to regulate its own affairs and to enact legislation, even if a law intrudes on state operations. Where the Court has wavered and at times reined Congress in is over its authority in relation to the other national institutions, particularly the executive. In other words, during certain periods of the nation's history, the Court has taken a hard line on the separation of powers doctrine, limiting both friendly and unfriendly relations between Congress and the president.

The Delegation of Powers

Almost all discussions of the ability of Congress to delegate its lawmaking power begin with the old Latin

19. Pritchett, *Constitutional Law of the Federal System*, 305.

20. Louis Henkin, *Foreign Affairs and the Constitution* (New York: W. W. Norton, 1975), 15.

21. See, for example, *South Carolina v. Katzenbach* (1966), which upheld the validity of the 1965 Voting Rights Act.

maxim: *delegata potestas non potest delegari,* which means "a power once delegated cannot be redelegated." We could apply this statement to Congress in the following way: Because the Constitution delegates to that institution all legislative powers—lawmaking authority—it cannot give such power to another body or person. No political institution has, however, fully accepted the principle expressed in the Latin maxim. From the First Congress on, the legislature has delegated its power to other branches or even to nongovernmental entities. But why would Congress want to give away some of its power? One reason is that Congress is often busy with other matters and must delegate some authority if it is to fulfill all of its responsibilities. Another is that Congress might be fully capable of formulating general policies, but might lack the time and expertise needed to develop specific methods for carrying out those policies. As the job of governance grows increasingly technical and complex, this reason becomes even more valid. *Curtiss-Wright* provides yet another reason: the need for flexibility. In *Curtiss-Wright* Congress gave the president authority to issue an arms embargo if such an action would help to bring peace to warring South American nations. Congress recognized that once it enacts legislation it may have difficulty amending it with sufficient speed to keep up with rapidly changing events. Finally, there are political reasons why Congress might want to delegate. To avoid dealing with certain "hot potato" issues, Congress might hand them off to others. The delegation of powers issue is tricky: It is accepted, theoretically, that Congress should not dole out its lawmaking authority, but it is a matter of practical and reasonable politics that it does so.

Wayman v. Southard (1825) was the Court's first major ruling on the delegation of domestic powers. This dispute involved a challenge to a provision of the Judiciary Act of 1789 in which Congress delegated to the courts authority to establish rules for the conduct of judicial business.

Writing for the Court in *Wayman,* Chief Justice Marshall responded pragmatically. He sought to balance the letter of the Constitution with the practical concerns facing Congress when he formulated the following standard: the legislature must itself "entirely" regulate "important

subjects"; but for "those of less interest," it can enact a general provision and authorize "those who are to act under such general provisions to fill up the details." Put simply, Marshall established a set of rules for the delegation of power that varied by the importance of the subject under regulation. Applying this standard to the delegation of power contained in the 1789 Judiciary Act, he found that Congress could grant courts authority to promulgate their own rules.

For more than a century following *Wayman* the Court continued to demonstrate a generally sympathetic attitude toward delegation, although it modified Marshall's standard. In **Hampton & Co. v. United States** (1928) the justices considered the validity of the Fordney-McCumber Act, in which Congress established a tariff commission within the executive branch and permitted the president to increase or decrease tariffs on imported goods by as much as 50 percent. Because Congress gave the president (and the commission) so much discretion to adjust rates, an import company challenged the act as a violation of the separation of powers doctrine. The company argued that Congress had provided the president with what was essentially lawmaking power. Writing for a unanimous Court, Chief Justice William Howard Taft—a former president of the United States—disagreed: "In determining what [Congress] may do in seeking assistance from another branch, the extent and character of that assistance must be fixed according to common sense and the inherent necessities of the governmental coordination." So long as Congress "shall lay down by legislative act an intelligible principle to which the person or body authorized to [exercise the delegated authority] is directed to conform," according to Taft, "such legislative action is not a forbidden delegation of legislative power."

For nearly a decade, the Court seemed quite willing to accept the so-called "intelligible principle" approach to congressional delegations. But in 1935 the Court dealt Congress and the president major blows when it struck down provisions of the National Industrial Recovery Act (NIRA) as excessive delegations of power. NIRA was a major piece of New Deal legislation designed to pull the nation out of the economic depression. In *Panama Refining* the focus was on Congress allowing the president to prohibit the shipment in interstate commerce of oil produced in excess of state quotas; in *Schechter Poultry v. United States* (1935) the issue was Congress authorizing the president to approve fair competition codes and standards if representatives of a particular industry recommended he do so. In both instances, the Court struck down the delegations of power as unconstitutional.

As we will see in chapter 7, these decisions were a part of a larger pattern of judicial actions hostile to the economic proposals of the Roosevelt administration. The justices may well have been using the excessive delegation of powers argument as an excuse to strike down New Deal legislation that they fundamentally and ideologically opposed. In the long run, *Panama Refining* and *Schechter Poultry* proved to be anomalies. In 1937 the Court shifted to a more sympathetic view of the New Deal and soon returned to its traditional position of giving Congress a great deal of latitude to delegate authority. In fact, since 1936 the Court has not struck down a single federal law explicitly on excessive delegation grounds (although a few of the more suspect laws never have reached the Court).

An interesting example is *Mistretta v. United States* (1989), in which the Court scrutinized an act of Congress designed to minimize judicial discretion in sentencing. The Court's decision takes us back to *Wayman v. Southard* and *Hampton v. United States.*

Mistretta v. United States

488 U.S. 361 (1989)
http://laws.findlaw.com/US/488/361.html
Oral arguments may be found at: http://www.oyez.org
Vote: 8 (Blackmun, Brennan,[22] Kennedy, Marshall, O'Connor,
    Rehnquist, Stevens, White)
        1 (Scalia)
Opinion of the Court: Blackmun
Dissenting opinion: Scalia

Concerned about wide discrepancies in sentences imposed by federal court judges, Congress enacted the Sen-

22. Brennan joined the majority in all but note 11 of its opinion, which dealt with the death penalty.

tencing Reform Act of 1984, which created the U.S. Sentencing Commission as "an independent commission in the judicial branch of government." The commission was empowered to create sentencing guidelines for all federal offenses, to which lower court judges generally would be bound. It was to have seven members, nominated by the president and confirmed by the Senate. Three of its members, at minimum, were to be federal court judges, and no more than four members could be of the same political party.

The commission fulfilled its charge, promulgating sentencing guidelines for federal offenses, but the federal courts were not in agreement over their constitutionality. More than 150 lower court judges found the guidelines constitutionally defective, while about 100 others upheld them.

In *Mistretta v. United States* the lower federal court judge had upheld the plan, but the arguments of John Mistretta, who had been convicted of three counts of selling cocaine, were similar to those proffered by judges who did not approve of the guidelines. Of particular relevance here was Mistretta's charge that the act violated delegation of powers principles by giving the commission "excessive legislative authority."

JUSTICE BLACKMUN delivered the opinion of the Court.

Petitioner argues that in delegating the power to promulgate sentencing guidelines for every federal criminal offense to an independent Sentencing Commission, Congress has granted the Commission excessive legislative discretion in violation of the constitutionally based nondelegation doctrine. We do not agree.

The nondelegation doctrine is rooted in the principle of separation of powers that underlies our tripartite system of government. The Constitution provides that "[a]ll legislative Powers herein granted shall be vested in a Congress of the United States," and we long have insisted that "the integrity and maintenance of the system of government ordained by the Constitution" mandate that Congress generally cannot delegate its legislative power to another Branch. We also have recognized, however, that the separation-of-powers principle, and the nondelegation doctrine in particular, do not prevent Congress from obtaining the assistance of its coordinate Branches. In a passage now enshrined in our jurisprudence, Chief Justice Taft, writing for the Court, explained our approach to such cooperative ventures: "In determining what [Congress] may do in seeking assistance from another branch, the extent and character of that assistance must be fixed according to common sense and the inherent necessities of the governmental coordination." *J. W. Hampton, Jr., & Co. v. United States* (1928). So long as Congress "shall lay down by legislative act an intelligible principle to which the person or body authorized to [exercise the delegated authority] is directed to conform, such legislative action is not a forbidden delegation of legislative power."

Applying this "intelligible principle" test to congressional delegations, our jurisprudence has been driven by a practical understanding that in our increasingly complex society, replete with ever changing and more technical problems, Congress simply cannot do its job absent an ability to delegate power under broad general directives. . . .

Until 1935, this Court never struck down a challenged statute on delegation grounds. . . . After invalidating in 1935 two statutes as excessive delegations, see *Schechter Poultry Corp. v. United States* and *Panama Refining Co. v. Ryan,* we have upheld, again without deviation, Congress' ability to delegate power under broad standards.

In light of our approval of . . . broad delegations, we harbor no doubt that Congress' delegation of authority to the Sentencing Commission is sufficiently specific and detailed to meet constitutional requirements. Congress charged the Commission with three goals: to "assure the meeting of the purposes of sentencing as set forth" in the Act; to "provide certainty and fairness in meeting the purposes of sentencing, avoiding unwarranted sentencing disparities among defendants with similar records . . . while maintaining sufficient flexibility to permit individualized sentences," where appropriate; and to "reflect to the extent practicable, advancement in knowledge of human behavior as it relates to the criminal justice process." Congress further specified four "purposes" of sentencing that the Commission must pursue in carrying out its mandate: "to reflect the seriousness of the offense, to promote respect for the law, and to provide just punishment for the offense"; "to afford adequate deterrence to criminal conduct"; "to protect the public from further crimes of the defendant"; and "to provide the defendant with needed . . . correctional treatment."

In addition, Congress prescribed the specific tool—the guidelines system—for the Commission to use in regulating sentencing. More particularly, Congress directed the Commission to develop a system of "sentencing ranges" applicable "for each category of offense involving each category of defendant." . . .

To guide the Commission in its formulation of offense categories, Congress directed it to consider seven factors: the grade of the offense; the aggravating and mitigating circumstances of the crime; the nature and degree of the harm caused by the crime; the community view of the gravity of the offense; the public concern generated by the crime; the deterrent effect that a particular sentence may have on others; and the current incidence of the offense. Congress set forth 11 factors for the Commission to consider in establishing categories of defendants. These include the offender's age, education, vocational skills, mental and emotional condition, physical condition (including drug dependence), previous employment record, family ties and responsibilities, community ties, role in the offense, criminal history, and degree of dependence upon crime for a livelihood. Congress also prohibited the Commission from considering the "race, sex, national origin, creed, and socio-economic status of offenders," and instructed that the guidelines should reflect the "general inappropriateness" of considering certain other factors, such as current unemployment, that might serve as proxies for forbidden factors.

In addition to these overarching constraints, Congress provided even more detailed guidance to the Commission about categories of offenses and offender characteristics. Congress directed that guidelines require a term of confinement at or near the statutory maximum for certain crimes of violence and for drug offenses, particularly when committed by recidivists. Congress further directed that the Commission assure a substantial term of imprisonment for an offense constituting a third felony conviction, for a career felon, for one convicted of a managerial role in a racketeering enterprise, for a crime of violence by an offender on release from a prior felony conviction, and for an offense involving a substantial quantity of narcotics. . . . In other words, although Congress granted the Commission substantial discretion in formulating guidelines, in actuality it legislated a full hierarchy of punishment—from near maximum imprisonment, to substantial imprisonment, to some imprisonment, to alternatives—and stipulated the most important offense and offender characteristics to place defendants within these categories.

We cannot dispute petitioner's contention that the Commission enjoys significant discretion in formulating guidelines. The Commission does have discretionary authority to determine the relative severity of federal crimes and to assess the relative weight of the offender characteristics that Congress listed for the Commission to consider.... The Commission also has significant discretion to determine which crimes have been punished too leniently, and which too severely. Congress has called upon the Commission to exercise its judgment about which types of crimes and which types of criminals are to be considered similar for the purposes of sentencing.

But our cases do not at all suggest that delegations of this type may not carry with them the need to exercise judgment on matters of policy....

... The Act sets forth more than merely an "intelligible principle" or minimal standards. One court has aptly put it: "The statute outlines the policies which prompted establishment of the Commission, explains what the Commission should do and how it should do it, and sets out specific directives to govern particular situations."

Developing proportionate penalties for hundreds of different crimes by a virtually limitless array of offenders is precisely the sort of intricate, labor-intensive task for which delegation to an expert body is especially appropriate. Although Congress has delegated significant discretion to the Commission to draw judgments from its analysis of existing sentencing practice and alternative sentencing models, "Congress is not confined to that method of executing its policy which involves the least possible delegation of discretion to administrative officers." We have no doubt that in the hands of the Commission "the criteria which Congress has supplied are wholly adequate for carrying out the general policy and purpose" of the Act....

The judgment . . . is affirmed.

JUSTICE SCALIA, dissenting.

While the products of the Sentencing Commission's labors have been given the modest name "Guidelines," they have the force and effect of laws, prescribing the sentences criminal defendants are to receive. A judge who disregards them will be reversed. I dissent from today's decision be-

cause I can find no place within our constitutional system for an agency created by Congress to exercise no governmental power other than the making of laws.

Congress and the Usurpation of Executive and Judicial Powers

The cases we discussed in the last section share a common thread: They involved cooperative relations between Congress and another branch of government, usually the executive. Congress was delegating some of its lawmaking authority to an executive who wanted, perhaps even requested, such authority. But Congress is not always so eager to give away its powers; indeed, on many occasions and through different devices, it has sought to exercise authority over the judicial or executive branch.

With respect to the judicial branch, Congress on occasion has attempted to tell the courts how to interpret the Constitution. It should not come as a surprise that the justices have cast a dim eye at such efforts. For example, Congress, upset with the Court's interpretation of the First Amendment's free exercise of religion clause, passed the Religious Freedom Restoration Act of 1993. This statute dictated that all government agencies, including the courts, apply an interpretation of the free exercise clause that ran contrary to the Supreme Court's decision in *Employment Division v. Smith* (1990). The Court, however, struck down the Religious Freedom Restoration Act in *City of Boerne v. Flores* (1997) largely on the ground that Congress had overstepped its authority and had infringed on the power of the judiciary to determine what the Constitution means. The Court took a similar action in *Dickerson v. United States* (2000) when it struck down a congressional statute that defined "voluntary confessions" in a manner at odds with the Supreme Court's decision in *Miranda v. Arizona* (1966).

The dispute over the legislative veto is an illustration of Congress violating separation of powers principles in its relations with the executive branch. This kind of veto is a constitutional oddity because it flips the mandated lawmaking process. Rather than follow Article I procedures—both houses of Congress pass bills and the president signs or vetoes them—under this practice, the executive branch makes policies that Congress can veto by a vote of both houses, one house, or even a committee. It should come as no surprise that the legislative veto has been the source of contention between presidents and Congresses, with the former suggesting that they violate constitutional principles and the latter arguing that they represent a way to check the lawmaking power Congress has delegated to the executive branch.

When it was first developed, the legislative veto was not all that contentious; to the contrary, it was part of a quid pro quo between Congress and President Herbert Hoover, who wanted authority to reorganize the executive branch without going through the normal legislative process. The legislature agreed to go along, but only on the condition that either house of Congress could block the president's reorganization plan by passing a resolution expressing opposition. When Congress passed the 1933 legislative appropriations bill with that condition attached to it, the legislative veto was born.

Although Hoover had agreed to it, he was less than pleased when Congress used it the following year to veto part of the reorganization plan. His attorney general, William D. Mitchell, decried the device as a violation of the separation of powers doctrine. That sort of sparring over the legislative veto continued through the early 1980s, but the patterns of debate were somewhat contradictory and confusing. On the one hand, until 1972 Congress had used the device rather sparingly, attaching it to only fifty-one laws.[23] On the other hand, presidents always complained about the legislative veto. Dwight D. Eisenhower loathed it, claiming that it violated "fundamental constitutional principles." Complaints grew louder after the presidency of Richard M. Nixon, when Congress sought to reassert itself over the executive and enacted sixty-two statutes with legislative vetoes between 1972 and 1979. In fact, in 1976 the House of Representatives "came within two votes of approving a proposal to make every rule and regulation of every executive agency subject to legislative review."[24]

This issue came to a head during the Carter administration. Jimmy Carter, like Eisenhower, despised legislative vetoes. Suggesting that he did not consider them

binding, he had the Justice Department join *Immigration and Naturalization Service v. Chadha*, to test it. The result was the first U.S. Supreme Court ruling centering specifically on the constitutionality of the legislative veto. On what grounds did the Court strike down the practice? Two justices dissented. Why did Justice White, in particular, believe that the Court had committed a grave error?

Immigration and Naturalization Service v. Chadha

462 U.S. 919 (1983)
http://laws.findlaw.com/US/462/919.html
Oral arguments may be found at: http://www.oyez.org
Vote: 7 (Blackmun, Brennan, Burger, Marshall, O'Connor,
    Powell, Stevens)
    2 (Rehnquist, White)
Opinion of the Court: Burger
Concurring opinion: Powell
Dissenting opinions: Rehnquist, White

Jagdish Rai Chadha, an East Indian born in Kenya and holder of a British passport, was admitted into the United States in 1966 on a six-year student visa. More than a year after his visa expired, in October 1973, the Immigration and Naturalization Service ordered Chadha to attend a deportation hearing and show cause why he should not be deported. After two hearings, an immigration judge in June 1974 ordered a suspension of Chadha's deportation, which meant that Chadha could stay in the United States, because he was of "good moral character" and would "suffer extreme hardship" if deported.

Acting under a provision of the Immigration and Nationality Act, the U.S. attorney general recommended to Congress that Chadha be allowed to remain in the United States in accordance with the judge's opinion. The act states:

Upon application by any alien who is found by the Attorney General to meet the requirements of . . . this section the Attorney General may in his discretion suspend deportation of such alien. If the deportation of any alien is suspended . . . a complete and detailed statement of the facts and pertinent provisions of the law in the case shall be reported to the Congress with the reasons for such suspension. Such reports shall be

---

23. Melvin I. Urofsky, *A March of Liberty* (New York: Knopf, 1988), 945.
24. Ibid., 946.

submitted on the first day of each calendar month in which Congress is in session.

Congress, in turn, had the authority to veto—by a resolution passed in either house—the attorney general's decision. The act specifies:

[I]f during the session of the Congress at which a case is reported, or prior to the close of the session of the Congress next following the session at which a case is reported, either the Senate or the House of Representatives passes a resolution stating in substance that it does not favor the suspension of such deportation, the Attorney General shall thereupon deport such alien or authorize the alien's voluntary departure at his own expense under the order of deportation in the manner provided by law. If, within the time above specified, neither the Senate nor the House of Representatives shall pass such a resolution, the Attorney General shall cancel deportation proceedings.

For a while it appeared as if Chadha's suspension of deportation was secure, but at the last moment Congress asserted its veto power. Congress had until December 19, 1975, to take action, and on December 12 the chair of a House committee introduced a resolution opposing the "granting of permanent residence in the United States to [six] aliens," including Chadha. Four days later the House of Representatives passed the motion. No debate or recorded vote occurred; indeed, it was never really clear why the chamber took the action.

That vote set the stage for a major showdown between Congress and the executive branch. Chadha filed a suit, first with the Immigration Court and then with a federal court of appeals, asking that they declare the legislative veto unconstitutional. The Carter administration joined him to argue likewise. The president agreed with Chadha's basic position, and administration attorneys thought his suit provided a great test case because it "pointed up the worst features of the legislative veto—no debate, no recorded vote, no approval by the other chamber, and no chance for presidential review."[25] Given the importance of the dispute, the court of appeals asked both the House and the Senate to file amicus curiae briefs supporting the veto practice, but in 1980 it ruled against their position, finding that the device violated separation of powers principles.

25. Ibid., 947.

Jagdish Chadha, shown here with his wife, Therese Lorentz, and their two daughters, successfully challenged the constitutionality of the legislative veto during his legal efforts to avoid deportation.

By the time the case was first argued before the Supreme Court in February 1982, the Carter administration was out and the Reagan administration was in. During his 1980 campaign, Ronald Reagan claimed to support the legislative veto, but, once in office, he instructed the attorney general to go forward with the *Chadha* case.

CHIEF JUSTICE BURGER delivered the opinion of the Court.

We granted certiorari [to consider] the constitutionality of the provision in §244(c)(2) of the Immigration and Nationality Act, authorizing one House of Congress, by resolution, to invalidate the decision of the Executive Branch, pursuant to authority delegated by Congress to the Attorney General of the United States, to allow a particular deportable alien to remain in the United States. . . .

. . . We begin, of course, with the presumption that the challenged statute is valid. Its wisdom is not the concern of the courts; if a challenged action does not violate the Constitution, it must be sustained. . . .

By the same token, the fact that a given law or procedure is efficient, convenient, and useful in facilitating functions of government, standing alone, will not save it if it is contrary to the Constitution. Convenience and efficiency are not the primary objectives—the hallmarks—of democratic government and our inquiry is sharpened rather than blunted by the fact that congressional veto provisions are appearing with increasing frequency in statutes which delegate authority to executive and independent agencies. . . .

Explicit and unambiguous provisions of the Constitution prescribe and define the respective functions of the Congress and of the Executive in the legislative process. . . .

Just as we relied on the textual provision of Art II, §2, cl 2, to vindicate the principle of separation of powers in *Buckley* [v. *Valeo*, 1976], we see that the purposes underlying the Presentment Clauses, Art I, §7, cls 2, 3, and the bicameral requirement of Art I, §1, and §7, cl 2, guide our resolution of the important question present in these cases. . . .

The records of the Constitutional Convention reveal that the requirement that all legislation be presented to the President before becoming law was uniformly accepted by the Framers. Presentment to the President and the Presidential veto were considered so imperative that the draftsmen took special pains to assure that these requirements could not be circumvented. . . .

The decision to provide the President with a limited and qualified power to nullify proposed legislation by veto was based on the profound conviction of the Framers that the powers conferred on Congress were the powers to be most carefully circumscribed. It is beyond doubt that lawmaking was a power to be shared by both Houses and the President. . . .

The bicameral requirement of Art I, §§1, 7, was of scarcely less concern to the Framers than was the Presidential veto and indeed the two concepts are interdependent. By providing that no law could take effect without the concurrence of the prescribed majority of the Members of both Houses, the Framers reemphasized their belief . . . that legislation should not be enacted unless it has been carefully and fully considered by the Nation's elected officials. . . .

We see therefore that the Framers were acutely conscious that the bicameral requirement and the Presentment Clauses would serve essential constitutional functions. The President's participation in the legislative process was to protect the Executive Branch from Congress and to protect the whole people from improvident laws. The division of the Congress into two distinctive bodies assures that the legislative power would be exercised only after opportunity for full study and debate in separate settings. The President's unilateral veto power, in turn, was limited by the power of two-thirds of both Houses of Congress to overrule a veto thereby precluding final arbitrary action of one person. It emerges clearly that the prescription for legislative action in Art I, §§1, 7, represents the Framers' decision that the legislative power of the Federal Government be exercised in accord with a single, finely wrought and exhaustively considered, procedure. . . .

Examination of the action taken here by one House pursuant to §244(c)(2) reveals that it was essentially legislative in purpose and effect. In purporting to exercise power defined in Art I, §8, cl 4, to "establish an uniform Rule of Naturalization," the House took action that had the purpose and effect of altering the legal rights, duties, and relations of persons, including the Attorney General, Executive Branch officials and Chadha, all outside the Legislative Branch. . . .

The legislative character of the one-House veto in these cases is confirmed by the character of the congressional action it supplants. Neither the House of Representatives nor the Senate contends that, absent the veto provision in §244(c)(2), either one of them, or both of them acting together, could effectively require the Attorney General to deport an alien once the Attorney General, in the exercise of legislatively delegated authority, had determined the alien should remain in the United States. Without the challenged provision in §244(c)(2), this could have been achieved, if at all, only by legislation requiring deportation. Similarly, a veto by one House of Congress . . . cannot be justified as an attempt at amending the standards set out in §244(c)(2), or as a repeal of §244 as applied to Chadha. Amendment and repeal of statutes, no less than enactment, must conform with Art I.

The nature of the decision implemented by the one-House veto in these cases further manifests its legislative character. . . . Congress made a deliberate choice to delegate to the Executive Branch . . . the authority to allow deportable aliens to remain in this country in certain specified circumstances. Congress must abide by its delegation of authority until that delegation is legislatively altered or revoked. . . .

Since it is clear that the action by the House . . . was an exercise of legislative power, that action was subject to the standards prescribed in Art I. . . . To accomplish what has been attempted by one House of Congress in this case requires action in conformity with the express procedures of the Constitution's prescription for legislative action: passage by a majority of both Houses and presentment to the President.

The veto authorized by §244(c)(2) doubtless has been in many respects a convenient shortcut; the "sharing" with the Executive by Congress of its authority over aliens in this manner is, on its face, an appealing compromise. In purely practical terms, it is obviously easier for action to be taken by one House without submission to the President; but it is crystal clear from the records of the Convention, contemporaneous writings and debates, that the Framers ranked other values higher than efficiency. . . .

The choices we discern as having been made in the Constitutional Convention impose burdens on governmental processes that often seem clumsy, inefficient, even unworkable, but those hard choices were consciously made by men who had lived under a form of government that permitted arbitrary governmental acts to go unchecked. There is no support in the Constitution or decisions of this Court for the proposition that the cumbersomeness and delays often encountered in complying with explicit constitutional standards may be avoided, either by the Congress or by the President. With all the obvious flaws of delay, untidiness, and potential for abuse, we have not yet found a better way to preserve freedom than by making the exercise of power subject to the carefully crafted restraints spelled out in the Constitution.

We hold that the congressional veto provision . . . is severable from the Act and that it is unconstitutional.

JUSTICE WHITE, dissenting.

Today the Court not only invalidates §244(c)(2) of the Immigration and Nationality Act, but also sounds the death knell for nearly 200 other statutory provisions in which Congress has reserved a "legislative veto." For this reason, the Court's decision is of surpassing importance. . . .

The prominence of the legislative veto mechanism in our contemporary political system and its importance to Congress can hardly be overstated. It has become a central means by which Congress secures the accountability of executive and independent agencies. Without the legislative veto, Congress is faced with a Hobson's choice: either to refrain from delegating the necessary authority, leaving itself with a hopeless task of writing laws with the requisite specificity to cover endless special circumstances across the entire policy landscape, or in the alternative, to abdicate its lawmaking function to the Executive Branch and independent agencies. To choose the former leaves major national problems unresolved; to opt for the latter risks unaccountable policymaking by those not elected to fill that role. Accordingly, over the past five decades, the legislative veto has been placed in nearly 200 statutes. The device is known in every field of governmental concern: reorganization, budgets, foreign affairs, war powers, and regulation of trade, safety, energy, the environment, and the economy. . . .

I do not suggest that all legislative vetoes are necessarily consistent with separation-of-powers principles. A legislative check on an inherently executive function . . . poses an entirely different question. But the legislative veto device here—and in many other settings—is far from an instance of legislative tyranny over the Executive. It is a necessary check on the unavoidably expanding power of the agencies, both Executive and independent, as they engage in exercising authority delegated by Congress.

I regret that I am in disagreement with my colleagues on the fundamental questions that these cases present. But even more I regret the destructive scope of the Court's holding. It reflects a profoundly different conception of the Constitution than that held by the courts which sanctioned the modern administrative state. Today's decision strikes down in one fell swoop provisions in more laws enacted by Congress than the Court has cumulatively invalidated in its history. I fear it will now be more difficult to "insur[e] that the fundamental policy decisions in our society will be made not by an appointed official but by the body immediately responsible to the people," *Arizona v. California* (1963) (Harlan, J., dissenting in part). I must dissent.

In theory, the Court banished legislative vetoes from the government system because they undermined the spirit and letter of the Constitution. In practice, however, the Court's decision had a negligible effect on congressional-executive relations. Since *Chadha*, Congress has passed new laws containing legislative vetoes. But even more important is that the practice continues even in the absence of specific legislation—agencies and departments still pay heed to congressional rejections of policy.[26]

Why has the Court's opinion resulted in such blatant noncompliance? More to the point, why do executive agencies and departments continue to respect the wishes of Congress, even though they need not? One reason is purely pragmatic: Because departments and agencies depend on Congress for fiscal support, they relent out of "fear of budgetary retaliation."[27] Another reason was implied by Justice White in his dissenting opinion: The legislative veto is a natural response to an executive branch that wants broad delegations of power and a legislature that desires the ability to control such delegations without needing to pass new legislation.

In this particular instance, then, the U.S. Supreme Court may have been the loser: Its decision settling the *Chadha* dispute was unacceptable to the political branches and was largely ignored by them. But this resistance has not stopped the Court from continuing to rule on important separation of powers questions. In the next chapter we examine how the Court has settled disputes over the executive branch and its role in the separation of powers scheme.

---

26. Louis Fisher, "The Legislative Veto: Invalidated, It Survives," *Law and Contemporary Problems* 56 (1993): 288.

27. Urofsky, *A March of Liberty*, 948.

READINGS

Adler, David Gray, and Larry N. George, eds. *The Constitution and the Conduct of American Foreign Policy.* Lawrence: University Press of Kansas, 1996.

Barber, Sotirios A. *The Constitution and the Delegation of Congressional Power.* Chicago: University of Chicago Press, 1975.

Barnes, Jeb. *Overruled? Legislative Overrides, Pluralism, and Contemporary Court-Congress Relations.* Palo Alto: Stanford University Press, 2004.

Craig, Barbara H. *Chadha: The Story of an Epic Constitutional Struggle.* New York: Oxford University Press, 1988.

Devins, Neal, and Keith E. Whittington, eds. *Congress and the Constitution.* Durham: Duke University Press, 2005.

Eskridge, William N., Jr., and John Ferejohn. "The Article I, Section 7 Game." *Georgetown Law Journal* 80 (1992): 523–563.

Goodman, Walter. *The Committee: The Extraordinary Career of the House Committee on Un-American Activities.* New York: Farrar, Straus and Giroux, 1968.

Henkin, Louis. *Foreign Affairs and the Constitution.* New York: W. W. Norton, 1975.

Ignagni, Joseph, and James Meernik. "Explaining Congressional Attempts to Reverse Supreme Court Decisions." *Political Research Quarterly* 47 (1994): 353–371.

Irons, Peter H. *The New Deal Lawyers.* Princeton: Princeton University Press, 1982.

Katzmann, Robert A., ed. *Judges and Legislators: Toward Institutional Comity.* Washington, D.C.: Brookings Institution, 1988.

Murphy, Walter F. *Congress and the Court.* Chicago: University of Chicago Press, 1962.

Pickerill, J. Mitchell. *Constitutional Deliberation in Congress: The Impact of Judicial Review in a Separated System.* Durham: Duke University Press, 2004.

Pritchett, C. Herman. *Congress Versus the Supreme Court, 1957–1960.* Minneapolis: University of Minnesota Press, 1961.

Schmidhauser, John R., and Larry L. Berg. *The Supreme Court and Congress.* New York: Free Press, 1972.

CHAPTER 5
THE EXECUTIVE

The framers would have great trouble recognizing today's presidency. The sentiment of the Philadelphia Convention was that the Articles of Confederation were flawed because they did not provide for an executive, but few delegates would have approved of the extent of the powers wielded by our modern presidents. After suffering under the British monarch, many delegates had serious reservations about awarding too much authority to the executive branch. Those who supported the New Jersey Plan even envisioned a plural executive arrangement under which two individuals would share the chief executive position so that excessive power would not accrue to a single person. The framers would be astonished at the vast military resources over which the president presides as commander in chief, to say nothing of the hundreds of departments, agencies, and bureaus that constitute the executive branch.

We can attribute some of this growth to the rather loose wording of Article II, which has neither the detail nor the precision of the framers' Article I description of the legislature. Instead, Article II is dominated by issues of selection and removal and devotes less attention to powers and limitations. The wording is quite broad: Presidents are given the undefined "executive power" of the United States and are admonished to take care that the laws are "faithfully executed." Other grants of authority, such as the president's role as "Commander in Chief of the Army and Navy" and the preferential position given the chief executive in matters of foreign policy, allow for significant expansion.

The presidency also has grown in response to the world's changing conditions. Over the years American society has increased in complexity, and the number of matters that require government action has mushroomed. Because Congress has been overwhelmed by the nation's demands, the legislature has delegated to the executive branch authority that the framers did not anticipate. In addition, the expanding importance of defense and foreign policy has demanded a more powerful presidency.

As these changes took place, the Supreme Court frequently was called upon to referee disputes over the constitutional limits of executive authority. The Court's decisions have contributed significantly to the way the presidency has evolved, allowing considerable growth in authority and yet imposing necessary restraints.

SELECTION AND FORMAL POWERS

In Article II the framers developed a novel way to select the chief executive. Until then, the executives of most nations were chosen by bloodline, military power, or legislative selection. No other country had experimented with a system like the Electoral College apparatus created at the Philadelphia convention. Perhaps because it had never been tried, the system was plagued with defects that required correction over time.

Presidential Selection and Constitutional Change

The framers designed the Electoral College system to allow the general electorate to have some influence on the selection of the chief executive without resorting to direct popular election. The original blueprint called for each state to select presidential electors equal in number to the state's delegates to the Senate and House of Representatives. The Constitution empowered the state legislatures to decide the method of choosing the electors. Popular election was always the most common method, but in the past some state legislatures voted for the electors. Article II disqualifies those who hold federal office, but otherwise there are no specified qualifications for being an elector. The Electoral College system was based on the theory that the states would select their most qualified citizens, who would exercise their best judgment in the selection of the president.

The Constitution mentions only three qualifications for presidential eligibility—citizenship, age, and residency. First, Article II requires that only individuals who are natural-born citizens may become president.[1] Naturalized citizens—those who attain citizenship after birth—may not hold the nation's highest office. Second, to be president a person must have reached the age of thirty-five. Third, the president must have been a resident of the United States for fourteen years. Although the original version of the Constitution made no mention of qualifications for vice president, this oversight was corrected with the 1804 ratification of the Twelfth Amendment, which says that no person can serve as vice president who is not eligible to be president.

Under the original procedures set forth in Article II, the electors were to assemble in their respective state capitals on election day and cast votes for their presidential preferences. Each elector had two votes, no more than one of which could be cast for a candidate from the elector's home state. The states' votes were sent to the federal capital, where the president of the Senate opened them. The candidate who received the most votes would be declared president, provided that the number of votes received was a majority of the number of electors. Article II anticipated two possible problems with this procedure. First, because the electors each cast two votes, it

1. The Constitution also allowed individuals who were citizens at the time the Constitution was adopted to be eligible to hold the presidency.

was possible for the balloting to result in a tie between two candidates. In this event, the Constitution stipulated that the House of Representatives should select one of the two. Second, if multiple candidates sought the presidency, it would be possible for no candidate to receive the required majority. In this case the House was to decide among the top five finishers in the Electoral College voting. In settling such disputed elections, each state delegation was to cast a single vote, rather than allowing the individual members to vote independently.

In the original scheme the vice president was selected right after the president. The formula for choosing the vice president was simple—the vice president was the presidential candidate who received the second highest number of electoral votes. If two or more candidates tied for second in the Electoral College voting, the Senate would select the vice president from among them.

The first two elections took place with no difficulty. In 1789 George Washington received one ballot from each of the 69 electors who participated and was elected president. John Adams became vice president because he got the next highest number of electoral votes (34). History repeated itself in the election of 1792, with Washington receiving one vote from each of the 132 electors. Adams again gathered the next highest number of votes (77) and returned to the vice presidency.

The first defects in the electoral system became apparent with the election of 1796. By this time political parties had begun to develop, and this election was a contest between the incumbent Federalists and the Democratic-Republicans. With Washington declining to run for a third term, John Adams became the candidate of the Federalists, and Thomas Jefferson was the choice of those who wanted political change. When the ballots were counted, Adams had won the presidency with seventy-one electoral votes; Jefferson, with sixty-eight, became vice president. For the first time, the nation had a divided executive branch, with the president and vice president of different political parties.

Matters got even worse with the 1800 election. The Democratic-Republicans were now the more popular of the two major parties, and they backed Jefferson for president and Aaron Burr for vice president. The electors committed to the Democratic-Republican Party candidates each cast one ballot for Jefferson and one for Burr. Although it was clear which man was running for which office, the method of selection did not allow for such distinctions. The result was that Jefferson and Burr each received seventy-three votes, and the election moved to the House of Representatives for settlement. Each of the sixteen states had a single vote, and a majority was required for election. On February 11, 1801, the first vote in the House was taken. Jefferson received eight votes, Burr six. Two states, Maryland and Vermont, were unable to register a preference because their state delegations were evenly divided. Votes continued to be taken over the next several days, until finally, on February 17, after thirty-six ballots, Jefferson received the support of ten state delegations and was named president, with Burr becoming vice president.

It was clear that the Constitution had to be changed to avoid such situations. Congress proposed the Twelfth Amendment in 1803, and the states ratified it the next year. The amendment altered the selection system by separating the offices of president and vice president. Rather than casting two votes for president, electors would vote for a presidential candidate and then vote separately for a vice-presidential candidate. The House and Senate continued to settle presidential and vice-presidential elections in which no candidate received a majority, although the amendment also modified the procedures for such elections.

Presidential and vice-presidential elections are still governed by the Twelfth Amendment, but the evolution of political parties and the reduction in the degree of independence exercised by presidential electors have resulted in huge changes in the way the system operates. The Electoral College persists, despite considerable support for replacing it with direct popular election. Proponents of this reform have never achieved enough strength to prompt Congress or the state legislatures to propose the necessary constitutional amendment. Historically, opposition to popular election has come from the smaller states, which enjoy more influence within the Electoral College system than they would under popular election reforms.

Tenure, Removal, and Succession

The Constitution sets the presidential term at four years. Originally, there was no restriction on the number of terms a president could serve; George Washington began the tradition of a two-term limit when he announced at the end of his second administration that he would not run again. This tradition was honored by every president until Franklin Roosevelt sought election to a third term in 1940 and further violated the custom by running for a fourth term in 1944. In reaction, Congress proposed the Twenty-second Amendment, which held that no person could run for president after having served more than six years in that office. The states ratified the amendment in 1951.

If an incumbent president or vice president abuses the office, the Constitution provides for impeachment as the method of removal. Impeachment is a two-stage process. First, the House of Representatives investigates the charges against the incumbent. The Constitution stipulates that impeachment can occur only upon charges of "Treason, Bribery, or other High Crimes and Misdemeanors." Once convinced that there is sufficient evidence of such misconduct, the House passes articles of impeachment specifying the crimes charged and authorizing a trial. The second stage, the trial, takes place in the Senate, with the chief justice of the United States presiding. Conviction requires the agreement of two-thirds of the voting senators. Congress can impose no penalties on a convicted official other than removal from office.

Only two presidents have been impeached—Andrew Johnson in 1868 and Bill Clinton in 1999. Both were acquitted in the Senate, with Johnson surviving by a single vote. The only other president who became the subject of serious impeachment efforts was Richard Nixon in 1974. The House of Representatives was well on its way to completing impeachment articles on Nixon, and a conviction in the Senate was almost assured. To spare himself and the nation the strain of such proceedings, Nixon resigned from office, the only American president ever to do so. Because both the Nixon and Clinton episodes led to several important constitutional rulings on executive power, we have more to say about the circumstances surrounding their impeachments in the coming pages.

Although presidential approval is not required for amendments to be proposed or ratified, here President Lyndon B. Johnson, surrounded by congressional leaders, signs the newly ratified Twenty-fifth Amendment on February 23, 1967. The Amendment authorized the president to nominate a new vice president when a vacancy in that office occurred and also provided for an orderly transition of authority should the president become disabled. At the time, the vice presidency was vacant. If Johnson had died or become disabled, seventy-five-year-old Speaker John McCormack *(far right)* would have assumed the presidency. Next in line of succession was president pro tempore of the Senate, eighty-nine-year-old Carl Hayden *(third from left, standing)*.

Eight other sitting presidents failed to complete their terms. Four (William Henry Harrison, Zachary Taylor, Warren G. Harding, and Franklin Roosevelt) died of natural causes, and four (Abraham Lincoln, James A. Garfield, William McKinley, and John F. Kennedy) were assassinated. The framers provided in Article II that in the event of the president's death or disability, the vice president assumes the powers and responsibilities of the office. In Section 1 of Article II, the Constitution authorizes Congress to determine presidential succession if there is no sitting vice president when a vacancy occurs.

In 1965 Congress recommended some additional changes in the Constitution to govern presidential succession. The need became apparent after Lyndon Johnson assumed the presidency following Kennedy's assassination in 1963. Johnson's ascension left the vice presidency vacant. If anything had happened to Johnson, the federal succession law dictated that next in line was the Speaker of the House, followed by the president pro tempore of the Senate *(see Box 5-1)*. In 1965 the Speaker was John McCormack, D-Mass., who was seventy-four years old, and the president pro tempore of the Senate was Carl Hayden, D-Ariz., who was eighty-eight. Neither was capable of handling the demands of the presidency. Congress proposed that the Constitution be amended to provide that when a vacancy occurs in the office of vice president, the president nominates a new vice president who takes office upon confirmation by majority vote in both houses of Congress. The proposal also clarified procedures governing those times when a president is temporarily unable to carry out the duties of the office. The change was ratified by the states as the Twenty-fifth Amendment in 1967.

BOX 5-1   LINE OF SUCCESSION

ON MARCH 30, 1981, President Ronald Reagan was shot by would-be assassin John Hinckley outside a Washington hotel and rushed to an area hospital for surgery. Vice President George H. W. Bush was on a plane returning to Washington from Texas. Presidential aides and cabinet members gathered at the White House, where questions arose among them and the press corps about who was "in charge."[1] Secretary of State Alexander M. Haig Jr. rushed to the press briefing room and, before an audience of reporters and live television cameras, said, "As of now, I am in control here in the White House, pending the return of the vice president. . . . Constitutionally, gentlemen, you have the president, the vice president, and the secretary of state."

Haig was, as many gleeful critics subsequently pointed out, wrong. The Constitution says nothing about who follows the vice president in the line of succession. The Succession Act of 1947 (later modified to reflect the creation of new departments) establishes congressional leaders and the heads of the departments, in the order the departments were created, as filling the line of succession that follows the vice president.

The line of succession is:

vice president	secretary of commerce
Speaker of the House of Representatives	secretary of labor
president pro tempore of the Senate	secretary of health and human services
secretary of state	secretary of housing and urban development
secretary of the Treasury	secretary of transportation
secretary of defense	secretary of energy
attorney general	secretary of education
secretary of the interior	secretary of veterans affairs
secretary of agriculture	secretary of homeland security

A different "line"—not of succession to the presidency, but of National Command Authority in situations of wartime emergency—was created according to the National Security Act of 1947. The command rules are detailed in secret presidential orders that each new president signs at the outset of the term. Among other things, the orders authorize the secretary of defense to act as commander in chief in certain specific, limited situations in which neither the president nor the vice president is available. Presumably, such situations would follow a nuclear attack on Washington.

SOURCE: *Guide to the Presidency*, 3rd ed., ed. Michael Nelson (Washington, D.C.: Congressional Quarterly, 2002), 409.
    1. "Confusion over Who Was in Charge Arose Following Reagan Shooting," *Wall Street Journal*, April 1, 1981.

It was not long before the country needed the procedures outlined in the Twenty-fifth Amendment. In 1973 Vice President Spiro Agnew resigned when he was charged with income tax evasion stemming from alleged corruption during his years as governor of Maryland. Nixon nominated, and Congress confirmed, Rep. Gerald R. Ford of Michigan to become vice president. Just one year later, Nixon resigned the presidency, and Ford became the nation's first unelected chief executive. Ford selected Nelson Rockefeller, former governor of New York, to fill the new vacancy in the vice presidency.

Constitutional Powers

Despite the constitutional changes dealing with presidential selection and succession, the president's formal powers are the same today as when they were drafted by the Philadelphia convention. The first section of Article II, the vesting clause, stipulates that "The executive

Power shall be vested in a President of the United States of America." After this general grant of authority, Sections 2 and 3 of Article II list specific, formal powers. Those formal grants of authority fall into four categories.

General Executive Powers
To execute and enforce the laws
To appoint and remove executive branch officials

Military and Foreign Policy Powers
To be commander in chief of the armed forces
To appoint ambassadors
To receive foreign ambassadors
To make treaties

Powers Related to the Legislative Branch
To veto bills passed by Congress
To convene special sessions of Congress
To advise Congress on the state of the nation

Powers Related to the Judicial Branch
To appoint federal judges
To grant pardons to those convicted of federal crimes

Many of the provisions conferring powers on the chief executive are vaguely worded and open to interpretation. For example, just what is included in the "executive power" that the Constitution grants to the president? The lack of precision in the wording of Article II has given rise to two opposing theories of presidential power. The first, called the "mere designation of office" theory, holds that the executive power includes no more than the tasks specifically included in Sections 2 and 3. This limited view of presidential authority was implied by James Madison in Federalist No. 51 and advocated by President William Howard Taft:

The true view of the Executive function is, as I conceive it, that the President can exercise no power which cannot be fairly and reasonably traced to some specific grant of power or justly implied and included within such express grant as proper and necessary to its exercise. Such specific grant must be either in the Federal Constitution or in an act of Congress passed in pursuance thereof. There is no undefined residuum of power which he can exercise because it seems to him to be in the public interest.[2]

The opposing viewpoint is called the "general grant of power" theory (sometimes called the stewardship theory, or the prerogative or inherent power approach, by modern-day scholars). This approach holds that the grant of executive power is a broad one, giving the president whatever is needed to run the country. President Theodore Roosevelt, a well-known adherent of this perspective, put it this way in his autobiography:

[When immediate and vigorous executive action is necessary] it is the duty of the President to act upon the theory that he is the steward of the people, and that the proper attitude for him to take is that he is bound to assume that he has the legal right to do whatever the needs of the people demand, unless the Constitution or laws explicitly forbid him to do it.[3]

It should not be surprising that these two very different views of presidential power have given rise to legal conflicts that ultimately found their way to the Supreme Court's doorstep. In no small way, the presidency has been shaped by how the justices have responded to these important conflicts.

THE DOMESTIC POWERS OF THE PRESIDENT

To understand the powers of the executive more thoroughly it is useful to consider the domestic and foreign policy roles of the president separately. This division reflects the perspective of political scientists who suggest that there are actually two "presidencies": one for domestic affairs and one for foreign relations. Today, we find it difficult to separate the two because of the many ways they affect each other, but differences between the two remain. The president is significantly more constrained— by the public, Congress, and even the Supreme Court— in domestic affairs than in the realm of foreign policy. As you read the material to come, consider whether this division makes sense.

The Faithful Execution of the Laws

At the heart of executive power is the enforcement of the law; Article II, Section 3, states that the president

2. William Howard Taft, *Our Chief Magistrate and His Powers* (New York: Columbia University, 1916), 139–140.

3. *Theodore Roosevelt: An Autobiography* (New York: Scribner's, 1920), 464.

shall be given the responsibility to "take Care that the Laws be faithfully executed." Undoubtedly, the take care clause means that the provisions of the Constitution and the laws enacted by Congress are entrusted to the president for administration and enforcement. Presidents may use the substantial powers of the executive branch to see that the law is followed.

In *In re Neagle* (1890) the Court held that presidential enforcement powers were to be interpreted broadly. *Neagle* stemmed from a disappointed litigant's threat to kill Justice Stephen Field. President Benjamin Harrison authorized the Justice Department to appoint a bodyguard to protect Field, although such appointments were not authorized by law. The Supreme Court upheld the appointment, thus endorsing the "general grant of power" view of presidential authority.

The Constitution obliges the president to enforce all the laws, not just those the administration supports. A number of presidents have been criticized for failing to carry out certain laws enthusiastically, but it would be difficult to prove that the chief executive had not satisfied the constitutional mandate of faithful execution. On rare occasions, however, a president has openly refused to execute a law validly passed by Congress. In such cases court challenges are to be expected.

One such incident occurred over the Federal Water Pollution Control Act Amendments of 1972, which made federal moneys available for local water projects. President Nixon opposed the law, which Congress had passed over his veto, and he ordered his administration not to allocate the money as required by the statute. In *Train v. City of New York* (1975) the Court held that the law allowed no discretion in the matter. The president's obligation was to carry out the terms of the statute. Faithful execution of the laws requires the executive branch to enforce and administer the policies enacted by the legislature even if the president opposes them.

The Constitution unambiguously gives the president the responsibility and authority to enforce the laws. But is this power given exclusively to the president, or may the other branches also exercise enforcement? This question has been at the root of several important battles between Congress and the president. In most instances the Court has held that powers clearly executive in nature must be carried out by the executive branch.

Bowsher v. Synar (1986) involved a challenge to the constitutionality of certain provisions of the Balanced Budget and Emergency Deficit Control Act of 1985, better known as the Gramm-Rudman-Hollings Act. The legislation attempted to control the federal budget deficit by imposing automatic budget cuts when members of Congress were unable or unwilling to exercise sufficient fiscal restraint. The law established maximum budget deficit levels for each year beginning in 1986. The size of the deficit was to decrease each year until fiscal 1991, when no deficit would be allowed. If the federal budget deficit in any year exceeded the maximum allowed, across-the-board budget cuts would automatically be imposed.

Triggering the cuts involved steps to be taken by several government officials, culminating in a final report by the U.S. comptroller general. If the comptroller general concluded that budget projections required spending cuts under the statute, the president would issue an order to curb spending. This provision gave the comptroller general an important role in the enforcement of the balanced budget law. But the comptroller general is an officer within the legislative branch, not the executive. The justices ruled in *Bowsher* that giving the comptroller general such authority violated the separation of powers principle. Executive authority is not to be exercised by the legislative branch.

The *Bowsher* decision supplied an authoritative declaration of the boundaries between legislative and executive authority. Once Congress makes its choice in enacting laws, its participation ends. Thereafter, Congress can control the execution of the law only indirectly—by passing new legislation. The execution and enforcement of the law must be left to the executive branch.

The Veto Power

Section 7 of Article I of the Constitution contains what has become known as the presentment clause:

Every Bill which shall have passed the House of Representatives and the Senate, shall, before it become a Law, be presented to the President of the United States; If he approve he shall sign it, but if not he shall return it, with his Objections to that House

President Bill Clinton uses new power under the Line Item Veto Act to cancel two spending provisions and a special tax break on August 11, 1997. Groups challenging the law won a Supreme Court ruling declaring the act unconstitutional.

in which it shall have originated. . . . If after . . . Reconsideration two thirds of that House shall agree to pass the Bill, it shall be sent . . . to the other House, by which it shall likewise be reconsidered, and if approved by two thirds of that House, it shall become a Law.

In other words, after Congress passes a piece of legislation, it is sent to the president. The chief executive, in turn, has three options: sign it, veto it, or do nothing. If the president signs the bill, it becomes law. If the president vetoes it, the bill does not become law unless Congress passes it again by a two-thirds majority in each house. If the president does nothing, the bill becomes law after ten days, provided Congress is in session. If Congress adjourns during the ten-day period, the bill is "pocket vetoed" and does not become law. Although presidents exercise the veto infrequently (over the nation's history the veto has been used about seven times per year), they understand the importance of this option. It allows the president to block legislation he considers unwise, and the very threat of its use is a considerable power in the give and take of legislative-executive politics.

The relatively clear wording of the Constitution has resulted in very few legal disputes regarding the veto power. Among the interpretations of the presentment clause over which there is little controversy is that presidents are not able to veto specific provisions of bills passed by Congress but must veto the entire bill if the power is to be exercised at all. A line item veto law would give the president the power to reject or cancel specific items within a larger bill while allowing the remaining portions to become law. Proponents of the line item veto argue that the president needs this power when considering complex appropriations bills, which inevitably contain numerous wasteful spending provisions that fund individual legislators' pet projects. Under the traditional interpretation of the Constitution, the president cannot reject these "pork barrel" projects or "earmarks" without vetoing the entire act.

Presidents, beginning with Ulysses Grant, have long advocated that Congress pass line item veto legislation. Congress continually refused to do so until 1996, when the legislature enacted the Line Item Veto Act:

[T]he President may, with respect to any bill or joint resolution that has been signed into law pursuant to Article I, section 7, of the Constitution of the United States, cancel in whole—(1) any dollar amount of discretionary budget authority; (2) any item of new direct spending; or (3) any limited tax benefit; if the President—

[A] determines that such cancellation will—(i) reduce the Federal budget deficit; (ii) not impair any essential Government functions; and (iii) not harm the national interest; and

[B] notifies the Congress of such cancellation by transmitting a special message . . . within five calendar days (excluding Sundays) after the enactment of the law [to which the cancellation applies].

The act contained another important provision. Although it gave the president the power to rescind various expenditures, it established a check on his ability to do so: Congress may consider "disapproval bills"—which would render the president's cancellation "null and void." In other words, Congress could restore appropriations cuts by the president; but, it is worth noting, new congressional legislation would be subject to a presidential veto.

On January 2, 1997, just one day after the act went into effect, it was challenged by six members of Congress who had voted against it. The Supreme Court dismissed this suit on standing to sue grounds (*Raines v. Byrd*, 1997), but then considered the constitutional merits of the line item veto in *Clinton v. City of New York* (1998).

Clinton v. City of New York

524 U.S. 417 (1998)
http://laws.findlaw.com/US/524/417.html
Oral arguments may be found at: http://www.oyez.org
Vote: 6 (Ginsburg, Kennedy, Rehnquist, Souter, Stevens, Thomas)
    3 (Breyer, O'Connor, Scalia)
Opinion of the Court: Stevens
Concurring opinion: Kennedy
Opinion concurring in part and dissenting in part: Scalia
Dissenting opinion: Breyer

Following the Court's decision in *Raines v. Byrd*, President Clinton began actively using his new power, canceling more than eighty provisions in taxing and spending bills passed by Congress. Among the canceled items were a provision of the Balanced Budget Act of 1997 that provided money for New York City hospitals and a section of the Taxpayer Relief Act of 1997 that gave a tax break to potato growers in Idaho. The president's action was immediately challenged in court by the affected parties. Those in the first case were New York City, two hospital associations, and two unions representing health care employees. The parties in the second were a farmers' cooperative and one of its members.

A federal district court consolidated the cases, determined that at least one party in each suit had standing to sue, and then ruled that the line item veto law violated the presentment clause. The administration then appealed to the U.S. Supreme Court.

JUSTICE STEVENS delivered the opinion of the Court:

Less than two months after our decision in [*Raines*], the President exercised his authority to cancel one provision in the Balanced Budget Act of 1997 and two provisions in the Taxpayer Relief Act of 1997. Appellees, claiming that they had been injured by two of those cancellations, filed these cases in the District Court. That Court again held the statute invalid and we again expedited our review. We now hold that these appellees have standing to challenge the constitutionality of the Act and, reaching the merits, we agree that the cancellation procedures set forth in the Act violate the Presentment Clause, Art. I, §7, cl. 2, of the Constitution. . . .

In both legal and practical effect, the President has amended two Acts of Congress by repealing a portion of each. "[R]epeal of statutes, no less than enactment, must conform with Art. I." *INS v. Chadha* (1983). There is no provision in the Constitution that authorizes the President to enact, to amend, or to repeal statutes. Both Article I and Article II assign responsibilities to the President that directly relate to the lawmaking process, but neither addresses the issue presented by these cases. The President "shall from time to time give to the Congress Information on the State of the Union, and recommend to their Consideration such Measures as he shall judge necessary and expedient. . . ." Art. II, §3. Thus, he may initiate and influence legislative proposals. Moreover, after a bill has passed both Houses of Congress, but "before it become[s] a Law," it must be presented to the President. If he approves it, "he shall sign it, but if not he shall return it, with his Objections to that House in which it shall have originated, who shall enter the Objections at large on their Journal, and proceed to reconsider it." Art. I, §7, cl. 2. His "return" of a bill, which is usually described as a "veto," is subject to being overridden by a two-thirds vote in each House.

There are important differences between the President's "return" of a bill pursuant to Article I, §7, and the exercise of the President's cancellation authority pursuant to the Line Item Veto Act. The constitutional return takes place *before* the bill becomes law; the statutory cancellation occurs *after* the bill becomes law. The constitutional return is of the entire bill; the statutory cancellation is of only a part. Although the Constitution expressly authorizes the President to play a role in the process of enacting statutes, it is silent on the subject of unilateral Presidential action that either repeals or amends parts of duly enacted statutes.

There are powerful reasons for construing constitutional silence on this profoundly important issue as equivalent to an express prohibition. The procedures governing the enactment of statutes set forth in the text of Article I were the product of the great debates and compromises that produced the Constitution itself. Familiar historical materials provide abundant support for the conclusion that the power to enact statutes may only "be exercised in accord with a single, finely wrought and exhaustively considered, procedure." *Chadha.* Our first President understood the text of the Presentment Clause as requiring that he either "approve all the parts of a Bill, or reject it in toto." What has emerged in these cases from the President's exercise of his statutory cancellation powers, however, are truncated versions of two bills that passed both Houses of Congress. They are not the product of the "finely wrought" procedure that the Framers designed. . . .

[O]ur decision rests on the narrow ground that the procedures authorized by the Line Item Veto Act are not authorized by the Constitution. The Balanced Budget Act of 1997 is a 500-page document that became "Public Law 105-33" after three procedural steps were taken: (1) a bill containing its exact text was approved by a majority of the Members of the House of Representatives; (2) the Senate approved precisely the same text; and (3) that text was signed into law by the President. The Constitution explicitly requires that each of those three steps be taken before a bill may "become a law." Art. I, §7. If one paragraph of that text had been omitted at any one of those three stages, Public Law 105-33 would not have been validly enacted. If the Line Item Veto Act were valid, it would authorize the President to create a different law—one whose text was not voted on by either House of Congress or presented to the President for signature. Something that might be known as "Public Law 105-33 as modified by the President" may or may not be desirable, but it is surely not a document that may "become a law" pursuant to the procedures designed by the Framers of Article I, §7, of the Constitution.

If there is to be a new procedure in which the President will play a different role in determining the final text of what may "become a law," such change must come not by legislation but through the amendment procedures set forth in Article V of the Constitution. Cf. *U. S. Term Limits, Inc. v. Thornton,* (1995).

The judgment of the District Court is affirmed.

It is so ordered.

JUSTICE KENNEDY, concurring.

A nation cannot plunder its own treasury without putting its Constitution and its survival in peril. The statute before us, then, is of first importance, for it seems undeniable the Act will tend to restrain persistent excessive spending. Nevertheless, for the reasons given by JUSTICE STEVENS in the opinion for the Court, the statute must be found invalid. Failure of political will does not justify unconstitutional remedies. . . .

The Constitution is not bereft of controls over improvident spending. Federalism is one safeguard, for political accountability is easier to enforce within the States than nationwide. The other principal mechanism, of course, is control of the political branches by an informed and responsible electorate. Whether or not federalism and control by the electorate are adequate for the problem at hand, they are two of the structures the Framers designed for the problem the statute strives to confront. The Framers of the Constitution could not command statesmanship. They could simply provide structures from which it might emerge. The fact that these mechanisms, plus the proper functioning of the separation of powers itself, are not employed, or that they prove insufficient, cannot validate an otherwise unconstitutional device. With these observations, I join the opinion of the Court.

JUSTICE SCALIA, with whom JUSTICE O'CONNOR joins, and with whom JUSTICE BREYER joins [in part,] concurring in part and dissenting in part.

I turn . . . to the crux of the matter: whether Congress's authorizing the President to cancel an item of spending gives him a power that our history and traditions show must reside exclusively in the Legislative Branch. . . .

Insofar as the degree of political, "law-making" power conferred upon the Executive is concerned, there is not a dime's worth of difference between Congress's authorizing the President to *cancel* a spending item, and Congress's authorizing money to be spent on a particular item at the President's discretion. And the latter has been done since the Founding of the Nation. From 1789–1791, the First Congress made lump-sum appropriations for the entire Government—"sum[s] not exceeding" specified amounts for broad purposes. From a very early date Congress also made permissive individual appropriations, leaving the decision whether to spend the money to the President's unfettered discretion. . . .

The short of the matter is this: Had the Line Item Veto Act authorized the President to "decline to spend" any item of spending contained in the Balanced Budget Act of 1997, there is not the slightest doubt that authorization would have been constitutional. What the Line Item Veto Act does instead—authorizing the President to "cancel" an item of spending—is technically different. But the technical difference does *not* relate to the technicalities of the Presentment Clause, which have been fully complied with; and the doctrine of unconstitutional delegation, which *is* at issue here, is preeminently *not* a doctrine of technicalities. The title of the Line Item Veto Act, which was perhaps designed to simplify for public comprehension, or perhaps merely to comply with the terms of a campaign pledge, has succeeded in faking out the Supreme Court. The President's action it authorizes in fact is not a line-item veto and thus does not offend Art. I, §7; and insofar as the substance of that action is concerned, it is no different from what Congress has permitted the President to do since the formation of the Union.

JUSTICE BREYER, with whom JUSTICE O'CONNOR and JUSTICE SCALIA join [in part], dissenting.

I agree with the Court that the parties have standing, but I do not agree with its ultimate conclusion. In my view the Line Item Veto Act does not violate any specific textual constitutional command, nor does it violate any implicit Separation of Powers principle. Consequently, I believe that the Act is constitutional. . . .

. . . I recognize that the Act before us is novel. In a sense, it skirts a constitutional edge. But that edge has to do with means, not ends. The means chosen do not amount literally to the enactment, repeal, or amendment of a law. Nor, for that matter, do they amount literally to the "line item veto" that the Act's title announces. Those means do not violate any basic Separation of Powers principle. They do not improperly shift the constitutionally foreseen balance of power from Congress to the President. Nor, since they comply with Separation of Powers principles, do they threaten the liberties of individual citizens. They represent an experiment that may, or may not, help representative government work better. The Constitution, in my view, authorizes Congress and the President to try novel methods in this way. Consequently, with respect, I dissent.

President Clinton issued a statement expressing his displeasure: "I am deeply disappointed with today's Supreme Court decision striking down the line-item veto. The decision is a defeat for all Americans—it deprives the President of a valuable tool for eliminating waste in the Federal budget and for enlivening the public debate over how to make the best use of public funds." Given the view of the six-person majority, however, it is unlikely that the Court will reverse itself any time in the near future.

Presidential Signing Statements

On occasion, presidents have expressed their opinions about particular bills at the time they sign them. Called "presidential signing statements," these opinions typically point to provisions within the law over which the president has some concern and

(1) provide the president's interpretation of the language of the law;

(2) announce constitutional limits on the implementation of some of its provisions; or

(3) indicate directions to executive branch officials as to how to administer the new law in an acceptable manner.[4]

4. Phillip J. Cooper, "George W. Bush, Edgar Allen Poe, and the Use and Abuse of Presidential Signing Statements," *Presidential Studies Quarterly* 35 (2005): 515–532. We adapt material in this section from this article. See also Phillip J. Cooper, *By Order of the President: The Use and Abuse of Executive Direct Action* (Lawrence: University Press of Kansas, 2002).

When Congress passed the Balanced Budget and Emergency Deficit Act of 1985, the law designed to reduce budget deficits, President Ronald Reagan issued a signing statement. He expressed his view that the law was constitutionally defective because it gave the comptroller general, an official removable only by Congress, power over the president. (The Court agreed with the president the following year.)

On what authority did Reagan and presidents before and after him issue these statements? Although the Constitution contains no specific authorization, some presidents have pointed to the take care clause of Article II, arguing that it counsels against executing provisions of a law that they believe are unconstitutional. "That, of course, means," as one commentator put it, that agencies charged with executing the law "are to act in the manner that the [president] considers appropriate as compared to the way the legislation sets forth the policy. In that sense, it is a kind of line-item veto."[5] It is also a form of constitutional interpretation on the part of the president. Well before the Supreme Court enters the picture, assuming it ever does, the president may have expressed his views on the constitutionality of particular portions of a law.

What have the justices had to say about this practice? Not much, as it turns out. Although signing statements have been the subject of lower court litigation, they have not faced a constitutional challenge in the Supreme Court. Moreover, the justices have virtually ignored these statements in their review of federal laws. In only a handful of cases has the Court cited, much less relied on, presidential signing statements to interpret legislation, even though some, such as in the case involving the Balanced Budget and Emergency Deficit Act, have been quite important.

But change may be in the wind. First, it is true that presidents since James Monroe have issued signing statements, but President George W. Bush's use of the device was, in some regards, unique. Although he issued fewer statements on an annual basis than many of his predecessors, he challenged far more statutory provisions within a single statement—by some counts, nearly six times as many as Bill Clinton.[6] In those statements, Bush raised scores of constitutional objections to various congressional enactments—some on the ground that they interfered with his "exclusive power over foreign affairs."

The frequency and purpose of President Bush's use of signing statements generated more awareness and commentary about the practice than ever before—with scholars coming down both in favor and in opposition. Whether legal challenges or congressional action will follow, we cannot say. But what does seem clear—and this brings us to a second development—is that pressure may be building from within the Court to pay greater heed to the practice. In critiquing the Court's use of legislative history to interpret a law, a practice he condemns, Justice Scalia chided the majority for "wholly ignor[ing] the President's signing statement, which explicitly set forth *his* understanding" of the law at issue.[7] An "understanding," we might add, with which Scalia agreed but the majority did not.

So far, we are left with more questions than answers. Will the justices now become more attentive to signing statements when they interpret or review the constitutionality of federal laws? Should they? And what about the practice itself, especially its implications? Prior to a federal court decision, are presidents obligated to execute statutory provisions they believe are unconstitutional? If so, then ought they never issue signing statements? We leave these for you to consider as you read the material and cases to follow.

The Powers of Appointment and Removal

For presidents to carry out the executive duties of the government effectively, they must be able to staff the various departments and offices with administrators who share their views and in whom they have confidence. This duty implies the power to appoint and the power to remove. The Constitution is relatively clear on the presi-

---

5. Cooper, "George W. Bush," 517.

6. Curtis A. Bradley and Eric A. Posner, "Presidential Signing Statements and Executive Power," July 2006, SSRN Electronic Paper Collection, http://ssrn.com/abstract=922400.

7. In *Hamdan v. Rumsfeld* (2006).

dent's appointment power but is silent on the right to remove.

Appointing Executive Officials. Article II, Section 2, contains what is known as the appointments clause. It details the president's authority to appoint major administrative and judicial officials, but it also allows Congress to allocate that authority to other bodies for minor administrative positions:

[The President] shall nominate, and by and with the Advice and Consent of the Senate, shall appoint Ambassadors, other public Ministers and Consuls, Judges of the supreme Court, and all other Officers of the United States, whose Appointments are not herein otherwise provided for, and which shall be established by Law: but the Congress may by Law vest the Appointment of such inferior Officers, as they think proper, in the President alone, in the Courts of Law, or in the Heads of Departments.

From time to time Congress has established government positions that, for various reasons, were to be filled by an appointing authority other than the president. When the executive has objected, legal disputes have arisen. In many cases the issue is whether the official holds a major position as an officer of the United States or is an inferior official. The former, according to the appointments clause, must be filled by presidential nomination and Senate confirmation, but the latter may be chosen by some other means as determined by Congress. Two Supreme Court decisions, reaching opposite conclusions, illustrate the differences between major and inferior officials.

Buckley v. Valeo (1976) involved a multi-issue challenge to the 1974 amendments to the Federal Election Campaign Act. The law enacted a complex scheme regulating federal election campaigns, including creation of the eight-member Federal Election Commission (FEC) to police the new regulations. Given the political importance of the FEC's duties, Congress created a selection system designed to ensure that no political party or branch of government would dominate it. The secretary of the Senate and the clerk of the House were ex officio members without the right to vote. The president pro tempore of the Senate, the Speaker of the House, and the

president each appointed two members, one Democrat and one Republican. The six voting members had to be confirmed by both houses of Congress.

The Supreme Court, unanimously on this point, found the FEC's selection system to be incompatible with the appointments clause. The commissioners were not inferior officers; they were officials entrusted with major enforcement and administrative duties. As such, they should be appointed by the president and confirmed by the Senate with no House involvement.

The Court reached a different conclusion in *Morrison v. Olson* (1988). In 1978 Congress included a provision in the Ethics in Government Act dealing with the position of special prosecutor. The law provided for a special prosecutor to investigate and, when necessary, to prosecute high-ranking officials of the government for violations of federal criminal laws.

Because the duties of the special prosecutor involved the investigation of wrongdoing in the executive branch, Congress did not want the president to have a role in the appointment of that official. Instead, the law established the following selection procedures: If, after a preliminary investigation, the attorney general concluded that a special prosecutor was needed, a "special division" was convened. The special division consisted of three federal judges appointed by the chief justice of the United States. The judges were empowered to appoint the special prosecutor. The selection of the prosecutor and a description of the prosecutor's tasks and jurisdiction were the special division's only function.

Once appointed, the special prosecutor could exercise all of the powers of the Justice Department. A prosecutor appointed under the act could be removed by the attorney general, but only for cause or disabilities that substantially impaired the counsel from completing the required duties. Such dismissals could be reviewed by the federal district court. The special prosecutor's tenure otherwise ended when he or she declared the work to be completed, or the special division concluded that the prosecutor's assigned tasks had been accomplished.

Theodore B. Olson and two other Justice Department officials suspected of presenting false information to Congress in 1985 challenged the authority of the special prosecutor on the ground that the prosecutor was a major official and, as such, could be appointed only by the president, not by a panel of judges.

In *Morrison* the Supreme Court upheld the law. The majority acknowledged that the line between inferior and principal officers is a blurred one, but found that the special prosecutor clearly fell into the inferior officer category. Chief Justice William Rehnquist's opinion cited four reasons. First, the special prosecutor could be removed by the attorney general. Second, the special prosecutor was authorized to perform only certain, limited duties. Third, the jurisdiction of the special prosecutor was limited to the investigation of specified federal officials. And finally, the special prosecutor's tenure was temporary; once the investigation was completed the special prosecutor left office. In addition, the Court could find no substantial reason to believe that the special prosecutor in any way infringed on the rights and powers of the president; nor was the law an attempt by Congress to increase its power at the expense of the president.

The special prosecutor statute, upheld in *Morrison*, expired at the end of 1992. Because of partisan differences at that time, it was not reenacted. In June 1994, however, a new independent counsel statute became law. The act received bipartisan support in Congress and was endorsed by President Clinton, the first chief executive to back independent counsel legislation. The new law imposed selection procedures modeled after the earlier statute.

It was under this new law that Independent Counsel Kenneth Starr investigated various activities of President Clinton that ultimately led to his 1998 impeachment by the House of Representatives. The revised law received even more criticism than the earlier version. The special prosecutor's open-ended term of office, nearly unconstrained prosecutorial power, and expensive operation doomed the prospects for renewing the statute without significant reform. The legislation expired without reauthorization in 1999.

Dismissing Executive Officials. The president's need to have executive branch officials who support the administration's policy goals is only partially satisfied by the power to appoint. What is also required is the corollary—the discretionary right to remove administrative officials from office. This need may arise when a president's appointees do not carry out their duties the way the president wishes. It also applies when an official appointed by a previous administration will not voluntarily step aside to make way for a nominee of the new president's choosing.

Although an established removal procedure is obviously necessary, the framers neglected to mention it in the Constitution. In the absence of constitutional guidelines, a lingering controversy has centered on whether administrative officials can be removed at the discretion of the president alone or whether Congress may play a role.

The argument supporting presidential discretion holds that the chief executive must be free to remove subordinates who fail to meet the president's expectations or who are not loyal to the administration's policy objectives. It would be unreasonable to require the approval of Congress before such officials could be dismissed. Such a requirement might well paralyze the executive branch, particularly when the legislature and the presidency are under the control of different political parties. Moreover, to proponents of a doctrine called the "unitary executive," this argument finds support in the vesting clause of Article II: "The executive Power shall be vested in a President of the United States of America." Only the president, they contend, is vested with the authority to execute the laws in the executive branch, and only he can remove officers in "his" branch.

The argument for legislative participation in the process holds that the Constitution anticipates Senate action. If the president can appoint major executive department officials only with senatorial approval, it is reasonable to infer that the chief executive can remove administrators only by going through the same process and obtaining the advice and consent of the Senate. Alexander Hamilton supported this view in *The Federalist Papers'* only reference to removal powers. Hamilton flatly stated in Federalist No. 77, "The consent of that body [the Senate] would be necessary to displace as well as to appoint." Hamilton argued that if the president and the Senate agreed that an official should be removed, the decision would be much better accepted than if the president acted alone. Furthermore, Hamilton asserted that a new president should be restrained from removing an experienced official who had conducted his duties satisfactorily just because the president preferred to have a different person in the position.

Historical practice generally has rejected Hamilton's position. From the very beginning, Congress allowed the chief executive to remove administrative officials without Senate consent. In the First Congress James Madison proposed that three executive departments be created: Foreign Affairs, Treasury, and War. The creation of the Foreign Affairs (later State) Department received the most legislative attention. According to Madison's recommendation, the department was to have a secretary to be appointed by the president with the approval of the Senate who could be removed by the president alone. The House and the Senate held long comprehensive debates on the removal power at that time and passed legislation allowing the secretary of state to be removed at the president's discretion without Senate approval.

At times, however, the legislature has asserted a right to participate in the process. The most notable example occurred with the passage of the Tenure of Office Act in 1867. This statute was enacted to restrict the powers of President Andrew Johnson, who took office after Lincoln's assassination in 1865. Following the Civil War, the Radical Republicans dominated Congress and had little use for Johnson, a Democrat from Tennessee. Congress did not want Johnson to be able to remove Lincoln's appointees. The Tenure of Office Act stipulated that the president could not remove high-ranking executive department heads without first obtaining the approval of the Senate. Johnson blatantly defied the statute by dismissing Secretary of War Edwin M. Stanton in August 1867 and appointing Ulysses S. Grant as interim secretary. The Senate reacted by ordering Stanton reinstated. Grant left office and Stanton returned in January 1868. The next month Johnson fired Stanton again. The president's failure to comply with the Tenure of Office Act constituted one of the grounds upon which the House impeached him.

The Tenure of Office Act never had a judicial test. Once Johnson's term expired, the statute was weakened by amendment and then repealed in 1887. Consequently, as the nation entered the twentieth century there had yet to be an authoritative declaration of the constitutional parameters of the removal power, although some statutes remaining on the books asserted a role for the Senate in the dismissal of administrative officials.

It was well into the twentieth century before the Supreme Court resolved the confusion over the president's removal powers. Its first and most important ruling came in *Myers v. United States* (1926), a lawsuit challenging the authority of President Woodrow Wilson to fire Frank Myers, a Portland, Oregon, postmaster. In a strongly worded opinion, Chief Justice William Howard Taft, a former U.S. president, upheld Wilson's power to remove.

Taft's opinion stressed that the power to remove is an incident of the power to appoint. It is an executive power that resides with the president. That the Constitution limits the appointment power by senatorial consent does not necessarily mean that the removal power is also to be limited by Senate participation. The president is entrusted with taking care that the laws are faithfully executed. To accomplish this goal, the president must have an administration in which he has confidence. To allow the Senate to participate in the removal of administrative officials would severely limit the chief executive's ability to carry out the constitutional obligations of the office. As a result of this reasoning, the Court declared unconstitutional the Tenure of Office Act of 1867 and any subsequent legislation having the same purpose.

Later, the Court qualified the president's removal power, partially backing away from the strong position expressed in *Myers*. In *Humphrey's Executor v. United States* (1935) and *Wiener v. United States* (1958), the Court distinguished between officials with purely executive responsibilities and those who exercise quasi-legislative or quasi-judicial power. In *Humphrey's Executor* the justices upheld the right of Congress to restrict the president's authority to remove commissioners serving on independent administrative agencies, such as the Federal Trade Commission. These officials are involved in administrative rulemaking and enforcement. Congress purposefully placed them outside the president's direct command. In *Wiener* the justices allowed the legislature to limit the president's power to remove members of a special war claims commission created to adjudicate war-related compensation claims. Because of its quasi-judicial responsibilities, the commission was not organized under the president's executive command. Consistent with *Myers,* however, officials that exercise purely executive power serve at the pleasure of the president and can be removed at the president's discretion.

Executive Privilege Protecting Presidential Confidentiality

Article II is silent on two potentially important and related questions pertaining to the president's role as chief executive. The first, executive privilege, asks whether the president can refuse to supply the other branches of government with information about his activities. The second, immunity (covered in the next section), asks whether and to what extent the president is protected from lawsuits while in office.

The executive privilege argument asserts that conversations, documents, and records that are closely tied to the sensitive duties of the president should remain confidential. Neither the legislature nor the judiciary should be allowed access to these materials without presidential consent; nor should the other branches be empowered to compel the president to hand over such items. Matters concerning national security or foreign policy, especially, fall under this protection. Executive privilege, it is argued, is inherent to the office of the president.

Although infrequently invoked, the privilege doctrine has been part of American history since the beginning of the nation. In some early disputes between the president and Congress, chief executives refused to provide certain information to the legislature. George Washington balked at giving the House of Representatives certain documents pertaining to negotiations over the Jay Treaty. During the investigation and trial of Aaron Burr, Thomas Jefferson cooperated with congressional information requests, but only up to a point. He refused to produce some items and later declined to testify at the trial even

though he was subpoenaed. Presidents through the years have refused to comply with congressional requests for testimony. It is generally accepted that Congress does not have the power to compel the president to come before it to answer questions. Other executive department officials generally are not covered by claims of privilege.

In most instances, disputes over executive privilege are handled through negotiation between the executive branch and the institution requesting information. Only rarely have such disputes led to major court cases. When pushed to the limit, executive privilege claims rarely prevail, but when sensitive military or diplomatic matters requiring secrecy are involved, a president can expect to be on relatively safe ground in asserting executive privilege.

No case involving executive privilege has been more important than *United States v. Nixon* (1974). It occurred at a time of great constitutional stress, when all three branches were locked in a fight about fundamental issues regarding the separation of powers. The conflict ultimately was resolved when Nixon resigned. Much of the impetus for breaking the constitutional deadlock came from the unanimous decision of the justices in the *Nixon* case. Chief Justice Warren Burger's opinion for the Court reviewed the issues surrounding the executive privilege controversy and then rejected Nixon's invocation of the doctrine.

United States v. Nixon

418 U.S. 683 (1974)
http://laws.findlaw.com/US/418/683.html
Oral arguments may be found at: http://www.oyez.org
Vote: 8 (Blackmun, Brennan, Burger, Douglas, Marshall,
　　Powell, Stewart, White)
　　0
Opinion of the Court: Burger
Not participating: Rehnquist

This case was one of many court actions spawned by the Watergate scandal. The controversy began on June 17, 1972, when seven men broke into Democratic National Committee headquarters located in the Watergate complex in Washington, D.C. The seven were appre-

This subpoena *duces tecum* was issued July 23, 1973. It ordered President Nixon or his representatives to appear before the federal grand jury on July 26 and to bring taped conversations relevant to the investigation of the Watergate affair.

hended and charged with criminal offenses. All had ties either to the White House or to the Committee to Re-elect the President. Five of the seven pleaded guilty, and two were convicted. At the end of the trial, one of the defendants, James McCord Jr., claimed that he had been pressured to plead guilty and that others had been involved in the break-in who had escaped prosecution. It was clear to many that the break-in was only the tip of a very large iceberg of shady dealings and cover-ups engaged in by influential persons closely tied to the Nixon administration.

In response to these events, the Senate began an investigation of the Watergate incident and the activities related to it. The star witness was John Dean III, special counsel to the president, who testified under a grant of immunity. Dean implicated high officials in the president's office, and he claimed that Nixon had known about the events and the subsequent cover-ups. As surprising as this testimony was, the most shocking revelation was made by presidential aide Alexander Butterfield, who testified that the president had installed a secret taping sys-

tem that automatically recorded all conversations in the Oval Office. Obviously, the tape recordings held information that would settle the dispute between the witnesses claiming White House involvement in the Watergate affair and the denial issued by administration officials.

In addition to the Senate investigation, a special prosecutor was appointed to look into the Watergate affair. The first person to hold this position, Archibald Cox, asked Nixon to turn over the tapes. When Nixon declined, Cox went to court to get an order compelling him to deliver the materials. The district and appeals courts ruled in favor of the prosecutor. Nixon then offered to release summaries of the recordings, but that did not satisfy Cox, who continued to pursue the tapes. Nixon ordered that Cox be fired. When the two highest officials in the Justice Department resigned rather than comply with the order, Solicitor General Robert Bork became the acting attorney general and dismissed Cox. The firing of the prosecutor, popularly known as the "Saturday Night Massacre," enraged the American people, and many began calling for the president's impeachment.

This drawing illustrates Richard Nixon's attorney, James St. Clair, arguing the president's case before the Supreme Court in *United States v. Nixon* (1974). The four justices are *(left to right):* Chief Justice Warren Burger, William J. Brennan Jr., Byron R. White, and Harry A. Blackmun. The empty chair at the far right belongs to Justice William Rehnquist, who disqualified himself from sitting on the case.

A new special prosecutor, Leon Jaworski, was appointed. The Houston attorney pursued the tapes with the same zeal as had Cox. Finally, Nixon relented and agreed to produce some of the materials. But when he did so, the prosecutor found that the tapes had been heavily edited. One contained eighteen and one-half minutes of mysterious buzzing at a crucial point, indicating that conversation had been erased.

Jaworski obtained criminal indictments against several Nixon aides. Although no criminal charges were brought against the president, he was named in the indictment as a co-conspirator. At about the same time, the House Judiciary Committee began an investigation into whether the president should be impeached.

Both the Judiciary Committee and Jaworski sought more of the tapes to review. Nixon steadfastly refused to comply, claiming that it was his right under executive privilege to decide what would be released and what would remain secret. The district court issued a final subpoena *duces tecum* (a judicial command to bring forth physical evidence); thus the president was ordered to produce the tapes and other documents. Both the United States and Nixon requested that the Supreme Court review the case, and the justices accepted the case on an expedited basis, bypassing the court of appeals.

Note that Justice William Rehnquist did not participate in this case. Immediately before joining the Court in 1971, Rehnquist had served in the Nixon Justice Department as an assistant attorney general in a period during which many of the incidents related to this case occurred. Because of a possible conflict of interest, Rehnquist excused himself from any role in resolving the dispute.

MR. CHIEF JUSTICE BURGER delivered the opinion of the Court.

[W]e turn to the claim that the subpoena should be quashed because it demands "confidential conversations between a President and his close advisors that it would be inconsistent with the public interest to produce." The first contention is a broad claim that the separation of powers doctrine precludes judicial review of a President's claim of privilege. The second contention is that if he does not prevail on the claim of absolute privilege, the court should hold as a matter of constitutional law that the privilege prevails over the subpoena *duces tecum.*

In the performance of assigned constitutional duties each branch of the Government must initially interpret the Constitution, and the interpretation of its powers by any branch is due great respect from the others. The President's counsel, as we have noted, reads the Constitution as providing an absolute privilege of confidentiality for all Presidential communications. Many decisions of this Court, however, have unequivocally reaffirmed the holding of *Marbury v. Madison* (1803) that "[i]t is emphatically the province and duty of the judicial department to say what the law is."

No holding of the Court has defined the scope of judicial power specifically relating to the enforcement of a subpoena for confidential Presidential communications for use in a criminal prosecution, but other exercises of power by the Executive Branch and the Legislative Branch have been found invalid as in conflict with the Constitution. *Powell v. McCormack* (1969); *Youngstown Sheet & Tube Co. v. Sawyer* (1952). . . .

Notwithstanding the deference each branch must accord the others, the "judicial Power of the United States" vested in the federal courts by Art. III, §1, of the Constitution can no more be shared with the Executive Branch than the Chief Executive, for example, can share with the Judiciary the veto power, or the Congress share with the Judiciary the power to override a Presidential veto. Any other conclusion would be contrary to the basic concept of separation of powers and the checks and balances that flow from the scheme of a tripartite government. We therefore reaffirm that it is the province and duty of this Court "to say what the law is" with respect to the claim of privilege presented in this case.

In support of his claim of absolute privilege, the President's counsel urges two grounds, one of which is common to all governments and one of which is peculiar to our system of separation of powers. The first ground is the valid need for protection of communications between high Government officials and those who advise and assist them in the performance of their manifold duties; the importance of this confidentiality is too plain to require further discussion. Human experience teaches that those who expect public dissemination of their remarks may well temper candor with a concern for appearances and for their own interests to the detriment of the decisionmaking process. Whatever

the nature of the privilege of confidentiality of Presidential communications in the exercise of Art. II powers, the privilege can be said to derive from the supremacy of each branch within its own assigned area of constitutional duties. Certain powers and privileges flow from the nature of enumerated powers; the protection of the confidentiality of Presidential communications has similar constitutional underpinnings.

The second ground asserted by the President's counsel in support of the claim of absolute privilege rests on the doctrine of separation of powers. Here it is argued that the independence of the Executive Branch within its own sphere insulates a President from a judicial subpoena in an ongoing criminal prosecution, and thereby protects confidential Presidential communications.

However, neither the doctrine of separation of powers, nor the need for confidentiality of high-level communications, without more, can sustain an absolute, unqualified Presidential privilege of immunity from judicial process under all circumstances. The President's need for complete candor and objectivity from advisers calls for great deference from the courts. However, when the privilege depends solely on the broad, undifferentiated claim of public interest in the confidentiality of such conversations, a confrontation with other values arises. Absent a claim of need to protect military, diplomatic, or sensitive national security secrets, we find it difficult to accept the argument that even the very important interest in confidentiality of Presidential communications is significantly diminished by production of such material for *in camera* inspection with all the protection that a district court will be obliged to provide.

The impediment that an absolute, unqualified privilege would place in the way of the primary constitutional duty of the Judicial Branch to do justice in criminal prosecutions would plainly conflict with the function of the courts under Art. III. In designing the structure of our Government and dividing and allocating the sovereign power among three co-equal branches, the Framers of the Constitution sought to provide a comprehensive system, but the separate powers were not intended to operate with absolute independence. . . . To read the Art. II powers of the President as providing an absolute privilege as against a subpoena essential to enforcement of criminal statutes on no more than a generalized claim of the public interest in confidentiality of nonmilitary and nondiplomatic discussions would upset the constitutional balance of "a workable government" and gravely impair the role of the courts under Art. III.

Since we conclude that the legitimate needs of the judicial process may outweigh Presidential privilege, it is necessary to resolve those competing interests in a manner that preserves the essential functions of each branch. The right and indeed the duty to resolve that question does not free the Judiciary from according high respect to the representations made on behalf of the President.

The expectation of a President to the confidentiality of his conversations and correspondence, like the claim of confidentiality of judicial deliberations, for example, has all the values to which we accord deference for the privacy of all citizens and, added to those values, is the necessity for protection of the public interest in candid, objective, and even blunt or harsh opinions in Presidential decisionmaking. A President and those who assist him must be free to explore alternatives in the process of shaping policies and making decisions and to do so in a way many would be unwilling to express except privately. These are the considerations justifying a presumptive privilege for Presidential communications. The privilege is fundamental to the operation of Government and inextricably rooted in the separation of powers under the Constitution. . . .

But this presumptive privilege must be considered in light of our historic commitment to the rule of law. This is nowhere more profoundly manifest than in our view that "the twofold aim [of criminal justice] is that guilt shall not escape or innocence suffer." We have elected to employ an adversary system of criminal justice in which the parties contest all issues before a court of law. The need to develop all relevant facts in the adversary system is both fundamental and comprehensive. The ends of criminal justice would be defeated if judgments were to be founded on a partial or speculative presentation of the facts. The very integrity of the judicial system and public confidence in the system depend on full disclosure of all the facts, within the framework of the rules of evidence. To ensure that justice is done, it is imperative to the function of courts that compulsory process be available for the production of evidence needed either by the prosecution or by the defense. . . .

In this case the President challenges a subpoena served on him as a third party requiring the production of materials for use in a criminal prosecution; he does so on the claim that he has a privilege against disclosure of confidential communications. He does not place his claim of privilege on the ground they are military or diplomatic secrets. As to these areas of Art. II duties the courts have traditionally shown the utmost deference to Presidential responsibilities. . . . No case of the Court, however, has extended this high degree of deference to a President's generalized interest in confidentiality. Nowhere in the Constitution, as we have noted earlier, is there any explicit reference to a privilege of confidentiality, yet to the extent this interest relates to the effective discharge of a President's powers, it is constitutionally based.

The right to the production of all evidence at a criminal trial similarly has constitutional dimensions. The Sixth Amendment explicitly confers upon every defendant in a criminal trial the right "to be confronted with the witnesses against him" and "to have compulsory process for obtaining witnesses in his favor." Moreover, the Fifth Amendment also guarantees that no person shall be deprived of liberty without due process of law. It is the manifest duty of the courts to vindicate those guarantees, and to accomplish that it is essential that all relevant and admissible evidence be produced.

In this case we must weigh the importance of the general privilege of confidentiality of Presidential communications in performance of the President's responsibilities against the inroads of such a privilege on the fair administration of criminal justice. The interest in preserving confidentiality is weighty indeed and entitled to great respect. However, we cannot conclude that advisers will be moved to temper the candor of their remarks by the infrequent occasions of disclosure because of the possibility that such conversations will be called for in the context of a criminal prosecution.

On the other hand, the allowance of the privilege to withhold evidence that is demonstrably relevant in a criminal trial would cut deeply into the guarantee of due process of law and gravely impair the basic function of the courts. A President's acknowledged need for confidentiality in the communications of his office is general in nature, whereas the constitutional need for production of relevant evidence in a criminal proceeding is specific and central to the fair adjudication of a particular criminal case in the administration of justice. Without access to specific facts a criminal prosecution may be totally frustrated. The President's broad interest in confidentiality of communications will not be vitiated by disclosure of a limited number of conversations

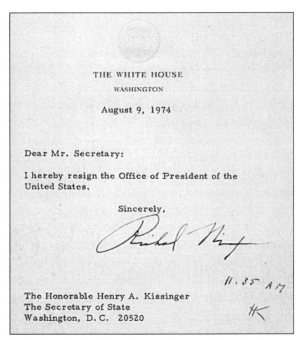

THE WHITE HOUSE
WASHINGTON

August 9, 1974

Dear Mr. Secretary:

I hereby resign the Office of President of the
United States.

Sincerely,

[signature: Richard Nixon]

11.35 AM

The Honorable Henry A. Kissinger
The Secretary of State
Washington, D.C. 20520

HK

With this one-sentence letter Richard Nixon became the first American president to resign from office.

preliminarily shown to have some bearing on the pending criminal cases.

We conclude that when the ground for asserting privilege as to subpoenaed materials sought for use in a criminal trial is based only on the generalized interest in confidentiality, it cannot prevail over the fundamental demands of due process of law in the fair administration of criminal justice. The generalized assertion of privilege must yield to the demonstrated, specific need for evidence in a pending criminal trial.

The Court's ruling was clear. The people's interest in the fair administration of criminal justice outweighed the president's interest in confidentiality. Executive privilege was rejected as a justification for refusing to make the tapes available to the prosecutor.

Nixon complied with the Court's ruling, knowing full well that it meant the end of his presidency. In obeying the Court order, he avoided provoking what many feared would be the most serious of all constitutional confrontations. What if Nixon had refused to comply? What

if he had destroyed the tapes rather than turn them over? Who could have enforced sanctions on the president for doing so? Impeachment and conviction of the president probably would have been the only way to handle such a crisis. Whatever Nixon's culpability in Watergate and related matters, he spared the nation an unprecedented crisis by bowing to the Supreme Court's interpretation of the Constitution.

The Nixon tapes revealed substantial wrongdoing. It was obvious to all that if Nixon had not voluntarily relinquished his position, the House of Representatives would have presented articles of impeachment, and a Senate trial would have taken place, resulting in his removal from office. Rather than put himself and the nation through such an ordeal, Nixon resigned.

Executive Immunity: Protecting the President from Lawsuit

Immunity is a variation of the notion of executive privilege. It deals with the extent to which the president is protected from lawsuits while in office, and the subject raises many interesting questions. May a president be ordered by a court to carry out certain executive actions, which are discretionary, or ministerial actions, which are performed as a matter of legal duty? Or, conversely, may a president be restrained by a court from taking such actions? May a private party sue the president for damages that might have been suffered because of the president's actions or omissions? If so, may a court order the president to pay damages or provide some other restitution? These questions place us in a quandary. To grant the president immunity from such legal actions may remove needed accountability. But to allow the chief executive to be subject to suit could make the execution of presidential duties impossible.

The Supreme Court's first significant venture into the area of executive immunity came in *Mississippi v. Johnson* (1867). Following the Civil War, Congress passed a number of laws "for the more efficient government of the rebel states." More commonly known as the Reconstruction Acts, they imposed military rule over the southern states until such time as loyal republican governments could be established. Andrew Johnson, a southerner from

Tennessee, who became president after Lincoln's assassination, vetoed the legislation, but the Radical Republicans in Congress had sufficient votes to override him. Once the acts were part of federal law, the president had little choice but to enforce them, despite his belief that they were unconstitutional.

The state of Mississippi joined the fray. Applying directly to the Supreme Court, Mississippi sued Johnson, asking the justices to issue an order prohibiting him from enforcing the laws, which the state argued were unconstitutional.

The Supreme Court rejected Mississippi's petition. The Court drew the distinction between ministerial and executive actions. A ministerial act is one over which there is no discretion. It occurs when a statute clearly directs the performance of a specific act. An executive act, by contrast, is one that allows discretion. The enforcement of a statute, such as the Reconstruction Act, is undoubtedly an executive action. A president enforces a law using judgment and discretion. It is not a simple ministerial act, but one that involves many political and administrative decisions. The judiciary is without power to enjoin the president in carrying out his executive authority. This stems not only from the separation of powers principle, but also as a practical matter. If the courts enjoined the president and he refused to comply, how would the judiciary enforce its order? The Court concluded, as Chief Justice Salmon P. Chase wrote, "this court has no jurisdiction of a bill to enjoin the President in the performance of his official duties."

The decision in *Johnson* settles the issue of whether the president may be personally sued with respect to executive functions, but it does not answer the question of civil suits brought by private individuals who have been harmed by a president's actions. If an incumbent president engages in unlawful activities that harm private individuals, can the president be held accountable in a court of law? Or is the president immune from such suits?

The Court answered these questions in **Nixon v. Fitzgerald** (1982). This legal action was initiated by A. Ernest Fitzgerald, who had been employed as a civilian management analyst for the U.S. Air Force. Fitzgerald blew the whistle in congressional testimony on some $2 billion in cost overruns for the development of the C-5A transport plane. His testimony was not well received by the Defense Department or military contractors. Thirteen months later Fitzgerald lost his job in what Defense officials claimed was a necessary departmental reorganization. Fitzgerald, however, believed the elimination of his job was an illegal retaliation for his congressional testimony. He was able to gather some evidence to support his claim, including Richard Nixon's admission that the president was aware of the firing and approved it. Fitzgerald sued several executive branch officials, including the president (who resigned during the early stages of the lower court proceedings). The former president's lawyers asserted that he should be removed from the suit on the ground of absolute executive immunity from legal actions based on his official conduct as president. The lower courts rejected the absolute immunity claim, and Nixon appealed.

By a 5–4 vote, the justices supported the president and extended immunity from lawsuit to cases such as this. Justice Powell explained:

Because of the singular importance of the President's duties, diversion of his energies by concern with private lawsuits would raise unique risks to the effective functioning of government. . . . In view of the special nature of the President's constitutional office and functions, we think it appropriate to recognize absolute Presidential immunity from damages liability for acts within the "outer perimeter" of his official responsibility.

Decisions such as *Mississippi v. Johnson* and *Nixon v. Fitzgerald* speak to immunity from lawsuits based on the president's official conduct, but they do not consider the problem of lawsuits filed against the president for behavior unrelated to his office. This issue was raised in 1994 when Paula Jones, a former Arkansas state employee, filed a civil suit against President Clinton, claiming that, while he was governor, he had made improper and illegal sexual advances toward her in a Little Rock hotel room. The charges led to heated public arguments over whether this was a case of inexcusable sexual harassment or a groundless, politically motivated lawsuit designed only to undermine and embarrass the president. Political rhetoric aside, the case presented a major constitutional issue: Can a sitting president be required to stand trial on allegations concerning his unofficial conduct? Jones's supporters argued that the president is not immune from lawsuit and that Jones, just like any other citizen, had the right to prompt judicial determination of her claims of being unlawfully treated. Clinton's supporters argued that the chief executive should not have to stand trial during his term of office. Allowing the trial to proceed would divert the president's attention from his official duties; the situation would be made worse by a potential rash of civil lawsuits that might follow.

Clinton v. Jones

520 U.S. 681 (1997)
http://laws.findlaw.com/US/520/681.html
Oral arguments may be found at: http://www.oyez.org
Vote: 9 (Breyer, Ginsburg, Kennedy, O'Connor, Rehnquist,
*   Scalia, Souter, Stevens, Thomas)*
*   0*
Opinion of the Court: Stevens
Concurring opinion: Breyer

Bill Clinton was elected to the presidency in 1992 and reelected in 1996. Prior to his elevation to the office of president, Clinton was the governor of Arkansas. In 1994 Paula Corbin Jones filed suit in federal district court in Arkansas against Clinton and Arkansas state trooper Danny Ferguson over an incident that was alleged to have occurred on May 8, 1991, at the Excelsior Hotel in Little Rock. On the day in question Jones, then an employee of the state Industrial Development Commission, was working at the registration desk for a management conference at which Governor Clinton had delivered a speech. According to her allegations, Trooper Ferguson approached Jones, indicating that the governor wanted to see her. Ferguson escorted her to Clinton's hotel suite. Jones and the governor were left alone in the room. The suit claimed that Clinton made "abhorrent" sexual advances to Jones, including exposing himself to her, touching her inappropriately, and making unwelcome sexual remarks. Jones said she rejected Clinton's suggestions, and the governor ceased his advances. As she was leaving the room, Jones alleged that the governor told her, "You are smart. Let's

Paula Corbin Jones, shown here at a 1998 news conference, brought a sexual harassment lawsuit against President Bill Clinton. The suit led the Supreme Court to confront the question of whether a president can be tried while still in office for conduct unrelated to his official duties.

keep this between ourselves." Jones's suit claimed that after she returned to her state job, her superiors began treating her rudely; she was ultimately transferred to another position that had little potential for advancement. She attributed this harsh treatment to retaliation for her rejection of the governor. The suit asked for actual damages of $75,000 and punitive damages of $100,000 in compensation for Clinton's violations of state and federal civil rights and sexual harassment laws.

Clinton denied the allegations and claimed the lawsuit was politically motivated. He filed motions asking the district court to dismiss the case on the ground of presidential immunity and to prohibit Jones from refiling the suit until after the end of his presidency. The district judge rejected the presidential immunity argument. Although she allowed pretrial discovery activities to proceed, the judge ordered that no trial would take place until Clinton was no longer president. Both Jones and Clinton appealed. Holding that "the President, like all other government officials, is subject to the same laws that apply to all other members of society," the court of appeals ruled that the trial should not be postponed. Clinton asked the Supreme Court to reverse the decision.

JUSTICE STEVENS delivered the opinion of the Court.

This case raises a constitutional and a prudential question concerning the Office of the President of the United States. Respondent, a private citizen, seeks to recover damages from the current occupant of that office based on actions allegedly taken before his term began. The President submits that in all but the most exceptional cases the Constitution requires federal courts to defer such litigation until his term ends and that, in any event, respect for the office warrants such a stay. Despite the force of the arguments supporting the President's submissions, we conclude that they must be rejected. . . .

Only three sitting Presidents have been defendants in civil litigation involving their actions prior to taking office. Complaints against Theodore Roosevelt and Harry Truman had been dismissed before they took office; the dismissals were affirmed after their respective inaugurations. Two companion cases arising out of an automobile accident were filed against John F. Kennedy in 1960 during the Presidential campaign. After taking office, he unsuccessfully argued that his status as Commander in Chief gave him a right to a stay under the Soldiers' and Sailors' Civil Relief Act of 1940. The motion for a stay was denied by the District Court, and the matter was settled out of court. Thus, none of those cases sheds any light on the constitutional issue before us.

The principal rationale for affording certain public servants immunity from suits for money damages arising out of their official acts is inapplicable to unofficial conduct. In cases involving prosecutors, legislators, and judges we have repeatedly explained that the immunity serves the public interest in enabling such officials to perform their designated functions effectively without fear that a particular decision may give rise to personal liability. . . .

That rationale provided the principal basis for our holding that a former President of the United States was "entitled to absolute immunity from damages liability predicated on his official acts," [*Nixon v.*] *Fitzgerald* [1982]. Our central concern was to avoid rendering the President "unduly cautious in the discharge of his official duties."

This reasoning provides no support for an immunity for *unofficial* conduct. As we explained in *Fitzgerald*, "the sphere of protected action must be related closely to the immunity's justifying purposes." Because of the President's broad responsibilities, we recognized in that case an immunity from damages claims arising out of official acts extending to the "outer perimeter of his authority." But we have never suggested that the President, or any other official, has an immunity that extends beyond the scope of any action taken in an official capacity.

Moreover, when defining the scope of an immunity for acts clearly taken *within* an official capacity, we have applied a functional approach. "Frequently our decisions have held that an official's absolute immunity should extend only to acts in performance of particular functions of his office." Hence, for example, a judge's absolute immunity does not extend to actions performed in a purely administrative capacity. As our opinions have made clear, immunities are grounded in "the nature of the function performed, not the identity of the actor who performed it."

Petitioner's effort to construct an immunity from suit for unofficial acts grounded purely in the identity of his office is unsupported by precedent.

We are also unpersuaded by the evidence from the historical record to which petitioner has called our attention. . . .

Petitioner's strongest argument supporting his immunity claim is based on the text and structure of the Constitution. He does not contend that the occupant of the Office of the President is "above the law," in the sense that his conduct is entirely immune from judicial scrutiny. The President argues merely for a postponement of the judicial proceedings that will determine whether he violated any law. His argument is grounded in the character of the office that was created by Article II of the Constitution, and relies on separation of powers principles that have structured our constitutional arrangement since the founding.

As a starting premise, petitioner contends that he occupies a unique office with powers and responsibilities so vast and important that the public interest demands that he devote his undivided time and attention to his public duties. He submits that—given the nature of the office—the doctrine of separation of powers places limits on the authority of the Federal Judiciary to interfere with the Executive Branch that would be transgressed by allowing this action to proceed.

We have no dispute with the initial premise of the argument. Former presidents, from George Washington to George Bush, have consistently endorsed petitioner's characterization of the office. . . .

It does not follow, however, that separation of powers principles would be violated by allowing this action to proceed. The doctrine of separation of powers is concerned with the allocation of official power among the three co-equal branches of our Government. . . .

Of course the lines between the powers of the three branches are not always neatly defined. But in this case there is no suggestion that the Federal Judiciary is being asked to perform any function that might in some way be described as "executive." Respondent is merely asking the courts to exercise their core Article III jurisdiction to decide cases and controversies. Whatever the outcome of this case, there is no possibility that the decision will curtail the scope of the official powers of the Executive Branch. The litigation of questions that relate entirely to the unofficial conduct of the individual who happens to be the President poses no perceptible risk of misallocation of either judicial power or executive power.

Rather than arguing that the decision of the case will produce either an aggrandizement of judicial power or a narrowing of executive power, petitioner contends that—as a by-product of an otherwise traditional exercise of judicial power—burdens will be placed on the President that will hamper the performance of his official duties. . . . As a factual matter, petitioner contends that this particular case—as well as the potential additional litigation that an affirmance of the Court of Appeals judgment might spawn—may impose an unacceptable burden on the President's time and energy, and thereby impair the effective performance of his office.

Petitioner's predictive judgment finds little support in either history or the relatively narrow compass of the issues raised in this particular case. As we have already noted, in the more than 200-year history of the Republic, only three sitting Presidents have been subjected to suits for their private actions. If the past is any indicator, it seems unlikely that a deluge of such litigation will ever engulf the Presidency. As for the case at hand, if properly managed by the District Court, it appears to us highly unlikely to occupy any substantial amount of petitioner's time.

Of greater significance, petitioner errs by presuming that interactions between the Judicial Branch and the Executive, even quite burdensome interactions, necessarily rise to the level of constitutionally forbidden impairment of the Executive's ability to perform its constitutionally mandated functions. . . . The fact that a federal court's exercise of its traditional Article III jurisdiction may significantly burden the time and attention of the Chief Executive is not sufficient to establish a violation of the Constitution. Two long-settled propositions, first announced by Chief Justice Marshall, support that conclusion.

First, we have long held that when the President takes official action, the Court has the authority to determine whether he has acted within the law. . . .

Second, it is also settled that the President is subject to judicial process in appropriate circumstances. Although Thomas Jefferson apparently thought otherwise, Chief Justice Marshall, when presiding in the treason trial of Aaron Burr, ruled that a subpoena *duces tecum* could be directed to the President. We unequivocally and emphatically endorsed Marshall's position when we held that President Nixon was obligated to comply with a subpoena commanding him to produce certain tape recordings of his conversations with his aides. *United States v. Nixon* (1974). As we explained, "neither the doctrine of separation of powers, nor the need for confidentiality of high-level communications, without more, can sustain an absolute, unqualified Presidential privilege of immunity from judicial process under all circumstances."

Sitting Presidents have responded to court orders to provide testimony and other information with sufficient frequency that such interactions between the Judicial and Executive Branches can scarcely be thought a novelty. President Monroe responded to written interrogatories, President Nixon—as noted above—produced tapes in response to a subpoena *duces tecum*, President Ford complied with an order to give a deposition in a criminal trial, and President Clinton has twice given videotaped testimony in criminal proceedings. Moreover, sitting Presidents have also voluntarily complied with judicial requests for testimony. . . .

In sum, "[i]t is settled law that the separation-of-powers doctrine does not bar every exercise of jurisdiction over the President of the United States." *Fitzgerald.* If the Judiciary may severely burden the Executive Branch by reviewing the legality of the President's official conduct, and if it may direct appropriate process to the President himself, it must follow that the federal courts have power to determine the legality of his unofficial conduct. The burden on the President's time and energy that is a mere by-product of such review surely cannot be considered as onerous as the direct burden imposed by judicial review and the occasional invalidation of his official actions. We therefore hold that the doctrine of separation of powers does not require federal courts to stay all private actions against the President until he leaves office. . . .

. . . [W]e are persuaded that it was an abuse of discretion for the District Court to defer the trial until after the President leaves office. Such a lengthy and categorical stay takes no account whatever of the respondent's interest in bringing the case to trial. The complaint was filed within the statutory limitations period—albeit near the end of that period—and delaying trial would increase the danger of prejudice resulting from the loss of evidence, including the inability of witnesses to recall specific facts, or the possible death of a party.

The decision to postpone the trial was, furthermore, premature. The proponent of a stay bears the burden of establishing its need. . . . We think the District Court may have given undue weight to the concern that a trial might generate unrelated civil actions that could conceivably hamper the President in conducting the duties of his office. If and when that should occur, the court's discretion would permit it to manage those actions in such fashion (including deferral of trial) that interference with the President's duties would not occur. But no such impingement upon the President's conduct of his office was shown here.

We add a final comment on two matters that are discussed at length in the briefs: the risk that our decision will generate a large volume of politically motivated harassing and frivolous litigation, and the danger that national security concerns might prevent the President from explaining a legitimate need for a continuance.

We are not persuaded that either of these risks is serious. Most frivolous and vexatious litigation is terminated at the pleading stage or on summary judgment, with little if any personal involvement by the defendant. Moreover, the availability of sanctions provides a significant deterrent to litigation directed at the President in his unofficial capacity for purposes of political gain or harassment. History indicates that the likelihood that a significant number of such cases will be filed is remote. Although scheduling problems may arise, there is no reason to assume that the District Courts will be either unable to accommodate the President's needs or unfaithful to the tradition—especially in matters involving national security—of giving "the utmost deference to Presidential responsibilities." Several Presidents, including petitioner, have given testimony without jeopardizing the Nation's security. In short, we have confidence in the ability of our federal judges to deal with both of these concerns.

If Congress deems it appropriate to afford the President stronger protection, it may respond with appropriate legislation. . . . If the Constitution embodied the rule that the President advocates, Congress, of course, could not repeal it. But our holding today raises no barrier to a statutory response to these concerns.

The Federal District Court has jurisdiction to decide this case. Like every other citizen who properly invokes that jurisdiction, respondent has a right to an orderly disposition of her claims. Accordingly, the judgment of the Court of Appeals is affirmed.

It is so ordered.

The Court's conclusion that Jones's sexual harassment suit could proceed was a blow to President Clinton, who was by that time heavily involved in more serious controversies that were leading toward a possible impeachment *(see Box 5-2).* In the end, Clinton and Jones reached an out-of-court monetary settlement of the dispute. Although the Jones case never went to trial, the Supreme Court's ruling that presidents while in office may be sued for unofficial conduct is a significant addition to the law of presidential immunity.

THE PRESIDENT AND FOREIGN AFFAIRS

Americans have always looked to the president for leadership in foreign affairs, whether in the normal conduct of political and economic relationships with other countries or leadership in times of war and national

BOX 5-2 AFTERMATH . . . PRESIDENT BILL CLINTON

IN *CLINTON V. JONES* (1997) the Supreme Court rejected President Clinton's request to postpone a trial on Paula Jones's sexual harassment charges until his presidency ended. Thus began two years of intense legal difficulties for the president. Clinton was already under investigation by Independent Counsel Kenneth Starr for possible financial improprieties in the Whitewater matter, an Arkansas land deal that occurred prior to his presidency. That investigation coupled with the Jones lawsuit subjected Clinton to more intense scrutiny than any previous president.

While preparing their case, Jones's attorneys were made aware of a possible illicit relationship between Clinton and a young White House intern, Monica Lewinsky. Attempting to establish a pattern of wrongdoing, Jones's lawyers subpoenaed Lewinsky and the president. Lewinsky initially denied any sexual relationship with Clinton. On January 17, 1998, President Clinton gave a sworn deposition claiming that he had not had a sexual relationship with Lewinsky. Nine days later he made the same denial to the American people on national television. Taped telephone conversations between Lewinsky and her friend Linda Tripp, who had given the tapes to the independent counsel's office, revealed that a sexual relationship between Lewinsky and Clinton had occurred. Starr expanded his investigation to include an inquiry into the Lewinsky matter.

After receiving immunity from prosecution, Lewinsky changed her testimony, acknowledging a past relationship with the president. In August Clinton admitted to "a critical lapse of judgment" that had led to his affair with Lewinsky. By this time, other women had come forward claiming that Clinton had acted inappropriately with them. In November the president settled his legal dispute with Jones for $850,000 with no apology or admission of guilt.

Settling the Jones case, however, did not end Clinton's troubles. In December the House of Representatives considered four articles of impeachment recommended by its Judiciary Committee. Two of the proposals passed: one charged Clinton with perjury, and the other alleged obstruction of justice. As a result, Bill Clinton became the second president in U.S. history to be impeached.

In January 1999, with Chief Justice William Rehnquist presiding and the senators acting as a jury, the U.S. Senate tried Clinton on the two articles of impeachment. On February 12 Clinton was acquitted on both counts. The senators voted 55–45 to acquit on the perjury charge, and 50–50 on the obstruction of justice charge, both votes falling far short of the sixty-seven required to remove Clinton from office. Throughout the impeachment process, public opinion ran decidedly against removing Clinton from office.

Clinton's legal problems continued. U.S. judge Susan Webber Wright, who presided over the Jones lawsuit, found Clinton in contempt and fined him $90,000 for undermining "the integrity of the judicial system" by "false, misleading, and evasive answers that were designed to obstruct justice." In May 2000, the Arkansas Supreme Court initiated disbarment proceedings. But on January 19, 2001, his last full day in office, Clinton reached an agreement with the independent counsel in which he admitted wrongdoing and accepted a $25,000 fine and a five-year suspension of his license to practice law, thus settling the disbarment question.

Throughout all of these difficulties, Bill Clinton's presidency was surprisingly unaffected. Polls indicated that the public perceived Clinton as a man with serious personal character flaws, but gave him historically high approval ratings for the job he was doing as president.

SOURCES: *Los Angeles Times*, May 23, 2000; *Omaha World-Herald*, February 13, 1999; *New York Times*, February 13, 1999, July 30, 1999; *San Francisco Chronicle*, February 13, 1999.

---

emergency. As with the exercise of power in other critical areas, the president's constitutional role in international affairs has occasionally required definition by the Supreme Court.

The President and Foreign Policy

There can be no doubt that the Constitution confers on the president special authority over matters of foreign policy. A review of the powers granted to the chief executive by the Constitution demonstrates why this is the case.

First, Article II, Section 2, assigns to the president the role of commander in chief of the army and navy. The military capability of a nation clearly is tied to its foreign policy. Military power not only enables a nation to deter hostile actions from other countries, but it also can be used as a credible threat to persuade other nations to follow certain preferred courses of action. Armed interventions and full-scale wars can be major elements in executing a nation's foreign policy. Modern military actions, both small and large, taken by the United States in Grenada, Panama, the Persian Gulf, Eastern Europe, Afghanistan, and Iraq, demonstrate the use of this power.

Second, Article II gives the president the sole authority to make treaties on behalf of the United States. These international agreements may cover almost any area of interaction among nations, including defense pacts, economic understandings, and human rights accords.

Third, the president selects the individuals to represent the United States in contacts with other nations. The power to appoint ambassadors and ministers influences U.S. relations with the leaders of other states.

Fourth, Article II, Section 3, provides that the president is the appropriate official to receive ambassadors and ministers from foreign nations. When the president accepts the credentials of foreign emissaries, the act confers U.S. recognition on the governments they represent. This provision also means that when foreign diplomats communicate with the United States, they must do so through the president.

The Supreme Court has endorsed the notion that by the sum of these powers the Constitution has entrusted the president with the primary responsibility for creating and implementing foreign policy. Perhaps the most definitive statement of the president's authority on matters of foreign relations occurred in *United States v. Curtiss-Wright Export Corp.* (1936). As you recall, we discussed this case in chapter 4 for what it demonstrated about the constitutional limits on the delegation of legislative power to the executive branch. But Justice George Sutherland's opinion for the Court also nicely develops the president's constitutional position in formulating foreign policy.

Curtiss-Wright Export Corporation challenged a congressional resolution granting the president discretionary power to prohibit U.S. companies from selling arms to the warring nations of Bolivia and Paraguay. The Court concluded that this delegation of power was appropriate because, in Justice Sutherland's words, the president is "the sole organ of the federal government in the field of international relations." And, "In this vast external realm, with its important, complicated, delicate and manifold problems, the President alone has the power to speak or listen as a representative of the nation." Because of this position the president must be given far greater latitude of action in foreign relations than in his governance of domestic affairs. The importance of foreign policy and military matters has grown substantially since 1936, making the Court's reasoning in *Curtiss-Wright* even more relevant today.

Still, the Constitution does not leave the president completely unfettered in the pursuit of the nation's foreign policy. In fact, the framers were sufficiently concerned about the distribution of these foreign policy prerogatives that they gave the legislative branch certain powers to counterbalance those of the executive.

Although the president is commander in chief of the military, Congress has the power to raise and support the army and the navy, to make rules for the military, and to call up the militia. According to Article I, only Congress may declare war. The president has the constitutional authority to make treaties, but a treaty cannot take effect unless the Senate ratifies it by a two-thirds vote. The president's appointments of ambassadors and other foreign policy ministers must be confirmed by the Senate. But, as *Curtiss-Wright* indicates, the Supreme Court generally has been sympathetic to the executive branch when deciding disputes over the president's foreign policy role.

Presidential Power during War and National Emergencies

Questions concerning the constitutional authority to make and wage war have plagued the nation from the very beginning. Even today many questions remain unresolved. Because war and conditions of national emergency customarily demand quick action, there is rarely sufficient time for the dispassionate consideration of legal questions. When national survival is at risk, the country is usually in an emotionally heightened state and may be willing to ignore the limitations on government power that would be insisted upon in peacetime.[8] Once the crisis has passed, the country turns to other matters, and

8. Clinton L. Rossiter, *Constitutional Dictatorship: Crisis Government in the Modern Democracies* (Princeton: Princeton University Press, 1948).

questions of war do not again capture the nation's attention until the next threat occurs.

The Constitutional War Powers. The constitutional authority to send troops into combat has always sparked controversy. The root of the problem is that both the legislative and the executive branches have powers that can be interpreted as controlling the commitment of military forces to combat.[9] The case for presidential control is based on the following passage from Article II, Section 2: "The President shall be Commander in Chief of the Army and Navy of the United States, and of the Militia of the several States, when called into actual Service of the United States." Proponents of congressional dominance over the making of war rest their case on these words from Article I, Section 8:

The Congress shall have Power . . . to declare War, grant Letters of Marque and Reprisal, and make Rules concerning Captures on Land and Water; To raise and support Armies, but no Appropriation of Money to that Use shall be for a longer Term than two Years; To provide and maintain a Navy; To make Rules for the Government and Regulation of the land and naval Forces; To provide for calling forth the Militia to execute the Laws of the Union, suppress Insurrections, and repel Invasions.

The distribution of war-making powers as determined by the framers envisioned a situation in which Congress would raise and support military forces when necessary and provide the general rules governing them. By granting Congress the power to declare war, the Constitution anticipates that the legislature should determine when military force is to be used. Once the military is raised and war is declared, executive power will be dominant, consistent with the philosophy that to wage war successfully requires that a single official be in charge.

This allocation of powers was more realistic at the end of the eighteenth century than it is today. At the time the framers considered these issues, the United States was a remote nation far removed from the frequent wars in Europe. It took weeks for vessels to cross the Atlantic, allowing plenty of time for Congress to debate the question of initiating hostilities. Most delegates at the Constitutional Convention did not even anticipate the establishment of a standing military.

Today, with the rapid deployment of troops, air power, and intercontinental missiles, hostile conditions demand quick and decisive actions. The nation expects the president to act immediately to repel a hostile attack and to worry about congressional approval later.

Hundreds of military actions have been initiated by the United States without a declaration of war. The first such action was taken by President John Adams when he authorized military strikes against French privateers.[10] Most such undeclared actions have been quick rather than prolonged conflicts. Two notable exceptions are the Korean War and the Vietnam War, major, long-term military efforts that were conducted without the benefit of Congress's having declared war. In fact, Congress has taken the positive action of declaring a state of war only five times in the nation's history.[11]

1. The War of 1812 against Great Britain
2. The Mexican War in 1846
3. The Spanish-American War in 1898
4. World War I in 1917
5. World War II in 1941

Occasionally, military force is begun and ended so quickly that the president's actions permit no opportunity for congressional approval. When military actions extend over greater periods of time, Congress often has given approval through means other than a formal declaration of war. This approval may come in the form of a resolution authorizing the president to conduct some form of military action, such as the 1964 Tonkin Gulf Resolution, which granted President Lyndon Johnson authority to use force to repel attacks on U.S. forces and to prevent future aggression. Similarly, on January 12, 1991, Congress passed a joint resolution authorizing President George H. W. Bush to use force against Iraq; Congress gave its approval of the Persian Gulf conflict in words

9. See Joan Biskupic, "Constitution's Conflicting Clauses Underscored by Iraq Crisis," *Congressional Quarterly Weekly Report*, January 5, 1991, 33–36.

10. For a good review of the history of undeclared military engagements, see Ronald D. Elving, "America's Most Frequent Fight Has Been the Undeclared War," *Congressional Quarterly Weekly Report*, January 5, 1991, 37–40.

11. Congress also declared a state of war during the Civil War, but this conflict is technically classified as an internal rebellion rather than a true war between independent nations.

just short of a formal declaration of war. Just days after the terrorist attacks of September 11, 2001, the legislature passed a joint resolution authorizing President George W. Bush to use "United States Armed Forces against those responsible for the recent attacks launched against the United States." A little over a year later, in October 2002, Congress voted in favor of a similar resolution enabling the president to employ military force against Iraq. Finally, Congress can give indirect approval to the president in the form of continuing congressional appropriations to support military action.

But Congress has not abdicated its constitutional authority to approve war; in fact, the legislature has been adamant that the president consult it on all military actions. In 1973 Congress passed the War Powers Act over Nixon's veto. This legislation acknowledges the right of the president to undertake limited military action without first obtaining formal approval from Congress. The statute requires the president to file a formal report with Congress within forty-eight hours of initiating hostilities. Military action under this act is limited to sixty days with a possible thirty-day extension. If the president wishes to pursue military activity beyond these limits, prior congressional consent is required. Although the legislature intended to impose restrictions on the president with the passage of the War Powers Act, most experts believe the law actually expands the chief executive's right to initiate military action.

Because the courts must wait for an appropriate case to be filed before acting, and because legal procedures are slow and deliberative, the judicial branch is least capable of taking a role in matters of war and national emergency. Furthermore, the Constitution gives the courts no specified authority in these areas. Sometimes, however, the judiciary is called upon to decide when government power is used legitimately and when constitutional limits have been exceeded. In times of war and national emergency the executive branch may find it necessary to take actions that would be unlawful at other times. The limits of the Constitution may be stretched to respond to the crisis. When legal disputes arise from such situations, the courts become active participants in determining the government's legitimate authority.

Civil War Disputes. It is a generally recognized constitutional doctrine that government may exercise more power during wars and national emergencies than during periods of peace and security. What is not evident is when the extraordinary powers of the government are to be activated. This question came to the Supreme Court in the *Prize Cases* in 1863, the first of several major constitutional rulings related to questionable actions taken by President Lincoln. The disputes giving rise to these cases present the most fundamental questions of the constitutional allocation of the war powers. When does war begin? Who has the power to initiate war? What war powers may the president pursue without a formal declaration from Congress?

Abraham Lincoln was elected president in November 1860. Before his inauguration on March 4, 1861, seven Southern states seceded from the Union, and Lincoln knew that he had to act quickly and decisively to restore the nation. Beginning in mid-April, shortly after the first shots were fired at Fort Sumter, Lincoln imposed a naval blockade of Southern ports. He took this action unilaterally without seeking the prior approval of Congress, which did not enact a formal declaration of hostilities until July 13. Before Congress could act, Union war vessels seized a number of ships that were trading with the Confederate states. The owners of the captured ships brought suit to recover their property, claiming that Lincoln had no authority to institute a blockade in the absence of a congressional declaration of war and that the seizures were illegal. Among other matters, the justices confronted this important constitutional issue: Did the president have the right to institute a blockade of ports under the control of persons in armed rebellion against the government?

The Court upheld the president's actions. It ruled that the chief executive is bound to resist force or invasion from any hostile party without waiting to receive special authorization from the legislature. Regardless of whether the military action is initiated by a foreign nation or a rebelling state, a condition of war exists when hostilities are initiated. The lack of a formal declaration does not mean that a war has not begun. In fulfilling his duties, the president is bound to suppress insurrections. The commander in chief is the appropriate person to determine when a military response is necessary.

The blockade was only the first of Lincoln's acts that were of questionable constitutionality. More severely criticized were his actions suppressing civil liberties. The Civil War was unlike other wars Americans had faced: The enemies were fellow Americans, not foreigners. The conflict touched every part of the nation, and Lincoln particularly worried about the presence of Confederate supporters in the Northern and Border states. These individuals were capable of aiding the Southern forces without joining the Confederate army. Of special concern were the large numbers of Southern sympathizers, known as Copperheads, who were especially active in Indiana, Illinois, Ohio, and Missouri. Combating these civilian enemies posed a difficult problem for the president. He decided that the Union was more important than the procedural rights of individuals. Consequently, Lincoln gave his military commanders broad powers to arrest civilians suspected of engaging in traitorous activities. These suspects were to be tried in military courts.

In those areas of the country where hostilities were not occurring, however, the army had no legal authority to arrest and try civilians. State and federal courts were in full operation and capable of trying civilians charged with treason or any other crime. To allow arrests and military trials for civilians, a state of martial law had to be declared, and to do that, the right of habeas corpus had to be suspended. Habeas corpus is a legal procedure with roots extending far back into English legal history; it permits an arrested person to have a judge determine whether the detention is legal. If the court determines that there are no legal grounds for the arrest, it may order the release of the detained individual. Habeas corpus is essential to the doctrine of checks and balances because it gives the judiciary the right to intervene if the executive branch abuses the law enforcement power.

Article I, Section 9, of the Constitution states: "The Privilege of the Writ of Habeas Corpus shall not be suspended, unless when in Cases of Rebellion or Invasion the public Safety may require it." This provision posed two problems for Lincoln. First, the suspension provision is found in Article I, which outlines legislative, not executive, powers. And second, if the civilian courts are in full operation and no armed hostilities are taking place in the area, the public safety probably does not demand a suspension of habeas corpus procedures.

These obstacles did not stop the president. Several times during the war he issued orders expanding military control of civilian areas, permitting military arrests and trials of civilians, and suspending habeas corpus. Congress later endorsed some of these actions. Arrests of suspected traitors and conspirators were common and often based on little evidence. Were such actions constitutional under the war powers doctrine? The Court addressed this question in *Ex parte Milligan* (1866), a decision of great importance in defining the wartime powers of the chief executive.[12]

Lambdin Milligan was an attorney living in southern Indiana. He had strong states' rights beliefs, and his sympathies lay with the Confederate cause during the war. He openly organized groups and gave speeches in support of the South. He also was involved in efforts to persuade men not to join the Union army. At one point Milligan and his fellow Copperheads were suspected of hatching a plan to raid prisoner of war camps in Illinois, Indiana, and Ohio and release the imprisoned Confederate soldiers, who would then take control of the three states. Federal military investigators followed Milligan closely and kept records of his activities and contacts.

On October 5, 1864, under orders from Gen. Alvin Hovey, commander of the Union armies in Indiana, federal agents arrested Milligan at his home. They also arrested four of Milligan's fellow Confederate sympathizers. Sixteen days later Hovey placed Milligan on trial before a military tribunal in Indianapolis. He was found guilty and sentenced to be hanged on May 19, 1865. On May 2, less than a month after the war ended with Gen. Robert E. Lee's surrender at Appomattox, President Andrew Johnson sustained the order that Milligan be executed. In response, Milligan's attorneys filed for a writ of habeas corpus in federal circuit court. Uncertain of how

12. For a description of the events leading up to the Court's decision, see Allan Nevins, "The Case of the Copperhead Conspirator," in *Quarrels That Have Shaped the Constitution*, ed. John A. Garraty (New York: Harper Colophon Books, 1964).

to apply the law, the circuit judges requested that the Supreme Court resolve certain questions regarding the legal authority of a military commission to try and sentence Milligan.

Nine months later, in March 1866, the Court heard the *Milligan* case. Oral arguments took place at a time of heightened political tension. Relations were strained between Johnson, who supported a moderate position toward the reintroduction of the Southern states into the Union, and the Radical Republicans in Congress, who demanded a more severe Reconstruction policy. A majority of the justices opposed the military trials at issue in *Milligan,* but there was concern about possible congressional retaliation if the justices struck a blow against military authority. The Court at this point was quite vulnerable, having suffered a decline in prestige following the infamous *Dred Scott* case. But the justices had a potential ally in Johnson. The president opposed the use of military tribunals, and the Radicals had not yet gained sufficient strength to override a veto of a congressional act. On April 3, 1866, the Court announced its decision in *Milligan,* but formal opinions were not issued until eight months later.

The Court condemned Lincoln's actions. It held that the military was without authority to try Milligan on the charges against him. The federal courts were in full operation in Indiana and open to adjudicate charges of criminal misconduct. Indiana was not in the theater of war, and Milligan was not a member of the military. Consequently, with the civilian courts in full operation and Milligan undeniably having civilian status, jurisdiction over his alleged misdeeds rested with the normal federal courts, not with a military tribunal. Milligan's constitutional rights had been violated.

Although the Court's decision was unanimous as to Milligan's claim of illegal imprisonment, the justices split on the power of the government to suspend habeas corpus under conditions presented in the case. A majority of five (Nathan Clifford, David Davis, Stephen Field, Robert Grier, and Samuel Nelson) held that neither the president nor Congress, acting separately or in agreement, could suspend the writ of habeas corpus as long as the civilian courts were in full operation and the area was

---

BOX 5-3 AFTERMATH . . . LAMBDIN P. MILLIGAN

BEGINNING with his October 1864 arrest for disloyal practices and continuing throughout the controversy over his activities, Lambdin Milligan claimed that the charges were a fantasy created by the Republicans for political gain. By the time the Supreme Court reversed his conviction and death sentence, Milligan had spent eighteen months in prison. Upon his release, he returned to his hometown of Huntington, Indiana, where he was received as a local hero. Two decades earlier Milligan had moved with his family to the Indiana town from Ohio to farm and practice law. He had also been active in local Democratic Party politics, unsuccessfully running for Congress and governor.

Milligan immediately sought revenge for the treatment he had received at the hands of the military. He filed suit for trespass and false imprisonment against James Slack, a local attorney who first urged that he be arrested; Gen. Alvin Hovey, who had ordered his arrest; and twenty-two others involved in his prosecution. The jury decided in favor of Milligan, but the law placed a $5 ceiling on damages awarded in such cases, limiting the satisfaction he received from his judicial victory.

Milligan ran a successful legal practice in Huntington for an additional thirty years. He retired in 1897 at the age of eighty-five. He died two years later, only three months after the death of his second wife.

SOURCE: *American National Biography,* Vol. 15 (New York: Oxford University Press, 1999), 529–530.

---

not a combat zone. In a concurring opinion joined by Samuel Miller, Noah Swayne, and James Wayne, Chief Justice Salmon Chase argued that although the president did not have the power to suspend habeas corpus and establish these military tribunals, Congress did.

Before the Court handed down its ruling in this case, President Johnson commuted Milligan's sentence to life in prison, a sentence he was serving under General Hovey in an Ohio prison when the case was decided. Milligan was released from custody in April 1866. *(See Box 5-3.)*

World War II. The restriction of civil liberties during time of war is not uncommon. Nations pressed for their very survival may feel compelled to deny basic liberties to insure against the efforts of traitors and saboteurs.

Early in the war against Germany, the Supreme Court faced another legal challenge to the use of military tribunals. In 1941 federal authorities captured eight Nazi saboteurs who had illegally entered the country. All had previously lived in the United States, and one claimed to be a U.S. citizen. President Franklin Roosevelt ordered them to be tried by a military tribunal. The Germans filed for a writ of habeas corpus, claiming that the president had no authority to subject them to military trial and that they, like Milligan, had the right to be tried in the civilian courts.

In *Ex parte Quirin* (1942), however, the justices unanimously upheld the government's authority to try these men by military tribunal. Why did the Court reach a decision seemingly inconsistent with the precedent set in *Milligan*? According to the justices, the Nazi saboteurs were unlawful combatants. Contrary to the laws of war, they secretly and illegally entered the country without uniform for the purpose of gathering military information or destroying life and property. As such, the saboteurs had no right to be treated as prisoners of war but could be subject to trial by military tribunal. Milligan, by comparison, was an American citizen, permanently residing in the United States, and not a military combatant in service to the enemy. It did not help the Nazis that they, unlike Milligan, were captured and tried during one of the most desperate times of the war when public opinion was especially hostile. Six of the eight saboteurs were sentenced to death, and the remaining two received long prison terms in return for their cooperation with federal authorities.[13]

The government engaged in more infamous restrictions of civil liberties in its wartime treatment of Japanese Americans. The Japanese bombing of Pearl Harbor on December 7, 1941, touched off a wave of anti-Japanese

hysteria. In the early weeks of the Pacific war the Japanese fleet showed remarkable strength and power, and the United States feared that Japanese forces were planning an invasion of the West Coast. Concern was growing about the large numbers of people of Japanese ancestry who lived on the coast. Many thought that among the Japanese American population were significant numbers of people sympathetic to the Japanese war effort, people who might aid the enemy in an invasion of the United States.

To prevent such an occurrence President Roosevelt on February 19, 1942, issued the first of several orders affecting all people of Japanese background residing on the West Coast. His initial command placed all Japanese Americans under a tight curfew that required them to stay in their homes between 8 P.M. and 6 A.M. and to register for future relocation. In *Hirabayashi v. United States* (1943) the Supreme Court upheld the constitutionality of the curfew program. For the Court, Justice Harlan Stone explained that the war powers doctrine gave the government ample authority to impose the restrictions. The grave and threatening conditions of war made the racially based program constitutionally acceptable, he said.

The following year the Court heard *Korematsu v. United States* (1944), an appeal attacking the most serious denial of the civil liberties of Japanese Americans—the orders removing them to inland detention camps. About 110,000 Japanese Americans were affected by this policy, some interned for as long as four years.[14] Read Justice Hugo Black's opinion carefully. Does he make a convincing case that the conditions of war stretch the Constitution to the point that exclusion orders based on national origin are permissible? How can you explain the fact that some of the justices most sympathetic to civil liberties causes—Black, Stone, William Douglas, and Wiley Rutledge—voted to approve the military orders? Compare Black's opinion with the dissents of Frank Murphy, who emphasizes the racial foundations of the policy, and of Robert Jackson, who states the case for preserving guarantees of civil liberties even in times of war or national emergency.

---

13. For more on this case, see William H. Rehnquist, *All the Laws but One* (New York: Knopf, 1998); Louis Fisher, *Nazi Saboteurs on Trial: A Military Tribunal and American Law* (Lawrence: University Press of Kansas, 2003).

14. See Peter H. Irons, *Justice at War: The Story of the Japanese-American Internment Cases* (New York: Oxford University Press, 1983).

Korematsu v. United States

323 U.S. 214 (1944)
http://laws.findlaw.com/US/323/214.html
Vote: 6 (Black, Douglas, Frankfurter, Reed, Rutledge, Stone)
    3 (Jackson, Murphy, Roberts)
Opinion of the Court: Black
Concurring opinion: Frankfurter
Dissenting opinions: Jackson, Murphy, Roberts

Fred Korematsu was arrested on May 30, 1942, by San Leandro, California, police for being on public streets in violation of the government's evacuation orders. Korematsu was a native-born American with Japanese American parents. He grew up in the San Francisco area. Rejected for military service for health reasons, he worked in the defense industry as a welder. When arrested, he tried to convince police that he was of Spanish-Hawaiian origin. He had undergone plastic surgery to make his racial characteristics less pronounced in an effort to avoid the anti-Japanese discrimination he feared because of his engagement to an Italian American woman.[15] After the arrest, representatives of the American Civil Liberties Union approached Korematsu and offered to defend him and challenge the validity of the evacuation program. The Japanese-American Citizens League also lent support.

MR. JUSTICE BLACK delivered the opinion of the Court.

It should be noted, to begin with, that all legal restrictions which curtail the civil rights of a single racial group are immediately suspect. That is not to say that all such restrictions are unconstitutional. It is to say that courts must subject them to the most rigid scrutiny. Pressing public necessity may sometimes justify the existence of such restrictions; racial antagonism never can. . . .

In the light of the principles we announced in the *Hirabayashi* case, we are unable to conclude that it was beyond the war power of Congress and the Executive to exclude those of Japanese ancestry from the West Coast war area at the time they did. True, exclusion from the area in which one's home is located is a far greater deprivation than constant confinement to the home from 8 P.M. to 6 A.M.

15. Ibid., 93–99.

Nothing short of apprehension by the proper military authorities of the gravest imminent danger to the public safety can constitutionally justify either. But exclusion from a threatened area, no less than curfew, has a definite and close relationship to the prevention of espionage and sabotage. The military authorities, charged with the primary responsibility of defending our shores, concluded that curfew provided inadequate protection and ordered exclusion. They did so, as pointed out in our *Hirabayashi* opinion, in accordance with Congressional authority to the military to say who should, and who should not, remain in the threatened areas.

In this case the petitioner challenges the assumptions upon which we rested our conclusions in the *Hirabayashi* case. He also urges that by May 1942, when Order No. 34 was promulgated, all danger of Japanese invasion of the West Coast had disappeared. After careful consideration of these contentions we are compelled to reject them.

Here, as in the *Hirabayashi* case, ". . . we cannot reject as unfounded the judgment of the military authorities and of Congress that there were disloyal members of that population, whose number and strength could not be precisely and quickly ascertained. We cannot say that the warmaking branches of the Government did not have ground for believing that in a critical hour such persons could not readily be isolated and separately dealt with, and constituted a menace to the national defense and safety, which demanded that prompt and adequate measures be taken to guard against it."

Like curfew, exclusion of those of Japanese origin was deemed necessary because of the presence of an unascertained number of disloyal members of the group, most of whom we have no doubt were loyal to this country. It was because we could not reject the finding of the military authorities that it was impossible to bring about an immediate segregation of the disloyal from the loyal that we sustained the validity of the curfew order as applying to the whole group. In the instant case, temporary exclusion of the entire group was rested by the military on the same ground. The judgment that exclusion of the whole group was for the same reason a military imperative answers the contention that the exclusion was in the nature of group punishment based on antagonism to those of Japanese origin. That there were members of the group who retained loyalties to Japan has been confirmed by investigations made subsequent to

Japanese American civilians with whatever possessions they could carry arrive at a Los Angeles pickup point from which they would be transferred by bus to inland detention centers in 1942. The evacuation of individuals of Japanese descent from the Pacific Coast states was upheld by the Supreme Court in *Korematsu v. United States* (1944).

the exclusion. Approximately five thousand American citizens of Japanese ancestry refused to swear unqualified allegiance to the United States and to renounce allegiance to the Japanese Emperor, and several thousand evacuees requested repatriation to Japan.

We uphold the exclusion order as of the time it was made and when the petitioner violated it. In doing so, we are not unmindful of the hardships imposed by it upon a large group of American citizens. But hardships are part of war, and war is an aggregation of hardships. All citizens alike, both in and out of uniform, feel the impact of war in greater or lesser measure. Citizenship has its responsibilities as well as its privileges, and in time of war the burden is always heavier. Compulsory exclusion of large groups of citizens from their homes, except under circumstances of direst emergency and peril, is inconsistent with our basic governmental institutions. But when under conditions of modern warfare our shores are threatened by hostile forces, the power to protect must be commensurate with the threatened danger. . . .

It is said that we are dealing here with the case of imprisonment of a citizen in a concentration camp solely because of his ancestry, without evidence or inquiry concerning his loyalty and good disposition towards the United States. Our task would be simple, our duty clear, were this a case involving the imprisonment of a loyal citizen in a concentration camp because of racial prejudice. Regardless of the true nature of the assembly and relocation centers—and we deem it unjustifiable to call them concentration camps with all the ugly connotations that term implies—we are dealing specifically with nothing but an exclusion order. To cast this case into outlines of racial prejudice, without reference to the real military dangers which were presented, merely confuses the issue. Korematsu was not excluded from the Military Area because of hostility to him or his race. He *was* excluded because we are at war with the Japanese Empire, because the properly constituted military authorities feared an invasion of our West Coast and felt constrained to take proper security measures, because they decided that the military urgency of the situation demanded that all citizens of Japanese ancestry be segregated from the West Coast temporarily, and finally, because Congress, reposing its confidence in this time of war in our military leaders—as inevitably it must—determined that they should have the power to do just this.

There was evidence of disloyalty on the part of some, the military authorities considered that the need for action was great, and time was short. We cannot—by availing ourselves of the calm perspective of hindsight—now say that at that time these actions were unjustified.

Affirmed.

MR. JUSTICE MURPHY, dissenting.

This exclusion of "all persons of Japanese ancestry, both alien and non-alien," from the Pacific Coast area on a plea of military necessity in the absence of martial law ought not to be approved. Such exclusion goes over "the very brink of constitutional power" and falls into the ugly abyss of racism.

In dealing with matters relating to the prosecution and progress of a war, we must accord great respect and consideration to the judgments of the military authorities who are on the scene and who have full knowledge of the military facts. The scope of their discretion must, as a matter of necessity and common sense, be wide. And their judgments ought not to be overruled lightly by those whose training and duties ill-equip them to deal intelligently with matters so vital to the physical security of the nation.

At the same time, however, it is essential that there be definite limits to military discretion, especially where martial law has not been declared. Individuals must not be left impoverished of their constitutional rights on a plea of military necessity that has neither substance nor support. Thus, like other claims conflicting with the asserted constitutional rights of the individual, the military claim must subject itself to the judicial process of having its reasonableness determined and its conflicts with other interests reconciled. "What are the allowable limits of military discretion, and whether or not they have been overstepped in a particular case, are judicial questions." *Sterling v. Constantin* [1932].

The judicial test of whether the Government, on a plea of military necessity, can validly deprive an individual of any of his constitutional rights is whether the deprivation is reasonably related to a public danger that is so "immediate, imminent, and impending" as not to admit of delay and not to permit the intervention of ordinary constitutional processes to alleviate the danger. Civilian Exclusion Order No. 34, banishing from a prescribed area of the Pacific Coast "all persons of Japanese ancestry, both alien and non-alien," clearly does not meet that test. Being an obvious racial discrimination, the order deprives all those within its scope of the equal protection of the laws as guaranteed by the Fifth Amendment. It further deprives these individuals of their constitutional rights to live and work where they will, to establish a home where they choose and to move about freely. In excommunicating them without benefit of hearings, this order also deprives them of all their constitutional rights to procedural due process. Yet no reasonable relation to an "immediate, imminent, and impending" public danger is evident to support this racial restriction which is one of the most sweeping and complete deprivations of constitutional rights in the history of this nation in the absence of martial law.

It must be conceded that the military and naval situation in the spring of 1942 was such as to generate a very real fear of invasion of the Pacific Coast, accompanied by fears of sabotage and espionage in that area. The military command was therefore justified in adopting all reasonable means necessary to combat these dangers. In adjudging the military action taken in light of the then apparent dangers, we must not erect too high or too meticulous standards; it is necessary only that the action have some reasonable relation to the removal of the dangers of invasion, sabotage and espionage. But the exclusion, either temporarily or permanently, of all persons with Japanese blood in their veins has no such reasonable relation. And that relation is lacking because the exclusion order necessarily must rely for its reasonableness upon the assumption that *all* persons of Japanese ancestry may have a dangerous tendency to commit sabotage and espionage and to aid our Japanese enemy in other ways. It is difficult to believe that reason, logic or experience could be marshalled in support of such an assumption.

That this forced exclusion was the result in good measure of this erroneous assumption of racial guilt rather than bona fide military necessity is evidenced by the Commanding General's Final Report on the evacuation from the Pacific Coast area. In it he refers to all individuals of Japanese descent as "subversive," as belonging to "an enemy race" whose "racial strains are undiluted," and as constituting "over 112,000 potential enemies . . . at large today" along the Pacific Coast. . . .

The main reasons relied upon by those responsible for the forced evacuation, therefore, do not prove a reasonable relation between the group characteristics of Japanese Americans and the dangers of invasion, sabotage and espionage. The reasons appear, instead, to be largely an accumulation of much of the misinformation, half-truths and insinuations that for years have been directed against Japanese Americans by people with racial and economic prejudices—the same people who have been among the foremost advocates of the evacuation. A military judgment based upon such racial and sociological considerations is not entitled to the great weight ordinarily given the judgments based upon strictly military considerations. Especially is this so when every charge relative to race, religion, culture, geographical location, and legal and economic status has been substantially discredited by independent studies made by experts in these matters.

The military necessity which is essential to the validity of the evacuation order thus resolves itself into a few intimations that certain individuals actively aided the enemy, from which it is inferred that the entire group of Japanese Americans could not be trusted to be or remain loyal to the United States. . . . To give constitutional sanction to that inference in this case, however well-intentioned may have been the military command on the Pacific Coast, is to adopt one of the cruelest of the rationales used by our enemies to destroy the dignity of the individual and to encourage and open the door to discriminatory actions against other minority groups in the passions of tomorrow. . . .

I dissent, therefore, from this legalization of racism. Racial discrimination in any form and in any degree has no justifiable part whatever in our democratic way of life. It is unattractive in any setting but it is utterly revolting among a free people who have embraced the principles set forth in the Constitution of the United States. All residents of this nation are kin in some way by blood or culture to a foreign land. Yet they are primarily and necessarily a part of the new and distinct civilization of the United States. They must accordingly be treated at all times as the heirs of the American experiment and as entitled to all the rights and freedoms guaranteed by the Constitution.

MR. JUSTICE JACKSON, dissenting.

Korematsu was born on our soil, of parents born in Japan. The Constitution makes him a citizen of the United States by nativity and a citizen of California by residence. No claim is made that he is not loyal to this country. There is no suggestion that apart from the matter involved here he is not law-abiding and well disposed. Korematsu, however, has been convicted of an act not commonly a crime. It consists merely of being present in the state whereof he is a citizen, near the place where he was born, and where all his life he has lived.

Even more unusual is the series of military orders which made this conduct a crime. They forbid such a one to remain, and they also forbid him to leave. They were so drawn that the only way Korematsu could avoid violation was to give himself up to the military authority. This meant submission to custody, examination, and transportation out of the territory, to be followed by indeterminate confinement in detention camps.

A citizen's presence in the locality, however, was made a crime only if his parents were of Japanese birth. Had Korematsu been one of four—the others being, say, a German alien enemy, an Italian alien enemy, and a citizen of American-born ancestors, convicted of treason but out on parole—only Korematsu's presence would have violated the order. The difference between their innocence and his crime would result, not from anything he did, said, or thought, different than they, but only in that he was born of different racial stock.

Now, if any fundamental assumption underlies our system, it is that guilt is personal and not inheritable. Even if all of one's antecedents had been convicted of treason, the Constitution forbids its penalties to be visited upon him, for it provides that "no attainder of treason shall work corruption of blood, or forfeiture except during the life of the person attainted." But here is an attempt to make an otherwise innocent act a crime merely because this prisoner is the son of parents as to whom he had no choice, and belongs to a race from which there is no way to resign. If Congress in peace-time legislation should enact such a criminal law, I should suppose this Court would refuse to enforce it.

But the "law" which this prisoner is convicted of disregarding is not found in an act of Congress, but in a military order. Neither the Act of Congress nor the Executive Order of the President, nor both together, would afford a basis for this conviction. It rests on the orders of General DeWitt. And it is said that if the military commander had reasonable military grounds for promulgating the orders, they are constitutional and become law, and the Court is required to enforce them. There are several reasons why I cannot subscribe to this doctrine. . . .

BOX 5-4   AFTERMATH . . . FRED KOREMATSU

FOLLOWING his arrest and conviction in 1942 for refusing to leave his Northern California home in compliance with President Roosevelt's evacuation orders, Fred T. Korematsu was sentenced to five years' probation. He was also sent with other Japanese Americans to an isolated internment camp in Topaz, Utah. After the war, he returned to his home in San Leandro, California, married, and continued his work as a welder.

Almost forty years later, documents were discovered providing evidence that officials of the U.S. Navy and the Justice Department had intentionally deceived the Supreme Court by suppressing information showing that Japanese Americans posed no threat during World War II. Basing their case on this new evidence, lawyers representing Korematsu filed a legal action to clear his name. In November 1983 a federal district court in San Francisco overturned Korematsu's conviction. Charges against Gordon Hirabayashi for violating a curfew imposed on Japanese Americans, upheld by the

President Bill Clinton stands with Fred Korematsu after awarding him the Presidential Medal of Freedom, January 15, 1998.

Supreme Court in 1943, were similarly reversed by a Seattle federal court in 1986. These legal actions helped fuel a movement that led Congress in 1988 to approve $20,000 in reparations for every living Japanese American who was interned during the war.

In 1998 President Clinton awarded Korematsu, then seventy-eight years old, the Presidential Medal of Freedom, the nation's highest civilian award. "In the long history of our country's constant search for justice," Clinton said, "some names of ordinary citizens stand for millions of souls. Plessy, Brown, Parks. To that distinguished list, today we add the name of Fred Korematsu." Korematsu died in Marin County, California, on March 30, 2005. He was eighty-six.

SOURCES: *New York Times,* January 31, 1983, November 11, 1983, August 11, 1988, February 19, 1992; *San Francisco Chronicle,* January 16, 1998, April 10, 2005.

Much is said of the danger to liberty from the Army program for deporting and detaining these citizens of Japanese extraction. But a judicial construction of the due process clause that will sustain this order is a far more subtle blow to liberty than the promulgation of the order itself. A military order, however unconstitutional, is not apt to last longer than the military emergency. Even during that period a succeeding commander may revoke it all. But once a judicial opinion rationalizes such an order to show that it conforms to the Constitution, or rather rationalizes the Constitution to show that the Constitution sanctions such an order, the Court for all time has validated the principle of racial discrimination in criminal procedure and of transplanting American citizens. The principle then lies about like a loaded weapon ready for the hand of any authority that can bring forward a plausible claim of an urgent need. . . .

I should hold that a civil court cannot be made to enforce an order which violates constitutional limitations even

if it is a reasonable exercise of military authority. The courts can exercise only the judicial power, can apply only law, and must abide by the Constitution, or they cease to be civil courts and become instruments of military policy. . . .

My duties as a justice as I see them do not require me to make a military judgment as to whether General DeWitt's evacuation and detention program was a reasonable military necessity. I do not suggest that the courts should have attempted to interfere with the Army in carrying out its task. But I do not think they may be asked to execute a military expedient that has no place in law under the Constitution. I would reverse the judgment and discharge the prisoner.

Legal scholars and civil libertarians have severely criticized the *Korematsu* decision. In 1988 the government, recognizing its mistakes, approved $20,000 in reparations for every living Japanese American who was interned during the war. And in 1998 Fred Korematsu was awarded the Presidential Medal of Freedom *(see Box 5-4)*.

The Korean Conflict. During the Korean conflict the justices were called upon to decide the constitutional validity of another executive action taken in the name of the war powers doctrine. This case involved property rights rather than civil liberties. As you read Justice Black's opinion for the Court in *Youngstown Sheet & Tube Co. v. Sawyer* (1952), compare it with *Korematsu*. Both involved actions taken by the president to strengthen war efforts. Does it make sense to you that the Court approved the detention of more than 110,000 individuals on the basis of national origin but ruled that the government could not take nominal possession of the steel mills? Note the analysis provided in Justice Jackson's concurring opinion, in which he lays out a formula for deciding questions of presidential power in relation to congressional action.

Youngstown Sheet & Tube Co. v. Sawyer

343 U.S. 579 (1952)
http://laws.findlaw.com/US/343/579.html
Vote: 6 (Black, Burton, Clark, Douglas, Frankfurter, Jackson)
*   3 (Minton, Reed, Vinson)*
Opinion of the Court: Black
Concurring opinions: Burton, Clark, Douglas, Frankfurter,
*   Jackson*
Dissenting opinion: Vinson

In 1951 a labor dispute began in the steel industry. In December the United Steelworkers Union announced that it would call a strike at the end of that month, when its contract with the steel companies expired. For the next several months the Federal Mediation and Conciliation Service and the Federal Wage Stabilization Board tried to work out a settlement, but the efforts were unsuccessful. On April 4, 1952, the union said that its strike would begin on April 9.

President Truman was not about to let a strike hit the steel industry. The nation was engaged in a war in Korea,

and steel production was necessary to produce weapons and other military equipment. Only hours before the strike was to begin, Truman issued an executive order commanding Secretary of Commerce Charles Sawyer to seize the nation's steel mills and keep them in operation. Sawyer in turn ordered the mill owners to continue to run their facilities as operators for the United States.

Truman's seizure order cited no statutory authority for his action because there was none. There were federal statutes permitting the seizure of industrial plants for certain specified reasons, but the settlement of a labor dispute was not one of them. In fact, the Taft-Hartley Act of 1947 rejected the idea that labor disputes could be resolved by such means. Instead, the act authorized the president to impose an eighty-day cooling-off period as a way to postpone any strike that seriously threatened the public interest. Truman, however, had little regard for the Taft-Hartley Act, which Congress had passed over his veto. The president ignored the cooling-off period alternative and took the direct action of seizing the mills. The inherent powers of the chief executive, he maintained, were enough to authorize the action.

Congress might have improved the president's legal ground by immediately passing legislation authorizing such seizures retroactively, but it did not. The mill owners complied with the seizure orders under protest and filed suit in federal court to have Truman's action declared unconstitutional. The district court ruled in favor of the steel industry, enjoining the secretary from seizing the plants, but the same day the court of appeals stayed the injunction.

MR. JUSTICE BLACK delivered the opinion of the Court.

We are asked to decide whether the President was acting within his constitutional power when he issued an order directing the Secretary of Commerce to take possession of and operate most of the Nation's steel mills. The mill owners argue that the President's order amounts to lawmaking, a legislative function which the Constitution has expressly confided to the Congress and not to the President. The Government's position is that the order was made on findings of the President that his action was necessary to avert a national catastrophe which would inevitably result from a

The attorney representing the steel industry, John W. Davis Jr. *(left)*, arriving at the Supreme Court May 13, 1952, with acting attorney general Philip B. Perlman. Davis was the Democratic nominee for the presidency in 1924, capturing 29 percent of the popular vote in a loss to Calvin Coolidge. He later represented the school board defendants in the 1954 school desegregation cases.

stoppage of steel production, and that in meeting this grave emergency the President was acting within the aggregate of his constitutional powers as the Nation's Chief Executive and the Commander in Chief of the Armed Forces of the United States. . . .

The President's power, if any, to issue the order must stem either from an act of Congress or from the Constitution itself. There is no statute that expressly authorizes the President to take possession of property as he did here. Nor is there any act of Congress to which our attention has been directed from which such a power can fairly be implied. Indeed, we do not understand the Government to rely on statutory authorization for this seizure. . . .

It is clear that if the President had authority to issue the order he did, it must be found in some provision of the Constitution. And it is not claimed that express constitutional language grants this power to the President. The contention is that presidential power should be implied from the aggregate of his powers under the Constitution. Particular reliance is placed on provisions in Article II which say that "The executive Power shall be vested in a President . . ."; that "he shall take Care that the Laws be faithfully executed"; and that he "shall be Commander in Chief of the Army and Navy of the United States."

The order cannot properly be sustained as an exercise of the President's military power as Commander in Chief of the Armed Forces. The Government attempts to do so by citing a number of cases upholding broad powers in military commanders engaged in day-to-day fighting in a theater of war. Such cases need not concern us here. Even though "theater of war" be an expanding concept, we cannot with faithfulness to our constitutional system hold that the Commander in Chief of the Armed Forces has the ultimate power as such to take possession of private property in order to keep labor disputes from stopping production. This is a job for the Nation's lawmakers, not for its military authorities.

Nor can the seizure order be sustained because of the several constitutional provisions that grant executive power to the President. In the framework of our Constitution, the President's power to see that the laws are faithfully executed refutes the idea that he is to be a lawmaker. The Constitution limits his functions in the lawmaking process to the recommending of laws he thinks wise and the vetoing of laws he thinks bad. And the Constitution is neither silent nor equivocal about who shall make laws which the President is to execute. The first section of the first article says that "All legislative Powers herein granted shall be vested in a Congress of the United States. . . ." After granting many powers to the Congress, Article I goes on to provide that Congress may "make all Laws which shall be necessary and proper for carrying into Execution the foregoing Powers, and all other Powers vested by this Constitution in the Government of the United States, or in any Department or Officer thereof."

The President's order does not direct that a congressional policy be executed in a manner prescribed by Congress—it directs that a presidential policy be executed in a manner prescribed by the President. The preamble of the order itself, like that of many statutes, sets out reasons why the President believes certain policies should be adopted, proclaims these policies as rules of conduct to be followed, and again, like a statute, authorizes a government official to promulgate additional rules and regulations consistent with the policy proclaimed and needed to carry that policy into execution. The power of Congress to adopt such public policies as those proclaimed by the order is beyond question. It can authorize the taking of private property for public use. It can make laws regulating the relationships between employers and employees, prescribing rules designed to settle labor disputes, and fixing wages and working conditions in certain fields of our economy. The Constitution does not subject this lawmaking power of Congress to presidential or military supervision or control.

It is said that other Presidents without congressional authority have taken possession of private business enterprises in order to settle labor disputes. But even if this be true, Congress has not thereby lost its exclusive constitutional authority to make laws necessary and proper to carry out the powers vested by the Constitution "in the Government of the United States, or any Department or Officer thereof."

The Founders of this Nation entrusted the lawmaking power to the Congress alone in both good and bad times. It would do no good to recall the historical events, the fears of power and the hopes for freedom that lay behind their choice. Such a review would but confirm our holding that this seizure order cannot stand.

The judgment of the District Court is

Affirmed.

MR. JUSTICE JACKSON, concurring in the judgment and opinion of the Court.

A judge, like an executive adviser, may be surprised at the poverty of really useful and unambiguous authority applicable to concrete problems of executive power as they actually present themselves. Just what our forefathers did envision, or would have envisioned had they foreseen modern conditions, must be divined from materials almost as enigmatic as the dreams Joseph was called upon to interpret for Pharaoh. A century and a half of partisan debate and scholarly speculation yields no net result but only supplies more or less apt quotations from respected sources on each side of any question. They largely cancel each other. And court decisions are indecisive because of the judicial practice of dealing with the largest questions in the most narrow way.

. . . We may well begin by a somewhat over-simplified grouping of practical situations in which a President may doubt, or others may challenge, his powers, and by distinguishing roughly the legal consequences of this factor of relativity.

1. When the President acts pursuant to an express or implied authorization of Congress, his authority is at its maximum, for it includes all that he possesses in his own right plus all that Congress can delegate. . . .

2. When the President acts in absence of either a congressional grant or denial of authority, he can only rely upon his own independent powers, but there is a zone of twilight in which he and Congress may have concurrent authority, or in which its distribution is uncertain. Therefore, congressional inertia, indifference or quiescence may sometimes, at least as a practical matter, enable, if not invite, measures on independent presidential responsibility. In this area, any actual test of power is likely to depend on the imperatives of events and contemporary imponderables rather than on abstract theories of law.

3. When the President takes measures incompatible with the expressed or implied will of Congress, his power is at its lowest ebb, for then he can rely only upon his own constitutional powers minus any constitutional powers of Congress over the matter. . . .

Into which of these classifications does this executive seizure of the steel industry fit? It is eliminated from the first by admission, for it is conceded that no congressional authorization exists for this seizure. That takes away also the support of the many precedents and declarations which were made in relation, and must be confined, to this category.

Can it then be defended under flexible tests available to the second category? It seems clearly eliminated from that class because Congress has not left seizure of private property an open field but has covered it by three statutory policies inconsistent with this seizure. . . .

This leaves the current seizure to be justified only by the severe tests under the third grouping, where it can be supported only by any remainder of executive power after subtraction of such powers as Congress may have over the subject. In short, we can sustain the President only by holding that seizure of such strike-bound industries is within his domain and beyond control by Congress. Thus, this Court's first review of such seizures occurs under circumstances which leave presidential power most vulnerable to attack and in the least favorable of possible constitutional postures. . . .

The Solicitor General, acknowledging that Congress has never authorized the seizure here, says practice of prior Presidents has authorized it. He seeks color of legality from claimed executive precedents, chief of which is President Roosevelt's seizure on June 9, 1941, of the California plant of the North American Aviation Company. Its superficial similarities with the present case, upon analysis, yield to distinctions so decisive that it cannot be regarded as even a precedent, much less an authority for the present seizure.

The appeal, however, that we declare the existence of inherent powers *ex necessitate* to meet an emergency asks us to do what many think would be wise, although it is something the forefathers omitted. They knew what emergencies were, knew the pressures they engender for authoritative action, knew, too, how they afford a ready pretext for usurpation. We may also suspect that they suspected that emergency powers would tend to kindle emergencies. Aside from suspension of the privilege of the writ of habeas corpus in time of rebellion or invasion, when the public safety may require it, they made no express provision for exercise of extraordinary authority because of a crisis. I do not think we rightfully may so amend their work, and, if we could, I am not convinced it would be wise to do so, although many modern nations have forthrightly recognized that war and economic crises may upset the normal balance between liberty and authority. . . .

The essence of our free Government is "leave to live by no man's leave, underneath the law"—to be governed by those impersonal forces which we call law. Our Government is fashioned to fulfill this concept so far as humanly possible. The Executive, except for recommendation and veto, has no legislative power. The executive action we have here originates in the individual will of the President and represents an exercise of authority without law. No one, perhaps not even the President, knows the limits of the power he may seek to exert in this instance and the parties affected cannot learn the limit of their rights. We do not know today what powers over labor or property would be claimed to flow from Government possession if we should legalize it, what rights to compensation would be claimed or recognized, or on what contingency it would end. With all its defects, delays and inconveniences, men have discovered no technique for long preserving free government except that the Executive be under the law, and that the law be made by parliamentary deliberations.

Such institutions may be destined to pass away. But it is the duty of the Court to be last, not first, to give them up.

MR. CHIEF JUSTICE VINSON, with whom MR. JUSTICE REED and MR. JUSTICE MINTON join, dissenting.

A review of executive action demonstrates that our Presidents have on many occasions exhibited the leadership contemplated by the Framers when they made the President Commander in Chief, and imposed upon him the trust to "take Care that the Laws be faithfully executed." With or without explicit statutory authorization, Presidents have at such times dealt with national emergencies by acting promptly and resolutely to enforce legislative programs, at least to save those programs until Congress could act. Congress and the courts have responded to such executive initiative with consistent approval. . . .

The broad executive power granted by Article II to an officer on duty 365 days a year cannot, it is said, be invoked to avert disaster. Instead, the President must confine himself to sending a message to Congress recommending action. Under this messenger-boy concept of the Office, the President cannot even act to preserve legislative programs from destruction so that Congress will have something left to act upon. . . .

. . . Presidents have been in the past, and any man worthy of the Office should be in the future, free to take at least interim action necessary to execute legislative programs essential to survival of the Nation. A sturdy judiciary should not be swayed by the unpleasantness or unpopularity of necessary executive action, but must independently determine for itself whether the President was acting, as required by the Constitution, to "take Care that the Laws be faithfully executed."

September 11 and the War on Terrorism. History repeated itself in the period following the September 11,

2001, terrorist attacks on the United States. Once again the nation found itself in the throes of military hostilities, as President Bush sent troops first into Afghanistan and then into Iraq. As it had in earlier conflicts, the federal government took a number of constitutionally questionable actions in the pursuit of the war. Among the more controversial was the government's policy on captured enemy combatants. The Bush administration took the position that supporters of the enemy could be detained indefinitely without access to the civilian courts. Such policies ultimately brought to the Supreme Court disputes similar to those the justices faced in *Ex parte Milligan* during the Civil War and *Ex parte Quirin* during World War II. One of the most important was *Hamdi v. Rumsfeld* (2004).

Hamdi v. Rumsfeld

542 U.S. 507 (2004)
http://laws.findlaw.com/US/542/507.html
Oral arguments may be found at: http://www.oyez.org
On the question of the validity of Hamdi's detention:
Vote: 5 (Breyer, Kennedy, O'Connor, Rehnquist, Thomas)
*   4 (Ginsburg, Scalia, Souter, Stevens)*
On the question of Hamdi's access to courts and lawyers:
Vote: 8 (Breyer, Ginsburg, Kennedy, O'Connor, Rehnquist,
*   Scalia, Souter, Stevens)*
*   1 (Thomas)*
Opinion announcing the judgment of the Court: O'Connor
Opinion concurring in part, dissenting in part, and concurring
*   in judgment: Souter*
Dissenting opinions: Scalia, Thomas

One week after the September 11, 2001, al Qaeda terrorist attacks on the United States, Congress passed the Authorization for Use of Military Force resolution (AUMF), which gave the president authority to "use all necessary and appropriate force against those nations, organizations, or persons he determines planned, authorized, committed, or aided the terrorist attacks" or "harbored such organizations or persons, in order to prevent any future acts of international terrorism against the United States." On the basis of this congressional grant

In 2004 the Supreme Court upheld the military detention of Yaser Hamdi, a U.S. citizen captured during hostilities in Afghanistan, but also ruled that Hamdi must be given an opportunity to rebut the government's designation of him as an "enemy combatant."

of authority, President Bush ordered American armed forces to Afghanistan to attack al Qaeda and the Taliban regime that supported it.

During this military effort, Afghan elements supporting the United States captured twenty-year-old Yaser Esam Hamdi and delivered him to U.S. forces. Hamdi was an American citizen by virtue of his birth in Louisiana, but his family had moved to Saudi Arabia when he was a child. After being interrogated in Afghanistan, Hamdi was transferred first to the U.S. Naval Base at Guantánamo Bay, Cuba, then to military prisons in Norfolk, Virginia, and Charleston, South Carolina. The government claimed that Hamdi was an "enemy combatant" and as such could be held indefinitely without formal charges, court proceedings, access to counsel, or the freedom to communicate with anyone beyond the prison walls.

In June 2002 Hamdi's father, Esam Fouad Hamdi, filed a petition for habeas corpus on behalf of his son against Secretary of Defense Donald Rumsfeld, claiming the continued detention without formal charges or access to lawyers or the courts violated the younger Hamdi's constitutional right to due process of law. Hamdi's father argued that his son was not engaged in military activity but had gone to Afghanistan as a relief worker. The United States countered that Hamdi had received military training in Afghanistan and had joined a Taliban unit prior to his capture in a theater of war. The government's allegations as to Hamdi's participation in Taliban activities were submitted in the form of a statement by Michael Mobbs, a Defense Department official. This document, referred to as the Mobbs Declaration, contained little in the way of direct factual evidence.

After a series of hearings at the district and circuit court levels, the U.S. Court of Appeals for the Fourth Circuit ruled in favor of the government's position, holding that Hamdi could be detained and was entitled only to the limited judicial determination of whether the government had acted properly under its war powers.

JUSTICE O'CONNOR announced the judgment of the Court and delivered an opinion, in which THE CHIEF JUSTICE, JUSTICE KENNEDY, and JUSTICE BREYER join.

At this difficult time in our Nation's history, we are called upon to consider the legality of the Government's detention of a United States citizen on United States soil as an "enemy combatant" and to address the process that is constitutionally owed to one who seeks to challenge his classification as such. . . . We hold that although Congress authorized the detention of combatants in the narrow circumstances alleged here, due process demands that a citizen held in the United States as an enemy combatant be given a meaningful opportunity to contest the factual basis for that detention before a neutral decisionmaker. . . .

The threshold question before us is whether the Executive has the authority to detain citizens who qualify as "enemy combatants." There is some debate as to the proper scope of this term, and the Government has never provided any court with the full criteria that it uses in classifying individuals as such. It has made clear, however, that, for purposes of this case, the "enemy combatant" that it is seeking

to detain is an individual who, it alleges, was "'part of or supporting forces hostile to the United States or coalition partners'" in Afghanistan and who "'engaged in an armed conflict against the United States'" there. We therefore answer only the narrow question before us: whether the detention of citizens falling within that definition is authorized.

The Government maintains that no explicit congressional authorization is required, because the Executive possesses plenary authority to detain pursuant to Article II of the Constitution. We do not reach the question whether Article II provides such authority, however, because we agree with the Government's alternative position, that Congress has in fact authorized Hamdi's detention, through the AUMF [the Authorization for Use of Military Force resolution]. . . .

The AUMF authorizes the President to use "all necessary and appropriate force" against "nations, organizations, or persons" associated with the September 11, 2001, terrorist attacks. There can be no doubt that individuals who fought against the United States in Afghanistan as part of the Taliban, an organization known to have supported the al Qaeda terrorist network responsible for those attacks, are individuals Congress sought to target in passing the AUMF. We conclude that detention of individuals falling into the limited category we are considering, for the duration of the particular conflict in which they were captured, is so fundamental and accepted an incident to war as to be an exercise of the "necessary and appropriate force" Congress has authorized the President to use.

The capture and detention of lawful combatants and the capture, detention, and trial of unlawful combatants, by "universal agreement and practice," are "important incident[s] of war." *Ex parte Quirin* [1942]. The purpose of detention is to prevent captured individuals from returning to the field of battle and taking up arms once again. . . .

There is no bar to this Nation's holding one of its own citizens as an enemy combatant. In *Quirin*, one of the detainees, Haupt, alleged that he was a naturalized United States citizen. We held that "[c]itizens who associate themselves with the military arm of the enemy government, and with its aid, guidance and direction enter this country bent on hostile acts, are enemy belligerents within the meaning of . . . the law of war." While Haupt was tried for violations of the law of war, nothing in *Quirin* suggests that his citizenship would have precluded his mere detention for the duration of the relevant hostilities. Nor can we see any reason for drawing such a line here. A citizen, no less than an alien, can be "part of or supporting forces hostile to the United States or coalition partners" and "engaged in an armed conflict against the United States"; such a citizen, if released, would pose the same threat of returning to the front during the ongoing conflict.

In light of these principles, it is of no moment that the AUMF does not use specific language of detention. Because detention to prevent a combatant's return to the battlefield is a fundamental incident of waging war, in permitting the use of "necessary and appropriate force," Congress has clearly and unmistakably authorized detention in the narrow circumstances considered here.

Hamdi objects, nevertheless, that Congress has not authorized the *indefinite* detention to which he is now subject. . . . As the Government concedes, "given its unconventional nature, the current conflict is unlikely to end with a formal cease-fire agreement." The prospect Hamdi raises is therefore not far-fetched. If the Government does not consider this unconventional war won for two generations, and if it maintains during that time that Hamdi might, if released, rejoin forces fighting against the United States, then the position it has taken throughout the litigation of this case suggests that Hamdi's detention could last for the rest of his life.

It is a clearly established principle of the law of war that detention may last no longer than active hostilities.

Hamdi contends that the AUMF does not authorize indefinite or perpetual detention. Certainly, we agree that indefinite detention for the purpose of interrogation is not authorized. Further, we understand Congress' grant of authority for the use of "necessary and appropriate force" to include the authority to detain for the duration of the relevant conflict, and our understanding is based on longstanding law-of-war principles. If the practical circumstances of a given conflict are entirely unlike those of the conflicts that informed the development of the law of war, that understanding may unravel. But that is not the situation we face as of this date. Active combat operations against Taliban fighters apparently are ongoing in Afghanistan. The United States may detain, for the duration of these hostilities, individuals legitimately determined to be Taliban combatants who "engaged in an armed conflict against the United States." If the record establishes that United States troops are still involved in active combat in Afghanistan, those detentions are part of the exercise of "necessary and appropriate force," and therefore are authorized by the AUMF.

Ex parte Milligan (1866) does not undermine our holding about the Government's authority to seize enemy combatants, as we define that term today. In that case, the Court made repeated reference to the fact that its inquiry into whether the military tribunal had jurisdiction to try and punish Milligan turned in large part on the fact that Milligan was not a prisoner of war, but a resident of Indiana arrested while at home there. That fact was central to its conclusion. Had Milligan been captured while he was assisting Confederate soldiers by carrying a rifle against Union troops on a Confederate battlefield, the holding of the Court might well have been different. The Court's repeated explanations that Milligan was not a prisoner of war suggest that had these different circumstances been present he could have been detained under military authority for the duration of the conflict, whether or not he was a citizen. . . .

Even in cases in which the detention of enemy combatants is legally authorized, there remains the question of what process is constitutionally due to a citizen who disputes his enemy-combatant status. . . .

Though they reach radically different conclusions on the process that ought to attend the present proceeding, the parties begin on common ground. All agree that, absent suspension, the writ of habeas corpus remains available to every individual detained within the United States. Only in the rarest of circumstances has Congress seen fit to suspend the writ. At all other times, it has remained a critical check on the Executive, ensuring that it does not detain individuals except in accordance with law. All agree suspension of the writ has not occurred here. . . .

. . . [A]s critical as the Government's interest may be in detaining those who actually pose an immediate threat to the national security of the United States during ongoing international conflict, history and common sense teach us that an unchecked system of detention carries the potential to become a means for oppression and abuse of others who do not present that sort of threat. See *Ex parte Milligan*. . . . We reaffirm today the fundamental nature of a citizen's right to be free from involuntary confinement by his own government without due process of law, and we weigh the opposing governmental interests against the curtailment of liberty that such confinement entails.

On the other side of the scale are the weighty and sensitive governmental interests in ensuring that those who have in fact fought with the enemy during a war do not return to battle against the United States. . . . [T]he law of war and the realities of combat may render such detentions both necessary and appropriate, and our due process analysis need not blink at those realities. Without doubt, our Constitution recognizes that core strategic matters of warmaking belong in the hands of those who are best positioned and most politically accountable for making them.

The Government also argues at some length that its interests in reducing the process available to alleged enemy combatants are heightened by the practical difficulties that would accompany a system of trial-like process. In its view, military officers who are engaged in the serious work of waging battle would be unnecessarily and dangerously distracted by litigation half a world away, and discovery into military operations would both intrude on the sensitive secrets of national defense and result in a futile search for evidence buried under the rubble of war. To the extent that these burdens are triggered by heightened procedures, they are properly taken into account in our due process analysis.

Striking the proper constitutional balance here is of great importance to the Nation during this period of ongoing combat. But it is equally vital that our calculus not give short shrift to the values that this country holds dear or to the privilege that is American citizenship. It is during our most challenging and uncertain moments that our Nation's commitment to due process is most severely tested; and it is in those times that we must preserve our commitment at home to the principles for which we fight abroad. . . .

We therefore hold that a citizen-detainee seeking to challenge his classification as an enemy combatant must receive notice of the factual basis for his classification, and a fair opportunity to rebut the Government's factual assertions before a neutral decisionmaker. These essential constitutional promises may not be eroded.

At the same time, the exigencies of the circumstances may demand that, aside from these core elements, enemy combatant proceedings may be tailored to alleviate their uncommon potential to burden the Executive at a time of ongoing military conflict. Hearsay, for example, may need to be accepted as the most reliable available evidence from the Government in such a proceeding. Likewise, the Constitution would not be offended by a presumption in favor of the Government's evidence, so long as that presumption remained a rebuttable one and fair opportunity for rebuttal were provided. Thus, once the Government puts forth credible evidence that the habeas petitioner meets the enemy-combatant criteria, the onus could shift to the petitioner to rebut that evidence with more persuasive evidence that he falls outside the criteria. A burden-shifting scheme of this sort would meet the goal of ensuring that the errant tourist, embedded journalist, or local aid worker has a chance to prove military error while giving due regard to the Executive once it has put forth meaningful support for its conclusion that the detainee is in fact an enemy combatant. . . .

We think it unlikely that this basic process will have the dire impact on the central functions of warmaking that the Government forecasts. The parties agree that initial captures on the battlefield need not receive the process we have discussed here; that process is due only when the determination is made to *continue* to hold those who have been seized. . . . While we accord the greatest respect and consideration to the judgments of military authorities in matters relating to the actual prosecution of a war, and recognize that the scope of that discretion necessarily is wide, it does not infringe on the core role of the military for the courts to exercise their own time-honored and constitutionally mandated roles of reviewing and resolving claims like those presented here. . . .

In so holding, we necessarily reject the Government's assertion that separation of powers principles mandate a heavily circumscribed role for the courts in such circumstances. Indeed, the position that the courts must forgo any examination of the individual case and focus exclusively on the legality of the broader detention scheme cannot be mandated by any reasonable view of separation of powers, as this approach serves only to *condense* power into a single branch of government. We have long since made clear that a state of war is not a blank check for the President when it comes to the rights of the Nation's citizens. . . . Likewise, we have made clear that, unless Congress acts to suspend it, the Great Writ of habeas corpus allows the Judicial Branch to play a necessary role in maintaining this delicate balance of governance, serving as an important judicial check on the Executive's discretion in the realm of detentions. . . .

. . . Plainly, the "process" Hamdi has received is not that to which he is entitled under the Due Process Clause.

There remains the possibility that the standards we have articulated could be met by an appropriately authorized and properly constituted military tribunal. . . .

Hamdi asks us to hold that the Fourth Circuit also erred by denying him immediate access to counsel upon his detention and by disposing of the case without permitting him to meet with an attorney. Since our grant of certiorari in this case, Hamdi has been appointed counsel, with whom he has met for consultation purposes on several occasions, and with whom he is now being granted unmonitored meetings. He unquestionably has the right to access to counsel in connection with the proceedings on remand. No further consideration of this issue is necessary at this stage of the case.

The judgment of the United States Court of Appeals for the Fourth Circuit is vacated, and the case is remanded for further proceedings.

It is so ordered.

JUSTICE SOUTER, with whom JUSTICE GINSBURG joins, concurring in part, dissenting in part, and concurring in the judgment.

The plurality [accepts] the Government's position that if Hamdi's designation as an enemy combatant is correct, his detention (at least as to some period) is authorized by an Act of Congress as required by . . . the Authorization for Use of Military Force. Here, I disagree and respectfully dissent. The Government has failed to demonstrate that the Force Resolution authorizes the detention complained of here even on the facts the Government claims. If the Government raises nothing further than the record now shows, the Non-Detention Act [prohibiting the detention of citizens except pursuant to an Act of Congress] entitles Hamdi to be released. . . .

. . . Since the Force Resolution was adopted one week after the attacks of September 11, 2001, it naturally speaks with some generality, but its focus is clear, and that is on the use of military power. It is fairly read to authorize the use of armies and weapons, whether against other armies or individual terrorists. But . . . it never so much as uses the word detention, and there is no reason to think Congress might have perceived any need to augment Executive power to deal with dangerous citizens within the United States, given the well-stocked statutory arsenal of defined criminal offenses covering the gamut of actions that a citizen sympathetic to terrorists might commit. . . .

Because I find Hamdi's detention . . . unauthorized by the Force Resolution, I would not reach any questions of what process he may be due in litigating disputed issues in a proceeding under the habeas statute or prior to the habeas enquiry itself. For me, it suffices that the Government has failed to justify holding him in the absence of a further Act of Congress, criminal charges, [or] a showing that the detention conforms to the laws of war. . . .

Since this disposition does not command a majority of the Court, however, the need to give practical effect to the conclusions of eight members of the Court rejecting the Government's position calls for me to join with the plurality in ordering remand on terms closest to those I would impose. Although I think litigation of Hamdi's status as an enemy combatant is unnecessary, the terms of the plurality's remand will allow Hamdi to offer evidence that he is not an enemy combatant, and he should at the least have the benefit of that opportunity.

It should go without saying that in joining with the plurality to produce a judgment, I do not adopt the plurality's resolution of constitutional issues that I would not reach. It is not that I could disagree with the plurality's determinations (given the plurality's view of the Force Resolution) that someone in Hamdi's position is entitled at a minimum to notice of the Government's claimed factual basis for holding him, and to a fair chance to rebut it before a neutral decision maker; nor, of course, could I disagree with the plurality's affirmation of Hamdi's right to counsel. On the other hand, I do not mean to imply agreement that the Government could claim an evidentiary presumption casting the burden of rebuttal on Hamdi or that an opportunity to litigate before a military tribunal might obviate or truncate enquiry by a court on habeas.

Subject to these qualifications, I join with the plurality in a judgment of the Court vacating the Fourth Circuit's judgment and remanding the case.

JUSTICE SCALIA, with whom JUSTICE STEVENS joins, dissenting.

This case brings into conflict the competing demands of national security and our citizens' constitutional right to personal liberty. Although I share the Court's evident unease as it seeks to reconcile the two, I do not agree with its resolution.

Where the Government accuses a citizen of waging war against it, our constitutional tradition has been to prosecute him in federal court for treason or some other crime. Where the exigencies of war prevent that, the Constitution's Suspension Clause, Art. I, §9, cl.2, allows Congress to relax the usual protections temporarily. Absent suspension, however, the Executive's assertion of military exigency has not been thought sufficient to permit detention without charge. No one contends that the congressional Authorization for Use of Military Force, on which the Government relies to justify its actions here, is an implementation of the Suspension Clause. Accordingly, I would reverse the decision below. . . .

JUSTICE O'CONNOR, writing for a plurality of this Court, asserts that captured enemy combatants (other than those suspected of war crimes) have traditionally been detained until the cessation of hostilities and then released. That is probably an accurate description of wartime practice with respect to enemy *aliens.* The tradition with respect to American citizens, however, has been quite different. Citizens aiding the enemy have been treated as traitors subject to the criminal process. . . .

There are times when military exigency renders resort to the traditional criminal process impracticable. English law accommodated such exigencies by allowing legislative suspension of the writ of habeas corpus for brief periods. . . .

Where the Executive has not pursued the usual course of charge, committal, and conviction, it has historically secured the Legislature's explicit approval of a suspension. In England, Parliament on numerous occasions passed temporary suspensions in times of threatened invasion or rebellion. . . .

Our Federal Constitution contains a provision explicitly permitting suspension, but limiting the situations in which it may be invoked: "The privilege of the Writ of Habeas Corpus shall not be suspended, unless when in Cases of Rebellion or Invasion the public Safety may require it." Art. I, §9, cl.2. Although this provision does not state that suspension must be effected by, or authorized by, a legislative act, it has been so understood, consistent with English practice and the Clause's placement in Article I. . . .

Writings from the founding generation also suggest that, without exception, the only constitutional alternatives are to charge the crime or suspend the writ. . . .

. . . [T]he reasoning and conclusion of [*Ex parte*] *Milligan* logically cover the present case. The Government justifies imprisonment of Hamdi on principles of the law of war and admits that, absent the war, it would have no such authority. But if the law of war cannot be applied to citizens where courts are open, then Hamdi's imprisonment without criminal trial is no less unlawful than Milligan's trial by military tribunal. . . .

The proposition that the Executive lacks indefinite wartime detention authority over citizens is consistent with the Founders' general mistrust of military power permanently at the Executive's disposal. . . .

. . . Hamdi is entitled to a habeas decree requiring his release unless (1) criminal proceedings are promptly brought, or (2) Congress has suspended the writ of habeas corpus. A suspension of the writ could, of course, lay down conditions for continued detention, similar to those that today's opinion prescribes under the Due Process Clause. But there is a world of difference between the people's representatives' determining the need for that suspension (and prescribing the conditions for it), and this Court's doing so.

The plurality finds justification for Hamdi's imprisonment in the Authorization for Use of Military Force. . . .

This is not remotely a congressional suspension of the writ, and no one claims that it is. . . . The Suspension Clause of the Constitution, which carefully circumscribes the conditions under which the writ can be withheld, would be a sham if it could be evaded by congressional prescription of requirements *other than the common-law requirement of committal for criminal prosecution* that render the writ, though available, unavailing. If the Suspension Clause does not guarantee the citizen that he will either be tried or released, unless the conditions for suspending the writ exist and the grave action of suspending the writ has been taken; if it merely guarantees the citizen that he will not be detained unless Congress by ordinary legislation says he can be detained; it guarantees him very little indeed. . . .

There is a certain harmony of approach in the plurality's making up for Congress's failure to invoke the Suspension Clause and its making up for the Executive's failure to apply what it says are needed procedures—an approach that reflects what might be called a Mr. Fix-it Mentality. The plurality seems to view it as its mission to Make Everything Come Out Right, rather than merely to decree the consequences, as far as individual rights are concerned, of the other two branches' actions and omissions. Has the Legislature failed to suspend the writ in the current dire emergency? Well, we will remedy that failure by prescribing the reasonable conditions that a suspension should have included. And has the Executive failed to live up to those reasonable conditions? Well, we will ourselves make that failure good, so that this dangerous fellow (if he is dangerous) need not be set free. The problem with this approach is not only that it steps out of the courts' modest and limited role in a democratic society; but that by repeatedly doing what it thinks the political branches ought to do it encourages their lassitude and saps the vitality of government by the people.

Several limitations give my views in this matter a relatively narrow compass. They apply only to citizens, accused of being enemy combatants, who are detained within the territorial jurisdiction of a federal court. This is not likely to be a numerous group. . . . Where the citizen is captured outside and held outside the United States, the constitutional requirements may be different. Moreover, even within the United States, the accused citizen-enemy combatant may lawfully be detained once prosecution is in progress or in contemplation. . . .

I frankly do not know whether these tools are sufficient to meet the Government's security needs, including the need to obtain intelligence through interrogation. It is far beyond my competence, or the Court's competence, to determine that. But it is not beyond Congress's. If the situation demands it, the Executive can ask Congress to authorize suspension of the writ—which can be made subject to whatever conditions Congress deems appropriate, including even the procedural novelties invented by the plurality today. To be sure, suspension is limited by the Constitution to cases of rebellion or invasion. But whether the attacks of September 11, 2001, constitute an "invasion," and whether those attacks still justify suspension several years later, are questions for Congress rather than this Court. If civil rights are to be curtailed during wartime, it must be done openly and democratically, as the Constitution requires, rather than by silent erosion through an opinion of this Court. . . .

Many think it not only inevitable but entirely proper that liberty give way to security in times of national crisis—that, at the extremes of military exigency, *inter arma silent leges.* Whatever the general merits of the view that war silences law or modulates its voice, that view has no place in the interpretation and application of a Constitution de-

signed precisely to confront war and, in a manner that accords with democratic principles, to accommodate it. Because the Court has proceeded to meet the current emergency in a manner the Constitution does not envision, I respectfully dissent.

JUSTICE THOMAS, dissenting.

The Executive Branch, acting pursuant to the powers vested in the President by the Constitution and with explicit congressional approval, has determined that Yaser Hamdi is an enemy combatant and should be detained. This detention falls squarely within the Federal Government's war powers, and we lack the expertise and capacity to second-guess that decision. As such, petitioners' habeas challenge should fail, and there is no reason to remand the case. The plurality reaches a contrary conclusion by failing adequately to consider basic principles of the constitutional structure as it relates to national security and foreign affairs. . . . I do not think that the Federal Government's war powers can be balanced away by this Court. Arguably, Congress could provide for additional procedural protections, but until it does, we have no right to insist upon them. But even if I were to agree with the general approach the plurality takes, I could not accept the particulars. The plurality utterly fails to account for the Government's compelling interests and for our own institutional inability to weigh competing concerns correctly. I respectfully dissent.

Hamdi answered questions about the rights of U.S. citizens who are captured during military conflict, but it did not address similar issues with respect to noncitizens. The justices considered this aspect of the president's war powers in *Rasul v. Bush* (2004), decided the same day as *Hamdi.*

The *Rasul* case centered on the status of some six hundred men who had been captured during hostilities in Afghanistan and transported to the naval detention facilities at Guantánamo Bay. The United States occupies and completely controls the naval base pursuant to a lease and treaty, but Cuba retains ultimate sovereignty over the land. The prisoners were detained without formal charges and without access to courts or attorneys. The relatives of two Australians and twelve Kuwaitis held at

Guantánamo filed habeas corpus petitions on the detainees' behalf claiming they were illegally incarcerated. The lower federal courts dismissed these lawsuits, holding that the federal courts have no jurisdiction outside the United States. The relatives of the detainees requested Supreme Court review.

A six-justice majority reversed, ruling that U.S. law confers jurisdiction on the federal courts over such habeas corpus petitions. Federal authority extends to areas under the control of the United States, such as the Guantánamo naval base, as well as to the military custodians of the detainees. Therefore, the incarcerated captives, whether American citizens or aliens, have the right to challenge their imprisonment in federal court.

The decision in *Rasul* was based on an interpretation of federal statutes, not on the Constitution. The ruling is important, however, because it allows access to the courts where the constitutional validity of the detainees' continued imprisonment may be challenged.

Hamdi and *Rasul* were not the Court's last words on the executive power in the war against terrorism. Just as Lincoln and Roosevelt resorted to military tribunals or commissions, so too did President Bush. And just as during those earlier wartime administrations—recall *Milligan* and *Quirin*—the president's actions were challenged. In *Hamdan v. Rumsfeld* (2006) the Court considered a military order issued by President Bush that subjected "enemy combatants" to military commissions. For purposes of the order, an enemy combatant is any noncitizen for whom the president determines there is reason to believe the individual (1) is or was a member of al Qaeda or (2) has engaged in activities aimed at or harmful to the United States.

In *Hamdan* the majority outlawed the use of these commissions, reiterating the view that even during wars the "Executive is bound to comply with the Rule of Law." The Court did not, however, entirely shut the door. Part of the majority's concern about the commissions was that Congress had not authorized them. But under the Court's ruling, as Justice Breyer noted, "Nothing prevents the President from returning to Congress to seek the authority he believes necessary." And, in fact, the administra-

tion took that step—with success. Within months of the Court's decision in *Hamdan,* Congress passed the Military Commissions Act (MCA), which authorized the use of military commissions for trying suspected terrorists and denied federal courts jurisdiction to hear the detainees' habeas corpus applications.

Basing their decision in part on their review of the history and origins of the writ of habeas corpus, the justices struck down parts of the MCA in ***Boumediene v. Bush*** (2008). In a closely divided vote, they held that the Guantánamo Bay detainees have a right to challenge their imprisonment in the federal courts. Writing for the majority, Justice Kennedy declared, "The laws and Constitution are designed to survive, and remain in force, in extraordinary times. Liberty and security can be reconciled; and in our system they are reconciled within the framework of the law. The Framers decided that habeas corpus, a right of first importance, must be a part of that framework, a part of that law." He held that "if the privilege of habeas corpus is to be denied to the detainees now before us, Congress must act in accordance with the requirements of the Suspension Clause"; that is, it must suspend the writ.

The four dissenters took issue with Kennedy's analysis; indeed, Justice Scalia went so far as to say, "The game of bait-and-switch that today's opinion plays upon the Nation's Commander in Chief will make the war harder on us. It will almost certainly cause more Americans to be killed." President Bush, not surprisingly, said that while his administration would "abide by the Court's decision," he did not agree with it.

What are the lessons of *Hamdi, Rasul, Hamdan,* and *Boumediene*—all of which the executive lost in part or in full? Are they in line with other cases we have read in this chapter? Is the central idea that in the interest of the nation's security, the justices may be willing to allow the president to take actions during times of war that they would otherwise prohibit, but generally only if the president has the backing of Congress? If so, do you agree that this is the appropriate way for the justices to proceed? On the one hand, why would legislative approval be so important if the president believes he is acting in the country's best interest? On the other, should the Court allow the president, even with Congress's support, to curtail rights and liberties? Keep in mind that in *Boumediene* the Court took the position that it should not: Congress had approved the detentions, but the Court still ruled against the executive. Whether this is an appropriate role for the Court to play in times of war remains an open question, and one the justices will no doubt continue to mull over in the decades to come.

READINGS

Berger, Raoul. *Executive Privilege: A Constitutional Myth.* Cambridge: Harvard University Press, 1974.

Calabresi, Steven G., and Christopher S. Yoo. *The Unitary Executive: Presidential Power from Washington to Bush.* New Haven: Yale University Press, 2008.

Cooper, Phillip J. *By Order of the President: The Use and Abuse of Executive Direct Action.* Lawrence: University Press of Kansas, 2002

Corwin, Edward S. *The President: Office and Powers.* 5th rev. ed. New York: New York University Press, 1984.

Ely, John Hart. *War and Responsibility: Constitutional Lessons of Vietnam and Its Aftermath.* Princeton: Princeton University Press, 1993.

Fisher, Louis. *Nazi Saboteurs on Trial: A Military Tribunal and American Law.* Lawrence: University Press of Kansas, 2003.

———. *Presidential War Power.* 2nd ed. Lawrence: University Press of Kansas, 2004.

Harriger, Katy J. *Independent Justice: The Federal Special Prosecutor in American Politics.* Lawrence: University Press of Kansas, 1992.

Henkin, Louis. *Foreign Affairs and the Constitution.* Mineola, N.Y.: Foundation Press, 1972.

Irons, Peter. *Justice at War: The Story of the Japanese-American Internment Cases.* New York: Oxford University Press, 1983.

Koenig, Louis. *The Chief Executive.* 3rd ed. New York: Harcourt Brace Jovanovich, 1975.

Korn, Jessica. *The Power of Separation: American Constitutionalism and the Myth of the Legislative Veto.* Princeton: Princeton University Press, 1998.

Marcus, Maeva. *Truman and the Steel Seizure Case: The Limits of Presidential Power.* New York: Columbia University Press, 1987.

May, Christopher. *In the Name of War: Judicial Review and the War Powers Since 1918.* Cambridge: Harvard University Press, 1989.

McKenzie, G. Calvin. *The Politics of Presidential Appointments.* New York: Free Press, 1981.

Randall, James. *Constitutional Problems Under Lincoln.* Urbana: University of Illinois Press, 1964.

Rehnquist, William H. *All the Laws but One: Civil Liberties in Wartime.* New York: Knopf, 1998.

Reveley, W. Taylor, III. *War Powers of the President and Congress.* Charlottesville: University Press of Virginia, 1981.

Sheffer, Martin S. *The Judicial Development of Presidential War Powers.* Westport, Conn.: Praeger, 1999.

Stone, Geoffrey R. *Perilous Times: Free Speech in Wartime from the Sedition Act of 1798 to the War on Terrorism.* New York: Norton, 2004.

Westin, Alan F. *Anatomy of a Constitutional Law Case.* New York: Macmillan, 1958.

Whittington, Keith E. *Constitutional Construction: Divided Powers and Constitutional Meaning.* Cambridge: Harvard University Press, 1999.

———. *Political Foundations of Judiciary Supremacy: The Presidency, the Supreme Court, and Constitutional Leadership in U.S. History.* Princeton: Princeton University Press, 2007.

PART III
NATION-STATE RELATIONS

AN INTRODUCTION TO NATION-STATE RELATIONS

If we cataloged the types of governments existing in the world today, we would have a fairly diverse list. Some are unitary systems in which power is located in a central authority that may or may not mete out some power to its subdivisions. Others are virtually the opposite: Authority rests largely with local governments with only certain powers reserved to national authority. When the framers drafted the Constitution, they had to make some basic decisions about the balance between the states and the national government they were creating. Their choice, generally speaking, was federalism: a system in which government power is divided between a national government and several subnational units with each given a sphere of authority.

Many commentators suggest that the framers' decision was a wise one, with benefits that Americans continue to enjoy today. Some examples: Because the government is multitiered, Americans have many points of access to the system. Because federal, state, and even local systems are all involved in making policy, the system provides for numerous checks on the exercise of government power. In addition, federalism encourages experimentation and provides for flexibility. Justice Louis Brandeis once wrote, "It is one of the happy incidents of the federal system that a single courageous State may, if its citizens choose, serve as a laboratory; and try novel social and economic experiments without risk to the rest of the country."[1] Local problems often can be remedied

1. Dissenting opinion in *New State Ice Co. v. Liebmann* (1932).

best by state officials who are better positioned than national leaders to understand local conditions and resources. The states were first to implement welfare reform, policies protecting workers' rights, and so forth.

But federalism is not perfect. For one thing, it can be costly. In some countries citizens pay a single (but often very large) tax; Americans may pay local property taxes, state sales and income taxes, as well as federal assessments. For another, the system lacks efficiency. The implementation of certain kinds of policies might require the coordination of the national government, fifty states, and numerous local governments, which inevitably slows down the process.

For our purposes, the most relevant concern about federalism is its complexity. Multiple layers of government with overlapping interests are difficult for most citizens to comprehend. People may not understand which level of government makes specific policies, and some citizens may have so little interest in government that they do not even know the names of their political leaders. At the other end of the spectrum, governments sometimes do not well understand the boundaries of their own power. Throughout American history, states have charged that the federal government has gone too far in regulating "their" business; indeed, this was one issue over which the Civil War, the most extreme disagreement, was fought.

Since the nation's founding, the U.S. Supreme Court has played the major role in delineating and defining the contours of American federalism. Why and how it has done so are the subjects of the chapters that follow. Chapter 6 focuses on the various and general theories of federal-state relations with which the Court has dealt. Chapters 7 and 8 consider the exercise of government power over the most contentious of issues: commerce, taxing, and spending.

But first, let us explore several issues emanating from our discussion so far: the kind of system the framers adopted, the amending of that system, and its complexity. The resulting conflicts often require the involvement of "neutral" arbiters—judges and Supreme Court justices.

THE FRAMERS AND FEDERALISM

We have already mentioned that the framers selected federalism from among several alternative forms of government, although the word *federalism* does not appear in the Constitution. The founders had a general vision of the sort of government they wanted—or, more aptly, of what they did not want. They rejected a unitary system as wholly incompatible with basic values and traditions already existing within the states. They also rejected a confederation in which power would reside with the states; after all, that is what existed under the Articles of Confederation, the charter they came to Philadelphia to revise.

How to divide power, then, became the delegates' central concern. In the end, they wrote into the document a rather elaborate allocation of political authority. Nevertheless, ambiguity resulted. A most important source of this confusion was the question of constitutional relationships; that is, in the parlance of the eighteenth century, the framers looked at the Constitution as a contract, but a contract between whom? Some commentators argue that it specifies the relationship between the people and the national government and that the former empower the latter. Justice Joseph Story wrote:

The constitution of the United States was ordained and established, not by the states in their sovereign capacities, but emphatically, as the preamble of the constitution declares, by "the people of the United States." . . . The constitution was not, therefore, necessarily carved out of existing state sovereignties, nor a surrender of powers already existing in state institutions.[2]

2. *Martin v. Hunter's Lessee* (1816).

Others suggest that the contract is between the states and the nation. In a 1798 resolution of the Virginia Assembly, James Madison wrote:

That this Assembly doth explicitly and peremptorily declare that it views the powers of the Federal Government as resulting from the compact, to which the States are parties, as limited by the plain sense and intention of the instrument constituting that compact; as no further valid than they are authorized by the grants enumerated in that compact; and that in case of deliberate, palpable, and dangerous exercise of other powers not granted by the said compact, the States, who are the parties thereto, have the right, and are in duty bound, to interpose for arresting the progress of the evil, and for maintaining within their respective limits, the authorities, rights, and liberties appertaining to them.[3]

This is not merely an abstract debate, but one with real consequences. In its most violent incarnation, the Civil War, southern leaders took Madison's logic to its limit. They argued that because the Constitution represented a contract between the states and the federal government, with the states creating the national government, when the latter abrogated its end of the contract, the contract was no longer valid. The Civil War ended that particular dispute, but the principle continued to flare up in less extreme, but no less important, forms. The refusal of some southern states to abide by federal civil rights laws is one example.

This problem continues to manifest itself largely because the Constitution supports both sides and therefore neither. Those who favor the argument that the national government is beholden to the people point to the document's preamble: "*We the people* of the United States . . . do ordain and establish this Constitution." To support the argument that the states create the national government, proponents turn to the language in Article VII, that the ratification of nine states "shall be sufficient for the Establishment of this Constitution *between the States* so ratifying." When the issue of the contractual nature of the Constitution arises, therefore, many look to the Supreme Court to resolve it. As we shall see in chapter 6, different Courts have approached this debate in varying

3. Reprinted in *Documents of American Constitutional and Legal History*, Vol. 1, ed. Melvin I. Urofsky (New York: Knopf, 1989), 159.

ways, adopting one view over the other at distinct points in American history.

THE ALLOCATION OF
GOVERNMENT POWER

Arguments over which entities are the parties to the contract, the U.S. Constitution, may never be fully resolved, but another point of ambiguity was thought so onerous that it could not be left up to mere interpretation. That area is the balance of power between the states and the federal government. The original charter, in the view of many, placed too much authority with the federal government. In particular, states' rights advocates pointed to two clauses in the Constitution as working against their interests.

The first is the necessary and proper clause: Congress has the power "[t]o make all Laws which shall be necessary and proper for carrying into Execution [its] Powers, and all other Powers vested by this Constitution in the Government of the United States, or in any Department or Officer thereof."

The second is the supremacy clause: "This Constitution, and the Laws of the United States which shall be made in Pursuance thereof; and all Treaties made, or which shall be made, under the Authority of the United States, shall be the supreme Law of the Land; and the Judges in every state shall be bound thereby, any Thing in the Constitution or Laws of any State to the Contrary notwithstanding." These clauses seem to allocate a great deal of power to the national government.

Yet, as Madison wrote in Federalist No. 45:

The powers delegated by the proposed Constitution to the Federal Government, are few and defined. Those which are to remain in the State Governments are numerous and indefinite. The former will be exercised principally on external objects, as war, peace, negotiation, and foreign commerce; with which last the power of taxation will for the most part be connected. The powers reserved to the several States will extend to all the objects, which, in the ordinary course of affairs, concern the lives, liberties and properties of the people; and the internal order, improvement, and prosperity of the State.

Nevertheless, states remained concerned that the national government would attempt to cut into their power

and sovereignty, and the language of the Constitution did little to allay their fears. At worst, it suggested that the federal institutions always would be supreme; at best, it was highly ambiguous. Even Madison recognized the document's lack of clarity when he wrote in Federalist No. 39:

The proposed Constitution therefore . . . is in strictness neither a national nor a federal Constitution; but a composition of both. In its foundation it is federal, not national; in the sources from which the ordinary powers of the Government are drawn, it is partly federal, and partly national: in the operation of these powers, it is national, not federal. In the extent of them, again, it is federal; not national: And finally in the authoritative mode of introducing amendments, it is neither wholly federal, nor wholly national.

Madison clearly thought this ambiguity was an asset of the new system of government, an advantage that made it fit compatibly into the overall philosophies of separation of powers and checks and balances. But his argument proved inadequate; when the perceived unfair balance of power proved to be an obstacle to the ratification of the Constitution, those favoring its adoption promised to remedy the inequality.

This remedy took the form of the Tenth Amendment, which—in relation to the rest of the Bill of Rights—is a constitutional oddity. The first nine amendments deal mainly with the rights of the people vis-à-vis the federal government (for example, the First Amendment: "Congress shall make no law respecting an establishment of religion," and so forth), but the Tenth Amendment states: "The powers not delegated to the United States by the Constitution, nor prohibited by it to the States, are reserved to the States respectively, or to the people." With these words in place, states' rights advocates were mollified, at least temporarily, and the American system of government—that unique brand of federalism—was established.

In the final analysis, what does the system look like? In other words, who gets what? Table III-1 depicts the allocation of powers emanating from the Constitution. As we can see, the different levels of government have some exclusive and some concurrent powers, but they are also prohibited from operating in certain spheres. The powers

TABLE III-1   The Constitutional Allocation of Government Power

Powers Specified within the Constitution or by Court Interpretation		
Powers exclusive to the federal government	Powers exclusive to state governments	Concurrent powers to both federal and state governments
Coin money	Run elections	Tax
Regulate interstate and foreign commerce	Regulate intrastate commerce	Borrow money
Tax imports	Establish republican forms of state and local governments	Establish courts
Make treaties	Protect public health, safety, and morals	Charter banks and corporations
Make all laws "necessary and proper"	All powers not delegated to the national government or denied to the states by the Constitution	Make and enforce laws
Make war		Take property (power of eminent domain)
Regulate postal system		

Powers Denied by the Constitution or by Court Interpretation		
Expressly prohibited to the federal government	Expressly prohibited to state governments	Expressly prohibited to both
Tax state exports	Tax imports and exports	Pass bills of attainder
Change state boundaries	Coin money	Pass ex post facto laws
	Enter into treaties	Grant titles of nobility
	Impair obligation of contracts	Impose religious tests
		Pass laws in conflict with the Bill of Rights and subsequent amendments

SOURCE: Adapted from J. W. Peltason and Sue Davis, *Corwin & Peltason's Understanding the Constitution*, 15th ed. (Belmont, Calif.: Wadsworth, 2000), chaps. 1–2; and C. Herman Pritchett, *Constitutional Law of the Federal System* (Englewood Cliffs, N.J.: Prentice-Hall, 1984), 58.

of the federal government are those that are enumerated in the Constitution, broadly defined according to provisions such as the necessary and proper clause. Unless otherwise restricted by the Constitution, the states retain broad governing authority, which includes the "police powers"—the general authority to regulate for the health, safety, morals, and general welfare of their citizens.

The elaborate system of American federalism depicted in Table III-1 seems to belie what we noted at the beginning of this essay, and you may be wondering how such a well-articulated division of power could be the center of so much controversy. In part, the answer takes us back to the contractual nature of the Constitution. As we shall see in Chapter 6, in which we explore general theoretical approaches to federalism, the Court has had some difficulty determining who the parties to the

contract are, and its confusion encouraged litigation. In more concrete terms, no matter how elaborate the design, the Constitution does not (and perhaps cannot) address the range of real disputes that arise between nation and state.

Indeed, the irony here is that the complexity of the system coupled with the language of the Constitution is what fosters the need for interpretation. Note the last column in Table III-1, which illustrates concurrent powers. Where do state powers begin and federal powers end and vice versa? States have the authority to regulate intrastate commerce, and the federal government regulates interstate commerce, but is it so easy to delineate those boundaries? Which entity controls the making and selling of goods manufactured in one state and shipped to another? And, more to the point, what happens when the national government and the states have different notions of how to regulate the manufacturing?

If that problem is not enough, compare the constitutional language of the Tenth Amendment with that of the necessary and proper and supremacy clauses. The last prohibits states from passing laws that directly conflict with the Constitution, federal laws, and so forth. But so often the issues are not clear. Is the federal authority supreme only in its sphere of operations—those activities where it has clear constitutional mandates—as some argue the Tenth Amendment states? Or is it the case that every time the federal government enters into a particular realm, it automatically preempts states from acting? Or does the answer depend on whether Congress intended to preempt state action?

It should be clear that American federalism is something of a double-edged sword. On the one side, the balance of power it created not only pacified those who were opposed to ratifying the Constitution but also continues to define the contours of the U.S. system of government. On the other, the complexity of the system has given rise to tensions between the levels of government in the form of disputes that require settlement by the courts. It may be that the system has been so resilient because the Constitution constantly requires interpretation. But we will leave that for you to decide as we now turn to the way the Supreme Court has formulated theories and specific rulings in response to two distinct but interrelated issues: the general contours of state-federal relations and the important powers of commerce and taxing and spending.

CHAPTER 6
FEDERALISM

When the framers created a new national government and at the same time left the existing state governments intact, the stage was set for continuing disputes over the allocation of political authority. In what areas should the federal government be dominant? To what extent are the states allowed autonomy to govern within their respective borders? Over the course of the nation's history, two competing theories have been advocated: dual federalism and cooperative federalism (see Table 6-1).

Proponents of dual federalism are advocates of states' rights. They would argue that the Constitution represents an agreement between the states and the federal government in which the states empower the central government. States, therefore, are not subservient to the federal government. Each is supreme within its own sphere. To back their theory, dual federalists invoke the Tenth Amendment, arguing that Congress cannot "invade" power reserved to the states and that courts should invalidate any congressional legislation touching traditional state functions.

Cooperative federalism proponents take precisely the opposite view. They argue that the people, not the states, created and animated the federal government. They hold that the supremacy clause and the necessary and proper clause should settle arguments, not the Tenth Amendment. That amendment, under cooperative federalism, grants no express power to the states.

The debate between advocates of cooperative and dual federalism has never been fully resolved. Instead, the nation has swung back and forth between different variations of these two opposing concepts of nation-state relations. As illustrated in Table 6-2, the swings of the federalism pendulum are clearly reflected in the history of Supreme Court decisions. This chapter examines the components of that cycle. As you read the cases, consider not only which doctrine governed each decision but also why the philosophies have grown stronger or weaker. What forces—legal, political, and historical—have led the justices to choose one approach over the other?

THE MARSHALL COURT AND THE RISE OF NATIONAL SUPREMACY

An ardent Federalist, Chief Justice John Marshall was true to his party's tenets over the course of his long career on the Court. In case after case, he was more than willing to elevate the powers of the federal government above those of the states. Perhaps his most significant statement on national supremacy came in *McCulloch v. Maryland* (1819). In chapter 4 we saw how he used this case to assert firmly that Congress has implied powers. Here, we shall see that *McCulloch* also served as his vehicle to expound the notion of national supremacy. A brief review of the essential facts is offered to remind you of the issues in this case.

TABLE 6-1   A Comparison of Dual and Cooperative Federalism

	Dual Federalism	Cooperative Federalism
General view	Operates under the assumption that the two levels of government are co-equal sovereigns, each supreme within its own sphere.	Operates under the assumption that the national government is supreme even if its actions touch state functions. States and the federal government are "partners," but the latter largely sets policy for the nation.
View of the Constitution	It is a compact among the states and a contract between the states and the federal government.	Rejects view of it as a compact; the people, not the states, empower the national government.
Constitutional support	Tenth Amendment reserves certain powers to the states and limits the national government to those powers specifically delegated to it.	Tenth Amendment does not provide additional powers to the states.
	Necessary and proper clause is to be read literally and narrowly.	Necessary and proper clause is to be read expansively and loosely.
		Supremacy clause means that the national government is supreme within its own sphere, even if its actions touch on state functions.

McCulloch v. Maryland

4 (17 U.S.) Wheat. 316 (1819)

http://laws.findlaw.com/US/17/316.html

Vote: 6 (Duvall, Johnson, Livingston, Marshall, Story, Washington)

0

Opinion of the Court: Marshall
Not participating: Todd

Congress established the second Bank of the United States in 1816. Because of inefficiency and corruption, the bank was very unpopular, and many went so far as to blame it for the nation's economic problems. To show its displeasure, the Maryland legislature passed a law saying that banks operating in the state that were not chartered by the state—in other words, the national bank—could issue bank notes only on special paper, which the state taxed.

When James McCulloch, the cashier of the Baltimore branch of the Bank of the United States, refused to pay the tax, Maryland took legal action to enforce its law. The United States challenged the constitutionality of the Maryland tax, and in return Maryland disputed the constitutionality of the bank.[1]

MR. CHIEF JUSTICE MARSHALL delivered the opinion of the court.

The constitution of our country, in its most interesting and vital parts, is to be considered; the conflicting powers of the government of the Union and of its members, as marked in that constitution, are to be discussed; and an opinion given, which may essentially influence the great operations of the government. . . .

In discussing this . . . the counsel for the state of Maryland have deemed it of some importance, in the construction of the constitution, to consider that instrument not as emanating from the people, but as the act of sovereign and independent states. The powers of the general government, it has been said, are delegated by the states, who alone are truly sovereign; and must be exercised in subordination to the states, who alone possess supreme dominion.

---

1. The first part of Marshall's opinion deals with whether Congress had the power to create the bank. (See the excerpt in chapter 4.) The second part, excerpted here, deals with the constitutionality of the Maryland tax. Marshall clearly delineates this division in his opinion.

TABLE 6-2 Doctrinal Cycles of Nation-State Relations

Court Era	General Approach Adopted
Marshall Court (1801–1835)	Cooperative federalism (National supremacy)
Taney Court (1835–1864)	Dual federalism
Civil War/Reconstruction Courts (1865–1895)	Cooperative federalism (National supremacy)
Laissez-faire Courts (1896–1936)	Dual federalism (Grounded in laissez-faire philosophy)
Post–New Deal Courts (1937–1975)	Cooperative federalism
Burger Court: *National League of Cities v. Usery* (1976)	Dual federalism (Traditional state functions)
Burger Court: *Garcia v. SAMTA* (1985)	Cooperative federalism
Rehnquist Court/Roberts Court (1972–)	Modified dual federalism (States cannot be treated as administrative units of the federal government)

It would be difficult to sustain this proposition. The convention which framed the constitution was indeed elected by the state legislatures. But the instrument, when it came from their hands, was a mere proposal, without obligation, or pretensions to it. It was reported to the then existing Congress of the United States, with a request that it might "be submitted to a convention of delegates, chosen in each state by the people thereof, under the recommendation of its legislature, for their assent and ratification." This mode of proceeding was adopted; and by the convention, by Congress, and by the state legislatures, the instrument was submitted to the people. They acted upon it in the only manner in which they can act safely, effectively, and wisely, on such a subject, by assembling in convention. It is true, they assembled in their several states—and where else should they have assembled? No political dreamer was ever wild enough to think of breaking down the lines which separate the states, and of compounding the American people into one common mass. Of consequence, when they act, they act in their states. But the measures they adopt do not, on that account, cease to be the measures of the people themselves, or become the measures of the state governments. . . .

The government of the Union, then . . . is, emphatically, and truly, a government of the people. . . .

It is the government of all; its powers are delegated by all; it represents all, and acts for all. Though any one state may be willing to control its operations, no state is willing to allow others to control them. The nation, on those subjects on which it can act, must necessarily bind its component parts. But this question is not left to mere reason; the people have, in express terms, decided it by saying, "this constitution, and the laws of the United States, which shall be made in pursuance thereof," "shall be the supreme law of the land," and by requiring that the members of the state legislatures, and the officers of the executive and judicial departments of the states shall take the oath of fidelity to it. The government of the United States, then, though limited in its powers, is supreme; and its laws, when made in pursuance of the constitution, form the supreme law of the land, "anything in the constitution or laws of any State to the contrary notwithstanding."

Among the enumerated powers, we do not find that of establishing a bank or creating a corporation. But there is no phrase in the instrument which, like the articles of confederation, excludes incidental or implied powers; and which requires that everything granted shall be expressly and minutely described. Even the 10th amendment, which was framed for the purpose of quieting the excessive jealousies which had been excited, omits the word "expressly," and declares only that the powers "not delegated to the United States, nor prohibited to the states, are reserved to the states or to the people;" thus leaving the question, whether the particular power which may become the subject of contest has been delegated to the one government, or prohibited to the other, to depend on a fair construction of the whole instrument. The men who drew and adopted this amendment had experienced the embarrassments resulting from the insertion of this word in the articles of confederation, and probably omitted it to avoid those embarrassments. A constitution, to contain an accurate detail of all the subdivisions of which its great powers will admit, and of all the means by which they may be carried into execution, would partake of a prolixity of a legal code, and could scarcely be embraced by the human mind. It would probably never be understood by the public. Its nature, therefore, requires, that only its great outlines should be marked, its important objects designated, and the minor ingredients which compose those objects be deduced from the nature of the objects themselves. That this idea was entertained by the framers of the American constitution, is not only to be inferred from the nature of the instrument, but from the language. . . .

After this declaration, it can scarcely be necessary to say that the existence of state banks can have no possible influence on the question. No trace is to be found in the constitution of an intention to create a dependence of the government of the Union on those of the states, for the execution of the great powers assigned to it. Its means are adequate to its ends; and on those means alone was it expected to rely for the accomplishment of its ends. To impose on it the necessity of resorting to means which it cannot control, which another government may furnish or withhold, would render its course precarious; the result of its measures uncertain, and create a dependence on other governments, which might disappoint its most important designs and is incompatible with the language of the constitution. But were it otherwise, the choice of means implies a right to choose a national bank in preference to state banks, and Congress alone can make the election.

After the most deliberate consideration, it is the unanimous and decided opinion of this court that the act to incorporate the bank of the United States is a law made in pursuance of the constitution, and is part of the supreme law of the land. . . .

It being the opinion of the court, that the act incorporating the bank is constitutional; and that the power of establishing a branch in the State of Maryland might be properly exercised by the bank itself, we proceed to inquire . . . whether the State of Maryland may, without violating the constitution, tax that branch? . . .

The argument on the part of the State of Maryland, is, not that the States may directly resist a law of Congress, but that they may exercise their acknowledged powers upon it, and that the constitution leaves them this right in the confidence that they will not abuse it.

That the power to tax involves the power to destroy; that the power to destroy may defeat and render useless the power to create; that there is a plain repugnance, in conferring on one government a power to control the constitutional measures of another, which other, with respect to those very measures, is declared to be supreme over that which exerts the control, are propositions not to be denied. But all inconsistencies are to be reconciled by the magic of the word CONFIDENCE. Taxation, it is said, does not necessarily and unavoidably destroy. To carry it to the excess of destruction would be an abuse, to presume which, would banish that confidence which is essential to all government.

But is this a case of confidence? Would the people of any one State trust those of another with a power to control the most insignificant operations of their State government? We know they would not. Why, then, should we suppose that the people of any one State should be willing to trust those of another with a power to control the operations of a government to which they have confided their most important and most valuable interests? In the legislature of the Union alone, are all represented. The legislature of the Union alone, therefore, can be trusted by the people with the power of controlling measures which concern all, in the confidence that it will not be abused. This, then, is not a case of confidence, and we must consider it as it really is.

If we apply the principle for which the State of Maryland contends, to the constitution generally, we shall find it capable of changing totally the character of that instrument. We shall find it capable of arresting all the measures of the government, and of prostrating it at the foot of the States. The American people have declared their constitution, and the laws made in pursuance thereof, to be supreme; but this principle would transfer the supremacy, in fact, to the States.

If the States may tax one instrument, employed by the government in the execution of its powers, they may tax any and every other instrument. They may tax the mail; they may tax the mint; they may tax patent rights; they may tax the papers of the custom-house; they may tax judicial process; they may tax all the means employed by the government, to an excess which would defeat all the ends of government. This was not intended by the American people. They did not design to make their government dependent on the States. . . .

It has also been insisted, that, as the power of taxation in the general and State governments is acknowledged to be concurrent, every argument which would sustain the right of the general government to tax banks chartered by the States, will equally sustain the right of the States to tax banks chartered by the general government.

But the two cases are not on the same reason. The people of all the States have created the general government, and have conferred upon it the general power of taxation. The people of all the States, and the States themselves, are represented in Congress, and, by their representatives, exercise this power. When they tax the chartered institutions of the States, they tax their constituents; and these taxes must be uniform. But, when a State taxes the operations of the government of the United States, it acts upon institutions created, not by their own constituents, but by people over whom they claim no control. It acts upon the measures of a government created by others as well as themselves, for the benefit of others in common with themselves. The difference is that which always exists, and always must exist, between the action of the whole on a part, and the action of a part on the whole—between the laws of a government declared to be supreme, and those of a government which, when in opposition to those laws, is not supreme.

But if the full application of this argument could be admitted, it might bring into question the right of Congress to tax the State banks, and could not prove the right of the States to tax the Bank of the United States.

The court has bestowed on this subject its most deliberate consideration. The result is a conviction that the states have no power, by taxation or otherwise, to retard, impede, burden, or in any manner control the operations of the constitutional laws enacted by Congress to carry into execution the powers vested in the general government. This is, we think, the unavoidable consequence of that supremacy which the constitution has declared.

We are unanimously of opinion that the law passed by the legislature of Maryland, imposing a tax on the Bank of the United States, is unconstitutional and void.

Constitutional scholars regard *McCulloch* as an unequivocal statement of national power over the states. Its strength lies in Marshall's treatment of the three relevant constitutional provisions: the necessary and proper clause, the Tenth Amendment, and the supremacy clause.

First, according to *McCulloch*, the necessary and proper clause permits Congress to pass legislation implied by its enumerated functions, bounded only in this way: "Let the end be legitimate, let it be within the scope of the constitution, and all means which are appropriate, which are plainly adapted to that end, which are not prohibited, but consist with the letter and spirit of the constitution, are constitutional."

Second, because the Tenth Amendment reserves to the states or to the people only power that has not been delegated to Congress (expressly or otherwise), it stands as no significant bar to congressional power. Rather, it simply serves to emphasize that Congress can exercise only those powers listed in Article I or that can be implied from the enumerated powers under a necessary and proper clause analysis. Given Marshall's treatment of the necessary and proper clause, implied powers are quite broad.

Third, the supremacy clause places the national government at the top within its sphere of operation, a sphere that, again according to Marshall's interpretation of the necessary and proper clause, is expansive. If the supremacy clause means anything, it means that no state may "retard, impede, burden, or in any manner control the operations of the constitutional laws enacted by Congress."

Note, too, Marshall's view of the constitutional arrangement; as one would expect, he fully endorsed the position that the charter represents a contract between the people—not the states—and the federal government.

McCulloch's holdings—supporting congressional creation of the bank and negating state taxation of it—were not particularly surprising. Most observers thought the Marshall Court would rule the way it did. It was the chief justice's language and the constitutional theories he offered that sparked a "fierce ideological" debate in a states' rights newspaper, the *Richmond Enquirer*. It began just weeks after *McCulloch* was decided, when a barrage of state rights' advocates wrote in to condemn the ruling. Apparently concerned that if their views took hold "the constitution would be converted into the old confederation," Marshall took an unusual step for a Supreme Court justice: He responded to his critics. Initially, he wrote two articles, carried by a Philadelphia newspaper, defending *McCulloch*. But when an old enemy, Spence Roane, a Virginia Supreme Court judge, launched an

TABLE 6-3   Selected Events Leading to the Civil War

Year	Event	Significance
November 1832	South Carolina ordinance of nullification.	Suggests that states can nullify acts of the federal government and, if necessary, secede from the Union.
December 1832	Jackson issues proclamation warning South Carolina against secession.	Temporarily halts secession crisis, as no state follows South Carolina's lead.
December 1835	Jackson nominates Taney to be chief justice of the United States.	Senate delays confirming Taney, a former slaveholder, until 1836.
May 1854	Congress repeals the Missouri Compromise.	Allows territories to enter the Union with or without slavery.
March 1857	*Scott v. Sandford.*	Increases tension between the North and South, as the former loudly denounces the decision.
November 1860	Lincoln is elected president.	South proclaims that secession is inevitable.
December 1860	South Carolina ordinance of secession.	South Carolina votes to secede from the Union. Within a few weeks, six other states follow suit.

unbridled attack, Marshall responded with nine "elaborate essays," published under the pseudonym "A Friend of the Constitution."[2]

THE TANEY COURT AND THE (RE)EMERGENCE OF STATES' RIGHTS

While Marshall was chief justice of the United States, his view of nation-state relations, not Roane's, prevailed. But their argument foreshadowed a series of events that took place between the 1830s and 1860s, events that would change the country forever (*see Table 6-3*). The first occurred in November 1832. After Congress passed a tariff act that the South thought unfairly burdensome, South Carolina adopted an ordinance that nullified the federal law. Several days later, the state said it was prepared to enforce its nullification by military force and, if necessary, secession from the Union. It is not surprising that South Carolina took the lead in the battle for state sovereignty. The state was the home of John C. Calhoun, a former vice president of the United States and a most outspoken proponent of slavery and states' rights. Indeed, Calhoun is best remembered as an advocate of the doctrine of concurrent majorities, a view that would provide states with a veto over federal policies. This doctrine was the underpinning for South Carolina's ordinance of nullification.

The president, Andrew Jackson, was no great nationalist; rather, he believed that states' rights were not incompatible with those of the federal government. But even he took issue with South Carolina's ordinance. As Table 6-3 illustrates, just a month after the state acted, Jackson issued a proclamation warning the state that it could not secede from the Union. The president's action infuriated South Carolina, but it temporarily averted a major crisis, as no other state attempted to act on the nullification doctrine.

Another event that would have major implications was Chief Justice Marshall's death in 1835 and Roger Taney's ascension to the chief justiceship (*see Box 6-1*). In contrast to Marshall, the Federalist, Taney was a Jacksonian Democrat, a full believer in those ideas espoused by President Jackson, under whom he had served as attorney general, secretary of war, and secretary of the Treasury, and who had appointed him chief justice. The two chief justices' views on the Bank of the United States

2. For records of Marshall's essays, see Gerald Gunther, ed., *John Marshall's Defense of* McCulloch v. Maryland (Stanford: Stanford University Press, 1969).

BOX 6-1   ROGER BROOKE TANEY (1836–1864)

ROGER TANEY was descended on both sides from prominent Maryland families. His mother's family, named Brooke, first arrived in the state in 1650, complete with fox hounds and other trappings of aristocracy. The first Taney arrived about 1660 as an indentured servant but was able to acquire a large amount of property and became a member of the landed Maryland tidewater gentry.

Taney was born March 17, 1777, on his father's tobacco plantation in Calvert County. He was educated in local rural schools and privately tutored by a Princeton student. In 1795, at the age of eighteen, he graduated first in his class from Dickinson College in Pennsylvania.

As his father's second son, Taney was not in line to inherit the family property and so decided on a career in law and politics. For three years, he was an apprentice lawyer in the office of Judge Jeremiah Chase of the Maryland General Court in Annapolis. He was admitted to the bar in 1799.

Taney married Anne Key, daughter of a prominent farmer and the sister of Francis Scott Key, on January 7, 1806. Since Taney was a devout Roman Catholic and his wife an Episcopalian, they agreed to raise their sons as Catholics and their daughters as Episcopalians. The couple had six daughters and a son who died in infancy. In 1855, the year *Scott v. Sandford* came before the Supreme Court, Taney's wife and youngest daughter died of yellow fever.

Taney began his political career as a member of the Federalist Party, serving one term in the Maryland legislature from 1799 to 1800. After being defeated for reelection, he moved from Calvert County to Frederick, where he began to develop a profitable law practice. In 1803 Taney was beaten again in an attempt to return to the House of Delegates. Despite this setback, he began to achieve prominence in the Frederick community as a lawyer and politician. He lived there for twenty years.

In supporting the War of 1812, Taney split with the majority of Maryland Federalists. But in 1816, as a result of shifting political loyalties, he was elected to the state senate and became a dominant figure in party politics. Taney's term expired in 1821. In 1823 he settled in Baltimore, where he continued his successful law practice and political activities. By this time, the Federalist Party had virtually disintegrated, and Taney threw his support to Andrew Jackson's Democrats. He led Jackson's 1828 presidential campaign in Maryland and served as the state's attorney general from 1827 until 1831. At that time, he was named U.S. attorney general for the Jackson administration and left Baltimore for Washington.

It was at this stage in his career that Taney played a leading role in the controversy over the second Bank of the United States, helping to write President Andrew Jackson's message in 1832 vetoing the bank's recharter. The next year, when Treasury secretary William Duane refused to withdraw federal deposits from the national bank, Duane was dismissed and replaced by Taney, who promptly carried out the action.

Taney held the Treasury job for nine months, presiding over a new system of state bank depositories called "pet banks." Jackson, who had delayed as long as he could, was eventually forced to submit Taney's nomination as Treasury secretary to the Senate, which rejected it. Taney was forced to resign.

In 1835 Jackson named Taney to replace aging Supreme Court justice Gabriel Duvall, but the nomination was indefinitely postponed by a close Senate vote. Ten months later, on December 28, Jackson proposed Taney's name again, this time to fill the seat left vacant by the death of Chief Justice John Marshall. To the horror of the Whigs, who considered him much too radical, Taney was confirmed as chief justice on March 15, 1836. He served until his death in Washington, October 12, 1864.

SOURCE: David Savage, *Guide to the U.S. Supreme Court*, 4th ed. (Washington, D.C.: CQ Press, 1997), 939–940.

provide a clear example of their political ideas in action. In 1819 in *McCulloch* Marshall lent his full support to the bank; in 1832 Taney helped write President Jackson's veto message in which he "condemned the Second Bank of the United States" and refused to recharter it.[3]

Had Taney been Jackson's only appointment to the Court, the course of federalism may have remained unchanged. But that was not the case. By 1841 Joseph Story was the only justice remaining from the Marshall Court that decided *McCulloch*. The others, like Taney, were schooled in Jacksonian democracy. It was, R. Kent Newmyer noted, no longer "the Marshall Court. But, then again it was not the age of Marshall."[4] This observation holds on two levels: doctrinally and politically. The Taney Court ushered in substantial legal changes, especially in federal-state relations. Although there is no true Taney corollary to Marshall's opinion in *McCulloch*, examples of his views abound. In many opinions he explicated the doctrine of dual federalism, that national and state government are equivalent sovereigns within their own spheres of operation. Unlike Marshall, he read the Tenth Amendment in a broad sense: that it did, in fact, reserve to the states certain powers and limited the authority of the federal government over them.

Although Jackson had his feuds with the states (as his battle with South Carolina illustrated), his general philosophical approach to federalism and to governance was consistent with popular opinion of that time. The issue of slavery was another matter. It was a cause of acrimony at the Philadelphia convention in 1787, and animosity between the North and the South continued. The country remained united only through compromises, such as the "three-fifths" plan in the U.S. Constitution, by which a slave was considered three-fifths of a person for taxation and representation purposes, and the Missouri Compromise of 1820, which provided a plan for slavery in newly admitted states and the territories. But by the 1850s old battles began heating up, and after California was admitted as a free state, South Carolina once again issued a secession call.

Slavery, therefore, represented the most immediate concern of the day, splitting the nation into two ideological camps. On a different level, it was a symptom of a larger problem: the growing resistance of Southern states to federal supremacy. As the North's criticism of slavery became more strident, calls for secession—or, at the very least, for adoption of Calhoun's "concurrent majority" doctrine—became more widespread in the South.

It was at this critical moment that the Taney-led Supreme Court interceded in both issues—slavery and federal supremacy. When, in the infamous case of *Scott v. Sandford* (1857), the Court planted its feet firmly in the states' rights camp, it may have contributed to the collapse of the Union.

Dred Scott, a slave bought in Missouri, was the property of Dr. John Emerson, an army surgeon. In 1834 Emerson took Scott to the free state of Illinois and in 1836 to the Upper Louisiana territory, which was to remain free of slavery under the Missouri Compromise of 1820. Eventually, Scott and Emerson returned to Missouri, but the doctor died shortly thereafter, leaving title to Scott to his brother-in-law, John Sanford, a citizen of New York.[5] Believing that he no longer had slave status because he had lived on free soil, Scott sued for his freedom in a Missouri state court in 1846. He received a favorable decision at the trial court level but lost in the Missouri Supreme Court. Several years later, Scott and his lawyer decided to try again. This time they brought the case to a federal district court, contending that they had a diversity suit—Scott was a citizen of Missouri and Sanford of New York. Sanford argued that the suit should be dismissed because blacks could not be citizens.

By the time the case arrived at the U.S. Supreme Court for final judgment in 1856, the facts and the political situation had become more complex. In 1854, under mounting pressure, Congress had repealed the Missouri Compromise, replacing it with legislation declaring congressional neutrality on the issue of slavery. Given this new law and the growing tensions between the North and the South and the free and the slave states, some ob-

---

3. R. Kent Newmyer, *The Supreme Court under Marshall and Taney* (New York: Crowell, 1968), 93.
4. Ibid., 94.

5. The party's name, Sanford, was misspelled "Sandford" in the official records.

servers speculated that the Court would decline to decide the case as it had become highly controversial and overtly political.

For at least a year, the Court chose that route. In fact, historians have suggested that after hearing the case the justices wanted simply to affirm the state court's decision, thereby evading the issue of slavery and citizenship for blacks. But when Justice James Wayne insisted that the Court deal with these concerns, the majority of the others—including Chief Justice Taney, a former slaveholder—went along.[6] Waiting until after the presidential election of 1856, a very divided Court (nine separate opinions were written) announced its decision.

At the end of the day, the Court held that Scott was still a slave. In his majority opinion, Taney offered several reasons for this holding.[7] First, although Scott could become a citizen of a state, he could not be considered, in a legal sense, to be a citizen of the United States; the nation's history and the words of the Constitution and other documents foreclosed that possibility. As a result, Scott could not sue in federal courts. As Taney put it, members of the slave class, emancipated or not, were considered from the beginning to be inferior and subordinate beings who "had no rights or privileges but such as those who held the power and the government might choose to grant them."

Second, Congress had no constitutional power to regulate slavery in the territories (in reaching this result, the Court struck down the Missouri Compromise, which already had been repealed by Congress), and the Constitution protects the right to property, a category into which slaves, according to Taney, fell.

Third, the status of slaves depended on the law of the state to which they voluntarily returned, regardless of where they had been. Because the Missouri Supreme Court ruled that Scott was a slave, the U.S. Supreme Court would follow suit.

Scott was decided as the nation was on the verge of collapse *(see Table 6-3)*. Taney's holding, coupled with his vision of the nature of the federal-state relationship, rather than calming matters, probably added fuel to the fire. From the perspective of Northerners and abolitionists, the opinion was among the most evil and heinous ever issued by the Court. Opponents of slavery used the ruling to rally support for their position; they took aim at Taney and the Court, claiming that the institution was so pro-South that it could not be taken seriously. Northern newspapers aroused anti-Court sentiment around the country, with stories about the decision. As one wrote, "The whole slavery agitation was reopened by the proceedings in the Supreme Court today, and that tribunal voluntarily introduced itself into the political arena. . . . Much feeling is excited by this decree, and the opinion is freely expressed that a new element of sectional strife has been wantonly imposed upon the country."[8] Members of Congress lambasted the Court for the raw and unnecessary display of judicial power it had exercised in striking down the Missouri Compromise. In short, historians of the day asserted that "never has the Supreme Court been treated with such ineffable contempt, and never has that tribunal so often cringed before the clamor of the mob."[9] As for the chief justice, his reputation was forever tarnished. Even after his death, Congress resisted commissioning a bust of him to sit beside those of other chief justices in the Capitol's Supreme Court room. At the time, Sen. Charles Sumner said: "I object that an emancipated country should make a bust to the author of the Dred Scott decision," because "the name of Taney is to be hooted down the page of history."[10]

To Southerners, *Scott* was a cause for celebration. Indeed, Taney's notions of slavery and dual federalism appeared in a more energized form just a few years later when South Carolina issued its Declaration of the Causes of Secession. President Abraham Lincoln presented precisely the opposite view—the Marshall approach—in his

6. Melvin I. Urofsky and Paul Finkelman, *A March of Liberty*, 2nd ed. (New York: Oxford University Press, 2002), 392.

7. For additional discussion, see ibid., 384–391, and Walter Ehrlich, "Scott v. Sandford," in *The Oxford Companion to the Supreme Court*, ed. Kermit L. Hall (New York: Oxford University Press, 1992), 760–761.

8. Quoted in Charles Warren, *The Supreme Court in United States History*, vol. 2 (Boston: Little, Brown, 1926), 304.

9. Quoted in Bernard Schwartz, *A History of the Supreme Court* (New York: Oxford University Press, 1993), 154.

10. It was not until 1874 that a bust of Taney was approved and approved "without debate." See Warren, *The Supreme Court in United States History*, 393–394.

1861 inaugural address, but his words were not enough to stop the outbreak of war.

Thus, at its core the Civil War was not only about slavery but also the supremacy of the national government over the states. It was the culmination of the debates between the Federalists and Anti-Federalists, between Marshall and Roane, and so forth. When the Union won the war, it seemed to have also won the debate over the nature of federal-state relations. In the immediate aftermath of the battle, the Court acceded, although not willingly, to congressional power over the defeated region.

DUAL FEDERALISM AND
LAISSEZ-FAIRE ECONOMICS

Did the end of the war and the rise of national supremacy mean that Taney's dual federalism had seen its last days? Indeed, the doctrine remained under wraps for several decades but then resurfaced in a somewhat different form in the courts from the 1890s to the 1930s. The most vivid example of its revival came in *Hammer v. Dagenhart* (1918). Some analysts think that this Court's version of dual federalism differed from Taney's in *Dred Scott*. Do you see the distinction? Or do Justice William R. Day's words echo the sentiment Taney expressed?

Hammer v. Dagenhart

247 U.S. 251 (1918)
http://laws.findlaw.com/US/247/251.html
Vote: 5 (Day, McReynolds, Pitney, Van Devanter, White)
    4 (Brandeis, Clarke, Holmes, McKenna)
Opinion of the Court: Day
Dissenting opinion: Holmes

In the 1880s America entered the industrial age, which was characterized by the unfettered growth of the private-sector economy. The Industrial Revolution changed the United States for the better in countless ways, but it also had a downside. Lacking any significant government controls, many businesses treated their workers less than benevolently. Some forced employees to work more than fourteen hours a day at absurdly low wages and under awful conditions. They also had no qualms about employing children under the age of sixteen, a practice that was bitterly opposed by reform groups, who urged state and federal governments to regulate the practice.

One of the first battles came in 1916 when Congress passed the Child Labor Act that prohibited the shipment in interstate commerce of factory products made by children under the age of fourteen or by children aged fourteen to sixteen who worked more than eight hours a day.[11] The act was supported by numerous progressive groups but opposed by employer associations, including the Executive Committee of Southern Cotton Manufacturers. This group, made up of militant mill owners, was headed by David Clark, who vowed to challenge the constitutionality of the law. To do so, Clark initiated legal action against Fidelity Manufacturing Company.

The case he brought was perfect for the committee's needs. Roland Dagenhart and his two minor sons were employed by Fidelity, a cotton mill in North Carolina. Under state law, both of Dagenhart's sons were permitted to work up to eleven hours a day. Under the new federal act, however, the older boy could work only eight hours, and the younger one could not work at all. Not only were the facts relating to the Dagenharts advantageous, but also Clark secured the cooperation of the company, which had equal disdain for the law, in planning the litigation. One month before the effective date of the law, the company posted the new federal regulations on its door and "explained" to affected employees that they would be unable to continue to work. A week later, having already secured the consent of the Dagenharts and of the factory, the committee's attorneys filed an injunction against Fidelity and William C. Hammer, a U.S. attorney, to prevent enforcement of the law.

The Supreme Court received the case after a federal district court ruled against the law. The Executive Committee argued that Congress had no authority to impose its policies on the states. Solicitor General John W. Davis led the government's defense. One of the great attorneys

---

11. For a discussion of this legal battle, see Lee Epstein, *Conservatives in Court* (Knoxville: University of Tennessee Press, 1985); and Stephen B. Wood, *Constitutional Politics in the Progressive Era* (Chicago: University of Chicago Press, 1968).

Young girls working in a clothing factory. Congressional attempts to curb child labor by taxing the items produced or prohibiting their interstate shipment initially were rebuffed by the Supreme Court.

of the day, Davis made a strong case for the law, although he probably opposed it. Not only did he argue that the regulation of child labor fell squarely within Congress's purview, but also he supplied the Court with data indicating that the states themselves had sought to eliminate such practices. His brief pointed out that only three states placed no age limit on factory employees, and only ten allowed those between the ages of fourteen and sixteen to work.

MR. JUSTICE DAY delivered the opinion of the court.

It is . . . contended that the authority of Congress may be exerted to control interstate commerce in the shipment of child-made goods because of the effect of the circulation of such goods in other states where the evil of this class of labor has been recognized by local legislation, and the right to thus employ child labor has been more rigorously restrained than in the state of production. In other words, that the unfair competition thus engendered may be controlled by closing the channels of interstate commerce to manufacturers in those states where the local laws do not meet what Congress deems to be the more just standard of other states.

There is no power vested in Congress to require the states to exercise their police power so as to prevent possible unfair competition. Many causes may co-operate to give one state, by reason of local laws or conditions, an economic advantage over others. The commerce clause was not intended to give to Congress a general authority to equalize such conditions. In some of the states laws have been passed fixing minimum wages for women; in others the local law regulates the hours of labor of women in various employments. Business done in such states may be at an economic disadvantage when compared with states which have no such regulations; surely, this fact does not give Congress the power to deny transportation in interstate commerce to those who carry on business where the hours of labor and the rate of compensation for women have not been fixed by a standard in use in other states and approved by Congress.

The grant of power to Congress over the subject of interstate commerce was to enable it to regulate such commerce, and not to give it authority to control the states in their exercise of the police power over local trade and manufacture.

The grant of authority over a purely Federal matter was not intended to destroy the local power always existing and carefully reserved to the states in the 10th Amendment to the Constitution. . . .

That there should be limitations upon the right to employ children in mines and factories in the interest of their own and the public welfare, all will admit. That such employment is generally deemed to require regulation is shown by the fact that the brief of counsel states that every state in the Union has a law upon the subject, limiting the right to thus employ children. In North Carolina, the state wherein is located the factory in which the employment was had in the present case, no child under twelve years of age is permitted to work.

. . . The maintenance of the authority of the states over matters purely local is as essential to the preservation of our institutions as is the conservation of the supremacy of the Federal power in all matters intrusted to the nation by the Federal Constitution.

In interpreting the Constitution it must never be forgotten that the nation is made up of states, to which are intrusted the powers of local government. And to them and to the people the powers not expressly delegated to the national government are reserved. The power of the states to regulate their purely internal affairs by such laws as seem wise to the local authority is inherent, and has never been surrendered to the general government. To sustain this statute would not be, in our judgment, a recognition of the lawful exertion of congressional authority over interstate commerce, but would sanction an invasion by the Federal power of the control of a matter purely local in its character, and over which no authority has been delegated to Congress in conferring the power to regulate commerce among the states.

We have neither authority nor disposition to question the motives of Congress in enacting this legislation. The purposes intended must be attained consistently with constitutional limitations, and not by an invasion of the powers of the states. This court has no more important function than that which devolves upon it the obligation to preserve inviolate the constitutional limitations upon the exercise of authority, Federal and state, to the end that each may continue to discharge, harmoniously with the other, the duties intrusted to it by the Constitution.

In our view the necessary effect of this act is, by means of a prohibition against the movement in interstate commerce of ordinary commercial commodities, to regulate the hours of labor of children in factories and mines within the states,—a purely state authority. Thus the act in a twofold sense is repugnant to the Constitution. It not only transcends the authority delegated to Congress over commerce, but also exerts a power as to a purely local matter to which the Federal authority does not extend. The far-reaching result of upholding the act cannot be more plainly indicated than by pointing out that if Congress can thus regulate matters intrusted to local authority by prohibition of the movement of commodities in interstate commerce, all freedom of commerce will be at an end, and the power of the states over local matters may be eliminated, and thus our system of government be practically destroyed.

For these reasons we hold that this law exceeds the constitutional authority of Congress. It follows that the decree of the District Court must be affirmed.

MR. JUSTICE HOLMES, dissenting.

The act does not meddle with anything belonging to the states. They may regulate their internal affairs and their domestic commerce as they like. But when they seek to send their products across the state line they are no longer within their rights. If there were no Constitution and no Congress their power to cross the line would depend upon their neighbors. Under the Constitution such commerce belongs not to the states, but to Congress to regulate. It may carry out its views of public policy whatever indirect effect they may have upon the activities of the states. Instead of being encountered by a prohibitive tariff at her boundaries, the state encounters the public policy of the United States which it is for Congress to express. The public policy of the United States is shaped with a view to the benefit of the nation as a whole. . . . The national welfare as understood by Congress may require a different attitude within its sphere from that of some self-seeking state. It seems to me entirely constitutional for Congress to enforce its understanding by all the means at its command.

The Supreme Court's decision was a total victory for the Executive Committee, but it meant little to the Dagenharts *(see Box 6-2)*. But Justice Day's opinion—a clear endorsement of dual federalism—rested on tenuous grounds. C. Herman Pritchett points out that Day misquoted the Tenth Amendment: It does not contain the word *expressly*.[12] In so doing, Day ignored Marshall's reasoning in *McCulloch*. It was critical to Marshall's interpretation of congressional powers that the word *expressly* did not appear. When Congress considered the Tenth Amendment, one representative proposed to "add the word 'expressly' so as to read 'the powers not expressly delegated by this Constitution.'" James Madison and others objected and the motion was defeated.[13] So Day assumed "a position that was historically inaccurate."[14]

Although this error seemed to undermine Day's logic, a more important question may be this: Was Day's explication of dual federalism the same as Taney's? Many scholars think not; in fact, they argue that *Hammer*—taken in conjunction with other opinions of that Court era—diverges from Taney's philosophy. Taney viewed dual federalism as a way to equalize state and federal power, but the Supreme Court between 1890 and 1930 did not seem to be concerned with the rights of states as states. Rather, the justices were bent on prohibiting any state *or* federal interference with the growth of the nation's booming private-sector economy. They used dual federalism as a vehicle to strike down federal regulation of the sort at issue in *Hammer*. At the same time, the Court limited the ability of states to pass similar legislation under the guise that it would restrict individual liberties. (See chapter 10 for a discussion of limits on state regulatory efforts during this time.) The Court's approach was quite distinct from Taney's. For the Courts from the 1890s through the 1930s, dual federalism and the Tenth Amendment were masks to hide their laissez-faire philosophy and strong support of business.

BOX 6-2   AFTERMATH . . .

HAMMER V. DAGENHART

FIVE YEARS after the Supreme Court's decision in *Hammer v. Dagenhart* striking down the child labor law, a journalist interviewed Reuben Dagenhart, whose father had sued to prevent Congress from interfering with his sons' jobs in a North Carolina cotton mill. Reuben was twenty when he was interviewed. Excerpts follow:

"What benefit . . . did you get out of the suit which you won in the United States Supreme Court?"

"I don't see that I got any benefit. I guess I'd be a lot better off if they hadn't won it.

"Look at me! A hundred and five pounds, a grown man, and no education. I may be mistaken, but I think the years I've put in the cotton mills have stunted my growth. They kept me from getting any schooling. I had to stop school after the third grade and now I need the education I didn't get."

"Just what did you and John get out of that suit then?" he was asked.

"Why, we got some automobile rides when them big lawyers from the North was down here. Oh yes, and they bought both of us a Coca-Cola! That's all we got out of it."

"What did you tell the judge when you were in court?"

"Oh, John and me was never in court. Just Paw was there. John and me was just little kids in short pants. I guess we wouldn't have looked like much in court. . . . We were working in the mill while the case was going on."

Reuben hasn't been to school in years, but his mind has not been idle.

"It would have been a good thing for all the kids in this state if that law they passed had been kept. Of course, they do better now than they used to. You don't see so many babies working in the factories, but you see a lot of them that ought to be going to school."

SOURCE: *Labor*, November 17, 1923, 3, quoted in Leonard F. James, *The Supreme Court in American Life*, 2nd ed. (Glenview, Ill.: Scott, Foresman, 1971), 74.

---

12. C. Herman Pritchett, *Constitutional Law of the Federal System* (Englewood Cliffs, N.J.: Prentice Hall, 1984), 60.

13. Daniel A. Farber and Suzanna Sherry, *A History of the American Constitution*, 2nd ed. (St. Paul: Thomson/West, 2005), 343.

14. Pritchett, *Constitutional Law of the Federal System*, 60–61.

THE (RE)EMERGENCE OF NATIONAL SUPREMACY: COOPERATIVE FEDERALISM

Despite the Court's language, the days of dual federalism were numbered. Amid increasing pressure for change, including President Franklin Roosevelt's Court-packing scheme, came the famous "switch in time that saved nine" and with it the demise of broad interpretations of the Tenth Amendment (see chapter 7). Although this process began in 1937, the death knell rang most loudly with the decision in *United States v. Darby Lumber* (1941).[15] As you read Chief Justice Harlan Fiske Stone's opinion, think about Marshall's in *McCulloch*. Are they making similar claims, or can you detect distinctions?

United States v. Darby Lumber

312 U.S. 100 (1941)
http://laws.findlaw.com/US/312/100.html
Vote: 8 (Black, Douglas, Frankfurter, Hughes, Murphy, Reed, Roberts, Stone)
      0
Opinion of the Court: Stone

In 1938 Congress, under its power to regulate interstate commerce, enacted an important piece of New Deal legislation, the Fair Labor Standards Act (FLSA). It provided that all employers "engaged in interstate commerce, or in the production of goods for that commerce" must pay all their employees a minimum wage of twenty-five cents per hour and not permit employees to work longer than forty-four hours per week without paying them one and one-half times their regular pay. In November 1939 the federal government sought and obtained an indictment against Fred W. Darby for violating the FLSA. The indictment alleged that Darby, the owner of a lumber company, was engaged in the production and manufacturing of goods shipped out of state and that he had not abided by either of the FLSA's major pay requirements.

15. See Joseph F. Kobylka, "The Court, Justice Blackmun, and Federalism," *Creighton Law Review* 19 (1985–1986): 21.

Darby did not dispute the charges. Rather, invoking the logic of *Hammer,* his brief argued: "The Fair Labor Standards Act . . . is an unconstitutional attempt to regulate conditions in production of goods and commodities and it can not be sustained as a regulation of interstate commerce within the delegated power of Congress under the commerce clause. It violated the Tenth Amendment."

The government responded more pragmatically than legally, stating:

State legislators, Congressional committees, federal commissions, and businessmen over a period of time have realized that no state, acting alone, could require labor standards substantially higher than those obtained in other states whose producers and manufacturers competed in the interstate market.

The reiterated conclusion that the individual states were helpless gained added force during the prolonged economic depression of the 1930's. The . . . National Industrial Recovery Act . . . and the Fair Labor Standards Act itself each reflect a great volume of testimony adduced at congressional hearings and elsewhere to the effect that employers with lower labor standards possess an unfair advantage in interstate competition, and that only the national government could deal with the problem.

The lumber industry, the government asserted, well illustrated "the inability of the particular states to ensure adequate labor standards; over 57 percent of the lumber produced enters into interstate or foreign commerce from 45 of the states."

MR. JUSTICE STONE delivered the opinion of the Court.

The motive and purpose of the present regulation are plainly to make effective the Congressional conception of public policy that interstate commerce should not be made the instrument of competition in the distribution of goods produced under substandard labor conditions, which competition is injurious to the commerce and to the states from and to which the commerce flows. The motive and purpose of a regulation of interstate commerce are matters for the legislative judgment upon the exercise of which the Constitution places no restriction and over which the courts are given no control. . . . Whatever their motive and purpose, regulations of commerce which do not infringe some constitutional prohibition are within the plenary power conferred on Congress by the Commerce Clause. Subject only to that limitation, presently to be considered, we conclude that the prohibition of the shipment interstate of goods produced under the forbidden substandard labor conditions is within the constitutional authority of Congress. . . .

Our conclusion is unaffected by the Tenth Amendment which provides: "The powers not delegated to the United States by the Constitution nor prohibited by it to the states are reserved to the states respectively or to the people." The amendment states but a truism that all is retained which has not been surrendered. There is nothing in the history of its adoption to suggest that it was more than declaratory of the relationship between the national and state governments as it had been established by the Constitution before the amendment or that its purpose was other than to allay fears that the new national government might seek to exercise powers not granted, and that the states might not be able to exercise fully their reserved powers.

From the beginning and for many years the amendment has been construed as not depriving the national government of authority to resort to all means for the exercise of a granted power which are appropriate and plainly adapted to the permitted end.

Reversed.

Justice Stone's opinion in *Darby Lumber* brought the Court full circle, from Marshall's nationalism to Taney's dual federalism and back. Not only did *Darby Lumber* explicitly overrule *Hammer* and uphold the FLSA, but also it gutted the Tenth Amendment, declaring it to be but a truism.

For the next thirty-five years dual federalism was out, and Stone's cooperative federalism was in. Under this doctrine, at least theoretically, the various levels of government shared policy-making responsibilities. In practice it meant, as Stone's opinion implies, that the national government took the lead in formulating policy goals, which it expected state and local officials to implement. Tremendous changes in government followed. As the federal government took advantage of its new constitutional freedom—creating more and more programs and projects covering all aspects of American life—it began to account for greater and greater percentages of government spending. By the 1960s the federal government reigned supreme.

Although federal supremacy was a fact of American life, it was not universally supported. During the 1950s and 1960s, for example, leaders of the southern states vehemently opposed federal actions to integrate schools and public facilities. Other opposition was more national in scope. President Richard Nixon lamented the tremendous growth of the federal government and the concomitant demise of states' authority over their own affairs. Advocating a "new federalism" policy, Nixon pledged to return more decision-making authority to the states. Nixon's new federalism, however, was not the dual federalism of earlier generations. He may have wanted to give the states and localities greater authority in certain policy arenas, but he was not one to argue that the federal government and the states were "co-equal sovereigns." Moreover, issues of federalism were never the most important items on the president's agenda, particularly when it came to nominations to the Supreme Court. Nixon looked for jurists who would be inclined toward judicial restraint generally and to a law and order posture, in particular.

When "Nixon's" Supreme Court handed down its decision in ***National League of Cities v. Usery*** (1976), therefore, it took many legal scholars by surprise. A greater concern with states' rights was certainly within the realm of the politics of the day, but the Court took that concern to a rather extreme level.

To understand why the *National League* ruling was so surprising and controversial, let us first consider the facts of the case. At issue was the Federal Labor Standards Act, which the Court had upheld in 1941 in *United States v. Darby Lumber.* Since then, Congress had amended the act to cover public employees. Those amendments, along with other attempts to regulate state employment, were themselves the subject of several major Supreme Court rulings. Consistent with the philosophy of cooperative federalism expressed in *Darby,* the justices generally upheld the regulations.[16]

National League crystallized when in 1974 Congress once again expanded the scope of the FLSA, this time

---

16. See, for example, *Maryland v. Wirtz* (1968) and *Fry v. United States* (1975).

bringing under its reach virtually all state public employees, who were excluded in the original legislation. As a result, various cities and states and two organizations representing their collective interests—the National League of Cities and the National Governors' Conference—challenged the constitutionality of the new amendments. In particular, they argued that the amendments represented a "collision" between federal expansion and states' rights in violation of the Tenth Amendment. In his opinion for the majority, consisting of the four Nixon appointees, plus Justice Potter Stewart, Justice William Rehnquist invoked the underlying "dual federalism" logic of cases like *Hammer* and *Scott* to hold for the National League of Cities. He suggested that the Court had "repeatedly recognized that there are attributes of sovereignty attaching to every state government which may not be impaired by Congress, not because Congress may lack an affirmative grant of legislative authority to reach the matter, but because the Constitution prohibits it from exercising the authority in that manner."

Yet Rehnquist's opinion did not and could not stop there because he needed to address this critical question: Where is the line separating constitutional from unconstitutional federal intrusions into state business? He provided one answer when he wrote: "Congress may not exercise that power so as to force directly upon the States its choices as to how essential decisions regarding the conduct of integral governmental functions are to be made."

To be sure, the majority believed that "[o]ne undoubted attribute of state sovereignty is the States' power to determine the wages which shall be paid to those whom they employ in order to carry out their governmental functions." That is why these five justices held for the National League of Cities. But were there other functions so "essential to [the] separate and independent existence of the states" that Congress could not "abrogate the States' otherwise plenary authority to make them"? While the Court did not clearly delineate these functions, it did provide some examples of activities outside congressional authority and within the area of "traditional operations of state and local governments, including fire-fighting, police protection, sanitation, public health, and parks and recreation."[17]

In his concurrence, Justice Harry A. Blackmun argued that the Court was adopting a moderate "balancing approach" to federal-state relations. But others saw it quite differently, and *National League* provoked numerous scholarly articles. Many agreed with points raised by Justice William Brennan's dissenting opinion in which he criticized the Court for elevating the Tenth Amendment and for reasserting the "discredited" doctrine of dual federalism. Others focused on the "uncertainties raised by the ruling." In particular, what would the justices define as "essential to the separate and independent existence of the states," beyond firefighting, police protection, sanitation, and so forth? This was not a mere academic question: Between 1976 and 1978 litigants filed numerous cases asking the Court to address it. The Court's response was to pull back from its ruling in *National League*, little by little chipping away at its central principles.[18]

In theory, *National League* remained on the books as good law, at least until 1985. In *Garcia v. San Antonio Metropolitan Transit Authority*, the justices officially overruled *National League*.

Garcia v. San Antonio Metropolitan Transit Authority

469 U.S. 528 (1985)
http://laws.findlaw.com/US/469/528.html
Oral arguments may be found at: http://www.oyez.org
Vote: 5 (Blackmun, Brennan, Marshall, Stevens, White)
    4 (Burger, O'Connor, Powell, Rehnquist)
Opinion of the Court: Blackmun
Dissenting opinions: Powell, O'Connor, Rehnquist

Garcia was virtually a carbon copy of *National League*. Once again litigation centered on amendments to the

---

17. Kobylka, "The Court, Justice Blackmun, and Federalism," 24–25.
18. See, for example, *Hodel v. Virginia Surface Mining & Reclamation Association* (1981), *United Transportation Union v. Long Island Rail Road* (1982), *Federal Energy Regulatory Commission v. Mississippi* (1982), and *Equal Employment Opportunity Commission v. Wyoming* (1983).

FLSA that required states to pay public employees minimum wages and overtime. The facts, however, were a bit more complicated.

The San Antonio Transit System (SATS) began operations in 1959. For almost a decade SATS was a money-making venture, but by 1969 it was operating at a loss and turned to the federal government for assistance. The federal Urban Mass Transit Administration (UMTA) provided a $4 million grant. In 1978 the city replaced SATS with SAMTA (San Antonio Metropolitan Transit Authority), and federal grants continued to subsidize it. Between 1970 and 1980 the transit system received more than $51 million, or 40 percent of its costs, from the federal government. The case started in 1979 when, in response to a specific inquiry about the applicability of the FLSA to employees of SAMTA, the Department of Labor issued an opinion holding that SAMTA must abide by the act's wage provisions. SAMTA filed a challenge to the department's holding, and Joe G. Garcia and other SAMTA employees, in turn, initiated a suit against their employer for overtime pay.

When the case and a companion, *Donovan v. San Antonio Metropolitan Transit Authority*, reached the U.S. Supreme Court, SAMTA relied heavily on *National League*. SAMTA argued that "transit is a traditional [city] function" and that, as the operator of that function, it was not covered by FLSA amendments. The U.S. government and Garcia countered by arguing that *National League* was not necessarily applicable. In their view, application of the FLSA to public transit did not violate the Tenth Amendment because (1) operation of a transit system is not a traditional government function, and (2) operation of a transit system is not a core government function that must be exempted from federal commerce power legislation to preserve the states' independence.

JUSTICE BLACKMUN delivered the opinion of the Court.

We revisit in these cases an issue raised in *National League of Cities v. Usery* (1976). In that litigation, this Court, by a sharply divided vote, ruled that the Commerce Clause does not empower Congress to enforce the minimum-wage and overtime provisions of the Fair Labor Standards Act

(FLSA) against the States "in areas of traditional government functions." Although *National League of Cities* supplied some examples of "traditional governmental functions," it did not offer a general explanation of how a "traditional" function is to be distinguished from a "nontraditional" one. Since then, federal and state courts have struggled with the task, thus imposed, of identifying a traditional function for purposes of state immunity under the Commerce Clause.

In the present cases, a Federal District Court concluded that municipal ownership and operation of a mass-transit system is a traditional governmental function and thus, under *National League of Cities*, is exempt from the obligations imposed by the FLSA. Faced with the identical question, three Federal Courts of Appeals and one state appellate court have reached the opposite conclusion.

Our examination of this "function" standard applied in these and other cases over the last eight years now persuades us that the attempt to draw the boundaries of state regulatory immunity in terms of "traditional governmental function" is not only unworkable but is also inconsistent with established principles of federalism and, indeed, with those very federalism principles on which *National League of Cities* purported to rest. That case, accordingly, is overruled. . . .

The central theme of *National League of Cities* was that the States occupy a special position in our constitutional system and that the scope of Congress' authority under the Commerce Clause must reflect that position. Of course, the Commerce Clause by its specific language does not provide any special limitation on Congress' actions with respect to the States. It is equally true, however, that the text of the Constitution provides the beginning rather than the final answer to every inquiry into questions of federalism, for "[b]ehind the words of the constitutional provisions are postulates which limit and control." *National League of Cities* reflected the general conviction that the Constitution precludes "the National Government [from] devour[ing] the essentials of state sovereignty." In order to be faithful to the underlying federal premises of the Constitution, courts must look for the "postulates which limit and control."

What has proved problematic is not the perception that the Constitution's federal structure imposes limitations on the Commerce Clause, but rather the nature and content of those limitations. One approach to defining the limits on Congress' authority to regulate the States under the Commerce Clause is to identify certain underlying elements of political sovereignty that are deemed essential to the States' "separate and independent existence." This approach obviously underlay the Court's use of the "traditional governmental function" concept in *National League of Cities.* It also has led to the separate requirement that the challenged federal statute "address matters that are indisputably 'attribute[s] of state sovereignty.'" In *National League of Cities* itself, for example, the Court concluded that decisions by a State concerning the wages and hours of its employees are an "undoubted attribute of state sovereignty." The opinion did not explain what aspects of such decisions made them such an "undoubted attribute," and the Court since then has remarked on the uncertain scope of the concept. The point of the inquiry, however, has remained to single out particular features of a State's internal governance that are deemed to be intrinsic parts of state sovereignty.

We doubt that courts ultimately can identify principled constitutional limitations on the scope of Congress' Commerce Clause powers over the States merely by relying on a priori definitions of state sovereignty. In part, this is because of the elusiveness of objective criteria for "fundamental" elements of state sovereignty, a problem we have witnessed in the search for "traditional governmental functions." There is, however, a more fundamental reason: the sovereignty of the States is limited by the Constitution itself. A variety of sovereign powers, for example, are withdrawn from the States by Article I, §10. Section 8 of the same Article works an equally sharp contraction of state sovereignty by authorizing Congress to exercise a wide range of legislative powers and (in conjunction with the Supremacy Clause of Article VI) to displace contrary state legislation. . . .

The States unquestionably do "retai[n] a significant measure of sovereign authority." They do so, however, only to the extent that the Constitution has not divested them of their original powers and transferred those powers to the Federal Government. In the words of James Madison to the Members of the First Congress: "Interference with the power of the States was no constitutional criterion of the power of Congress. If the power was not given, Congress could not exercise it; if given, they might exercise it, although it should interfere with the laws, or even the Constitution of the states." . . .

As a result, to say that the Constitution assumes the continued role of the States is to say little about the nature of that role. Only recently, this Court recognized that the purpose of the constitutional immunity recognized in *National League of Cities* is not to preserve "a sacred province of state autonomy." With rare exceptions, like the guarantee, in Article IV, §3, of state territorial integrity, the Constitution does not carve out express elements of state sovereignty that Congress may not employ its delegated powers to displace. . . . The power of the Federal Government is a "power to be respected" as well, and the fact that the States remain sovereign as to all powers not vested in Congress or denied them by the Constitution offers no guidance about where the frontier between state and federal power lies. In short, we have no license to employ freestanding conceptions of state sovereignty when measuring congressional authority under the Commerce Clause. . . .

Insofar as the present cases are concerned, then, we need go no further than to state that we perceive nothing in the overtime and minimum-wage requirements of the FLSA, as applied to SAMTA, that is destructive of state sovereignty or violative of any constitutional provision. SAMTA faces nothing more than the same minimum-wage and overtime obligations that hundreds of thousands of other employers, public as well as private, have to meet.

In these cases, the status of public mass transit simply underscores the extent to which the structural protections of the Constitution insulate the States from federally imposed burdens. When Congress first subjected state mass-transit systems to FLSA obligations in 1966, and when it expanded those obligations in 1974, it simultaneously provided extensive funding for state and local mass transit through UMTA. In the two decades since its enactment, UMTA has provided over $22 billion in mass-transit aid to States and localities. In 1983 alone, UMTA funding amounted to $3.7 billion. . . . In short, Congress has not simply placed a financial burden on the shoulders of States and localities that operate mass-transit systems, but has provided substantial countervailing financial assistance as well, assistance that may leave individual mass-transit systems better off than they would have been had Congress never intervened at all in the area. Congress' treatment of public mass transit reinforces our conviction that the national political process systematically protects States from the risk of having their functions in that area handicapped by Commerce Clause regulation.

This analysis makes clear that Congress' action in affording SAMTA employees the protections of the wage and hour provisions of the FLSA contravened no affirmative limit on Congress' power under the Commerce Clause. The judgment of the District Court therefore must be reversed.

Of course, we continue to recognize that the States occupy a special and specific position in our constitutional system and that the scope of Congress' authority under the Commerce Clause must reflect that position. But the principal and basic limit on the federal commerce power is that inherent in all congressional action—the built-in restraints that our system provides through state participation in federal governmental action. The political process ensures that laws that unduly burden the States will not be promulgated. In the factual setting of these cases the internal safeguards of the political process have performed as intended.

These cases do not require us to identify or define what affirmative limits the constitutional structure might impose on federal action affecting the States under the Commerce Clause. . . .

Though the separate concurrence providing the fifth vote in *National League of Cities* was "not untroubled by certain possible implications" of the decision, the Court in that case attempted to articulate affirmative limits on the Commerce Clause power in terms of core governmental functions and fundamental attributes of state sovereignty. But the model of democratic decisionmaking the Court there identified underestimated, in our view, the solicitude of the national political process for the continued vitality of the States. Attempts by other courts since then to draw guidance from this model have proved it both impracticable and doctrinally barren. In sum, in *National League of Cities* the Court tried to repair what did not need repair.

We do not lightly overrule recent precedent. We have not hesitated, however, when it has become apparent that a prior decision has departed from a proper understanding of congressional power under the Commerce Clause. Due respect for the reach of congressional power within the federal system mandates that we do so now.

National League of Cities v. Usery (1976) is overruled. The judgment of the District Court is reversed, and these cases are remanded to that court for further proceedings consistent with this opinion.

It is so ordered.

JUSTICE O'CONNOR, with whom JUSTICE POWELL and JUSTICE REHNQUIST join, dissenting.

The Court today surveys the battle scene of federalism and sounds a retreat. . . . I would prefer to hold the field and, at the very least, render a little aid to the wounded. . . . I . . . write separately to note my fundamental disagreement with the majority's views of federalism and the duty of this Court.

The Court overrules *National League of Cities v. Usery* (1976) on the grounds that it is not "faithful to the role of federalism in a democratic society." *National League of Cities* is held to be inconsistent with this narrow view of federalism because it attempts to protect only those fundamental aspects of state sovereignty that are essential to the States' separate and independent existence, rather than protecting all state activities "equally."

In my view, federalism cannot be reduced to the weak "essence" distilled by the majority today. There is more to federalism than the nature of the constraints that can be imposed on the States in "the realm of authority left open to them by the Constitution." The central issue of federalism, of course, is whether any realm is left open to the States by the Constitution—whether any area remains in which a State may act free of federal interference. "The issue . . . is whether the federal system has any *legal* substance, any core of constitutional right that courts will enforce." The true "essence" of federalism is that the States as States have legitimate interests which the National Government is bound to respect even though its laws are supreme. If federalism so conceived and so carefully cultivated by the Framers of our Constitution is to remain meaningful, this Court cannot abdicate its constitutional responsibility to oversee the Federal Government's compliance with its duty to respect the legitimate interests of the States.

Due to the emergence of an integrated and industrialized national economy, this Court has been required to examine and review a breathtaking expansion of the powers of Congress. In doing so the Court correctly perceived that the Framers of our Constitution intended Congress to have sufficient power to address national problems. . . .

It is worth recalling the cited passage in *McCulloch v. Maryland* (1819) that lies at the source of the recent expansion of the commerce power. "Let the end be legitimate, let it be within the scope of the constitution," Chief Justice

Marshall said, "and all means which are appropriate, which are plainly adapted to that end, which are not prohibited, but consist with the letter *and spirit* of the constitution, are constitutional" (emphasis added). The *spirit* of the Tenth Amendment, of course, is that the States will retain their integrity in a system in which the laws of the United States are nevertheless supreme.

It is not enough that the "end be legitimate"; the means to that end chosen by Congress must not contravene the spirit of the Constitution. Thus many of this Court's decisions acknowledge that the means by which national power is exercised must take into account concerns for state autonomy. . . . The operative language of these cases varies, but the underlying principle is consistent: state autonomy is a relevant factor in assessing the means by which Congress exercises its powers. . . .

. . . With the abandonment of *National League of Cities,* all that stands between the remaining essentials of state sovereignty and Congress is the latter's underdeveloped capacity for self-restraint. . . .

It has been difficult for this Court to craft bright lines defining the scope of the state autonomy protected by *National League of Cities.* Such difficulty is to be expected whenever constitutional concerns as important as federalism and the effectiveness of the commerce power come into conflict. Regardless of the difficulty, it is and will remain the duty of this Court to reconcile these concerns in the final instance. That the Court shuns the task today by appealing to the "essence of federalism" can provide scant comfort to those who believe our federal system requires something more than a unitary, centralized government. I would not shirk the duty acknowledged by *National League of Cities* and its progeny, and I share Justice Rehnquist's belief that this Court will in time again assume its constitutional responsibility.

I respectfully dissent.

With his opinion in *Garcia,* Justice Blackmun once again buried dual federalism and returned the Court to its posture in *Darby Lumber.*

DUAL FEDERALISM RETURNS
IN MODIFIED FORM

Given the cyclical history of debates over the proper form of American federalism, it should not be surprising that *Garcia* did not settle the issue. Justice Sandra Day O'Connor's prediction in *Garcia* that the principles of *National League of Cities* would return one day "to command the support of a majority of the Court" proved to be not entirely accurate but not entirely wrong either. In the early 1990s, five members left the Court, including William Brennan and Thurgood Marshall, two members of the five-justice *Garcia* majority. William Rehnquist, a strong supporter of state authority, assumed the chief justiceship. New members, appointed by Presidents Ronald Reagan and George H. W. Bush, sufficiently changed the makeup of the Court to prompt observers to look for a rekindling of the federalism debate.

The first indication that the balance of power had shifted occurred in **New York v. United States** (1992). At issue was the 1980 Low-Level Radioactive Waste Policy Act, a federal law designed to confront the difficult problem of disposing of radioactive waste from private industry, government, hospitals, and research institutions. The act provided incentives for state cooperation with certain waste disposal options, but states that failed to participate were required to "take title" to the radioactive waste generated inside the state and be responsible for it. A six-justice majority struck down the "take title" portion of the law. Justice O'Connor, writing for the Court, explained that although the federal government was free to use its spending power to offer incentives for state participation, it could not direct the states to provide for the disposal of radioactive waste generated within their borders. O'Connor's words were direct and hard hitting:

Some truths are so basic that, like the air around us, they are easily overlooked. . . . States are not mere political subdivisions of the United States. State governments are neither regional offices nor administrative agencies of the Federal Government. The positions occupied by state officials appear nowhere on the Federal Government's most detailed organization chart. The Constitution instead "leaves to the several States a residuary and inviolable sovereignty." . . . Whatever the outer limits of that sovereignty may be, one thing is clear: The Federal Government may not compel the States to enact or administer a federal regulatory program.

O'Connor's opinion was not a complete return to the logic of *National League of Cities,* but she did give a rather narrow reading to *Garcia*. Under her interpretation, *Garcia* simply held the states to the same standards as private employers. But when a problem is "uniquely governmental," as is the disposal of radioactive waste, the Tenth Amendment prohibits Congress from compelling the states to act, from "commandeering state legislatures."

The Court's decision in *New York* signaled that those sympathetic to the interests of the states now formed a majority. Five years later the same majority ruled when the Court handed down its decision in *Printz v. United States* (1997), which centered on the federal government's response to another difficult problem of society: violence and firearms.

Printz v. United States

521 U.S. 898 (1997)
http://laws.findlaw.com/US/521/898.html
Oral arguments may be found at: http://www.oyez.org
Vote: 5 (Kennedy, O'Connor, Rehnquist, Scalia, Thomas)
    4 (Breyer, Ginsburg, Souter, Stevens)
Opinion of the Court: Scalia
Concurring opinions: O'Connor, Thomas
Dissenting opinions: Breyer, Souter, Stevens

The Gun Control Act of 1968 forbids firearms dealers to transfer firearms to convicted felons, unlawful users of controlled substances, fugitives from justice, persons judged to be mentally defective, persons dishonorably discharged from the military, persons who have renounced their citizenship, and persons who have committed certain acts of domestic violence. In 1993 Congress amended the Gun Control Act with the Brady Handgun Violence Prevention Act. This act required the attorney general to establish by November 30, 1998, a national database allowing for instant background checks of those attempting to buy handguns. In the interim, the Brady Act allowed gun dealers to sell a firearm to buyers who already possessed a state handgun permit or who lived in states with existing instant background check systems.

In states where these two alternatives were not possible, the act required certain actions by the local chief law enforcement officer (CLEO). It mandated that CLEOs re-

James S. Brady, former press secretary for President Reagan, who was wounded during an assassination attempt on the president, listens as President Clinton speaks before signing the Brady Bill gun control legislation in 1993.

ceive firearm purchase forms from gun dealers and make a reasonable effort within five business days to verify that the proposed sale was not to a person unqualified under the law. Essentially this required local CLEOs to conduct a background check of all potential gun purchasers. When CLEOs determined that proposed sales would violate the law, they were required upon request to submit a written report to the proposed purchasers stating the reasons for that determination. If CLEOs found no reason for objecting to a sale, they were required to destroy all records pertaining to it. These mandated responsibilities were to terminate in 1998 once the federal instant background check program became operative.

Jay Printz, sheriff of Ravalli County, Montana, and Richard Mack, sheriff of Graham County, Arizona, filed separate suits challenging the constitutionality of the Brady Act's interim provisions. They argued that the federal government had no authority to command state or local officials to administer a federal program. In each case the district court declared the act unconstitutional to the extent that it forced state officers to carry out federal policies. Other provisions of the law were left untouched. The court of appeals disagreed, finding no provisions of the law to violate the Constitution. The Supreme Court consolidated the two cases and accepted them for review. Although the decision immediately affected only a temporary provision that was scheduled to become inoperative in 1998, the constitutional issue involved is a significant one.

JUSTICE SCALIA delivered the opinion of the Court.

The question presented in these cases is whether certain interim provisions of the Brady Handgun Violence Prevention Act, commanding state and local law enforcement officers to conduct background checks on prospective handgun purchasers and to perform certain related tasks, violate the Constitution. . . .

. . . [I]t is apparent that the Brady Act purports to direct state law enforcement officers to participate, albeit only temporarily, in the administration of a federally enacted regulatory scheme. Regulated firearms dealers are required to forward Brady Forms not to a federal officer or employee, but to the CLEOs, whose obligation to accept those forms is implicit in the duty imposed upon them to make "reasonable efforts" within five days to determine whether the sales reflected in the forms are lawful. While the CLEOs are subjected to no federal requirement that they prevent the sales determined to be unlawful (it is perhaps assumed that their state-law duties will require prevention or apprehension), they are empowered to grant, in effect, waivers of the federally prescribed 5-day waiting period for handgun purchases by notifying the gun dealers that they have no reason to believe the transactions would be illegal.

The petitioners here object to being pressed into federal service, and contend that congressional action compelling state officers to execute federal laws is unconstitutional. Be-

cause there is no constitutional text speaking to this precise question, the answer to the CLEOs' challenge must be sought in historical understanding and practice, in the structure of the Constitution, and in the jurisprudence of this Court. . . .

Petitioners contend that compelled enlistment of state executive officers for the administration of federal programs is, until very recent years at least, unprecedented. The Government contends, to the contrary, that "the earliest Congresses enacted statutes that required the participation of state officials in the implementation of federal laws." The Government's contention demands our careful consideration, since early congressional enactments "provid[e] 'contemporaneous and weighty evidence' of the Constitution's meaning." . . . Conversely if, as petitioners contend, earlier Congresses avoided use of this highly attractive power, we would have reason to believe that the power was thought not to exist. . . .

. . . The only early federal law the Government has brought to our attention that imposed duties on state executive officers is the Extradition Act of 1793, which required the "executive authority" of a State to cause the arrest and delivery of a fugitive from justice upon the request of the executive authority of the State from which the fugitive had fled. That was in direct implementation, however, of the Extradition Clause of the Constitution itself. . . .

To complete the historical record, we must note that there is not only an absence of executive-commandeering statutes in the early Congresses, but there is an absence of them in our later history as well, at least until very recent years. The Government points to the Act of August 3, 1882, which enlisted state officials "to take charge of the local affairs of immigration in the ports within such State, and to provide for the support and relief of such immigrants therein landing as may fall into distress or need of public aid"; to inspect arriving immigrants and exclude any person found to be a "convict, lunatic, idiot," or indigent; and to send convicts back to their country of origin "without compensation." The statute did not, however, *mandate* those duties, but merely empowered the Secretary of the Treasury "to *enter into contracts* with such State . . . officers as *may be designated* for that purpose *by the governor* of any State." (Emphasis added.). . . .

The Government points to a number of federal statutes enacted within the past few decades that require the participation of state or local officials in implementing federal regulatory schemes. Some of these are connected to federal funding measures, and can perhaps be more accurately described as conditions upon the grant of federal funding than as mandates to the States; others, which require only the provision of information to the Federal Government, do not involve the precise issue before us here, which is the forced participation of the States' executive in the actual administration of a federal program. . . .

The constitutional practice we have examined above tends to negate the existence of the congressional power asserted here, but is not conclusive. We turn next to consideration of the structure of the Constitution, to see if we can discern among its "essential postulate[s]," a principle that controls the present cases.

It is incontestible that the Constitution established a system of "dual sovereignty." Although the States surrendered many of their powers to the new Federal Government, they retained "a residuary and inviolable sovereignty," The Federalist No. 39 (J. Madison). . . . Residual state sovereignty was also implicit, of course, in the Constitution's conferral upon Congress of not all governmental powers, but only discrete, enumerated ones, which implication was rendered express by the Tenth Amendment's assertion that "[t]he powers not delegated to the United States by the Constitution, nor prohibited by it to the States, are reserved to the States respectively, or to the people."

The Framers' experience under the Articles of Confederation had persuaded them that using the States as the instruments of federal governance was both ineffectual and provocative of federal-state conflict. . . . [T]he Framers rejected the concept of a central government that would act upon and through the States, and instead designed a system in which the state and federal governments would exercise concurrent authority over the people—who were, in Hamilton's words, "the only proper objects of government," The Federalist No. 15. We have set forth the historical record in more detail elsewhere, see *New York v. United States* [1992] and need not repeat it here. It suffices to repeat the conclusion: "The Framers explicitly chose a Constitution that confers upon Congress the power to regulate individuals, not States." . . .

We have thus far discussed the effect that federal control of state officers would have upon the first element of the "double security" alluded to by Madison: the division of power between State and Federal Governments. It would also have an effect upon the second element: the separation and equilibration of powers between the three branches of the Federal Government itself. The Constitution does not leave to speculation who is to administer the laws enacted by Congress; the President, it says, "shall take Care that the Laws be faithfully executed," personally and through officers whom he appoints (save for such inferior officers as Congress may authorize to be appointed by the "Courts of Law" or by "the Heads of Departments" who are themselves presidential appointees). The Brady Act effectively transfers this responsibility to thousands of CLEOs in the 50 States, who are left to implement the program without meaningful Presidential control (if indeed meaningful Presidential control is possible without the power to appoint and remove). The insistence of the Framers upon unity in the Federal Executive—to insure both vigor and accountability—is well known. That unity would be shattered, and the power of the President would be subject to reduction, if Congress could act as effectively without the President as with him, by simply requiring state officers to execute its laws.

The dissent of course resorts to the last, best hope of those who defend *ultra vires* congressional action, the Necessary and Proper Clause. It reasons that the power to regulate the sale of handguns under the Commerce Clause, coupled with the power to "make all Laws which shall be necessary and proper for carrying into Execution the foregoing Powers," Art. I, §8, conclusively establishes the Brady Act's constitutional validity, because the Tenth Amendment imposes no limitations on the exercise of *delegated* powers but merely prohibits the exercise of powers "*not* delegated to the United States." What destroys the dissent's Necessary and Proper Clause argument, however, is not the Tenth Amendment but the Necessary and Proper Clause itself. When a "La[w] . . . for carrying into Execution" the Commerce Clause violates the principle of state sovereignty reflected in the various constitutional provisions we mentioned earlier, it is not a "La[w] . . . *proper* for carrying into Execution the Commerce Clause," and is thus, in the words of The Federalist, "merely [an] ac[t] of usurpation" which "deserve[s] to be treated as such." The Federalist No. 33 (A. Hamilton). We in fact answered the dissent's Necessary and Proper Clause argument in *New York:* "[E]ven where Congress has the authority under the Constitution to pass laws requiring or prohibiting certain acts, it lacks the power directly to compel the States to require or prohibit those acts. . . . [T]he Commerce Clause, for example, authorizes Congress to regulate interstate commerce directly; it does not authorize Congress to regulate state governments' regulation of interstate commerce." . . .

Finally, and most conclusively in the present litigation, we turn to the prior jurisprudence of this Court. . . .

When we were at last confronted squarely with a federal statute that unambiguously required the States to enact or administer a federal regulatory program, our decision should have come as no surprise. At issue in *New York v. United States* (1992) were the so-called "take title" provisions of the Low-Level Radioactive Waste Policy Amendments Act of 1985, which required States either to enact legislation providing for the disposal of radioactive waste generated within their borders, or to take title to, and possession of the waste—effectively requiring the States either to legislate pursuant to Congress's directions, or to implement an administrative solution. We concluded that Congress could constitutionally require the States to do neither. "The Federal Government," we held, "may not compel the States to enact or administer a federal regulatory program." . . .

. . . The mandatory obligation imposed on CLEOs to perform background checks on prospective handgun purchasers plainly runs afoul of that rule. . . .

. . . The Federal Government may neither issue directives requiring the States to address particular problems, nor command the States' officers, or those of their political subdivisions, to administer or enforce a federal regulatory program. It matters not whether policymaking is involved, and no case-by-case weighing of the burdens or benefits is necessary; such commands are fundamentally incompatible with our constitutional system of dual sovereignty. Accordingly, the judgment of the Court of Appeals for the Ninth Circuit is reversed.

It is so ordered.

JUSTICE STEVENS, with whom JUSTICE SOUTER, JUSTICE GINSBURG, and JUSTICE BREYER join, dissenting.

When Congress exercises the powers delegated to it by the Constitution, it may impose affirmative obligations on executive and judicial officers of state and local governments as well as ordinary citizens. This conclusion is firmly supported by the text of the Constitution, the early history of the Nation, decisions of this Court, and a correct understanding of the basic structure of the Federal Government.

These cases do not implicate the more difficult questions associated with congressional coercion of state legislatures addressed in *New York v. United States* (1992). Nor need we consider the wisdom of relying on local officials rather than federal agents to carry out aspects of a federal program, or even the question whether such officials may be required to perform a federal function on a permanent basis. The question is whether Congress, acting on behalf of the people of the entire Nation, may require local law enforcement officers to perform certain duties during the interim needed for the development of a federal gun control program. . . .

The text of the Constitution provides a sufficient basis for a correct disposition of this case.

Article I, §8, grants the Congress the power to regulate commerce among the States. . . . [T]here can be no question that that provision adequately supports the regulation of commerce in handguns effected by the Brady Act. Moreover, the additional grant of authority in that section of the Constitution "[t]o make all Laws which shall be necessary and proper for carrying into Execution the foregoing Powers" is surely adequate to support the temporary enlistment of local police officers in the process of identifying persons who should not be entrusted with the possession of handguns. In short, the affirmative delegation of power in Article I provides ample authority for the congressional enactment.

Unlike the First Amendment, which prohibits the enactment of a category of laws that would otherwise be authorized by Article I, the Tenth Amendment imposes no restriction on the exercise of delegated powers. . . .

The Amendment confirms the principle that the powers of the Federal Government are limited to those affirmatively granted by the Constitution, but it does not purport to limit the scope or the effectiveness of the exercise of powers that are delegated to Congress. Thus, the Amendment provides no support for a rule that immunizes local officials from obligations that might be imposed on ordinary citizens. . . .

There is not a clause, sentence, or paragraph in the entire text of the Constitution of the United States that supports the proposition that a local police officer can ignore a command contained in a statute enacted by Congress pursuant to an express delegation of power enumerated in Article I. . . .

The provision of the Brady Act that crosses the Court's newly defined constitutional threshold is more comparable to a statute requiring local police officers to report the identity of missing children to the Crime Control Center of the Department of Justice than to an offensive federal command to a sovereign state. If Congress believes that such a statute will benefit the people of the Nation, and serve the interests of cooperative federalism better than an enlarged federal bureaucracy, we should respect both its policy judgment and its appraisal of its constitutional power.

Accordingly, I respectfully dissent.

The *Printz* decision had little impact on gun control. After all, the challenged mandates to local law enforcement officers were to be phased out no later than November 1998 when the national instant background check system was scheduled to take over. Moreover, Congress passed additional gun control legislation after this decision. *Printz*, however, gave a clear indication of the Rehnquist Court's position on federalism. Five justices, all appointees of Republican presidents Reagan and Bush, were committed to maintaining at least a modified version of dual federalism: that the Tenth Amendment can serve as a barrier to the exercise of some congressional power over the states. Justice Antonin Scalia, for the majority, repeatedly invokes the term "dual sovereignty" to describe the constitutionally mandated division of power between the central government and the states. Justice John Paul Stevens, writing for the four justices in dissent, explicitly endorses "cooperative federalism."

The Court's tendency to support the interests of the states against federal encroachment was reinforced in *Alden v. Maine* (1999). At issue, once again, was the Fair Labor Standards Act. Sixty-five probation officers brought a legal action against their employer, the state of Maine, for allegedly violating the overtime provisions of the FLSA. The officers filed their suit in state court, as authorized under the federal statute. The trial court judge dismissed the suit on the ground of "sovereign immunity," a traditional principle that a government may not

be sued without its permission. On appeal to the Supreme Court, the question was whether Congress, by legislation, could subject nonconsenting states to lawsuits in their own courts.

By the same 5–4 division that occurred in *Printz*, the Court ruled that Congress was without authority to strip the state of its sovereign immunity by compelling the state courts to accept such lawsuits. Since the state of Maine had not consented to be sued, its courts were without jurisdiction to hear the case. Three years earlier, in *Seminole Tribe of Florida v. Florida* (1996), the justices handed down a similar ruling to protect nonconsenting states from being sued in federal court. As a consequence of these decisions, state employees have a hard time asserting their rights under certain federal labor laws unless the state agrees to be sued. Although the minority in *Alden* vigorously attacked the injustice that might result, the majority remained convinced that the principles of federalism left little room for Congress to eliminate a nonconsenting state's traditional immunity from lawsuit.

The Court's leaning toward state-centered notions of federalism should not be interpreted as a return to the pre–Civil War days of Roger Taney or to the laissez-faire philosophies that were popular prior to the New Deal. The contemporary Court has not used its revised interpretation of federalism to strike down any major law or to alter significantly how the United States is governed. Rather, in cases such as *New York, Printz,* and *Alden* the majority seems to be reminding us that under our constitutional system the states retain significant independent sovereignty and they cannot be treated by Congress as administrative units of the federal government. Congress may achieve its goals by cooperating with the states or by providing incentives to encourage states to participate in the administration of federally established policies. But the federal government may not commandeer the states and order them to carry out federal directives.

The swing of the pendulum back toward the dual federalism position is closely associated with the Court's personnel changes. Table 6-4 illustrates how the makeup of the Court has differed from *National League of Cities* to *Alden*. Note how individual justices rarely change their positions. A justice who favors cooperative federalism

TABLE 6-4 Changes in Court Personnel and Voting in Selected Federalism Cases, 1976–1999

Justice	Vote in *National League of Cities* (1976)	Vote in *Garcia* (1985)	Vote in *New York* (1992)	Vote in *Printz* (1997)	Vote in *Alden* (1999)
Blackmun	State	Federal	Federal	—	—
Brennan	Federal	Federal	—	—	—
Breyer	—	—	—	Federal	Federal
Burger	State	State	—	—	—
Ginsburg	—	—	—	Federal	Federal
Kennedy	—	—	State	State	State
Marshall	Federal	Federal	—	—	—
O'Connor	—	State	State	State	State
Powell	State	State	—	—	—
Rehnquist	State	State	State	State	State
Scalia	—	—	State	State	State
Souter	—	—	State	Federal	Federal
Stevens	Federal	Federal	Federal	Federal	Federal
Stewart	State	—	—	—	—
Thomas	—	—	State	State	State
White	Federal	Federal	Federal	—	—

Federal = Federal authority
State = State sovereignty
NOTE: Each of the cases in this table involved a clash between the authority of the federal government to act and the opposing interests of the states. The table reflects which interests the individual justices supported in each case.

tends consistently to support the interests of the national government over the states; and justices with ideologies sympathetic to dual federalism repeatedly side with the states. Whether this pattern continues in light of more liberal "experiments" emerging from the states—such as domestic partnership laws and green policies—remains to be seen. (For some possible answers, see the dicussion of *Gonzales v. Raich*, in chapter 7.)

Still, how the Supreme Court interprets the Constitution's core principle of federalism is highly dependent on the values of appointees to the bench. In subsequent chapters we will see the federalism debate fought out when national and state interests clash over issues such as commerce and taxation.

READINGS

Corwin, Edward S. "The Passing of Dual Federalism." *Virginia Law Review* 36 (1950): 1–24.

Gunther, Gerald, ed. *John Marshall's Defense of McCulloch v. Maryland.* Stanford: Stanford University Press, 1969.

Howard, A. E. Dick. "The States and the Supreme Court." *Catholic University Law Review* 31 (1982): 375–438.

Killenbeck, Mark R., ed. *The Tenth Amendment and State Sovereignty.* Lanham, Md.: Rowman and Littlefield, 2002.

Kobylka, Joseph F. "The Court, Justice Blackmun, and Federalism." *Creighton Law Review* 19 (1985–1986): 9–49.

Maltz, Earl M. *Dred Scott and the Politics of Slavery.* Lawrence: University Press of Kansas, 2007.

Mason, Alpheus. *The States' Rights Debate: Anti-Federalism and the Constitution.* New York: Oxford University Press, 1972.

Newmyer, R. Kent. *The Supreme Court under Marshall and Taney.* New York: Crowell, 1968.

Schecter, Stephen. "The State of American Federalism." *Publius* 10 (1980): 3–11.

Schmidhauser, John. *The Supreme Court as a Final Arbitrator of Federal-State Relations.* Chapel Hill: University of North Carolina Press, 1958.

Semonche, John E. *Charting the Future: The Supreme Court Responds to a Changing Society, 1890–1920.* Westport, Conn.: Greenwood Press, 1978.

Tarr, G. Alan, and Mary C. Porter. *State Supreme Courts in State and Nation.* New Haven: Yale University Press, 1988.

Waltenburg, Eric N., and Bill Swinford. *Litigating Federalism: The States Before the U.S. Supreme Court.* Westport, Conn.: Greenwood Press, 1999.

Wood, Stephen B. *Constitutional Politics in the Progressive Era: Child Labor and the Law.* Chicago: University of Chicago Press, 1968.

CHAPTER 7

THE COMMERCE POWER

Of all the powers granted to government, perhaps none has caused more controversies and resulted in more litigation than the power to regulate commerce. Concern over the exercise of this power was present at the Constitution's birth and continues today. At each stage of the nation's development from a former colony isolated from the world's commercial centers to a country of vast economic power, legal disputes of great significance tested the powers of government to regulate the economy.

During certain periods, such as John Marshall's chief justiceship, the decisions of the Supreme Court enhanced the role of the federal government in promoting economic development. At other times, such as in the early years of the Great Depression, the Court's interpretations thwarted the government's attempts to overcome economic collapse. From the earliest days of the nation, battles over the commerce power have raised basic questions. What is commerce? What is interstate commerce? What powers of commercial regulation did the Constitution grant to the federal government, and what role remains to be played by the states?

CONSTITUTIONAL FOUNDATIONS OF THE COMMERCE POWER

A primary reason for calling the Constitutional Convention was the inability of the government under the Articles of Confederation to control the country's commercial activity effectively. Economic conditions following the Revolutionary War were dismal. The national and state governments were deeply in debt. The tax base of the newly independent nation was minimal, and commerce was undeveloped, leaving property taxes and customs duties as the primary sources of government funds.

The states were almost exclusively in charge of economic regulation. To raise enough revenue to pay their debts, the states imposed substantial taxes on land, placing farmers in an economically precarious situation. The states also erected trade barriers and imposed duties on the importation of foreign goods. Although such policies were enacted in part to promote the states' domestic businesses, the result was a general strangulation of commercial activity. Several states printed their own money and passed statutes canceling debts. With each of the states working independently, the national economy continued to slide into stagnation; for all practical purposes, the central government was powerless to respond effectively.

When agrarian interests reached their economic breaking point—culminating in the 1787 march on the federal arsenal at Springfield, Massachusetts, by a makeshift army of farmers led by Daniel Shays and others—it was clear that something had to be done. Congress called for a convention to reconsider the status of the Articles of Confederation, a convention that ultimately resulted in the drafting of the U.S. Constitution.

Commerce and the Constitutional Convention

The delegates to the Constitutional Convention recognized the necessity of giving the power to regulate the economy to the central government. The condition of the nation could no longer allow the individual states to pursue independent policies, each having a different impact on the country's economic health. To that end Article I of the Constitution removed certain powers from the states and gave the federal government powers it did not have under the Articles of Confederation. States were stripped of the ability to print money, to impair the obligation of contracts, or to levy import duties. The federal government obtained the authority necessary to impose uniform regulations for the national economy. Among the powers granted to the central government were the authority to tax and impose customs duties, to spend and borrow, to develop and protect a single monetary system, and to regulate bankruptcies. Most important was the authority to regulate interstate and foreign commerce. Article I, Section 8, states: "The Congress shall have the power . . . to regulate Commerce with foreign Nations, and among the several States, and with the Indian Tribes."

The need for Congress to speak for the nation with a single voice on these matters was clear to the framers. Even Alexander Hamilton and James Madison, who disagreed on many questions of federalism, were in accord on the need for the central government to control interstate and foreign commerce. Hamilton wrote in Federalist No. 22:

In addition to the defects already enumerated in the existing federal system, there are others of not less importance which concur in rendering it altogether unfit for the administration of the affairs of the Union.

The want of a power to regulate commerce is by all parties allowed to be of the number.

Madison took a similar position in Federalist No. 42, arguing that the experience under the Articles of Confederation, as well as that of the European nations, demonstrated that a central government without broad powers over the nation's commerce was destined to fail.

Congress quickly seized upon the authority to regulate commerce with other nations. Almost immediately, it imposed import duties as a means of raising revenue. The constitutional grant in this area was clear: The power to regulate foreign commerce, as well as other matters of foreign policy, was given unambiguously to the national government, and the role of the states was eliminated. Only on rare occasions since ratification have the states challenged congressional supremacy over foreign commerce.

The power to regulate interstate commerce, however, was a different story. Congress was slow in responding to this grant of authority, despite its constitutional power to regulate commerce among the states. For the first several decades, federal officials continued to view business as an activity occurring within the borders of the individual states. In fact, Congress did not pass comprehensive legislation governing commerce among the states until the Interstate Commerce Act of 1887.

Marshall Defines Commerce

The history of the commerce clause is replete with disputes over definitions. For example, how do we distinguish between commercial activities and noncommercial activities? More important, what is the difference between *inter*state commerce, authority over which the Constitution gave to the federal government, and *intra*state commerce, over which the states retain regulatory power? Problems associated with such distinctions were difficult enough in the early years, but they became even more complex as the economy grew and the country changed from agrarian to industrialized. As many constitutional law cases illustrate, disputes over commercial regulatory authority often involve power struggles between the national government and the states.

Disputes over the meaning of the commerce clause came before the Supreme Court even during the early years of nationhood. The justices probed the constitutional definition of commerce and the proper division of federal and state power to regulate it. Of the commerce cases decided by the Supreme Court in those early decades, none was more important than *Gibbons v. Ogden* (1824). This dispute involved some of the nation's most prominent and powerful businessmen and attorneys. A great deal was at stake both economically and politically. In his opinion for the Court, Chief Justice John Marshall responded to the fundamental problems of defining commerce and allocating the power to control it. His answers

Aaron Ogden

Thomas Gibbons

to the questions presented in this case are still very much a part of the American constitutional fabric.

Gibbons v. Ogden

9 (22 U.S.) Wheat. 1 (1824)
http://laws.findlaw.com/US/22/1.html
Vote: 6 (Duvall, Johnson, Marshall, Story, Todd, Washington)
  0
Opinion of the Court: Marshall
Concurring opinion: Johnson
Not participating: Thompson

This complicated litigation can be traced back to 1798, when the New York legislature granted the wealthy and prominent Robert R. Livingston a monopoly to operate steamboats on all waters within the state, including the two most important commercial waterways, New York Harbor and the Hudson River. New York officials did not see the monopoly grant as particularly important because no one had yet developed a steamship that could operate reliably and profitably. But Livingston joined forces with Robert Fulton, and together they produced a commercially viable steamship. This mode of transportation became extremely popular and very profitable for the partners. When they obtained a similar monopoly over the port of New Orleans in 1811, they had significant control over the nation's two most important harbors.

The rapid westward expansion taking place at that time fueled the need for modern transportation systems. The Livingston-Fulton monopoly, however, put a damper on the use of steam in the evolution of such a system. The New York monopoly was so strong and so vigorously enforced that retaliatory laws were enacted by other states, which refused to let steam-powered vessels from New York use their waters. Especially hostile relations

Daniel Webster's 1821 handwritten note to Cornelius Vanderbilt acknowledging receipt of a $500 retainer to represent Thomas Gibbons in the case of *Gibbons v. Ogden.*

developed between New York and New Jersey, and violence between the crews of rival companies were common. Livingston died in 1813, followed two years later by Fulton, but their monopoly lived on.

In 1817 Aaron Ogden, a former governor of New Jersey, and Thomas Gibbons, a successful Georgia lawyer, entered into a partnership to carry passengers between New York City and Elizabethtown, New Jersey. Ogden had purchased the right to operate in New York waters from the Livingston-Fulton monopoly, and Gibbons had a federal permit issued under the 1793 Coastal Licensing Act to operate steamships along the coast. With these grants of authority the two partners could carry passengers between New York and New Jersey. The New York monopoly, however, pressured Ogden to terminate his relationship with Gibbons, and the partnership dissolved.

Gibbons then joined forces with Cornelius Vanderbilt, and they became fierce competitors with Ogden and the New York monopoly interests. Gibbons and Vanderbilt entered New York waters in violation of the monopoly whenever they could, picking up as much New York business as possible. In response, Ogden successfully persuaded the New York courts to enjoin Gibbons from entering New York waters. Gibbons appealed this ruling to the U.S. Supreme Court.

To press their case, Gibbons and Vanderbilt acquired the services of two of the best lawyers of the day, Daniel Webster and William Wirt, who later served as attorney general of the United States. Wirt argued that the federal permit issued to Gibbons took precedence over any state-issued monopoly and therefore Gibbons had the right to enter New York waters. Webster took a more radical position, explicitly stating that the commerce clause of the Constitution gave Congress exclusive power over commerce and that the state-granted monopoly was a violation of that clause. Ogden's lawyer responded that navigation was not commerce under the meaning of the Constitution but instead was an intrastate enterprise left to the states to regulate. The oral arguments in the case lasted four and a half days, an unusually long time.

MR. CHIEF JUSTICE MARSHALL delivered the opinion of the Court.

The appellant contends that this decree is erroneous, because the laws which purport to give the exclusive privilege it sustains, are repugnant to the constitution and laws of the United States.

They are said to be repugnant:

To that clause in the constitution which authorizes Congress to regulate commerce. . . .

The words are, "Congress shall have power to regulate commerce with foreign nations, and among the several States, and with the Indian tribes."

The subject to be regulated is commerce; and our constitution being . . . one of enumeration, and not of definition, to ascertain the extent of the power, it becomes necessary to settle the meaning of the word. The counsel for the appellee would limit it to traffic, to buying and selling, or the interchange of commodities, and do not admit that it comprehends navigation. This would restrict a general term, applicable to many objects, to one of its significations. Commerce, undoubtedly, is traffic, but it is something more: it is intercourse. It describes the commercial intercourse between nations, and parts of nations, in all its branches, and is regulated by prescribing rules for carrying on that intercourse. The mind can scarcely conceive a system for regulating commerce between nations, which shall exclude all laws concerning navigation, which shall be silent on the admission of the vessels of the one nation into the ports of the other, and be confined to prescribing rules for the conduct of individuals, in the actual employment of buying and selling, or of barter.

If commerce does not include navigation, the government of the Union has no direct power over that subject, and can make no law prescribing what shall constitute American vessels, or requiring that they shall be navigated by American seamen. Yet this power has been exercised from the commencement of the government, has been exercised with the consent of all, and has been understood by all to be a commercial regulation. All America understands, and has uniformly understood, the word "commerce," to comprehend navigation. It was so understood, and must have been so understood, when the constitution was framed. The power over commerce, including navigation, was one of the primary objects for which the people of America adopted their government, and must have been contemplated in forming it. The convention must have used the word in that sense, because all have understood it in that sense; and the attempt to restrict it comes too late. . . .

The word used in the constitution, then, comprehends, and has been always understood to comprehend, navigation within its meaning; and a power to regulate navigation, is as expressly granted, as if that term had been added to the word "commerce."

To what commerce does this power extend? The constitution informs us, to commerce "with foreign nations, and among the several States, and with the Indian tribes."

It has, we believe, been universally admitted, that these words comprehend every species of commercial intercourse between the United States and foreign nations. No sort of trade can be carried on between this country and any other, to which this power does not extend. It has been truly said, that commerce, as the word is used in the constitution, is a unit, every part of which is indicated by the term.

If this be the admitted meaning of the word, in its application to foreign nations, it must carry the same meaning throughout the sentence, and remain a unit, unless there be some plain intelligible cause which alters it.

The subject to which the power is next applied, is to commerce "among the several States." The word "among" means intermingled with. A thing which is among others, is intermingled with them. Commerce among the States, cannot stop at the external boundary line of each State, but may be introduced into the interior.

It is not intended to say that these words comprehend that commerce, which is completely internal, which is carried on between man and man in a State, or between different parts of the same State, and which does not extend to or affect other States. Such a power would be inconvenient, and is certainly unnecessary.

Comprehensive as the word "among" is, it may very properly be restricted to that commerce which concerns more States than one. The phrase is not one which would probably have been selected to indicate the completely interior traffic of a State, because it is not an apt phrase for that purpose; and the enumeration of the particular classes of commerce, to which the power was to be extended, would not have been made, had the intention been to extend the power to every description. The enumeration presupposes something not enumerated; and that something, if we regard the language or the subject of the sentence, must be the exclusively internal commerce of a State. The genius and character of the whole government seem to be, that its action is to be applied to all the external concerns of the nation, and to those internal concerns which affect the States generally; but not to those which are completely within a particular State, which do not affect other States, and with which it is not necessary to interfere, for the purpose of executing some of the general powers of the government. The completely internal commerce of a State, then, may be considered as reserved for the State itself.

But, in regulating commerce with foreign nations, the power of Congress does not stop at the jurisdictional lines of the several States. It would be a very useless power, if it could not pass those lines. The commerce of the United States with foreign nations, is that of the whole United States. Every district has a right to participate in it. The deep streams which penetrate our country in every direction, pass through the interior of almost every State in the Union, and furnish the means of exercising this right. If Congress has the power to regulate it, that power must be exercised whenever the subject exists. If it exists within the States, if a foreign voyage may commence or terminate at a port within a State, then the power of Congress may be exercised within a State.

This principle is, if possible, still more clear, when applied to commerce "among the several States." They either join each other, in which case they are separated by a mathematical line, or they are remote from each other, in which case other States lie between them. What is commerce "among" them; and how is it to be conducted? Can a trading expedition between two adjoining States, commence and terminate outside of each? And if the trading intercourse be between two States remote from each other, must it not commence in one, terminate in the other, and probably pass through a third? Commerce among the States must, of necessity, be commerce with the States. . . .

We are now arrived at the inquiry—What is this power?

It is the power to regulate; that is, to prescribe the rule by which commerce is to be governed. This power, like all others vested in Congress, is complete in itself, may be exercised to its utmost extent, and acknowledges no limitations, other than are prescribed in the constitution. . . . If, as has always been understood, the sovereignty of Congress, though limited to specified objects, is plenary as to those objects, the power over commerce with foreign nations, and among the several States, is vested in Congress as absolutely as it would be in a single government, having in its constitution the same restrictions on the exercise of the power as are found in the constitution of the United States. The wisdom and the discretion of Congress, their identity with the people, and the influence which their constituents possess at elections, are, in this, as in many other instances, as that, for example, of declaring war, the sole restraints on which they have relied, to secure them from its abuse. They are the restraints on which the people must often rely solely, in all representative governments.

The power of Congress, then, comprehends navigation, within the limits of every State in the Union; so far as that navigation may be, in any manner, connected with "commerce with foreign nations, or among the several States, or with the Indian tribes." It may, of consequence, pass the jurisdictional line of New-York, and act upon the very waters to which the prohibition now under consideration applies.

But it has been urged with great earnestness, that, although the power of Congress to regulate commerce with foreign nations, and among the several States, be co-extensive with the subject itself, and have no other limits than are prescribed in the constitution, yet the States may severally exercise the same power, within their respective jurisdictions. In support of this argument, it is said, that they possessed it as an inseparable attribute of sovereignty, before the formation of the constitution, and still retain it, except so far as they have surrendered it by that instrument; that this principle results from the nature of the government, and is secured by the tenth amendment; that an affirmative grant of power is not exclusive, unless in its own nature it be such that the continued exercise of it by the former possessor is inconsistent with the grant, and that this is not of that description.

The appellant, conceding these postulates, except the last, contends, that full power to regulate a particular subject, implies the whole power, and leaves no residuum; that a grant of the whole is incompatible with the existence of a right in another to any part of it. . . .

In discussing the question, whether this power is still in the States, in the case under consideration, we may dismiss from it the inquiry, whether it is surrendered by the mere grant to Congress, or is retained until Congress shall exercise the power. We may dismiss that inquiry, because it has been exercised, and the regulations which Congress deemed it proper to make, are now in full operation. The sole question is, can a State regulate commerce with foreign nations and among the States, while Congress is regulating it?

The counsel for the respondent answer this question in the affirmative, and rely very much on the restrictions in the 10th section, as supporting their opinion. . . .

It has been contended by the general counsel for the appellant, that, as the word "to regulate" implies in its nature, full power over the thing to be regulated, it excludes, necessarily, the action of all others that would perform the same operation on the same thing. That regulation is designed for the entire result, applying to those parts which remain as they were, as well as to those which are altered. It produces a uniform whole, which is as much disturbed and deranged by changing what the regulating power designs to leave untouched, as that on which it has operated.

There is great force in this argument, and the Court is not satisfied that it has been refuted.

Since, however, in exercising the power of regulating their own purely internal affairs, whether of trading or police, the States may sometimes enact laws, the validity of which depends on their interfering with, and being contrary to, an act of Congress passed in pursuance of the constitution, the Court will enter upon the inquiry, whether the laws of New-York, as expounded by the highest tribunal of that State, have, in their application to this case, come into collision with an act of Congress, and deprived a citizen of a right to which that act entitles him. Should this collision exist, it will be immaterial whether those laws were passed in virtue of a concurrent power "to regulate commerce with foreign nations and among the several States," or, in virtue of a power to regulate their domestic trade and police. In one case and the other, the acts of New-York must yield to the law of Congress; and the decision sustaining the privilege they confer, against a right given by a law of the Union, must be erroneous. . . .

But the framers of our constitution foresaw this state of things, and provided for it, by declaring the supremacy not only of itself, but of the laws made in pursuance of it. The nullity of any act, inconsistent with the constitution, is produced by the declaration, that the constitution is the supreme law. The appropriate application of that part of the clause which confers the same supremacy on laws and treaties, is to such acts of the State Legislatures as do not transcend their powers, but, though enacted in the execution of acknowledged State powers, interfere with, or are contrary to the laws of Congress, made in pursuance of the constitution, or some treaty made under the authority of the United States. In every such case, the act of Congress, or the treaty, is supreme; and the law of the State, though enacted in the exercise of powers not controverted, must yield to it. . . .

But all inquiry into this subject seems to the Court to be put completely at rest, by the act already mentioned, entitled, "An act for the enrolling and licensing of steam boats."

This act authorizes a steam boat employed, or intended to be employed, only in a river or bay of the United States, owned wholly or in part by an alien, resident within the United States, to be enrolled and licensed as if the same belonged to a citizen of the United States.

This act demonstrates the opinion of Congress, that steam boats may be enrolled and licensed, in common with vessels using sails. They are, of course, entitled to the same privileges, and can no more be restrained from navigating waters, and entering ports which are free to such vessels, than if they were wafted on their voyage by the winds, instead of being propelled by the agency of fire. The one element may be as legitimately used as the other, for every commercial purpose authorized by the laws of the Union; and the act of a State inhibiting the use of either to any vessel having a license under the act of Congress, comes, we think, in direct collision with that act.

Like his opinions in *Marbury v. Madison* and *McCulloch v. Maryland*, Marshall's opinion in *Gibbons* laid a constitutional foundation that remains in place today. The decision made several important points. First, commerce involves more than buying and selling. It includes the commercial intercourse between nations and states, and therefore transportation and navigation clearly fall within the definition of commerce. Second, the power to regulate commerce that occurs completely within the boundaries of a single state, and does not extend to or affect other states, is reserved for the states. Third, commerce among the states begins in one state and ends in another. It does not stop when the act of crossing a state border is completed. Consequently, commerce that occurs within a state may be part of a larger interstate process. Fourth, once an act is considered part of interstate commerce, Congress is empowered by the Constitution to regulate it. The power to regulate interstate commerce is complete and has no limitation other than what may be found in other constitutional provisions.

Gibbons v. Ogden was a substantial victory for national power. It broadly construed the definitions of both commerce and interstate commerce. But Marshall did not go as far as Daniel Webster had urged. The opinion asserts only that Congress has complete power to regulate interstate commerce and that federal regulations are superior to any state laws. The decision does not answer the question of the legitimacy of states regulating interstate commerce in the absence of federal action. That controversy was left for future justices to decide.

DEFINING INTERSTATE COMMERCE

The regulation of commerce by the federal government did not become a major item on the Supreme

Court's agenda until the latter half of the nineteenth century. By this time, small intrastate businesses were giving way to large interstate corporations. Industrialization was expanding, and the interstate railroad and pipeline systems were well under way. The infamous captains of industry were creating large monopolistic trusts that dominated huge segments of the national economy, squeezing out small businesses and discouraging new entrepreneurs. The industrial combines that controlled the railroads also, in effect, ruled agriculture and other interests that relied on the rails to transport goods to market. This commercial growth brought great prosperity to some but caused horrendous social problems. Unsafe working conditions, sweatshops, child labor, and low wages plagued employees, who eventually formed labor unions.

Shreveport Doctrine

In an effort to exert some control over interstate commerce, Congress passed two major laws based on the commerce power. The first was the Interstate Commerce Act of 1887, which established a mechanism for regulating the nation's interstate railroads. The second was the Sherman Anti-Trust Act of 1890, which was designed to break up monopolies that restrained trade. Critics immediately attacked Congress for exceeding its constitutional authority. Although the commerce clause and Marshall's interpretation of it clearly established congressional power, discriminating between interstate and intrastate commerce was not easy. The Supreme Court faced a significant number of appeals that asked the justices to clarify whether the national legislature had overstepped its bounds and regulated commerce that was purely intrastate. To say that the Court had difficulty developing a coherent doctrine is an understatement.

The regulation of the railroads provides a case in point. The first railroads were small local operations regulated by the states. But as the interstate systems developed, the justices held that their regulation was rightfully a federal responsibility.[1] Congress responded with the Interstate Commerce Act, which established the Interstate Commerce Commission (ICC) to regulate the railroads

and set rates. The Supreme Court approved the constitutionality of the commission but later stripped it of its rate-setting powers.[2] In 1906 Congress revised the authority and procedures of the commission and reestablished its power to set rates. The Court generally supported this amended version of the regulatory plan.[3]

The Court's decision in *Houston, E. & W. Texas Railway Co. v. United States* (1914), better known as the *Shreveport Rate Case*, firmly established congressional power over the nation's rails. This dispute arose from competition among three railroad companies to serve various cities in Texas. Two were based in Texas, one in Houston and the other in Dallas, and the third competitor operated out of Shreveport, Louisiana. The Texas Railroad Commission regulated the Texas companies because their operations were exclusively intrastate, but the Shreveport company came under the jurisdiction of the ICC. Difficulties arose when the Texas regulators set rates substantially lower than did the ICC. The motive behind these lower rates was clear: The Texas commission wanted to encourage intrastate trade and to discourage companies from taking their business to Shreveport. The rates placed the Shreveport railroad at a distinct disadvantage in competing for the Texas market. In response, the ICC ordered the intrastate Texas rates to be raised to the interstate levels. When the commission's authority to set intrastate rail rates was challenged, the Supreme Court ruled in favor of the ICC, articulating what became known as the Shreveport doctrine. The Court held that the federal government had the power to regulate intrastate commerce when a failure to regulate would cripple, retard, or destroy interstate commerce. According to Justice Charles Evans Hughes's opinion for the Court, whenever interstate and intrastate commercial activities are entwined so that the regulation of one controls the other, "it is Congress, and not the State, that is entitled to prescribe the final and dominant rule."

---

1. *Wabash, St. Louis & Pacific Railway Co. v. Illinois* (1886).

2. *Interstate Commerce Commission v. Brimson* (1894); *Interstate Commerce Commission v. Cincinnati, New Orleans, & Texas Pacific Railway Co.* (1897); and *Interstate Commerce Commission v. Alabama-Midland Railway Co.* (1897).

3. See *Illinois Central Railroad Co. v. Interstate Commerce Commission* (1907).

Manufacturing and Direct Effects on Interstate Commerce

The Court's endorsement of the federal power to regulate interstate transportation and distribution did not extend initially to the attempts by Congress to impose effective antitrust legislation. The target of the antitrust statutes were the monopolies that controlled basic industries and choked out all competition. During the late nineteenth century these trusts grew to capture and exercise dominance over many industries, including oil, meatpacking, sugar, and steel. The Sherman Act was Congress's first attempt to break up these anticompetitive combines. It outlawed all contracts and combinations of companies that had the effect of restraining trade and commerce or eliminating competition.

For the antitrust law to be fully effective, however, its provisions had to cover the manufacturing and processing stages of commercial activity, which raised a serious constitutional problem. In earlier cases the Court had ruled that manufacturing was essentially a local activity and not part of interstate commerce. In *Veazie v. Moor* (1853) the Court had labeled it a far-reaching "pretension" to suggest that the federal power over interstate commerce extended to manufacturing. In **Kidd v. Pearson** (1888) the Court took an even stronger stand, holding that the production of alcoholic beverages was an intrastate activity even if the resulting products were to be sold in interstate commerce.

Could the new antitrust law be applied to manufacturing? Or had Congress exceeded its constitutional authority in regulating production? These questions were answered in **United States v. E. C. Knight Co.** (1895), a battle over the federal government's attempts to break up the sugar trust. At the end of the nineteenth century six companies dominated the American sugar refining industry. American Sugar Refining Company was the largest, with control of about 65 percent of the nation's refining capacity. Four Pennsylvania refiners shared 33 percent of the market, and a Boston company had a scant 2 percent. In March 1892 American Sugar entered into agreements that allowed it to acquire the four Pennsylvania refineries, including the E. C. Knight Company, giving American

Sugar absolute control over 98 percent of the sugar refining business in the United States.

The federal government sued to have the acquisition agreements canceled. According to Justice Department attorneys, the sugar trust operated as a monopoly in restraint of trade in violation of the Sherman Anti-Trust Law. Attorneys for American Sugar and the acquired companies held that the law did not apply to sugar refining because that activity is manufacturing, subject to state, not federal, control.

With only John Marshall Harlan in dissent, the justices rejected the federal government's position and ruled that the antitrust law could not be imposed on the sugar refining industry. Refining was manufacturing. It was production that occurred within the boundaries of a single state. It made no difference that the sugar trust controlled 98 percent of the nation's sugar supply or that the processed sugar was destined to be sold in interstate commerce. Manufacturing was not interstate commerce. In Chief Justice Melville Fuller's words for the Court, "Commerce succeeds to manufacture, and is not a part of it."

In *E. C. Knight* the Court first expressed concern about the effects of various economic activities on interstate commerce. Proponents of federal regulation often argued that if an intrastate economic activity had an effect—any effect—on interstate commerce it could be regulated by Congress. The Court rejected this position in *E. C. Knight*, holding that federal authority is not activated unless the intrastate activity has a direct effect on interstate commerce. In the sugar trust case, Fuller concluded that the challenged monopoly had only an indirect effect on interstate commerce and therefore was not subject to federal regulation. The distinction between direct and indirect effects is not very clear and can be interpreted in various ways.

Although the decision in *E. C. Knight* removed manufacturing from the authority of the Sherman Act, it did not doom federal antitrust efforts. In fact, when manufacturing was not accused of monopolistic activity, the Court was quite willing to apply the law. For example, the Court held that companies engaged in production and interstate sale of pipe came under sections of the

Sherman Act.[4] In 1904 the Court went even further, ruling in ***Northern Securities Company v. United States*** that stock transactions creating a holding company (the result of an effective merger between the Northern Pacific and the Great Northern Railroad companies) were subject to Sherman Act scrutiny. In spite of these applications of the antitrust law, *E. C. Knight*, by declaring manufacturing to be outside the definition of interstate commerce, set an important precedent. The ruling later would be extended, with serious repercussions, to bar many of the New Deal programs passed to combat the Great Depression. Only when the economy collapsed did the wisdom expressed in Justice Harlan's *E. C. Knight* dissent become apparent: The federal government must be empowered to regulate economic evils that are injurious to the nation's commerce and that a single state is incapable of eradicating.

Stream of Commerce Doctrine

Government efforts to break up the meatpacking trust presented a different constitutional challenge. The corporations that dominated the meat industry, such as Armour, Cudahy, and Swift, ruled the nation's stockyards, which stood at the throat of the meat distribution process. Western ranchers sent their livestock to the stockyards to be sold, butchered, and packed for shipment to consumers in the East. Livestock brokers, known as commission men, received the animals at the stockyards and sold them to the meatpacking companies for the ranchers. Consequently, when the meatpacking trust acquired control of the stockyards and the commission men who worked there, it was in a position to direct where the ranchers sent their stock, fix meat prices, demand unreasonably low rates from those who transported stock, and decide when to withhold meat from the market. The government believed these actions constituted a restraint of trade in violation of the Sherman Act. The meatpackers argued that their control over the stockyards was an intrastate matter to be regulated by the states.

In ***Swift & Company v. United States*** (1905) Justice Oliver Wendell Holmes, speaking for a unanimous Court, held that the Sherman Act applied to the stockyards. The commercial sale of beef, Holmes reasoned, began when the cattle left the range and did not terminate until final sale. The fact that the cattle stopped at the stockyards, midpoint in this commercial enterprise, did not mean that they were removed from interstate commerce. Holmes's opinion develops what has become known as the stream of commerce doctrine, which allows federal regulation of interstate commerce from the point of its origin to the point of its termination. Interruptions in the course of that interstate commerce do not suspend the right of Congress to regulate. Seventeen years later, in *Stafford v. Wallace* (1922), the Court reaffirmed the stream of commerce doctrine when it upheld the constitutionality of the 1921 Packers and Stockyard Act, a comprehensive regulation of the stockyard industry.

The stream of commerce precedents set in the *Swift* and *Stafford* stockyards cases later were applied to other regulatory schemes. Most notable was *Chicago Board of Trade v. Olsen* (1923), which brought the grain exchanges under the rubric of interstate commerce. Such decisions broadened the power of the federal government to control the economy. But the Court still found that certain commercial activities exerted too little direct impact on interstate commerce to justify congressional control. The most prominent among these were manufacturing and processing. The 1895 sugar trust case of *E. C. Knight* established this principle, and it was reinforced in 1918 by *Hammer v. Dagenhart*, the child labor case discussed in Chapter 6.

As the nation enjoyed the prosperity of the 1920s, the federal government had more power to regulate the economy than it had ever had, but not enough to cope effectively with a full-scale economic collapse. When the stock market crashed, the central government did not have the constitutional authority to impose adequate corrective measures, and the justices of the Supreme Court, at least initially, were unwilling to provide the political branches with that authority. This situation touched off history's most dramatic confrontation be-

4. *Addystone Pipe and Steel Co. v. United States* (1899).

tween the Court and the president, an episode that permanently altered the distribution of government powers.

THE SUPREME COURT, THE NEW DEAL, AND BEYOND

The New York Stock Exchange crashed on October 29, 1929, and set in motion a series of events that shook the American economy and drove the nation into a deep depression. For the next two years, the stock market continued to tumble, with the Standard and Poor's Industrial Averages falling 75 percent. The gross national product declined 27 percent over three years, and the unemployment rate rose from a healthy 3.2 percent in 1929 to a catastrophic 24.9 percent in 1933.

The Republican Party, which had been victorious in the 1928 elections, controlled the White House and both houses of Congress. The party attempted to cope with the Depression by following philosophies of government that had been successful during the previous years of prosperity, with dismal results. The economic forces against which the Republicans fought were enormous. A different political approach was necessary to battle the

collapse, and the American people were demanding such a change.

The Depression and Political Change

In the 1932 presidential election, Democratic candidate Franklin D. Roosevelt was swept into office by a huge margin as the voters rejected the incumbent, Herbert Hoover. With new Democratic majorities in the House and Senate, the president began combating the Great Depression with his New Deal policies. The overwhelming Democratic margins in Congress gave Roosevelt all the political clout he needed to gain approval of his radical new approach to boosting the economy. His programs were so popular with the American people that in 1936 they reelected Roosevelt by an even greater margin and provided him with even larger Democratic majorities in Congress, reducing the Republicans almost to minor party status. *(See Table 7-1.)*

The U.S. Supreme Court, however, did not change. In 1929, just before the stock market crashed, the Court had six Republicans and three Democrats. The economic conservatives (William Howard Taft, Willis Van Devanter,

TABLE 7-1 The Great Depression and Political Change

	1929	1931	1933	1935	1937
House of Representatives					
No. of Democratic seats	163	216	313	332	333
No. of Republican seats	267	218	117	103	89
Senate					
No. of Democratic seats	39	47	59	69	75
No. of Republican seats	56	48	36	25	17
Presidency					
Incumbent	Hoover (R)	—	Roosevelt (D)	—	Roosevelt (D)
% of popular vote	58.2	—	57.4	—	60.8
Electoral vote margin	444-87	—	472-59	—	523-8
Supreme Court					
Republican justices	6	6	5	5	5
Number of new appointments over previous two years	0	2	1	0	0

NOTES: Data depict the change in political representation in the three branches of the federal government following the 1929 stock market crash and the deepening depression that continued over the next several years.

Members of the House and one-third of the senators were elected the previous November. Data on presidential election margins are based on previous November's elections. Supreme Court information is as of January of the designated years.

James C. McReynolds, Pierce Butler, George Sutherland, and Edward Sanford) held control and clearly outnumbered the justices more sympathetic to political and economic change (Oliver Wendell Holmes, Louis Brandeis, and Harlan Fiske Stone). By 1932 the Court had three new justices. Hughes succeeded Taft as chief justice, Benjamin Cardozo took Holmes's seat, and Owen Roberts replaced Sanford. Although these changes reduced the Republican majority to five, the ideological balance of the Court underwent no appreciable change. Hoover had filled all three of these vacancies, which occurred before Roosevelt took office. Inaugurated in March 1933, Roosevelt had no opportunity to name a Supreme Court justice until Van Devanter retired in June 1937. Roosevelt's first appointment, Hugo Black, assumed his seat in August of that year. Not until 1940 did the Court have a majority appointed from the period after Roosevelt's first election.

In the executive branch, Roosevelt assembled a cadre of young, creative people to devise novel ways of approaching the ailing economy, and these New Deal Democrats quickly set out to develop, enact, and implement their programs. Congress passed the first legislation, the Emergency Banking Act of 1933, just five days after Roosevelt's inauguration, and a string of statutes designed to control all major sectors of the nation's economy followed (see Box 7-1). In adopting these programs, Congress relied on a number of constitutional powers, including the powers to tax, spend, and regulate interstate and foreign commerce.

The new political majority that dominated the legislative and executive branches espoused philosophies that called for the government to take a significantly more active role in economic regulation. The Supreme Court remained firmly in the control of representatives of the old order, whose views on the relationship of government and the economy were at odds with those of the political branches. A clash between the president and the Court was inevitable.

The Court Attacks the New Deal

As soon as the New Deal programs came into being, conservative business interests began to challenge their

constitutional validity. In just two years the appeals started to reach the Court's doorstep. Beginning in 1935 and lasting for two long, tense years, the Court and the New Deal Democrats fought over the constitutionality of an expanded federal role in managing the economy.

BOX 7-1   NEW DEAL LEGISLATION

The Roosevelt Democrats moved on the nation's economic problems with great speed. Roosevelt took the oath of office on March 4, 1933. Listed below are the major economic actions passed during his first term. Note how many were enacted within the first 100 days of the new administration.

March 9, 1933	Emergency Banking Act
March 31, 1933	Civilian Conservation Corps created
May 12, 1933	Agricultural Adjustment Act
May 12, 1933	Federal Emergency Relief Act
May 18, 1933	Tennessee Valley Authority created
June 5, 1933	Nation taken off gold standard
June 13, 1933	Home Owners Loan Corporation created
June 16, 1933	Federal Deposit Insurance Corporation created
June 16, 1933	Farm Credit Administration created
June 16, 1933	National Industrial Recovery Act
January 30, 1934	Dollar devalued
June 6, 1934	Securities and Exchange Commission authorized
June 12, 1934	Reciprocal Tariff Act
June 19, 1934	Federal Communications Commission created
June 27, 1934	Railroad Retirement Act
June 28, 1934	Federal Housing Administration authorized
April 8, 1935	Works Progress Administration created
July 5, 1935	National Labor Relations Act
August 14, 1935	Social Security Act
August 26, 1935	Federal Power Commission created
August 30, 1935	National Bituminous Coal Conservation Act
February 19, 1936	Soil Conservation and Domestic Allotment Act

During this period, the justices struck down many important New Deal statutes. Of ten major programs, the Court approved only two—the Tennessee Valley Authority and the emergency monetary laws. Four hardline conservative justices, Van Devanter, McReynolds, Sutherland, and Butler, formed the heart of the Court's opposition. Many thought their obstruction of New Deal initiatives would bring about the nation's ruin. As a consequence, they became known as the Four Horsemen of the Apocalypse, a reference to the end of the world as depicted in the Bible's Book of Revelation. Two of the four, McReynolds and Butler, were Democrats *(see Box 7-2)*.

Naturally, these four justices by themselves could not declare void any act of Congress. They needed the vote of at least one other justice. As indicated in Box 7-3, they had little trouble attracting others to their cause. Of the eight major 1935–1936 decisions striking down congressional policies, three were by 5–4 votes in which the four were able to attract Justice Roberts to their side. In one additional case, Roberts and Hughes voted with the conservatives. But in three of these significant decisions, the Court was unanimous, with even the more liberal Brandeis, Cardozo, and Stone voting to strike down the challenged legislation.

The first salvo in the war between the two branches occurred on January 7, 1935, when the Supreme Court by an 8–1 vote in ***Panama Refining Company v. Ryan*** struck down a section of the National Industrial Recovery Act (NIRA) as an improper delegation of congressional power to the executive branch. The section in question was a major New Deal weapon in regulating the oil industry. It gave the president the power to prohibit interstate shipment of oil and petroleum products that were produced or stored in a manner illegal under state law. The justices found fault with the act because it did not provide sufficiently clear standards to guide the executive branch; rather, it gave the president almost unlimited discretion in applying the prohibitions. *Panama Refining* was the first case in which the Court struck down legislation because it was an improper delegation of power.

Although the decision in *Panama Refining* was restricted to the delegation question and did not focus on Congress's interstate commerce authority, it promised

---

BOX 7-2   THE FOUR HORSEMEN

Willis Van Devanter
(1910–1937)

Republican from Wyoming. Born 1859. University of Cincinnati Law School. Wyoming state legislator and state supreme court judge. Federal appeals court judge. Appointed by William Howard Taft.

James Clark McReynolds
(1914–1941)

Democrat from Tennessee. Born 1862. University of Virginia Law School. United States attorney general. Appointed by Woodrow Wilson.

George Sutherland
(1922–1938)

Republican from Utah. Born 1862. University of Michigan Law School. State legislator, U.S. representative, U.S. senator. Appointed by Warren G. Harding.

Pierce Butler
(1922–1939)

Democrat from Minnesota. Born 1866. No law school, studied privately. Corporate attorney. Appointed by Warren G. Harding.

---

bad days ahead for the administration. Not only was the decision a disappointment for the president, but the vote was lopsided. Only Justice Cardozo voted to approve the law.

The Court dropped its biggest bomb on the New Deal four months later, in May 1935. The justices voted 5–4 on May 6 to declare the Railroad Retirement Act an unconstitutional violation of the commerce clause and the due

BOX 7-3   THE SUPREME COURT AND THE NEW DEAL

Listed below are eight major decisions handed down by the Supreme Court in 1935 and 1936 declaring parts of the New Deal legislative program unconstitutional.

Case/Decision Date	Acts Ruled Unconstitutional/Grounds	Majority	Dissent
Panama Refining Co. v. Ryan (January 7, 1935)	Portions of the National Industrial Recovery Act (improper delegation of congressional powers)	Brandeis, Butler, Hughes, McReynolds, Roberts, Stone, Sutherland, Van Devanter	Cardozo
Railroad Retirement Board v. Alton Railroad Co. (May 6, 1935)	Railroad Retirement Act of 1934 (exceeded commerce clause powers; Fifth Amendment due process violations)	Butler, McReynolds, Roberts, Sutherland, Van Devanter	Brandeis, Cardozo, Hughes, Stone
Schechter Poultry Corp. v. United States (May 27, 1935)	Portions of the National Industrial Recovery Act (a regulation of intrastate commerce and improper delegation of congressional power)	Brandeis, Butler, Cardozo, Hughes, McReynolds, Roberts, Stone, Sutherland, Van Devanter	
Louisville Bank v. Radford (May 27, 1935)	Frazier-Lemke Act of 1934 extending bankruptcy relief (Fifth Amendment property rights)	Brandeis, Butler, Cardozo, Hughes, McReynolds, Roberts, Stone, Sutherland, Van Devanter	
Hopkins Savings Association v. Cleary (December 12, 1935)	Home Owners Loan Act of 1933 (Tenth Amendment)	Brandeis, Butler, Cardozo, Hughes, McReynolds, Roberts, Stone, Sutherland, Van Devanter	
United States v. Butler (January 6, 1936)	Agricultural Adjustment Act (taxing and spending power violations)	Butler, Hughes, McReynolds, Roberts, Sutherland, Van Devanter	Brandeis, Cardozo, Stone
Carter v. Carter Coal Co. (May 18, 1936)	Bituminous Coal Conservation Act (a regulation of intrastate commerce; improper delegation of congressional power)	Butler, McReynolds, Roberts, Sutherland, Van Devanter	Brandeis, Cardozo, Hughes, Stone
Ashton v. Cameron County District Court (May 25, 1936)	Municipal Bankruptcy Act (Tenth Amendment; Fifth Amendment property rights)	Butler, McReynolds, Roberts, Sutherland, Van Devanter	Brandeis, Cardozo, Hughes, Stone

process clause of the Fifth Amendment.[5] Then, on May 27, a date that became known as Black Monday, the justices dealt three significant blows to the administration's efforts to fight the Depression—all by unanimous votes. First, in *Humphrey's Executor v. United States* the Court declared that the president did not have the power to remove a member of the Federal Trade Commission. Second, the justices invalidated the Frazier-Lemke Act, which provided mortgage relief, especially to farmers.[6] Finally, in *Schechter Poultry Corp. v. United States* the Court handed the president his most stinging defeat when it declared major portions of the NIRA unconstitutional as an improper delegation of legislative power and a violation of the commerce clause.

Schechter Poultry Corp. v. United States

295 U.S. 495 (1935)
http://laws.findlaw.com/US/295/495.html
Vote: 9 (Brandeis, Butler, Cardozo, Hughes, McReynolds,
   Roberts, Stone, Sutherland, Van Devanter)
   0

Opinion of the Court: Hughes
Concurring opinion: Cardozo

Congress passed the NIRA, the most far-reaching and comprehensive of all the New Deal legislation, on June 16, 1933. Applying to every sector of American industry, the NIRA called for the creation of codes of fair competition for business. The codes would regulate trade practices, wages, hours, and other business activities within various industries. Trade associations and other industry groups had the responsibility for drafting the codes, which were submitted to the president for approval. In the absence of the private sector's recommendations, the president was authorized to draft codes himself. Once approved by the president, the codes had the force of law, and violators faced fines and even jail.

The NIRA was vulnerable to constitutional challenge on two grounds. First, it set virtually no standards for the

president in approving or drafting the codes. Congress had handed Roosevelt a blank check to bring all of American industry into line with his views of what was best for the recovery of the economy. Second, the law regulated what at that time was considered intrastate commerce.

The *Schechter* case involved a challenge to the NIRA poultry codes, focusing on the industry in New York, the nation's largest chicken market.[7] This market clearly was operating in interstate commerce; 96 percent of the poultry sold in New York came from out-of-state suppliers. The industry was riddled with graft and plagued by deplorable health and sanitary conditions. The Live Poultry Code approved by President Roosevelt set a maximum workweek of forty hours and a minimum hourly wage of fifty cents. In addition, the code established a health inspection system, regulations to govern slaughtering procedures, and compulsory record keeping.

A. L. A. Schechter Poultry Corporation, owned by Joseph, Martin, Aaron, and Alex Schechter, was a poultry slaughtering business in Brooklyn. Slaughterhouse operators, such as the Schechters, purchased large numbers of live chickens from local poultry dealers who imported the fowl from out of state to be killed and dressed for sale.

Government officials found the Schechters in violation of the Poultry Code on numerous counts. They ignored the code's wage and hour provisions, failed to comply with government record-keeping requirements, and did not conform to the slaughter regulations. Their worst offense, however, was selling unsanitary poultry that the government found unfit for human consumption. For this reason, *Schechter Poultry* became known as the Sick Chicken Case.

The government obtained indictments against Schechter Poultry Corporation and the four brothers on sixty counts of violating the code, and the jury found them guilty of nineteen. Each of the brothers was sentenced to a short jail term. They appealed unsuccessfully to the court of appeals and then pressed their case to the U.S. Supreme Court, asserting that the NIRA was unconstitu-

---

5. *Railroad Retirement Board v. Alton Railroad Co.* (1935).
6. *Louisville Bank v. Radford* (1935).

7. For an interesting discussion of the *Schechter* case, see chapter 5 in *The New Deal Lawyers*, by Peter H. Irons (Princeton: Princeton University Press, 1982).

A. L. A. Schechter (*center*) of Schechter Poultry Corporation with his attorneys Joseph Heller (*left*) and Frederick Wood, May 2, 1935.

tional because it called for improper delegation of powers and violated the commerce clause.

MR. CHIEF JUSTICE HUGHES delivered the opinion of the Court.

The question of the delegation of legislative power. We recently had occasion to review the pertinent decisions and the general principles which govern the determination of this question. The Constitution provides that "All legislative powers herein granted shall be vested in a Congress of the United States, which shall consist of a Senate and House of Representatives." Art. I, §1. And the Congress is authorized "To make all laws which shall be necessary and proper for carrying into execution" its general powers. Art. I, §8, par. 18. The Congress is not permitted to abdicate or to transfer to others the essential legislative functions with which it is thus vested. . . .

Section 3 of the Recovery Act is without precedent. It supplies no standards for any trade, industry or activity. It does not undertake to prescribe rules of conduct to be applied to particular states of fact determined by appropriate administrative procedure. Instead of prescribing rules of conduct, it authorizes the making of codes to prescribe them. For that legislative undertaking, §3 sets up no standards, aside from the statement of the general aims of rehabilitation, correction and expansion described in section

one. In view of the scope of that broad declaration, and of the nature of the few restrictions that are imposed, the discretion of the President in approving or prescribing codes, and thus enacting laws for the government of trade and industry throughout the country, is virtually unfettered. We think that the code-making authority thus conferred is an unconstitutional delegation of legislative power.

. . . *The question of the application of the provisions of the Live Poultry Code to intrastate transactions.* . . . This aspect of the case presents the question whether the particular provisions of the Live Poultry Code, which the defendants were convicted for violating and for having conspired to violate, were within the regulating power of Congress.

These provisions relate to the hours and wages of those employed by defendants in their slaughterhouses in Brooklyn and to the sales there made to retail dealers and butchers.

(1) Were these transactions *"in"* interstate commerce? Much is made of the fact that almost all the poultry coming to New York is sent there from other States. But the code provisions, as here applied, do not concern the transportation of the poultry from other States to New York, or the transactions of the commission men or others to whom it is consigned, or the sales made by such consignees to defendants. When defendants had made their purchases, whether at the West Washington Market in New York City or at the railroad terminals serving the City, or elsewhere, the poultry was trucked to their slaughterhouses in Brooklyn for local disposition. The interstate transactions in relation to that poultry then ended. Defendants held the poultry at their slaughterhouse markets for slaughter and local sale to retail dealers and butchers who in turn sold directly to consumers. Neither the slaughtering nor the sales by defendants were transactions in interstate commerce.

The undisputed facts thus afford no warrant for the argument that the poultry handled by defendants at their slaughterhouse markets was in a *"current"* or *"flow"* of interstate commerce and was thus subject to congressional regulation. The mere fact that there may be a constant flow of commodities into a State does not mean that the flow continues after the property has arrived and has become commingled with the mass of property within the State and is there held solely for local disposition and use. So far as the poultry here in question is concerned; the flow in interstate commerce had ceased. The poultry had come to a permanent rest within the State. It was not held, used, or sold by defendants in relation to any further transactions in interstate commerce and was not destined for transportation to other States. Hence, decisions which deal with a stream of interstate commerce—where goods come to rest within a State temporarily and are later to go forward in interstate commerce—and with the regulations of transactions involved in that practical continuity of movement, are not applicable here.

(2) Did the defendants' transactions directly *"affect"* interstate commerce so as to be subject to federal regulation? The power of Congress extends not only to the regulation of transactions which are part of interstate commerce, but to the protection of that commerce from injury. It matters not that the injury may be due to the conduct of those engaged in intrastate operations. Thus, Congress may protect the safety of those employed in interstate transportation "no matter what may be the source of the dangers which threaten it." We said in *Second Employers' Liability Cases*, that it is the "effect upon interstate commerce," not "the source of the injury," which is "the criterion of congressional power." We have held that, in dealing with common carriers engaged in both interstate and intrastate commerce, the dominant authority of Congress necessarily embraces the right to control their intrastate operations in all matters having such a close and substantial relation to interstate traffic that the control is essential or appropriate to secure the freedom of that traffic from interference or unjust discrimination and to promote the efficiency of the interstate service. And combinations and conspiracies to restrain interstate commerce, or to monopolize any part of it, are none the less within the reach of the Anti-Trust Act because the conspirators seek to attain their end by means of intrastate activities. . . .

In determining how far the federal government may go in controlling intrastate transactions upon the ground that they "affect" interstate commerce, there is a necessary and well-established distinction between direct and indirect effects. The precise line can be drawn only as individual cases arise, but the distinction is clear in principle. Direct effects are illustrated by the railroad cases we have cited, as *e.g.,* the effect of failure to use prescribed safety appliances on railroads which are the highways of both interstate and intrastate commerce, injury to an employee engaged in interstate transportation by the negligence of an employee

engaged in an intrastate movement, the fixing of rates for intrastate transportation which unjustly discriminate against interstate commerce. But where the effect of intrastate transactions upon interstate commerce is merely indirect, such transactions remain within the domain of state power. If the commerce clause were construed to reach all enterprises and transactions which could be said to have an indirect effect upon interstate commerce, the federal authority would embrace practically all the activities of the people and the authority of the State over its domestic concerns would exist only by sufferance of the federal government. Indeed, on such a theory, even the development of the State's commercial facilities would be subject to federal control. As we said in the *Minnesota Rate Cases:* "In the intimacy of commercial relations, much that is done in the superintendence of local matters may have an indirect bearing upon interstate commerce. The development of local resources and the extension of local facilities may have a very important effect upon communities less favored and to an appreciable degree alter the course of trade. The freedom of local trade may stimulate interstate commerce, while restrictive measures within the police power of the State enacted exclusively with respect to internal business, as distinguished from interstate traffic, may in their reflex or indirect influence diminish the latter and reduce the volume of articles transported into or out of the State."

The distinction between direct and indirect effects has been clearly recognized in the application of the Anti-Trust Act. Where a combination or conspiracy is formed, with the intent to restrain interstate commerce or to monopolize any part of it, the violation of the statute is clear. But where that intent is absent, and the objectives are limited to intrastate activities, the fact that there may be an indirect effect upon interstate commerce does not subject the parties to the federal statute, notwithstanding its broad provisions. . . .

[T]he distinction between direct and indirect effects of intrastate transactions upon interstate commerce must be recognized as a fundamental one, essential to the maintenance of our constitutional system. Otherwise, as we have said, there would be virtually no limit to the federal power and for all practical purposes we should have a completely centralized government. We must consider the provisions here in question in the light of this distinction.

The question of chief importance relates to the provisions of the Code as to the hours and wages of those employed in defendants' slaughterhouse markets. It is plain that these requirements are imposed in order to govern the details of defendants' management of their local business. The persons employed in slaughtering and selling in local trade are not employed in interstate commerce. Their hours and wages have no direct relation to interstate commerce. The question of how many hours these employees should work and what they should be paid differs in no essential respect from similar questions in other local businesses which handle commodities brought into a State and there dealt in as a part of its internal commerce. This appears from an examination of the considerations urged by the Government with respect to conditions in the poultry trade. Thus, the Government argues that hours and wages affect prices; that slaughterhouse men sell at a small margin above operating costs; that a slaughterhouse operator paying lower wages or reducing his cost by exacting long hours of work, translates his saving into lower prices; that this results in demands for a cheaper grade of goods; and that the cutting of prices brings about a demoralization of the price structure. Similar conditions may be adduced in relation to other businesses. The argument of the Government proves too much. If the federal government may determine the wages and hours of employees in the internal commerce of a State, because of their relation to cost and prices and their indirect effect upon interstate commerce, it would seem that a similar control might be exerted over other elements of cost, also affecting prices, such as the number of employees, rents, advertising, methods of doing business, etc. All the processes of production and distribution that enter into cost could likewise be controlled. If the cost of doing an intrastate business is in itself the permitted object of federal control, the extent of the regulation of cost would be a question of discretion and not of power.

The Government also makes the point that efforts to enact state legislation establishing high labor standards have been impeded by the belief that unless similar action is taken generally, commerce will be diverted from the States adopting such standards, and that this fear of diversion has led to demands for federal legislation on the subject of wages and hours. The apparent implication is that the federal authority under the commerce clause should be deemed to extend to the establishment of rules to govern wages and hours in intrastate trade and industry generally throughout the country, thus overriding the authority of the States to deal with domestic problems arising from labor conditions in their internal commerce.

It is not the province of the Court to consider the economic advantages or disadvantages of such a centralized system. It is sufficient to say that the Federal Constitution does not provide for it. Our growth and development have called for wide use of the commerce power of the federal government in its control over the expanded activities of interstate commerce, and in protecting that commerce from burdens, interferences, and conspiracies to restrain and monopolize it. But the authority of the federal government may not be pushed to such an extreme as to destroy the distinction, which the commerce clause itself establishes, between commerce "among the several States" and the internal concerns of a State. The same answer must be made to the contention that is based upon the serious economic situation which led to the passage of the Recovery Act,—the fall in prices, the decline in wages and employment, and the curtailment of the market for commodities. Stress is laid upon the great importance of maintaining wage distributions which would provide the necessary stimulus in starting "the cumulative forces making for expanding commercial activity." Without in any way disparaging this motive, it is enough to say that the recuperative efforts of the federal government must be made in a manner consistent with the authority granted by the Constitution.

We are of the opinion that the attempt through the provisions of the Code to fix the hours and wages of employees of defendants in their intrastate business was not a valid exercise of federal power.

The other violations for which defendants were convicted related to the making of local sales. Ten counts, for violation of the provision as to "straight killing," were for permitting customers to make "selections of individual chickens taken from particular coops and half coops." Whether or not this practice is good or bad for the local trade, its effect, if any, upon interstate commerce was only indirect. The same may be said of violations of the Code by intrastate transactions consisting of the sale "of an unfit chicken" and of sales which were not in accord with the ordinances of the City of New York. The requirement of reports as to prices and volumes of defendants' sales was incident to the effort to control their intrastate business. . . .

On both the grounds we have discussed, the attempted delegation of legislative power, and the attempted regulation of intrastate transactions which affect interstate commerce only indirectly, we hold the code provisions here in question to be invalid and that the judgment of conviction must be reversed.

The decision in *Schechter* closely paralleled the *E. C. Knight* ruling and rejected the application of the stream of commerce doctrine. In *E. C. Knight* the Court held that sugar refining was a manufacturing stage, not part of interstate commerce, and, therefore, the federal government could not regulate it. In *Schechter* the Court classified the slaughtering and local sale of chickens as intrastate commerce. The stream of commerce evident in the stockyards decisions did not apply. In *Schechter* the interstate movement of the poultry had ceased. Once the distributor had sold to local processors like the Schechter company, the chickens had reached their state of final destination and became a part of intrastate commerce. Also consistent with *E. C. Knight* was the justices' conclusion that the poultry slaughter business had only an indirect effect on interstate commerce.

Through the remaining months of 1935 and into 1936, the Court continued to strike down federal legislation designed to cope with the Depression. In some cases the Court found the statutes defective for violating the federal taxing and spending power or for depriving individuals of their right to property without due process of law, topics covered in later chapters. But throughout this period, the Court was concerned with congressional actions that went beyond constitutional authority to regulate interstate commerce. Congress could not constitutionally legislate local business activity, such as manufacturing, processing, or refining, unless it had a direct effect on interstate commerce. The Court supported congressional regulation when the commerce was in movement from one state to another, but, as demonstrated in *Schechter,* the justices were unwilling to allow Congress to act on commerce after it had completed its interstate journey. *Schechter* examined when interstate commerce ends; in May 1936, with its decision in **Carter v. Carter Coal Company**, the Court taught the administration a lesson in when interstate commerce begins.

Congress passed the Bituminous Coal Conservation Act in August 1935, following the *Schechter* decision. This law replaced the NIRA coal codes, which had been reasonably effective in bringing some stability to the depressed coal industry. The new act called for the establishment of a commission empowered to develop regulations regarding fair competition, production, wages, hours, and labor relations. The commission included representatives from the coal producers, coal miners, and the public. To fund the program, Congress imposed a tax at the mines of 15 percent of the value of the coal produced. As was not the case with the NIRA codes, compliance with the new code regulations was voluntary. There was, however, an incentive for joining the program. Companies who participated were given a rebate of 90 percent of the taxes levied by the act.

James W. Carter and other shareholders urged their company, Carter Coal, not to participate in the program. The board of directors did not want to join, but it believed that the company could not afford to pay the 15 percent tax and forgo the participation rebate. Carter and the stockholders sued to prevent the company from joining the program on the ground that the Coal Act was unconstitutional. Of Carter's several attacks on the law, the most deadly was the charge that coal mining was not interstate commerce.

By a 5–4 vote the justices struck down the law. The majority held that coal mining was not interstate commerce because the activity occurred within a single state. The stream of commerce doctrine was inapplicable because the movement of the coal to other states had not yet begun. Furthermore, the justices concluded that the production of coal did not have a direct effect on interstate commerce. For these reasons, the Court invalidated federal regulation of coal mining. But *Carter v. Carter Coal* was to be Roosevelt's last major defeat at the hands of the Four Horsemen and their allies.

The Court-Packing Plan

The Court entered its summer recess in 1936 having completed a year and a half of dealing with Roosevelt's legislative program and striking down several of the New Deal's most significant programs. The Four Horsemen

Editorial cartoon on President Roosevelt's Court-packing plan, *Washington Post*, February 6, 1937.

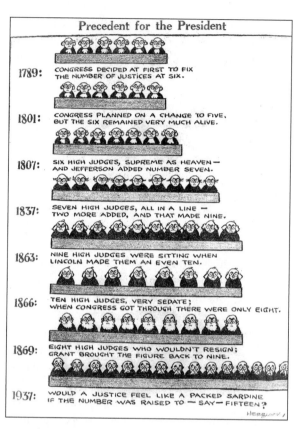

A *Washington Post* Herblock cartoon on the Court-packing plan, February 22, 1937.

constituted a solid bloc, and in important cases they could count on the support of at least one other member—usually Roberts. Roosevelt was understandably frustrated with what he viewed as the Court's obstructionism; he was also impatient that no vacancies had occurred that he might fill with appointees sympathetic to the New Deal.

The national elections took center stage in fall 1936, with little doubt that Roosevelt would be reelected and that the Democrats would continue to control Congress. The only question was how big the margin was going to be. Roosevelt won by a landslide, capturing 98 percent of the electoral votes. His Republican opponent, Alf Landon of Kansas, carried only Maine and Vermont. The congressional elections were another triumph for the Democrats. When the legislature reconvened in early

1937, they controlled approximately 80 percent of the seats in both houses. With such an impressive mandate from the people and such strong party support in Congress, Roosevelt was willing to proceed with his planned attack on the Court. If no vacancies on the Supreme Court occurred naturally, Roosevelt would try to create some.

On February 5, 1937, the president announced his plan to reorganize the federal court system. Among other proposals, the president asked Congress to authorize the creation of one new seat on the Court for every justice who had attained the age of seventy but remained in active service. These expanded positions would have an upper limit of six, bringing the potential size of the Court to a maximum of fifteen. At the time of his proposal, six sitting justices were older than seventy. If Roosevelt could appoint six New Deal advocates to the Court, they proba-

FIGURE 7-1 Public Support for Roosevelt's 1937 Court-Packing Plan

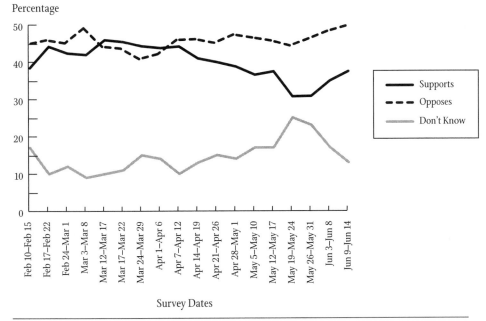

Survey Dates

DATA SOURCE: Lee Epstein, Jeffrey A. Segal, Harold Spaeth, and Thomas G. Walker, *The Supreme Court Compendium: Data, Decisions, and Developments,* 4th ed. (Washington, D.C.: CQ Press, 2007), Table 8-30.

bly could attract the votes of at least two others and form a majority that would give constitutional approval to the president's programs. Although Roosevelt attempted to justify his proposal on the ground that the advanced age of several sitting justices called for the addition of younger, more vigorous colleagues, everyone saw the plan for what it was—an attempt to pack the Court.

The reaction was not favorable.[8] Public opinion polls taken during the course of the debate over the plan revealed that at no time did a majority of Americans support Roosevelt's proposal *(see Figure 7-1)*. Members of the organized bar were overwhelmingly opposed. Even with large Democratic majorities in both houses of Congress, Roosevelt had difficulty selling his proposal to the legislature. Chief Justice Hughes wrote a public letter criticizing the proposal to Sen. Burton Wheeler of Montana, a leader of Democrats opposing the president.[9] The press expressed sharp disapproval. In spite of the general support the people gave Roosevelt and the New Deal, they did not appreciate his tampering with the structure of government to get his way.

The Switch in Time That Saved Nine

The battle in Congress over the president's plan was closely fought.[10] A continuation of the confrontation was averted in large measure by the actions of the Supreme Court itself. On March 29 the Court signaled that changes were in the making. The first indication was the 5–4 decision in *West Coast Hotel v. Parrish* (1937), which upheld the validity of a Washington State law regulating wages

8. See Gregory A. Caldeira, "Public Opinion and the U.S. Supreme Court: FDR's Court-Packing Plan," *American Political Science Review* 81 (December 1987): 1139–53.

9. The letter, dated March 21, 1937, is reprinted in *Guide to the U.S. Supreme Court,* 3rd ed., ed. Joan Biskupic and Elder Witt (Washington, D.C.: Congressional Quarterly, 1997), 1039–40.

10. See William E. Leuchtenburg, "The Origins of Franklin D. Roosevelt's 'Court-Packing' Plan," *Supreme Court Review* 1966 (Chicago: University of Chicago Press, 1966), 347–400; and Leuchtenburg, *Franklin D. Roosevelt and the New Deal, 1932–1940* (New York: Harper and Row, 1963).

and working conditions for women and children. Although this case involved a state law rather than a federal statute and focused on a Fourteenth Amendment issue rather than the commerce clause, it had great significance. The voting coalitions on the Court had changed. Justice Roberts, so long an ally of the Four Horsemen, deserted the conservatives and voted with the liberal bloc to approve the legislation. Just months earlier Roberts had voted with the conservatives in a 5–4 decision striking down a New York law that was nearly a carbon copy of the one he now approved.[11]

Two weeks later Roberts proved that his *West Coast Hotel* vote was not an aberration. On April 12 the Court issued its ruling in *National Labor Relations Board v. Jones & Laughlin Steel Corporation.* Once again Roberts joined Hughes, Brandeis, Cardozo, and Stone to form a majority, this time upholding a major piece of New Deal legislation. This decision may be the most significant economic ruling handed down during the twentieth century. In it the Court announced a break from the past and ushered in a new era in the constitutional relationship between the government and the economy.

National Labor Relations Board v. Jones & Laughlin Steel Corporation

301 U.S. 1 (1937)
http://laws.findlaw.com/US/301/1.html
Vote: 5 (Brandeis, Cardozo, Hughes, Roberts, Stone)
    4 (Butler, McReynolds, Sutherland, Van Devanter)
Opinion for the Court: Hughes
Dissenting opinion: McReynolds

In 1935 Congress passed the National Labor Relations Act, more commonly known as the Wagner Act. The purpose of the legislation was to help workers achieve gains in wages and working conditions through the collective-bargaining process. The act's primary aim was to protect the rights of employees to organize and join labor unions and to provide a means for the enforcement of those rights. The law authorized the creation of the National

Labor Relations Board (NLRB), which was empowered to hear complaints of unfair labor practices and impose certain corrective measures. The act was based on the power of Congress to regulate interstate commerce and upon the assertion that labor unrest and strikes caused an interruption in such commerce that Congress had the right to prevent.

Jones & Laughlin was one of the nation's largest steel producers. Its operations were fully integrated, extending into many states and involving every aspect of steel production from mining through production and distribution. Complaints were filed against the company for engaging in unfair labor practices at its plant in Aliquippa, Pennsylvania. The charges included discriminating against workers who wanted to join a labor union. The NLRB ruled against the company and ordered it to reinstate ten workers who had been dismissed because of their union activities. The company refused, claiming that the National Labor Relations Act was unconstitutional. Steel production facilities, according to the company, were engaged in a manufacturing activity that had been declared by the Supreme Court to be intrastate commerce outside the regulatory authority of Congress. The lower courts, applying existing Supreme Court precedent, ruled in favor of the company, and the NLRB appealed.

MR. CHIEF JUSTICE HUGHES delivered the opinion of the Court.

First. The scope of the Act.—The Act is challenged in its entirety as an attempt to regulate all industry, thus invading the reserved powers of the States over their local concerns. It is asserted that the references in the Act to interstate and foreign commerce are colorable at best; that the Act is not a true regulation of such commerce or of matters which directly affect it but on the contrary has the fundamental object of placing under the compulsory supervision of the federal government all industrial labor relations within the nation. . . .

If this conception of terms, intent and consequent inseparability were sound, the Act would necessarily fall by reason of the limitation upon the federal power which inheres in the constitutional grant, as well as because of the explicit reservation of the Tenth Amendment. The authority of the

---

11. *Morehead v. New York ex rel. Tipaldo* (1936).

federal government may not be pushed to such an extreme as to destroy the distinction, which the commerce clause itself establishes, between commerce "among the several States" and the internal concerns of a State. That distinction between what is national and what is local in the activities of commerce is vital to the maintenance of our federal system. . . .

We think it clear that the National Labor Relations Act may be construed so as to operate within the sphere of constitutional authority. The jurisdiction conferred upon the Board, and invoked in this instance, is found in §10 (a), which provides:

"Sec. 10 (a). The Board is empowered, as hereinafter provided, to prevent any person from engaging in any unfair labor practice (listed in section 8) affecting commerce."

The critical words of this provision, prescribing the limits of the Board's authority in dealing with the labor practices, are "affecting commerce." The Act specifically defines the "commerce" to which it refers (§2 (6)):

"The term 'commerce' means trade, traffic, commerce, transportation, or communication among the several States, or between the District of Columbia or any Territory of the United States and any State or other Territory, or between any foreign country and any State, Territory, or the District of Columbia, or within the District of Columbia or any Territory, or between points in the same State but through any other State or any Territory or the District of Columbia or any foreign country."

There can be no question that the commerce thus contemplated by the Act (aside from that within a Territory or the District of Columbia) is interstate and foreign commerce in the constitutional sense. The Act also defines the term "affecting commerce" (§2 (7)):

"The term 'affecting commerce' means in commerce, or burdening or obstructing commerce or the free flow of commerce or having led or tending to lead to a labor dispute burdening or obstructing commerce or the free flow of commerce."

This definition is one of exclusion as well as inclusion. The grant of authority to the Board does not purport to extend to the relationship between all industrial employees and employers. Its terms do not impose collective bargaining upon all industry regardless of effects upon interstate and foreign commerce. It purports to reach only what may be deemed to burden or obstruct that commerce and, thus qualified, it must be construed as contemplating the exercise of control within constitutional bounds. It is a familiar principle that acts which directly burden or obstruct interstate or foreign commerce, or its free flow, are within the reach of the congressional power. Acts having that effect are not rendered immune because they grow out of labor disputes. It is the effect upon commerce, not the source of the injury, which is the criterion. Whether or not particular action does affect commerce in such a close and intimate fashion as to be subject to federal control, and hence to lie within the authority conferred upon the Board, is left by the statute to be determined as individual cases arise. We are thus to inquire whether in the instant case the constitutional boundary has been passed.

Second. The unfair labor practices in question.— . . .

[T]he statute goes no further than to safeguard the right of employees to self-organization and to select representatives of their own choosing for collective bargaining or other mutual protection without restraint or coercion by their employer.

That is a fundamental right. Employees have as clear a right to organize and select their representatives for lawful purposes as the respondent has to organize its business and select its own officers and agents. Discrimination and coercion to prevent the free exercise of the right of employees to self-organization and representation is a proper subject for condemnation by competent legislative authority. Long ago we stated the reason for labor organizations. We said that they were organized out of the necessities of the situation; that a single employee was helpless in dealing with an employer; that he was dependent ordinarily on his daily wage for the maintenance of himself and family; that if the employer refused to pay him the wages that he thought fair, he was nevertheless unable to leave the employ and resist arbitrary and unfair treatment; that union was essential to give laborers opportunity to deal on an equality with their employer. We reiterated these views when we had under consideration the Railway Labor Act of 1926. Fully recognizing the legality of collective action on the part of employees in order to safeguard their proper interests, we said that Congress was not required to ignore this right but could safeguard it. Congress could seek to make appropriate collective action of employees an instrument of peace rather than of strife. We said that such collective action would be a mockery if representation were made futile by interference with freedom of choice. Hence the prohibition by Congress of interference with the selection of representatives for the purpose of negotiation and conference between employers and employees, "instead of being an invasion of the constitutional right of either, was based on the recognition of the rights of both." We have reasserted the same principle in sustaining the application of the Railway Labor Act as amended in 1934.

Third. The application of the Act to employees engaged in production.—The principle involved.—Respondent says that whatever may be said of employees engaged in interstate commerce, the industrial relations and activities in the manufacturing department of respondent's enterprise are not subject to federal regulation. The argument rests upon the proposition that manufacturing in itself is not commerce.

The Government distinguishes these cases. The various parts of respondent's enterprise are described as interdependent and as thus involving "a great movement of iron ore, coal and limestone along well-defined paths to the steel mills, thence through them, and thence in the form of steel products into the consuming centers of the country—a definite and well-understood course of business." It is urged that these activities constitute a "stream" or "flow" of commerce, of which the Aliquippa manufacturing plant is the focal point, and that industrial strife at that point would cripple the entire government. Reference is made to our decision sustaining the Packers and Stockyards Act. . . .

We do not find it necessary to determine whether these features of defendant's business dispose of the asserted analogy to the "stream of commerce" cases. The instances in which that metaphor has been used are but particular, and not exclusive, illustrations of the protective power which the Government invokes in support of the present Act. The congressional authority to protect interstate commerce from burdens and obstructions is not limited to transactions which can be deemed to be an essential part of a "flow" of interstate or foreign commerce. Burdens and obstructions may be due to injurious action springing from other sources. The fundamental principle is that the power to regulate commerce is the power to enact "all appropriate legislation" for "its protection and advancement"; to adopt measures "to promote its growth and insure its safety"; "to foster, protect, control and restrain." That power is plenary and may be exerted to protect interstate commerce "no matter what the source of the dangers which threaten it."

Although activities may be intrastate in character when separately considered, if they have such a close and substantial relation to interstate commerce that their control is essential or appropriate to protect that commerce from burdens and obstructions, Congress cannot be denied the power to exercise that control. . . .

It is thus apparent that the fact that the employees here concerned were engaged in production is not determinative. The question remains as to the effect upon interstate commerce of the labor practice involved. . . .

Fourth. Effects of the unfair labor practice in respondent's enterprise.—Giving full weight to respondent's contention with respect to a break in the complete continuity of the "stream of commerce" by reason of respondent's manufacturing operations, the fact remains that the stoppage of those operations by industrial strife would have a most serious effect upon interstate commerce. In view of respondent's far-flung activities, it is idle to say that the effect would be indirect or remote. It is obvious that it would be immediate and might be catastrophic. We are asked to shut our eyes to the plainest facts of our national life and to deal with the question of direct and indirect effects in an intellectual vacuum. Because there may be but indirect and remote effects upon interstate commerce in connection with a host of local enterprises throughout the country, it does not follow that other industrial activities do not have such a close and intimate relation to interstate commerce as to make the presence of industrial strife a matter of the most urgent national concern. When industries organize themselves on a national scale, making their relation to interstate commerce the dominant factor in their activities, how can it be maintained that their industrial labor relations constitute a forbidden field into which Congress may not enter when it is necessary to protect interstate commerce from the paralyzing consequences of industrial war? We have often said that interstate commerce itself is a practical conception. It is equally true that interferences with that commerce must be appraised by a judgment that does not ignore actual experience.

Experience has abundantly demonstrated that the recognition of the right of employees to self-organization and to have representatives of their own choosing for the purpose of collective bargaining is often an essential condition of industrial peace. Refusal to confer and negotiate has been one of the most prolific causes of strife. This is such an outstanding fact in the history of labor disturbances that it is a proper subject of judicial notice and requires no citation of instances. . . .

These questions have frequently engaged the attention of Congress and have been the subject of many inquiries. The steel industry is one of the great basic industries of the United States, with ramifying activities affecting interstate commerce at every point. The Government aptly refers to the steel strike of 1919–1920 with its far-reaching consequences. The fact that there appears to have been no major disturbance in that industry in the more recent period did not dispose of the possibilities of future and like dangers to interstate commerce which Congress was entitled to foresee and to exercise its protective power to forestall. It is not necessary again to detail the facts as to respondent's enterprise. Instead of being beyond the pale, we think that it presents in a most striking way the close and intimate relation which a manufacturing industry may have to interstate commerce and we have no doubt that Congress had constitutional authority to safeguard the right of respondent's employees to self-organization and freedom in the choice of representatives for collective bargaining.

Reversed.

MR. JUSTICE MCREYNOLDS delivered the following dissenting opinion in the cases preceding:

MR. JUSTICE VAN DEVANTER, MR. JUSTICE SUTHERLAND, MR. JUSTICE BUTLER and I are unable to agree with the decisions just announced. . . .

Considering the far-reaching import of these decisions, the departure from what we understand has been consistently ruled here, and the extraordinary power confirmed to a Board of three [the NLRB], the obligation to present our views becomes plain. . . .

The precise question for us to determine is whether in the circumstances disclosed Congress has power to authorize what the Labor Board commanded the respondents to do. Stated otherwise, in the circumstances here existing could Congress by statute direct what the Board has ordered? . . .

The argument in support of the Board affirms: "Thus the validity of any specific application of the preventive measures of this Act depends upon whether industrial strife resulting from the practices in the particular enterprise under consideration would be of the character which Federal power could control if it occurred. If strife in that enterprise could be controlled, certainly it could be prevented."

Manifestly that view of Congressional power would extend it into almost every field of human industry. . . .

The Constitution still recognizes the existence of states with indestructible powers; the Tenth Amendment was supposed to put them beyond controversy.

We are told that Congress may protect the "stream of commerce" and that one who buys raw material without the state, manufactures it therein, and ships the output to another state is in that stream. Therefore it is said he may be prevented from doing anything which may interfere with its flow.

This, too, goes beyond the constitutional limitations heretofore enforced. If a man raises cattle and regularly delivers them to a carrier for interstate shipment, may Congress prescribe the conditions under which he may employ or discharge helpers on the ranch? The products of a mine pass daily into interstate commerce; many things are brought to it from other states. Are the owners and miners within the power of Congress in respect of the miners' tenure and discharge? May a mill owner be prohibited from closing his factory or discontinuing his business because so to do would stop the flow of products to and from his plant in interstate commerce? May employees in a factory be restrained from quitting work in a body because this will close the factory and thereby stop the flow of commerce? May arson of a factory be made a Federal offense whenever this would interfere with such flow? If the business cannot continue with the existing wage scale, may Congress command a reduction? If the ruling of the Court just announced is adhered to these questions suggest some of the problems certain to arise. . . .

There is no ground on which reasonably to hold that refusal by a manufacturer, whose raw materials come from states other than that of his factory and whose products are regularly carried to other states, to bargain collectively with employees in his manufacturing plant, directly affects interstate commerce. In such business, there is not one but two distinct movements or streams in interstate transportation. The first brings in raw material and there ends. Then follows manufacture, a separate and local activity. Upon completion of this, and not before, the second distinct movement or stream in interstate commerce begins and the products go to other states. Such is the common course for small as well as large industries. It is unreasonable and unprecedented to say the commerce clause confers upon Congress power to govern the relations between employers and employees in these local activities. In *Schechter*'s case we condemned as unauthorized by the commerce clause assertion of federal power in respect of commodities which had come to rest after interstate transportation. And, in *Carter*'s case, we held Congress lacked the power to regulate labor relations in respect of commodities before interstate commerce has begun.

It is gravely stated that experience teaches that if an employer discourages membership in "any organization of any kind" "in which employees participate, and which exists for the purpose in whole or in part of dealing with employers concerning grievances, labor disputes, wages, rates of pay, hours of employment or conditions of work," discontent may follow and this in turn may lead to a strike, and as the outcome of the strike there may be a block in the stream of interstate commerce. Therefore Congress may inhibit the discharge! Whatever effect any cause of discontent may ultimately have upon commerce is far too indirect to justify Congressional regulation. Almost anything—marriage, birth, death—may in some fashion affect commerce.

That Congress has power by appropriate means, not prohibited by the Constitution, to prevent direct and material interference with the conduct of interstate commerce is settled doctrine. But the interference struck at must be direct and material, not some mere possibility contingent on wholly uncertain events; and there must be no impairment of rights guaranteed. . . .

The things inhibited by the Labor Act relate to the management of a manufacturing plant—something distinct from commerce and subject to the authority of the state. And this may not be abridged because of some vague possibility of distant interference with commerce. . . .

It seems clear to us that Congress has transcended the powers granted.

The decisions in *West Coast Hotel v. Parrish* and *NLRB v. Jones & Laughlin Steel* took the energy out of Roosevelt's drive to pack the Court. It no longer appeared necessary, as the Court was now looking with greater approval at state and federal legislation to correct the failing economy. In addition, on May 18, 1937, Justice Van Devanter,

Justice Owen Roberts. He cast critical votes in 1937 Supreme Court cases that expanded the authority of the federal government to regulate the economy.

a consistent foe of Roosevelt's New Deal programs, announced that he would retire from the Court at the end of the term. At long last the president would have an opportunity to put a justice of his own choosing on the Court.

Much has been said and written about Justice Roberts's change in position. At the time, it was described as "the switch in time that saved nine," because his move from the conservative to the liberal wing of the Court was largely responsible for killing the Court-packing plan and preserving the Court as a nine-justice institution. Such a characterization is not flattering for a judge, who is not supposed to make decisions on the basis of external political pressures. Nevertheless, it would certainly be understandable for a justice to rethink his views if the future of the Court as an institution were at stake.

More contemporary analyses of Roberts's switch assert that the notion that he caved in to the pressures of the president's plan is simplistic. Although the decision in *West Coast Hotel* was announced after Roosevelt sent his proposal to Congress, it was argued and initially voted upon weeks before the president made his plans public. Roosevelt had kept the Court-packing proposal carefully under wraps before he announced it, and there is little likelihood that the justices had advance knowledge of it. Furthermore, Owen Roberts was not a doctrinaire conservative. Although he joined the Court's right wing in several important decisions, he did not have the laissez-faire zeal of the Four Horsemen. In fact, Roberts had voted on many occasions in support of state efforts to combat economic problems.[12] Some observers now conclude that Roberts's change of position was primarily a matter of his growing disenchantment with the hardline conservative view and that he followed "his sound judicial intuition to a well-reasoned position in keeping with the public interest."[13] As for Roberts's own explanation, he maintained traditional judicial silence. When asked in a 1946 interview why he had altered his position, he deflected the question by responding, "Who knows what causes a judge to decide as he does? Maybe the breakfast he had has something to do with it."[14] Whatever the reasons for his switch, it broke the conservatives' domination of the Court.

Consolidating the New Interpretation of the Commerce Power

Van Devanter's retirement was followed over the next four years by the retirements of Justices Sutherland and Brandeis and the deaths of Justices Cardozo and Butler. By 1940 Franklin Roosevelt had appointed a majority of the sitting justices. And in 1941 Justice McReynolds, the last of the Four Horsemen, retired.

With *NLRB v. Jones & Laughlin Steel* showing the way, the increasingly liberal Court upheld many New Deal

programs. It also continued to expand the concept of interstate commerce. Gone were the old notions that production, manufacturing, mining, and processing were exclusively intrastate affairs with insufficient direct effects on interstate commerce to activate federal commerce powers. Precedents such as *E. C. Knight, Dagenhart, Panama Refining, Schechter Poultry,* and *Carter Coal* were substantially overruled, discredited, or severely limited *(see Box 7-4).*

Wickard v. Filburn (1942) illustrates how far the Court moved from its pre-1937 idea of interstate commerce. The 1938 Agricultural Adjustment Act, as amended, allowed the secretary of agriculture to establish production limits for various grains. Under these limits, acreage allotments were assigned to the individual farmer. The purpose of the law was to stop the wild swings in grain prices by eliminating both surpluses and shortfalls.

Roscoe Filburn owned a small farm in Montgomery County, Ohio. For many years he raised dairy cattle and chickens, selling the milk, poultry, and eggs the farm produced. He also raised winter wheat on a small portion of his farm. He sold some of the wheat and used the rest to feed his cattle and chickens, make flour for home consumption, and produce seeds for the next planting.

In July 1940 Secretary of Agriculture Claude R. Wickard set the wheat production limits for the 1941 crop. Filburn was allotted 11.1 acres to be planted in wheat with a yield of 20.1 bushels per acre. He planted not only his allotted acres but also some other land to produce the wheat for home consumption. In total Filburn planted 23 acres in wheat from which he harvested 239 bushels more than the government allowed him. For this excess planting Filburn was fined $117.11. He refused to pay the fine, claiming that Congress had exceeded its powers under the commerce clause by regulating an individual's planting wheat on his own property for on-farm consumption. The lower court ruled in Filburn's favor, and Secretary Wickard appealed.

The Supreme Court unanimously reversed and held that the act applied to Filburn's wheat production. The justices reasoned that wheat grown for on-farm consumption competes with wheat sold in commerce. Filburn's wheat combined with grain grown on other farms for

12. See, for example, his opinion for the Court in *Nebbia v. New York* (1934).
13. Merlo J. Pusey, "Justice Roberts' 1937 Turnaround," *Yearbook of the Supreme Court Historical Society* (Washington, D.C.: Supreme Court Historical Society, 1983), 107.
14. Quoted in ibid., 106.

BOX 7-4   SUPREME COURT EXPANSION OF THE COMMERCE POWERS, 1937–1941

Decision	Ruling
Helvering v. Davis (1937)	Old-age benefits provisions of the Social Security Act are constitutional.
NLRB v. Friedman-Harry Marks Clothing Company (1937)	The National Labor Relations Act applies to a company engaged in the manufacturing of clothing.
NLRB v. Fruehauf Trailer Company (1937)	The National Labor Relations Act applies to a company engaged in the manufacturing of trailers.
Steward Machine v. Davis (1937)	Unemployment provisions of the Social Security Act are constitutional.
Consolidated Edison Company v. NLRB (1938)	The National Labor Relations Act applies to a power company although all of its power is sold in state.
Santa Cruz Fruit Packing v. NLRB (1938)	The National Labor Relations Act applies to a fruit packing company although only 37 percent of its product is sold in interstate commerce.
Mulford v. Smith (1939)	Tobacco production quotas set by the secretary of agriculture under the Agricultural Adjustment Act of 1938 are constitutional.
NLRB v. Fainblatt (1939)	The National Labor Relations Act applies to a small garment manufacturer even though all of its goods are sold in state.
United States v. Rock Royal Cooperative (1939)	Legislation allowing the secretary of agriculture to set milk prices paid to farmers is constitutional.
United States v. Darby Lumber Company (1941)	Congressional action prohibiting shipment in interstate commerce of goods in violation of federal wage and hour laws is constitutional.

---

home consumption may have a considerable impact on interstate commerce. Therefore, Congress has the authority to regulate such production—even small amounts produced by individuals. How far the Court had come! Prior to 1937 the justices had held that the 98 percent of the nation's sugar supply and the country's coal production had only an indirect effect on interstate commerce.

With decisions such as *NLRB v. Jones & Laughlin Steel* and *Wickard v. Filburn,* the Court had entered a new era of commerce clause interpretation. No longer would the justices grapple with issues such as direct versus indirect effects or stream of commerce concerns. Under the mod-

ern interpretations very little commercial activity could be defined as purely intrastate.

Modern Limitations on the Commerce Power

That the Court remained loyal to this modern interpretation of the commerce power for six decades led constitutional scholars to conclude that it was "settled law." Perhaps that is why the Court's decision in *United States v. Lopez* (1995) was so shocking. For the first time since the battles over the New Deal, the justices struck down a federal statute for falling outside the authority granted to Congress by the commerce clause.

Roscoe Filburn, the Ohio farmer who unsuccessfully argued that Congress lacked the constitutional power to regulate the production of wheat intended for on-farm consumption.

United States v. Lopez

514 U.S. 549 (1995)
http://laws.findlaw.com/US/514/549.html
Oral arguments may be found at: http://www.oyez.org
Vote: 5 (Kennedy, O'Connor, Rehnquist, Scalia, Thomas)
*   4 (Breyer, Ginsburg, Souter, Stevens)*
Opinion of the Court: Rehnquist
Concurring opinions: Kennedy, Thomas
Dissenting opinions: Breyer, Souter, Stevens

On March 10, 1992, Alfonso Lopez Jr. came to Edison High School carrying a concealed .38 caliber handgun and five rounds of ammunition. Acting on an anonymous tip, officials at the San Antonio school confronted the twelfth-grade student, and he admitted having the weapon. Lopez claimed that he had been given the gun by a person who instructed him to deliver it to another individual. The gun was to be used in gang-related activities. Lopez was arrested for violating the federal Gun-Free School Zones Act.

Lopez, who had no record of previous criminal activity, was convicted in federal district court and sentenced to six months in prison, two years of supervised release, and a fifty-dollar fine. His attorneys appealed to the Fifth Circuit Court of Appeals, claiming that Congress had no constitutional authority to pass the Gun-Free School Zones Act. Attorneys for the United States countered by arguing that the law was an appropriate exercise of congressional power to regulate interstate commerce. The appeals court held in favor of Lopez, and the government asked the Supreme Court to review that ruling.

Congress passed the Gun-Free School Zones Act—section 922[q] of chapter 18 of the United States Code—in 1990. In passing the act, Congress did not issue any findings showing a relationship between gun possession on school property and commerce. The federal government argued that such findings should not be required, that it would be sufficient if Congress could reasonably conclude that gun-related violence in schools affects interstate commerce directly or indirectly. Lopez countered by arguing that the simple possession of a weapon on school grounds is not a commercial activity that reasonably falls under commerce clause jurisdiction. Furthermore, the regulation of crime and education are traditional areas of state, not federal, jurisdiction.

CHIEF JUSTICE REHNQUIST delivered the opinion of the Court.

In the Gun-Free School Zones Act of 1990, Congress made it a federal offense "for any individual knowingly to possess a firearm at a place that the individual knows, or has reasonable cause to believe, is a school zone." The Act neither regulates a commercial activity nor contains a requirement that the possession be connected in any way to interstate commerce. We hold that the Act exceeds the authority of Congress "[t]o regulate Commerce . . . among the several States." . . .

We start with first principles. The Constitution creates a Federal Government of enumerated powers. As James

Madison wrote, "[t]he powers delegated by the proposed Constitution to the federal government are few and defined. Those which are to remain in the State governments are numerous and indefinite." This constitutionally mandated division of authority "was adopted by the Framers to ensure protection of our fundamental liberties." *Gregory v. Ashcroft,* (1991). . . .

. . . The Court, through Chief Justice Marshall, first defined the nature of Congress' commerce power in *Gibbons v. Ogden* (1824):

"Commerce, undoubtedly, is traffic, but it is something more: it is intercourse. It describes the commercial intercourse between nations, and parts of nations, in all its branches, and is regulated by prescribing rules for carrying on that intercourse."

The commerce power "is the power to regulate; that is, to prescribe the rule by which commerce is to be governed. This power, like all others vested in Congress, is complete in itself, may be exercised to its utmost extent, and acknowledges no limitations, other than are prescribed in the constitution." Id. . . .

. . . [I]n the watershed case of *NLRB v. Jones & Laughlin Steel Corp.* (1937), the Court upheld the National Labor Relations Act against a Commerce Clause challenge, and in the process, departed from the distinction between "direct" and "indirect" effects on interstate commerce. The Court held that intrastate activities that "have such a close and substantial relation to interstate commerce that their control is essential or appropriate to protect that commerce from burdens and obstructions" are within Congress' power to regulate.

In *United States v. Darby* (1941), the Court upheld the Fair Labor Standards Act, stating:

"The power of Congress over interstate commerce is not confined to the regulation of commerce among the states. It extends to those activities intrastate which so affect interstate commerce or the exercise of the power of Congress over it as to make regulation of them appropriate means to the attainment of a legitimate end, the exercise of the granted power of Congress to regulate interstate commerce."

In *Wickard v. Filburn,* the Court upheld the application of amendments to the Agricultural Adjustment Act of 1938 to the production and consumption of homegrown wheat. The *Wickard* Court explicitly rejected earlier distinctions between direct and indirect effects on interstate commerce, stating:

"[E]ven if appellee's activity be local and though it may not be regarded as commerce, it may still, whatever its nature, be reached by Congress if it exerts a substantial economic effect on interstate commerce, and this irrespective of whether such effect is what might at some earlier time have been defined as 'direct' or 'indirect.' "

The *Wickard* Court emphasized that although Filburn's own contribution to the demand for wheat may have been trivial by itself, that was not "enough to remove him from the scope of federal regulation where, as here, his contribution, taken together with that of many others similarly situated, is far from trivial."

Jones & Laughlin Steel, Darby, and *Wickard* ushered in an era of Commerce Clause jurisprudence that greatly expanded the previously defined authority of Congress under that Clause. In part, this was a recognition of the great changes that had occurred in the way business was carried on in this country. Enterprises that had once been local or at most regional in nature had become national in scope. But the doctrinal change also reflected a view that earlier Commerce Clause cases artificially had constrained the authority of Congress to regulate interstate commerce.

But even these modern-era precedents which have expanded congressional power under the Commerce Clause confirm that this power is subject to outer limits. In *Jones & Laughlin Steel,* the Court warned that the scope of the interstate commerce power "must be considered in the light of our dual system of government and may not be extended so as to embrace effects upon interstate commerce so indirect and remote that to embrace them, in view of our complex society, would effectually obliterate the distinction between what is national and what is local and create a completely centralized government." See also *Darby* (Congress may regulate intrastate activity that has a "substantial effect" on interstate commerce); *Wickard* (Congress may regulate activity that "exerts a substantial economic effect on interstate commerce"). Since that time, the Court has heeded that warning and undertaken to decide whether a rational basis existed for concluding that a regulated activity sufficiently affected interstate commerce. . . .

Consistent with this structure, we have identified three broad categories of activity that Congress may regulate under its commerce power. First, Congress may regulate the use of the channels of interstate commerce. Second, Congress is empowered to regulate and protect the instrumentalities of interstate commerce, or persons or things in interstate commerce, even though the threat may come only from intrastate activities. Finally, Congress' commerce authority includes the power to regulate those activities having a substantial relation to interstate commerce.

Within this final category, admittedly, our case law has not been clear whether an activity must "affect" or "substantially affect" interstate commerce in order to be within Congress' power to regulate it under the Commerce Clause. We conclude, consistent with the great weight of our case law, that the proper test requires an analysis of whether the regulated activity "substantially affects" interstate commerce.

We now turn to consider the power of Congress, in the light of this framework, to enact §922(q). The first two categories of authority may be quickly disposed of: §922(q) is not a regulation of the use of the channels of interstate commerce, nor is it an attempt to prohibit the interstate transportation of a commodity through the channels of commerce; nor can §922(q) be justified as a regulation by which Congress has sought to protect an instrumentality of interstate commerce or a thing in interstate commerce. Thus, if §922(q) is to be sustained, it must be under the third category as a regulation of an activity that substantially affects interstate commerce.

First, we have upheld a wide variety of congressional Acts regulating intrastate economic activity where we have concluded that the activity substantially affected interstate commerce. . . . Where economic activity substantially affects interstate commerce, legislation regulating that activity will be sustained. . . .

Section 922(q) is a criminal statute that by its terms has nothing to do with "commerce" or any sort of economic enterprise, however broadly one might define those terms. Section 922(q) is not an essential part of a larger regulation of economic activity, in which the regulatory scheme could be undercut unless the intrastate activity were regulated. It cannot, therefore, be sustained under our cases upholding regulations of activities that arise out of or are connected with a commercial transaction, which viewed in the aggregate, substantially affects interstate commerce.

Second, §922(q) contains no jurisdictional element which would ensure, through case-by-case inquiry, that the firearm possession in question affects interstate commerce.

For example, in *United States v. Bass* (1971), the Court interpreted former 18 U.S.C. §1202(a), which made it a crime for a felon to "receiv[e], posses[s], or transpor[t] in commerce or affecting commerce . . . any firearm." The Court interpreted the possession component of §1202(a) to require an additional nexus to interstate commerce both because the statute was ambiguous and because "unless Congress conveys its purpose clearly, it will not be deemed to have significantly changed the federal-state balance." . . . Unlike the statute in *Bass,* §922(q) has no express jurisdictional element which might limit its reach to a discrete set of firearm possessions that additionally have an explicit connection with or effect on interstate commerce.

Although as part of our independent evaluation of constitutionality under the Commerce Clause we of course consider legislative findings, and indeed even congressional committee findings, regarding effect on interstate commerce, the Government concedes that "[n]either the statute nor its legislative history contain[s] express congressional findings regarding the effects upon interstate commerce of gun possession in a school zone." We agree with the Government that Congress normally is not required to make formal findings as to the substantial burdens that an activity has on interstate commerce. But to the extent that congressional findings would enable us to evaluate the legislative judgment that the activity in question substantially affected interstate commerce, even though no such substantial effect was visible to the naked eye, they are lacking here. . . .

The Government's essential contention, *in fine,* is that we may determine here that §922(q) is valid because possession of a firearm in a local school zone does indeed substantially affect interstate commerce. The Government argues that possession of a firearm in a school zone may result in violent crime and that violent crime can be expected to affect the functioning of the national economy in two ways. First, the costs of violent crime are substantial, and, through the mechanism of insurance, those costs are spread throughout the population. Second, violent crime reduces the willingness of individuals to travel to areas within the country that are perceived to be unsafe. The Government also argues that the presence of guns in schools poses a substantial threat to the educational process by threatening the learning environment. A handicapped educational process, in turn, will result in a less productive citizenry. That, in turn, would have an adverse effect on the Nation's economic well-being. As a result, the Government argues that Congress could rationally have concluded that §922(q) substantially affects interstate commerce.

We pause to consider the implications of the Government's arguments. The Government admits, under its "costs of crime" reasoning, that Congress could regulate not only all violent crime, but all activities that might lead to violent crime, regardless of how tenuously they relate to interstate commerce. Similarly, under the Government's "national productivity" reasoning, Congress could regulate any activity that it found was related to the economic productivity of individual citizens: family law (including marriage, divorce, and child custody), for example. Under the theories that the Government presents in support of §922(q), it is difficult to perceive any limitation on federal power, even in areas such as criminal law enforcement or education where States historically have been sovereign. Thus, if we were to accept the Government's arguments, we are hard pressed to posit any activity by an individual that Congress is without power to regulate. . . .

Admittedly, a determination whether an intrastate activity is commercial or noncommercial may in some cases result in legal uncertainty. But, so long as Congress' authority is limited to those powers enumerated in the Constitution, and so long as those enumerated powers are interpreted as having judicially enforceable outer limits, congressional legislation under the Commerce Clause always will engender "legal uncertainty." . . .

These are not precise formulations, and in the nature of things they cannot be. But we think they point the way to a correct decision of this case. The possession of a gun in a local school zone is in no sense an economic activity that might, through repetition elsewhere, substantially affect any sort of interstate commerce. Respondent was a local student at a local school; there is no indication that he had recently moved in interstate commerce, and there is no requirement that his possession of the firearm have any concrete tie to interstate commerce.

To uphold the Government's contentions here, we would have to pile inference upon inference in a manner that would bid fair to convert congressional authority under the Commerce Clause to a general police power of the sort retained by the States. Admittedly, some of our prior cases have taken long steps down that road, giving great deference to congressional action. The broad language in these opinions has suggested the possibility of additional expansion, but we decline here to proceed any further. To do so would require us to conclude that the Constitution's enumeration of powers does not presuppose something not enumerated, and that there never will be a distinction between what is truly national and what is truly local. This we are unwilling to do.

For the foregoing reasons the judgment of the Court of Appeals is

Affirmed.

JUSTICE BREYER, with whom JUSTICE STEVENS, JUSTICE SOUTER, and JUSTICE GINSBURG join, dissenting.

The issue in this case is whether the Commerce Clause authorizes Congress to enact a statute that makes it a crime to possess a gun in, or near, a school. In my view, the statute falls well within the scope of the commerce power as this Court has understood that power over the last half century.

In reaching this conclusion, I apply three basic principles of Commerce Clause interpretation. First, the power to "regulate Commerce . . . among the several States" encompasses the power to regulate local activities insofar as they significantly affect interstate commerce. . . . I use the word "significant" because the word "substantial" implies a somewhat narrower power than recent precedent suggests. But, to speak of "substantial effect" rather than "significant effect" would make no difference in this case.

Second, in determining whether a local activity will likely have a significant effect upon interstate commerce, a court must consider, not the effect of an individual act (a single instance of gun possession), but rather the cumulative effect of all similar instances (i.e., the effect of all guns possessed in or near schools). . . .

Third, the Constitution requires us to judge the connection between a regulated activity and interstate commerce, not directly, but at one remove. Courts must give Congress a degree of leeway in determining the existence of a significant factual connection between the regulated activity and interstate commerce—both because the Constitution delegates the commerce power directly to Congress and because the determination requires an empirical judgment of a kind that a legislature is more likely than a court to make with accuracy. The traditional words "rational basis" capture this leeway. Thus, the specific question before us, as the Court recognizes, is not whether the "regulated activity sufficiently affected interstate commerce," but, rather, whether Congress could have had "*a rational basis*" for so concluding. . . .

Applying these principles to the case at hand, we must ask whether Congress could have had a *rational basis* for finding a significant (or substantial) connection between gun-related school violence and interstate commerce. . . . As long as one views the commerce connection, not as a "technical legal conception," but as "a practical one," *Swift & Co. v. United States* (1905), the answer to this question must be yes. . . .

For one thing, reports, hearings, and other readily available literature make clear that the problem of guns in and around schools is widespread and extremely serious. . . . Congress obviously could have thought that guns and learning are mutually exclusive. Congress could therefore have found a substantial educational problem—teachers unable to teach, students unable to learn—and concluded that guns near schools contribute substantially to the size and scope of that problem.

Having found that guns in schools significantly undermine the quality of education in our Nation's classrooms, Congress could also have found, given the effect of education upon interstate and foreign commerce, that gun-related violence in and around schools is a commercial, as well as a human, problem. Education, although far more than a matter of economics, has long been inextricably intertwined with the Nation's economy. . . .

The economic links I have just sketched seem fairly obvious. Why then is it not equally obvious, in light of those links, that a widespread, serious, and substantial physical threat to teaching and learning *also* substantially threatens the commerce to which that teaching and learning is inextricably tied? . . .

Specifically, Congress could have found that gun-related violence near the classroom poses a serious economic threat (1) to consequently inadequately educated workers who must endure low paying jobs, and (2) to communities and businesses that might (in today's "information society") otherwise gain, from a well-educated work force, an important commercial advantage, of a kind that location near a railhead or harbor provided in the past. . . . The violence-related facts, the educational facts, and the economic facts, taken together, make this conclusion rational. And, because

under our case law, the sufficiency of the constitutionally necessary Commerce Clause link between a crime of violence and interstate commerce turns simply upon size or degree, those same facts make the statute constitutional.

The majority's holding—that §922 falls outside the scope of the Commerce Clause—creates three serious legal problems. First, the majority's holding runs contrary to modern Supreme Court cases that have upheld congressional actions despite connections to interstate or foreign commerce that are less significant than the effect of school violence. . . .

The second legal problem the Court creates comes from its apparent belief that it can reconcile its holding with earlier cases by making a critical distinction between "commercial" and noncommercial "transaction[s]." That is to say, the Court believes the Constitution would distinguish between two local activities, each of which has an identical effect upon interstate commerce, if one, but not the other, is "commercial" in nature. . . .

The third legal problem created by the Court's holding is that it threatens legal uncertainty in an area of law that, until this case, seemed reasonably well settled. . . .

. . . For these reasons, I would reverse the judgment of the Court of Appeals. Respectfully, I dissent.

There was considerable debate in legal circles over the meaning of *Lopez*. Some saw it as an isolated exception to the broad definition of interstate commerce that the Court had applied since 1937. Others viewed it as a significant shift in the Court's commerce clause jurisprudence.

Those who saw the decision as an anomaly were to be disappointed as the Court handed down subsequent commerce clause rulings. In **United States v. Morrison** (2000) the Court, by the same 5–4 voting split that occurred in *Lopez*, struck down the Violence Against Women Act of 1994. The majority found that Congress was without authority under the commerce clause to pass a criminal law against gender-motivated crimes of violence. Such crimes are in no sense economic activity. Therefore, the states, not the federal government, should exercise criminal law jurisdiction over such acts.

Morrison was quickly followed by *Jones v. United States* (2000), which held that a federal criminal statute against arson, passed pursuant to the commerce power, could not be applied to a man who tossed a Molotov cocktail into his cousin's house. Because the target of the arson was a private residence not used in any commercial activity, the Court concluded that Congress under the commerce clause had no authority to regulate.

The Court reinforced this revised view of the federal commerce power in *Solid Waste Agency of Northern Cook Cty. v. Army Corps of Engineers* (2001), a case presenting a very different factual story than those challenging the authority of Congress to regulate gun possession, rape, or arson. At issue was an application of the federal Clean Water Act. A consortium of twenty-three Chicago-area cities attempted to develop a solid waste facility on a 533-acre parcel of land that previously had been used as a sand and gravel pit operation. The site included a series of small ponds, some permanent and others seasonal. The Army Corps of Engineers claimed that federal approval was necessary before development could take place because the ponds were used as habitats by migratory birds that cross state lines. The Court, in another 5–4 ruling, held that action by the Corps impinged on the states' traditional power over land and water use and that there was no evidence that Congress's regulation of navigable waters extended to abandoned gravel pits.

The *Lopez, Morrison, Jones,* and *Solid Waste* cases, taken together with other Rehnquist Court federalism and taxation decisions, clearly demonstrate that the justices had modified their commerce clause jurisprudence *(see Box 7-5).* Following the New Deal revolution, the federal government was given wide latitude to regulate in the name of interstate commerce. But in more recent decisions the Court has cautioned that the commerce clause does not give Congress a blank check.

The importance of this evolution in doctrine remains to be seen. Although the Court has enunciated a revised interpretation of the commerce power, its application of that standard in no way resembles the breadth of the Court's attack on federal authority in the period prior to 1937. In fact, some of its decisions have been quite consistent with its earlier post–New Deal jurisprudence. Take, for example, *Gonzales v. Raich* (2005), a controversial ruling on the validity of state laws that allow the medical

use of marijuana. Despite a vigorous attack from the dissenters, the majority applied the precedent of *Wickard v. Filburn.*

Gonzales v. Raich

545 U.S. 1 (2005)
http://laws.findlaw.com/US/545/1.html
Oral arguments may be found at: http://www.oyez.org
Vote: 6 (Breyer, Ginsburg, Kennedy, Scalia, Souter, Stevens)
    3 (O'Connor, Rehnquist, Thomas)
Opinion of the Court: Stevens
Opinion concurring in judgment: Scalia
Dissenting opinions: O'Connor, Thomas

In 1996 California voters passed Proposition 215, commonly known as the Compassionate Use Act (CUA). The law allowed seriously ill state residents to use marijuana for medical purposes. The act also created an exemption from criminal prosecution for patients, physicians, and caregivers who cultivate and possess marijuana for medical reasons.

Californian Angel Raich suffered from more than ten serious and possibly life-threatening medical conditions, including an inoperable brain tumor. On the advice of her doctor she used marijuana to help ease her suffering. Too ill to produce her own supply, Raich depended on two caregivers to grow and provide marijuana without charge.

Diane Monson, another California resident following her physician's advice, had been using marijuana in compliance with the CUA for five years to combat chronic spinal pain. She grew about six cannabis plants to maintain a supply of the drug.

In 2002 county deputy sheriffs and federal drug agents came to Monson's home. After an investigation, the local officials found no evidence of illegal activity under California law. The federal agents, however, concluded that Monson's possession of marijuana violated the federal Controlled Substances Act (CSA). They seized and destroyed her marijuana plants.

Raich and Monson sued Attorney General Alberto Gonzales and the head of the Drug Enforcement Administration to bar enforcement of the CSA to the extent that

BOX 7-5   THE EVOLUTION OF INTERSTATE COMMERCE DOCTRINE

MARSHALL INTERPRETATION

Gibbons v. Ogden (1824)
Marshall opinion for a 6–0 Court

Commerce begins in one state and ends in another. It does not stop when the act of crossing a state border is completed. Commerce occurring within a state may be part of a larger interstate process.

SHREVEPORT DOCTRINE

Shreveport Rate Case (1914)
Hughes opinion for a 7–2 Court

Congress may regulate intrastate commerce when it is intertwined with interstate commerce and a failure to regulate intrastate commerce would injure interstate commerce.

STREAM OF COMMERCE DOCTRINE

Swift and Company v. United States (1905)
Holmes opinion for a 9–0 Court

Stafford v. Wallace (1922)
Taft opinion for a 7–1 Court

An article in interstate commerce does not lose its status until it reaches its final destination. Stopping along the way to its terminal sale does not remove an article from the stream of interstate commerce.

MANUFACTURING EXCLUDED FROM INTERSTATE COMMERCE

United States v. E. C. Knight Co. (1895)
Fuller opinion for an 8–1 Court

Schechter Poultry v. United States (1935)
Hughes opinion for a 9–0 Court

Carter v. Carter Coal Co. (1936)
Sutherland opinion for a 5–4 Court

Manufacturing, processing, and mining activities are local by nature and not a part of interstate commerce. Their effect on interstate commerce is indirect. That an article is intended for interstate commerce does not make its manufacture part of interstate commerce. Commerce succeeds to manufacture and is not a part of it.

MODERN INTERPRETATION OF INTERSTATE COMMERCE

NLRB v. Jones & Laughlin Steel Corp. (1937)
Hughes opinion for a 5–4 Court

Congress may enact all appropriate legislation to protect, advance, promote, and insure interstate commerce. Although activities may be intrastate in character when separately considered, if they have such a close and substantial relation to interstate commerce that their control is essential or appropriate to protect that commerce from burdens and obstructions, Congress cannot be denied the power to exercise that control.

COMMERCE POWER LIMITATIONS

United States v. Lopez (1995)
Rehnquist opinion for a 5–4 Court

United States v. Morrison (2000)
Rehnquist opinion for a 5–4 Court

Federal legislation is constitutionally suspect if it does not regulate an economic activity that, in the aggregate, substantially affects interstate commerce.

Angel Raich, shown here at a 2004 press conference, sued to block the U.S. attorney general from enforcing the federal Controlled Substances Act against her. Raich, suffering from a brain tumor and other serious medical conditions, used marijuana under California's Compassionate Use Act to combat the pain and discomfort.

Diane Monson joined Angel Raich in asking the Supreme Court to uphold California's medicinal marijuana law. Monson, under a physician's direction, regularly used marijuana to alleviate chronic back pain.

it prevented them from obtaining and possessing marijuana for medical purposes. The federal government claimed that its constitutional power to regulate commerce was sufficiently broad to regulate the use of the substance. Raich and Monson argued the federal commerce power does not extend to the medical use of marijuana, a purely local and noncommercial activity regulated by state law. They further claimed that their marijuana plants were grown and processed only with water, nutrients, supplies, and equipment originating in California. The court of appeals ruled in favor of Raich and Monson, and the federal government asked the Supreme Court to reverse.

JUSTICE STEVENS delivered the opinion of the Court.

California is one of at least nine States that authorize the use of marijuana for medicinal purposes. The question presented in this case is whether the power vested in Congress by Article I, §8, of the Constitution "[t]o make all Laws which shall be necessary and proper for carrying into Execution" its authority to "regulate Commerce with foreign Nations, and among the several States" includes the power to prohibit the local cultivation and use of marijuana in compliance with California law. . . .

Respondents in this case do not dispute that passage of the CSA, as part of the Comprehensive Drug Abuse Prevention and Control Act, was well within Congress' commerce power. Nor do they contend that any provision or section of the CSA amounts to an unconstitutional exercise of congressional authority. Rather, respondents' challenge is actually quite limited; they argue that the CSA's categorical prohibition of the manufacture and possession of marijuana as applied to the intrastate manufacture and possession of marijuana for medical purposes pursuant to California law exceeds Congress' authority under the Commerce Clause. . . .

Our case law firmly establishes Congress' power to regulate purely local activities that are part of an economic "class of activities" that have a substantial effect on interstate commerce. See, *e.g.*, *Perez* [*v. United States* (1971)]; *Wickard v. Filburn* (1942). As we stated in *Wickard*, "even if appellee's activity be local and though it may not be regarded as commerce, it may still, whatever its nature, be reached by Congress if it exerts a substantial economic effect on interstate commerce." We have never required Congress to legislate with scientific exactitude. When Congress decides that the "'total incidence'" of a practice poses a threat to a national market, it may regulate the entire class.

Our decision in *Wickard* is of particular relevance. In *Wickard*, we upheld the application of regulations promulgated under the Agricultural Adjustment Act of 1938, which were designed to control the volume of wheat moving in interstate and foreign commerce in order to avoid surpluses and consequent abnormally low prices. The regulations established an allotment of 11.1 acres for Filburn's 1941 wheat crop, but he sowed 23 acres, intending to use the excess by consuming it on his own farm. Filburn argued that even though we had sustained Congress' power to regulate the production of goods for commerce, that power did not authorize "federal regulation [of] production not intended in any part for commerce but wholly for consumption on the farm." *Wickard*. Justice Jackson's opinion for a unanimous Court rejected this submission. He wrote:

"The effect of the statute before us is to restrict the amount which may be produced for market and the extent as well to which one may forestall resort to the market by producing to meet his own needs. That appellee's own contribution to the demand for wheat may be trivial by itself is not enough to remove him from the scope of federal regulation where, as here, his contribution, taken together with that of many others similarly situated, is far from trivial."

Wickard thus establishes that Congress can regulate purely intrastate activity that is not itself "commercial," in that it is not produced for sale, if it concludes that failure to regulate that class of activity would undercut the regulation of the interstate market in that commodity.

The similarities between this case and *Wickard* are striking. Like the farmer in *Wickard*, respondents are cultivating, for home consumption, a fungible commodity for which there is an established, albeit illegal, interstate market. . . . In *Wickard*, we had no difficulty concluding that Congress had a rational basis for believing that, when viewed in the aggregate, leaving home-consumed wheat outside the regulatory scheme would have a substantial influence on price and market conditions. Here too, Congress had a rational basis for concluding that leaving home-consumed marijuana outside federal control would similarly affect price and market conditions.

More concretely, one concern prompting inclusion of wheat grown for home consumption in the 1938 Act was that rising market prices could draw such wheat into the interstate market, resulting in lower market prices. The parallel concern making it appropriate to include marijuana grown for home consumption in the CSA is the likelihood that the high demand in the interstate market will draw such marijuana into that market. While the diversion of homegrown wheat tended to frustrate the federal interest in stabilizing prices by regulating the volume of commercial transactions in the interstate market, the diversion of homegrown marijuana tends to frustrate the federal interest in eliminating commercial transactions in the interstate market in their entirety. In both cases, the regulation is squarely within Congress' commerce power because production of the commodity meant for home consumption, be it wheat or marijuana, has a substantial effect on supply and demand in the national market for that commodity. . . .

In assessing the scope of Congress' authority under the Commerce Clause, we stress that the task before us is a modest one. We need not determine whether respondents' activities, taken in the aggregate, substantially affect interstate commerce in fact, but only whether a "rational basis" exists for so concluding. Given the enforcement difficulties that attend distinguishing between marijuana cultivated locally and marijuana grown elsewhere and concerns about diversion into illicit channels, we have no difficulty concluding that Congress had a rational basis for believing that failure to regulate the intrastate manufacture and possession of marijuana would leave a gaping hole in the CSA. Thus, as in *Wickard*, when it enacted comprehensive legislation to regulate the interstate market in a fungible commodity, Congress was acting well within its authority to "make all Laws which shall be necessary and proper" to "regulate Commerce . . . among the several States." That the regulation ensnares some purely intrastate activity is of no moment. As we have done many times before, we refuse to excise individual components of that larger scheme.

To support their contrary submission, respondents rely heavily on two of our more recent Commerce Clause cases. In their myopic focus, they overlook the larger context of modern-era Commerce Clause jurisprudence preserved by those cases. Moreover, even in the narrow prism of respondents' creation, they read those cases far too broadly. Those two cases, of course, are [*United States v.*] *Lopez* [1995] and [*United States v.*] *Morrison* [2000]. . . .

Unlike those at issue in *Lopez* and *Morrison*, the activities regulated by the CSA are quintessentially economic. "Economics" refers to "the production, distribution, and consumption of commodities." Webster's Third New International Dictionary 720 (1966). The CSA is a statute that regulates the production, distribution, and consumption of commodities for which there is an established, and lucrative, interstate market. Prohibiting the intrastate possession or manufacture of an article of commerce is a rational (and commonly utilized) means of regulating commerce in that product. . . . Because the CSA is a statute that directly regulates economic, commercial activity, our opinion in *Morrison* casts no doubt on its constitutionality. . . .

The exemption for cultivation by patients and caregivers can only increase the supply of marijuana in the California market. The likelihood that all such production will promptly terminate when patients recover or will precisely match the patients' medical needs during their convalescence seems remote; whereas the danger that excesses will satisfy some of the admittedly enormous demand for recreational use seems obvious. Moreover, that the national and international narcotics trade has thrived in the face of vigorous criminal enforcement efforts suggests that no small number of unscrupulous people will make use of the California exemptions to serve their commercial ends whenever it is feasible to do so. Taking into account the fact that California is only one of at least nine States to have authorized the medical use of marijuana, . . . Congress could have rationally concluded that the aggregate impact on the national market of all the transactions exempted from federal supervision is unquestionably substantial.

. . . Thus the case for the exemption comes down to the claim that a locally cultivated product that is used domestically rather than sold on the open market is not subject to federal regulation. Given the findings in the CSA and the undisputed magnitude of the commercial market for marijuana, our decisions in *Wickard v. Filburn* and the later cases endorsing its reasoning foreclose that claim. . . .

. . . [T]he judgment of the Court of Appeals must be vacated. The case is remanded for further proceedings consistent with this opinion.

It is so ordered.

JUSTICE O'CONNOR, with whom the CHIEF JUSTICE and JUSTICE THOMAS join . . . , dissenting.

We enforce the "outer limits" of Congress' Commerce Clause authority not for their own sake, but to protect historic spheres of state sovereignty from excessive federal encroachment and thereby to maintain the distribution of power fundamental to our federalist system of government. One of federalism's chief virtues, of course, is that it promotes innovation by allowing for the possibility that "a single courageous State may, if its citizens choose, serve as a laboratory; and try novel social and economic experiments without risk to the rest of the country." *New State Ice Co. v. Liebmann* (1932) (Brandeis, J., dissenting).

This case exemplifies the role of States as laboratories. The States' core police powers have always included authority to define criminal law and to protect the health, safety, and welfare of their citizens. Exercising those powers, California (by ballot initiative and then by legislative codification) has come to its own conclusion about the difficult and sensitive question of whether marijuana should be available to relieve severe pain and suffering. Today the Court sanctions an application of the federal Controlled Substances Act that extinguishes that experiment, without any proof that the personal cultivation, possession, and use of marijuana for medicinal purposes, if economic activity in the first place, has a substantial effect on interstate commerce and is therefore an appropriate subject of federal regulation. In so doing, the Court announces a rule that gives Congress a perverse incentive to legislate broadly pursuant to the Commerce Clause—nestling questionable assertions of its authority into comprehensive regulatory schemes—rather than with precision. That rule and the result it produces in this case are irreconcilable with our decisions in *Lopez* and *Morrison*. . . .

The Government has not overcome empirical doubt that the number of Californians engaged in personal cultivation, possession, and use of medical marijuana, or the amount of marijuana they produce, is enough to threaten the federal regime. Nor has it shown that Compassionate Use Act marijuana users have been or are realistically likely to be responsible for the drug's seeping into the market in a significant way. . . .

Relying on Congress' abstract assertions, the Court has endorsed making it a federal crime to grow small amounts of marijuana in one's own home for one's own medicinal use. This overreaching stifles an express choice by some States, concerned for the lives and liberties of their people, to regulate medical marijuana differently. If I were a California citizen, I would not have voted for the medical marijuana ballot initiative; if I were a California legislator I would not have supported the Compassionate Use Act. But whatever the wisdom of California's experiment with medical marijuana, the federalism principles that have driven our Commerce Clause cases require that room for experiment be protected in this case. For these reasons I dissent.

JUSTICE THOMAS, dissenting.

Respondents Diane Monson and Angel Raich use marijuana that has never been bought or sold, that has never crossed state lines, and that has had no demonstrable effect on the national market for marijuana. If Congress can regulate this under the Commerce Clause, then it can regulate virtually anything—and the Federal Government is no longer one of limited and enumerated powers. . . .

Even the majority does not argue that respondents' conduct is itself "Commerce among the several States." Monson and Raich neither buy nor sell the marijuana that they consume. They cultivate their cannabis entirely in the State of California—it never crosses state lines, much less as part of a commercial transaction. Certainly no evidence from the founding suggests that "commerce" included the mere possession of a good or some purely personal activity that did not involve trade or exchange for value. In the early days of the Republic, it would have been unthinkable that Congress could prohibit the local cultivation, possession, and consumption of marijuana. . . .

Moreover, even a Court interested more in the modern than the original understanding of the Constitution ought to resolve cases based on the meaning of words that are actually in the document. Congress is authorized to regulate "Commerce," and respondents' conduct does not qualify under any definition of that term. The majority's opinion only illustrates the steady drift away from the text of the Commerce Clause. There is an inexorable expansion from " 'commerce,' " to "commercial" and "economic" activity, and finally to all "production, distribution, and consumption" of goods or services for which there is an "established . . . interstate market." Federal power expands, but never con-

tracts, with each new locution. The majority is not interpreting the Commerce Clause, but rewriting it. . . .

. . . I respectfully dissent.

The decision in *Raich* makes clear that *Lopez, Morrison, Jones,* and *Solid Waste* should not be seen as a wholesale repudiation of commerce clause jurisprudence as it has developed since 1937. Rather, the six-justice majority in *Raich*, which included the votes of conservatives Scalia and Kennedy, held fast to the precedent set in *Wickard v. Filburn:* The production of commercially viable items, when considered in the aggregate, has a sufficiently substantial relationship with interstate commerce to trigger the use of congressional regulatory authority. But, when Congress under the commerce clause attempts to regulate directly noneconomic activity (such as gun possession, rape, arson, or the flights of migratory birds) without showing the necessary connection to interstate commerce, it may impermissibly infringe on powers reserved for the states.

REGULATING COMMERCE AS A FEDERAL POLICE POWER

During the battle over the meaning of interstate commerce from *Gibbons v. Ogden* through the post–New Deal period, the stakes were almost exclusively economic. The regulation of interstate commercial enterprises can, however, have an impact on noneconomic activities, which potentially gives Congress the ability to use the commerce power to regulate for noneconomic purposes. For example, if Congress bans the interstate transportation of obscene materials, the law is clearly an exercise of the commerce power, but the legislators obviously are motivated by morality considerations. Is this an appropriate exercise of the commerce power? May Congress legitimately use the commerce clause as a means of exercising an authority at the national level similar to the states' police powers?

The Supreme Court's answer to such questions has been clear and relatively consistent. If an activity falls under the definition of commerce among the states, then Congress has the right to regulate it. The commerce clause itself imposes no limitations on the motivations for such legislation. As Chief Justice Marshall explained in *Gibbons v. Ogden,* "This power, like all others vested in Congress, is complete in itself, may be exercised to its utmost extent, and acknowledges no limitations, other than are prescribed in the Constitution." The commerce clause, therefore, gives Congress power to regulate some activities that would otherwise be outside the federal purview. An excellent example is Congress's ability to legislate in the field of civil rights.

The constitutional protections against discrimination are found primarily in the equal protection clause of the Fourteenth Amendment and the due process clause of the Fifth, which have erected powerful barriers against invidious discrimination. But their exclusive target is discrimination perpetuated by the government. The words of the Fourteenth Amendment are clear: "Nor shall any state . . . deny to any person within its jurisdiction the equal protection of the laws." Nothing in the Fifth or Fourteenth Amendments prohibits discrimination by private parties. They were not intended to prohibit a private citizen from being discriminatory, but only to bar discriminatory government action. Although the Fourteenth Amendment includes a clause giving Congress the authority to enforce the provision with appropriate legislation, the Supreme Court has ruled that such enforcement legislation may not extend beyond the scope of the amendment itself.[15] Consequently, the amendment does not empower Congress to regulate private discriminatory behavior.

When the civil rights movement of the 1950s and 1960s campaigned for the elimination of discriminatory conditions, high on the list was the eradication of discrimination by private parties who operated public accommodations. The movement targeted the owners of hotels, restaurants, movies, theaters, recreation areas, and transportation systems. In the aftermath of *Brown v. Board of Education* (1954), governments could not maintain laws mandating the segregation of such facilities, but private operators could still impose discrimination on their own. In the South, where racial segregation was

15. *The Civil Rights Cases* (1883).

the way of life, no one expected the states to pass civil rights statutes prohibiting private parties from discriminating. Therefore, civil rights advocates pressured Congress to do something about the situation.

Congress responded with passage of the Civil Rights Act of 1964, the most comprehensive legislation of its type ever passed. The act, as amended, is still the nation's most significant statute aimed at eliminating discrimination. The primary authority for passing this groundbreaking legislation was not a clause in the Bill of Rights or one of the Civil War amendments, but the commerce clause. Because the Court had treated commerce clause legislation favorably since 1937, members of Congress had confidence that the Civil Rights Act would withstand a legal challenge. Opponents of the legislation, however, argued that Congress had misused its power to regulate commerce by invoking it as justifying a civil rights law. Obviously, they said, the framers, many of whom owned slaves, did not intend the power to regulate commerce among the states to be used to enact civil rights legislation.

Was Congress on solid ground in doing so? The primary test of the law's constitutionality was *Heart of Atlanta Motel v. United States* (1964). As you read this case, note Justice Tom C. Clark's description of how racial discrimination has a negative impact on interstate commerce. Also note the Court's expansive view of interstate commerce and its conclusion that the commerce clause can be used to combat moral wrongs.

Heart of Atlanta Motel v. United States

379 U.S. 241 (1964)
http://laws.findlaw.com/US/379/241.html
Oral arguments may be found at: http://www.oyez.org
Vote: 9 (Black, Brennan, Clark, Douglas, Goldberg, Harlan, Stewart, Warren, White)
     0
Opinion of the Court: Clark
Concurring opinions: Black, Douglas, Goldberg

Title II of the 1964 Civil Rights Act in its original form prohibited discrimination on the basis of race, color, religion, or national origin by certain public accommodations that operated in or affected interstate commerce. The accommodations specifically included were:

1. Inns, hotels, motels, or other lodging facilities of five rooms or more. Because they served the traveling public, these facilities were considered part of interstate commerce by definition.

2. Restaurants and cafeterias, if they served interstate travelers or if a substantial portion of their food or other products had moved in interstate commerce.

3. Motion picture houses, if they presented films that had moved in interstate commerce.

4. Any facility physically located within any of the other covered accommodations, which included operations such as hotel shops and theater snack bars.

The Heart of Atlanta Motel was a 216-room facility in Atlanta, Georgia. Located near the commercial center of the city, it had easy access to two interstate highways and two major state roads. About three-quarters of its guests were interstate travelers. The motel advertised for business in national publications and maintained more than fifty billboards and highway signs around the state. Both the government and the motel agreed that the facility met the act's definition of a public accommodation in interstate commerce.

The motel admitted that it practiced a policy of racial discrimination prior to the enactment of the civil rights law, and it acknowledged that it intended to continue its policy of not serving blacks. To secure its right to do so, the motel filed suit to have the 1964 Civil Rights Act declared unconstitutional.

MR. JUSTICE CLARK delivered the opinion of the Court.

The Basis of Congressional Action.

While the Act as adopted carried no congressional findings the record of its passage through each house is replete with evidence of the burdens that discrimination by race or color places upon interstate commerce. This testimony included the fact that our people have become increasingly mobile with millions of people of all races traveling from State to State; that Negroes in particular have been the sub-

ject of discrimination in transient accommodations, having to travel great distances to secure the same; that often they have been unable to obtain accommodations and have had to call upon friends to put them up overnight; and that these conditions had become so acute as to require the listing of available lodging for Negroes in a special guidebook which was itself "dramatic testimony to the difficulties" Negroes encounter in travel. These exclusionary practices were found to be nationwide, the Under Secretary of Commerce testifying that there is "no question that this discrimination in the North still exists to a large degree" and in the West and Midwest as well. This testimony indicated a qualitative as well as a quantitative effect on interstate travel by Negroes. The former was the obvious impairment of the Negro traveler's pleasure and convenience that resulted when he continually was uncertain of finding lodging. As for the latter, there was evidence that this uncertainty stemming from racial discrimination had the effect of discouraging travel on the part of a substantial portion of the Negro community. This was the conclusion not only of the Under Secretary of Commerce but also of the Administrator of the Federal Aviation Agency who wrote the Chairman of the Senate Commerce Committee that it was his "belief that air commerce is adversely affected by the denial to a substantial segment of the traveling public of adequate and desegregated public accommodations." We shall not burden this opinion with further details since the voluminous testimony presents overwhelming evidence that discrimination by hotels and motels impedes interstate travel.

The Power of Congress Over Interstate Travel.

The power of Congress to deal with these obstructions depends on the meaning of the Commerce Clause. Its meaning was first enunciated 140 years ago by the great Chief Justice John Marshall in Gibbons v. Ogden (1824), in these words:

"The subject to be regulated is commerce; and . . . to ascertain the extent of the power, it becomes necessary to settle the meaning of the word. The counsel for the appellee would limit it to traffic, to buying and selling, or the interchange of commodities . . . but it is something more: it is intercourse . . . between nations, and parts of nations, in all its branches, and is regulated by prescribing rules for carrying on that intercourse.

"To what commerce does this power extend? The constitution informs us, to commerce 'with foreign nations and among the several States, and with the Indian tribes.'

"It has, we believe, been universally admitted, that these words comprehend every species of commercial intercourse. . . . No sort of trade can be carried on . . . to which this power does not extend.

"The subject to which the power is next applied, is to commerce 'among the several States.' The word 'among' means intermingled." . . .

In short, the determinative test of the exercise of power by the Congress under the Commerce Clause is simply whether the activity sought to be regulated is "commerce which concerns more States than one" and has a real and substantial relation to the national interest. Let us now turn to this facet of the problem.

That the "intercourse" of which the Chief Justice spoke included the movement of persons through more States than one was settled as early as 1849, in the Passenger Cases, where Mr. Justice McLean stated: "That the transportation of passengers is a part of commerce is not now an open question." Again in 1913 Mr. Justice McKenna, speaking for the Court, said: "Commerce among the States, we have said, consists of intercourse and traffic between their citizens, and includes the transportation of persons and property. . . . Nor does it make any difference whether the transportation is commercial in character." . . .

The same interest in protecting interstate commerce which led Congress to deal with segregation in interstate carriers and the white-slave traffic has prompted it to extend the exercise of its power to gambling; to criminal enterprises; to deceptive practices in the sale of products; to fraudulent security transactions; to misbranding of drugs; to wages and hours; to members of labor unions; to crop control; to discrimination against shippers; to the protection of small business from injurious price cutting; to resale price maintenance; to professional football; and to racial discrimination by owners and managers of terminal restaurants.

That Congress was legislating against moral wrongs in many of these areas rendered its enactments no less valid. In framing Title II of this Act Congress was also dealing with what it considered a moral problem. But that fact does not detract from the overwhelming evidence of the disrup-

tive effect that racial discrimination has had on commercial intercourse. It was this burden which empowered Congress to enact appropriate legislation, and, given this basis for the exercise of its power, Congress was not restricted by the fact that the particular obstruction to interstate commerce with which it was dealing was also deemed a moral and social wrong.

It is said that the operation of the motel here is of a purely local character. But . . . the power of Congress to promote interstate commerce also includes the power to regulate the local incidents thereof, including local activities in both the States of origin and destination, which might have a substantial and harmful effect upon that commerce. One need only examine the evidence which we have discussed above to see that Congress may—as it has—prohibit racial discrimination by motels serving travelers, however "local" their operations may appear. . . .

We, therefore, conclude that the action of the Congress in the adoption of the Act as applied here to a motel which concededly serves interstate travelers is within the power granted it by the Commerce Clause of the Constitution, as interpreted by this Court for 140 years. It may be argued that Congress could have pursued other methods to eliminate the obstructions it found in interstate commerce caused by racial discrimination. But this is a matter of policy that rests entirely with the Congress not with the courts. How obstructions in commerce may be removed—what means are to be employed—is within the sound and exclusive discretion of the Congress. It is subject only to one caveat—that the means chosen by it must be reasonably adapted to the end permitted by the Constitution. We cannot say that its choice here was not so adapted. The Constitution requires no more.

Affirmed.

Employing the same sweeping language as the Court used in *Wickard v. Filburn* to declare wheat grown for home consumption to be engaged in interstate commerce, Justice Clark's opinion gives Congress broad powers to use the commerce clause as authority to regulate moral wrongs that occur in interstate commerce. The Heart of Atlanta Motel complied with the Court's decision *(see Box 7-6),* and a new era of civil rights in public accommodations had begun. The Supreme Court's inter-

BOX 7-6 AFTERMATH . . . HEART OF ATLANTA MOTEL

The Heart of Atlanta Motel was built in 1956 and owned by a group of Atlanta investors. One of the co-owners was Moreton Rolleston Jr., a former lieutenant commander in the navy and a longtime Atlanta lawyer. Rolleston was a strong supporter of racial segregation. It was no coincidence, therefore, that the Heart of Atlanta Motel refused to serve black customers or that the motel did not cooperate with a consortium of fourteen downtown hotels who agreed in 1963 to accommodate conventions that included blacks.

When it appeared certain that Congress would pass the 1964 Civil Rights Act, Rolleston, who also

Moreton Rolleston Jr., a co-owner of the Heart of Atlanta Motel, who challenged the constitutionality of the Civil Rights Act of 1964.

served as the motel's attorney, prepared a lawsuit to challenge its constitutionality. He filed the suit just two hours after President Lyndon Johnson signed the bill into law.

In August 1964, after losing in the district court, the owners complied with the court's ruling and began operating the motel on an integrated basis. Still, they pressed an appeal to the U.S. Supreme Court. Rolleston, arguing before the justices, claimed that the Civil Rights Act was an unconstitutional intrusion by the federal government into an area reserved to the states and also a violation of the rights of business owners. When the Supreme Court unanimously upheld the law on December 14, 1964, Rolleston lamented: "The de-

cision opens the frightful door to unlimited power of a centralized government in Washington, in which the individual citizen and his personal liberty are of no importance."

Several years later Rolleston bought out his fellow investors and became the motel's sole owner. In 1973 the motel was sold and razed. A large, modern hotel now occupies the land where the Heart of Atlanta Motel once stood.

Rolleston continued to practice law in Atlanta well into his eighties. In 2000 he was briefly a Republican candidate for the U.S. Senate. Seven years later, the Georgia Supreme Court disbarred the eighty-nine year old Rolleston for abusing the legal process by excessive litigation in a property dispute that was ongoing for twenty-two years. In the midst of that legal battle Rolleston lost a $5.4 million malpractice ruling in 1995, and he suffered a $4.1 million judgment in 1998. In defiance of the disbarment action, Rolleston pledged to continue practicing law.

SOURCES: Richard C. Cortner, *Civil Rights and Public Accommodations: The Heart of Atlanta Motel and McClung Cases* (Lawrence: University Press of Kansas, 2001); *Atlanta Journal-Constitution*, May 14, 1991; May 16, 1991; December 25, 1991; March 23, 1995; February 8, 1996; March 5, 1998; August 8, 2000; October 10, 2007.

pretation of the commerce clause turned that provision into one of the most powerful weapons in the federal government's regulatory arsenal.

THE COMMERCE POWER
OF THE STATES

Resolving the question of federal power over interstate and foreign commerce leaves unsettled the question of state commercial regulation. Marshall wrote in *Gibbons v. Ogden* that the "completely internal commerce" of a state was reserved for state regulation. This grant of power was substantial prior to the Civil War when most commercial activity was distinctly local and subject to state regulation. But with the Industrial Revolution and improved transportation systems, business became increasingly interstate in nature. Finally, the Supreme Court's 1937 redefinition of interstate commerce left little that met Marshall's notion of commerce that is "completely internal."

If the regulation of any business activity that affects interstate commerce were the exclusive preserve of the federal government, the role of the states would be minimal indeed. But this is not the case. The decisions of the Supreme Court have left a substantial sphere of authority for the states to regulate commerce. The dividing line between federal and state power has varied over time, as the Supreme Court has struggled to build an appropriate doctrine to govern this difficult area of federal-state relations.

Perhaps the Court's most influential ruling on state commerce powers occurred in *Cooley v. Board of Wardens* (1852). Here the justices attempted to balance congressional supremacy over interstate and foreign commerce with the need for the states to regulate the local aspects of such activity. Justice Benjamin Curtis's opinion for the Court establishes a doctrine for handling federal-state commercial conflicts that is still used today.

Cooley v. Board of Wardens

12 (53 U.S.) How. 299 (1852)
http://laws.findlaw.com/US/53/299.html
Vote: 7 (Catron, Curtis, Daniel, Grier, McKinley, Nelson,
    Taney)
    2 (McLean, Wayne)
Opinion of the Court: Curtis
Concurring opinion: Daniel
Dissenting opinion: McLean

Using its power over interstate and foreign commerce, Congress passed a statute in 1789 pertaining to the regulation of ports. The legislation said that until Congress acted otherwise, state and local authorities would continue to control the nation's ports and harbors. In 1803 Pennsylvania passed a port regulation law requiring that all vessels hire a local pilot to guide ships in and out of the Port of Philadelphia. Ship owners who did not comply were fined. The money from these fines was placed in a "charitable fund for the distressed or decayed pilots, their widows and children."

Aaron Cooley owned a vessel that sailed into Philadelphia without hiring a local pilot. The port's Board of Wardens took legal action against him, and Cooley was fined. He responded by claiming that the Pennsylvania law was unconstitutional; only Congress, he asserted, could regulate the port because the harbor was an integral part of interstate and foreign commerce, and the states had no constitutional authority to set regulations for such commerce. By implication, Cooley also was challenging the 1789 act of Congress that had delegated such powers to the states. The Pennsylvania Supreme Court upheld the law and the fine, and Cooley pressed his case to the U.S. Supreme Court.

MR. JUSTICE CURTIS delivered the opinion of the Court.

That the power to regulate commerce includes the regulation of navigation, we consider settled. And when we look to the nature of the service performed by pilots, to the relations which that service and its compensations bear to navigation between the several States, and between the ports of the United States and foreign countries, we are brought to the conclusion, that the regulation of the qualifications of pilots, of the modes and times of offering and rendering their services, of the responsibilities which shall rest upon them, of the powers they shall possess, of the compensation they may demand, and of the penalties by which their rights and duties may be enforced, do constitute regulations of navigation, and consequently of commerce, within the just meaning of this clause of the Constitution. . . .

Nor should it be lost sight of, that this subject of the regulation of pilots and pilotage has an intimate connection with, and an important relation to the general subject of commerce with foreign nations and among the several States, over which it was one main object of the Constitution to create a national control. Conflicts between the laws of neighboring States, and discriminations favorable or adverse to commerce with particular foreign nations, might be created by State laws regulating pilotage, deeply affecting that equality of commercial rights, and that freedom from State interference, which those who formed the Constitution were so anxious to secure, and which the experience of more than half a century has taught us to value so highly. . . .

It becomes necessary, therefore, to consider whether this law of Pennsylvania, being a regulation of commerce, is valid.

The act of Congress of the 7th of August, 1789, sect. 4, is as follows:

"That all pilots in the bays, inlets, rivers, harbors, and ports of the United States shall continue to be regulated in conformity with the existing laws of the States, respectively, wherein such pilots may be, or with such laws as the States may respectively hereafter enact for the purpose, until further legislative provision shall be made by Congress."

If the law of Pennsylvania, now in question, had been in existence at the date of this act of Congress, we might hold it to have been adopted by Congress, and thus made a law of the United States, and so valid. Because this act does, in effect, give the force of an act of Congress, to the then existing State laws on this subject, so long as they should continue unrepealed by the State which enacted them.

But the law on which these actions are founded was not enacted till 1803. What effect then can be attributed to so much of the act of 1789, as declares, that pilots shall continue to be regulated in conformity, "with such laws as the States may respectively hereafter enact for the purpose, until further legislative provision shall be made by Congress"?

If the States were divested of the power to legislate on this subject by the grant of the commercial power to Congress, it is plain this act could not confer upon them power thus to legislate. If the Constitution excluded the States from making any law regulating commerce, certainly Congress cannot regrant, or in any manner reconvey to the States that power. And yet this act of 1789 gives its sanction only to laws enacted by the States. This necessarily implies a constitutional power to legislate; for only a rule created by the sovereign power of a State acting in its legislative capacity, can be deemed a law, enacted by a State; and if the State has so limited its sovereign power that it no longer extends to a particular subject, manifestly it cannot, in any proper sense, be said to enact laws thereon. Entertaining these views we are brought directly and unavoidably to the consideration of the question, whether the grant of the commercial power to Congress, did *per se* deprive the States of all power to regulate pilots. This question has never been decided by this court, nor, in our judgment, has any case depending upon all the considerations which must govern this one, come before this court. The grant of

commercial power to Congress does not contain any terms which expressly exclude the States from exercising an authority over its subject-matter. If they are excluded it must be because the nature of the power, thus granted to Congress, requires that a similar authority should not exist in the States. If it were conceded on the one side, that the nature of this power, like that to legislate for the District of Columbia, is absolutely and totally repugnant to the existence of similar power in the States, probably no one would deny that the grant of the power to Congress, as effectually and perfectly excludes the States from all future legislation on the subject, as if express words had been used to exclude them. And on the other hand, if it were admitted that the existence of this power in Congress, like the power of taxation, is compatible with the existence of a similar power in the States, then it would be in conformity with the contemporary exposition of the Constitution, (Federalist, No. 32), and with the judicial construction, given from time to time by this court, after the most deliberate consideration, to hold that the mere grant of such a power to Congress, did not imply a prohibition on the States to exercise the same power; that it is not the mere existence of such a power, but its exercise by Congress, which may be incompatible with the exercise of the same power by the States, and that the States may legislate in the absence of congressional regulations.

The diversities of opinion, therefore, which have existed on this subject, have arisen from the different views taken of the nature of this power. But when the nature of a power like this is spoken of, when it is said that the nature of the power requires that it should be exercised exclusively by Congress, it must be intended to refer to the subjects of that power, and to say they are of such a nature as to require exclusive legislation by Congress. Now the power to regulate commerce, embraces a vast field, containing not only many, but exceedingly various subjects, quite unlike in their nature; some imperatively demanding a single uniform rule, operating equally on the commerce of the United States in every port; and some, like the subject now in question, as imperatively demanding that diversity, which alone can meet the local necessities of navigation.

Either absolutely to affirm, or deny that the nature of this power requires exclusive legislation by Congress, is to lose sight of the nature of the subjects of this power, and to assert concerning all of them, what is really applicable but to a part. Whatever subjects of this power are in their nature national, or admit only of one uniform system, or plan of regulation, may justly be said to be of such a nature as to require exclusive legislation by Congress. That this cannot be affirmed of laws for the regulation of pilots and pilotage is plain. The act of 1789 contains a clear and authoritative declaration by the first Congress, that the nature of this subject is such, that until Congress should find it necessary to exert its power, it should be left to the legislation of the States; that it is local and not national; that it is likely to be the best provided for, not by one system, or plan of regulations, but by as many as the legislative discretion of the several States should deem applicable to the local peculiarities of the ports within their limits.

Viewed in this light, so much of this act of 1789 as declares that pilots shall continue to be regulated "by such laws as the States may respectively hereafter enact for that purpose," instead of being held to be inoperative, as an attempt to confer on the States a power to legislate, of which the Constitution had deprived them, is allowed an appropriate and important signification. It manifests the understanding of Congress, at the outset of the government, that the nature of this subject is not such as to require its exclusive legislation. The practice of the States, and of the national government, has been in conformity with this declaration, from the origin of the national government to this time; and the nature of the subject when examined, is such as to leave no doubt of the superior fitness and propriety, not to say the absolute necessity, of different systems of regulation, drawn from local knowledge and experience, and conformed to local wants. How then can we say, that by the mere grant of power to regulate commerce, the States are deprived of all the power to legislate on this subject, because from the nature of the power the legislation of Congress must be exclusive. . . .

It is the opinion of a majority of the court that the mere grant to Congress of the power to regulate commerce, did not deprive the States of power to regulate pilots, and that although Congress has legislated on this subject, its legislation manifests an intention, with a single exception, not to regulate this subject, but to leave its regulation to the several States. To these precise questions, which are all we are called on to decide, this opinion must be understood to be confined. It does not extend to the question what other sub-

jects, under the commercial power, are within the exclusive control of Congress, or may be regulated by the States in the absence of all congressional legislation; nor to the general question how far any regulation of a subject by Congress, may be deemed to operate as an exclusion of all legislation by the States upon the same subject. We decide the precise questions before us, upon what we deem sound principles, applicable to this particular subject in the state in which the legislation of Congress has left it. We go no further. . . .

We are of opinion that this State law was enacted by virtue of a power, residing in the State to legislate; that it is not in conflict with any law of Congress; that it does not interfere with any system which Congress has established by making regulations, or by intentionally leaving individuals to their own unrestricted action; that this law is therefore valid, and the judgment of the Supreme Court of Pennsylvania in each case must be affirmed.

Justice Curtis's opinion in *Cooley* nicely outlines the basic constitutional principles governing the states' power to regulate commerce. From this decision we can begin to build some understanding of how far the states may go in regulating commercial enterprise:

1. The states retain the power to regulate purely intrastate commerce.

2. Congress has the power to regulate interstate and foreign commerce. When it exercises this power any contrary state laws are preempted.

3. The power of Congress to regulate interstate and foreign commerce is exclusive over those elements of commercial activity that are national in scope or require uniform regulation.

4. Those elements of interstate and foreign commerce that are not national in scope or do not require uniformity, and which have not been regulated by Congress, may be subject to state authority, including the state's police powers.

This division of authority is known as the doctrine of selected exclusiveness. It designates certain aspects of interstate and foreign commerce over which the powers of Congress are exclusive, allowing no state action. This

BOX 7-7 SUPREME COURT DECISIONS STRIKING DOWN STATE RESTRICTIONS ON INTERSTATE COMMERCE

Case	State Law Declared Unconstitutional
Edwards v. California (1941)	California law making it a crime knowingly to bring an indigent into the state.
Southern Pacific Co. v. Arizona (1945)	Arizona regulation restricting the length of trains.
Dean Milk Company v. Madison (1951)	City ordinance discriminating against milk produced out of state.
Bibb v. Navajo Freight Lines (1959)	Illinois statute requiring a particular type of mudflap on all trucks and outlawing a conventional mudflap legal in forty-five other states.
Pike v. Bruce Church (1970)	Arizona law commanding that all Arizona-grown cantaloupes be packaged inside the state.
Great Atlantic and Pacific Tea Company v. Cottrell (1976)	Mississippi law banning milk produced in Louisiana in response to Louisiana's refusal to sign a reciprocity agreement.
Hunt v. Washington State Apple Advertising Commission (1977)	North Carolina law mandating an apple-grading system that discriminated against out-of-state producers.
Raymond Motor Transit v. Rice (1978)	Wisconsin regulation prohibiting from the state's highways double trucks exceeding sixty-five feet in length.
Philadelphia v. New Jersey (1978)	New Jersey ban on the importation and dumping of out-of-state garbage.
Hughes v. Oklahoma (1979)	Law outlawing the transportation of Oklahoma-grown minnows for out-of-state sale.
Kassell v. Consolidated Freightways (1981)	Iowa law banning sixty-five-foot double trucks.
New England Power Company v. New Hampshire (1982)	New Hampshire prohibition against selling domestically produced power to out-of-state interests.
Healy v. Beer Institute (1989)	Connecticut law requiring out-of-state beer distributors to show that the prices charged inside Connecticut are not higher than prices charged in bordering states.
State of Wyoming v. State of Oklahoma (1992)	Oklahoma law mandating that electrical utility companies purchase at least 10 percent of their coal from Oklahoma mining operations.
C & A Carbone, Inc. v. Town of Clarkstown, New York (1994)	City ordinance requiring that all nonhazardous solid waste within the town be sent to a local transfer station, forbidding such waste to be shipped to out-of-state facilities.
Camps Newfound/Owatoona v. Town of Harrison (1997)	Maine statute singling out institutions that served mostly state residents for beneficial tax treatment and penalizing those institutions that did primarily interstate business.
Granholm v. Heald (2005)	Michigan law allowing the state's wineries to ship alcohol directly to Michigan consumers, but prohibiting out-of-state wineries from doing so.

exclusiveness, however, is not complete; in the absence of federal legislation, states may regulate some business activity affecting interstate commerce. The regulation of the Philadelphia port is an obvious part of interstate and foreign commerce where local harbor conditions require state supervision.

Although the states are free to regulate within the general boundaries set in *Cooley,* twentieth-century justices have emphasized two important principles in their state commerce power decisions. First, state regulations, even on local commercial activities, may not place an undue burden on interstate commerce. And second, state regulations may not discriminate against interstate commerce by giving preference to local businesses or economic activities. In applying these principles, the Court often refers to the "dormant commerce clause" or the "negative commerce clause." This jurisprudence recognizes that although the commerce clause is a positive grant of power to the federal government, it carries with it a negative command as well: States may not unreasonably discriminate or burden interstate or foreign commerce. Many times during the Court's history the justices have declared unconstitutional state laws that do not comport with these dictates. *(See Box 7-7 for examples.)*

The rules of law developed by the Supreme Court generally have been faithful to the purposes of the commerce clause. After the period under the Articles of Confederation in which the national economy suffered because the individual states imposed trade and protective measures, the framers wanted a system that guaranteed a free flow of business and commerce among the states. State regulations that place undue burdens on interstate commerce or favor in-state enterprises over interstate competition are contrary to the intent of the commerce clause.

READINGS

Baker, Leonard. *Back to Back: The Duel Between FDR and the Supreme Court.* New York: Macmillan, 1967.

Baxter, Maurice G. *The Steamboat Monopoly: Gibbons v. Ogden.* New York: Knopf, 1972.

Benson, Paul R., Jr. *The Supreme Court and the Commerce Clause, 1937–1970.* New York: Dunellen, 1970.

Cortner, Richard. *Civil Rights and Public Accommodations: The Heart of Atlanta Motel and McClung Cases.* Lawrence: University Press of Kansas, 2001.

———. *The Wagner Act Cases.* Knoxville: University of Tennessee Press, 1964.

Corwin, Edward S. *The Commerce Power versus States' Rights.* Princeton: Princeton University Press, 1936.

Cushman, Barry. *Rethinking the New Deal: The Structure of a Constitutional Revolution.* New York: Oxford University Press, 1998.

Dawson, Nelson. *Louis D. Brandeis, Felix Frankfurter, and the New Deal.* Hamden, Conn.: Archon Books, 1980.

Frankfurter, Felix. *The Commerce Clause Under Marshall, Taney and Waite.* Chapel Hill: University of North Carolina Press, 1937.

Himmelberg, Robert. *The Origins of the National Recovery Administration.* New York: Fordham University Press, 1976.

Irons, Peter H. *New Deal Lawyers.* Princeton: Princeton University Press, 1982.

Leuchtenburg, William E. *The Supreme Court Reborn: The Constitutional Revolution in the Age of Roosevelt.* New York: Oxford University Press, 1995.

McClosky, Robert. *American Conservatism in the Age of Enterprise, 1865–1910.* Cambridge: Harvard University Press, 1951.

Pearson, Drew, and Robert S. Allen. *The Nine Old Men.* Garden City, N.Y.: Doubleday, 1936.

Pritchett, C. Herman. *The Roosevelt Court: A Study in Judicial Politics and Values.* New York: Macmillan, 1948.

Shamir, Ronen. *Managing Legal Uncertainty: Elite Lawyers in the New Deal.* Durham: Duke University Press, 1995.

Whalen, Charles W., and Barbara Whalen. *The Longest Debate: A Legislative History of the 1964 Civil Rights Act.* Washington, D.C.: Seven Locks Press, 1985.

Wood, Stephen B. *Constitutional Politics in the Progressive Era: Child Labor and the Law.* Chicago: University of Chicago Press, 1968.

CHAPTER 8
THE POWER TO TAX AND SPEND

Perhaps no government power affects Americans more directly than the authority to tax and spend. Each year federal, state, and local governments collect billions of dollars in taxes imposed on a wide variety of activities, transactions, and goods. The federal government reminds us of its power to tax when we receive our paychecks, to say nothing of every April 15, the deadline for filing tax returns. Many state governments lay taxes on our incomes as well, and a majority of them also impose a levy each time we make a retail purchase. If we own a house, we must annually pay a tax on its value. We pay state and/or federal excise taxes whenever we make a local phone call, put gas in the car, buy an airline ticket, or purchase from a long list of other products and services. When we buy goods from abroad, the price includes a duty imposed on imports.

Americans have strong opinions about the government's taxing and spending activities. Many people think they pay too much and receive too little from the government in return. The battles over spending priorities are never ending, especially when choices must be made between national defense spending and social programs. In addition, there are constant complaints about tax dollars wasted by inefficient and ineffective government agencies. The mere mention of the Internal Revenue Service strikes fear in the hearts of many. Minor tax revolts at the state and local level are not unusual. But, in spite of this general dissatisfaction, most Americans pay their taxes honestly and on time and accept that taxation is a fact of modern life.

Today the government's power to tax and spend is firmly established and has reasonably well-defined contours, but this was not always the case. Some of the country's greatest constitutional battles were fought over the fiscal powers. The results of these legal disputes have significantly shaped the powers and constraints of American political institutions. In this chapter, we examine the Supreme Court's interpretations of the twin fiscal powers of taxation and spending.

THE CONSTITUTIONAL POWER TO TAX AND SPEND

The power to tax was a fundamental issue at the Constitutional Convention. The government under the Articles of Confederation was ineffective in part because it had no authority to levy taxes. It could only request funds from the states and had no power to collect payment if the states refused to cooperate. The taxing authority resided solely with the states, which left the national government unable to execute public policies unless the states overwhelmingly supported them, a situation that did not often occur. It was clear that the central government would have to gain some revenue-gathering powers under the new constitution, while the states would retain concurrent authority to impose taxes.

Federal Taxation Authority

Article I, Section 8, of the Constitution enumerates the powers of the federal government, and the first of those listed is the power to tax and spend:

The Congress shall have the Power to lay and collect Taxes, Duties, Imposts and Excises, to pay the Debts and provide for the common Defence and general Welfare of the United States.

The wording of this grant of authority is quite broad. The revenue function breaks into three categories. The first is the general grant of taxation power. Second is the authority to collect duties and imposts, both of which are taxes levied on imports, the primary source of revenue at that time. The third is the power to impose excises, which are taxes on the manufacture, sale, or use of goods, or on occupational or other activities.

The power to spend is also broadly constructed. The revenues gathered through the various taxing mechanisms may be used to pay government debts, to fund the nation's defense, and to provide for the general welfare. Although James Madison (and others) argued that the framers intended the spending power to be limited to funding those government activities explicitly authorized in the Constitution, the wording of Article I, Section 8, does not impose any such restriction. The fact that Congress may spend federal funds to provide for the general welfare is indeed a broad grant of authority.

This is not to say that the federal power to tax and spend is without limits. The framers were sufficiently wary of the dangers of a strong central government that they imposed some restrictions.

First, Article I, Section 8, stipulates that "all Duties, Imposts and Excises shall be uniform throughout the United States." The purpose of this provision is to prevent Congress from imposing different tax rates on various regions or requiring the citizens of one state to pay a tax rate higher than the citizens of other states. Geographical uniformity is the only stated constitutional requirement for excise taxes and taxes on imports. If this standard is met, the tax is likely to be valid.

Second, Article I, Section 9, holds that "No Tax or Duty shall be laid on Articles exported from any State." Consistent with the prevailing philosophy of increased commerce and trade, the framers wanted to ensure that the products of the states would move freely without the burden of federal taxes being placed on them. Although this clause may appear absolute, the Supreme Court on occasion has been called upon to enforce it. In *United*

States v. United States Shoe Corporation (1998), the justices struck down the harbor maintenance tax imposed by the federal Water Resources Development Act of 1986. The law imposed a tax of 0.125 percent on the value of commercial cargo throughout the nation's ports. The proceeds were used for harbor maintenance and improvements. Rejecting the government's plea that the program imposed a legitimate user fee and not a tax, the Court unanimously found the law to be a direct violation of the constitutional prohibition against the taxation of exports.

Third, Article I, Section 9, also dictates that "No capitation, or other direct, Tax shall be laid, unless in Proportion to the Census or Enumeration herein before directed to be taken." This same admonition is found in Article I, Section 2, where the framers wrote, "[D]irect Taxes shall be apportioned among the several States . . . according to their respective Numbers" as determined by the national census. The term *direct tax* is not defined in the Constitution, and it is a difficult concept to understand. When the framers referred to direct taxes they most likely meant a head tax—a tax imposed on each person—or a tax on land. As we shall see in the next section of this chapter, the requirement that direct taxes be apportioned on the basis of population has proved troublesome, and Congress has not often resorted to such levies.

State Taxation Authority

The framers generally allowed the states to retain their taxing authority as it existed prior to the ratification of the Constitution. Consequently, state and local governments today tax a wide array of activities and goods, including individual and corporate incomes, personal property, real estate, retail sales, investment holdings, and inheritances. But the Constitution imposed some new restraints on state taxing authority. These limitations specifically removed from the states any power to place a tax on certain forms of commerce. Article I, Section 10, prohibits them from imposing any duty on imports or exports, as well as any tax on the cargo capacity of vessels using the nation's ports. The framers were interested in the promotion of commerce, and these provisions meant that states could not retard commerce by using foreign trade as a source of tax revenue. These provisions also reserved for the federal government the exclusive authority to tax goods coming into the United States from other countries.

In addition to these specific restrictions, state and federal taxation must be consistent with the other provisions of the Constitution. It would be a violation of the Constitution if a state or the federal government taxed the exercise of a constitutional right, such as the freedom of speech or the exercise of religion. By the same token, if the government imposed varying tax rates based on a person's sex or race, such levies would be in violation of the constitutional rights of due process and equal protection of the laws.

State taxation policies must also be consistent with the dictates of the commerce clause. Although states have the authority to tax commercial activity within their borders, they may not discriminate by taxing local aspects of interstate commerce at higher rates than purely intrastate business.[1] Nor may they devise taxation systems that protect intrastate businesses from interstate concerns.[2]

DIRECT TAXES AND THE POWER TO TAX INCOME

The Constitution stipulates two standards for assessing federal taxes. The first is geographical uniformity. Duties, imposts, and excise taxes all must be applied according to this standard. If Congress taxes a particular product entering the ports of the United States, the tax rate on the article must be the same regardless of the point of entry. Excise taxes also must be applied uniformly throughout the nation. If an excise is placed on automobiles, the amount assessed must be the same in California as it is in Tennessee.

The second standard for imposing taxes is population distribution. The Constitution says that all direct taxes must be apportioned among the states on the basis of population. The delegates from the sparsely populated states supported this provision because they feared that the larger states, with greater representation in the House of Representatives, would craft tax measures in such a way that the burden would fall disproportionately upon the citizens of the smaller states. Unfortunately, the framers did not explain what they meant by a direct tax. As illustrated in Box 8-1, whether a tax is levied uniformly or is apportioned on the basis of population greatly affects who pays how much. In Federalist No. 21, Alexander Hamilton claimed that direct taxes were only those imposed on land and buildings, but Hamilton's opinion did not settle the issue. It required a Supreme Court decision to do that.

Defining Direct Taxation

In one of the Court's earliest cases, **Hylton v. United States** (1796), the justices defined the term *direct tax*. The dispute stemmed from a carriage tax passed by Congress on June 5, 1794. The statute classified the tax as an excise and, therefore, applied the same rate on carriages nationwide. The Federalist majorities in Congress passed the statute over Anti-Federalist opposition, and the tax was completely partisan. The Federalists generally represented the states in the Northeast with large populations but relatively few carriages; the Anti-Federalist strongholds were the less densely populated and more agricultural states with larger numbers of carriages. Because the carriage tax was deemed an excise, the Anti-Federalist areas would pay a much greater share of it than would the residents of the Northeast. The Anti-Federalists would have preferred to classify the measure as a direct tax and apportion it on the basis of population.

Daniel Hylton, a resident of Virginia, challenged the constitutionality of the assessment, claiming that it was a direct tax, not an excise, and should have been apportioned on the basis of population. The government took the position that, as a tax on an article, the carriage tax was an excise.

By almost every rule of judicial authority developed since that time, the Court should have refused to hear the dispute.[3] The evidence showed that the case did not

---

1. See *Complete Auto Transit v. Brady* (1977).
2. See *Oregon Waste Systems v. Department of Environmental Quality of the State of Oregon* (1994); *West Lynn Creamery v. Healy* (1994).

3. See Melvin I. Urofsky and Paul Finkelman, *A March of Liberty: A Constitutional History of the United States,* 2nd ed. (New York: Oxford University Press, 2002), 160–162.

BOX 8-1   DIRECT AND INDIRECT TAXES: APPORTIONMENT
VERSUS GEOGRAPHICAL UNIFORMITY

This example demonstrates the difference between direct and indirect taxing methods. The facts and figures used are purely hypothetical.

Assume that Congress decides to raise $1 million through a tax on the nation's 100,000 thoroughbred horses. If this tax is considered an excise tax, it must conform to the constitutional requirement of geographical uniformity. Congress would have to require that all thoroughbred horse owners pay a tax of $10 per horse. The rate would be the same in Maine as in Oregon. If, however, the tax on thoroughbred horses is classified as a direct tax, a different set of calculations would have to be made to meet the constitutionally required apportionment standard. Three facts would need to be known: first, the amount of money Congress intends to raise; second, the proportion of the national population residing in each state; and, third, the number of thoroughbred horses in each state. *Apportionment* means that the proportion of the revenue obtained from a state must equal the proportion of the country's population living there.

The impact of apportionment can be seen by the following calculations in applying the $1 million horse tax to three states. State A is a densely populated, urban state with few horses. State B is a moderately populated state with some ranching areas. And State C is a sparsely populated, primarily agricultural state, with a relatively large number of thoroughbreds.

State	Percentage of National Population	Taxes Due from State	Number of Horses in State	Tax Rate per Horse
State A	10	$100,000	100	$1,000
State B	5	$50,000	1,000	$50
State C	1	$10,000	10,000	$1

Obviously, the horse owners in State A would be greatly disadvantaged if the horse tax were classified as a direct tax and apportioned among the states on the basis of population. State C, on the other hand, would be greatly benefited. Because State C has only 1 percent of the nation's population, it would be responsible for raising only 1 percent of the tax revenues. Furthermore, that smaller tax obligation would be distributed over a disproportionately large number of horses.

Horse owners in State A clearly would prefer the tax on thoroughbreds to be defined as an excise tax with its required geographical uniformity. State C's thoroughbred owners obviously would want the horse tax to be considered a direct tax and be apportioned among the states on the basis of population.

involve adverse parties. In fact, the suit appeared to be little more than a ploy by the government to obtain Court approval of its interpretation of the taxation provisions of the Constitution. Both sides to the dispute agreed that Hylton owned 125 carriages exclusively for his private use. In reality, he owned only one, but the tax due on a single carriage was insufficient to meet the threshold for federal court jurisdiction. If Hylton owned 125 carriages, the taxes and penalties due would reach $2,000, enough for federal court action. This jurisdic-

tional point was important because Federalist judges dominated the federal courts, and they were likely to give the law a sympathetic hearing. Administration officials also agreed that if the tax were found valid they would demand that Hylton pay only $16. Perhaps an even greater indication of collusion was that the government paid the fees of the attorneys for both sides.

Former secretary of the Treasury Alexander Hamilton presented the government's case. Hamilton was one of the most vigorous supporters of a strong national government and of broad federal taxation powers. He understood the problems associated with apportioning taxes on the basis of population and consequently wanted the Court to set down a very narrow definition of direct taxes.

Hamilton's side was victorious. The three judges who participated in the decision each voted in favor of the statute and in agreement with Congress's determination that the carriage tax was an excise tax.[4] As was the custom in the years before John Marshall became chief justice, each justice wrote a separate opinion explaining his vote.[5] The opinions of James Iredell and Samuel Chase stressed the inappropriateness of attempting to apportion a tax on carriages and the inevitable inequities that would result. William Paterson's opinion emphasized the intention of the framers. His opinion had particular credibility because Paterson, who had been a New Jersey delegate to the Constitutional Convention, was one of the framers.[6] All three agreed that only two kinds of taxes fell into the direct tax category: capitation (or head) taxes and taxes on land.

Apportioning taxes on the basis of population is very cumbersome and almost inevitably leads to unjust tax burdens. The *Hylton* decision, by limiting the kinds of taxes that fell into the direct taxation category, significantly strengthened federal taxation powers. It freed Congress from having to apply unpopular apportionment standards to most taxes. So difficult is the apportionment problem that Congress only rarely has attempted to use a direct tax, and such efforts generally have been unsatisfactory.

Hylton was the first case in which the Supreme Court heard a challenge to the constitutionality of a federal statute: The decision predated *Marbury v. Madison* by seven years. It is clear from the arguments before the Court and the justices' opinions that the law was tested for its constitutionality. *Hylton* is not as well known as *Marbury* because the act of Congress was found to be valid.

The Constitutionality of the Income Tax

From *Hylton* to the 1860s federal taxing authority remained generally unchanged. The government financed its activities largely through import duties and excise taxes. The Civil War, however, placed a tremendous financial strain on the federal government. Between 1858 and the end of the war, the government ran unusually high budget deficits and needed to find new sources of revenue to fund the war effort. In response, Congress in 1862 and 1864 imposed the first taxes on individual incomes. **Springer v. United States** (1881) involved a challenge to the validity of the 1864 income tax act. William M. Springer, an attorney, claimed that the income tax was a direct tax and should have been apportioned on the basis of population. The justices unanimously rejected this position, once again holding that only capitation taxes and taxes on land were direct taxes. Although the challenged tax was a levy on the income of individuals, it could not be considered a capitation tax (a "head" tax, or tax on people as individuals) within the normal meaning of that term. *Springer,* then, set the precedent that the federal government had the power to tax incomes.

As the government reduced its war debts, Congress in 1872 was able to repeal the income tax law.[7] But the issue of taxing incomes did not go away. The populist movement favored the use of the income tax as the primary method of raising federal revenues. In addition, labor groups and farm organizations began arguing that new revenue sources should be developed to shift the burden away from reliance on import duties.

---

4. The other three members of the Court were absent for various reasons. Oliver Ellsworth had just been sworn in as chief justice and, because he had missed some of the arguments, did not participate in the decision. Justice James Wilson heard arguments but did not vote in the case because he had participated in the lower court decision upholding the tax. Justice William Cushing was not present for the arguments and therefore did not vote on the merits.

5. Having each justice write a separate opinion explaining his views was a practice borrowed from the British courts. When John Marshall became chief justice, he moved away from the use of these seriatim opinions to the current practice of a single opinion explaining the views of the majority. Marshall believed that the presentation of a single opinion increased the Court's status and effectiveness.

6. Justice Wilson also was a delegate at the Constitutional Convention and, therefore, one of the framers. Although he did not participate at the Supreme Court level, Wilson had voted to uphold the tax as an excise in the lower court.

7. For an excellent review of the history of the income tax in the United States, see John F. Witte, *The Politics and Development of the Federal Income Tax* (Madison: University of Wisconsin Press, 1985).

Members of the Democratic Party criticized the regressive aspects of the tax structure of that time. In response to these demands, Congress enacted an income tax law in 1894. The statute, which was passed as part of the Wilson-Gorman Tariff Act, imposed a 2 percent tax on all corporate profits and on individual incomes.

Income derived from salaries and wages, gifts, inheritances, dividends, rents, and interest, including interest from state and municipal bonds, all were subject to this tax. People with incomes under $4,000 paid no tax. This exemption, set at a figure much higher than what the average worker earned, meant that most of the burden fell upon the wealthy. For this reason, the tax received overwhelming support from rank-and-file citizens and bitter opposition from businesses and high-income individuals. The wealthy classes, in fact, claimed that the income tax would destroy the very fabric of the nation, replacing the historical principle of respect for private property with communism and socialism.

The income tax law was promptly challenged in Court in an 1895 appeal, *Pollock v. Farmers' Loan & Trust Co.* One of the primary arguments of the law's opponents was that the income tax was a direct tax, and because Congress had not apportioned it, the law was unconstitutional. Given precedents such as *Hylton* and *Springer,* would you anticipate that this position would be successful?

Pollock v. Farmers' Loan & Trust Co.

158 U.S. 601 (1895)
http://laws.findlaw.com/US/158/601.html
Vote: 5 (Brewer, Field, Fuller, Gray, Shiras)
    4 (Brown, Harlan, Jackson, White)
Opinion of the Court: Fuller
Dissenting opinions: Brown, Harlan, Jackson, White

Charles Pollock, a shareholder in Farmers' Loan & Trust Company of New York, filed suit on behalf of himself and his fellow stockholders to block the company from paying the national income tax on the ground that the tax was unconstitutional. The lawsuit was obviously collusive: The company no more wanted to pay the tax than did its shareholders. Opponents of the law claimed

(1) that taxing income from state and city bonds was an unconstitutional encroachment on the state's power to borrow money; (2) that a tax on income from real property was a direct tax and must be apportioned on the basis of population; and (3) that these taxes were so integral to the entire tax act that the whole law should be declared unconstitutional.

The Court heard arguments on the *Pollock* case twice. In its first decision, the majority declared the tax on state and municipal bonds unconstitutional.[8] It further ruled that a tax on income from land was essentially the same as taxing land itself. Because a tax on land is a direct tax, so too is a tax on the income from land; therefore, such taxes must be apportioned on the basis of population. But the Court was unable to reach a decision on whether the entire law should be declared unconstitutional. On this question the justices divided 4–4 because Justice Howell Jackson, ill with tuberculosis, was absent.

Pollock filed a petition for a second hearing, and Jackson made it known that he would be present for it. The second decision reviewed much of what the Court concluded in the first, but this time the Court ruled on the question of the general constitutionality of the income tax act.

The *Pollock* decision was one of the most controversial and important of its day. It contained all the elements of high drama. The case pitted the interests of business and wealthy individuals against those supporting social and fiscal reform. Both sides believed that a victory for their opponents would have disastrous consequences for the nation. Newspapers editorialized with enthusiasm. The first decision having ended in a tie, the suspense surrounding the second hearing grew tremendously. The human interest factor was heightened when Justice Jackson was transported to Washington to cast what he thought would be the deciding vote in favor of the tax. (Jackson died three months later.) Oral arguments took place from May 6 to May 8. The justices did not act in a manner consistent with detached objectivity. As political science professor Loren Beth put it, Justice John Marshall "Harlan wrote privately that Justice Stephen J. Field

---

8. *Pollock v. Farmers' Loan & Trust Co.,* 157 U.S. 429 (1895).

acted like a 'madman' throughout the case, but the dissenters' own opinions were similarly emotional."[9] In the end the opponents of the tax were victorious. Although Jackson, as expected, voted to uphold the law, Justice George Shiras, who had supported the tax in the first hearing, changed positions and became the crucial fifth vote to strike it down.

MR. JUSTICE FULLER delivered the opinion of the Court.

Whenever this court is required to pass upon the validity of an act of Congress as tested by the fundamental law enacted by the people, the duty imposed demands in its discharge the utmost deliberation and care, and invokes the deepest sense of responsibility. And this is especially so when the question involves the exercise of a great governmental power, and brings into consideration, as vitally affected by the decision, that complex system of government, so sagaciously framed to secure and perpetuate "an indestructible Union, composed of indestructible States." . . .

As heretofore stated, the Constitution divided Federal taxation into two great classes, the class of direct taxes, and the class of duties, imposts and excises; and prescribed two rules which qualified the grant of power as to each class.

The power to lay direct taxes apportioned among the several States in proportion to their representation in the popular branch of Congress, a representation based on population as ascertained by the census, was plenary and absolute; but to lay direct taxes without apportionment was forbidden. The power to lay duties, imposts, and excises was subject to the qualification that the imposition must be uniform throughout the United States.

Our previous decision was confined to the consideration of the validity of the tax on the income from real estate, and on the income from municipal bonds. The question thus limited was whether such taxation was direct or not, in the meaning of the Constitution; and the court went no farther, as to the tax on the income from real estate, than to hold that it fell within the same class as the source whence the income was derived, that is, that a tax upon the realty and a tax upon the receipts therefrom were alike direct; while as to the income from municipal bonds, that could not be

taxed because of want of power to tax the source, and no reference was made to the nature of the tax as being direct or indirect.

We are now permitted to broaden the field of inquiry, and to determine to which of the two great classes a tax upon a person's entire income, whether derived from rents, or products, or otherwise, of real estate, or from bonds, stocks, or other forms of personal property, belongs; and we are unable to conclude that the enforced subtraction from the yield of all the owner's real or personal property, in the manner prescribed, is so different from a tax upon the property itself, that it is not a direct, but an indirect tax, in the meaning of the Constitution. . . .

The reasons for the clauses of the Constitution in respect of direct taxation are not far to seek. The States, respectively, possessed plenary powers of taxation. They could tax the property of their citizens in such manner and to such extent as they saw fit; they had unrestricted powers to impose duties or imposts on imports from abroad, and excises on manufactures, consumable commodities, or otherwise. They gave up the great sources of revenue derived from commerce; they retained the concurrent power o[f] levying excises, and duties if covering anything other than excises; but in respect of them the range of taxation was narrowed by the power granted over interstate commerce, and by the danger of being put at disadvantage in dealing with excises on manufactures. They retained the power of direct taxation, and to that they looked as their chief resource; but even in respect of that, they granted the concurrent power, and if the tax were placed by both governments on the same subject, the claim of the United States had preference. Therefore, they did not grant the power of direct taxation without regard to their own condition and resources as States; but they granted the power of apportioned direct taxation, a power just as efficacious to serve the needs of the general government, but securing to the States the opportunity to pay the amount apportioned, and to recoup from their own citizens in the most feasible way, and in harmony with their systems of local self-government. . . .

The founders anticipated that the expenditures of the States, their counties, cities, and towns, would chiefly be met by direct taxation on accumulated property, while they expected that those of the Federal government would be for the most part met by indirect taxes. And in order that the power of direct taxation by the general government should

9. Loren P. Beth, "*Pollock v. Farmers' Loan & Trust Co.*," in *The Oxford Companion to the Supreme Court*, ed. Kermit L. Hall (New York: Oxford University Press, 1992), 655.

not be exercised, except on necessity; and, when the necessity arose, should be so exercised as to leave the States at liberty to discharge their respective obligations, and should not be so exercised, unfairly and discriminatingly, as to particular States or otherwise, by a mere majority vote, possibly of those whose constituents were intentionally not subjected to any part of the burden, the qualified grant was made. . . .

It is said that a tax on the whole income of property is not a direct tax in the meaning of the Constitution, but a duty, and, as a duty, leviable without apportionment, whether direct or indirect. We do not think so. Direct taxation was not restricted in one breath, and the restriction blown to the winds in another. . . .

We have unanimously held in this case that, so far as this law operates on the receipts from municipal bonds, it cannot be sustained, because it is a tax on the power of the States, and on their instrumentalities to borrow money, and consequently repugnant to the Constitution. But if, as contended, the interest when received has become merely money in the recipient's pocket, and taxable as such without reference to the source from which it came, the question is immaterial whether it could have been originally taxed at all or not. This was admitted by the Attorney General with characteristic candor; and it follows that, if the revenue derived from municipal bonds cannot be taxed because the source cannot be, the same rule applies to revenue from any other source not subject to the tax; and the lack of power to levy any but an apportioned tax on real and personal property equally exists as to the revenue therefrom.

Admitting that this act taxes the income of property irrespective of its source, still we cannot doubt that such a tax is necessarily a direct tax in the meaning of the Constitution. . . .

We are not here concerned with the question whether an income tax be or be not desirable, nor whether such a tax would enable the government to diminish taxes on consumption and duties on imports, and to enter upon what may be believed to be a reform of its fiscal and commercial system. Questions of that character belong to the controversies of political parties, and cannot be settled by judicial decision. In these cases our province is to determine whether this income tax on the revenue from property does or does not belong to the class of direct taxes. If it does, it is, being unapportioned, in violation of the Constitution, and we must so declare. . . .

Being of opinion that so much of the sections of this law as lays a tax on income from real and personal property is invalid, we are brought to the question of the effect of that conclusion upon these sections as a whole.

It is elementary that the same statute may be in part constitutional and in part unconstitutional, and if the parts are wholly independent of each other, that which is constitutional may stand while that which is unconstitutional will be rejected. And in the case before us there is no question as to the validity of this act, except sections twenty-seven to thirty-seven, inclusive, which relate to the subject which has been under discussion; and as to them we think . . . that if the different parts "are so mutually connected with and dependent on each other, as to warrant a belief that the legislature intended them as a whole, and that, if all could not be carried into effect, the legislature would not pass the residue independently, and some parts are unconstitutional, all the provisions which are thus dependent, conditional or connected, must fall with them." . . .

According to the census, the true valuation of real and personal property in the United States in 1890 was $65,037,091,197, of which real estate with improvements thereon made up $39,544,544,333. Of course, from the latter must be deducted, in applying these sections, all unproductive property and all property whose net yield does not exceed four thousand dollars; but, even with such deductions, it is evident that the income from realty formed a vital part of the scheme for taxation embodied therein. If that be stricken out, and also the income from all invested personal property, bonds, stocks, investments of all kinds, it is obvious that by far the largest part of the anticipated revenue would be eliminated, and this would leave the burden of the tax to be borne by professions, trades, employments, or vocations; and in that way what was intended as a tax on capital would remain in substance a tax on occupations and labor. We cannot believe that such was the intention of Congress. We do not mean to say that an act laying by apportionment a direct tax on all real estate and personal property, or the income thereof, might not also lay excise taxes on business, privileges, employments, and vocations. But this is not such an act; and the scheme must be considered as a whole. Being invalid as to the greater part, and falling, as the tax would, if any part were held valid, in a direction which could not have been contemplated except in connection with the taxation considered as an entirety, we are constrained to conclude that sections twenty-seven to

This 1895 editorial cartoon, published after the Supreme Court's decision in *Pollock v. Farmers' Loan and Trust*, illustrates the defeat of the federal income tax law. In 1913, however, the situation reversed itself when the states ratified the Sixteenth Amendment, which gave the federal government the power to tax incomes regardless of source.

thirty-seven, inclusive, of the act, which became a law without the signature of the President on August 28, 1894, are wholly inoperative and void.

Our conclusions may, therefore, be summed up as follows:

First. We adhere to the opinion already announced, that, taxes on real estate being indisputably direct taxes, taxes on the rents or income of real estate are equally direct taxes.

Second. We are of opinion that taxes on personal property, or on the income of personal property, are likewise direct taxes.

Third. The tax imposed by sections twenty-seven to thirty-seven, inclusive, of the act of 1894, so far as it falls

on the income of real estate and of personal property, being a direct tax within the meaning of the Constitution, and, therefore, unconstitutional and void because not apportioned according to representation, all those sections, constituting one entire scheme of taxation, are necessarily invalid.

MR. JUSTICE HARLAN, dissenting.

Assuming it to be the settled construction of the constitution that the general government cannot tax lands, . . . except by apportioning the tax among the states according to their respective numbers, does it follow that a tax on incomes derived from rents is a direct tax on the real estate from which such rents arise?

In my judgment, a tax on income derived from real property ought not to be, and until now has never been, regarded by any court as a direct tax on such property, within the meaning of the constitution. As the great mass of lands in most of the states do not bring any rents, and as incomes from rents vary in the different states, such a tax cannot possibly be apportioned among the states, on the basis merely of numbers, with any approach to equality of right among taxpayers, any more than a tax on carriages or other personal property could be so apportioned. And in view of former adjudications, beginning with the *Hylton Case*, and ending with the *Springer Case*, a decision now that a tax on income from real property can be laid and collected only by apportioning the same among the states on the basis of numbers may not improperly be regarded as a judicial revolution that may sow the seeds of hate and distrust among the people of different sections of our common country. . . .

. . . While a tax on the land itself, whether at a fixed rate applicable to all lands, without regard to their value, or by the acre, or according to their market value, might be deemed a direct tax, within the meaning of the constitution, as interpreted in the *Hylton Case*, a duty on rents is a duty on something distinct and entirely separate from, although issuing out of, the land. . . .

But the court, by its judgment just rendered, goes far in advance, not only of its former decisions, but of any decision heretofore rendered by an American court. . . .

In my judgment,—to say nothing of the disregard of the former adjudications of this court, and of the settled practice of the government,—this decision may well excite the gravest apprehensions. It strikes at the very foundations of national authority, in that it denies to the general government a power which is or may become vital to the very existence and preservation of the Union in a national emergency, such as that of war with a great commercial nation, during which the collection of all duties upon imports will cease or be materially diminished. It tends to re-establish that condition of helplessness in which congress found itself during the period of the Articles of Confederation, when it was without authority, by laws operating directly upon individuals, to lay and collect, through its own agents, taxes sufficient to pay the debts and defray the expenses of government, but was dependent in all such matters upon the good will of the states, and their promptness in meeting requisitions made upon them by congress.

Why do I say that the decision just rendered impairs or menaces the national authority? The reason is so apparent that it need only be stated. In its practical operation this decision withdraws from national taxation not only all incomes derived from real estate, but tangible personal property, "invested personal property, bonds, stocks, investments of all kinds," and the income that may be derived from such property. This results from the fact that, by the decision of the court, all such personal property and all incomes from real estate and personal property are placed beyond national taxation otherwise than by apportionment among the states on the basis simply of population. No such apportionment can possibly be made without doing gross injustice to the many for the benefit of the favored few in particular states. Any attempt upon the part of congress to apportion among the states, upon the basis simply of their population, taxation of personal property or of incomes, would tend to arouse such indignation among the freemen of America that it would never be repeated. When, therefore, this court adjudges, as it does now adjudge, that congress cannot impose a duty or tax upon personal property, or upon income arising either from rents of real estate or from personal property, including invested personal property, bonds, stocks, and investments of all kinds, except by apportioning the sum to be so raised among the states according to population, it practically decides that, without an amendment of the constitution,—two-thirds of both houses of congress and three-fourths of the states concurring,—such property and incomes can never be made to contribute to the support of the national government. . . .

. . . I dissent from the opinion and judgment of the court.

The Sixteenth Amendment

The decision to invalidate the entire income tax act was quite unpopular. Because that statute had placed a greater obligation on the wealthy, the ruling convinced the middle and working classes that the Supreme Court was little more than the defender of the rich. Various political groups immediately began working to reverse the impact of the Court's decision either with a constitutional amendment or revised federal legislation. Labor and farming interests supported a new income tax, as did Progressive Republicans and Democratic populists. Opposition came primarily from conservative Republicans in the Northeast.

In 1909 Congress began serious work on an income tax measure. There were sufficient votes in the legislature to reform the tax structure, moving the federal government away from excessive reliance on regressive tariffs and excise taxes. The major question was whether to pass another income tax bill or to propose a constitutional amendment. Finding themselves in a minority, conservative Republicans threw their support to an amendment. They hoped the state legislatures would not ratify it; but, even if the states approved, the process would take several years to complete.

Congress proposed a constitutional amendment to authorize a federal income tax in July 1909 by overwhelming votes of 77–0 in the Senate and 318–14 in the House. The amendment received the required number of approvals from the state legislatures in February 1913 and became the Sixteenth Amendment to the United States Constitution:

The Congress shall have power to lay and collect taxes on incomes, from whatever source derived, without apportionment among the several States, and without regard to any census or enumeration.

The amendment, which effectively ended the debate over direct taxation, is one of only four designed to overturn a Supreme Court precedent. It gave Congress sufficient taxing authority to fund the federal government

TABLE 8-1 Federal Tax Revenues: The Impact of the Sixteenth Amendment

Source	1800	1850	1900	1950	2000	2010 (est.)
Customs duties	83.7	91.0	41.1	1.0	1.0	1.1
Excises	7.5	—	50.1	18.4	3.4	2.1
Gifts and inheritances	—	—	—	1.7	1.4	0.7
Individual incomes	—	—	—	38.5	49.6	48.4
Corporate incomes	—	—	—	25.5	10.2	11.6
Insurance trust (Social Security, etc.)	—	—	—	10.7	32.2	34.3
Other income	8.8	9.0	8.8	4.2	2.2	2.0

SOURCES: *Historical Statistics of the United States: Colonial Times to 1970* (Washington, D.C.: U.S. Bureau of the Census, 1975); *World Almanac and Book of Facts 2003* (New York: World Almanac Books, 2003), 116; *Budget of the United States, FY 2009* (Washington, D.C.: Government Printing Office, 2008).

NOTE: The data represent the proportion of total federal revenues for each of seven sources of taxation. The data prior to ratification of the Sixteenth Amendment in 1913 demonstrate the federal government's reliance on customs duties and excise taxes. Data from the period after 1913 illustrate the shift to income taxes as the primary sources for federal tax dollars.

without having to resort to direct taxes. The Constitution now made all sources of income subject to Congress's taxing power and removed any requirement that a tax on income be apportioned on the basis of population.

Congress wasted no time. In 1913 the legislature imposed a 1 percent tax rate on individual incomes in excess of $3,000 and on incomes of married couples over $4,000. Not surprisingly, the statute's constitutionality was challenged in Court, but the justices upheld the law three years later in *Brushaber v. Union Pacific Railroad* (1916) by a 7–2 vote. As shown in Table 8-1, the income tax is now the primary source of federal revenue.

INTERGOVERNMENTAL TAX IMMUNITY

The operation of a federal system carries within it inherent risks of conflict between the national government and the states. When both levels of government are authorized to tax, one government can use the power as a weapon against the other. No specific provision of the Constitution prohibits the federal government from taxing state governments or vice versa, but for the federal system to operate effectively, the entities need to avoid such conflicts.

Establishing the Tax Immunity Doctrine

The issue of intergovernmental tax immunity was first raised in *McCulloch v. Maryland* (1819), which tested the constitutional validity of the national bank. The Supreme Court's decision in *McCulloch* was tremendously important in many ways. We have already discussed its significance for the development of congressional power and the concept of federalism, but *McCulloch* also is relevant to the constitutional limitations on the power to tax.

McCulloch involved a challenge to a tax imposed by the state of Maryland on the national bank, a creation of the federal government. Supporters of federal power argued that the Union could not be maintained if the states were permitted to place debilitating taxes on any operations of the federal government they disapproved. States' rights advocates claimed that the power of the states to tax within their own borders was absolute and there was no constitutional bar to such taxes. The Court ruled in favor of the federal government, declaring the state tax unconstitutional. Chief Justice Marshall's hard-hitting opinion for a unanimous Court put an immediate stop to a conflict that would have desperately weakened the Union if allowed to continue.

In doing so, Marshall created the intergovernmental tax immunity doctrine. He wrote, "[T]he power to tax involves the power to destroy; . . . the power to destroy may defeat and render useless the power to create; . . . there is plain repugnance, in conferring on one government a power to control the constitutional measures of another." The ability of the states to tax the legitimate operations of the federal government is simply incompatible with the framers' intent of creating viable government units at both the national and state levels.

Marshall's decision in *McCulloch* was consistent with his general philosophy of favoring a strong national government. But was the doctrine of intergovernmental tax immunity a two-way street? Marshall's opinion fell short of proclaiming that the national government was prohibited from taxing the legitimate operations of the states. He was more concerned in this case with reinforcing principles of federal supremacy. Yet a strong case can be made that it would also violate the principles of the Constitution for the federal government to be permitted to destroy the states through its taxing power.

The first case that tested whether the states enjoyed immunity from federal taxation was **Collector v. Day** (1871), which stemmed from an application of the Civil War federal income tax law. Judge J. M. Day of the probate court in Massachusetts objected to paying a federal tax on his income on intergovernmental tax immunity grounds. Three decades earlier the Supreme Court had ruled that the state governments could not tax the income of federal officeholders.[10] Now Day was asking the Court to adopt the converse of that ruling. The Supreme Court, 8–1, held that Day's judicial income was immune from federal taxation. The Court reasoned that the Constitution protects the legitimate functions of the state. The federal government cannot use its taxation powers to curtail or destroy the operations or instruments of the state, and the probate court system is a legitimate and necessary agency of state government. To allow the federal government to tax the income of state judges would be to open the door for Congress to tax all state government functions.

For several decades the justices vigorously maintained the doctrine that the Constitution did not allow one government to tax the essential functions of another. In the *Pollock* income tax decisions, as we have already seen, the Court struck down a federal tax on interest income from state and municipal bonds as an unconstitutional burden on the state's authority to borrow. The Court struck down

state taxes on income from federal land leases and federally granted patents and copyrights, and on the sales of petroleum products to the federal government.[11] It also invalidated a federal tax on revenues derived from the sales of goods to state agencies.[12] The only significant standard imposed by the Court in this line of cases was that immunity covered only essential government functions. Consequently, the justices upheld a federal tax on the profits of South Carolina's state-run liquor stores.[13] As a merchant of alcoholic beverages, the state was acting as a private business, not exercising a government function, and therefore was not immune from federal taxation.

Erosion of the Tax Immunity Doctrine

During the New Deal period, support for the tax immunity doctrine began to wane. A series of Supreme Court decisions modified or reversed the earlier rulings that had established an almost impenetrable barrier against the taxation by one government of the instruments or operations of another.

In *Helvering v. Gerhardt* (1938) the Court overruled *Dobbins v. Commissioners of Erie County* (1842) and permitted states to tax the income of federal officials. The justices then overruled *Collector v. Day* in **Graves v. New York ex rel. O'Keefe** (1939) and held that there was no constitutional bar to the taxation by the federal government of the income of state employees. "The theory," said the Court, "that a tax on income is legally or economically a tax on its source, is no longer tenable." Also falling were bans on taxing profits from doing business with state or federal government agencies. The Supreme Court went so far as to allow a state to impose taxes on a federal contractor even when those taxes were passed on to the federal government through a cost-plus contract.[14]

Although these rulings seriously weakened the doctrine of intergovernmental tax immunity, the principle still has some vitality. It would be unconstitutional for a state to place a tax on cases filed in the federal courts op-

10. *Dobbins v. Commissioners of Erie County* (1842).

11. *Gillespie v. Oklahoma* (1922) and *Long v. Rockwood* (1928) concerned patents and copyrights; *Panhandle Oil Co. v. Mississippi* (1928) dealt with petroleum sales.

12. *Indian Motorcycle Co. v. United States* (1931).

13. *South Carolina v. United States* (1905).

14. *Alabama v. King and Boozer* (1941).

erating within its boundaries, or for the federal government to impose an excise tax on the tickets issued by a state highway patrol. But aside from these obvious examples, where is the line between permissible and impermissible taxation? The Supreme Court helped answer that question in *South Carolina v. Baker* (1988), which involved a challenge to a federal law taxing the income from long-term state and city bonds.

In 1982 Congress passed a tax act that removed the federal tax exemption for interest earned on publicly offered long-term bonds issued by state and local governments unless the bonds and their owners were registered. The registration requirement was intended to identify owners of such bonds so that capital gains and estate taxes could be better monitored. The taxing of interest from unregistered state and municipal bonds ran directly contrary to the *Pollock* decision. South Carolina objected to the law as a direct violation of the intergovernmental tax immunity doctrine. The federal tax, it argued, placed a direct burden on the ability of state and local governments to raise revenue.

By a 7–1 vote, with only Justice Sandra Day O'Connor in dissent, the Supreme Court upheld the law. For the Court, Justice William J. Brennan Jr. explained that precedents since *Pollock* had repudiated the position that a tax on those doing business with the state was the equivalent of a tax on the state. The justices could see no reason for treating persons who receive interest on state bonds any differently from persons receiving income from other kinds of contracts with the state.

The decision in *South Carolina v. Baker* continued a long-standing trend of the Court to erode the doctrine of intergovernmental tax immunity. A statement of the contemporary status of the doctrine, in Justice Brennan's words, is that "the States can never tax the United States directly but can tax any private parties with whom it does business, even though the financial burden falls on the United States, as long as the tax does not discriminate against the United States or those with whom it deals." A similar, although not quite as rigid, prohibition applies to federal taxes on the states.

Even in those cases, like *South Carolina v. Baker*, that have limited intergovernmental tax immunity, the Court

repeatedly has stressed the principle that taxes must be nondiscriminatory. If a state wishes to tax a company's profits from a business transaction with the federal government, for example, the tax obligation must be the same as that imposed on profits from business with nongovernmental parties. This bar against discriminatory taxation was reinforced in *Davis v. Michigan Department of Treasury* (1989), in which the Court struck down a state law that taxed income that residents received from federal retirement plans but exempted income from state retirement programs.

Fourteen other states had similar tax laws. As a result of this decision they were required to revise the laws, choosing between extending the tax exemptions to retired federal employees or eliminating the exemption granted to state and local retirees. The Court's decision in *Davis* reminds us that the tax immunity doctrine remains viable in spite of decisions that have imposed limitations on it.

TAXATION AS A REGULATORY POWER

Normally, we think of taxation as a method of funding the government. Yet Marshall's well-known statement that the "power to tax involves the power to destroy" was an early recognition that taxes can be used for purposes other than raising revenue. Excessive taxation can make the targeted activities so unprofitable that it is no longer feasible to engage in them. The converse also is true. Favorable tax status, including tax exemptions, can encourage a preferred activity. These observations lead us to several important constitutional questions regarding the taxation powers of the federal government. Is it proper for the United States to impose taxes for reasons other than revenue raising? Is it constitutional for the government to use taxation as a method of regulation? Is it valid for Congress to enact tax laws as a means of controlling activities not otherwise within the jurisdiction of the federal government?

From the beginning, Congress has used its authority to tax for purposes other than raising revenue. Before the ratification of the Sixteenth Amendment, the federal government relied heavily on customs duties. In deciding what imported products to tax and at what level, the legislators clearly were guided by their policy preferences. Certain industries received protection from imports and were able to grow with little foreign competition. The practice of combining revenue gathering with other policy objectives continues to this day.

Deciding that Congress may impose import duties with regulatory purposes does not necessarily answer a similar question with respect to excise taxes. Customs, after all, have a limited range. They can be applied only to those goods that are brought into the country from abroad. Excise taxes can be applied to the broad spectrum of domestic goods, services, and activities. The only restriction on such taxes explicitly mentioned in the Constitution is that they be geographically uniform. But is there an implied requirement that excise taxes be generated only for revenue purposes, or may Congress regulate through the use of the excise? If Congress is allowed to regulate domestic activities through the power to tax, does that not give the federal government the equivalent of a police power that the framers reserved to the states?

Initially, the Court took the position that Congress had wide latitude in exercising the taxing power. In *Veazie Bank v. Fenno* (1869) the justices upheld a 10 percent tax on notes issued by state banks. The law was intended to protect the newly chartered national bank from state competition by making notes far too costly for state banks to issue. In **McCray v. United States** (1904) the Court held valid a federal tax on oleomargarine designed primarily to protect the dairy industry from competition from the less expensive butter substitute. The justices refused to examine the motives of the legislators in passing the act. In the words of Justice Edward White, "The decisions of this court from the beginning lend no support whatever to the assumption that the judiciary may restrain the exercise of lawful power on the assumption that a wrongful purpose or motive has caused the power to be exerted." The tax was clearly an excise tax, and as such was subject to only one constitutional limitation—geographical uniformity. That requirement having been met, the federal tax on margarine was constitutional.

Later, in **Bailey v. Drexel Furniture Co.** (1922), the Court changed course. At issue was a federal tax on the profits of any company hiring child labor. In striking down the tax, the justices took into consideration the motives behind the legislation. They concluded that the legislature was using the power to tax as a means of regulating activities that were outside Congress's proper authority. As Chief Justice William Howard Taft explained, "So here the so-called tax is a penalty to coerce the people of a State to act as Congress wishes them to act in respect of a matter completely the business of the state government under the Federal Constitution."

The decision in *Drexel* was a reversal of the position on excise taxes the Court had held since the early 1800s. It generally proved to be out of line with Supreme Court rulings both before and after. The Court repeatedly has faced the question of taxation and regulation and generally has ruled in favor of the federal power to tax and even acknowledged that all taxes to some degree have regulatory effects. In *United States v. Doremus* (1919) and *Nigro v. United States* (1928) the Court upheld federal excise taxes on narcotics, and in *United States v. Sanchez* (1950) it upheld a tax on marijuana. Similarly, an excise tax on objectionable firearms was declared valid in *Sonzinsky v. United States* (1937), even though the Court admitted that the law had an unmistakable "legislative purpose to regulate rather than to tax." The justices found no constitutional defects with an excise levied on professional gamblers in *United States v. Kahriger* (1953). These taxes expand federal regulatory powers. If Congress has the power to impose the tax, then the federal government also has the power to enforce the tax laws, creating, to an extent, "police powers" within the federal government that originally resided with the states.

TAXING AND SPENDING FOR THE GENERAL WELFARE

The Constitution authorizes Congress to tax and spend for the general welfare. Whether the term *general welfare* was intended to expand the powers of Congress beyond those explicitly stated in the Constitution is subject to debate. James Madison argued that *general welfare* was only a reference to the other enumerated powers. Because the United States is a government of limited and specified powers, he asserted, the authority to tax and spend must be confined to those spheres of authority the

Constitution explicitly granted. Alexander Hamilton took the opposite position. He interpreted the power to tax and spend for the general welfare to be a separate power altogether. For Hamilton, taxing and spending authority was given in addition to the other granted powers, not limited by them. The conflict between these two opposing interpretations was the subject of legal disputes throughout much of the nation's history, and the last battle between them was waged during the constitutional crisis over legislation passed during the New Deal.

Many of the programs recommended by Franklin Roosevelt to reestablish the nation's economic strength involved regulatory activity far more extensive than ever before proposed. Several depended on the power of the federal government to tax and spend for the general welfare. Opponents of the New Deal claimed that these programs, while ostensibly based upon the taxing and spending authority, in reality were regulations of matters the Constitution reserved for the states.

During the Great Depression, agriculture was one of the hardest-hit sectors of the economy. The nation's farmers were overproducing, which caused prices for farm products to drop. In many cases the cost of production was higher than the income from crop sales, leaving farmers in desperate straits. Most of their farms were mortgaged, and all owed taxes on their lands. The more the farmers got behind economically, the more they attempted to produce to improve their situation. This strategy further increased production, making matters even worse. At that time agriculture was responsible for a much larger proportion of the nation's economy than it is today, and conditions in the farming sector had dire effects on the general welfare of the entire country.

In response, Roosevelt proposed and Congress passed the Agricultural Adjustment Act (AAA), a statute that combined the taxing and spending powers to combat the agricultural crisis. The central purpose of the plan was to reduce the amount of acreage being farmed. To accomplish this goal, the federal government would "rent" a percentage of the nation's farmland and leave this acreage unplanted. In effect, the government would pay the farmers not to farm. If the plan succeeded, production would drop, prices would rise, and the farmer

would have a sufficient income. Making payments to the nation's farmers was an expensive proposition, and to fund these expenditures the AAA imposed an excise tax on the processing of agricultural products.

The program was a success until William M. Butler challenged the constitutionality of the law. Butler was the bankruptcy receiver for Hoosac Mills Corporation, a cotton processor. When the government imposed the processing tax on Hoosac, Butler took legal action to avoid payment, claiming that the AAA exceeded the taxing and spending powers granted to the federal government.

In *United States v. Butler* (1936) the Court concluded that the federal government had broad powers to tax and spend for the general welfare. The justices decided, consistent with Hamilton's position, that Congress's fiscal authority was not limited to those subjects specifically enumerated in Article I. This philosophy did not, however, mean that congressional powers had no limits. The majority in *Butler* ruled that the law was unconstitutional because what it imposed was not truly a tax. Instead, the government was taking money from one group (the processors) to give to another (the farmers), and doing this to regulate farm production, a matter of intrastate commerce reserved for state regulation. The decision dealt a severe blow to the New Deal, but only temporarily.

Butler's impact was short-lived. Following the Court's dramatic change in position after Roosevelt's threat to add new members, the justices ruled that agriculture could be regulated under the commerce power.[15] As for the power to tax and spend for the general welfare, the position taken in *Butler* was reevaluated the very next year in *Steward Machine Co. v. Davis* (1937) and *Helvering v. Davis* (1937), challenges to the constitutionality of the newly formed Social Security system. The Social Security Act shared several characteristics with the AAA the Court had condemned in *Butler*. Both used the taxing and spending powers to combat the effects of the Depression; both took money from one group of people to give to another; and both regulated areas previously thought to be reserved to the states. The radical change in position occurred largely because Chief Justice Charles

15. See *Mulford v. Smith* (1939) and *Wickard v. Filburn* (1942).

William M. Butler, receiver for Hoosac Mills, objected to paying the federal tax on processing cotton. His lawsuit successfully challenged the constitutionality of the Agricultural Adjustment Act of 1933.

Since these 1937 decisions, Congress has used the spending authority to expand greatly the role of the federal government.

Serious challenges to a federal spending program are now unusual, but occasionally a battle erupts over federal and state authority with respect to spending programs. One such case was *South Dakota v. Dole* (1987). This dispute involved a conflict over federal spending power and the state's authority to regulate highway safety and alcoholic beverages. The use of federal funds to coerce the states into taking particular policy positions was attacked in much the same manner that *Steward Machine* attacked the establishment of state unemployment compensation programs. It is interesting to note that Chief Justice William Rehnquist, who was considered a strong defender of states' rights, wrote the majority opinion upholding the exercise of federal authority over the states. Not surprising was the stinging dissent registered by Justice O'Connor on behalf of state interests.

South Dakota v. Dole

483 U.S. 203 (1987)
http://laws.findlaw.com/US/483/203.html
Oral arguments may be found at: http://www.oyez.org
Vote: 7 (Blackmun, Marshall, Powell, Rehnquist, Scalia, Stevens, White)
    2 (Brennan, O'Connor)
Opinion of the Court: Rehnquist
Dissenting opinions: Brennan, O'Connor

Evans Hughes and Justice Owen Roberts deserted the *Butler* majority and joined with the liberal wing of the Court to forge a new constitutional interpretation.

The Social Security cases firmly established that the taxing and spending powers are to be broadly construed. If Congress decides that the general welfare of the United States demands a program requiring the use of these fiscal powers, the Supreme Court likely will find it constitutionally valid unless parts of the law violate specific provisions of the Constitution. In fact, *United States v. Butler* was the last major case in which the Supreme Court ruled that Congress had exceeded its spending powers.

In 1984 Congress passed a statute directing the secretary of transportation to withhold a portion of federal highway funds from any state that did not establish a minimum drinking age of twenty-one years. The purpose of the law was to decrease the number of serious automobile accidents among a group that statistics showed had a high percentage of accidents. The legislators correctly believed that withholding federal dollars would be an effective way of encouraging the states to comply with the federal program.

South Dakota, which allowed the purchase of beer containing 3.2 percent alcohol by persons nineteen years or older, objected to the statute, arguing that Congress was infringing on the rights of the states. The Twenty-first Amendment, which repealed Prohibition in 1933, gave full authority to the states to regulate alcoholic beverages; therefore, South Dakota claimed that Congress had no authority to set minimum drinking ages. According to the state, the federal government was using its considerable spending power to coerce the states into enacting laws that were otherwise outside congressional authority.

The state sued Secretary of Transportation Elizabeth Dole, asking the courts to declare the law unconstitutional. Both the district court and the court of appeals ruled against the state and upheld the law.

CHIEF JUSTICE REHNQUIST delivered the opinion of the Court.

The Constitution empowers Congress to "lay and collect Taxes, Duties, Imposts, and Excises, to pay the Debts and provide for the common Defence and general Welfare of the United States." Art. I, §8, cl. 1. Incident to this power, Congress may attach conditions on the receipt of federal funds, and has repeatedly employed the power "to further broad policy objectives by conditioning receipt of federal moneys upon compliance by the recipient with federal statutory and administrative directives." The breadth of this power was made clear in *United States v. Butler* (1936), where the Court, resolving a longstanding debate over the scope of the Spending Clause, determined that "the power of Congress to authorize expenditure of public moneys for public purposes is not limited by the direct grants of legislative power found in the Constitution." Thus, objectives not thought to be within Article I's "enumerated legislative fields" may nevertheless be attained through the use of the spending power and the conditional grant of federal funds.

The spending power is of course not unlimited, but is instead subject to several general restrictions articulated in our cases. The first of these limitations is derived from the language of the Constitution itself: the exercise of the spending power must be in pursuit of "the general welfare." In considering whether a particular expenditure is intended to serve general public purposes, courts should defer substantially to the judgment of Congress. Second, we have required that if Congress desires to condition the States' receipt of federal funds, it "must do so unambiguously . . . ,

enabl[ing] the States to exercise their choice knowingly, cognizant of the consequences of their participation." Third, our cases have suggested (without significant elaboration) that conditions on federal grants might be illegitimate if they are unrelated "to the federal interest in particular national projects or programs." Finally, we have noted that other constitutional provisions may provide an independent bar to the conditional grant of federal funds.

South Dakota does not seriously claim that §158 is inconsistent with any of the first three restrictions mentioned above. We can readily conclude that the provision is designed to serve the general welfare, especially in light of the fact that "the concept of welfare or the opposite is shaped by Congress. . . ." Congress found that the differing drinking ages in the States created particular incentives for young persons to combine their desire to drink with their ability to drive, and that this interstate problem required a national solution. The means it chose to address this dangerous situation were reasonably calculated to advance the general welfare. The conditions upon which States receive the funds, moreover, could not be more clearly stated by Congress. And the State itself, rather than challenging the germaneness of the condition to federal purposes, admits that it "has never contended that the congressional action was . . . unrelated to a national concern in the absence of the Twenty-first Amendment." Indeed, the condition imposed by Congress is directly related to one of the main purposes for which highway funds are expended—safe interstate travel. This goal of the interstate highway system had been frustrated by varying drinking ages among the States. . . . By enacting §158, Congress conditioned the receipt of federal funds in a way reasonably calculated to address this particular impediment to a purpose for which the funds are expended.

The remaining question about the validity of §158—and the basic point of disagreement between the parties—is whether the Twenty-first Amendment constitutes an "independent constitutional bar" to the conditional grant of federal funds. Petitioner, relying on its view that the Twenty-first Amendment prohibits *direct* regulation of drinking ages by Congress, asserts that "Congress may not use the spending power to regulate that which it is prohibited from regulating directly under the Twenty-first Amendment." But our cases show that this "independent constitutional bar" limitation on the spending power is not of the kind petitioner suggests. *United States v. Butler,* for example, established that the constitutional limitations on Congress when exercising its spending power are less exacting than those on its authority to regulate directly. . . .

[T]he "independent constitutional bar" limitation on the spending power is not, as petitioner suggests, a prohibition on the indirect achievement of objectives which Congress is not empowered to achieve directly. Instead, we think that the language in our earlier opinions stands for the unexceptionable proposition that the power may not be used to induce the States to engage in activities that would themselves be unconstitutional. Thus, for example, a grant of federal funds conditioned on invidiously discriminatory state action or the infliction of cruel and unusual punishment would be an illegitimate exercise of the Congress' broad spending power. But no such claim can be or is made here. Were South Dakota to succumb to the blandishments offered by Congress and raise its drinking age to 21, the State's action in so doing would not violate the constitutional rights of anyone.

Our decisions have recognized that in some circumstances the financial inducement offered by Congress might be so coercive as to pass the point at which "pressure turns into compulsion." Here, however, Congress has directed only that a State desiring to establish a minimum drinking age lower than 21 lose a relatively small percentage of certain federal highway funds. Petitioner contends that the coercive nature of this program is evident from the degree of success it has achieved. We cannot conclude, however, that a conditional grant of federal money of this sort is unconstitutional simply by reason of its success in achieving the congressional objective.

When we consider, for a moment, that all South Dakota would lose if she adheres to her chosen course as to a suitable minimum drinking age is 5% of the funds otherwise obtainable under specified highway grant programs, the argument as to coercion is shown to be more rhetoric than fact. . . .

Here Congress has offered relatively mild encouragement to the States to enact higher minimum drinking ages than they would otherwise choose. But the enactment of such laws remains the prerogative of the States not merely in theory but in fact. Even if Congress might lack the power to impose a national minimum drinking age directly, we conclude that encouragement to state action found in §158

is a valid use of the spending power. Accordingly, the judgment of the Court of Appeals is

Affirmed.

JUSTICE O'CONNOR, dissenting.

The Court today upholds the National Minimum Drinking Age Amendment, 23 U.S.C. §158, as a valid exercise of the spending power conferred by Article I, §8. But §158 is not a condition on spending reasonably related to the expenditure of federal funds and cannot be justified on that ground. Rather, it is an attempt to regulate the sale of liquor, an attempt that lies outside Congress' power to regulate commerce because it falls within the ambit of §2 of the Twenty-first Amendment. . . .

When Congress appropriates money to build a highway, it is entitled to insist that the highway be a safe one. But it is not entitled to insist as a condition of the use of highway funds that the State impose or change regulations in other areas of the State's social and economic life because of an attenuated or tangential relationship to highway use or safety. Indeed, if the rule were otherwise, the Congress could effectively regulate almost any area of a State's social, political, or economic life on the theory that use of the interstate transportation system is somehow enhanced. If, for example, the United States were to condition highway moneys upon moving the state capital, I suppose it might argue that interstate transportation is facilitated by locating local governments in places easily accessible to interstate highways—or, conversely, that highways might become overburdened if they had to carry traffic to and from the state capital. In my mind, such a relationship is hardly more attenuated than the one which the Court finds supports §158.

There is a clear place at which the Court can draw the line between permissible and impermissible conditions on federal grants. It is the line identified in the Brief for the National Conference of State Legislatures et al. as *Amici Curiae:*

"Congress has the power to spend for the general welfare, it has the power to legislate only for the delegated purposes." . . .

This approach harks back to *United States v. Butler* (1936), the last case in which this Court struck down an Act of Congress as beyond the authority granted by the Spending Clause. . . .

While *Butler*'s authority is questionable insofar as it assumes that Congress has no regulatory power over farm

THE POWER TO TAX AND SPEND

production, its discussion of the spending power and its description of both the power's breadth and its limitations remain sound. The Court's decision in *Butler* also properly recognizes the gravity of the task of appropriately limiting the spending power. If the spending power is to be limited only by Congress' notion of the general welfare, the reality, given the vast financial resources of the Federal Government, is that the Spending Clause gives "power to the Congress to tear down the barriers, to invade the states' jurisdiction, and to become a parliament of the whole people, subject to no restrictions save such as are self-imposed." This, of course, as *Butler* held, was not the Framers' plan and it is not the meaning of the Spending Clause. . . .

The immense size and power of the Government of the United States ought not obscure its fundamental character. It remains a Government of enumerated powers. Because 23 U.S.C. §158 cannot be justified as an exercise of any power delegated to the Congress, it is not authorized by the Constitution. The Court errs in holding it to be the law of the land, and I respectfully dissent.

Rehnquist's opinion gave strong support to the federal spending power. The majority held that there are only four basic requirements that must be met for a federal spending statute to be valid: (1) the expenditure must be for the general welfare; (2) any conditions imposed on the expenditure must be unambiguous; (3) the conditions must be reasonably related to the purpose of the expenditure; and (4) the legislation must not violate any independent constitutional provision. These are minimal requirements indeed, especially since the Court acknowledged a policy of deferring to the legislature's determinations of what promotes the general welfare. O'Connor's dissent, which praised much of what the Court concluded in *Butler,* is not likely to find a great deal of support today; rather, since 1937 the Court repeatedly has given approval to an expansive interpretation of the powers of the federal government to tax and spend for the general welfare.

Decisions such as *South Dakota v. Dole* give wide latitude to Congress to use the taxing and spending power to "encourage" states to comply with federal policy preferences. If Congress uses this power effectively, it can extend its policy influence well beyond the customary limits. Congress simply enlists the states to regulate areas where the federal government may not constitutionally act on its own. States may resent what they consider to be "coercive" federal action, and, as exemplified by South Dakota's opposition to the federal government's intrusion into alcohol regulation, it is not uncommon for states to challenge these federal incentive programs.

READINGS

Carson, Gerald. "The Income Tax and How It Grew." *American Heritage,* December 1973, 4–7, 79–88.

Corwin, Edward S. "The Spending Power of Congress—Apropos the Maternity Act." *Harvard Law Review* 36 (1923): 548–582.

Dakin, Melvin G. "The Protective Cloak of the Export-Import Clause: Immunity for the Goods or Immunity for the Process?" *Louisiana Law Review* 19 (1959): 747–776.

Dunne, Gerald T. *Monetary Decisions of the Supreme Court.* New Brunswick: Rutgers University Press, 1960.

Early, Alexander R., and Robert G. Weitzman. "A Century of Dissent: The Immunity of Goods Imported for Resale from Nondiscriminatory State Personal Property Taxes." *Southwestern University Law Review* 7 (1975): 247–272.

Hurst, James Willard. *A Legal History of Money in the United States, 1774–1970.* Lincoln: University of Nebraska Press, 1973.

Lund, Nelson. "Congressional Power over Taxation and Commerce: The Supreme Court's Lost Chance to Devise a Consistent Doctrine." *Texas Tech Law Review* 18 (1987): 729–760.

McCoy, Thomas R., and Barry Friedman. "Conditional Spending: Federalism's Trojan Horse." *Supreme Court Review* (1988): 85–127.

Powell, Thomas Reed. "State Taxation of Imports: When Does an Import Cease to Be an Import?" *Harvard Law Review* 58 (1945): 858–876.

Weisman, Steven R. *The Great Tax Wars: Lincoln to Wilson—The Fierce Battles over Money and Power.* New York: Simon and Schuster, 2001.

Witte, John F. *The Politics and Development of the Federal Income Tax.* Madison: University of Wisconsin Press, 1985.

PART IV
ECONOMIC LIBERTIES

ECONOMIC LIBERTIES AND INDIVIDUAL RIGHTS

If Americans were asked what they admire about the United States, many would say the freedoms of speech, press, and religion. But when asked to make political decisions—to choose elected officials, for example—Americans may put other considerations ahead of the cherished freedoms. As the old adage goes, people tend to vote their pocketbooks. Americans might not admit that the state of the economy drives their behavior, but it is perhaps the single most important determinant in their voting decisions.

That Americans hold economic well-being as a priority is not surprising. In Part III we saw that economic issues—commerce, taxing, and spending—were major sources of friction between the federal government and the states virtually from the beginning of U.S. history.

Economic questions, however, are not the exclusive domain of the Supreme Court's federalism cases. Quite the contrary. The Supreme Court often has heard constitutional challenges in which individuals claim that their personal economic liberties have been violated by government actions. In such cases the justices must determine how much power federal and state governments have to seize private property, to alter freely made contracts, and to restrict private employment agreements about wages and hours. Seen in this way, there is a strong relationship between civil liberties, such as the freedom of speech, and economic liberties, such as the right to own private property. Indeed, both provoke the same fundamental question: To what extent can government enact legislation that infringes on personal rights? Both

also involve the same perennial conflict between the interests of the individual and the common good.

Even so, most people, including elected officials and even Supreme Court justices, tend to separate economic liberties from other civil liberties. We consider the right to express our views as significantly different from the right to conduct business. The framers, however, viewed both as "vested" or fundamental rights that government should not violate. According to James Madison, one of the most important objectives of the framers was to provide "more effectively for the security of private rights and the steady dispensation of justice within the states. Interference with these were the evils which had, more perhaps than anything else, produced this convention."

But, as Madison's comment implies, the framers' conception of liberties and what interfered with their exercise was somewhat different from ours. They equated liberty with the protection of private property, and in their view the states, not the new government, posed the greater threat. Given the economic chaos under the Articles of Confederation, we can easily understand the founders' concerns. They believed the states had "crippled" both the government and the economy, and they wanted to create a national government strong enough to protect economic liberty from aggressive state governments. We must also keep in mind that many who attended the convention were wealthy men who wanted to protect their economic advantage. In short, the framers were concerned that the unpropertied masses might succeed in taking control of state legislatures and pass legislation that would jeopardize the economic advantages of the upper classes. Indeed, in an important (albeit controversial) work published in 1913, *An Economic Interpretation of the Constitution,* historian Charles A. Beard depicted the founders as self-serving, even greedy, men, who viewed the Constitution as a vehicle for the protection of their property interests.

Other analysts have taken issue with Beard's interpretation. Some contend that we cannot necessarily equate modern definitions of property with those used by the framers; that is, the property interests they sought to protect were probably more encompassing than those we envision today. Although we may consider property as something tangible, or of clear monetary value, the framers—at least some of them—thought of property as "shorthand for an expanse of personal freedoms that need only be tangentially related, if at all, to economic activity."[1]

To protect these paramount property rights, however conceptualized, the framers inserted several provisions into the Constitution. An important provision, which we examine in chapter 9, is the contract clause. Under Article I, Section 10, "No State shall . . . pass any . . . Law impairing the Obligation of Contracts." To understand the meaning of the clause, we must consider its language within the context of the day. As one source suggests:

For the generation of 1787–91, property was a natural right, though the constitutional text did not so label it. And, because the right to property included rights to use and increase property, that basic right included a cognate right to contract with other property holders. Thus did the right to contract borrow a measure of moral status from the broader right in which it originated: the obligation to keep one's contracts was a duty flowing from the natural right to property.[2]

If the contract clause was one of the ways the framers sought to protect property interests against the "evils" of government interference, it was effective, at least initially. For the Marshall Court the contract clause, in particular, was an effective vehicle for promoting federal supremacy and economic growth. That Court understood Article I, Section 10, to prohibit state action that infringed on property rights, which in turn impeded economic development.

But this interpretation was short-lived. With the end of the Marshall Court and the ascendancy of the Taney Court in the mid-1830s, use of the contract clause as a vehicle to protect property interests waned. Why that occurred is considered fully in chapter 9; for now, it is important to note that the "death" of the contract clause did not mean that courts were no longer interested in protecting economic liberties. They simply turned to another section of the Constitution to do so. The Fourteenth Amendment's due process clause says no state shall "deprive any person of life, liberty, or property, without due process of law." Under a doctrine called substantive due process, which is reviewed in chapter 10, between the 1890s and the 1930s the Supreme Court used the Fourteenth Amendment to prohibit states' interference with "liberty" interests. It struck down legislation mandating maximum work hours on the ground that such legislation interfered with the rights of employers to enter into contracts with their employees. Like the Court's interpretation of the contract clause, this treatment of the Fourteenth Amendment—at least in the economic realm—eventually fell into disrepute. In chapter 10 we examine the reasons for its decline (but see chapter 16 for its use in cases implicating the right to privacy).

More recently, the Court has taken a serious look at yet another provision of the Constitution designed to protect property interests—the takings clause of the Fifth Amendment. Whereas in the contract clause the framers sought to prevent governments from infringing on contractual agreements, in the takings clause they tried to protect private property from government seizure: "nor shall private property be taken for public use without just compensation." The founders recognized that the government could confiscate property, for example, to construct roads or erect government buildings and that property owners should have some form of protection from abusive government practices.

Although the heyday of the contract clause and economic substantive due process has long since passed, the takings clause is enjoying a renaissance. As described in

1. Walter F. Murphy, James E. Fleming, and William F. Harris II, *American Constitutional Interpretation,* 2nd ed. (Mineola, N.Y.: Foundation Press, 1985), 1071.

2. Ibid., 1073.

chapter 11, some justices, particularly Antonin Scalia and Clarence Thomas, have sought to revitalize the takings clause as a significant vehicle for protecting property rights. In fact, the Court seems to have taken an increased interest in economic questions of all kinds. Whether this represents a real trend or a minor historical blip is an important question because the kinds of cases the Court accepts speak to the role it plays in American society.[3] When the justices were deciding mostly economic cases, as they did for the first 150 years of the Court's history, it is not surprising that they exerted great influence in that arena and not in civil liberties, civil rights, or criminal justice. Moreover, if the Court is seeking to play a greater role in the economic realm, it will be forced to confront the fundamental issue that bedeviled its predecessors: the complex relationship between "vested rights" and "community interests." Although, as we have suggested, many of the founders were concerned about individual

liberty (such as the protection of private property), we now know that in a mature democratic society the pursuit of such individual interests may impinge on the collective good. For example, if a state enacts a law setting a minimum wage, that statute affects the individual liberty of employers, who believe it would be in their best interest, economically speaking, to pay their employees as little as possible. As a result, they may argue that minimum wage laws violate their constitutional guarantees. But is there another interest at stake? What are the results of paying workers a substandard wage? Does the state have a responsibility to enact legislation for the "health, safety, and welfare" of all its citizens?

The clash between the two interests—individual liberty (vested rights) and the state (community well being)—has been a primary reason for the Court's involvement in this area. As the current justices confront issues of economic liberty, the major questions center less on which interests are to be balanced than on the approaches different Courts have taken to balance them. As we shall see, during some eras the Court exalted liberty interests above those of the community; and during others it took precisely the opposite approach.

---

3. Richard L. Pacelle Jr., *The Transformation of the Supreme Court's Agenda* (Boulder: Westview Press, 1991); and Pacelle, "The Dynamics and Determinants of Agenda Change in the Rehnquist Court," in *Contemplating Courts*, ed. Lee Epstein (Washington, D.C.: CQ Press, 1995).

CHAPTER 9
THE CONTRACT CLAUSE

Suppose a friend of yours had accepted a position some years ago with a large corporation. One of the reasons she took this particular job was that the company offered an attractive savings plan as a fringe benefit. Under the terms of the savings plan contract, your friend regularly placed a portion of her income into the fund, and the company matched her contributions. Money deposited in the fund belonged to the individual savers, and the company had no authority to use the funds for any corporate purpose. Over the years her savings account grew steadily. Then, in a national recession, the company's fortunes reversed and it, along with many others, faced bankruptcy. The state rushed to the relief of the troubled businesses by passing a law that allowed them unilaterally to use the assets in employee savings plans to finance operations until the economy regained its strength. The company took advantage of this statute, but, after spending all of the savings plan funds, the company still went under.

This story raises some basic questions. How can the state pass a law that releases a company from its contractual obligations? The company's employees were cheated out of their money, and the state was involved. How can one participate in any investment or commercial activity without some protection against a state's granting similar special considerations to corporations or other parties?

If you were outraged by your friend's fate, your reaction would be understandable. One of the hallmarks of a society that values commercial activity is the right to enter into legally binding contracts. It would be hard to imagine a market-based economy that did not recognize and protect such agreements. In most instances, we would expect the government to enforce contracts and not encourage parties who wished to break them.

The individuals who drafted the Constitution felt much the same way. Disturbed by the actions of state governments in the economic upheaval that followed the Revolution, the delegates to the Constitutional Convention moved to block state interference with contractual obligations. They did this by drafting the contract clause, one of the most important provisions of the Constitution during the nation's formative years.

THE FRAMERS AND THE CONTRACT CLAUSE

In fact, it might be difficult to find a group of people more supportive of the right to enter into binding agreements than the delegates to the Constitutional Convention. For the most part, these individuals represented the propertied classes, and they assembled in Philadelphia at a time of economic turmoil. Many of them feared that as the nation coped with its economic problems it might suspend the obligation to honor contracts.

After the Revolutionary War, the economy was very unstable, and the government under the Articles of Confederation was powerless to correct the situation. Hardest hit were small farmers, many of whom had taken out large loans they could not repay. When creditors started foreclosing on real estate and debtors were jailed for failing to pay, farmers and others faced with unmanageable obligations began to agitate for relief. Several states responded by passing laws to help them. Among these acts were bankruptcy laws that erased certain debt obligations or extended the time to pay, legal obstacles that blocked creditors from asserting their contractual rights against their debtors. Also, state currencies of dubious value were declared legal tender to satisfy debt obligations.

These policies hurt the creditors, many of whom were wealthy landowners. They called for a strengthening of the national government to deal with economic problems and a ban on the state governments' practice of nullifying contractual obligations. In response, Congress authorized a convention to propose changes in the Articles of Confederation. Once assembled, the delegates went much further than originally authorized and created the Constitution of the United States. The document drafted in Philadelphia clearly reflected the economic interests of the delegates. Among the provisions they wrote was a protection of contracts against state government infringement. Article I, Section 10, declares: "No State shall . . . pass any . . . Law impairing the obligation of contracts."

The eighteenth century's understanding of the term *contract* was the same as today's. A contract is an agreement voluntarily entered into by two or more parties in which a promise is made and something of value is given or pledged. Contractual agreements are made in almost every commercial transaction, such as a mining company's promise to deliver a quantity of iron ore to a steel mill in return for a particular fee, or a lawyer's promise to represent a client at a specified rate of compensation.

For the framers, the right to enter into contracts was an important freedom closely tied to the right of private property. The ownership of private property implies the right to buy, sell, divide, occupy, lease, and use it; but one cannot effectively exercise these various property rights without the ability to enter into legally binding arrangements with others. In commercial transactions the parties rely on each other to carry out the contractual provisions. During the nation's formative years, those who failed to live up to contractual promises were dealt with harshly. In the minds of the propertied classes of the eighteenth century, this was correct, and the government should not be allowed to intervene in such private arrangements.

Evidence from the convention indicates that the framers adopted the contract clause as a means of protecting agreements between private parties from state interference. At that time, however, contracts also were a means of carrying out public policy. Because governments then were much more limited than they are today, the states regularly entered into contracts with individuals or corporations to carry out government policy or to distribute government benefits. These state actions included land grants, commercial monopolies, and licenses to construct roads and bridges. Individuals who entered into a contractual agreement with the state expected it to live up to its obligations and not abrogate the arrangement or unilaterally change the terms. In spite of what the framers might have intended, the contract clause is worded generally and therefore offers protection both to contracts among private parties and to agreements made between private parties and state governments.

The debates over ratification of the Constitution made little reference to the contract clause. In *The Federalist Papers,* Alexander Hamilton justified the prohibition against state impairment of contract obligations by claiming, "Laws in violation of private contracts . . . may be considered as another probable source of hostility."[1] James Madison declared in Federalist No. 44: "[L]aws impairing the obligation of contracts are contrary to the first principles of the social compact and to every principle of sound legislation."

The contract clause became an important legal force in the early years of the nation's development. As political majorities changed from election to election, it was not unusual for state legislatures to enter into contracts with private parties only to break or change those agreements in subsequent legislative sessions. In addition, state governments often would adopt policies that ran contrary to contracts among private individuals. When such actions occurred, injured parties would challenge the state in court. As a result, the contract clause was one of the most litigated constitutional provisions in the first decades of U.S. history. One study concluded that

---

1. Alexander Hamilton, "Federalist No. 7," in *The Federalist Papers,* ed. Clinton Rossiter (New York: New American Library, 1961).

roughly 40 percent of all Supreme Court cases prior to 1889 that attacked the validity of state legislation did so on the basis of contract clause arguments.[2]

JOHN MARSHALL AND THE CONTRACT CLAUSE

The significance of the contract clause increased dramatically through the Marshall Court's interpretations of its meaning. Chief Justice John Marshall had strong views on private property, economic development, and the role of the federal government. He consistently supported aggressive policies that would result in vigorous economic expansion. Underlying this position was a philosophy that elevated private property to the level of a natural right that government had little authority to limit. Furthermore, Marshall firmly believed that the nation's interests could be served best if the federal government rather than the states became the primary agent for economic policy making. As we have seen in the areas of federalism and commerce, Marshall could be counted on to uphold actions taken by the federal government and to favor it over competing state interests. Marshall's ideology predisposed him to champion the contract clause, which he viewed as essential to the right to private property. Moreover, the clause's restriction of state regulatory powers appealed to his views on federalism. Given Marshall's domination of the Court for more than three decades, it is not surprising that the contract clause achieved an elevated status during those years.

Establishing the Importance of the Contract Clause

The first major Supreme Court decision to consider the contract clause was *Fletcher v. Peck* (1810), which concerned whether a state could nullify a public contract. The suit flowed from one of the most notorious incidents of corruption and bribery in the nation's early history— the Yazoo River land fraud. In this litigation the beneficiaries of the scheme sought to use the contract clause to protect their gains.

2. Benjamin F. Wright, *The Contract Clause of the Constitution* (Cambridge: Harvard University Press, 1938).

This dispute had its roots in the 1795 session of the Georgia legislature. Clearly motivated by wholesale bribery, the legislators sold about 35 million acres of public lands to several land companies. The territory in question encompassed most of what is now Mississippi and Alabama. Some of the nation's most prominent public figures, including members of Congress, supported this transaction or invested in it. The citizens of Georgia were outraged by the sale and turned out most of their state legislators in the next election. In 1796 the newly elected legislature promptly rescinded the sales contract and moved to repossess the land. Unfortunately, by this time the land companies had sold numerous parcels to third-party investors and settlers. A massive and complicated set of legal actions ensued to determine ownership of the disputed lands. Attempts to negotiate a settlement proved unsuccessful. Even the president, Thomas Jefferson, was drawn into the controversy as he tried to work out a compromise settlement that would satisfy the state of Georgia as well as the investors.

Fletcher v. Peck was a lawsuit filed to obtain a judicial determination of the ownership question. John Peck acquired a parcel of the land in question from James Gunn, one of the original buyers in the Georgia land sales. Peck in turn sold the land to Robert Fletcher. When the state repealed the sale and resumed control of the land, Fletcher sued Peck for return of the purchase price. The real issue, however, rested squarely on the meaning of the contract clause: May a state that has entered into a valid contract later rescind that contract?

Joseph Story, who later became the youngest man ever appointed to the Supreme Court, represented those who had purchased the land and wanted clear title to it. He argued that the contract clause barred the state from rescinding the original sales agreements. Attorneys supporting Georgia's repudiation of the land sale held that the state was empowered to declare it void because the original transaction was based on fraud. Furthermore, they contended that the contract clause was intended to protect against the abrogation of private contracts, not those made by the states.

Chief Justice Marshall was caught in a bind. To give force to the contract clause would be to rule in favor of those who profited from state government corruption. To rule against the unpopular fraudulent transactions would be to hand down a precedent significantly curtailing the meaning of the provision.

Marshall's choice, supported by each of the other four justices participating in the decision, was to uphold the land sales. The Court did not question the general ability of a legislature to repeal what a previous legislature had done. But, when the law is in the form of "a contract, when absolute rights have vested under that contract, a repeal of the law cannot devest those rights." To do so would be to impair the obligation of contracts in violation of Article I, Section 10.

Marshall's opinion gave considerable force to the contract clause. Although he acknowledged that the original transactions were based on bribery and corruption, Marshall concluded that such matters are beyond the power of the courts to control. He concentrated instead on the validity of a state's rescinding a previously passed, binding agreement. According to the Court's holding in this case, the Constitution prohibits the states from impairing the obligation of any contract, even those contracts contrary to the public good. In striking down the 1796 Georgia statute, the Supreme Court for the first time nullified a state law on constitutional grounds. *Fletcher v. Peck* established the contract clause as an important provision of the new Constitution and encouraged its use in challenging the states' economic regulations. As illustrated in Box 9-1, however, it took several additional years for the legal confusion over the Yazoo land titles to be settled.

In 1819 the Marshall Court heard *Sturges v. Crowninshield,* an appeal that presented issues hitting squarely on the concerns expressed by the delegates at the Constitutional Convention. Richard Crowninshield, whose business enterprises had suffered hard times, received two loans from Josiah Sturges totaling approximately $1,500. The loans were secured by promissory notes. When Crowninshield became insolvent, he sought relief from his debts by invoking New York's recently passed bankruptcy law. Sturges objected, claiming that the New York law was a state impairment of the obligation of contracts in violation of the Constitution. The New York bankruptcy law was an example of just what the framers had

intended to prohibit—states interfering with agreements between debtors and creditors.

The case presented two issues to the Supreme Court. The first was whether a state may enact a bankruptcy law at all. Article I, Section 8, Clause 4, of the Constitution expressly gave the federal government power to enact such legislation. Did this power preclude the states' acting? A unanimous Court, again through an opinion written by Chief Justice Marshall, held that in the absence of any federal action the states were free to enact bankruptcy laws. The second issue was whether the New York law was invalid as an impairment of contracts. Here the Court found the law defective. The New York law discharged Crowninshield's contractual indebtedness entered into prior to the passage of the statute, which, according to the Court, was beyond the power of the state.[3]

Corporate Charters as Contracts

The same year the Court decided *Sturges,* the justices announced their decision in **Trustees of Dartmouth College v. Woodward** (1819), perhaps the most famous of the Marshall-era contract clause cases. The Dartmouth College case presented a question of particular significance to the business community: Is a corporation charter a contract protected against state impairment? The case had added intrigue because it involved a bitter partisan battle between the Republicans and the Federalists.

In 1769 King George III issued a corporate charter establishing Dartmouth College in New Hampshire. The charter designated a board of trustees as the ultimate governing body. The board was self-perpetuating with the power to fill its own vacancies. The founder and first president of Dartmouth was Eleazar Wheelock, who also had authority to designate his own successor. He chose his son, John Wheelock, who assumed the presidency upon Eleazar's death. John Wheelock was ill-suited for the position, and for years friction existed between him and the board of trustees.

To shore up his position, Wheelock made political alliances with the Jeffersonian Republicans, who had

---

3. Eight years later, however, the Court held in *Ogden v. Saunders* (1827) that state bankruptcy laws did not violate the contract clause if the contract was entered into after the enactment of the bankruptcy statute.

BOX 9-1   AFTERMATH . . . THE YAZOO LANDS CONTROVERSY

THE SUPREME COURT'S decision in *Fletcher v. Peck* (1810) provided a landmark ruling on the meaning of the contract clause, but it did not fully resolve the issues surrounding the Yazoo land claims. In the period between the original land sale by the Georgia legislature in 1795 and the state's voiding of the sale in 1796, parcels were bought and sold in a climate of feverish land speculation. About 60 percent of the purchasers were New England residents eager to participate in western land investments. After Georgia repealed the original sale, titles to the Yazoo lands were in considerable doubt. Not only did the actions by the Georgia legislature thoroughly confuse the issue, but also claims by Indian tribes, old Spanish interests, squatters, and those who had been granted lands by Georgia governors over the years clouded the issue. Bogus titles and sales of nonexistent land further complicated matters.

When purchasers learned that Georgia had passed legislation canceling the original sale, they pressured Congress to provide compensation if their titles proved to be invalid. Northern representatives favored a compensation program to provide relief to constituents who had purchased property, but southerners, especially representatives from Georgia, opposed any compensation as rewarding those who sought to benefit from the original acts of bribery and fraud. *Fletcher v. Peck* was first filed in federal circuit court in Massachusetts in 1803 in an attempt to have the judiciary settle the matter. Action on the lawsuit and subsequent appeals were delayed, with the parties hoping that Congress would resolve the dispute by passing a compensation act. When

legislation failed in 1804, 1805, and 1806, it appeared that the courts would have to answer the lingering questions. By the time the Supreme Court decided *Fletcher v. Peck*, fifteen years had elapsed since the original sales, and determining valid title to each parcel of land was next to impossible.

The decision in *Fletcher v. Peck* was unpopular in many circles. Some thought the Court should not uphold contracts based on wholesale corruption. Thomas Jefferson used the decision as an opportunity to renew his attacks on Marshall. He claimed the chief justice's opinion was filled with "twistifications," "cunning," and "sophistry." According to Jefferson, it illustrated once again "how dexterously [Marshall] can reconcile law to his personal biases."

The decision, however, put pressure on Congress to bring closure to the controversy. Northerners again demanded a compensation program, but southerners still resisted. In 1814 Congress appropriated $5 million from federal land sales to compensate those who held title to the Yazoo lands. Investors released their land claims in return for monetary compensation. It took four years for the claims to be settled. Northern representatives had obtained relief for their constituents, but southern interests also benefited. Resolving the confusion over the Yazoo lands cleared the way for organizing the Mississippi territory, which was admitted as a slave-holding state in 1817.

SOURCE: Peter Magrath, *Yazoo* (Providence: Brown University Press, 1966).

gained control of the state legislature in 1816. The Republicans gladly took his side in the dispute with the Federalist-dominated board of trustees and passed a law radically changing the governing structure of the college. The law called for an expansion of the board from twelve to twenty-one members to be appointed by the governor, and it created a supervisory panel with veto power over the actions of the trustees. The new officials removed the old trustees from office. In effect, the legislature had converted Dartmouth College, renamed Dartmouth University under the new law, from a private to a public institu-

tion. The result was chaos. The students and faculty for the most part remained loyal to the old trustees, but the state essentially took over the buildings and records of the college. As might be expected, the college soon found itself on the edge of fiscal collapse.

To resolve the situation, the old trustees hired Daniel Webster to represent them. Webster, an 1801 Dartmouth graduate, agreed to take the case for a fee of $1,000, a considerable sum of money in those days. The trustees sued William Woodward, the secretary of the college, who had in his possession the college charter, records,

BOX 9-2   DANIEL WEBSTER (1782–1852)

DANIEL WEBSTER played an influential role in the development of American law and politics during a public career that spanned almost fifty years. He was born in Salisbury, New Hampshire, January 18, 1782, and educated at Phillips Exeter Academy and Dartmouth College. He was admitted to the bar in 1805 and immediately began the practice of law in his home state.

In 1813 Webster was first elected to Congress as a Federalist representative from New Hampshire. This office was only the beginning of an illustrious series of important positions:

United States representative, New Hampshire,
   1813–1817
Monroe delegate to Electoral College, 1820
United States representative, Massachusetts,
   1823–1827
United States senator, Massachusetts, 1827–1841
Presidential candidate, 1836
Secretary of state (Harrison-Tyler administrations),
   1841–1843
United States senator, Massachusetts,
   1845–1850

Secretary of state (Fillmore
   administration), 1850–1852

Webster was perhaps best known for his role as an advocate before the Supreme Court and the brilliant oratorical skills he displayed in both Congress and the courts. Webster appeared before the Supreme Court in 168 cases, winning about half of them. In twenty-four of his appearances he was an advocate in a major constitutional dispute. Among his most celebrated cases were:

McCulloch v. Maryland (1819)
Dartmouth College v. Woodward (1819)
Cohens v. Virginia (1821)
Gibbons v. Ogden (1824)
Osborn v. Bank of the United States (1824)
Ogden v. Saunders (1827)
Wheaton v. Peters (1834)
Charles River Bridge v. Warren Bridge (1837)
Swift v. Tyson (1842)
West River Bridge v. Dix (1848)
Luther v. Borden (1849)

NOTE: For a review of Webster's legal career, see Maurice G. Baxter, *Daniel Webster and the Supreme Court* (Amherst: University of Massachusetts Press, 1966).

and seal. Webster and the old trustees lost in the state courts and then appealed to the U.S. Supreme Court. When the case was argued in March 1818, Webster engaged in four hours of brilliant oratory before the justices. At times his argument was quite emotional, and he is said to have brought tears to the eyes of those present when he spoke his often-quoted line, "It is, sir, as I have said, a small college, and yet there are those that love it." The justices did not act in the heat of emotion. Instead, it took almost a year before they announced their decision. By the time the opinion was released, both John Wheelock and William Woodward had died.

With only one justice dissenting, the Court supported Webster's position. The grant by the English Crown setting up the college was a contract, Marshall declared, and the governing structure of the college was part of that contract. When the state of New Hampshire restructured the college with the 1816 legislation, it impaired the original contract. The statute was repugnant to the contract clause and therefore void.

As a result of this decision, the old trustees regained control of the college, and Webster's reputation as one of the nation's leading legal advocates was firmly established. The decision was also a victory for business interests. By holding that corporate charters were contracts under the meaning of Article I, Section 10, the Court gave businesses considerable protection against state regulation. The decision, however, was not totally one-sided. Marshall acknowledged the power of the state to include in its contracts and charters provisions reserving the right to make future changes.

The importance of the contract clause reached its zenith under the Marshall Court. These early decisions protecting contractual agreements helped spur economic development and expansion. But an inevitable battle was on the horizon, a battle between the constitutional sanctity of contracts and a state's authority to regulate for the public good.

THE DECLINE OF THE CONTRACT CLAUSE

The Marshall years ended when the chief justice died July 6, 1835, at the age of seventy-nine. Marshall had been appointed in 1801 in one of the last acts of the once-dominant Federalist Party, and he had imposed his political philosophy on the Court's constitutional interpretations for more than three decades. His decisions in contract clause disputes, as well as in other areas of federalism and economic regulation, encouraged economic development and fostered entrepreneurial activity.

Elevating the Public Good

The days of the Federalist philosophy sympathetic to the interests of business and the economic elite had passed. Andrew Jackson now occupied the White House. Jackson came from the American frontier and was committed to policies beneficial to ordinary citizens; he had little sympathy for the moneyed classes of the Northeast. Within a short period, Jackson had the opportunity to change the course of the Supreme Court. During his presidency he filled not only the center chair left vacant by Marshall's death but also those of five associate justices. The new appointees all held ideologies consistent with principles of Jacksonian democracy, especially the new chief justice, Roger Brooke Taney, a Maryland Democrat who had served in several posts in the Jackson administration. Changes in constitutional interpretation

were inevitable, although in the final analysis the Taney Court did not veer as far from Marshall Court precedents as many had predicted.

Given the differences between Federalist and Jacksonian values, however, the Court was likely to reevaluate the contract clause. The Taney Court's first opportunity to do so came in *Proprietors of Charles River Bridge v. Proprietors of Warren Bridge* (1837). As you read the Court's opinion, compare it with the positions taken by the Court during the Marshall era. Although Taney certainly did not repudiate Marshall's rulings, his opinion in *Charles River Bridge* struck a new balance between the inviolability of contracts and the power of the state to legislate for the public good. The Court also held that contracts should be strictly construed, a position at odds with Marshall's rather expansive interpretations of contractual obligations. Justice Story, who had appeared as an attorney in *Fletcher* and had supported Marshall's views of the contract clause since he joined the Court in 1811, dissented from this change in doctrine.

Proprietors of Charles River Bridge v. Proprietors of Warren Bridge

36 U.S. (11 Pet.) 420 (1837)
http://laws.findlaw.com/US/36/420.html
Vote: 5 (Baldwin, Barbour, McLean, Taney, Wayne)
       2 (Story, Thompson)
Opinion of the Court: Taney
Concurring opinion: McLean
Dissenting opinions: Story, Thompson

In 1785 the Massachusetts legislature created by charter the Charles River Bridge Company. The charter gave the company the right to construct a bridge between Boston and Charlestown and to collect tolls for its use. This agreement replaced a ferry franchise between the two cities that the colonial legislature had granted to Harvard College in 1650. In 1792 the legislature extended the charter. Because of the population growth in the Boston area, the bridge received heavy use, and its investors prospered. In 1828, when traffic congestion on the bridge became a significant problem, the legislature decided

The Charles River Bridge ran from Prince Street in Boston to Charlestown. The bridge, considered a very advanced design at the time of its construction, was built on seventy-five oak piers and was more than 1,500 feet long.

that a second bridge was needed. Consequently, the state incorporated the Warren Bridge Company and authorized it to construct a bridge to be located about a hundred yards from the first. The Warren Bridge investors had authority to collect tolls to pay for the expense of construction plus an agreed-upon profit. In no more than six years the state was to assume ownership of the Warren Bridge and then operate it on a toll-free basis.

Charles River Bridge Company opposed the construction of a second bridge. It claimed that its charter conferred the exclusive right to build and operate a bridge between Boston and Charlestown. A second bridge, eventually to be operated without tolls, would deprive the company of the profits from its investment. The second charter, the company claimed, was a violation of the contract clause. To represent it, Charles River Bridge Company hired Daniel Webster, who had won the Dartmouth College case two decades earlier *(see Box 9-2)*. When the Massachusetts courts failed to grant relief, Charles River Bridge Company took its case to the U.S. Supreme Court.

The case was first argued in March 1831. John Marshall still led the Court at that time, and Webster under-

standably felt confident of victory. But the justices could not agree on a decision, and the case was scheduled for reargument in 1833. Once again, no decision was reached. Before a third hearing could be scheduled, deaths and resignations had changed the ideological complexion of the Court. When Jackson announced Taney as his choice for chief justice, Webster is said to have proclaimed, "The Constitution is gone." From Webster's perspective perhaps that was true. The Taney justices scheduled arguments on the bridge case in 1837, and Webster no longer had a sympathetic audience for his strong contract clause position.

MR. CHIEF JUSTICE TANEY delivered the opinion of the Court.

The plaintiffs in error insist. . . [t]hat. . . the acts of the legislature of Massachusetts. . . by their true construction, necessarily implied that the legislature would not authorize another bridge, and especially a free one, by the side of this, and placed in the same line of travel, whereby the franchise granted to the "proprietors of the Charles River Bridge" should be rendered of no value; and the plaintiffs in error contend, that the grant of the ferry to the college, and of the charter to the proprietors of the bridge, are both contracts on the part of the state; and that the law authorizing the erection of the Warren Bridge in 1828, impairs the obligation of one or both of these contracts. . . .

[W]e are not now left to determine, for the first time, the rules by which public grants are to be construed in this country. The subject has already been considered in this Court. . . and the principle recognized, that in grants by the public, nothing passes by implication. . . .

[T]he object and end of all government is to promote the happiness and prosperity of the community by which it is established; and it can never be assumed, that the government intended to diminish its power of accomplishing the end for which it was created. And in a country like ours, free, active, and enterprising, continually advancing in numbers and wealth; new channels of communication are daily found necessary, both for travel and trade; and are essential to the comfort, convenience, and prosperity of the people. A state ought never to be presumed to surrender this power, because, like the taxing power, the whole community have an interest in preserving it undiminished. And when a corporation alleges, that a state has surrendered for seventy years, its power of improvement, and public accommodation, in a great and important line of travel, along which a vast number of its citizens must daily pass; the community have a right to insist, in the language of this Court above quoted, "that its abandonment ought not to be presumed, in a case, in which the deliberate purpose of the state to abandon it does not appear." The continued existence of a government would be of no great value, if by implications and presumptions, it was disarmed of the powers necessary to accomplish the ends of its creation; and the functions it was designed to perform, transferred to the hands of privileged corporations. The rule of construction announced by the Court, was not confined to the taxing power; nor is it so limited in the opinion delivered. On the contrary, it was distinctly placed on the ground that the interests of the community were concerned in preserving, undiminished, the power then in question; and whenever any power of the state is said to be surrendered or diminished, whether it be the taxing power or any other affecting the public interest, the same principle applies, and the rule of construction must be the same. No one will question that the interests of the great body of the people of the state,

would, in this instance, be affected by the surrender of this great line of travel to a single corporation, with the right to exact toll, and exclude competition for seventy years. While the rights of private property are sacredly guarded, we must not forget that the community also have rights, and that the happiness and well being of every citizen depends on their faithful preservation.

Adopting the rule of construction above stated as the settled one, we proceed to apply it to the charter of 1785, to the proprietors of the Charles River Bridge. This act of incorporation is in the usual form, and the privileges such as are commonly given to corporations of that kind. It confers on them the ordinary faculties of a corporation, for the purpose of building the bridge; and establishes certain rates of toll, which the company are authorized to take. This is the whole grant. There is no exclusive privilege given to them over the waters of Charles river, above or below their bridge. No right to erect another bridge themselves, nor to prevent other persons from erecting one. No engagement from the state, that another shall not be erected; and no undertaking not to sanction competition, nor to make improvements that may diminish the amount of its income. Upon all these subjects the charter is silent; and nothing is said in it about a line of travel, so much insisted on in the argument, in which they are to have exclusive privileges. No words are used, from which an intention to grant any of these rights can be inferred. If the plaintiff is entitled to them, it must be implied, simply, from the nature of the grant; and cannot be inferred from the words by which the grant is made.

The relative position of the Warren Bridge has already been described. It does not interrupt the passage over the Charles River Bridge, nor make the way to it or from it less convenient. None of the faculties or franchises granted to that corporation, have been revoked by the legislature; and its right to take the tolls granted by the charter remains unaltered. In short, all the franchises and rights of property enumerated in the charter, and there mentioned to have been granted to it, remain unimpaired. But its income is destroyed by the Warren Bridge; which, being free, draws off the passengers and property which would have gone over it, and renders their franchise of no value. This is the gist of the complaint. For it is not pretended, that the erection of the Warren Bridge would have done them any injury, or in any degree affected their right of property; if it had not diminished the amount of their tolls. In order then to entitle themselves to relief, it is necessary to show, that the legislature contracted not to do the act of which they complain; and that they impaired, or in other words, violated that contract by the erection of the Warren Bridge.

The inquiry then is, does the charter contain such a contract on the part of the state? Is there any such stipulation to be found in that instrument? It must be admitted on all hands, that there is none—no words that even relate to another bridge or to the diminution of their tolls, or to the line of travel. If a contract on that subject can be gathered from the charter, it must be by implication; and cannot be found in the words used. Can such an agreement be implied? The rule of construction before stated is an answer to the question. In charters of this description, no rights are taken from the public, or given to the corporation, beyond those which the words of the charter, by their natural and proper construction, purport to convey. There are no words which import such a contract as the plaintiffs in error contend for, and none can be implied. . . .

Indeed, the practice and usage of almost every state in the Union, old enough to have commenced the work of internal improvement, is opposed to the doctrine contended for on the part of the plaintiffs in error. Turnpike roads have been made in succession, on the same line of travel; the later ones interfering materially with the profits of the first. These corporations have, in some instances, been utterly ruined by the introduction of newer and better modes of transportation, and travelling. In some cases, rail roads have rendered the turnpike roads on the same line of travel so entirely useless, that the franchise of the turnpike corporation is not worth preserving. Yet in none of these cases have the corporations supposed that their privileges were invaded, or any contract violated on the part of the state. Amid the multitude of cases which have occurred, and have been daily occurring for the last forty or fifty years, this is the first instance in which such an implied contract has been contended for, and this Court called upon to infer it from an ordinary act of incorporation, containing nothing more than the usual stipulations and provisions to be found in every such law. The absence of any such controversy, when there must have been so many occasions to give rise to it, proves that neither states, nor individuals, nor corporations, ever imagined that such a contract could be implied from such charters. It shows that the men who voted for these laws, never imagined that they were forming such a

contract; and if we maintain that they have made it, we must create it by a legal fiction, in opposition to the truth of the fact, and the obvious intention of the party. We cannot deal thus with the rights reserved to the states; and by legal intendments and mere technical reasoning, take away from them any portion of that power over their own internal police and improvement, which is so necessary to their well being and prosperity. . . .

The judgment of the supreme judicial court of the commonwealth of Massachusetts, dismissing the plaintiff's bill, must, therefore, be affirmed, with costs.

MR. JUSTICE STORY, dissenting.

I maintain, that, upon the principles of common reason and legal interpretation, the present grant carries with it a necessary implication that the legislature shall do no act to destroy or essentially to impair the franchise; that, (as one of the learned judges of the state court expressed it,) there is an implied agreement that the state will not grant another bridge between Boston and Charlestown, so near as to draw away the custom from the old one; and, (as another learned judge expressed it,) that there is an implied agreement of the state to grant the undisturbed use of the bridge and its tolls so far as respects any acts of its own, or of any persons acting under its authority. In other words, the state, impliedly, contracts not to resume its grant, or to do any act to the prejudice or destruction of its grant. I maintain, that there is no authority or principle established in relation to the construction of crown grants, or legislative grants; which does not concede and justify this doctrine. Where the thing is given, the incidents, without which it cannot be enjoyed, are also given. . . . I maintain that a different doctrine is utterly repugnant to all the principles of the common law, applicable to all franchises of a like nature; and that we must overturn some of the best securities of the rights of property, before it can be established. I maintain, that the common law is the birthright of every citizen of Massachusetts, and that he holds the title deeds of his property, corporeal, and incorporeal, under it. I maintain, that under the principles of the common law, there exists no more right in the legislature of Massachusetts, to erect the Warren Bridge, to the ruin of the franchise of the Charles River Bridge than exists to transfer the latter to the former, or to authorize the former to demolish the latter. If the legislature does not mean in its grant to give any exclusive rights, let it say so, expressly; directly; and in terms admitting of no misconstruction. The grantees will then take at their peril, and must abide the results of their overweening confidence, indiscretion, and zeal.

My judgment is formed upon the terms of the grant, its nature and objects, its design and duties; and, in its interpretation, I seek for no new principles, but I apply such as are as old as the very rudiments of the common law.

In spite of Justice Story's protest that the majority had rendered the contract clause meaningless, the Taney Court continued to allow the states more leeway in regulating for the public good. As Taney noted in *Charles River Bridge*, "While the rights of private property are sacredly guarded, we must not forget that the community also have rights, and that the happiness and well being of every citizen depends on their faithful preservation."

The Taney justices, however, did not totally abandon the Marshall Court's posture favoring business, nor did they repeal the contract clause by judicial fiat; instead, the Court took a more balanced position. In many cases, especially when the contractual provisions were clear, the Taney Court struck down state regulations on contract clause grounds.

Decline in the Post–Civil War Period

After the Taney years, the Court continued to move away from strong enforcement of the contract clause and to accord the states increased freedom to exercise their police powers. *Fertilizing Company v. Hyde Park* (1878) provides a good illustration. The Illinois state legislature passed a statute on March 8, 1867, creating Northwest Fertilizing Company. The charter authorized the company within a designated territory to operate a facility that converted dead animals to fertilizer and other products. The charter also gave the company the right to transport dead animals and animal parts (offal) through the territory. Acting on this authority, the company operated its plant in a sparsely populated, swampy area.

The facility was, however, located within the boundaries of the village of Hyde Park, which was beginning to experience considerable population growth. In 1869 the legislature upgraded the village charter, giving it full powers of local government, including the authority to "define or abate nuisances which are, or may be, injurious to the public health." Recognizing its charter with Northwest, the legislature stipulated that no village regulations could be applied to the company for at least two years. At the end of the two years, the village passed an ordinance that said, "No person shall transfer, carry, haul, or convey any offal, dead animals, or other offensive or unwholesome matter or material, into or through the village of Hyde Park." Parties in violation of the law were subject to fines. In 1873, following the arrest and conviction of railroad workers hauling dead animals to its plant, Northwest filed suit, claiming that its original charter was a contract that could not be abrogated by the state or its local governments. The company was unsuccessful in the state courts and appealed to the U.S. Supreme Court.

Justice Noah H. Swayne's opinion made clear at the outset that the company faced a difficult task in its attempt to convince the justices:

The rule of construction in this class of cases is that it shall be most strongly against the corporation. Every reasonable doubt is to be resolved adversely. Nothing is to be taken as conceded but what is given in unmistakable terms, or by an implication equally clear. The affirmative must be shown. Silence is negation, and doubt is fatal to the claim. This doctrine is vital to the public welfare.

The Court then went on to rule against the contract clause arguments of the company. The justices had no doubt that the transportation of offal was a public nuisance. Nor was there any doubt that the state had ample police power to combat such an offensive practice. According to Swayne:

That power belonged to the States when the Federal Constitution was adopted. They did not surrender it, and they all have it now. . . . It rests upon the fundamental principle that every one shall so use his own as not to wrong and injure another. To regulate and abate nuisances is one of its ordinary functions.

The states, the Court was implying, could not contract away their inherent powers to regulate for their citizens' health, safety, and welfare.

Two years later, the justices addressed a similar appeal, this time dealing with questions of public morality.

Stone v. Mississippi (1880) focused on the use of the state's police power to combat lotteries, a form of gambling that much of the population considered evil at that time.

In 1867 the post–Civil War provisional state legislature chartered the Mississippi Agricultural, Educational, and Manufacturing Aid Society. In spite of its name, the society's only purpose was to operate a lottery. The charter gave the society authority to run a lottery in Mississippi for twenty-five years, and, in return, the society paid an initial sum of cash to the state, an additional annual payment for each year of operation, plus a percentage of the lottery receipts. In 1868 a state convention drafted a new constitution, which the people ratified the next year. This constitution contained provisions explicitly outlawing lotteries. On July 16, 1870, the legislature passed a statute providing for enforcement of the antilottery provisions, and four years later, on March 17, 1874, the state attorney general filed charges against John B. Stone and others associated with the Mississippi Agricultural, Educational, and Manufacturing Aid Society for being in violation of state law. The state admitted that the company was operating within the provisions of its 1867 charter but contended that the new constitution and subsequent enforcement legislation effectively repealed that grant. Stone countered that the federal contract clause explicitly prohibits the state from negating the provisions of the charter.

A unanimous Supreme Court ruled in favor of the state. The states possess police powers that allow them to regulate for the health, safety, morals, and general welfare of their citizens. The legislature, by means of a contract, cannot bargain away a state's police powers. Lotteries are proper subjects for police power regulation. Anyone contracting with a state to conduct a lottery does so with the implied understanding that the people, through their properly constituted state agencies, may later exercise the power to regulate or even prohibit such gambling.

Following *Stone v. Mississippi* it was clear that the Court would no longer be sympathetic to contract clause attacks on state regulatory statutes. With contract clause avenues closing, opponents of the state regulation of business and commercial activities turned to another provision of the Constitution, the due process clause of the Fourteenth Amendment. From the late 1880s to the 1930s—a period of Court history discussed in chapter 10—the Court heard and often responded favorably to these substantive due process arguments.

The Depression and the Abrogation of Contracts

The contract clause reached its lowest status during the Great Depression of the 1930s. With the stock market crash of 1929, the nation entered its worst economic crisis; most Americans were placed in serious financial jeopardy. The 1932 election of Franklin Roosevelt ushered in the New Deal, and the federal government began innovative economic programs to combat the Depression. At the same time, various states were developing their own programs to protect their citizens against the economic ravages the country was experiencing.

What people feared most during the Depression was losing the family home. Homeowners did what they could to meet their mortgage obligations, but because so many were out of work, they were often unable to make their payments. Financial institutions had little choice but to foreclose on these properties as stipulated in the mortgage contracts. To provide relief, several states passed statutes to increase homeowners' chances of saving their houses. Banks and other creditors opposed these assistance measures. For them, intervention by the state was a direct violation of the constitutional ban against impairment of contracts.

The showdown between the contract clause and the government's authority to cope with economic crisis occurred in *Home Building and Loan Association v. Blaisdell* (1934). As you read Chief Justice Charles Evans Hughes's opinion for the Court, think about the Constitutional Convention and the concerns that led the framers to adopt the contract clause. Would they agree with the Court that the Constitution should bend in the face of national crises, or would they side with Justice George Sutherland's dissent that the provisions of the Constitution should be interpreted the same way regardless of the conditions of the times?

Home Building and Loan Association v. Blaisdell

290 U.S. 398 (1934)
http://laws.findlaw.com/US/290/398.html
Vote: 5 (Brandeis, Cardozo, Hughes, Roberts, Stone)
      4 (Butler, McReynolds, Sutherland, Van Devanter)
Opinion of the Court: Hughes
Dissenting opinion: Sutherland

During the Great Depression, people faced high unemployment, low prices for agricultural and manufactured products, a stagnation of business, and a scarcity of credit. In response to these conditions, the Minnesota legislature declared that a state of economic emergency existed that demanded the use of extraordinary police powers for the protection of the people. One of the legislature's actions was passage of the Minnesota Mortgage Moratorium Act, which was designed to protect homeowners when they could not make their mortgage payments. The act allowed homeowners who were behind in their payments to petition a state court for an extension of time to meet their mortgage obligations. During the period of the extension, the homeowners would not make normal mortgage payments but instead would pay a reasonable rental to the mortgage holder. The maximum extension was two years. The act was to be in effect only as long as the economic emergency continued. Its provisions applied to all mortgages, including those signed prior to the passage of the statute.

John and Rosella Blaisdell owned a house in Minneapolis that was mortgaged to Home Building and Loan Association. They lived in one part of the house and rented out the other part. When the Blaisdells were unable to keep their payments current or to obtain additional credit, they requested an extension in accordance with the moratorium law. After initially denying the request and then being reversed by the state supreme court, the trial court granted the Blaisdells a two-year moratorium on mortgage payments. During this period the Blaisdells were ordered to pay $40.00 per month, which would be applied to taxes, insurance, interest, and mortgage principal. Home Building and Loan Association opposed the extension and appealed to the Minnesota Supreme Court on the ground that the law was an impairment of contracts in violation of the contract clause of the federal Constitution. The Minnesota court conceded that the law impaired the obligation of contracts, but concluded that the statute was within the police powers of the state because of the severe economic emergency. Home Building and Loan appealed to the U.S. Supreme Court.

MR. CHIEF JUSTICE HUGHES delivered the opinion of the Court.

In determining whether the provision for this temporary and conditional relief exceeds the power of the State by reason of the clause in the Federal Constitution prohibiting impairment of the obligations of contracts, we must consider the relation of emergency to constitutional power, the historical setting of the contract clause, the development of the jurisprudence of this Court in the construction of that clause, and the principles of construction which we may consider to be established.

Emergency does not create power. Emergency does not increase granted power or remove or diminish the restrictions imposed upon power granted or reserved. The Constitution was adopted in a period of grave emergency. Its grants of power to the Federal Government and its limitations of the power of the States were determined in the light of emergency and they are not altered by emergency. What power was thus granted and what limitations were thus imposed are questions which have always been, and always will be, the subject of close examination under our constitutional system.

While emergency does not create power, emergency may furnish the occasion for the exercise of power. "Although an emergency may not call into life a power which has never lived, nevertheless emergency may afford a reason for the exertion of a living power already enjoyed." The constitutional question presented in the light of an emergency is whether the power possessed embraces the particular exercise of it in response to particular conditions. Thus, the war power of the Federal Government is not created by the emergency of war, but it is a power given to meet that emergency.

It is a power to wage war successfully, and thus it permits the harnessing of the entire energies of the people in a supreme cooperative effort to preserve the nation. But even the war power does not remove constitutional limitations safeguarding essential liberties. When the provisions of the Constitution, in grant or restriction, are specific, so particularized as not to admit of construction, no question is presented. Thus, emergency would not permit a State to have more than two Senators in the Congress, or permit the election of President by a general popular vote without regard to the number of electors to which the States are respectively entitled, or permit the States to "coin money" or to "make anything but gold and silver coin a tender in payment of debts." But where constitutional grants and limitations of power are set forth in general clauses, which afford a broad outline, the process of construction is essential to fill in the details. That is true of the contract clause. The necessity of construction is not obviated by the fact that the contract clause is associated in the same section with other and more specific prohibitions. Even the grouping of subjects in the same clause may not require the same application to each of the subjects, regardless of differences in their nature.

In the construction of the contract clause, the debates in the Constitutional Convention are of little aid. But the reasons which led to the adoption of that clause, and of the other prohibitions of Section 10 of Article I, are not left in doubt and have frequently been described with eloquent emphasis. The widespread distress following the revolutionary period, and the plight of debtors, had called forth in the States an ignoble array of legislative schemes for the defeat of creditors and the invasion of contractual obligations. Legislative interferences had been so numerous and extreme that the confidence essential to prosperous trade had been undermined and the utter destruction of credit was threatened. "The sober people of America" were convinced that some "thorough reform" was needed which would "inspire a general prudence and industry, and give a regular course to the business of society." The Federalist, No. 44. It was necessary to impose the restraining power of a central authority in order to secure the foundations even of "private faith." . . .

But full recognition of the occasion and general purpose of the clause does not suffice to fix its precise scope. Nor does an examination of the details of prior legislation in the States yield criteria which can be considered controlling. To ascertain the scope of the constitutional prohibition we examine the course of judicial decisions in its application. These put it beyond question that the prohibition is not an absolute one and is not to be read with literal exactness like a mathematical formula. . . .

The legislature cannot "bargain away the public health or the public morals." Thus, the constitutional provision against the impairment of contracts was held not to be violated by an amendment of the state constitution which put an end to a lottery theretofore authorized by the legislature. The lottery was a valid enterprise when established under express state authority, but the legislature in the public interest could put a stop to it. A similar rule has been applied to the control by the State of the sale of intoxicating liquors. The States retain adequate power to protect the public health against the maintenance of nuisances despite insistence upon existing contracts. Legislation to protect the public safety comes within the same category of reserved power. This principle has had recent and noteworthy application to the regulation of the use of public highways by common carriers and "contract carriers," where the assertion of interference with existing contract rights has been without avail. . . .

It is manifest from this review of our decisions that there has been a growing appreciation of public needs and of the necessity of finding ground for a rational compromise between individual rights and public welfare. The settlement and consequent contraction of the public domain, the pressure of a constantly increasing density of population, the interrelation of the activities of our people and the complexity of our economic interests, have inevitably led to an increased use of the organization of society in order to protect the very bases of individual opportunity. Where, in earlier days, it was thought that only the concerns of individuals or of classes were involved, and that those of the State itself were touched only remotely, it has later been found that the fundamental interests of the State are directly affected; and that the question is no longer merely that of one party to a contract as against another, but of the use of reasonable means to safeguard the economic structure upon which the good of all depends.

It is no answer to say that this public need was not apprehended a century ago, or to insist that what the provision of the Constitution meant to the vision of that day it must mean to the vision of our time. If by the statement that what the Constitution meant at the time of its adoption it means today, it is intended to say that the great clauses of the Constitution must be confined to the interpretation which the framers, with the conditions and outlook of their time, would have placed upon them, the statement carries its own refutation. It was to guard against such a narrow conception that Chief Justice Marshall uttered the memorable warning—"We must never forget that it is *a constitution* we are expounding": *(McCulloch v. Maryland)*—"a constitution intended to endure for ages to come, and consequently, to be adapted to the various *crises* of human affairs." When we are dealing with the words of the Constitution, said this Court in *Missouri v. Holland*, "we must realize that they have called into life a being the development of which could not have been foreseen completely by the most gifted of its begetters. . . . The case before us must be considered in the light of our whole experience and not merely in that of what was said a hundred years ago."

Nor is it helpful to attempt to draw a fine distinction between the intended meaning of the words of the Constitution and their intended application. When we consider the contract clause and the decisions which have expounded it in harmony with the essential reserved power of the States to protect the security of their peoples, we find no warrant for the conclusion that the clause has been warped by these decisions from its proper significance or that the founders of our Government would have interpreted the clause differently had they had occasion to assume that responsibility in the conditions of the later day. The vast body of law which has been developed was unknown to the fathers, but it is believed to have preserved the essential content and the spirit of the Constitution. With a growing recognition of public needs and the relation of individual right to public security, the court has sought to prevent the perversion of the clause through its use as an instrument to throttle the capacity of the States to protect their fundamental interests. This development is a growth from the seeds which the fathers planted. . . . The principle of this development is . . . that the reservation of the reasonable exercise of the protective power of the State is read into all contracts and there is no greater reason for refusing to apply this principle to Minnesota mortgages than to New York leases.

Applying the criteria established by our decisions we conclude:

1. An emergency existed in Minnesota which furnished a proper occasion for the exercise of the reserved power of the State to protect the vital interests of the community. . . .

2. The legislation was addressed to a legitimate end, that is, the legislation was not for the mere advantage of particular individuals but for the protection of a basic interest of society.

3. In view of the nature of the contracts in question—mortgages of unquestionable validity—the relief afforded and justified by the emergency, in order not to contravene the constitutional provision, could only be of a character appropriate to that emergency and could be granted only upon reasonable conditions.

4. The conditions upon which the period of redemption is extended do not appear to be unreasonable. . . .

5. The legislation is temporary in operation. It is limited to the exigency which called it forth. . . .

We are of the opinion that the Minnesota statute as here applied does not violate the contract clause of the Federal Constitution. Whether the legislation is wise or unwise as a matter of policy is a question with which we are not concerned. . . .

The judgment of the Supreme Court of Minnesota is affirmed.

MR. JUSTICE SUTHERLAND, dissenting.

Few questions of greater moment than that just decided have been submitted for judicial inquiry during this generation. He simply closes his eyes to the necessary implications of the decision who fails to see in it the potentiality of future gradual but ever-advancing encroachments upon the sanctity of private and public contracts. The effect of the Minnesota legislation, though serious enough in itself, is of trivial significance compared with the far more serious and dangerous inroads upon the limitations of the Constitution which are almost certain to ensue as a consequence naturally following any step beyond the boundaries fixed by that instrument. And those of us who are thus apprehensive of the effect of this decision would, in a matter so important, be neglectful of our duty should we fail to spread upon the permanent records of the court the reasons which move us to the opposite view.

A provision of the Constitution, it is hardly necessary to say, does not admit of two distinctly opposite interpretations. It does not mean one thing at one time and an entirely different thing at another time. If the contract impairment clause, when framed and adopted, meant that the terms of a contract for the payment of money could not be altered . . . by a state statute enacted for the relief of hardly pressed debtors to the end and with the effect of postponing payment or enforcement during and because of an economic or financial emergency, it is but to state the obvious to say that it means the same now. This view, at once so rational in its application to the written word, and so necessary to the stability of constitutional principles, though from time to time challenged, has never, unless recently, been put within the realm of doubt by the decisions of this court. . . .

The provisions of the Federal Constitution, undoubtedly, are pliable in the sense that in appropriate cases they have the capacity of bringing within their grasp every new condition which falls within their meaning. But, their *meaning* is changeless; it is only their *application* which is extensible. . . .

A statute which materially delays enforcement of the mortgagee's contractual right of ownership and possession does not modify the remedy merely; it destroys, for the period of delay, *all* remedy so far as the enforcement of that right is concerned. The phrase, "obligation of a contract," in the constitutional sense imports a legal duty to perform the specified obligation of *that* contract, not to substitute and perform, against the will of one of the parties, a different, albeit equally valuable, obligation. And a state, under the contract impairment clause, has no more power to accomplish such a substitution than has one of the parties to the contract against the will of the other. It cannot do so either by acting directly upon the contract, or by bringing about the result under the guise of a statute in form acting only upon the remedy. If it could, the efficacy of the constitutional restriction would, in large measure, be made to disappear. . . .

I quite agree with the opinion of the court that whether the legislation under review is wise or unwise is a matter with which we have nothing to do. Whether it is likely to work well or work ill presents a question entirely irrelevant to the issue. The only legitimate inquiry we can make is whether it is constitutional. If it is not, its virtues, if it have any, cannot save it; if it is, its faults cannot be invoked to accomplish its destruction. If the provisions of the Constitu-

tion be not upheld when they pinch as well as when they comfort, they may as well be abandoned. Being unable to reach any other conclusion than that the Minnesota statute infringes the constitutional restriction under review, I have no choice but to say so.

The Court upheld the Minnesota statute because the majority concluded that the economic emergency justified the state's use of extensive police powers. Does the contract clause retain any vitality under such an interpretation? Or did the *Home Building and Loan Association* decision render it virtually meaningless? After all, legislatures would have little reason to pass such a statute in good economic times.

CONTEMPOARY APPLICATIONS OF THE CONTRACT CLAUSE

For decades following the Minnesota Mortgage Moratorium Act decision, parties challenging state laws rarely rested their arguments on the contract clause. It made little practical sense to do so when the justices were reluctant to use the provision to strike down state legislation designed to promote the economic welfare of the citizens. Litigants who attempted to invoke the clause usually were unsuccessful.

But to conclude that the contract clause had been erased from the Constitution effectively and forever would be incorrect. In the decades following the New Deal, the Court was dominated by justices who took generally liberal positions on economic matters. They were philosophically opposed to allowing business interests to use the clause as a weapon to strike down legislation benefiting the people at large. The Court's liberal majority began to unravel when Chief Justice Earl Warren retired in 1969 and President Richard Nixon appointed Warren Burger to replace him. As succeeding appointments brought more conservative and business-oriented justices to the Court, the prospects for a revitalized contract clause grew. This fact was not lost on enterprising lawyers, who began to consider raising contract clause issues once again.

During the 1970s the justices handed down two decisions that struck down state actions for violating the contract clause. First, in **United States Trust v. New Jersey** (1977) the Court invalidated laws passed by New York and New Jersey repealing a 1962 contractual promise made to New York Port Authority bondholders that the authority's revenues pledged as security for existing bonds would never be used for railroad expenditures. Second, in **Allied Structural Steel v. Spannaus** (1978) the justices declared unconstitutional a Minnesota law that changed the contractual provisions of employee retirement plans retroactively.

Did these decisions signal that the contract clause, long thought to have been stripped of its contemporary relevance, was being resurrected? Not necessarily. Other decisions handed down by the Court turned away contract clause challenges to state actions. In **Energy Reserves Group, Inc. v. Kansas Power and Light** (1983) the Court upheld a state law that dictated an energy-pricing system that conflicted with existing contracts. And in **Keystone Bituminous Coal Association v. DeBenedictis** (1987) the justices gave constitutional approval to a state law that required coal mine operators to leave 50 percent of the coal in the ground beneath certain structures to provide support. The regulation was at odds with existing contracts between the mining companies and landowners that allowed the companies to extract a higher proportion of coal in the ground. In both cases the Court recognized the need of the states to use their police powers to remedy social or economic problems. The contract clause, according to the Court, prohibits only those state actions that "substantially impair the contractual arrangement." And even such substantial impairment can be justified if there is a significant and legitimate public purpose behind the regulation.

Decisions such as these have signaled potential litigants that successfully challenging state laws on contract clause grounds remains a difficult task, although success is more likely today than it was immediately following the New Deal. As a consequence, parties wishing to defend private property rights against state regulation have begun to turn to other constitutional provisions. Most often, the Fifth Amendment takings clause has served as a vehicle for such challenges. This subject is addressed in chapter 11.

READINGS

Ackerman, Bruce. *Private Property and the Constitution.* New Haven: Yale University Press, 1977.

Dowd, Morgan D. "Justice Story, the Supreme Court, and the Obligation of Contract." *Case Western Reserve Law Review* 19 (1968): 493–527.

Hagin, Horace H. *"Fletcher vs. Peck."* Georgetown Law Journal 16 (November 1927): 1–40.

Hall, Kermit L., ed. *Law, Economy, and the Power of Contract: Major Historical Interpretations.* New York: Garland, 1987.

Horowitz, Morton J. *The Transformation of American Law, 1780–1860.* Cambridge: Harvard University Press, 1977.

Hunting, Warren B. *The Obligation of Contracts Clause of the United States Constitution.* Baltimore: Johns Hopkins University Press, 1919.

Isaacs, Nathan. "John Marshall on Contracts: A Study in Early American Juristic Theory." *Virginia Law Review* 7 (March 1921): 413–428.

Kutler, Stanley I. *Privilege and Creative Destruction: The Charles River Bridge Case.* Philadelphia: J. B. Lippincott, 1971.

Magrath, C. Peter. *Yazoo: Law and Politics in the New Republic.* Providence: Brown University Press, 1966.

Scheiber, Harry N., ed. *The State and Freedom of Contract.* Stanford: Stanford University Press, 1999.

Schwartz, Bernard. "Old Wine in New Bottles? The Renaissance of the Contract Clause." *Supreme Court Review 1979* (1980): 95–121.

Stites, Francis N. *Private Interest and Public Gain: The Dartmouth College Case.* Amherst: University of Massachusetts Press, 1972.

Trimble, Bruce. "Chief Justice Waite and the Limitations on the Dartmouth College Decision." *University of Cincinnati Law Review* 9 (January 1935): 41–66.

Wright, Benjamin F. *The Contract Clause of the Constitution.* Cambridge: Harvard University Press, 1938.

CHAPTER 10

ECONOMIC SUBSTANTIVE DUE PROCESS

In the Fifth Amendment the framers imposed a restraint on the federal government that reads: "No person shall . . . be deprived of life, liberty, or property, without due process of law." Seven decades later the Fourteenth Amendment applied this prohibition to the actions of state governments with a similarly worded provision: "Nor shall any State deprive any person of life, liberty, or property, without due process of law."

Twenty-first-century Americans usually read these words as a guarantee of fundamental fairness, often with respect to criminal prosecutions. The federal and state governments cannot impose fines, put a person in jail, or impose capital punishment without following procedures that are fundamentally fair. Therefore, police must gather evidence in a lawful fashion, the accused must have the right to present a defense in open court, trials must be conducted fairly, and so on. Known as *procedural due process,* this is the traditional and most widely accepted understanding of the due process guarantee.

For a significant period of U.S. history, however, the due process clauses were given a second interpretation. Specifically, they were seen as prohibiting the government from imposing unjust or arbitrary laws. The Constitution not only required fair procedures, but the Fifth and Fourteenth Amendments also demanded that the substance of the laws be just and reasonable. This interpretation, known as *substantive due process,* normally was associated with economic liberties and prohibited the government from passing laws that infringed on economic rights—no matter how fair the regulatory procedures.

In this chapter we examine whether the substantive due process argument is a reasonable reading of the due process clauses. We shall see that in the modern era the Supreme Court for the most part has rejected substantive due process as it applies to laws governing economic relationships. But for approximately forty years between the 1890s and the 1930s, the Court read due process in substantive terms and used the principle to strike down many laws that allegedly infringed on economic rights.

If economic substantive due process is now a discredited doctrine, why should we devote an entire chapter to it? There are several reasons. First, its rise in and fall from the Court's grace are an intriguing part of legal history. The adoption of substantive due process came about gradually and resulted from the push and pull of the legal and political environment of the day.

Second, looking at economic substantive due process provides us with an opportunity to revisit the concept of judicial activism. Today, we usually associate judicial activism with liberalism, but the justices from the 1890s to the 1930s actively used the doctrine of substantive due process to impose their conservative ideology on American society. The Court overturned many laws that legislatures passed to regulate businesses for the general good. Substantive due process became associated with the Court's strong support of business interests.

Third, substantive due process is a way to reexamine the cycles of history we have already discussed. As depicted in Table 10-1, substantive due process was another weapon in the Court's laissez-faire arsenal. While it was

TABLE 10-1 The Legal Tools of the Laissez-Faire Courts, 1890s to 1930s: Some Examples

	1890–1899	1900–1909	1910–1919	1920–1929	1930–1939
Used to Strike State Laws					
Substantive Due Process	*Allgeyer v. Louisiana* (1897)	*Lochner v. New York* (1905)			*Morehead v. Tipaldo* (1936)
Used to Strike Federal Laws					
Delegation of Powers					*Panama Refining Co. v. Ryan* (1935)
					Schechter Poultry v. United States (1935)
Commerce Clause			*Hammer v. Dagenhart* (1918)		*Panama Refining Co. v. Ryan* (1935)
					Schechter Poultry v. United States (1935)
					Carter v. Carter Coal (1936)
Taxing and Spending				*Bailey v. Drexel Furniture* (1922)	*United States v. Butler* (1936)
Tenth Amendment			*Hammer v. Dagenhart* (1918)		

using delegation of power doctrines (chapter 4), the Tenth Amendment (chapter 6), the commerce clause (chapter 7), and taxing and spending provisions (chapter 8) to strike down federal regulation of business, the Court was also invoking substantive due process to hold against similar legislation passed by the states. This use was particularly ironic because, at the time, the Court was espousing notions of dual federalism and invoking the Tenth Amendment. In other words, the Court found ways to strike down all sorts of economic regulation, even though, in so doing, it often took contradictory stances. Therefore, substantive due process provides a way to tie together much of what has been covered in this book.

Finally, although the doctrine of substantive due process largely has been discredited, it continues to have some relevance today. The Court has used it to justify the protection of certain civil liberties, such as the right to privacy, and to nullify excessive monetary judgments awarded by juries in civil cases. We shall consider these issues at the end of the chapter, but first we review substantive due process chronologically—how it developed, why the Court embraced it, and what led to its demise.

THE DEVELOPMENT OF SUBSTANTIVE DUE PROCESS

Prior to the adoption of the Fourteenth Amendment, judges generally interpreted due process guarantees contained in the Fifth Amendment and in state constitutions as procedural in intent and nature. Historian Kermit L. Hall wrote, "Before the Civil War [due process] had essentially one meaning," that people were "entitled" to fair and orderly proceedings, particularly criminal proceedings.[1]

1. Kermit L. Hall, *The Magic Mirror* (New York: Oxford University Press, 1989), 232.

Initial Interpretation of the Fourteenth Amendment's Due Process Clause

The social ills that flowed from the nation's transition from an agrarian to an industrial economy after the Civil War prompted state legislatures to consider new regulations on commerce. But business interests saw a reduction in corporate profits as the necessary consequence of increased regulation. With the decline of the contract clause as a defense against state interference with business, it is not surprising that corporate interests looked to other parts of the Constitution for protection. The due process clause of the Fourteenth Amendment was seen as particularly promising.

The first attempt to invoke due process as a shield against government actions that business viewed as unreasonable occurred in *Butchers' Benevolent Association v. Crescent City Livestock Landing and Slaughter House Company* (1873), usually referred to as *The Slaughterhouse Cases*. Although industrialization had many benefits, it also had some unpleasant side effects. In this case the Louisiana state legislature claimed that the Mississippi River had become polluted because New Orleans butchers dumped garbage into it. To remedy this problem (or, as some have suggested, to use it as an excuse to create a monopolistic enterprise), the legislature created Crescent City Livestock Landing and Slaughterhouse Company and gave it the right to receive and slaughter all city livestock for twenty-five years.

Because the butchers were forced to use the company facilities and to pay top dollar for the privilege, they formed their own organization, the Butchers' Benevolent Association, and hired an attorney, former U.S. Supreme Court justice John A. Campbell, to sue the corporation. In his arguments, Campbell sought to apply the Fourteenth Amendment to the butchers' cause. In general terms, he asserted that the amendment, although passed in the wake of the Civil War, was not meant solely to protect former slaves. Rather, he said, its language was broad enough to encompass all citizens. In addition to presenting arguments based on the amendment's privileges and immunities and equal protection clauses, Campbell claimed that the Louisiana law violated the due process

clause because it arbitrarily deprived his clients of their fundamental right to pursue their business.

Writing for the Court's majority, Justice Samuel Miller rejected these claims. He relied on history to confirm the true purpose of the Fourteenth Amendment—to protect African Americans—and to refute Campbell's basic position. Miller focused his opinion on showing why the privileges and immunities claim was inapplicable, but he also rejected the due process clause argument. As he asserted:

[I]t is sufficient to say that under no construction of that provision that we have ever seen, or any that we deem admissible, can the restraint imposed by the state of Louisiana upon the exercise of their trade by the butchers of New Orleans be held to be a deprivation of property within the meaning of that provision.

Why did Miller take such a hard-line position? In large measure, he did not want to see the Court become a "super legislature," a censor imposing its own judgment on what laws were arbitrary or unreasonable. That was a job best left to elected state legislatures.

Two of the four dissenters, Justices Joseph Bradley and Stephen Field, wrote especially important opinions, taking issue with Miller's claims. Bradley, in particular, countered the majority's position that the due process clause was inapplicable to the dispute:

In my view, a law which prohibits a large class of citizens from adopting a lawful employment, or from following a lawful employment previously adopted, does deprive them of liberty as well as property, without due process of law. Their right of choice is a portion of their liberty; their occupation is their property.

It was Miller's view, however, that for the moment carried the day—that there was no substance in due process.

The Beginning of Substantive Due Process: The Court Opens a Window

Given the definitive nature of Miller's opinion in *The Slaughterhouse Cases*, we might suspect that it closed the book on substantive due process forever. But that was not the case. Miller observed just five years later:

It is not a little remarkable, that while [due process] has been in the Constitution . . . as a restraint upon the authority of the

Federal government, for nearly a century . . . its powers ha[ve] rarely been invoked in the judicial forum or the more enlarged theatre of public discussion. But while it has been a part of the Constitution, as a restraint upon the power of the States, only a very few years, the docket of this court is crowded with cases in which we are asked to hold that State courts and State legislatures have deprived their own citizens of life, liberty, or property without due process of law. There is here abundant evidence that there exists some strange misconception of the scope of this provision as found in the fourteenth amendment.[2]

Why did Miller feel it necessary to write this? Had not *Slaughterhouse* freed state regulatory authority from substantive due process concerns?

It had, but that did not prevent attorneys, representing increasingly desperate business interests, from continuing to make substantive due process arguments. From their perspective, the current environment held promise for the eventual adoption of such arguments. Within legal circles, for example, there was much discussion of several theories that lent themselves to Bradley's dissenting position in *Slaughterhouse.* One was expressed in a book by Thomas M. Cooley, a nineteenth-century legal scholar and jurist. His influential *Constitutional Limitations* singled out the word *liberty* within the due process clause as an important constitutional right. The protection of this right, in Cooley's eyes, required a substantive reading of the Fourteenth Amendment, which, in turn, would serve as a mechanism for protecting property rights and for restricting government regulation. Cooley's theory was specific, but nineteenth-century philosopher Herbert Spencer offered a more general view. Called social Darwinism, it treated social evolution in the same terms as Darwin wrote about biological evolution: "If left to themselves, the best of mankind, 'the fittest' would survive and prosper."[3] This proposition had a natural compatibility with laissez-faire economic theories: If government does not interfere, the best will prosper. Applying substantive due process would require government to leave business alone.

Social Darwinism may have influenced some scholars, the social elite, and business, but most Americans did not buy its tenets. Instead, the general public supported government regulation of commercial activities. The state legislatures responded to the people by continuing to pass legislation designed to alleviate the adverse social conditions brought about by America's rapid industrialization. And business reacted to these regulatory reforms by challenging them in court. This process resulted in the crowded docket to which Miller referred.

In addition, the Court itself contributed to the mounting number of substantive due process attacks on state regulation of business. Take, for example, the Court's ruling in **Munn v. Illinois** (1877). In this case, the justices considered an 1871 Illinois law that sought to regulate the grain storage industry, which had grown increasingly corrupt. The state justified the law as compatible with its constitution, which specified that public warehouses were subject to regulation. But companies forced to comply with the law disliked it. Ira Munn, co-owner of one of the more successful grain warehouses, challenged the law as a violation of the Fourteenth Amendment's due process clause.

In his opinion for the Court, Chief Justice Morrison Waite upheld the law and, in so doing, seemed to reject substantive due process completely, asserting that most regulatory legislation should be presumed valid. The decision, in fact, elicited an acrimonious dissent from Justice Field, which largely reflected Bradley's in *Slaughterhouse:* The law was "nothing less than a bold assertion of absolute power by the state to control at its discretion the property and business of the citizen." So it is not surprising that Waite's majority opinion "has generally been regarded as a great victory for liberalism and a judicial refusal to recognize due process as a limit on the substance of legislative regulatory power."[4]

But that description is not exactly accurate. Although Waite could have taken the same approach as Miller in *Slaughterhouse*—the complete rejection of the due process claim—he did not. Instead, Waite qualified his opinion,

2. *Davidson v. New Orleans* (1878).

3. Walter F. Murphy, James E. Fleming, and William F. Harris II, *American Constitutional Interpretation,* 2nd ed. (Mineola, N.Y.: Foundation Press, 1995), 1075.

4. C. Herman Pritchett, *The American Constitution* (New York: McGraw-Hill, 1959), 557.

asserting first that state regulations of private property were "not supposed" to deprive owners of their right to due process, but that "under some circumstances they may." What differentiated "some circumstances" from others? In Waite's opinion, the answer lay in the nature of the business being regulated: "We find that when private property is 'affected with a public interest it ceases to be [of private right] only.'" Waite used this doctrine, often called the business affected with a public interest doctrine, to find against Ira Munn's claim.

But holding that businesses affected with the public interest could be constitutionally regulated implied that businesses not meeting this description could raise a due process defense against unreasonable state regulation. Waite's opinion unwittingly provided the loophole that lawyers representing business clients who were unhappy with state regulation attempted to open even further. By avoiding a hard-line stance of the sort taken by Miller in *Slaughterhouse*, Waite's "maybe yes, maybe no" approach in the end provided some elbow room for the concept of substantive due process.

In two cases, coming a decade or so after *Munn*, the Court moved closer to the concession only implied by Waite. In the first, **Mugler v. Kansas** (1887), the Court considered a state law that prohibited the manufacture and sale of liquor. Although the majority upheld the regulation against a substantive due process challenge, the Court's opinion represented something of a break from *Munn*. First, it articulated the view that not "every statute enacted ostensibly for the promotion of [the public interest] is to be accepted as a legitimate exertion of police powers of the state." This opinion was far more explicit than Waite's: There were clear limits of state regulatory power. Second, and more important, it took precisely the opposite position from that of the majority in *Slaughterhouse*. Recall that Justice Miller wanted to avoid having the Court become a "super legislature," scrutinizing and perhaps censoring state action. But in *Mugler*, that is precisely what the Court said it would do:

There are . . . limits beyond which legislation cannot rightfully go. . . . If, therefore, a statute purporting to have been enacted to protect the public health, the public morals, or the public safety, has no real or substantial relation to those objects, or is a palpable invasion of rights secured by the fundamental law, *it*

is the duty of the courts to so adjudge, and thereby give effect to the Constitution. [Emphasis added.]

In *Mugler* the Court did not fully adopt the doctrine of substantive due process; it even upheld the state regulation on liquor. Yet the Court established its intent to review legislation to determine whether a law was a "reasonable" exercise of state power. In essence, the Court would balance the interests of the state against those of individual due process guarantees—a course of action *Slaughterhouse* rejected.

The legislation tested in *Mugler* was deemed reasonable, but in **Chicago, Milwaukee & St. Paul Railway v. Minnesota** (1890), decided three years later, the Court went the other way: The justices struck down a state regulation on the ground that it interfered with due process guarantees. At first glance, *Chicago, Milwaukee & St. Paul Railway* bears a distinct resemblance to *Munn v. Illinois*. Strong lobbying efforts by farm groups led Minnesota in 1887 to establish a railroad and warehouse commission to set "equal and reasonable" rates for railroad transportation of goods and for warehouse storage. When the commission, and later the state courts, ruled that Chicago, Milwaukee, and St. Paul Railway Company was charging dairy farmers unreasonable rates to ship their milk, the railroad took its case to the U.S. Supreme Court, where it argued that the commission had interfered with "its property" without providing it with due process of law.

Writing for the majority, Justice Samuel Blatchford examined the law in terms of the reasonableness standard promulgated in *Mugler:* "The question of the reasonableness of a rate of charge for transportation by a railroad company . . . is eminently a question for judicial investigation, requiring due process of law for its determination."

Blatchford found the law deprived the company of its property in an unfair way: "If the company is deprived of the power of charging reasonable rates . . . and such deprivation takes place in the absence of an investigation by judicial machinery, it is deprived of the lawful use of its property, and thus, in substance and effect, of the property itself, without due process of law."

Chicago, Milwaukee & St. Paul Railway was not extraordinary: It merely applied the standard articulated in *Mu-*

gler, a standard that obviously cut both ways. Sometimes the Court, in its attempt to inquire (balance interests), would find a law a "reasonable" use of state power (*Mugler*), and sometimes it would find that it violated substantive due process guarantees, as it did here. But this case and, to a lesser extent, *Mugler,* were remarkable if we consider how different they were from *Slaughterhouse.* Over a seventeen-year period, the Court had moved from a refusal to inject substance into due process to a near affirmation of the doctrine of substantive due process; it had moved from the assertion that it would not become a censor of legislative reasonableness to one arguing that judicial inquiry was necessary, if not mandated, by the Constitution. And although, as we shall see, the Court did not fully endorse Thomas Cooley's position defining due process "liberty" in economic terms until seven years later, Blatchford's opinion laid the groundwork for exactly that.

This change in position prompts us to ask why the Court did such a turnabout over two decades. The most obvious answer is personnel changes. By the time the Court decided *Mugler,* only one member of the *Slaughterhouse* majority, Miller, remained. By 1890 Miller also was gone, as was Chief Justice Waite, who, despite the loophole in the *Munn* opinion, generally favored state regulatory power. Their replacements were quite different. Some had been corporate attorneys schooled in the philosophies of Cooley and Spencer and quite willing to borrow from the briefs of their former colleagues who argued against state regulation. Given the backgrounds of the new appointees, it also is not surprising to find that the views of the *Slaughterhouse* dissenters went on to rule the day.

But there may have been more to it. By asserting the standard it did, the Court was engaging in extreme judicial activism, ruling against the strong public sentiment that prompted the state legislatures to pass regulatory policies.

It is fair to say that the justices did not see it this way; rather, they viewed these political pressures of the day as particularized, radical "socialistic" elements that did not reflect majority interests. If this was their perception, it had a solid foundation. Some legislation had resulted from the lobbying efforts of farm and labor movements

and later, as we shall see, of the Progressives and New Dealers. In the minds of many conservatives of the day, including some of the justices, such pressures were illegitimate because they sought to subvert the free enterprise system. In short, while the Populists, Progressives, and New Dealers, in the opinion of conservatives, tried to put the brakes on businesses and inculcate the government with socialistic legislation, the conservatives strongly believed that the best interests of the country lay with a free market, unregulated by the government.

A fundamental change was in the wind, and many point to the Court's decision in **Allgeyer v. Louisiana** (1897) as the turning point. This case involved a Louisiana law that barred its citizens and corporations from doing business with out-of-state insurance companies, unless the companies complied with a specified set of requirements. Allgeyer Company wanted insurance protection to cover one hundred bales of cotton it shipped to a foreign port. When the company secured such a policy from a New York insurer that was not approved to do business in Louisiana, state attorneys alleged that Allgeyer had violated the law.

The state argued that the purpose of the law was to prevent fraud. But Allgeyer did not see it that way, and it challenged the constitutionality of the law on Fourteenth Amendment due process grounds. In its view, the term *liberty* included the right to use and enjoy all "endowments" without constraint, and the term *property* included the right to acquire property and engage in business. Here, Allgeyer's attorney alleged, the law acts as a significant and unconstitutional curtailment of the legitimate business activity of the company.

In some ways, the opinion Justice Rufus Peckham wrote for the Court was not so different from the majority's opinion in *Chicago, Milwaukee & St. Paul Railway.* He struck down the state law in part on the ground that it was not reasonable. But he went much further: He merged substantive due process with freedom of contract, by reading the term *liberty* to mean economic liberty, encompassing the right to "enter into all contracts." As he wrote:

Has not a citizen of a state, under the [due process clause of the Fourteenth Amendment], a right to contract outside of the state for insurance on his property—a right of which state legislation cannot deprive him? . . . When we speak of the liberty to contract for insurance or to do an act to effectuate such a contract already existing, we refer to and have in mind the facts of this case, where the contract was made outside the state, and as such was a valid and proper contract. . . . To deprive the citizen of such a right as herein described without due process of law is illegal. Such a statute as this in question is not due process of law, because it prohibits an act which under the Federal Constitution the defendants had a right to perform. This does not interfere in any way with the acknowledged right of the state to enact such legislation in the legitimate exercise of its police or other powers as to it may seem proper. In the exercise of such right, however, care must be taken not to infringe upon those other rights of the citizen which are protected by the Federal Constitution.

In other words, Peckham adopted the position that businesses had been pressing since the demise of the contract clause as a source of protection. Now their right to do business, to set their own rates, and to enter into contracts with other businesses and perhaps even with employees had the highest level of legal protection.

THE ROLLER-COASTER RIDE OF SUBSTANTIVE DUE PROCESS: 1898–1923

However explicit *Allgeyer* was, the true test of its importance would come in its application. Some read the decision to mean that the Court would not uphold legislation that infringed on economic "liberty," but **Holden v. Hardy**, decided the very next year, dispelled this notion. In this case, the Court examined a Utah law prohibiting mining companies from working their employees more than eight hours a day, except in emergency situations. Attorneys challenging the law claimed that the legislature had no authority to prevent competent people from voluntarily entering into employment contracts even if the work to be performed was considered dangerous. The state asserted that the challenged statute was a "health regulation" and within the state's power because it was aimed at "preserving to a citizen his ability to work and support himself."

In *Holden* the Court reiterated its *Mugler* position: "The question in each case is whether the legislature has adopted the statute in exercise of a reasonable discretion or whether its actions be a mere excuse for an unjust discrimination." The Supreme Court, now acting as the nation's "super legislature," deemed the legislation "reasonable"; that is, it did not impinge on the liberty of contract because the state had a well-justified interest in protecting its citizens from the unique health problems caused by working in mines.

Holden was a victory for emerging labor groups and the still-forming progressive movement, which were vigorously lobbying state legislatures to pass laws protecting workers. As the Industrial Revolution wore on, they argued, the necessity for such laws was increasing because corporations were even more profit oriented and, as a result, more likely to exploit employees. While they succeeded in persuading many state legislatures to enact laws like Utah's, the possibility that courts would strike them down remained a threat. *Holden* had proven otherwise.

That ruling, however, took on a different gloss once the Court decided *Lochner v. New York* (1905). Although the law at issue varied only slightly from Utah's, the justices reached a wholly different conclusion. Why? Does the case fit compatibly with the logic of *Holden,* as Justice Peckham implies, or does it reveal the true reach of his opinion in *Allgeyer?*

Lochner v. New York

198 U.S. 45 (1905)
http://laws.findlaw.com/US/198/45.html
Vote: 5 (Brewer, Brown, Fuller, McKenna, Peckham)
    4 (Day, Harlan, Holmes, White)
Opinion of the Court: Peckham
Dissenting opinions: Harlan, Holmes

In 1897 New York enacted a law that limited employees of bakeries to no more than ten hours per day and sixty hours per week of work. The state justified the law on two grounds. First, New York had the authority under its police powers to regulate working conditions while taking into account local circumstances and community standards. Second, the state, through the police power, had the authority to regulate for the health of both consumers and workers.

After Joseph Lochner, the owner of a bakery located in Utica, New York, was convicted of violating a state maximum hour work law, he asked the U.S. Supreme Court to strike down the law as violative of his constitutional rights. In *Lochner v. New York* (1905), the justices agreed. The majority found that the law impermissibly interfered with the right of employers to enter into contracts with their employees.

After he was convicted of violating the law, Joseph Lochner, the owner of a New York bakery, challenged it on Fourteenth Amendment due process grounds. In part, he alleged the following:

1. Employees and employer have the right to agree upon hours and wages, and the use of the police power by New York to interfere with such agreements is so "paternal" as to violate the due process clause of the Fourteenth Amendment.

2. Regardless of the state's asserted interests, the "most cherished rights of American citizenship"—freedom of contract and property rights—"should be most closely and jealously scrutinized by this court." Since the interests here are not sufficiently "clear and apparent," the Court should strike the law.

MR. JUSTICE PECKHAM . . . delivered the opinion of the court.

The mandate of the statute, that "no employee shall be required or permitted to work," is the substantial equivalent of an enactment that "no employee shall contract or agree to work," more than ten hours per day; and, as there is no provision for special emergencies, the statute is mandatory in all cases. It is not an act merely fixing the number of hours which shall constitute a legal day's work, but an absolute prohibition upon the employer permitting, under any circumstances, more than ten hours' work to be done in his establishment. The employee may desire to earn the extra money which would arise from his working more than the prescribed time, but this statute forbids the employer from permitting the employee to earn it.

The statute necessarily interferes with the right of contract between the employer and employees, concerning the number of hours in which the latter may labor in the bakery of the employer. The general right to make a contract in relation to his business is part of the liberty of the individual protected by the 14th Amendment of the Federal Constitution. *Allgeyer v. Louisiana.* Under that provision no state can deprive any person of life, liberty, or property without due process of law. The right to purchase or to sell labor is part of the liberty protected by this amendment, unless there are circumstances which exclude the right. There are, however, certain powers, existing in the sovereignty of each state in the Union, somewhat vaguely termed police powers, the exact description and limitation of which have not been attempted by the courts. Those powers, broadly stated, and without, at present, any attempt at a more specific limitation, relate to the safety, health, morals, and general welfare of the public. Both property and liberty are held on such reasonable conditions as may be imposed by the governing power of the state in the exercise of those powers, and with such conditions the 14th Amendment was not designed to interfere.

The state, therefore, has power to prevent the individual from making certain kinds of contracts, and in regard to them the Federal Constitution offers no protection. If the contract be one which the state, in the legitimate exercise of its police power, has the right to prohibit, it is not prevented from prohibiting it by the 14th Amendment. Contracts in violation of a statute, either of the Federal or state government, or a contract to let one's property for immoral purposes, or to do any other unlawful act, could obtain no protection from the Federal Constitution, as coming under the liberty of person or of free contract. Therefore, when the state, by its legislature, in the assumed exercise of its police powers, has passed an act which seriously limits the right to labor or the right of contract in regard to their means of livelihood between persons who are *sui juris* (both employer and employee), it becomes of great importance to determine which shall prevail,—the right of the individual to labor for such time as he may choose, or the right of the state to prevent the individual from laboring, or from entering into any contract to labor, beyond a certain time prescribed by the state.

This court has recognized the existence and upheld the exercise of the police powers of the states in many cases which might fairly be considered as border ones, and it has, in the course of its determination of questions regarding the asserted invalidity of such statutes, on the ground of their violation of the rights secured by the Federal Constitution, been guided by rules of a very liberal nature, the application of which has resulted, in numerous instances, in upholding the validity of state statutes thus assailed. Among the later cases where the state law has been upheld by this court is that of *Holden v. Hardy.* A provision in the act of the legislature of Utah was there under consideration, the act limiting the employment of workmen in all underground mines or workings, to eight hours per day, "except in cases of emergency, where life or property is in imminent danger." It also limited the hours of labor in smelting and other institutions for the reduction or refining of ores or metals to eight hours

per day, except in like cases of emergency. The act was held to be a valid exercise of the police powers of the state . . . [because the] law applies only to the classes subjected by their employment to the peculiar conditions and effects attending underground mining and work in smelters, and other works for the reduction and refining of ores. Therefore it is not necessary to discuss or decide whether the legislature can fix the hours of labor in other employments. . . .

It must, of course, be conceded that there is a limit to the valid exercise of the police power by the state. There is no dispute concerning this general proposition. Otherwise the 14th Amendment would have no efficacy and the legislatures of the states would have unbounded power, and it would be enough to say that any piece of legislation was enacted to conserve the morals, the health, or the safety of the people; such legislation would be valid, no matter how absolutely without foundation the claim might be. The claim of the police power would be a mere pretext,—become another and delusive name for the supreme sovereignty of the state to be exercised free from constitutional restraint. This is not contended for. In every case that comes before this court, therefore, where legislation of this character is concerned, and where the protection of the Federal Constitution is sought, the question necessarily arises: Is this a fair, reasonable, and appropriate exercise of the police power of the state, or is it an unreasonable, unnecessary, and arbitrary interference with the right of the individual to his personal liberty, or to enter into those contracts in relation to labor which may seem to him appropriate or necessary for the support of himself and his family? Of course the liberty of contract relating to labor includes both parties to it. The one has as much right to purchase as the other to sell labor.

This is not a question of substituting the judgment of the court for that of the legislature. If the act be within the power of the state it is valid, although the judgment of the court might be totally opposed to the enactment of such a law. But the question would still remain: Is it within the police power of the state? and that question must be answered by the court.

The question whether this act is valid as a labor law, pure and simple, may be dismissed in a few words. There is no reasonable ground for interfering with the liberty of person or the right of free contract, by determining the hours of labor, in the occupation of a baker. There is no contention that bakers as a class are not equal in intelligence and capacity to men in other trades or manual occupations, or that they are not able to assert their rights and care for themselves without the protecting arm of the state, interfering with their independence of judgment and of action. They are in no sense wards of the state. Viewed in the light of a purely labor law, with no reference whatever to the question of health, we think that a law like the one before us involves neither the safety, the morals, nor the welfare, of the public, and that the interest of the public is not in the slightest degree affected by such an act. The law must be upheld, if at all, as a law pertaining to the health of the individual engaged in the occupation of a baker. It does not affect any other portion of the public than those who are engaged in that occupation. Clean and wholesome bread does not depend upon whether the baker works but ten hours per day or only sixty hours a week. The limitation of the hours of labor does not come within the police power on that ground.

It is a question of which of two powers or rights shall prevail,—the power of the state to legislate or the right of the individual to liberty of person and freedom of contract. The mere assertion that the subject relates, though but in a remote degree, to the public health, does not necessarily render the enactment valid. The act must have a more direct relation, as a means to an end, and the end itself must be appropriate and legitimate, before an act can be held to be valid which interferes with the general right of an individual to be free in his person and in his power to contract in relation to his own labor. . . .

We think the limit of the police power has been reached and passed in this case. There is, in our judgment, no reasonable foundation for holding this to be necessary or appropriate as a health law to safeguard the public health, or the health of the individuals who are following the trade of a baker. If this statute be valid, and if, therefore, a proper case is made out in which to deny the right of an individual, *sui juris,* as employer or employee, to make contracts for the labor of the latter under the protection of the provisions of the Federal Constitution, there would seem to be no length to which legislation of this nature might not go. The case differs widely, as we have already stated, from the expressions of this court in regard to laws of this nature, as stated in *Holden v. Hardy.* . . .

We think that there can be no fair doubt that the trade of a baker, in and of itself, is not an unhealthy one to that degree which would authorize the legislature to interfere with the right to labor, and with the right of free contract on the part of the individual, either as employer or employee. . . .

It is also urged, pursuing the same line of argument, that it is to the interest of the state that its population should be strong and robust, and therefore any legislation which may be said to tend to make people healthy must be valid as health laws, enacted under the police power. If this be a valid argument and a justification for this kind of legislation, it follows that the protection of the Federal Constitution from undue interference with liberty of person and freedom of contract is visionary, wherever the law is sought to be justified as a valid exercise of the police power. Scarcely any law but might find shelter under such assumptions, and conduct, properly so called, as well as contract, would come under the restrictive sway of the legislature. Not only the hours of employees, but the hours of employers, could be regulated, and doctors, lawyers, scientists, all professional men, as well as athletes and artisans, could be forbidden to fatigue their brains and bodies by prolonged hours of exercise, lest the fighting strength of the state be impaired. We mention these extreme cases because the contention is extreme. We do not believe in the soundness of the views which uphold this law. On the contrary, we think that such a law as this, although passed in the assumed exercise of the police power, and as relating to the public health, or the health of the employees named, is not within that power, and is invalid. . . .

It was further urged on the argument that restricting the hours of labor in the case of bakers was valid because it tended to cleanliness on the part of the workers, as a man was more apt to be cleanly when not overworked, and if cleanly then his "output" was also more likely to be so. What has already been said applies with equal force to this contention. We do not admit the reasoning to be sufficient to justify the claimed right of such interference. The state in that case would assume the position of a supervisor, or pater familias, over every act of the individual, and its right of governmental interference with his hours of labor, his hours of exercise, the character thereof, and the extent to which it shall be carried would be recognized and upheld. In our judgment it is not possible in fact to discover the connection between the number of hours a baker may work in the bakery and the healthful quality of the bread made by the workman. The connection, if any exist, is too shadowy and thin to build any argument for the interference of the legislature. If the man works ten hours a day it is all right, but if ten and a half or eleven his health is in danger and his bread may be unhealthy, and, therefore, he shall not be permitted to do it. This, we think, is unreasonable and entirely arbitrary. When assertions such as we have adverted to become necessary in order to give, if possible, a plausible foundation for the contention that the law is a "health law," it gives rise to at least a suspicion that there was some other motive dominating the legislature than the purpose to subserve the public health or welfare. . . .

It is impossible for us to shut our eyes to the fact that many of the laws of this character, while passed under what is claimed to be the police power for the purpose of protecting the public health or welfare, are, in reality, passed from other motives. . . .

It is manifest to us that the limitation of the hours of labor provided for in this section of the statute under which the indictment was found, and the plaintiff in error convicted, has no such direct relation to, and no such substantial effect upon, the health of the employee, as to justify us in regarding the section as really a health law. It seems to us that the real object and purpose were simply to regulate the hours of labor between the master and his employees (all being men, sui juris), in a private business, not dangerous in any degree to morals, or in any real and substantial degree to the health of the employees. Under such circumstances the freedom of master and employee to contract with each other in relation to their employment, and in defining the same, cannot be prohibited or interfered with, without violating the Federal Constitution.

The judgment of the Court of Appeals of New York, as well as that of the Supreme Court and the County Court of Oneida County, must be reversed and the case remanded to the County Court for further proceedings not inconsistent with this opinion.

Reversed.

MR. JUSTICE HOLMES dissenting.

This case is decided upon an economic theory which a large part of the country does not entertain. If it were a question whether I agreed with that theory I should desire to study it further and long before making up my mind. But I do not conceive that to be my duty, because I strongly be-

lieve that my agreement or disagreement has nothing to do with the right of a majority to embody their opinions in law. It is settled by various decisions of this court that state constitutions and state laws may regulate life in many ways which we as legislators might think as injudicious or if you like as tyrannical as this, and which equally with this interfere with the liberty to contract. . . . The Fourteenth Amendment does not enact Mr. Herbert Spencer's Social Statics. . . . United States and state statutes and decisions cutting down the liberty to contract by way of combination are familiar to this court. Two years ago we upheld the prohibition of sales of stock on margins or for future delivery in the constitution of California. *Otis v. Parker.* The decision sustaining an eight hour law for miners is still recent. *Holden v. Hardy.* Some of these laws embody convictions or prejudices which judges are likely to share. Some may not. But a constitution is not intended to embody a particular economic theory, whether of paternalism and the organic relation of the citizen to the State or of *laissez faire.* It is made for people of fundamentally differing views, and the accident of our finding certain opinions natural and familiar or novel and even shocking ought not to conclude our judgment upon the question whether statutes embodying them conflict with the Constitution of the United States.

General propositions do not decide concrete cases. The decision will depend on a judgment or intuition more subtle than any articulate major premise. But I think that the proposition just stated, if it is accepted, will carry us far toward the end. Every opinion tends to become a law. I think that the word liberty in the Fourteenth Amendment is perverted when it is held to prevent the natural outcome of a dominant opinion, unless it can be said that a rational and fair man necessarily would admit that the statute proposed would infringe fundamental principles as they have been understood by the traditions of our people and our law. It does not need research to show that no such sweeping condemnation can be passed upon the statute before us. A reasonable man might think it a proper measure on the score of health. Men whom I certainly could not pronounce unreasonable would uphold it as a first installment of a general regulation of the hours of work. Whether in the latter aspect it would be open to the charge of inequality I think it unnecessary to discuss.

Curt Muller (with arms folded) made constitutional history when he asked the U.S. Supreme Court to strike down as violative of his rights an Oregon law regulating the number of hours female laundry workers could work at his cleaning establishment. In *Muller v. Oregon* (1908), however, the Court held that states may constitutionally enact maximum hour work laws for women.

Many scholars have called *Lochner* the Court's strongest expression of economic substantive due process. Although the Court said the question to be asked in this case is the same one it had been addressing since *Mugler*—Is the law a fair, reasonable, and appropriate exercise of police power?—its answer is quite different. By distinguishing *Holden* to the point of nonexistence and by narrowing the scope of reasonable state regulations, the Court moved away from a strict "reasonableness" approach to one that reflected *Allgeyer:* An employer's right "to make a contract" with employees is virtually sacrosanct.

That the Court, although divided 5–4, accomplished this feat not by changing the legal question but by changing the answer creates something of a puzzle, particularly with regard to the immediate subject of the dispute—maximum work hours. Think about it this way: The

Court upheld the Utah law at issue in *Holden* on the ground that the kind of employment (underground mining) and the character of the employees (miners) were such as to make the law reasonable and proper; it struck the *Lochner* law because bakers can "care for themselves" and the production of "clean and wholesome bread" is not affected. Was this distinction significant? Or was it merely a way to mask what the Court wanted to do: narrow the grounds on which states could reasonably regulate and, thereby, strike protective legislation as a violation of the right to contract? Justice Oliver Wendell Holmes's dissent certainly implies the latter. He goes so far as to accuse the Court of using the Fourteenth Amendment to "enact Mr. Herbert Spencer's Social Statics." Although many scholars agree with Holmes's assessment and argue that the justices in the *Lochner* majority were "motivated by their own policy preferences favoring

BOX 10-1   LOUIS DEMBITZ BRANDEIS (1916–1939)

LOUIS DEMBITZ BRANDEIS, born November 13, 1856, in Louisville, Kentucky, was the son of Adolph and Fredericka Dembitz Brandeis, Jews who had emigrated from Bohemia after the unsuccessful democratic revolts of 1848. His father was a prosperous grain merchant who provided his family with comfort, education, and culture. Having completed two years of preparatory studies at the Annen-Realschule in Dresden, but without a college degree, Brandeis enrolled at Harvard Law School when he was eighteen years of age. He graduated in 1877 with the highest average in the law school's history. After eight months practicing law in St. Louis, Brandeis returned to Cambridge—for him "the world's center"—and with Bostonian Samuel D. Warren Jr., second in their law school class, opened a one-room office in Boston.

Warren and Brandeis and the successor firm Brandeis, Dunbar, and Nutter handled a variety of cases and were highly successful. By the time he was thirty-five, Brandeis was earning more than $50,000 a year. He married Alice Goldmark of New York, March 23, 1891, and the couple had two daughters. Despite his earnings, the family preferred to live simply, set-

ting a ceiling on their personal expenditures of $10,000 a year. As a young lawyer Brandeis devoted many hours to his alma mater. He helped raise funds for a teaching post for Oliver Wendell Holmes Jr. and was one of the founders of the *Harvard Law Review.*

The turn of the century marked the rapid growth in America of corporate monopolies—the "curse of bigness," as Brandeis described it. He chose to protect the rights not of special interest groups but of the general public, and usually without a fee for his services. Although Brandeis never held political office, his efforts as a lawyer resulted in sliding-scale gas rates in Boston that lowered consumer costs while raising corporate dividends and savings bank insurance policies, another reform later implemented in the rest of the country. He defended municipal control of Boston's subway system and opposed the monopolistic practices of the New Haven Railroad. He arbitrated labor disputes in New York's garment industry, serving as chairman of an arbitration board from 1910 to 1916. His legal strategies helped to establish the constitutionality of state maximum hour and minimum wage statutes. For thirty-seven years Brandeis devoted his time, energy, and talents to a host of public causes. He called himself an "attorney

---

laissez-faire economics and Social Darwinism," other analysts present a somewhat different picture.[5] They suggest that the Court was seeking to remain faithful to "a long-standing constitutional ideology that distinguished between valid economic regulation and invalid 'class,' or factional legislation."[6] In other words, *Lochner* repre-

sented a "principled effort" on the part of the justices to keep this area of the law consistent and coherent, and not merely a statement of their ideological predilections.

Regardless of who is right, these issues moved to the fore in ***Muller v. Oregon*** (1908). This case began when the state of Oregon brought charges against Curt Muller for working his female laundry workers longer than the state maximum of ten hours per day. Once convicted, Muller decided to challenge the law. In the view of his attorneys, Oregon's regulation, which prohibited the employment of women, but not men, in laundries for more than ten

5. Quotation from C. Ian Anderson, "Courts and the Constitution," *Michigan Law Review* 92 (1994): 1438. For the different viewpoint, see, especially, Howard Gillman, *The Constitution Besieged: The Rise and Demise of Lochner Era Police Powers Jurisprudence* (Durham: Duke University Press, 1993).

6. Anderson, "Courts and the Constitution," 1439.

for the situation," but the press adopted the popular title "people's attorney."

President Woodrow Wilson respected Brandeis and often sought his opinion. He nominated Brandeis associate justice of the Supreme Court on January 28, 1916, to fill the vacancy left by Justice Joseph R. Lamar's death. Vicious opposition to his appointment ensued. One particularly vituperative critic described Brandeis as a "business-baiter, stirrer up of strife, litigious lover of hate and unrest, destroyer of confidence, killer of values, commercial coyote, spoiler of pay envelopes."

Factory owners paying higher wages, New Haven Railroad stockholders, moguls in the Boston transit system, insurance and gas industries—in short, all the losers in court—united to voice their objections to the appointment. Among those seeking satisfaction for past injuries was former president William Howard Taft. His administration had been embarrassed by an investigation led in part by Brandeis of the conservation practices of Secretary of the Interior Richard A. Ballinger.

Ambitious for a justiceship himself, Taft described the nomination as "one of the deepest wounds that I have had as an American and a lover of the Constitution" and spoke of the "indelible stain" on the Wilson administration that confirmation would bring.

Another critic, Clarence W. Barron, editor and publisher of the *Wall Street Journal*, also felt the choice was unwise: "There is only one redeeming feature in the nomination and that is that it will assist to bury Mr. Wilson in the next Presidential election." The president viewed the political climate differently. He believed Brandeis was a smart choice who would attract the needed Progressive vote. Wilson could not count on a divided Republican Party to ensure his reelection.

During four months of acrimonious debate over his appointment, Brandeis quietly pursued his legal practice. He went to the office every day and did not resort to personal attacks against his opponents. "Your attitude while the wolves yelp is sublime," his young nephew wrote.

The hearings in the Senate Judiciary Committee turned up no valid grounds for rejection. According to Sen. Thomas J. Walsh, Brandeis's only "real crime" was that "he had not stood in awe of the majesty of wealth." Arthur Hill, one of his supporters from Harvard Law School, attributed the opposition to the fact that "Mr. Brandeis is an outsider, successful and a Jew."

Brandeis was confirmed by the Senate on June 1, 1916, by a vote of 47–22, becoming the first Jewish justice.

On February 13, 1939, Brandeis, age eighty-two, resigned from the Court but not from public service. After twenty-two years on the bench, he devoted the last years of his life to the Zionist movement and a boycott of German products. As the *New York Times* noted upon his retirement in 1939, "the storm against him . . . seems almost incredible now." He died on October 5, 1941, in Washington, D.C.

SOURCE: Adapted from David Savage, *Guide to the U.S. Supreme Court*, 4th ed. (Washington, D.C.: CQ Press, 2004), 982–983.

hours a day, violated his right to enter into a contract with his employees.

Recognizing that, in light of *Lochner*, Muller's argument rested on strong legal grounds, the National Consumers' League (NCL)—a group that had pressed states to pass maximum hour legislation—grew concerned. The organization was reluctant to see its hard work to attain passage of the Oregon law nullified by the Supreme Court. To defend the law, the NCL contacted Louis Brandeis, a well-known attorney of the day and a future U.S. Supreme Court justice *(see Box 10-1)*.

Because of the decision in *Lochner* and the lack of significant membership changes on the Court since that case was decided, Brandeis believed that bold action was necessary. Instead of filling his brief with legal arguments, he would provide the Court with "*facts*, published by anyone with expert knowledge of industry in its relation to women's hours of labor," which indicated the evils of Muller's actions. In particular, the brief pointed out that forcing women to work long hours affected their health and their reproductive systems. In the end, with the help of the NCL, Brandeis produced an incredible document. Known in legal history as the Brandeis Brief, it contained 113 pages of sociological data and only 2 pages of legal argument.

To the surprise of some, the justices ruled in the NCL's favor. Why, given *Lochner,* did the Court affirm the Oregon law? One answer is that, in its opinion, the Court did not depart from *Lochner:* It merely found that Oregon's regulations, unlike New York's, were a reasonable use of the state's power. But the Court applied the reasonableness approach in both *Lochner* and *Holden* and came to completely different conclusions. So, despite the Court's attempt to distinguish *Lochner,* how much can the application of that standard possibly explain about *Muller*'s outcome? Another possibility is that Brandeis forced the Court to see the reasonableness of the Oregon regulation. By presenting a mass of statistical data, he kept the justices riveted on the law and diverted their attention from a substantive due process approach. The strategy worked: The justices even commended the Brandeis Brief. Finally, *Muller* was different from *Lochner* in at least one important way: The law applied solely to women. This was a point stressed by Brandeis and by the Court. As the majority opinion put it:

That woman's physical structure and the performance of maternal functions place her at a disadvantage in the struggle for subsistence is obvious. This is especially true when the burdens of motherhood are upon her. Even when they are not, by abundant testimony of the medical fraternity continuance for a long time on her feet at work, repeating this from day to day, tends to injurious effects upon the body, and, as healthy mothers are essential to vigorous offspring, the physical well-being of woman becomes an object of public interest and care in order to preserve the strength and vigor of the race.

Winning *Muller* gave a big boost to organizations like the NCL. Those who favored maximum hour work laws worried, however, that the decision depended on the fact that the law covered only women and that, when the Court had an opportunity to review a law covering all workers, it would apply *Lochner.* Their fears were greatly relieved when the justices in **Bunting v. Oregon** (1917) upheld an Oregon law that barred employees of mills, factories, or manufacturing facilities from working more than ten hours per day.

Once again the Court failed even to mention *Lochner.* And, given the Court's holding, many predicted the death of that decision; after all, it was wholly incompatible with *Bunting.* Perhaps the demise of substantive due process would follow. Indeed, throughout the period between *Mugler* (1887) and up to about *Bunting,* it appeared that *Lochner* was more the exception than the rule. Between 1887 and 1910, the Court decided 558 cases involving due process claims challenging state regulations and upheld 83 percent of the laws. It seemed that *Lochner,* not *Muller,* was the unusual case.[7]

THE HEYDAY OF SUBSTANTIVE DUE PROCESS: 1923–1936

The *Bunting* funeral for *Lochner* proved to be premature. Within six years, not only did the Court virtually overrule *Bunting,* but also it seemed to be more committed to the *Lochner* version of due process than ever before. *Adkins v. Children's Hospital* (1923) provides an excellent illustration of the magnitude of this resurgence.

Adkins v. Children's Hospital

261 U.S. 525 (1923)
http://laws.findlaw.com/US/261/525.html
Vote: 5 (Butler, McKenna, McReynolds, Sutherland,
      Van Devanter)
   3 (Holmes, Sanford, Taft)
Opinion of the Court: Sutherland
Dissenting opinions: Holmes, Taft
Not participating: Brandeis

In 1918 Congress, with the support of the progressive-minded president, Woodrow Wilson, enacted a law that fixed minimum wages for women and children in the District of Columbia. The act authorized the establishment of the Minimum Wage Board to set pay rates. The board, staffed by Progressives, ordered that restaurants and hospitals pay women workers a minimum wage of 34.5 cents per hour, $16.50 per week, or $71.50 per month. Accord-

---

7. Alfred H. Kelly, Winfred A. Harbison, and Herman Belz, *The American Constitution,* 7th ed. (New York: W. W. Norton, 1991), 405.

In *Adkins v. Children's Hospital* the Supreme Court struck down a federal minimum wage law on substantive due process grounds. The legal action to enjoin enforcement of the law was filed by the corporation that managed the Children's Hospital of the District of Columbia *(left)*.

ing to the board, these rates would "supply the necessary cost of living to . . . women workers to maintain them in good health and morals."

Children's Hospital of the District of Columbia, which employed many women, refused to comply. In its opinion, the law violated the due process clause of the Fifth Amendment encompassing the liberty to enter into salary contracts with employees.[8]

Because of delay at the lower court level, the case did not reach the Supreme Court until 1923. An attorney for the wage board, assisted by NCL attorney (and future Supreme Court justice) Felix Frankfurter and other NCL staffers, sought to defend the 1918 law on grounds similar to Brandeis's in *Muller*. They offered the Court "impressive documentation on the cost of living and the desirability of good wages."

MR. JUSTICE SUTHERLAND delivered the opinion of the Court.

The statute now under consideration is attacked upon the ground that it authorizes an unconstitutional interference with the freedom of contract included within the

8. Because the District of Columbia is not a state, the due process clause of the Fourteenth Amendment did not apply.

guaranties of the due process clause of the 5th Amendment. That the right to contract about one's affairs is a part of the liberty of the individual protected by this clause is settled by the decisions of this court, and is no longer open to question. . . .

There is, of course, no such thing as absolute freedom of contract. It is subject to a great variety of restraints. But freedom of contract is, nevertheless, the general rule and restraint the exception; and the exercise of legislative authority to abridge it can be justified only by the existence of exceptional circumstances. . . .

[The statute under consideration] is simply and exclusively a price-fixing law, confined to adult women . . . who are legally as capable of contracting for themselves as men. It forbids two parties having lawful capacity—under penalties as to the employer—to freely contract with one another in respect of the price for which one shall render service to the other in a purely private employment. . . .

The feature of this statute which, perhaps more than any other, puts upon it the stamp of invalidity is that it exacts from the employer an arbitrary payment for a purpose and upon a basis having no causal connection with his business, or the contract, or the work the employee engages to do. The declared basis . . . is not the value of the service rendered, but the extraneous circumstance that the employee needs to get a prescribed sum of money to insure her subsistence, health, and morals. . . . The moral requirement, implicit in every contract of employment, viz., that the amount to be paid and the service to be rendered shall bear to each other some relation of just equivalence, is completely ignored. The necessities of the employee are alone considered, and these arise outside of the employment, are the same when there is no employment, and as great in one occupation as in another. Certainly the employer, by paying a fair equivalent for the service rendered, though not sufficient to support the employee, has neither caused nor contributed to her poverty. . . . A statute requiring an employer to pay in money, to pay at prescribed and regular intervals, to pay the value of the services rendered, even to pay with fair relation to the extent of the benefit obtained from the service, would be understandable. But a statute which prescribes payment without regard to any of these things, and solely with relation to circumstances apart from the contract of employment, the business affected by it, and the work done under it, is so clearly the product of a naked, arbitrary exercise of power, that it cannot be allowed to stand under the Constitution of the United States. . . .

It has been said that legislation of the kind now under review is required in the interest of social justice, for whose ends freedom of contract may lawfully be subjected to restraint. The liberty of the individual to do as he pleases, even in innocent matters, is not absolute. It must frequently yield to the common good, and the line beyond which the power of interference may not be pressed is neither definite nor unalterable, but may be made to move, within limits not well defined, with changing need and circumstance. Any attempt to fix a rigid boundary would be unwise as well as futile. But, nevertheless, there are limits to the power, and when these have been passed, it becomes the plain duty of the courts, in the proper exercise of their authority, to so declare. To sustain the individual freedom of action contemplated by the Constitution is not to strike down the common good, but to exalt it; for surely the good of society as a whole cannot be better served than by the preservation against arbitrary restraint of the liberties of its constituent members.

It follows from what has been said that the act in question passes the limit prescribed by the Constitution, and, accordingly, the decrees of the court below are affirmed.

MR. CHIEF JUSTICE TAFT, dissenting.

I regret much to differ from the court in these cases. . . .

The right of the Legislature under the Fifth and Fourteenth Amendments to limit the hours of employment on the score of the health of the employee, it seems to me, has been firmly established. As to that, one would think, the line had been pricked out so that it has become a well formulated rule. In *Holden v. Hardy* it was applied to miners and rested on the unfavorable environment of employment in mining and smelting. In *Lochner v. New York* it was held that restricting those employed in bakeries to 10 hours a day was an arbitrary and invalid interference with the liberty of contract secured by the Fourteenth Amendment. Then followed a number of cases beginning with *Muller v. Oregon*, sustaining the validity of a limit on maximum hours of labor for women to which I shall hereafter allude, and following these cases came *Bunting v. Oregon*. In that case, this court sustained a law limiting the hours of labor of any person, whether man or woman, working in any mill, factory, or manufacturing establishment to 10 hours a day with a proviso as to further hours to which I shall hereafter advert. The law covered the whole field of industrial employment and certainly covered the case of persons employed in bakeries. Yet the opinion in the *Bunting* Case does not mention the *Lochner* Case. No one can suggest any constitutional distinction between employment in a bakery and one in any other kind of a manufacturing establishment which should make a limit of hours in the one invalid, and the same limit in the other permissible. It is impossible for me to reconcile the *Bunting* Case and the *Lochner* Case, and I have always supposed that the *Lochner* Case was thus overruled *sub silentio*. . . .

I am authorized to say that Mr. Justice SANFORD concurs in this opinion.

MR. JUSTICE HOLMES, dissenting.

The question in this case is the broad one, whether Congress can establish minimum rates of wages for women in the District of Columbia, with due provision for special circumstances, or whether we must say that Congress has no power to meddle with the matter at all. To me, notwithstanding the deference due to the prevailing judgment of the court, the power of Congress seems absolutely free from doubt. The end—to remove conditions leading to ill health, immorality, and the deterioration of the race—no one would deny to be within the scope of constitutional legislation. The means are means that have the approval of Congress, of many states, and of those governments from which we have learned our greatest lessons. When so many intelligent persons, who have studied the matter more than any of us can, have thought that the means are effective and are worth the price, it seems to me impossible to deny that the belief reasonably may be held by reasonable men. . . . [T]he only objection that can be urged is found within the vague contours of the 5th Amendment, prohibiting the depriving any person of liberty or property without due process of law. To that I turn.

The earlier decisions upon the same words in the 14th Amendment began within our memory, and went no farther than an unpretentious assertion of the liberty to follow the ordinary callings. Later that innocuous generality was expanded into the dogma, Liberty of Contract. Contract is not specially mentioned in the text that we have to construe. It is merely an example of doing what you want to do, embodied in the word "liberty." But pretty much all law consists in forbidding men to do some things that they want to do, and contract is no more exempt from law than other acts. . . .

I confess that I do not understand the principle on which the power to fix a minimum for the wages of women can be denied by those who admit the power to fix a maximum for their hours of work. I fully assent to the proposition that here, as elsewhere, the distinctions of the law are distinctions of degree; but I perceive no difference in the kind or degree of interference with liberty, the only matter with which we have any concern, between the one case and the other. The bargain is equally affected whichever half you regulate. . . .

I am of opinion that the statute is valid.

Adkins represented the return of substantive due process; indeed, it made clear that *Muller* and *Bunting* were not major breaks from that doctrine. If anything, as Justice Holmes wrote in his *Adkins* dissent, it had come back stronger than ever with the term "due process of law" evolving into the "dogma, Liberty of Contract."

Why the change? In large measure, it can be traced back to the political climate of the day. Following World War I, the U.S. economy boomed, and voters elected one president after another committed to a free market

economy. These presidents, in turn, appointed justices, at least some of whom shared their economic point of view. Warren Harding made the first four of these new Supreme Court appointments. As scholar Clement E. Vose noted, "The most important single fact about the Harding appointments was that he named two ardent conservatives of the old school—Sutherland and Butler—to serve along with two justices similarly committed who were already sitting—Van Devanter and McReynolds."[9] By 1922 the Four Horsemen were all in place.

The entrenchment of substantive due process, as we mentioned at the beginning of this chapter, was but one manifestation of the impact of Supreme Court appointments by Republican presidents. With their stronger commitment to an utterly free market, these conservative justices also invoked creative theories of the limits of national power, especially dual federalism, to strike down federal regulatory efforts. In the hands of these business-oriented justices, the doctrines of dual federalism and substantive due process, along with a very restrictive view of the commerce clause, served as powerful weapons against state and federal regulatory legislation.

THE DEPRESSION, THE NEW DEAL, AND THE DECLINE OF SUBSTANTIVE DUE PROCESS

The laissez-faire approach of the Court through the 1920s was in keeping with the times. The nation continued to boom and to elect politicians—President Herbert Hoover, for example—who were committed to a private sector–based economy that they were convinced would remain successful if left free from regulation. The Great Depression, triggered by the stock market crash of 1929, and the subsequent election of Franklin Roosevelt demonstrate just how quickly that perception changed. Roosevelt's election indicated the desire of the citizenry for greater regulation to get the nation back on its feet.

At first, it appeared as if the Court, although dominated by Republican-appointed justices, might go along with the Depression-fighting regulatory efforts of the

---

9. Clement E. Vose, *Constitutional Change* (Lexington, Mass.: Lexington Books, 1972), 194.

new administration and of the states, which in part would require a repudiation of substantive due process. How could states exercise any control over employers if the Court continued to strike down the legislatures' efforts on "liberty of contract" grounds?

This was a central question in *Nebbia v. New York* (1934), and here the Court upheld a state law that created the Milk Control Board, which was empowered to fix retail milk prices. By a 5–4 vote, the justices rejected a substantive due process argument that the law unconstitutionally deprived the seller and the buyer of the freedom to negotiate the terms of a sale. Justice Owen Roberts, writing for the majority, seemed to invoke the spirit of Chief Justice Waite's opinion in *Munn v. Illinois:* Milk was so important to the life and health of the community that its sale was "affected with the public interest" and therefore subject to regulation.

But the Court was not yet ready to relent altogether from the substantive due process doctrines of *Lochner* and *Adkins.* Just two years after *Nebbia,* the Court heard arguments in *Morehead v. New York ex rel. Tipaldo* (1936), involving a challenge to a New York statute setting minimum wage standards for women. The Court struck down the law. Writing for a majority of five, Justice Butler was just as emphatic on the subject of substantive due process as the *Adkins* Court had been: "Freedom of contract is the general rule and restraint the exception." This decision strongly reinforced the doctrine of substantive due process, but the Court's rejection of that theory was just around the corner.

West Coast Hotel v. Parrish:
The End of Substantive Due Process

The Court's refusal to uphold federal New Deal legislation, as you recall from chapter 7, angered President Roosevelt. Its ruling in *Morehead* cut even deeper. Peter Irons wrote, "More than any other decision by the Court during the New Deal period, *Morehead* unleashed a barrage of criticism from conservatives as well as from liberals" who sympathized with the plight of women and children workers.[10] Even the Republican Party's 1936

platform included a plank supporting adoption of minimum wage and maximum hour laws of the sort struck in *Morehead.*

Amid all this pressure, including Roosevelt's Court-packing scheme, the Court did a major about-face on the constitutionality of New Deal programs. As part of that change came what would be the demise of the doctrine of substantive due process in *West Coast Hotel v. Parrish.*

West Coast Hotel v. Parrish

300 U.S. 379 (1937)
http://laws.findlaw.com/US/300/379.html
Vote: 5 *(Brandeis, Cardozo, Hughes, Roberts, Stone)*
      4 *(Butler, McReynolds, Sutherland, Van Devanter)*
Opinion of the Court: Hughes
Dissenting opinion: Sutherland

Elsie Parrish had worked as a chambermaid in a hotel in Washington State for a wage of 22 cents to 25 cents per hour.[11] When she was discharged in 1935, she asked the management for back pay of $216.19, the difference between what she had received and what she would have gotten if the hotel had abided by the Washington wage board's minimum wage rate of $14.30 per week.

The hotel offered her $17.00, but Parrish refused to settle and brought suit against it. She found an attorney willing to represent her, but the attorney could not generate much interest in her case among outside organizations. Even the National Consumers' League declined to participate, viewing the effort as a waste of time in light of *Morehead.*

MR. CHIEF JUSTICE HUGHES delivered the opinion of the Court.

This case presents the question of the constitutional validity of the minimum wage law of the State of Washington. . . .

---

10. Peter Irons, *The New Deal Lawyers* (Princeton: Princeton University Press, 1982), 278.

11. For a more thorough discussion of this case, see William E. Leuchtenburg, "The Case of the Wenatchee Chambermaid," in *Quarrels That Have Shaped the Constitution,* ed. John A. Garraty (New York: Harper and Row, 1987).

The appellant relies upon the decision of this Court in *Adkins v. Children's Hospital,* which held invalid the District of Columbia Minimum Wage Act which was attacked under the due process clause of the Fifth Amendment. . . .

. . . The Supreme Court of Washington has upheld the minimum wage statute of that State. It has decided that the statute is a reasonable exercise of the police power of the State. In reaching that conclusion the state court has invoked principles long established by this Court in the application of the Fourteenth Amendment. The state court has refused to regard the decision in the *Adkins* Case as determinative and has pointed to our decisions both before and since that case as justifying its position. We are of the opinion that this ruling of the state court demands on our part a reexamination of the *Adkins* Case. The importance of the question, in which many States having similar laws are concerned, the close division by which the decision in the *Adkins* Case was reached, and the economic conditions which have supervened, and in the light of which the reasonableness of the exercise of the protective power of the State must be considered, make it not only appropriate, but we think imperative, that in deciding the present case the subject should receive fresh consideration. . . .

The principle which must control our decision is not in doubt. The constitutional provision invoked is the due process clause of the Fourteenth Amendment governing the States, as the due process clause invoked in the *Adkins* Case governed Congress. In each case the violation alleged by those attacking minimum wage regulation for women is deprivation of freedom of contract. What is this freedom? The Constitution does not speak of freedom of contract. It speaks of liberty and prohibits the deprivation of liberty without due process of law. In prohibiting that deprivation the Constitution does not recognize an absolute and uncontrollable liberty. Liberty in each of its phases has its history and connotation. But the liberty safeguarded is liberty in a social organization which requires the protection of law against the evils which menace the health, safety, morals and welfare of the people. Liberty under the Constitution is thus necessarily subject to the restraints of due process, and regulation which is reasonable in relation to its subject and is adopted in the interests of the community is due process.

This essential limitation of liberty in general governs freedom of contract in particular. More than twenty-five years ago we set forth the applicable principle in these words

after referring to the cases where the liberty guaranteed by the Fourteenth Amendment had been broadly described:

"But it was recognized in the cases cited, as in many others, that freedom of contract is a qualified and not an absolute right. There is no absolute freedom to do as one wills or to contract as one chooses. The guaranty of liberty does not withdraw from legislative supervision that wide department of activity which consists of the making of contracts, or deny to government the power to provide restrictive safeguards. Liberty implies the absence of arbitrary restraint, not immunity from reasonable regulations and prohibitions imposed in the interests of the community."

This power under the Constitution to restrict freedom of contract has had many illustrations. That it may be exercised in the public interest with respect to contracts between employer and employee is undeniable. . . . In dealing with the relation of employer and employed, the legislature has necessarily a wide field of discretion in order that there may be suitable protection of health and safety, and that peace and good order may be promoted through regulations designed to insure wholesome conditions of work and freedom from oppression.

The point that has been strongly stressed that adult employees should be deemed competent to make their own contracts was decisively met nearly forty years ago in *Holden v. Hardy,* where we pointed out the inequality in the footing of the parties. . . .

It is manifest that this established principle is peculiarly applicable in relation to the employment of women in whose protection the State has a special interest. That phase of the subject received elaborate consideration in *Muller v. Oregon* (1908). . . . In later rulings this Court sustained the regulation of hours of work of women employees.

This array of precedents and the principles they applied were thought by the dissenting Justices in the *Adkins* Case to demand that the minimum wage statute be sustained. The validity of the distinction made by the Court between a minimum wage and a maximum of hours in limiting liberty of contract was especially challenged. That challenge persists and is without any satisfactory answer. . . .

One of the points which was pressed by the Court in supporting its ruling in the *Adkins* Case was that the standard set up by the District of Columbia Act did not take appropriate account of the value of the services rendered. In the *Morehead* Case, the minority thought that the New York statute had met that point in its definition of a "fair wage" and that it accordingly presented a distinguishable feature which the Court could recognize within the limits which the *Morehead* petition for certiorari was deemed to present. The Court, however, did not take that view and the New York Act was held to be essentially the same as that for the District of Columbia. The statute now before us is like the latter, but we are unable to conclude that in its minimum wage requirement the State has passed beyond the boundary of its broad protective power.

The minimum wage to be paid under the Washington statute is fixed after full consideration by representatives of employers, employees and the public. It may be assumed that the minimum wage is fixed in consideration of the services that are performed in the particular occupations under normal conditions. Provision is made for special licenses at less wages in the case of women who are incapable of full service. The statement of Mr. Justice Holmes in the *Adkins* Case is pertinent: "This statute does not compel anybody to pay anything. It simply forbids employment at rates below those fixed as the minimum requirement of health and right living. It is safe to assume that women will not be employed at even the lowest wages allowed unless they earn them, or unless the employer's business can sustain the burden. In short the law in its character and operation is like hundreds of so-called police laws that have been upheld." . . .

We think that the views thus expressed are sound and that the decision in the *Adkins* Case was a departure from the true application of the principles governing the regulation by the State of the relation of employer and employed. Those principles have been reenforced by our subsequent decisions. . . .

With full recognition of the earnestness and vigor which characterize the prevailing opinion in the *Adkins* Case, we find it impossible to reconcile that ruling with these well-considered declarations. What can be closer to the public interest than the health of women and their protection from unscrupulous and overreaching employers? And if the protection of women is a legitimate end of the exercise of state power, how can it be said that the requirement of the payment of a minimum wage fairly fixed in order to meet the very necessities of existence is not an admissible means to that end? The legislature of the State was clearly entitled to

consider the situation of women in employment, the fact that they are in the class receiving the least pay, that their bargaining power is relatively weak, and that they are the ready victims of those who would take advantage of their necessitous circumstances. The legislature was entitled to adopt measures to reduce the evils of the "sweating system," the exploiting of workers at wages so low as to be insufficient to meet the bare cost of living, thus making their very helplessness the occasion of a most injurious competition. The legislature had the right to consider that its minimum wage requirements would be an important aid in carrying out its policy of protection. The adoption of similar requirements by many States evidences a deep-seated conviction both as to the presence of the evil and as to the means adapted to check it. Legislative response to the conviction cannot be regarded as arbitrary or capricious and that is all we have to decide. Even if the wisdom of the policy be regarded as debatable and its effects uncertain, still the legislature is entitled to its judgment.

There is an additional and compelling consideration which recent economic experience has brought into a strong light. The exploitation of a class of workers who are in an unequal position with respect to bargaining power and are thus relatively defenceless against the denial of a living wage is not only detrimental to their health and well-being but casts a direct burden for their support upon the community. What these workers lose in wages the taxpayers are called upon to pay. The bare cost of living must be met. We may take judicial notice of the unparalleled demands for relief which arose during the recent period of depression and still continue to an alarming extent despite the degree of economic recovery which has been achieved. It is unnecessary to cite official statistics to establish what is of common knowledge through the length and breadth of the land. While in the instant case no factual brief has been presented, there is no reason to doubt that the State of Washington has encountered the same social problem that is present elsewhere. The community is not bound to provide what is in effect a subsidy for unconscionable employers. The community may direct its law-making power to correct the abuse which springs from their selfish disregard of the public interest. The argument that the legislation in question constitutes an arbitrary discrimination, because it does not extend to men, is unavailing. This Court has frequently held that the legislative authority, acting within its proper field, is not bound to extend its regulation to all cases which it might possibly reach. The legislature "is free to recognize degrees of harm and it may confine its restrictions to those classes of cases where the need is deemed to be clearest." . . .

Our conclusion is that the case of *Adkins v. Children's Hospital* should be, and it is, overruled. The judgment of the Supreme Court of the State of Washington is affirmed.

MR. JUSTICE SUTHERLAND, dissenting:

MR. JUSTICE VAN DEVANTER, MR. JUSTICE MCREYNOLDS, MR. JUSTICE BUTLER, and I think the judgment of the court below should be reversed. . . .

Coming, then, to a consideration of the Washington statute, it first is to be observed that it is in every substantial respect identical with the statute involved in the *Adkins* Case. Such vices as existed in the latter are present in the former. And if the *Adkins* Case was properly decided, as we who join in this opinion think it was, it necessarily follows that the Washington statute is invalid. . . .

That the clause of the Fourteenth Amendment which forbids a state to deprive any person of life, liberty, or property without due process of law includes freedom of contract is so well settled as to be no longer open to question. Nor reasonably can it be disputed that contracts of employment of labor are included in the rule. . . .

In the *Adkins* Case we referred to this language, and said that while there was no such thing as absolute freedom of contract, but that it was subject to a great variety of restraints, nevertheless, freedom of contract was the general rule and restraint the exception; and that the power to abridge that freedom could only be justified by the existence of exceptional circumstances. This statement of the rule has been many times affirmed; and we do not understand that it is questioned by the present decision.

The Washington statute, like the one for the District of Columbia, fixes minimum wages for adult women. Adult men and their employers are left free to bargain as they please; and it is a significant and an important fact that all state statutes to which our attention has been called are of like character. The common-law rules restricting the power of women to make contracts have, under our system, long since practically disappeared. Women today stand upon a

legal and political equality with men. There is no longer any reason why they should be put in different classes in respect of their legal right to make contracts; nor should they be denied, in effect, the right to compete with men for work paying lower wages which men may be willing to accept. And it is an arbitrary exercise of the legislative power to do so.

The Aftermath of West Coast Hotel

West Coast Hotel was an explicit repudiation of economic substantive due process. In one fell swoop, the justices overruled *Adkins* and changed the way the Court would view state regulatory efforts.

The modern Court has adopted a rational basis test that "starts with the assumption that legislation bears some rational relation to a state's legitimate powers and places the burden on opponents to prove there is no conceivable rational relationship between the statute or regulation and a legitimate function of government." [12] Indeed, since 1937 the Court has rejected virtually all due process challenges to state economic regulatory efforts. One reason for these decisions is the nature of the current legal test: It is extremely difficult for attorneys to demonstrate "no conceivable rational relationship" between a challenged law and legitimate government function. The contemporary Court generally refuses to determine what is and is not in the public interest or what is and is not rational.

Williamson v. Lee Optical Company (1955) provides a good example of how the Court now treats Fourteenth Amendment economic claims. Here, the Court upheld a 1953 Oklahoma law that made it "unlawful for any person . . . to fit, adjust, adapt, or to apply . . . lenses, frames . . . or any other optical appliances to the face," unless that person was a licensed ophthalmologist, "a physician who specializes in the care of eyes," or an optometrist, "one who examines eyes for refractory error . . . and fills prescriptions." It did so even though the justices

12. Malcolm M. Feeley and Samuel Krislov, *Constitutional Law,* 2nd ed. (Glenview, Ill.: Scott, Foresman, 1990), 336.

thought that the "law may exact a needless, wasteful requirement in many cases." But, as Justice William O. Douglas noted in his majority opinion, "[I]t is for the legislature, not the courts, to balance the advantages and disadvantages of the new requirement." Moreover, he said "The day is gone when this Court uses the Due Process Clause of the Fourteenth Amendment to strike down state laws, regulatory of business and industrial conditions, because they may be unwise, improvident, or out of harmony with a particular school of thought." The Court even quoted from Waite's opinion in *Munn:* "For protection against abuses by legislatures the people must resort to the polls, not to the courts."

Although *Williamson* was decided in 1955, it continues to characterize the Court's thinking on substantive due process. In **Pennell v. City of San Jose** (1988) the Court rejected the claims of a landlord who sought to invalidate a city rent control scheme on substantive due process grounds. In applying a rational basis standard, Chief Justice William Rehnquist concluded, "We have long recognized that a legitimate and rational goal of price or rate regulation is the protection of consumer welfare."

This is not to say that substantive due process has disappeared altogether. In fact, we have seen it reemerge in at least two different contexts. The first is the issue of excessive monetary damages awarded by juries. In **BMW of North America v. Gore** (1996) the justices reviewed the outcome of a dispute between an automobile company and the purchaser of one of its cars. Ira Gore bought a new BMW from a dealership in Alabama. He later discovered that his car had been repainted prior to his purchase. He sued the manufacturer, claiming that it had failed to disclose the repainting and therefore should make a reasonable adjustment to the sales price. The jury decided in his favor, finding that the automobile was worth $4,000 less than if it had not been repainted. In addition to the $4,000 in compensatory damages, the jury awarded Gore another $4,000,000 because it found that BMW's nondisclosure policy amounted to "gross, oppressive, or malicious" fraud. The state supreme court reduced these punitive damages to $2,000,000, and

BMW appealed to the Supreme Court, arguing that the jury award was so excessive as to violate due process of law. Over the objections of four dissenters who criticized the Court's use of substantive due process as a guide, the majority held that grossly unreasonable jury awards are contrary to the Fourteenth Amendment. The Court has continued to apply this reasoning to subsequent jury award appeals.

The second context in which the doctrine of substantive due process retains some relevance is in the Court's interpretation of personal privacy rights. Indeed, at least some of the justices in the majority of *Griswold v. Connecticut* (1965), in which the Court struck a Connecticut law prohibiting the disbursement of birth control and established a right to privacy, did so on substantive due process grounds. Justice John Harlan wrote in a concurring opinion:

In my view, the proper constitutional inquiry in this case is whether this Connecticut statute infringes the Due Process Clause of the Fourteenth Amendment because the enactment violates basic values "implicit in the concept of ordered liberty." . . . The Due Process Clause of the Fourteenth Amendment stands, in my opinion, on its own bottom.

Furthermore, Justice Harry A. Blackmun's 1973 opinion in *Roe v. Wade* legalizing abortion during the first two trimesters of pregnancy also invoked the due process clause:

[The] right of privacy, whether it be founded in the Fourteenth Amendment's concept of personal liberty and restrictions upon state action, as we feel it is, or [another clause] . . . is broad enough to encompass a woman's decision whether or not to terminate her pregnancy.

That the *Roe* right rests, in part, on the due process clause has been a source of contention among legal scholars. Some, such as John Hart Ely, accuse Blackmun of "*Lochner*-ing," of returning to a discredited theory of individual rights as the peg on which to hang abortion rights. Others point out the difference between *Lochner* and *Roe* in the nature of the rights at issue.

Either way, it is true that the doctrine—so exalted at the beginning of the twentieth century and so rejected in the post–New Deal period—has had a significant effect on the course of the law. What could have simply faded out of existence with Miller's *Slaughterhouse* opinion became the source of one of the most interesting episodes in constitutional law.

READINGS

Barnett, Randy E. *Restoring the Lost Constitution: The Presumption of Liberty.* Princeton: Princeton University Press, 2003.

Berger, Raoul. *Government by Judiciary.* Cambridge: Harvard University Press, 1977.

Cortner, Richard C. *The Iron Horse and the Constitution: The Railroads and the Transformation of the Fourteenth Amendment.* Westport, Conn.: Greenwood Press, 1993.

Gillman, Howard. *The Constitution Besieged: The Rise and Demise of Lochner Era Police Powers Jurisprudence.* Durham: Duke University Press, 1993.

Hovenkamp, Herbert. *Enterprise and American Law, 1836–1937.* Cambridge: Harvard University Press, 1991.

Jacobs, Clyde E. *Law Writers and the Courts.* Berkeley: University of California Press, 1954.

Keller, Morton. *Affairs of State.* Cambridge: Harvard University Press, 1977.

Kens, Paul. *Judicial Power and Reform Politics: The Anatomy of Lochner v. New York.* Lawrence: University Press of Kansas, 1990.

Keynes, Edward. *Liberty, Property, and Privacy: Toward a Jurisprudence of Substantive Due Process.* University Park: Pennsylvania State University Press, 1996.

Paul, Arnold M. *Conservative Crisis and the Rule of Law.* Ithaca: Cornell University Press, 1960.

Phillips, Michal J. *The Lochner Court, Myth and Reality: Substantive Due Process from the 1890s to the 1930s.* Westport, Conn.: Praeger, 2001.

Strong, Frank R. *Substantive Due Process of Law: A Dichotomy of Sense and Nonsense.* Durham: Carolina Academic Press, 1986.

Swindler, William F. *Court and Constitution in the Twentieth Century.* 3 vols. Indianapolis: Bobbs-Merrill, 1970.

Vose, Clement E. *Constitutional Change.* Lexington, Mass.: Lexington Books, 1972.

Wolfe, Christopher. *The Rise of Modern Judicial Review.* New York: Basic Books, 1986.

CHAPTER 11
THE TAKINGS CLAUSE

One day a certified letter arrives at your house informing you that the government has decided to construct a new highway and your property lies directly in its path. The letter further states that in return for your property the government will pay you $200,000—an amount it considers "fair market value" for your home. Finally, the letter instructs you to vacate the house within six months.

Does the government have the right to seize your property in this fashion? What if this house has been in your family for five generations and you do not want to sell? What if this is your dream house, just completed after years of saving and sacrificing? If you believe the government has offered much less than the property is worth, can you challenge the amount offered? What about your rights to private property? Do they mean anything?

The general answer to these questions is that the government indeed has the right to seize private property for a public purpose, such as a new road. This authority is referred to as the power of eminent domain. When federal, state, or local governments embark on new construction projects for roads, schools, military bases, or government offices, private property usually must be acquired. Sometimes only a single parcel or two needs to be obtained, but at other times a massive condemnation of property is necessary. Although the property owner may feel mistreated when the government seizes the land, such government power is generally regarded as justified. Moreover, property owners have an important protection. The

Constitution contains a provision, known as the takings clause, that checks the authority of the government against the individual's right to property.

PROTECTING PRIVATE POVERTY FROM GOVERNMENT SEIZURE

When the Bill of Rights is mentioned, we almost automatically think of liberties such as freedom of speech, press, and religion, or the protections against unfair criminal procedures. But when the members of the First Congress proposed a listing of those rights considered important enough to merit constitutional protection, they included in the Fifth Amendment a significant private property guarantee—the takings clause—which states, "nor shall private property be taken for public use, without just compensation."

That the framers would have protected private property in this way is not surprising. The men who fashioned the U.S. Constitution were firm believers in private property rights, but they also supported a national government that would be stronger than it had been under the Articles of Confederation. The takings clause acknowledges that government projects sometimes require the seizure of private property. Without the power of eminent domain, individuals could block government programs, such as the interstate highway system, by refusing to sell property to the government or demanding unreasonable compensation, holding the government project for ransom. But James Madison, the primary author of the Bill of Rights, rejected the notion that government should have the absolute power to confiscate private property.[1] The takings clause was intended to moderate that authority by ensuring that property owners would not be unduly disadvantaged when the government seized their land. It guarantees that the owner will be fairly compensated for the loss. As Justice Hugo Black explained, the takings clause "was designed to bar Government from forcing some people to bear public burdens which, in all fairness and justice, should be borne by the public as a whole."[2]

Because many states already protected private property against state government seizures, the takings clause was intended to apply only to federal government confiscations. This interpretation was endorsed by the Supreme Court in the case of **Barron v. Baltimore** in 1833. The dispute arose when the city of Baltimore initiated a series of street improvements, which also necessitated the alteration of several small streams. As a result, large amounts of sand and dirt were swept downstream into Baltimore Harbor, causing serious problems for the owners of wharves operating there. John Barron and John Craig were particularly damaged. Their wharf had been very profitable because its deep water location enabled them to service large ships. The accumulation of silt and waste near their wharf was so great that the water became too shallow for large vessels, and Barron and Craig lost considerable business. They demanded compensation from the city for their loss. When the city refused, they sued, asking for $20,000 in damages. The local court awarded them $4,500, but a state appellate court reversed the decision of the lower court. Barron and Craig appealed to the U.S. Supreme Court.

They claimed that the city's construction caused their wharf's loss of profitability. That constituted a "taking" under the meaning of the Fifth Amendment, and they deserved "just compensation." The justices, however, were not concerned with questions of whether a taking had occurred or what constituted just compensation. Instead, the Court focused on a more fundamental issue: Did the Fifth Amendment apply to state actions at all?

The Court concluded that it did not. In the words of Chief Justice John Marshall:

We are of opinion that the provision in the fifth amendment to the constitution, declaring that private property shall not be taken for public use without just compensation, is intended solely as a limitation on the exercise of power by the government of the United States, and is not applicable to the legislation of the states.[3]

For the next half century this interpretation remained the law of the land. The takings clause applied only to the federal government. If states did not impose similar restraints on themselves, they were free to exercise the power of eminent domain without providing adequate compensation to landowners whose property had been seized.

In the late 1800s, prompted by the ratification of the Fourteenth Amendment, the Court began to reconsider this position. The due process clause of the Fourteenth Amendment, you will recall, states, "nor shall any state deprive any person of life, liberty, or property, without due process of law." Lawyers began arguing that when states confiscated private property without giving the owners adequate compensation they were depriving the owners of property without due process of law, a violation of the Fourteenth Amendment.

The Supreme Court adopted this position in **Chicago, Burlington, and Quincy Railroad Company v. Chicago** (1897). The justices held that the takings clause of the U.S. Constitution was binding not only upon the federal government but also upon state and local governments. It affirmed the government's power of eminent domain, but required the payment of adequate compensation whenever that power was exercised.[4] With this ruling, the takings clause became the first provision of the Bill of Rights to be made binding on the states.

---

1. James W. Ely Jr., *The Guardian of Every Other Right: A Constitutional History of Property Rights* (New York: Oxford University Press, 1992), 55.

2. *Armstrong v. United States* (1960).

3. The implications of this decision went far beyond the takings clause issue. In ruling as it did, the Supreme Court held that the states did not have to abide by any of the provisions of the Bill of Rights, that those sections of the Constitution limited federal government actions only. The states were governed only by their own bills of rights. Over time the Court incrementally changed its position (through a process known as "selective incorporation"), but it took more than 130 years for it to conclude that the states were bound by *almost* all the provisions of the Bill of Rights.

4. See David A. Schultz, *Property, Power, and American Democracy* (New Brunswick, N.J.: Transaction, 1992).

The authority of government to take private property in order to carry out legitimate projects is now well established. The most common issue that flows from government takings cases is what constitutes "just compensation." In the normal course of events, the government attempts to buy the necessary land from the owners. If negotiations fail, the government may declare the power of eminent domain and take the property, giving the owners what it thinks is a fair price. Fair market value is usually the appropriate standard, but it is not uncommon for owners to argue that the government's offer is inadequate. In such situations the owners may go to court to challenge the amount. Questions of just compensation normally are settled through negotiation or trial court action and rarely involve issues of significance beyond the specific land under dispute.[5] Although legal battles may be fought over whether the offered compensation is just, there is no doubt about the power of the government to seize the property.

Of greater importance are two questions of more general significance in understanding the meaning of the Fifth Amendment takings clause: What is a taking and what constitutes a public use? Both questions have required authoritative answers by the Supreme Court.

WHAT CONSTITUTES A TAKING?

In most cases it is relatively easy to determine that a taking has occurred. If the federal government decides to build a new post office and must acquire a piece of privately owned property upon which to build, a taking is necessary if a voluntary sale is not negotiated. Similarly, a taking occurs when, to complete a water control project, the government will need to dam certain streams and cause privately owned land to become permanently flooded. In these situations private land is totally taken by the government and is used for a public purpose.

There is no question that the individual has been deprived of ownership rights over the property.

But a taking may also occur if the government engages in some activity that destroys the use of private property without physically seizing it. **United States v. Causby** (1946) arose when the federal government built a military airfield within 2,300 feet of a North Carolina chicken farm. The planes flew just sixty-seven feet above the farmhouse. The constant noise and commotion as the planes took off and landed caused considerable disruption on the farm. The chickens became less productive, and many died when they flew into the walls of their coops out of fear and panic. In short, the property was no longer suitable for raising chickens.

The Supreme Court held that the government had "taken" this property. The path of the airplanes was so low and so close to the farm and residence as to deprive the owners of the use and enjoyment of their land. There was a diminution of the property's value that was directly and immediately attributable to the government's actions. Under such circumstances a taking has occurred and the landowners deserve compensation.

How far can the definition of a taking be legitimately extended? After all, every time the government passes a law regulating the use of property, the rights of owners are diminished. Does regulation constitute a taking? Justice Oliver Wendell Holmes addressed this question in **Pennsylvania Coal Co. v. Mahon** (1922). For Holmes, the answer depended upon the extent of the regulation: "The general rule at least is, that while property may be regulated to a certain extent, if regulation goes too far it will be recognized as a taking." Holmes feared that given too much discretion the government might regulate "until the last private property disappears."[6]

Generally, government regulation that only incidentally infringes on the owner's use of property is not considered a taking; nor is regulation that outlaws the noxious or dangerous use of property. Obvious examples are zoning laws or other regulatory ordinances that make certain uses unlawful.[7] Owners may be distressed that they can no longer use their property in particular ways, but the Supreme Court has held that such statutes do not

---

5. Although disputes over compensation levels normally are settled at the trial court level, occasionally such controversies involve significant issues and large amounts of money. In *United States v. Sioux Nation of Indians* (1980) the Supreme Court settled a long-standing dispute over the abrogation of the Fort Laramie Treaty of 1868. The treaty had established the right of the Sioux nation to the Black Hills, but an 1877 act of Congress essentially took back those lands. The Court ruled that the treaty abrogation was governed by the takings clause and that the Sioux were entitled to the value of the land in 1877 plus 5 percent annual interest since that year, amounting to a total claim of some $100 million.

6. See Ely, *The Guardian of Every Other Right*, chap. 6.
7. See *Agins v. City of Tiburon* (1980).

constitute a Fifth Amendment taking that deserves compensation. For example, the justices ruled that takings did not occur when a state ordered property owners to cut down standing cedar trees because a disease carried by the cedars threatened nearby apple orchards; when a local government passed an ordinance removing an individual's right to use his land as a brickyard, a use seen as inconsistent with the surrounding neighborhood; and when for safety reasons a city prohibited a person from mining sand and gravel on his land.[8] In these and numerous similar cases the government's action significantly reduced the way the land could be used and decreased its commercial value, yet the Court held that a taking had not occurred. Instead, these government policies were instituted in response to social, economic, or environmental problems that could be addressed through the use of the government's police powers.

The questions of how far such regulation may go and for what reasons were addressed in *Penn Central Transportation Company v. City of New York* (1978). The issue is important. If the government imposes regulations that seriously curtail the economic use of the property, has a taking occurred? Although Justice William Brennan's opinion acknowledges that this area of the law has proved to be one of "considerable difficulty," it presents a good review of the principles the Court has developed to determine when a taking has occurred.

Penn Central Transportation Company v. City of New York

438 U.S. 104 (1978)
http://laws.findlaw.com/US/438/104.html
Oral arguments may be found at: http://www.oyez.org
Vote: 6 (Blackmun, Brennan, Marshall, Powell, Stewart, White)
   3 (Burger, Rehnquist, Stevens)
Opinion of the Court: Brennan
Dissenting opinion: Rehnquist

New York City passed the Landmarks Preservation Law in 1965 as part of an effort to protect historic buildings and districts. Each of the fifty states and more than

8. *Miller v. Schoene* (1928); *Hadacheck v. Los Angeles* (1915); and *Goldblatt v. Hempstead* (1962), respectively.

five hundred cities had similar statutes. The Landmarks Preservation Commission administered the law, and the commission's task was to identify buildings and areas that held special historic or aesthetic value. The buildings were then discussed in hearings to determine whether landmark status should be conferred. If a building or area was designated as historic, the owner's ability to change the property was restricted. Owners of landmark buildings were required to keep the exterior in good repair and not alter the building without securing approval from the commission. Owners of such buildings received no direct compensation, but they were accorded enhanced development rights for other properties.

This case involved the application of the preservation law to Grand Central Terminal, owned by Penn Central Transportation Company. The station opened in 1913 and is widely regarded as an example of ingenious engineering in response to problems presented by modern urban rail stations. It is also cited as a magnificent example of French beaux-arts style. The terminal was designated a historic landmark in 1967, although Penn Central initially opposed the action.

In 1968, to increase revenue, Penn Central entered into an agreement with UGP Properties to build a multistory office building above the terminal. UGP and Penn Central presented two separate plans to the commission for its approval. One of the plans proposed a change in the facade of the building and the construction of a fifty-three-story office tower above it. The other envisioned a fifty-five-story office building cantilevered above the existing facade and resting on the roof of the terminal. The commission rejected both proposals.

In response, Penn Central and UGP filed suit claiming that the application of the Landmark Preservation Law to the terminal constituted a taking of their property without just compensation. The New York courts denied their claims, with the state's highest court rejecting the notion that the property had been "taken" under the meaning of the Fifth Amendment.

MR. JUSTICE BRENNAN delivered the opinion of the Court.

Before considering appellants' specific contentions, it will be useful to review the factors that have shaped the

Artist's conception of a fifty-five story office building to be floated over the waiting room of New York's Grand Central Terminal, which had been designated a historic landmark. Plans for this building, and several others, were rejected by the Landmarks Preservation Commission, and the Supreme Court ruled that such a rejection did not constitute a taking.

jurisprudence of the Fifth Amendment injunction "nor shall private property be taken for public use, without just compensation." The question of what constitutes a "taking" for purposes of the Fifth Amendment has proved to be a problem of considerable difficulty. . . . [T]his Court, quite simply, has been unable to develop any "set formula" for determining when "justice and fairness" require that economic injuries caused by public action be compensated by the government, rather than remain disproportionately concentrated on a few persons. Indeed, we have frequently observed that whether a particular restriction will be rendered invalid by the government's failure to pay for any losses proximately caused by it depends largely "upon the particular circumstances [in that] case."

In engaging in these essentially ad hoc, factual inquiries, the Court's decisions have identified several factors that have particular significance. The economic impact of the regulation on the claimant and, particularly, the extent to which the regulation has interfered with distinct investment-backed expectations are, of course, relevant considerations. So, too, is the character of the government action. A "taking" may more readily be found when the interference with property can be characterized as a physical invasion by the government than when interference arises from some public program adjusting the benefits and burdens of economic life to promote the common good.

"Government hardly could go on if to some extent values incident to property could not be diminished without paying for every such change in the general law," *Pennsylvania Coal Co. v. Mahon* (1922), and this Court has accordingly recognized, in a wide variety of contexts, that government may execute laws or programs that adversely affect recognized economic values. Exercises of the taxing power are one obvious example. A second are the decisions in which this Court has dismissed "taking" challenges on the ground that, while the challenged government action caused economic harm, it did not interfere with interests that were sufficiently bound up with the reasonable expectations of the claimant to constitute "property" for Fifth Amendment purposes.

More importantly for the present case, in instances in which a state tribunal reasonably concluded that "the health, safety, morals, or general welfare" would be promoted by prohibiting particular contemplated uses of land, this Court has upheld land-use regulations that destroyed or adversely affected recognized real property interests. Zoning laws are, of course, the classic example. . . .

Zoning laws generally do not affect existing uses of real property, but "taking" challenges have also been held to be without merit in a wide variety of situations when the challenged governmental actions prohibited a beneficial use to which individual parcels had previously been devoted and thus caused substantial individualized harm. . . .

Pennsylvania Coal Co. v. Mahon (1922) is the leading case for the proposition that a state statute that substantially furthers important public policies may so frustrate distinct investment-backed expectations as to amount to a "taking." There the claimant had sold the surface rights to particular parcels of property, but expressly reserved the right to remove the coal thereunder. A Pennsylvania statute, enacted after the transactions, forbade any mining of coal that caused the subsidence of any house, unless the house was the property of the owner of the underlying coal and was more than 150 feet from the improved property of another. Because the statute made it commercially impracticable to mine the coal, and thus had nearly the same effect as the complete destruction of rights claimant had reserved from the owners of the surface land, the Court held that the statute was invalid as effecting a "taking" without just compensation. . . .

In contending that the New York City law has "taken" their property in violation of the Fifth and Fourteenth Amendments, appellants make a series of arguments, which, while tailored to the facts of this case, essentially urge that any substantial restriction imposed pursuant to a landmark law must be accompanied by just compensation if it is to be constitutional. Before considering these, we emphasize what is not in dispute. Because this Court has recognized in a number of settings, that States and cities may enact land-use restrictions or controls to enhance the quality of life by preserving the character and desirable aesthetic features of a city, appellants do not contest that New York City's objective of preserving structures and areas with special historic, architectural, or cultural significance is an entirely permissible governmental goal. They also do not dispute that the restrictions imposed on its parcel are appropriate means of securing the purposes of the New York City law. Finally, appellants do not challenge any of the specific factual premises of the decision below. They accept for present purposes both that the parcel of land occupied by Grand Central Terminal

must, in its present state, be regarded as capable of earning a reasonable return, and that the transferable development rights afforded the appellants by virtue of the Terminal's designation as a landmark are valuable, even if not as valuable as the rights to construct above the Terminal. In appellants' view none of these factors derogate from their claim that New York City's law has effected a "taking."

They first observe that the airspace above the Terminal is a valuable property interest, citing *United States v. Causby.* They urge that the Landmarks Law has deprived them of any gainful use of their "air rights" above the Terminal and that, irrespective of the value of the remainder of their parcel, the city has "taken" their right to this superadjacent airspace, thus entitling them to "just compensation" measured by the fair market value of these air rights.

Apart from our own disagreement with appellants' characterization of the effect of the New York City law, the submission that appellants may establish a "taking" simply by showing that they have been denied the ability to exploit a property interest that they heretofore had believed was available for development is quite simply untenable. . . . "Taking" jurisprudence does not divide a single parcel into discrete segments and attempt to determine whether rights in a particular segment have been entirely abrogated. In deciding whether a particular governmental action has effected a taking, this Court focuses rather both on the character of the action and on the nature and extent of the interference with rights in the parcel as a whole—here, the city tax block designated as the "landmark site."

Secondly, appellants, focusing on the character and impact of the New York City law, argue that it effects a "taking" because its operation has significantly diminished the value of the Terminal site. Appellants concede that the decisions sustaining other land-use regulations, which, like the New York City law, are reasonably related to the promotion of the general welfare, uniformly reject the proposition that diminution in property value, standing alone, can establish a "taking." . . . [B]ut appellants argue that New York City's regulation of individual landmarks is fundamentally different from zoning or from historic-district legislation because the controls imposed by New York City's law apply only to individuals who own selected properties.

Stated baldly, appellants' position appears to be that the only means of ensuring that selected owners are not singled out to endure financial hardship for no reason is to hold that any restriction imposed on individual landmarks pursuant to the New York City scheme is a "taking" requiring the payment of "just compensation." Agreement with this argument would, of course, invalidate not just New York City's law, but all comparable landmark legislation in the Nation. We find no merit in it. . . .

Equally without merit is the related argument that the decision to designate a structure as a landmark "is inevitably arbitrary or at least subjective, because it is basically a matter of taste," thus unavoidably singling out individual landowners for disparate and unfair treatment. The argument has a particularly hollow ring in this case. . . . [A] landmark owner has a right to judicial review of any Commission decision, and, quite simply, there is no basis whatsoever for a conclusion that courts will have any greater difficulty identifying arbitrary or discriminatory action in the context of landmark regulation than in the context of classic zoning or indeed in any other context. . . .

In any event, appellants' repeated suggestions that they are solely burdened and unbenefited is factually inaccurate. This contention overlooks the fact that the New York City law applies to vast numbers of structures in the city in addition to the Terminal—all the structures contained in the 31 historic districts and over 400 individual landmarks, many of which are close to the Terminal. Unless we are to reject the judgment of the New York City Council that the preservation of landmarks benefits all New York citizens and all structures, both economically and by improving the quality of life in the city as a whole—which we are unwilling to do—we cannot conclude that the owners of the Terminal have in no sense been benefited by the Landmarks Law. . . .

. . . [T]he New York City law does not interfere in any way with the present uses of the Terminal. Its designation as a landmark not only permits but contemplates that appellants may continue to use the property precisely as it has been used for the past 65 years: as a railroad terminal containing office space and concessions. So the law does not interfere with what must be regarded as Penn Central's primary expectation concerning the use of the parcel. More importantly, on this record, we must regard the New York City law as permitting Penn Central not only to profit from the Terminal but also to obtain a "reasonable" return on its investment. . . .

On this record, we conclude that the application of New York City's Landmarks Law has not effected a "taking" of appellants' property. The restrictions imposed are substantially related to the promotion of the general welfare and not only permit reasonable beneficial use of the landmark site but also afford appellants opportunities further to enhance not only the Terminal site proper but also other properties.

Affirmed.

MR. JUSTICE REHNQUIST, with whom the CHIEF JUSTICE, and MR. JUSTICE STEVENS join, dissenting.

Of the over one million buildings and structures in the city of New York, appellees have singled out 400 for designation as official landmarks. The owner of a building might initially be pleased that his property has been chosen by a distinguished committee of architects, historians, and city planners for such a singular distinction. But he may well discover, as appellant Penn Central Transportation Co. did here, that the landmark designation imposes upon him a substantial cost, with little or no offsetting benefit except for the honor of the designation. The question in this case is whether the cost associated with the city of New York's desire to preserve a limited number of "landmarks" within its borders must be borne by all of its taxpayers or whether it can instead be imposed entirely on the owners of the individual properties. . . .

The Fifth Amendment provides in part: "nor shall private property be taken for public use, without just compensation." In a very literal sense, the actions of appellees violated this constitutional prohibition. Before the city of New York declared Grand Central Terminal to be a landmark, Penn Central could have used its "air rights" over the Terminal to build a multistory office building, at an apparent value of several million dollars per year. Today, the Terminal cannot be modified in any form, including the erection of additional stories, without the permission of the Landmark Preservation Commission, a permission which appellants, despite good-faith attempts, have so far been unable to obtain. . . .

As Mr. Justice Holmes pointed out in *Pennsylvania Coal Co. v. Mahon,* "the question at bottom" in an eminent domain case "is upon whom the loss of the changes desired should fall." The benefits that appellees believe will flow from preservation of the Grand Central Terminal will accrue to all the citizens of New York City. There is no reason to believe that appellants will enjoy a substantially greater share of these benefits. If the cost of preserving Grand Central Terminal were spread evenly across the entire population of the city of New York, the burden per person would be in cents per year—a minor cost appellees would surely concede for the benefit accrued. Instead, however, appellees would impose the entire cost of several million dollars per year on Penn Central. But it is precisely this sort of discrimination that the Fifth Amendment prohibits. . . .

Over 50 years ago, Mr. Justice Holmes, speaking for the Court, warned that the courts were "in danger of forgetting that a strong public desire to improve the public condition is not enough to warrant achieving the desire by a shorter cut than the constitutional way of paying for the change." The Court's opinion in this case demonstrates that the danger thus foreseen has not abated. The city of New York is in a precarious financial state, and some may believe that the costs of landmark preservation will be more easily borne by corporations such as Penn Central than the overburdened individual taxpayers of New York. But these concerns do not allow us to ignore past precedents construing the Eminent Domain Clause to the end that the desire to improve the public condition is, indeed, achieved by a shorter cut than the constitutional way of paying for the change.

Although Justice Brennan's majority opinion in *Penn Central* represented the accepted view of regulatory takings at that time, Justice Rehnquist's dissent signaled that the more conservative justices on the Court preferred to give greater weight to the interests of property owners. Eight years later the ideological balance on the Court shifted when Rehnquist was elevated to the chief justiceship and Antonin Scalia joined the Court as an associate justice. Both were strong advocates of private property rights and adhered to a much broader conception of what constitutes a taking. In addition, the new chief justice had a special interest in takings clause issues. *(See Box 11-1.)*

The first signs of change appeared in 1987, when the Court handed down three takings clause decisions. The first, decided in March, was **Keystone Bituminous Coal Association v. DeBenedictis**. The majority upheld a state regulation of coal mining operations against takings clause and contract clause attacks, but a dissenting opinion by Chief Justice Rehnquist attracted the support of three other justices, indicating that the conservative-minded members of the Court were poised to make a major assault on existing takings clause interpretations.

The second 1987 decision, *First English Evangelical Lutheran Church of Glendale v. County of Los Angeles,* was decided in June. Although this case involved a relatively minor point regarding the recovery of damages, the Court voted 6–3 to support the property owners who claimed compensation. Rehnquist wrote the majority opinion in support of the property rights position. This decision was a clear invitation to private property interests that the Rehnquist Court was open to new takings clause appeals. Justice John Paul Stevens's dissenting opinion acknowledged this point: "One thing is certain. The Court's decision today will generate a great deal of litigation."

The final 1987 decision, **Nollan v. California Coastal Commission**, decided in late June, was the most important indication that the Rehnquist Court was about to resurrect property rights under the takings clause. James and Marilyn Nollan owned a beachfront lot in Ventura County, California, located between two public beaches. The Nollans' property included a small bungalow that they rented to summer vacationers. When the house fell into serious disrepair and could no longer be rented, the couple decided to replace it with a new structure. To do so, they needed a building permit from the California Coastal Commission.

The commission granted the Nollans permission to build their new house, but with one significant condition: A strip of land across the Nollan property was to be set aside for public use as a passageway between the two public beaches. The Nollans protested, but the commission remained firm. The Nollans then filed suit claiming that the public access condition constituted a taking under the Fifth Amendment. The Court, in an opinion by Justice Scalia for the 5–4 majority, ruled that the condition attached to the building permit was in fact a taking for which the Nollans must be compensated. In dissent, Justice Brennan condemned the decision as being out of

BOX 11-1   WILLIAM HUBBS REHNQUIST (1971–2005)

WILLIAM HUBBS REHNQUIST was born in Milwaukee, Wisconsin, October 1, 1924. After serving in World War II, Rehnquist received B.A. and M.A. degrees in political science from Stanford University. He earned an additional master's degree in government at Harvard, before returning to Stanford to study law. He graduated first in his class in 1952. One of his classmates, Sandra Day, would later join him on the Supreme Court.

After completing law school, Rehnquist clerked for Justice Robert Jackson. In 1952 he wrote a memorandum favoring separate but equal schools for blacks and whites. When questioned about these views at his confirmation hearings, he said they were Jackson's beliefs at that time, not his own.

Following his clerkship, Rehnquist moved to Arizona to practice law. He married Natalie Cornell, whom he had met at Stanford, and they had three children. Rehnquist, a conservative, immersed himself in Republican Party politics. In 1957 he wrote an article for *U.S. News and World Report* in which he criticized the Warren Court's liberal rulings and suggested that they might be the result of undue influence exerted by the Court's law clerks.

After Richard Nixon was elected to the presidency in 1968, Rehnquist received an appointment to the Justice Department's Office of Legal Counsel, largely because of his association with Deputy Attorney General Richard Kliendienst, a fellow Phoenix lawyer. Nixon nominated Rehnquist to be an associate justice on the Supreme Court in 1971 to replace the retiring John Marshall Harlan. Rehnquist was only forty-seven years old at the time and not politically well known. He was confirmed, 68–26. As an associate justice, Rehnquist voted in a predictably conservative fashion, favoring state interests in federalism disputes and law enforcement in criminal cases. He was frequently in the minority.

In 1986 President Ronald Reagan nominated Rehnquist to replace the retiring chief justice, Warren Burger, but the nomination sparked controversy. Rehnquist's views on civil rights were questioned. He was accused of harassing black voters in Phoenix during the 1950s and early 1960s and was criticized for owning property with racially restrictive covenants. Liberals branded him too extreme to lead the Court. In the end, the Senate majority considered the charges against him to be unproven or "ancient history." There was no evidence of misconduct during his tenure as associate justice. Rehnquist was confirmed, 65–33, becoming only the third sitting justice to be promoted to chief.

As chief justice, Rehnquist continued to vote conservatively on federalism, civil liberties, criminal justice, and private property issues. With the Court gradually shifting to the right, he more often than not found himself in the majority.

Rehnquist wrote several books on Supreme Court history, including *The Supreme Court: How It Was, How It Is* (1988), *Grand Inquests: The Historic Impeachments of Justice Samuel Chase and President Andrew Johnson* (1992), *Civil Liberty and the Civil War* (1996), and *All the Laws but One: Civil Liberties in Wartime* (1998). Rehnquist's research and writing on federal impeachments proved propitious when he was called upon to preside over the 1999 Senate impeachment trial of President Bill Clinton.

Rehnquist died on September 3, 2005, just weeks before his eighty-first birthday. He had served on the Court for thirty-three years, nineteen as chief justice. President George W. Bush appointed federal court of appeals judge John Roberts to replace him.

SOURCES: David Savage, *Guide to the U.S. Supreme Court*, 4th ed. (Washington, D.C.: CQ Press, 2004), 1015–1016; Clare Cushman, ed., *The Supreme Court Justices: Illustrated Biographies, 1789–1993*, 2nd ed. (Washington, D.C.: Congressional Quarterly, 1995); updated by the authors.

step with the complex reality of natural resource protection in the twentieth century.

Brennan's hope that *Nollan* would be an aberration did not come to pass. In the years following *Nollan,* the personnel on the Court continued to change. Justices Brennan and Thurgood Marshall retired. Both had been firm supporters of public interests over private property rights. Two supporters of private property joined the Court, Anthony Kennedy in 1988 and Clarence Thomas in 1991, and they strengthened Chief Justice Rehnquist's efforts to breathe new life into the Constitution's private property protections.

The importance of these personnel changes can be seen in *Lucas v. South Carolina Coastal Council* (1992), a case that pitted private property rights against a state's attempts to protect its coastal environment. As might be predicted, the Court's conservative majority sided with the landowner, holding that the state may not deprive the owner of the value of his property without proper compensation. In dissent, Justice Harry A. Blackmun decried the Court's changing policies.

Lucas v. South Carolina Coastal Council

505 U.S. 1003 (1992)
http://laws.findlaw.com/US/505/1003.html
Oral arguments may be found at: http://www.oyez.org
Vote: 6 *(Kennedy, O'Connor, Rehnquist, Scalia, Thomas, White)*
        3 *(Blackmun, Souter, Stevens)*
Opinion of the Court: Scalia
Opinion concurring in the judgment: Kennedy
Dissenting opinions: Blackmun, Stevens
Separate statement: Souter

In 1986 David Lucas paid $975,000 for two vacant oceanfront lots on the Isle of Palms, a barrier island near Charleston, South Carolina. He acquired the property with the intention of building single-family homes similar to those already built on adjacent lots. When Lucas bought the land there were no regulations prohibiting such use. Shortly thereafter, however, the state passed the Beachfront Management Act, an environmental law that gave the state coastal council increased authority to protect certain shoreline areas against erosion and other dangers. The council decided that the Lucas lots were in a "critical area" and prohibited any new construction.

There is no doubt that under its police powers the state has the right to pass such legislation, but Lucas claimed that the new regulations amounted to a taking of his property for a public purpose. The Fifth Amendment, he argued, required the state to pay him for the loss of his property. A state trial judge agreed that the regulations had made the Lucas property essentially worthless and ordered the state to pay him $1.23 million as just compensation for the loss. On appeal the South Carolina Supreme Court reversed the decision, holding that the environmental legislation was not a taking under the meaning of the Constitution. Lucas appealed to the U.S. Supreme Court.

JUSTICE SCALIA delivered the opinion of the Court.

We think . . . that there are good reasons for our frequently expressed belief that when the owner of real property has been called upon to sacrifice *all* economically beneficial uses in the name of the common good, that is, to leave his property economically idle, he has suffered a taking.

The trial court found Lucas's two beachfront lots to have been rendered valueless by respondent's enforcement of the coastal-zone construction ban. Under Lucas's theory of the case, which rested upon our "no economically viable use" statements, that finding entitled him to compensation. . . . The South Carolina Supreme Court, however, thought otherwise. In its view, the Beachfront Management Act was no ordinary enactment, but involved an exercise of South Carolina's "police powers" to mitigate the harm to the public interest that petitioner's use of his land might occasion. . . .

It is correct that many of our prior opinions have suggested that "harmful or noxious uses" of property may be proscribed by government regulation without the requirement of compensation. For a number of reasons, however, we think the South Carolina Supreme Court was too quick to conclude that that principle decides the present case. The "harmful or noxious uses" principle was the Court's early attempt to describe in theoretical terms why government may, consistent with the Takings Clause, affect property values by

One of two lots on the Isle of Palms that David Lucas purchased with the intention of building houses on them. Shortly after the sale was completed the South Carolina Coastal Council determined that building would be detrimental to the environment and prohibited future development. In 1992 the Supreme Court agreed with Lucas that the state's action violated the takings clause.

regulation without incurring an obligation to compensate— a reality we nowadays acknowledge explicitly with respect to the full scope of the State's police power.... "Harmful or noxious use" analysis was, in other words, simply the progenitor of our more contemporary statements that "land-use regulation does not effect a taking if it 'substantially advance[s] legitimate state interests'...."

The transition from our early focus on control of "noxious" uses to our contemporary understanding of the broad realm within which government may regulate without compensation was an easy one, since the distinction between "harm-preventing" and "benefit-conferring" regulation is often in the eye of the beholder. It is quite possible, for example, to describe in *either* fashion the ecological, economic, and aesthetic concerns that inspired the South Carolina legislature in the present case. One could say that imposing a servitude on Lucas's land is necessary in order to prevent his use of it from "harming" South Carolina's ecological resources; or, instead, in order to achieve the "benefits" of an ecological preserve.... Whether Lucas's construction of single-family residences on his parcels should be described as bringing "harm" to South Carolina's adjacent ecological resources thus depends principally upon whether the describer believes that the State's use interest in nurturing those resources is so important that any competing adjacent use must yield.

When it is understood that "prevention of harmful use" was merely our early formulation of the police power justification necessary to sustain (without compensation) *any* regulatory diminution in value; and that the distinction between regulation that "prevents harmful use" and that which "confers benefits" is difficult, if not impossible, to discern on an objective, value-free basis; it becomes self-evident that noxious-use logic cannot serve as a touchstone to distinguish regulatory "takings"—which require compensation—from regulatory deprivations that do not require compensation. A fortiori the legislature's recitation of a noxious-use justification cannot be the basis for departing from our categorical rule that total regulatory takings must be compensated. If it were, departure would virtually always be allowed....

Where the State seeks to sustain regulation that deprives land of all economically beneficial use, we think it may resist compensation only if the logically antecedent inquiry into the nature of the owner's estate shows that the proscribed use interests were not part of his title to begin with. This accords, we think, with our "takings" jurisprudence, which has traditionally been guided by the understandings of our citizens regarding the content of, and the State's power over, the "bundle of rights" that they acquire when they obtain title to property. It seems to us that the property owner necessarily expects the uses of his property to be restricted, from time to time, by various measures newly enacted by the State in legitimate exercise of its police powers; "[a]s long recognized, some values are enjoyed under an implied limitation and must yield to the police power." And in the case of personal property, by reason of the State's traditionally high degree of control over commercial dealings, he ought to be aware of the possibility that new regulation might even render his property economically worthless (at least if the property's only economically productive use is sale or manufacture for sale). In the case of land, however, we think the notion pressed by the Council that title is somehow held subject to the "implied limitation" that the State may subsequently eliminate all economically valuable use is inconsistent with the historical compact recorded in the Takings Clause that has become part of our constitutional culture.

Where "permanent physical occupation" of land is concerned, we have refused to allow the government to decree it anew (without compensation), no matter how weighty the asserted "public interests" involved. . . . We believe similar treatment must be accorded confiscatory regulations, *i.e.,* regulations that prohibit all economically beneficial use of land: Any limitation so severe cannot be newly legislated or decreed (without compensation), but must inhere in the title itself, in the restrictions that background principles of the State's law of property and nuisance already place upon land ownership. A law or decree with such an effect must, in other words, do no more than duplicate the result that could have been achieved in the courts—by adjacent landowners (or other uniquely affected persons) under the State's law of private nuisance, or by the State under its complementary power to abate nuisances that affect the public generally, or otherwise.

On this analysis, the owner of a lake bed, for example, would not be entitled to compensation when he is denied the requisite permit to engage in a landfilling operation that would have the effect of flooding others' land. Nor the corporate owner of a nuclear generating plant, when it is directed to remove all improvements from its land upon discovery that the plant sits astride an earthquake fault. Such regulatory action may well have the effect of eliminating the land's only economically productive use, but it does not proscribe a productive use that was previously permissible under relevant property and nuisance principles. The use of these properties for what are now expressly prohibited purposes was always unlawful, and (subject to other constitu-

tional limitations) it was open to the State at any point to make the implication of those background principles of nuisance and property law explicit. . . . When, however, a regulation that declares "off-limits" all economically productive or beneficial uses of land goes beyond what the relevant background principles would dictate, compensation must be paid to sustain it.

The "total taking" inquiry we require today will ordinarily entail (as the application of state nuisance law ordinarily entails) analysis of, among other things, the degree of harm to public lands and resources, or adjacent private property, posed by the claimant's proposed activities, the social value of the claimant's activities and their suitability to the locality in question, and the relative ease with which the alleged harm can be avoided through measures taken by the claimant and the government (or adjacent private landowners) alike. The fact that a particular use has long been engaged in by similarly situated owners ordinarily imports a lack of any common-law prohibition (though changed circumstances or new knowledge may make what was previously permissible no longer so). So also does the fact that other landowners, similarly situated, are permitted to continue the use denied to the claimant.

. . . We emphasize that to win its case South Carolina must do more than proffer the legislature's declaration that the uses Lucas desires are inconsistent with the public interest, or the conclusory assertion that they violate a common-law maxim. . . . Instead, as it would be required to do if it sought to restrain Lucas in a common-law action for public nuisance, South Carolina must identify background principles of nuisance and property law that prohibit the uses he now intends in the circumstances in which the property is presently found. Only on this showing can the State fairly claim that, in proscribing all such beneficial uses, the Beachfront Management Act is taking nothing.

The judgment is reversed and the cause remanded for proceedings not inconsistent with this opinion.

So ordered.

JUSTICE BLACKMUN, dissenting.

Today the Court launches a missile to kill a mouse. . . .

The Court makes sweeping and, in my view, misguided and unsupported changes in our takings doctrine. While it limits these changes to the most narrow subset of govern-

IN 1986 DAVID LUCAS, a developer of residential properties, purchased two lots on the Isle of Palms in South Carolina for $975,000. He intended to build two houses on the land, keeping one for himself and selling the other. Because of environmental concerns, however, the state coastal council denied Lucas permission to build. In response, Lucas took legal action, demanding compensation for his economic loss. He won a $1.23 million judgment in the state trial court, but the state supreme court reversed that ruling. In 1992 the U.S. Supreme Court found that Lucas had been deprived of property for a public purpose and was entitled to be compensated. The justices remanded the case back to the South Carolina courts for further proceedings.

Additional court action was not required, however. The state had lost the essential issue presented in the case, and only the determination of adequate compensation remained to be decided. South Carolina was understandably eager to settle the dispute rather than to prolong the legal battle. Lucas and the state came to a quick out-of-court settlement, in which the state agreed to pay Lucas $1.5 million in return for the property.

To recoup the funds lost in the Lucas settlement and related litigation costs, the state decided to sell the properties. Ironically, to increase their value prior to sale, the state announced that the new owners would be allowed to build houses on the lots.

SOURCES: *Arizona Republic*, November 2, 1994; *Chicago Sun-Times*, July 28, 1995; *Christian Science Monitor*, September 27, 1993; *San Diego Union-Tribune*, July 21, 1993.

ment regulation—those that eliminate all economic value from land—these changes go far beyond what is necessary to secure petitioner Lucas' private benefit. One hopes they do not go beyond the narrow confines the Court assigns them to today. I dissent.

Following *Lucas*, the Court continued to support takings clause claims against government regulations. In *Dolan v. City of Tigard* (1994) the Court considered a challenge to a municipality that had required the owner of a small store to devote a portion of her land to public green space and allow a pedestrian/ bicycle path to cross her property in return for permission to expand her store and pave her parking lot. The justices, divided 5–4, ruled that the property owner's Fifth Amendment rights had been violated because the requirements for obtaining the permit were insufficiently related to the proposed store improvements.

But not all recent cases have been decided in favor of property owners. In *Tahoe-Sierra Preservation Council v. Tahoe Regional Planning Agency* (2002) the Court, 6–3, ruled against private property interests. A regional planning agency had imposed a "temporary" moratorium on new construction in the Lake Tahoe Basin while it conducted a study of appropriate land-use regulations. When the moratorium had lasted thirty-two months, the landowners objected, claiming that a taking had occurred. The Supreme Court held otherwise, ruling that the moratorium did not constitute a taking that required compensation.

PUBLIC USE REQUIREMENT

Although the Fifth Amendment recognizes the government's power to take private property, it does not allow all such seizures. The takings clause stipulates quite explicitly that the government may take private property only for a "public use." Even if the government provides adequate compensation, it may not take property against the owner's will for the sole benefit of a private individual or organization. When the government plans to build a new courthouse, road, or park, the public use is clear; but it would be of doubtful constitutionality if a state seized a piece of private property under the power of eminent domain and gave it to a fraternal organization to construct a new lodge.

Throughout most of the nation's history, the justices were relatively insistent about the public use requirement.[9] Beginning in the New Deal period, however, the Court initiated a policy of deferring to Congress's authority to determine what constitutes a public purpose. In *Berman v. Parker* (1954) the Court upheld a federal urban

---

9. See Schultz, *Property, Power, and American Democracy.*

renewal project in Washington, D.C., in which private property was seized, improved, and then transferred to another private party. The program's objective was to ameliorate conditions in a particularly blighted section of the city. Even though private property was taken and given to another private party, the Court accepted the conclusion of Congress that the program had a public purpose.

The Court's deference to the legislature on public use questions was extended to the state level in *Hawaii Housing Authority v. Midkiff* (1984). Attacked here was Hawaii's plan to redistribute land, using the power of eminent domain to force large landowners to sell their properties to the people who leased them. The transfer of land was clearly from one private owner to another. The land distribution program was the state legislature's response to social and economic problems that had their origins in Hawaii's unusual past.

The Hawaiian Islands were settled by Polynesians who developed an economic system based upon principles of feudalism. Ownership and control of the land rested with the islands' high chief, who distributed parcels to various lower-ranking chiefs. At the end of the chain, tenant farmers and their families lived on the land and worked it. Private ownership of real property was not permitted. Ultimate ownership of all lands rested with the royal family.

The monarchy was overthrown in 1893, and, after a brief period as a republic, the islands were annexed by the United States in 1898. When Hawaii became the fiftieth state in 1959, the land still remained in the hands of a few. In the mid-1960s the federal government owned 49 percent of the land, and just seventy-two private landowners held another 47 percent. On Oahu, the most commercially developed island, twenty-two landowners controlled more than 72 percent of the private real estate. The Hawaiian legislature determined that this concentration of land ownership was detrimental to the state's economy and general welfare.

The legislature first decided to compel landowners to sell a large portion of their holdings to those individuals who leased the land from them. The landowners opposed this plan because it would result in exceedingly high capital gains taxes. The legislature revised its plans and enacted the Land Reform Act of 1967. This legislation al-

lowed the state to condemn tracts of residential real estate. The Hawaii Housing Authority (HHA) would then seize the condemned property, compensate the landowners for their loss, and resell the parcels to the private individuals who had been leasing the land. Compensation for land seized by the government enjoyed a more favorable tax status than did profits from outright sales, making the legislation more acceptable to the landowners.

Frank Midkiff and others owned a large tract of land that was condemned under the land reform program, but Midkiff and the HHA could not agree on a fair price. He and his co-owners filed suit in federal district court to have the Land Reform Act declared unconstitutional as a violation of the takings clause. Their primary argument was that taking land from one private owner to transfer to another private owner did not meet the Constitution's requirement that takings be for a public purpose.

A unanimous Supreme Court upheld the Hawaii program. Using much of the same logic as it did in *Berman,* the Court concluded that the land reform plan was done for a public purpose. The crucial issue was not the transfer from one private party to another; rather, it was whether the program was rationally related to a public purpose. The justices conceded that the legislature was in the best position to determine public use and that the Court would normally defer to the legislature's judgment on that question.

Decisions such as *Berman* and *Midkiff* made significant changes in the way the Court dealt with takings clause appeals. No longer did the justices examine the nature of the public purpose of the taking. Instead, the Court gave wide latitude to legislatures to determine what constitutes public use. To this extent, private property rights became political as well as legal questions, increasing the power of the legislature at the expense of traditional property considerations. These decisions also reduced the extent to which "public use" objections could be employed to thwart the legislative redistribution of wealth and property for the public good.[10]

The Court's announced policy of deferring to the elected branches on the question of public use encouraged governments to expand their exercise of eminent

10. Ibid., 73–74.

domain, especially at the local level. Cities and towns faced with declining economies and dwindling tax revenues saw economic redevelopment as a means of expanding job opportunities, revitalizing local business activity, and increasing tax revenues. Many attempted to lure new businesses, create industrial parks, and develop areas that combined commercial and residential facilities. Often these polices required the local government to acquire significant tracts of land either by purchasing the necessary property or seizing it under eminent domain if owners refused to sell.

Although cities saw such policies as benefiting the entire community, the targeted owners who did not want to give up their property did not see it that way. To them, the city was using the power of eminent domain in an unconstitutional fashion. Their homes and land were being taken not because their property was blighted or being misused, but because the city ultimately wanted to turn the seized parcels over to private businesses who were willing to build new stores, hotels, factories, or higher priced residences. Advocates of private property rights believed that such development policies violated the Fifth Amendment because no true public purpose was advanced. To them it was nothing more than local officials taking private property from individual owners and giving it to corporate business interests to raise city tax revenues. A major confrontation between municipalities and private property owners was inevitable. The Supreme Court tackled the issue in the controversial case of *Kelo v. City of New London* (2005).

Kelo v. City of New London

545 U.S. 469 (2005)
http://laws.findlaw.com/US/000/04-108.html
Oral arguments may be found at: http://www.oyez.org
Vote: 5 (Breyer, Ginsburg, Kennedy, Souter, Stevens)
        4 (O'Connor, Rehnquist, Scalia, Thomas)
Opinion of the Court: Stevens
Concurring opinion: Kennedy
Dissenting opinions: O'Connor, Thomas

For decades the city of New London, Connecticut, suffered significant economic decline. By 1998 the unem-

ployment rate was double that of the state, and the population had declined to 24,000, the same number of residents the city had in 1920. In response, state and local officials created the New London Development Corporation (NLDC) to devise strategies for economic advancement. Efforts to revitalize the city resulted in a tentative commitment by the Pfizer drug company to build a $300 million research facility in the city's Fort Trumbull area. Officials believed that this new development would not only bring jobs and tax revenues to the city but also encourage other economic revitalization efforts.

The NLDC developed a master plan for the area surrounding the proposed Pfizer operation. This plan called for a hotel, conference center, museum, restaurants, shops, office space, marina, river walk, and new residential housing. In 2000 the city adopted the development plan. To begin the development, the city had to acquire approximately 115 privately owned parcels of land. The city successfully negotiated the purchase of most of this land, but some landowners refused to sell. The city responded by condemning their properties through the use of eminent domain.

Nine landowners, unwilling to sell their homes, filed suit, claiming the city's actions violated the Fifth Amendment's takings clause. Among them were Susette Kelo, who had owned a water-view house since 1997 and had spent considerable time and money renovating it, and Wilhelmina Dery, who had lived in her Fort Trumbull home since her birth in 1918. The properties involved were not blighted or in poor condition. The city condemned them only because they stood in the path of the redevelopment plan. The petitioners claimed that the plan failed to meet the Fifth Amendment's "public use" requirement. After the Connecticut Supreme Court ruled in favor of the city, Kelo and her fellow petitioners requested review by the U.S. Supreme Court.

JUSTICE STEVENS delivered the opinion of the Court.

Two polar propositions are perfectly clear. On the one hand, it has long been accepted that the sovereign may not take the property of A for the sole purpose of transferring it to another private party B, even though A is paid just compensation. On the other hand, it is equally clear that a State

The home of Susette Kelo is shown here in February 2005, just four months before the Supreme Court ruled that the city of New London could seize it as part of an economic revitalization program.

may transfer property from one private party to another if future "use by the public" is the purpose of the taking; the condemnation of land for a railroad with common-carrier duties is a familiar example. Neither of these propositions, however, determines the disposition of this case.

As for the first proposition, the City would no doubt be forbidden from taking petitioners' land for the purpose of conferring a private benefit on a particular private party. . . . Nor would the City be allowed to take property under the mere pretext of a public purpose, when its actual purpose was to bestow a private benefit. The takings before us, however, would be executed pursuant to a "carefully considered" development plan. The trial judge and all the members of the Supreme Court of Connecticut agreed that there was no evidence of an illegitimate purpose in this case. Therefore, as was true of the statute challenged in [*Hawaii Housing Authority v.*] *Midkiff*, the City's development plan was not adopted "to benefit a particular class of identifiable individuals."

On the other hand, this is not a case in which the City is planning to open the condemned land—at least not in its entirety—to use by the general public. Nor will the private lessees of the land in any sense be required to operate like common carriers, making their services available to all comers. But although such a projected use would be suffi-

cient to satisfy the public use requirement, this "Court long ago rejected any literal requirement that condemned property be put into use for the general public." [*Midkiff.*] Indeed, while many state courts in the mid-19th century endorsed "use by the public" as the proper definition of public use, that narrow view steadily eroded over time. Not only was the "use by the public" test difficult to administer (*e.g.,* what proportion of the public need have access to the property? at what price?), but it proved to be impractical given the diverse and always evolving needs of society. . . .

The disposition of this case therefore turns on the question whether the City's development plan serves a "public purpose." Without exception, our cases have defined that concept broadly, reflecting our longstanding policy of deference to legislative judgments in this field.

In *Berman v. Parker* (1954), this Court upheld a redevelopment plan targeting a blighted area of Washington, D.C., in which most of the housing for the area's 5,000 inhabitants was beyond repair. Under the plan, the area would be condemned and part of it utilized for the construction of streets, schools, and other public facilities. The remainder of the land would be leased or sold to private parties for the purpose of redevelopment, including the construction of low-cost housing. . . .

In *Hawaii Housing Authority v. Midkiff* (1984), the Court considered a Hawaii statute whereby fee title was taken from lessors and transferred to lessees (for just compensation) in order to reduce the concentration of land ownership. We unanimously upheld the statute and rejected the Ninth Circuit's view that it was "a naked attempt on the part of the state of Hawaii to take the property of A and transfer it to B solely for B's private use and benefit." Reaffirming *Berman's* deferential approach to legislative judgments in this field, we concluded that the State's purpose of eliminating the "social and economic evils of a land oligopoly" qualified as a valid public use. Our opinion also rejected the contention that the mere fact that the State immediately transferred the properties to private individuals upon condemnation somehow diminished the public character of the taking. "[I]t is only the taking's purpose, and not its mechanics," we explained, that matters in determining public use. . . .

. . . For more than a century, our public use jurisprudence has wisely eschewed rigid formulas and intrusive scrutiny in favor of affording legislatures broad latitude in determining what public needs justify the use of the takings power.

Those who govern the City were not confronted with the need to remove blight in the Fort Trumbull area, but their determination that the area was sufficiently distressed to justify a program of economic rejuvenation is entitled to our deference. The City has carefully formulated an economic development plan that it believes will provide appreciable benefits to the community, including—but by no means limited to—new jobs and increased tax revenue. As with other exercises in urban planning and development, the City is endeavoring to coordinate a variety of commercial, residential, and recreational uses of land, with the hope that they will form a whole greater than the sum of its parts. To effectuate this plan, the City has invoked a state statute that specifically authorizes the use of eminent domain to promote economic development. Given the comprehensive character of the plan, the thorough deliberation that preceded its adoption, and the limited scope of our review, it is appropriate for us, as it was in *Berman,* to resolve the challenges of the individual owners, not on a piecemeal basis, but rather in light of the entire plan. Because that plan unquestionably serves a public purpose, the takings challenged here satisfy the public use requirement of the Fifth Amendment.

To avoid this result, petitioners urge us to adopt a new bright-line rule that economic development does not qualify as a public use. Putting aside the unpersuasive suggestion that the City's plan will provide only purely economic benefits, neither precedent nor logic supports petitioners' proposal. Promoting economic development is a traditional and long accepted function of government. There is, moreover, no principled way of distinguishing economic development from the other public purposes that we have recognized. . . . Clearly, there is no basis for exempting economic development from our traditionally broad understanding of public purpose.

Petitioners contend that using eminent domain for economic development impermissibly blurs the boundary between public and private takings. Again, our cases foreclose this objection. Quite simply, the government's pursuit of a public purpose will often benefit individual private parties. . . . "We cannot say that public ownership is the sole method of promoting the public purposes of community redevelopment projects."

It is further argued that without a bright-line rule nothing would stop a city from transferring citizen A's property to citizen B for the sole reason that citizen B will put the property to a more productive use and thus pay more taxes. Such a one-to-one transfer of property, executed outside the confines of an integrated development plan, is not presented in this case. While such an unusual exercise of government power would certainly raise a suspicion that a private purpose was afoot, the hypothetical cases posited by petitioners can be confronted if and when they arise. They do not warrant the crafting of an artificial restriction on the concept of public use. . . .

Just as we decline to second-guess the City's considered judgments about the efficacy of its development plan, we also decline to second-guess the City's determinations as to what lands it needs to acquire in order to effectuate the project. "It is not for the courts to oversee the choice of the boundary line nor to sit in review on the size of a particular project area. Once the question of the public purpose has been decided, the amount and character of land to be taken for the project and the need for a particular tract to complete the integrated plan rests in the discretion of the legislative branch."

In affirming the City's authority to take petitioners' properties, we do not minimize the hardship that condemnations may entail, notwithstanding the payment of just compensation. We emphasize that nothing in our opinion precludes any State from placing further restrictions on its exercise of the takings power. Indeed, many States already impose "public use" requirements that are stricter than the federal baseline. Some of these requirements have been established as a matter of state constitutional law, while others are expressed in state eminent domain statutes that carefully limit the grounds upon which takings may be exercised. As the submissions of the parties and their *amici* make clear, the necessity and wisdom of using eminent domain to promote economic development are certainly matters of legitimate public debate. This Court's authority, however, extends only to determining whether the City's proposed condemnations are for a "public use" within the meaning of the Fifth Amendment to the Federal Constitution. Because over a century of our case law interpreting that provision dictates an affirmative answer to that question, we may not grant petitioners the relief that they seek.

The judgment of the Supreme Court of Connecticut is affirmed.

It is so ordered.

JUSTICE KENNEDY, concurring.

I join the opinion for the Court and add these further observations.

This Court has declared that a taking should be upheld as consistent with the Public Use Clause as long as it is "rationally related to a conceivable public purpose." *Hawaii Housing Authority v. Midkiff* (1984); see also *Berman v. Parker* (1954). This deferential standard of review echoes the rational-basis test used to review economic regulation under the Due Process and Equal Protection Clauses. The determination that a rational-basis standard of review is appropriate does not, however, alter the fact that transfers intended to confer benefits on particular, favored private entities, and with only incidental or pretextual public benefits, are forbidden by the Public Use Clause.

A court applying rational-basis review under the Public Use Clause should strike down a taking that, by a clear showing, is intended to favor a particular private party, with only incidental or pretextual public benefits. . . .

This is not the occasion for conjecture as to what sort of cases might justify a more demanding standard, but it is

appropriate to underscore aspects of the instant case that convince me no departure from *Berman* and *Midkiff* is appropriate here. This taking occurred in the context of a comprehensive development plan meant to address a serious city-wide depression, and the projected economic benefits of the project cannot be characterized as *de minimus*. The identity of most of the private beneficiaries were unknown at the time the city formulated its plans. The city complied with elaborate procedural requirements that facilitate review of the record and inquiry into the city's purposes. In sum, while there may be categories of cases in which the transfers are so suspicious, or the procedures employed so prone to abuse, or the purported benefits are so trivial or implausible, that courts should presume an impermissible private purpose, no such circumstances are present in this case.

JUSTICE O'CONNOR, with whom the CHIEF JUSTICE, JUSTICE SCALIA, and JUSTICE THOMAS join, dissenting.

Over two centuries ago, just after the Bill of Rights was ratified, Justice Chase wrote:

"An act of the Legislature (for I cannot call it a law) contrary to the great first principles of the social compact, cannot be considered a rightful exercise of legislative authority. . . . A few instances will suffice to explain what I mean. . . . [A] law that takes property from A. and gives it to B: It is against all reason and justice, for a people to entrust a Legislature with such powers; and, therefore, it cannot be presumed that they have done it." *Calder v. Bull* (1798).

Today the Court abandons this long-held, basic limitation on government power. Under the banner of economic development, all private property is now vulnerable to being taken and transferred to another private owner, so long as it might be upgraded—*i.e.*, given to an owner who will use it in a way that the legislature deems more beneficial to the public—in the process. To reason, as the Court does, that the incidental public benefits resulting from the subsequent ordinary use of private property render economic development takings "for public use" is to wash out any distinction between private and public use of property—and thereby effectively to delete the words "for public use" from the Takings Clause of the Fifth Amendment. Accordingly I respectfully dissent. . . .

This case returns us for the first time in over 20 years to the hard question of when a purportedly "public purpose" taking meets the public use requirement. It presents an issue of first impression: Are economic development takings constitutional? I would hold that they are not. We are guided by two precedents about the taking of real property by eminent domain. In *Berman*, we upheld takings within a blighted neighborhood of Washington, D.C. The neighborhood had so deteriorated that, for example, 64.3% of its dwellings were beyond repair. It had become burdened with "overcrowding of dwellings," "lack of adequate streets and alleys," and "lack of light and air." Congress had determined that the neighborhood had become "injurious to the public health, safety, morals, and welfare" and that it was necessary to "eliminat[e] all such injurious conditions by employing all means necessary and appropriate for the purpose," including eminent domain. Mr. Berman's department store was not itself blighted. Having approved of Congress' decision to eliminate the harm to the public emanating from the blighted neighborhood, however, we did not second-guess its decision to treat the neighborhood as a whole rather than lot-by-lot.

In *Midkiff*, we upheld a land condemnation scheme in Hawaii whereby title in real property was taken from lessors and transferred to lessees. At that time, the State and Federal Governments owned nearly 49% of the State's land, and another 47% was in the hands of only 72 private landowners. Concentration of land ownership was so dramatic that on the State's most urbanized island, Oahu, 22 landowners owned 72.5% of the fee simple titles. The Hawaii Legislature had concluded that the oligopoly in land ownership was "skewing the State's residential fee simple market, inflating land prices, and injuring the public tranquility and welfare," and therefore enacted a condemnation scheme for redistributing title. . . .

The Court's holdings in *Berman* and *Midkiff* were true to the principle underlying the Public Use Clause. In both those cases, the extraordinary, precondemnation use of the targeted property inflicted affirmative harm on society—in *Berman* through blight resulting from extreme poverty and in *Midkiff* through oligopoly resulting from extreme wealth. And in both cases, the relevant legislative body had found that eliminating the existing property use was necessary to remedy the harm. Thus a public purpose was realized when the harmful use was eliminated. Because each taking directly achieved a public benefit, it did not matter that the property was turned over to private use. Here, in contrast, New London does not claim that Susette Kelo's and Wilhelmina

Dery's well-maintained homes are the source of any social harm. Indeed, it could not so claim without adopting the absurd argument that any single-family home that might be razed to make way for an apartment building, or any church that might be replaced with a retail store, or any small business that might be more lucrative if it were instead part of a national franchise, is inherently harmful to society and thus within the government's power to condemn.

In moving away from our decisions sanctioning the condemnation of harmful property use, the Court today significantly expands the meaning of public use. It holds that the sovereign may take private property currently put to ordinary private use, and give it over for new, ordinary private use, so long as the new use is predicted to generate some secondary benefit for the public—such as increased tax revenue, more jobs, maybe even aesthetic pleasure. But nearly any lawful use of real private property can be said to generate some incidental benefit to the public. Thus, if predicted (or even guaranteed) positive side-effects are enough to render transfer from one private party to another constitutional, then the words "for public use" do not realistically exclude any takings, and thus do not exert any constraint on the eminent domain power. . . .

Finally, . . . the Court suggests that property owners should turn to the States, who may or may not choose to impose appropriate limits on economic development takings. This is an abdication of our responsibility. States play many important functions in our system of dual sovereignty, but compensating for our refusal to enforce properly the Federal Constitution (and a provision meant to curtail state action, no less) is not among them. . . .

Any property may now be taken for the benefit of another private party, but the fallout from this decision will not be random. The beneficiaries are likely to be those citizens with disproportionate influence and power in the political process, including large corporations and development firms. As for the victims, the government now has license to transfer property from those with fewer resources to those with more. The Founders cannot have intended this perverse result.

JUSTICE THOMAS, dissenting.

Today's decision is simply the latest in a string of our cases construing the Public Use Clause to be a virtual nullity,

---

BOX 11-3   AFTERMATH . . . *KELO V. CITY OF NEW LONDON*

THE *KELO* decision touched off a storm of protest by private property rights advocates, and public opinion ran decidedly against the decision. Taking the Court's admonishment that nothing in the decision prohibits the states from imposing their own limits, thirty state legislatures immediately introduced bills and constitutional amendments to restrict local government's use of eminent domain. Ten states already had laws barring government seizures of nonblighted private property for economic development purposes. Supporters of eminent domain, including the National League of Cities, were able to convince legislators to modify many of the more extreme anti-*Kelo* proposals.

Two months after the decision, *Kelo*'s author, Justice John Paul Stevens, acknowledged that the ruling was "unwise" and that he would have opposed it had he been a legislator and not a federal judge bound by precedent.

Some protests were directed at the justices themselves. In Weare, New Hampshire, private property activists secured sufficient petition signatures to place a proposal on the ballot to have the town seize the two-hundred-year-old farmhouse home of Justice David Souter, who voted with the majority in *Kelo*. Under the proposal the property would be turned over to private investors who would build an inn to be named the "Lost Liberty Hotel," featuring the "Just Desserts" cafe. One of the proposal's supporters said, "It would be more like a bed and breakfast. . . . There would be nine suites, with a black robe in each of the closets." In March 2006 the Weare voters rejected the proposal 1,167 to

493, endorsing instead a resolution asking the state legislature to forbid the use of eminent domain approved in the *Kelo* decision.

In a related but also unsuccessful effort, members of the state Libertarian Party urged the city of Plainfield, New Hampshire, to seize a 167-acre vacation retreat owned by Justice Stephen Breyer. In its place they planned to create a "Constitution Park" including monuments to the U.S. and New Hampshire constitutions.

In a reversal of sorts, the city of Hercules, California, in 2006 used *Kelo* in an attempt to stop development. Wal-Mart had purchased a $15-million, 17-acre parcel near the town's waterfront intending to construct a store on the property. The city council opposed the development and voted to seize the land to "ward off urban blight." Wal-Mart resisted the city's eminent domain efforts, and a long legal battle between the city and the corporation was predicted.

Susette Kelo continued the fight to save her home from government seizure. During the summer of 2006, she reached a compromise solution with New London. The city agreed to fund the physical relocation of the house to a nearby lot. Kelo lost her waterview location but saved the 1893 house she had spent many years renovating.

SOURCES: Associated Press, March 14, 2006; *Financial Times*, January 26, 2006; *Los Angeles Times*, May 25, 2006; *Money*, September 2006; *New York Times*, February 21, 2006, March 14, 2006; *San Francisco Chronicle*, May 25, 2006, May 30, 2006; *Valley News*, July 28, 2005.

---

without the slightest nod to its original meaning. In my view, the Public Use Clause, originally understood, is a meaningful limit on the government's eminent domain power. . . .

. . . I would revisit our Public Use Clause cases and consider returning to the original meaning of the Public Use Clause: that the government may take property only if it actually uses or gives the public a legal right to use the property.

The consequences of today's decision are not difficult to predict, and promise to be harmful. So-called "urban renewal" programs provide some compensation for the properties they take, but no compensation is possible for the

subjective value of these lands to the individuals displaced and the indignity inflicted by uprooting them from their homes. Allowing the government to take property solely for public purposes is bad enough, but extending the concept of public purpose to encompass any economically beneficial goal guarantees that these losses will fall disproportionately on poor communities. Those communities are not only systematically less likely to put their lands to the highest and best social use, but are also the least politically powerful. If ever there were justification for intrusive judicial review of constitutional provisions that protect "discrete and insular minorities," *United States v. Carolene Products Co.* (1938), surely that principle would apply with great force to the powerless groups and individuals the Public Use Clause protects. The deferential standard this Court has adopted for the Public Use Clause is therefore deeply perverse. It encourages "those citizens with disproportionate influence and power in the political process, including large corporations and development firms" to victimize the weak. (O'Connor, J., dissenting). . . .

The Court relies almost exclusively on this Court's prior cases to derive today's far-reaching, and dangerous, result. But the principles this Court should employ to dispose of this case are found in the Public Use Clause itself. . . . When faced with a clash of constitutional principle and a line of unreasoned cases wholly divorced from the text, history, and structure of our founding document, we should not hesitate to resolve the tension in favor of the Constitution's original meaning. For the reasons I have given, and for the reasons given in Justice O'Connor's dissent, the conflict of principle raised by this boundless use of the eminent domain power should be resolved in petitioners' favor. I would reverse the judgment of the Connecticut Supreme Court.

In its takings clause decisions the Court has consistently favored neither private property interests nor the government's power of eminent domain. With respect to defining a "taking," the justices have tended to favor property owners by expanding the range of government actions that come under the authority of the Fifth Amendment. The Court has, however, given broad latitude to the government to define what constitutes a "public use." The Court's decisions have revealed deep internal divisions between those justices who place primary value on the rights of individual property owners and those who accord greater value to the interests of the larger community.

Decisions such as *Kelo* have turned a once obscure constitutional provision into a subject of intense political controversy *(see Box 11-3)*. Local governments have stepped up their use of the power of eminent domain as a method of spurring economic development and raising tax revenues. With each such action groups dedicated to private property rights have become more organized and politically involved. This political conflict ensures that takings clause disputes will continue to find their way to the Supreme Court's docket for some time to come.

READINGS

Ackerman, Alan T. *Current Condemnation Law: Takings, Compensation, and Benefits.* Chicago: American Bar Association, 1994.

Ackerman, Bruce. *Economic Foundations of Property Law.* Boston: Little, Brown, 1975.

———— *Private Property and the Constitution.* New Haven: Yale University Press, 1977.

Coyle, Dennis J. *Property Rights and the Constitution: Shaping Society through Land Regulation.* Albany: State University of New York Press, 1993.

Eagle, Steven J. *Regulatory Takings.* Charlottesville, Va.: Lexis Publishing, 2001.

Ely, James W., Jr. *The Guardian of Every Other Right: A Constitutional History of Property Rights.* New York: Oxford University Press, 1992.

Epstein, Richard A. *Takings: Private Property and the Power of Eminent Domain.* Cambridge: Harvard University Press, 1985.

Fischel, William A. *Regulatory Takings: Law, Economics, and Politics.* Cambridge: Harvard University Press, 1995.

Greenhut, Steven. *Abuse of Power: How the Government Misuses Eminent Domain.* Santa Ana, Calif.: Seven Locks Press, 2004.

Mercuro, Nicholas. *Taking Property and Just Compensation.* Boston: Kluwer, 1992.

Miceli, Thomas J., and Kathleen Segerson. *Compensation for Regulatory Takings.* Greenwich, Conn.: JAI Press, 1996.

Nedelsky, Jennifer. *Private Property and the Limits of American Constitutionalism: The Madisonian Framework and Its Legacy.* Chicago: University of Chicago Press, 1990.

Olivetti, Alfred M. *This Land Is Your Land, This Land Is My Land: The Property Rights Movement and Regulatory Takings.* New York: LFB Scholarly Publishing, 2003.

Paul, Ellen Frankel. *Liberty, Property, and the Foundations of the American Constitution.* Albany: State University of New York Press, 1988.

————. *Property Rights and Eminent Domain.* New Brunswick, N.J.: Transaction, 1987.

Roberts, Thomas E., ed. *Taking Sides on Takings Issues: The Impact of Tahoe-Sierra.* Chicago: American Bar Association, 2003.

Schultz, David A. *Property, Power, and American Democracy.* New Brunswick, N.J.: Transaction, 1992.

Stoebuck, William B. *Nontrespassory Takings in Eminent Domain.* Charlottesville, Va.: Michie, 1977.

PART V
CIVIL LIBERTIES

APPROACHING CIVIL LIBERTIES

The next five chapters explore Supreme Court interpretation of the guarantees contained in the First and Second Amendments and those that have been seen as relating to the right of privacy. These constitutional provisions allow Americans to live their lives as they please, to worship in whatever manner they wish, to hold and express political and social views of their own conviction, to place demands upon the government, to join with others, to print and read what satisfies them, and to keep government out of those areas of human life that are considered private and personal. Yet in contemporary society few freedoms are absolute. To maintain order, the government must regulate in ways that may restrict some of these liberties. The history of the Supreme Court is a chronicle of how it has played its role as an interpreter of these fundamental rights and an umpire between the often contradictory values of freedom and order.

As a student approaching civil liberties, perhaps for the first time, you might be wondering why we devote so much space in chapter 12 (religion) and chapters 13 (speech) and 14 (press) to the following few phrases:

Congress shall make no law respecting an establishment of religion, or prohibiting the free exercise thereof; or abridging the freedom of speech, or of the press; or the right of the people peaceably to assemble, and to petition the Government for a redress of grievances.

After all, the guarantees contained in the First Amendment seem specific enough—or do they? Suppose we read about a religion that required its members to ingest LSD before religious services, or about students who expressed their opposition to university policies by burning down the administration building, or about a radio station that regularly allowed its announcers to use profanity. Taking the words of the First Amendment, "Congress shall make *no* law," to heart, we might conclude that its language—the guarantees of freedom of religion, speech, and press—protects these activities. Is that conclusion correct? Is society obliged to condone forms of expression such as those in our examples? What these and the subsequent case examples illustrate is that a gap sometimes exists between the words of the First Amendment and reality. Although the language of the amendment may seem straightforward, its meaning can be elusive and therefore difficult to apply to actual circumstances.

In contrast, the constitutional problems presented by the Second Amendment center on what exactly the amendment covers. Some argue that it creates only a narrow right—that of the states to maintain "a well regulated militia"; others suggest that it creates a broader right that enables citizens to "keep and bear" guns. In chapter 15, we sort through these competing approaches, as well as the Supreme Court's most recent and definitive statement on the subject— its decision in *District of Columbia v. Heller* (2008), in which the majority came down on the side of those who have long argued for a broad interpretation.

The Supreme Court's formulation and interpretation of a right to privacy, as we shall see in chapter 16, present even more difficulties, primarily because the Constitution contains no explicit mention of such a guarantee. Even though most justices agree that a right to privacy exists, they have disagreed over various questions, including from what provision of the Constitution the right arises and how far it extends.

It is the gap between what the Constitution says (or does not say) and the kinds of questions litigants ask the Court to address that explains why we devote so much space to civil liberties. Because the meaning of those rights is less than crystal clear, the institution charged with interpreting and applying them—the Supreme Court of the United States—has approached its task in a somewhat erratic way. Throughout the Court's history, different justices have brought different modes of interpretation to the guarantees of freedom of religion, expression, and the press, and to the right to privacy, which in turn have significantly affected the way citizens enjoy those rights.

The Supreme Court has interpreted basic civil liberties either broadly or narrowly, depending upon the tenor of the times and the philosophies of the Court's sitting justices. Since the 1950s we have seen two distinct Court periods. From 1953 to 1969 the Court was led by Chief Justice Earl Warren. It was a period in which civil liberties flourished, as the Supreme Court expanded the rights of individuals to engage in political association and expression with limited government restrictions. Similarly, the Court created greater protections for the press to publish a wide variety of materials. The justices moved to impose a greater separation of church and state and created a right to privacy that was not explicitly written into the Constitution. In over two-thirds of the civil liberties cases brought to the Court, the justices ruled in favor of the individuals or groups claiming that the government had unconstitutionally limited their freedoms.

The Warren Court era was followed by a period of more conservative Courts, under the leadership of Warren Burger (1969–1986), William Rehnquist (1986–2004), and John G. Roberts, appointed in 2005. This Republican Court era came about in part because the nation as a whole began to adopt more conservative political positions. In addition, the public reacted negatively to many of the Warren Court's rulings. The protection of various

forms of political expression, expansion of rights to publish and distribute sexually oriented literature and films, and elimination of prayer in the public schools were among the actions that large segments of the population disapproved. As we will see in subsequent sections of this book, similar reactions occurred with respect to Warren Court opinions in the areas of discrimination and the rights of the criminally accused. As a consequence of the nation's turn to the right, four Republicans (Richard Nixon, Gerald Ford, Ronald Reagan, and George H. W. Bush) ascended to the presidency and between 1969 and 1993 appointed more politically conservative individuals to the Court. It was not until Bill Clinton's presidency (1993–2001) and his two appointments to the Court that this conservative trend was interrupted, but not stopped. In 2005 and 2006 George W. Bush made two conservative appointments: Roberts and Associate Justice Samuel Alito.

Changing times and new justices brought about a Court less sympathetic to those claiming that the government had deprived them of rights guaranteed by the Constitution. The Burger-Rehnquist years—and, as it seems likely, the Roberts Court era—show a reluctance to expand civil liberties and a greater deference to the actions taken by the government. But this does not mean that the Court always rejected those who brought civil liberties claims to it. After all, it was the Burger Court that handed down the decision in *Roe v. Wade* (1973) that expanded women's reproductive rights and the Rehnquist Court that held that desecrating the American flag as a means of political protest was expression protected by the First Amendment. And, as we discussed in chapter 5, the Roberts justices (but not Roberts or Alito) ruled that prisoners detained at Guantánamo Bay have the right to file habeas corpus petitions in federal court.

Civil liberties issues occupy a prominent position on the Supreme Court's docket. About 10 percent of the decisions handed down by the justices in recent years have involved appeals based on the First Amendment or the right to privacy. This percentage is much higher than it was in the pre–Warren Court eras. Even more important is the impact of the Court's civil liberties rulings. Disputes involving aid to religious institutions, prayer in schools, the rights of protesters, hate speech, censorship of the press, libel, obscenity, and reproductive rights fall into this category. The Court's response to these issues determines the extent to which the government can constitutionally impose regulations that impinge on personal freedom.

Each decade brings to the Court new questions regarding these fundamental freedoms, as well as novel approaches to more traditional issues. In the coming pages, we examine major controversies that the justices have been asked to settle. In some areas they have been successful in developing coherent and settled doctrine. In others the Court has repeatedly returned to the same conflicts between personal freedoms and government authority without reaching conclusions that stand the test of time. This is not surprising. As you read the coming chapters you will discover that these are not issues easy to resolve. Instead, they present perplexing conflicts among values that go to the very core of what it means to be an American citizen.

CHAPTER 12
RELIGION: EXERCISE AND ESTABLISHMENT

O n my arrival in the United States," wrote Alexis de Tocqueville in the 1830s,

the religious aspect of the country was the first thing that struck my attention; and the longer I stayed there, the more I perceived the great political consequences resulting from this new state of things. In France I had almost always seen the spirit of religion and the spirit of freedom marching in opposite directions. But in America I found they were intimately united and that they reigned in common over the same country.[1]

More than a century and a half later, political commentator Garry Wills asserted:

We may not realize that we live in the most religious nation in the developed world. But nine out of ten Americans say that they have never doubted the existence of God, and internationally, Americans rank second (behind only Malta) when rating the importance of God in their lives. So why is it surprising when the decisions we make in the voting booth reflect our basic religious values?[2]

Two of the most astute observers of American politics, writing in different historical periods, reached similar conclusions: Religion plays an important role in the lives of most Americans. In a nation where 68 percent of the population belong to one of more than 350,000 churches, temples, mosques, and synagogues, it is not surprising to find chaplains reading invocations before legislative sessions or cities erecting Christmas displays.[3]

Indeed, as Tocqueville observed, Americans have always been a religious people. Americans learn in elementary school that the first settlers came to the New World to escape religious persecution in Europe and to practice their religion freely in a new land. What Americans often forget, however, is that as the colonies developed during the seventeenth century, they too became intolerant toward "minority" religions: Many passed anti-Catholic laws or imposed ecclesiastical views on their citizens. Prior to the adoption of the Constitution, only two states (Maryland and Rhode Island, later joined by Virginia) provided full religious freedoms—the remaining eleven had some restrictive laws, and six of those had established state religions. Puritanism was the official faith of the Massachusetts Bay Colony, as was the Church of England in Virginia.

More tolerant attitudes toward religious liberty developed with time. After independence was declared, some states adopted constitutions that contained guarantees of religious freedom. North Carolina's 1776 constitution proclaimed that "[a]ll men have a natural and unalienable right to worship Almighty God according to the dictates of their own consciences." But other constitutions

---

1. Alexis de Tocqueville, *Democracy in America*, Vol. 1 (New York: Vintage Books, 1954), 319.

2. Gary Wills, *Under God* (New York: Simon and Schuster, 1990), book jacket.

3. Religious membership and organization statistics are taken from *Statistical Abstract of the United States* (Washington, D.C.: U.S. Bureau of the Census, 2001), and *The New York Times 2001 Almanac* (New York: Penguin Putnam, 2000).

continued to favor some religions over others. Although Delaware provided that "[t]here shall be no establishment of any religious sect in this State in preference to another," it forced all state officers to "profess faith in God the Father, and in Jesus Christ His Only Son."

It would be fair to say that when the framers gathered in Philadelphia, they—like modern-day Americans—held divergent views about the relationship between religion and the state. Even so, the subject of religion arose only occasionally during the course of the debates. After one particularly difficult session, Benjamin Franklin moved that the delegates pray "for the assistance of Heaven, and its blessings on our deliberations." With virtual unanimity, the delegates attacked Franklin, arguing that a prayer session might offend some members and that it would require them to pay a minister "to officiate in [the] service."[4] In the end, the founders mentioned religion only once in the Constitution. Article VI provides that all government officials must take an oath to "support this Constitution; but no religious Test shall ever be required as a Qualification to any Office or public Trust under the United States."

Opponents of the proposed Constitution objected to its lack of any guarantees of religious liberty. New York Anti-Federalists, for example, condemned the document for "not securing the rights of conscience in matters of religion, of granting the liberty of worshipping God agreeable to the mode thereby dictated."[5] Many states proposed amendments to the Constitution that centered on religious liberty.

In response to such criticism, the first Congress took up the question of religious liberty in developing a proposed bill of rights. At the conclusion of congressional debate and the state ratification process, the establishment and the free exercise clauses became the first two guarantees contained in the First Amendment of the Constitution: "Congress shall make no law respecting an establishment of religion, or prohibiting the free exercise thereof. . . ."

But how has the Court interpreted the establishment and free exercise clauses? Are their meanings the same today as when the framers wrote them? In this chapter, we examine these and other questions associated with the First Amendment's religion clauses.

FREE EXERCISE OF RELIGION

The First Amendment ("Congress shall make no law . . . prohibiting the free exercise" of religion) appears to erect a solid barrier against government regulation of religious practice. But imagine a religious sect whose members handle poisonous snakes in the belief that such activity demonstrates their faith in God. Should government prohibit such activity because it is dangerous? Or should snake handling fall under the umbrella of the free exercise of religion and therefore constitute constitutionally protected behavior?

A literal approach to the free exercise clause would suggest the latter; that is, religious denominations can pursue any exercise of their religion they desire. It seems clear, however, that the majority of Americans did not think the free exercise of religion meant any such thing at the time the clause was framed. Although we do not know specifically what the framers intended by the words "free exercise" (congressional debates over religious guarantees tended to focus on the establishment clause, rather than the free exercise clause), writings and documents of the day point to a universally accepted limit.[6] As Thomas Jefferson set it out in 1802 in a letter to the Danbury Baptist Association: "[I believe] that religion is a matter which lies solely between man and his God; that he owes account to none other for his faith or his worship; that the legislative powers of the Government reach actions only, and not opinion."[7] In other words, the free exercise of religion is not limitless, as a literal reading of the amendment would suggest. Rather, at least under Jefferson's interpretation, governments can regulate "actions."

---

4. Quoted by Adam Clymer in "Congress Moves to Ease Curb on Religious Acts," *New York Times*, May 10, 1993, A9.

5. Address of the Albany Antifederal Committee, April 26, 1788, excerpted in Daniel A. Farber and Suzanna Sherry, *A History of the American Constitution*, 2nd ed. (St. Paul: Thomson/West, 2005), 256.

6. Michael W. McConnell, "Free Exercise as the Framers Understood It," in *The Bill of Rights: Original Meaning and Current Understanding*, ed. Eugene W. Hickok Jr. (Charlottesville: University Press of Virginia, 1991).

7. Letter to the Danbury Baptist Association, 1802, quoted in *Reynolds v. United States* (1879).

The Belief/Action Distinction and the Valid Secular Policy Test

Like Jefferson, the Supreme Court has never taken a literal approach to the free exercise clause. Rather, in its first major decision in this area, it seized on his words to proclaim that some religious activities lie beyond First Amendment protection. That case was **Reynolds v. United States** (1879), which involved the Mormon practice of polygamy. Mormons at that time believed that men "had the duty . . . to practice polygamy" and that failure to do so would result in "damnation in the life to come." Word of this practice found its way to the U.S. Congress, which was charged with governing the Utah territory, where many Mormons lived. In 1874 Congress outlawed polygamy. After he took his second wife, George Reynolds, a Mormon, was charged with violating the law. In his defense, Reynolds argued that he was following the dictates of his faith. Punishing him, Reynolds argued, would be a direct violation of the First Amendment, which prohibits Congress from making any law prohibiting free exercise of religion.

The U.S. Supreme Court disagreed. In a unanimous opinion, the justices rejected an absolutist interpretation of the clause and instead sought to draw a distinction between behavior it did and did not protect. Chief Justice Morrison Waite's opinion for the Court asserted: "Congress was deprived of all legislative power over mere opinion, but was left free to reach actions which were in violation of social duties or subversive of the good order." This distinction between opinions (or beliefs) and actions (or practices) became, as we shall see, the centerpiece for several future religion cases.

In **Cantwell v. Connecticut** (1940) the Court embellished the belief-action dichotomy. Here, the Court considered a Connecticut law that required those who wanted to solicit money to obtain a "certificate of approval" from the state's secretary of the Public Welfare Council. The state charged this official with determining whether "the cause is a religious one" or one of a "*bona fide* object of charity." If the official found neither, he was authorized to withhold the necessary certificate.

Although this law was neutral—that is, it applied to all those engaging in solicitation for any religious or

Russell Cantwell raising funds for the Jehovah's Witnesses in Brooklyn in 1991. He, his brother Jesse, and his father, Newton Cantwell, were convicted for soliciting without a license; the Supreme Court overturned the convictions in 1940.

charitable cause—the Jehovah's Witnesses challenged it as a restriction on their free exercise rights. This denomination considers itself "ministers of the gospel to the 'gentiles,'" and, as such, distributes pamphlets and solicits money, activities regulated by the Connecticut law. Accordingly the Witnesses argued that the state regulation deprived them of "their right of freedom to worship Almighty God."

In a unanimous decision, the Court held for the Witnesses. Yet Justice Owen Roberts's majority opinion was something less than a complete victory for them. Not only did Roberts rely on the belief-action dichotomy—he claimed that the free exercise clause covered belief and action—"[t]he first is absolute but, in the nature of things, the second cannot be"—but he went further, explaining how the Court distinguishes protected action from illegal action. He said that the Court looks at the particular legislation or policy adopted by the government. If the policy serves a legitimate nonreligious governmental goal, not directed at any particular religion, the Court upholds it, even if the legislation has the effect of conflicting with religious practices. Applying this principle, which some analysts refer to as the "valid secular policy" test, to *Cantwell*, Roberts asserted that the state could regulate the collection of funds, even if those funds were for a religious purpose, because it has a valid interest in protecting its citizens from fraudulent solicitation. The major defect in the law? It empowered a single administrative official to determine if a cause was religious. Had the law not contained such a provision, the Court probably would have upheld it as a legitimate secular policy.

If the Court had upheld the law, the Jehovah's Witnesses would have found it more difficult to carry out the dictates of their religion. By the same token, all other would-be solicitors—charitable organizations and the like—would have been similarly affected. In other words, the religious and the nonreligious would have been subject to the regulations. Looking at *Cantwell* this way reveals an important underpinning of the logic of the valid secular policy test: neutrality. If the government has a valid secular reason for its policy, then in the eyes of the justices, religions should not be exempt from its coverage simply because they are religions. Exempting them would be to give religion an elevated position in society. One could argue that there is a difference between making it more difficult for a religion to carry out its mandate and for a charity to collect funds. But by adopting the valid secular policy test, the Court suggested that the effect on the Jehovah's Witnesses would amount to only an incidental intrusion on religion that would come about as the government pursued a legitimate interest.

How has this test worked? In particular, what constitutes a valid secular policy, a legitimate state interest? In *Cantwell* Justice Roberts provided some clues about what these concepts might encompass: the prevention of

fraud, the regulation of the time and manner of solicitation, and actions involving the interest of "public safety, peace, comfort or convenience." Shortly after *Cantwell*, the Court added to Roberts's list when it reviewed cases involving mandatory flag salutes and child labor laws.

At issue in the first flag salute case, ***Minersville School District v. Gobitis*** (1940), were the recitation of the Pledge of Allegiance and the hand gesture or salute that accompanied it. For most individuals, particularly schoolchildren, the pledge and salute are noncontroversial routines that illustrate their loyalty to the basic tenets of American society. Such is not the case for the Jehovah's Witnesses, who exalt religious laws over all others. They claim that the salute and the pledge violate a teaching from Exodus: "Thou shalt not make unto thee any graven image, or any likeness of anything that is in heaven above, or that is in earth beneath, or that is in the water under the earth; thou shalt not bow down thyself to them, nor serve them."

Accordingly, Jehovah's Witnesses do not want their children to recite the pledge and salute the flag. The problem, at the time of this case, was that states made the pledge and salute to the flag mandatory for all public school children. Flag salute laws became particularly pervasive after World War I as a show of patriotism. Before the war only five states required flag salutes; by 1935 that figure had risen to eighteen, with many local school boards compelling the salute in the absence of state legislation.[8]

Some members of the Jehovah's Witnesses asked their children not to salute the flag. Among these was Walter Gobitas,[9] whose two children—twelve-year-old Lillian and her younger brother William—attended a Pennsylvania public school with a mandatory flag salute policy. When they refused to salute the flag, they were expelled. Represented by attorneys from the Witnesses, Gobitas brought suit against the school board, arguing that the expulsion violated his children's free speech and free exercise of religion rights. Writing for the Court, Justice Felix Frankfurter used the valid secular policy rationale to

8. See Peter Irons, *The Courage of Their Convictions* (New York: Free Press, 1988), 16–24.

9. The family name, Gobitas, was misspelled in the records.

Walter Gobitas sued the Minersville, Pennsylvania, school district after his children, William and Lillian, were expelled for refusing to salute the flag because of their Jehovah's Witnesses faith.

uphold the flag salute requirement. Frankfurter claimed that the state had a legitimate secular reason for requiring flag salutes: to foster patriotism. That the law affected the religious practice of the Jehovah's Witnesses did not, in Frankfurter's view, detract from its constitutionality.[10]

Prince v. Massachusetts (1944) provides a second example of the valid secular policy test, this time applied in the area of child welfare. *Prince* involved a Massachusetts law that said minors (girls under eighteen and boys under twelve) could not sell "upon the streets or in other public places, any newspaper, magazines, periodicals, or other articles of merchandise." It further specified that any parent or guardian who allowed a minor to perform such activity would be engaging in criminal behavior. Sarah Prince, a Jehovah's Witness, allowed her nine-year-old niece, Betty Simmons, for whom Prince was the legal guardian, to help her distribute religious pamphlets. Prince knew she was violating the law—she had been warned by school authorities—but she continued and was arrested.

At the trial court level, there was some doubt about whether the child actually had sold materials, but the Supreme Court dealt exclusively with this question: Did the state law violate First Amendment principles? A divided Court held that it did not. Writing for a five-person majority, Justice Wiley Rutledge asserted:

The State's authority over children's activities is broader than over like actions of adults. This is peculiarly true of public activities and in matters of employment. A democratic society rests . . . upon the healthy, well-rounded growth of young people into full maturity as citizens. . . . It may secure this against impeding restraints and dangers, within a broad range of selection. Among evils most appropriate for such action are the crippling effects of child employment . . . and the possible harms arising from other activities subject to all the diverse influences of the street. It is too late now to doubt that legislation appropriately designed to reach such evils is within the state's police power, whether against the parent's claim to control of the child or one that religious scruples dictate contrary action.

10. Three years later, in *West Virginia Board of Education v. Barnette* (1943), after the initial intensity of the war years had subsided and criticism of the decision from the legal community had made their mark, the justices overruled *Gobitis*. As we will see in chapter 13, however, *Barnette* was primarily based on freedom of speech grounds rather than on religious exercise. As such, the overruling of *Gobitis* had little direct effect on the valid secular purpose test.

Clearly, legislatures can regulate religious practices of potential harm to children as well as those of questionable morality and safety. Such laws, in the eyes of the justices, present a reasonable use of state police power, which is the ability of states to regulate in the best interests of their citizens. In other words, child labor laws represent a valid secular policy and, when in opposition to a free exercise claim, the free exercise claim falls.

The Sherbert-Yoder *Compelling Interest Test*

Cantwell, Gobitis, and *Prince* have several traits in common: They were brought by a minority religion (Jehovah's Witnesses); they were decided during the 1940s, a period when the Court was neither particularly conservative nor liberal in ideological outlook; and they often involved free exercise arguments combined with other constitutional claims, such as freedom of expression. In addition, the Court's approaches to the cases were relatively consistent. The Court remained true to the belief-action dichotomy set out in *Reynolds.* Religious beliefs were not questioned, but when a religion's actions were in question, the Court invoked the valid secular policy test to resolve the disputes. These approaches occasionally led the justices to strike down state policies (*Cantwell*), as well as to uphold them (*Gobitis, Prince*).

In the 1960s, however, major changes began to occur in the Supreme Court's religious exercise jurisprudence. The first signs of change came in **Braunfeld v. Brown,** which was one of several cases the Court heard in 1961 involving "blue," or Sunday closing, laws. At issue in *Braunfeld* was Pennsylvania's blue law, which allowed only certain kinds of stores considered essential to remain open on Sunday. Abraham Braunfeld, an Orthodox Jew, owned a retail clothing and home furnishings store in Philadelphia. Because such stores were not among those permitted to remain open on Sunday, Braunfeld wanted the Court to issue a permanent injunction against the law. His religious principles dictated that he could not work on Saturday, the Jewish Sabbath, but he needed to be open six days a week for his store to survive economically. He challenged the law as a violation of, among other things, his right to exercise his religion.

In an opinion for a plurality of the justices, Chief Justice Earl Warren upheld the constitutionality of the Sunday closing laws. He did so on the basis of the belief-action dichotomy and the valid secular purpose test. His explanation of the latter, however, contained a new twist. It is constitutional for the government to pursue a valid secular policy even if it incidentally restricts religious exercise, Warren wrote, but only if there is no alternative means available that does not burden religious liberty. In other words, government could restrict religious exercise only if doing so was the least restrictive means available to achieve a valid government interest.

In opposition to Warren's new interpretation of the valid secular policy test, Justices William Brennan and Potter Stewart wrote powerful dissents, criticizing not only the outcome in *Braunfeld* but also the standard the Court used to decide the case. The valid secular policy test, they argued, provided inadequate protection of individual religious liberties.

The divided opinion over *Braunfeld* created something of a quandary for legal scholars: Was the Court signaling a change in the way it would resolve free exercise disputes? Or was *Braunfeld* an aberration? In *Sherbert v. Verner* (1963) the Court provided some answers.

Sherbert v. Verner

374 U.S. 398 (1963)
http://laws.findlaw.com/US/374/398.html
Oral arguments may be found at: http://www.oyez.org
Vote: 7 (Black, Brennan, Clark, Douglas, Goldberg, Stewart, Warren)
    2 (Harlan, White)
Opinion of the Court: Brennan
Concurring opinions: Douglas, Stewart
Dissenting opinion: Harlan

Adell Sherbert was a spool tender in a Spartanburg, South Carolina, textile mill—a job she had held for thirty-five years. Sherbert worked Monday through Friday from 7 A.M. to 3 P.M. She had the option of working Saturdays but chose not to. Sherbert was a member of the Seventh-day Adventist Church, which held that no work be performed between sundown on Friday and sundown on Saturday. In other words, Saturday was her church's Sabbath.

On June 5, 1959, Sherbert's employer informed her that starting the next day, work on Saturdays would no longer be voluntary: To retain her job she would need to report to the mill every Saturday. Sherbert continued to work Monday through Friday but, in accord with her religious beliefs, failed to show up on six successive Saturdays. Her employer fired her July 27.

Between June 5 and July 27, Sherbert had tried to find a job at three other textile mills, but they too operated on Saturdays. Sherbert filed for state unemployment benefits. Under South Carolina law, a claimant who is eligible for benefits must be "able to work . . . and available for work"; a claimant is ineligible for benefits if he or she has "failed, without good cause . . . to accept available suitable work when offered . . . by the employment office or the employer." The benefits examiner in charge of Sherbert's claim turned her down on the ground that she failed, without good cause, to accept "suitable work when offered" by her employer. In other words, her religious preference was an insufficient justification for her refusal of a job.

Sherbert and her lawyers filed suit, asserting that the rejection of the unemployment benefits claim amounted to a violation of the free exercise clause. After unsuccessfully arguing this point in the state courts, Sherbert's attorneys asked the U.S. Supreme Court to review the case. The appeal presented a fundamental question to the justices: May a state deny unemployment benefits to persons whose religious beliefs preclude working on Saturdays?

MR. JUSTICE BRENNAN delivered the opinion of the Court.

The door of the Free Exercise Clause stands tightly closed against any governmental regulation of religious beliefs as such, *Cantwell v. Connecticut.* . . . On the other hand, the Court has rejected challenges under the Free Exercise Clause to governmental regulation of certain overt acts prompted by religious beliefs or principles, for "even when the action is in accord with one's religious convictions, [it] is not totally free from legislative restrictions." *Braunfeld v. Brown.* The conduct or actions so regulated have invariably posed some substantial threat to public safety, peace or order. See, e.g., *Reynolds v. United States; Prince v. Massachusetts.* . . .

Plainly enough, appellant's conscientious objection to Saturday work constitutes no conduct prompted by religious principles of a kind within the reach of state legislation. If, therefore, the decision of the South Carolina Supreme Court is to withstand appellant's constitutional challenge, it must be either because her disqualification as a beneficiary represents no infringement by the State of her constitutional rights of free exercise, or because any incidental burden on the free exercise of appellant's religion may be justified by a "compelling state interest in the regulation of a subject within the State's constitutional power to regulate. . . ."

We turn first to the question whether the disqualification for benefits imposes any burden on the free exercise of appellant's religion. We think it is clear that it does. In a sense the consequences of such a disqualification to religious principles and practices may be only an indirect result of welfare legislation within the State's general competence to enact; it is true that no criminal sanctions directly compel appellant to work a six-day week. But this is only the beginning, not the end, of our inquiry. For "if the purpose or effect of a law is to impede the observance of one or all religions or is to discriminate invidiously between religions, that law is constitutionally invalid even though the burden may be characterized as being only indirect." *Braunfeld v. Brown.* Here not only is it apparent that appellant's declared ineligibility for benefits derives solely from the practice of her religion, but the pressure upon her to forego that practice is unmistakable. The ruling forces her to choose between following the precepts of her religion and forfeiting benefits, on the one hand, and abandoning one of the precepts of her religion in order to accept work, on the other hand. Governmental imposition of such a choice puts the same kind of burden upon the free exercise of religion as would a fine imposed against appellant for her Saturday worship.

Nor may the South Carolina court's construction of the statute be saved from constitutional infirmity on the ground that unemployment compensation benefits are not appellant's "right" but merely a "privilege." It is too late in the day to doubt that the liberties of religion and expression may be infringed by the denial of or placing of conditions upon a benefit or privilege. . . .

We must next consider whether some compelling state interest enforced in the eligibility provisions of the South Carolina statute justifies the substantial infringement of appellant's First Amendment right. It is basic that no showing merely of a rational relationship to some colorable state interest would suffice; in this highly sensitive constitutional area, "[o]nly the gravest abuses, endangering paramount interests, give occasion for permissible limitation." . . . No such abuse or danger has been advanced in the present case. The appellees suggest no more than a possibility that the filing of fraudulent claims by unscrupulous claimants feigning religious objections to Saturday work might not only dilute the unemployment compensation fund but also hinder the scheduling by employers of necessary Saturday work. But that possibility is not apposite here because no such objection appears to have been made before the South Carolina Supreme Court, and we are unwilling to assess the importance of an asserted state interest without the views of the state court. Nor, if the contention had been made below, would the record appear to sustain it; there is no proof whatever to warrant such fears of malingering or deceit as those which the respondents now advance. Even if consideration of such evidence is not foreclosed by the prohibition against judicial inquiry into the truth or falsity of religious beliefs, *United States v. Ballard*, . . . it is highly doubtful whether such evidence would be sufficient to warrant a substantial infringement of religious liberties. For even if the possibility of spurious claims did threaten to dilute the fund and disrupt the scheduling of work, it would plainly be incumbent upon the appellees to demonstrate that no alternative forms of regulation would combat such abuses without infringing First Amendment rights. . . .

In these respects, then, the state interest asserted in the present case is wholly dissimilar to the interests which were found to justify the less direct burden upon religious practices in *Braunfeld v. Brown*. The Court recognized that the Sunday closing law which that decision sustained undoubtedly served "to make the practice of [the Orthodox Jewish merchants'] . . . religious beliefs more expensive." But the statute was nevertheless saved by a countervailing factor which finds no equivalent in the instant case—a strong state interest in providing one uniform day of rest for all workers. That secular objective could be achieved, the Court found, only by declaring Sunday to be that day of rest. Requiring exemptions for Sabbatarians, while theoretically possible, appeared to present an administrative problem of such magnitude, or to afford the exempted class so great a competitive advantage, that such a requirement would have rendered the entire statutory scheme unworkable. In the present case no such justifications underlie the determination of the state court that appellant's religion makes her ineligible to receive benefits. . . .

The judgment of the South Carolina Supreme Court is reversed and the case is remanded for further proceedings not inconsistent with this opinion.

It is so ordered.

MR. JUSTICE DOUGLAS, concurring.

Some have thought that a majority of a community can, through state action, compel a minority to observe their particular religious scruples so long as the majority's rule can be said to perform some valid secular function. That was the essence of the Court's decision in the Sunday Blue Law Cases . . . a ruling from which I then dissented and still dissent.

That ruling of the Court travels part of the distance that South Carolina asks us to go now. She asks us to hold that when it comes to a day of rest a Sabbatarian must conform with the scruples of the majority in order to obtain unemployment benefits.

The result turns not on the degree of injury, which may indeed be nonexistent by ordinary standards. The harm is the interference with the individual's scruples or conscience—an important area of privacy which the First Amendment fences off from government.

MR. JUSTICE STEWART, concurring in the result.

My . . . difference with the Court's opinion is that I cannot agree that today's decision can stand consistently with *Braunfeld v. Brown*. The Court says that there was a "less direct burden upon religious practices" in that case than in this. With all respect, I think the Court is mistaken, simply as a matter of fact. The *Braunfeld* case involved a state criminal statute. The undisputed effect of that statute, as pointed out by MR. JUSTICE BRENNAN in his dissenting opinion in that case, was that " 'Plaintiff, Abraham Braunfeld, will be unable to continue in his business if he may not stay open on Sunday and he will thereby lose his capital investment.' In other words, the issue in this case—and we do not understand either appellees or the Court to contend otherwise—is whether a State may put an individual to a choice between his business and his religion."

The impact upon the appellant's religious freedom in the present case is considerably less onerous. We deal here not with a criminal statute, but with the particularized administration of South Carolina's Unemployment Compensation Act. Even upon the unlikely assumption that the appellant could not find suitable non-Saturday employment, the appellant at the worst would be denied a maximum of 22 weeks of compensation payments. I agree with the Court that the possibility of that denial is enough to infringe upon the appellant's constitutional right to the free exercise of her religion. But it is clear to me that in order to reach this conclusion the Court must explicitly reject the reasoning of *Braunfeld v. Brown.* I think the *Braunfeld* case was wrongly decided and should be overruled, and accordingly I concur in the result reached by the Court in the case before us.

MR. JUSTICE HARLAN, whom MR. JUSTICE WHITE joins, dissenting.

Today's decision is disturbing both in its rejection of existing precedent and in its implications for the future. . . .

. . . What the Court is holding is that if the State chooses to condition unemployment compensation on the applicant's availability for work, it is constitutionally compelled to *carve out an exception*—and to provide benefits—for those whose unavailability is due to their religious convictions. Such a holding has particular significance in two respects.

First, despite the Court's protestations to the contrary, the decision necessarily overrules *Braunfeld v. Brown,* which held that it did not offend the "Free Exercise" Clause of the Constitution for a State to forbid a Sabbatarian to do business on Sunday. . . .

Second, the implications of the present decision are far more troublesome than its apparently narrow dimensions would indicate at first glance. The meaning of today's holding, as already noted, is that the State must furnish unemployment benefits to one who is unavailable for work if the unavailability stems from the exercise of religious convictions. The State, in other words, must *single out* for financial assistance those whose behavior is religiously motivated, even though it denies such assistance to others whose identical behavior (in this case, inability to work on Saturdays) is not religiously motivated. . . .

. . . I cannot subscribe to the conclusion that the State is constitutionally compelled to carve out an exception to its general rule of eligibility in the present case. Those situations in which the Constitution may require special treatment on account of religion are, in my view, few and far between, and this view is amply supported by the course of constitutional litigation in this area. . . . Such compulsion in the present case is particularly inappropriate in light of the indirect, remote, and insubstantial effect of the decision below on the exercise of appellant's religion and in light of the direct financial assistance to religion that today's decision requires.

For these reasons I respectfully dissent from the opinion and judgment of the Court.

Brennan's majority opinion represents a significant break from past free exercise claims. No longer would a secular legislative purpose suffice as a justification for restricting religious exercise; rather, under *Sherbert,* when the government enacts a law that burdens the free exercise of religion, it must show that it is protecting a compelling government interest and in the least restrictive manner possible. *Sherbert* also represents a step away from previous free exercise cases in which the Court insisted on neutrality, for here the Court was striking down a law that was neutral in application on the ground that it burdened the free exercise of religion with a less than compelling interest at stake. As such, the *Sherbert* approach is much more favorable to religious exercise claims and much less sympathetic to government efforts to regulate religious practice.

The Warren Court ushered in the change in free exercise standards in *Sherbert,* but that Court heard very few free exercise cases after *Sherbert.* It was up to the justices of the Court led by Chief Justice Warren Burger to apply those standards.

The opportunity for the Burger Court to put its stamp on this area of the law arose early in the new chief's tenure. In 1972 the Court decided **Wisconsin v. Yoder**. At issue here was a Wisconsin law mandating that children attend public or private schools until the age of sixteen. This kind of compulsory education law violated the norms of the Amish, who had been among the first religious groups to arrive in the United States. As a simple people, who eschew technology, including automobiles and electricity, the Amish do not permit their children to attend school after the eighth grade, believing that they would be adversely exposed to worldly influences in regard to attitudes, goals, and values contrary to their beliefs.

In challenging the Wisconsin law, attorneys representing the parents of Amish children raised two fundamental claims. First, they asserted that the Amish did not want their children to be uneducated or ignorant. In fact, the teenagers pursued rigorous home study after their public school education. Second, because education was continuing at home, the state could demonstrate no compelling reason to require the children to attend public school. In contrast, the attorney general of Wisconsin compared this case with *Prince v. Massachusetts*, in which the Court upheld child labor regulations. He claimed that the two laws were similar because both were enacted out of a legitimate concern for the welfare of children.

Chief Justice Burger's opinion for the Court held for the Amish. In so doing, he cited *Sherbert* with approval:

The essence of all that has been said and written on the subject is that only those interests of the highest order and those not otherwise served can overbalance legitimate claims of free exercise of religion. We can accept it as settled, therefore, that, however strong the State's interest in universal compulsory education, it is by no means absolute to the exclusion or subordination of all other interests. *E.g., Sherbert v. Verner* (1963).

Burger invoked *Sherbert*'s approach to find that the state's interest was not sufficiently compelling to outweigh the free exercise claim. In doing so, the Court eliminated any doubt that *Sherbert* represented a major change in free exercise jurisprudence. The Sherbert-Yoder test, as it became known, was now firmly established. A law prohibiting individuals from engaging in religious exercise can withstand constitutional challenge only if the government has a compelling interest in doing so and uses the least restrictive means possible to achieve that end. It should not be surprising that when this test is used, the religious liberty claimant almost always is victorious.

The Burger Court continued to apply the Sherbert-Yoder compelling interest test in subsequent cases. Less than a decade after *Yoder*, the justices decided **Thomas v. Review Board of Indiana Employment Security Division** (1981), the facts of which bore a marked resemblance to *Sherbert*. Eddie Thomas was a Jehovah's Witness who worked in a steel mill. When the owners closed the mill down, they transferred Thomas to another plant. Because his new job required him to make tanks for use by the military, Thomas quit on religious grounds and filed for unemployment benefits, which the state denied. Writing for the Court, Chief Justice Burger acknowledged the parallels between *Sherbert* and this dispute: "Here, as in *Sherbert*, the employee was put to a choice between fidelity to his religious beliefs or cessation of work; the coercive impact on Thomas is indistinguishable from *Sherbert*." Accordingly, he said, "Unless we are prepared to overrule *Sherbert*, Thomas can not be denied the benefits due him."

The Smith Test

Despite the Burger Court's apparent adoption of the compelling interest standard, some of the justices wanted to rethink that standard or, at the very least, make it easier for the state to respond to free exercise challenges. As a result, in the 1980s the Court was deeply divided over the wisdom of retaining the Sherbert-Yoder test with its compelling state interest/least restrictive means standard, or returning to a position that would allow more government regulation of religious activity.

The debate began in 1982 with the Court's decision in **United States v. Lee**. This dispute began when Edwin Lee, a member of the Amish faith and owner of a farm and carpentry shop, refused to withhold Social Security taxes or pay the employer's share of those taxes. He argued that the payment of taxes and the receipt of Social Security benefits violated his religious tenets.

In a short opinion for the Court, Chief Justice Burger disagreed. To be sure, Burger conceded, "compulsory participation" in the Social Security system interferes with the free exercise rights of the Amish. But the government was able to justify that burden on religion by showing that compulsory participation is "essential to accomplish an overriding governmental interest" in the maintenance of the Social Security system in the United States. As Burger put it: "To maintain an organized society that guarantees religious freedom to a great variety of faiths requires that some religious practices yield to the common good."

To many observers, *Lee* appeared inconsistent with the Sherbert-Yoder standard. After all, the Court had previously used that test to exempt Amish children from compulsory education laws. Why was an exemption from Social Security requirements not also required by the First Amendment's free exercise clause?

Four years later, in *Goldman v. Weinberger* (1986), the Court provided even more evidence that the justices were beginning to stray from the Sherbert-Yoder test. At issue was the claim of Simcha Goldman, an Air Force psychologist and ordained Orthodox rabbi, that the military dress requirements violated his First Amendment rights. Goldman's superior officers at March Air Force Base in California had prohibited him from wearing a yarmulke (skullcap) while in uniform. Goldman's Jewish faith required him to keep his head covered at all times, but wearing the yarmulke violated the "Air Force Dress Code," a 190-page regulation that describes in minute detail all of the various items of apparel that constitute the air force uniform.

Goldman's attorneys argued that because the religious skullcap in no way interfered with his performance or created any other problem of compelling interest to the air force, Goldman's religious exercise should not be infringed. Lawyers for the military saw the issue differently. They argued that strict uniform regulations helped maintain discipline, morale, and esprit de corps. Granting an exemption to Goldman, they claimed, would lead others to request permission to wear turbans, dreadlocks, kum kums (red dots on foreheads), and so forth.

Writing for the majority, Justice William Rehnquist agreed with the government and ruled against Goldman. As he said:

Petitioner argues that AFR 35-10, as applied to him, prohibits religiously motivated conduct and should therefore be analyzed under the standard enunciated in *Sherbert v. Verner* (1963). . . . But we have repeatedly held that "the military is, by necessity, a specialized society separate from civilian society." . . . "[T]he military must insist upon a respect for duty and a discipline without counterpart in civilian life" . . . in order to prepare for and perform its vital role. . . .

Our review of military regulations challenged on First Amendment grounds is far more deferential than constitutional review of similar laws or regulations designed for civilian society. . . .

These aspects of military life do not, of course, render entirely nugatory in the military context the guarantees of the First Amendment. . . . But "within the military community there is simply not the same [individual] autonomy as there is in the larger civilian community." . . . In the context of the present case, when evaluating whether military needs justify a particular restriction on religiously motivated conduct, courts must give great deference to the professional judgment of military authorities concerning the relative importance of a particular military interest.

The Court's decision in *Goldman* fueled debate in political and academic circles. Taking up an invitation issued by Justice Brennan in a dissenting opinion ("The Court and the military have refused these servicemen their constitutional rights; we must hope that Congress will correct this wrong"), members of Congress introduced legislation to overturn the ruling. The bill allowed members of the armed forces "to wear an item of religious apparel while in uniform" so long as the item is "neat and conservative" and does not "interfere with the performance" of military duties. Congress passed the law in September 1987. *Goldman* was effectively overturned.

Debate in academic and legal circles centered less on the Court's holding in *Goldman* than on the rationale the Court invoked to resolve the dispute. Was *Goldman* a substantial break from the Sherbert standard? Clearly, the four dissenters (Harry Blackmun, Brennan, Thurgood Marshall, and Sandra Day O'Connor) saw it that way. Justice O'Connor's opinion is particularly interesting. After noting that Court cases in this area adopted slightly different versions of a similar standard, she set out the "two consistent themes" running through Court precedent from *Sherbert* to *Lee*. First, the government "must show that an unusually important interest is at stake, whether that interest is denominated 'compelling.'" Second, "the government must show that granting the requested exemption will do substantial harm to that interest, whether by showing that the means adopted is the 'least restrictive' or 'essential.'" O'Connor saw no reason to jettison this two-pronged standard—as she thought the majority had done—simply because the military was involved. In contrast, some scholars (along with a few members of the Court) did not think *Goldman* represented a significant shift in Court opinion. They argued that *Goldman* was an exceptional case: It involved the interests of the armed forces, interests to which the justices traditionally defer. Accordingly, they predicted that the Court would return to the compelling interest–least restrictive means standard, mentioned in the dissents, in future cases.

Predictions of a return to the Sherbert-Yoder standard proved to be inaccurate. In 1986 William Rehnquist, the author of the majority opinion in *Goldman*, became chief justice. Rehnquist's promotion was quickly followed by the appointments of conservative justices Antonin Scalia and Anthony Kennedy. The shift in the ideological balance of the Court set the stage for a serious rethinking of the Court's free exercise jurisprudence.

In 1990 the justices not only reconsidered their previous free exercise rulings but also completely rejected the Sherbert-Yoder standard. In *Employment Division, Department of Human Resources of Oregon v. Smith* (1990) the Court seemed to turn its back on nearly three decades of free exercise cases and adopt a new standard. How did the majority justify its position? Do you find its logic compelling? Keep these questions in mind as you read the facts and excerpts in this highly controversial case.

Employment Division, Department of Human Resources of Oregon v. Smith

494 U.S. 872 (1990)
http://laws.findlaw.com/US/494/872.html
Oral arguments may be found at: http://www.oyez.org
Vote: 6 (Kennedy, O'Connor, Rehnquist, Scalia, Stevens, White)
    3 (Blackmun, Brennan, Marshall)

Opinion of the Court: Scalia
Concurring opinion: O'Connor
Dissenting opinion: Blackmun

This case centers on the use of peyote, which is a controlled substance under Oregon law. It is illegal to possess the drug unless it is prescribed by a physician. Peyote is a hallucinogen produced by certain cactus plants found in the southwestern United States and northern Mexico. Unlike other hallucinogenic drugs (such as LSD), peyote has never been widely used. One reason is that peyote is taken by eating the buds of certain cactus plants, which have an unpleasant taste and may cause nausea and vomiting.

There is, however, one group of citizens who regularly ingest peyote—members of a bona fide religion, the Native American Church. To them peyote is a sacramental substance, an object of worship, and a source of divine protection. They use the substance during religious rituals.

The spiritual nature of the church's use of peyote has been acknowledged by various governments. Although they have laws criminalizing the general use of peyote, twenty-three states—those with large Native American populations—and the federal government exempt the religious use of peyote from such laws. The federal government even provides licenses to grow peyote for sacramental purposes.

The dispute at issue in *Smith* arose when two members of the Native American Church, Alfred Smith and Galen Black, were fired from their jobs as counselors at a private drug and alcohol abuse clinic for ingesting peyote at a religious ceremony. Smith and Black applied for unemployment benefits, but the state turned them down. Oregon found them ineligible because they had been fired for "misconduct"; under state law, workers discharged for that reason cannot obtain benefits.

Smith and Black brought suit in state court, arguing that under the U.S. Supreme Court's precedents of *Sherbert* and *Thomas* the state could not deny them benefits. The issue for them was not that the state had criminalized peyote because they had not been charged with committing a criminal offense. Rather, they pointed to the Supreme Court's previous rulings, which indicated that states may not deny unemployment benefits because of an individual's unwillingness to forgo activity mandated by religion. The state argued that it could deny the benefits—regardless of Smith and Black's free exercise claim—because the use of peyote was prohibited by a general criminal statute, which was not aimed at inhibiting religion. Oregon also noted that it—like all other government entities—has a compelling interest in regulating drug use and that the state's law represented the least intrusive means of achieving that interest.

The Oregon Supreme Court thought otherwise, and relied on *Sherbert* and *Thomas* to find in favor of Smith and Black. The decision was appealed to the U.S. Supreme Court, where both sides assumed that the Court would use the Sherbert-Yoder standard to resolve the dispute.

JUSTICE SCALIA delivered the opinion of the Court.

The free exercise of religion means, first and foremost, the right to believe and profess whatever religious doctrine one desires. Thus, the First Amendment obviously excludes all "governmental regulation of religious beliefs as such." . . .

But the "exercise of religion" often involves not only belief and profession but the performance of (or abstention from) physical acts: assembling with others for a worship service, participating in sacramental use of bread and wine, proselytizing, abstaining from certain foods or certain modes of transportation. It would be true, we think (though no case of ours has involved the point), that a state would be "prohibiting the free exercise [of religion]" if it sought to ban such acts or abstentions only when they are engaged in for religious reasons, or only because of the religious belief that they display. It would doubtless be unconstitutional, for example, to ban the casting of "statues that are to be used for worship purposes," or to prohibit bowing down before a golden calf.

Respondents in the present case, however, seek to carry the meaning of "prohibiting the free exercise [of religion]" one large step further. They contend that their religious motivation for using peyote places them beyond the reach of a criminal law that is not specifically directed at their religious practice, and that is concededly constitutional as applied to those who use the drug for other reasons. . . .

. . . We have never held that an individual's religious beliefs excuse him from compliance with an otherwise valid law prohibiting conduct that the State is free to regulate. On the contrary, the record of more than a century of our free exercise jurisprudence contradicts that proposition. . . . We first had occasion to assert that principle in *Reynolds v.*

United States (1879), where we rejected the claim that criminal laws against polygamy could not be constitutionally applied to those whose religion commanded the practice. . . .

Subsequent decisions have consistently held that the right of free exercise does not relieve an individual of the obligation to comply with a "valid and neutral law of general applicability on the ground that the law proscribes (or prescribes) conduct that his religion prescribes (or proscribes)." *United States v. Lee* (1982). . . . In *Prince v. Massachusetts* (1944) we held that a mother could be prosecuted under the child labor laws for using her children to dispense literature in the streets, her religious motivation notwithstanding. We found no constitutional infirmity in "excluding [these children] from doing there what no other children may do." In *Braunfeld v. Brown* (1961) (plurality opinion) we upheld Sunday-closing laws against the claim that they burdened the religious practices of persons whose religions compelled them to refrain from work on other days. . . .

The only decisions in which we have held that the First Amendment bars application of a neutral, generally applicable law to religiously motivated action have involved not the Free Exercise Clause alone, but the Free Exercise Clause in conjunction with other constitutional protections, such as freedom of speech and of the press, see *Cantwell v. Connecticut*. . . .

The present case does not present such a hybrid situation, but a free exercise claim unconnected with any communicative activity or parental right. Respondents urge us to hold, quite simply, that when otherwise prohibitable conduct is accompanied by religious convictions, not only the convictions but the conduct itself must be free from governmental regulation. We have never held that, and decline to do so now. There being no contention that Oregon's drug law represents an attempt to regulate religious beliefs, the communication of religious beliefs, or the raising of one's children in those beliefs, the rule to which we have adhered ever since *Reynolds* plainly controls. "Our cases do not at their farthest reach support the proposition that a stance of conscientious opposition relieves an objector from any colliding duty fixed by a democratic government." . . .

Respondents argue that even though exemption from generally applicable criminal laws need not automatically be extended to religiously motivated actors, at least the claim for a religious exemption must be evaluated under the balancing test set forth in *Sherbert v. Verner* (1963). Under the *Sherbert* test, governmental actions that substantially burden a religious practice must be justified by a compelling governmental interest. . . . Applying that test we have, on three occasions, invalidated state unemployment compensation rules that conditioned the availability of benefits upon an applicant's willingness to work under conditions forbidden by his religion. See *Sherbert v. Verner; Thomas v. Review Bd. of Indiana Employment Security Div.* (1981); *Hobbie v. Unemployment Appeals Comm'n of Florida* (1987). We have never invalidated any governmental action on the basis of the *Sherbert* test except the denial of unemployment compensation. Although we have sometimes purported to apply the *Sherbert* test in contexts other than that, we have always found the test satisfied. . . . In recent years we have abstained from applying the *Sherbert* test (outside the unemployment compensation field) at all. . . . In *Goldman v. Weinberger* (1986) we rejected application of the *Sherbert* test to military dress regulations that forbade the wearing of yarmulkes. . . .

Even if we were inclined to breathe into *Sherbert* some life beyond the unemployment compensation field, we would not apply it to require exemptions from a generally applicable criminal law. The *Sherbert* test, it must be recalled, was developed in a context that lent itself to individualized governmental assessment of the reasons for the relevant conduct. . . .

Whether or not the decisions are that limited, they at least have nothing to do with an across-the-board criminal prohibition on a particular form of conduct. Although, as noted earlier, we have sometimes used the *Sherbert* test to analyze free exercise challenges to such laws . . . we have never applied the test to invalidate one. We conclude today that the sounder approach, and the approach in accord with the vast majority of our precedents, is to hold the test inapplicable to such challenges. The government's ability to enforce generally applicable prohibitions of socially harmful conduct, like its ability to carry out other aspects of public policy, "cannot depend on measuring the effects of a governmental action on a religious objector's spiritual development." . . . To make an individual's obligation to obey such a law contingent upon the law's coincidence with his religious beliefs, except where the State's interest is "compelling"—permitting him, by virtue of his beliefs, "to become a law unto himself," *Reynolds v. United States*—contradicts both constitutional tradition and common sense.

The "compelling government interest" requirement seems benign, because it is familiar from other fields. But using it as the standard that must be met before the government may accord different treatment on the basis of race . . . or before the government may regulate the content of speech . . . is not remotely comparable to using it for the purpose asserted here. What it produces in those other fields—equality of treatment and an unrestricted flow of contending speech—are constitutional norms; what it would produce here—a private right to ignore generally applicable laws—is a constitutional anomaly.

Nor is it possible to limit the impact of respondents' proposal by requiring a "compelling state interest" only when the conduct prohibited is "central" to the individual's religion. . . . It is no more appropriate for judges to determine the "centrality" of religious beliefs before applying a "compelling interest" test in the free exercise field, than it would be for them to determine the "importance" of ideas before applying the "compelling interest" test in the free speech field. What principle of law or logic can be brought to bear to contradict a believer's assertion that a particular act is "central" to his personal faith? Judging the centrality of different religious practices is akin to the unacceptable "business of evaluating the relative merits of differing religious claims." . . . Repeatedly and in many different contexts, we have warned that courts must not presume to determine the place of a particular belief in a religion or the plausibility of a religious claim. . . .

If the "compelling interest" test is to be applied at all, then, it must be applied across the board, to all actions thought to be religiously commanded. Moreover, if "compelling interest" really means what it says (and watering it down here would subvert its rigor in the other fields where it is applied), many laws will not meet the test. Any society adopting such a system would be courting anarchy, but that danger increases in direct proportion to the society's diversity of religious beliefs, and its determination to coerce or suppress none of them. Precisely because "we are a cosmopolitan nation made up of people of almost every conceivable religious preference," *Braunfeld v. Brown*, and precisely because we value and protect that religious divergence, we cannot afford the luxury of deeming *presumptively invalid,* as applied to the religious objector, every regulation of conduct that does not protect an interest of the highest order. The rule respondents favor would open the prospect of constitutionally required religious exemptions from civic obligations of almost every conceivable kind—ranging from compulsory military service . . . to the payment of taxes . . . to health and safety regulation such as manslaughter and child neglect laws . . . compulsory vaccination laws . . . drug laws . . . and traffic laws . . . to social welfare legislation such as minimum wage laws . . . child labor laws . . . animal cruelty laws . . . environmental protection laws . . . and laws providing for equality of opportunity for the races. . . . The First Amendment's protection of religious liberty does not require this.

Values that are protected against government interference through enshrinement in the Bill of Rights are not thereby banished from the political process. Just as a society that believes in the negative protection accorded to the press by the First Amendment is likely to enact laws that affirmatively foster the dissemination of the printed word, so also a society that believes in the negative protection accorded to religious belief can be expected to be solicitous of that value in its legislation as well. It is therefore not surprising that a number of States have made an exception to their drug laws for sacramental peyote use. . . . But to say that a nondiscriminatory religious-practice exemption is permitted, or even that it is desirable, is not to say that it is constitutionally required, and that the appropriate occasions for its creation can be discerned by the courts. It may fairly be said that leaving accommodation to the political process will place at a relative disadvantage those religious practices that are not widely engaged in; but that unavoidable consequence of democratic government must be preferred to a system in which each conscience is a law unto itself or in which judges weigh the social importance of all laws against the centrality of all religious beliefs.

Because respondents' ingestion of peyote was prohibited under Oregon law, and because that prohibition is constitutional, Oregon may, consistent with the Free Exercise Clause, deny respondents unemployment compensation when their dismissal results from use of the drug. The decision of the Oregon Supreme Court is accordingly reversed.

It is so ordered.

JUSTICE O'CONNOR, with whom JUSTICE BRENNAN, JUSTICE MARSHALL, and JUSTICE BLACKMUN join as to Parts I and II, concurring in the judgment.[11]

Although I agree with the result the Court reaches in this case, I cannot join its opinion. In my view, today's holding dramatically departs from well-settled First Amendment jurisprudence, appears unnecessary to resolve the question presented, and is incompatible with our Nation's fundamental commitment to individual religious liberty.

[Part I omitted]

II

The Court today extracts from our long history of free exercise precedents the single categorical rule that "if prohibiting the exercise of religion . . . is . . . merely the incidental effect of a generally applicable and otherwise valid provision, the First Amendment has not been offended." Indeed, the Court holds that where the law is a generally applicable criminal prohibition, our usual free exercise jurisprudence does not even apply. To reach this sweeping result, however, the Court must not only give a strained reading of the First Amendment but must also disregard our consistent application of free exercise doctrine to cases involving generally applicable regulations that burden religious conduct.

The Free Exercise Clause of the First Amendment commands that "Congress shall make no law . . . prohibiting the free exercise [of religion]." In *Cantwell v. Connecticut* (1940) we held that this prohibition applies to the States by incorporation into the Fourteenth Amendment and that it categorically forbids government regulation of religious beliefs. As the Court recognizes, however, the "free *exercise*" of religion often, if not invariably, requires the performance of (or abstention from) certain acts. . . . Because the First Amendment does not distinguish between religious belief and religious conduct, conduct motivated by sincere religious belief, like the belief itself, must be at least presumptively protected by the Free Exercise Clause.

The Court today, however, interprets the Clause to permit the government to prohibit, without justification, conduct mandated by an individual's religious beliefs, so long

11. Although JUSTICE BRENNAN, JUSTICE MARSHALL, and JUSTICE BLACKMUN join parts I and II of this opinion, they do not concur in the judgment.

as that prohibition is generally applicable. But a law that prohibits certain conduct—conduct that happens to be an act of worship for someone—manifestly does prohibit that person's free exercise of his religion. A person who is barred from engaging in religiously motivated conduct is barred from freely exercising his religion. Moreover, that person is barred from freely exercising his religion regardless of whether the law prohibits the conduct only when engaged in for religious reasons, only by members of that religion, or by all persons. It is difficult to deny that a law that prohibits religiously motivated conduct, even if the law is generally applicable, does not at least implicate First Amendment concerns.

The Court responds that generally applicable laws are "one large step" removed from laws aimed at specific religious practices. The First Amendment, however, does not distinguish between laws that are generally applicable and laws that target particular religious practices. Indeed, few States would be so naive as to enact a law directly prohibiting or burdening a religious practice as such. Our free exercise cases have all concerned generally applicable laws that had the effect of significantly burdening a religious practice. If the First Amendment is to have any vitality, it ought not be construed to cover only the extreme and hypothetical situation in which a State directly targets a religious practice. . . .

To say that a person's right to free exercise has been burdened, of course, does not mean that he has an absolute right to engage in the conduct. Under our established First Amendment jurisprudence, we have recognized that the freedom to act, unlike the freedom to believe, cannot be absolute. See, e.g., Cantwell; Reynolds v. United States (1879). Instead, we have respected both the First Amendment's express textual mandate and the governmental interest in regulation of conduct by requiring the government to justify any substantial burden on religiously motivated conduct by a compelling state interest and by means narrowly tailored to achieve that interest. . . .

The Court attempts to support its narrow reading of the Clause by claiming that "[w]e have never held that an individual's religious beliefs excuse him from compliance with an otherwise valid law prohibiting conduct that the State is free to regulate." But as the Court later notes, as it must, in cases such as Cantwell and Yoder we have in fact interpreted the Free Exercise Clause to forbid application of a generally applicable prohibition to religiously motivated conduct. . . .

Indeed, in Yoder we expressly rejected the interpretation the Court now adopts. . . .

The Court endeavors to escape from our decisions in Cantwell and Yoder by labeling them "hybrid" decisions, but there is no denying that both cases expressly relied on the Free Exercise Clause . . . and that we have consistently regarded those cases as part of the mainstream of our free exercise jurisprudence. Moreover, in each of the other cases cited by the Court to support its categorical rule, we rejected the particular constitutional claims before us only after carefully weighing the competing interests. See Prince v. Massachusetts . . . Braunfeld v. Brown. . . . That we rejected the free exercise claims in those cases hardly calls into question the applicability of First Amendment doctrine in the first place. Indeed, it is surely unusual to judge the vitality of a constitutional doctrine by looking to the win-loss record of the plaintiffs who happen to come before us.

Respondents, of course, do not contend that their conduct is automatically immune from all governmental regulation simply because it is motivated by their sincere religious beliefs. The Court's rejection of that argument might therefore be regarded as merely harmless dictum. Rather, respondents invoke our traditional compelling interest test to argue that the Free Exercise Clause requires the State to grant them a limited exemption from its general criminal prohibition against the possession of peyote. The Court today, however, denies them even the opportunity to make that argument, concluding that "the sounder approach, and the approach in accord with the vast majority of our precedents, is to hold the [compelling interest] test inapplicable to" challenges to general criminal prohibitions.

In my view, however, the essence of a free exercise claim is relief from a burden imposed by government on religious practices or beliefs, whether the burden is imposed directly through laws that prohibit or compel specific religious practices, or indirectly through laws that, in effect, make abandonment of one's own religion or conformity to the religious beliefs of others the price of an equal place in the civil community. . . . A State that makes criminal an individual's religiously motivated conduct burdens that individual's free exercise of religion in the severest manner possible, for it "results in the choice to the individual of either abandoning his religious principle or facing criminal prosecution." . . . I would have thought it beyond argument that such laws implicate free exercise concerns.

Indeed, we have never distinguished between cases in which a State conditions receipt of a benefit on conduct prohibited by religious beliefs and cases in which a State affirmatively prohibits such conduct. The *Sherbert* compelling interest test applies in both kinds of cases. . . . I would reaffirm that principle today: a neutral criminal law prohibiting conduct that a State may legitimately regulate is, if anything, *more* burdensome than a neutral civil statute placing legitimate conditions on the award of a state benefit.

Legislatures, of course, have always been "left free to reach actions which were in violation of social duties or subversive of good order." . . . Yet because of the close relationship between conduct and religious belief, "[i]n every case the power to regulate must be so exercised as not, in attaining a permissible end, unduly to infringe the protected freedom." . . . Once it has been shown that a government regulation or criminal prohibition burdens the free exercise of religion, we have consistently asked the Government to demonstrate that unbending application of its regulation to the religious objector "is essential to accomplish an overriding governmental interest," or represents "the least restrictive means of achieving some compelling state interest." . . . To me, the sounder approach—the approach more consistent with our role as judges to decide each case on its individual merits—is to apply this test in each case to determine whether the burden on the specific plaintiffs before us is constitutionally significant and whether the particular criminal interest asserted by the State before us is compelling. Even if, as an empirical matter, a government's criminal laws might usually serve a compelling interest in health, safety, or public order, the First Amendment at least requires a case-by-case determination of the question, sensitive to the facts of each particular claim. . . . Given the range of conduct that a State might legitimately make criminal, we cannot assume, merely because a law carries criminal sanctions and is generally applicable, that the First Amendment *never* requires the State to grant a limited exemption for religiously motivated conduct. . . .

The Court today gives no convincing reason to depart from settled First Amendment jurisprudence. There is nothing talismanic about neutral laws of general applicability or general criminal prohibitions, for laws neutral toward religion can coerce a person to violate his religious conscience or intrude upon his religious duties just as effectively as laws aimed at religion. Although the Court suggests that the compelling interest test, as applied to generally applicable laws, would result in a "constitutional anomaly," the First Amendment unequivocally makes freedom of religion, like freedom from race discrimination and freedom of speech, a "constitutional nor[m]," not an "anomaly." . . . The Court's parade of horribles not only fails as a reason for discarding the compelling interest test, it instead demonstrates just the opposite: that courts have been quite capable of applying our free exercise jurisprudence to strike sensible balances between religious liberty and competing state interests.

Finally, the Court today suggests that the disfavoring of minority religions is an "unavoidable consequence" under our system of government and that accommodation of such religions must be left to the political process. In my view, however, the First Amendment was enacted precisely to protect the rights of those whose religious practices are not shared by the majority and may be viewed with hostility. The history of our free exercise doctrine amply demonstrates the harsh impact majoritarian rule has had on unpopular or emerging religious groups such as the Jehovah's Witnesses and the Amish. . . .

III

The Court's holding today not only misreads settled First Amendment precedent; it appears to be unnecessary to this case. I would reach the same result applying our established free exercise jurisprudence.

There is no dispute that Oregon's criminal prohibition of peyote places a severe burden on the ability of respondents to freely exercise their religion. Peyote is a sacrament of the Native American Church and is regarded as vital to respondents' ability to practice their religion. . . .

There is also no dispute that Oregon has a significant interest in enforcing laws that control the possession and use of controlled substances by its citizens. . . .

Thus, the critical question in this case is whether exempting respondents from the State's general criminal prohibition "will unduly interfere with fulfillment of the governmental interest." . . . Although the question is close, I would conclude that uniform application of Oregon's criminal prohibition is "essential to accomplish" . . . its overriding interest in preventing the physical harm caused by the use of a . . . controlled substance. Oregon's criminal prohibition represents that State's judgment that the possession and use of controlled substances, even by only one person, is inherently harmful and dangerous. Because the health effects caused by the use of controlled substances exist regardless of the motivation of the user, the use of such substances, even for religious purposes, violates the very purpose of the laws that prohibit them. . . . Moreover, in view of the societal interest in preventing trafficking in controlled substances, uniform application of the criminal prohibition at issue is essential to the effectiveness of Oregon's stated interest in preventing any possession of peyote. . . .

I would therefore adhere to our established free exercise jurisprudence and hold that the State in this case has a compelling interest in regulating peyote use by its citizens and that accommodating respondents' religiously motivated conduct "will unduly interfere with fulfillment of the governmental interest." . . .

Accordingly, I concur in the judgment of the Court.

JUSTICE BLACKMUN, with whom JUSTICE BRENNAN and JUSTICE MARSHALL join, dissenting.

This Court over the years painstakingly has developed a consistent and exacting standard to test the constitutionality of a state statute that burdens the free exercise of religion. Such a statute may stand only if the law in general, and the State's refusal to allow a religious exemption in particular, are justified by a compelling interest that cannot be served by less restrictive means.

Until today, I thought this was a settled and inviolate principle of this Court's First Amendment jurisprudence. The majority, however, perfunctorily dismisses it as a "constitutional anomaly." As carefully detailed in Justice O'Connor's concurring opinion, the majority is able to arrive at this view only by mischaracterizing this Court's precedents. The Court discards leading free exercise cases such as *Cantwell v. Connecticut* (1940) and *Wisconsin v. Yoder* (1972), as "hybrid." The Court views traditional free exercise analysis as somehow inapplicable to criminal prohibitions (as opposed to conditions on the receipt of benefits), and to state laws of general applicability (as opposed, presumably, to laws that expressly single out religious practices). The Court cites cases in which, due to various exceptional circumstances, we found strict scrutiny inapposite, to hint that the Court has repudiated that standard altogether. In short, it effectuates a wholesale overturning of settled law concerning the Religion Clauses of our Constitution. One

hopes that the Court is aware of the consequences, and that its result is not a product of overreaction to the serious problems the country's drug crisis has generated.

This distorted view of our precedents leads the majority to conclude that strict scrutiny of a state law burdening the free exercise of religion is a "luxury" that a well-ordered society cannot afford, and that the repression of minority religions is an "unavoidable consequence of democratic government." I do not believe the Founders thought their dearly bought freedom from religious persecution a "luxury," but an essential element of liberty—and they could not have thought religious intolerance "unavoidable," for they drafted the Religion Clauses precisely in order to avoid that intolerance. . . .

In weighing respondents' clear interest in the free exercise of their religion against Oregon's asserted interest in enforcing its drug laws, it is important to articulate in precise terms the state interest involved. It is not the State's broad interest in fighting the critical "war on drugs" that must be weighed against respondents' claim, but the State's narrow interest in refusing to make an exception for the religious, ceremonial use of peyote. . . .

The State's interest in enforcing its prohibition, in order to be sufficiently compelling to outweigh a free exercise claim, cannot be merely abstract or symbolic. The State cannot plausibly assert that unbending application of a criminal prohibition is essential to fulfill any compelling interest, if it does not, in fact, attempt to enforce that prohibition. In this case, the State actually has not evinced any concrete interest in enforcing its drug laws against religious users of peyote. Oregon has never sought to prosecute respondents, and does not claim that it has made significant enforcement efforts against other religious users of peyote. The State's asserted interest thus amounts only to the symbolic preservation of an unenforced prohibition. But a government interest in "symbolism, even symbolism for so worthy a cause as the abolition of unlawful drugs," cannot suffice to abrogate the constitutional rights of individuals. . . .

Similarly, this Court's prior decisions have not allowed a government to rely on mere speculation about potential harms, but have demanded evidentiary support for a refusal to allow a religious exception. . . . In this case, the State's justification for refusing to recognize an exception to its criminal laws for religious peyote use is entirely speculative. . . .

I dissent.

Smith represents a significant change in the standards governing free exercise disputes. For the first time since it was articulated, the Court explicitly rejected the Sherbert test. To be sure, the justices had failed to apply it in cases such as *Goldman,* but here the Court was eradicating the Sherbert-Yoder lineage of cases and returning to the kind of analysis it used in *Reynolds v. United States.* As Scalia wrote:

To make an individual's obligation to obey . . . a law contingent upon the law's coincidence with his religious beliefs, except where the State's interest is "compelling"—permitting him, by virtue of his beliefs, "to become a law unto himself," *Reynolds v. United States*—contradicts both constitutional tradition and common sense.

In place of the Sherbert-Yoder test, the Court now held that the free exercise clause does not relieve an individual from the obligation to comply with a valid and neutral law of general applicability on the ground that the law commands behavior inconsistent with a person's religious teachings. The articulation of this new standard meant, as one scholar put it, that the Court had "brought free exercise jurisprudence full circle by reaffirming the . . . doctrine of *Reynolds*" and rejecting the compelling interest approach of *Sherbert.*[12]

As you might expect, *Smith* was the subject of enormous controversy. O'Connor's concurrence and Blackmun's dissent joined by Brennan and Marshall expressed displeasure with the majority's break from precedent, asserting that the Court should stick with the compelling interest–least restrictive means approach of *Sherbert* and *Yoder.* Congress also voiced its disapproval. Soon after the justices handed down their opinion on *Smith,* interest groups began to lobby Congress to overturn the decision. As Sen. Edward M. Kennedy, D-Mass., put it, these groups feared that, under the new standard, "dry commu-

nities could ban the use of wine in communion services, Government meat inspectors could require changes in the preparation of kosher food and school boards could force children to attend sex education classes [contrary to their religious beliefs]."[13] With support from politicians as varied in ideological approach as Sens. Kennedy and Orrin Hatch, R-Utah, Congress began debating legislative options to counteract the Supreme Court's newly articulated position on religious liberty.

Before Congress could arrive at a legislative response to *Smith,* the Supreme Court heard yet another free exercise case. In ***Church of the Lukumi Babalu Aye v. City of Hialeah*** (1993) the justices considered whether the ordinances prohibiting animal sacrifice for religious purposes in Hialeah, Florida, violated the free exercise clause. The particular targets of the law were adherents of the Santeria religion. Central to this religion is animal sacrifice. Practitioners sacrifice chickens, pigeons, doves, ducks, guinea pigs, goats, sheep, and turtles at various events, including the initiations of new priests, weddings, births, and deaths, and as cures for the ailing. The animals, which are killed by cutting the carotid arteries in the neck, are cooked and eaten after some of the rituals. Santerians sacrifice as many as thirty animals during a given ritual.

Members of the Hialeah community—who apparently were less than enthusiastic about the practice of animal sacrifice—enacted six ordinances limiting animal sacrifice, which it defined as "to unnecessarily kill, torment, or mutilate an animal in a public or private ritual or ceremony not for the primary purpose of food consumption."

The Supreme Court struck down the Hialeah ordinance by a 9–0 vote. Although the justices were no more in agreement over the appropriate standard to use than they were in *Smith,* they unanimously concluded that the city had violated the free exercise clause. Despite the general wording of the ordinances, they were clearly passed to prohibit the practices of a particular religious group, the Santerians. As such, the statutes would fall under

---

12. Frederick Mark Gedicks, "Religion," in *The Oxford Companion to the Supreme Court,* ed. Kermit L. Hall (New York: Oxford University Press, 1992), 725.

13. Quoted by Adam Clymer in "Congress Moves to Ease Curb on Religious Acts," *New York Times,* May 10, 1993, A9.

Santeria priest Rigoberto Zamora cooks the lamb and goat he sacrificed in a religious ritual the previous day. Zamora and other members of his church celebrated the Supreme Court's decision striking down city attempts to prohibit animal sacrifices in religious worship.

either the Sherbert-Yoder or Smith tests. As Justice Blackmun put it in a concurring opinion, "Because the respondent [Hialeah] here does single out religion in this way, the present case is an easy one to decide."[14]

That the Court unanimously had supported a religious practice over state regulation did not stop Congress from continuing to consider ways to blunt the impact of the *Smith* decision. In spite of the Court's finding for the Santerians, the majority opinion liberally cited *Smith* as the governing standard in religious liberty cases. Almost no one viewed *Lukumi Babalu* as a retreat from the Smith test. As a consequence, in November 1993 Congress passed the Religious Freedom Restoration Act (RFRA). The purpose of the statute was to counteract the Court's more pro-regulatory policies as manifested in *Smith*. The

law's most important provision, which applied to both state and federal governments, reads as follows:

Government shall not substantially burden a person's exercise of religion even if the burden results from a rule of general applicability [unless the government can show that the burden] (1) is in furtherance of a compelling governmental interest; and (2) is the least restrictive means of furthering that compelling governmental interest.

The language should sound familiar. The statute codified the compelling interest–least restrictive means test used in *Sherbert* and *Yoder*. It explicitly rejected the general applicability approach ushered in by *Smith*. Congress was extending more protection to religious exercise rights than the Court was offering through its interpretation of the First Amendment, and it was commanding that all government officials, federal and state, use this standard.

Although RFRA was praised by most religious groups, it troubled state and local officials. Did the act mean that a city would violate federal civil rights laws if it enforced an antinoise ordinance against a religious group that used sound trucks to spread its message, or arrested for disorderly conduct a group of religious zealots who paraded

14. In *Locke v. Davey* (2004) the Court demonstrated that singling out religion for unfavorable treatment does not always run afoul of the Constitution. Here the Court approved a Washington State scholarship program that funded advanced studies for especially promising students. Although students could use the scholarships to go to public, private, or religious colleges, state moneys could not be used to attend programs for the training of clergy. The Court found that excepting such devotional studies from the scholarship program did not violate the precedent set in *Church of the Lukumi Babalu Aye v. City of Hialeah.*

down streets blocking traffic, or failed to make religious accommodations for jail inmates? What did the statute mean when it prohibited a government from imposing a substantial burden on a person's religious exercise? What standards would be used to determine a compelling government interest and the least restrictive means?

It did not take long for the statute to be challenged. A dispute arose between St. Peter the Apostle Catholic Church and the city of Boerne, Texas. Based on its historic preservation policies, the city had denied the church permission to tear down its existing building and erect a new structure large enough to serve its expanding congregation. The Catholic archdiocese claimed that under RFRA the city was without power to block construction. Did Congress act constitutionally when it passed a statute substituting its own preferred free exercise test for the one handed down by the Court in *Smith*?

The Court answered this question in *City of Boerne v. Flores* (1997). The justices struck down RFRA as applied to the states, finding that the law violated both the separation of powers and the principles of federalism. First, Congress had intruded on the powers of the judicial branch. The judiciary, not the legislature, is given authority to determine what the Constitution means. Congress violated principles of the separation of powers when it attempted to replace the Court's interpretation of the Constitution (i.e., the Smith test) with its own (i.e., the Sherbert-Yoder standard). Second, the national legislature had no authority to command the state governments to adopt the compelling interest–least restrictive means test.

The Court's decision in *City of Boerne* did not stop members of Congress from trying to reimpose the Sherbert-Yoder test. Three years after the Court issued *City of Boerne,* President Bill Clinton signed into law the Religious Land Use and Institutionalized Persons Act (RLUIPA), a scaled-back version of RFRA applying primarily to zoning issues and the religious rights of prisoners. Congress based this law on the power of the federal government to regulate interstate commerce and to spend for the general welfare. Specifically, the provisions of the law applied to any zoning activity or prison facility that received federal financial assistance or affected inter-

state or foreign commerce. Under the law, the religious exercise rights could not be restricted without a compelling reason to do so using the least restrictive means possible.

Shortly after RLUIPA was enacted, a group of inmates sued the Ohio Department of Rehabilitation and Correction for violating their rights under the statute. The prisoners, members of the Satanist, Wicca, and Asatru sects, along with adherents of the Church of Jesus Christ Christian, claimed that Ohio authorities discriminated against them. They were not allowed access to religious literature, opportunities for group worship, freedom to engage in religious dress, and access to ceremonial items that members of mainstream religions were given. In *Cutter v. Wilkinson* (2005) the Court unanimously upheld the law. The justices ruled that Congress was within its authority to require accommodation of the religious liberty of persons institutionalized in prisons systems receiving federal assistance.

In spite of the Court's willingness to allow government to provide additional protections for religious liberty, the justices have not changed their view of the free exercise clause. The Smith test prevails. Under this approach, the government, if it wishes to do so, is free to make and enforce valid and neutral laws of general applicability even if they restrict religious exercise.

RELIGIOUS ESTABLISHMENT

In a letter he wrote in 1802 to the Danbury Baptist Association, Thomas Jefferson proclaimed that the First Amendment built "a wall of separation between Church and State." But what sort of wall did Jefferson imagine? Was it to be flimsy, connoting, as some suggest, that commingling between church and state is constitutional so long as government does not establish a national religion? Or was it to be a solid wall that bars all cooperative interactions between church and state? Or something in between?

Underlying the cases involving the religious establishment clause is that question: What is the nature of the wall that separates church from state? The answer is not clear, but three alternative interpretations have been advanced over the years:

1. The religious establishment clause erects a solid wall of separation between church and state, prohibiting most, if not all, forms of public aid for or support of religion.

2. The religious establishment clause may erect a wall of separation between church and state, but that wall of separation forbids only the favoring by the state of one religion over another—not nondiscriminatory support or aid for all religions.

3. The religious establishment clause prohibits only the establishment of an official national religion.

In a detailed analysis of the intent of the framers, Michael J. Malbin found that the *majority* of the founders ascribed to views 2 or 3 (*accommodationist* positions), but not view 1 (a *separationist* position), which erects the highest wall.[15] Some scholars, however, describe two of the most influential figures during the founding, Jefferson and James Madison, as leaning toward view 1, believing that government should have very little to do with religion. Because the framers did not speak with one clear voice on the matter, Supreme Court justices have frequently come to very different conclusions regarding the intent of the framers in proposing the establishment clause. Generally speaking, the decisions of the Court have fluctuated between views 1 and 2.

In the remaining portions of this chapter we deal first with the Court's struggle for an appropriate standard to use in establishment clause cases and then examine some of the recurring issues that have faced the justices.

The Search for a Standard

The Supreme Court began its search for the meaning of the establishment clause in 1899. Since that time the justices have had great difficulty developing a coherent and consistent establishment clause jurisprudence. As one scholar explained, "From a lawyer's point of view, the Establishment Clause is the most frustrating part of First Amendment law. The cases are an impossible tangle of divergent doctrines and seemingly conflicting results."[16]

Initial Attempts. *Bradfield v. Roberts* (1899) was the Court's first establishment clause dispute. It involved a $30,000 appropriation to a hospital in Washington, D.C., for the construction of facilities to be used to treat indigent patients. The appropriation was challenged because the hospital was operated by Roman Catholic nuns. The justices, however, unanimously rejected the challenge. The Court found little relevance in the fact that Catholic nuns administered the hospital. It was the purpose of the facility that was important to the Court; and in this case the justices found the hospital to have a secular, not religious, purpose.

Bradfield was important because it demonstrated from the start that the Court was willing to allow some aid to religious institutions, especially if the aid was intended to advance a clear secular purpose. But the Court certainly did not offer a comprehensive legal standard by which to adjudicate future claims.

Almost fifty years elapsed between *Bradfield* and the next important religious establishment case, ***Everson v. Board of Education*** (1947). This litigation involved a 1941 New Jersey law authorizing local school boards that provided "any transportation for public school children to and from school" also to supply transportation to schoolchildren living in the district who attended nonprofit private schools. Ewing Township decided to use tax dollars to reimburse parents for transportation costs incurred in sending their children to school. Because the township had no public high schools of its own, the reimbursement policy covered transportation expenses to parents sending their children to three neighboring public high schools. It also covered four private schools, all of which were affiliated with the Roman Catholic Church. In addition to normal secular subjects, these schools provided regular religious instruction conforming to the religion's tenets and modes of worship of the Catholic faith. The average payment to parents sending their chil-

15. Michael J. Malbin, *Religion and Politics: The Intentions of the Authors of the First Amendment* (New York: Oxford University Press, 1988); Leonard W. Levy, *Constitutional Opinions* (New York: Oxford University Press, 1986) and *The Establishment Clause*, 2nd ed. (Chapel Hill: University of North Carolina Press, 1994); and Garry Wills, *Under God* (New York: Simon and Schuster, 1990).

16. Daniel A. Farber, *The First Amendment* (New York: Foundation Press, 1998), 263.

dren to public or Catholic schools was $40 per student. Arch Everson, a taxpayer living in the district, challenged the reimbursements to parents sending their children to private religious schools. He argued that they supported religion in violation of the establishment clause of the First Amendment.

In his opinion for a divided Court, Justice Hugo Black held for the state. As he wrote:

[W]e cannot say that the First Amendment prohibits New Jersey from spending tax-raised funds to pay the bus fares of parochial school pupils as a part of a general program under which it pays the fares of pupils attending public and other schools. It is undoubtedly true that children are helped to get to church schools. There is even a possibility that some of the children might not be sent to the church schools if the parents were compelled to pay their children's bus fares out of their own pockets when transportation to a public school would have been paid for by the State. The same possibility exists where the state requires a local transit company to provide reduced fares to school children including those attending parochial schools, or where a municipally owned transportation system undertakes to carry all school children free of charge. Moreover, state-paid policemen, detailed to protect children going to and from church schools from the very real hazards of traffic, would serve much the same purpose and accomplish much the same result as state provisions intended to guarantee free transportation of a kind which the state deems to be best for the school children's welfare. And parents might refuse to risk their children to the serious danger of traffic accidents going to and from parochial schools, the approaches to which were not protected by policemen. Similarly, parents might be reluctant to permit their children to attend schools which the state had cut off from such general government services as ordinary police and fire protection, connections for sewage disposal, public highways and sidewalks. Of course, cutting off church schools from these services, so separate and so indisputably marked off from the religious function, would make it far more difficult for the schools to operate. But such is obviously not the purpose of the First Amendment. That Amendment requires the state to be a neutral in its relations with groups of religious believers and non-believers; it does not require the state to be their adversary. State power is no more to be used so as to handicap religions, than it is to favor them.

Beyond this basic holding, the Court's decision in *Everson* is notable for several reasons. First, even though Black ruled for the state, his opinion etches into law that interpretation of Madison's and Jefferson's philosophies that suggests their desire for a strong wall of separation of church and state. As he noted, in an often-cited passage from the opinion:

The "establishment of religion" clause of the First Amendment means at least this: Neither a state nor the Federal Government can set up a church. Neither can pass laws which aid one religion, aid all religions, or prefer one religion over another. Neither can force nor influence a person to go to or to remain away from church against his will or force him to profess a belief or disbelief in any religion. No person can be punished for entertaining or professing religious beliefs or disbeliefs, for church attendance or non-attendance. No tax in any amount, large or small, can be levied to support any religious activities or institutions, whatever they may be called, or whatever form they may adopt to teach or practice religion. Neither a state nor the Federal Government can, openly or secretly, participate in the affairs of any religious organizations or groups and vice versa. In the words of Jefferson, the clause against establishment of religion by law was intended to erect "a wall of separation between Church and State."

Second, although Black's opinion does not lay down a concrete legal standard, it stresses several fundamental ideas, most notably that the aid was secular in purpose (to provide safe transportation for students); that the aid was indirect (it was not paid directly to a religious institution); that the beneficiaries of the aid were children and their parents (not churches); and that the state was "neutral in its relations with groups of religious believers and non-believers" (all schoolchildren were eligible for aid). As we shall see, these themes recur in later Court opinions and foreshadow aspects of a legal standard the Court eventually formulated.

Finally, and perhaps most important, *Everson* indicates the divisive and complex nature of religious establishment questions. On the one hand, all the justices—the majority and dissenters alike—agreed with Black's portrayal of the intent of the framers. In other words, the entire Court believed that Jefferson and Madison preferred strict separation of church and state. On the other hand—and this is the crux of the matter—the justices applied that historical framework to reach wholly disparate conclusions about the reimbursement plan. The majority, as Frank Sorauf put it, "succeeded . . . in combining

TABLE 12-1 Major Religious Establishment Cases from *Everson* through the Warren Court

Case	Issue	Vote (outcome)	Rationale
Everson v. Board of Education (1947)	Reimbursement for transportation costs incurred by parents sending their children to private schools	5-4 (accommodationist; program upheld)	Secular purpose; child benefits; neutral
Illinois ex rel. McCollum v. Board of Education (1948)	Time-release program in which religious instructors come to public school weekly and provide religious training	8-1 (separationist; program struck down)	State provides "invaluable aid" to religion
Zorach v. Clauson (1952)	Time-release program in which students are released an hour or so early each week to obtain religious instruction off school premises	6-3 (accommodationist; program upheld)	State and religion need not be "hostile, suspicious, and even unfriendly"
Engel v. Vitale (1962)	Prayer, recited by public school children each morning, written by state's board of regents	8-1 (separationist; program struck down)	Government cannot be in the prayer-writing business
School District of Abington Township v. Schempp (1963)	Reading of the Lord's Prayer and verses from the Bible in public schools	8-1 (separationist; program struck down)	Public school prayer does not have (1) a secular legislative purpose or (2) a primary purpose that neither advances nor inhibits religion
Board of Education v. Allen (1968)	Public school loans of secular textbooks to students attending private schools	6-3 (accommodationist; program upheld)	Primary purpose of the law furthers education, not religion
Epperson v. Arkansas (1968)	Barring the teaching of evolutionary theory in public schools	9-0 (separationist; program struck down)	Not neutral; nonsecular purpose

the strictest separationist rhetoric with an accommodationist outcome."[17] That is, Black's opinion, although adopting Jefferson's metaphor, found in favor of the township. The dissenters also advocated the same general approach, but they thought it led to a disposition against the township. Indeed, they took Black to task for heading in one direction and landing in another.

That the adoption of a similar historical vision of religious establishment could lead to such disparate outcomes is a problem that continued to confound this area

of the law at least through the Warren Court (and, as we shall see, crops up today). As illustrated in Table 12-1, between 1947 and 1968 the Court decided seven major cases involving the establishment clause. Three led to an accommodationist outcome (upholding a government policy challenged as a violation of the establishment clause), and four to a separationist outcome (striking down a government policy as a violation of the establishment clause). These decisions underscore several points.

The first is a reiteration: Although the Court continued to adhere to Black's historical account of the separation between church and state, it was willing to uphold some kinds of support for religion, as it had in *Everson*, while

17. Frank J. Sorauf, *The Wall of Separation* (Princeton: Princeton University Press, 1976), 20.

ruling others unconstitutional. But, as shown in Table 12-1, a pattern began to emerge from the Court's rulings. The justices seemed more willing to tolerate *some* public support of private education, such as transporting children to school (*Everson*) and loaning textbooks (*Board of Education v. Allen*, 1968), than to legitimize the entry of religion into public education, such as prayer in school (*Abington Township, School District v. Schempp*, 1963) and the teaching of creationism (*Epperson v. Arkansas*, 1968).

Another point highlighted in Table 12-1 is this: After *Everson*, the Court began to formulate a test, flowing from Jefferson's metaphor and Black's decision in *Everson*, to determine whether government actions violated the establishment clause. During the Warren Court era, that test received its fullest articulation in the school prayer case of *Abington Township, School District v. Schempp*. (Near the end of this chapter, we examine in some detail the Court's important decisions involving prayer in school.) Writing for the majority, Justice Tom C. Clark explained that standard:

The test may be stated as follows: What are the purpose and primary effect of the enactment? If either is the advancement or inhibition of religion then the enactment exceeds the scope of legislative power as circumscribed by the Constitution. That is to say that to withstand the strictures of the Establishment Clause there must be a secular legislative purpose and a primary effect that neither advances nor inhibits religion.

With these words, Clark did what Black had failed to do in *Everson*—provide attorneys and lower court judges with a benchmark for future litigation and decisions.

Early on, some analysts argued that this standard would always lead to separationist outcomes. These scholars thought it would be difficult for government attorneys to show that their policies met the two-pronged standard reached in *Abington*: that the policy had a secular legislative purpose and that its primary effect neither advanced nor inhibited religion. But, as shown in Table 12-1, those commentators were wrong. In *Board of Education v. Allen* the Court considered a New York state requirement that public schools lend, upon request, secular subject textbooks to private school students in the seventh through twelfth grades. Attorneys challenging

the state argued that the requirement violated the establishment clause, but the Court disagreed. Writing for a six-person majority, Justice Byron R. White asserted:

The express purpose [of the law] was stated by the New York legislature to be furtherance of the educational opportunities available to the young. Appellants have shown us nothing about the necessary effects of the statute that is contrary to this stated purpose. The law merely makes available to all children the benefits of a general program to lend school books free of charge. Perhaps free books make it more likely that some children choose to attend a sectarian school, but that was true of the state-paid bus fare in *Everson* and does not alone demonstrate an unconstitutional degree of support for a religious institution.

In other words, White used *Abington*'s "purpose" prong to reach an accommodationist outcome. Three justices, William O. Douglas, Abe Fortas, and Hugo Black (the author of *Everson*), dissented. Both Black and Douglas differentiated the kind of aid at issue in *Everson* (reimbursement for transportation costs) from that in *Allen* (book loans). As Douglas put it:

Whatever may be said of *Everson*, there is nothing ideological about a bus. . . . [But] the textbook goes to the very heart of education in a parochial school. It is the chief, although not solitary, instrumentality for propagating a particular religious creed or faith. How can we possibly approve such state aid to a religion?

The third point about the Warren Court's handling of religious establishment cases is that although the justices generally adopted Jefferson's "wall of separation" metaphor and agreed on the test for adjudicating establishment clause cases, they continued to split on case outcomes. As Table 12-1 illustrates, the justices were unanimous in only one of the seven major establishment clause decisions handed down by the Warren Court.

The Lemon Test. By the time Warren Burger became chief justice in 1969, observers predicted that the Court would change its approach to adjudicating establishment clause cases. Although the justices generally coalesced around the Everson historical understanding and the Abington standard, they were divided over how to apply those approaches to particular disputes. Moreover, some analysts expected that the new chief justice would be more inclined than his predecessor, Earl Warren, to rule with the government in many areas of the law. As it turned out, the new chief justice had a strong interest in taking a leadership role in religion cases. In fact, Burger was so determined to exert influence over this area of the law that during his tenure on the Court (1969–1985 terms) he wrote 69 percent (eighteen of twenty-six) of the Court's majority opinions dealing with religion, a much higher percentage than his overall rate of 20 percent in all formally decided cases.[18] *(See Box 12-1.)*

What was Burger's "understanding" of the establishment clause? How did he seek to change the law? Was he successful? We can begin to address these questions by considering Burger's first two religious establishment cases, *Walz v. Tax Commission of the City of New York* (1970) and *Lemon v. Kurtzman* (1971).

Walz involved the property tax exemptions enjoyed by religious institutions. Frederick Walz bought a small, useless lot on Staten Island, New York, for the sole purpose of challenging the state's tax laws, which gave religious organizations exemptions from property taxes. Walz contended that the tax exemptions in effect forced property owners to make involuntary contributions to churches in violation of the establishment clause. After losing in the lower courts, Walz appealed to the U.S. Supreme Court.

Writing for a seven-person majority (only Justice Douglas dissented), Chief Justice Burger found in favor of the state. The outcome was not so surprising; after all, had the Court ruled the other way, the tax status of every religious institution in the United States would have been dramatically altered. The startling aspect of *Walz* was that Burger, in his first writing on the establishment clause, sought to usher in a major change. The opinion started traditionally enough, with an examination of the "purpose" prong of *Abington*:

The legislative purpose of property tax exemptions is neither the advancement nor the inhibition of religion; it is neither sponsorship nor hostility. New York, in common with the

other States, has determined that certain entities that exist in a harmonious relationship to the community at large, and that foster its "moral or mental improvement," should not be inhibited in their activities by property taxation or the hazard of loss of those properties for nonpayment of taxes.

But instead of exploring whether the effect of the legislation inhibited or advanced religion, as the Abington standard specified, Burger suggested the following:

Determining that the legislative purpose of tax exemption is not aimed at establishing, sponsoring, or supporting religion does not end the inquiry, however. We must also be sure that the end result—the effect—is not *an excessive government entanglement* with religion. [Emphasis added.]

He went on to hold that property tax exemptions did not create an excessive entanglement with religion: To the contrary, even though tax exemptions to churches "necessarily operate to afford an indirect economic benefit," involvement with religion would be far greater if the exemptions did not exist. State officials might occasionally want to examine church records, or they might need to speak with clergy about expenditures, and so forth. As Burger concluded, the tax exemption "restricts the fiscal relationship between church and state, and tends to complement and reinforce the desired separation insulating each from the other."

In the end, then, *Walz* probably raised more questions about Burger and the fate of establishment clause litigation than it answered. Did Burger seek to redesign the Abington standard—through adoption of an "excessive entanglement" criterion—as a way to bring down the wall of separation between church and state? Would excessive entanglement now become a part of the Court's analytic toolbag for examining establishment claims? Or would the majority of the justices favor a return to a strict reading of *Abington?* Consider these questions as you read *Lemon v. Kurtzman* and its companion case, *Earley v. DiCenso.*

---

18. Joseph F. Kobylka, "Leadership in the Supreme Court: Chief Justice Burger and Establishment Clause Litigation," *Western Political Quarterly* 42 (December 1989): 545.

BOX 12-1 WARREN EARL BURGER (1969–1986)

WARREN BURGER was born on September 17, 1907, in St. Paul, Minnesota, the fourth of seven children. His Swiss-German-Austrian grandparents had come to the Middle West before the Civil War. Financially unable to attend college full time, Burger spent the years following his graduation from high school in 1925 attending college and law school evening classes—two years at the University of Minnesota and four at St. Paul College of Law, now William Mitchell College of Law. To support himself, Burger worked full time as an accountant for a life insurance company.

He graduated magna cum laude from law school in 1931 and joined a respected law firm in Minnesota, where he practiced until 1953. He also taught part time at Mitchell from 1931 to 1948.

Burger married Elvera Stromberg, November 8, 1933. They had one son and one daughter.

As a boy, Burger developed a deep interest in art and was an accomplished sculptor. As chief justice, he served as chairman of the board of the National Gallery of Art. He was an antiques buff and a connoisseur of fine wines. He also served as chancellor of the Smithsonian Institution.

Soon after beginning his law career in Minnesota, Burger became involved in Republican state politics. In 1938 he helped in Harold E. Stassen's successful campaign for governor of Minnesota.

During Stassen's unsuccessful bid for the Republican presidential nomination ten years later, Burger met a man who was to figure prominently in his future—Herbert Brownell, then campaign manager for GOP presidential nominee Thomas E. Dewey. Brownell, who became attorney general during the Eisenhower administration, brought Burger to Washington in 1953 to serve as assistant attorney general in charge of the Justice Department's Civil Division.

Burger's stint as assistant attorney general from 1953 to 1956 was not without controversy. His decision to defend the government's action in the dismissal of John F. Peters, a part-time federal employee, on grounds of disloyalty—after Solicitor General Simon E. Sobeloff had refused to do so on grounds of conscience—won Burger the enmity of many liberals.

But Burger's overall record as assistant attorney general apparently met with President Dwight D. Eisenhower's approval, and in 1956 Burger was appointed to the U.S. Court of Appeals for the District of Columbia circuit. As an appeals court judge, Burger developed a reputation as a conservative, especially in criminal justice cases.

Off the bench, Burger became increasingly outspoken in his support of major administrative reform of the judicial system—a cause he continued to advocate as chief justice. During Burger's years as chief justice, Congress approved many measures to modernize the operations of the federal judiciary.

President Richard Nixon's appointment of Burger as chief justice on May 21, 1969, caught most observers by surprise. Despite Burger's years of service in the Justice Department and the court of appeals, he was little known outside the legal community. But Nixon apparently was impressed by Burger's consistent argument as an appeals judge that the Constitution should be read narrowly—a belief Nixon shared. Burger was confirmed by the Senate, 74–3, on June 9, 1969.

Burger served for seventeen years as chief justice, retiring in 1986 to devote full time to the chairmanship of the commission that planned the bicentennial celebration of the Constitution in 1987. He continued to speak and write about judicial administration and reform of the legal system until his death in Washington on June 25, 1995. A few months before he died, Burger published a book entitled *It Is So Ordered: A Constitution Unfolds.*

SOURCE: Adapted from David Savage, *Guide to the U.S. Supreme Court,* 4th ed. (Washington, D.C.: CQ Press, 2004), 1012–1013.

Lemon v. Kurtzman; Earley v. DiCenso

403 U.S. 602 (1971)
http://laws.findlaw.com/US/403/602.html
Oral arguments may be found at: http://www.oyez.org
Vote in Lemon: 8 (Black, Blackmun, Brennan, Burger, Douglas,
        Harlan, Stewart, White)

                        0

Opinion of the Court: Burger
Concurring opinions: Brennan, White
Not participating: Marshall

Vote in DiCenso: 8 (Black, Blackmun, Brennan, Burger,
            Douglas, Harlan, Marshall, Stewart)
                1 (White)
Opinion of the Court: Burger
Concurring opinion: Douglas
Dissenting opinion: White

In *Lemon v. Kurtzman,* which tested a Pennsylvania law, Alton Lemon brought suit against David Kurtzman, state superintendent of schools. Lemon wanted the court to declare unconstitutional the law that authorized Kurtzman to "purchase" secular educational services from nonpublic schools. Under this law, the superintendent would use state taxes levied on cigarettes to reimburse nonpublic schools for expenses incurred for teachers' salaries, textbooks, and instructional materials. The state authorized such funding with certain restrictions: It would pay for secular expenses only—that is, secular books and teachers' salaries for the same courses taught in public schools. To receive payments, schools had to keep separate records, identifying secular and nonsecular expenses.

The act took effect in July 1968. Up to the time the Supreme Court heard the case, Pennsylvania had spent about $5 million annually. It reimbursed expenses at 1,181 nonpublic elementary and secondary schools attended by about a half million students, around 20 percent of the school population. About 96 percent of the nonpublic school students attended religious schools, primarily Roman Catholic.

The other case, *Earley v. DiCenso,* involved a challenge to the Rhode Island Salary Supplement Act. Aimed at improving the quality of private education, this law supplemented the salaries of teachers of secular subjects in private elementary schools by up to 15 percent of their current salaries; payments could be made only to those who agreed in writing not to teach religious subjects, and salaries could not exceed the maximum salaries paid to public school instructors. The plaintiffs claimed that this law violated the establishment clause, in part because 95 percent of the schools falling under the terms of the act were affiliated with the Roman Catholic Church. Moreover, all of the 250 teachers who had applied for salary supplements worked at Roman Catholic schools. And, as evidence submitted at trial indicated, about two-thirds of them were nuns of various religious orders.

MR. CHIEF JUSTICE BURGER delivered the opinion of the Court.

These two appeals raise questions as to Pennsylvania and Rhode Island statutes providing state aid to church-related elementary and secondary schools. Both statutes are challenged as violative of the Establishment and Free Exercise Clauses of the First Amendment and the Due Process Clause of the Fourteenth Amendment. . . .

In *Everson v. Board of Education* (1947), this Court upheld a state statute that reimbursed the parents of parochial school children for bus transportation expenses. There Mr. Justice Black, writing for the majority, suggested that the decision carried to "the verge" of forbidden territory under the Religion Clauses. Candor compels acknowledgment, moreover, that we can only dimly perceive the lines of demarcation in this extraordinarily sensitive area of constitutional law.

The language of the Religion Clauses of the First Amendment is at best opaque, particularly when compared with other portions of the Amendment. Its authors did not simply prohibit the establishment of a state church or a state religion, an area history shows they regarded as very important and fraught with great dangers. Instead they commanded that there should be "no law *respecting* an establishment of religion." A law may be one "respecting" the forbidden objective while falling short of its total realization. A law "respecting" the proscribed result, that is, the establishment of religion, is not always easily identifiable as one violative of the Clause. A given law might not establish a state religion but nevertheless be one "respecting" that end in the sense of being a step that could lead to such establishment and hence offend the First Amendment.

In the absence of precisely stated constitutional prohibitions, we must draw lines with reference to the three main evils against which the Establishment Clause was intended to afford protection: "sponsorship, financial support, and active involvement of the sovereign in religious activity." *Walz v. Tax Commission* (1970).

Every analysis in this area must begin with consideration of the cumulative criteria developed by the Court over many years. Three such tests may be gleaned from our cases. First, the statute must have a secular legislative purpose; second, its principal or primary effect must be one that neither advances nor inhibits religion; finally, the statute must not foster "an excessive government entanglement with religion."

Inquiry into the legislative purposes of the Pennsylvania and Rhode Island statutes affords no basis for a conclusion that the legislative intent was to advance religion. On the contrary, the statutes themselves clearly state that they are intended to enhance the quality of the secular education in all schools covered by the compulsory attendance laws. There is no reason to believe the legislatures meant anything else. A State always has a legitimate concern for maintaining minimum standards in all schools it allows to operate. As in *Allen*, we find nothing here that undermines the stated legislative intent; it must therefore be accorded appropriate deference.

In *Allen* the Court acknowledged that secular and religious teachings were not necessarily so intertwined that secular textbooks furnished to students by the State were in fact instrumental in the teaching of religion. The legislatures of Rhode Island and Pennsylvania have concluded that secular and religious education are identifiable and separable. In the abstract we have no quarrel with this conclusion.

The two legislatures, however, have also recognized that church-related elementary and secondary schools have a significant religious mission and that a substantial portion of their activities is religiously oriented. They have therefore sought to create statutory restrictions designed to guarantee the separation between secular and religious educational functions and to ensure that State financial aid supports only the former. All these provisions are precau-

tions taken in candid recognition that these programs approached, even if they did not intrude upon, the forbidden areas under the Religion Clauses. We need not decide whether these legislative precautions restrict the principal or primary effect of the programs to the point where they do not offend the Religion Clauses, for we conclude that the cumulative impact of the entire relationship arising under the statutes in each State involves excessive entanglement between government and religion.

In *Walz v. Tax Commission,* the Court upheld state tax exemptions for real property owned by religious organizations and used for religious worship. That holding, however, tended to confine rather than enlarge the area of permissible state involvement with religious institutions by calling for close scrutiny of the degree of entanglement involved in the relationship. The objective is to prevent, as far as possible, the intrusion of either into the precincts of the other. . . .

In order to determine whether the government entanglement with religion is excessive, we must examine the character and purposes of the institutions that are benefited, the nature of the aid that the State provides, and the resulting relationship between the government and the religious authority. . . . Here we find that both statutes foster an impermissible degree of entanglement.

Rhode Island program

The District Court made extensive findings on the grave potential for excessive entanglement that inheres in the religious character and purpose of the Roman Catholic elementary schools of Rhode Island, to date the sole beneficiaries of the Rhode Island Salary Supplement Act.

The church schools involved in the program are located close to parish churches. This understandably permits convenient access for religious exercises since instruction in faith and morals is part of the total educational process. The school buildings contain identifying religious symbols such as crosses on the exterior and crucifixes, and religious paintings and statues either in the classrooms or hallways. Although only approximately 30 minutes a day are devoted to direct religious instruction, there are religiously oriented extracurricular activities. Approximately two-thirds of the teachers in these schools are nuns of various religious orders. Their dedicated efforts provide an atmosphere in which religious instruction and religious vocations are natural and proper parts of life in such schools. Indeed, as the District Court found, the role of teaching nuns in enhancing the religious atmosphere has led the parochial school authorities to attempt to maintain a one-to-one ratio between nuns and lay teachers in all schools rather than to permit some to be staffed almost entirely by lay teachers.

On the basis of these findings the District Court concluded that the parochial schools constituted "an integral part of the religious mission of the Catholic Church." The various characteristics of the schools make them "a powerful vehicle for transmitting the Catholic faith to the next generation." This process of inculcating religious doctrine is, of course, enhanced by the impressionable age of the pupils, in primary schools particularly. In short, parochial schools involve substantial religious activity and purpose. . . .

The dangers and corresponding entanglements are enhanced by the particular form of aid that the Rhode Island Act provides. Our decisions from *Everson* to *Allen* have permitted the States to provide church-related schools with secular, neutral, or nonideological services, facilities, or materials. Bus transportation, school lunches, public health services, and secular textbooks supplied in common to all students were not thought to offend the Establishment Clause. We note that the dissenters in *Allen* seemed chiefly concerned with the pragmatic difficulties involved in ensuring the truly secular content of the textbooks provided at state expense. . . .

In our view the record shows these dangers are present to a substantial degree. The Rhode Island Roman Catholic elementary schools are under the general supervision of the Bishop of Providence and his appointed representative, the Diocesan Superintendent of Schools. In most cases, each individual parish, however, assumes the ultimate financial responsibility for the school, with the parish priest authorizing the allocation of parish funds. With only two exceptions, school principals are nuns appointed either by the Superintendent or the Mother Provincial of the order whose members staff the school. By 1969 lay teachers constituted more than a third of all teachers in the parochial elementary schools, and their number is growing. They are first interviewed by the superintendent's office and then by the school principal. The contracts are signed by the parish priest, and he retains some discretion in negotiating salary levels. Religious authority necessarily pervades the school system.

The schools are governed by the standards set forth in a "Handbook of School Regulations," which has the force of synodal law in the diocese. It emphasizes the role and importance of the teacher in parochial schools: "The prime factor for the success or the failure of the school is the spirit and personality, as well as the professional competency, of the teacher. . . ." The Handbook also states that: "Religious formation is not confined to formal courses; nor is it restricted to a single subject area." Finally, the Handbook advises teachers to stimulate interest in religious vocations and missionary work. Given the mission of the church school, these instructions are consistent and logical.

Several teachers testified, however, that they did not inject religion into their secular classes. And the District Court found that religious values did not necessarily affect the content of the secular instruction. But what has been recounted suggests the potential if not actual hazards of this form of state aid. The teacher is employed by a religious organization, subject to the direction and discipline of religious authorities, and works in a system dedicated to rearing children in a particular faith. These controls are not lessened by the fact that most of the lay teachers are of the Catholic faith. Inevitably some of a teacher's responsibilities hover on the border between secular and religious orientation. . . .

We do not assume, however, that parochial school teachers will be unsuccessful in their attempts to segregate their religious beliefs from their secular educational responsibilities. But the potential for impermissible fostering of religion is present. The Rhode Island Legislature has not, and could not, provide state aid on the basis of a mere assumption that secular teachers under religious discipline can avoid conflicts. The State must be certain, given the Religion Clauses, that subsidized teachers do not inculcate religion—indeed the State here has undertaken to do so. To ensure that no trespass occurs, the State has therefore carefully conditioned its aid with pervasive restrictions. An eligible recipient must teach only those courses that are offered in the public schools and use only those texts and materials that are found in the public schools. In addition the teacher must not engage in teaching any course in religion.

A comprehensive, discriminating, and continuing state surveillance will inevitably be required to ensure that these restrictions are obeyed and the First Amendment otherwise respected. Unlike a book, a teacher cannot be inspected once so as to determine the extent and intent of his or her personal beliefs and subjective acceptance of the limitations imposed by the First Amendment. These prophylactic contacts will involve excessive and enduring entanglement between state and church. . . .

Pennsylvania program

The Pennsylvania statute also provides state aid to church-related schools for teachers' salaries. The complaint describes an educational system that is very similar to the one existing in Rhode Island. According to the allegations, the church-related elementary and secondary schools are controlled by religious organizations, have the purpose of propagating and promoting a particular religious faith, and conduct their operations to fulfill that purpose. . . .

As we noted earlier, the very restrictions and surveillance necessary to ensure that teachers play a strictly non-ideological role give rise to entanglements between church and state. The Pennsylvania statute, like that of Rhode Island, fosters this kind of relationship. Reimbursement is not only limited to courses offered in the public schools and materials approved by state officials, but the statute excludes "any subject matter expressing religious teaching, or the morals or forms of worship of any sect." In addition, schools seeking reimbursements must maintain accounting procedures that require the State to establish the cost of the secular as distinguished from the religious instruction.

The Pennsylvania statute, moreover, has the further defect of providing state financial aid directly to the church-related schools. This factor distinguishes both *Everson* and *Allen*, for in both those cases the Court was careful to point out that state aid was provided to the student and his parents—not to the church-related school. . . . The history of government grants of a continuing cash subsidy indicates that such programs have almost always been accompanied by varying measures of control and surveillance. The government cash grants before us now provide no basis for predicting that comprehensive measures of surveillance and controls will not follow. In particular the government's post-audit power to inspect and evaluate a church-related school's financial records and to determine which expenditures are religious and which are secular creates an intimate and continuing relationship between church and state. . . .

The sole question is whether state aid to these schools can be squared with the dictates of the Religion Clauses. Under our system the choice has been made that government is to be entirely excluded from the area of religious instruction and churches excluded from the affairs of government. The Constitution decrees that religion must be a private matter for the individual, the family, and the institutions of private choice, and that while some involvement and entanglements are inevitable, lines must be drawn.

The judgment of the Rhode Island District Court . . . is affirmed. The judgment of the Pennsylvania District Court . . . is reversed, and the case is remanded for further proceedings consistent with this opinion.

MR. JUSTICE DOUGLAS, whom MR. JUSTICE BLACK joins, concurring.

We said in unequivocal words in *Everson v. Board of Education* [1947], "No tax in any amount, large or small, can be levied to support any religious activities or institutions, whatever they may be called, or whatever form they may adopt to teach or practice religion." We reiterated the same idea in *Zorach v. Clauson* [1952] and in *McGowan v. Maryland* [1961] and in *Torcaso v. Watkins* [1961]. We repeated the same idea in *McCollum v. Board of Education* [1948] and added that a State's tax-supported public schools could not be used "for the dissemination of religious doctrines" nor could a State provide the church "pupils for their religious classes through use of the State's compulsory public school machinery."

Yet in spite of this long and consistent history there are those who have the courage to announce that a State may nonetheless finance the *secular* part of a sectarian school's educational program. That, however, makes a grave constitutional decision turn merely on cost accounting and bookkeeping entries. A history class, a literature class, or a science class in a parochial school is not a separate institute; it is part of the organic whole which the State subsidizes. The funds are used in these cases to pay or help pay the salaries of teachers in parochial schools; and the presence of teachers is critical to the essential purpose of the parochial school, *viz.*, to advance the religious endeavors of the particular church. It matters not that the teacher receiving taxpayers' money only teaches religion a fraction of the time. Nor does it matter that he or she teaches no religion. The school is an organism living on one budget. What the taxpayers give for salaries of those who teach only the humanities or science without any trace of proselytizing enables the school to use all of its own funds for religious training. . . .

In my view, the taxpayers' forced contribution to the parochial schools in the present cases violates the First Amendment.

Lemon and *DiCenso* cleared up some of the confusion created by *Walz* over legal standards governing establishment clause cases. It now seemed that the justices planned to adhere to a three-pronged test, usually called the Lemon test: First, the statute must have a secular legislative purpose; second, the statute's primary effect must be one that neither advances nor inhibits religion; and third, the statute must not foster an excessive government entanglement with religion. None of these prongs is new; all had their genesis in early Supreme Court cases.

Still, the enunciation of a legal standard by which to judge religious establishment claims raises questions: Would the justices of the Burger Court and their successors continue to apply the Lemon test? Would it stand the test of time? The answer seems to be yes. The Lemon test has remained the justices' official standard for evaluating establishment clause claims. But they have interpreted and applied it in many different ways, and its critics have been many, both on and off the Court.

Lemon hangs on because a majority of justices have yet to coalesce behind an alternative standard, even though other standards have been proposed *(see Table 12-2)*. You will have further opportunities to consider these alternative standards and their proponents. In the pages to come, we explore how the Court has approached several areas in which repeated disputes have arisen. Because the Court delved into some of these areas prior to *Lemon*, you will discover trends in Court decision making in particular issues, such as prayer, over the past six decades.

Recurring Establishment Clause Issues

Certain areas of establishment clause law have generated repeated disputes that have found their way to the Supreme Court's doorstep. In this section we examine five of them: aid to religious schools, the use of public school facilities and funds for religious purposes, religious instruction in the public schools, school prayer, and religious displays.

Aid to Religious Schools. Questions concerning "parochiaid"—aid to religious schools—are among the most enduring of those raised in religious establishment litigation. Since *Everson*, when the Court signaled that some government aid programs to private schools is constitutionally permissible, state legislatures have responded by developing creative assistance programs. Each time the Court ruled in favor of such policies, states were encouraged to develop even more comprehensive programs. When the Court found fault with some of these programs, states returned to the drawing board to devise policies that would pass constitutional muster.

Complicating this process is that the Supreme Court has had a great deal of difficulty developing a consistent and coherent interpretation of the establishment clause for parochiaid cases. The adoption of the Lemon test did not result in a coherent legal policy. Rather, the justices continued to spar over the application of *Lemon* to specific disputes as well as over whether the Lemon test should be retained at all.

Between the *Lemon* decision in 1971 and the mid-1980s, the justices, although sharply divided, tended to take a more separationist approach to the school aid cases. They struck down government funding of programs such as the administration of state-required examinations, counseling and therapy services, instructional materials, teachers' salaries, and remedial instruction.[19] Aid that went directly to the religious school (rather than to the child or the parents) and state programs that supported church-related schools at the primary level were particularly vulnerable. Some decisions during this period did interpret *Lemon* in a way that led to accommodationist outcomes. The Court approved programs that supported transportation, textbook loans, college building construction, and certain tax deductions for private school tuition.[20]

In 1986, however, the Court began to change positions, a shift that coincided with the appointment of more conservative justices to the Court. Although the Court was

---

19. See *Levitt v. CPEARL* (1973), *CPEARL v. Nyquist* (1973), *Meek v. Pittenger* (1975), *New York v. Cathedral Academy* (1977), *Grand Rapids School District v. Ball* (1985), and *Aguilar v. Felton* (1985).

20. See *Tilton v. Richardson* (1971), *Roemer v. Maryland Public Works Board* (1976), *CPEARL v. Regan* (1980), and *Mueller v. Allen* (1983).

TABLE 12-2 Religious Establishment Standards Offered as Alternatives to the Lemon Test

Standard	Definition	Chief Supporters
Nonpreferentialism	"The Framers intended the Establishment Clause to prohibit the designation of any church as a 'national' one. The Clause was also designed to stop the Federal Government from asserting a preference for one religious denomination or sect over others." (Rehnquist, dissenting in *Wallace v. Jaffree*)	Rehnquist
Endorsement	"The Establishment Clause prohibits government from making adherence to a religion relevant in any person's standing in the political community. Government can run afoul of that prohibition in two principal ways. One is excessive entanglement with religious institutions. . . . The second and more direct infringement is government endorsement or disapproval of religion." "Under this view, *Lemon*'s inquiry as to the purpose and effect of a statute requires courts to examine whether government's purpose is to endorse religion and whether the statute actually conveys a message of endorsement." (O'Connor, concurring in *Lynch v. Donnelly* and in *Wallace v. Jaffree*)	O'Connor
Coercion	"Our cases disclose two limiting principles: government may not coerce anyone to support or participate in any religion or its exercise; and it may not, in the guise of avoiding hostility or callous indifference, give direct benefits to a religion in such a degree that it in fact 'establishes a religion or religious faith, or tends to do so.'" (Kennedy, concurring and dissenting in *County of Allegheny v. American Civil Liberties Union*)	Kennedy
Social conflict	"In a society composed of many different religious creeds, I fear that this present departure from the Court's earlier understanding risks creating a form of religiously based conflict potentially harmful to the Nation's social fabric. Because I believe the Establishment Clause was written in part to avoid this kind of conflict . . . I respectfully dissent." (Breyer, dissenting in *Zelman v. Simmons-Harris*)	Breyer

still internally divided, the balance of power now favored accommodationist positions. The Court began to approve a number of aid programs in ways that seemed inconsistent with previous rulings. The justices allowed government aid to pay tuition for disabled students to attend religious schools, to support special education programs and services, to fund library services, and to purchase computer hardware, software, and instructional materials.[21]

As the Court's rulings signaled greater sympathy for programs that aided religious schools, states supporting such policies became more aggressive in developing more expansive aid programs. This set the stage for a legal battle over the most controversial form of such aid—school vouchers—which the justices confronted in 2002 in *Zelman v. Simmons-Harris*.

Zelman v. Simmons-Harris

536 U.S. 639 (2002)
http://laws.findlaw.com/US/536/639.html
Oral arguments may be found at: http://www.oyez.org
Vote: 5 (Kennedy, O'Connor, Rehnquist, Scalia, Thomas)
       4 (Breyer, Ginsburg, Souter, Stevens)
Opinion of the Court: Rehnquist
Concurring opinions: O'Connor, Thomas
Dissenting opinions: Breyer, Ginsburg, Souter, Stevens

In the 1990s the Cleveland School District faced a crisis. The district served some seventy-five thousand

21. *Witters v. Washington Services for the Blind* (1986), *Zobrest v. Catalina Foothills School District* (1993), *Agostini v. Felton* (1997), and *Mitchell v. Helms* (2000).

children, most of them from low-income, minority families. Evaluation studies found it to be one of the worst-performing school districts in the nation. The district failed to meet any of the eighteen state standards for minimal acceptable performance. Only 10 percent of ninth graders could pass basic proficiency examinations. More than two-thirds of high school students either failed or dropped out before graduation. In 1995 the state assumed control over the district.

In order to improve performance, the state enacted its Pilot Project Scholarship Program. This program allowed parents to choose among the following alternatives:

1. to continue in Cleveland public schools as before;

2. to receive a scholarship (up to $2,250 per year) to attend an accredited, private, nonreligious school;

3. to receive a scholarship (up to $2,250 per year) to attend an accredited, private, religious school;

4. to remain in the Cleveland public schools and receive up to $500 in tutorial assistance; or

5. to attend a public school outside the district. Other public school districts accepting Cleveland students would receive $2,250 from the Cleveland district in addition to normal state funding for each student enrolled.

Scholarship levels were adjusted according to family income levels. Tuition assistance checks went directly to the parents who then endorsed the check to the participating private school that accepted their child. Parents were required to copay a small portion of the private school tuition expense. Private schools participating in the program could not charge more than $2,500 for tuition, and they retained their own admissions standards, although they were prohibited from discriminating on the basis of race, religion, or ethnic background. In separate actions the state created two additional educational alternatives: magnet public schools that specialized in certain subject areas and community schools that were governed by local boards independent of the regular public school district.

Although no public schools from adjacent districts opted to participate in the program, fifty-six private schools, 80 percent of them religious, did. Religious schools were the choice of the parents of 96.7 percent of the students who used tuition vouchers to attend private schools. A majority of students who used the scholarship program to attend religious schools were not of the same faith as the school's sponsoring religious organization.

Doris Simmons-Harris and other local citizens filed suit against Susan Tave Zelman, Ohio's superintendent of public instruction, charging that the voucher program violated the First Amendment's establishment clause. Both the federal district court and the court of appeals struck down the program. The state asked for Supreme Court review.

CHIEF JUSTICE REHNQUIST delivered the opinion of the Court.

The State of Ohio has established a pilot program designed to provide educational choices to families with children who reside in the Cleveland City School District. The question presented is whether this program offends the Establishment Clause of the United States Constitution. We hold that it does not. . . .

The Establishment Clause of the First Amendment, applied to the States through the Fourteenth Amendment, prevents a State from enacting laws that have the "purpose" or "effect" of advancing or inhibiting religion. *Agostini v. Felton* (1997). There is no dispute that the program challenged here was enacted for the valid secular purpose of providing educational assistance to poor children in a demonstrably failing public school system. Thus, the question presented is whether the Ohio program nonetheless has the forbidden "effect" of advancing or inhibiting religion.

To answer that question, our decisions have drawn a consistent distinction between government programs that provide aid directly to religious schools, *Mitchell v. Helms* (2000) (plurality opinion); *Agostini; Rosenberger v. Rector and Visitors of Univ. of Va.* (1995), and programs of true private choice, in which government aid reaches religious schools only as a result of the genuine and independent choices of private individuals, *Mueller v. Allen* (1983); *Witters v. Washington Dept. of Servs. for Blind* (1986); *Zobrest v. Catalina Foothills School Dist.* (1993). While our jurisprudence with respect to the constitutionality of direct aid programs has "changed significantly" over the past two decades, *Agostini*, our jurisprudence with respect to true private choice programs has remained consistent and unbroken. Three times

Roberta Kitchen, right, and Rosa-Linda Demore-Brown, executive director of Cleveland Parents for School Choice, celebrate the Supreme Court's ruling in favor of school voucher programs that endorsed a six-year-old pilot program in inner-city Cleveland and provided parents with tax-supported education stipends.

we have confronted Establishment Clause challenges to neutral government programs that provide aid directly to a broad class of individuals, who, in turn, direct the aid to religious schools or institutions of their own choosing. Three times we have rejected such challenges.

In *Mueller*, we rejected an Establishment Clause challenge to a Minnesota program authorizing tax deductions for various educational expenses, including private school tuition costs, even though the great majority of the program's beneficiaries (96%) were parents of children in religious schools. We began by focusing on the class of beneficiaries, finding that because the class included "*all* parents," including parents with "children [who] attend nonsectarian private schools or sectarian private schools" (emphasis in original), the program was "not readily subject to challenge under the Establishment Clause." Then, viewing the

program as a whole, we emphasized the principle of private choice, noting that public funds were made available to religious schools "only as a result of numerous, private choices of individual parents of school-age children." This, we said, ensured that "'no imprimatur of state approval' can be deemed to have been conferred on any particular religion, or on religion generally." We thus found it irrelevant to the constitutional inquiry that the vast majority of beneficiaries were parents of children in religious schools. . . . That the program was one of true private choice, with no evidence that the State deliberately skewed incentives toward religious schools, was sufficient for the program to survive scrutiny under the Establishment Clause.

In *Witters*, we used identical reasoning to reject an Establishment Clause challenge to a vocational scholarship program that provided tuition aid to a student studying at a religious institution to become a pastor. . . . We further re-marked that, as in *Mueller*, "[the] program is made available generally without regard to the sectarian-nonsectarian, or public-nonpublic nature of the institution benefited." In light of these factors, we held that the program was not in-consistent with the Establishment Clause. . . .

Finally, in *Zobrest*, we applied *Mueller* and *Witters* to re-ject an Establishment Clause challenge to a federal program that permitted sign-language interpreters to assist deaf chil-dren enrolled in religious schools. Reviewing our earlier de-cisions, we stated that "government programs that neutrally provide benefits to a broad class of citizens defined without reference to religion are not readily subject to an Establish-ment Clause challenge." Looking once again to the chal-lenged program as a whole, we observed that the program "distributes benefits neutrally to any child qualifying as 'dis-abled.'" Its "primary beneficiaries," we said, were "disabled children, not sectarian schools."

We further observed that "[b]y according parents free-dom to select a school of their choice, the statute ensures that a government-paid interpreter will be present in a sec-tarian school only as a result of the private decision of indi-vidual parents." Our focus again was on neutrality and the principle of private choice, not on the number of program beneficiaries attending religious schools. Because the pro-gram ensured that parents were the ones to select a reli-gious school as the best learning environment for their handicapped child, the circuit between government and re-ligion was broken, and the Establishment Clause was not implicated.

Mueller, Witters, and *Zobrest* thus make clear that where a government aid program is neutral with respect to religion, and provides assistance directly to a broad class of citizens who, in turn, direct government aid to religious schools wholly as a result of their own genuine and independent private choice, the program is not readily subject to chal-lenge under the Establishment Clause. A program that shares these features permits government aid to reach reli-gious institutions only by way of the deliberate choices of numerous individual recipients. The incidental advance-ment of a religious mission, or the perceived endorsement of a religious message, is reasonably attributable to the indi-vidual recipient, not to the government, whose role ends with the disbursement of benefits. . . .

We believe that the program challenged here is a pro-gram of true private choice, consistent with *Mueller, Witters,* and *Zobrest,* and thus constitutional. As was true in those cases, the Ohio program is neutral in all respects toward re-ligion. It is part of a general and multifaceted undertaking by the State of Ohio to provide educational opportunities to the children of a failed school district. It confers educational assistance directly to a broad class of individuals defined without reference to religion, *i.e.,* any parent of a school-age child who resides in the Cleveland City School District. The program permits the participation of *all* schools within the district, religious or nonreligious. Adjacent public schools also may participate and have a financial incentive to do so. Program benefits are available to participating families on neutral terms, with no reference to religion. The only pref-erence stated anywhere in the program is a preference for low-income families, who receive greater assistance and are given priority for admission at participating schools.

There are no "financial incentive[s]" that "ske[w]" the program toward religious schools. . . . The program here in fact creates financial *dis*incentives for religious schools, with private schools receiving only half the government assis-tance given to community schools and one-third the assis-tance given to magnet schools. Adjacent public schools, should any choose to accept program students, are also eli-gible to receive two to three times the state funding of a pri-vate religious school. Families too have a financial disincen-tive to choose a private religious school over other schools. Parents that choose to participate in the scholarship pro-gram and then to enroll their children in a private school (religious or nonreligious) must copay a portion of the school's tuition. Families that choose a community school, magnet school, or traditional public school pay nothing. Although such features of the program are not necessary to its constitutionality, they clearly dispel the claim that the program "creates . . . financial incentive[s] for parents to choose a sectarian school." *Zobrest.*

Respondents suggest that even without a financial incen-tive for parents to choose a religious school, the program creates a "public perception that the State is endorsing reli-gious practices and beliefs." But we have repeatedly recog-nized that no reasonable observer would think a neutral program of private choice, where state aid reaches religious schools solely as a result of the numerous independent decisions of private individuals, carries with it the *imprimatur* of government endorsement. . . .

There also is no evidence that the program fails to provide genuine opportunities for Cleveland parents to select secular educational options for their school-age children. . . . That 46 of the 56 private schools now participating in the program are religious schools does not condemn it as a violation of the Establishment Clause. The Establishment Clause question is whether Ohio is coercing parents into sending their children to religious schools, and that question must be answered by evaluating *all* options Ohio provides Cleveland schoolchildren, only one of which is to obtain a program scholarship and then choose a religious school. . . .

Respondents . . . claim that even if we do not focus on the number of participating schools that are religious schools, we should attach constitutional significance to the fact that 96% of scholarship recipients have enrolled in religious schools. They claim that this alone proves parents lack genuine choice, even if no parent has ever said so. We need not consider this argument in detail, since it was flatly rejected in *Mueller*, where we found it irrelevant that 96% of parents taking deductions for tuition expenses paid tuition at religious schools. Indeed, we have recently found it irrelevant even to the constitutionality of a direct aid program that a vast majority of program benefits went to religious schools. See *Agostini*. The constitutionality of a neutral educational aid program simply does not turn on whether and why, in a particular area, at a particular time, most private schools are run by religious organizations, or most recipients choose to use the aid at a religious school. . . .

This point is aptly illustrated here. The 96% figure upon which the respondents . . . rely discounts entirely (1) the more than 1,900 Cleveland children enrolled in alternative community schools, (2) the more than 13,000 children enrolled in alternative magnet schools, and (3) the more than 1,400 children enrolled in traditional public schools with tutorial assistance. Including some or all of these children in the denominator of children enrolled in nontraditional schools during the 1999–2000 school year drops the percentage enrolled in religious schools from 96% to under 20%. . . .

In sum, the Ohio program is entirely neutral with respect to religion. It provides benefits directly to a wide spectrum of individuals, defined only by financial need and residence in a particular school district. It permits such individuals to exercise genuine choice among options public and private, secular and religious. The program is therefore a program of true private choice. In keeping with an unbroken line of decisions rejecting challenges to similar programs, we hold that the program does not offend the Establishment Clause.

The judgment of the Court of Appeals is reversed.

It is so ordered.

JUSTICE THOMAS, concurring.

Ten States have enacted some form of publicly funded private school choice as one means of raising the quality of education provided to underprivileged urban children. These programs address the root of the problem with failing urban public schools that disproportionately affect minority students. Society's other solution to these educational failures is often to provide racial preferences in higher education. Such preferences, however, run afoul of the Fourteenth Amendment's prohibition against distinctions based on race. By contrast, school choice programs that involve religious schools appear unconstitutional only to those who would twist the Fourteenth Amendment against itself by expansively incorporating the Establishment Clause. Converting the Fourteenth Amendment from a guarantee of opportunity to an obstacle against education reform distorts our constitutional values and disserves those in the greatest need.

JUSTICE O'CONNOR, concurring.

[T]oday's decision [does not] signal a major departure from this Court's prior Establishment Clause jurisprudence. A central tool in our analysis of cases in this area has been the *Lemon* test. As originally formulated, a statute passed this test only if it had "a secular legislative purpose," if its "principal or primary effect" was one that "neither advance[d] nor inhibit[ed] religion," and if it did "not foster an excessive government entanglement with religion." *Lemon v. Kurtzman* (1971). In *Agostini v. Felton* (1997), we folded the entanglement inquiry into the primary effect inquiry. This made sense because both inquiries rely on the same evidence, and the degree of entanglement has implications for whether a statute advances or inhibits religion. The test to-day is basically the same as that set forth in *School Dist. of Abington Township v. Schempp* (1963) over 40 years ago.

The Court's opinion in these cases focuses on a narrow question related to the *Lemon* test: how to apply the primary effects prong in indirect aid cases? Specifically, it clarifies the basic inquiry when trying to determine whether a program that distributes aid to beneficiaries, rather than directly to service providers, has the primary effect of advancing or inhibiting religion, *Lemon v. Kurtzman*, or, as I have put it, of "endors[ing] or disapprov[ing] . . . religion." Courts are instructed to consider two factors: first, whether the program administers aid in a neutral fashion, without differentiation based on the religious status of beneficiaries or providers of services; second, and more importantly, whether beneficiaries of indirect aid have a genuine choice among religious and nonreligious organizations when determining the organization to which they will direct that aid. If the answer to either query is "no," the program should be struck down under the Establishment Clause. . . .

In my view the . . . significant finding in these cases is that Cleveland parents who use vouchers to send their children to religious private schools do so as a result of true private choice. The Court rejects, correctly, the notion that the high percentage of voucher recipients who enroll in religious private schools necessarily demonstrates that parents do not actually have the option to send their children to nonreligious schools. . . .

Based on the reasoning in the Court's opinion, which is consistent with the realities of the Cleveland educational system, I am persuaded that the Cleveland voucher program affords parents of eligible children genuine nonreligious options and is consistent with the Establishment Clause.

JUSTICE BREYER, with whom JUSTICE STEVENS and JUSTICE SOUTER join, dissenting.

I write separately . . . to emphasize the risk that publicly financed voucher programs pose in terms of religiously based social conflict. I do so because I believe that the Establishment Clause concern for protecting the Nation's social fabric from religious conflict poses an overriding obstacle to the implementation of this well-intentioned school voucher program. . . .

. . . [T]he Court's 20th century Establishment Clause cases—both those limiting the practice of religion in public schools and those limiting the public funding of private religious education—focused directly upon social conflict, potentially created when government becomes involved in religious education. . . .

School voucher programs differ . . . in both kind and degree from aid programs upheld in the past. They differ in kind because they direct financing to a core function of the church: the teaching of religious truths to young children. For that reason the constitutional demand for "separation" is of particular constitutional concern. . . .

Vouchers also differ in degree. The aid programs recently upheld by the Court involved limited amounts of aid to religion. But the majority's analysis here appears to permit a considerable shift of taxpayer dollars from public secular schools to private religious schools. . . .

I do not believe that the "parental choice" aspect of the voucher program sufficiently offsets the concerns I have mentioned. Parental choice cannot help the taxpayer who does not want to finance the religious education of children. It will not always help the parent who may see little real choice between inadequate nonsectarian public education and adequate education at a school whose religious teachings are contrary to his own. It will not satisfy religious minorities unable to participate because they are too few in number to support the creation of their own private schools. It will not satisfy groups whose religious beliefs preclude them from participating in a government-sponsored program, and who may well feel ignored as government funds primarily support the education of children in the doctrines of the dominant religions. And it does little to ameliorate the entanglement problems or the related problems of social division. . . . Consequently, the fact that the parent may choose which school can cash the government's voucher check does not alleviate the Establishment Clause concerns associated with voucher programs.

. . . In a society composed of many different religious creeds, I fear that this present departure from the Court's earlier understanding risks creating a form of religiously based conflict potentially harmful to the Nation's social fabric. Because I believe the Establishment Clause was written in part to avoid this kind of conflict, and for reasons set forth by JUSTICE SOUTER and JUSTICE STEVENS, I respectfully dissent.

JUSTICE SOUTER, with whom JUSTICE STEVENS, JUSTICE GINSBURG, and JUSTICE BREYER join, dissenting.

The occasion for the legislation . . . upheld is the condition of public education in the city of Cleveland. The record indicates that the schools are failing to serve their objective, and the vouchers in issue here are said to be needed to provide adequate alternatives to them. If there were an excuse for giving short shrift to the Establishment Clause, it would probably apply here. But there is no excuse. Constitutional limitations are placed on government to preserve constitutional values in hard cases, like these. "[C]onstitutional lines have to be drawn, and on one side of every one of them is an otherwise sympathetic case that provokes impatience with the Constitution and with the line. But constitutional lines are the price of constitutional government." *Agostini v. Felton* (1997) (SOUTER, J., dissenting). I therefore respectfully dissent.

The applicability of the Establishment Clause to public funding of benefits to religious schools was settled in *Everson v. Board of Ed. of Ewing* (1947), which inaugurated the modern era of establishment doctrine. The Court stated the principle in words from which there was no dissent:

"No tax in any amount, large or small, can be levied to support any religious activities or institutions, whatever they may be called, or whatever form they may adopt to teach or practice religion."

The Court has never in so many words repudiated this statement, let alone, in so many words, overruled *Everson.*

Today, however, the majority holds that the Establishment Clause is not offended by Ohio's Pilot Project Scholarship Program, under which students may be eligible to receive as much as $2,250 in the form of tuition vouchers transferable to religious schools. In the city of Cleveland the overwhelming proportion of large appropriations for voucher money must be spent on religious schools if it is to be spent at all, and will be spent in amounts that cover almost all of tuition. The money will thus pay for eligible students' instruction not only in secular subjects but in religion as well, in schools that can fairly be characterized as founded to teach religious doctrine and to imbue teaching in all subjects with a religious dimension. Public tax money will pay at a systemic level for teaching the covenant with Israel and Mosaic law in Jewish schools, the primacy of the Apostle Peter and the Papacy in Catholic schools, the truth of reformed Christianity in Protestant schools, and the revelation to the Prophet in Muslim schools, to speak only of major religious groupings in the Republic.

How can a Court consistently leave *Everson* on the books and approve the Ohio vouchers? The answer is that it cannot. It is only by ignoring *Everson* that the majority can claim to rest on traditional law in its invocation of neutral aid provisions and private choice to sanction the Ohio law. It is, moreover, only by ignoring the meaning of neutrality and private choice themselves that the majority can even pretend to rest today's decision on those criteria. . . .

. . . *Everson*'s statement is still the touchstone of sound law, even though the reality is that in the matter of educational aid the Establishment Clause has largely been read away. True, the majority has not approved vouchers for religious schools alone, or aid earmarked for religious instruction. But no scheme so clumsy will ever get before us, and in the cases that we may see, like these, the Establishment Clause is largely silenced. I do not have the option to leave it silent, and I hope that a future Court will reconsider today's dramatic departure from basic Establishment Clause principle.

JUSTICE STEVENS, dissenting.

For the reasons stated by JUSTICE SOUTER and JUSTICE BREYER, I am convinced that the Court's decision is profoundly misguided. Admittedly, in reaching that conclusion I have been influenced by my understanding of the impact of religious strife on the decisions of our forbears to migrate to this continent, and on the decisions of neighbors in the Balkans, Northern Ireland, and the Middle East to mistrust one another. Whenever we remove a brick from the wall that was designed to separate religion and government, we increase the risk of religious strife and weaken the foundation of our democracy.

I respectfully dissent.

In *Zelman* the Court extended its recent pattern of taking accommodationist positions on aid to religious schools. Emphasizing the program's neutrality, its dependence on the private, independent choices of parents, and the availability of numerous other education options, the majority found no violation of the establishment clause.

The Cleveland program did not provide just incidental support for expenses such as transportation and secular textbooks. Instead, it provided actual tuition money to pay for instruction, including religious education, at church-related schools. Furthermore, after parents signified their school choice by endorsement, the appropriated moneys went directly to the religious schools. There is little doubt that the program approved in *Zelman* was more extensive both in kind and degree than had been found constitutionally acceptable in earlier rulings.

Does *Zelman* mean that the Court will now approve almost any variety of government aid to religious schools? It is too early to reach such a conclusion. *Zelman* was a significant accommodation position, but it was decided by the barest of majorities, and the four dissenters expressed strong opposition to the Court's ruling. Such deep divisions reflect inherent instability in the Court's position. The continued close votes on religion cases highlight the vulnerability of the Court's establishment clause jurisprudence to future personnel changes.

Public Facilities and Funds. The Court has settled a number of cases involving access by religious groups to public resources. Most commonly these cases have presented the question of whether public schools that generally make their facilities or funds available to student groups or community organizations are prohibited by the establishment clause from extending the same privileges to religious organizations.

In the first of these cases, *Widmar v. Vincent* (1981), the Court struck down a University of Missouri at Kansas City policy that denied a student religious group the use of meeting rooms when nonreligous groups were granted such access. In doing so, the justices rejected the school's position that allowing the group to conduct their religious activities in campus rooms would cross the constitutional line between church and state.

Justice Lewis F. Powell applied the Lemon rule, concluding that equal access policies have the secular purpose of encouraging the exchange of ideas. Further, he asserted that if the university retained its closed access policy, it would risk excessive entanglement with religion, as it would have to determine whether groups were engaging in religious speech or worship. Finally, Powell claimed that equal access policies do not have the primary effect of advancing religion; rather they encourage "all forms of discourse."

The *Widmar* decision dealt exclusively with colleges and universities, asserting that "equal access" policies at these institutions would not violate the establishment clause. In 1984, with passage of the Equal Access Act, Congress built on *Widmar*. The act required all public secondary schools with "limited open forum" policies to give equal access to "any students who wish to conduct a meeting within that limited open forum," regardless of the "religious, political, philosophical, or other content of the speech at such meetings." A "limited open forum" is in effect if a school permits "one or more non-curriculum related student groups to meet in school premises during non-instructional times."

Some observers speculated that the Court might strike down the Equal Access Act as a violation of the establishment clause because the justices might be reluctant to apply a university policy to less mature secondary school students. In *Board of Education of Westside Community School v. Mergens* (1990), however, a divided Court voted to uphold the law. In a plurality opinion representing the views of only four members of the Court, Justice O'Connor held that the law did not have the primary effect of advancing religion. In her argument, O'Connor adopted the logic of the endorsement test, which itself built on *Lemon (see Table 12-2)*: Religion was not advanced because it was private, not governmental, speech endorsing religion. Private endorsements of religion (such as those that might occur during a group meeting), as she noted, were protected by the free speech and free exercise clauses of the First Amendment, but government endorsements violated the establishment clause.

Justices Kennedy and Scalia agreed that the act was constitutional, but they took issue with O'Connor's endorsement approach. They advocated a standard emphasizing the relative "coercive" nature of government policies *(see Table 12-2)*. Justice Kennedy wrote:

[N]o constitutional violation occurs if the school's action is based upon a recognition of the fact that membership in a religious club is one of many permissible ways for a student to further his or her own personal enrichment. The inquiry with respect to coercion must be whether the government imposes pressure upon a student to participate in a religious activity. This inquiry, of course, must be undertaken with sensitivity to the special circumstances that exist in a secondary school where the line between voluntary and coerced participation may be difficult to draw. No such coercion . . . has been shown to exist as a necessary result of this statute.

Mergens indicates the Court's willingness to uphold government policies that allow religious groups equal access to school facilities. It also shows just how divided the Court is over the appropriate standard by which to adjudicate religious establishment cases. That is why observers anxiously awaited the Court's decision in **Lamb's Chapel v. Center Moriches Union Free School District** (1993). Some thought that by 1993 the justices would coalesce around a particular test, but the Court's decision revealed continued division.

Lamb's Chapel concerned the policies of Long Island's Center Moriches School District with respect to circumstances under which school property may be used by outside groups and for purposes other than education. Consistent with state law, the school board issued rules allowing use of school property only for social, civic, or recreational purposes or by political organizations. Its rules prohibited use by groups for religious purposes.

Lamb's Chapel, an evangelical church located in the Center Moriches community, twice asked the school board for permission to show a film series in school buildings. The series contained lectures by a psychologist on "the undermining influences of the media [which] could only be counterbalanced by returning to traditional, Christian family values instilled at an early age." Believing that the films were church-related, the school district denied both requests.

Lamb's Chapel took the school district to court, asserting that the denial violated the church's First Amendment guarantees of free speech and religious liberty. It presented evidence that district officials had permitted other religious groups to use school facilities, including a New Age religious group known as the Mind Center, the Southern Harmonize Gospel Singers, and the Hampton Council of Churches. The school district countered that

it could deny use of its property to a "radical" church "for the purpose of proselytizing," which might lead to violence. Just as the University of Missouri had said in *Widmar*, the school board claimed that it had a compelling interest in restricting the church's First Amendment rights: Use of its property for religious purposes would violate the establishment clause.

After a federal district court and a court of appeals rejected its claims, the church appealed to the U.S. Supreme Court, where the justices unanimously struck down the school board's policy. Writing for the majority, Justice White found that the school board's denial of permission to show the film violated the free speech provisions of the First Amendment. Refusing access based on the religious content of the film constituted government regulation of speech "in ways that favor some viewpoints or ideas at the expense of others."

White next rejected the school board's defense that its policies were required by the establishment clause. Using a combination of the Lemon test and O'Connor's endorsement approach, he explained:

Under these circumstances, as in *Widmar*, there would have been no realistic danger that the community would think that the District was endorsing religion or any particular creed, and any benefit to religion or to the Church would have been no more than incidental. As in *Widmar*, permitting District property to be used to exhibit the film involved in this case would not have been an establishment of religion under the three-part test articulated in *Lemon v. Kurtzman* (1971). The challenged governmental action has a secular purpose, does not have the principal or primary effect of advancing or inhibiting religion, and does not foster an excessive entanglement with religion.

Although the vote was unanimous, disagreements over the appropriate standard to use continued to divide the justices, and their rhetoric became more extreme. Consider this portion of Justice Scalia's concurring opinion in which he attacks the majority's use of the Lemon test:

Like some ghoul in a late-night horror movie that repeatedly sits up in its grave and shuffles abroad, after being repeatedly killed and buried, *Lemon* stalks our Establishment Clause jurisprudence once again, frightening the little children and school attorneys of Center Moriches Union Free School District. . . . Over the years, however, no fewer than five of the currently sitting Justices [Scalia, O'Connor, Rehnquist, White, and Kennedy] have, in their own opinions, personally driven pencils through the creature's heart (the author of today's opinion repeatedly), and a sixth [Thomas] has joined an opinion doing so.

Two years later the Court heard arguments in ***Rosenberger v. University of Virginia*** (1995). *Rosenberger* presented a different twist to the access issue. Here the question was not access to public buildings, but instead to public funding programs for student activities. In this dispute, Ronald Rosenberger, a member of a recognized organization of Christian students at the University of Virginia, objected to a denial of student activity funds to support the printing of the group's newspaper, *Wide Awake: A Christian Perspective.* Other student groups received funding to support their publications, but the university's rules prohibited support for religious activities.

A closely divided Supreme Court ruled in favor of Rosenberger. Relying on decisions such as *Lamb's Chapel,* Justice Kennedy, writing for the Court, found the university's policies to be an unconstitutional form of "viewpoint discrimination." He explained that "it does not violate the Establishment Clause for a public university to grant access to its facilities on a religion-neutral basis to a wide spectrum of student groups." Ruling otherwise, according to Kennedy, would require the university to scrutinize all student speech to ensure that it did not contain excessively religious content. Four justices dissented from this view, condemning the majority for approving for the first time direct government expenditures to support core religious activities.

Clearly, *Rosenberger* did little to settle the disagreements within the Court over the governing standard to use in this line of establishment clause cases. Although many thought the Court might use *Rosenberger* to overrule *Lemon,* that did not occur. In fact, the majority opinion largely avoided any direct mention of *Lemon,* although the opinion certainly rested on precedents based on that decision. The justices seem to have left this battle for another day.

Religion in the Public Schools. Some public schools have sought to disseminate tenets held by particular

Ronald Rosenberger, right, cofounder of the religious newspaper *Wide Awake,* holds a copy outside the Supreme Court after oral arguments. At left is cofounder Robert Prince.

religions by slanting the curriculum to favor religious views about secular subjects. The best-known and most enduring example is the way teachers address the origins of human life. Did humankind evolve, as scientists suggest (evolutionary theory), or did it come about as a result of some divine intervention, as various religions argue (creationism)?

This debate received an unusual amount of attention in 1925 when the "Scopes Monkey Trial" was held in Dayton, Tennessee.[22] The case centered on a twenty-four-year-old high school science teacher, John T. Scopes, charged with violating state law by denying the biblical account of creation and instead teaching that man de-

22. For an account of this case see Bernard Schwartz, *The Law in America* (New York: McGraw Hill, 1974).

scended from a lower order of animals. The trial featured two of the nation's most prominent lawyers pitted against each other, William Jennings Bryan as prosecutor and Clarence Darrow for the defense. The case was tried amid great national publicity, as the law, based on fundamentalist religious belief, clashed with the findings of modern science. The trial, which culminated in Scopes's conviction, never made it to the Supreme Court, but two other similar challenges did.

The first was *Epperson v. Arkansas*, a 1968 case in which the Court considered the constitutionality of a 1928 state "anti-evolution" law that was an "adaptation" of Tennessee's 1925 version. The Arkansas law made it a crime for any state university or public school instructor "to teach the theory or doctrine that mankind ascended or descended from a lower order of animals" or to "adopt or use . . . a textbook that teaches" evolutionary theory. The history of the law's adoption makes it clear that its purpose was to further religious beliefs about the beginning of life. An advertisement placed in an Arkansas newspaper to drum up support for the act said: "The Bible or atheism, which? All atheists favor evolution. . . . Shall conscientious church members be forced to pay taxes to support teachers to teach evolution which will undermine the faith of their children?"

Epperson began in the mid-1960s when the school system in Little Rock, Arkansas, decided to adopt a biology book that contained a chapter on evolutionary theory. Susan Epperson, a biology teacher in a Little Rock high school, wanted to use the new book but was afraid—in light of the 1928 law—that she could face criminal prosecution if she did so. She asked the Arkansas courts to nullify the law, and, when the Arkansas Supreme Court turned down her request, she appealed her case to the U.S. Supreme Court.

Writing for a unanimous Court, Justice Abe Fortas reversed the state supreme court's ruling. Relying heavily on *Everson* (the Lemon test had yet to be established), Fortas said:

Arkansas' law cannot be defended as an act of religious neutrality. Arkansas did not seek to excise from the curricula of its

schools . . . all discussion of the origin of man. The law's effort was confined to an attempt to blot out a particular theory because of its supposed conflict with the Biblical account, literally read. Plainly, the law is contrary to the mandate of the First . . . Amendment.

Despite the Court's clear statement about the constitutional violation posed by anti-evolutionary laws, some states devised other ways to teach creationism. In *Edwards v. Aguillard* (1987) the Court reviewed one of these attempts. The case arose following Louisiana's 1981 adoption of the Balanced Treatment for Creation-Science and Evolution-Science in Public School Instruction Act. The law did not ban the teaching of evolution, but it prohibited schools from teaching evolutionary principles unless theories of creationism were also taught. The state tried to justify the law by claiming that both creationism and evolutionary theory were a mixture of science and religion and that both deserved to be treated equally in the classroom. Don Aguillard, an assistant principal in Scott, Louisiana, and other teachers and parents thought differently and challenged the law's constitutionality.

By a 7–2 vote, the Supreme Court struck down the law as a violation of the establishment clause. For the majority, Justice Brennan demonstrated from the legislative debates that advancing religious beliefs was the clear intent of the law's sponsors. Using the Lemon test, Brennan had little trouble ruling against the state. The law lacked a secular purpose; rather, its purpose was to endorse a particular religious view.

Prayer in the Public Schools. Throughout most of the nation's history, almost all public schools engaged in religious practices of some kind. They may have held devotional services, distributed Bibles, or taught about religion. Particularly prevalent was prayer. Even into the 1960s, as indicated in Table 12-3, the Bible was read regularly in most public schools in the South and East; in some schools, students recited state-written prayers. Separationist groups, such as the American Civil Liberties Union (ACLU), that oppose intermingling between church and state, believed that these practices violated

TABLE 12-3 Variations in Incidence of Bible Reading in Public School by Region, 1960 and 1966

	Percentage of schools reporting Bible reading	
Region	1960	1966
East	67.6	4.3
Midwest	18.3	5.2
South	76.8	49.5
West	11.0	2.3

SOURCE: Frank J. Sorauf, *The Wall of Separation* (Princeton: Princeton University Press, 1976), 297.

the establishment clause and set out to persuade the Court to eradicate them.

Their first significant suit, ***Engel v. Vitale*** (1962), challenged a New York practice that each morning had public school children reciting a prayer written by the state's board of regents: "Almighty God, we acknowledge our dependence upon Thee, and we beg Thy blessings upon us, our parents, our teachers and our country." New York representatives argued that this prayer was innocuous and purposefully drafted so that it would not favor one religion over another. They also argued that recitation was voluntary: Students who did not want to participate could remain silent or leave the room. The New York Civil Liberties Union, representing parents from a Long Island school district, claimed the religious neutrality of the prayer and the voluntary aspect were irrelevant. What mattered was that the state had written it and made its recitation in the classroom mandatory. Therefore, it violated the establishment clause.

Writing for the Court, Justice Black adopted the separationist argument:

We think the constitutional prohibition against laws respecting the establishment of religion must at least mean that in this country it is no part of the business of government to compose official prayers for any group of the American people to recite as a part of a religious program carried out by the government.

Only Justice Stewart dissented from the Court's opinion. After citing many examples of congressional approval of religion, including the legislation placing the words "In God We Trust" on currency, he quoted Justice Douglas's statement, written a decade before in *Illinois ex rel. McCollum v. Board of Education* (1948): "We are a religious people whose institutions presuppose a Supreme Being." What New York "has done has been to recognize and to follow the deeply entrenched and highly cherished spiritual traditions of our Nation," he said.

Despite the majority's strong words, the decision was not a complete victory for separationists. The Court failed to enunciate a strict legal definition of establishment (it announced no standard), and it dealt with only one aspect of prayer in school—state-written prayers—and not the more widespread practice of Bible readings. Moreover, *Engel* generated a tremendous public backlash. Less than 20 percent of the public supported the Court's decision; Congress considered constitutional amendments to overturn it; and church leaders condemned it. Most of the justices described themselves as "surprised and pained" by the negative reaction. Chief Justice Warren later wrote: "I vividly remember one bold newspaper headline, 'Court outlaws God.' Many religious leaders in this same spirit condemned the Court." Justice Clark defended the Court's opinion in a public address:

Here was a state-written prayer circulated by the school district to state-employed teachers with instructions to have their pupils recite it. [The Constitution] provides that both state and Federal governments shall take no part respecting the establishment of religion. . . . "No" means "No." That was all the Court decided.[23]

With all this uproar, it is no wonder that separationist groups were concerned in 1963 when the Court agreed to hear arguments in *School District of Abington Township v. Schempp* and its companion case, *Murray v. Curlett*. These appeals involved the more prevalent public school practices of reciting the Lord's Prayer and listening to Bible readings. Supporters of church-state separation questioned whether the justices would cave in to public pressure and reverse their stance in *Engel*. But, as it turned out, their fears were misplaced, for the Court used *Abington* to reinforce its *Engel* decision.

23. Quotes from the justices come from Bernard Schwartz, *Super Chief* (New York: New York University Press, 1983), 441–442.

School District of Abington Township v. Schempp; Murray v. Curlett

374 U.S. 203 (1963)
http://laws.findlaw.com/US/374/203.html
Oral arguments may be found at: http://www.oyez.org
Vote: 8 (Black, Brennan, Clark, Douglas, Goldberg, Harlan, Warren, White)
    1 (Stewart)
Opinion of the Court: Clark
Concurring opinions: Brennan, Douglas, Goldberg
Dissenting opinion: Stewart

Sydney Schempp holds the Bible as her husband, Edward, and their children Roger and Donna look on at their home in Roslyn, Pennsylvania, on June 18, 1963, one day after the Supreme Court announced its decision in *School District of Abington Township v. Schempp.* The Court agreed with the Schempps that compulsory Bible reading in public schools violates the establishment clause.

Pennsylvania law mandated that "at least ten verses from the Holy Bible shall be read, without comment, at the opening of each public school on each school day." Edward Lewis Schempp and his wife, Sydney, were not atheists; in fact, they were members of a Unitarian church, where they regularly attended services. But they did not want their children, Roger and Donna, to engage in Bible reading at Abington Senior High School. To them "specific religious doctrines purveyed by a literal reading of the Bible" were not in accord with their particular religious beliefs. Following the law, Abington High held opening exercises each morning while the students were in their homerooms. The required number of Bible verses were read over the school's public address system, and the reading was followed by a recitation of the Lord's Prayer, during which students stood and repeated the prayer in unison. Those students whose parents did not want them to participate could, under the Pennsylvania law, leave the room.

Edward Schempp decided to challenge the practice. The reasons he gave were that teachers and classmates would label Donna and Roger as "oddballs," or "atheists"—a term with "very bad" connotations to Schempp; Roger and Donna would miss hearing morning announcements that were read after the religious readings; and other students, seeing Donna and Roger in the halls, would think they were being punished for "bad conduct."

Separationist groups presented Schempp's reasons to the trial court. They also brought in religious leaders and other religious experts to support the claim that Bible readings inherently favored some religions over others and violated principles of religious establishment. Attorneys for the school board, on the other hand, sought to frame the case in moral rather than religious terms. They also found their own expert witnesses to testify that the Bible was nonsectarian.

Murray v. Curlett, which the Court consolidated with the Schempp appeal, involved a similar challenge to a Maryland law that required daily readings of the Bible or the recitation of the Lord's Prayer in public schools. The suit was brought by prominent atheist Madalyn Murray on behalf of her son, William J. Murray III. *(See Box 12-2.)*

MR. JUSTICE CLARK delivered the opinion of the Court.

[T]his Court has rejected unequivocally the contention that the Establishment Clause forbids only governmental preference of one religion over another. Almost 20 years ago in *Everson* the Court said that "[n]either a state nor the Federal Government can set up a church. Neither can pass laws which aid one religion, aid all religions, or prefer one religion over another.". . .

. . . In short, the Court held that the Amendment

"requires the state to be a neutral in its relations with groups of religious believers and non-believers; it does not require the state to be their adversary. State power is no more to be used so as to handicap religions than it is to favor them."

. . . The wholesome "neutrality" of which this Court's cases speak . . . stems from a recognition of the teachings of history that powerful sects or groups might bring about a fusion of governmental and religious functions or a concert or dependency of one upon the other to the end that official support of the State or Federal Government would be placed behind the tenets of one or of all orthodoxies. This the Establishment Clause prohibits. And a further reason for neutrality is found in the Free Exercise Clause, which recognizes the value of religious training, teaching and observance and, more particularly, the right of every person to freely choose his own course with reference thereto, free of any compulsion from the state. This the Free Exercise Clause guarantees. Thus, as we have seen, the two clauses may overlap. As we have indicated, the Establishment Clause has been directly considered by this Court eight times in the past score of years and, with only one Justice dissenting on the point, it has consistently held that the clause withdrew all legislative power respecting religious belief or the expression thereof. The test may be stated as follows: what are the purpose and the primary effect of the enactment? If either is the advancement or inhibition of religion then the enactment exceeds the scope of legislative power as circumscribed by the Constitution. That is to say that to withstand the strictures of the Establishment Clause there must be a secular legislative purpose and a primary effect that neither advances nor inhibits religion. *Everson v. Board of Education.* . . . The Free Exercise Clause, likewise considered many times here, withdraws from legislative power, state and federal, the exertion of any restraint on the free exercise of religion. Its purpose is to secure religious liberty in the individual by prohibiting any invasions thereof by civil authority. Hence it is necessary in a free exercise case for one to show the coercive effect of the enactment as it operates against him in the practice of his religion. The distinction between the two clauses is appar-

ent—a violation of the Free Exercise Clause is predicated on coercion while the Establishment Clause violation need not be so attended.

Applying the Establishment Clause principles to the cases at bar we find that the States are requiring the selection and reading at the opening of the school day of verses from the Holy Bible and the recitation of the Lord's Prayer by the students in unison. These exercises are prescribed as part of the curricular activities of students who are required by law to attend school. They are held in the school buildings under the supervision and with the participation of teachers employed in those schools. None of these factors, other than compulsory school attendance, was present in the program upheld in *Zorach v. Clauson.* The trial court in [*Schempp*] has found that such an opening exercise is a religious ceremony and was intended by the State to be so. We agree with the trial court's finding as to the religious character of the exercises. Given that finding, the exercises and the law requiring them are in violation of the Establishment Clause. . . .

The conclusion follows that . . . the [law] require[s] religious exercises and such exercises are being conducted in direct violation of the rights of the appellees and petitioners. Nor are these required exercises mitigated by the fact that individual students may absent themselves upon parental request, for that fact furnishes no defense to a claim of unconstitutionality under the Establishment Clause. Further, it is no defense to urge that the religious practices here may be relatively minor encroachments on the First Amendment. The breach of neutrality that is today a trickling stream may all too soon become a raging torrent and, in the words of Madison, "it is proper to take alarm at the first experiment on our liberties."

It is insisted that unless these religious exercises are permitted a "religion of secularism" is established in the schools. We agree of course that the State may not establish a "religion of secularism" in the sense of affirmatively opposing or showing hostility to religion, thus "preferring those who believe in no religion over those who do believe." . . . We do not agree, however, that this decision in any sense has that effect. In addition, it might well be said that one's education is not complete without a study of comparative religion or the history of religion and its relationship to the advancement of civilization. It certainly may be said that the Bible is worthy of study for its literary and historic qualities.

BOX 12-2 AFTERMATH . . . MADALYN MURRAY O'HAIR

In 1963 the U.S. Supreme Court, in *School District of Abington Township v. Schempp* and its companion case, *Murray v. Curlett,* declared Bible reading and the recitation of the Lord's Prayer in public schools to be unconstitutional. *Murray v. Curlett* was a lawsuit brought by Madalyn Murray on behalf of her son William, then a fourteen-year-old student in Baltimore. Madalyn Murray O'Hair, as she became known after her marriage to Richard O'Hair, was no stranger to controversy or the courts. Dubbed by *Life* magazine in 1964 "the most hated woman in America," O'Hair initiated several lawsuits based on First Amendment claims, including legal actions to have the words "In God We Trust" removed from U.S. currency and to prohibit astronauts from praying in space. She described the Bible as "nauseating, historically inaccurate and replete with the ravings of madmen." O'Hair, an abrasive, profane woman, attempted to defect to the Soviet Union in 1960 and later became associated with Larry Flynt, the publisher of *Hustler* magazine. But she is probably best known as the founder of American Atheists, Inc., a national organization devoted to advancing the interests of atheists, headquartered in Austin, Texas.

On August 28, 1995, O'Hair, age seventy-six and in declining health, mysteriously vanished, along with her second son, Jon Murray, and granddaughter Robin. Nothing appeared to be missing from their house—clothes were in the closet and food on the table. Many thought that O'Hair and her family were fleeing from her organization's declining membership and troubled financial condition. Speculation was fueled by evidence that more than $500,000 of American Atheists funds, most in gold coins, was missing and allegations that O'Hair had hidden organization funds in bank accounts in New Zealand.

Law enforcement authorities, however, were convinced that O'Hair and the others were victims of foul play. The chief suspects were David Waters, Gary Karr, and Danny Fry. Waters, a former American Atheists employee, had pleaded guilty to stealing $54,000 from the organization and had a grudge against O'Hair. Karr and Fry were associates of Waters; all three had criminal records. Evidence mounted that the three suspects kidnapped the O'Hair family members, held them hostage, and extorted $500,000 before murdering them. Fry was removed from the suspect list when a body discovered on the banks of the Trinity River was identified as his. The head and hands had been severed in an obvious attempt to block identification.

Madalyn Murray O'Hair with son Jon and granddaughter Robin.

Police put continued pressure on Waters and Karr, both of whom had been imprisoned for crimes related to the O'Hair disappearance. Finally, in 2001 Waters agreed to cooperate with authorities as part of a plea bargain on the murder charges. He led police to a remote ranch west of San Antonio, where three dismembered and burned bodies were found in a shallow grave along with a head and hands presumed to be Fry's. The bodies were identified through dental records and O'Hair's metal artificial hip. Police believe that the three victims had been held and killed in a North Austin storage unit and the remains discarded at the burial site.

In February 2003 Waters died in prison. Karr continues to serve a life sentence.

Another twist to the O'Hair story involves her son William Murray. After being treated for alcoholism, Murray publicly rejected atheism in May 1980 and became a Southern Baptist. Later, as a Christian activist, he chaired Religious Coalition USA, a conservative organization that supports, among other things, the reintroduction of prayer in the public schools. As might be expected, Murray and his mother had been estranged for many years.

SOURCES: *Arizona Republic,* May 15, 2000; *Atlanta Journal-Constitution,* June 3, 2000; *Houston Chronicle,* December 29, 1996, March 3, 2000, March 16, 2001, February 5, 2003; *Washington Post,* March 28, 1999, August 16–17, 1999; *Buffalo News,* April 25, 1999; *San Diego Union-Tribune,* October 22, 1999; and *New York Times,* December 8, 1999, March 16, 2001.

Nothing we have said here indicates that such study of the Bible or of religion, when presented objectively as part of a secular program of education, may not be effected consistently with the First Amendment. But the exercises here do not fall into those categories. They are religious exercises, required by the States in violation of the command of the First Amendment that the Government maintain strict neutrality, neither aiding nor opposing religion.

Finally, we cannot accept that the concept of neutrality, which does not permit a State to require a religious exercise even with the consent of the majority of those affected, collides with the majority's right to free exercise of religion. While the Free Exercise Clause clearly prohibits the use of state action to deny the rights of free exercise to anyone, it has never meant that a majority could use the machinery of the State to practice its beliefs. . . .

The place of religion in our society is an exalted one, achieved through a long tradition of reliance on the home, the church and the inviolable citadel of the individual heart and mind. We have come to recognize through bitter experience that it is not within the power of government to invade that citadel, whether its purpose or effect be to aid or oppose, to advance or retard. In the relationship between man and religion, the State is firmly committed to a position of neutrality. Though the application of that rule requires interpretation of a delicate sort, the rule itself is clearly and concisely stated in the words of the First Amendment. Applying that rule to the facts of these cases, we affirm the judgment in [*Schempp*]. In [*Murray*] the judgment is reversed and the cause remanded to the Maryland Court of Appeals for further proceedings consistent with this opinion.

It is so ordered.

MR. JUSTICE DOUGLAS, concurring.

These regimes violate the Establishment Clause in two different ways. In each case, the State is conducting a religious exercise; and, as the Court holds, that cannot be done without violating the "neutrality" required of the State by the balance of power between individual, church and state that has been struck by the First Amendment. But the Establishment Clause is not limited to precluding the State itself from conducting religious exercises. It also forbids the State to employ its facilities or funds in a way that gives any

church, or all churches, greater strength in our society than it would have by relying on its members alone. Thus, the present regimes must fall under that clause for the additional reason that public funds, though small in amount, are being used to promote a religious exercise. Through the mechanism of the State, all of the people are being required to finance a religious exercise that only some of the people want and that violates the sensibilities of others.

MR. JUSTICE BRENNAN, concurring.

I join fully in the opinion and the judgment of the Court. I see no escape from the conclusion that the exercises called in question in these two cases violate the constitutional mandate. The reasons we gave only last Term in *Engel v. Vitale* for finding in the New York Regents' prayer an impermissible establishment of religion compel the same judgment of the practices at bar. The involvement of the secular with the religious is no less intimate here; and it is constitutionally irrelevant that the State has not composed the material for the inspirational exercises presently involved. It should be unnecessary to observe that our holding does not declare that the First Amendment manifests hostility to the practice or teaching of religion, but only applies prohibitions incorporated in the Bill of Rights in recognition of historic needs shared by Church and State alike. While it is my view that not every involvement of religion in public life is unconstitutional, I consider the exercises at bar a form of involvement which clearly violates the Establishment Clause.

MR. JUSTICE GOLDBERG, with whom MR. JUSTICE HARLAN joins, concurring.

The practices here involved do not fall within any sensible or acceptable concept of compelled or permitted accommodation, and involve the state so significantly and directly in the realm of the sectarian as to give rise to those very divisive influences and inhibitions of freedom which both religion clauses of the First Amendment preclude. The state has ordained and has utilized its facilities to engage in unmistakably religious exercises—the devotional reading and recitation of the Holy Bible—in a manner having substantial and significant import and impact. That it has selected, rather than written, a particular devotional liturgy seems to me without constitutional import. The pervasive religiosity and direct governmental involvement inhering in the prescription of prayer and Bible reading in the public schools, during and as part of the curricular day, involving young impressionable children whose school attendance is statutorily compelled, and utilizing the prestige, power, and influence of school administration, staff, and authority, cannot realistically be termed simply accommodation, and must fall within the interdiction of the First Amendment.

MR. JUSTICE STEWART, dissenting.

It is important to stress that, strictly speaking, what is at issue here is a privilege rather than a right. In other words, the question presented is not whether exercises such as those at issue here are constitutionally compelled, but rather whether they are constitutionally invalid. And that issue, in my view, turns on the question of coercion.

It is clear that the dangers of coercion involved in the holding of religious exercises in a schoolroom differ qualitatively from those presented by the use of similar exercises or affirmations in ceremonies attended by adults. Even as to children, however, the duty laid upon government in connection with religious exercises in the public schools is that of refraining from so structuring the school environment as to put any kind of pressure on a child to participate in those exercises; it is not that of providing an atmosphere in which children are kept scrupulously insulated from any awareness that some of their fellows may want to open the school day with prayer, or of the fact that there exist in our pluralistic society differences of religious belief. . . .

Viewed in this light, it seems to me clear that the records in both of the cases before us are wholly inadequate to support an informed or responsible decision. Both cases involve provisions which explicitly permit any student who wishes, to be excused from participation in the exercises. There is no evidence . . . as to whether there would exist any coercion of any kind upon a student who did not want to participate. . . . In the *Schempp* case the record shows no more than a subjective prophecy by a parent of what he thought would happen if a request were made to be excused from participation in the exercises under the amended statute. No such request was ever made, and there is no evidence whatever as to what might or would actually happen, nor of what administrative arrangements the school actually might or could make to free from pressure of any kind those who do not want to participate in the exercises. . . .

What our Constitution indispensably protects is the freedom of each of us, be he Jew or Agnostic, Christian or Atheist, Buddhist or Freethinker, to believe or disbelieve, to worship or not worship, to pray or keep silent, according to his own conscience, uncoerced and unrestrained by government. It is conceivable that these school boards, or even all school boards, might eventually find it impossible to administer a system of religious exercises during school hours in such a way as to meet this constitutional standard—in such a way as completely to free from any kind of official coercion those who do not affirmatively want to participate. But I think we must not assume that school boards so lack the qualities of inventiveness and good will as to make impossible the achievement of that goal.

I would remand both cases for further hearings.

The *Schempp* and *Murray* decisions, following on the heels of *Engel v. Vitale,* set firmly in American jurisprudence the principle that state-sponsored prayers in public schools violate the establishment clause. In addition, these decisions set a standard of law that served as the forerunner of *Lemon.* But take note of Justice Stewart's dissent: His coercion approach provided fodder for justices of the Rehnquist Court—particularly Anthony Kennedy—who would later attempt to etch some version of it into law. In 1963 it represented the position of one justice.

But, if the justices thought that *Abington* would quell the prayer-in-school controversy they had ignited in *Engel,* they could not have been more wrong. Opinion polls taken after *Abington* indicated that only 24 percent of the public supported the Court's decision, and that number has not changed much since then. Polls in 2004 showed that 35 percent of the population favored the Court's ban on prayer and Bible reading in public schools.[24] Given the public antipathy to *Engel* and *Abington,* it is not surprising to find widespread noncompliance with the Court's decisions. Note the data in Table 12-3 showing

24. Lee Epstein, Jeffrey A. Segal, Harold J. Spaeth, and Thomas G. Walker, *The Supreme Court Compendium: Data, Decisions, and Developments,* 4th ed. (Washington, D.C.: CQ Press, 2007), Table 8-26.

that almost half of the schools in the South continued to allow Bible readings three years after the Court's decision in *Abington.* Responding to public opposition to *Engel, Abington,* and *Murray,* over the years members of Congress have introduced close to 150 constitutional amendments to return prayer to the nation's classrooms. None has been successful.

Supporters of school prayer were hopeful that the Supreme Court under the leadership of conservative chief justices Warren Burger and William Rehnquist would eventually permit the reintroduction of religious affirmation in the public schools. They were encouraged when the Court in *Marsh v. Chambers* (1983) found nothing unconstitutional about the Nebraska legislature hiring a Presbyterian minister to say a public prayer before each daily session. Chief Justice Burger's opinion for the Court rested primarily on original intent, as demonstrated by the long tradition of American legislatures, starting with the First Congress, of beginning their sessions with a prayer. The Court largely ignored the precedents set in the school prayer cases and did not apply the Lemon test, which quite probably would have led to a different result.

The *Marsh* decision prompted school prayer advocates to press their position, hoping for a reversal of the ban on devotional expressions. Time after time, however, they were disappointed. The justices remained firm in their view that prayer in public schools violated the establishment clause. Three important cases, decided over a span of fifteen years, illustrate the Court's consistent response in school prayer disputes.

The first case was **Wallace v. Jaffree** (1985), which involved a challenge to an Alabama law authorizing a daily period of silence in all public schools "for meditation or voluntary prayer." Opponents of the law argued that it was unconstitutional because it lacked a secular purpose as required by *Lemon;* its legislative sponsors clearly viewed it as a way to return prayer to school. The state countered that the law does not "in any way offend the constitution" because it "neither proscribes prayer; nor affirms religious belief; nor coerces religious exercise." On behalf of the Reagan administration, the solicitor general argued that the law was "perfectly neutral with

respect to religious practices. It neither favors one religion over another nor conveys endorsement of religion."

Despite public opinion and political pressure, the Court did not overturn *Engel* or *Abington.* To the contrary, by invoking the Lemon test to strike down the Alabama law, it reaffirmed its commitment to those decisions and to the standards of law on which they were based—the forerunners of *Lemon.* Specifically, the Court found that the Alabama law's primary purpose was not secular. In fact, the law, according to the Court, had *no* secular purpose at all. The Constitution would not be offended by a period of rest or quiet designed to promote a proper learning environment or other legitimate goal, but here the explicit objective was to encourage "meditation or voluntary prayer."

Still, although the majority opinion invoked *Lemon,* the justices were not unanimous in their support for the three-pronged test. Powell expressed concern over some justices' criticism of the test, and O'Connor continued to press for her endorsement approach to *Lemon.* In dissent, Burger lamented that the majority's "extended treatment" of the Lemon test "suggests a naive preoccupation with an easy, bright-line approach for addressing constitutional issues." But it was Rehnquist's dissenting opinion that raised the most eyebrows because it questioned the Court's entire approach to establishment clause cases beginning with *Everson.* He said the Court was wrong to "concede" Jefferson's metaphor of a "wall of separation," or to etch into law such a strict separation. In other words, he asserted that for the four decades since *Everson,* the Court had operated under a misguided understanding of what the framers meant by religious establishment. The truth, according to Rehnquist, was that the founders, particularly Madison, intended something more in line with the nonpreferential position that the establishment clause simply "forbade the establishment of a national religion and forbade preference among religious sects or denominations. . . . [I]t did not prohibit the federal government from providing nondiscriminatory aid to religion." Justice White, who admitted that he had "been out of step" with the Court's rulings in this area, was happy to "appreciate" Rehnquist's reexamination of history.

Daniel Weisman and his daughter, Deborah, challenged the practice of having a member of the clergy deliver invocation and benediction prayers at public junior high school graduation exercises in Providence, Rhode Island. The Supreme Court ruled in their favor in *Lee v. Weisman.*

In the second case, ***Lee v. Weisman*** (1992), the Rehnquist Court faced its first school prayer controversy. The dispute arose over the 1989 graduation ceremonies at Nathan Bishop Middle School in Providence, Rhode Island. The school had traditionally arranged to have a member of the local clergy say a prayer at the beginning and end of the ceremony. Well in advance of the graduation date participating clergy were given a pamphlet entitled "Guidelines for Civic Occasions." Prepared by the National Conference of Christians and Jews, the guidelines stressed inclusiveness and sensitivity in writing nonsectarian prayers.

For the June 1989 graduation the school invited Rabbi Leslie Gutterman to give the invocation and benediction. The rabbi wrote and delivered prayers that were consistent with the guidelines provided by the school. Daniel Weisman, whose daughter Deborah was in the graduating class, challenged as a violation of the First Amendment the school's allowing invocations and benedictions at graduation exercises.

Justice Kennedy reaffirmed the Court's position that state-sponsored prayer violates the establishment clause. In this case, the school principal had decided to have prayers at the ceremony, selected the clergyman to deliver those prayers, and provided guidelines controlling the content of the prayers. Although participating in the prayer is voluntary, the sponsorship of the public school officials creates pressure to conform or at least to act respectfully during the designated prayer period. Kennedy took particular offense at such forms of coercion, no matter how subtle. There was far too much state involvement with prayer to survive an establishment clause challenge.

The third case, ***Santa Fe Independent School District v. Doe*** (2000), concerned a tradition of long standing in many communities: public prayer at high school football games. At issue was the policy of a Texas public school district that allowed student-led invocations to be delivered on the public address system during pregame ceremonies. To ensure continuing support for this practice, the school district required an annual vote of students, by secret ballot, on whether they wanted public prayers at the games. If the vote favored the invocations, a second election took place to select a single student who would deliver the prayers at all home games for that season. The school required that the prayers be consistent with the district's policy goals: to solemnize the event, to promote sportsmanship and safety, and to establish the appropriate environment for competition. Otherwise the content of the message was left to the discretion of the student delivering it.

Two families, one Mormon and the other Catholic, challenged the district's policy. Local sentiment strongly supported the pregame prayers, and as a consequence the lower courts allowed the individuals filing the challenge to proceed anonymously to protect them from intimidation and harassment.

The school district defended its policy on several grounds. First, it argued that because the invocations were controlled by the students and not by the district administration, the prayers constituted private expression, not government-mandated expression. Second, the two-stage election system ensured that the prayers would

Youth group members from the Santa Fe and Bayou Drive Baptist churches conduct a prayer circle under the Santa Fe High School scoreboard. A student's prayer delivered over the loudspeaker prior to the kickoff of a high school football game became the subject of a Supreme Court case.

not be said without the support of the majority of the students. Third, the school district only permitted the process to take place—it was not in any way involved in the writing or presentation of the prayers. Finally, the prayers were said at a completely voluntary, extracurricular event. Attendance was not required, nor was participation in the recitation of the prayers. There was no coercion to participate.

Looking back to precedents such as *Weisman* and *Lemon*, a six-justice majority struck down the district's prayer practices as violations of the establishment clause. In an uncommon expression of unity, all six members of the majority subscribed to a single opinion written by Justice Stevens. No concurring opinions were issued. The majority found the district policy unconstitutional on several grounds. First, the practice constituted an endorsement of religion. The invocations were authorized by a government policy and took place on government property at a government-sponsored, school-related event. The school district clearly invited and encouraged the religious activity. The prayers sent a constitutionally impermissible message that nonadherents are "outsiders, not full members of the political community, and an accompanying message to adherents that they are insiders, favored members of the political community."

Second, the policy contained an element of coercion. Although generally voluntary, for some students (players, cheerleaders, and band members) attendance was not optional. In addition, in many communities high school football games are important social events with strong peer pressure to attend. The majority found it constitutionally unacceptable to force students to forgo attending such school-sponsored events to avoid conforming with a state-sponsored religious practice.

Finally, the majority found the district's policy to be in direct violation of the Lemon test's requirement that government policies have a secular purpose. In spite of the district's arguments to the contrary, the Court concluded that the primary purpose of the prayers was religious.

Chief Justice Rehnquist, joined by Justices Scalia and Thomas, dissented. They objected not only to the outcome, but also to the tone of the Court's opinion, which, Rehnquist said, "bristles with hostility to all things religious in public life." According to the minority, the country's traditions allow voluntary religious expressions by private individuals at public events such as football games.

The *Santa Fe* decision is the most recent in a long line of decisions in which the justices have found various forms of school prayer constitutionally impermissible. In an area of the law that is characterized by inconsistencies, the school prayer decisions stand out as remarkably stable. Although justices have squabbled over the most appropriate test to apply, the outcomes have never been in serious doubt—prayer in public schools is unconstitutional.

Religious Displays. Government-supported religious displays have led to objections on establishment clause grounds. Such displays occur most often during the Christmas season when local governments decorate their main streets and municipal buildings to encourage the holiday spirit.

Lynch v. Donnelly (1984) was the Court's first significant ruling on this issue. The case involved a holiday display in Pawtucket, Rhode Island, that the Retail Merchants Association had been erecting every Christmas for four decades in a park owned by a nonprofit organization. The display featured many different elements, including a Santa Claus house, reindeer, a Christmas tree, a clown, colored lights, a season's greetings banner, and a crèche [nativity scene] with the Christ child, Mary and Joseph, angels, animals, and so forth. The city had purchased the crèche for $1,365 in 1973, and the city spent about $20 annually to set it up and take it down. Believing these expenditures to constitute a violation of the establishment clause, the ACLU of Rhode Island sued the city. City officials and area business people countered that the display had a secular purpose, which was to attract customers to the city's downtown shopping area.

Chief Justice Burger, speaking for a five-person majority, found that the display was not an impermissible breach of the establishment clause. In one of his more strongly worded accommodationist opinions, he pointed to many examples indicating "an unbroken history of official acknowledgment by all three branches of government of the role of religion in American life": executive

orders proclaiming Christmas and Thanksgiving as national holidays, "In God We Trust" on currency, and publicly supported art galleries full of religious paintings.

Of special importance to the majority was the fact that the crèche was only one part of the display. It was one passive symbol, along with several other scenes, depicting American traditions during the winter holiday season. In short, Burger implied that Christmas was so much a part of our heritage that it came close to representing a national, nonsectarian celebration, rather than a religious holiday.

Five years later, the Court revisited the holiday display issue. *County of Allegheny v. ACLU* (1989) presented a challenge to two public holiday displays in Pittsburgh, Pennsylvania. The first was a crèche that belonged to a Roman Catholic group, the Holy Name Society. Beginning with the Christmas season of 1981, the city allowed Holy Name to place the crèche on the grand staircase of the county courthouse, which is, by all accounts, the "main," "most beautiful," and "most public" part of the courthouse. The second challenged display was a Hanukkah menorah located outside the City-County Building, where the mayor and other city officials have their offices. For much of its history, the city erected only a Christmas tree outside this building, but, beginning in the 1980s, it included the menorah. By 1986 the entire display included a forty-five-foot Christmas tree complete with lights and ornaments and an eighteen-foot menorah, owned by a Jewish group but stored and erected by the city.

Did these displays violate the establishment clause? This question gave the Court a good deal of trouble: A majority of justices could not agree over the appropriate standard by which to answer it. In the end, the Court issued a judgment written by Justice Blackmun.

Blackmun explained the plurality's approach to the case:

Our . . . decisions [subsequent to *Lemon*] further have refined the definition of governmental action that unconstitutionally advances religion. In recent years, we have paid particularly close attention to whether the challenged governmental practice either has the purpose or effect of "endorsing" religion, a concern that has long had a place in our Establishment Clause jurisprudence.

Applying these principles, the Court concluded that given its physical setting, the display of the crèche violated the establishment clause. It stood alone, in a place of particular prominence, communicating the unmistakable message that the county supported and promoted all that the nativity scene represented. But the Court found that the Christmas tree and menorah did not run afoul of the Constitution. Because the display included side-by-side symbols of two religious traditions celebrated during the winter holiday period, there was little to indicate government endorsement of a particular religious message.

Throughout this chapter, we have noted that scholars criticize the Court for reaching inconsistent, puzzling, and even amusing decisions. *County of Allegheny* provided ammunition for these critics. Because Blackmun's judgment centers on the kinds of objects, in juxtaposition to one another, that holiday displays may or may not contain, it has been the source of some ridicule. As a 1993 newspaper article put it:

Pity the public school principal in December. Between Hanukkah, Christmas and Kwanzaa, this long last month lays a minefield of grand proportions for educators trying to acknowledge the holidays without bridging the separation of church and state. Every decoration is fraught with peril. Every lesson and every song must pass the "does not promote religion" test. Red and green cookies? Maybe. "A Christmas Carol?" Maybe. "Silent Night?" Definitely not.[25]

Controversies over religious displays are, however, not confined to holiday symbols; they have also erupted over public exhibition of the Ten Commandments. In *Stone v. Graham* (1980) the Court struck down a Kentucky law that required the Ten Commandments to be posted in every public schoolroom. A five-justice majority concluded that the law had a religious purpose violating the first prong of the Lemon test. In 2005 the Ten Commandments issue returned to the Court with *Van Orden v. Perry*, a challenge to a Ten Commandments monument erected on the grounds of the Texas state capitol. As you read the opinion in this case, pay attention not only to how the majority treats the issue of a reli-

gious display, but also to the controversy over the appropriate standard to use in establishment clause cases.

Van Orden v. Perry

545 U.S. 677 (2005)
http://laws.findlaw.com/US/000/03-1500.html
Oral arguments may be found at: http://www.oyez.org
Vote: 5 (Breyer, Kennedy, Rehnquist, Scalia, Thomas)
    4 (Ginsburg, O'Connor, Souter, Stevens)
Opinion of the Court: Rehnquist
Concurring opinions: Kennedy, Scalia, Thomas
Opinion concurring in judgment: Breyer
Dissenting opinions: Ginsburg, O'Connor, Souter, Stevens

The twenty-two-acre park surrounding the Texas capitol contains seventeen monuments and twenty-one historical markers commemorating the "people, ideals, and events that compose Texan identity." One of these is a six-foot-high monument displaying the text of the Ten Commandments. The Fraternal Order of Eagles gave the monument to the people of Texas in 1961 and paid for its construction and dedication.

Thomas Van Orden, a lawyer by training and a resident of Austin, frequently saw the monument on his walks through the capitol grounds. After doing so for about six years, he filed suit against Gov. Rick Perry and other state officials asking the court to order the removal of the monument because its presence on the capitol grounds violated the establishment clause. The trial court judge rejected Van Orden's request, finding that the monument had a secular purpose and that no reasonable observer would conclude that the state was endorsing religion by allowing this passive monument to be placed on state property. The court of appeals affirmed, and the Supreme Court granted review.

CHIEF JUSTICE REHNQUIST announced the judgment of the Court and delivered an opinion, in which JUSTICE SCALIA, JUSTICE KENNEDY, and JUSTICE THOMAS join.

The question here is whether the Establishment Clause of the First Amendment allows the display of a monument

25. Kimberly J. McLarin, "Holiday Dilemma at Schools: Is That a Legal Decoration?" *New York Times*, December 16, 1993, 1, 15.

This six-foot-tall stone slab bearing the Ten Commandments was the focal point of the Supreme Court's decision in *Van Orden v. Perry* (2005). The justices ruled that the placement of this monument on the state capitol grounds in Austin, Texas, did not violate the First Amendment's establishment clause.

inscribed with the Ten Commandments on the Texas State Capitol grounds. We hold that it does. . . .

Our cases, Janus-like, point in two directions in applying the Establishment Clause. One face looks toward the strong role played by religion and religious traditions throughout our Nation's history. . . .

The other face looks toward the principle that governmental intervention in religious matters can itself endanger religious freedom.

This case, like all Establishment Clause challenges, presents us with the difficulty of respecting both faces. Our institutions presuppose a Supreme Being, yet these institutions must not press religious observances upon their citizens. One face looks to the past in acknowledgment of our Nation's heritage, while the other looks to the present in demanding a separation between church and state. Reconciling these two faces requires that we neither abdicate our responsibility to maintain a division between church and state nor evince a hostility to religion by disabling the government from in some ways recognizing our religious heritage. . . .

These two faces are evident in representative cases both upholding and invalidating laws under the Establishment Clause. Over the last 25 years, we have sometimes pointed to *Lemon v. Kurtzman* (1971) as providing the governing test in Establishment Clause challenges. Yet, just two years after *Lemon* was decided, we noted that the factors identified in *Lemon* serve as "no more than helpful signposts." *Hunt v. McNair* (1973). Many of our recent cases simply have not applied the *Lemon* test. See, *e.g., Zelman v. Simmons-Harris* (2002); *Good News Club v. Milford Central School* (2001). Others have applied it only after concluding that the challenged practice was invalid under a different Establishment Clause test.

Whatever may be the fate of the *Lemon* test in the larger scheme of Establishment Clause jurisprudence, we think it not useful in dealing with the sort of passive monument that Texas has erected on its Capitol grounds. Instead, our analysis is driven both by the nature of the monument and by our Nation's history.

As we explained in *Lynch v. Donnelly* (1984): "There is an unbroken history of official acknowledgment by all three branches of government of the role of religion in American life from at least 1789." . . .

Recognition of the role of God in our Nation's heritage has also been reflected in our decisions. We have acknowledged, for example, that "religion has been closely identified with our history and government," *School Dist. of Abington Township v. Schempp* [1963], and that "[t]he history of man is inseparable from the history of religion," *Engel v.*

Vitale (1962). This recognition has led us to hold that the Establishment Clause permits a state legislature to open its daily sessions with a prayer by a chaplain paid by the State. *Marsh v. Chambers* [1983]. . . . With similar reasoning, we have upheld laws, which originated from one of the Ten Commandments, that prohibited the sale of merchandise on Sunday. *McGowan v. Maryland* (1961).

In this case we are faced with a display of the Ten Commandments on government property outside the Texas State Capitol. Such acknowledgments of the role played by the Ten Commandments in our Nation's heritage are common throughout America. We need only look within our own Courtroom. Since 1935, Moses has stood, holding two tablets that reveal portions of the Ten Commandments written in Hebrew, among other lawgivers in the south frieze. Representations of the Ten Commandments adorn the metal gates lining the north and south sides of the Courtroom as well as the doors leading into the Courtroom. Moses also sits on the exterior east facade of the building holding the Ten Commandments tablets.

Similar acknowledgments can be seen throughout a visitor's tour of our Nation's Capital. . . .

Of course, the Ten Commandments are religious—they were so viewed at their inception and so remain. The monument, therefore, has religious significance. According to Judeo-Christian belief, the Ten Commandments were given to Moses by God on Mt. Sinai. But Moses was a lawgiver as well as a religious leader. And the Ten Commandments have an undeniable historical meaning. . . . Simply having religious content or promoting a message consistent with a religious doctrine does not run afoul of the Establishment Clause.

There are, of course, limits to the display of religious messages or symbols. For example, we held unconstitutional a Kentucky statute requiring the posting of the Ten Commandments in every public schoolroom. *Stone v. Graham* (1980). In the classroom context, we found that the Kentucky statute had an improper and plainly religious purpose. As evidenced by *Stone's* almost exclusive reliance upon two of our school prayer cases, *School Dist. of Abington Township v. Schempp* (1963) and *Engel v. Vitale* (1962), it stands as an example of the fact that we have "been particularly vigilant in monitoring compliance with the Establishment Clause in elementary and secondary schools," *Edwards v.*

Aguillard (1987). Indeed, *Edwards v. Aguillard* recognized that *Stone*—along with *Schempp* and *Engel*—was a consequence of the "particular concerns that arise in the context of public elementary and secondary schools." Neither *Stone* itself nor subsequent opinions have indicated that *Stone's* holding would extend to a legislative chamber or to capitol grounds.

The placement of the Ten Commandments monument on the Texas State Capitol grounds is a far more passive use of those texts than was the case in *Stone*, where the text confronted elementary school students every day. Indeed, Van Orden, the petitioner here, apparently walked by the monument for a number of years before bringing this lawsuit. The monument is therefore also quite different from the prayers involved in *Schempp* and *Lee v. Weisman* [1992]. Texas has treated her Capitol grounds monuments as representing the several strands in the State's political and legal history. The inclusion of the Ten Commandments monument in this group has a dual significance, partaking of both religion and government. We cannot say that Texas' display of this monument violates the Establishment Clause of the First Amendment.

The judgment of the Court of Appeals is affirmed.

It is so ordered.

JUSTICE SCALIA, concurring.

I join the opinion of the Chief Justice because I think it accurately reflects our current Establishment Clause jurisprudence—or at least the Establishment Clause jurisprudence we currently apply some of the time. I would prefer to reach the same result by adopting an Establishment Clause jurisprudence that is in accord with our Nation's past and present practices, and that can be consistently applied—the central relevant feature of which is that there is nothing unconstitutional in a State's favoring religion generally, honoring God through public prayer and acknowledgment, or, in a nonproselytizing manner, venerating the Ten Commandments.

JUSTICE THOMAS, concurring.

The Court holds that the Ten Commandments monument found on the Texas State Capitol grounds does not violate the Establishment Clause. Rather than trying to suggest meaninglessness where there is meaning, the Chief Justice rightly recognizes that the monument has "religious significance." He properly recognizes the role of religion in this Nation's history and the permissibility of government displays acknowledging that history. For those reasons, I join the Chief Justice's opinion in full.

This case would be easy if the Court were willing to abandon the inconsistent guideposts it has adopted for addressing Establishment Clause challenges, and return to the original meaning of the Clause. I have previously suggested that the Clause's text and history "resis[t] incorporation" against the States. See *Elk Grove Unified School Dist. v. Newdow* (2004) (opinion concurring in judgment). If the Establishment Clause does not restrain the States, then it has no application here, where only state action is at issue.

Even if the Clause is incorporated, or if the Free Exercise Clause limits the power of States to establish religions, our task would be far simpler if we returned to the original meaning of the word "establishment" than it is under the various approaches this Court now uses. The Framers understood an establishment "necessarily [to] involve actual legal coercion." "In other words, establishment at the founding involved, for example, mandatory observance or mandatory payment of taxes supporting ministers." And "government practices that have nothing to do with creating or maintaining . . . coercive state establishments" simply do not "implicate the possible liberty interest of being free from coercive state establishments."

JUSTICE BREYER, concurring in the judgment.

The case before us is a borderline case. It concerns a large granite monument bearing the text of the Ten Commandments located on the grounds of the Texas State Capitol. On the one hand, the Commandments' text undeniably has a religious message, invoking, indeed emphasizing, the Diety. On the other hand, focusing on the text of the Commandments alone cannot conclusively resolve this case. Rather, to determine the message that the text here conveys, we must examine how the text is used. And that inquiry requires us to consider the context of the display. . . .

Here the tablets have been used as part of a display that communicates not simply a religious message, but a secular message as well. The circumstances surrounding the display's placement on the capitol grounds and its physical setting suggest that the State itself intended the latter, nonreligious aspects of the tablets' message to predominate. And the monument's 40-year history on the Texas state grounds indicates that that has been its effect. . . .

The physical setting of the monument, moreover, suggests little or nothing of the sacred. The monument sits in a large park containing 17 monuments and 21 historical markers, all designed to illustrate the "ideals" of those who settled in Texas and of those who have lived there since that time. The setting does not readily lend itself to meditation or any other religious activity. But it does provide a context of history and moral ideals. It (together with the display's inscription about its origin) communicates to visitors that the State sought to reflect moral principles, illustrating a relation between ethics and law that the State's citizens, historically speaking, have endorsed. That is to say, the context suggests that the State intended the display's moral message—an illustrative message reflecting the historical "ideals" of Texans—to predominate. . . .

For these reasons, I believe that the Texas display—serving a mixed but primarily nonreligious purpose, not primarily "advanc[ing]" or "inhibit[ing]" religion," and not creating an "excessive government entanglement with religion,"—might satisfy this Court's more formal Establishment Clause tests. But, as I have said, in reaching the conclusion that the Texas display falls on the permissible side of the constitutional line, I rely less upon a literal application of any particular test than upon consideration of the basic purposes of the First Amendment's Religion Clauses themselves. This display has stood apparently uncontested for nearly two generations. That experience helps us understand that as a practical matter of degree this display is unlikely to prove divisive. And this matter of degree is, I believe, critical in a borderline case such as this one.

At the same time, to reach a contrary conclusion here, based primarily upon on the religious nature of the tablets' text would, I fear, lead the law to exhibit a hostility toward religion that has no place in our Establishment Clause traditions. Such a holding might well encourage disputes concerning the removal of longstanding depictions of the Ten Commandments from public buildings across the Nation. And it could thereby create the very kind of religiously based divisiveness that the Establishment Clause seeks to avoid. . . .

I concur in the judgment of the Court.

JUSTICE STEVENS, with whom JUSTICE GINSBURG joins, dissenting.

Government's obligation to avoid divisiveness and exclusion in the religious sphere is compelled by the Establishment and Free Exercise Clauses, which together erect a wall of separation between church and state. This metaphorical wall protects principles long recognized and often recited in this Court's cases. The first and most fundamental of these principles, one that a majority of this Court today affirms, is that the Establishment Clause demands religious neutrality—government may not exercise a preference for one religious faith over another. This essential command, however, is not merely a prohibition against the government's differentiation among religious sects. We have repeatedly reaffirmed that neither a State nor the Federal Government "can constitutionally pass laws or impose requirements which aid all religions as against non-believers, and neither can aid those religions based on a belief in the existence of God as against those religions founded on different beliefs." *Torcaso v. Watkins* (1961). This principle is based on the straightforward notion that governmental promotion of orthodoxy is not saved by the aggregation of several orthodoxies under the State's banner. . . .

The monolith displayed on Texas Capitol grounds cannot be discounted as a passive acknowledgment of religion, nor can the State's refusal to remove it upon objection be explained as a simple desire to preserve a historic relic. This Nation's resolute commitment to neutrality with respect to religion is flatly inconsistent with the plurality's wholehearted validation of an official state endorsement of the message that there is one, and only one, God. . . .

The judgment of the Court in this case stands for the proposition that the Constitution permits governmental displays of sacred religious texts. This makes a mockery of the constitutional ideal that government must remain neutral between religion and irreligion. If a State may endorse a particular deity's command to "have no other gods before me," it is difficult to conceive of any textual display that would run afoul of the Establishment Clause. . . .

I respectfully dissent.

JUSTICE SOUTER, with whom JUSTICE STEVENS and JUSTICE GINSBURG join, dissenting.[26]

26. In a separate statement, Justice O'Connor also expressed agreement with Souter's opinion.

[A] pedestrian happening upon the monument at issue here needs no training in religious doctrine to realize that the statement of the Commandments, quoting God himself, proclaims that the will of the divine being is the source of obligation to obey the rules, including the facially secular ones. In this case, moreover, the text is presented to give particular prominence to the Commandments' first sectarian reference, "I am the Lord thy God." That proclamation is centered on the stone and written in slightly larger letters than the subsequent recitation. To ensure that the religious nature of the monument is clear to even the most casual passerby, the word "Lord" appears in all capital letters (as does the word "am"), so that the most eye-catching segment of the quotation is the declaration "I AM the LORD thy God." What follows, of course, are the rules against other gods, graven images, vain swearing, and Sabbath breaking. And the full text of the fifth Commandment puts forward filial respect as a condition of long life in the land "which the Lord thy God giveth thee." These "[w]ords . . . make [the] . . . religious meaning unmistakably clear." *County of Allegheny v. American Civil Liberties Union, Greater Pittsburgh Chapter* (1989).

To drive the religious point home, and identify the message as religious to any viewer who failed to read the text, the engraved quotation is framed by religious symbols: two tablets with what appears to be ancient script on them, two Stars of David, and the superimposed Greek letters Chi and Rho as the familiar monogram of Christ. Nothing on the monument, in fact, detracts from its religious nature, and the plurality does not suggest otherwise. It would therefore be difficult to miss the point that the government of Texas is telling everyone who sees the monument to live up to a moral code because God requires it, with both code and conception of God being rightly understood as the inheritances specifically of Jews and Christians. . . .

Texas . . . says that the Capitol grounds are like a museum for a collection of exhibits, the kind of setting that several Members of the Court have said can render the exhibition of religious artifacts permissible, even though in other circumstances their display would be seen as meant to convey a religious message forbidden to the State. . . .

But 17 monuments with no common appearance, history, or esthetic role scattered over 22 acres is not a museum, and anyone strolling around the lawn would surely take each memorial on its own terms without any dawning sense that some purpose held the miscellany together more coherently than fortuity and the edge of the grass. One monument expresses admiration for pioneer women. One pays respect to the fighters of World War II. And one quotes the God of Abraham whose command is the sanction for moral law. The themes are individual grit, patriotic courage, and God as the source of Jewish and Christian morality; there is no common denominator. . . .

. . . The monument in this case sits on the grounds of the Texas State Capitol. There is something significant in the common term "statehouse" to refer to a state capitol building: it is the civic home of every one of the State's citizens. If neutrality in religion means something, any citizen should be able to visit that civic home without having to confront religious expressions clearly meant to convey an official religious position that may be at odds with his own religion, or with rejection of religion. . . .

I would reverse the judgment of the Court of Appeals.

Van Orden illustrates the continuing divisions among the justices.[27] Chief Justice Rehnquist's plurality opinion again belittles the importance of *Lemon*. He argues that *Lemon* is no more than a "helpful signpost" and that the Court has often ignored it or applied different tests in its place. Justices Breyer, Scalia, and Thomas offer concurring views. Breyer concludes that the Texas display was just one of many monuments on the capitol grounds and that there was no evidence that the state was emphasizing the religious (over the secular) nature of the Ten Commandments. Scalia posits that there is nothing unconstitutional about venerating the Ten Commandments in a nonproselytizing manner. Thomas offers the most extreme position: He questions the validity of incorporating the establishment clause and making it applicable to the states.

The dissenters focus on the religious nature of the Ten Commandments. They claim that there is no place under the U.S. Constitution for the state to erect a monument to a divinely given code of law. Neutrality means not only

that one denomination cannot be favored over another but also that believers cannot be favored over nonbelievers. Here the state endorsed a specific religious text. In Justice Stevens's words, this makes a "mockery of the constitutional ideal that government must remain neutral."

What can we conclude about the Court's handling of establishment clause litigation in general? At the very least, we can say that this area of the law is unstable, with the justices sharply divided and professing very different approaches to resolve the cases. As we have observed, each time the Court seems on the verge of eliminating the Lemon test, it reappears, as Justice Scalia put it in *Lamb's Chapel*, "like some ghoul in a late-night horror movie." Whether the Court rejects *Lemon* once and for all seems to hinge on the justices' ability to agree on a replacement standard, which so far they have been unable to do.

Establishment clause cases are rife with contradictions and inconsistencies, and the justices fully acknowledge the problems they have had in this area. As Chief Justice Burger admitted, "[W]e can only dimly perceive the lines of demarcation in this extraordinarily sensitive area of constitutional law." Scalia characterized the Court's record as "embarrassing," Kennedy labeled the decisions as "tangled," and Thomas described the Court's establishment clause jurisprudence as "in hopeless disarray."

Will the Court seek to resolve the law's inconsistencies in the religious establishment area? What standard or test will it invoke to do so? Will *Lemon* survive or be modified, overruled, or simply ignored? Will the Court adopt any of the competing standards, such as coercion, endorsement, or nonpreferentialism—or will a new standard emerge? Now that you have read about many of the significant cases of the past, you probably realize that there are no easy answers.

READINGS

Alley, Robert S. *The Supreme Court on Church and State.* New York: Oxford University Press, 1988.

Carter, Stephen L. *The Culture of Disbelief.* New York: Basic Books, 1993.

Choper, Jesse H. *Securing Religious Liberty: Principles for Judicial Interpretation of the Religion Clauses.* Chicago: University of Chicago Press, 1995.

Cookson, Catharine. *Regulating Religion: The Courts and the Free Exercise Clause.* New York: Oxford University Press, 2001.

---

27. To add to the confusion over such religious displays, the Court on the same day it decided *Van Orden* came to a completely different result in *McCreary County, Kentucky v. American Civil Liberties Union of Kentucky* (2005). In *McCreary* the justices, in a 5–4 decision, struck down the county's posting of the Ten Commandments in the local courthouse. In large measure the decision was based on a long history of county actions demonstrating a religious purpose motivating the Ten Commandments exhibit.

Currey, Thomas J. *The First Amendment Freedoms: Church and State in America to the Passage of the First Amendment.* New York: Oxford University Press, 1986.

Dolbeare, Kenneth M., and Phillip E. Hammond. *The School Prayer Decision.* Chicago: University of Chicago Press, 1971.

Dreisbach, Daniel L. *Thomas Jefferson and the Wall of Separation between Church and State.* New York: New York University Press, 2002.

Fisher, Louis. *Religious Liberty in America: Political Safeguards.* Lawrence: University Press of Kansas, 2002.

Greenawalt, Kent. *Does God Belong in Public Schools?* Princeton: Princeton University Press, 2004.

Hamburger, Philip. *Separation of Church and State.* Cambridge: Harvard University Press, 2002.

Howe, Mark Dewolfe. *The Garden and the Wilderness: Religion and Government in American Constitutional History.* Chicago: University of Chicago Press, 1965.

Ivers, Gregg. *Redefining the First Freedom.* New Brunswick, N.J.: Transaction, 1993.

Levy, Leonard W. *The Establishment Clause,* 2nd ed. Chapel Hill: University of North Carolina Press, 1994.

Long, Carolyn N. *Religious Freedom and Indian Rights: The Case of Oregon v. Smith.* Lawrence: University Press of Kansas, 2000.

Manwaring, David B. *Render unto Caesar: The Flag Salute Controversy.* Chicago: University of Chicago Press, 1962.

McGarvie, Mark Douglas. *One Nation under Law: America's Early National Struggles to Separate Church and State.* DeKalb: Northern Illinois University Press, 2004.

Miller, William Lee. *The First Liberty: America's Foundation in Religious Freedom.* Washington, D.C.: Georgetown University Press, 2003.

Monsma, Steven V. *When Sacred and Secular Mix.* Lanham, Md.: Rowman and Littlefield, 1996.

Noonan, John T., Jr. *The Lustre of Our Country: The American Experience of Religious Freedom.* Berkeley: University of California Press, 1998.

O'Brien, David M. *Animal Sacrifice and Religious Freedom: Church of Lukumi Babalu Aye v. City of Hialeah.* Lawrence: University Press of Kansas, 2004.

Peters, Shawn Francis. *Judging Jehovah's Witnesses: Religious Persecution and the Dawn of the Rights Revolution.* Lawrence: University Press of Kansas, 2002.

———. *The Yoder Case: Religion, Freedom, Education, and Parental Rights.* Lawrence: University Press of Kansas, 2003.

Pfeffer, Leo. *Religion, State, and the Burger Court.* Buffalo: Prometheus Books, 1985.

Sheffer, Martin S. *God versus Caesar: Belief, Worship, and Proselytizing under the First Amendment.* Albany: State University of New York Press, 1999.

Smith, Steven D. *Foreordained Failure: The Quest for a Constitutional Principle of Religious Freedom.* New York: Oxford University Press, 1995.

Sorauf, Frank J. *The Wall of Separation.* Princeton: Princeton University Press, 1976.

Wills, Garry. *Under God.* New York: Simon and Schuster, 1990.

CHAPTER 13

FREEDOM OF SPEECH, ASSEMBLY, AND ASSOCIATION

At one time or another, each of us has criticized someone in government. The president, the mayor, or some other public official has said or done something we thought was wrong. We may have been polite, simply noting our displeasure, or we may have used more colorful language to voice our criticism. Either way, we expressed our views. Speaking our minds is a privilege we enjoy in the United States, a privilege guaranteed by the First Amendment against government infringement.

While the Bill of Rights was making its way through Congress and the state legislatures, the First Amendment's freedom of expression provisions were hardly debated. The framers had a fundamental commitment to speech and press freedoms, especially as they related to public discussion of political and social issues. After all, vigorous public oratory had fueled the Revolution and helped shape the contours of the new government.

The language of the First Amendment is very bold: "Congress shall make no law . . . abridging the freedom of speech, or of the press; or the right of the people peaceably to assemble, and to petition the Government for a redress of grievances." These words would seem to provide an impregnable shield against government actions that would restrict any of the four components of freedom of expression: speech, press, assembly, and petition. But to what extent *does* the Constitution protect these rights? May mischievous patrons stand up in a crowded movie theater and shout "fire!" when they know there is no fire? May a publisher knowingly print lies

about a member of the community and try to destroy that person's reputation? May a political group attempt to spread its message by driving sound trucks through residential neighborhoods at all hours? May protesters storm onto the floor of the United States Senate to bring attention to their demands?

Despite the strong wording of the First Amendment, the answer to each of these questions is no. The Supreme Court never has adhered to a literal interpretation of the expression guarantees; rather, it has ruled that certain expressions—whether communicated verbally, in print, or by actions—may be restricted because of the effect they may have.

This chapter is the first of two dealing with the right of expression. Here we examine the development of constitutional standards for freedom of expression and then the application of those standards to various kinds of expression. In the next we look at issues specific to the freedom of the press and discuss forms of expression that traditionally have been considered outside First Amendment protection.

THE DEVELOPMENT OF LEGAL STANDARDS: THE EMERGENCE OF LAW IN TIMES OF CRISIS

In the period immediately following the September 11, 2001, terrorist attacks on the World Trade Center in New York City and the Pentagon just outside Washington, D.C., the balance between freedom and security shifted. The government placed a high priority on identifying possible terrorists and preventing future assaults. Although the reasons for taking such actions may seem logical, the price was a restriction on personal liberties. Among other actions, the government restricted the right to move about freely by increasing security precautions at airports, expanded its authority to monitor telephone and Internet usage, and asserted greater powers of search and seizure.

Such actions should not be surprising. History teaches that governments tend to respond to times of crisis in a particular way. Emergencies may be the result of war, economic collapse, natural catastrophes, or internal rebellion. During these times a nation's survival may be at stake, the government may be unstable, and political dissent and opposition to the government may increase. The responses of political leaders are predictable: They will place a priority on national security and unity and take firm action against subversive and opposition criticism. Often these reactions take the form of policies that restrict the right of the people to speak, publish, and organize.

The United States is no exception to this rule. In times of peace and general prosperity, there is little reason to restrict freedom of expression. The government and the nation are secure, and the people are relatively content. In times of crisis, however, the president and Congress may react harshly, contending that some forms of expression must be curtailed to protect national security.

This tendency manifested itself shortly after the nation's founding. In its early years the government was weak and vulnerable, the economy was in disarray, and Europe continued to pose a threat. The ruling Federalist Party was the target of much political criticism. In response, Congress passed one of the most restrictive laws in American history, the Sedition Act of 1798. This statute made it a crime to write, print, utter, or publish malicious material that would defame the federal government, the president, or the members of Congress, that would bring them into disrepute, or that could excite the hatred of the people against them. Violations of the act were punishable by imprisonment of up to two years. The act expired in 1801 without any court challenges to its validity. Yet it serves today as a lesson that threatened regimes, even in nations with a fundamental commitment to political freedom, are capable of repressive measures.

The justices of the Supreme Court are called upon to decide where constitutional protections end and the government's right to restrict expression begins. Because expression rights are most severely threatened during times of war and national crisis, the Court often has found itself searching for an appropriate constitutional standard in response to conflicts over government policies designed to protect national security. For this reason we turn to the national security cases in the first part of this chapter to see how the justices have developed general theories of the freedom of expression. In later sections we address the ways the Court has responded to more specific expression controversies.

Clear and Present Danger Test

The Supreme Court faced no significant freedom of expression disputes during the nation's first century. Certainly there were periods of national emergency, most notably the Civil War. And during these periods of stress, the government took oppressive actions. President Abraham Lincoln pursued a number of policies to suppress "treacherous" behavior, believing "that the nation must be able to protect itself in war against utterances which actually cause insubordination."[1] But the Supreme Court had no opportunity to rule on the constitutionality of the president's actions, at least on First Amendment grounds.

Significant changes occurred with the outbreak of war in Europe in 1914 and the Russian Revolution in 1917. The United States turned its attention away from domestic programs and toward defense of the American system of government. The growing threat of communism and socialism touched off a wave of nationalism that led to many attacks against suspected subversives.

The patriotic fervor unleashed by World War I was strong and pervasive. No American was immune, not even Supreme Court justices. Consider Chief Justice Edward D. White's response to an attorney who argued that the military draft, enacted by Congress in 1917, lacked public support: "I don't think your statement has anything to do with legal arguments and should not have

---

1. Zechariah Chafee Jr., *Free Speech in the United States* (Cambridge: Harvard University Press, 1941), 266.

been said in this Court. It is a very unpatriotic statement to make."[2] Members of Congress, too, were caught up in the patriotic fervor gripping the nation. They, like the founders, felt it necessary to enact legislation to ensure that Americans presented a unified front to the world. The Espionage Act of 1917 prohibited any attempt to "interfere with the operation or success of the military or naval forces of the United States . . . to cause insubordination . . . in the military or naval forces . . . or willfully obstruct the recruiting or enlistment service of the United States." A year later, Congress passed the Sedition Act, which prohibited the uttering, writing, or publishing of anything disloyal to the government, flag, or military forces of the United States.

Although the majority of Americans probably supported these laws, some groups and individuals thought they constituted intolerable infringements on civil liberties guarantees contained in the First Amendment. The dissenters, however, did not speak with one political voice: Some, most notably the American Union Against Militarism (a predecessor of the American Civil Liberties Union), were blatantly pacifist; others, primarily leaders of the progressive movement, were pure civil libertarians, opposed to any government intrusion into free expression; and finally there were the radicals—individuals who hoped to see the United States undergo a Socialist or Communist revolution. Regardless of their motivation, these individuals and groups brought legal challenges to the repressive laws and pushed the Supreme Court into freedom of expression cases for the first time. The Court decided the first of the World War I cases, *Schenck v. United States*, in 1919, followed by three others the same year.

As you read *Schenck*, keep in mind the circumstances surrounding the Court's decision. The United States had just successfully completed a war effort in which more than 4 million troops were in uniform and more than a million had been sent to fight in Europe. The number of Americans killed or seriously wounded exceeded 300,000. The national fervor and support for the war effort had been tremendous. In the face of this national unity, Charles Schenck, a Socialist, engaged in active opposition to America's participation in the war. His appeal of an espionage conviction allowed the Supreme Court to make its first major doctrinal statement on freedom of expression. What did the Court decide? What standard did it develop to adjudicate future claims?

Schenck v. United States

249 U.S. 47 (1919)
http://laws.findlaw.com/US/249/47.html
Vote: 9 (Brandeis, Clarke, Day, Holmes, McKenna,
        McReynolds, Pitney, Van Devanter, White)
        0
Opinion of the Court: Holmes

In 1917 Charles Schenck, the general secretary of the Socialist Party, had fifteen thousand pamphlets printed, urging resistance to the draft. He sent these leaflets, described by the government's case as "frank, bitter, passionate appeal[s] for resistance to the Selective Service Law," to men listed in a local newspaper as eligible for service. Federal authorities charged him with violating the Espionage Act; specifically, the United States alleged that Schenck had attempted to obstruct recruitment and illegally used the mail to do so.

John Henry Nelson and Henry J. Gibbons, Schenck's attorneys, did not dispute the government's charges; rather, they argued that the Espionage Act violated the First Amendment's freedom of speech clause. The law imposed criminal penalties on the expression of political opposition to a government policy. This was precisely the type of expression, they claimed, that the First Amendment was designed to protect.

MR. JUSTICE HOLMES delivered the opinion of the Court.

The document in question upon its first printed side recited the first section of the Thirteenth Amendment, said that the idea embodied in it was violated by the Conscription Act and that a conscript is little better than a convict. In impassioned language it intimated that conscription was despotism in its worst form and a monstrous wrong against humanity in the interest of Wall Street's chosen few. It said

---

2. Quoted by John R. Schmidhauser in *Constitutional Law in American Politics* (Monterey, Calif.: Brooks/Cole, 1984), 325.

"Do not submit to intimidation," but in form at least confined itself to peaceful measures such as a petition for the repeal of the act. The other and later printed side of the sheet was headed "Assert Your Rights." It stated reasons for alleging that any one violated the Constitution when he refused to recognize "your right to assert your opposition to the draft," and went on "If you do not assert and support your rights, you are helping to deny or disparage rights which it is the solemn duty of all citizens and residents of the United States to retain." It described the arguments on the other side as coming from cunning politicians and a mercenary capitalist press, and even silent consent to the conscription law as helping to support an infamous conspiracy. It denied the power to send our citizens away to foreign shores to shoot up the people of other lands, and added that words could not express the condemnation such cold-blooded ruthlessness deserves, &c., &c., winding up "You must do your share to maintain, support and uphold the rights of the people of this country." Of course the document would not have been sent unless it had been intended to have some effect, and we do not see what effect it could be expected to have upon persons subject to the draft except to influence them to obstruct the carrying of it out. The defendants do not deny that the jury might find against them on this point.

But it is said, suppose that that was the tendency of this circular, it is protected by the First Amendment to the Constitution. Two of the strongest expressions are said to be quoted respectively from well-known public men. It may well be that the prohibition of laws abridging the freedom of speech is not confined to previous constraints, although to prevent them may have been the main purpose. We admit that in many places and in ordinary times the defendants in saying all that was said in the circular would have been within their constitutional rights. But the character of every act depends upon the circumstances in which it is done. The most stringent protection of free speech would not protect a man in falsely shouting fire in a theatre and causing a panic. It does not even protect a man from an injunction against uttering words that may have all the effect of force. The question in every case is whether the words used are used in such circumstances and are of such a nature as to create a clear and present danger that they will bring about the substantive evils that Congress has a right to prevent. It is a question of proximity and degree. When a nation is at war many things that might be said in time of peace are such a hindrance to its effort that their utterance will not be endured so long as men fight and that no Court could regard them as protected by any constitutional right. It seems to be admitted that if an actual obstruction of the recruiting service were proved, liability for words that produced that effect might be enforced. The statute of 1917 in §4 punishes conspiracies to obstruct as well as actual obstruction. If the act, (speaking, or circulating a paper), its tendency and the intent with which it is done are the same, we perceive no ground for saying that success alone warrants making the act a crime. Indeed that case might be said to dispose of the present contention if the precedent covers all *media concludendi* [the steps of an argument]. But as the right to free speech was not referred to specifically, we have thought fit to add a few words.

It was not argued that a conspiracy to obstruct the draft was not within the words of the Act of 1917. The words are "obstruct the recruiting or enlistment service," and it might be suggested that they refer only to making it hard to get volunteers. Recruiting heretofore usually having been accomplished by getting volunteers the word is apt to call up that method only in our minds. But recruiting is gaining fresh supplies for the forces, as well by draft as otherwise. It is put as an alternative to enlistment or voluntary enrollment in this act. . . .

Judgments affirmed.

Justice Oliver Wendell Holmes's opinion in *Schenck* represents the first important and substantial explication of the freedom of speech. Holmes provided the Court with a mechanism, known as the clear and present danger test, for framing such cases and a standard by which to adjudicate future claims:

The question in every case is whether the words used are used in such circumstances and are of such a nature as to create a clear and present danger that they will bring about the substantive evils that Congress has a right to prevent.

This test requires a consideration not only of the content of the expression but also of the context in which the words are uttered, the consequences of those words, and the time when those consequences may occur.

In addition, Holmes's opinion was a politically astute compromise. On the one hand, the clear and present danger test was a rather liberal interpretation of expression rights. On the other, the justices recognized that free speech rights were not absolute, and they found room within the clear and present danger test to uphold the conviction of an unpopular opponent of the war effort. In *Schenck* Holmes was able to write into law a test favorable to expression rights without arousing the ire of Congress. Immediately after *Schenck,* the Court used the clear and present danger rationale to decide two other challenges to the Espionage Act, seemingly designating the test as the approved standard for interpreting the First Amendment.[3]

Bad Tendency Test

The perceived permanence of the clear and present danger test proved to be an illusion. Just eight months after *Schenck,* a majority of the justices banished the test to a legal exile that would last for almost two decades. This abrupt change occurred in **Abrams v. United States** (1919), a case in which Jacob Abrams and a group of his political associates challenged their convictions under the 1918 Sedition Act. They had published and distributed leaflets, written in English and Yiddish, criticizing President Woodrow Wilson for sending U.S. troops into Russia. The leaflets were written in language characteristic of the anticapitalist rhetoric of the Russian Revolution, calling Wilson a "Kaiser" and urging workers to go on strike.

Writing for the Supreme Court, Justice John Clarke upheld the convictions, but, in doing so, he moved away from the clear and present danger test and instead asserted:

[T]he plain purpose of their propaganda was to excite, at the supreme crisis of the war, disaffection, sedition, riots, and, as they hoped, revolution, in this country for the purpose of embarrassing and if possible defeating the military plans of the Government in Europe. A technical distinction may perhaps be taken between disloyal and abusive language applied to the *form* of our government or language intended to bring the *form* of our government into contempt and disrepute, and language of like character and intended to produce like results directed against the President and Congress, the agencies through

Samuel Lipman, Hyman Lychowsky, Mollie Steimer, and Jacob Abrams, World War I–era anarchists and revolutionaries, were found guilty of attempting to hinder the war effort. The Supreme Court upheld the convictions in *Abrams v. United States.*

which that form of government must function in time of war. *But it is not necessary to a decision of this case to consider whether such distinction is vital or merely formal, for the language of these circulars was obviously intended to provoke and to encourage resistance to the United States in the war. . . .* [Emphasis added.]

Justice Holmes, joined by Justice Louis D. Brandeis, wrote a vigorous dissent to counter Clarke's approach. Arguing that clear and present danger was the more appropriate approach, he emphasized that government should only be allowed to punish speech that creates "a present danger of immediate evil." Under the First Amendment, Holmes claimed, the government is not permitted to repress "a silly leaflet by an unknown man."

That the *Abrams* decision marked a turning away from the clear and present danger standard was evident to Holmes. In his dissent he tried to refine the test to show how the *Schenck* rationale could work in a variety of contexts. Many view this dissent as one of Holmes's finest, helping earn him the sobriquet "the Great Dissenter." *(See Box 13-1.)*

---

3. See, for example, *Frohwerk v. United States* (1919) and *Debs v. United States* (1919).

BOX 13-1   OLIVER WENDELL HOLMES JR. (1902–1932)

OLIVER WENDELL HOLMES JR. was born March 8, 1841, in Boston. He was named after his father, a professor of anatomy at Harvard Medical School as well as a poet, essayist, and novelist in the New England literary circle that included Longfellow, Emerson, Lowell, and Whittier. Dr. Holmes's wife, Amelia Lee Jackson Holmes, was the third daughter of Justice Charles Jackson of the Supreme Judicial Court of Massachusetts. Young Holmes attended a private Latin school in Cambridge and received his undergraduate education at Harvard, graduating as class poet in 1861 as had his father thirty-two years before him.

Commissioned a second lieutenant in the Massachusetts Twentieth Volunteers, known as the Harvard Regiment, Holmes was wounded three times in battle. Serving three years, he was mustered out a captain in recognition of his bravery and gallant service. After the Civil War, Holmes returned to Harvard to study law despite his father's conviction that "a lawyer can't be a great man."

He was admitted to the Massachusetts bar in 1867 and practiced in Boston for fifteen years, beginning with the firm of Chandler, Shattuck, and Thayer and later forming his own partnership with Shattuck. In 1872 Holmes married Fanny Bowdich Dixwell, the daughter of his former schoolmaster and a friend since childhood. They were married fifty-seven years.

During his legal career Holmes taught constitutional law at his alma mater, edited the *American Law Review,* and lectured on common law at the Lowell Institute. His twelve lectures were compiled in a book called *The Common Law* and published shortly before his fortieth birthday. The London *Spectator* heralded Holmes's treatise as the most original work of legal speculation in decades. *The Common Law* was translated into German, Italian, and French.

IN 1882 THE GOVERNOR of Massachusetts appointed Holmes—then a full professor at the Harvard Law School in a chair established by Boston lawyer Louis D. Brandeis—an associate justice of the Massachusetts Supreme Court. Holmes served on the state court for twenty years, the last three as chief justice, and wrote more than 1,000 opinions, many of them involving labor disputes. Holmes's progressive labor views, criticized by railroad and other corporate interests, were considered favorably by President Theodore Roosevelt during his search in 1902 for someone to fill the "Massachusetts seat" on the U.S. Supreme Court, vacated by Bostonian Horace Gray. Convinced of Holmes's compatibility with the administration's national policies, Roosevelt nominated him associate justice on December 2, and he was confirmed without objection two days later.

Holmes's twenty-nine years of service on the Supreme Court spanned the tenures of Chief Justices Fuller, White, Taft, and Hughes and the administrations of Presidents Roosevelt, Taft, Wilson, Harding, Coolidge, and Hoover.

For twenty-five years he never missed a session and daily walked the two and a half miles from his home to the Court. Like Justice Brandeis, Holmes voluntarily paid an income tax despite the majority's ruling that exempted federal judges. Unlike the idealistic and often moralistic Brandeis, with whom he is frequently compared, Holmes was pragmatic, approaching each case on its own set of facts without a preconceived notion of the proper result.

Although a lifelong Republican, on the Court Holmes did not fulfill Roosevelt's expectations as a loyal party man. His dissent shortly after his appointment from the Court's decision to break up the railroad trust of the Northern Securities Company surprised the nation and angered the president.

At the suggestion of Chief Justice Hughes and his colleagues on the bench, Holmes retired on January 12, 1932, at the age of ninety. A widower since 1929, he continued to spend his winters in Washington, D.C., and his summers in Beverly Farms, Massachusetts. He died at his Washington home March 6, 1935, two days before his ninety-fourth birthday.

SOURCE: Adapted from David Savage, *Guide to the U.S. Supreme Court,* 4th ed. (Washington, D.C.: CQ Press, 2004), 971–972.

Holmes had failed to convince his colleagues in *Abrams*. Instead, Clarke's majority opinion used a standard known as the bad tendency test, an approach derived from English common law. It asks, "Do the words have a *tendency* to bring about something evil?" rather than, "Do the words bring about an immediate substantive evil?" Why the majority shifted constitutional standards is a matter of speculation.

Regardless of their motivation, by the early 1920s it was obvious that a majority of justices rejected the clear and present danger standard in favor of more stringent constitutional interpretations, such as the bad tendency test. Two cases, *Gitlow v. New York* (1925) and *Whitney v. California* (1927), exemplify this shift, but with a slightly different twist. *Gitlow* and *Whitney* involved violations of state laws. Just as the federal government wanted to foster patriotism during wartime, the states also felt the need to promulgate their own versions of nationalism. The result was the so-called state criminal syndicalism laws, which made it a crime to advocate, teach, aid, or abet in any activity designed to bring about the overthrow of the government by force or violence. The actual effect of such laws was to outlaw any association with views "abhorrent" to the interests of the United States, such as communism and socialism. Would the Court be willing to tolerate such state intrusions into free speech?

In *Gitlow* the Court heard the appeal of a Socialist leader, Benjamin Gitlow, who had been convicted under a state criminal anarchy law for distributing a pamphlet that called for mass action to overthrow the capitalist system in the United States. The majority upheld the conviction, ruling that the state had the authority to punish expression that might lead to the violent overthrow of the government. In dissent, Holmes continued to press his clear and present danger standard, finding that Gitlow's actions posed no immediate danger.

The majority in *Gitlow*, however, made an enduring contribution to constitutional law with its statement that for "present purposes we may and do assume that freedom of speech and of the press—which are protected by the First Amendment from abridgment by Congress—are among the fundamental personal rights and 'liberties' protected by the due process clause of the Four-

William Foster, left, and Benjamin Gitlow, presidential and vice presidential candidates for the Workers (Communist) Party, at Madison Square Garden in 1928. Gitlow's publication of a "Left Wing Manifesto" led to his arrest and conviction under New York's criminal anarchy act. The Supreme Court upheld the conviction but ruled that states were bound by the freedom of speech provision of the First Amendment.

teenth Amendment from impairment by the States." This sweeping incorporation vastly expanded constitutional guarantees for freedom of expression by ensuring that the states had to abide by guarantees contained in the First Amendment.

In *Whitney v. California* the Court again used the bad tendency test to uphold the conviction of a political radical.[4] Charlotte Whitney, a well-known California heiress and niece of former Supreme Court justice Stephen J. Field, was active in a number of Socialist organizations and a founding member of the California Communist Labor Party. In 1919 she was arrested and later sentenced to fourteen years in prison for being a member of an

4. For more on this 1927 case, see Thomas I. Emerson, *The System of Freedom of Expression* (New York: Vintage Books, 1970), 105–107.

Charlotte Anita Whitney, who devoted her life to socialist and communist causes, was convicted in 1920 of violating the California criminal syndicalism act. Her conviction was upheld by the U.S. Supreme Court in *Whitney v. California* (1927).

organization that was dedicated to overthrowing the United States government, a violation of the state syndicalism law.

On appeal to the Supreme Court, her attorneys from the newly formed American Civil Liberties Union (ACLU) argued that the state law violated the freedom of speech provision of the First Amendment. The majority rejected that argument:

That the freedom of speech which is secured by the Constitution does not confer an absolute right to speak . . . whatever one may choose . . . and that a State in the exercise of its police power may punish those who abuse this freedom by utterances inimical to the public welfare, tending to incite crime, disturb the public peace, or endanger the foundations of organized government and threaten its overthrow by unlawful means, is not open to question.

The Court's decision in *Whitney* went a step beyond previous decisions upholding the convictions of those with unpopular political views. There was no evidence that Whitney had ever taken concrete actions to bring down the government. Her conviction was based exclusively on her membership in a subversive organization. Never before had the Court approved criminal charges based on mere membership alone.

Throughout these cases Holmes and Brandeis continued to distance themselves from the majority by arguing in favor of the clear and present danger test in their dissenting and concurring opinions. But the majority refused to back away from the position that the restriction of expression that might produce evils was constitutionally permissible.

Regardless of the philosophical debates triggered by the series of cases from *Schenck* to *Whitney*, one fact remains clear: The justices seemed swept away by the wave of nationalism and patriotism in the aftermath of World War I. They generally acceded to the wishes of Congress and the states—wishes that centered on the complementary goals of promoting nationalism and suppressing radicalism.

Preferred Freedoms Doctrine

As the pressures of World War I and its aftermath faded, the national debate over seditious speech was argued in calmer voices. As part of this general trend, the Supreme Court began to reevaluate its decisions from *Schenck* to *Whitney*.

The Court's greater willingness to consider the message of civil liberties advocates was first signaled in **Stromberg v. California** (1931). Yetta Stromberg, a nineteen-year-old member of the Young Communist League, served as a counselor at a summer camp for children ages ten to fifteen. She regularly introduced her campers to Marxist theory. In addition, she would raise a red banner and lead the children in reciting a workers' pledge of allegiance. She was convicted of violating a state statute making it a crime to raise publicly a red flag or banner as a symbol of opposition to organized government or in support of anarchy. The Supreme Court reversed the conviction, holding that the California statute was excessively broad, applying not only to those who advocated violent overthrow of the government but also to those who supported political change by orderly and peaceful means.

Stromberg was followed six years later by *DeJonge v. Oregon* (1937). Dirk DeJonge, a member of the Communist Party, distributed handbills in Portland, Oregon, calling for a meeting to protest police raids on the homes of party members. The meeting attracted between 160 and 200 individuals, some of whom were members of the party. Police raided the gathering and arrested DeJonge for violating the state syndicalism act, which prohibited the organization of the Communist Party.

The Supreme Court overturned DeJonge's conviction on this charge. The justices unanimously held that the state violated the First Amendment. The meeting was peaceful and orderly. DeJonge had not engaged in any "forcible subversion." According to the majority opinion by Chief Justice Charles Evans Hughes, written in language closely resembling the clear and present danger test, "peaceable assembly for lawful discussion cannot be made a crime." Certainly, such reasoning turned *Whitney* on its head.

Even more dramatic was a seemingly insignificant bit of writing—a footnote contained in Justice Harlan F. Stone's opinion in *United States v. Carolene Products* (1938). This case dealt with a federal ban on the shipment of a certain kind of milk—an economic, not a First Amendment, issue. Stone wrote in footnote 4:

There may be narrower scope for operation of the presumption of constitutionality when legislation appears on its face to be within a specific prohibition of the Constitution, such as those of the first ten Amendments, which are deemed equally specific when held to be embraced by the Fourteenth Amendment. . . .

It is unnecessary to consider now whether legislation which restricts those political processes which can ordinarily be expected to bring about repeal of undesirable legislation, is to be subjected to more exacting judicial scrutiny under the general prohibitions of the Fourteenth Amendment than are most other types of legislation. . . .

Nor need we enquire whether similar considerations enter into the review of statutes directed at particular religious, or national, or racial minorities; whether prejudice against discrete and insular minorities may be a special condition, which tends seriously to curtail the operation of those political

processes ordinarily to be relied upon to protect minorities, and which may call for a correspondingly more searching judicial inquiry.

What appeared to be an obscure footnote in a relatively insignificant case took on tremendous importance for civil liberties claims, especially those based on First Amendment expression rights. As Alpheus Mason and Donald Grier Stephenson explain, each of the footnote's three paragraphs contained powerful ideas regarding the status of constitutional rights.[5] The first paragraph holds that whenever a government regulation appears on its face to be in conflict with the Bill of Rights, the usual presumption that laws are constitutional should be reduced or waived altogether. The second paragraph hints that the judiciary has a special responsibility to defend rights that are essential to the effective functioning of the political process, a class of liberties that clearly includes free expression rights. The third paragraph suggests a special role for the Court in protecting the rights of minorities and unpopular groups. The standard expressed in footnote 4 has become known as the preferred freedoms doctrine. This doctrine has special significance for First Amendment claims, for it means that the judiciary will proceed with a special scrutiny when faced with laws that restrict freedom of expression, especially as those laws may relate to the articulation of unpopular political views. Put another way, "Laws restricting fundamental rights . . . would be regarded as suspect and potentially dangerous to the functioning of democracy."[6]

The importance of Justice Stone's footnote goes beyond its obvious declaration of a new standard for evaluating First Amendment claims. In *Carolene Products* Stone announces a modification in the fundamental role of the Court. He declares that the Court will assume a special responsibility for protecting civil rights and civil liberties and be particularly vigilant in guarding the rights of minorities and the politically unpopular. Stone's statement marked a major change in direction for an

5. Alpheus Thomas Mason and Donald Grier Stephenson Jr., *American Constitutional Law*, 11th ed. (Englewood Cliffs, N.J.: Prentice Hall, 1996), 307–308.
6. Stanley I. Kutler, ed., *The Supreme Court and the Constitution* (New York: W. W. Norton, 1984), 429.

institution that had, for its entire history, been tilted toward settling private economic disputes and wrestling with questions of government power. From this point forward the civil liberties docket began to grow, and the Court rapidly began to evolve into an institution with a primary focus on civil liberties issues.[7]

But would the majority of the justices adopt Stone's preferred freedoms approach to First Amendment claims? Moreover, how would such an approach square with the clear and present danger standard, to which most of the justices seemed to want to return? Attorneys, states, and civil libertarians had to wait only a year until the Court addressed these questions in **Schneider v. State of New Jersey (Town of Irvington)** (1939). *Schneider* was one of four cases the Court grouped together for a single decision. The cases involved municipal ordinances from New Jersey, Wisconsin, California, and Massachusetts that limited free expression. The Wisconsin, California, and Massachusetts laws restricted public handbill distribution to keep the streets uncluttered and free of litter. The New Jersey law, designed to reduce incidents of fraud, required the approval of a police official before an individual or group could solicit, canvass, or distribute printed materials door-to-door. In an 8 to 1 decision, the Court struck down each municipal regulation as an unconstitutional burden on free speech. Justice Owen Roberts stated:

We are of the opinion that the purpose to keep the streets clean [is] insufficient to justify an ordinance which prohibits a person rightfully on a public street from handing literature to one willing to receive it. Any burden imposed upon the city authorities in cleaning ... the streets ... results from the constitutional protection of the freedom of speech.

And

... a municipality cannot ... require all who wish to disseminate ideas to present them first to police authorities for their consideration and approval, with a discretion in the police to say some ideas may, while others may not, be carried to the homes of citizens; some persons may, while others may not, disseminate information from house to house.

7. Richard L. Pacelle, *The Transformation of the Supreme Court's Agenda: From the New Deal to the Reagan Administration* (Boulder: Westview Press, 1991).

BOX 13-2   THE PREFERRED FREEDOMS DOCTRINE

JUSTICE HARLAN FISKE STONE'S famous Footnote Four in *United States v. Carolene Products* (1938) gave birth to the preferred freedoms doctrine. This doctrine holds that some constitutional rights, particularly those protected by the First Amendment, are so fundamental to a free society that they deserve an especially high degree of judicial protection.

Stone's position built on theories advanced by earlier justices. Oliver Wendell Holmes Jr., for example, contended in several cases that government regulation of the economy required only a rational basis to establish its constitutionality, but that regulation of speech could take place only if a "clear and present danger" could be shown. Justice Benjamin Cardozo argued in *Palko v. Connecticut* (1937) that certain rights are so fundamental as to be indispensable for our system of liberty. Stone expanded these arguments to enlarge the role of the judiciary as a protector of freedom and to carve out a special responsibility for the protection of minority rights.

The preferred freedoms doctrine became more prominent in the years immediately after *Carolene Products.* Several justices who wanted expanded protection for First Amendment rights based their argument on the doctrine. In *Murdock v. Pennsylvania* (1943), Justice William O. Douglas declared, "Freedom of press, freedom of speech, freedom of religion are in a preferred position." Justice Hugo Black frequently stated that the rights contained in the First Amendment are the very heart of our government.

In contemporary times, the preferred freedoms doctrine is rarely applied in its original form, but its spirit lives on in subsequently adopted rules of judicial interpretation. The Court today often distinguishes between fundamental rights and other liberties, designating certain rights as deserving "strict scrutiny." Government may restrict such rights only if there is a compelling reason to do so. These doctrines directly flow from Stone's assertion in 1938 that the rights most central to our system of liberty deserve special status and protection.

SOURCE: C. Herman Pritchett, "Preferred Freedoms Doctrine," in *The Oxford Companion to the Supreme Court of the United States,* ed. Kermit L. Hall (New York: Oxford University Press, 1992), 663–664.

The Court's decision demonstrated that the justices were beginning to favor a preferred freedoms approach. They were giving a priority to First Amendment expression rights over otherwise legitimate government interests.

Six years later, in *Thomas v. Collins* (1945), the Court moved even closer to embracing the preferred freedoms test. The case arose when R. J. Thomas, president of the United Automobile, Aircraft and Agricultural Workers (UAW) and vice president of the Congress of Industrial Organizations (CIO), arrived in Houston, Texas, to deliver a speech to a group of workers that a regional CIO affiliate wanted to organize. Six hours before Thomas was to speak, Texas authorities served him with a restraining order, prohibiting him from making his scheduled address. Believing that the order constituted a violation of his free speech guarantees, Thomas delivered his speech anyway to an audience of three hundred people. The meeting was described as "peaceful and orderly," but authorities arrested Thomas. He was sentenced to three days in jail and a $100 fine. Thomas appealed, claiming the state had violated his First Amendment rights.

In a 6–3 opinion, the Supreme Court agreed with Thomas and ruled against the state. Most significant, the Court used a preferred freedoms approach to reach that conclusion. Justice Wiley Rutledge, writing for the majority, asserted:

[This] case confronts us again with the duty our system places on this Court to say where the individual's freedom ends and the State's power begins. Choice of that border, now as always delicate, is perhaps more so where the usual presumptive supporting legislation is balanced *by the preferred place given in our scheme to the great, the indispensable democratic freedoms secured by the First Amendment*. . . . For [this] reason any attempt to restrict those liberties must be justified by clear public interest, threatened not . . . remotely, but by a *clear and present danger.* [Emphasis added.]

Constitutional experts claim that this decision represented another major breakthrough in the area of freedom of speech, but why? First, it reinforces the position that the preferred freedoms doctrine provides an appropriate solution to First Amendment problems. Second, Rutledge's language—"[A]ny attempt to restrict [the lib-

erties of speech and assembly] must be justified . . . by a clear and present danger"—indicates that the Court, instead of abandoning Holmes's standard, had combined the clear and present danger standard with the preferred freedoms framework. The preferred freedoms "concept was never a repudiation of the notion of clear and present danger, but was seen as giving its purposes a firmer base and texture—incorporating it much as Einsteinian physics incorporates Newtonian."[8]

Aftermath of World War II: Competing Tests and a Divided Court

As *Thomas* indicates, by the mid-1940s it seemed as if the Court had finally settled on an approach to solve First Amendment problems. Stone's preferred freedoms doctrine had gained acceptance among the justices, even though it served as a vehicle by which to overturn many laws restricting speech. But, like previous tests, the preferred freedoms doctrine was short-lived. In the early 1950s the Court began to turn back toward more conservative interpretations of the First Amendment. What caused this sudden shift in direction? Three factors may explain it.

First, several changes in Court membership occurred between 1945 and 1952. Chief Justice Frederick M. Vinson replaced Stone, the author of footnote 4, and two relatively conservative justices, Tom C. Clark and Sherman Minton, took the place of two liberals, Francis W. Murphy and Wiley Rutledge. As we have seen, such changes in personnel can have a substantial impact on Court outcomes.

Second, by 1949 it became evident that some of the justices were not satisfied with the preferred freedoms framework. Keep in mind that several dissented in *Thomas*, but at the time they offered no alternative standard. This situation changed dramatically in 1949 with *Kovacs v. Cooper*, when the Court applied the preferred freedoms approach to approve a local ordinance prohibiting the use of sound and amplifying devices on city streets. In a long concurring opinion, Justice Felix

---

8. Malcolm M. Feeley and Samuel Krislov, *Constitutional Law* (Boston: Little, Brown, 1985), 427.

Frankfurter agreed with the outcome in *Kovacs,* but not with the Court's reasoning. Calling the preferred freedoms doctrine a "mischievous phrase," Frankfurter articulated a new standard by which to review First Amendment claims. He argued that a "wise accommodation between liberty and order always has been, and ever will be, indispensable for a democratic society" and urged his colleagues to strike a "wise balance" between the two.

Often called the ad hoc balancing test, Frankfurter's approach wants the Court to balance, on a case-by-case basis, the individual's free speech claim against the government's reason for regulating the behavior. But, in Frankfurter's judgment, these competing claims were not of equal merit; the latter should be taken more seriously because legislators had already determined that the law in question met a compelling government interest.

A third reason for the Court's dramatic turnaround in the 1950s was a change in the external environment. After World War II the United States entered into a cold war with the Soviet Union. This period was characterized by an intense fear of communism, not unlike the time just after World War I. Some politicians, led by Sen. Joseph R. McCarthy, R-Wis., fed the fear by alleging that Communist Party sympathizers had infiltrated the upper echelon of government. Others asserted Communists were exercising considerable influence in public education, labor, the arts, and other important sectors of American society. The fear of communism manifested itself in many ways, including congressional enactment of several pieces of legislation designed to suppress Communist and other forms of subversive activity in the United States.

In *American Communication Associations v. Douds* (1950) the Court considered a challenge to a section of the Labor Management Relations Act that required union leaders to file sworn statements proclaiming nonaffilliation with the Communist Party before they could receive federal recognition of their union. Writing for the Court, Chief Justice Vinson upheld the law and rejected the clear and present danger standard, the heart of the preferred freedoms approach, noting: "It is the considerations that gave birth to the phrase clear and present danger, not the phrase itself, that are vital in our deci-

sions of questions involving . . . the First Amendment." In his view, the ad hoc balancing approach fully encapsulated that genesis: Because Congress has determined that communism constitutes harmful conduct, then it may regulate subversive activity in the public interest.

Vinson's standard is akin to the bad tendency test of the 1920s. Both operate under the assumption that the First Amendment protects the public good, as defined by legislatures, rather than individual expression.

The Court's movement toward more conservative approaches took another turn in *Dennis v. United States* (1951). At issue in *Dennis* was the Smith Act. Enacted in 1940, this statute prohibited anyone from knowingly or willfully advocating or teaching the overthrow of any government of the United States by force; from organizing any society to teach, advocate, or encourage the overthrow of the United States by force; or from becoming a member of any such society. By covering so many kinds of activities, the law provided authorities with a significant weapon to stop the spread of communism in the United States.

The justices upheld the Smith Act against a First Amendment challenge. The majority supported this conclusion by applying what has become known as the clear and probable danger test. This standard adopts much of the clear and present danger approach, but it does not require that the danger be proximate. In other words, the activities of individuals who desire to bring about the fall of the government can be suppressed long before the revolution gathers enough support to succeed; the evil need not be immediately present. Therefore, the government may regulate rights of subversives to organize and express their opinions even though no violent or illegal act against the government has yet occurred.

The Court's broad grant of discretion to the government to regulate expression prompted a hostile reaction from Justices Hugo Black and William O. Douglas. Both posted vigorous dissenting opinions. These two civil libertarians consistently opposed almost any regulation of speech and press rights. They often articulated what has become known as the absolute freedoms test. This standard, never adopted by a majority of the Court, endorses a literal reading of the First Amendment. When the framers wrote, "Congress shall make no law" abridging speech or press, they meant exactly that: No law means no law. When the Court in case after case upheld federal and state regulation of the expression rights of Communists and other revolutionaries, Douglas and Black were consistently in the minority.

In sum, during the 1950s we once again see the Supreme Court responding to perceived threats to national security. As was the case during the 1920s, when the justices moved from a clear and present danger test to a bad tendency standard, in the 1950s they moved from a preferred freedoms approach to a revisionist interpretation of the Holmes standard, clear and probable danger, which itself "marked a return to the 'bad tendency' views of the post–World War I period."[9]

Speech and Association during the Warren Court Era

In his dissenting opinion in *Dennis*, Justice Black wrote the following:

Public opinion being what it now is, few will protest the conviction of these Communist petitioners. There is hope, however, that in calmer times, when present pressures, passions and fears subside, this or some later Court will restore the First Amendment liberties to the high preferred place where they belong in a free society.

Black's words were indeed prophetic. As the 1950s drew to a close, the high emotions of the anti-Communist, postwar period dissipated. Senator McCarthy, whose campaign against domestic communism had fueled much of the repressive legislation, was discredited and censured by the Senate. While the nation remained concerned about the Communist threat and the possibility of nuclear war, the hysteria died down.

Once the red scare was over, the Supreme Court, now under the leadership of Chief Justice Earl Warren, began taking positions defending freedom of expression and association against the repressive legislation passed during the McCarthy era. It handed down a series of decisions upholding the constitutional rights of Communists and other so-called subversives. For example, in *Communist*

9. Kutler, *The Supreme Court and the Constitution*, 429.

Party v. United States (1963) and *Albertson v. Subversive Activities Control Board* (1965) the justices repudiated federal laws requiring Communist organizations to register with the government. In *Elfbrandt v. Russell* (1966) and *Whitehill v. Elkins* (1967) loyalty oath requirements directed at subversives were found constitutionally defective. The Court also struck down laws and enforcement actions barring Communists from holding office in labor unions (*United States v. Brown*, 1965), prohibiting Communists from working in defense plants (*United States v. Robel*, 1967), and stripping passports from Communist Party leaders (*Aptheker v. Secretary of State*, 1964). Clearly, these decisions and others handed down during more tranquil years would have been unheard of during the times of strong anti-Communist feelings.

By the end of the 1960s, then, the Court had turned away from many of its cold war rulings. It struck down as being in violation of the freedom to speak, publish, or associate much of the federal and state anti-Communist legislation still on the books. An important representative of this era was **Brandenburg v. Ohio** (1969), one of the Warren Court's last major rulings. Ironically, the *Brandenburg* decision had nothing to do with the Communist Party or other groups dedicated to violent overthrow of the U.S. government. Instead, the dispute involved a group with a much different purpose, the racist Ku Klux Klan.

Clarence Brandenburg, the leader of an Ohio affiliate of the KKK, sought to obtain publicity for the group's goals by inviting a Cincinnati reporter and camera crew to attend a rally. Subsequently, local and national television stations aired some of the events that occurred at this gathering; one film "showed 12 hooded figures, some of whom carried firearms. They were gathered around a large wooden cross, which they burned." In another, Brandenburg delivered a speech to the group in which he said, "Personally I believe the nigger should be returned to Africa, the Jew returned to Israel." Based on these films, Ohio authorities arrested Brandenburg for violating the Ohio Criminal Syndicalism law, which was passed in 1919 to prevent the spread of unpatriotic views. Similar to many other state laws of the sort upheld in *Gitlow*, the Ohio act prohibited the advocacy and assembly of individuals to teach criminal syndicalism.

In a *per curiam* (unsigned) opinion, the Court claimed that "the constitutional guarantees of free speech and free press do not permit a State to forbid or proscribe advocacy of the use of force or of law violation except where such advocacy is directed to inciting or producing imminent lawless action and is likely to incite or produce such action." The opinion said that "measured by this test," the Ohio law could not be sustained, for it punishes "mere advocacy."

In so ruling, the justices closed the door on the long series of repressive expression rulings. Indeed, as if to underscore the point, *Whitney v. California* was explicitly overruled by *Brandenburg*.

Vietnam, the Civil Rights Movement, and Beyond

As the nation's fear of Communist infiltration ebbed, a new international crisis was brewing in Vietnam. Although U.S. involvement in that conflict dated back to the Truman administration, it grew significantly in 1964 when President Lyndon Johnson announced that the North Vietnamese had attacked American ships in the Gulf of Tonkin. Johnson launched a massive military buildup, and by 1968, 541,000 U.S. troops had been sent to Vietnam. Initially, many Americans approved of Johnson's pursuit of the war, but by the late 1960s, approval had turned to criticism. A peace movement, centered on college campuses, arose throughout the country.

In addition, another cause was gathering strength. The civil rights movement, which in the 1950s was isolated in the South, by the 1960s had taken hold in all major urban centers. Because of these two social currents, and the resistance to them, the decade was marked by domestic upheaval and turmoil. These protest movements generated many free expression cases. Some involved the constitutionality of mass demonstrations, the chief weapon of the civil rights and peace movements. Others involved the issues of political expression associated with that decade—flag desecrations, draft card burnings, and so forth.

The freedom of expression cases flowing from the Vietnam War protests and civil rights movement presented the Court with a host of novel constitutional claims. The character of the Court was also undergoing change. In 1969 Warren Burger, a conservative Nixon appointee, replaced the retiring Earl Warren as chief justice. Burger was soon followed by three additional Nixon appointees—William H. Rehnquist, Harry A. Blackmun, and Lewis F. Powell Jr. With these appointments the Court began to take on a more conservative posture. This trend continued without interruption for the next twenty-three years as Republican presidents Gerald Ford, Ronald Reagan, and George H. W. Bush filled vacancies with an eye to moving the Court to the right. It was not until the mid-1990s, with President Bill Clinton's appointments of Justices Ruth Bader Ginsburg and Stephen G. Breyer, that a Democratic president had an opportunity to fill Court vacancies. But in 2005 and 2006 the conservative wing of the Court was reinforced when George W. Bush appointed John G. Roberts Jr. to replace William Rehnquist as chief justice and Samuel A. Alito Jr. to fill a vacancy created by the retirement of Sandra Day O'Connor.

In confronting the new disputes over expression rights, the justices had at their disposal a half-century of doctrinal development. The internal security cases beginning with *Schenck* and continuing into the 1960s had given birth to six major tests of how the First Amendment should be interpreted and applied *(see Table 13-1)*. In the years that followed, the justices created no significant additions to this list of competing approaches to First Amendment interpretation but continued to debate their relative merits as applied to various expressive forms and contexts. Borrowing primarily from the clear and present danger test and the preferred freedoms doctrine, the Court today remains wedded to the principle that freedom of expression is a fundamental right and that only a compelling government interest can justify restraints upon it. Thus, just as the justices before them, modern members of the Court have had to struggle with the perennial conflict between the need for an ordered society and the desire for individual liberty.

The history of freedom of expression demonstrates great variation in the government's response to unpopular and opposition opinion. When the nation is secure and prosperous, the government tends to be tolerant of dissenting views; but in times of crisis, the regulation of

TABLE 13-1 Summary of Legal Standards Governing Free Speech

Standard	Major Proponents	Court Usage: Examples
Clear and Present Danger Test "Whether the words are used in such circumstances and are of such a nature as to create a clear and present danger that they will bring about substantive evils that Congress has a right to prevent."	Holmes, Brandeis	*Schenck v. United States*, 1919
Bad Tendency Test Do the words have a tendency to bring about something evil?	Clarke, Sanford	*Abrams v. United States*, 1919
Preferred Freedoms "There may be a narrower scope for operation of the presumption of constitutionality when legislation appears on its face to be within a specific prohibition of the Constitution, such as those of the first ten Amendments."	Douglas, Stone, Rutledge	*United States v. Carolene Products*, 1938; *Thomas v. Collins*, 1945
Absolutism "The First Amendment, its prohibition in terms absolute, was designed to preclude courts as well as legislatures from weighing values of speech against silence."	Black, Douglas	Never adopted. See Black's dissent in *Dennis v. United States*, 1951; Douglas's dissent in *Roth v. United States*, 1957
Ad Hoc Balancing "On a case by case basis, the government's interest in regulation is weighed against the individual's interest in expression. Because the legislative process naturally involves a consideration of a wide range of societal interests, the courts normally defer to the government and presume that the regulation is valid."	Frankfurter, Harlan	Frankfurter's concurrence in *Kovacs v. Cooper*, 1949; Harlan's opinion in *Barenblatt v. United States* (1959)
Clear and Probable Danger "Whether the gravity of the 'evil,' discounted by its improbability, justifies such an invasion of free speech as is necessary to avoid danger."	Vinson	*Dennis v. United States*, 1951

expression veers toward the restrictive. As more repressive policies are enforced and people object, the judiciary is called upon to determine how far the government may go in restricting free speech.

The events of the recent past show that this cyclical pattern of tolerance and restriction continues to operate. From the end of the Vietnam War to the turn of the twenty-first century, Americans enjoyed relative peace and prosperity. As a consequence the government placed few new restrictions on expression rights. All of that ended with the September 2001 terrorist attacks and the subsequent military actions in Afghanistan and Iraq.

President Bush and Congress responded with the war on terrorism that included legislation designed to protect the nation against future terrorist attacks. At the forefront of this effort was the USA PATRIOT Act of 2001. This statute, among other things, expanded the power of the government to monitor and intercept telephone, face-to-face, and electronic communications. It also liberalized search and seizure, arrest, and detention authority.

In addition to the USA PATRIOT Act, Congress passed laws expanding and redefining the powers of government agencies to combat terrorism. Most important was the creation of the Department of Homeland Security (DHS) in 2002. This new cabinet-level department combined twenty-two federal agencies with more than 170,000 employees. It was given primary responsibility for protecting the nation's ports, borders, airports, and infrastructure—including utilities, the Internet, telecommunications, and financial networks—from terrorist attacks. DHS also assumed the former duties of the Immigration and Naturalization Service and has primary responsibility for emergency preparedness. The agency has broad intelligence-gathering authority to help it carry out its mission.

Civil libertarians were quick to criticize these laws for jeopardizing privacy and other fundamental rights, as well as for placing a chilling effect on the expression of opposition viewpoints. Undoubtedly, this period of national stress will spawn disputes that will once again require the federal courts to determine the line that separates legitimate government policy from unconstitutional regulation of civil liberties.

REGULATING EXPRESSION: CONTENT AND CONTEXTS

Justice Holmes noted in *Schenck* that the legitimacy of expression often depends upon the nature of the words and the conditions under which they are uttered. The major tests of the First Amendment, developed in the national security cases, provide broad guidelines for determining the boundaries of constitutional protection. Yet even if the justices could agree on a controlling philosophy of what the First Amendment means, they would still have to wrestle with the task of applying that doctrine to specific cases. In the remaining portion of this chapter, we present some of the recurring expression issues the justices have confronted and the rules of law they developed as a response.

Guiding Principles

Before we turn our attention to specific types of expression, we set forth some of the principles the Court has deemed relevant in deciding freedom of expression issues. Keep in mind that these principles are flexible and may be applied in slightly different ways depending upon the nature of the expression and the forum in which it occurs.

When the framers drafted the First Amendment they had specific purposes in mind. The goal was to create a society in which expression would thrive and the government could not use its power to repress individuals' expression by speech, publication, or in association with others of similar mind. The Supreme Court has accepted the duty to interpret the First Amendment with these purposes in mind: Over the years the justices often have referred to the goal of creating a free marketplace of ideas and a society in which a robust exchange of views occurs without government censorship.

Although the vibrant exchange of thoughts and opinions might be the goal, the justices have never concluded that the First Amendment absolutely protects all forms of speech. Instead, the Court's decisions have acknowledged that freedom of expression has certain limitations. These limitations are in response to the need for an ordered society that functions well. In general, the Court has recognized that freedom of expression must be balanced against the need to safeguard the rights of others and the right of the government to carry out its legitimate functions in a reasonable fashion.

Although the First Amendment does not make distinctions, the framers approached freedom of expression with a definite hierarchy in mind. Of primary concern was the need to protect political and social speech. Other forms of expression, such as those primarily for entertainment or commercial gain, ranked lower in the hierarchy. Still others, like libel and obscenity, were viewed as illegitimate and occupied a position outside the scope of First Amendment protections. As we shall see in this section and the next chapter, the Court has often approached freedom of expression disputes with this hierarchy in mind. It is especially vigilant in protecting political and social communication, but it allows greater deference to government in regulating other forms.

Under what conditions, then, may the government regulate expression? In general, government may encroach on speech rights if the expression itself or its consequences involve matters of legitimate government concern. Holmes may have defined it best when he referred to "substantive evils that Congress has a right to prevent." The Court has applied this admittedly vague standard by designating certain conditions that justify government's authority to intervene. Although not exhaustive, the following list includes the major categories of conditions that may trigger valid government regulation of expression.

Violence. The government has authority to protect citizens from personal injury. If expression takes a violent form or incites others to violence, the government may regulate it.

Property Damage. The government has the right to protect private and public property from being destroyed or damaged. Antiwar protesters who express themselves by setting fire to a National Guard armory have gone beyond their First Amendment protections and can be arrested for their conduct.

Criminal Speech. Some forms of expression are crimes by their very nature. For example, the Constitution does not protect those who give military secrets to the enemy or engage in conspiracies to violate valid criminal laws.

Encroaching on the Rights of Others. Freedom of expression does not provide a license to infringe on the rights of others. If animal rights protesters block an entrance to a zoo or pro-life groups prevent access to an abortion clinic, the government may intervene. In both cases, the protesters have curtailed the right of the public to move about without interference.

Burdens on Government Functions. Regulation is permissible if expression places a burden on a legitimate government function. If environmentalists opposed to the construction of a Corps of Engineers dam lie down in front of bulldozers, the government may arrest them.

Trespass. The freedom of expression does not include the right to speak anywhere one wishes. A campaign worker does not have the right to come into another person's home without permission to promote the candidate's cause. Similarly, some public facilities are not legitimate places for groups of demonstrators to congregate.

It would be legitimate, for example, to prohibit antiwar protesters from demonstrating inside a defense facility.

Forms of Expression Considered Outside the Scope of the First Amendment. As indicated previously, certain classes of expression from the very beginning have been considered unprotected by the Constitution. Chief among these are obscenity and libel. As we shall see in chapter 14, if expression meets the Court's rather strict definitions of libel or obscenity, the First Amendment does not bar government regulation.

Time, Place, and Manner Restrictions. These various conditions of legitimate government concern have given rise to the Court's "time, place, and manner" doctrine. By this standard the Court acknowledges that government has the general authority to impose reasonable time, place, and manner restrictions on the freedom of expression. Therefore, the Court would certainly uphold the arrest of demonstrators who gathered in the middle of an expressway or of political zealots who promoted their candidate by driving a sound truck through a residential area in the middle of the night.

Restraints on Government Power

Although the Court has been sympathetic to the government's need to regulate expression under certain carefully defined conditions, the justices also have been careful to place restraints on the government to ensure against abuse. The Court has constructed certain generally accepted criteria to hold the government's power within acceptable bounds. We list here some of the more frequently invoked of those standards.

Appropriate Purpose. Any government restriction on freedom of expression must have a clearly defined, legitimate government purpose. A law that makes inciting to riot a crime would rest on the legitimate government purpose of curtailing violence. A law prohibiting criticism of the president, motivated by an interest in keeping incumbents in power, would clearly fail this test. In some areas the Court has demanded that the government's purpose be legitimate; in others, the justices have required a higher standard—that the purpose be a compelling one.

Narrow Construction/Overbreadth. Any regulation of expression must be narrowly tailored to meet the government's objectives. If a legislature, concerned with protests that cause violence, passed a law prohibiting all public demonstrations, the statute would fail the narrow construction requirement. This regulatory scheme would be overbroad, going far beyond what is necessary to deal with the legislature's legitimate concern.

Vagueness. Legislatures must draft laws restricting freedom of expression with sufficient precision to give fair notice of what is being regulated. If normally intelligent people have to guess what a statute means and come to different conclusions about what is prohibited by it, the statute is unconstitutionally vague.

Chilling Effect. A law intended to regulate certain forms of illegitimate expression cannot be written in a way that makes people fearful of engaging in legitimate activity. Often such a "chilling effect" stems from statutes that are vague or overbroad. Assume that a state legislature, concerned about sexual activities that occur in certain nightclubs, passes a statute making it illegal to serve alcoholic beverages in any establishment that also offers nude entertainment. In response to that law, museum officials may be fearful of sponsoring a gathering at which patrons would sip wine while viewing an exhibit of paintings that include some nude figures. Here a statute designed to curb obscenity creates a chilling effect on the exercise of legitimate activities.

Prior Restraint. Government may prosecute individuals who violate legitimate restrictions on expression, but, absent extraordinary circumstances, may not intervene before the fact. For example, the government may not constitutionally require a speaker to submit for review a copy of the speech before its delivery in order to make sure that nothing in it may incite the audience to riot.

Content/Viewpoint Discrimination. Laws regulating expression should be content and viewpoint neutral. A local ordinance that allows public gatherings for all groups except political organizations would be guilty of content discrimination. Similarly, city officials permitting demonstrations by groups in favor of a war, but not allowing similar gatherings by antiwar organizations, would violate the principle against viewpoint discrimination.

As you read the cases and commentary in the remaining portion of this chapter and the next, keep these principles in mind. You will observe many examples of cases in which the justices debated whether the expression in question merited regulation and whether the methods of regulation were proper. You will witness the flexibility of these standards as the Court adjusted them to different contexts. Finally, you will see how individual justices differed in the way they applied these standards based upon their own ideologies and preferences.

Symbolic Speech

The First Amendment specifically protects the freedoms of speech and press, two forms of expression with which the framers were thoroughly familiar. In the days of the Revolution, political protest customarily took the form of eloquent addresses, sharply worded editorials, and fiery publications. Verbal expression and published communication were the methods of political debate, and the framers unambiguously sought to protect them from government encroachment by drafting and ratifying the First Amendment.

But what if someone wishes to communicate a message by means other than word of mouth or printed copy? If a point is made by action rather than by verbal expression, does the First Amendment still grant immunity from government regulation? These questions deal with symbolic speech and whether expressive conduct qualifies as speech under the meaning of the First Amendment.

Most of the symbolic speech cases have occurred in the modern period, but the debate over expressive conduct began much earlier. Recall the discussion of *Stromberg v. California.* In that 1931 case, a camp counselor was convicted not because of anything she said, but because of an expressive act that was in conflict with California law. In reversing her conviction on First Amendment grounds, the Supreme Court acknowledged that at

On March 31, 1966, David O'Brien and three other anti-war protestors demonstrated their opposition to U.S. military action in Vietnam by burning their draft cards on the steps of the South Boston courthouse. Their convictions for violating the Selective Service Act were affirmed in *United States v. O'Brien.*

least some forms of symbolic speech merit constitutional protection.

In the years that followed, the Court had to decide whether the same principles applied to various forms of picketing in labor disputes. Some states sought to hinder the development and success of labor unions by passing laws prohibiting workers from carrying placards and walking picket lines to protest allegedly unfair labor practices. The most significant case of this era was *Thornhill v. Alabama* (1940). Byron Thornhill was arrested for violating an Alabama law that made picketing a crime. Supporters of the law argued that picketing was conduct and not speech, but the Supreme Court reversed the conviction on First Amendment grounds. For the Court, Justice Frank Murphy concluded, "In the circumstances of our times the dissemination of information concerning the facts of a labor dispute must be regarded as within that area of free discussion that is guaranteed by the Constitution."

Decisions such as these established the principle that symbolic actions can qualify as speech and be accorded First Amendment protection. This principle does not mean, however, that the First Amendment shields from

government regulation *any* act committed to express an idea or opinion. No one, for example, would seriously claim that assassination is a protected form of expressing political opposition. Perhaps even more than verbal expression, symbolic speech presents especially difficult questions of drawing constitutional boundaries.

The turbulence of the late 1960s brought many difficult symbolic expression issues before the Court. The civil rights movement and the Vietnam War protests expanded the ways of communicating political messages. Traditional forms of speech and press gave way to demonstrations, sit-ins, flag desecration, and other varieties of conduct designed to present the protesters' political messages in a graphic manner. The first of such cases was *United States v. O'Brien* (1968). On March 31, 1966, David O'Brien and three other antiwar activists burned their draft cards on the steps of a South Boston courthouse. These actions violated the Selective Service Act, which made it illegal to destroy or mutilate a draft card.

After a federal court ruled that O'Brien's expressive conduct was constitutionally protected, the United States asked the Supreme Court to hear the case. Solicitor General Thurgood Marshall argued that O'Brien's actions

Mary Beth Tinker, pictured here with her mother, Lorena Tinker, and younger brother Paul, took part in a Vietnam War protest by wearing black armbands in school—an action that got Mary Beth and her older brother, John, suspended in 1965. In *Tinker v. Des Moines* (1969) the Supreme Court ruled that the suspensions violated the students' First Amendment rights.

thwarted a valid business of government—to draft men into the armed forces—because his purpose was "to influence others to adopt his anti-war beliefs."[10] The solicitor general also tried to negate the chief argument made by O'Brien's ACLU attorney that his action constituted symbolic speech of the kind upheld by the Court in *Stromberg*. To this, the government argued, "Terming [O'Brien's] conduct 'symbolic speech' does not transform it into activity entitled to the same kind of constitutional protection given to words and other modes of expression."

Writing for the Court, Chief Justice Warren explicitly rejected the notion that conduct used to express an idea automatically merits First Amendment protection. Rather, he wrote that whenever "speech" and "non-speech" elements are combined, a sufficiently important government interest in regulating the nonspeech element can justify limitations on First Amendment rights. As applied in this case, the Court found that O'Brien's conduct (burning the draft card) placed a burden on a le-

10. Solicitor General Marshall filed the petition for certiorari. After Marshall's elevation to the Supreme Court, Erwin Griswold took over the litigation, writing the major brief.

gitimate government activity (the power to raise and support armies). The government had a substantial interest in exercising its military authority, and the draft registration system was a reasonable means of achieving that end. The government regulations challenged in this case were directed at achieving these military interests; they were not designed to curtail freedom of expression. Consequently, the government had the constitutional power to prosecute individuals who violated the Selective Service laws even if the acts in question communicated a message of political protest.

One year later the Court heard another symbolic speech case stemming from protests against the Vietnam War, ***Tinker v. Des Moines*** (1969). In December 1965 a group of Des Moines, Iowa, adults and secondary school students devised two strategies to demonstrate their opposition to the Vietnam War: They would fast on December 16 and New Year's Day, and they would wear black armbands every day in between. Principals of the students' schools learned of the plan and agreed to suspend any students who wore armbands. Despite the warning, the parents of five children, among them John Tinker and Mary Beth Tinker, allowed them to wear black armbands to school. All five were suspended. Representing the students, ACLU attorneys argued that the armbands constituted legitimate symbolic speech that the principals could not suppress.

The Court ruled in favor of the Tinkers' expression claim, declaring that students and teachers do not "shed their constitutional rights to freedom of speech or expression at the schoolhouse gate." Important to the Court was that the protest was peaceful: There was no violence, no property damage, and no significant disruption of the school day. On this count, *Tinker* differed from *O'Brien*, in which the justices found that the burning of Selective Service documents placed a burden on a legitimate government function.

Tinker provided strong support for student expression, but the Court made it clear in subsequent rulings that to be protected such speech must be compatible with the purpose and goals of public education. In *Bethel School District No. 403 v. Fraser* (1986) the Court upheld the disciplining of Matthew Fraser, a student whose speech at a school assembly used a graphic and explicit sexual metaphor. The Court distinguished between the Tinkers' political message and the sexual content of Fraser's speech, holding that school boards have the authority to determine the manner of speech that is appropriate in a classroom or assembly hall. Similarly, in ***Morse v. Frederick*** (2007) the justices rejected the First Amendment plea of a student suspended for displaying a banner at a student gathering that was interpreted as advocating the use of illegal drugs.

Although *Tinker* and *O'Brien* are important cases in the development of symbolic expression doctrine, they did not seem to give the Court much trouble. Only one justice dissented in *O'Brien* and two in *Tinker.* Such agreement was not the case for the flag desecration cases; indeed, among all symbolic expression issues none has caused the Court greater difficulty. As a national symbol, the American flag evokes intense emotional feelings, especially among those, like members of the Supreme Court, who have long histories of public service. Even the justices who were most committed to freedom of speech indicated their discomfort in extending First Amend-

ment protection to those who destroy the flag as a method of political expression.

The justices had two important opportunities to deal with the flag desecration issue during the days of civil rights and antiwar protests.[11] But they faced their most significant flag case in 1989 in *Texas v. Johnson.* How would the justices respond? On the one hand, 1989 was a time of relative calm with few pressures to repress radical expression. On the other, the Court was dominated by justices with quite conservative ideologies. We would not expect them to be eager to extend constitutional protection to the desecration of the flag.

═══════════════════

Texas v. Johnson

491 U.S. 397 (1989)
http://laws.findlaw.com/US/491/397.html
Oral arguments may be found at: http://www.oyez.org
Vote: 5 (Blackmun, Brennan, Kennedy, Marshall, Scalia)
    4 (O'Connor, Rehnquist, Stevens, White)

Opinion of the Court: Brennan
Concurring opinion: Kennedy
Dissenting opinions: Rehnquist, Stevens

The Republican Party held its 1984 national convention in Dallas, Texas, and overwhelmingly supported President Ronald Reagan's reelection bid. While the party was meeting, a group of demonstrators marched through the city to protest the Reagan administration's policies. One of the demonstrators gave an American flag to Gregory Lee Johnson, who also was marching. When the march ended, Johnson "unfurled the flag, doused it with kerosene and set it on fire." As it burned, others chanted, "America, the red, white, and blue, we spit on you." Authorities arrested Johnson, charging him with violating the Texas flag desecration law. He was convicted and sentenced to a one-year prison term and a $2,000 fine.

───────────────

JUSTICE BRENNAN delivered the opinion of the Court.

Johnson was convicted of flag desecration for burning the flag rather than for uttering insulting words. This fact

11. *Street v. New York* (1969) and *Spence v. Washington* (1974).

somewhat complicates our consideration of his conviction under the First Amendment. We must first determine whether Johnson's burning of the flag constituted expressive conduct, permitting him to invoke the First Amendment in challenging his conviction. If his conduct was expressive, we next decide whether the State's regulation is related to the suppression of free expression. If the State's regulation is not related to expression, then the less stringent standard we announced in *United States v. O'Brien* for regulations of noncommunicative conduct controls. If it is, then we are outside of *O'Brien*'s test, and we must ask whether this interest justifies Johnson's conviction under a more demanding standard. A third possibility is that the State's asserted interest is simply not implicated on these facts, and in that event the interest drops out of the picture.

The First Amendment literally forbids the abridgement only of "speech," but we have long recognized that its protection does not end at the spoken or written word. While we have rejected "the view that an apparently limitless variety of conduct can be labeled 'speech' whenever the person engaging in the conduct intends thereby to express an idea," we have acknowledged that conduct may be "sufficiently imbued with elements of communication to fall within the scope of the First and Fourteenth Amendments."

In deciding whether particular conduct possesses sufficient communicative elements to bring the First Amendment into play, we have asked whether "[a]n intent to convey a particularized message was present, and [whether] the likelihood was great that the message would be understood by those who viewed it." Hence, we have recognized the expressive nature of students' wearing of black armbands to protest American military involvement in Vietnam. . . .

Especially pertinent to this case are our decisions recognizing the communicative nature of conduct relating to flags. Attaching a peace sign to the flag, saluting the flag, and displaying a red flag, we have held, all may find shelter under the First Amendment. That we have had little difficulty identifying an expressive element in conduct relating to flags should not be surprising. The very purpose of a national flag is to serve as a symbol of our country; it is, one might say, "the one visible manifestation of two hundred years of nationhood." . . .

We have not automatically concluded, however, that any action taken with respect to our flag is expressive. Instead, in characterizing such action for First Amendment

Gregory Johnson, who has a record of flag burning, speaks to reporters outside the Supreme Court on March 21, 1989. The justices would rule in December that the conviction of Johnson for burning a flag during a demonstration in Dallas violated his First Amendment expression rights.

purposes, we have considered the context in which it occurred. . . .

Johnson burned an American flag as part—indeed, as the culmination—of a political demonstration that coincided with the convening of the Republican Party and its renomination of Ronald Reagan for President. In these circumstances, Johnson's burning of the flag was conduct "sufficiently imbued with elements of communication" to implicate the First Amendment.

The Government generally has a freer hand in restricting expressive conduct than it has in restricting the written or spoken word. . . . "A law *directed at* the communicative nature of conduct must, like a law directed at speech itself, be justified by the substantial showing of need that the First Amendment requires." It is, in short, not simply the verbal or nonverbal nature of the expression, but the governmental interest at stake, that helps to determine whether a restriction on that expression is valid.

Thus, although we have recognized that where " 'speech' and 'nonspeech' elements are combined in the same course of conduct, a sufficiently important governmental interest in regulating the nonspeech element can justify incidental limitations on First Amendment freedoms," we have limited the applicability of *O'Brien*'s relatively lenient standard to those cases in which "the governmental interest is unrelated to the suppression of free expression." In stating, moreover, that *O'Brien*'s test "in the last analysis is little, if any, different from the standard applied to time, place, or manner restrictions," we have highlighted the requirement that the governmental interest in question be unconnected to expression in order to come under *O'Brien*'s less demanding rule.

In order to decide whether *O'Brien*'s test applies here, therefore, we must decide whether Texas has asserted an interest in support of Johnson's conviction that is unrelated to the suppression of expression. If we find that an interest asserted by the State is simply not implicated on the facts before us, we need not ask whether *O'Brien*'s test applies. The State offers two separate interests to justify this conviction: preventing breaches of the peace, and preserving the flag as a symbol of nationhood and national unity. We hold that the first interest is not implicated on this record and that the second is related to the suppression of expression.

Texas claims that its interest in preventing breaches of the peace justifies Johnson's conviction for flag desecration. However, no disturbance of the peace actually occurred or threatened to occur because of Johnson's burning of the flag. . . .

The State's position, therefore, amounts to a claim that an audience that takes serious offense at a particular expression is necessarily likely to disturb the peace and that the expression may be prohibited on this basis. Our precedents do not countenance such a presumption. On the contrary, they recognize that a principal "function of free speech under our system of government is to invite dispute. It may indeed best serve its high purpose when it induces a condition of unrest, creates dissatisfaction with conditions as they are, or even stirs people to anger." . . .

Nor does Johnson's expressive conduct fall within that small class of "fighting words" that are "likely to provoke the average person to retaliation, and thereby cause a breach of the peace." No reasonable onlooker would have regarded Johnson's generalized expression of dissatisfaction with the policies of the Federal Government as a direct personal insult or an invitation to exchange fisticuffs.

We thus conclude that the State's interest in maintaining order is not implicated on these facts. The State need not worry that our holding will disable it from preserving the peace. We do not suggest that the First Amendment forbids a State to prevent "imminent lawless action." . . .

The State also asserts an interest in preserving the flag as a symbol of nationhood and national unity. In *Spence* [v. *Washington*, 1974], we acknowledged that the Government's interest in preserving the flag's special symbolic value "is directly related to expression in the context of activity" such as affixing a peace symbol to a flag. We are equally persuaded that this interest is related to expression in the case of Johnson's burning of the flag. The State, apparently, is concerned that such conduct will lead people to believe either that the flag does not stand for nationhood and national unity, but instead reflects other, less positive concepts, or that the concepts reflected in the flag do not in fact exist, that is, we do not enjoy unity as a Nation. These concerns blossom only when a person's treatment of the flag communicates some message, and thus are related "to the suppression of free expression" within the meaning of *O'Brien*. We are thus outside of *O'Brien*'s test altogether.

It remains to consider whether the State's interest in preserving the flag as a symbol of nationhood and national unity justifies Johnson's conviction. . . .

Johnson's political expression was restricted because of the content of the message he conveyed. We must therefore subject the State's asserted interest in preserving the special symbolic character of the flag to "the most exacting scrutiny."

Texas argues that its interest in preserving the flag as a symbol of nationhood and national unity survives this close analysis. Quoting extensively from the writings of this Court chronicling the flag's historic and symbolic role in our society, the State emphasizes the " 'special place' " reserved for the flag in our Nation. The State's argument is not that it has an interest simply in maintaining the flag as a symbol of *something*, no matter what it symbolizes; indeed, if that were the State's position, it would be difficult to see how that interest is endangered by highly symbolic conduct such as Johnson's. Rather, the State's claim is that it has an interest in preserving the flag as a symbol of *nationhood* and *national unity,* a symbol with a determinate range of meanings. According to Texas, if one physically treats the flag in a way that would tend to cast doubt on either the idea that nationhood and national unity are the flag's referents or that national unity actually exists, the message conveyed thereby is a harmful one and therefore may be prohibited.

If there is a bedrock principle underlying the First Amendment, it is that the Government may not prohibit the expression of an idea simply because society finds the idea itself offensive or disagreeable.

We have not recognized an exception to this principle even where our flag has been involved. In *Street v. New York* we held that a State may not criminally punish a person for uttering words critical of the flag. . . .

In short, nothing in our precedents suggests that a State may foster its own view of the flag by prohibiting expressive conduct relating to it. To bring its argument outside our precedents, Texas attempts to convince us that even if its interest in preserving the flag's symbolic role does not allow it to prohibit words or some expressive conduct critical of the flag, it does permit it to forbid the outright destruction of the flag. The State's argument cannot depend here on the distinction between written or spoken words and nonverbal conduct. That distinction, we have shown, is of no moment where the nonverbal conduct is expressive, as it is here, and where the regulation of that conduct is related to expression, as it is here. . . .

Texas' focus on the precise nature of Johnson's expression, moreover, misses the point of our prior decisions: their enduring lesson, that the Government may not prohibit expression simply because it disagrees with its message, is not dependent on the particular mode in which one chooses to express an idea. If we were to hold that a State may forbid flag-burning wherever it is likely to endanger the flag's symbolic role, but allow it wherever burning a flag promotes that role—as where, for example, a person ceremoniously burns a dirty flag—we would be saying that when it comes to impairing the flag's physical integrity, the flag itself may be used as a symbol—as a substitute for the written or spoken word or a "short cut from mind to mind"—only in one direction. We would be permitting a

State to "prescribe what shall be orthodox" by saying that one may burn the flag to convey one's attitude toward it and its referents only if one does not endanger the flag's representation of nationhood and national unity. . . .

There is, moreover, no indication—either in the text of the Constitution or in our cases interpreting it—that a separate juridical category exists for the American flag alone. Indeed, we would not be surprised to learn that the persons who framed our Constitution and wrote the Amendment that we now construe were not known for their reverence for the Union Jack. The First Amendment does not guarantee that other concepts virtually sacred to our Nation as a whole—such as the principle that discrimination on the basis of race is odious and destructive—will go unquestioned in the marketplace of ideas. We decline, therefore, to create for the flag an exception to the joust of principles protected by the First Amendment. . . .

We are fortified in today's conclusion by our conviction that forbidding criminal punishment for conduct such as Johnson's will not endanger the special role played by our flag or the feelings it inspires. To paraphrase Justice Holmes, we submit that nobody can suppose that this one gesture of an unknown man will change our Nation's attitude towards its flag. See *Abrams v. United States* (1919) (Holmes, J., dissenting). Indeed, Texas' argument that the burning of an American flag " 'is an act having a high likelihood to cause a breach of the peace,' " and its statute's implicit assumption that physical mistreatment of the flag will lead to "serious offense," tend to confirm that the flag's special role is not in danger; if it were, no one would riot or take offense because a flag had been burned.

We are tempted to say, in fact, that the flag's deservedly cherished place in our community will be strengthened, not weakened, by our holding today. Our decision is a reaffirmation of the principles of freedom and inclusiveness that the flag best reflects, and of the conviction that our toleration of criticism such as Johnson's is a sign and source of our strength. Indeed, one of the proudest images of our flag, the one immortalized in our own national anthem, is of the bombardment it survived at Fort McHenry. It is the Nation's resilience, not its rigidity, that Texas sees reflected in the flag—and it is that resilience that we reassert today.

The way to preserve the flag's special role is not to punish those who feel differently about these matters. It is to persuade them that they are wrong. . . . And, precisely because it is our flag that is involved, one's response to the flag-burner may exploit the uniquely persuasive power of the flag itself. We can imagine no more appropriate response to burning a flag than waving one's own, no better way to counter a flag-burner's message than by saluting the flag that burns, no surer means of preserving the dignity even of the flag that burned than by—as one witness here did—according its remains a respectful burial. We do not consecrate the flag by punishing its desecration, for in doing so we dilute the freedom that this cherished emblem represents.

Johnson was convicted for engaging in expressive conduct. The State's interest in preventing breaches of the peace does not support his conviction because Johnson's conduct did not threaten to disturb the peace. Nor does the State's interest in preserving the flag as a symbol of nationhood and national unity justify his criminal conviction for engaging in political expression. The judgment of the Texas Court of Criminal Appeals is therefore

Affirmed.

CHIEF JUSTICE REHNQUIST, with whom JUSTICE WHITE and JUSTICE O'CONNOR join, dissenting.

In holding this Texas statute unconstitutional, the Court ignores Justice Holmes' familiar aphorism that "a page of history is worth a volume of logic." *New York Trust Co. v. Eisner* (1921). For more than 200 years, the American flag has occupied a unique position as the symbol of our Nation, a uniqueness that justifies a governmental prohibition against flag burning in the way respondent Johnson did here. . . .

The American flag . . . has come to be the visible symbol embodying our Nation. It does not represent the views of any particular political party, and it does not represent any particular political philosophy. The flag is not simply another "idea" or "point of view" competing for recognition in the marketplace of ideas. Millions and millions of Americans regard it with an almost mystical reverence regardless of what sort of social, political, or philosophical beliefs they may have. I cannot agree that the First Amendment invalidates the Act of Congress, and the laws of 48 of the 50 States, which make criminal the public burning of the flag. . . .

. . . [T]he public burning of the American flag by Johnson was no essential part of any exposition of ideas, and at the same time it had a tendency to incite a breach of the

peace. Johnson was free to make any verbal denunciation of the flag that he wished; indeed, he was free to burn the flag in private. He could publicly burn other symbols of the Government or effigies of political leaders. He did lead a march through the streets of Dallas, and conducted a rally in front of the Dallas City Hall. He engaged in a "die-in" to protest nuclear weapons. He shouted out various slogans during the march, including: "Reagan, Mondale which will it be? Either one means World War III"; "Ronald Reagan, killer of the hour, Perfect example of U.S. power"; and "red, white and blue, we spit on you, you stand for plunder, you will go under." For none of these acts was he arrested or prosecuted; it was only when he proceeded to burn publicly an American flag stolen from its rightful owner that he violated the Texas statute. . . .

. . . The Texas statute deprived Johnson of only one rather inarticulate symbolic form of protest—a form of protest that was profoundly offensive to many—and left him with a full panoply of other symbols and every conceivable form of verbal expression to express his deep disapproval of national policy. Thus, in no way can it be said that Texas is punishing him because his hearers—or any other group of people—were profoundly opposed to the message that he sought to convey. Such opposition is no proper basis for restricting speech or expression under the First Amendment. It was Johnson's use of this particular symbol, and not the idea that he sought to convey by it or by his many other expressions, for which he was punished. . . .

. . . Uncritical extension of constitutional protection to the burning of the flag risks the frustration of the very purpose for which organized governments are instituted. The Court decides that the American flag is just another symbol, about which not only must opinions pro and con be tolerated, but for which the most minimal public respect may not be enjoined. The government may conscript men into the Armed Forces where they must fight and perhaps die for the flag, but the government may not prohibit the public burning of the banner under which they fight. I would uphold the Texas statute as applied in this case.

The Court's decision in *Johnson* is intriguing for several reasons. Note, for example, the rather odd alignments: Two of the more conservative members of the Rehnquist Court, Antonin Scalia and Anthony M. Kennedy, voted with the majority; John Paul Stevens, usually found with the liberal wing of the Court, dissented.

Perhaps most important was the tremendous—and, to some, surprising—uproar created by the Court's ruling. President George H. W. Bush immediately condemned it, and public opinion polls indicated that Americans generally favored a constitutional amendment overturning *Johnson*. But, after some politicking by civil liberties groups, senators, and representatives, Congress did not propose an amendment. Instead, it passed the Flag Protection Act of 1989, which penalized by a one-year jail sentence and a $1,000 fine anyone who "knowingly mutilates, defaces, physically defiles, burns, maintains on the floor or ground, or tramples upon any flag of the United States."

Because the federal act differed from the Texas law at issue in *Johnson*—it banned flag desecration regardless of the motivation of the burner, whereas the Texas law did so only if a jury found the activity to be offensive—some thought it would meet approval in the Supreme Court. Others saw this difference as relatively insignificant, and, as it turned out, they were correct. In *United States v. Eichman* (1990) the Court, using the same reasoning expressed in *Johnson* and by the same vote, struck down this law as a violation of the First Amendment *(see Box 13-3)*.

Public Forums and the Preservation of Order

Preserving public order and protecting citizens from injury caused by violence are among the essential duties of government. The Preamble to the Constitution includes to "insure domestic Tranquility" among the six basic purposes for which the new government was formed. Yet in some instances free expression can threaten order. Such a breakdown of public order may take the form of bodily injury, property destruction, restricting the free movement of the public, or impeding the government from carrying out its duties. In such cases a conflict arises between the nation's commitment to freedom of expression and the government's duty to maintain order. At what point is the government constitutionally justified in repressing expression in order to stop or prevent violence?

The Court began to develop criteria to handle such expression in 1942 with *Chaplinsky v. New Hampshire*, but

---

**BOX 13-3   AFTERMATH . . .
GREGORY LEE JOHNSON**

SHORTLY AFTER the Supreme Court decided that Gregory Lee Johnson's burning of the American flag during the 1984 Republican National Convention was political expression protected by the First Amendment, Congress responded. The legislature passed the Flag Protection Act of 1989.

On October 30, two days after the new law took effect, a small group of demonstrators gathered on the steps of the Capitol in Washington to protest. Because the press had been informed that the protesters would burn flags, reporters, police, and curious passersby crowded the area. Suddenly four men separated themselves from the crowd and began to set fire to American flags.

Police reacted quickly—too quickly for one of the protesters. Gregory Lee Johnson was stopped before he could ignite his flag. Authorities arrested and prosecuted the other three demonstrators, but ignored Johnson.

Represented by William Kunstler, an attorney well known for defending radical causes, the three protestors argued that the new flag desecration law was just as constitutionally flawed as the Texas statute struck down earlier. When the justices issued their opinion in *United States v. Eichman*, the protesters prevailed, defeating the government's case presented by Solicitor General Kenneth Starr.

In the end, it was Shawn Eichman's name, not Johnson's, that was attached to the Supreme Court's decision. Johnson, who had hoped to win another place in legal history, sharply criticized police and prosecutors, claiming that his failure to be prosecuted with the others was a "gross miscarriage of justice."

SOURCES: *Washington Post*, October 31, 1989, November 1, 1989; and *New York Times*, April 11, 1990.

---

the majority of public order cases did not come to it until the 1960s and 1970s. As you read Justice Murphy's opinion in *Chaplinsky*, try to ascertain the legal standard he articulates and remember it as we look at the later Court decisions in these areas. Did Murphy's approach continue to permeate future Court decisions, or did the Court revise it to fit changing times?

Chaplinsky v. New Hampshire

315 U.S. 568 (1942)
http://laws.findlaw.com/US/315/568.html
Vote: 9 *(Black, Byrnes, Douglas, Frankfurter, Jackson, Murphy, Reed, Roberts, Stone)*

0

Opinion of the Court: Murphy

On April 6, 1940, Jehovah's Witness member Walter Chaplinsky was selling biblical pamphlets and literature, including *Watchtower* and *Consolation,* on a public street in New Hampshire. While he was announcing the sale of his pamphlets, a crowd began to gather. After one person tried to attack Chaplinsky, the rest joined in. When the police arrived and handcuffed a very agitated Chaplinsky, he demanded to know why they had arrested him and not the mob. An officer replied, "Shut up, you damn bastard," and Chaplinsky in turn called the officer a "damned fascist and a God damned racketeer." For those words, the state charged him with breaking a law prohibiting the use of "any offensive, derisive, or annoying word to any other person who is lawfully in the street."

On appeal to the Supreme Court, Chaplinsky's attorneys asked the Court to overturn the state statute on free speech grounds, arguing that "the fact that speech is likely to cause violence is no grounds for suppressing it." The state countered that the law constituted a valid exercise of its police powers.

MR. JUSTICE MURPHY delivered the opinion of the Court.

Allowing the broadest scope to the language and purpose of the Fourteenth Amendment, it is well understood that the right of free speech is not absolute at all times and under all circumstances. There are certain well-defined and narrowly limited classes of speech, the prevention and punishment of which have never been thought to raise any Constitutional problem. These include the lewd and obscene, the profane, the libelous, and the insulting or "fighting" words—those which by their very utterance inflict injury or tend to incite an immediate breach of the peace. It has been well observed that such utterances are no essential part of any exposition of ideas, and are of such slight social value as a step to truth that any benefit that may be derived from them is clearly outweighed by the social interest in order and morality. . . .

The state statute here challenged comes to us authoritatively construed by the highest court of New Hampshire. It has two provisions—the first relates to words or names addressed to another in a public place; the second refers to noises and exclamations. The court said: "the two provisions are distinct. One may stand separately from the other. Assuming, without holding, that the second were unconstitutional, the first could stand if constitutional." We accept that construction of severability and limit our consideration to the first provision of the statute.

On the authority of its earlier decisions, the state court declared that the state's purpose was to preserve the public peace, no words being "forbidden except such as have a direct tendency to cause acts of violence by the persons to whom, individually, the remark is addressed." It was further said: "The word 'offensive' is not to be defined in terms of what a particular addressee thinks. . . . The test is what men of common intelligence would understand would be words likely to cause an average addressee to fight. . . . The English language has a number of words and expressions which by general consent are 'fighting words' when said without a disarming smile. . . . Such words, as ordinary men know, are likely to cause a fight. So are threatening, profane or obscene revilings. Derisive and annoying words can be taken as coming within the purview of the statute as heretofore interpreted only when they have this characteristic of plainly tending to excite the addressee to a breach of the peace. . . . The statute, as construed, does no more than prohibit the face-to-face words plainly likely to cause a breach of the peace by the addressee, words whose speaking constitutes a breach of the peace by the speaker—including 'classical fighting words,' words in current use less 'classical' but equally likely to cause violence, and other disorderly words, including profanity, obscenity and threats."

We are unable to say that the limited scope of the statute as thus construed contravenes the Constitutional right of free expression. It is a statute narrowly drawn and limited to define and punish specific conduct lying within the domain of state power, the use in a public place of words likely to cause a breach of the peace.

In unanimously affirming Chaplinsky's conviction, the Court agreed with Murphy's enunciation of the "fighting words" doctrine: The government can regulate expressions that are likely to cause a fight. Or, to put it another way, fighting words are those whose mere utterance are likely to provoke an immediate violent response by or inflict injury on the person to whom the remarks have been directed.

Chaplinsky involved an individual who expressed himself in a way that caused local officials to be concerned about a breakdown in order. Public safety interests become even more acute when the expression takes the form of a mass demonstration rather than speech directed to one individual or a small group. In addition to the hostility the group's message may provoke, the presence of significant numbers of people raises the potential danger of personal injury and property damage. Large crowds may interfere with the free movement of individuals along streets, sidewalks, or other public areas. A demonstration that occurs near a government facility may place a burden on legitimate government activity. For these reasons, local police tend to watch such gatherings with great care. If the police believe that a breakdown in order is about to occur and move to end the demonstration, the protesters may feel that their First Amendment rights are being violated. This scenario was replayed time after time during the civil rights and anti-war protest era of the 1960s. Numerous disputes worked their way to the Supreme Court, giving the justices an opportunity to develop coherent rules of constitutional law governing public demonstrations.

To help maintain public order, local governments may require permits to be issued prior to the holding of mass demonstrations, protests, and parades. Such permits may not be denied based on the content of the group's message. Instead, the permit procedure must rest on legitimate time, place, and manner considera-

tions. Permits give local officials advance notice of mass gatherings so that adequate police protection is present. They also allow a local government to make sure that public facilities are properly used, that unlawful activities are not planned, and that financially responsible parties are identified should damages occur during the event.[12]

Additionally, local governments may place certain restrictions on the conduct of public gatherings. Again, these restraints must be content neutral and narrowly tailored to serve a significant government interest. In *Ward v. Rock Against Racism* (1989), the justices upheld a New York regulation that required groups performing in the Central Park band shell to use city-supplied amplification equipment supervised by a city-authorized sound technician. The purpose of the regulation was to ensure that concert music was played at a volume level sufficient for audience enjoyment but not so loud as to disturb local residents unreasonably. The Court concluded that this was a valid time, place, and manner restriction.

What new public forum issues will arise in the twenty-first century, and what direction will the Court take? One way to address these questions is to consider public forum cases decided over the last quarter century. Table 13-2 provides the facts of several of those disputes, their outcomes, and a synopsis of the Court's reasoning. As you can see, the Court continued to face questions of how far the government may go in restricting the manner and place of protests. We also see that civil rights, religion, and foreign policy protests still dominated First Amendment litigation. But the 1990s cases included a new protest issue: abortion. These cases usually involved a clash between pro-life advocates who protested at women's clinics and pro-choice groups who wanted the courts to curtail the demonstrations.[13]

Given that Americans today remain politically polarized, it is inevitable that protests over issues such as sending U.S. troops abroad, immigrants' rights, and global

---

12. See *Thomas v. Chicago Park District* (2002).

13. *Bray v. Alexandria Women's Health Clinic* (1993), *National Organization for Women v. Scheidler* (1994), *Madsen v. Women's Health Center, Inc.* (1994), *Schenck v. Pro-Choice Network of Western New York* (1997), and *Hill v. Colorado* (2000).

TABLE 13-2 Examples of Public Forum Cases Decided since 1988

Case	Facts	Outcome
Boos v. Barry (1988)	Challenge to a District of Columbia ordinance prohibiting the display of any sign within 500 feet of a foreign embassy that brings that foreign government into public disrepute, and prohibiting the congregation of three or more persons within 500 feet of an embassy.	The sign-display provision is an unconstitutional, content-based restriction on political expression. The congregation provision is a constitutional manner and place restriction.
Frisby v. Schultz (1988)	Challenge to a city ordinance prohibiting picketing before a particular residence of an individual.	Ordinance serves a legitimate governmental interest. It does not violate the First Amendment.
Ward v. Rock Against Racism (1989)	Challenge to a city regulation requiring bands playing in a city park to use sound-amplification equipment and sound technician provided by the city.	Ordinance is valid under the First Amendment as a reasonable regulation of place and manner of speech.
United States v. Kokinda (1990)	Challenge to a postal service regulation prohibiting the solicitation of contributions on sidewalks outside a post office.	Sidewalk outside a post office is not a traditional public forum. The regulation does not violate the First Amendment.
International Society for Krishna Consciousness v. Lee (1992)	Challenge to a New York Port Authority regulation forbidding the repetitive solicitation of money or distribution of literature in airport terminals.	An airport terminal is not a public forum. Repetitive, face-to-face solicitation may be disruptive, impede the normal flow of the public, and be fraudulent. The regulation is reasonable. However, the ban on the distribution of literature violates the First Amendment.
Forsyth County, Georgia v. Nationalist Movement (1992)	Challenge to a county ordinance allowing an official to fix the cost of a parade permit based on the estimated cost of providing sufficient security to maintain public order during the gathering.	The ordinance is unconstitutional because it gives excessive discretion to the official and allows the fee to be fixed on the content of the message and the projected public response to it.
Bray v. Alexandria Women's Health Clinic (1993)	An abortion clinic and its supporters sued to enjoin anti-abortion protesters from demonstrating at clinics in the Washington, D.C., area, claiming that such protests are in violation of the Civil Rights Act of 1871 because they reflect an "animus" against women and restrict freedom of interstate travel.	The protests were not directed at women as a class but were intended to protect victims of abortion, stop its practice, and reverse its legalization. Although many women travel interstate to obtain abortion services, the right to interstate travel was not the focus of the protesters' activity.
Madsen v. Women's Health Center, Inc. (1994)	Anti-abortion groups challenged a state court injunction prohibiting them from protesting within 36 feet of an abortion clinic, restricting noise levels during times abortion surgeries were being conducted, prohibiting protesters from physically approaching clinic clients within 300 feet of the facility, and prohibiting protests within 300 feet of the residences of clinic workers.	The injunction against protests within 36 feet of a clinic is generally upheld, as are the noise level restrictions. Banning protest activity within 300 feet of a clinic or private residences, however, is unconstitutional.
Schenck v. Pro-Choice Network of Western New York (1997)	Injunction issued to protect access rights of abortion clinic patients by 1) creating a fixed 15-foot buffer zone around clinic entrances and driveways, and 2) creating a floating 15-foot buffer zone around all individuals and vehicles entering and leaving the clinic.	Floating buffer zone violates First Amendment as excessively regulating the speech rights of the protesters, but fixed buffer zone is a valid restriction to protect access rights of clinic patients.
Thomas v. Chicago (2002)	City requirement that groups holding mass gatherings must apply for and be issued a meeting permit. Ordinance contains thirteen grounds for denial of the permit.	The ordinance is a content-neutral time, place, and manner regulation of the use of a public forum and includes adequate procedural safeguards.

warming will spawn significant legal disputes. Although issues may vary, the task of the Supreme Court will be the same as always: to decide where to draw the line between constitutionally protected speech and the government's obligation to preserve public order.

Hate Speech

The cases we have discussed so far demonstrate a great diversity in the content and method of communication. Individuals in some of these cases have used conventional forms of protest, such as speeches, parades, and published documents; others have used unconventional methods that are offensive to many, such as O'Brien's burning his draft card and Johnson's desecrating the American flag. Their expressions have included a wide array of philosophies and causes—communism, socialism, civil rights, religious beliefs, and opposition to war. In spite of this diversity, these cases share some common elements. Each case has involved an individual or group communicating a political or social message, usually expressing dissatisfaction with certain government policies. This speech is the traditional form of political expression that the framers sought to protect when they wrote the First Amendment.

Since the mid-1970s, however, another form of communication, which differs markedly from the traditional, has come before the Court. Expression based on hatred goes well beyond offending our standards of appropriateness or good taste. It arises from hostile, discriminatory, and prejudicial attitudes toward another person's innate characteristics: sex, race, ethnicity, religion, or sexual orientation. When directed at a member of the targeted group, such expression is demeaning and hurtful. Hate speech tends to be devoid of traditional commentary on political issues or on the need for changes in public policy. Instead, its central theme is hostility toward individuals belonging to the target group. May hate speech be banned, or does the First Amendment protect it? If regulation is permissible, under what conditions? And what standard should control?

One of the first modern cases involving these issues was *National Socialist Party v. Skokie* (1977). The National Socialist Party was a minor political party with no hope of gaining electoral victories. Minor parties often set their sights a bit lower, viewing activities such as public education and awareness as important tools in achieving their desired policy objectives. *Skokie* concerned the party's desire to exercise its First Amendment right to assemble. More specifically, the party wanted to "educate" the public by marching in Skokie, Illinois, a suburb of Chicago.

Such marches are commonplace in America; almost daily, a political party or other group stages a demonstration or protest somewhere. But this proposed march was anything but commonplace. The National Socialist Party is an American version of the Nazi Party, which came into power under Adolf Hitler in Germany. A large number of Jews, including survivors of Hitler's concentration camps, live in Skokie. Together the two groups formed a potentially lethal combination. In fact, as soon as the town heard of the Nazis' plan to march in full regalia, it passed a variety of ordinances aimed specifically at stopping it. Believing that these measures abridged their First Amendment rights, party leaders turned to the ACLU for legal assistance. Many of its members objected to representing Nazi interests, but the ACLU agreed to participate because Skokie's prohibitions symbolized just the sorts of laws the organization was founded to fight—abridgements of the First Amendment. Skokie residents saw the matter in a much different light; they felt the presence of Nazi uniforms in their town constituted fighting words.[14] Therefore, Skokie argued that it could legitimately regulate such speech to prevent a riot.

A state circuit court agreed with the town and entered an injunction prohibiting the Nazis from marching in Skokie. The ACLU asked the Illinois Supreme Court for a stay and for an expedited appeal. When both requests were denied, the matter came before the U.S. Supreme Court.

---

14. Many ACLU members also agreed with the town, and almost half of them resigned in protest of its decision to defend Nazis. For an interesting account of this episode, see Aryeh Neier's *Defending My Enemy* (New York: Dutton, 1979).

In a short *per curiam* opinion, five members of the Court reversed the Illinois Supreme Court's denial of the stay, finding that the town had denied the Nazis their First Amendment rights. The Court refused to uphold ordinances regulating speech before it occurred, claiming that such laws amounted to censorship. In the Court's eyes, governments can prohibit such expression only after it occurs, an opportunity the town of Skokie never had, as the Nazis chose instead to march in Chicago.

In the *Skokie* case, and in *Brandenburg* before it, the justices struck down government regulation of hate speech based on race and religion. In both cases, however, the Court's decision rested on defects in the way the government attempted to block the unacceptable expression. In *Brandenburg* the Court found constitutional problems with Ohio's Criminal Syndicalism Act upon which the prosecution of a Ku Klux Klan leader was based. In *Skokie* the Court found that the local government was unconstitutionally attempting to repress speech before it occurred, a form of prior restraint. In neither case did the Court directly confront the question whether the First Amendment allows government to punish expression based on hatred.

In response to an increase in hate speech incidents, many state and local governments, as well as colleges and universities, passed ordinances making hate speech punishable. Although most Americans consider hate-based expression reprehensible, opinion is deeply divided over whether it can be constitutionally banned. Individuals concerned with minority rights and elimination of bigotry have argued that laws making hate speech illegal are both necessary and constitutionally permissible.

Free speech advocates contend that such laws run in direct contradiction to the First Amendment. Often this issue has divided groups that have been traditional allies in the attempt to expand personal rights and liberties. *(See Box 13-4.)* The issue first found its way to the Supreme Court in the case of *R. A. V. v. City of St. Paul, Minnesota* (1992).

R. A. V. v. City of St. Paul, Minnesota

505 U.S. 377 (1992)
http://laws.findlaw.com/US/505/377.html
Oral arguments may be found at: http://www.oyez.org
Vote: 9 (Blackmun, Kennedy, O'Connor, Rehnquist, Scalia, Souter, Stevens, Thomas, White)

0

Opinion of the Court: Scalia
Concurring opinions: Blackmun, O'Connor, Stevens, White

St. Paul, Minnesota, alleged that between 1 A.M. and 3 A.M. on June 21, 1990, R. A. V., a seventeen-year-old high school dropout, and several other teen-agers "assembled a crudely made cross by taping together broken chair legs" and then burned the cross inside the fenced front yard of a black family who lived across the street from R. A. V.'s house. St. Paul could have prosecuted R. A. V. under several severe criminal laws, such as arson, which carries a maximum penalty of five years in prison and a $10,000 fine. Instead, it charged him with violating two laws, including the St. Paul Bias-Motivated Crime Ordinance. This law stated:

Whoever places on public or private property a symbol, object, appellation, characterization or graffiti, including, but not limited to, a burning cross or Nazi swastika, which one knows or has reasonable grounds to know arouses anger, alarm, or resentment in others on the basis of race, color, creed, religion, or gender commits disorderly conduct and shall be guilty of a misdemeanor.

Before R. A. V.'s trial, his attorney asked the judge to dismiss the charge, arguing that the ordinance violated the First Amendment because it was "substantially overbroad and impermissibly content-based." The trial court judge granted the motion, and the city appealed to the Minnesota Supreme Court.

The Minnesota high court reversed the trial court's decision, holding that the ordinance did not violate freedom of expression guarantees contained in the First Amendment. The court found that the ordinance prohibits conduct equivalent to "fighting words," unprotected expression under the First Amendment. It also

BOX 13-4   HATE SPEECH AND THE CIVIL LIBERTIES COMMUNITY

REGULATING HATE SPEECH is an issue that divides the civil liberties community. Groups that historically have worked together to advance civil liberties and civil rights have found themselves in the uncomfortable position of fighting against each other over the hate speech controversy. Listed below are short excerpts from amicus curiae briefs submitted by traditionally liberal groups in the case of *R.A.V. v. City of St. Paul* (1992). Notice how the briefs emphasize different values. Those in favor of striking down the St. Paul ordinance stress the primacy of the First Amendment. Supporters of the law focus on the significance of equality considerations.

IN SUPPORT OF R.A.V.:

[T]he antibias ordinance cannot be defended on the ground that the State has a compelling interest in banning messages of racial and religious bigotry and intolerance. Although these messages are inconsistent with the Nation's highest aspirations, the Court has repeatedly held that the First Amendment does not permit a State to prohibit the communication of ideas simply because they are offensive or at odds with national policies.

> —*Center for Individual Rights*

It is quite clear from the Court's First Amendment jurisprudence that government cannot criminalize such speech simply because it arouses anger, alarm and resentment.

> —*Association of American Publishers and the Freedom to Read Foundation*

This society has rested its faith on the proposition that "the remedy [for speech] is more speech, not enforced silence." [Justice Brandeis concurring in *Whitney v. California*] Accordingly, our constitutional tradition demands that even a message of racial supremacy is entitled to be heard so long as it remains in the realm of advocacy. Those who articulated this faith in public debate were not naive about the power of words or symbols. To the contrary, they believed that pernicious ideas were more dangerous when suppressed than when exposed.

> —*American Civil Liberties Union, Minnesota Civil Liberties Union, and the American Jewish Congress*

IN SUPPORT OF THE ST. PAUL ORDINANCE:

Crossburnings, of which defendant R.A.V. is accused, should be recognized as a terrorist hate practice of intimidation and harassment, which, contrary to the purposes of the Fourteenth Amendment, works to institutionalize the civil inequality of protected groups.... [T]he statute in question does not violate the First Amendment because social inequality, including through expressive conduct, is a harm for which states are entitled leeway in regulation.

> —*National Black Women's Health Project*

When not used in a personally threatening or assaultive manner, these symbols [burning cross and Nazi swastika] are part of the marketplace of ideas of which our society is justifiably tolerant; however, when used as a form of a bias-motivated personal attack, they cease to symbolize ideas and become violent tools that inflict injury. This Court has consistently recognized that this type of "expression" should not be afforded First Amendment protection.

> —*Anti-Defamation League of B'nai B'rith*

Cross burning is an especially invidious act. A burning cross is an insult and a threat; it carries with it the historical baggage of past terrorism and physical attacks. When a cross burning is targeted against an individual and his family, it is more than just expression; it is a form of violence itself—symbolic violence.

> —*Asian American Legal Defense and Education Fund, the Asian Law Caucus, the Asian Pacific American Legal Center, and the National Asian Pacific American Bar Association*

In his brief, [R.A.V.] intones principles of freedom of speech with which, in the abstract, no one will disagree. But the State of Minnesota was not indulging in theory when it charged [him] with a violation of the ordinance in controversy. It was dealing with what can only fairly be described as an act of terrorism. This conduct cannot rationally be viewed as protected by the First Amendment.

> —*National Association for the Advancement of Colored People and the Clarendon Foundation*

Russell and Laura Jones and their children. The Jones family awoke in the middle of the night to find a cross burning in their yard. The incident led to the Supreme Court's decision in *R. A. V. v. City of St. Paul.*

ruled that the ordinance was not impermissibly content-based because it was "a narrowly tailored means toward accomplishing the compelling governmental interest in protecting the community against bias-motivated threats to public safety and order."

JUSTICE SCALIA delivered the opinion of the Court.

In construing the St. Paul ordinance, we are bound by the construction given to it by the Minnesota court. Accordingly, we accept the Minnesota Supreme Court's authorita-

tive statement that the ordinance reaches only those expressions that constitute "fighting words" within the meaning of *Chaplinsky.* Petitioner . . . urge[s] us to modify the scope of the *Chaplinsky* formulation, thereby invalidating the ordinance as "substantially overbroad." We find it unnecessary to consider this issue. Assuming, *arguendo,* that all of the expression reached by the ordinance is proscribable under the "fighting words" doctrine, we nonetheless conclude that the ordinance is facially unconstitutional in that it prohibits otherwise permitted speech solely on the basis of the subjects the speech addresses.

The First Amendment generally prevents government from proscribing speech, *Cantwell v. Connecticut* (1940), or even expressive conduct, see *Texas v. Johnson* (1989), because of disapproval of the ideas expressed. Content-based regulations are presumptively invalid. From 1791 to the present, however, our society, like other free but civilized societies, has permitted restrictions upon the content of speech in a few limited areas, which are "of such slight social value as a step to truth that any benefit that may be derived from them is clearly outweighed by the social interest in order and morality." *Chaplinsky.* We have recognized that "the freedom of speech" referred to by the First Amendment does not include a freedom to disregard these traditional limitations. See, *e.g., Roth v. United States* (1957) (obscenity); *Beauharnais v. Illinois* (1952) (defamation); *Chaplinsky v. New Hampshire* ("fighting words"). Our decisions since the 1960's have narrowed the scope of the traditional categorical exceptions for defamation and for obscenity, but a limited categorical approach has remained an important part of our First Amendment jurisprudence.

We have sometimes said that these categories of expression are "not within the area of constitutionally protected speech" or that the "protection of the First Amendment does not extend" to them. Such statements must be taken in context, however, and are no more literally true than is the occasionally repeated shorthand characterizing obscenity "as not being speech at all." What they mean is that these areas of speech can, consistently with the First Amendment, be regulated *because of their constitutionally proscribable content* (obscenity, defamation, etc.)—not that they are categories of speech entirely invisible to the Constitution, so that they may be made the vehicles for content discrimination unrelated to their distinctively proscribable content.

Thus, the government may proscribe libel; but it may not make the further content discrimination of proscribing *only* libel critical of the government. We recently acknowledged this distinction in [*New York v.*] *Ferber* [1982], where, in upholding New York's child pornography law, we expressly recognized that there was no "question here of censoring a particular literary theme. . . ."

Our cases surely do not establish the proposition that the First Amendment imposes no obstacle whatsoever to regulation of particular instances of such proscribable expression, so that the government "may regulate [them] freely." That would mean that a city council could enact an ordinance prohibiting only those legally obscene works that contain criticism of the city government or, indeed, that do not include endorsement of the city government. Such a simplistic, all-or-nothing-at-all approach to First Amendment protection is at odds with common sense and with our jurisprudence as well. It is not true that "fighting words" have at most a *"de minimis"* expressive content, or that their content is *in all respects* "worthless and undeserving of constitutional protection"; sometimes they are quite expressive indeed. We have not said that they constitute *"no* part of the expression of ideas," but only that they constitute "no *essential* part of any exposition of ideas."

The proposition that a particular instance of speech can be proscribable on the basis of one feature (*e.g.,* obscenity) but not on the basis of another (*e.g.,* opposition to the city government) is commonplace, and has found application in many contexts. We have long held, for example, that nonverbal expressive activity can be banned because of the action it entails, but not because of the ideas it expresses—so that burning a flag in violation of an ordinance against outdoor fires could be punishable, whereas burning a flag in violation of an ordinance against dishonoring the flag is not. . . .

In other words, the exclusion of "fighting words" from the scope of the First Amendment simply means that, for purposes of that Amendment, the unprotected features of the words are, despite their verbal character, essentially a "nonspeech" element of communication. Fighting words are thus analogous to a noisy sound truck: Each is, as Justice Frankfurter recognized, a "mode of speech"; both can be used to convey an idea; but neither has, in and of itself, a claim upon the First Amendment. As with the sound truck, however, so also with fighting words: The government may

not regulate use based on hostility—or favoritism—towards the underlying message expressed. . . .

Even the prohibition against content discrimination that we assert the First Amendment requires is not absolute. It applies differently in the context of proscribable speech than in the area of fully protected speech. The rationale of the general prohibition, after all, is that content discrimination "rais[es] the specter that the Government may effectively drive certain ideas or viewpoints from the marketplace." *Simon & Schuster* [*v. Members of the New York State Crime Victims Board*] (1991). But content discrimination among various instances of a class of proscribable speech often does not pose this threat.

When the basis for the content discrimination consists entirely of the very reason the entire class of speech at issue is proscribable, no significant danger of idea or viewpoint discrimination exists. Such a reason, having been adjudged neutral enough to support exclusion of the entire class of speech from First Amendment protection, is also neutral enough to form the basis of distinction within the class. To illustrate: A State might choose to prohibit only that obscenity which is the most patently offensive *in its prurience—i.e.,* that which involves the most lascivious displays of sexual activity. But it may not prohibit, for example, only that obscenity which includes offensive *political* messages. . . .

Another valid basis for according differential treatment to even a content-defined subclass of proscribable speech is that the subclass happens to be associated with particular "secondary effects" of the speech, so that the regulation is *"justified* without reference to the content of the . . . speech." A State could, for example, permit all obscene live performances except those involving minors. Moreover, since words can in some circumstances violate laws directed not against speech but against conduct (a law against treason, for example, is violated by telling the enemy the nation's defense secrets), a particular content-based subcategory of a proscribable class of speech can be swept up incidentally within the reach of a statute directed at conduct rather than speech. Thus, for example, sexually derogatory "fighting words," among other words, may produce a violation of Title VII's general prohibition against sexual discrimination in employment practices. Where the government does not target conduct on the basis of its expressive content, acts are not shielded from regulation merely because they express a discriminatory idea or philosophy. . . .

Applying these principles to the St. Paul ordinance, we conclude that, even as narrowly construed by the Minnesota Supreme Court, the ordinance is facially unconstitutional. Although the phrase in the ordinance, "arouses anger, alarm or resentment in others," has been limited by the Minnesota Supreme Court's construction to reach only those symbols or displays that amount to "fighting words," the remaining, unmodified terms make clear that the ordinance applies only to "fighting words" that insult, or provoke violence, "on the basis of race, color, creed, religion or gender." Displays containing abusive invective, no matter how vicious or severe, are permissible unless they are addressed to one of the specified disfavored topics. Those who wish to use "fighting words" in connection with other ideas—to express hostility, for example, on the basis of political affiliation, union membership, or homosexuality—are not covered. The First Amendment does not permit St. Paul to impose special prohibitions on those speakers who express views on disfavored subjects.

In its practical operation, moreover, the ordinance goes even beyond mere content discrimination, to actual viewpoint discrimination. Displays containing some words—odious racial epithets, for example—would be prohibited to proponents of all views. But "fighting words" that do not themselves invoke race, color, creed, religion, or gender—aspersions upon a person's mother, for example—would seemingly be usable *ad libitum* in the placards of those arguing *in favor* of racial, color, etc. tolerance and equality, but could not be used by that speaker's opponents. One could hold up a sign saying, for example, that all "anti-Catholic bigots" are misbegotten; but not that all "papists" are, for that would insult and provoke violence "on the basis of religion." St. Paul has no such authority to license one side of a debate to fight freestyle, while requiring the other to follow Marquis of Queensbury Rules.

What we have here, it must be emphasized, is not a prohibition of fighting words that are directed at certain persons or groups (which would be *facially* valid if it met the requirements of the Equal Protection Clause); but rather, a prohibition of fighting words that contain (as the Minnesota Supreme Court repeatedly emphasized) messages of "bias-motivated" hatred and in particular, as applied to this case, messages "based on virulent notions of racial supremacy." One must wholeheartedly agree with the Minnesota Supreme Court that "[i]t is the responsibility, even the obligation, of diverse communities to confront such notions in whatever form they appear," but the manner of that confrontation cannot consist of selective limitations upon speech. St. Paul's brief asserts that a general "fighting words" law would not meet the city's needs because only a content-specific measure can communicate to minority groups that the "group hatred" aspect of such speech "is not condoned by the majority." The point of the First Amendment is that majority preferences must be expressed in some fashion other than silencing speech on the basis of its content. . . .

The content-based discrimination reflected in the St. Paul ordinance comes within neither any of the specific exceptions to the First Amendment prohibition we discussed earlier, nor within a more general exception for content discrimination that does not threaten censorship of ideas. It assuredly does not fall within the exception for content discrimination based on the very reasons why the particular class of speech at issue (here, fighting words) is proscribable. . . . [T]he reason why fighting words are categorically excluded from the protection of the First Amendment is not that their content communicates any particular idea, but that their content embodies a particularly intolerable (and socially unnecessary) *mode* of expressing *whatever* idea the speaker wishes to convey. St. Paul has not singled out an especially offensive mode of expression—it has not, for example, selected for prohibition only those fighting words that communicate ideas in a threatening (as opposed to a merely obnoxious) manner. Rather, it has proscribed fighting words of whatever manner that communicate messages of racial, gender, or religious intolerance. Selectivity of this sort creates the possibility that the city is seeking to handicap the expression of particular ideas. That possibility would alone be enough to render the ordinance presumptively invalid, but St. Paul's comments and concessions in this case elevate the possibility to a certainty. . . .

Finally, St. Paul . . . defend[s] the conclusion of the Minnesota Supreme Court that, even if the ordinance regulates expression based on hostility towards its protected ideological content, this discrimination is nonetheless justified because it is narrowly tailored to serve compelling state interests. Specifically, they assert that the ordinance helps to ensure the basic human rights of members of groups that have historically been subjected to discrimination, including the right of such group members to live in peace where they wish. We do not doubt that these interests are compelling, and that the ordinance can be said to promote them. But the "danger of censorship" presented by a facially content-based statute requires that that weapon be employed only where it is *"necessary* to serve the asserted [compelling] interest." ... The dispositive question in this case, therefore, is whether content discrimination is reasonably necessary to achieve St. Paul's compelling interests; it plainly is not. An ordinance not limited to the favored topics, for example, would have precisely the same beneficial effect. In fact the only interest distinctively served by the content limitation is that of displaying the city council's special hostility towards the particular biases thus singled out. That is precisely what the First Amendment forbids. The politicians of St. Paul are entitled to express that hostility—but not through the means of imposing unique limitations upon speakers who (however benightedly) disagree.

Let there be no mistake about our belief that burning a cross in someone's front yard is reprehensible. But St. Paul has sufficient means at its disposal to prevent such behavior without adding the First Amendment to the fire.

The judgment of the Minnesota Supreme Court is reversed, and the case is remanded for proceedings not inconsistent with this opinion.

It is so ordered.

JUSTICE WHITE, with whom JUSTICE BLACKMUN, JUSTICE O'CONNOR and . . . JUSTICE STEVENS join . . . concurring in the judgment.

Although I disagree with the Court's analysis, I do agree with its conclusion: The St. Paul ordinance is unconstitutional. However, I would decide the case on overbreadth grounds. . . .

In the First Amendment context, "[c]riminal statutes must be scrutinized with particular care; those that make unlawful a substantial amount of constitutionally protected conduct may be held facially invalid even if they also have legitimate application." The St. Paul antibias ordinance is such a law. Although the ordinance reaches conduct that is unprotected, it also makes criminal expressive conduct that causes only hurt feelings, offense, or resentment, and is protected by the First Amendment. The ordinance is therefore fatally overbroad and invalid on its face.

The Supreme Court unanimously declared the St. Paul hate speech ordinance to be unconstitutional. The justices found the law defective because it singled out a particular kind of hate speech. The ordinance, therefore, violated the principle that laws regulating expression must not discriminate on the basis of content. The concurring justices also found the law unacceptable, but they preferred to strike it down for being unconstitutionally overbroad.

It would be incorrect to generalize from *R. A. V.* that the Court will strike down any law that imposes a penalty for hateful expression. In two other cases the Court has held that properly constructed laws can constitutionally regulate behavior motivated by hate. First, in **Wisconsin v. Mitchell** (1993) the justices unanimously held that states are free to impose more severe sentences for crimes that are racially motivated—in this case a physical assault—than for otherwise identical crimes motivated by other factors. And second, in **Virginia v. Black** (2003) a divided Court held that a state could criminally prosecute cross burning if it could prove that the act was conducted with an intent to intimidate.

Commercial Expression

Traditionally, commercial expression has been accorded a very low level of First Amendment protection. Advertising was always considered part of commerce rather than a form of protected speech, and governments have been relatively free to regulate it. Clearly, the framers did not have advertising in mind when they drafted and ratified the First Amendment. In addition, advertising can involve false and fraudulent claims that are legitimate targets of commercial regulation.

Beginning in the 1970s, however, the Supreme Court began expanding constitutional protections for commercial expression. A series of four decisions radically changed the traditional approach, starting with **Bigelow v. Virginia** (1975), in which the justices struck down a state law that made it a crime to advertise legal abortion services. Then, in **Virginia State Board of Pharmacy v. Virginia Citizens Consumer Council** (1976) the Court declared unconstitutional a state regulation that prohibited the advertising of prescription drug prices. In **Linmark**

Associates v. Township of Willingboro (1977) a city's ban on residential "For Sale" signs was invalidated. Finally, in **Bates v. State Bar of Arizona** (1977) the justices found state bans on the advertising of legal services to be at odds with the First Amendment.

This is not to say that the Court has elevated advertising to the same level of protection enjoyed by political and social expression. The justices have acknowledged that there are legitimate reasons for placing restraints on commercial expression that would be unconstitutional if applied to political and social speech. States are, for example, free to regulate against false, deceptive, fraudulent, and misleading advertising.

The Right Not to Speak

So far we have discussed the constitutionality of government attempts to restrict or prohibit certain kinds of expression. Although curtailing expression is the most common form of government regulation, at times the government requires citizens to speak or write. Americans may be ordered to appear as witnesses before a court, grand jury, or legislative investigating committee. The government compels people to provide information on income tax returns. It may be necessary to take an oath when we become citizens, provide court testimony, take public office, or apply for a gun permit. Americans generally consider these regulations to be reasonable requirements relevant to legitimate government functions. But what if an individual refuses to comply with a government regulation that requires expression? Other than the Fifth Amendment's protection against the government's compelling self-incriminating testimony, is there any restraint on the government's authority to coerce expression? Put another way, does the First Amendment's guarantee of freedom of speech carry with it the freedom not to speak?

To understand this issue we need once again to turn our attention to the famous "flag salute" cases discussed in Chapter 12. As you recall, in 1940 the Court in **Minersville School District v. Gobitis** upheld flag salute regulations against claims that the school system was violating the children's right to free exercise of religion. Three years later, in *West Virginia Board of Education v. Barnette*

(1943), the Court again considered the constitutionality of the compulsory flag salute laws, once again in a case brought by Jehovah's Witnesses.

By this time some conditions had changed. First, the war had begun to turn in the Allies' favor, and the fear of defeat and the feverishly patriotic mood so strong at the beginning of World War II had moderated somewhat. Second, the Court had undergone some personnel changes that strengthened its civil libertarian wing. Third, the *Gobitis* decision had been roundly criticized in legal circles. These circumstances encouraged the Jehovah's Witnesses to be more optimistic about their chances of winning in *Barnette*.

But one additional factor distinguished *Gobitis* from *Barnette*. Lawyers supporting the challenge made a significant strategy decision to base it not so much on freedom of religion as on the freedom of speech. As you read Justice Jackson's majority opinion in *Barnette*, notice how he weaves religion and expression rights into his explanation for striking down the flag salute laws.

West Virginia Board of Education v. Barnette

319 U.S. 624 (1943)
http://laws.findlaw.com/US/319/624.html
Vote: 6 (Black, Douglas, Jackson, Murphy, Rutledge, Stone)
    3 (Frankfurter, Reed, Roberts)
Opinion of the Court: Jackson
Concurring opinions: Black and Douglas (joint), Murphy
Dissenting opinions: Frankfurter, Reed and Roberts (joint)

Following the *Gobitis* decision, the West Virginia legislature amended its laws to require that all public schools teach courses intended to increase students' knowledge of the American system of government and to foster the spirit of Americanism. In support of this policy, the state board of education required that the American flag be saluted and the Pledge of Allegiance be recited each day. Students who refused to participate could be charged with insubordination and expelled. Not attending school because of such an expulsion was grounds for the child's being declared delinquent. Parents of delinquent children were subject to fines and jail penalties of up to thirty days. In some cases officials threatened noncomplying students with reform school.

The Jehovah's Witnesses challenged these regulations in the name of the Barnette family, church members who had been harassed by the school system for failure to participate in the flag salute ritual. One of the Barnette children, in fact, had been expelled.[15]

Despite the Supreme Court's decision in *Gobitis,* a three-judge district court sympathized with the Barnette family's plight. According to the well-respected circuit court judge John J. Parker: "The salute to the United States' flag is an expression of the homage of the soul. To force it upon one who has conscientious scruples against giving it is petty tyranny unworthy of the spirit of the Republic, and forbidden, we think, by the United States Constitution." After the decision, the West Virginia School Board appealed to the U.S. Supreme Court.

MR. JUSTICE JACKSON delivered the opinion of the Court.

As the present Chief Justice said in dissent in the *Gobitis* case, the State may "require teaching by instruction and study of all in our history and in the structure and organization of our government, including the guaranties of civil liberty which tend to inspire patriotism and love of country." Here, however, we are dealing with a compulsion of students to declare a belief. They are not merely made acquainted with the flag salute so that they may be informed as to what it is or even what it means. The issue here is whether this slow and easily neglected route to aroused loyalties constitutionally may be short-cut by substituting a compulsory salute and slogan. . . .

There is no doubt that, in connection with the pledges, the flag salute is a form of utterance. Symbolism is a primitive but effective way of communicating ideas. The use of an emblem or flag to symbolize some system, idea, institution, or personality, is a short cut from mind to mind. Causes and nations, political parties, lodges and ecclesiastical groups seek to knit the loyalty of their following to a flag or banner, a color or design. The State announces rank, func-

tion, and authority through crowns and maces, uniforms and black robes; the church speaks through the Cross, the Crucifix, the altar and shrine, and clerical raiment. Symbols of State often convey political ideas just as religious symbols come to convey theological ones. Associated with many of these symbols are appropriate gestures of acceptance or respect: a salute, a bowed or bared head, a bended knee. A person gets from a symbol the meaning he puts into it, and what is one man's comfort and inspiration is another's jest and scorn.

Over a decade ago Chief Justice Hughes led this Court in holding that the display of a red flag as a symbol of opposition by peaceful and legal means to organized government was protected by the free speech guaranties of the Constitution. *Stromberg v. California* [1931]. Here it is the State that employs a flag as a symbol of adherence to government as presently organized. It requires the individual to communicate by word and sign his acceptance of the political ideas it thus bespeaks. Objection to this form of communication when coerced is an old one, well known to the framers of the Bill of Rights.

It is also to be noted that the compulsory flag salute and pledge requires affirmation of a belief and an attitude of mind. It is not clear whether the regulation contemplates that pupils forego any contrary convictions of their own and become unwilling converts to the prescribed ceremony or whether it will be acceptable if they simulate assent by words without belief and by a gesture barren of meaning. It is now a commonplace that censorship or suppression of expression of opinion is tolerated by our Constitution only when the expression presents a clear and present danger of action of a kind the State is empowered to prevent and punish. It would seem that involuntary affirmation could be commanded only on even more immediate and urgent grounds than silence. But here the power of compulsion is invoked without any allegation that remaining passive during a flag salute ritual creates a clear and present danger that would justify an effort even to muffle expression. To sustain the compulsory flag salute we are required to say that a Bill of Rights which guards the individual's right to speak his own mind, left it open to public authorities to compel him to utter what is not in his mind.

Whether the First Amendment to the Constitution will permit officials to order observance of ritual of this nature does not depend upon whether as a voluntary exercise we

---

15. For more details on this case, see David Manwaring, *Render unto Caesar: The Flag Salute Controversy* (Chicago: University of Chicago Press, 1962).

would think it to be good, bad or merely innocuous. Any credo of nationalism is likely to include what some disapprove or to omit what others think essential, and to give off different overtones as it takes on different accents or interpretations. If official power exists to coerce acceptance of any patriotic creed, what it shall contain cannot be decided by courts, but must be largely discretionary with the ordaining authority, whose power to prescribe would no doubt include power to amend. Hence validity of the asserted power to force an American citizen publicly to profess any statement of belief or to engage in any ceremony of assent to one presents questions of power that must be considered independently of any idea we may have as to the utility of the ceremony in question.

Nor does the issue as we see it turn on one's possession of particular religious views or the sincerity with which they are held. While religion supplies appellees' motive for enduring the discomforts of making the issue in this case, many citizens who do not share these religious views hold such a compulsory rite to infringe constitutional liberty of the individual. It is not necessary to inquire whether nonconformist beliefs will exempt from the duty to salute unless we first find power to make the salute a legal duty.

The *Gobitis* decision, however, *assumed*, as did the argument in that case and in this, that power exists in the State to impose the flag salute discipline upon school children in general. The Court only examined and rejected a claim based on religious beliefs of immunity from an unquestioned general rule. The question which underlies the flag salute controversy is whether such a ceremony so touching matters of opinion and political attitude may be imposed upon the individual by official authority under powers committed to any political organization under our Constitution. We examine rather than assume existence of this power and, against this broader definition of issues in this case, re-examine specific grounds assigned for the *Gobitis* decision.

1. It was said that the flag-salute controversy confronted the Court with "the problem which Lincoln cast in memorable dilemma: 'Must a government of necessity be too *strong* for the liberties of its people, or too *weak* to maintain its own existence?' " and that the answer must be in favor of strength. *Minersville School District v. Gobitis.*

We think these issues may be examined free of pressure or restraint growing out of such considerations.

It may be doubted whether Mr. Lincoln would have thought that the strength of government to maintain itself would be impressively vindicated by our confirming power of the state to expel a handful of children from school. Such oversimplification, so handy in political debate, often lacks the precision necessary to postulates of judicial reasoning. If validly applied to this problem, the utterance cited would resolve every issue of power in favor of those in authority and would require us to override every liberty thought to weaken or delay execution of their policies.

Government of limited power need not be anemic government. Assurance that rights are secure tends to diminish fear and jealousy of strong government, and by making us feel safe to live under it makes for its better support. Without promise of a limiting Bill of Rights it is doubtful if our Constitution could have mustered enough strength to enable its ratification. To enforce those rights today is not to choose weak government over strong government. It is only to adhere as a means of strength to individual freedom of mind in preference to officially disciplined uniformity for which history indicates a disappointing and disastrous end.

The subject now before us exemplifies this principle. Free public education, if faithful to the ideal of secular instruction and political neutrality, will not be partisan or enemy of any class, creed, party, or faction. If it is to impose any ideological discipline, however, each party or denomination must seek to control, or failing that, to weaken the influence of the educational system. Observance of the limitations of the Constitution will not weaken government in the field appropriate for its exercise.

2. It was also considered in the *Gobitis* case that functions of educational officers in states, counties and school districts were such that to interfere with their authority "would in effect make us the school board for the country."

The Fourteenth Amendment, as now applied to the States, protects the citizen against the State itself and all of its creatures—Boards of Education not excepted. These have, of course, important, delicate, and highly discretionary functions, but none that they may not perform within the limits of the Bill of Rights. That they are educating the young for citizenship is reason for scrupulous protection of Constitutional freedoms of the individual, if we are not to strangle the free mind at its source and teach youth to discount important principles of our government as mere platitudes.

Such Boards are numerous and their territorial jurisdiction often small. But small and local authority may feel less sense of responsibility to the Constitution, and agencies of publicity may be less vigilant in calling it to account. The action of Congress in making flag observance voluntary and respecting the conscience of the objector in a matter so vital as raising the Army contrasts sharply with these local regulations in matters relatively trivial to the welfare of the nation. There are village tyrants as well as village Hampdens, but none who acts under color of law is beyond reach of the Constitution.

3. The *Gobitis* opinion reasoned that this is a field "where courts possess no marked and certainly no controlling competence," that it is committed to the legislatures as well as the courts to guard cherished liberties and that it is constitutionally appropriate to "fight out the wise use of legislative authority in the forum of public opinion and before legislative assemblies rather than to transfer such a contest to the judicial arena," since all the "effective means of inducing political changes are left free."

The very purpose of a Bill of Rights was to withdraw certain subjects from the vicissitudes of political controversy, to place them beyond the reach of majorities and officials and to establish them as legal principles to be applied by the courts. One's right to life, liberty, and property, to free speech, a free press, freedom of worship and assembly, and other fundamental rights may not be submitted to vote; they depend on the outcome of no elections.

In weighing arguments of the parties it is important to distinguish between the due process clause of the Fourteenth Amendment as an instrument for transmitting the principles of the First Amendment and those cases in which it is applied for its own sake. The test of legislation which collides with the Fourteenth Amendment, because it also collides with the principles of the First, is much more definite than the test when only the Fourteenth is involved. Much of the vagueness of the due process clause disappears when the specific prohibitions of the First become its standard. The right of a State to regulate, for example, a public utility may well include, so far as the due process test is concerned, power to impose all of the restrictions which a legislature may have a "rational basis" for adopting. But freedoms of speech and of press, of assembly, and of worship may not be infringed on such slender grounds. They are susceptible of restriction only to prevent grave and immedi-

ate danger to interests which the state may lawfully protect. It is important to note that while it is the Fourteenth Amendment which bears directly upon the State it is the more specific limiting principles of the First Amendment that finally govern this case. . . .

4. Lastly, and this is the very heart of the *Gobitis* opinion, it reasons that "National unity is the basis of national security," that the authorities have "the right to select appropriate means for its attainment," and hence reaches the conclusion that such compulsory measures toward "national unity" are constitutional. Upon the verity of this assumption depends our answer in this case.

National unity as an end which officials may foster by persuasion and example is not in question. The problem is whether under our Constitution compulsion as here employed is a permissible means for its achievement.

Struggles to coerce uniformity of sentiment in support of some end thought essential to their time and country have been waged by many good as well as by evil men. Nationalism is a relatively recent phenomenon but at other times and places the ends have been racial or territorial security, support of a dynasty or regime, and particular plans for saving souls. As first and moderate methods to attain unity have failed, those bent on its accomplishment must resort to an ever-increasing severity. . . . Those who begin coercive elimination of dissent soon find themselves exterminating dissenters. Compulsory unification of opinion achieves only the unanimity of the graveyard.

It seems trite but necessary to say that the First Amendment to our Constitution was designed to avoid these ends by avoiding these beginnings. There is no mysticism in the American concept of the State or of the nature or origin of its authority. We set up government by consent of the governed, and the Bill of Rights denies those in power any legal opportunity to coerce that consent. Authority here is to be controlled by public opinion, not public opinion by authority.

The case is made difficult not because the principles of its decision are obscure but because the flag involved is our own. Nevertheless, we apply the limitations of the Constitution with no fear that freedom to be intellectually and spiritually diverse or even contrary will disintegrate the social organization. To believe that patriotism will not flourish if patriotic ceremonies are voluntary and spontaneous instead of a compulsory routine is to make an unflattering estimate of the appeal of our institutions to free minds. We can have intellectual individualism and the rich cultural diversity that we owe to exceptional minds only at the price of occasional eccentricity and abnormal attitudes. When they are so harmless to others or to the State as those we deal with here, the price is not too great. But freedom to differ is not limited to things that do not matter much. That would be a mere shadow of freedom. The test of its substance is the right to differ as to things that touch the heart of the existing order.

If there is any fixed star in our constitutional constellation, it is that no official, high or petty, can prescribe what shall be orthodox in politics, nationalism, religion, or other matters of opinion or force citizens to confess by word or act their faith therein. If there are any circumstances which permit an exception, they do not now occur to us.

We think the action of the local authorities in compelling the flag salute and pledge transcends constitutional limitations on their power and invades the sphere of intellect and spirit which it is the purpose of the First Amendment to our Constitution to reserve from all official control.

The decision of this Court in *Minersville School District v. Gobitis* and the holdings of those few *per curiam* decisions which preceded and foreshadowed it are overruled, and the judgment enjoining enforcement of the West Virginia Regulation is affirmed.

Affirmed.

MR. JUSTICE FRANKFURTER, dissenting.

One who belongs to the most vilified and persecuted minority in history is not likely to be insensible to the freedoms guaranteed by our Constitution. Were my purely personal attitude relevant I should wholeheartedly associate myself with the general libertarian views in the Court's opinion, representing as they do the thought and action of a lifetime. But as judges we are neither Jew nor Gentile, neither Catholic nor agnostic. We owe equal attachment to the Constitution and are equally bound by our judicial obligations whether we derive our citizenship from the earliest or latest immigrants to these shores. As a member of this Court I am not justified in writing my private notions of policy into the Constitution, no matter how deeply I may cherish them or how mischievous I may deem their disregard. The duty of a judge who must decide which of two claims before the Court shall prevail, that of a State to enact and enforce laws within its general competence or that of an individual to refuse obedience because of the demands of his conscience, is not that of the ordinary person. It can never be emphasized too much that one's own opinion about the wisdom or evil of a law should be excluded altogether when one is doing one's duty on the bench. . . . [I]t would require more daring than I possess to deny that reasonable legislators could have taken the action which is before us for review. Most unwillingly, therefore, I must differ from my brethren with regard to legislation like this. I cannot bring my mind to believe that the "liberty" secured by the Due Process Clause gives this Court authority to deny to the State of West Virginia the attainment of that which we all recognize as a legitimate legislative end, namely, the promotion of good citizenship, by employment of the means here chosen.

In striking down the West Virginia compulsory flag salute law, the Court ruled that the individual has at least a qualified right to be free of government coercion to express views he or she disavows. This decision does not go so far as to hold that a person's First Amendment rights can be used to avoid obligations such as testifying in a court case or providing information on a tax return, but it does preclude certain forms of coerced expression.

Take the case of *Wooley v. Maynard* (1977). George and Maxine Maynard, members of the Jehovah's Witnesses faith, were repeatedly stopped by local police for driving an automobile with a defaced license plate. The New Hampshire couple had covered the state slogan "Live Free or Die" on their plates. George Maynard explained, "I refuse to be coerced by the state into advertising a slogan which I find morally, ethically, religiously, and politically abhorrent." The Supreme Court ruled in favor of the Maynards, holding that the interests of the state in promoting New Hampshire's image were insufficiently compelling to outweigh the First Amendment liberties at stake. Certainly, if the Maynards had also covered the identifying numbers and letters on the license plate, the state's interests would have been more substantial and the decision likely would have gone in the other direction.

Not all decisions have favored the claims of litigants who attacked what they considered to be unconstitutionally compelled speech. In **Board of Regents of the University of Wisconsin v. Southworth** (2000) the justices were presented with a claim made by a group of conservative students challenging a compulsory student activity fee that in part funded groups with purposes they opposed—specifically, gay, Socialist, labor, women's, and other liberal causes. The Court unanimously ruled in favor of the university, holding that the school was pursuing a legitimate educational policy of encouraging the free and open exchange of ideas. Because the fees were available to all types of registered student groups on a viewpoint-neutral basis, they were constitutionally acceptable.

More recently an organization of law schools and law school faculty members challenged a federal statute, known as the Solomon Amendment, that required universities receiving federal funds to treat recruiters for the U.S. armed forces on an equal basis with other recruiting employers. The group's membership objected to the government's position on homosexuals in the military and believed that the Solomon Amendment unconstitutionally mandated that universities provide a forum for an employer with whose policies they disagreed. The justices unanimously rejected the challenge in **Rumsfeld v. Forum for Academic and Institutional Rights** (2006), finding that the federal regulation mandating equal treatment did not require the universities to express any position or to endorse military policies.

Expressive Association

Essential to the exercise of political and social expression is the ability to join with like-minded individuals to advance mutual goals. The Supreme Court has long recognized that the right of association is implicit in the First Amendment's freedoms of speech, press, assembly, and petition.[16]

Protecting the right of individuals to form groups for political or social purposes often means extending constitutional guarantees to organizations that hold unpopular or even dangerous views. In several cases during the 1960s the justices struck down government attempts to

regulate membership in the Communist Party. Similarly, the Court has been vigilant in protecting the association rights of minority groups. In the early years of the civil rights movement, the justices struck down efforts by southern states to interfere with the National Association for the Advancement of Colored People and its organizational activities.

Since then, conflicts have arisen between groups asserting First Amendment association rights and states enforcing legislation to reduce discrimination. Most frequently at issue are the policies of private organizations that restrict membership or services based on characteristics such as race, sex, sexual orientation, or religion. Country clubs, businessmen's clubs, fraternal organizations, and civic groups often have such membership restrictions. Do the members of private organizations have the constitutional right to impose whatever membership qualifications they desire? Or may the state, concerned that the exclusion of people could deprive them of opportunities for business and professional networking and advancement, enforce antidiscrimination statutes that make such membership restrictions unlawful?

The justices addressed this question in **Roberts v. United States Jaycees** (1984). The Jaycees, established in 1920 as the Junior Chamber of Commerce, is a private civic organization that helps young men participate in the affairs of their community. This dispute centered on the Jaycees' policy of restricting regular membership to men between the ages of eighteen and thirty-five. The Minnesota Department of Human Rights claimed that the organization's exclusion of women violated a state law prohibiting sex-based discrimination in public accommodations. The United States Jaycees argued that applying the Minnesota antidiscrimination law to its membership policies was a violation of the First Amendment freedom of association.

In a 7–0 decision, the Supreme Court ruled against the Jaycees. While acknowledging that freedom of association is a necessary component of the First Amendment, the Court said that the right is not absolute and does apply equally to all private organizations. The greatest degree of protection goes to small, intimate relationships, such as marriage and family, and to those organizations

---

16. In addition, the Court has invoked the relevance of association rights to the protection of intimate human relationships (marriage, family, and childbearing).

expressing sincerely held political or ideological messages. Large groups with nonideological or commercial purposes and nonselective membership policies are less deserving. The Jaycees, according to the Court, is a large, national organization, with no firm ideological views and membership selectivity based only on age and sex. As such, the group merited a level of First Amendment protection inferior to the state's interest in reducing arbitrary discrimination.

The Court in *Roberts* not only considered the nature of the organization itself but also the relationship between the expressive activities of the group and the effect of the government regulation. Two important questions, the Court said, must be answered: Is the group an expressive organization that attempts to communicate its viewpoints either publicly or privately? And does the state regulation significantly burden the expression of those viewpoints?

The scheme adopted in the Jaycees' case subsequently was applied in two similar disputes, *Board of Directors of Rotary International v. Rotary Club of Duarte* (1987) and *New York State Club Association v. City of New York* (1988). The results were identical—the state's interest in promoting antidiscrimination trumped the freedom of association. Again, the Court emphasized that as groups grew larger, more commercial, less ideological, and less selective, First Amendment protections decreased.

Roberts, Rotary, and *New York State Club Association* were unanimous rulings, creating the impression that the law was relatively settled: Freedom of association rights must give way to state interests in combating discrimination. That impression was weakened in 1995, however, when the justices decided **Hurley v. Irish-American Gay, Lesbian and Bisexual Group of Boston.** This dispute arose when a private association organizing a Saint Patrick's Day parade in Boston rejected the application of a gay rights group to march in the celebration. The gay rights group sued, claiming that its exclusion from the parade violated the Massachusetts antidiscrimination statute. The Supreme Court unanimously ruled in favor of the parade organizers. The justices held that the First Amendment is violated by a state law requiring private sponsors of a parade to include a group imparting a message that

The Boy Scouts revoked the adult membership of James Dale because of his admitted homosexuality. In *Boy Scouts of America v. Dale,* the Court determined that the organization had the right to exclude him.

the organizers do not wish to convey. The Court applied the principles set in *Roberts* but came to quite a different result. Here the forced inclusion of the gay rights group was found to place a significant burden on the expression rights of the parade organizers.

This decision set the stage for the next major freedom of association dispute, *Boy Scouts of America v. Dale* (2000), a challenge to the dismissal of a scout leader on sexual orientation grounds. Would the Court find the facts in this case similar to the exclusion of women in *Roberts, Rotary,* and *New York State Club Association,* or would the justices conclude that the Boy

Scouts' membership policies were protected by the First Amendment's freedom of association guarantee?

Boy Scouts of America v. Dale

530 U.S. 640 (2000)
http://laws.findlaw.com/US/530/640.html
Oral arguments may be found at: http://www.oyez.org
Vote: 5 (Kennedy, O'Connor, Rehnquist, Scalia, Thomas)
　　　4 (Breyer, Ginsburg, Souter, Stevens)
Opinion of the Court: Rehnquist
Dissenting opinions: Souter, Stevens

James Dale began his involvement in the Boy Scout organization in 1978, when, at the age of eight, he joined Cub Scout Pack 142 in Monmouth, New Jersey. He became a Boy Scout in 1981 and remained an active scout until he turned eighteen. Dale was an exemplary member of the organization, being admitted to the prestigious Order of the Arrow and achieving the rank of Eagle Scout, scouting's highest honor. In 1989 he became an adult member of the organization and was an assistant scoutmaster.

Around the same time, Dale left home to attend Rutgers University. At college, Dale first acknowledged to himself and to others that he was gay. He joined and later became copresident of Rutgers University Gay/Lesbian Alliance. After attending a seminar devoted to gay/lesbian health issues in 1990, he was interviewed and photographed for a newspaper story. He discussed the need for gay teenagers to have appropriate role models.

Shortly after the publication of the newspaper article, Dale received a letter from the Monmouth Council revoking his adult membership in the Boy Scouts. When he requested a reason for this action, the Council informed him that the Scouts "specifically forbid membership to homosexuals." In 1992 Dale filed a complaint against the Boy Scouts claiming that the revocation of his membership violated a New Jersey law prohibiting discrimination based on sexual orientation in public accommodations. The Boy Scouts countered that as a private, nonprofit organization it had the right under the freedom of association guarantees of the First Amendment to deny membership to individuals whose views are not consistent with the group's values. The New Jersey Supreme Court ruled in favor of Dale, and the Boy Scouts asked for review by the U.S. Supreme Court.

CHIEF JUSTICE REHNQUIST delivered the opinion of the Court.

In *Roberts v. United States Jaycees* (1984), we observed that "implicit in the right to engage in activities protected by the First Amendment" is "a corresponding right to associate with others in pursuit of a wide variety of political, social, economic, educational, religious, and cultural ends." This right is crucial in preventing the majority from imposing its views on groups that would rather express other, perhaps unpopular, ideas. Government actions that may unconstitutionally burden this freedom may take many forms, one of which is "intrusion into the internal structure or affairs of an association" like a "regulation that forces the group to accept members it does not desire." Forcing a group to accept certain members may impair the ability of the group to express those views, and only those views, that it intends to express. Thus, "[f]reedom of association . . . plainly presupposes a freedom not to associate."

The forced inclusion of an unwanted person in a group infringes the group's freedom of expressive association if the presence of that person affects in a significant way the group's ability to advocate public or private viewpoints. *New York State Club Assn., Inc. v. City of New York* (1988). But the freedom of expressive association, like many freedoms, is not absolute. We have held that the freedom could be overridden "by regulations adopted to serve compelling state interests, unrelated to the suppression of ideas, that cannot be achieved through means significantly less restrictive of associational freedoms." *Roberts.*

To determine whether a group is protected by the First Amendment's expressive associational right, we must determine whether the group engages in "expressive association." The First Amendment's protection of expressive association is not reserved for advocacy groups. But to come within its ambit, a group must engage in some form of expression, whether it be public or private. . . .

. . . [T]he general mission of the Boy Scouts is clear: "[T]o instill values in young people." The Boy Scouts seeks to instill these values by having its adult leaders spend time with the youth members, instructing and engaging them in activities like camping, archery, and fishing. During the time spent with the youth members, the scoutmasters and assistant scoutmasters inculcate them with the Boy Scouts' values—both expressly and by example. It seems indisputable that an association that seeks to transmit such a system of values engages in expressive activity.

Given that the Boy Scouts engages in expressive activity, we must determine whether the forced inclusion of Dale as an assistant scoutmaster would significantly affect the Boy Scouts' ability to advocate public or private viewpoints. This inquiry necessarily requires us first to explore, to a limited extent, the nature of the Boy Scouts' view of homosexuality.

The values the Boy Scouts seeks to instill are "based on" those listed in the Scout Oath and Law. The Boy Scouts explains that the Scout Oath and Law provide "a positive moral code for living; they are a list of 'do's' rather than 'don'ts.' " The Boy Scouts asserts that homosexual conduct is inconsistent with the values embodied in the Scout Oath and Law, particularly with the values represented by the terms "morally straight" and "clean."

Obviously, the Scout Oath and Law do not expressly mention sexuality or sexual orientation. And the terms "morally straight" and "clean" are by no means self-defining. Different people would attribute to those terms very different meanings. For example, some people may believe that engaging in homosexual conduct is not at odds with being "morally straight" and "clean." And others may believe that engaging in homosexual conduct is contrary to being "morally straight" and "clean." The Boy Scouts says it falls within the latter category.

The New Jersey Supreme Court analyzed the Boy Scouts' beliefs and found that the "exclusion of members solely on the basis of their sexual orientation is inconsistent with Boy Scouts' commitment to a diverse and 'representative' membership . . . [and] contradicts Boy Scouts' overarching objective to reach 'all eligible youth.' " The court concluded that the exclusion of members like Dale "appears antithetical to the organization's goals and philosophy." But our cases reject this sort of inquiry; it is not the role of the courts to reject a group's expressed values because they disagree with those values or find them internally inconsistent.

The Boy Scouts asserts that it "teach[es] that homosexual conduct is not morally straight," and that it does "not want to promote homosexual conduct as a legitimate form

of behavior." We accept the Boy Scouts' assertion. We need not inquire further to determine the nature of the Boy Scouts' expression with respect to homosexuality. But because the record before us contains written evidence of the Boy Scouts' viewpoint, we look to it as instructive, if only on the question of the sincerity of the professed beliefs.

A 1978 position statement to the Boy Scouts' Executive Committee . . . expresses the Boy Scouts' "official position" with regard to "homosexuality and Scouting":

". . . The Boy Scouts of America is a private, membership organization and leadership therein is a privilege and not a right. We do not believe that homosexuality and leadership in Scouting are appropriate. We will continue to select only those who in our judgment meet our standards and qualifications for leadership."

Thus, at least as of 1978—the year James Dale entered Scouting—the official position of the Boy Scouts was that avowed homosexuals were not to be Scout leaders.

A position statement promulgated by the Boy Scouts in 1991 (after Dale's membership was revoked but before this litigation was filed) also supports its current view:

"We believe that homosexual conduct is inconsistent with the requirement in the Scout Oath that a Scout be morally straight and in the Scout Law that a Scout be clean in word and deed, and that homosexuals do not provide a desirable role model for Scouts."

This position statement was redrafted numerous times but its core message remained consistent. . . .

. . . We cannot doubt that the Boy Scouts sincerely holds this view.

We must then determine whether Dale's presence as an assistant scoutmaster would significantly burden the Boy Scouts' desire to not "promote homosexual conduct as a legitimate form of behavior." As we give deference to an association's assertions regarding the nature of its expression, we must also give deference to an association's view of what would impair its expression. That is not to say that an expressive association can erect a shield against antidiscrimination laws simply by asserting that mere acceptance of a member from a particular group would impair its message. But here Dale, by his own admission, is one of a group of gay Scouts who have "become leaders in their community and are open and honest about their sexual orientation." Dale was the copresident of a gay and lesbian organization at college and remains a gay rights activist. Dale's presence in the Boy Scouts would, at the very least, force the organization to send a message, both to the youth members and the world, that the Boy Scouts accepts homosexual conduct as a legitimate form of behavior. . . .

The New Jersey Supreme Court determined that the Boy Scouts' ability to disseminate its message was not significantly affected by the forced inclusion of Dale as an assistant scoutmaster. . . .

We disagree with the New Jersey Supreme Court's conclusion. . . .

First, associations do not have to associate for the "purpose" of disseminating a certain message in order to be entitled to the protections of the First Amendment. An association must merely engage in expressive activity that could be impaired in order to be entitled to protection. . . .

Second, even if the Boy Scouts discourages Scout leaders from disseminating views on sexual issues—a fact that the Boy Scouts disputes with contrary evidence—the First Amendment protects the Boy Scouts' method of expression. If the Boy Scouts wishes Scout leaders to avoid questions of sexuality and teach only by example, this fact does not negate the sincerity of its belief discussed above.

Third, the First Amendment simply does not require that every member of a group agree on every issue in order for the group's policy to be "expressive association." The Boy Scouts takes an official position with respect to homosexual conduct, and that is sufficient for First Amendment purposes. . . . The fact that the organization does not trumpet its views from the housetops, or that it tolerates dissent within its ranks, does not mean that its views receive no First Amendment protection.

Having determined that the Boy Scouts is an expressive association and that the forced inclusion of Dale would significantly affect its expression, we inquire whether the application of New Jersey's public accommodations law to require that the Boy Scouts accept Dale as an assistant scoutmaster runs afoul of the Scouts' freedom of expressive association. We conclude that it does. . . .

. . . The state interests embodied in New Jersey's public accommodations law do not justify such a severe intrusion on the Boy Scouts' rights to freedom of expressive association. That being the case, we hold that the First Amendment prohibits the State from imposing such a requirement through the application of its public accommodations law. . . .

We are not, as we must not be, guided by our views of whether the Boy Scouts' teachings with respect to homosexual conduct are right or wrong; public or judicial disapproval of a tenet of an organization's expression does not justify the State's effort to compel the organization to accept members where such acceptance would derogate from the organization's expressive message. . . .

The judgment of the New Jersey Supreme Court is reversed, and the cause remanded for further proceedings not inconsistent with this opinion.

It is so ordered.

JUSTICE STEVENS, with whom JUSTICE SOUTER, JUSTICE GINSBURG, and JUSTICE BREYER join, dissenting.

The majority holds that New Jersey's law violates BSA's [Boy Scouts of America's] right to associate and its right to free speech. But that law does not "impos[e] any serious burdens" on BSA's "collective effort on behalf of [its] shared goals," *Roberts v. United States Jaycees* (1984), nor does it force BSA to communicate any message that it does not wish to endorse. New Jersey's law, therefore, abridges no constitutional right of the Boy Scouts. . . .

In this case, Boy Scouts of America contends that it teaches the young boys who are Scouts that homosexuality is immoral. Consequently, it argues, it would violate its right to associate to force it to admit homosexuals as members, as doing so would be at odds with its own shared goals and values. This contention, quite plainly, requires us to look at what, exactly, are the values that BSA actually teaches.

. . . BSA describes itself as having a "representative membership," which it defines as "boy membership [that] reflects proportionately the characteristics of the boy population of its service area." In particular, the group emphasizes that "[n]either the charter nor the bylaws of the Boy Scouts of America permits the exclusion of any boy. . . . To meet these responsibilities we have made a commitment that our membership shall be representative of *all* the population in every community, district, and council." . . .

To bolster its claim that its shared goals include teaching that homosexuality is wrong, BSA directs our attention to two terms appearing in the Scout Oath and Law. The first is the phrase "morally straight," which appears in the Oath ("On my honor I will do my best . . . To keep myself . . .

morally straight"); the second term is the word "clean," which appears in a list of 12 characteristics together comprising the Scout Law. . . .

It is plain as the light of day that neither one of these principles—"morally straight" and "clean"—says the slightest thing about homosexuality. Indeed, neither term in the Boy Scouts' Law and Oath expresses any position whatsoever on sexual matters.

BSA's published guidance on that topic underscores this point. Scouts, for example, are directed to receive their sex education at home or in school, but not from the organization. . . . In light of the BSA's self-proclaimed ecumenism, furthermore, it is even more difficult to discern any shared goals or common moral stance on homosexuality. . . .

BSA's claim finds no support in our cases. We have recognized "a right to associate for the purpose of engaging in those activities protected by the First Amendment—speech, assembly, petition for the redress of grievances, and the exercise of religion." *Roberts.* And we have acknowledged that "when the State interferes with individuals' selection of those with whom they wish to join in a common endeavor, freedom of association . . . may be implicated." But "[t]he right to associate for expressive purposes is not . . . absolute"; rather, "the nature and degree of constitutional protection afforded freedom of association may vary depending on the extent to which . . . the constitutionally protected liberty is at stake in a given case." Indeed, the right to associate does not mean "that in every setting in which individuals exercise some discrimination in choosing associates, their selective process of inclusion and exclusion is protected by the Constitution." *New York State Club Assn., Inc. v. City of New York* (1988). . . .

. . . [T]he majority insists that we must "give deference to an association's assertions regarding the nature of its expression" and "we must also give deference to an association's view of what would impair its expression." . . .

This is an astounding view of the law. I am unaware of any previous instance in which our analysis of the scope of a constitutional right was determined by looking at what a litigant asserts in his or her brief and inquiring no further. . . . But the majority insists that our inquiry must be "limited" because "it is not the role of the courts to reject a group's expressed values because they disagree with those values or find them internally inconsistent."

But nothing in our cases calls for this Court to do any such thing. An organization can adopt the message of its choice, and it is not this Court's place to disagree with it. But we must inquire whether the group is, in fact, expressing a message (whatever it may be) and whether that message (if one is expressed) is significantly affected by a State's antidiscrimination law. More critically, that inquiry requires our *independent* analysis, rather than deference to a group's litigating posture. . . .

There is, of course, a valid concern that a court's independent review may run the risk of paying too little heed to an organization's sincerely held views. But unless one is prepared to turn the right to associate into a free pass out of antidiscrimination laws, an independent inquiry is a necessity. . . .

In this case, no such concern is warranted. It is entirely clear that BSA in fact expresses no clear, unequivocal message burdened by New Jersey's law. . . .

. . . Over the years, BSA has generously welcomed over 87 million young Americans into its ranks. In 1992 over one million adults were active BSA members. The notion that an organization of that size and enormous prestige implicitly endorses the views that each of those adults may express in a non-Scouting context is simply mind boggling. . . .

Unfavorable opinions about homosexuals "have ancient roots." *Bowers v. Hardwick* (1986). . . .

That such prejudices are still prevalent and that they have caused serious and tangible harm to countless members of the class New Jersey seeks to protect are established matters of fact that neither the Boy Scouts nor the Court disputes. That harm can only be aggravated by the creation of a constitutional shield for a policy that is itself the product of a habitual way of thinking about strangers. As Justice Brandeis so wisely advised, "we must be ever on our guard, lest we erect our prejudices into legal principles."

If we would guide by the light of reason, we must let our minds be bold. I respectfully dissent.

In *Dale* the justices were sharply divided, with the outcome turning on a single vote. The division had little to do with the principles the Court had established to guide the resolution of such disputes. The standards set in *Roberts v. United States Jaycees* remained firmly in place. The government's authority to regulate the membership of private, voluntary groups depends on the nature of the group and the extent of the government's restrictions. At odds in *Dale* were the answers to questions about the actual beliefs of the Boy Scouts and the extent to which New Jersey's antidiscrimination law inhibited the right of expressive association.

Having discussed the constitutional protections given to the freedom of speech as well as to the rights of assembly, association, and petition, we turn next to the final component in the freedom of expression—the right to a free press.

READINGS

Bell, Jeannine. *Policing Hatred: Law Enforcement, Civil Rights, and Hate Crime.* New York: New York University Press, 2002.

Bosmajian, Haig. *The Freedom Not to Speak.* New York: New York University Press, 1999.

Chafee, Zechariah, Jr. *Free Speech in the United States.* Cambridge: Harvard University Press, 1941.

Cleary, Edward J. *Beyond the Burning Cross: The First Amendment and the Landmark R. A. V. Case.* New York: Random House, 1994.

Cox, Archibald. *Freedom of Expression.* Cambridge: Harvard University Press, 1981.

Easton, Susan. *The Case for the Right to Silence,* 2nd ed. Brookfield, Vt.: Ashgate Publishing, 1998.

Emerson, Thomas I. *The System of Freedom of Expression.* New York: Vintage Books, 1970.

Epstein, Lee, Daniel E. Ho, Gary King, and Jeffrey A. Segal. "The Supreme Court During Crisis: How War Affects Only Nonwar Cases." *New York University Law Review* 80 (April 2005): 1–116.

Farber, Daniel A. *The First Amendment.* New York: Foundation Press, 1998.

Fish, Stanley. *There's No Such Thing as Free Speech, and It's a Good Thing, Too.* New York: Oxford University Press, 1994.

Goldstein, Robert Justin. *Burning the Flag: The Great 1989–1990 American Flag Desecration Controversy.* Kent: Kent State University Press, 1996.

Gould, Jon B. *Speak No Evil: The Triumph of Hate Speech Regulation.* Chicago: University of Chicago Press, 2005.

Gower, Karla K. *Liberty and Authority in Free Expression Law: The United States and Canada.* New York: LFB Scholarly Publishing, 2002.

Graber, Mark A. *Transforming Free Speech.* Berkeley: University of California Press, 1991.

Heumann, Milton, and Thomas Church, with David Redlawsk. *Hate Speech on Campus: Cases, Case Studies, and Commentary.* Boston: Northeastern University Press, 1997.

Inglehart, Louis Edward, ed. *Press and Speech Freedoms in America, 1619–1995: A Chronology.* Westport, Conn.: Greenwood Press, 1997.

Johnson, John W. *The Struggle for Student Rights: Tinker v. Des Moines and the 1960s.* Lawrence: University Press of Kansas, 1997.

Kersch, Ken I. *Freedom of Speech: Rights and Liberties under the Law.* Santa Barbara, Calif.: ABC-CLIO, 2003.

Lawrence, Frederick M. *Punishing Hate: Bias Crimes under American Law.* Cambridge: Harvard University Press, 2002.

Levy, Leonard W. *Legacy of Suppression.* Cambridge: Harvard University Press, 1960.

Nielson, Laura Beth. *License to Harass: Law, Hierarchy, and Offensive Public Speech.* Princeton: Princeton University Press, 2004.

Rabban, David M. *Free Speech in Its Forgotten Years.* New York: Cambridge University Press, 1997.

Schweber, Howard. *Speech, Conduct, and the First Amendment.* New York: Peter Lang, 2003.

Shiner, Roger A. *Freedom of Commercial Expression.* New York: Oxford University Press, 2003.

Smolla, Rodney A. *Free Speech in an Open Society.* New York: Knopf, 1992.

Stone, Geoffrey B. *Perilous Times: Free Speech and Wartime from the Sedition Act of 1789 to the War on Terrorism.* New York: W. W. Norton, 2004.

Strum, Philippa. *When the Nazis Came to Skokie: Freedom for Speech We Hate.* Lawrence: University Press of Kansas, 1999.

Sunstein, Cass A. *Democracy and the Problem of Free Speech.* New York: Free Press, 1993.

Walker, Samuel. *Hate Speech: The History of an American Controversy.* Lincoln: University of Nebraska Press, 1994.

Washburn, Patrick S. *A Question of Sedition.* New York: Oxford University Press, 1986.

Wolfson, Nicholas. *Hate Speech, Sex Speech, Free Speech.* Westport, Conn.: Praeger, 1997.

CHAPTER 14
FREEDOM OF THE PRESS

F reedom of the press is perhaps the most visible manifestation of Americans' expression of their rights. Each day the print and broadcast media bombard the nation with news, editorials, and entertainment from almost every conceivable perspective. Newsstands and bookstores flourish by offering periodicals and books devoted to every imaginable interest. With the emergence of interactive media, such as talk radio, op-ed pages, and letters to the editor, citizens have become participants in the press rather than merely consumers. The result is a robust exchange of information and opinion.

Much of what appears in the press is critical of government and government policies. In contrast to the citizens of some other countries, however, Americans who criticize officials do not face government censorship or possible retaliation. They enjoy protection provided by the First Amendment's stipulation that "Congress shall make no law . . . abridging the freedom . . . of the press."

This constitutional provision reflects the framers' strong commitment to the rights of the press. They saw the right to publish freely not only as important for its own sake, but also as a significant protection for other political and personal liberties. The press is the watchdog that sounds a warning when other rights are threatened. The founders believed that the rights of speech and religion would be meaningless without a free press. Thomas Jefferson was so certain of this precept that in 1816 he proclaimed, "When the press is free, and every man is able to read, all is safe."

As British colonists, the framers were well schooled in the values of a free press. But history also taught them that this right could not be taken for granted. They knew that England had controlled the press from the fifteenth through the seventeenth centuries and that repressive measures from that period had become common law. After the introduction of printing into England in the 1400s, Britain developed a licensing system under which nothing could be printed without prior approval from the government.[1] Once the licensing laws expired in 1695, the right to publish materials, free from censorship, became recognized under common law, leading William Blackstone, the English jurist, to write: "The liberty of the press . . . consists in laying no previous restraints upon publications, and not in freedom from censure for criminal matter when published."[2]

Blackstone's words, although not fully embraced by the U.S. Supreme Court, convey a significant message about freedom of the press that the framers of the Constitution understood. They recognized that for a society to remain free, it must tolerate divergent views and opinions, which can be formed only through the open exchange of ideas. Unless protected from government interference, the press is vulnerable to becoming an extension of the political regime, not an independent observer, a check, or even a source of information.

1. Thomas I. Emerson, *The System of Freedom of Expression* (New York: Vintage Books, 1970), 504.
2. *Blackstone's Commentaries on the Laws of England*, Vol. 4 (London: 1765–1769), 151–152.

Why is this state of affairs so dangerous? Consider one of the most heinous regimes in the history of the world—Nazi Germany. How the Nazis came to power and carried out their deeds is still being debated, but certainly their ability to control the press and to use it as a propaganda tool is part of the explanation. The danger of government control of the press also can be seen closer to home. The Watergate scandal involved political manipulation and illegal behavior at the highest levels of government and led to the resignation of President Richard Nixon in 1974. We should remember that it was the press that first discovered the wrongdoing and brought it to light. If we allowed government to censor—to place restraints on—the press, the Watergate story never would have been published.

In the first part of this chapter, we examine the right of the press to be free from government control prior to publication. This is known as the doctrine of prior restraint. Under what conditions, if any, may the government enjoin the press from freely printing and distributing its material? In the second part of this chapter, we explore special privileges claimed by the media. Reporters argue that they should enjoy a unique set of guarantees to perform their jobs. How has the Court reacted to such claims? We then analyze those forms of expression that the Supreme Court historically has considered outside the free press protections of the First Amendment: obscenity and libel. To what extent can the government penalize those who distribute sexually explicit material or material that contains falsehoods? We conclude with a look at the rapidly expanding opportunities for free expression made available by the Internet and the constitutional issues surrounding it.

PRIOR RESTRAINT

The concept of prior restraint is central to a proper understanding of the freedom of the press. Prior restraint occurs when the government reviews material to determine whether publication will be allowed. The practice is a form of government censorship and is antithetical to freedom of the press. If the First Amendment means anything, it means that no government has the authority to decide what may and may not be published.

The government may punish press activity that violates legitimate criminal laws, but such government sanctions may take place only *after* publication, not before.

The principle that prior restraint runs contrary to the Constitution was established in the formative case of *Near v. Minnesota* (1931). The justices took a strong stance against such censorship. But does their decision imply that the government may never block the publication of material it considers inappropriate or harmful? Are there exceptions to the constitutional prohibition against prior restraint? As you read Chief Justice Charles Evans Hughes's opinion in *Near,* pay close attention to how the justices develop the general principle against prior restraint, and look for any indication that the Court might allow exceptions to it.

Near v. Minnesota

283 U.S. 697 (1931)
http://laws.findlaw.com/US/283/697.html
Vote: 5 (Brandeis, Holmes, Hughes, Roberts, Stone)
      4 (Butler, McReynolds, Sutherland, Van Devanter)
Opinion of the Court: Hughes
Dissenting opinion: Butler

A 1925 Minnesota law provided for "the abatement, as a public nuisance, of a 'malicious, scandalous and defamatory newspaper, magazine, or other periodical.' " In fall 1927 a county attorney asked a state judge to issue a restraining order banning publication of the *Saturday Press.* In the attorney's view, the newspaper, partly owned by Jay Near, was the epitome of a malicious, scandalous, and defamatory publication.[3] The *Saturday Press* committed itself to exposing corruption, bribery, gambling, and prostitution in Minneapolis. It attacked specific city officials for being in league with gangsters and chided the established press for refusing to uncover the corruption. These attacks were colored by Near's racist, anti-Semitic attitudes. In one issue, Near wrote:

---

3. For an in-depth account of this case, see Fred W. Friendly, *Minnesota Rag* (New York: Random House, 1981).

The only known photograph of *Saturday Press* editor Jay Near appeared April 19, 1936, in the Minneapolis *Tribune*. Near's successful appeal to the Supreme Court in 1931 marked the first time the Court enforced the First Amendment's guarantee of freedom of the press to strike a state law that imposed a prior restraint on a newspaper.

I simply state a fact when I say that ninety per cent of the crimes committed against society in this city are committed by Jew gangsters. . . . It is Jew, Jew, Jew, as long as one cares to comb over the records. I am launching no attack against the Jewish people AS A RACE. I am merely calling attention to a FACT. And if people of that race and faith wish to rid themselves of the odium and stigma THE RODENTS OF THEIR OWN RACE HAVE BROUGHT UPON THEM, they need only to step to the front and help the decent citizens of Minneapolis rid the city of these criminal Jews.[4]

In a piece attacking establishment journalism, Near proclaimed: "Journalism today isn't prostituted so much as it is disgustingly flabby. I'd rather be a louse in the cotton shirt of a nigger than be a journalistic prostitute."[5] Based on the paper's past record, a judge issued a temporary restraining order prohibiting the sale of printed and future editions of the paper.

Upset by this action, Near contacted the American Civil Liberties Union (ACLU), which agreed to take his case. But he grew uncomfortable with the organization and instead obtained assistance from the publisher of the *Chicago Tribune*. Together, they challenged the Minnesota

4. Ibid., 47.
5. Ibid., 43.

law as a violation of the First Amendment freedom of press guarantee, arguing that the law was tantamount to censorship. In their view, states could not issue gag orders to keep newspapers from publishing future issues; newspapers could be punished only after publication through libel or defamation proceedings. The state's attorney thought otherwise, arguing that freedom of the press does not give publishers an unrestricted right to print anything and everything, that they must act responsibly.

MR. CHIEF JUSTICE HUGHES delivered the opinion of the Court.

Chapter 285 of the Session Laws of Minnesota for the year 1925 provides for the abatement, as a public nuisance, of a "malicious, scandalous and defamatory newspaper, magazine, or other periodical." . . .

This statute, for the suppression as a public nuisance of a newspaper or periodical, is unusual, if not unique, and raises questions of grave importance transcending the local interests involved in the particular action. It is no longer open to doubt that the liberty of the press and of speech is within the liberty safeguarded by the due process clause of the Fourteenth Amendment from invasion by state action. It was found impossible to conclude that this essential personal liberty of the citizen was left unprotected by the general guaranty of fundamental rights of person and property. *Gitlow v. New York, Whitney v. California, Fiske v. Kansas.* In maintaining this guaranty, the authority of the state to enact laws to promote the health, safety, morals, and general welfare of its people is necessarily admitted. The limits of this sovereign power must always be determined with appropriate regard to the particular subject of its exercise. . . .

It is thus important to note precisely the purpose and effect of the statute as the state court has construed it.

First. The statute is not aimed at the redress of individual or private wrongs. Remedies for libel remain available and unaffected. . . . It is aimed at the distribution of scandalous matter as "detrimental to public morals and to the general welfare," tending "to disturb the peace of the community" and "to provoke assaults and the commission of crime." In order to obtain an injunction to suppress the future publication of the newspaper or periodical, it is not necessary to prove the falsity of the charges that have been made in the publication condemned. In the present action there was no allegation that the matter published was not true. It is alleged, and the statute requires the allegation that the publication was "malicious." But, as in prosecutions for libel, there is no requirement of proof by the state of malice in fact as distinguished from malice inferred from the mere publication of the defamatory matter. The judgment in this case proceeded upon the mere proof of publication. The statute permits the defense, not of the truth alone, but only that the truth was published with good motives and for justifiable ends. It is apparent that under the statute the publication is to be regarded as defamatory if it injures reputation, and that it is scandalous if it circulates charges of reprehensible conduct, whether criminal or otherwise, and the publication is thus deemed to invite public reprobation and to constitute a public scandal. . . .

Second. The statute is directed not simply at the circulation of scandalous and defamatory statements with regard to private citizens, but at the continued publication by newspapers and periodicals of charges against public officers of corruption, malfeasance in office, or serious neglect of duty. Such charges by their very nature create a public scandal. They are scandalous and defamatory within the meaning of the statute, which has its normal operation in relation to publications dealing prominently and chiefly with the alleged derelictions of public officers.

Third. The object of the statute is not punishment, in the ordinary sense, but suppression of the offending newspaper or periodical. The reason for the enactment, as the state court has said, is that prosecutions to enforce penal statutes for libel do not result in "efficient repression or suppression of the evils of scandal." Describing the business of publication as a public nuisance does not obscure the substance of the proceeding which the statute authorizes. It is the continued publication of scandalous and defamatory matter that constitutes the business and the declared nuisance. In the case of public officers, it is the reiteration of charges of official misconduct, and the fact that the newspaper or periodical is principally devoted to that purpose, that exposes it to suppression. . . .

This suppression is accomplished by enjoining publication, and that restraint is the object and effect of the statute.

Fourth. The statute not only operates to suppress the offending newspaper or periodical, but to put the publisher under an effective censorship. When a newspaper or periodical is found to be "malicious, scandalous and defamatory," and is suppressed as such, resumption of publication is punishable as a contempt of court by fine or imprisonment. Thus, where a newspaper or periodical has been suppressed because of the circulation of charges against public officers of official misconduct, it would seem to be clear that the renewal of the publication of such charges would constitute a contempt, and that the judgment would lay a permanent restraint upon the publisher, to escape which he must satisfy the court as to the character of a new publication. Whether he would be permitted again to publish matter deemed to be derogatory to the same or other public officers would depend upon the court's ruling. . . .

If we cut through mere details of procedure, the operation and effect of the statute in substance is that public authorities may bring the owner or publisher of a newspaper or periodical before a judge upon a charge of conducting a business of publishing scandalous and defamatory matter—in particular that the matter consists of charges against public officers of official dereliction—and, unless the owner or publisher is able and disposed to bring competent evidence to satisfy the judge that the charges are true and are published with good motives and for justifiable ends, his newspaper or periodical is suppressed and further publication is made punishable as a contempt. This is of the essence of censorship.

The question is whether a statute authorizing such proceedings in restraint of publication is consistent with the conception of the liberty of the press as historically conceived and guaranteed. In determining the extent of the constitutional protection, it has been generally, if not universally, considered that it is the chief purpose of the guaranty to prevent previous restraints upon publication. The struggle in England, directed against the legislative power of the licenser, resulted in renunciation of the censorship of the press. The liberty deemed to be established was thus described by Blackstone: "The liberty of the press is indeed essential to the nature of a free state; but this consists in laying no *previous* restraints upon publications, and not in freedom from censure for criminal matter when published. Every freeman has an undoubted right to lay what sentiments he pleases before the public; to forbid this, is to destroy the freedom of the press; but if he publishes what is improper, mischievous or illegal, he must take the consequence of his own temerity." The distinction was early pointed out between the extent of the freedom with respect to censorship under our constitutional system and that enjoyed in England. Here, as Madison said, "the great and essential rights of the people are secured against legislative as well as against executive ambition. They are secured, not by laws paramount to prerogative, but by constitutions paramount to laws. This security of the freedom of the press requires that it should be exempt not only from previous restraint by the Executive, as in Great Britain, but from legislative restraint also." . . .

The criticism upon Blackstone's statement has not been because immunity from previous restraint upon publication has not been regarded as deserving of special emphasis, but chiefly because that immunity cannot be deemed to exhaust the conception of the liberty guaranteed by State and Federal Constitutions. The point of criticism has been "that the mere exemption from previous restraints cannot be all that is secured by the constitutional provisions," and that "the liberty of the press might be rendered a mockery and a delusion, and the phrase itself a by-word, if, while every man was at liberty to publish what he pleased, the public authorities might nevertheless punish him for harmless publications." But it is recognized that punishment for the abuse of the liberty accorded to the press is essential to the protection of the public, and that the common-law rules that subject the libeler to responsibility for the public offense, as well as for the private injury, are not abolished by the protection extended in our Constitutions. The law of criminal libel rests upon that secure foundation. There is also the conceded authority of courts to punish for contempt when publications directly tend to prevent the proper discharge of judicial functions. In the present case, we have no occasion to inquire as to the permissible scope of subsequent punishment. For whatever wrong the appellant has committed or may commit, by his publications, the state appropriately affords both public and private redress by its libel laws. As has been noted, the statute in question does not deal with punishments; it provides for no punishment, except in case of contempt for violation of the court's order, but for suppression and injunction—that is, for restraint upon publication.

The objection has also been made that the principle as to immunity from previous restraint is stated too broadly, if every such restraint is deemed to be prohibited. That is undoubtedly true; the protection even as to previous restraint is not absolutely unlimited. But the limitation has been recognized only in exceptional cases. "When a nation is at war many things that might be said in time of peace are such a hindrance to its effort that their utterance will not be endured so long as men fight and that no Court could regard them as protected by any constitutional right." No one would question but that a government might prevent actual obstruction to its recruiting service or the publication of the sailing dates of transports or the number and location of troops. On similar grounds, the primary requirements of decency may be enforced against obscene publications. The security of the community life may be protected against incitements to acts of violence and the overthrow by force of orderly government. The constitutional guaranty of free speech does not "protect a man from an injunction against uttering words that may have all the effect of force." These limitations are not applicable here. Nor are we now concerned with questions as to the extent of authority to prevent publications in order to protect private rights according to the principles governing the exercise of the jurisdiction of courts of equity.

The exceptional nature of its limitations places in a strong light the general conception that liberty of the press, historically considered and taken up by the Federal Constitution, has meant, principally although not exclusively, immunity from previous restraints or censorship. The conception of the liberty of the press in this country had broadened with the exigencies of the colonial period and with the efforts to secure freedom from oppressive administration. That liberty was especially cherished for the immunity it afforded from previous restraint of the publication of censure of public officers and charges of official misconduct. . . .

The fact that for approximately one hundred and fifty years there has been almost an entire absence of attempts to impose previous restraints upon publications relating to the malfeasance of public officers is significant of the deep-seated conviction that such restraints would violate constitutional right. Public officers, whose character and conduct remains open to debate and free discussion in the press, find their remedies for false accusations in actions under libel laws providing for redress and punishment, and not in proceedings to restrain the publication of newspapers and periodicals. The general principle that the constitutional guaranty of the liberty of the press gives immunity from previous restraints has been approved in many decisions under the provisions of state constitutions.

The importance of this immunity has not lessened. While reckless assaults upon public men, and efforts to bring obloquy upon those who are endeavoring faithfully to discharge official duties, exert a baleful influence and deserve the severest condemnation in public opinion, it cannot be said that this abuse is greater, and it is believed to be less, than that which characterized the period in which our institutions took shape. Meanwhile, the administration of government has become more complex, the opportunities for malfeasance and corruption have multiplied, crime has grown to most serious proportions, and the danger of its protection by unfaithful officials and of the impairment of the fundamental security of life and property by criminal alliances and official neglect, emphasizes the primary need of a vigilant and courageous press, especially in great cities. The fact that the liberty of the press may be abused by miscreant purveyors of scandal does not make any the less necessary the immunity of the press from previous restraint in dealing with official misconduct. Subsequent punishment for such abuses as may exist is the appropriate remedy, consistent with constitutional privilege.

In attempted justification of the statute, it is said that it deals not with publication per se, but with the "business" of publishing defamation. If, however, the publisher has a constitutional right to publish, without previous restraint, an edition of his newspaper charging official derelictions, it cannot be denied that he may publish subsequent editions for the same purpose. He does not lose his right by exercising it. If his right exists, it may be exercised in publishing nine editions, as in this case, as well as in one edition. If previous restraint is permissible, it may be imposed at once; indeed, the wrong may be as serious in one publication as in several. Characterizing the publication as a business, and the business as a nuisance, does not permit an invasion of the constitutional immunity against restraint. Similarly, it does not matter that the newspaper or periodical is found to be "largely" or "chiefly" devoted to the publication of such derelictions. If the publisher has a right, without previous restraint, to publish them, his right cannot be deemed to be dependent upon his publishing something else, more or less, with the matter to which objection is made.

Nor can it be said that the constitutional freedom from previous restraint is lost because charges are made of derelictions which constitute crimes. With the multiplying provisions of penal codes, and of municipal charters and ordinances carrying penal sanctions, the conduct of public officers is very largely within the purview of criminal statutes. The freedom of the press from previous restraint has never been regarded as limited to such animadversions as lay outside the range of penal enactments. Historically, there is no such limitation; it is inconsistent with the reason which underlies the privilege, as the privilege so limited would be of slight value for the purposes for which it came to be established.

The statute in question cannot be justified by reason of the fact that the publisher is permitted to show, before injunction issues, that the matter published is true and is published with good motives and for justifiable ends. If such a statute, authorizing suppression and injunction on such a basis, is constitutionally valid, it would be equally permissible for the Legislature to provide that at any time the publisher of any newspaper could be brought before a court, or even an administrative officer (as the constitutional protection may not be regarded as resting on mere procedural details), and required to produce proof of the truth of his publication, or of what he intended to publish and of his motives, or stand enjoined. If this can be done, the Legislature may provide machinery for determining in the complete exercise of its discretion what are justifiable ends and restrain publication accordingly. And it would be but a step to a complete system of censorship. The recognition of authority to impose previous restraint upon publication in order to protect the community against the circulation of charges of misconduct, and especially of official misconduct, necessarily would carry with it the admission of the authority of the censor against which the constitutional barrier was erected. The preliminary freedom, by virtue of the very reason for its existence, does not depend, as this court has said, on proof of truth.

Equally unavailing is the insistence that the statute is designed to prevent the circulation of scandal which tends to disturb the public peace and to provoke assaults and the commission of crime. Charges of reprehensible conduct, and in particular of official malfeasance, unquestionably create a public scandal, but the theory of the constitutional guaranty is that even a more serious public evil would be caused by authority to prevent publication. . . . There is nothing new in the fact that charges of reprehensible conduct may create resentment and the disposition to resort to violent means of redress, but this well-understood tendency did not alter the determination to protect the press against censorship and restraint upon publication. As was said in *New Yorker Staats-Zeitung v. Nolan,* "If the township may prevent the circulation of a newspaper for no reason other than that some of its inhabitants may violently disagree with it, and resent its circulation by resorting to physical violence, there is no limit to what may be prohibited." The danger of violent reactions becomes greater with effective organization of defiant groups resenting exposure, and, if this consideration warranted legislative interference with the initial freedom of publication, the constitutional protection would be reduced to a mere form of words.

For these reasons we hold the statute, so far as it authorized the proceedings in this action under clause (b) of section 1, to be an infringement of the liberty of the press guaranteed by the Fourteenth Amendment. We should add that this decision rests upon the operation and effect of the statute, without regard to the question of the truth of the charges contained in the particular periodical. The fact that the public officers named in this case, and those associated with the charges of official dereliction, may be deemed to be impeccable, cannot affect the conclusion that the statute imposes an unconstitutional restraint upon publication.

Judgment reversed.

Chief Justice Hughes's opinion appears definitive. Note his words: "The statute not only operates to suppress the offending newspaper . . . but to put the publisher under an effective censorship." Although Hughes takes a strong position against prior censorship in *Near,* he acknowledges that the protection against "previous restraint is not absolutely unlimited." There may be exceptional circumstances under which government restraint is necessary. Hughes cites three vital interests that may justify the imposition of censorship by the government: protecting national security, regulating obscenity, and prohibiting expression that would incite acts of violence.

In *Near,* Hughes explains that the government may legitimately prohibit the publication of certain material in times of war that it might not constitutionally regulate in times of peace. For example, suppose that during World War II a major newspaper received advanced classified information about the Allied invasion of Normandy, and

the editors announced that they would publish that information so the American people would be fully informed about the war effort. Military officials would understandably be concerned because publication would give the enemy advance knowledge of the military operation. Could the government take action to prohibit publication, or would it be confined only to pursuing criminal charges against the paper for illegal dissemination of classified documents after publication? According to *Near,* the courts would likely rule in favor of the government.

Fortunately, the United States has rarely faced a situation in which the press threatened to publish material that would seriously jeopardize vital national security interests. But the national security issue has come before the justices. The most notable example is *New York Times v. United States* (1971), which concerned the government's attempt to stop the *New York Times* and the *Washington Post* from publishing classified documents pertaining to the Vietnam War.

The case began in June 1971, when the *Times* and the *Post* began publishing articles based on two government documents: a 1965 Defense Department depiction of the Gulf of Tonkin incident and the 1968 "History of U.S. Decision-Making Process on Viet Nam Policy," a Pentagon study that ran to seven thousand pages in forty-seven volumes. Known as the Pentagon Papers, the documents constituted a massive history of how the United States went to war in Indochina, a subject of acute interest in the early 1970s.

After the newspapers published several installments, the U.S. government brought action against them, asking a district court judge to restrain them from publishing any more. The government argued that the articles would cause "irreparable injury" to the country's national security. To support this assertion, the government said that the entire 1968 study was top secret, a classification "applied only to that information or material the defense aspect of which is paramount, and the unauthorized disclosure of which could result in *exceptionally grave* damage to the Nation." The newspapers disagreed; they argued that the material was largely of historical, not current, interest, and that nothing in the documents related "to a time period subsequent to early 1968." As such, the government's

Katharine Graham, publisher of the *Washington Post*, and Ben Bradlee, executive editor of the *Washington Post*, leave U.S. District Court in Washington, D.C., in 1971, following the initial hearing on their legal challenge to the government's attempt to block publication of the Pentagon Papers. The Supreme Court ultimately ruled that the government's efforts to prohibit publication amounted to an unconstitutional prior restraint on the press.

attempt to enjoin publication amounted to nothing less than prior restraint.

Because the issues in this case were so important and the public controversy so intense, the judicial system responded to the dispute in a very unusual manner. The government first requested that the district court prohibit publication on June 15, 1971. The lower courts handled the case in an expedited fashion, and only nine days later the issue was before the Supreme Court. By then the justices had completed their work for the term and were about to go into their summer recess. But they extended their session and heard arguments on June 26 and announced their decision four days later. Because of its hurried consideration of the dispute, the Court issued only a short *per curiam* (unsigned or collectively written) opinion announcing that the majority had voted to reject the government's demands. Then each of the justices submitted an opinion expressing his view. From start to finish, it took the federal judiciary only two weeks to decide this major constitutional dispute.

Six justices supported the claim of the newspapers, but they hardly agreed on the reasons for doing so. Justices Hugo Black and William O. Douglas took the most extreme position. Consistent with their views that First Amendment protections are absolute, they argued that the censorship requested by the government was inappropriate. In Justice Black's words:

I believe that every moment's continuance of the injunctions against these newspapers amounts to a flagrant, indefensible, and continuing violation of the First Amendment. . . . Both the history and language of the First Amendment support the view that the press must be left free to publish news, whatever the source, without censorship, injunctions, or prior restraints.

Justices William Brennan and Thurgood Marshall also strongly condemned the injunctions, but without completely foreclosing the possibility that under extreme circumstances such censorship might be allowable. The government simply had failed to show that it was necessary in this case. Brennan wrote: "[T]he First Amendment stands as an absolute bar to the imposition of judicial restraints in circumstances of the kind presented by these cases. . . . Unless and until the Government has clearly made out its case, the First Amendment commands that no injunction may issue."

Justices Byron White and Potter Stewart took the most moderate position of those in the majority. They agreed that the injunctions should not be issued in Pentagon Papers cases, but only because the government had not proven that publication would "result in direct, immediate, and irreparable damage to our Nation or its people." Both expressed concerns about letting the executive branch intervene against the press in this way. They explained that they would have been more open to the action requested by the executive if Congress had passed legislation authorizing prior restraints in circumstances such as those presented by this case.

The three dissenting justices, Harry Blackmun, Warren Burger, and John Harlan, stressed two major points. First, they condemned the speed with which the case was decided. The Court, in their view, had been unable to give careful consideration to the difficult issues raised because the justices were rushed to arrive at a judgment. Second, they took the position that in matters of foreign policy, the Constitution rested primary authority in the executive branch. Therefore, when the executive branch, for foreign policy reasons, claims that it is necessary to impose certain limits on the press, deference should be given to that position. The dissenters would have preferred to have the case sent back to the lower courts for more lengthy study and with instructions that the courts should give considerable latitude to the executive branch when it is "operating within the field of its constitutional prerogative."

New York Times has generated a great deal of debate among legal scholars. Some suggest that it was the Court's, or at least individual justices', strongest statement to date on freedom of the press, that the justices virtually eradicated Hughes's national security exception to prior restraint. Others disagree. C. Herman Pritchett noted, "While the result in *New York Times* was clear enough, the Court's opinions do not add up to a sound defense of freedom of the press."[6] At the very least, the justices were divided in their views.

Since *New York Times* the Court has had no other important cases dealing with prior restraint and national security concerns. Nevertheless, during contemporary military efforts, the government has not hesitated to impose constraints on the media. Depending on one's perspective, the 1991 Gulf War was either a high point or a low point in government-media relations: The government simply circumvented the need to censor the press by limiting its access to certain information.[7] During the war in Iraq that began in December 2003, six hundred embedded journalists enjoyed more, but not absolute, freedom. For example, the Department of Defense requested that journalists refrain from publishing information that could harm America's national security and did not rule out the possibility of demanding to review reports before they were published or aired. Later, the George W. Bush administration asked the media to use "caution" in broadcasting videotapes from Osama bin Laden or others associated with the al Qaeda organization.

No one has yet to mount a serious legal challenge to these types of restrictions. But, given responses from journalists—including complaints that it is impossible for them to know whether coverage of particular military operations would, in fact, jeopardize national security—it seems likely that some will arise. How do you think the Court would rule in such cases?

THE MEDIA AND SPECIAL RIGHTS

Challenging restraints on First Amendment rights is not the only battle the media have fought. For many years, the media have asked courts for "special rights" not normally accorded average citizens, but that the press considered necessary to provide "full and robust" coverage of local, national, and world events. The most important of these special rights is known as the reporter's privilege, a protection that prohibits the government from compelling reporters to supply information about their sources. While reading about the controversy surrounding this issue, ask yourself whether you believe the media should enjoy a special legal status.

---

6. C. Herman Pritchett, *Constitutional Civil Liberties* (Englewood Cliffs, N.J.: Prentice Hall, 1984), 65.

7. See, e.g., Kevin A. Smith, "The Media at the Tip of the Spear," *Michigan Law Review* 102 (2004): 1329–1372.

As far back as 1840, reporters asserted the need for unusual legal privileges. That year the Senate held a secret meeting to debate a proposed treaty to end the Mexican-American War. John Nugent, a reporter for the *New York Herald,* managed to obtain a copy of the proposed draft and mailed it to his editor. The Senate subpoenaed Nugent, and, when he refused to reveal his source of information, it held him in contempt. Nugent was later sent to prison for protecting his source.[8]

Although from time to time others faced the same fate as Nugent, during the 1960s and 1970s a marked increase occurred in the frequency of claims of reporter's privilege. Some credit this increase to the trial of the Chicago Seven, in which the government charged individuals with starting a riot in the streets outside of the Democratic Party's 1968 convention. The United States served subpoenas on the major networks, newspapers, and magazines to obtain any information they had on the disturbances. Others suggest that it was the Nixon administration's disdain for the press that led to the increase, and still others argue that the rise in investigative reporting ushered in by Watergate led reporters to assert their right to protect sources absolutely and unconditionally.

Whatever the cause, the debate over reporter's privilege reached its climax in 1972, when the Supreme Court agreed to hear several cases involving such claims. The cases presented somewhat different issues, but the points of view were clear on both sides. The government asserted that reporters were entitled to no special rights or privileges; if ordinary citizens were forced to testify upon subpoena, then so should reporters. In response, the media argued that the law traditionally has recognized the existence of certain privileged relationships. Doctors, for example, cannot be forced to reveal information about their patients. Reporters also argued that if they were forced to answer questions about their sources, those sources would dry up, a result that would have a chilling effect on their ability to do their jobs and would violate their free press guarantee.

8. Mark Neubauer, "The Newsmen's Privilege after *Branzburg,*" *UCLA Law Review* 24 (1976): 160–192.

Branzburg v. Hayes

408 U.S. 665 (1972)
http://laws.findlaw.com/US/408/665.html
Oral arguments may be found at: http://www.oyez.org
Vote: 5 (Blackmun, Burger, Powell, Rehnquist, White)
    4 (Brennan, Douglas, Marshall, Stewart)
Opinion of the Court: White
Concurring opinion: Powell
Dissenting opinions: Douglas, Stewart

This case involved two articles written by Paul M. Branzburg, a reporter for the Louisville *Courier-Journal.* In the first article, Branzburg detailed his observations of two individuals, "synthesizing hashish from Marijuana, an activity which they asserted earned them about $5,000 in three weeks." The article contained this statement:

"I don't know why I am letting you do this story," [one of the individuals] said quietly. "To make the narcs mad, I guess. That's the main reason." However, [the two individuals] *asked for and received a promise that their names would be changed.*" [Emphasis added.]

The second piece contained interviews Branzburg conducted with drug users in Frankfort, Kentucky. Branzburg was subpoenaed by a grand jury. He appeared but refused to answer the following questions:

1. Who was the person or persons you observed in possession of Marijuana, about which you wrote an article?

2. Who was the person or persons you observed compounding Marijuana, producing same to a compound known as hashish?

Branzburg was cited for contempt for failure to answer the grand jury's questions. He challenged this action claiming that the First Amendment gave reporters the right to protect their sources.

MR. JUSTICE WHITE delivered the opinion of the Court.

The issue in these cases is whether requiring newsmen to appear and testify before state or federal grand juries abridges the freedom of speech and press guaranteed by the First Amendment. We hold that it does not. . . .

Petitioner . . . Branzburg . . . press[es] First Amendment claims that may be simply put: that to gather news it is often necessary to agree either not to identify the source of information published or to publish only part of the facts revealed, or both; that if the reporter is nevertheless forced to reveal these confidences to a grand jury, the source so identified and other confidential sources of other reporters will be measurably deterred from furnishing publishable information, all to the detriment of the free flow of information protected by the First Amendment. Although the newsmen in these cases do not claim an absolute privilege against official interrogation in all circumstances, they assert that the reporter should not be forced either to appear or to testify before a grand jury or at trial until and unless sufficient grounds are shown for believing that the reporter possesses information relevant to a crime the grand jury is investigating, that the information the reporter has is unavailable from other sources, and that the need for the information is sufficiently compelling to override the claimed invasion of First Amendment interests occasioned by the disclosure. Principally relied upon are prior cases emphasizing the importance of the First Amendment guarantees to individual development and to our system of representative government, decisions requiring that official action with adverse impact on First Amendment rights be justified by a public interest that is "compelling" or "paramount," and those precedents establishing the principle that justifiable governmental goals may not be achieved by unduly broad means having an unnecessary impact on protected rights of speech, press, or association. The heart of the claim is that the burden on news gathering resulting from compelling reporters to disclose confidential information outweighs any public interest in obtaining the information.

We do not question the significance of free speech, press, or assembly to the country's welfare. Nor is it suggested that news gathering does not qualify for First Amendment protection; without some protection for seeking out the news, freedom of the press could be eviscerated. But these cases involve no intrusions upon speech or assembly, no prior restraint or restriction on what the press may publish, and no express or implied command that the press publish what it prefers to withhold. No exaction or tax for the privilege of publishing, and no penalty, civil or criminal, related to the content of published material is at issue here. The use of confidential sources by the press is not forbidden or restricted; reporters remain free to seek news from any source by means within the law. No attempt is made to require the press to publish its sources of information or indiscriminately to disclose them on request.

The sole issue before us is the obligation of reporters to respond to grand jury subpoenas as other citizens do and to answer questions relevant to an investigation into the commission of crime. Citizens generally are not constitutionally immune from grand jury subpoenas; and neither the First Amendment nor any other constitutional provision protects the average citizen from disclosing to a grand jury information that he has received in confidence. The claim is, however, that reporters are exempt from these obligations because if forced to respond to subpoenas and identify their sources or disclose other confidences, their informants will refuse or be reluctant to furnish newsworthy information in the future. This asserted burden on news gathering is said to make compelled testimony from newsmen constitutionally suspect and to require a privileged position for them. . . .

The prevailing constitutional view of the newsman's privilege is very much rooted in the ancient role of the grand jury that has the dual function of determining if there is probable cause to believe that a crime has been committed and of protecting citizens against unfounded criminal prosecutions. Grand jury proceedings are constitutionally mandated for the institution of federal criminal prosecutions for capital or other serious crimes, and "its constitutional prerogatives are rooted in long centuries of Anglo-American history." . . . Although state systems of criminal procedure differ greatly among themselves, the grand jury is similarly guaranteed by many state constitutions and plays an important role in fair and effective law enforcement in the overwhelming majority of the States. Because its task is to inquire into the existence of possible criminal conduct and to return only well-founded indictments, its investigative powers are necessarily broad. "It is a grand inquest, a body with powers of investigation and inquisition, the scope of whose inquiries is not to be limited narrowly by questions of propriety or forecasts of the probable result of the investigation, or by doubts whether any particular individual will be found properly subject to an accusation of crime." Hence the grand jury's authority to subpoena witnesses is not only historic but essential to its task. Although the powers of the grand jury are not unlimited and are subject to the supervision of a judge, the longstanding principle that "the public . . . has a right to every man's evidence," except for those persons protected by a constitutional, common-law, or statutory privilege, is particularly applicable to grand jury proceedings.

A number of States have provided newsmen a statutory privilege of varying breadth, but the majority have not done so, and none has been provided by federal statute. Until now the only testimonial privilege for unofficial witnesses that is rooted in the Federal Constitution is the Fifth Amendment privilege against compelled self-incrimination. We are asked to create another by interpreting the First Amendment to grant newsmen a testimonial privilege that other citizens do not enjoy. This we decline to do. Fair and effective law enforcement aimed at providing security for the person and property of the individual is a fundamental function of government, and the grand jury plays an important, constitutionally mandated role in this process. On the records now before us, we perceive no basis for holding that the public interest in law enforcement and in ensuring effective grand jury proceedings is insufficient to override the consequential, but uncertain, burden on news gathering that is said to result from insisting that reporters, like other citizens, respond to relevant questions put to them in the course of a valid grand jury investigation or criminal trial.

This conclusion itself involves no restraint on what newspapers may publish or on the type or quality of information reporters may seek to acquire, nor does it threaten the vast bulk of confidential relationships between reporters and their sources. Grand juries address themselves to the issues of whether crimes have been committed and who committed them. Only where news sources themselves are implicated in crime or possess information relevant to the grand jury's task need they or the reporter be concerned about grand jury subpoenas. Nothing before us indicates that a large number or percentage of *all* confidential news sources falls into either category and would in any way be deterred by our holding that the Constitution does not, as it never has, exempt the newsman from performing the citizen's normal duty of appearing and furnishing information relevant to the grand jury's task.

The preference for anonymity of those confidential informants involved in actual criminal conduct is presumably a product of their desire to escape criminal prosecution, and this preference, while understandable, is hardly deserving of constitutional protection. It would be frivolous to assert— and no one does in these cases—that the First Amendment, in the interest of securing news or otherwise, confers a license on either the reporter or his news sources to violate valid criminal laws. Although stealing documents or private wiretapping could provide newsworthy information, neither reporter nor source is immune from conviction for such conduct, whatever the impact on the flow of news. Neither is immune, on First Amendment grounds, from testifying against the other, before the grand jury or at a criminal trial. The Amendment does not reach so far as to override the interest of the public in ensuring that neither reporter nor source is invading the rights of other citizens through reprehensible conduct forbidden to all other persons. . . .

Thus, we cannot seriously entertain the notion that the First Amendment protects a newsman's agreement to conceal the criminal conduct of his source, or evidence thereof, on the theory that it is better to write about crime than to do something about it. Insofar as any reporter in these cases undertook not to reveal or testify about the crime he witnessed, his claim of privilege under the First Amendment presents no substantial question. The crimes of news sources are no less reprehensible and threatening to the public interest when witnessed by a reporter than when they are not. . . .

The argument that the flow of news will be diminished by compelling reporters to aid the grand jury in a criminal investigation is not irrational, nor are the records before us silent on the matter. But we remain unclear how often and to what extent informers are actually deterred from furnishing information when newsmen are forced to testify before a grand jury. The available data indicate that some newsmen rely a great deal on confidential sources and that some informants are particularly sensitive to the threat of exposure and may be silenced if it is held by this Court that, ordinarily, newsmen must testify pursuant to subpoenas, but the evidence fails to demonstrate that there would be a significant constriction of the flow of news to the public if this Court reaffirms the prior common-law and constitutional rule regarding the testimonial obligations of newsmen. Estimates of the inhibiting effect of such subpoenas on the willingness of informants to make disclosures to newsmen are widely divergent and to a great extent speculative. It would be difficult to canvass the views of the informants themselves: surveys of reporters on this topic are chiefly opinions of predicted informant behavior and must be viewed in the light of the professional self-interest of the interviewees. Reliance by the press on confidential informants does not mean that all such sources will in fact dry up because of the later possible appearance of the newsman before a grand jury. The reporter may never be called and if he objects to testifying, the prosecution may not insist. Also, the relationship of many informants to the press is a symbiotic one which is unlikely to be greatly inhibited by the threat of subpoena: quite often, such informants are members of a minority political or cultural group that relies heavily on the media to propagate its views, publicize its aims, and magnify its exposure to the public. Moreover, grand juries characteristically conduct secret proceedings, and law enforcement officers are themselves experienced in dealing with informers, and have their own methods for protecting them without interference with the effective administration of justice. There is little before us indicating that informants whose interest in avoiding exposure is that it may threaten job security, personal safety, or peace of mind, would in fact be in a worse position, or would think they would be, if they risked placing their trust in public officials as well as reporters. We doubt if the informer who prefers anonymity but is sincerely interested in furnishing evidence of crime will always or very often be deterred by the prospect of dealing with those public authorities characteristically charged with the duty to protect the public interest as well as his.

Accepting the fact, however, that an undetermined number of informants not themselves implicated in crime will nevertheless, for whatever reason, refuse to talk to newsmen if they fear identification by a reporter in an official investigation, we cannot accept the argument that the public interest in possible future news about crime from undisclosed, unverified sources must take precedence over the public interest in pursuing and prosecuting those crimes reported to the press by informants and in thus deterring the commission of such crimes in the future.

We note first that the privilege claimed is that of the reporter, not the informant, and that if the authorities independently identify the informant, neither his own reluctance to testify nor the objection of the newsman would shield him from grand jury inquiry, whatever the impact on the flow of news or on his future usefulness as a secret source of information. More important, it is obvious that agreements to conceal information relevant to commission of crime

have very little to recommend them from the standpoint of public policy. . . . It is apparent . . . from our history and that of England, that concealment of crime and agreements to do so are not looked upon with favor. Such conduct deserves no encomium, and we decline now to afford it First Amendment protection by denigrating the duty of a citizen, whether reporter or informer, to respond to grand jury subpoena and answer relevant questions put to him.

Of course, the press has the right to abide by its agreement not to publish all the information it has, but the right to withhold news is not equivalent to a First Amendment exemption from the ordinary duty of all other citizens to furnish relevant information to a grand jury performing an important public function. Private restraints on the flow of information are not so favored by the First Amendment that they override all other public interests. . . .

We are admonished that refusal to provide a First Amendment reporter's privilege will undermine the freedom of the press to collect and disseminate news. But this is not the lesson history teaches us. As noted previously, the common law recognized no such privilege, and the constitutional argument was not even asserted until 1958. From the beginning of our country the press has operated without constitutional protection for press informants, and the press has flourished. The existing constitutional rules have not been a serious obstacle to either the development or retention of confidential news sources by the press.

It is said that currently press subpoenas have multiplied, that mutual distrust and tension between press and officialdom have increased, that reporting styles have changed, and that there is now more need for confidential sources, particularly where the press seeks news about minority cultural and political groups or dissident organizations suspicious of the law and public officials. These developments, even if true, are treacherous grounds for a far-reaching interpretation of the First Amendment fastening a nationwide rule on courts, grand juries, and prosecuting officials everywhere. The obligation to testify in response to grand jury subpoenas will not threaten these sources not involved with criminal conduct and without information relevant to grand jury investigations, and we cannot hold that the Constitution places the sources in these two categories either above the law or beyond its reach.

The argument for such a constitutional privilege rests heavily on those cases holding that the infringement of protected First Amendment rights must be no broader than necessary to achieve a permissible governmental purpose. We do not deal, however, with a governmental institution that has abused its proper function, as a legislative committee does when it "expose[s] for the sake of exposure." Nothing in the record indicates that these grand juries were "prob[ing] at will and without relation to existing need." Nor did the grand juries attempt to invade protected First Amendment rights by forcing wholesale disclosure of names and organizational affiliations for a purpose that was not germane to the determination of whether crime has been committed, and the characteristic secrecy of grand jury proceedings is a further protection against the undue invasion of such rights. The investigative power of the grand jury is necessarily broad if its public responsibility is to be adequately discharged. . . .

At the federal level, Congress has freedom to determine whether a statutory newsman's privilege is necessary and desirable and to fashion standards and rules as narrow or broad as deemed necessary to deal with the evil discerned and, equally important, to refashion those rules as experience from time to time may dictate. There is also merit in leaving state legislatures free, within First Amendment limits, to fashion their own standards in light of the conditions and problems with respect to the relations between law enforcement officials and press in their own areas. It goes without saying, of course, that we are powerless to bar state courts from responding in their own way and construing their own constitutions so as to recognize a newsman's privilege, either qualified or absolute.

In addition, there is much force in the pragmatic view that the press has at its disposal powerful mechanisms of communication and is far from helpless to protect itself from harassment or substantial harm. Furthermore, if what the newsman urged in these cases is true—that law enforcement cannot hope to gain and may suffer from subpoenaing newsmen before grand juries—prosecutors will be loath to risk so much for so little. Thus, at the federal level the Attorney General has already fashioned a set of rules for federal officials in connection with subpoenaing members of the press to testify before grand juries or at criminal trials. These rules are a major step in the direction the reporters herein desire to move. They may prove wholly sufficient to resolve the bulk of disagreements and controversies between press and federal officials.

Finally, as we have earlier indicated, news gathering is not without its First Amendment protections, and grand jury investigations if instituted or conducted other than in good faith, would pose wholly different issues for resolution under the First Amendment. Official harassment of the press undertaken not for the purposes of law enforcement but to disrupt a reporter's relationship with his news sources would have no justification. Grand juries are subject to judicial control and subpoenas to motions to quash. We do not expect courts will forget that grand juries must operate within the limits of the First Amendment as well as the Fifth.

The decision . . . in *Branzburg v. Hayes* . . . must be affirmed. Here, petitioner refused to answer questions that directly related to criminal conduct that he had observed and written about. The Kentucky Court of Appeals noted that marijuana is defined as a narcotic drug by statute and that unlicensed possession or compounding of it is a felony punishable by both fine and imprisonment. It held that petitioner "saw the commission of the statutory felonies of unlawful possession of marijuana and the unlawful conversion of it into hashish." . . . [I]f what the petitioner wrote was true, he had direct information to provide the grand jury concerning the commission of serious crimes.

Affirmed.

MR. JUSTICE DOUGLAS, dissenting.

Today's decision will impede the wide-open and robust dissemination of ideas and counterthought which a free press both fosters and protects and which is essential to the success of intelligent self-government. Forcing a reporter before a grand jury will have two retarding effects upon the ear and the pen of the press. Fear of exposure will cause dissidents to communicate less openly to trusted reporters. And, fear of accountability will cause editors and critics to write with more restrained pens. . . .

A reporter is no better than his source of information. Unless he has a privilege to withhold the identity of his source, he will be the victim of governmental intrigue or aggression. If he can be summoned to testify in secret before a grand jury, his sources will dry up and the attempted exposure, the effort to enlighten the public, will be ended. If what the Court sanctions today becomes settled law, then the reporter's main function in American society will be to pass on to the public the press releases which the various departments of government issue. . . .

Today's decision is more than a clog upon news gathering. It is a signal to publishers and editors that they should exercise caution in how they use whatever information they can obtain. Without immunity they may be summoned to account for their criticism. Entrenched officers have been quick to crash their powers down upon unfriendly commentators.

The intrusion of government into this domain is symptomatic of the disease of this society. As the years pass the power of government becomes more and more pervasive. It is a power to suffocate both people and causes. Those in power, whatever their politics, want only to perpetuate it. Now that the fences of the law and the tradition that has protected the press are broken down, the people are the victims. The First Amendment, as I read it, was designed precisely to prevent that tragedy.

MR. JUSTICE STEWART, with whom MR. JUSTICE BRENNAN and MR. JUSTICE MARSHALL join, dissenting.

The Court's crabbed view of the First Amendment reflects a disturbing insensitivity to the critical role of an independent press in our society. The question whether a reporter has a constitutional right to a confidential relationship with his source is of first impression here, but the principles that should guide our decision are as basic as any to be found in the Constitution. . . . [T]he Court . . . holds that a newsman has no First Amendment right to protect his sources when called before a grand jury. The Court thus invites state and federal authorities to undermine the historic independence of the press by attempting to annex the journalistic profession as an investigative arm of government. Not only will this decision impair performance of the press' constitutionally protected functions, but it will, I am convinced, in the long run harm rather than help the administration of justice. . . .

Accordingly, when a reporter is asked to appear before a grand jury and reveal confidences, I would hold that the government must (1) show that there is probable cause to believe that the newsman has information that is clearly relevant to a specific probable violation of law; (2) demonstrate that the information sought cannot be obtained by alternative means less destructive of First Amendment rights; and (3) demonstrate a compelling and overriding interest in the information.

In *Branzburg* the majority emphatically denied the existence of the reporter's privilege. The dissenters were distraught: Justice Stewart, who in his youth had worked as a reporter for a Cincinnati newspaper and while in college had edited the *Yale Daily News*, condemned the "Court's crabbed view of the First Amendment." Some legal scholars later criticized the Court for invoking contradictory premises about the role of the press. In *Branzburg* the majority refused to recognize the reporter's privilege even against arguments that its absence would hamper the ability of the press to cover events of public concern because it would deter informants from speaking with reporters.

The reaction of the media was an outpouring of condemnation of *Branzburg* and calls for federal and state statutes that would shield reporters from revealing their sources. The states—either by statute or judicial decision—responded to these calls, with almost all now recognizing a privilege for reporters to refuse to divulge information about certain news-gathering activities. But because these shield laws often limit protections to specific circumstances, they may not be particularly effective. Kentucky already had a shield law on the books at the time of Branzburg's grand jury proceedings. Unfortunately for the reporter, it covered only sources of information and not personal observation. Journalists still face the threat of imprisonment if they refuse to answer questions pertaining to their stories—as Branzburg himself learned only a few months after the Supreme Court handed down the decision in his case (*see Box 14-1*). In addition, Congress has yet to enact a federal shield law, despite immense pressure from a range of organized interests.

Immunity from testifying was not the only privilege for which reporters pressed. In *Zurcher v. Stanford Daily* (1978) they also asserted a need for special treatment under the Fourth Amendment. This case stemmed from a demonstration at the university's hospital that turned into a riot. Reporters for the *Stanford Daily* covered the

BOX 14-1 AFTERMATH . . .
PAUL BRANZBURG

BETWEEN 1969 AND 1971 Paul M. Branzburg, an investigative reporter for the Louisville *Courier-Journal*, wrote a series of articles on illegal drug activities in central Kentucky. He was subpoenaed by two different grand juries and asked to provide information about his sources. When he refused to answer, contempt citations were issued. He appealed to the United States Supreme Court, which ruled on June 29, 1972, that the First Amendment confers no special privilege on reporters who do not answer grand jury questions.

In the aftermath of the Supreme Court ruling, Kentucky prosecutors again sought information from Branzburg concerning the drug users and dealers he had observed while researching his stories. Branzburg, who by this time had moved to Michigan to do investigative reporting for the *Detroit Free Press*, again declined to answer questions. On September 1, 1972, Branzburg was found in contempt of the Jefferson County court and was sentenced to six months in prison. When Branzburg refused to return to Kentucky voluntarily, state officials requested that Michigan authorities extradite him. Michigan's governor, William G. Milliken, denied the request, and Branzburg never served the six-month sentence.

SOURCES: Louisville *Courier-Journal*, June 30, 1972; Contemporary Authors On Line, Gale Group, 2000.

incident and took photographs. When police were unable to identify those responsible for injuries to officers who responded to the riot, they obtained a warrant to search the *Daily*'s office for pictures. None was found, but the newspaper took legal action, claiming that the First Amendment prohibited government searches of the press. The Supreme Court rejected this argument, holding that the press did not enjoy any special immunity from reasonable search and seizures.

Several months after *Zurcher*, the Court decided **Houchins v. KQED** (1978), which raised yet another issue involving the press. Of concern in *Houchins* was the right of reporters to have access to inmates in a county jail, which ordinarily would be denied to individuals. Although this case is different from *Zurcher*, it poses a similar question: Should the justices accord the press rights and privileges beyond those enjoyed by average citizens?

A divided Court ruled that it should not. As Chief Justice Burger explained for the majority:

The media are not a substitute for or an adjunct of the government, and like the courts, are "ill equipped" to deal with the problems of prison administration. We must not confuse the role of the media with that of government; each has special, crucial functions, each complementing—and sometimes conflicting with—the other.

Burger said that the Court would be no more amenable to special access claims than it was to the reporter's privilege; indeed, relying on past decisions such as *Branzburg*, Burger called the media's arguments flawed. He held that the First Amendment did not mandate "a right of access to government information or sources of information within the government's control." This was strong language, which could be understood to limit press access to a wide range of state and federal proceedings.

In cases following *Houchins*, however, the Court has not gone so far as Burger's words suggested. Burger also wrote the opinion in *Richmond Newspapers v. Virginia* (1980), overruling a trial court judge who had denied the press access to a highly publicized murder trial: "The right to attend criminal trials is implicit within the guarantees of the First Amendment," and, if such access were denied, "important aspects of freedom of speech and of the press could be eviscerated."

THE BOUNDARIES OF FREE PRESS: OBSCENITY AND LIBEL

One of the Supreme Court's consistent teachings is that the First Amendment is not absolute. This lesson began in *Schenck v. United States* (1919), in which Oliver Wendell Holmes noted that the First Amendment would not protect a person who falsely yelled "fire" in a crowded theater. Periodically, other justices have reminded us of the limits of First Amendment protection as the Court developed its freedom of expression doctrines.

First Amendment protection does not mean that people are shielded from government regulation of anything published or expressed verbally. Some varieties of expression are illegitimate and may be punished. Several examples immediately come to mind. One may not communicate military secrets to the enemy or make terrorist threats. One may not provide fraudulent information in commercial transactions or engage in discussions that amount to criminal conspiracies. One may not tell falsehoods under oath, or exchange "insider information" in securities transactions. In each of these cases the expression falls outside the boundaries of First Amendment protection.

In this section we explore the limits of First Amendment protection by examining two varieties of expression, obscenity and libel, that have presented the justices with perplexing freedom of the press questions. There is almost universal agreement that the framers considered neither to be legitimate expression and did not intend the First Amendment to protect them from government regulation. Accepting this proposition, however, does not settle the matter because other questions remain. How do we define obscenity and libel? What distinguishes obscene and libelous expression from protected speech and press? What standards of evidence should be imposed? How can government regulate obscenity and libel without imposing a "chilling effect" on protected expression?

Obscenity

According to Justice Harlan, "The subject of obscenity has produced a variety of views among the members of the Court unmatched in any other course of constitutional interpretation."[9] Justice Brennan, the member of the Court most associated with the subject, was even more candid *(see Box 14-2)*. Discussing service on the Court, Brennan noted, "It takes a while before you can become even calm about approaching a job like this. Which is not to say you do not make mistakes. In my case, there has been the obscenity area."[10]

What is it about obscenity that has produced such extraordinary statements from these justices? After all, the Court uniformly has held that obscenity is not entitled to First Amendment protection. The problem is determining what makes a work obscene. In other words, how should we define the term *obscenity*? The answer is important because how we differentiate protected from unprotected expression has broad implications for what we see, read, and hear. Consider the movie industry: In the not-so-distant past, strict definitions of obscenity required an actor to keep one foot on the floor when performing a bedroom scene. Imagine the number of contemporary movies the courts would ban under such a standard! Today, the issues are no less important: Groups throughout the country try to bar certain books from public schools, to prohibit the sale of particular records to minors, and to stop libraries from subscribing to certain magazines—all on obscenity grounds.

Given the task involved, one might think the Court has set definitive policy in this area, but nothing could be further from reality. For five decades the Court has grappled with the issue, particularly with fashioning a definition of obscenity. Why has this issue caused such problems? Is there a reasonable solution? Or will the Court continue to flounder among competing schools of thought?

The adjudication of obscenity claims is a modern phenomenon. Before the 1950s the Court generally avoided the issue by adopting the British definition of obscenity. In *Regina v. Hicklin* (1868), which involved a pamphlet questioning the morals of Catholic priests, a British court promulgated the following test: "Whether the tendency of the matter charged as obscenity is to deprave and corrupt those whose minds are open to such

---

9. *Interstate Circuit v. Dallas* (1968).
10. Nat Hentoff, "Profiles: The Constitutionalists," *New Yorker*, March 12, 1990, 54.

BOX 14-2   WILLIAM JOSEPH BRENNAN JR. (1956–1990)

WILLIAM J. BRENNAN JR. was born on April 25, 1906, in Newark, New Jersey. He was the second of eight children of Irish parents who immigrated to the United States in 1890. Brennan displayed impressive academic abilities early in life. He was an outstanding student in high school, an honors student at the University of Pennsylvania's Wharton School of Finance, and in the top 10 percent of his Harvard Law School class in 1931.

Brennan married Marjorie Leonard on May 5, 1928, and they had two sons and one daughter. (Marjorie Brennan died in 1982, and Brennan married Mary Fowler on March 9, 1983.) After law school Brennan returned to Newark, where he joined a prominent law firm. Following passage of the Wagner Labor Act in 1935, Brennan began to specialize in labor law.

With the outbreak of World War II, Brennan entered the army, serving as a manpower troubleshooter on the staff of the undersecretary of war, Robert B. Patterson. At the conclusion of the war, Brennan returned to his old law firm. But as his practice swelled, Brennan, a dedicated family man, began to resent the demands it placed on his time.

A DESIRE TO TEMPER the pace of his work was one of the reasons Brennan accepted an appointment to the newly created New Jersey Superior Court in 1949. Brennan had been a leader in the movement to establish the court as part of a large program of judicial reform. It came as no surprise when Republican governor Alfred E. Driscoll named Brennan, a registered but inactive Democrat, to the court.

During Brennan's tenure on the superior court, his use of pretrial procedures to speed up the disposition of cases brought him to the attention of New Jersey Supreme Court justice Arthur T. Vanderbilt. It was reportedly at Vanderbilt's suggestion that Brennan was moved first in 1950 to the appellate division of the superior court and then in 1952 to the state supreme court.

Late in 1956, when President Dwight D. Eisenhower was looking for a justice to replace Sherman Minton, Vanderbilt and others strongly recommended Brennan for the post, and Eisenhower gave him a recess appointment in October. There was some criticism that Eisenhower was currying favor with voters by nominating a Roman Catholic Democrat to the bench so close to the election, but Brennan's established integrity and nonpolitical background minimized the impact of the charges. He was confirmed by the Senate on March 19, 1957. Brennan retired from the Court on July 20, 1990. He died on July 24, 1997.

SOURCE: Adapted from David Savage, *Guide to the U.S. Supreme Court*, 4th ed. (Washington, D.C.: CQ Press, 2004), 1005.

---

immoral influences and into whose hands a publication of this sort might fall."

Under this standard, commonly referred to as the Hicklin test, the British court found the pamphlet obscene. That it did so is not surprising: Three aspects of the Hicklin test make it particularly difficult to overcome. First, the test targets "those whose minds are open to such immoral influences and into whose hands a publication of this sort might fall." Although this standard is vague, in practice, prosecutors often asked, What if this material were to fall into the hands of a child? In other words, the Hicklin test used a stringent level of acceptability—whether the material would be appropriate if a child were exposed to it. Second, the Hicklin test did not require that the publication be considered as a whole. Instead, a work could be declared obscene based upon one of its parts. Third, the Hicklin test did not direct the courts to consider the social value of the work; rather, it only provided that the effect of the offensive sections be examined. As a result, the Hicklin standard left a wide range of expression unprotected.

The U.S. Supreme Court not only adopted the standard; it also strengthened it. In *Ex parte Jackson* (1878) the Court upheld the Comstock Act, which made it a crime to send obscene materials, including information on abortion and birth control, through the U.S. mail. The justices applied the Hicklin test and extended its coverage to reproduction.

While the Supreme Court clung to *Hicklin*, some lower courts were attempting to liberalize it or even reject it. Among the examples cited most often is *United States v. One Book Called Ulysses* (1933), in which Judge Augustus Hand argued that the proper standard should be whether the author intended to produce obscenity. The promulgations of diverse rulings from the lower courts, coupled with the Supreme Court's silence on the issue, started to have an effect. By the 1950s the pornography business was flourishing in the United States, with little restriction on who could buy or view it. This situation led to a backlash, with irate citizens clamoring for tighter controls. Others, particularly the ACLU, pressured courts to move in precisely the opposite direction—to rule that the First Amendment covers all materials, including those previously adjudged obscene. By the late 1950s these interests, however diverse, were sending the same signal to the justices: The time had come to deal with the issue.

The Court responded in **Butler v. Michigan** (1957), an appeal challenging a state statute that defined obscenity along Hicklin test lines. Specifically, the law made it a crime to distribute material "found to have a potentially deleterious influence on youth." The justices struck down the statute, finding fault with the child standard. It is incompatible with the First Amendment, the justices said, to reduce the reading material available to adults to that which is fit for children. To do so, according to Justice Felix Frankfurter's opinion, is "to burn the house to roast the pig."

The *Butler* decision mortally wounded the Hicklin test, but the justices failed to provide an alternative until later

that year when the Court took its first stab at creating a contemporary American obscenity standard. The case was **Roth v. United States** (1957). This appeal stemmed from charges that Samuel Roth had sent "obscene, indecent, and filthy matter" through the mail. At Roth's trial the judge instructed the jury with this definition of obscenity: The material

must be calculated to debauch the minds and morals of those into whose hands it may fall and . . . the test in each case is the effect of the book, picture or publication considered as a whole, not upon any particular class, but upon all those whom it is likely to reach. In other words, you determine its impact upon the average person in the community.

The jury found Roth guilty on four of the counts, and the judge sentenced him to the maximum punishment: five years in prison and a $5,000 fine. Roth challenged his conviction, arguing that the standard imposed was inconsistent with First Amendment freedoms.

Although they were badly divided, a majority of the justices in *Roth* supported a new standard articulated by Justice Brennan in his opinion of the Court. Now known as the Roth test, Brennan's obscenity standard posed the following: "Whether to the average person applying contemporary community standards, the dominant theme of the material, taken as a whole, appeals to prurient interests."

At first glance, Brennan's opinion seems to forge a compromise between competing views. On the one hand, he appeased "decency" advocates by rejecting the view that nothing is obscene; on the other, he set a new standard of obscenity that was far less restrictive than *Hicklin*. The new Roth test was a significant departure from the Hicklin standard. First, *Roth* imposed an "average person" test, replacing *Hicklin*'s child standard with that of an adult. Second, the "contemporary community standards" criterion recognized the evolving nature of society's views of sexual morality. Third, the "dominant theme of the material taken as a whole" approach rejected *Hicklin*'s notion that a work can be declared obscene based on the content of a single part. And finally, the "prurient interests" element ensured that only material with sexual content would potentially fall under the obscenity rubric.

Although a majority of the Court supported Brennan's opinion, the Court remained divided over the proper way to handle the obscenity issue. In the following years, the Court confronted several appeals that provided opportunities for the justices to improve upon *Roth*. Attempts to replace *Roth* were unsuccessful. The justices simply could not agree on an acceptable substitute.

Although *Roth* survived, the justices did amplify and build upon its meaning. Perhaps the most significant of the post-*Roth* decisions were **Jacobellis v. Ohio** (1964) and **Memoirs v. Massachusetts** (1966). In *Jacobellis* the Court considered the appeal of Nico Jacobellis, the manager of a movie theater, who had been charged by Ohio authorities with showing an obscene film. Called *Les Amants* (*The Lovers*), the movie depicts the love affair of an archeologist and a woman who leaves her husband and child. *Les Amants* contains one "explicit love scene."

Brennan's opinion in *Jacobellis* is noteworthy for several reasons. First, Brennan refined his *Roth* test: He stated that contemporary community standards were those of the nation, not of a local community. In doing so, he not only held the film to be protected speech but also substantially liberalized the Roth test. It is bound to be the case that communities seeking to ban obscenity have stricter standards than those of the country at large. Under Brennan's refinement, Tulsa, Oklahoma, would be bound by the same obscenity standards as New York City. Second, Brennan added a new provision to the Roth test. Not only must material meet all of the provisions of the test to be legally obscene, but it also must be found to be "utterly without redeeming social importance."

In *Memoirs v. Massachusetts* the Court further explained what was required under its new social importance standard. This case reviewed the attempts of Massachusetts to declare obscene John Cleland's *Memoirs of a Woman of Pleasure*. This book, popularly known as *Fanny Hill*, dated from 1749. A concededly erotic novel, *Memoirs* traces the escapades of a London prostitute. The Massachusetts Supreme Court held that a book need not be "unqualifiedly worthless before it could be deemed obscene"; that is, just because *Memoirs* contained some nonerotic passages did not mean that it had redeeming value. Although divided, the U.S. Supreme Court disagreed. In his judgment for the Court, Brennan expanded

---

BOX 14-3   *ROTH, JACOBELLIS,* AND *MEMOIRS,* COMPARED

ROTH: Whether to the average person applying contemporary community standards, the dominant theme of the material, taken as a whole, appeals to prurient interests.

ROTH and *JACOBELLIS:* Whether to the average person applying standards of the society at large, the material is utterly without redeeming social importance.

ROTH, JACOBELLIS, and *MEMOIRS:* Whether to the average person applying standards of the society at large, the material is utterly without redeeming social importance, possessing not a modicum of social value.

---

the parameters of *Roth*. If a work had a "modicum of social value" it could not be adjudged obscene.

By 1966, then, a divided Court had substantially altered the Roth test, as shown in Box 14-3, which compares the test in 1957 to that articulated in 1966. Would anything be defined as obscene under the Roth-Jacobellis-Memoirs test? We might think that hard-core pornography would fall outside of it, but could not a clever moviemaker, author, or publisher circumvent it? If a short passage of some merit appears in the middle of an erotic book or pornographic movie, does the product have redeeming value?

The impact of these decisions was predictable. Expanded First Amendment protection prompted an explosion in sexually oriented materials. Adult movies, magazines, and books were more widely distributed than ever before. The reaction to these developments was also predictable. A backlash developed primarily among more conservative citizens who were not pleased with the growing numbers of adult bookstores, theaters, and nightclubs and that sexually explicit materials had become so widely available.

In the election of 1968, the Republican candidate, Richard Nixon, delivered a campaign message that was quite critical of the Supreme Court. His expressed discontent with the justices covered a wide array of decisions, but the Court's obscenity decisions were primary targets for his campaign rhetoric. He promised the voters that if he became president he would appoint justices to the Court who were more conservative in their orientation. When he took office he kept his promise. He had the opportunity to appoint four new justices to the Court, including a new chief justice, Warren Burger. Nixon's appointments turned the Court in a more conservative direction, and observers knew that eventually the justices would reconsider the line of liberal obscenity rulings that had begun with *Roth*. The anticipated change became apparent on June 21, 1973, when the justices announced their decision in *Miller v. California*.

Miller v. California

413 U.S. 15 (1973)
http://laws.findlaw.com/US/413/15.html
Oral arguments may be found at: http://www.oyez.org
Vote: 5 (Blackmun, Burger, Powell, Rehnquist, White)
  4 (Brennan, Douglas, Marshall, Stewart)
Opinion of the Court: Burger
Dissenting opinions: Douglas, Brennan

Marvin Miller, a vendor of so-called adult material, conducted a mass-mail campaign to drum up sales for his books. The pamphlets were fairly explicit: Some contained pictures of men and women in groups of two or more engaging in a variety of sexual activities, with genitals often prominently displayed.

Had Miller sent the brochures to interested individuals only, he might not have been caught. But because he did a mass mailing, some pamphlets ended up in the hands of people who did not want them. Indeed, Miller's arrest came when the manager of a restaurant and his mother opened one of the envelopes and complained to the police.

MR. CHIEF JUSTICE BURGER delivered the opinion of the Court.

This is one of a group of "obscenity-pornography" cases being reviewed by the Court in a re-examination of standards enunciated in earlier cases involving what Mr. Justice Harlan called "the intractable obscenity problem." . . .

This case involves the application of a State's criminal obscenity statute to a situation in which sexually explicit materials have been thrust by aggressive sales action upon unwilling recipients who had in no way indicated any desire to receive such materials. This Court has recognized that the States have a legitimate interest in prohibiting dissemination or exhibition of obscene material when the mode of dissemination carries with it a significant danger of offending the sensibilities of unwilling recipients or of exposure to juveniles. It is in this context that we are called on to define the standards which must be used to identify obscene material that a State may regulate without infringing on the First Amendment as applicable to the States through the Fourteenth Amendment. . . .

. . . [O]bscene material is unprotected by the First Amendment. We acknowledge, however, the inherent dangers of undertaking to regulate any form of expression. State statutes designed to regulate obscene materials must be carefully limited. As a result, we now confine the permissible scope of such regulation to works which depict or describe sexual conduct. That conduct must be specifically defined by the applicable state law, as written or authoritatively construed. A state offense must also be limited to works which, taken as a whole, appeal to the prurient interest in sex, which portray sexual conduct in a patently offensive way, and which, taken as a whole, do not have serious literary, artistic, political, or scientific value.

The basic guidelines for the trier of fact must be: (a) whether "the average person, applying contemporary community standards" would find that the work, taken as a whole, appeals to the prurient interest; (b) whether the work depicts or describes, in a patently offensive way, sexual conduct specifically defined by the applicable state law; and (c) whether the work, taken as a whole, lacks serious literary, artistic, political, or scientific value. We do not adopt as a constitutional standard the "*utterly* without redeeming social value" test of *Memoirs v. Massachusetts;* that concept has never commanded the adherence of more than three Justices at one time. If a state law that regulates obscene material is thus limited, as written or construed, the First Amendment values applicable to the States through the Fourteenth Amendment are adequately protected by the ultimate power of appellate courts to conduct an independent review of constitutional claims when necessary.

We emphasize that it is not our function to propose regulatory schemes for the States. That must await their concrete legislative efforts. It is possible, however, to give a few plain examples of what a state statute could define for regulation under part (b) of the standard announced in this opinion.

(a) Patently offensive representations or descriptions of ultimate sexual acts, normal or perverted, actual or simulated.

(b) Patently offensive representation or descriptions of masturbation, excretory functions, and lewd exhibition of the genitals.

Sex and nudity may not be exploited without limit by films or pictures exhibited or sold in places of public accommodation any more than live sex and nudity can be exhibited or sold without limit in such public places. At a minimum, prurient, patently offensive depiction or description of sexual conduct must have serious literary, artistic, political, or scientific value to merit First Amendment protection. . . .

Under the holdings announced today, no one will be subject to prosecution for the sale or exposure of obscene materials unless these materials depict or describe patently offensive "hard core" sexual conduct specifically defined by the regulating state law, as written or construed. We are satisfied that these specific prerequisites will provide fair notice to a dealer in such materials that his public and commercial activities may bring prosecution. If the inability to define regulated materials with ultimate, god-like precision altogether removes the power of the States or the Congress to regulate, then "hard core" pornography may be exposed without limit to the juvenile, the passerby, and the consenting adult alike. . . .

It is certainly true that the absence, since *Roth*, of a single majority view of this Court as to proper standards for testing obscenity has placed a strain on both state and federal courts. But today, for the first time since *Roth* was decided in 1957, a majority of this Court has agreed on concrete guidelines to isolate "hard core" pornography from expression protected by the First Amendment. Now we . . . attempt to provide positive guidance to federal and state courts alike.

This may not be an easy road, free from difficulty. But no amount of "fatigue" should lead us to adopt a convenient "institutional" rationale—an absolutist, "anything goes" view of the First Amendment—because it will lighten our burdens. "Such an abnegation of judicial supervision in this

field would be inconsistent with our duty to uphold the constitutional guarantees." Nor should we remedy "tension between state and federal courts" by arbitrarily depriving the States of a power reserved to them under the Constitution, a power which they have enjoyed and exercised continuously from before the adoption of the First Amendment to this day. "Our duty admits of no 'substitute for facing up to the tough individual problems of constitutional judgment involved in every obscenity case.' "

Under a National Constitution, fundamental First Amendment limitations on the powers of the States do not vary from community to community, but this does not mean that there are, or should or can be, fixed, uniform national standards of precisely what appeals to the "prurient interest" or is "patently offensive." These are essentially questions of fact, and our Nation is simply too big and too diverse for this Court to reasonably expect that such standards could be articulated for all 50 States in a single formulation, even assuming the prerequisite consensus exists. When triers of fact are asked to decide whether "the average person, applying contemporary community standards" would consider certain materials "prurient," it would be unrealistic to require that the answer be based on some abstract formulation. The adversary system, with lay jurors as the usual ultimate fact-finders in criminal prosecutions, has historically permitted triers of fact to draw on the standards of their community, guided always by limiting instructions on the law. To require a State to structure obscenity proceedings around evidence of a *national* "community standard" would be an exercise in futility.

. . . [T]his case was tried on the theory that the California obscenity statute sought to incorporate the tripartite test of *Memoirs*. This, a "national" standard of First Amendment protection enumerated by a plurality of this Court, was correctly regarded at the time of trial as limiting state prosecution under the controlling case law. The jury, however, was explicitly instructed that, in determining whether the "dominant theme of the material as a whole . . . appeals to the prurient interest" and in determining whether the material "goes substantially beyond customary limits of candor and affronts contemporary community standards of decency," it was to apply "contemporary community standards of the State of California."

During the trial, both the prosecution and the defense assumed that the relevant "community standards" in making the factual determination of obscenity were those of the State of California, not some hypothetical standard of the entire United States of America. Defense counsel at trial never objected to the testimony of the State's expert on community standards or to the instructions of the trial judge on "statewide" standards. On appeal to the Appellate Department, Superior Court of California, County of Orange, appellant for the first time contended that application of state, rather than national, standards violated the First and Fourteenth Amendments.

We conclude that neither the State's alleged failure to offer evidence of "national standards," nor the trial court's charge that the jury consider state community standards, were constitutional errors. Nothing in the First Amendment requires that a jury must consider hypothetical and unascertainable "national standards" when attempting to determine whether certain materials are obscene as a matter of fact. . . . It is neither realistic nor constitutionally sound to read the First Amendment as requiring that the people of Maine or Mississippi accept public depiction of conduct found tolerable in Las Vegas, or New York City. People in different States vary in their tastes and attitudes, and this diversity is not to be strangled by the absolutism of imposed uniformity. . . . We hold that the requirement that the jury evaluate the materials with reference to "contemporary standards of the State of California" serves this protective purpose and is constitutionally adequate.

The dissenting Justices sound the alarm of repression. But, in our view, to equate the free and robust exchange of ideas and political debate with commercial exploitation of obscene material demeans the grand conception of the First Amendment and its high purposes in the historic struggle for freedom. It is a "misuse of the great guarantees of free speech and free press. . . ." The First Amendment protects works which, taken as a whole, have serious literary, artistic, political, or scientific value, regardless of whether the government or a majority of the people approve of the ideas these works represent. . . . But the public portrayal of hardcore sexual conduct for its own sake, and for the ensuing commercial gain, is a different matter. . . .

In sum, we (a) reaffirm the *Roth* holding that obscene material is not protected by the First Amendment; (b) hold that such material can be regulated by the States, subject to the specific safeguards enunciated above, without a showing that the material is "*utterly* without redeeming social

value"; and (c) hold that obscenity is to be determined by applying "contemporary community standards," not "national standards." . . .

Vacated and remanded.

MR. JUSTICE DOUGLAS, dissenting.

Today we leave open the way for California to send a man to prison for distributing brochures that advertise books and a movie under freshly written standards defining obscenity which until today's decision were never the part of any law. . . .

Today the Court retreats from the earlier formulations of the constitutional test and undertakes to make new definitions. This effort, like the earlier ones, is earnest and well intentioned. The difficulty is that we do not deal with constitutional terms, since "obscenity" is not mentioned in the Constitution or Bill of Rights. And the First Amendment makes no such exception from "the press" which it undertakes to protect nor, as I have said on other occasions, is an exception necessarily implied for there was no recognized exception to the free press at the time the Bill of Rights was adopted which treated "obscene" publications differently from other types of papers, magazines, and books. So there are no constitutional guidelines for deciding what is and what is not "obscene." The Court is at large because we deal with tastes and standards of literature. What shocks me may be sustenance for my neighbor. What causes one person to boil up in rage over one pamphlet or movie may reflect only his neurosis, not shared by others. We deal here with a regime of censorship which, if adopted, should be done by constitutional amendment after full debate by the people. . . .

We deal with highly emotional, not rational, questions. To many the Song of Solomon is obscene. I do not think we, the judges, were ever given the constitutional power to make definitions of obscenity. If it is to be defined, let the people debate and decide by a constitutional amendment what they want to ban as obscene and what standards they want the legislatures and the courts to apply. Perhaps the people will decide that the path towards a mature, integrated society requires that all ideas competing for acceptance must have no censor. Perhaps they will decide otherwise. Whatever the choice, the courts will have some guidelines. Now we have none except our own predilections.

MR. JUSTICE BRENNAN, with whom MR. JUSTICE STEWART and MR. JUSTICE MARSHALL join, dissenting.

In the case before us, appellant was convicted of distributing obscene matter in violation of California Penal Code §311.2, on the basis of evidence that he had caused to be mailed unsolicited brochures advertising various books and a movie. I need not now decide whether a statute might be drawn to impose, within the requirements of the First Amendment, criminal penalties for the precise conduct at issue here. For it is clear that . . . the statute under which the prosecution was brought is unconstitutionally overbroad, and therefore invalid on its face.

The same day, the Court also handed down a decision in *Paris Adult Theatre I v. Slaton*, which involved a 1970 complaint filed by Atlanta, Georgia, against the Paris Adult Theatre, asserting that the theater was showing obscene films. The trial court judge viewed two of the offending films, which depicted simulated fellatio, cunnilingus, and group sexual intercourse. The judge ruled in favor of the theater, mainly because the owners did not admit anyone under the age of twenty-one. After the Georgia Supreme Court reversed, the owners appealed to the U.S. Supreme Court. The justices, however, affirmed the ruling, refusing to extend the theater First Amendment protection, even though only consenting adults could see the films.

Miller (and *Paris Adult Theatre I*) substantially changed the constitutional definition of obscenity. In Table 14-1 we compare the Roth test (and its expansions) with the new Miller standard. Although the Court retained three important elements of the Roth test (the adult standard, the work taken as a whole, and the restriction of obscenity to sexually oriented materials), two major changes stand out. First, the Miller test specifically gives the states the authority to define what is obscene. The Court, therefore, emphasized local values rather than the national standard articulated in *Jacobellis*. Second, the Court did away with the notion that a work merited protection as long as it did not meet the "utterly without redeeming social value" criterion. Instead, the justices held that to receive First Amendment protection, sexually oriented materials had to have serious literary, artistic, political, or scientific value. As a consequence, the new Miller test permitted much greater regulation of sexually explicit materials than the Roth standard had.

In addition to the significant change in obscenity law ushered in by *Miller* and its companion case, *Paris Adult Theatre I*, liberals from the Warren Court era also expressed a change in approach. Justice Brennan wrote in his dissenting opinion in *Paris Adult Theatre I*:

Our experience since *Roth* requires us not only to abandon the effort to pick out obscene materials on a case-by-case basis, but also to reconsider a fundamental postulate of *Roth:* that there exists a definable class of sexually oriented expression that may be totally suppressed by the Federal and State Governments.

TABLE 14-1 The Obscenity Standards of the Warren and Burger Courts, Compared

	Warren Court	Burger Court
Relevant audience:	Average person	Average person
Scope of consideration:	Work taken as a whole	Work taken as a whole
Standard:	Sexual material found patently offensive by the national standards of society at large	Sexual conduct found patently offensive by contemporary community standards as specifically defined by applicable state law
Value of the work:	Utterly without redeeming social importance	Lacks serious literary, artistic, political, or scientific value

Assuming that such a class of expression does in fact exist, I am forced to conclude that the concept of "obscenity" cannot be defined with sufficient specificity and clarity to provide fair notice to persons who create and distribute sexually oriented materials, to prevent substantial erosion of protected speech as a byproduct of the attempt to suppress unprotected speech, and to avoid very costly institutional harms. Given these inevitable side effects of state efforts to suppress what is assumed to be *unprotected* speech, we must scrutinize with care the state interest that is asserted to justify the suppression. For in the absence of some very substantial interest in suppressing such speech, we can hardly condone the ill effects that seem to flow inevitably from the effort. . . .

In short, while I cannot say that the interests of the State—apart from the question of juveniles and unconsenting adults—are trivial or nonexistent, I am compelled to conclude that these interests cannot justify the substantial damage to constitutional rights and to this Nation's judicial machinery that inevitably results from state efforts to bar the distribution even of unprotected material to consenting adults. . . . I would hold, therefore, that at least in the absence of distribution to juveniles or obtrusive exposure to unconsenting adults, the First and Fourteenth Amendments prohibit the State and Federal Governments from attempting wholly to suppress sexually oriented materials on the basis of their allegedly "obscene" contents.

Brennan's opinion, joined by Justices Marshall and Stewart, is remarkable for three reasons. First, after almost two decades of leading the Court in attempts to define obscenity, the author of *Roth* decided finally that it could not be done. Second, the three liberals argued that efforts to regulate "obscene" material inevitably led to unacceptable restrictions on protected expression. Third, Brennan and the others concluded that, except for protecting juveniles and unconsenting adults, state and federal authorities should be banned from regulating sexually oriented expression altogether.

While it would be difficult to imagine two more different positions than those taken by the majority and the dissenters in these obscenity cases, they are remarkably alike in one respect: Both sides wanted to extricate the Court from the obscenity business. Brennan and the other dissenters advocated an almost total end to government regulation of obscenity. The *Miller* majority wanted to put an end to federal obscenity cases by shifting authority to the states.

Since 1973 the Miller test has remained the authoritative definition of obscenity. The justices generally have refused to accept cases that have asked them to reconsider the definition of obscenity. The *Miller* majority successfully removed the Court from the obscenity area and allowed the state and local governments greater leeway in dealing with it.

The Miller test, like the Roth test before it, was designed to distinguish between protected and unprotected expression that is read or viewed by adults. The Court has always acknowledged that government may make more restrictive laws with respect to materials that are presented to juveniles. Similarly, government can regulate the production and distribution of materials that depict sexual activity by children, even if those materials do not meet the Miller test definition of obscenity. In *New York v. Ferber* (1982), for example, the Court reaffirmed government's authority to prohibit child pornography. The decision was unanimous, indicating that liberals and conservatives alike recognize the legitimate interest of the state in prohibiting sexual exploitation and abuse of children.

Libel

On any given day in the United States, people can buy a newspaper or turn on the television and find information on the activities of public officials, well-known figures, and even private citizens who, for various reasons, have made news. Sometimes the reports imply criticism, such as a newspaper article about a public official accused of wrongdoing. In other cases, the reports are blatantly false. To see this phenomenon we need go no farther than a supermarket checkout and read the tabloid headlines about the doings of celebrities.

We know from our readings on prior restraint that government generally cannot censor material before it is published. But once a story containing falsehoods is published or broadcast, do the people who have been damaged by it have any recourse? Under U.S. law they do: They can bring a libel action against the offender. That is, if individuals believe that falsehoods contained in an article resulted in monetary losses or the defamation of their character, they can attempt to have a court hold the media responsible for their actions. The reason is that, like obscenity, libelous statements remain outside the reach of the First Amendment.

The lack of First Amendment protection does not mean that libel is a simple area of law. The Supreme Court has had a difficult time developing standards for the application of libel. Why? One reason is that before 1964 libel was an undeveloped area of law. In chapter 13, we discussed the Sedition Act of 1798, which the Federalist Congress enacted to outlaw seditious libel—criticism of the government and of government officials. Under this act, the government could bring criminal charges against those who made "false, scandalous, and malicious" statements that brought the United States or its representatives into "contempt or disrepute." Because President Thomas Jefferson later pardoned all those who had been convicted under it, the Supreme Court never had an opportunity to rule on the law's constitutionality. For most of our nation's history, therefore, it was unclear whether seditious libel was protected or unprotected speech. Indeed, some scholars argued that the purpose of the First Amendment was to "abolish seditious libel," whereas others contended the contrary.[11]

What is clear is that until 1964 states were free to determine their own standards for the more typical version of libel: civil actions brought by individuals against other individuals—for example, those running a newspaper. Some variation existed among state laws, but most allowed defamed individuals to seek two kinds of damages: compensatory, which provide money for actual financial loss (if, for example, an individual loses a job because of the story), and punitive, which punish the offender. To collect compensatory damages, all the plaintiff generally had to demonstrate was that the story was false—truth is always a defense against claims of libel—and damaging.

These criteria might sound like simple standards for plaintiffs to meet. In fact, the simplicity further com-

pounded the Court's problems. Many newspapers, television stations, and other media argued that the traditional standard had a chilling effect on their First Amendment guarantee of a free press. They feared printing anything critical of government or public officials, in particular, because if the story contained even the smallest factual error, they could face a costly lawsuit. Therefore, they felt constrained in their reporting of news.

Until 1964 the Supreme Court ignored this complaint and allowed states to formulate their own libel laws. In the seminal case of *New York Times v. Sullivan*, however, the Court radically departed from this position. What standard did the Court articulate? How did it alter existing libel law?

New York Times v. Sullivan

376 U.S. 254 (1964)
http://laws.findlaw.com/US/376/254.html
Oral arguments may be found at: http://www.oyez.org
Vote: 9 (Black, Brennan, Clark, Douglas, Goldberg, Harlan, Stewart, Warren, White)
        0

Opinion of the Court: Brennan
Concurring opinions: Black, Goldberg

The March 29, 1960, edition of the *New York Times* ran an advertisement to publicize the struggle for civil rights and to raise money for the cause. L. B. Sullivan, an elected commissioner of the City of Montgomery, Alabama, took offense at the ad. It did not mention his name, but it gave an account of a racial incident that had occurred in the city. The ad suggested that the police, of whom Sullivan was in charge, participated in some wrongdoing.

Sullivan brought a libel action against the paper, alleging that the ad contained falsehoods—which, in fact, it did. The ad claimed that demonstrating students sang "My Country, 'Tis of Thee," when they actually sang the "Star-Spangled Banner," and so forth. In his charge to the jury, the judge said that the ad was "libelous per se," meaning that because it contained lies, it was unprotected speech, and that if the jury found that the state-

---

11. See Zechariah Chafee Jr., *Free Speech in the United States* (Cambridge: Harvard University Press, 1941); and Leonard W. Levy, *Legacy of Suppression* (Cambridge: Harvard University Press, 1960). See also Levy's revised and enlarged edition of *Emergence of a Free Press* (New York: Oxford University Press, 1985). See also Pritchett, *Constitutional Civil Liberties*, for an interesting review of these debates.

ments were made "of and concerning" Sullivan, it could hold the *Times* liable. Taking these words to heart, the jury awarded Sullivan $500,000 in damages.

The Supreme Court of Alabama affirmed this judgment. In doing so, it specified that words are libelous per se when they "tend to injure a person labeled by them in his reputation, profession, trade or business, or charge him with an indictable offense, or tend to bring the individual into public contempt." This definition was fairly typical. The *New York Times* challenged the decision, arguing that the libel standard "presumes malice and falsity. . . . Such a rule of liability works an abridgment of the free press." The newspaper's attorneys added, "It is implicit in this Court's decisions that speech which is critical of governmental action may not be repressed upon the ground that it diminishes the reputation of those officers whose conduct it deplores."

MR. JUSTICE BRENNAN delivered the opinion of the Court.

We are required in this case to determine for the first time the extent to which the constitutional protections for speech and press limit a State's power to award damages in a libel action brought by a public official against critics of his official conduct. . . .

Because of the importance of the constitutional issues involved, we granted the separate petitions for certiorari of the individual petitioners and of the *Times*. We reverse the judgment. We hold that the rule of law applied by the Alabama courts is constitutionally deficient for failure to provide the safeguards for freedom of speech and of the press that are required by the First and Fourteenth Amendments in a libel action brought by a public official against critics of his official conduct. We further hold that under the proper safeguards the evidence presented in this case is constitutionally insufficient to support the judgment for respondent.

We may dispose at the outset of [t]he . . . contention . . . that the constitutional guarantees of freedom of speech and of the press are inapplicable here, at least so far as the *Times* is concerned, because the allegedly libelous statements were published as part of a paid, "commercial" advertisement. . . .

The publication here was not a "commercial" advertisement in the sense in which the word was used in [*Valentine*

v.] *Chrestensen* [1942]. It communicated information, expressed opinion, recited grievances, protested claimed abuses, and sought financial support on behalf of a movement whose existence and objectives are matters of the highest public interest and concern. That the *Times* was paid for publishing the advertisement is as immaterial in this connection as is the fact that newspapers and books are sold. Any other conclusion would discourage newspapers from carrying "editorial advertisements" of this type, and so might shut off an important outlet for the promulgation of information and ideas by persons who do not themselves have access to publishing facilities—who wish to exercise their freedom of speech even though they are not members of the press. The effect would be to shackle the First Amendment in its attempt to secure "the widest possible dissemination of information from diverse and antagonistic sources." To avoid placing such a handicap upon the freedoms of expression, we hold that if the allegedly libelous statements would otherwise be constitutionally protected from the present judgment, they do not forfeit that protection because they were published in the form of a paid advertisement.

Under Alabama law as applied in this case, a publication is "libelous per se" if the words "tend to injure a person . . . in his reputation" or to "bring [him] into public contempt"; the trial court stated that the standard was met if the words are such as to "injure him in his public office, or impute misconduct to him in his office, or want of official integrity, or want of fidelity to a public trust. . . ." The jury must find that the words were published "of and concerning" the plaintiff, but where the plaintiff is a public official his place in the governmental hierarchy is sufficient evidence to support a finding that his reputation has been affected by statements that reflect upon the agency of which he is in charge. Once "libel per se" has been established, the defendant has no defense as to stated facts unless he can persuade the jury that they were true in all their particulars. His privilege of "fair comment" for expressions of opinion depends on the truth of the facts upon which the comment is based. Unless he can discharge the burden of proving truth, general damages are presumed, and may be awarded without proof of pecuniary injury. A showing of actual malice is apparently a prerequisite to recovery of punitive damages, and the defendant may in any event forestall a punitive award by a retraction meeting the statutory requirements. Good motives and belief in truth do not negate an inference of malice, but are

> **"** *The growing movement of peaceful mass demonstrations by Negroes is something new in the South, something understandable. . . . Let Congress heed their rising voices, for they will be heard.* **"**
>
> —New York Times editorial
> Saturday, March 19, 1960

Heed Their Rising Voices

As the whole world knows by now, thousands of Southern Negro students are engaged in widespread non-violent demonstrations in positive affirmation of the right to live in human dignity as guaranteed by the U. S. Constitution and the Bill of Rights. In their efforts to uphold these guarantees, they are being met by an unprecedented wave of terror by those who would deny and negate that document which the whole world looks upon as setting the pattern for modern freedom…

In Orangeburg, South Carolina, when 400 students peacefully sought to buy doughnuts and coffee at lunch counters in the business district, they were forcibly ejected, tear-gassed, soaked to the skin in freezing weather with fire hoses, arrested en masse and herded into an open barbed-wire stockade to stand for hours in the bitter cold.

In Montgomery, Alabama, after students sang "My Country, 'Tis of Thee" on the State Capitol steps, their leaders were expelled from school, and truckloads of police armed with shotguns and tear-gas ringed the Alabama State College Campus. When the entire student body protested to state authorities by refusing to re-register, their dining hall was padlocked in an attempt to starve them into submission.

In Tallahassee, Atlanta, Nashville, Savannah, Greensboro, Memphis, Richmond, Charlotte, and a host of other cities in the South, young American teen-agers, in face of the entire weight of official state apparatus and police power, have boldly stepped forth as pro-tagonists of democracy. Their courage and amazing restraint have inspired millions and given a new dignity to the cause of freedom.

Small wonder that the Southern violators of the Constitution fear this new, non-violent brand of freedom fighter… even as they fear the upswelling right-to-vote movement. Small wonder that they are determined to destroy the one man who, more than any other, symbolizes the new spirit now sweeping the South—the Rev. Dr. Martin Luther King, Jr., world-famous leader of the Montgomery Bus Protest. For it is his doctrine of non-violence which has inspired and guided the students in their widening wave of sit-ins; and it is this same Dr. King who founded and is president of the Southern Christian Leadership Conference—the organization which is spearheading the surging right-to-vote movement. Under Dr. King's direction the Leadership Conference conducts Student Workshops and Seminars in the philosophy and techniques of non-violent resistance.

Again and again the Southern violators have answered Dr. King's peaceful protests with intimidation and violence. They have bombed his home almost killing his wife and child. They have assaulted his person. They have arrested him seven times—for "speeding," "loitering" and similar "offenses." And now they have charged him with "perjury"—a *felony* under which they could imprison him for *ten years.* Obviously, their real purpose is to remove him physically as the leader to whom the students and millions of others—look for guidance and support, and thereby to intimidate *all* leaders who may rise in the South. Their strategy is to behead this affirmative movement, and thus to demoralize Negro Americans and weaken their will to struggle. The defense of Martin Luther King, spiritual leader of the student sit-in movement, clearly, therefore, is an integral part of the total struggle for freedom in the South.

Decent-minded Americans cannot help but applaud the creative daring of the students and the quiet heroism of thousands of others. But this is one of those moments in the stormy history of Freedom when men and women of good will must do more than applaud the rising-to-glory of others. The America whose good name hangs in the balance before a watchful world, the America whose heritage of Liberty these Southern Upholders of the Constitution are defending, is *our* America as well as theirs…

We must heed their rising voices—yes—but we must add our own.

We must extend ourselves above and beyond moral support and render the material help so urgently needed by those who are taking the risks, facing jail, and <u>even death</u> in a glorious re-affirmation of our Constitution and its Bill of Rights.

We urge you to join hands with our fellow Americans in the South by supporting, with your dollars, this combined appeal for all three needs—the defense of Martin Luther King—the support of the embattled students—and the struggle for the right-to-vote.

Your Help Is Urgently Needed . . . NOW!!

Stella Adler	Dr. Alan Knight Chalmers	Anthony Franciosa	John Killens	L. Joseph Overton	Maureen Stapleton
Raymond Pace Alexander	Richard Coe	Lorraine Hansbury	Eartha Kitt	Clarence Pickett	Frank Silvera
Harry Van Arsdale	Nat King Cole	Rev. Donald Harrington	Rabbi Edward Klein	Shad Polier	Hope Stevens
Harry Belafonte	Cheryl Crawford	Nat Hentoff	Hope Lange	Sidney Poitier	George Tabor
Julie Belafonte	Dorothy Dandridge	James Hicks	John Lewis	A. Philip Randolph	Rev. Gardner C.
Dr. Algernon Black	Ossie Davis	Mary Hinkson	Viveca Lindfors	John Raitt	Taylor
Marc Blitzstein	Sammy Davis, Jr.	Van Heflin	Carl Murphy	Elmer Rice	Norman Thomas
William Branch	Ruby Dee	Langston Hughes	Don Murray	Jackie Robinson	Kenneth Tynan
Marlon Brando	Dr. Philip Elliott	Morris Iushewitz	John Murray	Mrs. Eleanor Roosevelt	Charles White
Mrs. Ralph Bunche	Dr. Harry Emerson	Mahalia Jackson	A. J. Muste	Bayard Rustin	Shelley Winters
Diahann Carroll	Fosdick	Mordecai Johnson	Frederick O'Neal	Robert Ryan	Max Youngstein

We in the south who are struggling daily for dignity and freedom warmly endorse this appeal

Rev. Ralph D. Abernathy *(Montgomery, Ala.)*	Rev. Matthew D. McCollom *(Orangeburg, S.C.)*	Rev. Walter L. Hamilton *(Norfolk, Va.)*	Rev. A. L. Davis *(New Orleans, La.)*
Rev. Fred L. Shuttlesworth *(Birmingham, Ala.)*	Rev. William Holmes Borders *(Atlanta, Ga.)*	I. S. Levy *(Columbia, S.C.)*	Mrs. Katie E. Whickham *(New Orleans, La.)*
Rev. Kelley Miller Smith *(Nashville, Tenn.)*		Rev. Martin Luther King, Sr. *(Atlanta, Ga.)*	Rev. W. H. Hall *(Hattiesburg, Miss.)*
Rev. W. A. Dennis *(Chattanooga, Tenn.)*	Rev. Douglas Moore *(Durham, N.C.)*	Rev. Henry C. Bunton *(Memphis, Tenn.)*	Rev. J. E. Lowery *(Mobile, Ala.)*
Rev. C. K. Steele *(Tallahassee, Fla.)*	Rev. Wyatt Tee Walker *(Petersburg, Va.)*	Rev. S.S. Seay, Sr. *(Montgomery, Ala.)*	Rev. T. J. Jemison *(Baton Rouge, La.)*
		Rev. Samuel W. Williams *(Atlanta, Ga.)*	

COMMITTEE TO DEFEND MARTIN LUTHER KING AND THE STRUGGLE FOR FREEDOM IN THE SOUTH

312 West 125th Street, New York 27, N.Y. UNiversity 6-1700

Chairmen: A. Philip Randolph, Dr. Gardner C. Taylor; *Chairmen of Cultural Division:* Harry Belafonte, Sidney Poitier; *Treasurer:* Nat King Cole; *Executive Director:* Bayard Rustin; *Chairmen of Church Division:* Father George B. Ford, Rev. Harry Emerson Fosdick, Rev. Thomas Kilgore, Jr., Rabbi Edward E. Klein; *Chairman of Labor Division:* Morris Iushewitz.

Please mail this coupon TODAY!

Committee To Defend Martin Luther King
and
The Struggle For Freedom in The South

312 West 125th Street, New York 27, N.Y.
UNiversity 6-1700

I am enclosing my contribution of $_____ for the work of the Committee.

Name _____

Address _____

City_____ Zone_____ State_____

☐ I want to help   ☐ Please send further information

Please make checks payable to:
Committee to Defend Martin Luther King

relevant only in mitigation of punitive damages if the jury chooses to accord them weight.

The question before us is whether this rule of liability, as applied to an action brought by a public official against critics of his official conduct, abridges the freedom of speech and of the press that is guaranteed by the First and Fourteenth Amendments.

Respondent relies heavily, as did the Alabama courts, on statements of this Court to the effect that the Constitution does not protect libelous publications. Those statements do not foreclose our inquiry here. None of the cases sustained the use of libel laws to impose sanctions upon expression critical of the official conduct of public officials. . . . In deciding the question now, we are compelled by neither precedent nor policy to give any more weight to the epithet "libel" than we have to other "mere labels" of state law. Like insurrection, contempt, advocacy of unlawful acts, breach of the peace, obscenity, solicitation of legal business, and the various other formulae for the repression of expression that have been challenged in this Court, libel can claim no talismanic immunity from constitutional limitations. It must be measured by standards that satisfy the First Amendment. . . .

. . . [W]e consider this case against the background of a profound national commitment to the principle that debate on public issues should be uninhibited, robust, and wide-open, and that it may well include vehement, caustic, and sometimes unpleasantly sharp attacks on government and public officials. The present advertisement, as an expression of grievance and protest on one of the major public issues of our time, would seem clearly to qualify for the constitutional protection. The question is whether it forfeits that protection by the falsity of some of its factual statements and by its alleged defamation of respondent.

Authoritative interpretations of the First Amendment guarantees have consistently refused to recognize an exception for any test of truth—whether administered by judges, juries, or administrative officials—and especially one that puts the burden of proving truth on the speaker. The constitutional protection does not turn upon "the truth, popularity, or social utility of the ideas and beliefs which are offered." . . . That erroneous statement is inevitable in free debate, and that it must be protected if the freedoms of expression are to have the "breathing space" that they "need . . . to survive," was . . . recognized by the Court of Appeals for the District of Columbia Circuit in *Sweeney v. Patterson*. . . .

Injury to official reputation error affords no more warrant for repressing speech that would otherwise be free than does factual error. Where judicial officers are involved, this Court has held that concern for the dignity and reputation of the courts does not justify the punishment as criminal contempt of criticism of the judge or his decision. This is true even though the utterance contains "half-truths" and "misinformation." Such repression can be justified, if at all, only by a clear and present danger of the obstruction of justice. If judges are to be treated as "men of fortitude, able to thrive in a hardy climate," surely the same must be true of other government officials, such as elected city commissioners. Criticism of their official conduct does not lose its constitutional protection merely because it is effective criticism and hence diminishes their official reputations.

If neither factual error nor defamatory content suffices to remove the constitutional shield from criticism of official conduct, the combination of the two elements is no less inadequate. This is the lesson to be drawn from the great controversy over the Sedition Act of 1798, which first crystallized a national awareness of the central meaning of the First Amendment. That statute made it a crime, punishable by a $5,000 fine and five years in prison, "if any person shall write, print, utter or publish . . . any false, scandalous and malicious writing or writings against the government of the United States, or either House of the Congress . . . or the President . . . , with intent to defame . . . or to bring them, or either of them, into contempt or disrepute; or to excite against them, or either or any of them, the hatred of the good people of the United States." . . .

Although the Sedition Act was never tested in this Court, the attack upon its validity has carried the day in the court of history. Fines levied in its prosecution were repaid by Act of Congress on the ground that it was unconstitutional. Calhoun, reporting to the Senate on February 4, 1836, assumed that its invalidity was a matter "which no one now doubts." Jefferson, as President, pardoned those who had been convicted and sentenced under the Act and remitted their fines, stating: "I discharged every person under punishment or prosecution under the sedition law, because I considered, and now consider, that law to be a nullity, as absolute and as palpable as if Congress had ordered us to fall down and worship a golden image." [This view reflects] a broad consensus that the Act, because of the restraint it imposed upon criticism of government and public officials, was inconsistent with the First Amendment.

There is no force in respondent's argument that the constitutional limitations implicit in the history of the Sedition Act apply only to Congress and not to the States. It is true that the First Amendment was originally addressed only to action by the Federal Government, and that Jefferson, for one, while denying the power of Congress "to controul the freedom of the press," recognized such a power in the States. But this distinction was eliminated with the adoption of the Fourteenth Amendment and the application to the States of the First Amendment's restrictions.

What a State may not constitutionally bring about by means of a criminal statute is likewise beyond the reach of its civil law of libel. The fear of damage awards under a rule such as that invoked by the Alabama courts here may be markedly more inhibiting than the fear of prosecution under a criminal statute. Alabama, for example, has a criminal libel law which subjects to prosecution "any person who speaks, writes, or prints of and concerning another any accusation falsely and maliciously importing the commission by such person of a felony, or any other indictable offense involving moral turpitude," and which allows as punishment upon conviction a fine not exceeding $500 and a prison sentence of six months. Presumably a person charged with violation of this statute enjoys ordinary criminal-law safeguards such as the requirements of an indictment and of proof beyond a reasonable doubt. These safeguards are not available to the defendant in a civil action. The judgment awarded in this case—without the need for any proof of actual pecuniary loss—was one thousand times greater than the maximum fine provided by the Alabama criminal statute, and one hundred times greater than that provided by the Sedition Act. And since there is no double-jeopardy limitation applicable to civil lawsuits, this is not the only judgment that may be awarded against petitioners for the same publication. Whether or not a newspaper can survive a succession of such judgments, the pall of fear and timidity imposed upon those who would give voice to public criticism is an atmosphere in which the First Amendment freedoms cannot survive. Plainly the Alabama law of civil libel is "a form of regulation that creates hazards to protected freedoms markedly greater than those that attend reliance upon the criminal law."

The state rule of law is not saved by its allowance of the defense of truth. A defense for erroneous statements honestly made is no less essential here than was the requirement of proof of guilty knowledge which we held indispensable to a valid conviction of a bookseller for possessing obscene writings for sale.... A rule compelling the critic of official conduct to guarantee the truth of all his factual assertions—and to do so on pain of libel judgments virtually unlimited in amount—leads to a comparable "self-censorship." Allowance of the defense of truth, with the burden of proving it on the defendant, does not mean that only false speech will be deterred. Even courts accepting this defense as an adequate safeguard have recognized the difficulties of adducing legal proofs that the alleged libel was true in all its factual particulars. Under such a rule, would-be critics of official conduct may be deterred from voicing their criticism, even though it is believed to be true and even though it is in fact true, because of doubt whether it can be proved in court or fear of the expense of having to do so. They tend to make only statements which "steer far wider of the unlawful zone." The rule thus dampens the vigor and limits the variety of public debate. It is inconsistent with the First and Fourteenth Amendments.

The constitutional guarantees require, we think, a federal rule that prohibits a public official from recovering damages for a defamatory falsehood relating to his official conduct unless he proves that the statement was made with "actual malice"—that is, with knowledge that it was false or with reckless disregard of whether it was false or not....

... [A] privilege for criticism of official conduct is appropriately analogous to the protection accorded a public official when *he* is sued for libel by a private citizen.... The reason for the official privilege is said to be that the threat of damage suits would otherwise "inhibit the fearless, vigorous, and effective administration of policies of government" and "dampen the ardor of all but the most resolute, or the most irresponsible, in the unflinching discharge of their duties." Analogous considerations support the privilege for the citizen-critic of government. It is as much his duty to criticize as it is the official's duty to administer. As Madison said, "the censorial power is in the people over the Government, and not in the Government over the people." It would give public servants an unjustified preference over the public they serve, if critics of official conduct did not have a fair equivalent of the immunity granted to the officials themselves.

We conclude that such a privilege is required by the First and Fourteenth Amendments.

We hold today that the Constitution delimits a State's power to award damages for libel in actions brought by public officials against critics of their official conduct. Since this is such an action, the rule requiring proof of actual malice is applicable. While Alabama law apparently requires proof of actual malice for an award of punitive damages, where general damages are concerned malice is "presumed." Such a presumption is inconsistent with the federal rule. . . . Since the trial judge did not instruct the jury to differentiate between general and punitive damages, it may be that the verdict was wholly an award of one or the other. But it is impossible to know, in view of the general verdict returned. Because of this uncertainty, the judgment must be reversed and the case remanded.

Since respondent may seek a new trial, we deem that considerations of effective judicial administration require us to review the evidence in the present record to determine whether it could constitutionally support a judgment for respondent. This Court's duty is not limited to the elaboration of constitutional principles; we must also in proper cases review the evidence to make certain that those principles have been constitutionally applied. This is such a case, particularly since the question is one of alleged trespass across "the line between speech unconditionally guaranteed and speech which may legitimately be regulated." In cases where that line must be drawn, the rule is that we "examine for ourselves the statements in issue and the circumstances under which they were made to see . . . whether they are of a character which the principles of the First Amendment, as adopted by the Due Process Clause of the Fourteenth Amendment, protect." We must "make an independent examination of the whole record," so as to assure ourselves that the judgment does not constitute a forbidden intrusion on the field of free expression.

Applying these standards, we consider that the proof presented to show actual malice lacks the convincing clarity which the constitutional standard demands, and hence that it would not constitutionally sustain the judgment for respondent under the proper rule of law. The case of the individual petitioners requires little discussion. Even assuming that they could constitutionally be found to have authorized the use of their names on the advertisement, there was no evidence whatever that they were aware of any erroneous statements or were in any way reckless in that regard. The judgment against them is thus without constitutional support.

As to the *Times,* we similarly conclude that the facts do not support a finding of actual malice. The statement by the *Times'* Secretary that . . . he thought the advertisement was "substantially correct," affords no constitutional warrant for the Alabama Supreme Court's conclusion that it was a "cavalier ignoring of the falsity of the advertisement from which, the jury could not have but been impressed with the bad faith of the *Times,* and its maliciousness inferable therefrom." The statement does not indicate malice at the time of the publication; even if the advertisement was not "substantially correct"—although respondent's own proofs tend to show that it was—that opinion was at least a reasonable one, and there was no evidence to impeach the witness' good faith in holding it. The *Times'* failure to retract upon respondent's demand, although it later retracted upon the demand of Governor Patterson, is likewise not adequate evidence of malice for constitutional purposes. . . .

Finally, there is evidence that the *Times* published the advertisement without checking its accuracy against the news stories in the *Times'* own files. The mere presence of the stories in the files does not, of course, establish that the *Times* "knew" the advertisement was false, since the state of mind required for actual malice would have to be brought home to the persons in the *Times'* organization having responsibility for the publication of the advertisement. With respect to the failure of those persons to make the check, the record shows that they relied upon their knowledge of the good reputation of many of those whose names were listed as sponsors of the advertisement, and upon the letter from A. Philip Randolph, known to them as a responsible individual, certifying that the use of the names was authorized. There was testimony that the persons handling the advertisement saw nothing in it that would render it unacceptable under the *Times'* policy of rejecting advertisements containing "attacks of a personal character"; their failure to reject it on this ground was not unreasonable. We think the evidence against the *Times* supports at most a finding of negligence in failing to discover the misstatements, and is constitutionally insufficient to show the recklessness that is required for a finding of actual malice.

We also think the evidence was constitutionally defective in another respect: it was incapable of supporting the jury's finding that the allegedly libelous statements were made "of and concerning" respondent. Respondent relies on the words of the advertisement and the testimony of six witnesses to establish a connection between it and himself. . . . There was no reference to respondent in the advertisement, either by name or official position. A number of the allegedly libelous statements—the charges that the dining hall was padlocked and that Dr. King's home was bombed, his person assaulted, and a perjury prosecution instituted against him—did not even concern the police; despite the ingenuity of the arguments which would attach this significance to the word "They," it is plain that these statements could not reasonably be read as accusing respondent of personal involvement in the acts in question. The statements upon which respondent principally relies as referring to him are the two allegations that did concern the police or police functions: that "truckloads of police . . . ringed the Alabama State College Campus" after the demonstration on the State Capitol steps, and that Dr. King had been "arrested . . . seven times." These statements were false only in that the police had been "deployed near" the campus but had not actually "ringed" it and had not gone there in connection with the State Capitol demonstration, and in that Dr. King had been arrested only four times. The ruling that these discrepancies between what was true and what was asserted were sufficient to injure respondent's reputation may itself raise constitutional problems, but we need not consider them here. Although the statements may be taken as referring to the police, they did not on their face make even an oblique reference to respondent as an individual. . . .

The judgment of the Supreme Court of Alabama is reversed and the case is remanded to that court for further proceedings not inconsistent with this opinion.

Reversed and remanded.

MR. JUSTICE BLACK, with whom MR. JUSTICE DOUGLAS joins, concurring.

I concur in reversing this half-million-dollar judgment against the New York Times Company and the four individual defendants. In reversing the Court holds that "the Constitution delimits a State's power to award damages for libel in actions brought by public officials against critics of their official conduct." I base my vote to reverse on the belief that the First and Fourteenth Amendments not merely "delimit" a State's power to award damages to "public officials against critics of their official conduct" but completely prohibit a State from exercising such a power. The Court goes on to hold that a State can subject such critics to damages if "actual malice" can be proved against them. "Malice," even as defined by the Court, is an elusive, abstract concept, hard to prove and hard to disprove. The requirement that malice be proved provides at best an evanescent protection for the right critically to discuss public affairs and certainly does not measure up to the sturdy safeguard embodied in the First Amendment. Unlike the Court, therefore, I vote to reverse exclusively on the ground that the *Times* and the individual defendants had an absolute, unconditional constitutional right to publish in the *Times* advertisement their criticisms of the Montgomery agencies and officials.

Many consider Brennan's opinion a tour de force on the subject of libel. By holding the Sedition Act of 1798 unconstitutional, however belatedly, Brennan said that the First Amendment protects seditious libel, that the government cannot criminally punish individuals who speak out, in a true or false manner, against it. But more important was the part of the opinion that dealt with civil actions. The concurring justices, Black and Douglas, argued that the press had an absolute and unconditional right to criticize government officials, that states could not permit civil actions in such cases. Brennan's opinion did not go that far, but it radically altered the standards that *public officials* acting in a *public capacity* had to meet before they could prove libel and receive damages. Calling previous rules of falsehood and defamation "constitutionally deficient," Brennan asserted that if plaintiffs were public officials, they had to demonstrate that the statement was false, damaging, *and* "made with 'actual malice'—that is, with knowledge that it was false or with reckless disregard of whether it was false or not." In his view, such an exacting standard—now called the New York Times test—was necessary because of a "profound national commitment to the principle that debate on public issues should be uninhibited, robust, and wide-open."

L. B. Sullivan, second from right, poses with his attorneys after winning his libel suit against the *New York Times*. The Supreme Court overturned the decision in 1964. Justice Brennan's opinion stated that public officials are held to a higher standard than private citizens when proving libel.

Brennan's opinion significantly altered the course of libel law, making it more difficult for public officials to bring actions against the media. But the decision had some gaps. First, who constitutes a public official? In a footnote Brennan wrote, "We have no occasion here to determine how far down into lower ranks of government employees the 'public official' designation would extend." Obviously, such an occasion would present itself shortly, and the Court would have to draw some distinctions. How it did so would have significant ramifications because, under the New York Times test, only public officials had to prove actual malice; other plaintiffs were bound only to the traditional standards that the statements were false and damaging. Second, how could a public official prove actual malice? What did that term encompass?

In 1967 the Supreme Court decided two cases, ***Curtis Publishing Company v. Butts*** and ***Associated Press v. Walker***, in hopes of clarifying its ruling in *New York Times*. At issue in *Curtis* was an article entitled "The Story of a College Football Fix," published by the *Saturday Evening Post*. The author asserted that Wally Butts, the athletic director of the University of Georgia's sports program, had given Paul Bryant, the football coach at the University of

Alabama, "the plays, defensive patterns, and all the significant secrets Georgia's football team possessed." He did so, according to the article, to fix a 1962 game between the two schools. The author claimed he had obtained this information from an Atlanta insurance salesman, who accidentally overheard the conversation between Butts and Bryant. Butts initiated a libel suit against the publishing company, arguing that the article was false and damaging. Further, although the Court had yet to hand down the *New York Times* decision, Butts's suit also alleged that actual malice had occurred because the *Saturday Evening Post* "had departed greatly from the standards of good investigation and reporting." The magazine's attorneys "were aware of the progress" of the *New York Times* case, but they offered only a defense of truth. A jury awarded Butts $3,060,000, which was later reduced by an appeals court. The *Post* asked for a new trial on *New York Times* grounds—that Butts was a public figure and should have to prove malice. The judge refused, asserting that Butts was not a public official and, even if he were, the magazine had demonstrated a "reckless disregard for the truth."

Associated Press v. Walker concerned a 1962 AP story, an eyewitness account of the riots at the University of

Mississippi over the government-ordered admission of James Meredith, a black student. According to the story, retired army general Edwin Walker "took command of the violent crowd and . . . led a charge against federal marshals," who were in Mississippi to oversee the desegregation process. It also alleged that Walker gave the segregationists "lessons" on the use of tear gas. Walker sued the Associated Press for $2 million in compensatory and punitive damages, arguing that the article was false and damaging. The jury awarded $500,000 in compensation and $300,000 in punishment, but the judge set aside the latter on the ground that Walker, while not a public official, was a public figure—his views on integration were well known and, as such, he had to prove actual malice under the New York Times standard.

Writing for the Court, Justice Harlan ruled in favor of Butts's claim and against Walker's. In reaching those conclusions, Harlan used the differences between the two cases to clarify *New York Times.* On the one hand, he made it somewhat less burdensome for public officials to demonstrate malice: If the media engaged in "highly unreasonable conduct constituting an extreme departure from the standards of investigation and reporting," they could be held liable for their actions. On the other, the Court expanded the coverage of the New York Times test to include public figures. That is, even though Walker and Butts were not officials of the government, they would have to meet the New York Times test to win their suits because they were individuals in the public eye. Butts met this burden—he demonstrated that the magazine had abandoned professional standards and exhibited a reckless disregard for the truth. Walker failed to prove such press improprieties.

The result of these cases has been special protection given to the press from libel suits filed by public officials or public figures. Before such persons can win a libel case they must show that the press published or broadcast falsehoods and that such publication was done with actual malice. This allows the press greater latitude in covering public persons about whom the people have a legitimate interest.

Private individuals remained covered by traditional libel rules. A person who does not qualify as a public offi-

cial or public figure must prove only that the published statements were false. A showing of malice is not required. Drawing a line between public and private persons is not easy. The Court itself has had a difficult time doing so. In two cases, however, the justices helped draw the line between the two categories. In *Gertz v. Welch* (1974) the justices held that an attorney in private practice was not a public figure even though he represented a plaintiff in a controversial wrongful death suit. And in *Time, Inc. v. Firestone* (1976) the Court ruled that a prominent socialite involved in a scandalous divorce suit retained her status as a private person and had not become a public figure under the New York Times test approach to libel.

In essence, the Court has taken a middle position. It has given the media a significant shield against libel actions when they are carrying out their historic mission of reporting news about public persons. Yet the Court has not imposed any additional burden on private individuals who are damaged by published falsehoods and turn to the judicial system for redress.

NEW METHODS OF EXPRESSION: THE INTERNET

The development of the Internet and other forms of electronic expression has created an entirely new method of communication, combining elements of both speech and press. Initiated in 1969 as a military project, the Internet has grown into a vast international network of interconnected computers. Its effect on the expansion of opportunities for expression ranks with the development of the printing press and radio/television. Unlike traditional speech, with its audience limited by the power of the microphone, electronic expression can be communicated to the entire world with a few keystrokes. Internet communication is instantaneous and interactive. Unlike radio, the electronic media can carry text and graphics, as well as sound. Unlike a television station, the Internet does not reside in a single location but is a network of communicators not confined by state or national boundaries. Unlike the broadcast media, which are restricted by the number of frequencies available, the number of people who can communicate via the Internet is potentially infinite. And unlike many other forms of expression, it does not require large expenditures to participate in electronic speech. It can facilitate a wide variety of expression: personal messages, political and social commentary, commercial transactions, advertising, information, and entertainment. These factors make electronic communication potentially the most effective and participatory method of expression yet devised. The Internet carries the promise of creating a truly robust, free marketplace of ideas.

Yet electronic expression also carries certain dangers. Readily available computers allow children access to materials that might be inappropriate for them. The potential for fraud and deception is perhaps even greater in electronic communication than in more traditional forms of speech and press. The ability to collect and catalogue masses of data allows for possible invasions of privacy. Open access to the Internet means that there is no supervising authority to ensure the veracity of posted messages. Harassment based on sex, race, ethnicity, or sexual orientation can easily occur in an electronic world. Groups with political or social messages repugnant to the majority have an equal voice with mainstream organizations in spite of small numbers and minimal funds.

There is little doubt that confronting the Internet will provide significant challenges to government regulators at all levels. Congress and the state legislatures have already passed many laws in an attempt to reduce electronic wrongdoing. Although designed to curb undesirable activity on the Internet, these laws may also restrict legitimate and protected expression. Regulations have been proposed, and in some cases passed, restricting the use of pseudonyms. If such laws were in effect in earlier times, they would have prohibited Samuel Clemens from making his stories available on the Internet. Even more disturbing to free speech advocates, these laws would have stopped James Madison, Alexander Hamilton, and John Jay from publishing *The Federalist Papers* electronically because their essays were written under the pen name Publius.

It should not be surprising that with the passage of each state or federal law restricting expression on the Internet has come an immediate legal challenge. Newly formed organizations devoted to keeping the Internet

free have joined with traditional civil liberties groups, such as the ACLU, to attack these regulations as violations of the First Amendment.

Initial lower court decisions have overwhelmingly supported freedom of expression claims against such laws, but how has the Supreme Court responded? Its first major ruling on the regulation of the Internet came in *Reno v. American Civil Liberties Union* (1997). The case involved a challenge to the Communications Decency Act of 1996.

Reno v. American Civil Liberties Union

521 U.S. 844 (1997)
http://laws.findlaw.com/US/521/844.html
Oral arguments may be found at: http://www.oyez.org
Vote: 7 (Breyer, Ginsburg, Kennedy, Scalia, Souter, Stevens, Thomas)
  2 (O'Connor, Rehnquist)
Opinion of the Court: Stevens
Opinion concurring in the judgment in part and dissenting in part: O'Connor

On February 8, 1996, immediately after President Bill Clinton signed the Communications Decency Act (CDA) into law, a coalition of groups and individuals, led by the ACLU, filed suit asking the federal district court to declare it unconstitutional. The CDA was part of a larger legislative package regulating the telecommunications industry. It was passed to control the access of children to sexually explicit material transmitted electronically, especially via the Internet. The ACLU lawsuit challenged two provisions of the act, the "indecent transmission" provision and the "patently offensive display" provision.

The "indecent transmission" section made it unlawful knowingly to transmit by any telecommunications device any obscene or indecent message to any recipient under eighteen years of age, or knowingly to permit any telecommunications facility to be used for sending such messages. The "patently offensive display" provision prohibited using any interactive computer service to send to a person under eighteen years of age or to display in a manner available to any person under eighteen material that describes sexual or excretory activities or organs in patently offensive terms as measured by contemporary community standards. It also barred any person from permitting any telecommunications facility under his or her control to be used for that purpose. Violations of the law were punishable by imprisonment of not more than two years. The law recognized as legitimate defenses that the accused person took "good faith, reasonable, effective and appropriate actions" to restrict access by minors to the prohibited communications, and that the accused individual restricted access to the covered material by requiring proof of age.

Those attacking the law charged that terms such as *indecent* and *patently offensive* were unconstitutionally vague. They also argued the law was not narrowly tailored to accomplish the goal of protecting minors; rather, it also unconstitutionally restricted adult access to sexually explicit communications.

A three-judge district court unanimously agreed that the law was unconstitutional. Attorney General Janet Reno, representing the United States, appealed to the Supreme Court.

JUSTICE STEVENS delivered the opinion of the Court.

At issue is the constitutionality of two statutory provisions enacted to protect minors from "indecent" and "patently offensive" communications on the Internet. Notwithstanding the legitimacy and importance of the congressional goal of protecting children from harmful materials, we agree with the three-judge District Court that the statute abridges "the freedom of speech" protected by the First Amendment. . . .

In arguing for reversal, the Government contends that the CDA is plainly constitutional under three of our prior decisions: (1) *Ginsberg v. New York* (1968); (2) *FCC v. Pacifica Foundation* (1978); and (3) *Renton v. Playtime Theatres, Inc.* (1986). A close look at these cases, however, raises—rather than relieves—doubts concerning the constitutionality of the CDA.

In *Ginsberg,* we upheld the constitutionality of a New York statute that prohibited selling to minors under 17 years of age material that was considered obscene as to them even if not obscene as to adults. . . . In four important respects, the statute upheld in *Ginsberg* was narrower than the CDA.

First, we noted in *Ginsberg* that "the prohibition against sales to minors does not bar parents who so desire from purchasing the magazines for their children." Under the CDA, by contrast, neither the parents' consent—nor even their participation—in the communication would avoid the application of the statute. Second, the New York statute applied only to commercial transactions, whereas the CDA contains no such limitation. Third, the New York statute cabined its definition of material that is harmful to minors with the requirement that it be "utterly without redeeming social importance for minors." The CDA fails to provide us with any definition of the term "indecent" . . . and, importantly, omits any requirement that the "patently offensive" material . . . lack serious literary, artistic, political, or scientific value. Fourth, the New York statute defined a minor as a person under the age of 17, whereas the CDA, in applying to all those under 18 years, includes an additional year of those nearest majority.

In *Pacifica,* we upheld a declaratory order of the Federal Communications Commission, holding that the broadcast of a recording of a 12-minute monologue entitled "Filthy Words" that had previously been delivered to a live audience "could have been the subject of administrative sanctions." The Commission had found that the repetitive use of certain words referring to excretory or sexual activities or organs "in an afternoon broadcast when children are in the audience was patently offensive" and concluded that the monologue was indecent "as broadcast." . . .

As with the New York statute at issue in *Ginsberg,* there are significant differences between the order upheld in *Pacifica* and the CDA. First, the order in *Pacifica,* issued by an agency that had been regulating radio stations for decades, targeted a specific broadcast that represented a rather dramatic departure from traditional program content in order to designate when—rather than whether—it would be permissible to air such a program in that particular medium. The CDA's broad categorical prohibitions are not limited to particular times and are not dependent on any evaluation by an agency familiar with the unique characteristics of the Internet. Second, unlike the CDA, the Commission's declaratory order was not punitive; we expressly refused to decide whether the indecent broadcast "would justify a criminal prosecution." Finally, the Commission's order applied to a medium which as a matter of history had "received the most limited First Amendment protection," in large part because warnings could not adequately protect the listener from unexpected program content. The Internet, however, has no comparable history. Moreover, the District Court found that the risk of encountering indecent material by accident is remote because a series of affirmative steps is required to access specific material.

In *Renton,* we upheld a zoning ordinance that kept adult movie theatres out of residential neighborhoods. The ordinance was aimed, not at the content of the films shown in the theaters, but rather at the "secondary effects"—such as crime and deteriorating property values—that these theaters fostered. . . . According to the Government, the CDA is constitutional because it constitutes a sort of "cyberzoning" on the Internet. But the CDA applies broadly to the entire universe of cyberspace. And the purpose of the CDA is to protect children from the primary effects of "indecent" and "patently offensive" speech, rather than any "secondary" effect of such speech. Thus, the CDA is a content-based blanket restriction on speech, and, as such, cannot be "properly analyzed as a form of time, place, and manner regulation."

These precedents, then, surely do not require us to uphold the CDA and are fully consistent with the application of the most stringent review of its provisions.

In *Southeastern Promotions, Ltd. v. Conrad* (1975), we observed that "[e]ach medium of expression . . . may present its own problems." Thus, some of our cases have recognized special justifications for regulation of the broadcast media that are not applicable to other speakers, see *Red Lion Broadcasting Co. v. FCC* (1969); *FCC v. Pacifica Foundation* (1978). In these cases, the Court relied on the history of extensive government regulation of the broadcast medium, the scarcity of available frequencies at its inception, and its "invasive" nature.

Those factors are not present in cyberspace. Neither before nor after the enactment of the CDA have the vast democratic fora of the Internet been subject to the type of government supervision and regulation that has attended the broadcast industry. Moreover, the Internet is not as "invasive" as radio or television. The District Court specifically found that "[c]ommunications over the Internet do not 'invade' an individual's home or appear on one's computer screen unbidden. Users seldom encounter content 'by accident.' " It also found that "[a]lmost all sexually explicit im-

ages are preceded by warnings as to the content," and cited testimony that " 'odds are slim' that a user would come across a sexually explicit sight by accident." . . .

Finally, unlike the conditions that prevailed when Congress first authorized regulation of the broadcast spectrum, the Internet can hardly be considered a "scarce" expressive commodity. It provides relatively unlimited, low-cost capacity for communication of all kinds. The Government estimates that "[a]s many as 40 million people use the Internet today, and that figure is expected to grow to 200 million by 1999." This dynamic, multifaceted category of communication includes not only traditional print and news services, but also audio, video, and still images, as well as interactive, real-time dialogue. Through the use of chat rooms, any person with a phone line can become a town crier with a voice that resonates farther than it could from any soapbox. Through the use of Web pages, mail exploders, and newsgroups, the same individual can become a pamphleteer. As the District Court found, "the content on the Internet is as diverse as human thought." We agree with its conclusion that our cases provide no basis for qualifying the level of First Amendment scrutiny that should be applied to this medium.

Regardless of whether the CDA is so vague that it violates the Fifth Amendment, the many ambiguities concerning the scope of its coverage render it problematic for purposes of the First Amendment. For instance, each of the two parts of the CDA uses a different linguistic form. The first uses the word "indecent," while the second speaks of material that "in context, depicts or describes, in terms patently offensive as measured by contemporary community standards, sexual or excretory activities or organs." Given the absence of a definition of either term, this difference in language will provoke uncertainty among speakers about how the two standards relate to each other and just what they mean. . . .

The vagueness of the CDA is a matter of special concern for two reasons. First, the CDA is a content-based regulation of speech. The vagueness of such a regulation raises special First Amendment concerns because of its obvious chilling effect on free speech. Second, the CDA is a criminal statute. In addition to the opprobrium and stigma of a criminal conviction, the CDA threatens violators with penalties including up to two years in prison for each act of violation. The severity of criminal sanctions may well cause speakers to remain silent rather than communicate even arguably unlawful words, ideas, and images. . . .

. . . Given the vague contours of the coverage of the statute, it unquestionably silences some speakers whose messages would be entitled to constitutional protection. That danger provides further reason for insisting that the statute not be overly broad. The CDA's burden on protected speech cannot be justified if it could be avoided by a more carefully drafted statute.

We are persuaded that the CDA lacks the precision that the First Amendment requires when a statute regulates the content of speech. In order to deny minors access to potentially harmful speech, the CDA effectively suppresses a large amount of speech that adults have a constitutional right to receive and to address to one another. That burden on adult speech is unacceptable if less restrictive alternatives would be at least as effective in achieving the legitimate purpose that the statute was enacted to serve.

In evaluating the free speech rights of adults, we have made it perfectly clear that "[s]exual expression which is indecent but not obscene is protected by the First Amendment." *Sable [Communications of California, Inc. v. FCC, 1994]. . . .*

It is true that we have repeatedly recognized the governmental interest in protecting children from harmful materials. But that interest does not justify an unnecessarily broad suppression of speech addressed to adults. As we have explained, the Government may not "reduc[e] the adult population . . . to . . . only what is fit for children." . . .

In arguing that the CDA does not so diminish adult communication, the Government relies on the incorrect factual premise that prohibiting a transmission whenever it is known that one of its recipients is a minor would not interfere with adult-to-adult communication. The findings of the District Court make clear that this premise is untenable. Given the size of the potential audience for most messages, in the absence of a viable age verification process, the sender must be charged with knowing that one or more minors will likely view it. Knowledge that, for instance, one or more members of a 100-person chat group will be minor— and therefore that it would be a crime to send the group an indecent message—would surely burden communication among adults.

The District Court found that at the time of trial existing technology did not include any effective method for a sender to prevent minors from obtaining access to its communications on the Internet without also denying access to adults. The Court found no effective way to determine the age of a user who is accessing material through e-mail, mail exploders, newsgroups, or chat rooms. As a practical matter, the Court also found that it would be prohibitively expensive for noncommercial—as well as some commercial— speakers who have Web sites to verify that their users are adults. These limitations must inevitably curtail a significant amount of adult communication on the Internet. . . .

The breadth of the CDA's coverage is wholly unprecedented. Unlike the regulations upheld in *Ginsberg* and *Pacifica*, the scope of the CDA is not limited to commercial speech or commercial entities. Its open-ended prohibitions embrace all nonprofit entities and individuals posting indecent messages or displaying them on their own computers in the presence of minors. The general, undefined terms "indecent" and "patently offensive" cover large amounts of nonpornographic material with serious educational or other value. Moreover, the "community standards" criterion as applied to the Internet means that any communication available to a nation-wide audience will be judged by the standards of the community most likely to be offended by the message. The regulated subject matter includes any of the seven "dirty words" used in the *Pacifica* monologue, the use of which the Government's expert acknowledged could constitute a felony. It may also extend to discussions about prison rape or safe sexual practices, artistic images that include nude subjects, and arguably the card catalogue of the Carnegie Library.

For the purposes of our decision, we need neither accept nor reject the Government's submission that the First Amendment does not forbid a blanket prohibition on all "indecent" and "patently offensive" messages communicated to a 17-year-old—no matter how much value the message may contain and regardless of parental approval. It is at least clear that the strength of the Government's interest in protecting minors is not equally strong throughout the coverage of this broad statute. Under the CDA, a parent allowing her 17-year-old to use the family computer to obtain information on the Internet that she, in her parental judgment, deems appropriate could face a lengthy prison term. Similarly, a parent who sent his 17-year-old college freshman information on birth control via e-mail could be incarcerated even though neither he, his child, nor anyone in their home community, found the material "indecent" or "patently offensive," if the college town's community thought otherwise.

The breadth of this content-based restriction of speech imposes an especially heavy burden on the Government to explain why a less restrictive provision would not be as effective as the CDA. It has not done so. The arguments in this Court have referred to possible alternatives such as requiring that indecent material be "tagged" in a way that facilitates parental control of material coming into their homes, making exceptions for messages with artistic or educational value, providing some tolerance for parental choice, and regulating some portions of the Internet—such as commercial web sites—differently than others, such as chat rooms. Particularly in the light of the absence of any detailed findings by the Congress, or even hearings addressing the special problems of the CDA, we are persuaded that the CDA is not narrowly tailored if that requirement has any meaning at all.

In an attempt to curtail the CDA's facial overbreadth, the Government advances three additional arguments for sustaining the Act's affirmative prohibitions. . . .

The Government first contends that, even though the CDA effectively censors discourse on many of the Internet's modalities—such as chat groups, newsgroups, and mail exploders—it is nonetheless constitutional because it provides a "reasonable opportunity" for speakers to engage in the restricted speech on the World Wide Web. This argument is unpersuasive because the CDA regulates speech on the basis of its content. A "time, place, and manner" analysis is therefore inapplicable. . . . The Government's position is equivalent to arguing that a statute could ban leaflets on certain subjects as long as individuals are free to publish books. . . .

The Government also asserts that the "knowledge" requirement . . . especially when coupled with the "specific child" element . . . saves the CDA from overbreadth. Because both sections prohibit the dissemination of indecent messages only to persons known to be under 18, the Government argues, it does not require transmitters to "refrain from communicating indecent material to adults; they need only refrain from disseminating such materials to persons they know to be under 18." This argument ignores the fact that most Internet fora—including chat rooms, newsgroups, mail exploders, and the Web—are open to all comers. The Government's assertion that the knowledge requirement somehow protects the communications of adults is therefore untenable. . . .

Finally, we find no textual support for the Government's submission that material having scientific, educational, or other redeeming social value will necessarily fall outside the CDA's "patently offensive" and "indecent" prohibitions.

The Government's three remaining arguments focus on the defenses provided in [the act]. First, relying on the "good faith, reasonable, effective, and appropriate actions" provision, the Government suggests that "tagging" provides a defense that saves the constitutionality of the Act. The suggestion assumes that transmitters may encode their indecent communications in a way that would indicate their contents, thus permitting recipients to block their reception with appropriate software. It is the requirement that the good faith action must be "effective" that makes this defense illusory. The Government recognizes that its proposed screening software does not currently exist. Even if it did, there is no way to know whether a potential recipient will actually block the encoded material. Without the impossible knowledge that every guardian in America is screening for the "tag," the transmitter could not reasonably rely on its action to be "effective."

For its second and third arguments concerning defenses—which we can consider together—the Government relies on the latter half of [the act], which applies when the transmitter has restricted access by requiring use of a verified credit card or adult identification. Such verification is not only technologically available but actually is used by commercial providers of sexually explicit material. These providers, therefore, would be protected by the defense. Under the findings of the District Court, however, it is not economically feasible for most noncommercial speakers to employ such verification. Accordingly, this defense would not significantly narrow the statute's burden on noncommercial speech. . . . Given that the risk of criminal sanctions "hovers over each content provider, like the proverbial sword of Damocles," the District Court correctly refused to rely on unproven future technology to save the statute. The Government thus failed to prove that the proffered defense would significantly reduce the heavy burden on adult speech produced by the prohibition on offensive displays.

We agree with the District Court's conclusion that the CDA places an unacceptably heavy burden on protected speech, and that the defenses do not constitute the sort of "narrow tailoring" that will save an otherwise patently invalid unconstitutional provision. In *Sable*, we remarked that the speech restriction at issue there amounted to " 'burn[ing] the house to roast the pig.' " The CDA, casting a far darker shadow over free speech, threatens to torch a large segment of the Internet community. . . .

For the foregoing reasons, the judgment of the district court is affirmed.

It is so ordered.

Despite the Court's strong defense of First Amendment interests, reaction to its decision, at least among the act's congressional supporters, was harsh. As Sen. Christopher Bond, R-Mo., put it, the ruling was "an unfortunate blow to those of us who want to protect our children from sexual predators using the Internet. . . . I believe Congress will try again, and that we'll get it right next time." [12]

Congress did try again. In 1998 it passed the Child Online Protection Act (COPA, sometimes called CDA II), which prohibits distribution of "any communication for commercial purposes that is available to any minor and that includes any material that is harmful to minors" (in distinction to the CDA, which forbade "indecent" and "patently offensive" communications in a manner accessible to minors). Violators can face criminal penalties of up to $50,000 a day.

To determine whether material is "harmful to minors" the act relies on the Miller test, including the "community standards" measure. A federal district court struck down COPA on much the same grounds as the Supreme Court used in *Reno,* and a U.S. court of appeals agreed, concluding that the Supreme Court's community standards jurisprudence "has no applicability to the Internet and the Web" because Web publishers are currently without the ability to control the geographic scope of the recipients of their communications. This logic seems to reflect the Court's words in *Reno* that "the 'community standards' criterion as applied to the Internet means that any communication available to a nationwide audience will be judged by the standards of the community most likely to be offended by the message." In *Ashcroft v. American Civil Liberties Union [I]* (2002) the Court disagreed. Writing for the majority (or plurality, depending on the section of the

opinion) Justice Clarence Thomas, declared that the use of COPA's "community standards" to identify material harmful to children did not render the statute facially invalid in part because COPA applies to a narrower class of material than did the CDA.

This decision did not settle the matter. By its own reckoning, *Ashcroft* was "quite limited," stating only that the community standards criterion itself does not necessarily run afoul of the First Amendment. Indeed, the Court did not express an opinion on questions such as whether the law is unconstitutionally vague or would fail to surmount strict scrutiny and, instead, sent the case back to the court of appeals.

That court once again held that COPA violated the First Amendment, this time on the ground that it was not the "least restrictive" alternative available to accomplish Congress's goal of shielding children from harmful materials. Writing for a five-person majority in *Ashcroft v. American Civil Liberties Union [II]* (2004), Justice Kennedy agreed. To Kennedy, the government had not made its case that COPA was the least restrictive alternative.

In this line of cases—all of which center on shielding children from access to sexually explicit material—the Court generally has been protective of First Amendment principles in evaluating Internet regulation. The justices do, however, seem open to well-defined laws that accomplish legitimate objectives without overly restricting expression rights. In *United States v. American Library Association* (2003) a divided Court upheld a provision of the Children's Internet Protection Act of 2000 that withheld federal funds from any public library that did not use computer filtering devices to block young users from accessing inappropriate Internet material.

Moreover, in cases involving child pornography and the Internet, the Court has given Congress some leeway. That was not always the case. In *Ashcroft v. Free Speech Coalition* (2002), the first major suit in this area, the justices considered a challenge to the constitutionality of the Child Pornography Prevention Act of 1996 (CPPA). Although *New York v. Ferber* (1982) gave strong support for legislative prohibitions against producing and distributing materials depicting children engaged in sexual activity, the CPPA had much greater breadth than the state statute upheld in that decision. Not only did the

---

12. Quoted in the *St. Louis Post Dispatch,* June 27, 1997, A16.

federal law prohibit using minors to create such materials, but also it barred the use of adult actors who looked like children as well as the use of computer-generated images of youngsters. The law outlawed such virtual pornography even if it did not meet the *Miller* definition of obscenity.

These provisions, according to the Court, went too far. The use of child actors engaging in real or simulated sexual activity is a crime of sexual abuse that can be punished. But similar activity involving adult actors or computer images is not a crime. Unless the material is legally obscene or purposefully marketed to children, such regulation crosses First Amendment boundaries.

Congress "went back to the drawing board," as Justice Scalia put it, and enacted the PROTECT Act of 2003 to respond to ***Ashcroft v. Free Speech Coalition***. (PROTECT stands for Prosecutorial Remedies and Other Tools to end the Exploitation of Children Today.) Congress attempted to remedy the defects in the 1996 law in part by limiting the commission of crime to the "pandering" and solicitation of child pornography; that is, the law applies to anyone who knowingly "advertises, promotes, presents, distributes, or solicits . . . any material or purported material that reflects the belief, or that is intended to cause another to believe, that the material or purported material" contains illegal child pornography.

When a challenge reached the Court in 2008 in ***United States v. Williams***, Justices David Souter and Ruth Bader Ginsburg argued that the new law was just as problematic as the old one: It continued to criminalize virtual or "fake child pornography," which *Free Speech Coalition* had held came under First Amendment protection. Souter and Ginsburg accused Congress of evading the Court's earlier decision. The majority disagreed. Writing for the Court, Justice Scalia noted: "The statute's definition of the material or purported material that may not be pandered or solicited precisely tracks the material held constitutionally proscribable in *Ferber* and *Miller*: obscene material depicting (actual or virtual) children engaged in sexually explicit conduct, and any other material depicting actual children engaged in sexually explicit conduct." In response to the dissenters' claim that by upholding the 2003 law the majority had overturned *Free Speech Coalition*, Scalia wrote:

An offer to provide or request to receive virtual child pornography is not prohibited by the statute. A crime is committed only when the speaker believes or intends the listener to believe that the subject of the proposed transaction depicts *real* children. It is simply not true that this means "a protected category of expression [will] inevitably be suppressed." Simulated child pornography will be as available as ever, so long as it is offered and sought *as such,* and not as real child pornography.

What does the future hold? To date, as our discussion suggests, federal regulation of Internet content has focused on matters related to sexually explicit materials and the welfare of children. Potentially, however, legislation may touch upon many other aspects of Internet-based expression. Some such laws may stem from the government's battle against terrorism and others may involve more traditional subjects such as commercial regulation. It goes without saying that almost every Internet regulation will be legally challenged by groups that want this contemporary method of communication to remain as free and open as possible. Such challenges will require the nation's judges to apply constitutional principles to a medium of expression not even within the framers' imagination when they penned the First Amendment.

READINGS

Adler, Renata. *Reckless Disregard.* New York: Vintage Books, 1986.

Anderson, David A. "The Origins of the Press Clause." *UCLA Law Review* 30 (1983): 456–541.

Berger, Ronald. *Feminism and Pornography.* New York: Praeger, 1991.

Bollinger, Lee C. *Images of a Free Press.* Chicago: University of Chicago Press, 1991.

Chappell, Joseph. *Building the Fourth Estate: Democratization and the Rise of a Free Press.* Berkeley: University of California Press, 2002.

Downs, Donald Alexander. *The New Politics of Pornography.* Chicago: University of Chicago Press, 1989.

Forer, Lois G. *A Chilling Effect.* New York: W. W. Norton, 1987.

Friendly, Fred W. *Minnesota Rag.* New York: Random House, 1981.

Garry, Patrick M. *Scrambling for Protection: The New Media and the First Amendment.* Pittsburgh: University of Pittsburgh Press, 1994.

Gertz, Elmer. *Gertz v. Robert Welch, Inc.: The Story of a Landmark Libel Case.* Carbondale: Southern Illinois University Press, 1992.

Gillmor, Donald M. *Power, Publicity, and the Abuse of Libel Law.* New York: Oxford University Press, 1992.

Godwin, Mike. *Cyber Rights: Defending Free Speech in the Digital Age.* Cambridge: MIT Press, 2003.

Gubar, Susan. *For Adult Use Only: The Dilemmas of Violent Pornography.* Bloomington: Indiana University Press, 1989.

Heins, Marjorie. *Not in Front of the Children: "Indecency," Censorship, and the Innocence of Youth.* New York: Hill and Wang, 2001.

Hopkins, W. Wat. *Actual Malice.* New York: Praeger, 1989.

Jenkins, Philip. *Beyond Tolerance: Child Pornography Online.* New York: New York University Press, 2001.

Kane, Peter E. *Errors, Lies, and Libel.* Carbondale: Southern Illinois University Press, 1992.

Kirby, James. *Fumble: Bear Bryant, Wally Butts, and the Great College Football Scandal.* San Diego: Harcourt Brace Jovanovich, 1986.

Kobylka, Joseph F. *The Politics of Obscenity: Group Litigation in a Time of Legal Change.* New York: Greenwood Press, 1991.

Lessig, Lawrence. *Code and Other Laws of Cyberspace.* New York: Basic Books, 2000.

Levy, Leonard W. *Emergence of a Free Press.* New York: Oxford University Press, 1985.

Lewis, Anthony. *Make No Law: The Sullivan Case and the First Amendment.* New York: Random House, 1991.

Mackey, Thomas C. *Pornography on Trial.* Santa Barbara, Calif.: ABC-CLIO, 2002.

MacKinnon, Catherine A. *Only Words.* Cambridge: Harvard University Press, 1993.

Martin, Robert W. T. *The Founding of American Press Liberty, 1640–1880.* New York: New York University Press, 2001.

Neubauer, Mark. "The Newsmen's Privilege after *Branzburg.*" *UCLA Law Review* 24 (1976): 160–192.

Reeves, Richard. *What the People Know: Freedom and the Press.* Cambridge: Harvard University Press, 1999.

Rozenberg, Joshua. *Privacy and the Press.* Oxford: Oxford University Press, 2004.

Rudenstine, David. *The Day the Presses Stopped: A History of the Pentagon Papers Case.* Berkeley: University of California Press, 1996.

Shapiro, Martin. *The Pentagon Papers and the Courts.* San Francisco: Chandler, 1972.

Sunstein, Cass. *Republic.com.* Princeton: Princeton University Press, 2001.

Weaver, Russell L., Andrew T. Kenyon, David F. Partlett, and Clive P. Walker. *The Right to Speak Ill: Defamation, Reputation, and Free Speech.* Durham: Carolina Academic Press, 2006.

CHAPTER 15

THE RIGHT TO KEEP AND BEAR ARMS

Prominently displayed in the literature distributed by the National Rifle Association (NRA) and similar groups are statements invoking the Second Amendment. Advocates of gun ownership rights assert that this amendment protects the fundamental right for individuals to keep and bear arms; supporters of gun control legislation claim that the amendment guarantees no such thing. The conflict between these two points of view has continued without interruption since the earliest government attempts to limit gun ownership rights. In large measure the controversy rests on the ambiguity of the amendment's wording.

The Second Amendment states in full: "A well regulated Militia, being necessary to the security of a free State, the right of the people to keep and bear arms shall not be infringed." The form of this amendment makes it something of an oddity compared to other provisions of the Bill of Rights because it comes with its own preamble. The structure gives rise to the question of the extent to which the preamble conditions the right itself.

As a result, two distinctly different interpretations of the amendment have been advanced. The first, often expressed by those who favor government restrictions on private gun ownership, emphasizes the first half of the amendment. According to this view, the amendment guarantees only a *collective* right of the states to arm their militias. No individual right to own firearms exists, unless it is in conjunction with a state militia. This position, therefore, interprets the amendment's prefatory clause as significantly controlling the meaning of the right to keep and bear arms.

If, as gun control supporters argue, the amendment was intended as a barrier against the federal government disarming state militias, then the amendment has little relevance today. In the nation's early years, the states, with no standing armies in place, responded to emergencies by calling private persons to serve in their militias. When called into service, these individuals were often expected to bring their weapons with them. But states no longer do so. Whatever roles the state militias played in the nation's first century are now carried out by other institutions such as the states' national guard units.

The second interpretation, advocated by pro-gun interests, emphasizes the second half the amendment. It concludes that the Constitution guarantees an *individual* right to keep and bear arms. The preamble's reference to well-regulated state militias does not in any way limit the amendment's operative clause that explicitly guarantees "the right of the people" to own and carry weapons. The freedom to keep and bear arms, among other purposes, supports the inalienable right of individuals to engage in self-defensive behavior when necessary. As such, the Second Amendment is no less relevant today than it was when it was ratified in 1791.

The ambiguous wording of the Second Amendment provides significant obstacles to understanding its meaning. Further complicating matters is the fact that historical records allow different interpretations of what

Congress intended by proposing the amendment and what the state legislatures thought it meant when they ratified it. Until recently the Supreme Court has not offered much assistance, rarely accepting cases that call for an interpretation of gun ownership rights.

Perhaps because of the Second Amendment's lack of clarity and the scarcity of Supreme Court decisions interpreting it, few constitutional law texts discuss this provision of the Bill of Rights. But we believe the subject is worthy of treatment for two reasons. First, the split between gun control advocates and gun ownership interests is a political issue with important consequences for society. Gun control supporters cite the social problems associated with the irresponsible use of firearms. These include gun-related crimes of violence and domestic abuse, as well as accidental injuries and deaths, often involving children. On the other side, advocates of gun ownership rights argue that the prevalence of violent crime only underscores the need for responsible citizens to arm themselves for their personal protection. The political controversy also divides the nation geographically. Urban areas, particularly in the East, tend to support comprehensive gun regulation, while residents of rural areas, especially in the South and far West, tend to support individual gun ownership.

The second reason is that recently lawyers and historians have taken a new look at the meaning of the Second Amendment and have drawn some surprising conclusions. Earlier generations of scholars generally sided with the position that the Second Amendment guarantees only the collective right to keep and bear arms. Examining additional historical records, however, has led several contemporary scholars to conclude that the NRA and its allies may have a stronger legal argument than previously thought.[1] Or, as Justice Clarence Thomas put it in a footnote to his concurring opinion in *Printz v. United States* (1997): "Marshalling an impressive array of historical evidence, a growing body of scholarly commentary indicates that the 'right to keep and bear arms' is, as the amendment's texts suggests, a personal right."

INITIAL INTERPRETATIONS

Congress did little to regulate firearms prior to the twentieth century. Support for the federal weapons restrictions began to grow in the 1920s, largely because of the growth of organized crime that occurred during Prohibition and into the Great Depression. Particularly significant in raising public awareness of the misuse of guns was a violent confrontation between warring criminal organizations in Chicago in the infamous 1929 Valentine's Day Massacre. Congress responded by first imposing a ban on the use of the postal service to transport certain weapons and then by passing the National Firearms Act of 1934 (NFA), the first significant piece of federal gun control legislation.

The NFA was not a direct regulation of weapons. Instead, because the federal regulation of firearms was constitutionally suspect, Congress used its authority to levy taxes to justify the legislation. The law imposed an excise tax on certain particularly lethal weapons and required their registration. It further prohibited the interstate transportation of any unregistered firearm covered by act.

The legitimacy of the 1934 law was challenged in **United States v. Miller** (1939).[2] The case began when Jack Miller and Frank Layton, two relatively insignificant career criminals with histories of bank robbery, were arrested for transporting a sawed-off shotgun from Oklahoma to Arkansas. Taxes had not been paid on the gun, which was not registered.

The facts surrounding *Miller* allow the inference that it was a federally orchestrated test case.[3] The government was interested in expanding its gun control efforts, but needed an authoritative decision by the Supreme Court to alleviate any Second Amendment concerns. Miller, the

---

1. See, for example, Joyce Lee Malcolm, *To Keep and Bear Arms: The Origins of an Anglo-American Right* (Cambridge: Harvard University Press, 1996); Stephen P. Halbrook, *That Every Man Be Armed: The Evolution of a Constitutional Right*, 2nd ed. (Oakland, Calif.: The Independent Institute, 1994); William Van Alstyne, "The Second Amendment and the Personal Right to Arms," *Duke Law Journal* 43 (1994): 1236–55; Sanford Levinson, "The Embarrassing Second Amendment," *Yale Law Journal* 99 (1989): 637–659; Don B. Kates, "Handgun Prohibition and the Original Meaning of the Second Amendment," *Michigan Law Review* 82 (1983): 204–273.

2. For an interesting analysis of this case see, Brian L. Frye, "The Peculiar Story of United States v. Miller," *NYU Journal of Law and Liberty* 3 (2008): 48–82.

3. Ibid.

primary defendant, had a history cooperating with the government as an informant in criminal cases. Federal district judge Heartsill Ragon, a former member of Congress who heard the case, was a strong proponent of gun regulation. Judge Ragon refused to accept guilty pleas from Miller and Layton, thereby ensuring that the case would be tried. Although the Miller and Layton put up little defense, Ragon used the case to strike down the NFA for violating the Second Amendment. He did so by way of a memorandum opinion that provided no reasoning or argument to justify his decision. His opinion nicely set the stage for the federal government to ask the Supreme Court to reverse.

When the appeal reached the justices, only the federal government's position was argued. No one represented the other side, so the position that the NFA violated the Second Amendment was not defended either by a coherent opinion from the lower court or briefs and oral arguments on behalf of the defendants. One could hardly imagine more favorable conditions for the federal government's position to prevail.

Attorneys for the United States argued that the NFA was a constitutional use of the federal taxing power. In addition, the act of transporting an unregistered gun across state lines was a matter of interstate commerce over which Congress had authority. The government also claimed that the Second Amendment was not applicable because that provision was designed only to cover weapons of the kind used by a state militia. The sawed-off, double-barreled shotgun in question had no relevance to any militia activity.

Not surprisingly, a unanimous Supreme Court reversed the lower court ruling that the NFA was unconstitutional. Through an opinion by Justice James C. McReynolds, the justices endorsed the government's claim that the law was a valid use of the power to tax. The Court further concluded that the Second Amendment was designed to cover only military-style weapons associated with the state militias. In rather direct language McReynolds wrote:

In the absence of any evidence tending to show that possession or use of a "shotgun having a barrel of less than eighteen inches in length" at this time has some reasonable relationship to the preservation or efficiency of a well regulated militia, we cannot say that the Second Amendment guarantees the right to keep and bear such an instrument. . . . With obvious purpose to assure the continuation and render possible the effectiveness of such forces the declaration and guarantee of the Second Amendment were made. It must be interpreted and applied with that end in view.

On its face, the ruling seems unambiguous. The Court's opinion clearly interprets the right to keep and bear arms in light of the amendment's preamble. It protects a collective right associated with militia service, not a personal right to be exercised by all individuals.

THE SECOND AMENDMENT REVISITED

As clear as the Miller decision appears at first glance, it did not end the controversy over the Second Amendment. Gun rights groups continued to argue that a correct reading of the historical record proves that the Supreme Court got it wrong. In addition, Miller left some important questions unanswered: May Congress regulate firearms directly or only under the authority of the power to tax? What are the implications of McReynolds's position that the Second Amendment protects only the ownership of arms useful to military service? Could that possibly mean that individuals have a constitutionally protected right to possess the destructive weapons of today's military?

For decades the Supreme Court avoided cases that presented difficult Second Amendment issues. The lower courts, however, did rule on such cases and often reached contradictory conclusions on the meaning of the amendment. In District of Columbia v. Heller (2008) the Court addressed these differing interpretations by taking another look at the amendment's meaning. As you read the opinions in this case, pay close attention to the justices' reasoning, especially their attempts to use historical analyses to establish the common understanding of the wording of the amendment at the time it was proposed and ratified.

District of Columbia v. Heller

554 U.S. __ (2008)

http://laws.findlaw.com/US/000/07-290.html
Oral arguments may be found at: http://www.oyez.org
Vote: 5 (Alito, Kennedy, Roberts, Scalia, Thomas)
    4 (Breyer, Ginsburg, Souter, Stevens)
Opinion of the Court: Scalia
Dissenting opinions: Breyer, Stevens

In 1976 the District of Columbia, concerned with the high levels of gun-related crime, passed the nation's most restrictive gun control ordinance. The law essentially banned the private possession of handguns. Shotguns and rifles could be owned, but only if the weapons were registered, kept unloaded, and disassembled or restricted by trigger locks. The law allowed the chief of police, under certain circumstances, to issue a one-year certificate to carry a handgun.

Dick Heller, a D.C. police officer, had been granted a license to carry a handgun while on duty providing security at the Federal Judicial Center. Heller applied for permission to own a handgun for self-defense, but he was refused. Claiming that the District's statute violated his Second Amendment right to bear arms, Heller brought a suit against the city. The district court dismissed his case, but the U.S. Court of Appeals for the District of Columbia reversed, holding that the Second Amendment protected Heller's right to possess a firearm for self-defense.

Heller's case did not occur spontaneously, but was orchestrated by Florida attorney Robert Levy, who wanted to test the constitutionality of the District's gun control law. Levy had become a wealthy man in his first career as a money manager. At age forty-nine, he entered George Mason Law School and graduated first in his class. After clerking for two federal judges, he devoted his professional life to libertarian causes. Levy, who had never owed a gun, saw the District's law as a violation of personal freedom and private property rights. He recruited six possible plaintiffs to challenge the law, but only Heller met the strict standing requirements to pursue legal ac-

tion. To eliminate any possible influence over the case by the NRA or any other gun rights group, Levy funded the litigation out of his own pocket.

JUSTICE SCALIA delivered the opinion of the Court.

The Second Amendment is naturally divided into two parts: its prefatory clause and its operative clause. The former does not limit the latter grammatically, but rather announces a purpose. The Amendment could be rephrased, "Because a well regulated Militia is necessary to the security of a free State, the right of the people to keep and bear Arms shall not be infringed." . . .[O]ther legal documents of the founding era . . . commonly included a prefatory statement of purpose.

Logic demands that there be a link between the stated purpose and the command. The Second Amendment would be nonsensical if it read, "A well regulated Militia, being necessary to the security of a free State, the right of the people to petition for redress of grievances shall not be infringed." That requirement of logical connection may cause a prefatory clause to resolve an ambiguity in the operative clause. . . . But apart from that clarifying function, a prefatory clause does not limit or expand the scope of the operative clause. . . .

1. Operative Clause.

a. "Right of the People." The first salient feature of the operative clause is that it codifies a "right of the people." The unamended Constitution and the Bill of Rights use the phrase "right of the people" two other times, in the First Amendment's Assembly-and-Petition Clause and in the Fourth Amendment's Search-and-Seizure Clause. . . . All . . . of these instances unambiguously refer to individual rights, not "collective" rights, or rights that may be exercised only through participation in some corporate body. . . .

This contrasts markedly with the phrase "the militia" in the prefatory clause. As we will describe below, the "militia" in colonial America consisted of a subset of "the people"— those who were male, able bodied, and within a certain age range. Reading the Second Amendment as protecting only the right to "keep and bear Arms" in an organized militia therefore fits poorly with the operative clause's description of the holder of that right as "the people."

We start therefore with a strong presumption that the Second Amendment right is exercised individually and belongs to all Americans.

b. "Keep and bear Arms." We move now from the holder of the right—"the people"—to the substance of the right: "to keep and bear Arms."

Before addressing the verbs "keep" and "bear," we interpret their object: "Arms." The 18th-century meaning is no different from the meaning today. . . .

The term was applied, then as now, to weapons that were not specifically designed for military use and were not employed in a military capacity. . . .

. . . We turn to the phrases "keep arms" and "bear arms." [Dictionaries] defined "keep" as, most relevantly, "[t]o retain; not to lose," and "[t]o have in custody." Webster defined it as "[t]o hold; to retain in one's power or possession." No party has apprised us of an idiomatic meaning of "keep Arms." Thus, the most natural reading of "keep Arms" in the Second Amendment is to "have weapons." . . .

At the time of the founding, as now, to "bear" meant to "carry." When used with "arms," however, the term has a meaning that refers to carrying for a particular purpose—confrontation. In *Muscarello v. United States* (1998), in the course of analyzing the meaning of "carries a firearm" in a federal criminal statute, Justice Ginsburg wrote that "[s]urely a most familiar meaning is, as the Constitution's Second Amendment . . . indicate[s]: 'wear, bear, or carry . . . upon the person or in the clothing or in a pocket, for the purpose . . . of being armed and ready for offensive or defensive action in a case of conflict with another person.' " . . . Although the phrase implies that the carrying of the weapon is for the purpose of "offensive or defensive action," it in no way connotes participation in a structured military organization.

. . . In numerous instances, "bear arms" was unambiguously used to refer to the carrying of weapons outside of an organized militia. The most prominent examples are those most relevant to the Second Amendment: Nine state constitutional provisions written in the 18th century or the first two decades of the 19th, which enshrined a right of citizens to "bear arms in defense of themselves and the state" or "bear arms in defense of himself and the state." It is clear from those formulations that "bear arms" did not refer only to carrying a weapon in an organized military unit. . . .

These provisions demonstrate—again, in the most analogous linguistic context—that "bear arms" was not limited to the carrying of arms in a militia. . . .

. . . In any event, the meanings of "bear arms" that petitioners and Justice Stevens propose is *not even* the (sometimes) idiomatic meaning. Rather, they manufacture a hybrid definition, whereby "bear arms" connotes the actual carrying of arms (and therefore is not really an idiom) but only in the service of an organized militia. . . . Giving "bear Arms" its idiomatic meaning would cause the protected right to consist of the right to be a soldier or to wage war—an absurdity that no commentator has ever endorsed. Worse still, the phrase "keep and bear Arms" would be incoherent. The word "Arms" would have two different meanings at once: "weapons" (as the object of "keep") and (as the object of "bear") one-half of an idiom. It would be rather like saying "He filled and kicked the bucket" to mean "He filled the bucket and died." Grotesque. . . .

c. Meaning of the Operative Clause. Putting all of these textual elements together, we find that they guarantee the individual right to possess and carry weapons in case of confrontation. This meaning is strongly confirmed by the historical background of the Second Amendment. We look to this because it has always been widely understood that the Second Amendment, like the First and Fourth Amendments, codified a *pre-existing* right. . . .

. . .There seems to us no doubt, on the basis of both text and history, that the Second Amendment conferred an individual right to keep and bear arms. . . .

2. Prefatory Clause.

The prefatory clause reads: "A well regulated Militia, being necessary to the security of a free State. . . ."

a. "Well-Regulated Militia." In *United States v. Miller* (1939), we explained that "the Militia comprised all males physically capable of acting in concert for the common defense." That definition comports with founding-era sources.

Petitioners take a seemingly narrower view of the militia, stating that "[m]ilitias are the state- and congressionally-regulated military forces described in the Militia Clauses. Although we agree with petitioners' interpretive assumption that "militia" means the same thing in Article I and the Second Amendment, we believe that petitioners identify the wrong thing, namely, the organized militia. Unlike armies and navies, which Congress is given the power to create, the militia is assumed by Article I already to be *in existence. . . .*

3. Relationship between Prefatory Clause and Operative Clause

We reach the question, then: Does the preface fit with an operative clause that creates an individual right to keep and bear arms? It fits perfectly, once one knows the history that the founding generation knew and that we have described above. That history showed that the way tyrants had eliminated a militia consisting of all the able-bodied men was not by banning the militia but simply by taking away the people's arms, enabling a select militia or standing army to suppress political opponents. . . .

The debate with respect to the right to keep and bear arms, as with other guarantees in the Bill of Rights, was not over whether it was desirable (all agreed that it was) but over whether it needed to be codified in the Constitution. During the 1788 ratification debates, the fear that the federal government would disarm the people in order to impose rule through a standing army or select militia was pervasive in Antifederalist rhetoric. . . . Federalists responded that because Congress was given no power to abridge the ancient right of individuals to keep and bear arms, such a force could never oppress the people. It was understood across the political spectrum that the right helped to secure the ideal of a citizen militia, which might be necessary to oppose an oppressive military force if the constitutional order broke down. . . .

. . . If, as the [petitioners] believe, the Second Amendment right is no more than the right to keep and use weapons as a member of an organized militia—if, that is, the *organized* militia is the sole institutional beneficiary of the Second Amendment's guarantee—it does not assure the existence of a "citizens' militia" as a safeguard against tyranny. For Congress retains plenary authority to organize the militia, which must include the authority to say who will belong to the organized force. . . . Thus, if petitioners are correct, the Second Amendment protects citizens' right to use a gun in an organization from which Congress has plenary authority to exclude them. . . .

Our interpretation is confirmed by analogous arms-bearing rights in state constitutions that preceded and immediately followed adoption of the Second Amendment. Four States adopted analogues to the Federal Second Amendment in the period between independence and the ratification of the Bill of Rights. . . .

We therefore believe that the most likely reading of [some] pre-Second Amendment state constitutional provisions is that they secured an individual right to bear arms for defensive purposes. Other States did not include rights to bear arms in their pre-1789 constitutions. . . .

The historical narrative that petitioners must endorse would thus treat the Federal Second Amendment as an odd outlier, protecting a right unknown in state constitutions or at English common law, based on little more than an over-reading of the prefatory clause.

We conclude that nothing in our precedents forecloses our adoption of the original understanding of the Second Amendment. It should be unsurprising that such a significant matter has been for so long judicially unresolved. For most of our history, the Bill of Rights was not thought applicable to the States, and the Federal Government did not significantly regulate the possession of firearms by law-abiding citizens. Other provisions of the Bill of Rights have similarly remained unilluminated for lengthy periods. . . .

Like most rights, the right secured by the Second Amendment is not unlimited. From Blackstone through the 19th-century cases, commentators and courts routinely explained that the right was not a right to keep and carry any weapon whatsoever in any manner whatsoever and for whatever purpose. . . . Although we do not undertake an exhaustive historical analysis today of the full scope of the Second Amendment, nothing in our opinion should be taken to cast doubt on longstanding prohibitions on the possession of firearms by felons and the mentally ill, or laws forbidding the carrying of firearms in sensitive places such as schools and government buildings, or laws imposing conditions and qualifications on the commercial sale of arms.

We also recognize another important limitation on the right to keep and carry arms. *Miller* said, as we have explained, that the sorts of weapons protected were those "in common use at the time." We think that limitation is fairly supported by the historical tradition of prohibiting the carrying of "dangerous and unusual weapons." . . .

. . . [T]he inherent right of self-defense has been central to the Second Amendment right. The handgun ban amounts to a prohibition of an entire class of "arms" that is overwhelmingly chosen by American society for that lawful purpose. The prohibition extends, moreover, to the home,

THE RIGHT TO KEEP AND BEAR ARMS

where the need for defense of self, family, and property is most acute. Under any of the standards of scrutiny that we have applied to enumerated constitutional rights, banning from the home "the most preferred firearm in the nation to 'keep' and use for protection of one's home and family," would fail constitutional muster.

Few laws in the history of our Nation have come close to the severe restriction of the District's handgun ban. And some of those few have been struck down. . . .

. . . [T]he American people have considered the handgun to be the quintessential self-defense weapon. There are many reasons that a citizen may prefer a handgun for home defense: It is easier to store in a location that is readily accessible in an emergency; it cannot easily be redirected or wrestled away by an attacker; it is easier to use for those without the upper-body strength to lift and aim a long gun; it can be pointed at a burglar with one hand while the other hand dials the police. Whatever the reason, handguns are the most popular weapon chosen by Americans for self-defense in the home, and a complete prohibition of their use is invalid.

We must also address the District's requirement (as applied to respondent's handgun) that firearms in the home be rendered and kept inoperable at all times. This makes it impossible for citizens to use them for the core lawful purpose of self-defense and is hence unconstitutional. The District argues that we should interpret this element of the statute to contain an exception for self-defense. But we think that is precluded by the unequivocal text, and by the presence of certain other enumerated exceptions: "Except for law enforcement personnel . . . , each registrant shall keep any firearm in his possession unloaded and disassembled or bound by a trigger lock or similar device unless such firearm is kept at his place of business, or while being used for lawful recreational purposes within the District of Columbia." The nonexistence of a self-defense exception is also suggested by the D.C. Court of Appeals' statement that the statute forbids residents to use firearms to stop intruders. . . .

. . . We know of no other enumerated constitutional right whose core protection has been subjected to a freestanding "interest-balancing" approach. The very enumeration of the right takes out of the hands of government— even the Third Branch of Government—the power to decide on a case-by-case basis whether the right is *really worth* insisting upon. A constitutional guarantee subject to future judges' assessments of its usefulness is no constitutional guarantee at all. Constitutional rights are enshrined with the scope they were understood to have when the people adopted them, whether or not future legislatures or (yes) even future judges think that scope too broad. We would not apply an "interest-balancing" approach to the prohibition of a peaceful neo-Nazi march through Skokie. The First Amendment contains the freedom-of-speech guarantee that the people ratified, which included exceptions for obscenity, libel, and disclosure of state secrets, but not for the expression of extremely unpopular and wrong-headed views. The Second Amendment is no different. Like the First, it is the very *product* of an interest-balancing by the people. . . .

In sum, we hold that the District's ban on handgun possession in the home violates the Second Amendment, as does its prohibition against rendering any lawful firearm in the home operable for the purpose of immediate self-defense. Assuming that Heller is not disqualified from the exercise of Second Amendment rights, the District must permit him to register his handgun and must issue him a license to carry it in the home.

We are aware of the problem of handgun violence in this country, and we take seriously the concerns raised by the many *amici* who believe that prohibition of handgun ownership is a solution. The Constitution leaves the District of Columbia a variety of tools for combating that problem, including some measures regulating handguns. But the enshrinement of constitutional rights necessarily takes certain policy choices off the table. These include the absolute prohibition of handguns held and used for self-defense in the home. Undoubtedly some think that the Second Amendment is outmoded in a society where our standing army is the pride of our Nation, where well-trained police forces provide personal security, and where gun violence is a serious problem. That is perhaps debatable, but what is not debatable is that it is not the role of this Court to pronounce the Second Amendment extinct.

We affirm the judgment of the Court of Appeals.

It is so ordered.

JUSTICE STEVENS, with whom JUSTICE SOUTER, JUSTICE GINSBURG, and JUSTICE BREYER join, dissenting.

The Second Amendment was adopted to protect the right of the people of each of the several States to maintain a well-regulated militia. It was a response to concerns raised during the ratification of the Constitution that the power of Congress to disarm the state militias and create a national standing army posed an intolerable threat to the sovereignty of the several States. Neither the text of the Amendment nor the arguments advanced by its proponents evidenced the slightest interest in limiting any legislature's authority to regulate private civilian uses of firearms. Specifically, there is no indication that the Framers of the Amendment intended to enshrine the common-law right of self-defense in the Constitution.

. . . The view of the Amendment we took in *Miller*—that it protects the right to keep and bear arms for certain military purposes, but that it does not curtail the Legislature's power to regulate the nonmilitary use and ownership of weapons—is both the most natural reading of the Amendment's text and the interpretation most faithful to the history of its adoption.

Since our decision in *Miller*, hundreds of judges have relied on the view of the Amendment we endorsed there. . . . No new evidence has surfaced . . . supporting the view that the Amendment was intended to curtail the power of Congress to regulate civilian use or misuse of weapons. Indeed, a review of the drafting history of the Amendment demonstrates that its Framers *rejected* proposals that would have broadened its coverage to include such uses.

The opinion the Court announces today fails to identify any new evidence supporting the view that the Amendment was intended to limit the power of Congress to regulate civilian uses of weapons. . . .

Even if the textual and historical arguments on both sides of the issue were evenly balanced, respect for the well-settled views of all of our predecessors on this Court, and for the rule of law itself would prevent most jurists from endorsing such a dramatic upheaval in the law. . . .

. . . Until today, it has been understood that legislatures may regulate the civilian use and misuse of firearms so long as they do not interfere with the preservation of a well-regulated militia. The Court's announcement of a new constitutional right to own and use firearms for private purposes upsets that settled understanding, but leaves for future cases the formidable task of defining the scope of permissible regulations. Today judicial craftsmen have confidently asserted that a policy choice that denies a "law-abiding, responsible citize[n]" the right to keep and use weapons in the home for self-defense is "off the table." Given the presumption that most citizens are law abiding, and the reality that the need to defend oneself may suddenly arise in a host of locations outside the home, I fear that the District's policy choice may well be just the first of an unknown number of dominoes to be knocked off the table. . . .

The Court properly disclaims any interest in evaluating the wisdom of the specific policy choice challenged in this case, but it fails to pay heed to a far more important policy choice—the choice made by the Framers themselves. The Court would have us believe that over 200 years ago, the Framers made a choice to limit the tools available to elected officials wishing to regulate civilian uses of weapons, and to authorize this Court to use the common-law process of case-by-case judicial lawmaking to define the contours of acceptable gun control policy. Absent compelling evidence that is nowhere to be found in the Court's opinion, I could not possibly conclude that the Framers made such a choice.

For these reasons, I respectfully dissent.

JUSTICE BREYER, with whom JUSTICE STEVENS, JUSTICE SOUTER, and JUSTICE GINSBURG join, dissenting.

[T]he protection the [Second] Amendment provides is not absolute. The Amendment permits government to regulate the interests that it serves. Thus, irrespective of what those interests are—whether they do or do not include an independent interest in self-defense—the majority's view cannot be correct unless it can show that the District's regulation is unreasonable or inappropriate in Second Amendment terms. This the majority cannot do. . . .

. . . The law is tailored to the urban crime problem in that it is local in scope and thus affects only a geographic area both limited in size and entirely urban; the law concerns handguns, which are specially linked to urban gun deaths and injuries, and which are the overwhelmingly favorite weapon of armed criminals; and at the same time, the law imposes a burden upon gun owners that seems proportionately no greater than restrictions in existence at the time the Second Amendment was adopted. In these circumstances, the District's law falls within the zone that the Second Amendment leaves open to regulation by legislatures.

The majority in *Heller* rejected the collective-right interpretation of the Second Amendment and held that the Constitution guarantees an individual right to keep and bear arms. Justice Scalia's majority opinion, however, strongly states that the personal right to possess weapons is not absolute. It is a right subject to reasonable regulation. In the majority's view, the outright banning of handguns by the District of Columbia exceeded the degree of regulation the Second Amendment permits.

HELLER AND THE STATES

The Court's position in *Heller* that the Second Amendment protects an individual's right to keep and bear arms was a sharp break from the past. We should be mindful, however, that the case dealt only with the very restrictive gun control ordinance in Washington, D.C. The District of Columbia is not a state, and it is ultimately controlled by the federal government.

This distinction is important. The Second Amendment is one of the few provisions of the Bill of Rights that has not been incorporated. *(See chapter 1, especially Table 1-3.)* Therefore, the amendment restricts the legislative power of the federal government, but not the authority of state or local governments. The Supreme Court reminded us of this fact as early as 1875 in *United States v. Cruikshank*, in which Chief Justice Morrison Waite for the majority wrote, "This is one of the amendments that has no other effect than to restrict the powers of the national government." And again in *Presser v. Illinois* (1886), the Court held that ". . . the amendment is a limitation only upon the power of congress and the national government, and not upon that of the state."

The Court's interpretation of the Second Amendment in *Heller* has no direct effect on the authority of the states to regulate firearms as they see fit. Instead, the states are bound primarily by the gun ownership and usage provisions of their own constitutions and laws.

Naturally, this state of affairs is subject to change. The *Heller* ruling has energized pro-gun organizations. Already in place are litigation strategies to convince the courts to incorporate the Second Amendment making it binding upon the states through the due process clause of the Fourteenth Amendment. This strategy will succeed only if the justices of the Supreme Court can be persuaded that the right to keep and bear arms is a fundamental freedom, a right so important that neither liberty nor justice would exist if it were sacrificed. Given the Court's 5–4 vote in *Heller* and the high probably of significant membership change over the next several years, the outcome for the incorporation issue is far from certain.

READINGS

Amar, Akhil Reed. "The Bill of Rights as a Constitution." *Yale Law Journal* 100 (1991): 1131–75.

Barnett, Randy E., and Don B. Kates. "Under Fire: The New Consensus on the Second Amendment." *Emory Law Journal* 45 (1996): 1140–1259.

Cornell, Saul. "Commonplace or Anachronism: The Standard Model, the Second Amendment, and the Problem of History in Contemporary Constitutional Theory." *Constitutional Commentary* 16 (1999): 221–246.

———. *Whose Right to Bear Arms Did the Second Amendment Protect?* New York: St. Martin's, 2000.

Cottrol, Robert, and Raymond Diamond. "The Second Amendment: Toward an Afro-Americanist Reconsideration." *Georgetown Law Journal* 80 (1991): 309–361.

Davidson, Osha Gray. *Under Fire: The NRA and the Battle for Gun Control.* Iowa City: University of Iowa Press, 1998.

Dowlut, Robert. "Federal and State Constitutional Guarantees to Arms." *University of Dayton Law Review* 15 (1989): 1–89.

Halbrook, Stephen P. "The Right of the People or the Power of the State: Bearing Arms, Arming Militias, and the Second Amendment." *Valpraiso University Law Review* 26 (1991): 131–207.

Herz, Andrew D. "Gun Crazy: Constitutional False Consciousness and Dereliction of Dialogic Responsibility." *Boston University Law Review* 75 (1995): 57–153.

Jacobs, James B. *Can Gun Control Work?* New York: Oxford University Press, 2002.

Kates, Don B. "Handgun Prohibition and the Original Meaning of the Second Amendment." *Michigan Law Review* 82 (1983): 204–273.

Levinson, Sanford. "The Embarrassing Second Amendment." *Yale Law Journal* 99 (1989): 637–659.

Lott, John R. *More Guns, Less Crime: Understanding Crime and Gun-Control Laws.* Chicago: University of Chicago Press, 1998.

Malcolm, Joyce Lee. *To Keep and Bear Arms: The Origins of an Anglo-American Right.* Cambridge: Harvard University Press, 1996.

McClurg, Andrew J., et al., eds. *Gun Control and Gun Rights.* New York: New York University Press, 2002.

Reynolds, Glenn Harlan. "A Critical Guide to the Second Amendment." *Tennessee Law Review* 62 (1995): 461–512.

Shalhope, Robert E. "The Ideological Origins of the Second Amendment." *Journal of American History* 6 (1982): 599–614.

Uviller, H. Richard, and William G. Merkel. *Militia and the Right to Arms: Or How the Second Amendment Fell Silent.* Durham: Duke University Press, 2002.

Van Alstyne, William. "The Second Amendment and the Personal Right to Arms." *Duke Law Journal* 43 (1994): 1236–1255.

Volokh, Eugene. "The Amazing Vanishing Second Amendment." *New York University Law Review* 73 (1998): 831–840.

———— "The Commonplace Second Amendment." *New York University Law Review* 73 (1998): 793–821.

Williams, David C. *Mythic Landscape of the Second Amendment: Taming Political Violence in a Constitutional Republic.* New Haven: Yale University Press, 2003.

Wills, Garry. "To Keep and Bear Arms." *New York Review of Books,* September 21, 1995.

CHAPTER 16

THE RIGHT TO PRIVACY

Americans place a high value on personal privacy. We believe that people have the right to be let alone; unnecessary government intrusion into people's private lives is generally unwelcome. But are the privacy interests of Americans protected by the Constitution?

Many are surprised to learn that privacy was not among the many liberties that the framers explicitly included in the Bill of Rights. In fact, the word *privacy* appears nowhere in the Constitution. Instead, the right to privacy became included among our protected liberties through judicial interpretation. In this chapter we discuss the right to privacy—its origins, constitutional status, and scope.

THE RIGHT TO PRIVACY: FOUNDATIONS

In today's legal and political context, the right to privacy has become more or less synonymous with reproductive freedom, particularly abortion. The reason may be that the case in which the Court articulated a constitutional right to privacy, *Griswold v. Connecticut* (1965), involved birth control, and a decision that depended on *Griswold*, *Roe v. Wade* (1973), legalized abortion.

Prior to these decisions, members of the Court had contemplated privacy in somewhat different contexts. Following the common law dictates that "a man's home is his castle" and all "have the right to be let alone," future Supreme Court justice Louis Brandeis coauthored an 1890 *Harvard Law Review* article asserting that privacy

rights should be applied to civil law cases of libel.[1] The article had enormous long-term influence in no small part because it argued for the creation of a new legal "wrong," the invasion of privacy.

After Brandeis ascended to the bench, he continued his quest to see a right to privacy etched into law. Among his most famous attempts was a dissent in ***Olmstead v. United States*** (1928), which involved the ability of federal agents to place wiretaps on telephones without warrants. The majority of the justices ruled that neither the Fifth Amendment's protection against self-incrimination nor the Fourth Amendment's search and seizure provision protected individuals against wiretaps. Brandeis, however, thought that the Fourth and Fifth Amendments prohibited such activity. He noted that the makers of the Constitution conferred on Americans "the right to be let alone—the most comprehensive of rights and the right most valued by civilized men."

No matter how persuasive Brandeis's logic might appear, for nearly thirty years it was the only serious mention of a right to privacy. The justices consistently ignored his dissent in *Olmstead*. Courts of earlier eras did, however, pay attention to a concept that would later become associated with privacy—the concept of liberty. The word *liberty* appears in the due process clauses of the

---

1. Samuel D. Warren and Louis D. Brandeis, "The Right of Privacy," *Harvard Law Review* 4 (1890): 192–220. William L. Prosser notes that they wrote this piece in response to the yellow journalism of the day. See "Privacy," *California Law Review* 48 (1960): 383–423.

Fifth and Fourteenth Amendments. The Fifth Amendment states that Congress shall not deprive any person of "life, liberty, or property, without due process of law," and the Fourteenth Amendment uses the same wording to apply to the states. In the early 1900s the Supreme Court created a doctrine, called substantive due process, to guide its interpretation of some government policies challenged as violations of the guarantees contained in the due process clauses. *(See chapter 10.)*

Under the doctrine of substantive due process, the Court stressed the word *liberty* in the due process clauses to prevent governments from enacting certain kinds of laws, particularly those that regulated business practices. *Lochner v. New York* (1905) illustrates the point. In this case, the Court struck down an 1897 New York law that limited the hours per day and per week that bakery employees could work. The Court said the law was an unreasonable interference with an employer's right of contract protected in the liberty guarantee of the Fourteenth Amendment. (An excerpt of *Lochner* appears in chapter 10.)

The Court also applied the doctrine of substantive due process to regulations outside of business. In *Meyer v. Nebraska* (1923) the justices considered a state law, enacted after World War I, that forbade schools to teach German and other foreign languages to students below the eighth grade. They invoked a substantive due process approach to strike down the law, reasoning that the word *liberty* in the Fourteenth Amendment protects more than the right to enter into contracts. It also covers

the right of the individual . . . to engage in any of the common occupations of life, to acquire useful knowledge, to marry, establish a home and bring up children, to worship God according to the dictates of his own conscience, and generally to enjoy those privileges long recognized at common law as essential to the orderly pursuit of happiness by free men.

According to the Court, government cannot interfere with these liberties, "under the guise of protecting the public interest, by legislative action which is arbitrary or without reasonable relation to some purpose within the competency of the State to that effect." *Lochner* and *Meyer* provide examples of substantive due process in action: Under this approach, the Court is free to strike down leg-

islation that interferes with liberty unless governments can demonstrate that they are seeking to achieve an end that is not "arbitrary," "capricious," or "unreasonable."

Through the 1930s the Court used the doctrine of substantive due process to strike down many laws, particularly those—as in *Lochner*—that sought to regulate businesses. The justices subscribed to the principle of laissez-faire; they believed that the government should not interfere with the business of business. During the New Deal, however, substantive due process fell into disrepute because the public demanded that the government attempt to straighten out the economy. As a result, the Court changed its approach: The federal and state governments would be free to adopt whatever economic policy they wanted so long as it may reasonably be deemed to promote public welfare. If an economic policy was related to a legitimate government interest, the Court would not strike it down. This reasoning is called the "rational basis" approach to the Fourteenth Amendment. It differs significantly from substantive due process because, under it, courts generally defer to governments and presume the validity of their policies.

Application of the rational basis test led the Court to uphold legislation such as maximum hour and minimum wage laws, which it had previously struck down on liberty grounds, even if the laws did not necessarily seem reasonable to the justices. In one case, in fact, the justices characterized a particular state's economic policy as "needless" and "wasteful." They upheld the law anyway, proclaiming that "[t]he day is gone when this Court uses the due process clause of the Fourteenth Amendment to strike down state laws, regulatory of business and industrial conditions, because they may be unwise, improvident, or out of harmony with a particular school of thought."[2] The majority added that if the people did not like the legislation their governments passed they should "resort to the polls, not to the courts." With this declaration, the Court seemed to strike the death knell for substantive due process. It would no longer substitute its

---

2. The case was *Williamson v. Lee Optical Company* (1955). The law at issue prohibited persons other than ophthalmologists and optometrists from fitting, adjusting, adapting, or applying lenses and frames.

"social and economic beliefs for the judgment of legislative bodies, who are elected to pass laws."[3]

What, then, does the discredited doctrine of substantive due process have to do with the right to privacy? It was Justice John Harlan who tied these two concepts together. Neither an activist nor a liberal, he took great offense at the Court's handling of a 1961 case, *Poe v. Ullman*. At issue in *Poe* was the constitutionality of an 1879 Connecticut law prohibiting the use of any method of birth control, even by married couples. A physician challenged the act on behalf of two women who wanted to use contraceptives for health reasons.

The majority of the Court voted to dismiss the case on procedural grounds. Several other justices disagreed with the Court, but Harlan's dissent was memorable. He argued that the Fourteenth Amendment's due process clause could be used to strike the law:

I consider that this Connecticut legislation . . . violates the Fourteenth Amendment. . . . [It] involves what, by common understanding throughout the English-speaking world, must be granted to be the fundamental aspect of "liberty," the privacy of the home in its most basic sense, and it is this which requires that the statute be subjected to "strict scrutiny."

In making this claim, Harlan sought to demonstrate that the concepts of liberty and privacy were constitutionally bound together, that the word *liberty*, as used in the due process clauses, "embraced" a right to privacy. And, because that right was fundamental, laws that touched on liberty/privacy interests, such as the one at issue in *Poe*, must be subjected to "strict scrutiny," meaning that the Court should presume that laws infringing on liberty/privacy were unconstitutional unless the state could show that the policies were the least restrictive means to accomplish a *compelling* interest.

Harlan's opinion was extraordinary in two ways. First, some scholars have pointed out that it resurrected the dead (and discredited) doctrine of substantive due process, which the Court had buried in the 1930s. Now Harlan wanted to reinject some substance into the word *liberty*, but with a twist. Rather than protecting economic rights, in his view, due process protects fundamental rights, those the Court believes to be important in the concept of ordered liberty.

It is one of these fundamental liberties—privacy—that provides the second novel aspect of Harlan's opinion. As we have indicated, he was not writing on a blank slate; Brandeis had written about a right to privacy in the contexts of libel and search and seizure. In fact, Harlan cited—with approval—Brandeis's dissent in *Olmstead*. Still, Harlan's application of the doctrine to marital sexual relations was bold. As he wrote, "It is difficult to imagine what is more private or more intimate than a husband and wife's marital relations."

Harlan's assertion of a constitutional right to privacy proved too much, too soon for the Court; the majority was not yet willing to adopt it. But just four years later in *Griswold v. Connecticut*, a dramatic change took place.[4] Why did the justices suddenly alter their views? More important is what the Court said about the right to privacy: The majority agreed that it existed, but they disagreed over where it resided in the Constitution.

Griswold v. Connecticut

381 U.S. 479 (1965)
http://laws.findlaw.com/US/381/479.html
Oral arguments may be found at: http://www.oyez.org
Vote: 7 (Brennan, Clark, Douglas, Goldberg, Harlan, Warren, White)
     2 (Black, Stewart)
Opinion of the Court: Douglas
Concurring opinions: Goldberg, Harlan, White
Dissenting opinions: Black, Stewart

Griswold was virtually a carbon copy of *Poe v. Ullman*. Estelle Griswold, the executive director of the Planned Parenthood League of Connecticut, and Dr. C. Lee Buxton, the physician involved in *Poe*, opened a birth control clinic in 1961 with the intent of being arrested for violating the Connecticut law that had been at issue in *Poe*.

---

3. *Ferguson v. Skrupa* (1963).

4. For an interesting account of *Griswold*, see Fred W. Friendly and Martha J. H. Elliot, *The Constitution: That Delicate Balance* (New York: Random House, 1984).

Estelle Griswold opened a birth control clinic in New Haven in violation of an 1879 Connecticut law prohibiting the use of contraceptives. She challenged the constitutionality of the statute, and in *Griswold v. Connecticut* (1965) the Supreme Court struck down the law and established a constitutionally protected right to privacy.

Three days after the clinic opened, Griswold was arrested for dispensing contraceptives to a married couple.

In the U.S. Supreme Court, Griswold's attorney, Yale Law School professor Thomas Emerson, challenged the Connecticut law on some of the same grounds as had been set forth in the *Poe* dissent. Emerson took a substantive due process approach to the Fourteenth Amendment, arguing that the law infringed on individual liberty. He strengthened the privacy argument by asserting that it could be found in five amendments: the First, Third, Fourth, Ninth, and Fourteenth.

MR. JUSTICE DOUGLAS delivered the opinion of the Court.

[W]e are met with a wide range of questions that implicate the Due Process Clause of the Fourteenth Amendment. . . . We do not sit as a super-legislature to determine the wisdom, need, and propriety of laws that touch economic problems, business affairs, or social conditions. This law, however, operates directly on an intimate relation of husband and wife and their physician's role in one aspect of that relation.

The association of people is not mentioned in the Constitution nor in the Bill of Rights. The right to educate a child in a school of the parents' choice—whether public or private or parochial—is also not mentioned. Nor is the right to study any particular subject or any foreign language. Yet the First Amendment has been construed to include certain of those rights. . . .

Without those peripheral rights the specific rights would be less secure. . . .

. . . [Previous] cases suggest that specific guarantees in the Bill of Rights have penumbras, formed by emanations from those guarantees that help give them life and substance. Various guarantees create zones of privacy. The right of association contained in the penumbra of the First Amendment is one. . . . The Third Amendment in its prohibition against the quartering of soldiers "in any house" in time of peace without the consent of the owner is another facet of that privacy. The Fourth Amendment explicitly affirms the "right of the people to be secure in their persons, houses, papers, and effects, against unreasonable searches and seizures." The Fifth Amendment in its Self-Incrimination Clause enables the citizen to create a zone of privacy which government may not force him to surrender to his detriment. The Ninth Amendment provides: "The enumeration in the Constitution, of certain rights, shall not be construed to deny or disparage others retained by the people."

The Fourth and Fifth Amendments were described in *Boyd v. United States* as protection against all governmental invasions "of the sanctity of a man's home and the privacies of life." We recently referred to the Fourth Amendment as creating a "right to privacy, no less important than any other right carefully and particularly reserved to the people."

We have had many controversies over these penumbral rights of "privacy and repose." These cases bear witness that the right of privacy which presses for recognition here is a legitimate one.

The present case, then, concerns a relationship lying within the zone of privacy created by several fundamental constitutional guarantees. And it concerns a law which, in forbidding the *use* of contraceptives rather than regulating their manufacture or sale, seeks to achieve its goals by means having a maximum destructive impact upon that relationship. Such a law cannot stand in light of the familiar principle, so often applied by this Court, that a "governmental purpose to control or prevent activities constitutionally subject to state regulation may not be achieved by means which sweep unnecessarily broadly and thereby invade the area of protected freedoms." Would we allow the police to search the sacred precincts of marital bedrooms for telltale signs of the use of contraceptives? The very idea is repulsive to the notions of privacy surrounding the marriage relationship.

We deal with a right of privacy older than the Bill of Rights—older than our political parties, older than our school system. Marriage is a coming together for better or for worse, hopefully enduring, and intimate to the degree of being sacred. It is an association that promotes a way of life, not causes; harmony in living, not political faiths; bilateral loyalty, not commercial or social projects. Yet it is an association for as noble a purpose as any involved in our prior decisions.

Reversed.

MR. JUSTICE GOLDBERG, whom the CHIEF JUSTICE and MR. JUSTICE BRENNAN join, concurring.

The language and history of the Ninth Amendment reveal that the Framers of the Constitution believed that there are additional fundamental rights, protected from governmental infringement, which exist alongside those fundamental rights specifically mentioned in the first eight constitutional amendments.

The Ninth Amendment reads, "The enumeration in the Constitution, of certain rights, shall not be construed to deny or disparage others retained by the people." The Amendment is almost entirely the work of James Madison. It was introduced in Congress by him and passed the House and Senate with little or no debate and virtually no change in language. It was proffered to quiet expressed fears that a bill of specifically enumerated rights could not be sufficiently broad to cover all essential rights and that the specific mention of certain rights would be interpreted as a denial that others were protected. . . .

While this Court has had little occasion to interpret the Ninth Amendment, "it cannot be presumed that any clause in the constitution is intended to be without effect." The Ninth Amendment to the Constitution may be regarded by some as a recent discovery and may be forgotten by others, but since 1791 it has been a basic part of the Constitution which we are sworn to uphold. To hold that a right so basic and fundamental and so deep-rooted in our society as the right of privacy in marriage may be infringed because that right is not guaranteed in so many words by the first eight amendments to the Constitution is to ignore the Ninth Amendment and to give it no effect whatsoever. Moreover, a judicial construction that this fundamental right is not protected by the Constitution because it is not mentioned in explicit terms by one of the first eight amendments or elsewhere in the Constitution would violate the Ninth Amendment, which specifically states that "the enumeration in the Constitution, of certain rights shall not be *construed* to deny or disparage others retained by the people." (Emphasis added.) . . .

Nor am I turning somersaults with history in arguing that the Ninth Amendment is relevant in a case dealing with a State's infringement of a fundamental right. While the Ninth Amendment—and indeed the entire Bill of Rights—originally concerned restrictions upon federal power, the subsequently enacted Fourteenth Amendment prohibits the States as well from abridging fundamental personal liberties. And, the Ninth Amendment, in indicating that not all such liberties are specifically mentioned in the first eight amendments, is surely relevant in showing the existence of other fundamental personal rights, now protected from state, as well as federal, infringement. . . .

In sum, I believe that the right of privacy in the marital relation is fundamental and basic—a personal right "retained by the people" within the meaning of the Ninth Amendment. Connecticut cannot constitutionally abridge this fundamental right, which is protected by the Fourteenth Amendment from infringement by the States. I agree with the Court that petitioners' convictions must therefore be reversed.

MR. JUSTICE HARLAN, concurring in the judgment.

I fully agree with the judgment of reversal, but find myself unable to join the Court's opinion. . . .

In my view, the proper constitutional inquiry in this case is whether this Connecticut statute infringes the Due Process Clause of the Fourteenth Amendment because the enactment violates basic values "implicit in the concept of ordered liberty." For reasons stated at length in my dissenting opinion in *Poe v. Ullman*, I believe that it does. While the relevant inquiry may be aided by resort to one or more of the provisions of the Bill of Rights, it is not dependent on them or any of their radiations. The Due Process Clause of the Fourteenth Amendment stands, in my opinion, on its own bottom.

MR. JUSTICE BLACK, with whom MR. JUSTICE STEWART joins, dissenting.

The Court talks about a constitutional "right of privacy" as though there is some constitutional provision or provisions forbidding any law ever to be passed which might abridge the "privacy" of individuals. But there is not. There are, of course, guarantees in certain specific constitutional provisions which are designed in part to protect privacy at certain times and places with respect to certain activities. Such, for example, is the Fourth Amendment's guarantee against "unreasonable searches and seizures." But I think it belittles that Amendment to talk about it as though it protects nothing but "privacy." To treat it that way is to give it a niggardly interpretation, not the kind of liberal reading I think any Bill of Rights provision should be given. The average man would very likely not have his feelings soothed any more by having his property seized openly than by having it seized privately and by stealth. He simply wants his property left alone. And a person can be just as much, if not more, irritated, annoyed and injured by an unceremonious public arrest by a policeman as he is by a seizure in the privacy of his office or home.

One of the most effective ways of diluting or expanding a constitutionally guaranteed right is to substitute for the crucial word or words of a constitutional guarantee another word or words, more or less flexible and more or less restricted in meaning. This fact is well illustrated by the use of the term "right of privacy" as a comprehensive substitute for the Fourth Amendment's guarantee against "unreason-able searches and seizures." "Privacy" is a broad, abstract and ambiguous concept which can easily be shrunken in meaning but which can also, on the other hand, easily be interpreted as a constitutional ban against many things other than searches and seizures. I have expressed the view many times that First Amendment freedoms, for example, have suffered from a failure of the courts to stick to the simple language of the First Amendment in construing it, instead of invoking multitudes of words substituted for those the Framers used. . . . For these reasons I get nowhere in this case by talk about a constitutional "right of privacy" as an emanation from one or more constitutional provisions. I like my privacy as well as the next one, but I am nevertheless compelled to admit that government has a right to invade it unless prohibited by some specific constitutional provision. For these reasons I cannot agree with the Court's judgment and the reasons it gives for holding this Connecticut law unconstitutional. . . .

. . . I think that if properly construed neither the Due Process Clause nor the Ninth Amendment, nor both together, could under any circumstances be a proper basis for invalidating the Connecticut law. I discuss the due process and Ninth Amendment arguments together because on analysis they turn out to be the same thing—merely using different words to claim for this Court and the federal judiciary power to invalidate any legislative act which the judges find irrational, unreasonable or offensive.

The due process argument . . . is based . . . on the premise that this Court is vested with power to invalidate all state laws that it considers to be arbitrary, capricious, unreasonable, or oppressive, or on this Court's belief that a particular state law under scrutiny has no "rational or justifying" purpose, or is offensive to a "sense of fairness and justice." If these formulas based on "natural justice," or others which mean the same thing, are to prevail, they require judges to determine what is or is not constitutional on the basis of their own appraisal of what laws are unwise or unnecessary. The power to make such decisions is of course that of a legislative body. Surely it has to be admitted that no provision of the Constitution specifically gives such blanket power to courts to exercise such a supervisory veto over the wisdom and value of legislative policies and to hold unconstitutional those laws which they believe unwise or dangerous. . . . While . . . our Court has constitutional power to strike down statutes, state or federal, that violate commands of the Federal Constitution, I do not believe that we are granted power by the Due Process Clause or any other constitutional provision or provisions to measure constitutionality by our belief that legislation is arbitrary, capricious or unreasonable, or accomplishes no justifiable purpose, or is offensive to our own notions of "civilized standards of conduct." Such an appraisal of the wisdom of legislation is an attribute of the power to make laws, not of the power to interpret them. The use by federal courts of such a formula or doctrine or whatnot to veto federal or state laws simply takes away from Congress and States the power to make laws based on their own judgment of fairness and wisdom and transfers that power to this Court for ultimate determination—a power which was specifically denied to federal courts by the convention that framed the Constitution. . . .

My Brother GOLDBERG has adopted the recent discovery that the Ninth Amendment as well as the Due Process Clause can be used by this Court as authority to strike down all state legislation which this Court thinks violates "fundamental principles of liberty and justice," or is contrary to the "traditions and [collective] conscience of our people." He also states, without proof satisfactory to me, that in making decisions on this basis judges will not consider "their personal and private notions." One may ask how they can avoid considering them. Our Court certainly has no machinery with which to take a Gallup Poll. And the scientific miracles of this age have not yet produced a gadget which the Court can use to determine what traditions are rooted in the "[collective] conscience of our people." Moreover, one would certainly have to look far beyond the language of the Ninth Amendment to find that the Framers vested in this Court any such awesome veto powers over lawmaking, either by the States or by the Congress. Nor does anything in the history of the Amendment offer any support for such a shocking doctrine. The whole history of the adoption of the Constitution and Bill of Rights points the other way. . . . That Amendment was passed, not to broaden the powers of this Court or any other department of "the General Government," but, as every student of history knows, to assure the people that the Constitution in all its provisions was intended to limit the Federal Government to the powers granted expressly or by necessary implication. . . . [F]or a period of a century and a half no serious suggestion was ever made that the Ninth Amendment, enacted to protect state powers against federal invasion, could be used as a weapon of federal power to prevent state legislatures from passing laws they consider appropriate to govern local affairs. Use of any such broad, unbounded judicial authority would make of this Court's members a day-to-day constitutional convention. . . .

I realize that many good and able men have eloquently spoken and written, sometimes in rhapsodical strains, about the duty of this Court to keep the Constitution in tune with the times. The idea is that the Constitution must be changed from time to time and that this Court is charged with a duty to make those changes. For myself, I must with all deference reject that philosophy. The Constitution makers knew the need for change and provided for it. Amendments suggested by the people's elected representatives can be submitted to the people or their selected agents for ratification. That method of change was good for our Fathers, and being somewhat old-fashioned I must add it is good enough for me. And so, I cannot rely on the Due Process Clause or the Ninth Amendment or any mysterious and uncertain natural law concept as a reason for striking down this state law. The Due Process Clause with an "arbitrary and capricious" . . . formula was liberally used by this Court to strike down economic legislation in the early decades of this century, threatening, many people thought, the tranquility and stability of the Nation. See, e.g., *Lochner v. New York*. That formula, based on subjective considerations of "natural justice," is no less dangerous when used to enforce this Court's views about personal rights than those about economic rights. I had thought that we had laid that formula, as a means for striking down state legislation, to rest once and for all.

MR. JUSTICE STEWART, whom MR. JUSTICE BLACK, joins dissenting.

Since 1879 Connecticut has had on its books a law which forbids the use of contraceptives by anyone. I think this is an uncommonly silly law. As a practical matter, the law is obviously unenforceable, except in the oblique context of the present case. As a philosophical matter, I believe the use of contraceptives in the relationship of marriage should be left to personal and private choice, based upon each individual's moral, ethical, and religious beliefs. As a matter of social policy, I think professional counsel about methods of birth control should be available to all, so that each individual's choice can be meaningfully made. But we are not asked in this case to say whether we think this law is unwise, or even asinine. We are asked to hold that it violates the United States Constitution. And that I cannot do.

In the course of its opinion the Court refers to no less than six Amendments to the Constitution: the First, the Third, the Fourth, the Fifth, the Ninth, and the Fourteenth. But the Court does not say which of these Amendments, if any, it thinks is infringed by this Connecticut law. . . .

What provision of the Constitution, then, does make this state law invalid? The Court says it is the right of privacy "created by several fundamental constitutional guarantees." With all deference, I can find no such general right of privacy in the Bill of Rights, in any other part of the Constitution, or in any case ever before decided by this Court.

At the oral argument in this case we were told that the Connecticut law does not "conform to current community standards." But it is not the function of this Court to decide cases on the basis of community standards. We are here to decide cases "agreeably to the Constitution and laws of the United States." It is the essence of judicial duty to subordinate our own personal views, our own ideas of what legislation is wise and what is not. If, as I should surely hope, the law before us does not reflect the standards of the people of Connecticut, the people of Connecticut can freely exercise their true Ninth and Tenth Amendment rights to persuade their elected representatives to repeal it. That is the constitutional way to take this law off the books.

Griswold was a landmark decision because it created a constitutional right to privacy and deemed that right fundamental. But the justices disagreed about where that right existed within the Constitution *(see Table 16-1).* William O. Douglas's opinion for the Court asserted that specific guarantees in the Bill of Rights have penumbras, formed by emanations from First, Third, Fourth, Fifth, and Ninth Amendment guarantees "that help give them life and substance." In other words, Douglas claimed that even though the Constitution failed to mention privacy, clauses within the document created zones that gave rise to the right. Note that in making this argument, Douglas avoided reliance on the Fourteenth Amendment's due process clause. He apparently believed that grounding

TABLE 16-1 The *Griswold* Splits

Location of the Privacy Right	Justices
First, Third, Fourth, Fifth, and Ninth Amendments	Douglas, Clark
Ninth Amendment	Goldberg, Brennan, Warren
Fourteenth Amendment (Due Process Clause)	Harlan, White
No general right to privacy in the Constitution	Black, Stewart

privacy in that clause would hark back to the days of *Lochner* and substantive due process, a doctrine he explicitly rejected.[5]

Justice Arthur Goldberg, writing for Earl Warren and William Brennan, did not dispute Douglas's penumbra theory but chose to emphasize the relevance of the Ninth Amendment. In Goldberg's view that amendment, which states, "The enumeration in the Constitution, of certain rights, shall not be construed to deny or disparage others retained by the people," could be read to contain a right to privacy. His logic was simple: The wording of the amendment, coupled with its history, suggested that it was "proffered to quiet expressed fears that a bill of specifically enumerated rights could not be sufficiently broad to cover all essential rights," including the right to privacy. Harlan took the opportunity to reiterate his stance in *Poe* that the due process clause of the Fourteenth Amendment prohibits such legislation. In holding to his *Poe* opinion, however, Harlan went one step beyond the Goldberg concurrers; he rejected the Douglas penumbra theory, asserting, "While the relevant inquiry may be aided by resort to one or more of the provisions of the Bill of Rights, it is not dependent on them or any of their radiations." Justice Byron White also filed a concurring opinion lending support to Harlan's due process view of privacy.

5. For an inside view of the Court's decision-making process in *Griswold,* see Bernard Schwartz, *The Unpublished Opinions of the Warren Court* (New York: Oxford University Press, 1985).

As important as *Griswold* was and still is, it is clear that the justices did not speak with one voice. Seven agreed, more or less, that a right to privacy existed, but they located that right in three distinct constitutional spheres. The other two—Hugo Black and Potter Stewart—argued that the Constitution did not contain a general right to privacy, but they did more than that. They took their colleagues to task for, in their view, reverting back to the days of *Lochner* and substantive due process. From Black and Stewart's vantage point, it should be the people, not the courts, that pressure legislatures to change "unwise" laws.

Whether a right to privacy existed and where the right was located, however, were not the only questions raised by *Griswold*. Another important issue concerned the areas covered by this newly found right. Clearly, it protected "notions of privacy surrounding the marriage relationship," but beyond that observers could only speculate.

In this chapter we examine the other areas where the Court has applied *Griswold*. We look first at its role in the issue of abortion and then into its extensions into other private activities. Keep the *Griswold* precedent in mind. To which interpretation of the right to privacy has the Court subscribed in the cases that follow? Has the Court's approach changed with its increasing conservatism? Or do the majority of justices continue to adopt its basic tenets?

REPRODUCTIVE FREEDOM AND THE RIGHT TO PRIVACY

Although all right-to-privacy issues tend to engender controversy, few have caused emotional reactions of such intensity and duration as has the debate over abortion initiated by the Court's decision in *Roe v. Wade* in 1973. Views on abortion have affected the outcome of many political races; occupied preeminent places on legislative, executive, and judicial agendas; and played a role in the nomination proceedings for Supreme Court and lower federal court judges.

What is particularly intriguing about the issue is that the Court generated the furor. Prior to 1973 abortion was not an especially important political issue. As shown in Figure 16-1, many states had on their books laws that permitted abortion only to save the life of the mother; many

of these laws were enacted in the late 1800s. Other states had reformed their legislation in the 1960s to allow for abortion when pregnancy had resulted from incest or when the baby was likely to be severely deformed. The majority of states defined performing or obtaining an abortion, under all other circumstances, as a criminal offense. These conditions do not mean that states were not under pressure to change their laws. During the 1960s a growing pro-choice movement, led by groups such as the American Civil Liberties Union (ACLU) and NARAL, which at that time stood for the National Association for Repeal of Abortion Laws, sought to persuade states to legalize the procedure fully, that is, to allow abortion on demand.

When only a handful of states even considered taking such action, attorneys and leaders of the pro-choice movement supplemented their legislative lobbying with litigation, initiating dozens of suits in federal and state courts. These cases challenged restrictive abortion laws on several grounds, including the First Amendment's freedoms of association and speech for doctors (and patients) and the Fourteenth Amendment's equal protection clause (alleging discrimination against women). But the most commonly invoked legal ground was *Griswold*'s right to privacy. Because it was unclear to attorneys which clause of the Constitution generated the right to privacy, in many cases, pro-choice lawyers covered their bases by arguing on all three specific grounds. But their larger point was clear: The right to privacy was broad enough to encompass the right to obtain an abortion. And, because the right to privacy was "fundamental," logic would hold that the right to obtain an abortion was also fundamental, meaning that states could proscribe the procedure only with a compelling interest. Such an interest, pro-choice attorneys asserted, did not exist.

The result of this legal activity was an avalanche of litigation. Pro-choice groups flooded the U.S. courts with lawsuits—some on behalf of doctors, some for women—challenging both major kinds of abortion laws: those that permitted abortion only to save the life of the mother and those that allowed abortion in cases of rape or incest or to save the life of the mother. They were hoping that the Supreme Court would hear at least one.

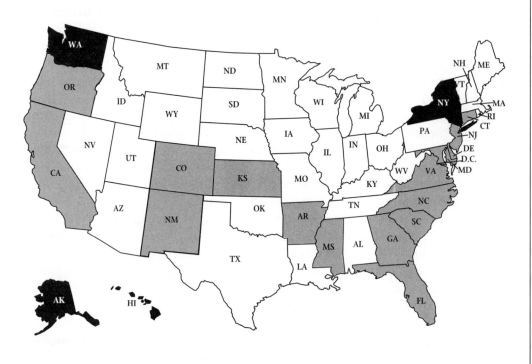

FIGURE 16-1 Legislative Action on Abortion through the Early 1970s

Key:

States in white: retained existing law, which generally permitted abortions to save the life of the mother only.

States in gray: altered existing abortion law, between 1966 and 1970, to permit abortion under certain circumstances, such as pregnancies resulting from rape or incest.

States in black: repealed existing abortion law in 1970 to allow for some form of "abortion on demand."

Their wish was granted when the Court agreed to hear arguments in December 1971 in two cases, *Roe v. Wade,* a challenge to a Texas law, representing the most restrictive kinds of abortion laws, and *Doe v. Bolton,* a challenge to a Georgia law, representing the newer, less restrictive laws. The justices had problems resolving these cases, so heard them again at the beginning of the next term.

In the meantime, the Court handed down a decision that had some bearing on the debate. In 1972 it struck down a Massachusetts law that prohibited the sale of contraceptives to unmarried people. Writing for a six-person majority (with only Chief Justice Warren Burger dissenting) in *Eisenstadt v. Baird,* Justice Brennan asserted that the law violated the "rights of single people" under the Fourteenth Amendment's equal protection clause. But, in *dicta,* he went much further:

If under *Griswold* the distribution of contraceptives to married persons cannot be prohibited, a ban on distribution to unmarried persons would be equally impermissible. It is true that in *Griswold* the right of privacy in question inhered in the marital relationship. Yet the marital couple is not an independent entity with a mind and heart of its own, but an association of two individuals each with separate intellectual and emotional makeup. If the right of privacy means anything, it is the right of the individual, married or single, to be free from unwarranted governmental intrusion into matters so fundamentally affecting a person as the decision whether to bear or beget a child.

Whether Brennan wrote this with *Roe* and *Doe* in mind we do not know, but clearly *Eisenstadt* heartened pro-choice forces. Their optimism was not misplaced, for, on January 22, 1973, when the Court handed down its decisions in *Roe* and *Doe,* they had won. As you read *Roe,* pay particular attention to the Court's logic: On what grounds did it strike down the Texas law?

Roe v. Wade

410 U.S. 113 (1973)
http://laws.findlaw.com/US/410/113.html
Oral arguments may be found at: http://www.oyez.org
Vote: 7 (Blackmun, Brennan, Burger, Douglas, Marshall,
        Powell, Stewart)
    2 (Rehnquist, White)
Opinion of the Court: Blackmun
Concurring opinions: Burger, Douglas, Stewart
Dissenting opinions: Rehnquist, White

In August 1969, twenty-one-year-old carnival worker Norma McCorvey was pregnant and claimed that the pregnancy was the result of rape.[6] Her doctor refused to perform an abortion, citing an 1857 Texas law, revised in 1879, that made it a crime to "procure an abortion" unless it was necessary to save the life of a mother. He provided her with the name of a lawyer who handled adoptions. The lawyer, in turn, sent her to two other attorneys, Linda Coffee and Sarah Weddington, whom he knew to be interested in challenging the Texas law.

Coffee and Weddington went after the Texas law with a vengeance, challenging it on all possible grounds: privacy, women's rights, due process, and so forth. Their efforts paid off; a three-judge district court ruled in their favor, mostly on Ninth Amendment privacy grounds. But because the court would not issue an injunction to the state law, McCorvey, using the pseudonym Jane Roe, and her attorneys appealed to the U.S. Supreme Court.

6. We draw this discussion from the papers of William J. Brennan Jr., Manuscript Division, Library of Congress; Lee Epstein and Joseph F. Kobylka, *The Supreme Court and Legal Change* (Chapel Hill: University of North Carolina Press, 1992); Lee Epstein and Jack Knight, *The Choices Justices Make* (Washington, D.C.: CQ Press, 1998); and Marion Faux, *Roe v. Wade* (New York: Macmillan, 1988). For other accounts, see Eva Rubin, *Abortion, Politics, and the Courts* (Westport, Conn.: Greenwood Press, 1987); and Richard C. Cortner, *The Supreme Court and Civil Liberties Policy* (Palo Alto, Calif.: Mayfield, 1975).

Once the Supreme Court agreed to hear the case, pro-choice and pro-life sides mobilized their forces. On the pro-choice side, the ACLU and other groups helped Weddington and Coffee, who had never appeared before the Court, prepare their briefs and arguments. These groups also lined up numerous amici, including the American College of Obstetricians and Gynecologists, Planned Parenthood Federation, and the American Association of University Women.

In general, the pro-choice side wanted to convince the Court that abortion was a fundamental right under the *Griswold* doctrine. So unless the state could provide a compelling and narrowly drawn interest, the Texas law should fall. It also presented a mass of data indicating that physical and mental health risks are associated with restrictive abortion laws.

The state countered with arguments concerning the rights of fetuses. Its brief devoted twenty-four pages, along with nine photographs of fetuses at various stages of development, to depict the "humanness" of the unborn and to support its argument that a state has a compelling interest in protecting human life. The state's position was supported by several pro-life organizations, including the National Right to Life Committee and the League for Infants, Fetuses, and the Elderly, and groups of doctors and nurses.

On December 13, 1971, the Supreme Court heard oral arguments in *Roe v. Wade* and *Doe v. Bolton,* and three days later it met to decide the abortion cases. Only seven justices were present because President Richard Nixon's newest appointees, Lewis F. Powell Jr. and William H. Rehnquist, had not participated in oral arguments. Of the seven participating justices, a four-person majority (Douglas, Brennan, Marshall, and Stewart) thought the abortion laws should be struck down, although for somewhat different reasons. Moreover, they were unsure about the "time problem"—whether a woman could obtain an abortion any time during her pregnancy or over a more limited period, such as the first six months. White came down most definitively in favor of the pro-life position. Warren Burger and Harry Blackmun, who had joined the Court in 1969 and 1970, respectively, were less decisive; the chief justice leaned toward upholding laws

BOX 16-1   HARRY ANDREW BLACKMUN (1970–1994)

HARRY A. BLACKMUN was born November 12, 1908, in Nashville, Illinois. He spent most of his early life in the Minneapolis-St. Paul area, where his father was an official of the Twin Cities Savings and Loan Company. In grade school Blackmun began a friendship with Warren Burger, with whom he was later to serve on the Supreme Court.

Showing an early aptitude for mathematics, Blackmun attended Harvard University on a scholarship. He majored in mathematics and thought briefly of becoming a physician, but chose law instead. He graduated Phi Beta Kappa from Harvard in 1929 and entered Harvard Law School, graduating in 1932. During his law school years, Blackmun supported himself with a variety of odd jobs, including tutoring in math and driving the launch for the college crew team.

After law school, Blackmun returned to St. Paul, where he served for a year and a half as a law clerk to Judge John B. Sanborn, whom Blackmun was to succeed on the U.S. Circuit Court twenty-six years later. He left the clerkship in 1933 to enter private practice with a Minneapolis law firm, where he remained for sixteen years. During that time he also taught at the Mitchell College of Law in St. Paul, Chief Justice Burger's alma mater, and at the University of Minnesota Law School.

Blackmun married Dorothy E. Clark, June 21, 1941; the couple had three daughters.

In 1950 he accepted a post as "house counsel" for the world-famous Mayo Clinic in Rochester, Minnesota. There, Blackmun quickly developed a reputation among his colleagues as a serious man totally engrossed in his profession.

BLACKMUN'S reputation followed him to the bench of the U.S. Court of Appeals for the Eighth Circuit, to which he was appointed by President Dwight D. Eisenhower in 1959. As an appeals court judge, Blackmun became known for his scholarly and thorough opinions.

Blackmun's nomination to the Supreme Court was President Richard Nixon's third try to fill the seat vacated by Justice Abe Fortas's resignation. The Senate had refused to confirm Nixon's first two nominees—Clement F. Haynesworth Jr. of South Carolina and G. Harrold Carswell of Florida. Nixon remarked that he had concluded from the rejection of his first two nominees that the Senate "as it is presently constituted" would not confirm a southern nominee who was also a judicial conservative.

Nixon then turned to Blackmun, who was confirmed without opposition. During his first years on the Court, Blackmun was frequently linked with Burger as the "Minnesota Twins," who thought and voted alike, but, beginning with his authorship of the Court's 1973 ruling in *Roe v. Wade,* which legalized abortion, Blackmun moved in a steadily more liberal direction, leaving Burger behind in the Court's conservative wing.

Blackmun retired from the Court August 3, 1994. He died March 4, 1999.

SOURCE: Adapted from David Savage, *Guide to the U.S. Supreme Court,* 4th ed. (Washington, D.C.: CQ Press, 2004), 1012–1013.

prohibiting abortion, and Blackmun leaned toward the pro-choice camp. Despite the disagreement about the reason why the laws were unconstitutional and about the time frame for abortions, the result was clear: The pro-choice side would win by a 5–2 or 4–3 vote, depending on how Blackmun voted. Although the Court's conference ended with some ambiguity over Blackmun's position, Burger assigned the *Roe* and *Doe* opinions to him. *(See Box 16-1.)*

This assignment triggered a series of events. The first was an irate letter from Douglas to Burger, in which Douglas had two bones to pick: First, as the senior member of the majority, he, not Burger, should have assigned the opinion; second, Blackmun should not have received the assignment in any event because Douglas's vote tallies had recorded Blackmun as voting with the minority. Burger responded that he would not change the assignment. He said, "At the close of discussion of this case, I remarked to the Conference that there were, literally, not enough columns to mark up an accurate reflection of the voting. . . . I therefore marked down no votes and said this was a case that would have to stand or fall on the writing, when it was done. . . . This is still my view of how to handle . . . this sensitive case."

Still uncertain of how Blackmun would dispose of the cases and of what rationale he would use, some of the justices began preparing opinions. Indeed, it took Douglas only a few weeks to circulate a memorandum to Brennan, who responded with some suggestions for revision and the admonition that Douglas hold onto the opinion until Blackmun circulated his.

It was a long wait. In mid-May 1972 Blackmun sent around his first draft in *Roe*—a draft that came to the "right" result in Brennan's and Douglas's minds but did so for the wrong (that is, narrowest possible) reasons: The restrictive Texas abortion law was void for vagueness and not because it interfered with any fundamental right. The four pro-choice justices were disappointed and urged Blackmun to recast his draft. In so doing, they raised the opinion assignment issue again. Douglas wrote to Blackmun:

In *Roe v. Wade*, my notes confirm what Bill Brennan wrote yesterday in his memo to you—that abortion statutes were invalid save as they required that an abortion be performed by a licensed physician within a limited time after conception.

That was the clear view of a majority of the seven who heard argument. My notes also indicate that the Chief had the opposed view, which made it puzzling as to why he made the assignment at all except that he indicated he might affirm on vagueness. My notes indicate that Byron [Justice White] was not firmly settled and that you might join the majority of four.

So I think we should meet what Bill Brennan calls the "core constitutional issue."

At the same time, Douglas and the others were ready to sign Blackmun's draft, believing that it represented the

best they could do. They were happier with Blackmun's effort in *Doe v. Bolton*, the Georgia abortion case, because it adopted much of Douglas's and Brennan's beliefs about the importance of privacy and women's rights. Where they thought Blackmun went astray was in exploring the state's interest in protecting life. In this version, he stressed the point that somewhere around quickening a woman's right to privacy is no longer "unlimited. It must be balanced against the state. We cannot automatically strike down . . . features of the Georgia statute simply because they restrict any right on the part of the woman to have an abortion at will." Despite the qualms Brennan and Douglas had over such a balancing approach, they planned to sign the opinion; it led Blackmun to the "right" result. Douglas went so far as to "congratulate" Blackmun on his "fine job" and expressed the hope that "we can agree to get the cases down this Term, so that we can spend our energies next Term on other matters."

Just when it appeared that a five-person majority would coalesce around Blackmun's opinion, on May 31 Burger initiated efforts to have *Roe* and *Doe* reargued. Ostensibly, his reason was that "[t]hese cases . . . are not as simple for me as they appear for the others." He also "complained that part of his problem . . . resulted from the poor quality of oral argument." Brennan, Douglas, Stewart, and Marshall disagreed. In their view, Burger pushed for reargument because he was displeased with Blackmun's opinion in *Doe* and thought his side would stand a better chance of victory next term when Powell and Rehnquist would participate in the decision. Douglas later suggested that Burger believed the *Doe* opinion would prove embarrassing to President Nixon's reelection campaign and sought to minimize the damage. The same day Burger issued his memo, Blackmun also suggested that the cases be reargued. In a memo to conference, he wrote: "Although it would prove costly to me personally, in the light of energy and hours expended, I have now concluded, somewhat reluctantly, that reargument in both cases at an early date in the next term, would perhaps be advisable." Despite Brennan's and Douglas's attempts to thwart this action, after White and the two new appointees voted with Burger, on the last day of the 1971 term the Court ordered rearguments in both *Roe* and *Doe*.[7] Three months after the after the reargument took place, the Court issued its decision with Justice Blackmun again having been assigned the task of writing for the majority.

MR. JUSTICE BLACKMUN delivered the opinion of the Court.

We forthwith acknowledge our awareness of the sensitive and emotional nature of the abortion controversy, of the vigorous opposing views, even among physicians, and of the deep and seemingly absolute convictions that the subject inspires. One's philosophy, one's experiences, one's exposure to the raw edges of human existence, one's religious training, one's attitudes toward life and family and their values, and the moral standards one establishes and seeks to observe, are all likely to influence and to color one's thinking and conclusions about abortion.

In addition, population growth, pollution, poverty, and racial overtones tend to complicate and not to simplify the problem.

Our task, of course, is to resolve the issue by constitutional measurement, free of emotion and of predilection. We seek earnestly to do this, and, because we do, we have inquired into, and in this opinion place some emphasis upon, medical and medical-legal history and what that history reveals about man's attitudes toward the abortion procedure over the centuries. . . .

The principal thrust of appellant's attack on the Texas statutes is that they improperly invade a right, said to be possessed by the pregnant woman, to choose to terminate her pregnancy. Appellant would discover this right in the concept of personal "liberty" embodied in the Fourteenth Amendment's Due Process Clause in personal, marital, familial, and sexual privacy said to be protected by the Bill of Rights or its penumbras, see *Griswold v. Connecticut* (1965), or among those rights reserved to the people by the Ninth

Amendment, *Griswold v. Connecticut.* Before addressing this claim, we feel it desirable briefly to survey, in several aspects, the history of abortion, for such insight as that history may afford us, and then to examine the state purposes and interests behind the criminal abortion laws.

It perhaps is not generally appreciated that the restrictive criminal abortion laws in effect in a majority of States today are of relatively recent vintage. Those laws, generally proscribing abortion or its attempt at any time during pregnancy except when necessary to preserve the pregnant woman's life, are not of ancient or even of common-law origin. Instead, they derive from statutory changes effected, for the most part, in the latter half of the 19th century. . . .

Three reasons have been advanced to explain historically the enactment of criminal abortion laws in the 19th century and to justify their continued existence.

It has been argued occasionally that these laws were the product of a Victorian social concern to discourage illicit sexual conduct. Texas, however, does not advance this justification in the present case, and it appears that no court or commentator has taken the argument seriously. . . .

A second reason is concerned with abortion as a medical procedure. When most criminal abortion laws were first enacted, the procedure was a hazardous one for the woman. This was particularly true prior to the development of antisepsis. . . . Thus, it has been argued that a State's real concern in enacting a criminal abortion law was to protect the pregnant woman, that is, to restrain her from submitting to a procedure that placed her life in serious jeopardy.

The modern medical techniques have altered this situation. . . . Consequently, any interest of the State in protecting the woman from an inherently hazardous procedure, except when it would be equally dangerous for her to forgo it, has largely disappeared. Of course, important state interests in the areas of health and medical standards do remain. The State has a legitimate interest in seeing to it that abortion, like any other medical procedure, is performed under circumstances that insure maximum safety for the patient. . . . Moreover, the risk to the woman increases as her pregnancy continues. Thus, the State retains a definite interest in protecting the woman's own health and safety when an abortion is proposed at a late stage of pregnancy.

The third reason is the State's interest—some phrase it in terms of duty—in protecting prenatal life. Some of the argument for this justification rests on the theory that a

---

7. Both Brennan and Douglas wrote letters to Blackmun attempting to convince him that the cases should not be reargued. When they failed to convince Blackmun, Douglas warned Burger, saying, "If the vote of Conference is to reargue, then I will file a statement telling what is happening to us and the tragedy it entails." He also accused Burger, in a memo to conference, of trying "to bend the Court to his will" and imperiling "the integrity of the institution." Douglas never carried through on his threat to take the matter public, but the *Washington Post* carried a story about it.

new human life is present from the moment of conception. The State's interest and general obligation to protect life then extends, it is argued, to prenatal life. Only when the life of the pregnant mother herself is at stake, balanced against the life she carries within her, should the interest of the embryo or fetus not prevail. Logically, of course, a legitimate state interest in this area need not stand or fall on acceptance of the belief that life begins at conception or at some other point prior to live birth. In assessing the State's interest, recognition may be given to the less rigid claim that as long as at least *potential* life is involved, the State may assert interests beyond the protection of the pregnant woman alone. . . .

It is with these interests, and the weight to be attached to them, that this case is concerned.

The Constitution does not explicitly mention any right of privacy. In a line of decisions, however, the Court has recognized that a right of personal privacy, or a guarantee of certain areas or zones of privacy, does exist under the Constitution. In varying contexts, the Court or individual Justices have, indeed, found at least the roots of that right in the First Amendment, in the Fourth and Fifth Amendments, in the penumbras of the Bill of Rights, in the Ninth Amendment, or in the concept of liberty guaranteed by the first section of the Fourteenth Amendment. These decisions make it clear that only personal rights that can be deemed "fundamental" or "implicit in the concept of ordered liberty" are included in this guarantee of personal privacy. They also make it clear that the right has some extension to activities relating to marriage, procreation, family relationships, and child rearing and education.

This right of privacy, whether it be founded in the Fourteenth Amendment's concept of personal liberty and restrictions upon state action, as we feel it is, or, as the District Court determined, in the Ninth Amendment's reservation of rights to the people, is broad enough to encompass a woman's decision whether or not to terminate her pregnancy. The detriment that the State would impose upon the pregnant woman by denying this choice altogether is apparent. Specific and direct harm medically diagnosable even in early pregnancy may be involved. Maternity, or additional offspring, may force upon the woman a distressful life and future. Psychological harm may be imminent. Mental and physical health may be taxed by child care. There is also the distress, for all concerned, associated

with the unwanted child, and there is the problem of bringing a child into a family already unable, psychologically and otherwise, to care for it. In other cases, as in this one, the additional difficulties and continuing stigma of unwed motherhood may be involved. All these are factors the woman and her responsible physician necessarily will consider in consultation.

On the basis of elements such as these, appellant and some *amici* argue that the woman's right is absolute and that she is entitled to terminate her pregnancy at whatever time, in whatever way, and for whatever reason she alone chooses. With this we do not agree. Appellant's arguments that Texas either has no valid interest at all in regulating the abortion decision, or no interest strong enough to support any limitation upon the woman's sole determination, are unpersuasive. The Court's decisions recognizing a right of privacy also acknowledge that some state regulation in areas protected by that right is appropriate. As noted above, a State may properly assert important interests in safeguarding health, in maintaining medical standards, and in protecting potential life. At some point in pregnancy, these respective interests become sufficiently compelling to sustain regulation of the factors that govern the abortion decision. The privacy right involved, therefore, cannot be said to be absolute. . . .

We, therefore, conclude that the right of personal privacy includes the abortion decision, but that this right is not unqualified and must be considered against important state interests in regulation. . . .

The District Court held that the appellee failed to meet his burden of demonstrating that the Texas statute's infringement upon Roe's rights was necessary to support a compelling state interest, and that, although the appellee presented "several compelling justifications for state presence in the area of abortions," the statutes outstripped these justifications and swept "far beyond any areas of compelling state interest." Appellant and appellee both contest that holding. Appellant, as has been indicated, claims an absolute right that bars any state imposition of criminal penalties in the area. Appellee argues that the State's determination to recognize and protect prenatal life from and after conception constitutes a compelling state interest. As noted above, we do not agree fully with either formulation.

A. The appellee and certain *amici* argue that the fetus is a "person" within the language and meaning of the Fourteenth Amendment. . . .

The Constitution does not define "person" in so many words. Section 1 of the Fourteenth Amendment contains three references to "person." The first, in defining "citizens," speaks of "persons born or naturalized in the United States." The word also appears both in the Due Process Clause and in the Equal Protection Clause. "Person" is used in other places in the Constitution: in the listing of qualifications for Representatives and Senators, Art. I, §2, cl. 2, and §3, cl. 3; in the Apportionment Clause, Art. I, §2, §3. . . . But in nearly all these instances, the use of the word is such that it has application only postnatally. None indicates, with any assurance, that it has any possible prenatal application.

All this, together with our observation that throughout the major portion of the 19th century prevailing legal abortion practices were far freer than they are today, persuades us that the word "person," as used in the Fourteenth Amendment, does not include the unborn. . . .

This conclusion, however, does not of itself fully answer the contentions raised by Texas, and we pass on to other considerations.

B. The pregnant woman cannot be isolated in her privacy. She carries an embryo and, later, a fetus, if one accepts the medical definitions of the developing young in the human uterus. The situation therefore is inherently different from marital intimacy, or bedroom possession of obscene material, or marriage, or procreation. . . . As we have intimated above, it is reasonable and appropriate for a State to decide that at some point in time another interest, that of health of the mother or that of potential human life, becomes significantly involved. The woman's privacy is no longer sole and any right of privacy she possesses must be measured accordingly.

Texas urges that, apart from the Fourteenth Amendment, life begins at conception and is present throughout pregnancy, and that, therefore, the State has a compelling interest in protecting that life from and after conception. We need not resolve the difficult question of when life begins. When those trained in the respective disciplines of medicine, philosophy, and theology are unable to arrive at any consensus, the judiciary, at this point in the development of man's knowledge, is not in a position to speculate as to the answer. . . .

In view of all this, we do not agree that, by adopting one theory of life, Texas may override the rights of the pregnant woman that are at stake. We repeat, however, that the State does have an important and legitimate interest in preserving and protecting the health of the pregnant woman, whether she be a resident of the State or a non-resident who seeks medical consultation and treatment there, and that it has still another important and legitimate interest in protecting the potentiality of human life. These interests are separate and distinct. Each grows in substantiality as the woman approaches term and, at a point during pregnancy, each becomes "compelling."

With respect to the State's important and legitimate interest in the health of the mother, the "compelling" point, in the light of present medical knowledge, is at approximately the end of the first trimester. This is so because of the now-established medical fact . . . that until the end of the first trimester mortality in abortion may be less than mortality in normal childbirth. It follows that, from and after this point, a State may regulate the abortion procedure to the extent that the regulation reasonably relates to the preservation and protection of maternal health. Examples of permissible state regulation in this area are requirements as to the qualifications of the person who is to perform the abortion; as to the licensure of that person; as to the facility in which the procedure is to be performed, that is, whether it must be a hospital or may be a clinic or some other place of less-than-hospital status; as to the licensing of the facility; and the like.

This means, on the other hand, that, for the period of pregnancy prior to this "compelling" point, the attending physician, in consultation with his patient, is free to determine, without regulation by the State, that, in his medical judgment, the patient's pregnancy should be terminated. If that decision is reached, the judgment may be effectuated by an abortion free of interference by the State.

With respect to the State's important and legitimate interest in potential life, the "compelling" point is at viability. This is so because the fetus then presumably has the capability of meaningful life outside the mother's womb. State regulation protective of fetal life after viability thus has both logical and biological justifications. If the State is interested in protecting fetal life after viability, it may go so far as to proscribe abortion during that period, except when it is necessary to preserve the life or health of the mother.

Measured against these standards, . . . the Texas [law] . . . , in restricting legal abortions to those "procured or attempted by medical advice for the purpose of saving the life of the mother," sweeps too broadly. The statute makes no distinction between abortions performed early in pregnancy and those performed later, and it limits to a single reason, "saving" the mother's life, the legal justification for the procedure. The statute, therefore, cannot survive the constitutional attack made upon it here. . . .

To summarize and to repeat:

1. A state criminal abortion statute of the current Texas type, that excepts from criminality only a *life-saving* procedure on behalf of the mother, without regard to pregnancy stage and without recognition of the other interests involved, is violative of the Due Process Clause of the Fourteenth Amendment.

(a) For the stage prior to approximately the end of the first trimester, the abortion decision and its effectuation must be left to the medical judgment of the pregnant woman's attending physician.

(b) For the stage subsequent to approximately the end of the first trimester, the State, in promoting its interest in the health of the mother, may, if it chooses, regulate the abortion procedure in ways that are reasonably related to maternal health.

(c) For the stage subsequent to viability, the State in promoting its interest in the potentiality of human life may, if it chooses, regulate, and even proscribe, abortion except where it is necessary, in appropriate medical judgment, for the preservation of the life or health of the mother. . . .

This holding, we feel, is consistent with the relative weights of the respective interests involved, with the lessons and examples of medical and legal history, with the lenity of the common law, and with the demands of the profound problems of the present day. The decision leaves the State free to place increasing restrictions on abortion as the period of pregnancy lengthens, so long as those restrictions are tailored to the recognized state interests. The decision vindicates the right of the physician to administer medical treatment according to his professional judgment up to the points where important state interests provide compelling justifications for intervention. Up to those points, the abortion decision in all its aspects is inherently, and primarily, a medical decision, and basic responsibility for it must rest with the physician. If an individual practitioner abuses the privilege of exercising proper medical judgment, the usual remedies, judicial and intra-professional, are available.[8]

MR. JUSTICE REHNQUIST, dissenting.

I have difficulty in concluding, as the Court does, that the right of "privacy" is involved in this case. Texas, by the statute here challenged, bars the performance of a medical abortion by a licensed physician on a plaintiff such as Roe. A transaction resulting in an operation such as this is not "private" in the ordinary usage of that word. Nor is the "privacy" that the Court finds here even a distant relative of the freedom from searches and seizures protected by the Fourth Amendment to the Constitution, which the Court has referred to as embodying a right to privacy. *Katz v. United States* (1967).

If the Court means by the term "privacy" no more than that the claim of a person to be free from unwanted state regulation of consensual transactions may be a form of "liberty" protected by the Fourteenth Amendment, there is no doubt that similar claims have been upheld in our earlier decisions on the basis of that liberty. I agree . . . that the "liberty," against deprivation of which without due process the Fourteenth Amendment protects, embraces more than the rights found in the Bill of Rights. But that liberty is not guaranteed absolutely against deprivation, only against deprivation without due process of law. The test traditionally applied in the area of social and economic legislation is whether or not a law such as that challenged has a rational relation to a valid state objective. . . . The Due Process Clause of the Fourteenth Amendment undoubtedly does place a limit, albeit a broad one, on legislative power to enact laws such as this. If the Texas statute were to prohibit an abortion even where the mother's life is in jeopardy, I have little doubt

8. *Authors' note:* In *Doe*, decided the same day as *Roe*, the Court reviewed a challenge to newer abortion laws enacted by some states in the 1960s. Whereas Texas permitted abortions only to save a mother's life, Georgia allowed them under the following circumstances: (1) when a "duly licensed Georgia physician" determines in "his best clinical judgment" that carrying the baby to term would injure the mother's life or health; (2) when a high likelihood existed that the fetus would be born with a serious deformity; and (3) when the pregnancy was the result of rape. The law contained other requirements, the most stringent of which was that two other doctors agree with the judgment of the one performing the abortion. Reiterating his opinion in *Roe*, Blackmun struck down the Georgia law as a violation of Fourteenth Amendment guarantees. Once again, six other members of the Court agreed with his conclusion.

that such a statute would lack a rational relation to a valid state objective. . . . But the Court's sweeping invalidation of any restrictions on abortion during the first trimester is impossible to justify under that standard, and the conscious weighing of competing factors that the Court's opinion apparently substitutes for the established test is far more appropriate to a legislative judgment than to a judicial one.

The Court eschews the history of the Fourteenth Amendment in its reliance on the "compelling state interest" test. . . . But the Court adds a new wrinkle to this test by transposing it from the legal considerations associated with the Equal Protection Clause of the Fourteenth Amendment to this case arising under the Due Process Clause of the Fourteenth Amendment. Unless I misapprehend the consequences of this transplanting of the "compelling state interest test," the Court's opinion will accomplish the seemingly impossible feat of leaving this area of the law more confused than it found it. . . .

. . . As in *Lochner* and similar cases applying substantive due process standards to economic and social welfare legislation, the adoption of the compelling state interest standard will inevitably require this Court to examine the legislative policies and pass on the wisdom of these policies in the very process of deciding whether a particular state interest put forward may or may not be "compelling." The decision here to break pregnancy into three distinct terms and to outline the permissible restrictions the State may impose in each one, for example, partakes more of judicial legislation than it does of a determination of the intent of the drafters of the Fourteenth Amendment.

The fact that a majority of the States reflecting, after all, the majority sentiment in those States, have had restrictions on abortions for at least a century is a strong indication, it seems to me, that the asserted right to an abortion is not "so rooted in the traditions and conscience of our people as to be ranked as fundamental." . . . Even today, when society's views on abortion are changing, the very existence of the debate is evidence that the "right" to an abortion is not so universally accepted as the appellant would have us believe.

To reach its result, the Court necessarily has had to find within the scope of the Fourteenth Amendment a right that was apparently completely unknown to the drafters of the Amendment. As early as 1821, the first state law dealing directly with abortion was enacted by the Connecticut Legislature. By the time of the adoption of the Fourteenth Amendment in 1868, there were at least 36 laws enacted by state or territorial legislatures limiting abortion. While many States have amended or updated their laws, 21 of the laws on the books in 1868 remain in effect today. Indeed, the Texas statute struck down today was, as the majority notes, first enacted in 1857 and "has remained substantially unchanged to the present time."

There apparently was no question concerning the validity of this provision or of any of the other state statutes when the Fourteenth Amendment was adopted. The only conclusion possible from this history is that the drafters did not intend to have the Fourteenth Amendment withdraw from the States the power to legislate with respect to this matter. . . .

For all of the foregoing reasons, I respectfully dissent.

MR. JUSTICE WHITE, with whom MR. JUSTICE REHNQUIST joins, dissenting.

The Court for the most part sustains this position: During the period prior to the time the fetus becomes viable, the Constitution of the United States values the convenience, whim, or caprice of the putative mother more than the life or potential life of the fetus; the Constitution, therefore, guarantees the right to an abortion as against any state law or policy seeking to protect the fetus from an abortion not prompted by more compelling reasons of the mother.

With all due respect, I dissent. I find nothing in the language or history of the Constitution to support the Court's judgment. The Court simply fashions and announces a new constitutional right for pregnant women and, with scarcely any reason or authority for its action, invests that right with sufficient substance to override most existing state abortion statutes. The upshot is that the people and the legislatures of the 50 States are constitutionally disentitled to weigh the relative importance of the continued existence and development of the fetus, on the one hand, against a spectrum of possible impacts on the mother, on the other hand. As an exercise of raw judicial power, the Court perhaps has authority to do what it does today; but in my view its judgment is an improvident and extravagant exercise of the power of judicial review that the Constitution extends to this Court.

The Court apparently values the convenience of the pregnant mother more than the continued existence and development of the life or potential life that she carries.

Whether or not I might agree with that marshaling of values, I can in no event join the Court's judgment because I find no constitutional warrant for imposing such an order of priorities on the people and legislatures of the States. In a sensitive area such as this, involving as it does issues over which reasonable men may easily and heatedly differ, I cannot accept the Court's exercise of its clear power of choice by interposing a constitutional barrier to state efforts to protect human life and by investing mothers and doctors with the constitutionally protected right to exterminate it. This issue, for the most part, should be left with the people and to the political processes the people have devised to govern their affairs.

Justice Blackmun's decisions in *Roe* and *Doe* were a tour de force on the subject of abortion. They provided a comprehensive history of government regulation of abortion and reviewed in some detail arguments for and against the procedure. Most important was his conclusion: The right to privacy "is broad enough to encompass a woman's decision whether or not to terminate a pregnancy." Behind this assertion are several important ideas. First, the Court, while not rejecting a Ninth Amendment theory of privacy, preferred to locate the right in the Fourteenth Amendment's due process clause, an approach suggested by Justices Harlan and White in their

concurring opinions in *Griswold* (see Table 16-1). Second, the Court found the abortion right fundamental and, therefore, would use a compelling state interest test to assess the constitutionality of restrictions on that right—but with something of a twist. For the reasons Blackmun gave in his opinion, the state's interests in protecting the woman's health and in protecting the "potentiality of human life" grow "in substantiality as the woman approaches term and, at a point during pregnancy . . . become compelling." This point led the majority to adopt the trimester scheme *(see Table 16-2).* Under this scheme, the state's compelling interest arises at the point of viability. It may, however, regulate second trimester abortions in ways that "are reasonably related to the mother's health."

In their dissents, Justices White and Rehnquist lambasted the trimester scheme, as well as almost every other aspect of the opinion. They thought it relied on "raw judicial power" to reach an "extravagant" and "improvident" decision. Rehnquist found that the Court's use of a compelling state interest test to assess statutes under the Fourteenth Amendment's due process clause represented a return to the discredited doctrine of substantive due process as expressed in *Lochner,* a complaint that echoed Black's dissent in *Griswold.* Rehnquist would have preferred that the Court adopt a "rational basis"

TABLE 16-2   The *Roe v. Wade* Trimester Scheme

Stage of Pregnancy	Degree of Permissible State Regulation of the Decision to Terminate Pregnancy
Prior to the end of the first trimester (approximately months 1–3)	Almost none: "the abortion and its effectuation must be left to [the woman and] the medical judgment of the pregnant woman's attending physician."
The end of the first trimester through "viability" (approximately months 4–6)	Some: "the state, in promoting its interest in the health of the mother, may, if it chooses, regulate the abortion procedure in ways that are reasonably related to maternal health." But it may not prohibit abortions.
Subsequent to viability (approximately months 7–9)	High: "the state, in promoting its interest in the potentiality of human life, may, if it chooses, regulate, and even proscribe, abortion except where necessary, in appropriate medical judgment, for the preservation of the life or health of the mother."

approach to the abortion right as it had to regulations challenged on due process grounds after the fall of substantive due process. Under this approach, the Court would have to decide only whether the government had acted reasonably to achieve a legitimate government objective. Using a rational basis approach, as you can imagine, the Court generally defers to the government and presumes the validity of the government's action. Had the Court adopted this approach to the abortion right, it would have upheld the Texas and Georgia restrictions. White, joined by Rehnquist, thought the Court had gone well beyond the scope of its powers and of the text and history of the Constitution to generate a policy statement that smacked of judicial activism. To White, it was up to the people and their elected officials to determine the fate of abortion, not the Court.

As Blackmun's opinion was nearly two years in the making, the other justices knew that, if nothing else, it would be a comprehensive statement. Outsiders, however, were shocked; few expected such an opinion from a Nixon appointee and Warren Burger's childhood friend. But Blackmun's opinion was not the only surprise; Burger's decision to go along with the majority startled many observers. Moreover, White and Stewart cast rather puzzling votes in light of their opinions in *Griswold*. Stewart had dissented in *Griswold*, asserting that the Constitution did not guarantee a general right to privacy. If he believed that to be so, then how could he agree to the creation of the right to obtain legal abortions, a right that rested on privacy? White, on the other hand, had been in the majority in *Griswold*, but apparently for him, the right to privacy was not broad enough to cover abortion.

The factors that explain the justices' position in *Roe* and *Doe* are matters of speculation, for, as Justice Blackmun once noted, it is always hard to predict how a new justice will come down on the abortion issue. What is not a matter of speculation is that the responses of Americans to *Roe*—both positive and negative—were (and still are) perhaps some of the strongest in the Court's history.

Reaction came from all quarters of American life. Some legal scholars applauded the *Roe* opinion, asserting that it indicated the Court's sensitivity to changing times. Others ripped it to shreds. They called the trimester scheme unworkable and said that, as medical technology advanced, viability would come increasingly earlier in pregnancy. Others attacked the decision's use of the Fourteenth Amendment, agreeing with Justice Rehnquist that the application represented a retreat to pre–New Deal days. Still others claimed that the decision usurped the intention of *Griswold*. Even Norma McCorvey (the Jane Roe in *Roe v. Wade*) surprisingly became an active critic of the decision *(see Box 16-2)*.

Roe also divided the political community. Some legislators were pleased that the Court, and not they, had handled a political hot potato. Others were outraged on moral grounds ("abortion is murder") and on constitutional grounds (this is a matter of public policy for legislators, not judges, to determine).

There is little evidence to indicate that the Court's decision in *Roe* significantly changed how Americans view abortion. Public opinion polls have consistently shown that people were and still are split on the question. But the decision did intensify the divisions. If one was pro-choice before *Roe*, one became even more so; the converse held true for those favoring the pro-life side.[9]

Although *Roe* may not have changed public opinion on abortion, it had the important effect of mobilizing the right-to-life movement. Before 1973 groups opposed to legalized abortion had lobbied successfully against efforts to liberalize state laws. When *Roe* nullified these legislative victories, these groups vowed to see the decision overturned. In short, *Roe* and *Doe* fanned the fire rather than quenched it.

The Aftermath of Roe: *Attempts to Limit the Decision*

Right-to-life groups dedicated to the eradication of *Roe v. Wade* could achieve their goal in one of two ways: They could persuade Congress to propose an amendment to the Constitution or persuade the Court to overrule its decision. In the immediate aftermath of *Roe*, neither option was viable. Despite the public's mixed view of abortion, during the 1970s only about a third of Americans supported a constitutional amendment to proscribe it. The lack of support may explain why Congress, ever

9. Charles Franklin and Liane Kosaki, "The Republican Schoolmaster: The Supreme Court, Public Opinion, and Abortion," *American Political Science Review* 83 (1989): 751–772.

BOX 16-2   AFTERMATH . . . NORMA McCORVEY

THE LIFE OF NORMA MCCOR-
VEY, the pregnant carnival worker
who, as Jane Roe, challenged Texas's
abortion laws in the Supreme Court,
took several interesting turns after *Roe
v. Wade* was handed down.

At first, McCorvey's personal life
was relatively untouched by the decision. She did not have an abortion, but
gave her baby up for adoption. She remained anonymous, continuing to lead
a life that included poverty, homeless-
ness, drug and alcohol addiction, petty
crimes, and attempted suicide. Then, in
the 1980s McCorvey went public and
announced that she was the real "Jane
Roe." She also confessed that she had
lied at the time of her case when she
claimed that her pregnancy was the result of rape.

McCorvey worked for several years
in Dallas abortion clinics, using her
wages to help support her drug habit.
She also dabbled in New Age religions and the occult and entered a romantic relationship with a store clerk who had
caught her shoplifting.

In 1995 Operation Rescue, the Christian-based anti-
abortion activist group, moved its headquarters to Dallas,
taking office space next door to the abortion clinic where
McCorvey worked. Rev. Philip "Flip" Benham, an Operation
Rescue leader, and other members of the group befriended
McCorvey. Subsequently, she underwent a religious conversion, became an evangelical Christian, and joined Benham's

Norma McCorvey stands with nine-year-old
Meredith Champion at an Operation Rescue rally
in downtown Dallas in January 1997. McCorvey,
the real "Jane Roe" of *Roe v. Wade* (1973), is now
pro-life and works with the anti-abortion group.

nondenominational Hillcrest Church.
Her 1995 baptism in a backyard swimming pool was nationally televised.
McCorvey left the abortion clinic and
began working for Operation Rescue,
proclaiming, "I don't have to go to
the death camps anymore, to earn
six bucks an hour." McCorvey also
founded an organization, Roe No More
Ministry, that provides information to
anti-abortion groups. She experienced
a second religious conversion in 1998
when she became a Roman Catholic. In
2000 McCorvey signed her name to a
lawsuit asking the federal courts to declare that women seeking abortions
have the right to be told that they are
carrying a human being and to be
shown a sonogram of the fetus. The
lawsuit was unsuccessful.

Looking back at her participation in
Roe v. Wade, McCorvey now says that
she feels exploited by the pro-choice
movement. She claims she met her lawyers in the case only
twice, the first time over pizza and beer, and that she did not
even know what the word "abortion" meant. "All I simply did
was sign," she says. "I never appeared in any court. I never
testified in front of any jury or judge."

SOURCES: *St. Louis Post Dispatch*, June 12, 1998; *Chicago Sun-Times*, July 27,
1998; *Boston Globe*, October 19, 1998; *Omaha World-Herald*, October 29 and
30, 1998; *Los Angeles Times*, December 8, 1999; *Houston Chronicle*, January 13,
2000; and *Independent* (London), March 16, 2000.

---

cognizant of the polls, did not pass any of the "human
life" amendments it considered in the 1970s. And, given
the 7–2 vote in *Roe*, wholesale changes in the Court's
membership would be required before the Court would
reconsider its stance on abortion.

Faced with this situation, pro-life groups determined
that their best course of action was to seek limitations
on the ways women could obtain and pay for abortions.
They lobbied legislatures to enact restrictions on *Roe*.

Two types of restrictions predominated—those that required the consent of a woman's parents or husband and
those that limited government funding for abortion services. These efforts were quite successful. During the
1970s, eighteen states required some form of consent and
thirty (along with the federal government) restricted
funding. To put it another way, by 1978 only about fifteen
states had not enacted laws requiring consent or restricting funding.

As you might suspect, pro-choice groups responded with legal challenges to these limits on the abortion right. But, for the most part, these efforts failed. The first major post-*Roe* battle, **Planned Parenthood v. Danforth** (1976), involved consent, a subject the Court had not considered in *Roe*. The state of Missouri had passed legislation that required the written consent of a pregnant woman and her spouse or, for an unmarried minor, her parents, before an abortion could be performed.

Although the Court found no constitutional violation in requiring a woman to give her own consent to the procedure, it struck down parental and spousal consent provisions as violative of the Constitution and inconsistent with *Roe*. But Justice Blackmun's majority opinion gave pro-life movements a little hope. It struck down Missouri's parental consent requirement, but it also stated: "We emphasize that our holding that parental consent is invalid does not suggest that every minor, regardless of age or maturity, may give effective consent for the termination of her pregnancy." With these words, Blackmun opened the door to the possibility of some form of required parental consent.

As illustrated in Table 16-3, pro-life forces took advantage of Blackmun's statement, persuading states to enact various parental and other consent requirements, many of which were tested by the Court. And, although the Court has continued to strike down laws forcing a woman to obtain the consent of or to notify her spouse/partner prior to obtaining an abortion, as shown in Table 16-3, it has generally allowed states to require parental consent or notification, especially if the law allowed a minor to bypass the parent and instead seek the consent of a judge.

The Court has been even less unequivocal about funding. In a trio of 1977 decisions, the Court upheld state or local restrictions on the funding of abortions.[10] Three

10. *Beal v. Doe* (upholding a Pennsylvania law limiting Medicaid funding "to those abortions that are certified by physicians as medically necessary"); *Maher v. Roe* (upholding a Connecticut Welfare Department regulation limiting state Medicaid "benefits for first trimester abortions . . . that are 'medically necessary.'"); *Poelker v. Doe* (upholding a St. Louis policy directive that barred city-owned hospitals from performing abortions). In all three cases, the Court rejected constitutional claims that the restrictions at issue interfered with the fundamental right to obtain an abortion as articulated in *Roe* and that they discriminated on the basis of socioeconomic status and against those choosing abortion over childbirth.

years later, an even bigger battle brewed over the Hyde Amendment, which limited federal Medicaid funding of abortions to those "where the life of the mother would be endangered if the fetus were carried to term." Pro-choice groups quickly challenged the regulation on the grounds that it violated due process (it impinges on a fundamental right), equal protection (it discriminates against women, especially poor women), and First Amendment (it burdens religious exercise and constitutes religious establishment) guarantees. In **Harris v. McCrae** (1980), however, a 5–4 Court rejected all three arguments and upheld the regulation. Writing for majority, Justice Stewart asserted that the Court "cannot overturn duly enacted statutes simply because they may be unwise, improvident or out of harmony with a particular school of thought." More important, however, was its legal rationale:

[R]egardless of whether the freedom of a woman to choose to terminate her pregnancy for health reasons lies at the core or the periphery of the due process liberty recognized in [*Roe v.*] *Wade*, it simply does not follow that a woman's freedom of choice carries with it a constitutional entitlement to the financial resources to avail herself of the full range of protected choices. . . . [A]lthough government may not place obstacles in the path of a woman's exercise of her freedom of choice, it need not remove those not of its own creation. Indigency falls in the latter category.

Justice Marshall, a dissenter in the case, along with Justice Blackmun, summarized accurately the greatest fears of the pro-choice movement when he wrote:

The denial of Medicaid benefits to individuals who meet all the statutory criteria for eligibility, solely because the treatment that is medically necessary involves the exercise of the fundamental right to choose abortion, is a form of discrimination repugnant to the equal protection of the laws guaranteed by the Constitution. The Court's decision today marks a retreat from *Roe v. Wade* and represents a cruel blow to the most powerless members of our society.

Attempts to Overturn Roe: Akron, Webster, and Casey

In the early 1980s pro-life forces had several reasons to feel optimistic. First, they had achieved considerable success in the funding decisions. Second, the 1980 elections placed Ronald Reagan, a pro-life advocate, in the White

TABLE 16-3 *Cases Involving Consent to Abortions, 1976–Present*

Case	Consent Provision at Issue	Court Holding
Planned Parenthood v. Danforth (1976)	Written consent required of the (1) pregnant woman, (2) her spouse, or (3) her parents.	The Court struck spousal and parental requirements. It upheld the provision requiring the woman's consent.
Bellotti v. Baird II (1979)	Parental consent required prior to abortions performed on unmarried women under eighteen. If one or both parents refuse, the "abortion may be obtained by order of a judge . . . for good cause shown."	The Court struck the law, but claimed that it was not "persuaded as a general rule" that parental consent "unconstitutionally burdens a minor's right to seek an abortion."
H. L. v. Matheson (1981)	Doctors should "notify, if possible" a minor's parents prior to performing an abortion.	The Court upheld the law on the ground that "the Constitution does not compel a state to fine-tune its statutes as to encourage or facilitate abortions."
Akron v. Akron Center for Reproductive Health (1983)	Parental notification and consent required prior to abortions performed on unmarried minors under fifteen. Doctors must make "certain specified statements" to ensure that consent for all those seeking abortions is "truly informed." Requires a twenty-four-hour waiting period "between the time a woman signs a consent form and the time the abortion is performed."	The Court invalidated all three provisions.
Planned Parenthood v. Ashcroft (1983)	Parental or judicial consent required prior to abortions performed on unmarried minors.	The Court upheld the provision, asserting that judges may give their consent to abortions.
Hodgson v. Minnesota (1990)	Requirement that both parents be notified prior to the performance of an abortion (unless a court orders otherwise). Abortions cannot be performed on minors until forty-eight hours after both parents have been notified.	The Court upheld the two-parent requirement with an exemption option. It upheld the forty-eight-hour waiting period.
Ohio v. Akron Center for Reproductive Health (1990)	Requirement that one parent be notified prior to the performance of an abortion on an unmarried, unemancipated minor (unless a court authorizes it).	The Court upheld the law.
Planned Parenthood of Southeastern Pennsylvania v. Casey (1992)	Required three kinds of consent: (1) informed consent of the woman; (2) statement from woman indicating that she has notified her spouse; and (3) in the case of minors, informed consent of one parent.	The Court upheld informed consent, struck spousal notifications, and upheld parental consent.
Lambert v. Wicklund (1997)	Required that the physician performing the abortion notify one of the minor's parents or legal guardian forty-eight hours in advance of performing an abortion. Minor could obtain a judicial bypass by demonstrating to a state youth court that either (1) the minor was sufficiently mature to decide whether to have an abortion, (2) there was evidence of abuse of the minor, or (3) the notification of a parent or guardian was not in the "best interests" of the minor.	Without hearing oral arguments, the Court (in a *per curiam* opinion) upheld the statute by a 9–0 vote. Justice Stevens, joined by Justices Ginsburg and Breyer, concurred in the judgment.
Ayotte v. Planned Parenthood of Northern New England (2006)	Requires parental notification of a minor's parents prior to abortion. Contains an exception if the minor's life is in danger but not if her health is at risk.	Held that the law must include an exception for medical emergencies but that the lower court erred by striking it down in its entirety. Remanded.

House. It was almost assured that Reagan's appointees would be proponents of the pro-life position. And third, personnel changes, damaging to the pro-choice position, were already taking place. John Paul Stevens had replaced William Douglas. While Stevens appeared to lean toward the pro-choice position, he could hardly embrace that view any more enthusiastically than the man he replaced. Douglas wrote the opinion in *Griswold* and supported the pro-choice position in every abortion-related case. Sandra Day O'Connor, Reagan's first appointment, replaced Potter Stewart, who had voted with the *Roe* majority. O'Connor's position on abortion was not clear. Some pro-life groups alleged that O'Connor supported the pro-choice side because of votes she had cast in the Arizona state legislature. But during her confirmation proceedings, she refused to answer pointed questions on abortion, saying only that it was "a practice in which [she] would not have engaged," but that she was "over the hill" and "not going to be pregnant any more . . . so perhaps it's easy for me to speak."

Given the changing context, pro-life forces began mounting a more direct attack on *Roe,* still hoping to overturn it. The first major battle occurred in **Akron v. Akron Center for Reproductive Health** (1983). At issue was a 1978 ordinance passed by the city council of Akron, Ohio, that contained five restrictions on the abortion right, including the following requirements: (1) all post–first trimester abortions must be performed in a hospital; (2) minors under the age of fifteen must obtain written consent of a parent (or a court) prior to an abortion; (3) women must give informed consent (she must be told by a physician that the "unborn child is a human life form from the moment of conception") prior to an abortion; (4) twenty-four hours must elapse between the time pregnant woman signs the consent form and the abortion; and (5) doctors who perform abortions "shall insure that the remains of the unborn child are disposed of in a humane and sanitary manner."

Invoking the *Roe* precedent, the Court, in an opinion written by Justice Powell and supported by five other justices, struck down the Akron law. The first four provisions were seen as unnecessary and unconstitutional impediments placed in the way of a woman's right to

choose; and the fifth provision was struck down as unconstitutionally vague.

What is noteworthy, however, is that the pro-choice forces had lost a vote. The 7–2 *Roe* majority was now 6–3, with Justice O'Connor writing the dissenting opinion in *Akron.* O'Connor's opinion was a scathing critique of *Roe.* She was especially critical of the trimester plan because it was at odds with advances in medical science that were progressively moving the point of fetal viability earlier in the pregnancy. O'Connor urged that the trimester framework be abandoned and replaced with one that "protects the woman from unduly burdensome interference with her freedom to decide whether to terminate her pregnancy."

Thus, as displayed in Box 16-3, by 1983 the justices had proposed three different approaches to restrictive abortion laws. Although the majority of the justices continued to support *Roe's* strict scrutiny standard, and White and Rehnquist remained loyal to the rational basis approach, O'Connor's dissent in *Akron* proposed an entirely different alternative.

Six years later, in **Webster v. Reproductive Health Services** (1989), the Court faced squarely the question of whether *Roe* should be overruled. In the interim, additional personnel changes on the Court had weakened *Roe's* prospects for survival. William Rehnquist, who had consistently voted for pro-life outcomes, replaced Warren Burger as chief justice. Joining the Court were Antonin Scalia, taking Rehnquist's associate justice position, and Anthony Kennedy, replacing the retiring Lewis Powell. Scalia and Kennedy, both Reagan appointees, were seen as two probable pro-life votes. Was *Roe* doomed? Justice Blackmun thought so. He wondered out loud: "Will *Roe v. Wade* go down the drain? I think that there is a very distinct possibility that it will, this term. You can count the votes."[11]

At issue in *Webster* was a Missouri law that prohibited state employees and public facilities from being used to perform abortions unless the mother's life was in jeopardy, banned state employees from encouraging or counseling a woman to have an abortion not necessary to save

---

11. "Justice Fears for *Roe* Ruling," *New York Times,* September 14, 1988.

BOX 16-3   PROPOSED APPROACHES TO RESTRICTIVE ABORTION LAWS

APPROACH	EXEMPLARY OPINIONS	DEFINITION
Strict scrutiny	Blackmun in *Roe;* Powell in *Akron*	The right to abortion is fundamental. So laws restricting that right must be the least restrictive means available to achieve a compelling state interest. In the abortion context, a state's interest grows more compelling as the pregnancy passes from the first to second to third trimesters.
Undue burden	O'Connor in *Akron*	The right to decide whether to terminate a pregnancy is fundamental. So laws placing an undue burden on the women's decision to terminate her pregnancy may be subject to strict scrutiny; other kinds of laws need only be rationally related to a legitimate state interest (rational basis test).
Rational basis	Rehnquist in *Roe*	The right to abortion is no different from economic rights claimed under the Fourteenth Amendment due process clause. So the law must be a reasonable measure designed to achieve a legitimate state interest.

her life, and required physicians, prior to performing an abortion, to perform a viability test on the fetus of any woman thought to be twenty weeks or more pregnant. In addition, the statute's preamble declared that human life begins at conception.

The possibility that *Webster* would overturn *Roe* was not lost on pro-choice and pro-life forces, who filed seventy-eight amicus curiae briefs (to that time the largest number ever submitted to the Court in a single case), representing more than five thousand individual groups and interests. The Bush administration's solicitor general not only filed a brief supporting state regulation of abortions but also participated in oral argument, asking the Court to overrule *Roe.*

A badly fractured Court in a 5–4 vote refused to strike down any of the provisions of the Missouri law. The justices held that it was consistent with the Court's funding decisions for Missouri to ban public facilities from being used for abortions and state employees from performing or encouraging abortions. The state's interest in preserving viable human life was also judged as sufficient to jus-

tify the viability tests. The justices did not rule on the declaration in the law's preamble that life begins at conception on the ground that the language amounted to little more than a statement of philosophy with no enforceable effect.

Although the pro-life forces were able to attract five votes to uphold the Missouri law, those who hoped the Court would dismantle *Roe* were disappointed. The Court explicitly declared that it would not revisit that issue. Additionally, the majority could not agree on a single opinion deciding the case. Chief Justice Rehnquist wrote the primary opinion and was joined by White and Kennedy. Justices Scalia and O'Connor joined parts of Rehnquist's opinion but also staked out their own views. Scalia explicitly called for overruling *Roe,* and O'Connor continued to push for her "undue burden" approach to abortion restrictions. The four liberal justices (Brennan, Marshall, Blackmun, and Stevens) remained loyal to *Roe* and dissented.

In *Planned Parenthood of Southeast Pennsylvania v. Casey* (1992) the justices were presented with yet another

BOX 16-4   COURT'S ACTION IN *PLANNED PARENTHOOD OF SOUTHEASTERN PENNSYLVANIA V. CASEY* (1992)

Provisions of Law Upheld on the Ground That They Do Not Place an Undue Burden on the Abortion Right

Informed consent/twenty-four-hour waiting period. At least twenty-four hours before a physician performs an abortion, he or she must inform the woman of "the nature of the procedure, the health risks of the abortion and of childbirth, and the 'probable gestational age of the unborn child.'" The physician also must provide the woman with a list of adoption agencies. Abortions may not be performed unless the woman "certifies in writing" that she has given her informed consent. Twenty-four hours must elapse between the time the woman gives her consent and the abortion procedure is performed.

Parental consent. Unless she exercises a judicial by-pass option, a woman under the age of eighteen must obtain the informed consent of one parent prior to obtaining an abortion.

Reporting and recordkeeping. All facilities performing abortions must file reports containing information about the procedure, including: the physician, the woman's age, the number of prior pregnancies or abortions she has had, "pre-existing medical conditions that would complicate the pregnancy," "the weight and age of the aborted fetus, whether or not the woman was married. . . . " If the abortion is performed in a facility funded by the state, the information becomes public. Patient identities, however, remain confidential.

Provisions of Law Struck Down on the Ground That They Place an Undue Burden on the Abortion Right

Spousal notice. Before performing an abortion on a married woman, a physician must receive a statement from her stating that she has notified her spouse that she "is about to undergo an abortion." Alternatively, the woman may "provide a statement certifying that her husband is not the man who impregnated her; that her husband could not be located; that the pregnancy is the result of spousal sexual assault which she has reported; or that the women believes that notifying her husband will cause him or someone else to inflict bodily injury upon her."

Reporting and recordkeeping. All facilities performing abortions must file reports containing information about the procedure, including . . . if relevant, the reason(s) the woman has failed to notify her spouse.

---

opportunity to dismantle *Roe.* By this time, two additional steadfast defenders of *Roe,* Brennan and Marshall, had retired and were replaced by two appointees of George H. W. Bush: David Souter and Clarence Thomas. Did the conservatives now have the votes necessary to overturn *Roe?*

Casey involved a challenge to a Pennsylvania law that required (1) informed consent and a twenty-four-hour waiting period before abortions could be performed; (2) parental consent with a judicial by-pass provision for minors; (3) spousal notification; and (4) comprehensive recordkeeping and reporting. A splintered Court upheld the informed consent, waiting period, parental consent, and most of the recordkeeping provisions, but struck down the spousal notification requirement. *(See Box 16-4.)*

More important, however, was the Court's response to attacks on *Roe.* Controlling the decision was a moderate coalition consisting of three justices, O'Connor, Kennedy, and Souter. Citing the importance of adhering to precedent, the trio declared in a jointly written opinion for the Court that the essential holding in *Roe* should be retained and reaffirmed. Before viability, a woman has the constitutional right to decide whether to continue or terminate a pregnancy.

The joint opinion explicitly rejected the trimester plan, holding that it was not essential to the central principle set by *Roe.* In place of the abandoned trimester formula, the Court place substituted O'Connor's "undue burden" test: "Only where state regulation imposes an undue burden on a woman's ability to make this decision does the power of the State reach into the heart of the liberty protected by the Due Process Clause." An undue burden occurs when the state places a substantial obstacle in the path of a woman seeking an abortion before the fetus attains viability. Therefore, the constitutional right to choose an abortion was preserved, but states can regulate that right up to the point of placing an undue burden on it. After viability, the state, because of its interest in protecting potential human life, may regulate or even proscribe abortion except where the procedure may be necessary to preserve the life or health of the mother.

The three dissenters in *Casey*—Rehnquist, Thomas, and Scalia—continued to criticize *Roe,* as well as O'Connor's newly adopted undue burden test. They urged the Court to reject the idea of a fundamental right to abortion and instead to allow the people on a state-by-state basis to decide abortion policy. Justice Scalia summarized this position by stating, "We should get out of this area, where we have no right to be, and where we do neither ourselves nor the country any good by remaining."

In the immediate aftermath of *Casey,* the Court seemed to have reached an uneasy truce on the abortion issue. At least some of the Court's conservatives appeared willing to accept abortion rights with reasonable state regulation, and the liberal justices seemed satisfied that the central right proclaimed in *Roe* remains alive. Moreover, the *Casey* approach appeared to meet the approval of the American public as well. Polls taken immediately after *Casey* found that a large majority of Americans (up to 82 percent) favor legalized abortions, but significant numbers also support reasonable restrictions on that right.[12]

This is not to say that the abortion issue is settled. Questions related to abortion continue to come before the Court. In *Stenberg v. Carhart* (2000), the justices were presented with a challenge to a Nebraska law banning "partial birth abortion"—a phrase its critics use to describe one of several different kinds of controversial procedures for terminating pregnancies. The challenged Nebraska statute explicitly declared that a crime is committed when a physician "partially delivers vaginally a living unborn child before killing the unborn child and completing the delivery." The law applied to both the pre- and post-viability stages. It allowed an exception

only if the procedure was necessary to preserve the life of the mother. Physicians who violated the law faced criminal penalties of up to twenty-five years in prison and the loss of the right to practice medicine.

Writing for a five-justice majority, Stephen Breyer struck down the law on two grounds. First, it did not allow an exception for the preservation of the health of the mother. This was consistent with the Court's long-held position that abortion bans had to allow exceptions for preserving both the life and the health of the mother. Second, the Court found that the law placed an undue burden on the right to abortion because it limited a woman's choice of abortion procedures. In addition, the harsh penalties for violating the law were seen as placing a chilling effect on the willingness of physicians to provide abortion services.

But that was 2000. Seven years later, with two new George W. Bush appointees on the Court—John Roberts and Samuel Alito—a 5–4 Court upheld a federal law banning partial birth abortions in *Gonzales v. Carhart.* Writing for the majority, Justice Kennedy ruled that the law did not impose "an unconstitutional burden on the abortion right." While not overturning *Stenberg,* Kennedy distinguished it on the ground that the federal law "is more specific concerning the instances to which it applies and in this respect more precise in its coverage." Crucial to the decision, many commentators have argued, was Alito. He voted with the majority in *Gonzales* to uphold the law, while his predecessor, O'Connor, had voted with the majority in *Stenberg* to strike it down. Justice Ginsburg's dissent alluded to the effect of this membership change when she claimed, "Though today's opinion does not go so far as to discard *Roe* or *Casey,* the Court, differently composed than it was when we last considered a restrictive abortion regulation, is hardly faithful to our earlier invocations of 'the rule of law' and the principles of *stare decisis.*"

Pro-life and pro-choice organizations continue to campaign to have their preferences written into law. Advances in medical technology may cause us to reconsider the current state of the law. Actions by Congress or the state legislatures could ignite additional rounds of litigation. Personnel changes in the coming years could alter

---

12. Polls cited in Barbara Hinkson Craig and David M. O'Brien, *Abortion and American Politics* (Chatham, N.J.: Chatham House, 1993), 327.

the Court's ideological balance, tipping it in one direction or another. It is doubtful that we have heard the last of the abortion controversy; and, as has consistently been the case, there are no easy answers.

PRIVATE ACTIVITIES AND THE APPLICATION OF *GRISWOLD*

Many Americans now equate *Griswold*'s right to privacy with reproductive freedom, especially the right to abortion, but one of the first important applications came in a criminal procedure case, **Katz v. United States** (1967). FBI agents suspected Charles Katz of engaging in illegal bookmaking; in particular, they thought he was "transmitting wagering information by telephone from Los Angeles to Miami and Boston." To gather evidence, they placed listening and recording devices outside the telephone booth where Katz made his calls and used the transcripts of his conversations to obtain an eight-count indictment.

Katz challenged the use of the transcripts as evidence against him, asserting that his conversations were private and that the government had violated his rights under the Fourth Amendment. The government argued that in previous Fourth Amendment search and seizure cases, the justices had permitted the use of concealed microphones as long as agents did not "physically penetrate" an individual's constitutionally protected space. Here, the FBI had attached listening devices to the *outside* of the booth and claimed that it had not invaded Katz's space.

The Court disagreed. In his majority opinion, Justice Stewart dealt primarily with existing precedent governing searches and seizures, a topic covered in chapter 17. But Stewart touched on the privacy issue, stating: "What a person knowingly exposes to the public, even in his own home or office, is not a subject of Fourth Amendment protection. But what he seeks to preserve as private, even in an area accessible to the public, may be constitutionally protected." Justice Harlan, in a concurring opinion, put it in these terms: If a person has "exhibited an actual (subjective) expectation of privacy," and "the expectation . . . [is] one that society is prepared to recog-

nize as 'reasonable,' " then he or she comes under the protection of the Fourth Amendment. In other words, the justices—even Stewart, who dissented in *Griswold*—were willing to apply the right to privacy to searches and seizures. If citizens expect privacy, as Charles Katz did when he entered the telephone booth, then they are entitled to it. This position was not wholly different from what Justice Louis Brandeis had advocated in *Olmstead v. United States*—about forty years before *Katz!*

Two years later, in **Stanley v. Georgia**, the Court had another occasion to examine the privacy doctrine and its relationship to searches and seizures. While the police were investigating Robert Stanley for illegal bookmaking, they obtained a warrant to search his home. Authorities found little evidence of gambling activity, but they did find three reels of film. They watched the movies and arrested Stanley for possessing obscene material. Stanley's attorney challenged the seizure and arrest on the ground that the law should not "punish mere private possession of obscene material"—that his client had a right of privacy to view whatever he wished in his own home. The state argued that it had the right to seize obscene materials because they are illegal to possess. Indeed, in previous decisions, the Court had said that states could regulate the dissemination of obscene movies, magazines, and so forth.

In a unanimous opinion for the Court, Justice Thurgood Marshall accepted Stanley's argument. As he put it: "If the First Amendment means anything, it means that a State has no business telling a man, sitting alone in his house, what books he may read or films he may watch." Put somewhat differently, states can regulate obscenity, but cannot prohibit such activity inside someone's house. The First Amendment and privacy rights simply prohibit this kind of intrusion into the home.

Private Sexual Activity

The decision in *Stanley* hinged on the privacy concerns combined with an infringement of a fundamental liberty—in this case, the First Amendment. But would the Court reach the same conclusion if activities forbidden by the state did not fall under the First Amendment? Of spe-

---

BOX 16-5   AFTERMATH . . . *BOWERS V. HARDWICK*

BY A SINGLE VOTE the Supreme Court rejected Michael Hardwick's arguments that the Constitution bars state regulation of consensual homosexual activity between adults in the privacy of their own homes. Crucial to the outcome was the vote of Justice Lewis F. Powell Jr., who initially joined the four justices who favored striking down the Georgia antisodomy law, but changed his mind. Four years after the decision, while speaking to law students at New York University, Powell said he "probably made a mistake" in voting to uphold the Georgia law. Although Powell admitted that "the dissent had the better of the argument," he thought the case was "not very important" and was somewhat "frivolous" because Hardwick was never prosecuted.

In 1998, in another challenge to the state's antisodomy law, the Georgia Supreme Court struck down the statute on state constitutional grounds, saying, "We cannot think of any other activity that reasonable persons would rank as more private and more deserving of protection from government interference than consensual, private adult sexual activity." Although the case arose from sexual relations between a man and a woman, the justices found that the privacy protections in the state constitution made no distinction between homosexuals and heterosexuals.

Even before the Supreme Court handed down its decision in *Bowers v. Hardwick*, Michael Hardwick moved from Atlanta to Miami, where he made a living tending bar. He died of an AIDS-related illness in 1991 at the age of thirty-seven.

SOURCES: *Washington Post*, August 21, 1986; *St. Louis Post Dispatch*, November 7, 1990; *San Francisco Chronicle*, January 14, 1991; *New Orleans Times-Picayune*, July 3, 1996; and *New York Times*, November 25, 1998.

---

cial concern was the question whether laws criminalizing certain forms of sexual activity would now be unconstitutional given decisions such as *Katz* and *Stanley*—especially if the activity in question took place in private and involved only consenting adults.

Bowers v. Hardwick (1986) raised this exact question. This dispute began in 1982 when an Atlanta police officer arrived at Michael Hardwick's home to serve an arrest warrant. When he entered with the permission of a housemate, the officer witnessed Hardwick engaging in sodomy with another man. Hardwick was arrested for violating a Georgia law that prohibited the practice of oral or anal sex. The law applied both to same-sex and opposite-sex couples. Although the prosecutor dropped the charge, Hardwick, with the help of the ACLU, challenged the validity of the sodomy law.

Splitting 5–4, the Supreme Court upheld the Georgia law. For the majority, Justice Byron White wrote that the Constitution conferred no right to engage in homosexual sodomy. Led by Harry Blackmun, the dissenters objected to the Court's characterization of the issue. It was not,

Blackmun argued, a matter of the right to engage in sodomy, but instead a question of privacy rights.

The Court's decision in *Bowers* was quite controversial. It politically energized the gay community. Organizations dedicated to advancing gay rights launched major efforts to change state laws that regulated private sexual behavior. In addition, overturning *Bowers* became a high priority. The importance of this goal became even more salient to the gay community when the retired Lewis Powell, who had cast the swing vote in *Bowers*, admitted that he probably had made a mistake in siding with the majority *(see Box 16-5)*.

It took seventeen years for the Court to reconsider the question presented in *Bowers v. Hardwick*. When it did, in *Lawrence v. Texas* (2003), supporters of gay rights scored a significant legal victory.

Lawrence v. Texas

539 U.S. 558 (2003)
http://laws.findlaw.com/US/539/558.html
Oral arguments may be found at: http://www.oyez.org
Vote: 6 (Breyer, Ginsburg, Kennedy, O'Connor, Souter, Stevens)
*   3 (Rehnquist, Scalia, Thomas)*
Opinion of the Court: Kennedy
Opinion concurring in the judgment: O'Connor
Dissenting opinions: Scalia, Thomas

In many ways, *Lawrence* is quite similar to *Bowers.* Like *Bowers* this case began with a police visit to a private residence. After receiving a phone call about a possible weapons disturbance, police officers in Houston, Texas, entered the apartment of John Geddes Lawrence, where they observed Lawrence and another man, Tyron Garner, engaging in a sexual act. The two men were arrested and eventually convicted of violating a Texas law that made it a crime for two persons of the same sex to engage in sodomy. This law, unlike the one at issue in *Bowers,* applied only to participants of the same sex.

Lawrence and Garner challenged the statute as a violation of the equal protection clause of the Fourteenth Amendment, a similar provision of the Texas Constitution, and the due process clause of the Fourteenth Amendment. After Texas courts, relying on the Supreme Court's decision in *Bowers,* rejected these claims, the two appealed to the U.S. Supreme Court.

Once the Court granted certiorari in *Lawrence,* numerous amici entered the dispute asking the Court to strike down the law. In some of the briefs, scholars criticized the historical premises on which the majority opinion in *Bowers* relied. Others pointed to the changing circumstances of the two cases. For example, at the time the Court decided *Bowers* half of the states outlawed sodomy; by 2003 that number was reduced to thirteen, of which four enforced their laws only against homosexual conduct.

JUSTICE KENNEDY delivered the opinion of the Court.

Liberty protects the person from unwarranted government intrusions into a dwelling or other private places. In our tradition the State is not omnipresent in the home. And there are other spheres of our lives and existence, outside the home, where the State should not be a dominant presence. Freedom extends beyond spatial bounds. Liberty presumes an autonomy of self that includes freedom of thought, belief, expression, and certain intimate conduct. The instant case involves liberty of the person both in its spatial and more transcendent dimensions. . . .

We granted certiorari to consider three questions:

"1. Whether Petitioners' criminal convictions under the Texas "Homosexual Conduct" law—which criminalizes sexual intimacy by same-sex couples, but not identical behavior by different-sex couples—violate the Fourteenth Amendment guarantee of equal protection of laws?

"2. Whether Petitioners' criminal convictions for adult consensual sexual intimacy in the home violate their vital interests in liberty and privacy protected by the Due Process Clause of the Fourteenth Amendment?

"3. Whether *Bowers v. Hardwick* (1986), should be overruled?"

The petitioners were adults at the time of the alleged offense. Their conduct was in private and consensual.

We conclude the case should be resolved by determining whether the petitioners were free as adults to engage in the private conduct in the exercise of their liberty under the Due Process Clause of the Fourteenth Amendment to the Constitution. For this inquiry we deem it necessary to reconsider the Court's holding in *Bowers.*

There are broad statements of the substantive reach of liberty under the Due Process Clause in earlier cases but the most pertinent beginning point is our decision in *Griswold v. Connecticut* (1965).

In *Griswold* the Court invalidated a state law prohibiting the use of drugs or devices of contraception and counseling or aiding and abetting the use of contraceptives. The Court described the protected interest as a right to privacy and placed emphasis on the marriage relation and the protected space of the marital bedroom.

After *Griswold* it was established that the right to make certain decisions regarding sexual conduct extends beyond the marital relationship. In *Eisenstadt v. Baird* (1972), the Court invalidated a law prohibiting the distribution of contraceptives to unmarried persons. . . .

Tyron Garner *(left)* and John Geddes Lawrence greet supporters at Houston City Hall who had gathered to celebrate the Court's landmark decision in *Lawrence v. Texas.* The justices struck down a Texas sodomy law, a decision applauded by gay rights advocates as a historic ruling that overturned sodomy laws in thirteen states.

The opinions in *Griswold* and *Eisenstadt* were part of the background for the decision in *Roe v. Wade* (1973). . . . *Roe* recognized the right of a woman to make certain fundamental decisions affecting her destiny and confirmed once more that the protection of liberty under the Due Process Clause has a substantive dimension of fundamental significance in defining the rights of the person.

. . . This was the state of the law with respect to some of the most relevant cases when the Court considered *Bowers v. Hardwick.* . . .

The Court began its substantive discussion in *Bowers* as follows: "The issue presented is whether the Federal Constitution confers a fundamental right upon homosexuals to engage in sodomy and hence invalidates the laws of the many States that still make such conduct illegal and have done so for a very long time." That statement, we now conclude, discloses the Court's own failure to appreciate the extent of the liberty at stake. To say that the issue in *Bowers* was simply the right to engage in certain sexual conduct demeans the claim the individual put forward, just as it would demean a married couple were it to be said marriage is simply about the right to have sexual intercourse. The laws involved in *Bowers* and here are, to be sure, statutes that pur-

port to do no more than prohibit a particular sexual act. Their penalties and purposes, though, have more far-reaching consequences, touching upon the most private human conduct, sexual behavior, and in the most private of places, the home. The statutes do seek to control a personal relationship that, whether or not entitled to formal recognition in the law, is within the liberty of persons to choose without being punished as criminals.

This, as a general rule, should counsel against attempts by the State, or a court, to define the meaning of the relationship or to set its boundaries absent injury to a person or abuse of an institution the law protects. It suffices for us to acknowledge that adults may choose to enter upon this relationship in the confines of their homes and their own private lives and still retain their dignity as free persons. When sexuality finds overt expression in intimate conduct with another person, the conduct can be but one element in a personal bond that is more enduring. The liberty protected by the Constitution allows homosexual persons the right to make this choice.

Having misapprehended the claim of liberty there presented to it, and thus stating the claim to be whether there is a fundamental right to engage in consensual sodomy, the

Bowers Court said: "Proscriptions against that conduct have ancient roots." In academic writings, and in many of the scholarly *amicus* briefs filed to assist the Court in this case, there are fundamental criticisms of the historical premises relied upon by the majority and concurring opinions in *Bowers*. We need not enter this debate in the attempt to reach a definitive historical judgment, but the following considerations counsel against adopting the definitive conclusions upon which *Bowers* placed such reliance.

At the outset it should be noted that there is no longstanding history in this country of laws directed at homosexual conduct as a distinct matter. Beginning in colonial times there were prohibitions of sodomy derived from the English criminal laws passed in the first instance by the Reformation Parliament of 1533. The English prohibition was understood to include relations between men and women as well as relations between men and men. The absence of legal prohibitions focusing on homosexual conduct may be explained in part by noting that according to some scholars the concept of the homosexual as a distinct category of person did not emerge until the late 19th century. Thus early American sodomy laws were not directed at homosexuals as such but instead sought to prohibit nonprocreative sexual activity more generally. This does not suggest approval of homosexual conduct. It does tend to show that this particular form of conduct was not thought of as a separate category from like conduct between heterosexual persons.

Laws prohibiting sodomy do not seem to have been enforced against consenting adults acting in private. A substantial number of sodomy prosecutions and convictions for which there are surviving records were for predatory acts against those who could not or did not consent, as in the case of a minor or the victim of an assault. As to these, one purpose for the prohibitions was to ensure there would be no lack of coverage if a predator committed a sexual assault that did not constitute rape as defined by the criminal law. Thus the model sodomy indictments presented in a 19th-century treatise addressed the predatory acts of an adult man against a minor girl or minor boy. Instead of targeting relations between consenting adults in private, 19th-century sodomy prosecutions typically involved relations between men and minor girls or minor boys, relations between adults involving force, relations between adults implicating disparity in status, or relations between men and animals. . . .

. . . American laws targeting same-sex couples did not develop until the last third of the 20th century. The reported decisions concerning the prosecution of consensual, homosexual sodomy between adults for the years 1880–1995 are not always clear in the details, but a significant number involved conduct in a public place.

It was not until the 1970's that any State singled out same-sex relations for criminal prosecution, and only nine States have done so. . . .

In summary, the historical grounds relied upon in *Bowers* are more complex than the majority opinion . . . indicate[s]. Their historical premises are not without doubt and, at the very least, are overstated. . . .

. . . In all events we think that our laws and traditions in the past half century are of most relevance here. These references show an emerging awareness that liberty gives substantial protection to adult persons in deciding how to conduct their private lives in matters pertaining to sex.

This emerging recognition should have been apparent when *Bowers* was decided. In 1955 the American Law Institute promulgated the Model Penal Code and made clear that it did not recommend or provide for "criminal penalties for consensual sexual relations conducted in private." In 1961 Illinois changed its laws to conform to the Model Penal Code. Other States soon followed.

In *Bowers* the Court referred to the fact that before 1961 all 50 States had outlawed sodomy, and that at the time of the Court's decision 24 States and the District of Columbia had sodomy laws. Justice Powell pointed out that these prohibitions often were being ignored, however. Georgia, for instance, had not sought to enforce its law for decades. . . .

. . . [A]lmost five years before *Bowers* was decided the European Court of Human Rights considered a case with parallels to *Bowers* and to today's case. An adult male resident in Northern Ireland alleged he was a practicing homosexual who desired to engage in consensual homosexual conduct. The laws of Northern Ireland forbade him that right. He alleged that he had been questioned, his home had been searched, and he feared criminal prosecution. The court held that the laws proscribing the conduct were invalid under the European Convention on Human Rights. Authoritative in all countries that are members of the Council of Europe (21 nations then, 45 nations now), the decision is at odds with the premise in *Bowers* that the claim put forward was insubstantial in our Western civilization.

In our own constitutional system the deficiencies in *Bowers* became even more apparent in the years following its announcement. The 25 States with laws prohibiting the relevant conduct referenced in the *Bowers* decision are reduced now to 13, of which 4 enforce their laws only against homosexual conduct. In those States where sodomy is still proscribed, whether for same-sex or heterosexual conduct, there is a pattern of nonenforcement with respect to consenting adults acting in private. The State of Texas admitted in 1994 that as of that date it had not prosecuted anyone under those circumstances.

Two principal cases decided after *Bowers* cast its holding into even more doubt. In *Planned Parenthood of Southeastern Pa. v. Casey* (1992), the Court reaffirmed the substantive force of the liberty protected by the Due Process Clause. The *Casey* decision again confirmed that our laws and tradition afford constitutional protection to personal decisions relating to marriage, procreation, contraception, family relationships, child rearing, and education. . . .

Persons in a homosexual relationship may seek autonomy for these purposes, just as heterosexual persons do. The decision in *Bowers* would deny them this right.

The second post-*Bowers* case of principal relevance is *Romer v. Evans* (1996). There the Court struck down class-based legislation directed at homosexuals as a violation of the Equal Protection Clause. *Romer* invalidated an amendment to Colorado's constitution which named as a solitary class persons who were homosexuals, lesbians, or bisexual either by "orientation, conduct, practices or relationships," and deprived them of protection under state antidiscrimination laws. . . .

As an alternative argument in this case, counsel for the petitioners and some *amici* contend that *Romer* provides the basis for declaring the Texas statute invalid under the Equal Protection Clause. That is a tenable argument, but we conclude the instant case requires us to address whether *Bowers* itself has continuing validity. Were we to hold the statute invalid under the Equal Protection Clause some might question whether a prohibition would be valid if drawn differently, say, to prohibit the conduct both between same-sex and different-sex participants.

Equality of treatment and the due process right to demand respect for conduct protected by the substantive guarantee of liberty are linked in important respects, and a decision on the latter point advances both interests. If protected conduct is made criminal and the law which does so remains unexamined for its substantive validity, its stigma might remain even if it were not enforceable as drawn for equal protection reasons. When homosexual conduct is made criminal by the law of the State, that declaration in and of itself is an invitation to subject homosexual persons to discrimination both in the public and in the private spheres. The central holding of *Bowers* has been brought in question by this case, and it should be addressed. Its continuance as precedent demeans the lives of homosexual persons.

The stigma this criminal statute imposes, moreover, is not trivial. The offense, to be sure, is but a class C misdemeanor, a minor offense in the Texas legal system. Still, it remains a criminal offense with all that imports for the dignity of the persons charged. The petitioners will bear on their record the history of their criminal convictions. Just this Term we rejected various challenges to state laws requiring the registration of sex offenders. *Smith v. Doe* (2003); *Connecticut Dept. of Public Safety v. Doe* (2003). We are advised that if Texas convicted an adult for private, consensual homosexual conduct under the statute here in question the convicted person would come within the registration laws of a least four States were he or she to be subject to their jurisdiction. . . .

The foundations of *Bowers* have sustained serious erosion from our recent decisions in *Casey* and *Romer.* When our precedent has been thus weakened, criticism from other sources is of greater significance. In the United States criticism of *Bowers* has been substantial and continuing, disapproving of its reasoning in all respects, not just as to its historical assumptions. . . .

The doctrine of *stare decisis* is essential to the respect accorded to the judgments of the Court and to the stability of the law. It is not, however, an inexorable command. In *Casey* we noted that when a Court is asked to overrule a precedent recognizing a constitutional liberty interest, individual or societal reliance on the existence of that liberty cautions with particular strength against reversing course. The holding in *Bowers*, however, has not induced detrimental reliance comparable to some instances where recognized individual rights are involved. Indeed, there has been no individual or societal reliance on *Bowers* of the sort that could counsel against overturning its holding once there are compelling reasons to do so. *Bowers* itself causes uncertainty, for the precedents before and after its issuance contradict its central holding.

The rationale of *Bowers* does not withstand careful analysis. . . . JUSTICE STEVENS' analysis, [in his dissenting opinion in *Bowers*], in our view, should have been controlling in *Bowers* and should control here.

Bowers was not correct when it was decided, and it is not correct today. It ought not to remain binding precedent. *Bowers v. Hardwick* should be and now is overruled.

The present case does not involve minors. It does not involve persons who might be injured or coerced or who are situated in relationships where consent might not easily be refused. It does not involve public conduct or prostitution. It does not involve whether the government must give formal recognition to any relationship that homosexual persons seek to enter. The case does involve two adults who, with full and mutual consent from each other, engaged in sexual practices common to a homosexual lifestyle. The petitioners are entitled to respect for their private lives. The State cannot demean their existence or control their destiny by making their private sexual conduct a crime. Their right to liberty under the Due Process Clause gives them the full right to engage in their conduct without intervention of the government. "It is a promise of the Constitution that there is a realm of personal liberty which the government may not enter." The Texas statute furthers no legitimate state interest which can justify its intrusion into the personal and private life of the individual. . . .

The judgment of the Court of Appeals for the Texas Fourteenth District is reversed, and the case is remanded for further proceedings not inconsistent with this opinion.

It is so ordered.

JUSTICE O'CONNOR, concurring in the judgment.

The Court today overrules *Bowers v. Hardwick* (1986). I joined *Bowers,* and do not join the Court in overruling it. Nevertheless, I agree with the Court that Texas' statute banning same-sex sodomy is unconstitutional. Rather than relying on the substantive component of the Fourteenth Amendment's Due Process Clause, as the Court does, I base my conclusion on the Fourteenth Amendment's Equal Protection Clause.

The Equal Protection Clause of the Fourteenth Amendment "is essentially a direction that all persons similarly situated should be treated alike." Under our rational basis standard of review, "legislation is presumed to be valid and will be sustained if the classification drawn by the statute is rationally related to a legitimate state interest." . . .

The statute at issue here makes sodomy a crime only if a person "engages in deviate sexual intercourse with another individual of the same sex." Sodomy between opposite-sex partners, however, is not a crime in Texas. That is, Texas treats the same conduct differently based solely on the participants. Those harmed by this law are people who have a same-sex sexual orientation and thus are more likely to engage in behavior prohibited by [the law]. . . .

Texas attempts to justify its law, and the effects of the law, by arguing that the statute satisfies rational basis review because it furthers the legitimate governmental interest of the promotion of morality. In *Bowers,* we held that a state law criminalizing sodomy as applied to homosexual couples did not violate substantive due process. We rejected the argument that no rational basis existed to justify the law, pointing to the government's interest in promoting morality. The only question in front of the Court in *Bowers* was whether the substantive component of the Due Process Clause protected a right to engage in homosexual sodomy. *Bowers* did not hold that moral disapproval of a group is a rational basis under the Equal Protection Clause to criminalize homosexual sodomy when heterosexual sodomy is not punished.

This case raises a different issue than *Bowers:* whether, under the Equal Protection Clause, moral disapproval is a legitimate state interest to justify by itself a statute that bans homosexual sodomy, but not heterosexual sodomy. It is not. Moral disapproval of this group, like a bare desire to harm the group, is an interest that is insufficient to satisfy rational basis review under the Equal Protection Clause. Indeed, we have never held that moral disapproval, without any other asserted state interest, is a sufficient rationale under the Equal Protection Clause to justify a law that discriminates among groups of persons. . . .

A law branding one class of persons as criminal solely based on the State's moral disapproval of that class and the conduct associated with that class runs contrary to the values of the Constitution and the Equal Protection Clause, under any standard of review. I therefore concur in the Court's judgment that Texas' sodomy law banning "deviate sexual intercourse" between consenting adults of the same sex, but not between consenting adults of different sexes, is unconstitutional.

JUSTICE SCALIA, with whom THE CHIEF JUSTICE and JUSTICE THOMAS join, dissenting.

I begin with the Court's surprising readiness to reconsider a decision rendered a mere 17 years ago in *Bowers v. Hardwick*. I do not myself believe in rigid adherence to *stare decisis* in constitutional cases; but I do believe that we should be consistent rather than manipulative in invoking the doctrine. Today's opinions in support of reversal do not bother to distinguish—or indeed, even bother to mention—the paean to *stare decisis* coauthored by three Members of today's majority in *Planned Parenthood v. Casey*. There, when *stare decisis* meant preservation of judicially invented abortion rights, the widespread criticism of *Roe* was strong reason to *reaffirm* it. . . .

Today, however, the widespread opposition to *Bowers*, a decision resolving an issue as "intensely divisive" as the issue in *Roe*, is offered as a reason in favor of *overruling* it. Gone, too, is any "enquiry" (of the sort conducted in *Casey*) into whether the decision sought to be overruled has "proven 'unworkable.' "

Today's approach to *stare decisis* invites us to overrule an erroneously decided precedent (including an "intensely divisive" decision) if: (1) its foundations have been "eroded" by subsequent decisions, (2) it has been subject to "substantial and continuing" criticism, and (3) it has not induced "individual or societal reliance" that counsels against overturning. The problem is that *Roe* itself—which today's majority surely has no disposition to overrule—satisfies these conditions to at least the same degree as *Bowers*. . . .

To tell the truth, it does not surprise me, and should surprise no one, that the Court has chosen today to revise the standards of *stare decisis* set forth in *Casey*. It has thereby exposed *Casey's* extraordinary deference to precedent for the result-oriented expedient that it is.

Having decided that it need not adhere to *stare decisis*, the Court still must establish that *Bowers* was wrongly decided and that the Texas statute, as applied to petitioners, is unconstitutional.

[The Texas law] undoubtedly imposes constraints on liberty. So do laws prohibiting prostitution, recreational use of heroin, and, for that matter, working more than 60 hours per week in a bakery. But there is no right to "liberty" under the Due Process Clause, though today's opinion repeatedly makes that claim. The Fourteenth Amendment *expressly allows* States to deprive their citizens of "liberty," *so long as "due process of law" is provided*. . . .

Our opinions applying the doctrine known as "substantive due process" hold that the Due Process Clause prohibits States from infringing *fundamental* liberty interests, unless the infringement is narrowly tailored to serve a compelling state interest. We have held repeatedly, in cases the Court today does not overrule, that *only* fundamental rights qualify for this so-called "heightened scrutiny" protection—that is, rights which are " 'deeply rooted in this Nation's history and tradition.' " All other liberty interests may be abridged or abrogated pursuant to a validly enacted state law if that law is rationally related to a legitimate state interest.

Bowers held, first, that criminal prohibitions of homosexual sodomy are not subject to heightened scrutiny because they do not implicate a "fundamental right" under the Due Process Clause. Noting that "[p]roscriptions against that conduct have ancient roots," that "[s]odomy was a criminal offense at common law and was forbidden by the laws of the original 13 States when they ratified the Bill of Rights," and that many States had retained their bans on sodomy, *Bowers* concluded that a right to engage in homosexual sodomy was not " 'deeply rooted in this Nation's history and tradition.' "

The Court today does not overrule this holding. Not once does it describe homosexual sodomy as a "fundamental right" or a "fundamental liberty interest," nor does it subject the Texas statute to strict scrutiny. Instead, having failed to establish that the right to homosexual sodomy is " 'deeply rooted in this Nation's history and tradition,' " the Court concludes that the application of Texas's statute to petitioners' conduct fails the rational-basis test, and overrules *Bowers'* holding to the contrary. "The Texas statute furthers no legitimate state interest which can justify its intrusion into the personal and private life of the individual." . . .

. . . This proposition is so out of accord with our jurisprudence—indeed, with the jurisprudence of *any* society we know—that it requires little discussion.

The Texas statute undeniably seeks to further the belief of its citizens that certain forms of sexual behavior are "immoral and unacceptable"—the same interest furthered by criminal laws against fornication, bigamy, adultery, adult incest, bestiality, and obscenity. *Bowers* held that this was a legitimate state interest. The Court today reaches the opposite conclusion. The Court embraces instead JUSTICE STEVENS' declaration in his *Bowers* dissent, that "the fact that the governing majority in a State has traditionally viewed a particular practice as immoral is not a sufficient reason for upholding a law prohibiting the practice." This effectively decrees the end of all morals legislation. If, as the Court asserts, the promotion of majoritarian sexual morality is not even a *legitimate* state interest, none of the above-mentioned laws can survive rational-basis review. . . .

Today's opinion is the product of a Court, which is the product of a law-profession culture, that has largely signed on to the so-called homosexual agenda, by which I mean the agenda promoted by some homosexual activists directed at eliminating the moral opprobrium that has traditionally attached to homosexual conduct. . . .

One of the most revealing statements in today's opinion is the Court's grim warning that the criminalization of homosexual conduct is "an invitation to subject homosexual persons to discrimination both in the public and in the private spheres." It is clear from this that the Court has taken sides in the culture war, departing from its role of assuring, as neutral observer, that the democratic rules of engagement are observed. Many Americans do not want persons who openly engage in homosexual conduct as partners in their business, as scoutmasters for their children, as teachers in their children's schools, or as boarders in their home. They view this as protecting themselves and their families from a lifestyle that they believe to be immoral and destructive. The Court views it as "discrimination" which it is the function of our judgments to deter. So imbued is the Court with the law profession's anti-anti-homosexual culture, that it is seemingly unaware that the attitudes of that culture are not obviously "mainstream"; that in most States what the Court calls "discrimination" against those who engage in homosexual acts is perfectly legal; that proposals to ban such "discrimination" under Title VII [of the Civil Rights Act of 1964] have repeatedly been rejected by Congress; that in some cases such "discrimination" is *mandated* by federal statute; and that in some cases such "discrimination" is a constitutional right, see *Boy Scouts of America v. Dale* (2000).

Let me be clear that I have nothing against homosexuals, or any other group, promoting their agenda through normal democratic means. Social perceptions of sexual and other morality change over time, and every group has the right to persuade its fellow citizens that its view of such matters is the best. That homosexuals have achieved some success in that enterprise is attested to by the fact that Texas is one of the few remaining States that criminalize private, consensual homosexual acts. But persuading one's fellow citizens is one thing, and imposing one's views in absence of democratic majority will is something else. I would no more *require* a State to criminalize homosexual acts—or, for that matter, display *any* moral disapproval of them—than I would *forbid* it to do so. What Texas has chosen to do is well within the range of traditional democratic action, and its hand should not be stayed through the invention of a brand-new "constitutional right" by a Court that is impatient of democratic change. It is indeed true that "later generations can see that laws once thought necessary and proper in fact serve only to oppress; and when that happens, later generations can repeal those laws. But it is the premise of our system that those judgments are to be made by the people, and not imposed by a governing caste that knows best.

One of the benefits of leaving regulation of this matter to the people rather than to the courts is that the people, unlike judges, need not carry things to their logical conclusion. The people may feel that their disapprobation of homosexual conduct is strong enough to disallow homosexual marriage, but not strong enough to criminalize private homosexual acts—and may legislate accordingly. The Court today pretends that it possesses a similar freedom of action, so that we need not fear judicial imposition of homosexual marriage, as has recently occurred in Canada (in a decision that the Canadian Government has chosen not to appeal). At the end of its opinion—after having laid waste the foundations of our rational-basis jurisprudence—the Court says that the present case "does not involve whether the government must give formal recognition to any relationship that homosexual persons seek to enter." Do not believe it. . . .

The matters appropriate for this Court's resolution are only three: Texas's prohibition of sodomy neither infringes a "fundamental right" (which the Court does not dispute), nor is unsupported by a rational relation to what the Constitution considers a legitimate state interest, nor denies the equal protection of the laws. I dissent.

JUSTICE THOMAS, dissenting.

I join JUSTICE SCALIA's dissenting opinion. I write separately to note that the law before the Court today "is . . . uncommonly silly." *Griswold v. Connecticut* (1965) (Stewart, J., dissenting). If I were a member of the Texas Legislature, I would vote to repeal it. Punishing someone for expressing his sexual preference through noncommercial consensual conduct with another adult does not appear to be a worthy way to expend valuable law enforcement resources.

Notwithstanding this, I recognize that as a member of this Court I am not empowered to help petitioners and others similarly situated. My duty, rather, is to "decide cases 'agreeably to the Constitution and laws of the United States.' " And, just like Justice Stewart, I "can find [neither in the Bill of Rights nor any other part of the Constitution a] general right of privacy," or as the Court terms it today, the "liberty of the person both in its spatial and more transcendent dimensions."

The Court in *Lawrence* overruled *Bowers*, holding that the Constitution does not permit the criminalization of private homosexual acts between consenting adults. The majority based its decision on the right to privacy as a liberty interest protected under the due process clause of the Fourteenth Amendment. The justices declined the opportunity to rest the decision on the equal protection clause. As a result, although *Lawrence* is a major victory for privacy advocates, it does not significantly expand the meaning or scope of protection of the equal protection clause, the constitutional provision most frequently used to combat claims of discrimination. On the other hand, as we note in chapter 19, the Massachusetts Supreme Judicial Court's decision in *Goodridge v. Department of Public Health* (2003), which legalized same-sex marriage in the state, came down only five months after *Lawrence*. *Goodridge* may rest on the state's own constitutional provisions, but the court cited *Lawrence v. Texas* in the second paragraph of its opinion.

The Right to Die

The disputes involving the right to privacy have become thornier over time. One of the most perplexing set of issues to be faced by the justices is found in the right-to-die cases. These cases involve fundamental questions of medicine, morality, and ethics as well as law. Does an individual have the right to refuse medical treatment that will result in death? May family members decide to remove life support from patients who cannot make such a decision on their own? Should a physician (or even a nonphysician) have the right to assist a consenting individual in the commission of suicide? These are questions that faced the Rehnquist Court, beginning with *Cruzan v. Director, Missouri Department of Health* (1990).

Cruzan v. Director, Missouri Department of Health

497 U.S. 261 (1990)
http://laws.findlaw.com/US/497/261.html
Oral arguments may be found at: http://www.oyez.org
Vote: 5 (Kennedy, O'Connor, Rehnquist, Scalia, White)
    4 (Blackmun, Brennan, Marshall, Stevens)
Opinion of the Court: Rehnquist
Concurring opinions: O'Connor, Scalia
Dissenting opinions: Brennan, Stevens

In January 1983 Nancy Beth Cruzan was in a serious car accident. When paramedics found her, she was "lying face down in a ditch without detectable respiratory or cardiac function." Although they were able to restore her breathing and heartbeat, Cruzan remained unconscious and was taken to a hospital. Both short- and long-term medical efforts failed, and, as a result, Cruzan degenerated to a persistent vegetative state, "a condition in which a person exhibits motor reflexes but evinces no indications of significant cognitive function." She required feeding and hydration tubes to stay alive. In short, when her case was before the Court, Nancy Cruzan was not dead, and some experts suggested that she could live another thirty years, but no one predicted any improvement in her condition.

Her parents, Lester and Joyce Cruzan, asked doctors to remove her feeding tubes, a step that would lead to Nancy's death. The hospital staff refused, and the

Cruzans sought permission from a state court. They argued that "a person in Nancy's condition had a fundamental right to refuse or direct the withdrawal of 'death prolonging procedures.'" The Cruzans presented as evidence that when Nancy was twenty-five, she had told a friend that "she would not wish to continue her life unless she could live it at least halfway normally."

The trial court ruled in their favor, but the state supreme court reversed. It found no support in common law for a right to die, and it refused to apply privacy doctrines to the Cruzan situation. It also held that because the state had a strong interest in preserving life, the Cruzans would have to provide "clear and convincing evidence" that Nancy would have wanted her feeding tubes withdrawn.

CHIEF JUSTICE REHNQUIST delivered the opinion of the Court.

We granted certiorari to consider the question of whether Cruzan has a right under the United States Constitution which would require the hospital to withdraw life-sustaining treatment from her under these circumstances. . . .

The Fourteenth Amendment provides that no state shall "deprive any person of life, liberty, or property, without due process of law." The principle that a competent person has a constitutionally protected liberty interest in refusing unwanted medical treatment may be inferred from our prior decisions. . . .

But determining that a person has a "liberty interest" under the Due Process Clause does not end the inquiry; "whether respondent's constitutional rights have been violated must be determined by balancing his liberty interests against the relevant state interests."

Petitioners insist that under the general holdings of our cases, the forced administration of life-sustaining medical treatment, and even of artificially-delivered food and water essential to life, would implicate a competent person's liberty interest. Although we think the logic of the cases . . . would embrace such a liberty interest, the dramatic consequences involved in refusal of such treatment would inform the inquiry as to whether the deprivation of that interest is constitutionally permissible. But for purposes of this case,

we assume that the United States Constitution would grant a competent person a constitutionally protected right to refuse lifesaving hydration and nutrition.

Petitioners go on to assert that an incompetent person should possess the same right in this respect as is possessed by a competent person. . . .

The difficulty with petitioners' claim is that in a sense it begs the question: an incompetent person is not able to make an informed and voluntary choice to exercise a hypothetical right to refuse treatment or any other right. Such a "right" must be exercised for her, if at all, by some sort of surrogate. Here, Missouri has in effect recognized that under certain circumstances a surrogate may act for the patient in electing to have hydration and nutrition withdrawn in such a way as to cause death, but it has established a procedural safeguard to assure that the action of the surrogate conforms as best it may to the wishes expressed by the patient while competent. Missouri requires that evidence of the incompetent's wishes as to the withdrawal of treatment be proved by clear and convincing evidence. The question, then, is whether the United States Constitution forbids the establishment of this procedural requirement by the State. We hold that it does not.

Whether or not Missouri's clear and convincing evidence requirement comports with the United States Constitution depends in part on what interests the State may properly seek to protect in this situation. Missouri relies on its interest in the protection and preservation of human life, and there can be no gainsaying this interest. As a general matter, the States—indeed, all civilized nations—demonstrate their commitment to life by treating homicide as a serious crime. Moreover, the majority of States in this country have laws imposing criminal penalties on one who assists another to commit suicide. We do not think a State is required to remain neutral in the face of an informed and voluntary decision by a physically-able adult to starve to death.

But in the context presented here, a State has more particular interests at stake. The choice between life and death is a deeply personal decision of obvious and overwhelming finality. We believe Missouri may legitimately seek to safeguard the personal element of this choice through the imposition of heightened evidentiary requirements. It cannot be disputed that the Due Process Clause protects an interest in life as well as an interest in refusing life-sustaining medical treatment. Not all incompetent patients will have loved ones available to serve as surrogate decision-makers. And even where family members are present, "there will, of course, be some unfortunate situations in which family members will not act to protect a patient." A State is entitled to guard against potential abuses in such situations. Similarly, a State is entitled to consider that a judicial proceeding to make a determination regarding an incompetent's wishes may very well not be an adversarial one, with the added guarantee of accurate factfinding that the adversary process brings with it. Finally, we think a State may properly decline to make judgments about the "quality" of life that a particular individual may enjoy, and simply assert an unqualified interest in the preservation of human life to be weighed against the constitutionally protected interests of the individual.

In our view, Missouri has permissibly sought to advance these interests through the adoption of . . . "an intermediate standard of proof—'clear and convincing evidence'—when the individual interests at stake in a state proceeding are both 'particularly important' and 'more substantial than mere loss of money.' "

We think it self-evident that the interests at stake in the instant proceedings are more substantial, both on an individual and societal level, than those involved in a run-of-the-mine civil dispute. But not only does the standard of proof reflect the importance of a particular adjudication, it also serves as "a societal judgment about how the risk of error should be distributed between the litigants." The more stringent the burden of proof a party must bear, the more that party bears the risk of an erroneous decision. We believe that Missouri may permissibly place an increased risk of an erroneous decision on those seeking to terminate an incompetent individual's life-sustaining treatment. An erroneous decision not to terminate results in a maintenance of the status quo; the possibility of subsequent developments such as advancements in medical science, the discovery of new evidence regarding the patient's intent, changes in the law, or simply the unexpected death of the patient despite the administration of life-sustaining treatment, at least create the potential that a wrong decision will eventually be corrected or its impact mitigated. An erroneous decision to withdraw life-sustaining treatment, however, is not susceptible of correction. . . .

It is also worth noting that most, if not all, States simply forbid oral testimony entirely in determining the wishes of parties in transactions which, while important, simply do not have the consequences that a decision to terminate a person's life does. At common law and by statute in most States, the parole evidence rule prevents the variations of the terms of a written contract by oral testimony. The statute of frauds makes unenforceable oral contracts to leave property by will, and statutes regulating the making of wills universally require that those instruments be in writing. There is no doubt that statutes requiring wills to be in writing, and statutes of frauds which require that a contract to make a will be in writing, on occasion frustrate the effectuation of the intent of a particular decedent, just as Missouri's requirement of proof in this case may have frustrated the effectuation of the not-fully-expressed desires of Nancy Cruzan. But the Constitution does not require general rules to work faultlessly; no general rule can.

In sum, we conclude that a State may apply a clear and convincing evidence standard in proceedings where a guardian seeks to discontinue nutrition and hydration of a person diagnosed to be in a persistent vegetative state. . . .

The Supreme Court of Missouri held that in this case the testimony adduced at trial did not amount to clear and convincing proof of the patient's desire to have hydration and nutrition withdrawn. In so doing, it reversed a decision of the Missouri trial court which had found that the evidence "suggest[ed]" Nancy Cruzan would not have desired to continue such measures, but which had not adopted the standard of "clear and convincing evidence" enunciated by the Supreme Court. The testimony adduced at trial consisted primarily of Nancy Cruzan's statements made to a housemate about a year before her accident that she would not want to live should she face life as a "vegetable," and other observations to the same effect. The observations did not deal in terms [of] withdrawal of medical treatment or of hydration and nutrition. We cannot say that the Supreme Court of Missouri committed constitutional error in reaching the conclusion that it did.

Petitioners alternatively contend that Missouri must accept the "substituted judgment" of close family members even in the absence of substantial proof that their views reflect the views of the patient. . . . Here again petitioners would seek to turn a decision which allowed a State to rely on family decisionmaking into a constitutional requirement that the State recognize such decisionmaking. But constitutional law does not work that way.

No doubt is engendered by anything in this record but that Nancy Cruzan's mother and father are loving and caring parents. If the State were required by the United States Constitution to repose a right of "substituted judgment" with anyone, the Cruzans would surely qualify. But we do not think the Due Process Clause requires the State to repose judgment on these matters with anyone but the patient herself. Close family members may have a strong feeling—a feeling not at all ignoble or unworthy, but not entirely disinterested, either—that they do not wish to witness the continuation of the life of a loved one which they regard as hopeless, meaningless, and even degrading. But there is no automatic assurance that the view of close family members will necessarily be the same as the patient's would have been had she been confronted with the prospect of her situation while competent. All of the reasons previously discussed for allowing Missouri to require clear and convincing evidence of the patient's wishes lead us to conclude that the State may choose to defer only to those wishes, rather than confide the decision to close family members.

The judgment of the Supreme Court of Missouri is

Affirmed.

JUSTICE O'CONNOR, concurring.

I agree that a protected liberty interest in refusing unwanted medical treatment may be inferred from our prior decisions ... and that the refusal of artificially delivered food and water is encompassed within that liberty interest. ...

I ... write separately to emphasize that the Court does not today decide the issue whether a State must also give effect to the decisions of a surrogate decisionmaker. In my view, such a duty may well be constitutionally required to protect the patient's liberty interest in refusing medical treatment. Few individuals provide explicit oral or written instructions regarding their intent to refuse medical treatment should they become incompetent. States which decline to consider any evidence other than such instructions may frequently fail to honor a patient's intent. Such failures might be avoided if the State considered an equally probative source of evidence: the patient's appointment of a proxy to make health care decisions on her behalf. Delegating the authority to make medical decisions to a family member or friend is becoming a common method of plan-

ning for the future. Several States have recognized the practical wisdom of such a procedure by enacting durable power of attorney statutes that specifically authorize an individual to appoint a surrogate to make medical treatment decisions. ...

Today's decision, holding only that the Constitution permits a State to require clear and convincing evidence of Nancy Cruzan's desire to have artificial hydration and nutrition withdrawn, does not preclude a future determination that the Constitution requires the States to implement the decisions of a patient's duly appointed surrogate. Nor does it prevent States from developing other approaches for protecting an incompetent individual's liberty interest in refusing medical treatment. ... [N]o national consensus has yet emerged on the best solution for this difficult and sensitive problem. Today we decide only that one State's practice does not violate the Constitution; the more challenging task of crafting appropriate procedures for safeguarding incompetents' liberty interests is entrusted to the "laboratory" of the States.

JUSTICE SCALIA, concurring.

The various opinions in this case portray quite clearly the difficult, indeed agonizing, questions that are presented by the constantly increasing power of science to keep the human body alive for longer than any reasonable person would want to inhabit it. The States have begun to grapple with these problems through legislation. I am concerned, from the tenor of today's opinions, that we are poised to confuse that enterprise as successfully as we have confused the enterprise of legislating concerning abortion—requiring it to be conducted against a background of federal constitutional imperatives that are unknown because they are being newly crafted from Term to Term. That would be a great misfortune.

While I agree with the Court's analysis today, and therefore join in its opinion, I would have preferred that we announce, clearly and promptly, that the federal courts have no business in this field; that American law has always accorded the State the power to prevent, by force if necessary, suicide—including suicide by refusing to take appropriate measures necessary to preserve one's life; that the point at which life becomes "worthless," and the point at which the means necessary to preserve it become "extraordinary" or "inappropriate," are neither set forth in the Constitution nor known to the nine Justices of this Court any better than they are known to nine people picked at random from the Kansas City telephone directory; and hence, that even when it is demonstrated by clear and convincing evidence that a patient no longer wishes certain measures to be taken to preserve her life, it is up to the citizens of Missouri to decide, through their elected representatives, whether that wish will be honored.

. . . This Court need not, and has no authority to, inject itself into every field of human activity where irrationality and oppression may theoretically occur, and if it tries to do so it will destroy itself.

JUSTICE BRENNAN, with whom JUSTICE MARSHALL and JUSTICE BLACKMUN join, dissenting.

Today the Court, while tentatively accepting that there is some degree of constitutionally protected liberty interest in avoiding unwanted medical treatment, including life-sustaining medical treatment such as artificial nutrition and hydration, affirms the decision of the Missouri Supreme Court. The majority opinion, as I read it, would affirm that decision on the ground that a State may require "clear and convincing" evidence of Nancy Cruzan's prior decision to forgo life-sustaining treatment under circumstances such as hers in order to ensure that her actual wishes are honored. Because I believe that Nancy Cruzan has a fundamental right to be free of unwanted artificial nutrition and hydration, which right is not outweighed by any interests of the State, and because I find that the improperly biased procedural obstacles imposed by the Missouri Supreme Court impermissibly burden that right, I respectfully dissent. Nancy Cruzan is entitled to choose to die with dignity. . . .

The question before this Court is a relatively narrow one: whether the Due Process Clause allows Missouri to require a now-incompetent patient in an irreversible persistent vegetative state to remain on life-support absent rigorously clear and convincing evidence that avoiding the treatment represents the patient's prior, express choice. . . .

A State's inability to discern an incompetent patient's choice still need not mean that a State is rendered powerless to protect that choice. But I would find that the Due Process Clause prohibits a State from doing more than that. A State may ensure that the person who makes the decision on the patient's behalf is the one whom the patient himself would have selected to make that choice for him. And a State may exclude from consideration anyone having improper motives. But a State generally must either repose the choice with the person whom the patient himself would most likely have chosen as proxy or leave the decision to the patient's family.

As many as 10,000 patients are being maintained in persistent vegetative states in the United States, and the number is expected to increase significantly in the near future. . . . The 80% of Americans who die in hospitals are "likely to meet their end . . . 'in a sedated or comatose state; betubed nasally, abdominally and intravenously; and far more like manipulated objects than like moral subjects.'" A fifth of all adults surviving to age 80 will suffer a progressive dementing disorder prior to death.

. . . The new medical technology can reclaim those who would have been irretrievably lost a few decades ago and restore them to active lives. For Nancy Cruzan, it failed, and for others with wasting incurable disease it may be doomed to failure. In these unfortunate situations, the bodies and preferences and memories of the victims do not escheat to the State; nor does our Constitution permit the State or any other government to commandeer them. No singularity of feeling exists upon which such a government might confidently rely as *parens patriae*. . . . Missouri and this Court have displaced Nancy's own assessment of the processes associated with dying. They have discarded evidence of her will, ignored her values, and deprived her of the right to a decision as closely approximating her own choice as humanly possible. They have done so disingenuously in her name, and openly in Missouri's own. That Missouri and this Court may truly be motivated only by concern for incompetent patients makes no matter. . . .

I respectfully dissent.

In August 1990, two months after the Court's decision, the Cruzans petitioned a Missouri court for a new hearing. Three of Nancy's former coworkers testified that she had said she would not want to live "like a vegetable." Despite protests from right-to-life groups, a state court judge ruled on December 14 that the Cruzans could have Nancy's feeding tube removed. She died on December 26. The family's tragedies continued, however. Six years after

Nancy's death, her father, Lester Cruzan, committed suicide, an act perhaps related to the stress of dealing with his daughter's ordeal.[13]

Although the courts finally settled the "right to die" question as it pertained to Nancy Cruzan, there are approximately ten thousand other "Nancy Cruzans" in the United States, a figure that may increase tenfold as medical technology advances. Does the Court's opinion provide guidance for them and their families? Yes and no. On the one hand, the Court clearly ruled that the Fourteenth Amendment's due process clause permits a competent individual to terminate medical treatment. As to incompetent patients, the majority of the justices suggested that states may fashion their own standards, including those that require "clear and convincing evidence" of the patient's interests. Living wills, as Justice O'Connor suggested in a concurring opinion, may be the best form of such evidence.

On the other hand, the case did not call for the Court to address squarely another dimension of the right-to-die question, suicides or "assisted suicides" for the terminally ill. May a person take his or her own life or arrange an assisted suicide when suffering from an illness that will surely result in death?

In 1997 two cases came to the Court dealing with the assisted suicide issue. Both *Washington v. Glucksberg* (1997) and *Vacco v. Quill* (1997) involved state laws making it a crime to assist another to commit suicide. By 9–0 votes, the justices rejected claims that such statutes violate the due process and equal protection clauses. In addition to identifying long-standing traditions against assisted suicide, the Court found that the state had legitimate interests in preserving human life, protecting the integrity and ethics of the medical profession, safeguarding the vulnerable from coercion, and ensuring the value of life even of the elderly and terminally ill.

What should we learn from these decisions? Surely, the justices made it crystal clear that states may maintain their existing bans on assisted suicides. But they did not foreclose the possibility of future constitutional claims. In a concurring opinion, O'Connor left open the possibil-

ity that the Court might respond positively to the question of "whether a mentally competent person who is experiencing great suffering has a constitutionally cognizable interest in controlling the circumstances of his or her imminent death."

O'Connor turned out to be prophetic. In *Gonzales v. Oregon* (2006) the Court took up the Oregon Death with Dignity Act, which permits state-licensed physicians to dispense or prescribe a lethal dose of drugs upon the request of a terminally ill patient. Although the law had been in effect since 1994 and, in fact, survived a ballot initiative designed to repeal it, in 2001 U.S. Attorney General John Ashcroft issued a rule asserting that the statute was unlawful. He claimed that the Controlled Substances Act (CSA) of 1970, enacted by Congress to regulate the legitimate and illegitimate trafficking of drugs, criminalizes the use of controlled substances to assist suicide. Physicians dispensing drugs for this purpose, he declared, were not engaging in the legitimate practice of medicine and could lose their privilege to write prescriptions.

The state, a physician, a pharmacist, and some terminally ill state residents challenged the rule. By the time the case reached the Supreme Court, Ashcroft was no longer attorney general, but his successor, Alberto Gonzales, stood by Ashcroft's interpretation of the CSA.

In a 6–3 decision, the Supreme Court expressed its firm disagreement with the Gonzales/Ashcroft rule. Writing for the majority, Justice Kennedy explained:

In deciding whether the CSA can be read as prohibiting physician-assisted suicide, we look to the statute's text and design. The statute and our case law amply support the conclusion that Congress regulates medical practice insofar as it bars doctors from using their prescription-writing powers as a means to engage in illicit drug dealing and trafficking as conventionally understood. Beyond this, however, the statute manifests no intent to regulate the practice of medicine generally. The silence is understandable given the structure and limitations of federalism, which allow the States " 'great latitude under their police powers to legislate as to the protection of the lives, limbs, health, comfort, and quiet of all persons.' "

The new chief justice, John Roberts, did not write an opinion, but he and Justice Thomas joined a dissent by Justice Scalia. Scalia wrote that it was "easy to sympathize" with the position he thought the majority opinion

---

13. Eric Pace, "Lester Cruzan Is Dead at 62; Fought to Let His Daughter Die," *New York Times*, August 19, 1996.

reflected—"a feeling that the subject of assisted suicide is none of the Federal Government's business." But, unlike majority, he believed that "unless we were to repudiate a long and well-established principle of our jurisprudence," it was well within Congress's power to prevent assisted suicide.

No doubt, *Gonzales v. Oregon* will not be the last word on this subject. Indeed, Chief Justice Rehnquist's words in *Washington v. Glucksberg* remain as true today as when he wrote them: "Throughout the Nation, Americans are engaged in an earnest and profound debate about the morality, legality, and practicality of physician-assisted suicide." He further noted that the Court's decision "permits this debate to continue, as it should in a democratic society." We might say the same about *Gonzales*.

Drug Testing

As the Court and the public continue to wrestle with the right to die, another privacy-related issue has moved to the fore: drug testing. Many public and private employers have initiated drug-screening or testing programs for job applicants or employees, and some schools have started them for students. Under many of these programs, individuals must submit to a urine test even if the examiner has no reason to suspect illegal drug use.

Those who support drug testing assert that the nation has a legitimate concern with drug abuse and the social problems that flow from illegal drug operations. Drug testing, they argue, is an effective method of identifying individuals who have consumed illegal substances. Finally, proponents suggest that a urinalysis is a minor intrusion into an individual's privacy rights and a minor incursion into the body.

Opponents respond that, under *Katz*, when the federal and state governments engage in drug testing programs they intrude on reasonable privacy expectations. Such testing, they argue, should not be conducted unless there is a reasonable suspicion of criminal activity; suspicionless, random testing violates the right to privacy.

Beginning in 1989 the Court began to sort through these competing claims. Initially the justices appeared sympathetic to drug testing programs if legitimate government interests were advanced. Three decisions are particularly important in this regard. First, in *Skinner v. Railway Labor Executives' Association* (1989), the Court allowed drug testing of railroad employees who had been involved in accidents. Evidence that drug use among railroad personnel may have contributed to previous accidents and the interests of public safety provided a reasonable rationale for the program. Second, in **National Treasury Union v. Von Raab** (1989), the Court approved the suspicionless drug testing of customs officials who carried arms and were involved in drug interdiction duties. Preserving the integrity of law enforcement forces that protect the nation's borders was seen as ample justification for drug testing. And third, in **Vernonia School District 47J v. Acton** (1995), the justices allowed the random drug testing of public school students engaged in athletics as a means of ensuring child health and welfare.

Soon, however, the Court confronted testing programs that crossed the constitutional line. In **Chandler v. Miller** (1997) the Court struck down a Georgia law that required drug testing of all candidates for statewide political office. The state failed to prove a convincing need for such a program. Then, in **Ferguson v. City of Charleston** (2001), the Court condemned a South Carolina program that required obstetrical patients in a public hospital to undergo drug testing as a prerequisite for receiving medical care. The justices were particularly offended by the fact that positive drug results were turned over to law enforcement officials.

Private sexual behavior, the right to die, and drug testing are only three of the many privacy issues about which Americans have become concerned. Many fear the development of computer technology that can store and analyze unlimited amounts of information about our personal, financial, and medical affairs. Others worry that the need to combat the threat of terrorism has prompted Congress to pass legislation, such as the USA PATRIOT Act, that enlarges the authority of the government to investigate the private lives of individuals suspected of having connections to terrorist activities or organizations. Such developments pose real issues for many Americans. Certainly the collection of information for business, research, or even national security purposes may be legitimate, but privacy rights also need to be preserved. Disputes will inevitably arise, and the justices of the Supreme Court will once again be asked to interpret constitutional protections in light of newly emerging conflicts.

READINGS

Behuniak, Susan M., and Arthur G. Svenson. *Physician-Assisted Suicide: The Anatomy of a Constitutional Law Issue.* Lanham, Md., Rowman and Littlefield, 2003.

Craig, Barbara Hinkson, and David M. O'Brien. *Abortion and American Politics.* Chatham, N.J.: Chatham House, 1993.

Decew, Judith Wagner. *In Pursuit of Privacy: Law, Ethics, and the Rise of Technology.* Ithaca, N.Y.: Cornell University Press, 1997.

Diffie, Whitfield, and Susan Landau. *Privacy on the Line: The Politics of Wiretapping and Encryption.* Cambridge: MIT Press, 2007.

Dworkin, Ronald. *An Argument about Abortion, Euthanasia, and Individual Freedom.* New York: Knopf, 1993.

Ely, John Hart. "The Wages of Crying Wolf: A Comment on *Roe v. Wade.*" *Yale Law Journal* 82 (1973): 920–949.

Emerson, Thomas I. "Nine Justices in Search of a Doctrine." *Michigan Law Review* 64 (1965): 219–234.

Epstein, Lee, and Joseph F. Kobylka. *The Supreme Court and Legal Change: Abortion and the Death Penalty.* Chapel Hill: University of North Carolina Press, 1992.

Epstein, Richard A. "Substantive Due Process by Any Other Name." *Supreme Court Review* (1973): 159–186.

Eskridge, William N., Jr. *Gaylaw: Challenging the Apartheid of the Closet.* Cambridge: Harvard University Press, 1999.

Etzioni, Amitai. *The Limits of Privacy.* New York: Basic Books, 1999.

Faux, Marian. *Roe v. Wade.* New York: Macmillan, 1988.

Gailey, Elizabeth Atwood. *Write to Death: News Framing of the Right-to-Die Conflict from Quinlan's Coma to Kevorkian's Conviction.* Westport, Conn.: Praeger, 2003.

Garrow, David J. *Liberty and Sexuality: The Right to Privacy and the Making of Roe v. Wade.* Berkeley: University of California Press, 1998.

Gillion, John. *Surveillance, Privacy, and the Law: Employee Drug Testing and the Politics of Social Control.* Ann Arbor: University of Michigan Press, 1994.

Glick, Henry R. *The Right to Die: Policy Innovation and Its Consequences.* New York: Columbia University Press, 1992.

Graber, Mark A. *Rethinking Abortion: Equal Choice, the Constitution, and Reproductive Politics.* Princeton: Princeton University Press, 1996.

Hull, N. E. H., and Peter Charles Hoffer. *Roe v. Wade: The Abortion Rights Controversy in American History.* Lawrence: University Press of Kansas, 2001.

Humphry, Derek, and Mary Clement. *Freedom to Die: People, Politics, and the Right-to-Die Movement.* New York: St. Martin's Press, 1998.

Johnson, John W. *Griswold v. Connecticut: Birth Control and the Constitutional Right of Privacy.* Lawrence: University Press of Kansas, 2005.

Luker, Kristen. *Abortion and the Politics of Motherhood.* Berkeley: University of California Press, 1984.

McDonagh, Eileen L. *Breaking the Abortion Deadlock.* New York: Oxford University Press, 1996.

Mezey, Susan Gluck. *Queers in Court: Gay Rights Law and Public Policy.* Lanham, Md.: Rowman and Littlefield, 2007.

Pacelle, Richard L., Jr. *Between Law and Politics: The Solicitor General and the Structuring of Race, Gender, and Reproductive Rights Litigation.* College Station: Texas A&M University Press, 2003.

Pinello, Daniel R. *Gay Rights and American Law.* New York: Cambridge University Press, 2003.

Richards, David A. J. *The Case for Gay Rights: From Bowers to Lawrence and Beyond.* Lawrence: University Press of Kansas, 2005.

Rubin, Eva R. *Abortion, Politics, and the Courts.* Westport, Conn.: Greenwood Press, 1987.

Silverstein, Helena. *Girls on the Stand.* New York: New York University Press, 2007.

Solove, Daniel J. *The Future of Reputation: Gossip, Rumor, and Privacy on the Internet.* New Haven: Yale University Press, 2007.

Tribe, Laurence H. *Abortion: The Clash of Absolutes.* New York: W. W. Norton, 1990.

Urofsky, Melvin I. *Lethal Judgments: Assisted Suicide and American Law.* Lawrence: University Press of Kansas, 2000.

Whiting, Raymond. *A Natural Right to Die: Twenty-Three Centuries of Debate.* Westport, Conn.: Greenwood Press, 2002.

THE CRIMINAL JUSTICE SYSTEM AND CONSTITUTIONAL RIGHTS

Americans regard the Bill of Rights as an enumeration of the nation's most cherished freedoms. The right to speak freely and to practice religion without undue interference from government are the guarantees to which politicians and citizens refer most often when they describe the unique character of the United States. Americans may need to be reminded, therefore, that four of the first eight amendments explicitly guarantee rights for the *criminally accused.* The framers of the Constitution emphasized criminal rights because they had grown to despise the abusive practices of British criminal procedure. The founders believed that agents of government should not enter private homes and search personal property without proper justification and that the accused should not be tried without the benefit of public scrutiny.

Consequently, the Fourth Amendment protects Americans from unreasonable searches and prescribes the procedures by which law enforcement officials can obtain warrants. The Fifth Amendment protects individuals from having to testify against themselves and from being tried more than once on the same charges; it provides for grand juries and ensures due process of law. The Sixth Amendment governs criminal proceedings. It calls for speedy and public jury trials during which defendants can call witnesses and face their accusers. It also provides for the assistance of counsel. The Eighth Amendment prohibits excessive bail and monetary fines as well as "cruel and unusual" punishments. The framers insisted on constitutional guarantees that would protect the guilty as well as the innocent against the potentially abusive prosecutorial powers of the government.

Just because these rights are not the first that come to mind when we think about the Bill of Rights does not mean that they are any less important or less relevant to society. At least once during your life, you are likely to be a participant in the criminal justice system. You may be the victim of a crime. You may serve as a juror in a criminal trial or become involved as a witness. You may even be accused of a crime. We all need to understand the rights the founders established and the procedures that invoke such guarantees.

The two chapters that follow explore the constitutional rights of the criminally accused and the Supreme Court's interpretation of them. To appreciate their importance, however, we first take a brief look at the stages of the criminal justice process. Following that discussion, we describe trends in Supreme Court decision making in this area.

OVERVIEW OF THE CRIMINAL JUSTICE SYSTEM

In Table VI-1 we provide a general overview of the criminal justice system and the constitutional rights effective at each stage. Keep two things in mind. First, because the states are given a degree of latitude in developing their criminal justice systems, these procedures vary from jurisdiction to jurisdiction. Second, fewer than 10 percent of all criminal cases actually proceed through every stage of the system. At some point during the

TABLE VI-1 The American Criminal Justice System

Stage	Governing Amendment[a]
Reported or suspected crime	
↓	
Investigation by law enforcement officials	Fourth Amendment search and seizure rights
	Fifth Amendment self-incrimination clause
↓	
Arrest	
	Sixth Amendment right to counsel clause
↓	
Booking	
↓	
Decision to prosecute	
↓	
Pretrial hearings (initial appearance, bail hearing, preliminary hearing, arraignment)	Fifth Amendment grand jury clause
	Sixth Amendment notification clause
	Eighth Amendment bail clause
↓	Fifth Amendment self-incrimination clause
Trial	Sixth Amendment speedy and public trial, jury, confrontation, and compulsory process clauses
↓	
Sentencing	Eighth Amendment cruel and unusual punishment clause
↓	
Appeals, postconviction stages	Fifth Amendment double jeopardy clause

[a]The right to due process of law is in effect throughout the process.

process, most criminal defendants plead guilty, thereby waiving their right to a jury trial, and proceed directly to sentencing. Most of these guilty pleas are the result of plea-bargaining arrangements in which the accused agrees to admit guilt in exchange for reduced charges or a lenient sentence.

This qualification noted, the process normally begins with an alleged or suspected violation of a state or federal criminal law. The first step in the criminal justice system is the response of law enforcement officials to the reporting of the offense. Many scholars and lawyers consider this part of the process to be of the utmost importance. The way police conduct their investigation and gather evidence affects all subsequent decisions made by lawyers, judges, and juries. Americans expect police officers to act lawfully, within the confines of the Constitution. We do not want them to break down doors and search houses without proper cause. But society

also expects effective law enforcement. The police must make arrests and enforce laws. No one wants to see heinous crimes go unpunished—and criminals out on the streets—because constitutional guarantees have unreasonably tied the hands of police. Law enforcement officers must understand the rules well enough to act without violating them because, when they make mistakes, the consequences can be enormous.

Once police make an arrest and take an individual into custody, the prosecuting attorney joins the process. The prosecutor of state-level crimes, commonly known as the district attorney, is an elected official who has jurisdiction over criminal matters in a particular local jurisdiction, usually a county. The prosecutor of federal offenses is called a United States attorney. U.S. attorneys are appointed by the president and confirmed by the Senate. Their assignments correspond to the geographical jurisdiction of the federal district courts, and they serve at the president's pleasure. State and federal prosecutors decide whether the government will bring charges against the accused. Prosecutors consider, among other factors, whether police acted properly in gathering evidence and making the arrest. If the prosecutor decides not to press charges, the police must release the suspect, and the process ends. If prosecution is indicated, the government brings the individual before a judge, who ensures that the accused has legal representation and understands the charges. The judge also must verify that police were justified in holding the accused in the first place. Further, the judge sets bail, a monetary guarantee that the accused will appear for trial.

The system next provides a step to ensure that the prosecutor is not abusing the power to charge persons with crimes. This check on prosecutorial discretion takes place in one of two ways. Individuals accused of committing federal offenses or of violating the laws of some states will receive grand jury hearings in accordance with the Fifth Amendment. Composed of ordinary citizens, grand juries hear from the prosecutor alone. The defense is not entitled to be present. The grand jurors examine the strength of the prosecutor's case to determine whether the government's evidence can support formal charges. If the grand jury decides that the prosecutor has satisfied the legal requirements, it will issue a formal document, known as an *indictment*, ordering the accused to stand trial on specified charges. If the grand jury concludes that the prosecutor's case is too weak, the defendant will be released.

The right to a grand jury hearing is not one of the provisions of the Bill of Rights that has been incorporated into the due process clause of the Fourteenth Amendment. Accordingly, the states are free to develop other methods of checking the prosecutor. As an alternative to the grand jury, many states use preliminary hearings. Such proceedings more closely resemble trials than does the grand jury process. Both prosecution and defense may present their cases to a judge, who evaluates the adequacy of the government's evidence. If the judge agrees that the prosecutor's case justifies a trial, a formal document known as an *information* is issued. The information

is roughly the equivalent of an indictment and orders the accused to stand trial on certain specified violations of the criminal code. If the prosecutor's case is found inadequate to justify a trial, the judge may order the release of the defendant.

After being formally charged, the defendant proceeds to the arraignment stage. At arraignment, a judge reads the indictment or information to ensure that the defendant understands the charges and the applicable constitutional rights. The judge makes sure the defendant is represented by counsel. Because the specific criminal accusations may have changed in seriousness or number of counts since the defendant's initial appearance, the judge reviews and perhaps modifies the bail amount. Finally, the judge accepts the defendant's plea: guilty, *nolo contendere* (no contest), or not guilty. Should the defendant plead either of the first two, a trial is not necessary, and the accused proceeds to sentencing.

A plea of not guilty normally leads to a full trial governed by constitutional provisions found in the Fifth and Sixth Amendments. The accused is entitled to a fair, public, and speedy trial by jury. The judge presides over the trial, and the two opposing lawyers question witnesses and summarize case facts. When both sides have presented their cases, the jury deliberates to reach a verdict. If the individual is found guilty, the judge issues a sentence, which under Eighth Amendment protections cannot be cruel and unusual.

If the defendant is found not guilty, the process ends. The Fifth Amendment prohibition against double jeopardy means that the government cannot try an acquitted defendant a second time for the same offense. The prosecution has no right to appeal an acquittal verdict reached by the trial court. Should the verdict be guilty, however, the defendant has the right to appeal the conviction to a higher court. The appeals court reviews the trial procedures to determine whether any significant errors in law or procedure occurred. If dissatisfied with the findings of the appeals court, either side—the prosecution or the defense—may try for a review by an even higher court. These requests may be denied because the system generally provides for only one appeal as a matter of right.

Subsequent appeals are left to the discretion of the appellate courts.

TRENDS IN COURT DECISION MAKING

In the chapters that follow, we examine each stage in the criminal justice system in regard to the constitutional rights of the criminally accused. While reading the narrative and cases, keep in mind that the four amendments governing criminal proceedings do not work in isolation. Rather, they fit into a larger scheme that includes law, politics, local custom, and the practical necessities of coping with crime in a contemporary society.

The rights accorded the criminally accused in the four amendments set limits that, in tandem with the legal system, define the criminal justice process. The system depends heavily upon Supreme Court interpretation of the several clauses contained in the amendments. As we have seen in other legal areas, however, the way the Court interprets constitutional rights is not determined exclusively by traditional legal factors such as precedent, the plain language of the law, or the intent of the framers. Historical circumstances, ideological stances, and pressure from other institutions and private groups also affect the course of law, which explains why jurisprudence varies from one Court era to the next or even from term to term.

Perhaps no issue illustrates this intersection of law and politics better than criminal rights. In the 1960s the Court under Chief Justice Earl Warren reformed criminal law by expanding the protections accorded those charged with crimes (see Box VI-1). The extent to which the Warren Court altered existing law was nothing short of revolutionary. As you read the cases in the following two chapters, you will see how the Warren Court changed the criminal process from one that was dominated by the interests of police and prosecutors to one in which the rights of the accused took center stage.

This liberal trend did not go unnoticed. President Richard Nixon was among the first to recognize that expanded rights for the criminally accused alarmed many Americans. During his presidential campaign of 1968 (and after his election), Nixon emphasized the law and order theme, proclaiming to the voters that the liberal Warren Court had gone too far.

In a 1968 speech Nixon said, "And tonight it's time for some honest talk about the problem of order in the United States. Let us always respect, as I do, our courts and those who serve on them, but let us also recognize that some of our courts in their decisions have gone too far in weakening the peace forces as against the criminal forces in this country." All of those who heard these words knew that Nixon was referring only to the Warren Court. Apparently, many voters agreed with the future president. Public opinion polls taken in 1968 show that nearly two-thirds of Americans believed that the courts were not dealing with criminals harshly enough, compared with about 50 percent just three years earlier.[1] In short, Nixon had hit a nerve with U.S. citizens; he placed crime on the public agenda, where it remains.

Nixon also had the opportunity to keep his promise to restore law and order to American communities by changing the composition of the Supreme Court. One year before Nixon took office, Earl Warren resigned to give President Lyndon Johnson the chance to appoint his successor. When Johnson's choice for that position, Associate Justice Abe Fortas, failed to obtain Senate confirmation, the chief justiceship remained vacant for Nixon to fill. His choice was Warren Burger, a court of appeals judge who agreed with Nixon's stance on criminal law.

During the 1970s those who sympathized with the liberal decisions of the Warren Court watched in horror as Nixon appointed three more justices to the Court. The American Civil Liberties Union and various legal aid societies predicted that this new Court not only would stop any expansion of criminal rights but also would begin to overturn Warren Court precedents.

There may be some truth to this view. During the Warren Court (1953–1969), the justices ruled in favor of the interests of the accused in 58 percent of the criminal cases they decided. Under Chief Justice Burger's leadership (1969–1986), the justices were far less supportive of criminal rights, supporting the position of the accused in about 35 percent of the criminal cases they heard. The Court's preference for law enforcement interests

1. Harold Stanley and Richard G. Niemi, *Vital Statistics on American Politics, 2005–2006* (Washington, D.C.: CQ Press, 2006), 164.

BOX VI-1   EARL WARREN (1953–1969)

EARL WARREN, the son of Scandinavian immigrant parents, was born on March 19, 1891, in Los Angeles, California. Soon after his birth, the family moved to Bakersfield, where his father worked as a railroad car repairman.

Warren worked his way through college and law school at the University of California. After graduating in 1914, he worked in law offices in San Francisco and Oakland, the only time in his career that he engaged in private practice.

Warren married Nina P. Meyers, October 14, 1925. They had three daughters and three sons.

In 1938, after Warren had become active in politics, his father was bludgeoned to death in a crime that was never solved.

At first viewed as a conservative governor—he denounced "communist radicals" and supported the wartime federal order to move all persons of Japanese ancestry away from the West Coast—Warren developed a progressive image after the war. In 1945 he proposed a state program of prepaid medical insurance and later championed liberal pension and welfare benefits.

Warren made two bids for national political office. In 1948 he ran for vice president on the Republican ticket with Gov. Thomas E. Dewey of New York. In 1952 he sought the Republican presidential nomination. But with little chance to win he threw his support at a crucial moment behind Gen. Dwight D. Eisenhower, helping him win the battle with Sen. Robert A. Taft of Ohio for the nomination.

FROM 1919 UNTIL his resignation from the Supreme Court in 1969, Warren served without interruption in public office. His first post was deputy city attorney for Oakland. Then he was named a deputy district attorney for Alameda County, which embraces the cities of Oakland, Alameda, and Berkeley.

In 1925 Warren was appointed district attorney when the incumbent resigned. He won election to the post in his own right in 1926, 1930, and 1934. During his fourteen years as district attorney, Warren developed a reputation as a crime fighter, sending a city manager and several councilmen to jail on graft charges and smashing a crooked deal on garbage collection.

A Republican, Warren decided in 1938 to run for state attorney general. He cross-filed and won three primaries—his own party's as well as the Democratic and Progressive party contests.

In 1942 Warren ran for governor of California. Although he was an underdog, he wound up defeating incumbent Democratic governor Culbert Olson by a margin of 342,000 votes, winning 57.1 percent of the total votes cast. He was twice reelected, winning the Democratic as well as the Republican nomination in 1946 and defeating Democrat James Roosevelt, son of President Franklin D. Roosevelt, by an almost two-to-one margin in 1950.

That support resulted in Eisenhower's political indebtedness to Warren, which the president repaid in 1953 with a recess appointment to the Supreme Court. Warren replaced Chief Justice Fred M. Vinson, who had died. Warren was confirmed by the Senate on March 1, 1954, by a voice vote. Eisenhower, reflecting on his choice years later in the light of the Warren Court's liberal record, called the appointment "the biggest damn-fool mistake I ever made."

In addition to his work on the Court, Warren headed the commission that investigated the assassination of President John F. Kennedy.

In 1968 Warren submitted his resignation, conditional on confirmation of a successor. But the Senate got bogged down in the fight to confirm President Lyndon B. Johnson's nomination of Justice Abe Fortas to succeed Warren, so Warren agreed to serve another year. In 1969, when Richard Nixon assumed office, he chose Warren E. Burger as the new chief justice, and Warren stepped down. He died July 9, 1974.

SOURCE: Adapted from David Savage, *Guide to the U.S. Supreme Court*, 4th ed. (Washington, D.C.: CQ Press, 2004), 1003–1004.

continued at about the same rate after Ronald Reagan's appointment of William Rehnquist to be chief justice in 1986.[2] During the first few terms of the Court under Chief Justice John G. Roberts, the justices have shown a slightly greater propensity to hold for criminal defendants—but only slightly. Defendants prevailed in 40 percent of such cases, a far cry from the nearly 60 percent during the Warren Court era.

These statistics alone, however, do not tell the entire story. Not only did the Burger and Rehnquist Courts and now the Roberts Court support the criminally accused at a lower rate than did the Warren Court, but the decisions moved the Court sharply away from the liberal path set by the Warren Court justices. Although the most significant Warren Court precedents remain standing, the Burger Court in particular chipped away at those rulings, often limiting their application or granting exceptions to the newly created rights. Whether these changes seriously damaged the elements of fairness introduced by the Warren Court or instead brought the system back into balance after the liberal excesses of the Warren era is for you to decide as you read the cases and discussion that follow.

2. For annual statistics on the Supreme Court's support of the accused in criminal cases, see Lee Epstein, Jeffrey A. Segal, Harold J. Spaeth, and Thomas G. Walker, *The Supreme Court Compendium: Data, Decisions, and Developments*, 4th ed. (Washington, D.C.: CQ Press, 2007), Table 3-8.

CHAPTER 17
INVESTIGATIONS AND EVIDENCE

T he investigation is a critical stage in most criminal cases. It is during this early portion of the criminal process that police collect evidence of the crime. How strongly that evidence points to the accused and how lawfully it was obtained largely dictate what will occur at subsequent phases of the criminal process. If the police work is sound and the evidence of guilt is strong, a guilty plea or conviction is likely to result. But if the evidence is weak or gathered illegally, criminal charges may be dropped altogether.

The framers understood the importance of the investigatory stage. They realized that effective law enforcement required that the police be able to collect evidence of criminal behavior, but they also had experienced abusive investigation tactics on the part of law enforcement agents in England and other European countries. As a consequence, the framers included in the Bill of Rights certain protections for the criminally accused, protections that were meant to safeguard individual liberties without significantly weakening the ability of the police to investigate and solve crimes.

Most evidence of criminal behavior is either physical or testimonial. The collection of physical evidence is controlled by the Fourth Amendment, which prohibits unreasonable searches and seizures by the police. The gathering of testimonial evidence is limited by the Fifth Amendment, which protects suspects from having to give testimony against themselves. In this chapter we focus on these two crucial rights and on how the Supreme Court has interpreted and enforced them.

SEARCHES AND SEIZURES

To build a case against a criminal suspect a prosecutor often relies on physical evidence gathered by the police. This evidence may assume many different forms: the money or goods taken during a theft, the weapons or tools used to carry out the crime, the clothing worn during the offense, illegal drugs, hair or blood samples, and so forth. Physical evidence can be a powerful indicator of the guilt or innocence of a suspect. Given contemporary advances in technology, such as DNA testing, physical evidence today can yield much more information than was the case even in fairly recent times.

The founders recognized the importance of physical evidence to the criminal process, but they also understood that people's rights could be abused by overzealous law enforcement efforts to obtain it. As a consequence, the Fourth Amendment, which deals exclusively with searches and seizures, became part of the Bill of Rights.

The Fourth Amendment has its genesis in the framers' resentment of an English institution, the writs of assistance. These writs were general search warrants that did not specify the places or things to be searched. They were authorized by the crown in England beginning in the mid-1600s; by the early 1700s they were used in the colonies primarily to allow customs officials to conduct unrestricted searches. By authorizing these searches, Britain hoped to discourage smuggling by colonial merchants and to enforce existing restrictions on colonial trade.[1]

As general searches grew more common, some colonists began to express their distaste for what they felt were major intrusions on their personal privacy and political liberty. Right before the Declaration of Independence was issued, Samuel Adams said that opposition to the general searches was the "Commencement of the Controversy between Great Britain and America."[2] By the time Madison proposed the Bill of Rights to Congress, it was clear that most Americans shared a contempt for general search warrants. Almost all of the newly adopted state constitutions restricted government searches and seizures.

The Fourth Amendment contains two provisions, the first stating the basic right against unreasonable searches and seizures, and the second detailing the requirements for search warrants:

[1] The right of the people to be secure in their persons, houses, papers, and effects, against unreasonable searches and seizures, shall not be violated, and [2] no Warrants shall issue, but upon probable cause, supported by Oath or affirmation, and particularly describing the place to be searched, and the persons or things to be seized.

The amendment clearly balances the government's need to gather evidence with the citizen's right not to suffer unnecessary government intrusions. The amendment does not stop police from searching and seizing, it simply outlaws such activities as are deemed "unreasonable." But what distinguishes a reasonable from an unreasonable search and seizure? As in so many other areas, the task has fallen to the Supreme Court to apply important principles to concrete cases, that is, to give meaning to the Constitution.

The Supreme Court and the Fourth Amendment

Throughout the twentieth century the justices have struggled to develop rules to govern searches and seizures. To be sure, the Court has wanted to be true to the spirit of the Fourth Amendment, providing protection for all citizens against abusive intrusions by the government, but not restricting police to the extent that effective law enforcement becomes impossible.

In grappling with these often conflicting goals, the Court has been guided by one important principle: The Fourth Amendment requires that searches be *reasonable.* Over the years the justices have designated as reasonable several types of searches and seizures. For each type, the Court has drafted procedures that must be followed for the search and seizure to be valid.

Searches with Warrants. The warrant procedure is the only search authorization method mentioned in the Constitution. Clause 2 of the Fourth Amendment outlines the steps to be followed. A police officer must go before a judge or magistrate and swear under oath that reason exists to believe that a crime has been committed and that evidence of the crime is located in a particular place. This information often is in the form of a sworn written statement called an affidavit. The judge then must determine whether probable cause exists to issue the warrant. If such cause is present, the judge authorizes a search by issuing a warrant that carefully describes the area to be searched and the items that may be seized. Police may then execute the warrant by searching in the area prescribed and seizing the designated evidence, if found.

Warrant-based searches are the preferred method of gathering physical evidence. Because a detached and objective judge issues the warrant, this method ensures the greatest protection of individual rights. The warrant procedure is, however, cumbersome. Time constraints or special circumstances may prevent police from going to a judge to apply for a warrant. Immediate action may be necessary. Recognizing this, the Supreme Court has defined certain circumstances under which a search may be deemed reasonable even without a warrant.

---

1. For more on the origins of the Fourth Amendment see Melvin I. Urofsky and Paul Finkelman, *A March of Liberty,* 2nd ed. (New York: Oxford University Press, 2002), 43–44.

2. Ira Glasser, *Visions of Liberty* (New York: Arcade, 1991), 166.

Searches Incident to a Valid Arrest. As a general principle of law, the police may conduct a search when placing a suspect under a valid arrest. For example, if a law enforcement official checks an apprehended suspect for weapons, the officer is engaging in a search incident to a valid arrest. The Supreme Court has allowed such searches for three reasons: to protect the safety of the police officer in case the suspect is armed, to remove any means of escape, and to prevent the suspect from disposing of evidence.

The Court has imposed two types of limits—temporal and spatial—on searches incident to a valid arrest. The temporal limit means that the police can conduct such a search only at the time of the arrest. If the arresting officers forget to check something or someone, they cannot later return to conduct a search unless they have some other justification. This rule makes sense in light of the original purposes for allowing searches incident to arrest: An individual can place a police officer in jeopardy or attempt escape at the time of an arrest, but no danger exists once the police have removed the individual from the scene. The spatial limitation means that searches made incident to a valid arrest may include only the arrested suspect and the area under the suspect's immediate control.

Loss of Evidence Searches. The Supreme Court has held that the police can conduct warrantless searches and seizures to prevent the loss of evidence. Frequently, officers come upon situations in which they must act quickly to preserve evidence that is in danger of being destroyed, such as when a drug dealer is about to flush narcotics down the toilet or an armed robber is intent on throwing the weapon into the river. It would not be reasonable to require an officer faced with such a situation to find a judge to issue a search warrant. By the time the law enforcement official complied with this requirement, the evidence would be gone. Therefore, the Supreme Court has allowed the police considerable latitude in acting without a warrant under such circumstances.

Like other searches and seizures, evidence-loss searches are limited: The search and seizure may extend no farther than necessary to preserve the evidence from loss or destruction. Searches justified under evidence-loss conditions may not be full evidence-seeking procedures because they must focus exclusively on securing the evidence at risk.

Consent Searches. As a rule, law enforcement officials may conduct searches upon consent. To be considered valid, consent searches must satisfy two criteria. First, permission must be freely and voluntarily granted. Second, the individual granting consent must have the authority to do so. Once permission is obtained the police may legitimately search, but the search may not extend beyond the limits imposed by the person giving consent. The required voluntary nature of the consent means that permission cannot be granted as a result of coercion. If the police extract consent by actual or threatened physical force or by means of trickery, the permission is invalid and so is the resulting search.

The second requirement is that only an authorized person can give permission to search. Normally such permission can be granted only by an adult who owns, occupies, or otherwise legally controls the house, automobile, office, or any other area the police desire to search. But the Court held in *Illinois v. Rodriguez* (1990) that this requirement may be satisfied if the police have reason to believe that the person granting permission has authority over the place to be searched, even if it later turns out that the individual had no such authority.

Safety Searches. The Court's decisions have recognized that in the conduct of their duties, police officers frequently find themselves in dangerous situations. What action may a police officer take upon confronting a person who may pose a danger to the officer or to the public? Suppose the officer fears the person may be armed, but none of the conditions justifying a search and seizure is present—that is, no warrant, insufficient evidence to justify an arrest, no consent, and so on? The response of the Court has been to allow safety searches. The Court first permitted such searches in *Terry v. Ohio* (1968); consequently, safety searches are often referred to as Terry stops.

Under the Court's safety search rulings, a police officer may stop and pat down a suspect believed to be dangerous in order to find and remove any weapons or other threatening objects. Similar to the other justifications we have discussed, safety searches are limited by the reasons the Court has allowed them. For such searches to be valid, two conditions must be met. First, there must be reason to believe that the suspect poses a threat to safety. And second, the search may be only for the purposes of removing the danger. As a consequence, the officer may not probe beyond a place where a hidden weapon is likely to be.

Hot Pursuit. Suppose a police officer observes the robbery of a jewelry store and chases the fleeing robber. The robber runs into a house. Must the police officer obtain a warrant to enter the building? As a general rule of law, the answer is no, and the reason is that the Supreme Court has carved out yet another exception to the Fourth Amendment's warrant requirement. This exception is known as hot pursuit. In other words, the Court has said that it would be reasonable for the police officer to enter the house without a search warrant, because evidence could be destroyed and lives could be endangered. And, if the officer found evidence of a crime—for example, the jewelry taken from the store—under the hot pursuit exception, the evidence could be used against the defendant.

As with all other exceptions to the warrant requirement, the Court has placed limits on the hot pursuit exception—limits that, as always, reflect the original justifications for permitting the exception. Granting police the power to engage in hot pursuit is based on the unusual circumstances the officers face. There are the real dangers that the suspect will avoid arrest, that evidence will be lost, and that the suspect will pose a threat to the safety of innocent people. These exigencies justify a warrantless search and seizure. But the search must focus only on the apprehension of the fleeing suspect.

Plain View Doctrine. Our discussion so far has described circumstances under which police may search and the guidelines the Court has established to determine reasonableness. Under each justification for a search

there are limitations: Searches based on a warrant must be confined to the place specified in the document; consent searches may go no farther than the grant of permission stipulates; and safety searches can extend only far enough to discover or remove the possible danger. But what if, while conducting a valid search, police come upon seizable articles that are outside the scope of the search authorization? Suppose law enforcement officials have a valid warrant to search a house for stolen goods and, in the course of their investigation, come across illegal narcotics. What should they do? Must they ignore such items? Or may they seize the drugs? These questions are addressed by the plain view doctrine, a controversial rule that expands the powers of police to gather evidence. This doctrine holds that if police officers are lawfully present and they come upon openly visible items subject to seizure, the officers may take possession of those articles without additional authorization.

Some analysts refer to the plain view doctrine as yet another exception to the Fourth Amendment's warrant requirement. This interpretation is reasonable because the doctrine provides officers with some freedom to seize contraband and other evidence of a crime without having a warrant. Still, it is important to understand that at the heart of the doctrine is the requirement that police must be acting lawfully when seizable items come into plain view.

The Fourth Amendment and the War against Terrorism

As noted in chapters 5 and 13, governments tend to repress civil liberties during times of war and crisis. Actions to preserve order, safety, and security often take priority over basic freedoms. This fact is well illustrated in the government's response to the problems posed by terrorism following the 2001 attacks on the World Trade Center and the Pentagon. Legislation passed by Congress and executive orders issued by the president have reduced the restraints on government investigations of potential terrorist activities. Fourth Amendment rights have been particularly affected.

For most individuals the added security at the nation's airports has been the most obvious example of governmental intrusion. Depending upon the level of alert declared, security personnel are authorized to search automobiles driven onto airport property, conduct full body scans of passengers, and search luggage, all without individualized suspicion or judicial supervision.

Less apparent to most Americans have been changes in the law that have streamlined the government's ability to engage in electronic surveillance. Under provisions of the USA PATRIOT Act, government agents investigating terrorism can trace electronic mail messages with less than probable cause, and the requirements for obtaining authority to wiretap have been significantly lowered. The act also expands the government's ability to obtain warrants for such investigations from the Foreign Intelligence Surveillance Court, a special judicial tribunal used for national security matters. This court operates in almost complete secrecy, and the government is normally the only party appearing before it.

In addition, the government has seized, without the usual Fourth Amendment safeguards, individuals suspected of having terrorist connections. Under normal conditions individuals must be brought before a judge within forty-eight hours of arrest for determination of whether the detention meets probable cause standards. The government, however, has held numerous detainees for extended periods without prompt judicial supervision and often without access to counsel, while investigations for possible terrorist activities have been conducted.

Justice Oliver Wendell Holmes noted in his dissent in *Abrams v. United States* (1919) that the government's power "is greater in time of war than in time of peace because war opens dangers that do not exist at other times." Based on a similar argument, the government claims that it cannot effectively secure the safety of Americans without having great latitude to investigate and prevent terrorist activities. Advocates of civil liberties, however, argue that the government has gone too far, that it has excessively circumvented Americans' basic liberties beyond what is necessary to combat terrorism. Debates over these issues have occurred in Congress, where controversies over the need to extend or expand the special powers of the government to combat terrorism have been an ongoing source of contention. Undoubtedly, litigation

flowing from the government's war on terrorism will continue to reach the Supreme Court, where the justices will attempt to resolve this important debate.

Enforcing the Fourth Amendment: The Exclusionary Rule

So far, we have focused on the constitutional rules governing searches and seizures. We showed that the Court has carved out numerous exceptions to the general principle that police should obtain warrants to conduct searches. At the same time, we saw that the Court has placed limits on those exceptions. For example, assume that the police arrest a person at his home. If they wish to use the incident-to-arrest exception to conduct the warrantless search of the person and his immediate surroundings, then they must conduct that search at the time of the arrest. If police officers return after the suspect has been removed to the police station and conduct a warrantless search of his house, the Court would not allow them to use the incident-to-arrest exception to justify their search. The search would fail the requirement that such searches be contemporaneous with the arrest. The search would be declared unconstitutional.

But suppose that the police did go back to the house a day later, found evidence, and tried to justify the search under the incident-to-arrest exception. We know that such a search would be illegal, but what is to prevent the police from doing it anyway? In England, if the police conduct an illegal search and seizure, the evidence they obtain may be used in court against the accused, although the person whose search and seizure rights have been violated can sue the police for damages. This system of police liability enables the British to enforce search and seizure rights.

The United States imposes a different remedy for police infractions. In this country the Fourth Amendment is enforced through the application of the exclusionary rule, a judicially created principle that removes any incentive the police might otherwise have for violating search and seizure rights. The exclusionary rule holds that evidence gathered illegally may not be admitted into court. It is excluded from use by prosecutors in attempting to establish the suspect's guilt. The rationale behind the rule is straightforward: If the police know that evidence produced by an illegal search will be of no use, they have no motive for violating the Constitution.

At one time, law enforcement officials faced no federal punitive measures for conducting illegal searches and seizures. Unless individual state laws imposed some form of redress, the police were not held liable for their activities, nor was evidence obtained unconstitutionally excluded from trials. In 1914, however, the Supreme Court decided *Weeks v. United States*, a case that arose from a federal investigation into the business practices of Freemont Weeks. Police officers went to Weeks's office, placed him under arrest, and conducted a search. Later, the police and a U.S. marshal went to Weeks's house and, without a warrant, carried off boxes of his papers and documents, a clear violation of search and seizure rules. In addition, the materials seized were not narrowly selected for their relevance but were voluminous business records and personal items on which authorities could conduct a fishing expedition in search of possible incriminating evidence.

Should the documents be used as evidence against Weeks, even though the police and the marshal had gathered the materials in an illegal manner? Writing for the Court, Justice William R. Day proclaimed:

If letters and private documents can thus be seized and held and used as evidence against a citizen accused of an offense, the protection of the Fourth Amendment declaring his right to be secure against such searches and seizures is of no value, and, so far as those thus placed are concerned, might as well be stricken from the Constitution.

With this conclusion, the Court, through Justice Day, created the exclusionary rule: Judges must exclude from trial any evidence gathered in violation of the Fourth Amendment. Although *Weeks* constituted a major decision, it was limited in scope, applying only to federal agents and federal judges in federal criminal cases. It was clear, however, that eventually the Court would be asked to apply the exclusionary rule to the states because that is where most criminal prosecutions take place. But it was also the case that many states or their judges resisted adopting an exclusionary rule. *People v. Defore* (1926) provides perhaps the most famous example. In

that case, Benjamin Cardozo, then a judge on the New York Court of Appeals, rejected expanding the *Weeks* rule to apply to state criminal cases. In his opinion he wrote the now-famous lines disparaging the exclusionary rule: "The criminal is to go free because the constable has blundered. . . . A room is searched against the law, and the body of a murdered man is found. . . . The privacy of the home has been infringed, and the murderer goes free."

The issue of applying the exclusionary rule to the states first reached the Supreme Court in 1949 in *Wolf v. Colorado*. This case involved a Colorado physician who was suspected of performing illegal abortions. Because the police were unable to obtain any solid evidence against him, a deputy sheriff surreptitiously took Dr. Wolf's appointment book and followed up on the names in it. The police gathered enough evidence to convict him. Wolf's attorney argued that because the case against his client rested on illegally obtained evidence, the Court should dismiss it. To implement his arguments, the justices would have to apply or incorporate the Fourth Amendment and impose the exclusionary rule on the states.

Writing for the Court, Justice Felix Frankfurter agreed that the states had to obey the Fourth Amendment. The right to be secure from unreasonable searches and seizures was deemed fundamental—"basic to a free society"—and the provisions of the amendment were applied to the states through the due process clause of the Fourteenth Amendment. The Court, however, refused to hold that the exclusionary rule was a necessary part of the Fourth Amendment. The rule was one method of enforcing search and seizure rights, but not the only one. In other words, although state law enforcement officials must abide by the guarantees contained in the Fourth Amendment, judges need not use a particular mechanism, such as the exclusionary rule, to ensure compliance. Frankfurter noted that the law in England, where there was no exclusionary rule, and in the states, the majority of which rejected the rule, proved that justice could be served without this check on police behavior. States were left free to adopt whatever procedures they wished to enforce search and seizure rights. The exclusionary rule was not mandatory.

Growing conflicts between state and federal search and seizure rules, coupled with changes in Court personnel, caused the Court to reconsider the applicability of the exclusionary rule to the states. As you read *Mapp v. Ohio* (1961), can you discern why it is such a significant, yet controversial, opinion? Does Justice Tom Clark's majority opinion leave any room for exceptions?

Mapp v. Ohio

367 U.S. 643 (1961)
http://laws.findlaw.com/US/367/643.html
Oral arguments may be found at: http://www.oyez.org
Vote: 6 (Black, Brennan, Clark, Douglas, Stewart, Warren)
    3 (Frankfurter, Harlan, Whittaker)
Opinion of the Court: Clark
Concurring opinions: Black, Douglas, Stewart
Dissenting opinion: Harlan

Dollree Mapp, a woman in her early twenties, was involved in myriad illegal activities, which she carried on in her Cleveland home. For several months the police had attempted to shut down her operations, but apparently Mapp was tipped off because each time the police planned a raid, she managed to elude them.

On May 23, 1957, police officers, led by Sgt. Carl Delau, tried to enter Mapp's house, this time on the ground that she was harboring a fugitive from justice. (The fugitive was suspected of bombing the house of an alleged Cleveland numbers racketeer, Don King, who later became a prominent boxing promoter.[3]) When the police arrived, Mapp refused to let them in because they did not have a search warrant. Delau returned to his car, radioed for a search warrant, and kept the house under surveillance. Three hours later, and with additional police officers, Delau again tried to enter. This time Mapp did not come to the door, so police forced it open.

At this point several events occurred almost simultaneously. Mapp's attorney, whom she had called when police first appeared, arrived and tried to see her. Police would not let him in. Hearing the police break in, Mapp came downstairs and began arguing with them. Delau held up a piece of paper, which he claimed was a search warrant. Mapp grabbed it and stuffed it down her blouse. A fight broke out, during which police handcuffed Mapp, retrieved the paper, and searched the house. The police did not find any fugitive from justice, but they did seize some allegedly obscene pictures, which were illegal to possess under Ohio law. The existence of a valid search warrant was never established by the state. Mapp was found guilty of possession of obscene materials and sentenced to prison. Her attorney appealed to the U.S. Supreme Court, asking the justices to review Mapp's claim on First Amendment grounds, but the justices were more interested in exploring the search and seizure issue.[4]

MR. JUSTICE CLARK delivered the opinion of the Court.

Seventy-five years ago, in *Boyd v. United States* ... [t]he Court noted that "constitutional provisions for the security of person and property should be liberally construed.... It is the duty of courts to be watchful for the constitutional rights of the citizen, and against any stealthy encroachments thereon."

In this jealous regard for maintaining the integrity of individual rights, the Court gave life to Madison's prediction that "independent tribunals of justice ... will be naturally led to resist every encroachment upon rights expressly stipulated for in the Constitution by the declaration of rights." ...

Less than 30 years after *Boyd*, this Court, in *Weeks v. United States*, 1914, ... stated that use of the seized evidence involved "a denial of the constitutional rights of the accused." Thus, in the year 1914, in the *Weeks* case, this Court "for the first time" held that "in a federal prosecution the Fourth Amendment barred the use of evidence secured through an illegal search and seizure." This Court has ever since required of federal law officers a strict adherence to

---

3. See Fred W. Friendly and Martha J. H. Elliott, *The Constitution: That Delicate Balance* (New York: Random House, 1984), 128–133.

4. Indeed, both Mapp's and the state's attorneys argued this case on First Amendment grounds because she was convicted for possessing obscene material. Neither side asked the court to overrule *Wolf* or reaffirm it. It was The ACLU, in an amicus curiae brief, that briefly raised the Fourth Amendment issue on which the Court ultimately decided. *Mapp*, therefore, presents an excellent illustration of the effect amicus curiae briefs can have. It also illustrates how the justices can reach for an issue they want to decide even if it is not presented by the parties to the dispute.

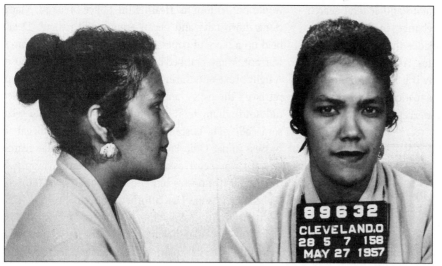

In 1957 Dollree Mapp was arrested for possession of obscene materials. The police seized vital evidence against her during an unconstitutional search. In *Mapp v. Ohio* (1961) the Supreme Court reversed her conviction, holding that evidence obtained through an illegal search could not be admitted in court.

that command which this Court has held to be a clear, specific, and constitutionally required—even if judicially implied—deterrent safeguard without insistence upon which the Fourth Amendment would have been reduced to "a form of words." It meant, quite simply, that "conviction by means of unlawful seizures and enforced confessions . . . should find no sanction in the judgments of the courts . . . ," that such evidence "shall not be used at all."

There are in the cases of this Court some passing references to the *Weeks* rule as being one of evidence. But the plain and unequivocal language of *Weeks*—and its later paraphrase in *Wolf*—to the effect that the *Weeks* rule is of constitutional origin, remains entirely undisturbed. . . .

In 1949, 35 years after *Weeks* was announced, this Court, in *Wolf v. People of State of Colorado*, again for the first time, discussed the effect of the Fourth Amendment upon the states through the operation of the Due Process Clause of the Fourteenth Amendment. It said: "[W]e have no hesitation in saying that were a State affirmatively to sanction such police incursion into privacy it would run counter to the guaranty of the Fourteenth Amendment."

Nevertheless, after declaring that the "security of one's privacy against arbitrary intrusion by the police" is "implicit in 'the concept of ordered liberty' and as such enforceable against the States through the Due Process Clause," and announcing that it "stoutly adhere[d]" to the *Weeks* decision, the Court decided that the *Weeks* exclusionary rule

would not then be imposed upon the States as "an essential ingredient of the right." The Court's reasons for not considering essential to the right to privacy, as a curb imposed upon the States by the Due Process Clause, that which decades before had been posited as part and parcel of the Fourth Amendment's limitation upon federal encroachment of individual privacy, were bottomed on factual considerations.

While they are not basically relevant to a decision that the exclusionary rule is an essential ingredient of the Fourth Amendment as the right it embodies is vouchsafed against the States by the Due Process Clause, we will consider the current validity of the factual grounds upon which *Wolf* was based.

The Court in *Wolf* first stated that "[t]he contrariety of views of the States" on the adoption of the exclusionary rule of *Weeks* was "particularly impressive" and, in this connection that it could not "brush aside the experience of States which deem the incidence of such conduct by the police too slight to call for a deterrent remedy . . . by overriding the [States'] relevant rules of evidence." While in 1949, prior to the *Wolf* case, almost two-thirds of the States were opposed to the use of the exclusionary rule, now, despite the *Wolf* case, more than half of those since passing upon it, by their own legislative or judicial decision, have wholly or partly adopted or adhered to the *Weeks* rule. Significantly, among those now following the rule is California, which, according to its highest court, was "compelled to reach that conclusion because other remedies have completely failed to secure compliance with the constitutional provisions. . . ." In connection with this California case, we note that the second basis elaborated in *Wolf* in support of its failure to enforce the exclusionary doctrine against the States was that "other means of protection" have been afforded "the right to privacy." The experience of California that such other remedies have been worthless and futile is buttressed by the experience of other States. . . .

Likewise, time has set its face against . . . *Wolf*. . . . [T]he force of that reasoning has been largely vitiated by later decisions of this Court. These include the recent discarding of the "silver platter" doctrine which allowed federal judicial use of evidence seized in violation of the Constitution by state agents; the relaxation of the formerly strict requirements as to standing to challenge the use of evidence thus seized, so that now the procedure of exclusion, "ultimately referable to constitutional safeguards," is available to anyone even "legitimately on [the] premises" unlawfully searched; and finally, the formulation of a method to prevent state use of evidence unconstitutionally seized by federal agents. Because there can be no fixed formula, we are admittedly met with "recurring questions of the [r]easonableness of searches," but less is not to be expected when dealing with a Constitution, and, at any rate, "reasonableness is in the first instance for the [trial court] to determine."

It, therefore, plainly appears that the factual considerations supporting the failure of the *Wolf* Court to include the *Weeks* exclusionary rule when it recognized the enforceability of the right to privacy against the States in 1949, while not basically relevant to the constitutional consideration, could not, in any analysis, now be deemed controlling.

Some five years after *Wolf*, in answer to a plea made here Term after Term that we overturn its doctrine on applicability of the *Weeks* exclusionary rule, this Court indicated that such should not be done until the States had "adequate opportunity to adopt or reject the [*Weeks*] rule." . . . Today we once again examine *Wolf*'s constitutional documentation of the right to privacy free from unreasonable state intrusion, and, after its dozen years on our books, are led by it to close the only courtroom door remaining open to evidence secured by official lawlessness in flagrant abuse of that basic right, reserved to all persons as a specific guarantee against that very same unlawful conduct. We hold that all evidence obtained by searches and seizures in violation of the Constitution is, by that same authority, inadmissible in a state court.

Since the Fourth Amendment's right of privacy has been declared enforceable against the States through the Due Process Clause of the Fourteenth, it is enforceable against them by the same sanction of exclusion as is used against the Federal Government. Were it otherwise, then just as without the *Weeks* rule the assurance against unreasonable federal searches and seizures would be "a form of words," valueless and undeserving of mention in a perpetual charter of inestimable human liberties, so too, without that rule the freedom from state invasions of privacy would be so ephemeral and so neatly severed from its conceptual nexus with the freedom from all brutish means of coercing evidence as not to merit this Court's high regard as a freedom "implicit in 'the concept of ordered liberty.' " At the time that the Court held in *Wolf* that the Amendment was applicable to the States through the Due Process Clause, the cases of this Court, as we have seen, had steadfastly held that as to federal officers the Fourth Amendment included the exclusion of the evidence seized in violation of its provisions. Even *Wolf* "stoutly adhered" to that proposition. The right to privacy, when conceded operatively enforceable against the States, was not susceptible of destruction by avulsion of the sanction upon which its protection and enjoyment had always been deemed dependent. . . . Therefore, in extending the substantive protections of due process to all constitutionally unreasonable searches—state or federal—it was logically and constitutionally necessary that the exclusion doctrine—an essential part of the right to privacy—be also insisted upon as an essential ingredient of the right newly recognized by the *Wolf* case. In short, the admission of the new constitutional right by *Wolf* could not consistently tolerate denial of its most important constitutional privilege, namely, the exclusion of the evidence which an accused had been forced to give by reason of the unlawful seizure. To hold otherwise is to grant the right but in reality to withhold its privilege and enjoyment. Only last year the Court itself recognized that the purpose of the exclusionary rule "is to deter—to compel respect for the constitutional guaranty in the only effectively available way—by removing the incentive to disregard it."

Indeed, we are aware of no restraint, similar to that rejected today, conditioning the enforcement of any other basic constitutional right. The right to privacy, no less important than any other right carefully and particularly reserved to the people, would stand in marked contrast to all other rights declared as "basic to a free society." This Court has not hesitated to enforce as strictly against the States as it does against the Federal Government the rights of free speech and of a free press, the rights to notice and to a fair, public trial, including, as it does, the right not to be convicted by use of a coerced confession, however logically relevant it be, and without regard to its reliability. And nothing could be more certain than that when a coerced confession is involved, "the relevant rules of evidence" are overridden without regard to "the incidence of such conduct by the police," slight or frequent. Why should not the same rule apply to what is tantamount to coerced testimony by way of unconstitutional seizure of goods, papers, effects, documents, etc.? We find that, as to the Federal Government, the Fourth and Fifth Amendments and, as to the States, the freedom from unconscionable invasions of privacy and the freedom from convictions based upon coerced confessions do enjoy an "intimate relation" in their perpetuation of "principles of humanity and civil liberty [secured] . . . only after years of struggle." The philosophy of each Amendment and of each freedom is complementary to, although not dependent upon, that of the other in its sphere of influence—the very least that together they assure in either sphere is that no man is to be convicted on unconstitutional evidence.

Moreover, our holding that the exclusionary rule is an essential part of both the Fourth and Fourteenth Amendments is not only the logical dictate of prior cases, but it also makes very good sense. There is no war between the Constitution and common sense. Presently, a federal prosecutor may make no use of evidence illegally seized, but a State's attorney across the street may, although he supposedly is operating under the enforceable prohibitions of the same Amendment. Thus the State, by admitting evidence unlawfully seized, serves to encourage disobedience to the Federal Constitution which it is bound to uphold. Moreover, "[t]he very essence of a healthy federalism depends upon the avoidance of needless conflict between state and federal courts." Such a conflict, hereafter needless, arose this very Term, in *Wilson v. Schnettler,* in which . . . we gave full recognition to our practice in this regard by refusing to restrain a federal officer from testifying in a state court as to evidence unconstitutionally seized by him in the performance of his duties. Yet the double standard recognized un-

til today hardly put such a thesis into practice. In nonexclusionary States, federal officers, being human, were by it invited to and did, as our cases indicate, step across the street to the State's attorney with their unconstitutionally seized evidence. Prosecution on the basis of that evidence was then had in a state court in utter disregard of the enforceable Fourth Amendment. If the fruits of an unconstitutional search had been inadmissible in both state and federal courts, this inducement to evasion would have been sooner eliminated. There would be no need to reconcile such cases as . . . *Schnettler,* pointing up the hazardous uncertainties of our heretofore ambivalent approach. . . .

There are those who say, as did Justice (then Judge) Cardozo, that under our constitutional exclusionary doctrine "[t]he criminal is to go free because the constable has blundered." *People v. Defore.* In some cases this will undoubtedly be the result. But . . . "there is another consideration—the imperative of judicial integrity." The criminal goes free, if he must, but it is the law that sets him free. Nothing can destroy a government more quickly than its failure to observe its own laws, or worse, its disregard of the character of its own existence. Nor can it lightly be assumed that, as a practical matter, adoption of the exclusionary rule fetters law enforcement. Only last year this Court expressly considered that contention and found that "pragmatic evidence of a sort" to the contrary was not wanting. . . . Moreover, the experience of the states is impressive. . . . The movement towards the rule of exclusion has been halting but seemingly inexorable.

The ignoble shortcut to conviction left open to the State tends to destroy the entire system of constitutional restraints on which the liberties of the people rest. Having once recognized that the right to privacy embodied in the Fourth Amendment is enforceable against the States, and that the right to be secure against rude invasions of privacy by state officers is, therefore, constitutional in origin, we can no longer permit that right to remain an empty promise. Because it is enforceable in the same manner and to like effect as other basic rights secured by the Due Process Clause, we can no longer permit it to be revocable at the whim of any police officer who, in the name of law enforcement itself, chooses to suspend its enjoyment. Our decision, founded on reason and truth, gives to the individual no more than that which the Constitution guarantees him, to the police officer no less than that to which honest law enforcement is entitled, and, to the courts, that judicial integrity so necessary in the true administration of justice.

The judgment of the Supreme Court of Ohio is reversed and the cause remanded for further proceedings not inconsistent with this opinion.

Reversed and remanded.

MR. JUSTICE BLACK, concurring.

I am still not persuaded that the Fourth Amendment, standing alone, would be enough to bar the introduction into evidence against an accused of papers and effects seized from him in violation of its commands. For the Fourth Amendment does not itself contain any provision expressly precluding the use of such evidence, and I am extremely doubtful that such a provision could properly be inferred from nothing more than the basic command against unreasonable searches and seizures. Reflection on the problem, however, in the light of cases coming before the Court since *Wolf,* has led me to conclude that when the Fourth Amendment's ban against unreasonable searches and seizures is considered together with the Fifth Amendment's ban against compelled self-incrimination, a constitutional basis emerges which not only justifies but actually requires the exclusionary rule.

The close interrelationship between the Fourth and Fifth Amendments, as they apply to this problem, has long been recognized and, indeed, was expressly made the ground for this Court's holding in *Boyd v. United States* [1866]. There the Court fully discussed this relationship and declared itself "unable to perceive that the seizure of a man's private books and papers to be used in evidence against him is substantially different from compelling him to be a witness against himself." It was upon this ground that Mr. Justice Rutledge largely relied in his dissenting opinion in the *Wolf* case. And, although I rejected the argument at that time, its force has, for me at least, become compelling with the more thorough understanding of the problem brought on by recent cases. In the final analysis, it seems to me that the *Boyd* doctrine, though perhaps not required by the express language of the Constitution strictly construed, is amply justified from an historical standpoint, soundly based in reason, and entirely consistent with what I regard to be the proper approach to interpretation of our Bill of Rights.

MR. JUSTICE HARLAN, whom MR. JUSTICE FRANKFURTER, and MR. JUSTICE WHITTAKER join, dissenting.

In overruling the *Wolf* case the Court, in my opinion, has forgotten the sense of judicial restraint which, with due regard for *stare decisis,* is one element that should enter into deciding whether a past decision of this Court should be overruled. Apart from that I also believe that the *Wolf* rule represents sounder Constitutional doctrine than the new rule which now replaces it.

From the Court's statement of the case one would gather that the central, if not controlling, issue on this appeal is whether illegally state-seized evidence is Constitutionally admissible in a state prosecution, an issue which would of course face us with the need for re-examining *Wolf.* However, such is not the situation. For, although that question was indeed raised here and below among appellant's subordinate points, the new and pivotal issue brought to the Court by this appeal is whether . . . [the Ohio law] making criminal the *mere* knowing possession or control of obscene material, and under which appellant has been convicted, is consistent with the rights of free thought and expression assured against state action by the Fourteenth Amendment. That was the principal issue which was decided by the Ohio Supreme Court, which was tendered by appellant's Jurisdictional Statement, and which was briefed* and argued in this Court.

In this posture of things, I think it fair to say that five members of this Court have simply "reached out" to overrule *Wolf.* With all respect for the views of the majority, and recognizing that *stare decisis* carries different weight in Constitutional adjudication than it does in nonconstitutional decision, I can perceive no justification for regarding this case as an appropriate occasion for re-examining *Wolf.* . . .

Since the demands of the case before us do not require us to reach the question of the validity of *Wolf,* I think this case furnishes a singularly inappropriate occasion for consideration of that decision, if reconsideration is indeed warranted. . . .

I am bound to say that what has been done is not likely to promote respect either for the Court's adjudicatory process or for the stability of its decisions. Having been unable, however, to persuade any of the majority to a different

* The appellant's brief did not urge the overruling of *Wolf.* Indeed it did not even cite the case. The brief of the appellee merely relied on *Wolf* in support of the State's contention that appellant's conviction was not vitiated by the admission in evidence of the fruits of the alleged unlawful search and seizure by the police. The brief of the American Civil Liberties Union, as *amici,* did in one short concluding paragraph of its argument "request" the Court to re-examine and overrule *Wolf,* but without argumentation.

procedural course, I now turn to the merits of the present decision. . . .

I would not impose upon the States this federal exclusionary remedy. The reasons given by the majority for now suddenly turning its back on *Wolf* seem to me notably unconvincing.

First, it is said that "the factual grounds upon which *Wolf* was based" have since changed, in that more States now follow the *Weeks* exclusionary rule than was so at the time *Wolf* was decided. While that is true, a recent survey indicates that at present one-half of the States still adhere to the common-law non-exclusionary rule, and one, Maryland, retains the rule as to felonies. But in any case surely all this is beside the point, as the majority itself indeed seems to recognize. Our concern here, as it was in *Wolf,* is not with the desirability of that rule but only with the question whether the States are Constitutionally free to follow it or not as they may themselves determine, and the relevance of the disparity of views among the States on this point lies simply in the fact that the judgment involved is a debatable one. Moreover, the very fact on which the majority relies, instead of lending support to what is now being done, points away from the need of replacing voluntary state action with federal compulsion.

The preservation of a proper balance between state and federal responsibility in the administration of criminal justice demands patience on the part of those who might like to see things move faster among the States in this respect. Problems of criminal law enforcement vary widely from State to State. One State, in considering the totality of its legal picture, may conclude that the need for embracing the *Weeks* rule is pressing because other remedies are unavailable or inadequate to secure compliance with the substantive Constitutional principle involved. Another, though equally solicitous of Constitutional rights, may choose to pursue one purpose at a time, allowing all evidence relevant to guilt to be brought into a criminal trial, and dealing with Constitutional infractions by other means. Still another may consider the exclusionary rule too rough-and-ready a remedy, in that it reaches only unconstitutional intrusions which eventuate in criminal prosecution of the victims. Further, a State after experimenting with the *Weeks* rule for a time may, because of unsatisfactory experience with it, decide to revert to a non-exclusionary rule. And so on. From the standpoint of Constitutional permissibility in pointing

a State in one direction or another, I do not see at all why "time has set its face against" the considerations which led Mr. Justice Cardozo, then chief judge of the New York Court of Appeals, to reject for New York in *People v. Defore,* the *Weeks* exclusionary rule. For us the question remains, as it has always been, one of state power, not one of passing judgment on the wisdom of one state course or another. In my view this Court should continue to forbear from fettering the States with an adamant rule which may embarrass them in coping with their own peculiar problems in criminal law enforcement.

Further, we are told that imposition of the *Weeks* rule on the States makes "very good sense," in that it will promote recognition by state and federal officials of their "mutual obligation to respect the same fundamental criteria" in their approach to law enforcement, and will avoid " 'needless conflict between state and federal courts.' " . . .

An approach which regards the issue as one of achieving procedural symmetry or of serving administrative convenience surely disfigures the boundaries of this Court's functions in relation to the state and federal courts. Our role in promulgating the *Weeks* rule . . . was quite a different one than it is here. There, in implementing the Fourth Amendment, we occupied the position of a tribunal having the ultimate responsibility for developing the standards and procedures of judicial administration within the judicial system over which it presides. Here we review state procedures whose measure is to be taken not against the specific substantive commands of the Fourth Amendment but under the flexible contours of the Due Process Clause. I do not believe that the Fourteenth Amendment empowers this Court to mould state remedies effectuating the right to freedom from "arbitrary intrusion by the police" to suit its own notions of how things should be done. . . .

In conclusion, it should be noted that the majority opinion in this case is in fact an opinion only for the *judgment* overruling *Wolf,* and not for the basic rationale by which four members of the majority have reached that result. For my Brother Black is unwilling to subscribe to their view that the *Weeks* exclusionary rule derives from the Fourth Amendment itself. . . .

I regret that I find so unwise in principle and so inexpedient in policy a decision motivated by the high purpose of increasing respect for Constitutional rights. But in the last analysis I think this Court can increase respect for the Con-

BOX 17-1   AFTERMATH . . .
DOLLREE MAPP

DOLLREE MAPP was a free woman following the Supreme Court's reversal of her obscenity conviction in 1961. As a consequence of the decision, state courts were obliged to use the exclusionary rule as a means of enforcing Fourth Amendment search and seizure rights.

In 1968 Mapp moved from Cleveland to New York City. She did not give up her life of crime. In November 1970 police arrested Mapp on charges of possession of and trafficking in stolen property. Pursuing the investigation, detectives obtained a warrant to search her home. They found stolen goods valued at more than $100,000 and 50,000 envelopes of heroin. Although she claimed that the search warrant was defective, New York courts did not agree. After her trial she was sentenced to a term of twenty years to life in the New York Correctional Institution for Women.

On New Year's Eve 1980, Gov. Hugh Carey of New York commuted Mapp's sentence to time served, and she became eligible for release on parole.

SOURCES: *New York Times*, May 27, 1971, December 15, 1975, January 1, 1981; and James A. Inciardi, *Criminal Justice*, 4th ed. (Fort Worth: Harcourt Brace Jovanovich, 1993).

with Cardozo and argue that letting a guilty person go free is too great a price for society to pay just because a police officer violated search and seizure guidelines (*see Box 17-1*).

Disagreement over the exclusionary rule, expressed in academic circles and the public, also was evident among the justices. Six voted to overturn Mapp's conviction, but only five expressed full support for the exclusionary rule. Potter Stewart, who voted with the majority, explicitly did so on other grounds. When Chief Justice Earl Warren left the Court and was replaced by law-and-order-minded Warren Burger in 1969, legal scholars predicted that the Court might well overrule *Mapp*. With each additional Court appointment by Richard Nixon and then later by Ronald Reagan, speculation on the end of the exclusionary rule increased.

At first, the predictions of the reversal of *Mapp* were proven unfounded, but by the mid-1980s the situation had changed. The Court became dominated by conservative justices appointed during the Nixon, Ford, and Reagan administrations. In addition, the national mood had turned quite conservative, and pressure was mounting to alter liberal, Warren Court rulings. The time seemed ripe for change, and in 1984 the Court imposed a major exception to the exclusionary rule.

stitution only if it rigidly respects the limitations which the Constitution places upon it, and respects as well the principles inherent in its own processes. In the present case I think we exceed both, and that our voice becomes only a voice of power, not of reason.

The application of the exclusionary rule provides yet another example of the Warren Court's revolutionary treatment of the rights of the criminally accused. It also illustrates the highly politicized nature of criminal law. Since 1961, when the Court informed states that they must adopt it, the rule has been attacked and defended by scholars, lawyers, and judges. Supporters fear that if the exclusionary rule is eliminated, police will have no incentive to respect the law. Opponents of the rule agree

United States v. Leon

468 U.S. 897 (1984)
http://laws.findlaw.com/US/468/897.html
Oral arguments may be found at: http://www.oyez.org
Vote: 6 (Blackmun, Burger, O'Connor, Powell, Rehnquist, White)
      3 (Brennan, Marshall, Stevens)
Opinion of the Court: White
Concurring opinion: Blackmun
Dissenting opinions: Brennan, Stevens

In 1981 Burbank, California, police received a tip from a person of unproven reliability, identifying two individuals, Patsy Stewart and Armando Sanchez, as drug dealers. According to the informant, the pair kept small quantities of drugs in their house on Price Drive in Burbank and a larger inventory at another residence in the same city. Police began a surveillance of the Burbank residence, where they spotted a car belonging to Ricardo Del Castillo, who had a history of drug possession. Del Castillo's probation records led police to Alberto Leon, a known drug dealer. Based on observation, continued surveillance of various residences, and information from a second informant, Burbank narcotics investigator Cyril Rombach drew up an affidavit to obtain a search warrant, which a judge issued. With the warrant, police searched several residences and seized large quantities of drugs. Leon, Stewart, Sanchez, and Del Castillo were arrested.

At the trial stage, attorneys for the defendants argued that the search warrant was invalid. They claimed that because the original informant lacked established credibility, the judge did not have probable cause to issue the warrant. The government's lawyers admitted that the defendants had a valid point but argued that the courts should decline to throw out the entire case because of a defective warrant. They claimed that the officers had acted in "good faith"; the police believed they had a legitimate warrant and acted accordingly.

JUSTICE WHITE delivered the opinion of the Court.

This case presents the question whether the Fourth Amendment exclusionary rule should be modified so as not to bar the use in the prosecution's case in chief of evidence obtained by officers acting in reasonable reliance on a search warrant issued by a detached and neutral magistrate but ultimately found to be unsupported by probable cause. To resolve this question, we must consider once again the tension between the sometimes competing goals of, on the one hand, deterring official misconduct and removing inducements to unreasonable invasions of privacy and, on the other, establishing procedures under which criminal defendants are "acquitted or convicted on the basis of all the evidence which exposes the truth." . . .

The Fourth Amendment contains no provision expressly precluding the use of evidence obtained in violation of its commands, and an examination of its origin and purposes makes clear that the use of fruits of a past unlawful search or seizure "work[s] no new Fourth Amendment wrong." The wrong condemned by the Amendment is "fully accomplished" by the unlawful search or seizure itself, and the

exclusionary rule is neither intended nor able to "cure the invasion of the defendant's rights which he has already suffered." The rule thus operates as "a judicially created remedy designed to safeguard Fourth Amendment rights generally through its deterrent effect, rather than a personal constitutional right of the person aggrieved."

Whether the exclusionary sanction is appropriately imposed in a particular case, our decisions make clear, is "an issue separate from the question whether the Fourth Amendment rights of the party seeking to invoke the rule were violated by police conduct." Only the former question is currently before us, and it must be resolved by weighing the costs and benefits of preventing the use in the prosecution's case in chief of inherently trustworthy tangible evidence obtained in reliance on a search warrant issued by a detached and neutral magistrate that ultimately is found to be defective.

The substantial social costs exacted by the exclusionary rule for the vindication of Fourth Amendment rights have long been a source of concern. "Our cases have consistently recognized that unbending application of the exclusionary sanction to enforce ideals of governmental rectitude would impede unacceptably the truth-finding functions of judge and jury." An objectionable collateral consequence of this interference with the criminal justice system's truth-finding function is that some guilty defendants may go free or receive reduced sentences as a result of favorable plea bargains. Particularly when law enforcement officers have acted in objective good faith or their transgressions have been minor, the magnitude of the benefit conferred on such guilty defendants offends basic concepts of the criminal justice system. Indiscriminate application of the exclusionary rule, therefore, may well "generat[e] disrespect for the law and administration of justice." Accordingly, "[a]s with any remedial device, the application of the rule has been restricted to those areas where its remedial objectives are thought most efficaciously served."

Close attention to those remedial objectives has characterized our recent decisions concerning the scope of the Fourth Amendment exclusionary rule. The Court has, to be sure, not seriously questioned, "in the absence of a more efficacious sanction, the continued application of the rule to suppress evidence from the [prosecution's] case where a Fourth Amendment violation has been substantial and deliberate. . . ." Nevertheless, the balancing approach that has evolved in various contexts—including criminal trials—"forcefully suggest[s] that the exclusionary rule be more generally modified to permit the introduction of evidence obtained in the reasonable good-faith belief that a search or seizure was in accord with the Fourth Amendment." . . .

The same attention to the purposes underlying the exclusionary rule also has characterized decisions not involving the scope of the rule itself. We have not required suppression of the fruits of a search incident to an arrest made in good-faith reliance on a substantive criminal statute that subsequently is declared unconstitutional. Similarly, although the Court has been unwilling to conclude that new Fourth Amendment principles are always to have only prospective effect, no Fourth Amendment decision marking a "clear break with the past" has been applied retroactively. . . .

As yet, we have not recognized any form of good-faith exception to the Fourth Amendment exclusionary rule. But the balancing approach that has evolved during the years of experience with the rule provides strong support for the modification currently urged upon us. As we discuss below, our evaluation of the costs and benefits of suppressing reliable physical evidence seized by officers reasonably relying on a warrant issued by a detached and neutral magistrate leads to the conclusion that such evidence should be admissible in the prosecution's case in chief.

Because a search warrant "provides the detached scrutiny of a neutral magistrate, which is a more reliable safeguard against improper searches than the hurried judgment of a law enforcement officer 'engaged in the often competitive enterprise of ferreting out crime,' " we have expressed a strong preference for warrants and declared that "in a doubtful or marginal case a search under a warrant may be sustainable where without one it would fall." Reasonable minds frequently may differ on the question whether a particular affidavit establishes probable cause, and we have thus concluded that the preference for warrants is most appropriately effectuated by according "great deference" to a magistrate's determination.

Deference to the magistrate, however, is not boundless. It is clear, first, that the deference accorded to a magistrate's finding of probable cause does not preclude inquiry into the knowing or reckless falsity of the affidavit on which that determination was based. Second, the courts must also insist that the magistrate purport to "perform his 'neutral and detached' function and not serve merely as a rubber stamp for the police." . . .

Third, reviewing courts will not defer to a warrant based on an affidavit that does not "provide the magistrate with a substantial basis for determining the existence of probable cause." . . . Even if the warrant application was supported by more than a "bare bones" affidavit, a reviewing court may properly conclude that, notwithstanding the deference that magistrates deserve, the warrant was invalid because the magistrate's probable-cause determination reflected an improper analysis of the totality of the circumstances or because the form of the warrant was improper in some respect.

Only in the first of these three situations, however, has the Court set forth a rationale for suppressing evidence obtained pursuant to a search warrant; in the other areas, it has simply excluded such evidence without considering whether Fourth Amendment interests will be advanced. To the extent that proponents of exclusion rely on its behavioral effects on judges and magistrates in these areas, their reliance is misplaced. First, the exclusionary rule is designed to deter police misconduct rather than to punish the errors of judges and magistrates. Second, there exists no evidence suggesting that judges and magistrates are inclined to ignore or subvert the Fourth Amendment or that lawlessness among these actors requires application of the extreme sanction of exclusion.

Third, and most important, we discern no basis, and are offered none, for believing that exclusion of evidence seized pursuant to a warrant will have a significant deterrent effect on the issuing judge or magistrate. Many of the factors that indicate that the exclusionary rule cannot provide an effective "special" or "general" deterrent for individual offending law enforcement officers apply as well to judges or magistrates. And, to the extent that the rule is thought to operate as a "systemic" deterrent on a wider audience, it clearly can have no such effect on individuals empowered to issue search warrants. Judges and magistrates are not adjuncts to the law enforcement team; as neutral judicial officers, they have no stake in the outcome of particular criminal prosecutions. The threat of exclusion thus cannot be expected significantly to deter them. Imposition of the exclusionary sanction is not necessary meaningfully to inform judicial officers of their errors, and we cannot conclude that admitting evidence obtained pursuant to a warrant while at the same time declaring that the warrant was somehow defective will in any way reduce judicial officers' professional incentives to comply with the Fourth Amendment, encourage them to repeat their mistakes, or lead to the granting of all colorable warrant requests.

If exclusion of evidence obtained pursuant to a subsequently invalidated warrant is to have any deterrent effect, therefore, it must alter the behavior of individual law enforcement officers or the policies of their departments. One could argue that applying the exclusionary rule in cases where the police failed to demonstrate probable cause in the warrant application deters future inadequate presentations or "magistrate shopping" and thus promotes the ends of the Fourth Amendment. Suppressing evidence obtained pursuant to a technically defective warrant supported by probable cause also might encourage officers to scrutinize more closely the form of the warrant and to point out suspected judicial errors. We find such arguments speculative and conclude that suppression of evidence obtained pursuant to a warrant should be ordered only on a case-by-case basis and only in those unusual cases in which exclusion will further the purposes of the exclusionary rule.

We have frequently questioned whether the exclusionary rule can have any deterrent effect when the offending officers acted in the objectively reasonable belief that their conduct did not violate the Fourth Amendment. . . . But even assuming that the rule effectively deters some police misconduct and provides incentives for the law enforcement profession as a whole to conduct itself in accord with the Fourth Amendment, it cannot be expected, and should not be applied, to deter objectively reasonable law enforcement activity. . . .

We conclude that the marginal or nonexistent benefits produced by suppressing evidence obtained in objectively reasonable reliance on a subsequently invalidated search warrant cannot justify the substantial costs of exclusion. We do not suggest, however, that exclusion is always inappropriate in cases where an officer has obtained a warrant and abided by its terms. "[S]earches pursuant to a warrant will rarely require any deep inquiry into reasonableness," for "a warrant issued by a magistrate normally suffices to establish" that a law enforcement officer has "acted in good faith in conducting the search." Nevertheless, the officer's reliance on the magistrate's probable-cause determination

and on the technical sufficiency of the warrant he issues must be objectively reasonable, and it is clear that in some circumstances the officer will have no reasonable grounds for believing that the warrant was properly issued.

Suppression therefore remains an appropriate remedy if the magistrate or judge in issuing a warrant was misled by information in an affidavit that the affiant knew was false or would have known was false except for his reckless disregard of the truth. The exception we recognize today will also not apply in cases where the issuing magistrate wholly abandoned his judicial role. . . . [I]n such circumstances, no reasonably well trained officer should rely on the warrant. Nor would an officer manifest objective good faith in relying on a warrant based on an affidavit "so lacking in indicia of probable cause as to render official belief in its existence entirely unreasonable." Finally, depending on the circumstances of the particular case, a warrant may be so facially deficient—*i.e.*, in failing to particularize the place to be searched or the things to be seized—that the executing officers cannot reasonably presume it to be valid.

In so limiting the suppression remedy, we leave untouched the probable-cause standard and the various requirements for a valid warrant. Other objections to the modification of the Fourth Amendment exclusionary rule we consider to be insubstantial. The good-faith exception for searches conducted pursuant to warrants is not intended to signal our unwillingness strictly to enforce the requirements of the Fourth Amendment, and we do not believe that it will have this effect. As we have already suggested, the good-faith exception, turning as it does on objective reasonableness, should not be difficult to apply in practice. . . .

When the principles we have enunciated today are applied to the facts of this case, it is apparent that the judgment of the Court of Appeals cannot stand. The Court of Appeals applied the prevailing legal standards to Officer Rombach's warrant application and concluded that the application could not support the magistrate's probable-cause determination. In so doing, the court clearly informed the magistrate that he had erred in issuing the challenged warrant. This aspect of the court's judgment is not under attack in this proceeding. . . .

In the absence of an allegation that the magistrate abandoned his detached and neutral role, suppression is appropriate only if the officers were dishonest or reckless in preparing their affidavit or could not have harbored an objectively reasonable belief in the existence of probable cause. . . .

Accordingly, the judgment of the Court of Appeals is

Reversed.

JUSTICE BRENNAN, with whom JUSTICE MARSHALL joins, dissenting.

Ten years ago in *United States v. Calandra* (1974), I expressed the fear that the Court's decision "may signal that a majority of my colleagues have positioned themselves to reopen the door [to evidence secured by official lawlessness] still further and abandon altogether the exclusionary rule in search-and-seizure cases." [BRENNAN, J., dissenting.] Since then, in case after case, I have witnessed the Court's gradual but determined strangulation of the rule. It now appears that the Court's victory over the Fourth Amendment is complete. That today's decision represents the *pièce de résistance* of the Court's past efforts cannot be doubted, for today the Court sanctions the use in the prosecution's case in chief of illegally obtained evidence against the individual whose rights have been violated—a result that had previously been thought to be foreclosed.

The Court seeks to justify this result on the ground that the "costs" of adhering to the exclusionary rule in cases like those before us exceed the "benefits." But the language of deterrence and of cost/benefit analysis, if used indiscriminately, can have a narcotic effect. It creates an illusion of technical precision and ineluctability. It suggests that not only constitutional principle but also empirical data support the majority's result. When the Court's analysis is examined carefully, however, it is clear that we have not been treated to an honest assessment of the merits of the exclusionary rule, but have instead been drawn into a curious world where the "costs" of excluding illegally obtained evidence loom to exaggerated heights and where the "benefits" of such exclusion are made to disappear with a mere wave of the hand.

The majority ignores the fundamental constitutional importance of what is at stake here. While the machinery of law enforcement and indeed the nature of crime itself have changed dramatically since the Fourth Amendment became part of the Nation's fundamental law in 1791, what the Framers understood then remains true today—that the task of combating crime and convicting the guilty will in every era seem of such critical and pressing concern that we may be lured by the temptations of expediency into forsaking our commitment to protecting individual liberty and privacy. It was for that very reason that the Framers of the Bill of Rights insisted that law enforcement efforts be permanently and unambiguously restricted in order to preserve personal freedoms. In the constitutional scheme they ordained, the sometimes unpopular task of ensuring that the government's enforcement efforts remain within the strict boundaries fixed by the Fourth Amendment was entrusted to the courts. . . . If those independent tribunals lose their resolve, however, as the Court has done today, and give way to the seductive call of expediency, the vital guarantees of the Fourth Amendment are reduced to nothing more than a "form of words." . . . .

When the public, as it quite properly has done in the past as well as in the present, demands that those in government increase their efforts to combat crime, it is all too easy for those government officials to seek expedient solutions. . . . In the long run, however, we as a society pay a heavy price for such expediency, because as Justice Jackson observed, the rights guaranteed in the Fourth Amendment "are not mere second-class rights but belong in the catalog of indispensable freedoms." Once lost, such rights are difficult to recover. There is hope, however, that in time this or some later Court will restore these precious freedoms to their rightful place as a primary protection for our citizens against overreaching officialdom.

I dissent.

In *Leon* the Court authorized a good faith exception to the exclusionary rule. If the police act in good faith, reasonably believing that they are following all of the appropriate rules and exhibiting no intent to violate the suspect's Fourth Amendment rights, then the evidence gathered will not be excluded should it later be determined that technical violations of the search and seizure rules occurred. Civil libertarians were dismayed by the *Leon* ruling. They agreed with Justice William Brennan's dissent that the Court had truly undermined the Fourth Amendment by allowing the good faith exception to the exclusionary rule. Others, however, sided with Justice By-ron White's majority opinion, believing that the decision did nothing more than bring a degree of reasonableness to the application of the rule.

In the end, the adoption of the "good faith exception" did much to quiet the debate over the exclusionary rule. Liberals did not favor the exception, but were relieved that *Mapp v. Ohio* was not overturned. Conservatives were disappointed that *Mapp* remained good law, but were pleased that the rule was modified. The exclusionary rule, as modified by decisions such as *Leon,* remains the primary means by which Fourth Amendment rights are enforced.

THE FIFTH AMENDMENT AND SELF-INCRIMINATION

As we now know, the Fourth Amendment governs the procedures by which police obtain evidence—generally physical evidence. But evidence used to make an arrest is not always physical or material. Very often arrests, and ultimately convictions, hinge on verbal evidence—testimony, confessions, and the like—the gathering of which is governed by the Fifth Amendment's self-incrimination clause: "No person . . . shall be compelled in any criminal case to be a witness against himself." Taken together, the Fourth (physical) and Fifth (verbal) Amendments dictate the procedures police use to gather most evidence against individuals.

The self-incrimination clause is violated by the presence of two elements. First, there must be some form of testimonial evidence that incriminates the person who provides it, and, second, the testimonial evidence must somehow be compelled by the government.

The protection against self-incrimination most commonly applies in two situations. First, it means that no person may be forced to give testimony in any court case or other governmental hearing in which the truthful answering of questions will implicate the witness in a criminal act. For this reason a witness may decline to answer any questions that would lead to self-incriminating answers. Furthermore, a defendant in a criminal case is exempt from testifying at all, and no inferences of guilt may be made on the basis of a decision not to speak in court.

The second common situation for which the Fifth Amendment is relevant involves police interrogation of suspects prior to trial. Certainly, police must be able to ask questions during the investigation of crimes, but constitutional disputes may arise if their interrogation tactics involve compulsion. The resulting legal challenges can require the Court to address difficult and controversial issues.

Even before the 1960s, the Supreme Court had established certain guidelines for police interrogations. For the most part, they dealt with the concept of coercion. Principles of self-incrimination and due process of law are violated, the Court held, when confessions are forced from a suspect by physical torture or psychological coercion.[5] These traditional guidelines curtailed the most blatant forms of police misconduct, but they left considerable latitude for investigators to pry confessions out of poorly educated or naive suspects.

Several of the justices on the Warren Court felt that the balance was tipped decidedly in favor of the police. There were too many opportunities for police to obtain self-incriminating statements from unsuspecting defendants. As a consequence, the justices handed down two particularly important decisions in the mid-1960s designed to provide additional protections to the criminally accused, *Escobedo v. Illinois* (1964) and *Miranda v. Arizona* (1966).

Danny Escobedo, a twenty-two-year-old of Mexican extraction and limited formal education, was accused of murder. The case began when Escobedo's brother-in-law was found fatally shot in a Chicago alley on January 19, 1960. The police quickly identified three potential suspects: Escobedo, his friend Benedict DiGerlando, and his sister. The crime was motivated, police believed, by the deceased's long history of physically abusing his wife.

In the ten days following the murder all three suspects at various times were taken into custody for questioning. Finally, on January 30, DiGerlando told police that Escobedo had fired the fatal shots. As a consequence, police arrested Escobedo, told him what DiGerlando had said, and began a lengthy interrogation. Escobedo, feeling overpowered by the situation, asked to have his attorney present. Police told Escobedo that his attorney did

---

5. See, for example, *Brown v. Mississippi* (1936); *Spano v. New York* (1959).

Danny Escobedo's 1960 arrest and conviction for the murder of his brother-in-law led to a Supreme Court decision that expanded constitutional protections for criminal defendants during police interrogations. This photograph of Escobedo was taken as he awaited processing on charges of burglarizing a hot dog stand not long after the Supreme Court issued its landmark ruling in *Escobedo v. Illinois* in 1964.

not want to see him, even though the lawyer had arrived at the police station and asked to meet with his client. The questioning lasted more than fourteen hours, at the end of which Escobedo made statements that implicated him in the crime. There was no overt physical or psychological coercion during this period. Against his attorney's objections, the incriminating statements, along with other evidence, were introduced at Escobedo's trial, and he was convicted of murder.

On appeal, Escobedo argued that his rights had been violated. The atmosphere at the police station surrounding the interrogation had been overpowering. Without having his attorney present to provide advice, Escobedo broke down and made incriminating statements. Under

such conditions, the incriminating statements could be considered the product of coercion in violation of the Fifth Amendment.

By a 5–4 vote the Warren Court ruled that Escobedo's statements had been compelled. Coercion, the majority concluded, may take place even if overt physical or psychological pressure is not present. When arrested and brought to the police station for questioning, a suspect does not stand on equal footing with the law enforcement authorities. There is a clear power imbalance in favor of the police. Poor and uneducated defendants are especially at a disadvantage. Under such circumstances, the suspect may break down and make incriminating statements.

The justices decided to remedy this situation by using the right to counsel as a method of protecting the defendant's Fifth Amendment rights. The Court held that suspects have the right to have an attorney present during any custodial interrogation. As stated in Justice Arthur Goldberg's opinion for the Court:

We hold, therefore, that where, as here, the investigation is no longer a general inquiry into an unsolved crime but has begun to focus on a particular suspect, the suspect has been taken into police custody, the police carry out a process of interrogations that lends itself to eliciting incriminating statements, the suspect has requested and been denied an opportunity to consult with his lawyer, and the police have not effectively warned him of his absolute constitutional right to remain silent, the accused has been denied "the Assistance of Counsel" in violation of the Sixth Amendment to the Constitution as "made obligatory upon the States by the Fourteenth Amendment," and that no statement elicited by the police during the interrogation may be used against him at a criminal trial.

Danny Escobedo had been denied his right to counsel, and the majority found this right to be a primary defense against violations of the self-incrimination clause. If an attorney is present, it is unlikely that the police will employ even subtle methods to coerce confessions from a suspect. Escobedo was freed *(see Box 17-2)*.

The *Escobedo* majority held that the right to counsel begins at the accusatory stage of the process, defined as the point at which the investigation ceases to be general and focuses on a specific individual. The right is in effect for every critical stage of the process, which includes all interrogations. But once the Court ruled this way, it

---

BOX 17-2   AFTERMATH . . . DANNY ESCOBEDO

DANNY ESCOBEDO's brush with the law for the murder of his brother-in-law, Manuel Valtierra, was neither his first nor his last encounter with the criminal justice system. In 1953 Escobedo, then sixteen, was incarcerated in a juvenile facility on theft charges. He was convicted of theft again in 1957 and of assault with a deadly weapon in 1958.

Escobedo had served four years of a twenty-year sentence for Valtierra's murder when the Supreme Court reversed his conviction. He then drifted from job to job in Chicago, at various times a plumber, dock worker, security guard, carpenter, and printer. He also had difficulty staying out of trouble with the law, a situation he blamed on police officers trying to advance their careers at his expense. Shortly after his release he was arrested for weapons violations, selling drugs to an undercover police officer, and robbing a hot dog stand. Each of these cases ended with dropped charges or acquittals. But in 1967 Escobedo was convicted on narcotics charges, for which he spent seven years in federal prisons.

Escobedo was arrested again in 1984 when his thirteen-year-old stepdaughter claimed that he had molested her six different times. Escobedo denied the charges, alleging that they stemmed from a bitter custody battle over the girl. He was convicted of two counts of taking indecent liberties with a minor and sentenced to twelve years in prison. He appealed his conviction, claiming that after his arrest police handcuffed him to a wall for more than eight hours before allowing him to call his attorney.

While free on a $50,000 bond pending the appeal of his indecency conviction, Escobedo shot a man in a bar. He pleaded guilty to attempted murder and was sentenced to eleven years in prison. He was also under investigation for a 1983 stabbing death.

Escobedo disappeared and was placed on the U.S. Marshals Service's "fifteen most wanted fugitives" list. In 2001 a combined effort by the U.S. Marshals Service and Mexican police tracked Escobedo to an area outside Mexico City where the sixty-four-year-old fugitive was arrested.

Escobedo's sister remarried after the famous decision of *Escobedo v. Illinois.* Her husband was later found shot to death by an unknown assailant.

SOURCES: *New York Times,* September 17, 1984, October 29, 1984, September 27, 1985, June 22, 2001; *Washington Post,* September 28, 1985; *San Diego Union-Tribune,* October 22, 1985; and Rocco J. Tresolini, *These Liberties* (Philadelphia: J. B. Lippincott, 1968).

---

was faced, in *Miranda v. Arizona,* with a more difficult and far-reaching question: How should this new right be enforced?

Miranda v. Arizona

384 U.S. 436 (1966)
http://laws.findlaw.com/US/384/436.html
Oral arguments may be found at: http://www.oyez.org
Vote: 5 (Black, Brennan, Douglas, Fortas, Warren)
        4 (Clark, Harlan, Stewart, White)
Opinion of the Court: Warren
Opinion dissenting in part: Clark
Dissenting opinions: Harlan, White

Ernesto Miranda, a twenty-three-year-old indigent, nearly illiterate truck driver, allegedly kidnapped and raped a young woman outside of Phoenix, Arizona. Ten days after the incident, police arrested him, took him to the station, and interrogated him. Within two hours of questioning, Miranda confessed. There was no evidence of any police misbehavior during the interrogation, and at no point during questioning did Miranda request an attorney. Because of the decision in *Gideon v. Wainwright* (1963) *(see chapter 18),* which mandated that all indigent criminal defendants receive a defense attorney at government expense, the trial judge appointed a lawyer to defend Miranda against the charges. Miranda was convicted and received a sentence of twenty to thirty years. The conviction was based not only on the confession but also on other evidence, including the victim's positive identification of Miranda as her assailant.

Miranda obtained new attorneys, who presented wholly different arguments to the Supreme Court, where Miranda's appeal was combined with three others presenting similar issues.[6] The attorneys claimed that be-

---

6. Along with *Miranda,* the Court decided *Vignera v. New York, Westover v. United States,* and *California v. Stewart.*

cause the entire interrogation process is so inherently coercive that any individual will eventually break down, the Court should affirmatively protect the right against self-incrimination by adding to those protections already extended in *Escobedo.*

MR. CHIEF JUSTICE WARREN delivered the opinion of the Court.

The cases before us raise questions which go to the roots of our concepts of American criminal jurisprudence: the restraints society must observe consistent with the Federal Constitution in prosecuting individuals for crime. More specifically, we deal with the admissibility of statements obtained from an individual who is subjected to custodial police interrogation and the necessity for procedures which assure that the individual is accorded his privilege under the Fifth Amendment to the Constitution not to be compelled to incriminate himself.

We dealt with certain phases of this problem recently in *Escobedo v. State of Illinois* (1964). . . .

This case has been the subject of judicial interpretation and spirited legal debate since it was decided two years ago. Both state and federal courts, in assessing its implications, have arrived at varying conclusions. A wealth of scholarly material has been written tracing its ramifications and underpinnings. Police and prosecutor have speculated on its range and desirability. We granted certiorari in these cases in order further to explore some facets of the problems, thus exposed, of applying the privilege against self-incrimination to in-custody interrogation, and to give concrete constitutional guidelines for law enforcement agencies and courts to follow.

We start here, as we did in *Escobedo,* with the premise that our holding is not an innovation in our jurisprudence, but is an application of principles long recognized and applied in other settings. We have undertaken a thorough reexamination of the *Escobedo* decision and the principles it announced, and we reaffirm it. That case was but an explication of basic rights that are enshrined in our Constitution—that "No person . . . shall be compelled in any criminal case to be a witness against himself," and that "the accused shall . . . have the Assistance of Counsel"—rights which were put in jeopardy in that case through official overbearing. . . .

Ernesto Miranda waits as the jury deliberates his case before finding him guilty of kidnapping and rape after he confessed to the crimes while in police custody. In a landmark ruling, *Miranda v. Arizona* (1966), the Supreme Court reversed the conviction because Miranda had not been told he had the right to remain silent and to have an attorney present during questioning.

It was necessary in *Escobedo,* as here, to insure that what was proclaimed in the Constitution had not become but a "form of words" in the hands of government officials. And it is in this spirit, consistent with our role as judges, that we adhere to the principles of *Escobedo* today.

Our holding will be spelled out with some specificity in the pages which follow but briefly stated it is this: the prosecution may not use statements, whether exculpatory or inculpatory, stemming from custodial interrogation of the defendant unless it demonstrates the use of procedural safeguards effective to secure the privilege against self-incrimination. By custodial interrogation, we mean questioning initiated by law enforcement officers after a person has been taken into custody or otherwise deprived of his freedom of action in any significant way. As for the procedural safeguards to be employed, unless other fully effective means are devised to inform accused persons of their right of silence and to assure a continuous opportunity to exercise it, the following measures are required. Prior to any questioning, the person must be warned that he has a right to remain silent, that any statement he does make may be used as evidence against him, and that he has a right to the presence of an attorney, either retained or appointed. The defendant may waive effectuation of these rights, provided the waiver is made voluntarily, knowingly and intelligently. If, however, he indicates in any manner and at any stage of the process that he wishes to consult with an attorney before speaking there can be no questioning. Likewise, if the individual is alone and indicates in any manner that he does not wish to be interrogated, the police may not question him. The mere fact that he may have answered some questions or volunteered some statements on his own does not deprive him of the right to refrain from answering any further inquiries until he has consulted with an attorney and thereafter consents to be questioned.

The constitutional issue we decide in each of these cases is the admissibility of statements obtained from a defendant questioned while in custody or otherwise deprived of his freedom of action in any significant way. . . .

An understanding of the nature and setting of this in-custody interrogation is essential to our decisions today. The difficulty in depicting what transpires at such interrogations stems from the fact that in this country they have largely taken place incommunicado. From extensive factual studies undertaken in the early 1930's, including the famous Wickersham Report to Congress by a Presidential Commission, it is clear that police violence and the "third degree" flourished at that time. In a series of cases decided by this Court long after these studies, the police resorted to physical brutality—beatings, hanging, whipping—and to sustained and protracted questioning incommunicado in order to extort confessions. The Commission on Civil Rights in 1961 found much evidence to indicate that "some policemen still resort to physical force to obtain confessions. . . ." Only recently in Kings County, New York, the police brutally beat, kicked and placed lighted cigarette butts on the back of a potential witness under interrogation for the purpose of securing a statement incriminating a third party.

The examples given above are undoubtedly the exception now, but they are sufficiently widespread to be the object of concern. Unless a proper limitation upon custodial interrogation is achieved—such as these decisions will advance—there can be no assurance that practices of this nature will be eradicated in the foreseeable future. . . .

Again we stress that the modern practice of in-custody interrogation is psychologically rather than physically oriented. As we have stated before, "[T]his Court has recognized that coercion can be mental as well as physical, and that the blood of the accused is not the only hallmark of an unconstitutional inquisition." *Blackburn v. State of Alabama* (1960). Interrogation still takes place in privacy. Privacy results in secrecy and this in turn results in a gap in our knowledge as to what in fact goes on in the interrogation rooms. A valuable source of information about present police practices, however, may be found in various police manuals and texts which document procedures employed with success in the past, and which recommend various other effective tactics. These texts are used by law enforcement agencies themselves as guides. It should be noted that these texts professedly present the most enlightened and effective means presently used to obtain statements through custodial interrogation. By considering these texts and other data, it is possible to describe the procedures observed and noted around the country.

The officers are told by the manuals that the "principal psychological factor contributing to a successful interrogation is privacy—being alone with the person under interrogation." . . .

To highlight the isolation and unfamiliar surroundings, the manuals instruct the police to display an air of confidence in the suspect's guilt and from outward appearance to maintain only an interest in confirming certain details. The guilt of the subject is to be posited as a fact. The interrogator should direct his comments toward the reasons why the subject committed the act, rather than court failure by asking the subject whether he did it. Like other men, perhaps the subject has had a bad family life, had an unhappy childhood, had too much to drink, had an unrequited desire for women. The officers are instructed to minimize the moral seriousness of the offense, to cast blame on the victim or on society. These tactics are designed to put the subject in a psychological state where his story is but an elaboration of what the police purport to know already—that he is guilty. Explanations to the contrary are dismissed and discouraged.

The texts thus stress that the major qualities an interrogator should possess are patience and perseverance. . . .

The manuals suggest that the suspect be offered legal excuses for his actions in order to obtain an initial admission of guilt. . . .

When the techniques described above prove unavailing, the texts recommend they be alternated with a show of some hostility. . . .

The interrogators sometimes are instructed to induce a confession out of trickery. . . .

Even without employing brutality, the "third degree" or the specific stratagems described above, the very fact of custodial interrogation exacts a heavy toll on individual liberty and trades on the weakness of individuals. . . .

In the cases before us today, given this background, we concern ourselves primarily with this interrogation atmosphere and the evils it can bring. In No. 759, *Miranda v. Arizona*, the police arrested the defendant and took him to a special interrogation room where they secured a confession. . . .

In these cases, we might not find the defendants' statements to have been involuntary in traditional terms. Our concern for adequate safeguards to protect precious Fifth Amendment rights is, of course, not lessened in the slightest. In each of the cases, the defendant was thrust into an unfamiliar atmosphere and run through menacing police interrogation procedures. The potentiality for compulsion is forcefully apparent, for example, in *Miranda*, where the indigent Mexican defendant was a seriously disturbed individual with pronounced sexual fantasies. . . . To be sure, the records do not evince overt physical coercion or patent psychological ploys. The fact remains that in none of these cases did the officers undertake to afford appropriate safeguards at the outset of the interrogation to insure that the statements were truly the product of free choice.

It is obvious that such an interrogation environment is created for no purpose other than to subjugate the individual to the will of his examiner. This atmosphere carries its own badge of intimidation. To be sure, this is not physical intimidation, but it is equally destructive of human dignity. The current practice of incommunicado interrogation is at odds with one of our Nation's most cherished principles—that the individual may not be compelled to incriminate himself. Unless adequate protective devices are employed to dispel the compulsion inherent in custodial surroundings, no statement obtained from the defendant can truly be the product of his free choice.

From the foregoing, we can readily perceive an intimate connection between the privilege against self-incrimination and police custodial questioning. . . .

Today, then, there can be no doubt that the Fifth Amendment privilege is available outside of criminal court proceedings and serves to protect persons in all settings in which their freedom of action is curtailed in any significant way from being compelled to incriminate themselves. We have concluded that without proper safeguards the process of in-custody interrogation of persons suspected or accused of crime contains inherently compelling pressures which work to undermine the individual's will to resist and to compel him to speak where he would not otherwise do so freely. In order to combat these pressures and to permit a full opportunity to exercise the privilege against self-incrimination, the accused must be adequately and effectively apprised of his rights and the exercise of those rights must be fully honored. . . .

At the outset, if a person in custody is to be subjected to interrogation, he must first be informed in clear and unequivocal terms that he has the right to remain silent. For those unaware of the privilege, the warning is needed simply to make them aware of it—the threshold requirement for an intelligent decision as to its exercise. More important, such a warning is an absolute prerequisite in overcoming the inherent pressures of the interrogation atmosphere. . . . Further, the warning will show the individual that his interrogators are prepared to recognize his privilege should he choose to exercise it.

The Fifth Amendment privilege is so fundamental to our system of constitutional rule and the expedient of giving an adequate warning as to the availability of the privilege so simple, we will not pause to inquire in individual cases whether the defendant was aware of his rights without a warning being given. Assessments of the knowledge the defendant possessed, based on information as to his age, education, intelligence, or prior contact with authorities, can never be more than speculation; a warning is a clearcut fact. More important, whatever the background of the person interrogated, a warning at the time of the interrogation is indispensable to overcome its pressures and to insure that the individual knows he is free to exercise the privilege at that point in time.

The warning of the right to remain silent must be accompanied by the explanation that anything said can and will be used against the individual in court. This warning is needed in order to make him aware not only of the privilege, but also of the consequences of forgoing it. It is only through an awareness of these consequences that there can be any assurance of real understanding and intelligent exercise of the privilege. Moreover, this warning may serve to make the individual more acutely aware that he is faced with a phase of the adversary system—that he is not in the presence of persons acting solely in his interest.

The circumstances surrounding in-custody interrogation can operate very quickly to overbear the will of one merely made aware of his privilege by his interrogators. Therefore, the right to have counsel present at the interrogation is indispensable to the protection of the Fifth Amendment privilege under the system we delineate today. Our aim is to assure that the individual's right to choose between silence and speech remains unfettered throughout the interrogation process. A once-stated warning, delivered by those who will conduct the interrogation, cannot itself suffice to that end among those who most require knowledge of their rights. A mere warning given by the interrogators is not alone sufficient to accomplish that end. Prosecutors themselves claim that the admonishment of the right to remain silent without more "will benefit only the recidivist and the professional." Even preliminary advice given to the accused by his own attorney can be swiftly overcome by the secret interrogation process. Thus, the need for counsel to protect the Fifth Amendment privilege comprehends not merely a right to consult with counsel prior to questioning, but also to have counsel present during any questioning if the defendant so desires.

The presence of counsel at the interrogation may serve several significant subsidiary functions as well. If the accused decides to talk to his interrogators, the assistance of counsel can mitigate the dangers of untrustworthiness. With a lawyer present the likelihood that the police will practice coercion is reduced, and if coercion is nevertheless exercised the lawyer can testify to it in court. The presence of a lawyer can also help to guarantee that the accused gives a fully accurate statement to the police and that the statement is rightly reported by the prosecution at trial.

An individual need not make a pre-interrogation request for a lawyer. While such request affirmatively secures his right to have one, his failure to ask for a lawyer does not constitute a waiver. No effective waiver of the right to counsel during interrogation can be recognized unless specifically made after the warnings we here delineate have been given. The accused who does not know his rights and therefore does not make a request may be the person who most needs counsel. . . .

Accordingly we hold that an individual held for interrogation must be clearly informed that he has the right to consult with a lawyer and to have the lawyer with him during interrogation under the system for protecting the privilege we delineate today. As with the warnings of the right to remain silent and that anything stated can be used in evidence against him, this warning is an absolute prerequisite to interrogation. No amount of circumstantial evidence that the person may have been aware of this right will suffice to stand in its stead. Only through such a warning is there ascertainable assurance that the accused was aware of this right.

If an individual indicates that he wishes the assistance of counsel before any interrogation occurs, the authorities cannot rationally ignore or deny his request on the basis that the individual does not have or cannot afford a retained attorney. The financial ability of the individual has no relationship to the scope of the rights involved here. The privilege against self-incrimination secured by the Constitution applies to all individuals. The need for counsel in order to protect the privilege exists for the indigent as well as the affluent. In fact, were we to limit these constitutional rights to those who can retain an attorney, our decisions today would be of little significance. The cases before us as well as the vast majority of confession cases with which we have dealt in the past involve those unable to retain counsel. While authorities are not required to relieve the accused of his poverty, they have the obligation not to take advantage of indigence in the administration of justice. Denial of counsel to the indigent at the time of interrogation while allowing an attorney to those who can afford one would be no more supportable by reason or logic than the similar situation at trial and on appeal struck down in *Gideon v. Wainwright* (1963).

In order fully to apprise a person interrogated of the extent of his rights under this system then, it is necessary to warn him not only that he has the right to consult with an attorney, but also that if he is indigent a lawyer will be appointed to represent him. Without this additional warning, the admonition of the right to consult with counsel would often be understood as meaning only that he can consult with a lawyer if he has one or has the funds to obtain one. The warning of a right to counsel would be hollow if not couched in terms that would convey to the indigent—the person most often subjected to interrogation—the knowledge that he too has a right to have counsel present. As with the warnings of the right to remain silent and of the general right to counsel, only by effective and express explanation to the indigent of this right can there be assurance that he was truly in a position to exercise it.

Once warnings have been given, the subsequent procedure is clear. If the individual indicates in any manner, at any time prior to or during questioning, that he wishes to remain silent, the interrogation must cease. At this point he has shown that he intends to exercise his Fifth Amendment privilege; any statement taken after the person invokes his privilege cannot be other than the product of compulsion, subtle or otherwise. Without the right to cut off questioning, the setting of in-custody interrogation operates on the individual to overcome free choice in producing a statement after the privilege has been once invoked. If the individual states that he wants an attorney, the interrogation must cease until an attorney is present. At that time, the individual must have an opportunity to confer with the attorney and to have him present during any subsequent questioning. If the individual cannot obtain an attorney and he indicates that he wants one before speaking to police, they must respect his decision to remain silent. . . .

If the interrogation continues without the presence of an attorney and a statement is taken, a heavy burden rests on the government to demonstrate that the defendant knowingly and intelligently waived his privilege against self incrimination and his right to retained or appointed counsel. . . .

The warnings required and the waiver necessary in accordance with our opinion today are, in the absence of a fully effective equivalent, prerequisites to the admissibility of any statement made by a defendant. No distinction can be drawn between statements which are direct confessions and statements which amount to "admissions" of part or all of an offense. The privilege against self-incrimination protects the individual from being compelled to incriminate himself in any manner; it does not distinguish degrees of incrimination. . . .

To summarize, we hold that when an individual is taken into custody or otherwise deprived of his freedom by the authorities in any significant way and is subjected to questioning, the privilege against self-incrimination is jeopardized. Procedural safeguards must be employed to protect the privilege and unless other fully effective means are adopted to notify the person of his right of silence and to assure that the exercise of the right will be scrupulously honored, the following measures are required. He must be warned prior to any questioning that he has the right to remain silent, that anything he says can be used against him in a court of law, that he has the right to the presence of an attorney, and that if he cannot afford an attorney one will be appointed for him prior to any questioning if he so desires. Opportunity to exercise these rights must be afforded to him throughout the interrogation. After such warnings have been given, and such opportunity afforded him, the individual may knowingly and intelligently waive these rights and agree to answer questions or make a statement. But unless and until such warnings and waiver are demonstrated by the prosecution at trial, no evidence obtained as a result of interrogation can be used against him. . . .

In announcing these principles, we are not unmindful of the burdens which law enforcement officials must bear, often under trying circumstances. We also fully recognize the obligation of all citizens to aid in enforcing the criminal laws. This Court, while protecting individual rights, has always given ample latitude to law enforcement agencies in the legitimate exercise of their duties. The limits we have placed on the interrogation process should not constitute an undue interference with a proper system of law enforcement. . . . [O]ur decision does not in any way preclude police from carrying out their traditional investigatory functions. Although confessions may play an important role in some convictions, the cases before us present graphic examples of the overstatement of the "need" for confessions. . . .

Over the years the Federal Bureau of Investigation has compiled an exemplary record of effective law enforcement while advising any suspect or arrested person, at the outset of an interview, that he is not required to make a statement, that any statement may be used against him in court, that the individual may obtain the services of an attorney of his own choice and, more recently, that he has a right to free counsel if he is unable to pay. . . .

The practice of the FBI can readily be emulated by state and local enforcement agencies. The argument that the FBI deals with different crimes than are dealt with by state authorities does not mitigate the significance of the FBI experience. . . .

Judicial solutions to problems of constitutional dimension have evolved decade by decade. As courts have been presented with the need to enforce constitutional rights, they have found means of doing so. That was our responsibility when *Escobedo* was before us and it is our responsibility today. Where rights secured by the Constitution are involved, there can be no rule making or legislation which would abrogate them.

Reversed.

MR. JUSTICE WHITE, with whom MR. JUSTICE HARLAN and MR. JUSTICE STEWART join, dissenting.

The obvious underpinning of the Court's decision is a deep-seated distrust of all confessions. As the Court declares that the accused may not be interrogated without counsel present, absent a waiver of the right to counsel, and as the Court all but admonishes the lawyer to advise the accused to remain silent, the result adds up to a judicial judgment that evidence from the accused should not be used against him in any way, whether compelled or not. This is the not so subtle overtone of the opinion—that it is inherently wrong for the police to gather evidence from the accused himself. And this is precisely the nub of this dissent. I see nothing wrong or immoral, and certainly nothing unconstitutional, in the police's asking a suspect whom they have reasonable cause to arrest whether or not he killed his wife or in confronting him with the evidence on which the arrest was based, at least where he has been plainly advised that he may remain completely silent. Until today, "the admissions or confessions of the prisoner, when voluntarily and freely made, have always ranked high in the scale of incriminating evidence." Particularly when corroborated, as where the police have confirmed the accused's disclosure of the hiding place of implements or

fruits of the crime, such confessions have the highest reliability and significantly contribute to the certitude with which we may believe the accused is guilty. Moreover, it is by no means certain that the process of confessing is injurious to the accused. To the contrary it may provide psychological relief and enhance the prospects for rehabilitation.

This is not to say that the value of respect for the inviolability of the accused's individual personality should be accorded no weight or that all confessions should be indiscriminately admitted. This Court has long read the Constitution to proscribe compelled confessions, a salutary rule from which there should be no retreat. But I see no sound basis, factual or otherwise, and the Court gives none, for concluding that the present rule against the receipt of coerced confessions is inadequate for the task of sorting out inadmissible evidence and must be replaced by the per se rule which is now imposed. Even if the new concept can be said to have advantages of some sort over the present law, they are far outweighed by its likely undesirable impact on other very relevant and important interests.

The most basic function of any government is to provide for the security of the individual and of his property. These ends of society are served by the criminal laws which for the most part are aimed at the prevention of crime. Without the reasonably effective performance of the task of preventing private violence and retaliation, it is idle to talk about human dignity and civilized values. . . .

The rule announced today will measurably weaken the ability of the criminal law to perform [its] tasks. It is a deliberate calculus to prevent interrogations, to reduce the incidence of confessions and pleas of guilty and to increase the number of trials. Criminal trials, no matter how efficient the police are, are not sure bets for the prosecution, nor should they be if the evidence is not forthcoming. Under the present law, the prosecution fails to prove its case in about 30% of the criminal cases actually tried in the federal courts. But it is something else again to remove from the ordinary criminal case all those confessions which heretofore have been held to be free and voluntary acts of the accused and to thus establish a new constitutional barrier to the ascertainment of truth by the judicial process. There is, in my view, every reason to believe that a good many criminal defendants who otherwise would have been convicted on what this Court has previously thought to be the most satisfactory kind of evidence will now, under this new version of

---

BOX 17-3 AFTERMATH . . . ERNESTO MIRANDA

IN FEBRUARY 1967, following the Supreme Court's decision overturning his conviction on kidnapping and rape charges, Ernesto Miranda was retried, this time with his incriminating statements excluded. To mask his identity from the jurors, Miranda stood trial as "José Gomez." He was convicted and sentenced to twenty to thirty years in prison. Most damning was the testimony of his common-law wife, who claimed that Miranda had admitted to her that he had kidnapped and raped the victim. He was also convicted of an unrelated robbery of a woman at knifepoint and was sentenced to a concurrent term of twenty to twenty-five years.

In December 1972 Miranda was released on parole. Only two years later he was arrested on drug and firearms charges after being stopped for a routine traffic violation. These charges were dropped because of Fourth Amendment violations and insufficient evidence. In 1975 he returned to prison for a short time on a parole violation.

Miranda's life ended in 1976. While drinking and playing cards in a Phoenix skid row bar, he became involved in a fight with two illegal aliens. Miranda got the best of the fight and went to the rest room to wash his bloodied hands. When he returned, the two attacked him with a knife. Miranda was stabbed once in the chest and once in the abdomen. He collapsed and died. Miranda was thirty-four years old. Upon arresting his assailants, police read them their Miranda warnings.

SOURCES: *New York Times*, October 12, 1974; *Atlanta Journal*, December 13, 1972, February 1, 1976, February 2, 1976; and James A. Inciardi, *Criminal Justice*, 4th ed. (Fort Worth: Harcourt Brace Jovanovich, 1993).

---

the Fifth Amendment, either not be tried at all or will be acquitted if the State's evidence, minus the confession, is put to the test of litigation.

I have no desire whatsoever to share the responsibility for any such impact on the present criminal process.

Chief Justice Warren's majority opinion requires that police read the so-called Miranda warnings to suspects before any custodial interrogation. The *Miranda* deci-

sion, in combination with subsequent rulings, means that whenever a criminal suspect is taken into custody for any crime, the police are required to precede interrogations with the warnings.[7] By "custody" the Court means any situation in which the suspect is under police control and may not freely leave—no matter where this may occur. Custody, therefore, is not confined to formal interrogation rooms at the police station.[8] Similarly, the justices have given a relatively broad interpretation of what is meant by "interrogation." Although most interrogations conform to the standard question-answer format, the justices have ruled that any police action designed to elicit statements from a suspect falls under the definition of interrogation and must be preceded by Miranda warnings.[9]

The Warren Court premised its decision in *Miranda* on the unavoidable inequities between the accused and the police during custodial interrogations. In 1966 the justices thought the likelihood was too high to ignore that individuals would forgo their privilege against self-incrimination under intense and ultimately coercive police questioning.

Miranda triggered an enormous amount of litigation as individuals who had made incriminating statements to police claimed that their rights had been violated. In addition, the decision left many questions to be answered in future cases. By the time these follow-up cases reached the Supreme Court, Earl Warren had retired and a more conservative Court under Chief Justice Burger was in place.

Beginning in 1971 and extending into the twenty-first century, the Court frequently heard difficult appeals questioning the meaning of *Miranda*. The justices responded by interpreting the precedent quite narrowly or by creating exceptions to it. Table 17-1 provides a review of some of the more important of these decisions.

Individuals favoring law enforcement interests supported these rulings as preserving the general spirit of *Miranda* without excessively curtailing police investigations. Civil libertarians, however, were critical. They

---

7. *Berkemer v. McCarty* (1984).
8. *Orozco v. Texas* (1969).
9. See *Brewer v. Williams* (1977); *Rhode Island v. Innis* (1980).

METROPOLITAN POLICE DEPARTMENT
WARNING AS TO YOUR RIGHTS

You are under arrest. Before we ask you any questions, you must understand what your rights are.

You have the right to remain silent. You are not required to say anything to us at any time or to answer any questions. Anything you say can be used against you in court.

You have the right to talk to a lawyer for advice before we question you and to have him with you during questioning.

If you cannot afford a lawyer and want one, a lawyer will be provided for you.

If you want to answer questions now without a lawyer present you will still have the right to stop answering at any time. You also have the right to stop answering at any time until you talk to a lawyer.

WAIVER

1. Have you read or had read to you the warning as to your rights? _____

2. Do you understand these rights? _____

3. Do you wish to answer any questions? _____

4. Are you willing to answer questions without having an attorney present? _____

5. Signature of defendant on line below.

   _____

6. Time _____   Date _____

7. Signature of Officer _____

8. Signature of Witness _____

TABLE 17-1 Exceptions to *Miranda*: Some Examples

Case	Facts	Ruling
Harris v. New York (1971)	Arrested drug suspect made incriminating statements without the benefit of Miranda warnings. At trial he gave an alibi at odds with his earlier statements. To impeach his credibility, the prosecutor introduced the suspect's initial statements.	Statements made without Miranda warnings may be used for the narrow purpose of counteracting perjury.
Michigan v. Tucker (1974)	Rape suspect who had not been given Miranda warnings claimed he was with a friend at the time of the crime. Police questioned the friend who did not corroborate the story, and testimony was used as evidence.	Although police were led to the witness by the defendant's statements made without the required warnings, the reliability of the witness's testimony is not affected and may be used.
New York v. Quarles (1984)	Rape suspect was apprehended after a chase through a supermarket. Police discovered an empty holster and asked, "Where's the gun?" Suspect revealed where he dropped it. Police then read Miranda warnings.	When there is a danger to public safety, police may ask questions to remove that danger prior to reading Miranda warnings. Answers to such questions may be used as evidence.
Oregon v. Elstad (1985)	Burglary suspect made an incriminating statement prior to receiving Miranda warnings. He later was given his warnings at the police station and confessed. The confession was used in court over his attorney's objection that the initial self-incriminating statement tainted all future interrogations.	Confession may be used as evidence because it was preceded by Miranda warnings. Initial statements made prior to warnings may not be used.

TABLE 17-1 *(continued)*

Case	Facts	Ruling
Moran v. Burbine (1986)	Murder suspect in custody made incriminating statements after receiving Miranda warnings and waiving his right to have an attorney present during questioning. Suspect's lawyer had previously contacted police and indicated a desire to advise his client. Police did not inform suspect of his lawyer's wishes.	Statements may be used as evidence. Defendant knew he had a right to an attorney and a right to remain silent. His waiver of these rights was not coerced.
Illinois v. Perkins (1990)	Undercover police agent obtained incriminating statements from a prison inmate without first providing Miranda warnings.	Miranda warnings are not required when suspect is unaware he is speaking to a law enforcement official and gives a voluntary statement.
New York v. Harris (1990)	Police unlawfully entered the home of a murder suspect without a warrant and without permission. They arrested the suspect and took him to the police station. He was read his Miranda warnings and subsequently signed a written confession.	The fact that police enter a home illegally to make an arrest does not taint a subsequent confession at the police station that takes place after Miranda warnings are given.
Arizona v. Fulminante (1991)	An inmate, a suspected child murderer, was under threat of physical attack from other prisoners. A fellow inmate, in reality a federal informant, said he would protect the suspect in return for the truth about the murder charge. The suspect confessed.	The confession was coerced by the threat of physical attack. But if such tainted testimony is erroneously admitted as evidence, a conviction need not be overturned if sufficient independent evidence supporting a guilty verdict is also introduced.
Davis v. United States (1994)	In the middle of an interrogation session a murder suspect, who had received proper Miranda warnings, commented, "Maybe I should talk to a lawyer." The questioning continued for about another hour at which time the suspect said, "I think I want a lawyer before I say anything else." At that point the investigators terminated the interview.	*Miranda* does not require police to stop questioning when the suspect makes an ambiguous reference to an attorney.
United States v. Patane (2004)	An arrested suspect, who did not receive full Miranda warnings, was questioned at his home by police officers about a possible firearms violation. The suspect voluntarily admitted to having the pistol in question and gave the officers permission to retrieve it from his bedroom.	The failure to give full Miranda warnings does not require suppression of physical evidence obtained from information voluntarily supplied by the suspect in custody.

argued that the justices were excessively stripping *Miranda* of its effectiveness as a protector of Fifth Amendment rights. Many even predicted that such decisions were a prelude to the Court overruling *Miranda* altogether. The extent to which *Miranda* continued to have the support of the justices was tested in **Dickerson v. United States** (2000).

Dickerson presented the Court with a constitutional challenge to a long-ignored congressional statute. The law, passed in 1968 in response to the *Miranda* decision, stated that a suspect's confession could be admitted as evidence in federal court as long as it was "voluntarily given." The statute listed several factors that might establish the voluntary nature of a confession, one of which was a suspect's statement made after being given Miranda warnings. The law made it clear, however, that the absence of any particular factor "need not be conclusive on the issue of voluntariness of the confession." In short, a confession could be voluntary, and therefore admissible, even if Miranda warnings were not given.

Thomas Dickerson, a bank robbery suspect, made incriminating statements without receiving Miranda warnings. Citing the statute, a lower appeals court ruled that although Dickerson was not informed of his rights, the statements were voluntarily made and could be used against him. Dickerson appealed to the Supreme Court, arguing that the 1968 statute was unconstitutional. Ruling against Dickerson and upholding the law would render the *Miranda* precedent largely meaningless.

With only Justices Scalia and Thomas dissenting, the Court reaffirmed the *Miranda* ruling. The majority held that *Miranda* rested firmly on the Fifth Amendment and Congress had no authority to alter by statute the Court's interpretation. Furthermore, the justices rejected arguments to overrule *Miranda* on their own, describing the required warnings as having become part of the national culture. Chief Justice Rehnquist's majority opinion acknowledged that the justices had made certain exceptions to *Miranda* to ease its burdens on legitimate law enforcement efforts, but declared that the core of the decision remained unchanged: "[U]nwarned statements may not be used as evidence in the prosecution's case in chief."

With decisions such as *Dickerson,* it appears that *Miranda* is firmly in place and will not be overruled in the foreseeable future. Perhaps the justices have achieved an appropriate compromise similar that that reached on the exclusionary rule. Liberal justices are pleased that *Miranda* has not been overturned, and conservatives are satisfied that sufficient changes in the application of the doctrine have been imposed to make it acceptable to them.

Now that you have a good understanding of how the Fifth Amendment's self-incrimination clause governs out-of-court "testimony," why do you think *Miranda* is so controversial? Some individuals continue to argue that the decision binds the hands of police. Yet supporters make equally strong arguments in its favor. As Marvin

Zalman and Larry Siegel point out, *Miranda* has not, in fact, made it more difficult for police to obtain incriminating statements. Empirical investigations of the effect of *Miranda* in cities—both large and small—indicate that "equivalent proportions of confessions were obtained in the post-*Miranda* period as before and that police effectiveness did not appear to suffer."[10] Why this is the case is a matter of speculation, but the answer, in part, lies with the pervasiveness of *Miranda* in our society, as anyone who watches police dramas on television can confirm. Police and suspects alike have come to view *Miranda* as part and parcel of the criminal justice system.

10. Marvin Zalman and Larry Siegel, *Criminal Procedure,* 2nd ed. (St. Paul, Minn.: West, 1997), 518. For a review of some of these studies, see Welsh S. White, "Defending *Miranda:* A Reply to Professor Caplan," *Vanderbilt Law Review* 39 (1986): 1–22.

READINGS

Baker, Liva. *Miranda: Crime, Law, and Politics.* New York: Atheneum, 1983.

Bradley, Craig M. *The Failure of the Criminal Procedure Revolution.* Philadelphia: University of Pennsylvania Press, 1993.

Creamer, J. Shane. *The Law of Arrest, Search, and Seizure.* New York: Holt, Rinehart and Winston, 1980.

Dash, Samuel. *The Intruders: Unreasonable Searches and Seizures from King John to John Ashcroft.* New Brunswick, N.J.: Rutgers University Press, 2004.

Eisenstein, James, Roy B. Fleming, and Peter F. Nardulli. *The Contours of Justice: Communities and Their Courts.* Boston: Little, Brown, 1988.

Helmholz, R. H., Charles M. Gray, John H. Langbein, Eben Moglen, Henry E. Smith, and Albert W. Alschuler. *The Privilege against Self-Incrimination: Its Origins and Development.* Chicago: University of Chicago Press, 1997.

Jacob, Herbert. *Law and Politics in the United States.* Boston: Little, Brown, 1988.

Landynski, Jacob W. *Search and Seizure and the Supreme Court.* Baltimore: Johns Hopkins University Press, 1966.

Leo, Richard A., and George C. Thomas III. *The Miranda Debate: Law, Justice, and Policing.* Boston: Northeastern University Press, 1998.

Levy, Leonard W. *Against the Law: The Nixon Court and Criminal Justice.* New York: Harper and Row, 1974.

Long, Carolyn N. *Mapp v. Ohio: Guarding against Unreasonable Searches and Seizures.* Lawrence: University Press of Kansas, 206.

McWhirter, Darien A. *Search, Seizure, and Privacy: Exploring the Constitution.* Phoenix: Oryx Press, 1994.

Medalie, Richard J. *From Escobedo to Miranda.* Washington, D.C.: Lerner Law Books, 1966.

Neubauer, David W. *America's Courts and the Criminal Justice System,* 3rd ed. Pacific Grove, Calif.: Brooks/Cole, 1988.

Scheingold, Stuart. *The Politics of Law and Order.* New York: Longman, 1984.

Taslitz, Andrew E. *Reconstructing the Fourth Amendment: A History of Search and Seizure, 1789–1868.* New York: New York University Press, 2006.

Taylor, John B. *The Right to Counsel and Privilege against Self-Incrimination: Rights and Liberties under the Law.* Santa Barbara, Calif.: ABC-CLIO, 2004.

CHAPTER 18
ATTORNEYS, TRIALS, AND PUNISHMENTS

T he framers clearly recognized the importance of fairness in evidence gathering, and they also realized the need to protect the integrity of the entire criminal process. Consequently, the Bill of Rights included specific guarantees to protect prosecuted defendants from abuse by the government. These rights are among those we most value, such as the right to be represented by counsel, to be tried by an impartial jury of peers, and to be protected against punishments that are cruel and unusual. Other guarantees, less well known but no less important, also enjoy constitutional status—such as the right to a speedy and public trial and to confront an accuser in open court. Taken as a whole, these rights were designed to help achieve a universally valued goal— fair criminal trials.

THE RIGHT TO COUNSEL

The Sixth Amendment guarantees that "in all criminal prosecutions, the accused shall enjoy the right . . . to have the Assistance of Counsel for his defence." At the time these words were written, the law was relatively uncomplicated, and lawyers in the new nation were scarce. Some individuals charged with crimes sought the advice of counsel, but most handled their own cases. Still, the framers understood the importance of legal representation well enough to include the right to counsel in the Bill of Rights.

Today, probably no other right guaranteed to the criminally accused is more important than the right to counsel. Until the 1960s, a lawyer representing a criminal

client could do the job by appearing at trial and dealing with well-established principles of evidence and procedure. That has changed, and appearing at the trial is now only a small part of what a criminal defense attorney must do. As the Supreme Court emphasized repeatedly in the Fifth Amendment cases we reviewed in chapter 17, the role of the defense attorney begins when police first interrogate a suspect. From arrest through appeal, there are critical and complicated stages during which a defendant's rights might be violated. It is the responsibility of counsel to ensure that the interests of the defendant are not jeopardized. The presence of the defense attorney, therefore, is the primary guarantee that all of the other rights of the criminal due process will be observed.

The provisions of the Sixth Amendment are clear, and there has been little controversy over the right of an individual to have legal representation throughout the various stages of the criminal process. Historically, however, it was the responsibility of the accused person to secure a lawyer and to pay for the services. Most controversy over legal representation in criminal matters has centered on the rights of those who cannot pay for legal assistance.

As the complexity of the U.S. system of justice increased, more people retained lawyers to handle their cases. But as soon as this practice took hold, complaints of economic discrimination were heard. Civil libertarians and reformers throughout the country argued that only those who could afford it were guaranteed the right to counsel; indigent defendants were denied their constitutional guarantee. Reformers claimed that the only way to

The plight of the nine "Scottsboro boys," arrested in rural Alabama in 1931 for raping two white females, spawned numerous legal actions including *Powell v. Alabama* (1932), which expanded the rights of indigents to legal representation. Samuel Leibowitz, a prominent attorney and later a judge, handled the defendants' cases after their original conviction. He is shown here conferring with seven of his clients. Deputy Sheriff Charles McComb stands to the left.

eliminate this injustice was a Supreme Court decision that would force governments to appoint free counsel for poor defendants.

In *Powell v. Alabama* (1932) the Supreme Court scrutinized this claim for the first time.[1] The case began when nine young black men were charged with raping two white women while riding a freight train through Alabama. The defendants had little chance of avoiding a conviction. They were uneducated, poor, and far away from home, with no friends or relatives to help them. Because of the nature of the charges, they faced a hostile en-

vironment. Much was at stake. Rape in Alabama at that time was punishable by death.

The young men did not have the funds to secure the services of an attorney, but under state law defendants in capital cases were entitled to a lawyer at government expense.[2] Instead of appointing a specific attorney to prepare a defense, the trial court judge assigned all the lawyers in the town to represent the defendants. Not surprisingly, no one lawyer would accept the responsibility. When the trial was about to begin, the defendants were

---

1. For more on this case, see Dan T. Carter, *Scottsboro: A Tragedy of the American South* (New York: Oxford University Press, 1969).

2. Many states had laws mandating the appointment of counsel for capital crimes such as rape. In *Coker v. Georgia* (1977) the Supreme Court outlawed the use of the death penalty in rape cases.

BOX 18-1   AFTERMATH . . . THE SCOTTSBORO BOYS

THEIR CONVICTIONS were reversed by the Supreme Court in 1932, but the subsequent lives of the nine defendants, known as the "Scottsboro Boys," were filled with tragedy and additional criminal accusations. Even though one of the alleged rape victims later admitted that she had not been raped, the defendants were convicted following their second trial. This time the convictions were overturned by the Supreme Court in *Norris v. Alabama* (1935) because of racial discrimination in jury selection. Between 1936 and 1937, additional retrials took place leading to the conviction of four of the original defendants, with sentences ranging from seventy-five years in prison to death.

In 1937 the rape charges were dropped against Olen Montgomery, Willie Roberson, and Eugene Williams. They subsequently fell into obscurity.

Charges against Roy Wright also were dismissed. In 1959 Wright stabbed his wife to death and then took his own life.

Rape charges against Ozie Powell were dropped. He was later convicted of shooting a law enforcement officer in the head. He received a long prison sentence, but was paroled in 1946.

Charlie Weems, Andrew Wright, Haywood Patterson, and Clarence Norris were convicted of the rape charges on retrial. Weems and Patterson were sentenced to seventy-five years in prison, Wright to a term of ninety-nine years, and Norris to death.

Three of the convicted men were subsequently released from prison, and one escaped. Weems was paroled in 1943. Wright was paroled in 1944, but was returned to prison three times for parole violations. In 1951 Wright was accused of raping a thirteen-year-old girl, but was acquitted and released. Patterson escaped from prison and fled to Michigan. In 1951 he was convicted of manslaughter and sentenced to prison. Shortly thereafter he died of lung cancer.

Norris had his death sentence commuted to life in prison in 1938. He was paroled in 1944, but was sent back to prison for leaving the state in violation of his parole agreement. Norris was paroled again in 1946, and almost immediately fled the state in violation of parole a second time. He lived undercover in New York City for many years. In 1976 the attorney general of Alabama acknowledged that subsequent studies of the case had concluded that Norris was not guilty of the original rape charge, and Gov. George Wallace pardoned him. A bill to compensate Norris for wrongful conviction was defeated in the Alabama legislature. Norris died in 1989 at the age of seventy-six.

SOURCE: James A. Inciardi, *Criminal Justice*, 4th ed. (Fort Worth: Harcourt Brace Jovanovich, 1993), 372.

still without meaningful representation. An out-of-town lawyer who was present at the time finally agreed to serve as counsel. His first request was for additional time to prepare. The request was denied, and the trial began. It should come as no surprise that the young men were convicted and sentenced to death.

With the assistance of civil rights groups and political organizations, the defendants appealed to the Supreme Court. The Court reversed the conviction, holding that the young men did not receive effective counsel. For the first time the justices held that the Constitution requires meaningful legal representation for indigent defendants. But the Court's decision was quite limited. Justice George Sutherland's opinion for the Court stressed that the right to government-provided attorneys was restricted to extreme situations. *Powell* certainly presented extreme circumstances: capital case, racially hostile environment, illiterate and indigent defendants with no family or friends in the area. It is easy to see why the Court concluded that under such conditions a fair trial was not possible if the defendants were not provided with a competent lawyer. (For the fate of the "Scottsboro boys," see Box 18-1.)

Six years after *Powell*, the Court went one step further. In *Johnson v. Zerbst* it ruled that indigent defendants involved in federal criminal prosecutions have the right to be represented by counsel. Federal criminal prosecutions account for only a small portion of all criminal cases. Therefore, although the *Johnson* decision was important, it did not affect most criminal defendants. Understandably, criminal defense attorneys wanted the Court to extend *Johnson* to state criminal courts, where the vast majority of prosecutions take place. The Court's first opportunity to do so occurred in ***Betts v. Brady*** (1942).

Indicted for robbery in Maryland, Smith Betts—a poor, uneducated (but literate) white man—requested that an attorney be provided him at government expense. Like many states, Maryland provided indigents with counsel only in rape and murder cases. Betts conducted his own defense and was convicted. On appeal he asked the Supreme Court to apply *Johnson* to the states. The Court refused, 6–3. Writing for the majority, Justice Owen Roberts compared Betts's claim with that of the *Powell* defendants and found that it came up short. Betts was not helpless or illiterate, and he could not have received the death penalty for his offense.

Justice Hugo Black dissented. He wrote:

Denial to the poor of the request for counsel in proceedings based on charges of serious crime has been long regarded as shocking to the "universal sense of justice" throughout this country. . . . Most . . . states have shown their agreement [and] assure that no man shall be deprived of counsel merely because of his poverty. Any other practice seems to me to defeat the promise of our democratic society to provide equal justice under law.

More than twenty years later, a Court more sympathetic to the rights of the criminally accused reevaluated the wisdom of *Betts v. Brady.* As you read the landmark case of *Gideon v. Wainwright,* think about these questions: Why did the Court extend the right to government-provided attorneys to indigents accused of state crimes? Did something distinguish *Gideon* from *Betts,* or did other factors come into play?

Gideon v. Wainwright

372 U.S. 335 (1963)
http://laws.findlaw.com/US/372/335.html
Oral arguments may be found at: http://www.oyez.org
Vote: 9 (Black, Brennan, Clark, Douglas, Goldberg, Harlan,
      Stewart, Warren, White)

      0

Opinion of the Court: Black
Concurring opinions: Clark, Douglas, Harlan

Florida officials charged Clarence Earl Gideon with breaking and entering a poolroom.[3] The trial court refused to appoint counsel for him because Florida did not provide free lawyers to those charged with less than a capital offense. Gideon (like Betts a poor, uneducated white man) tried to defend himself but failed. After studying the law in a prison library and attempting several lower court actions, Gideon filed a petition for a writ of certiorari with the U.S. Supreme Court. The petition was handwritten on prison notepaper, but the justices granted it a review.

Because Gideon was without counsel, the Court appointed Abe Fortas, a well-known attorney (and future Supreme Court justice) to represent him. Twenty-two states filed an amicus curiae brief, which was written by Walter Mondale (attorney general of Minnesota and later vice president of the United States), supporting Gideon's argument. Clarence Gideon went from being a poor convict facing a lonely court battle to a man represented by some of the country's finest legal minds.

MR. JUSTICE BLACK delivered the opinion of the Court.

Since 1942, when *Betts v. Brady* was decided by a divided Court, the problem of a defendant's federal constitutional right to counsel in a state court has been a continuing source of controversy and litigation in both state and federal courts. To give this problem another review here, we granted certiorari. Since Gideon was proceeding in forma pauperis, we appointed counsel to represent him and requested both sides to discuss in their briefs and oral arguments the following: "Should this Court's holding in *Betts v. Brady* be reconsidered?"

The facts upon which Betts claimed that he had been unconstitutionally denied the right to have counsel appointed to assist him are strikingly like the facts upon which Gideon here bases his federal constitutional claim. . . . Since the facts and circumstances of the two cases are so nearly indistinguishable, we think the *Betts v. Brady* holding if left standing would require us to reject Gideon's claim that the Constitution guarantees him the assistance of counsel. Upon

---

3. For a full account of this case see Anthony Lewis, *Gideon's Trumpet* (New York: Vintage Books, 1964).

(left) Clarence Earl Gideon's handwritten petition to the Supreme Court. The Court ruled unanimously that indigent defendants must be provided counsel in state trials.

(above) Clarence Earl Gideon.

full reconsideration we conclude that *Betts v. Brady* should be overruled.

The Sixth Amendment provides, "In all criminal prosecutions, the accused shall enjoy the right . . . to have the Assistance of Counsel for his defence." We have construed this to mean that in federal courts counsel must be provided for defendants unable to employ counsel unless the right is competently and intelligently waived. Betts argued that this right is extended to indigent defendants in state courts by the Fourteenth Amendment. In response the Court stated that, while the Sixth Amendment laid down "no rule for the conduct of the states, the question recurs whether the constraint laid by the amendment upon the national courts expresses a rule so fundamental and essential to a fair trial, and so, to due process of law, that it is made obligatory upon the states by the Fourteenth Amendment." In order to decide whether the Sixth Amendment's guarantee of counsel is of this fundamental nature, the Court in *Betts* set out and considered "[r]elevant data on the subject . . . afforded by constitutional and statutory provisions subsisting in the colonies and the states prior to the inclusion of the Bill of Rights in the national Constitution, and in the constitutional, legislative, and judicial history of the states to the present date." On the basis of this historical data the Court concluded that "appointment of counsel is not a fundamental right, essential to a fair trial." . . .

We accept *Betts v. Brady*'s assumption, based as it was on our prior cases, that a provision of the Bill of Rights which is "fundamental and essential to a fair trial" is made obligatory upon the States by the Fourteenth Amendment. We think the Court in *Betts* was wrong, however, in concluding that the Sixth Amendment's guarantee of counsel is not one of these fundamental rights. Ten years before *Betts v. Brady*, this Court, after full consideration of all the historical data examined in *Betts*, had unequivocally declared that "the right to the aid of counsel is of this fundamental character." *Powell v. Alabama* (1932). While the Court at the close of its *Powell* opinion did by its language, as this Court frequently does, limit its holding to the particular facts and circumstances of that case, its conclusions about the fundamental nature of the right to counsel are unmistakable. Several years later, in 1936, the Court reemphasized what it had said about the fundamental nature of the right to counsel in this language:

"We concluded that certain fundamental rights, safeguarded by the first eight amendments against federal action, were also safeguarded against state action by the due process of law clause of the Fourteenth Amendment, and among them the fundamental right of the accused to the aid of counsel in a criminal prosecution." *Grosjean v. American Press Co.* (1936). . . .

In light of these and many other prior decisions of the Court, it is not surprising that the *Betts* Court, when faced with the contention that "one charged with crime, who is unable to obtain counsel, must be furnished counsel by the state," conceded that "[e]xpressions in the opinions of this court lend color to the argument. . . ." The fact is that in deciding as it did—that "appointment of counsel is not a fundamental right, essential to a fair trial"—the Court in *Betts v. Brady* made an abrupt break with its own well-considered precedents. In returning to these old precedents, sounder we believe than the new, we but restore constitutional principles established to achieve a fair system of justice. Not only these precedents but also reason and reflection require us to recognize that in our adversary system of criminal justice, any person haled into court, who is too poor to hire a lawyer, cannot be assured a fair trial unless counsel is provided for him. This seems to us to be an obvious truth. Governments, both state and federal, quite properly spend vast sums of money to establish machinery to try defendants accused of crime. Lawyers to prosecute are everywhere deemed essential to protect the public's interest in an orderly society. Similarly, there are few defendants charged with crime, few indeed, who fail to hire the best lawyers they can get to prepare and present their defenses. That government hires lawyers to prosecute and defendants who have the money hire lawyers to defend are the strongest indications of the widespread belief that lawyers in criminal courts are necessities, not luxuries. The right of one charged with crime to counsel may not be deemed fundamental and essential to fair trials in some countries, but it is in ours. From the very beginning, our state and national constitutions and laws have laid great emphasis on procedural and substantive safeguards designed to assure fair trials before impartial tribunals in which every defendant stands equal before the law. This noble ideal cannot be realized if the poor man charged with crime has to face his accusers without a lawyer to assist him. A defendant's need for a lawyer is nowhere better stated than in the moving words of Mr. Justice Sutherland in *Powell v. Alabama:*

"The right to be heard would be, in many cases, of little avail if it did not comprehend the right to be heard by counsel. Even the intelligent and educated layman has small and sometimes no skill in the science of law. If charged with crime, he is incapable, generally, of determining for himself whether the indictment is good or bad. He is unfamiliar with the rules of evidence. Left without the aid of counsel he may be put on trial without a proper charge, and convicted upon incompetent evidence, or evidence irrelevant to the issue or otherwise inadmissible. He lacks both the skill and knowledge adequately to prepare his defense, even though he have a perfect one. He requires the guiding hand of counsel at every step in the proceedings against him. Without it, though he be not guilty, he faces the danger of conviction because he does not know how to establish his innocence."

The Court in *Betts v. Brady* departed from the sound wisdom upon which the Court's holding in *Powell v. Alabama* rested. Florida, supported by two other States, has asked that *Betts v. Brady* be left intact. Twenty-two States, as friends of the Court, argue that *Betts* was "an anachronism when handed down" and that it should now be overruled. We agree. The judgment is reversed and the cause is remanded to the Supreme Court of Florida for further action not inconsistent with this opinion.

Reversed.

MR. JUSTICE HARLAN, concurring.

I agree that *Betts v. Brady* should be overruled, but consider it entitled to a more respectful burial than has been accorded. . . .

I cannot subscribe to the view that *Betts v. Brady* represented "an abrupt break with its own well-considered precedents." In 1932, in *Powell v. Alabama,* a capital case, this Court declared that under the particular facts there presented—"the ignorance and illiteracy of the defendants, their youth, the circumstances of public hostility . . . and above all that they stood in deadly peril of their lives"—the state court had a duty to assign counsel for the trial as a necessary requisite of due process of law. It is evident that these limiting facts were not added to the opinion as an afterthought; they were repeatedly emphasized and were clearly regarded as important to the result.

Thus when this Court, a decade later, decided *Betts v. Brady,* it did no more than to admit of the possible existence of special circumstances in noncapital as well as capital trials, while at the same time insisting that such circumstances be shown in order to establish a denial of due process. . . . The declaration that the right to appointed counsel in state prosecutions, as established in *Powell v. Alabama,* was not limited to capital cases was in truth not a departure from, but an extension of, existing precedent.

The principles declared in *Powell* and in *Betts,* however, have had a troubled journey throughout the years. . . .

In noncapital cases, the "special circumstances" rule has continued to exist in form while its substance has been substantially and steadily eroded. . . . The Court has come to recognize, in other words, that the mere existence of a serious criminal charge constituted in itself special circumstances requiring the services of counsel at trial. In truth the *Betts v. Brady* rule is no longer a reality. . . .

The special circumstances rule has been formally abandoned in capital cases, and the time has now come when it should be similarly abandoned in noncapital cases, at least as to offenses which, as the one involved here, carry the possibility of a substantial prison sentence. (Whether the rule should extend to *all* criminal cases need not now be decided.) This indeed does no more than to make explicit something that has long since been foreshadowed in our decisions. . . .

On these premises I join in the judgment of the Court.

Beyond the legal significance of *Gideon,* the case is interesting for several reasons. First, *Gideon* is another example of the Warren Court's revolution in criminal rights. The Court of 1963 took a carbon copy of *Betts* and came up with a radically different solution. *Gideon* completed a process of constitutional evolution in which the Court first applied a rule of law to the federal government, refused to extend that rule to the states, and then reversed its position and brought the states under the rule's applicability.

Second, *Gideon* is a classic example of the importance of dissents. Justice Hugo Black's minority position in *Betts* was finally written into law when the Court reversed itself in *Gideon.* How fitting it was that Black was still on the Court twenty-one years later and was given the opportunity to write the majority opinion in *Gideon.*

Finally, *Gideon v. Wainwright* has had a tremendous impact on the U.S. criminal justice system, in which 75 percent of the criminally accused are indigent. To comply with the Court's ruling, states had to alter laws, creating mechanisms to provide lawyers for the accused. Many localities have a public defender's office, which employs a staff of attorneys who are available to represent indigent defendants. Other areas use a system of court-appointed attorneys in which judges assign members of the legal community to represent the underprivileged.

For all its importance, *Gideon* left several questions unanswered. First, what crimes does the ruling cover? Does it cover only serious offenses—felonies, such as the one Gideon was accused of committing—or does it apply to minor crimes as well? The Court answered this question in **Argersinger v. Hamlin** (1972) and **Scott v. Illinois** (1979). In these cases the Court developed the "loss of liberty" rule: An indigent charged with a crime that upon conviction will lead to incarceration for even one day is entitled to be represented by counsel at government expense. As a consequence, regardless of the range of penalties available to a judge, indigent criminal defendants may not be sentenced to incarceration unless they have been offered legal representation at government expense.

Twenty-three years after *Scott v. Illinois,* in **Alabama v. Shelton** (2002) the justices of the Rehnquist Court reinforced this basic premise. LeReed Shelton, convicted of third-degree assault, was sentenced to a jail term of thirty days, which the trial court immediately suspended, placing Shelton on probation for two years. The question the Court addressed was whether the Sixth Amendment right to appointed counsel, as delineated in *Argersinger* and *Scott*, applies to a defendant in Shelton's situation. The majority answered in the affirmative, holding that "a suspended sentence that may 'end up in the actual deprivation of a person's liberty' may not be imposed unless the defendant was accorded 'the guiding hand of counsel' in the prosecution for the crime charged." To the four dissenters—Antonin Scalia, William Rehnquist, Anthony Kennedy, and Clarence Thomas—this logic turned *Argersinger* and *Scott* upside down: "Today's decision ignores this long and consistent jurisprudence, extending the misdemeanor right to counsel to cases bearing the mere threat of imprisonment," Scalia wrote. "Respondent's 30-day suspended sentence, and the accompanying 2-year term of probation, are invalidated for lack of appointed counsel even though respondent has not suffered, and may never suffer, a deprivation of liberty."

A second unanswered question flowing from *Gideon* was to what stages of the process does the right to government-provided counsel apply? In his opinion in *Gideon*, Justice Black said that an indigent accused of a criminal offense must be represented by counsel at trial. What Black did not address was whether that right extended through the appellate process. And if so, did such a right apply only to obligatory appeals (usually the first appeal after a trial) or also to discretionary appeals (subsequent appeals that the appellate court may or may not agree to hear)?

In *Douglas v. California* (1963) the Court answered part of this question, holding that the right indeed extended through the first obligatory appeal. Eleven years later, however, in *Ross v. Moffitt* (1974), the Burger Court refused to extend the right to state-provided counsel for indigents to subsequent appeals.

FAIR TRIALS

From a quantitative perspective, trials are insignificant; only about 5 percent to 10 percent of all criminal prosecutions go to trial. In the majority of cases the defendant pleads guilty, usually after arriving at a plea-bargaining agreement with the prosecutor. In such arrangements, the defendant waives the right to a jury trial and agrees to plead guilty in return for certain concessions made by the prosecutor. These concessions normally involve a reduction in the seriousness of the crimes charged, a reduction in the number of counts, or a recommendation for a lenient sentence. Although many citizens look at such arrangements unfavorably, the Supreme Court has sanctioned the practice, and it remains the most common way criminal prosecutions are settled.

Qualitatively, trials are significant; the most serious crimes go to trial. In addition, trials serve a symbolic function and educate the public about crime and justice in the community. Furthermore, trials come closer than any other stage in the criminal process to reaching the goal of open and objective fairness.

The framers clearly intended American trials to be the epitome of justice. They drafted the Sixth Amendment to correct the weaknesses they had observed in the English justice system, weaknesses that included closed proceedings, long delays, and few safeguards for defendants. Specifically, Sixth Amendment provisions governing trials state:

In all criminal prosecutions, the accused shall enjoy the right to a speedy and public trial, by an impartial jury of the State and district wherein the crime shall have been committed, which district shall have been previously ascertained by law, and to be informed of the nature and cause of the accusation; to be confronted with the witnesses against him; to have compulsory process for obtaining witnesses in his favor, and to have the Assistance of Counsel for his defence.

These fair trial provisions of the Sixth Amendment are supported by two important rights found in the Fifth: the right against self-incrimination and the right to due process of law. The Constitution's fair trial guarantees provide strict guidelines for trial proceedings.

Speedy and Public Trials

Individuals accused of crimes have the right to their day in court. But if justice is to be meaningful, trials must be scheduled in a timely fashion. The framers considered it unfair for the government to levy criminal charges against suspects and then delay their trials for months, or even years. Consequently, the Sixth Amendment states that trials must be speedy.

But what constitutes "speedy"? In responding to this question the Supreme Court has refused to hold that a fixed number of days or months can be used to define what is a speedy trial. Instead, each case must be considered on its own merits. The Court has held that in determining whether the speedy trial provision has been violated, judges need to seek the answers to four basic questions: (1) How long was the delay? (2) What was the reason for the delay? (3) At what point did the defense begin objecting to the delay? and (4) Did the delay prejudice the defendant's case?[4] Balancing the answers to these questions will guide courts in determining whether the constitutional right to a speedy trial has been violated.[5]

Trials in the United States also must take place in public. The Sixth Amendment's right to a public trial was in direct reaction to the use of secret trials in England and other European countries. The underlying rationale for public trials is that abuse of authority is much less likely to occur when important proceedings can be witnessed by the public and the press. As a consequence, trials in the United States cannot be closed affairs.

Jury Trials

Like many other aspects of law and procedure, the framers incorporated the British jury system into the U.S. Constitution. A jury trial means that the determination of whether a defendant is guilty is made by individuals drawn from the community, not by a government official. A jury that represents a cross-section of the community is what we Americans consider a "jury of our peers."

To select a jury that is fair and representative, most jurisdictions follow a procedure that works this way:

1. Individuals living within a specified geographical area are called for jury duty. Most localities randomly select names from voter registration, property tax, or driver's license lists.

2. Those selected form the jury pool or venire, the group from which attorneys choose the actual jury.

3. The judge may conduct initial interviews excusing certain classes of people (felons, illiterates, the mentally ill) and certain occupational groups, as allowed under the laws of the particular jurisdiction.

4. The remaining individuals are available to be chosen to serve on a trial (petit) jury. In the final selection phase, the opposing attorneys interview the prospective jurors. This process is called voir dire. During voir dire, attorneys can dismiss those individuals they believe would not vote in the best interests of their clients. The attorneys, therefore, select the jury.

During voir dire, attorneys use two mechanisms or challenges to eliminate potential jurors. When a prospective juror appears to be unqualified to carry out the obligations of service, attorneys can *challenge for cause.* To do so they must explain to the judge their reason, such as conflict of interest or expressions of extreme prejudice, for eliminating that individual, and the judge must agree. Challenges for cause are unlimited. Attorneys also have a fixed number of *peremptory challenges,* which they may use to excuse jurors without stating a reason.

Traditionally, attorneys have been able to use their peremptory challenges in whatever way and for whatever reason they choose. Although that general rule remains in effect, the Supreme Court has intervened to limit lawyers' discretion in two important ways: Lawyers may not use their peremptory challenges to dismiss prospective jurors on account of race or sex.[6] To exclude potential jurors systematically on the basis of race or sex violates the equal protection clause of the Fourteenth Amendment.

Generally, juries consist of twelve individuals, and all jury decisions must be unanimous. Most jurisdictions follow this traditional format in major cases, but the Supreme Court has ruled that the Constitution requires

---

4. *Barker v. Wingo* (1972).

5. Congress and many state legislatures have passed speedy trial laws that compel the prosecution to be ready to proceed with a trial within a specified number of days. The federal Speedy Trial Act of 1974 requires indictment within thirty days of arrest, arraignment within ten days after indictment, and trial within sixty days after arraignment. Failure to meet the requirements of the speedy trial law can lead to the dismissal of charges against the defendant.

6. Race: *Batson v. Kentucky* (1986), *Powers v. Ohio* (1991), and *Georgia v. McCullum* (1992); sex: *J. E. B. v. Alabama ex rel. T. B.* (1994).

neither juries of twelve persons nor unanimous verdicts.[7] In response, many states have begun using six-person juries in minor cases, and some states have even experimented with less than unanimous decision-making rules.

Regardless of the specific configuration of the jury, however, it is fundamental to fair trials that juries deliberate and reach decisions in an atmosphere that allows detached and objective consideration of the evidence. Of particular concern are situations in which media coverage of criminal trials becomes so intense and extensive that the ends of justice are compromised. Given the constitutional guarantees of a public trial and freedom of the press, how can judges see to it that defendants receive fair, impartial jury trials? This question has major constitutional importance because it forces courts to deal with conflicting rights. The Sixth Amendment requires judges to regulate trials, ensuring, among other things, that the jury is impartial. In a highly publicized case, the judge's task can become arduous. The judge must deal with the media, who are exercising their constitutional guarantee of a free press. How can judges keep trials fair without interfering with the rights of the press and the public?

Before the mid-1960s no balance existed between freedom of the press and the right to an impartial jury—the former far outweighed the latter. In cases involving well-known individuals or otherwise of interest to the public, the press descended on courtrooms and often behaved in a disruptive manner. Without well-defined rules, reporters, accompanied by crews carrying bulky, noisy equipment, simply showed up and interviewed and photographed witnesses and other participants at will. These activities often breached normal courtroom decorum and made objective, dispassionate analysis of evidence almost impossible for the jurors.

Not surprisingly, the Warren Court placed limitations on the media. In two important cases, *Estes v. Texas* (1965) and *Sheppard v. Maxwell* (1966), the Court reversed convictions on the basis of media misbehavior and chastised lower court judges for allowing the press to jeopardize the integrity of the trial. As a result, judges around the

country policed their courtrooms more vigilantly to ensure that the press did not compromise the right of the defendant to receive a fair trial.

Although judges have the obligation to impose limitations on the activities of the press in covering trials, they cannot go too far. The press is still protected by the First Amendment in gathering and reporting the news. The justices have supported free press rights as long as they are compatible with the right to a fair trial.

Confronting Witnesses

Among the Sixth Amendment protections is the right to confront witnesses. This provision includes several guarantees. First, it means that defendants have the right to be present during their trials. Unlike some countries, the United States does not permit trials in absentia.

Second, the confrontation clause requires that prosecution witnesses appear in open court in the presence of the defendant to give their testimony under oath. As a consequence, the prosecution typically cannot obtain a conviction based on anonymous testimony or upon information provided by witnesses who are unwilling to appear in court. Although this requirement appears to be both reasonable and necessary for most crimes, it has received considerable criticism for crimes such as rape and child abuse. Rape victims may refuse to report the crimes, knowing that if they do so they may be required to give their testimony in open court. Similarly, many fear that children who have been abused will be traumatized by having to tell their stories in court with the person who abused them visibly present.

Although the justices have generally adhered to the requirement that prosecution witnesses appear in court, they have been sympathetic to the situation facing children who may have been the victims of abuse. In *Maryland v. Craig* (1990) the Supreme Court upheld a Maryland procedure that allowed child abuse victims to testify via closed-circuit television. This procedure permitted the defendant to see the testimony of the alleged victim but protected the child witness from the trauma of face-to-face interaction with her accused abuser. For the majority, Sandra Day O'Connor outlined the Court's reasoning:

---

7. See *Williams v. Florida* (1970), *Johnson v. Louisiana* (1972), and *Apodaca v. Oregon* (1972).

In sum, we conclude that where necessary to protect a child witness from trauma that would be caused by testifying in the physical presence of the defendant, at least where such trauma would impair the child's ability to communicate, the Confrontation Clause does not prohibit use of a procedure that, despite the absence of face-to-face confrontation, ensures the reliability of the evidence by subjecting it to rigorous adversarial testing and thereby preserves the essence of effective confrontation. Because there is no dispute that the child witnesses in this case testified under oath, were subject to full cross-examination, and were able to be observed by the judge, jury, and defendant as they testified, we conclude that, to the extent that a proper finding of necessity has been made, the admission of such testimony would be consonant with the Confrontation Clause.

A third component of the right to confrontation is cross-examination. The prosecution must produce witnesses who testify under oath in open court before the defendant, and those witnesses are subject to questioning by the defense. This requirement is based on the theory that a jury will best be able to discern the truth if testimony is tested by vigorous examination from the opposing side. Some exceptions exist, as *Washington v. Davis* (2006) illustrates. Perhaps taking to heart the plight of crime victims, the justices agreed that prosecutors could introduce as evidence victims' emergency phone calls to 911, even if the victims are not in court for cross-examination. But in the same case, the Court refused to allow the victim's statement to police, given at the crime scene, to be used at trial unless the victim was willing to be cross-examined. The difference between the two, according to Justice Scalia's majority opinion, was that the phone call is not a "testimonial statement" covered by the confrontation clause, whereas the on-the-scene statement to police investigating a crime is.

Self-Incrimination and Testimony

Because the Fifth Amendment's self-incrimination clause prohibits the government from compelling a criminal defendant to give testimony, the defendant in such a case cannot be required to take the witness stand. The Constitution does not preclude the defendant from giving testimony voluntarily, but whether to speak in court is the defendant's choice.

If a witness refuses to answer questions on Fifth Amendment grounds, no inference of guilt may be made. Judges may not instruct jurors to consider a defendant's refusal to take the witness stand and deny guilt under oath; nor may prosecutors argue that a defendant's decision not to testify is evidence of wrongdoing. Such actions by judges or prosecutors would be clear violations of the Fifth Amendment. An individual's decision to invoke the Fifth Amendment privilege and not answer questions can be interpreted as nothing more than a decision to remain silent.

Furthermore, individuals must be free to exercise their Fifth Amendment rights. Governments may not coerce a person to testify. A prosecutor may not threaten a defendant that if he or she does not testify, the government will ask for a more severe sentence. Nor may the government use economic pressure to coerce an individual to waive the Fifth Amendment privilege. In *Garrity v. New Jersey* (1967) and *Gardner v. Broderick* (1968) the Supreme Court ruled that public employees could not be threatened with the loss of their jobs if they did not testify in government investigations of corruption and wrongdoing. Citizens must be given the choice of exercising their rights against self-incrimination.

SENTENCING AND THE EIGHTH AMENDMENT

If a criminal defendant is convicted or pleads guilty, the next stage of consequence is sentencing. The framers included many provisions in the Bill of Rights dealing with fair trials, but only one section that focuses specifically on sentencing. The Eighth Amendment states: "Excessive bail shall not be required, nor excessive fines imposed, nor cruel and unusual punishment inflicted."

The most significant section of this amendment is its cruel and unusual punishment provision. Those who adopted the Bill of Rights clearly wanted to outlaw sentences that were not viewed as appropriate for a civilized society, those that were cruel and unusual. As a consequence, crucifixion, the rack, drawing and quartering, tarring and feathering, dismemberment, or the stocks are not practiced in the United States. By our standards of decency today, these would violate the prohibition against cruel and unusual punishments.

Defining Cruel and Unusual

The meaning of *cruel and unusual* is open to interpretation. The Supreme Court turned its attention to this critical question in *Solem v. Helm* (1983). In 1979 Jerry Helm was convicted of writing a $100 bad check. He had been convicted six previous times for crimes such as obtaining money under false pretenses and driving while intoxicated. None of his crimes was violent, none was a crime against a person, and all were related to a history of alcohol abuse. The judge, believing Helm to be beyond rehabilitation, invoked the South Dakota recidivism law and sentenced him to life in prison without possibility of parole. After two years of trying to get the governor to commute his sentence, Helm turned to the courts, claiming that his punishment was cruel and unusual.

By a 5–4 vote, the justices found the life sentence violated the cruel and unusual punishment clause. Justice Lewis F. Powell's majority opinion held that the Eighth Amendment proscribes not only barbaric punishments but also sentences that are *disproportionate to the crime committed.* Factors to be considered in determining whether the punishment is unconstitutionally disproportionate include not only the severity of the sentence relative to the seriousness of the offense, but also the sentences given to other offenders for the same crime. As applied in this case, life in prison without parole (the same penalty regularly handed out to murderers) was out of proportion to the string of relatively minor crimes Helm had committed. With this case the Court provided a working definition of cruel and unusual. The justices seemed to abide by the old adage "let the punishment fit the crime."

The use of the proportionality concept, however, has not been accepted by all the justices, and its application has not always been easy. In *Harmelin v. Michigan* (1991) the justices rejected a convict's claim that a sentence of life in prison without possibility of parole for a first-time offense of cocaine possession violated the cruel and unusual punishment clause. Members of the Court, however, could not agree on a reason why this sentence was not grossly disproportionate.

The issue returned to the Court in *Ewing v. California* (2003), which concerned the constitutionality of sentencing statutes popularly known as "three strikes and you're out" laws. Under this scheme, defendants convicted of their third serious or violent felony can be sentenced to long prison terms, including the possibility of life without parole. Such laws are designed both to deter crimes and to protect the public from habitual criminals by imprisoning them for long periods of time. In 1993 Washington became the first state to enact a three-strikes law when its voters approved such a proposal by a three-to-one margin. Over the next two years twenty-four states and the federal government adopted similar measures.

Ewing was a constitutional challenge to California's three-strikes law. Gary Ewing had previously committed three burglaries and a robbery when he was arrested in 2000 for shoplifting three expensive golf clubs. Under California law, the prosecutor had the option of charging Ewing with a felony or a misdemeanor. The prosecutor decided that a felony grand theft charge was the most appropriate alternative. Upon conviction on that charge, Ewing was eligible for sentencing under the state's three-strikes statute. The judge sentenced him to a term of twenty-five years to life in prison. Ewing appealed, claiming that the sentence was disproportionate to the triggering offense of stealing three golf clubs.

The Supreme Court upheld the state law. In doing so, the justices gave wide deference to the state legislature's determination that recidivism is a matter of great state concern and that interests of public safety justify this harsh sentencing option. In considering whether the punishment as meted out to Ewing violated the proportionality standard, Justice O'Connor, announcing the judgment of the Court, explained that the long prison term was not imposed because Ewing stole three golf clubs. Rather, the penalty was based on the grand theft violation as part of a long history of criminal activity. Consequently, the sentence was not grossly disproportionate and did not violate the Eighth Amendment's prohibition on cruel and unusual punishment.

The Death Penalty

The issue most frequently brought to the Court on Eighth Amendment grounds is the constitutionality of capital punishment. The death penalty cases have perplexed the Court for decades, presenting the justices with emotionally charged and legally complex questions.

The opinions in the death penalty cases tell us a great deal about what cruel and unusual punishment does and does not mean. Since 1947 the Court has held that the death penalty is inherently neither cruel nor unusual.[8] Never has a majority of the justices agreed that it is, but why not? The answer lies with the intent of the framers (at the time of ratification, death penalties were in use) and with the due process clauses of the Fifth and Fourteenth Amendments, which state that no person can be deprived of life without due process of law. Presumably, if due process is observed, life can be taken.

The majority of Americans also support use of the death penalty, but many interest groups are working to eliminate it. These groups believe that the death penalty constitutes cruel and unusual punishment; but, recognizing the Court's unwillingness to agree, they have tried to convince the justices that the way the death penalty is applied violates due process norms.

One of the first attempts to implement a due process strategy was undertaken by the NAACP Legal Defense and Educational Fund (LDF) in *Furman v. Georgia* (1972). This case involved William Furman, a black man accused of murdering a white man, the father of five children. Under Georgia law, it was completely up to the jury to determine whether a convicted murderer should be put to death. This system, the LDF argued, led to unacceptable disparities in sentencing; specifically, blacks convicted of murdering whites were far more likely to receive the death penalty than whites convicted of the same crime.

A divided Supreme Court agreed with the LDF. In a short *per curiam* opinion deciding *Furman* and two companion cases, the justices said, "The Court holds that the imposition and carrying out of the death penalty in these cases constitutes cruel and unusual punishment." Following this terse statement, however, were nine separate

opinions (five in favor of the LDF's position and four against, running 243 pages—one of the longest in Court history).[9]

The views presented in the opinions of the five-member majority varied considerably—three justices (Byron White, Potter Stewart, and William Douglas) thought capital punishment, as it was then imposed, violated the Constitution, and two (William Brennan and Thurgood Marshall) said it would be unconstitutional under all circumstances. Beyond these general groupings, the five justices agreed on only one major point of law: The states that used capital punishment did so in an arbitrary manner, particularly with regard to race.

The dissenters—Harry Blackmun, Warren Burger, William Rehnquist, and Lewis Powell (the four Nixon appointees)—were more uniform in their critiques. To a lesser or greater extent, all expressed the view that the Court was encroaching on legislative turf and that Americans had not "repudiated" the death penalty.

Chief Justice Burger's opinion raised a unique issue: He noted that the plurality (Douglas, Stewart, and White) had not ruled that capital punishment under all circumstances was unconstitutional and that it may be possible for states to rewrite their laws to meet their objections. Privately, however, Burger thought his suggestion futile, lamenting later, "There will never be another execution in this country."[10]

This view was echoed in many quarters. A University of Washington law professor wrote, "My hunch is that *Furman* spells the complete end of capital punishment in this country."[11] LDF attorneys, predictably, were ecstatic. One called it "the biggest step forward criminal justice has taken in 1,000 years."[12]

As it turned out, the abolitionist celebration was a bit premature, for the Supreme Court was not finished with

---

8. See *Louisiana ex rel. Frances v. Resweber* (1947).

9. We adopt this discussion from Lee Epstein and Joseph F. Kobylka, *The Supreme Court and Legal Change* (Chapel Hill: University of North Carolina Press, 1992), 78–80.

10. Quoted in Bob Woodward and Scott Armstrong, *The Brethren* (New York: Simon and Schuster, 1979), 219.

11. John M. Junker, "The Death Penalty Cases: A Preliminary Comment," *Washington Law Review* 48 (1972): 109.

12. Quoted in Frederick Mann, "Anthony Amsterdam," *Juris Doctor* 3 (1973): 31–32.

the death penalty. Just three years after *Furman*, the Court agreed to hear *Gregg v. Georgia* to consider the constitutionality of a new breed of death penalty laws written to overcome the defects of the old laws. Did these new laws reduce the chance for "wanton and freakish" punishment of the sort the Court found so distasteful in *Furman?* Consider this question as you read the facts and opinions in *Gregg v. Georgia*.

Gregg v. Georgia

428 U.S. 153 (1976)
http://laws.findlaw.com/US/428/153.html
Oral arguments may be found at: http://www.oyez.org
Vote: 7 (Blackmun, Burger, Powell, Rehnquist, Stevens, Stewart, White)
　　2 (Brennan, Marshall)

Opinion announcing the judgment of the Court: Stewart
Concurring opinions: Blackmun, Burger and Rehnquist, White
Dissenting opinions: Brennan, Marshall

Taking cues from the justices' opinions in *Furman*, many states set out to revise their death penalty laws. Among the new plans was one proposed by Georgia (and other states). At the heart of this law was the "bifurcated trial," which consisted of two stages—the trial and the sentencing phase. The trial would proceed as usual, with a jury finding the defendant guilty or not guilty. If the verdict was guilty, the prosecution could seek the death penalty at the sentencing stage, when the defense attorney would present the mitigating facts and the prosecution would present the aggravating facts. Mitigating facts might include the individual's age, record, family responsibility, psychiatric reports, and chances for rehabilitation.[13] Such factors are not specified in law. The prosecu-

---

13. In *Eddings v. Oklahoma* (1982) the Court agreed that the age of a youthful offender constitutes a relevant mitigating factor that jurors should consider in reaching a sentencing recommendation in a capital case. Six years later in *Oklahoma v. Thompson* (1988) the justices expanded the constitutional protection for minors by holding that the Eighth Amendment prohibits the execution of juveniles who commit murder before turning sixteen years of age. Finally, in 2005, after having ruled to the contrary in earlier cases, the Court held in *Roper v. Simmons* that the execution of any person who commits a capital offense before the age of eighteen violates the Constitution's ban on cruel and unusual punishment.

tion, in contrast, would have to demonstrate that at least one codified aggravating factor existed.

The Georgia law specified ten aggravating factors, including: murders committed "while the offender was engaged in the commission of another capital offense," the murder of "a judicial officer . . . or . . . district attorney because of the exercise of his official duty," and murders that are "outrageously or wantonly vile, horrible, or inhumane." After hearing arguments in mitigation and aggravation, the jury would determine whether the individual would receive the death penalty. By spelling out the conditions that must be present before a death penalty can be imposed, the law sought to reduce the jury's discretion and eliminate the arbitrary application of the death penalty that the Court in *Furman* found unacceptable. As a further safeguard, the Georgia Supreme Court was to review all jury determinations of death. This new law was applied to Troy Gregg and abolitionist interests quickly challenged it.

Gregg and a friend were hitchhiking north in Florida. Two men picked them up, and later another passenger joined the foursome and rode with them as far as Atlanta. The four then continued to a rest stop on the highway. The next day, the bodies of the two drivers were found in a nearby ditch. The individual let off in Atlanta identified Gregg and his friend as possible assailants. Gregg was tried under Georgia's new death penalty system. He was convicted of murder and sentenced to death, a penalty the state's highest court upheld.

Judgment of the Court, and opinions of MR. JUSTICE STEWART, MR. JUSTICE POWELL, and MR. JUSTICE STEVENS announced by MR. JUSTICE STEWART.

The issue in this case is whether the imposition of the sentence of death for the crime of murder under the law of Georgia violates the Eighth and Fourteenth Amendments. . . .

We address initially the basic contention that the punishment of death for the crime of murder is, under all circumstances, "cruel and unusual" in violation of the Eighth and Fourteenth Amendments of the Constitution. . . . [W]e will consider the sentence of death imposed under the Georgia statutes at issue in this case.

The Court on a number of occasions has both assumed and asserted the constitutionality of capital punishment. In several cases that assumption provided a necessary foundation for the decision, as the Court was asked to decide whether a particular method of carrying out a capital sentence would be allowed to stand under the Eighth Amendment. But until *Furman v. Georgia* (1972), the Court never confronted squarely the fundamental claim that the punishment of death always, regardless of the enormity of the offense or the procedure followed in imposing the sentence, is cruel and unusual punishment in violation of the Constitution. Although this issue was presented and addressed in *Furman,* it was not resolved by the Court. Four Justices would have held that capital punishment is not unconstitutional *per se;* two Justices would have reached the opposite conclusion; and three Justices, while agreeing that the statutes then before the Court were invalid as applied, left open the question whether such punishment may ever be imposed. We now hold that the punishment of death does not invariably violate the Constitution.

The history of the prohibition of "cruel and unusual" punishment already has been reviewed at length. The phrase first appeared in the English Bill of Rights of 1689, which was drafted by Parliament at the accession of William and Mary. The English version appears to have been directed against punishments unauthorized by statute and beyond the jurisdiction of the sentencing court, as well as those disproportionate to the offense involved. The American draftsmen, who adopted the English phrasing in drafting the Eighth Amendment, were primarily concerned, however, with proscribing "tortures" and other "barbarous" methods of punishment.

In the earliest cases raising Eighth Amendment claims, the Court focused on particular methods of execution to determine whether they were too cruel to pass constitutional muster. The constitutionality of the sentence of death itself was not at issue, and the criterion used to evaluate the mode of execution was its similarity to "torture" and other "barbarous" methods.

But the Court has not confined the prohibition embodied in the Eighth Amendment to "barbarous" methods that were generally outlawed in the 18th century. Instead, the Amendment has been interpreted in a flexible and dynamic manner. The Court early recognized that "a principle to be vital, must be capable of wider application than the mischief which gave it birth." *Weems v. United States* (1910). Thus the Clause forbidding "cruel and unusual" punishments "is not fastened to the obsolete but may acquire meaning as public opinion becomes enlightened by a humane justice." . . .

It is clear from . . . these precedents that the Eighth Amendment has not been regarded as a static concept. As Mr. Chief Justice Warren said, in an oft-quoted phrase, "[t]he Amendment must draw its meaning from the evolving standards of decency that mark the progress of a maturing society." Thus, an assessment of contemporary values concerning the infliction of a challenged sanction is relevant to the application of the Eighth Amendment. As we develop below more fully, this assessment does not call for a subjective judgment. It requires, rather, that we look to objective indicia that reflect the public attitude toward a given sanction.

But our cases also make clear that public perceptions of standards of decency with respect to criminal sanctions are not conclusive. A penalty also must accord with "the dignity of man," which is the "basic concept underlying the Eighth Amendment." This means, at least, that the punishment not be "excessive." When a form of punishment in the abstract (in this case, whether capital punishment may ever be imposed as a sanction for murder) rather than in the particular (the propriety of death as a penalty to be applied to a specific defendant for a specific crime) is under consideration, the inquiry into "excessiveness" has two aspects. First, the punishment must not involve the unnecessary and wanton infliction of pain. Second, the punishment must not be grossly out of proportion to the severity of the crime.

Of course, the requirements of the Eighth Amendment must be applied with an awareness of the limited role to be played by the courts. This does not mean that judges have no role to play, for the Eighth Amendment is a restraint upon the exercise of legislative power. . . .

But, while we have an obligation to insure that constitutional bounds are not overreached, we may not act as judges as we might as legislators. . . .

Therefore, in assessing a punishment selected by a democratically elected legislature against the constitutional measure, we presume its validity. We may not require the legislature to select the least severe penalty possible so long as the penalty selected is not cruelly inhumane or disproportionate to the crime involved. And a heavy burden rests on those who would attack the judgment of the representatives of the people. . . .

In the discussion to this point we have sought to identify the principles and considerations that guide a court in addressing an Eighth Amendment claim. We now consider specifically whether the sentence of death for the crime of murder is a *per se* violation of the Eighth and Fourteenth Amendments to the Constitution. We note first that history and precedent strongly support a negative answer to this question.

The imposition of the death penalty for the crime of murder has a long history of acceptance both in the United States and in England. . . .

It is apparent from the text of the Constitution itself that the existence of capital punishment was accepted by the Framers. At the time the Eighth Amendment was ratified, capital punishment was a common sanction in every State. . . . The Fifth Amendment, adopted at the same time as the Eighth, contemplated the continued existence of the capital sanction by imposing certain limits on the prosecution of capital cases. . . .

And the Fourteenth Amendment, adopted over three quarters of a century later, similarly contemplates the existence of the capital sanction in providing that no State shall deprive any person of "life, liberty, or property" without due process of law.

For nearly two centuries, this Court, repeatedly and often expressly, has recognized that capital punishment is not invalid *per se*. . . .

Four years ago, the petitioners in *Furman* and its companion cases predicated their argument primarily upon the asserted proposition that standards of decency had evolved to the point where capital punishment no longer could be tolerated. The petitioners in those cases said, in effect, that the evolutionary process had come to an end, and that standards of decency required that the Eighth Amendment be construed finally as prohibiting capital punishment for any crime regardless of its depravity and impact on society. This view was accepted by two Justices. Three other Justices were unwilling to go so far; focusing on the procedures by which convicted defendants were selected for the death penalty rather than on the actual punishment inflicted, they joined in the conclusion that the statutes before the Court were constitutionally invalid.

The petitioners in the capital cases before the Court today renew the "standards of decency" argument, but developments during the four years since *Furman* have undercut substantially the assumptions upon which their argument rested. Despite the continuing debate, dating back to the 19th century, over the morality and utility of capital punishment, it is now evident that a large proportion of American society continues to regard it as an appropriate and necessary criminal sanction.

The most marked indication of society's endorsement of the death penalty for murder is the legislative response to *Furman*. The legislatures of at least 35 States have enacted new statutes that provide for the death penalty for at least some crimes that result in the death of another person. And the Congress of the United States, in 1974, enacted a statute providing the death penalty for aircraft piracy that results in death. These recently adopted statutes have attempted to address the concerns expressed by the Court in *Furman* primarily (i) by specifying the factors to be weighed and the procedures to be followed in deciding when to impose a capital sentence, or (ii) by making the death penalty mandatory for specified crimes. But all of the post-*Furman* statutes make clear that capital punishment itself has not been rejected by the elected representatives of the people.

In the only statewide referendum occurring since *Furman* and brought to our attention, the people of California adopted a constitutional amendment that authorized capital punishment, in effect negating a prior ruling by the Supreme Court of California that the death penalty violated the California Constitution.

The jury also is a significant and reliable objective index of contemporary values because it is so directly involved. . . . It may be true that evolving standards have influenced juries in recent decades to be more discriminating in imposing the sentence of death. But the relative infrequency of jury verdicts imposing the death sentence does not indicate rejection of capital punishment *per se*. Rather, the reluctance of juries in many cases to impose the sentence may well reflect the humane feeling that this most irrevocable of sanctions should be reserved for a small number of extreme cases. Indeed, the actions of juries in many States since *Furman* are fully compatible with the legislative judgments, reflected in the new statutes, as to the continued utility and necessity of capital punishment in appropriate cases. At the close of 1974 at least 254 persons had been sentenced to death since *Furman*, and by the end of March 1976, more than 460 persons were subject to death sentences.

As we have seen, however, the Eighth Amendment demands more than that a challenged punishment be acceptable to contemporary society. The Court also must ask whether it comports with the basic concept of human dignity at the core of the Amendment. . . . [T]he sanction imposed cannot be so totally without penological justification that it results in the gratuitous infliction of suffering.

The death penalty is said to serve two principal social purposes: retribution and deterrence of capital crimes by prospective offenders.

In part, capital punishment is an expression of society's moral outrage at particularly offensive conduct. This function may be unappealing to many, but it is essential in an ordered society that asks its citizens to rely on legal processes rather than self-help to vindicate their wrongs. . . . "Retribution is no longer the dominant objective of the criminal law," but neither is it a forbidden objective nor one inconsistent with our respect for the dignity of men. . . .

Statistical attempts to evaluate the worth of the death penalty as a deterrent to crimes by potential offenders have occasioned a great deal of debate. The results simply have been inconclusive. . . .

Although some of the studies suggest that the death penalty may not function as a significantly greater deterrent than lesser penalties, there is no convincing empirical evidence either supporting or refuting this view. We may nevertheless assume safely that there are murderers, such as those who act in passion, for whom the threat of death has little or no deterrent effect. But for many others, the death penalty undoubtedly is a significant deterrent. There are carefully contemplated murders, such as murder for hire, where the possible penalty of death may well enter into the cold calculus that precedes the decision to act. And there are some categories of murder, such as murder by a life prisoner, where other sanctions may not be adequate.

The value of capital punishment as a deterrent of crime is a complex factual issue the resolution of which properly rests with the legislatures, which can evaluate the results of statistical studies in terms of their own local conditions and with a flexibility of approach that is not available to the courts. Indeed, many of the post-*Furman* statutes reflect just such a responsible effort to define those crimes and those criminals for which capital punishment is most probably an effective deterrent.

In sum, we cannot say that the judgment of the Georgia Legislature that capital punishment may be necessary in some cases is clearly wrong. Considerations of federalism, as well as respect for the ability of a legislature to evaluate, in terms of its particular State, the moral consensus concerning the death penalty and its social utility as a sanction, require us to conclude, in the absence of more convincing evidence, that the infliction of death as a punishment for murder is not without justification and thus is not unconstitutionally severe.

Finally, we must consider whether the punishment of death is disproportionate in relation to the crime for which it is imposed. There is no question that death as a punishment is unique in its severity and irrevocability. When a defendant's life is at stake, the Court has been particularly sensitive to insure that every safeguard is observed. But we are concerned here only with the imposition of capital punishment for the crime of murder, and when a life has been taken deliberately by the offender, we cannot say that the punishment is invariably disproportionate to the crime. It is an extreme sanction, suitable to the most extreme of crimes.

We hold that the death penalty is not a form of punishment that may never be imposed, regardless of the circumstances of the offense, regardless of the character of the offender, and regardless of the procedure followed in reaching the decision to impose it.

We now consider whether Georgia may impose the death penalty on the petitioner in this case.

While *Furman* did not hold that the infliction of the death penalty *per se* violates the Constitution's ban on cruel and unusual punishments, it did recognize that the penalty of death is different in kind from any other punishment imposed under our system of criminal justice. Because of the uniqueness of the death penalty, *Furman* held that it could not be imposed under sentencing procedures that created a substantial risk that it would be inflicted in an arbitrary and capricious manner. . . .

Furman mandates that where discretion is afforded a sentencing body on a matter so grave as the determination of whether a human life should be taken or spared, that discretion must be suitably directed and limited so as to minimize the risk of wholly arbitrary and capricious action. . . .

Jury sentencing has been considered desirable in capital cases in order "to maintain a link between contemporary community values and the penal system—a link without which the determination of punishment could hardly reflect 'the evolving standards of decency that mark the progress of a maturing society.' " But it creates special problems. Much of the information that is relevant to the sentencing decision may have no relevance to the question of guilt, or may even be extremely prejudicial to a fair determination of that question. This problem, however, is scarcely insurmountable. Those who have studied the question suggest that a bifurcated procedure—one in which the question of sentence is not considered until the determination of guilt has been made—is the best answer. . . . When a human life is at stake and when the jury must have information prejudicial to the question of guilt but relevant to the question of penalty in order to impose a rational sentence, a bifurcated system is more likely to ensure elimination of the constitutional deficiencies identified in *Furman*.

But the provision of relevant information under fair procedural rules is not alone sufficient to guarantee that the information will be properly used in the imposition of punishment, especially if sentencing is performed by a jury. Since the members of a jury will have had little, if any, previous experience in sentencing, they are unlikely to be skilled in dealing with the information they are given. To the extent that this problem is inherent in jury sentencing, it may not be totally correctable. It seems clear, however, that the problem will be alleviated if the jury is given guidance regarding the factors about the crime and the defendant that the State, representing organized society, deems particularly relevant to the sentencing decision.

The idea that a jury should be given guidance in its decisionmaking is also hardly a novel proposition. Juries are invariably given careful instructions on the law and how to apply it before they are authorized to decide the merits of a lawsuit. It would be virtually unthinkable to follow any other course in a legal system that has traditionally operated by following prior precedents and fixed rules of law. When erroneous instructions are given, retrial is often required. It is quite simply a hallmark of our legal system that juries be carefully and adequately guided in their deliberations.

While some have suggested that standards to guide a capital jury's sentencing deliberations are impossible to formulate, the fact is that such standards have been developed. . . . While such standards are by necessity somewhat general, they do provide guidance to the sentencing authority and thereby reduce the likelihood that it will impose a sentence that fairly can be called capricious or arbitrary. Where the sentencing authority is required to specify the factors it relied upon in reaching its decision, the further safeguard of meaningful appellate review is available to ensure that death sentences are not imposed capriciously or in a freakish manner.

In summary, the concerns expressed in *Furman* that the penalty of death not be imposed in an arbitrary or capricious manner can be met by a carefully drafted statute that ensures that the sentencing authority is given adequate information and guidance. As a general proposition these concerns are best met by a system that provides for a bifurcated proceeding at which the sentencing authority is apprised of the information relevant to the imposition of sentence and provided with standards to guide its use of the information.

We do not intend to suggest that only the above-described procedures would be permissible under *Furman* or that any sentencing system constructed along these general lines would inevitably satisfy the concerns of *Furman*, for each distinct system must be examined on an individual basis. Rather, we have embarked upon this general exposition to make clear that it is possible to construct capital-sentencing systems capable of meeting *Furman*'s constitutional concerns.

We now turn to consideration of the constitutionality of Georgia's capital-sentencing procedures. In the wake of *Furman*, Georgia amended its capital punishment statute, but chose not to narrow the scope of its murder provisions. Thus, now as before *Furman*, in Georgia "[a] person commits murder when he unlawfully and with malice aforethought, either express or implied, causes the death of another human being." All persons convicted of murder "shall be punished by death or by imprisonment for life."

Georgia did act, however, to narrow the class of murderers subject to capital punishment by specifying 10 statutory aggravating circumstances, one of which must be found by the jury to exist beyond a reasonable doubt before a death sentence can ever be imposed. In addition, the jury is authorized to consider any other appropriate aggravating or mitigating circumstances. The jury is not required to find any mitigating circumstance in order to make a recommendation of mercy that is binding on the trial court, but it must find a *statutory* aggravating circumstance before recommending a sentence of death.

These procedures require the jury to consider the circumstances of the crime and the criminal before it recommends sentence. No longer can a Georgia jury do as *Furman*'s jury did: reach a finding of the defendant's guilt and then, without guidance or direction, decide whether he should live or die. Instead, the jury's attention is directed to the specific circumstances of the crime. . . .In addition, the jury's attention is focused on the characteristics of the person who committed the crime. . . . As a result, while some jury discretion still exists, "the discretion to be exercised is controlled by clear and objective standards so as to produce nondiscriminatory application."

As an important additional safeguard against arbitrariness and caprice, the Georgia statutory scheme provides for automatic appeal of all death sentences to the State's Supreme Court. That court is required by statute to review each sentence of death and determine whether it was imposed under the influence of passion or prejudice, whether the evidence supports the jury's finding of a statutory aggravating circumstance, and whether the sentence is disproportionate compared to those sentences imposed in similar cases.

In short, Georgia's new sentencing procedures require as a prerequisite to the imposition of the death penalty, specific jury findings as to the circumstances of the crime or the character of the defendant. Moreover, to guard further against a situation comparable to that presented in *Furman*, the Supreme Court of Georgia compares each death sentence with the sentences imposed on similarly situated defendants to ensure that the sentence of death in a particular case is not disproportionate. On their face these procedures seem to satisfy the concerns of *Furman*. No longer should there be "no meaningful basis for distinguishing the few cases in which [the death penalty] is imposed from the many cases in which it is not." . . .

The basic concern of *Furman* centered on those defendants who were being condemned to death capriciously and arbitrarily. Under the procedures before the Court in that case, sentencing authorities were not directed to give attention to the nature or circumstances of the crime committed or to the character or record of the defendant. Left unguided, juries imposed the death sentence in a way that could only be called freakish. The new Georgia sentencing procedures, by contrast, focus the jury's attention on the particularized nature of the crime and the particularized

characteristics of the individual defendant. While the jury is permitted to consider any aggravating or mitigating circumstances, it must find and identify at least one statutory aggravating factor before it may impose a penalty of death. In this way the jury's discretion is channeled. No longer can a jury wantonly and freakishly impose the death sentence; it is always circumscribed by the legislative guidelines. In addition, the review function of the Supreme Court of Georgia affords additional assurance that the concerns that prompted our decision in *Furman* are not present to any significant degree in the Georgia procedure applied here.

For the reasons expressed in this opinion, we hold that the statutory system under which Gregg was sentenced to death does not violate the Constitution. Accordingly, the judgment of the Georgia Supreme Court is affirmed.

MR. JUSTICE WHITE, with whom THE CHIEF JUSTICE and MR. JUSTICE REHNQUIST join, concurring in the judgment.

The Georgia Legislature has plainly made an effort to guide the jury in the exercise of its discretion, while at the same time permitting the jury to dispense mercy on the basis of factors too intangible to write into a statute, and I cannot accept the naked assertion that the effort is bound to fail. As the types of murders for which the death penalty may be imposed become more narrowly defined and are limited to those which are particularly serious or for which the death penalty is peculiarly appropriate as they are in Georgia by reason of the aggravating-circumstance requirement, it becomes reasonable to expect that juries—even given discretion *not* to impose the death penalty—will impose the death penalty in a substantial portion of the cases so defined. If they do, it can no longer be said that the penalty is being imposed wantonly and freakishly or so infrequently that it loses its usefulness as a sentencing device. There is, therefore, reason to expect that Georgia's current system would escape the infirmities which invalidated its previous system under *Furman*. However, the Georgia Legislature was not satisfied with a system which might, but also might not, turn out in practice to result in death sentences being imposed with reasonable consistency for certain serious murders. Instead, it gave the Georgia Supreme Court the power and the obligation to perform precisely the task which three Justices of this Court, whose opinions were necessary to the result, performed in *Furman:* namely, the task of deciding whether in fact the death penalty was being administered for any given class of crime in a discriminatory, standardless, or rare fashion.

. . . Indeed, if the Georgia Supreme Court properly performs the task assigned to it under the Georgia statutes, death sentences imposed for discriminatory reasons or wantonly or freakishly for any given category of crime will be set aside. Petitioner has wholly failed to establish, and has not even attempted to establish, that the Georgia Supreme Court failed properly to perform its task in this case or that it is incapable of performing its task adequately in all cases; and this Court should not assume that it did not do so.

MR. JUSTICE BRENNEN, dissenting.

The fatal constitutional infirmity in the punishment of death is that it treats "members of the human race as nonhumans, as objects to be toyed with and discarded. [It is] thus inconsistent with the fundamental premise of the Clause that even the vilest criminal remains a human being possessed of common human dignity." As such it is a penalty that "subjects the individual to a fate forbidden by the principle of civilized treatment guaranteed by the [clause]." I therefore would hold, on that ground alone, that death is today a cruel and unusual punishment prohibited by the Clause.

MR. JUSTICE MARSHALL, dissenting.

An excessive penalty is invalid under the Cruel and Unusual Punishments Clause "even though popular sentiment may favor." The inquiry here, then, is simply whether the death penalty is necessary to accomplish the legitimate legislative purposes in punishment, or whether a less severe penalty—life imprisonment—would do as well.

The two purposes that sustain the death penalty as nonexcessive in the Court's view are general deterrence and retribution. In *Furman,* I canvassed the relevant data on the deterrent effect of capital punishment. . . . The available evidence, I concluded in *Furman,* was convincing that "capital punishment is not necessary as a deterrent to crime in our society." . . .

The other principal purpose said to be served by the death penalty is retribution. The notion that retribution can serve as a moral justification for the sanction of death finds credence in the opinion of my Brothers Stewart, Powell, and Stevens, and that of my Brother White. . . . It is this notion that I find to be the most disturbing aspect of today's unfortunate decisions.

The concept of retribution is a multifaceted one, and any discussion of its role in the criminal law must be undertaken with caution. On one level, it can be said that the notion of retribution or reprobation is the basis of our insistence that only those who have broken the law be punished, and in this sense the notion is quite obviously central to a just system of criminal sanctions. But our recognition that retribution plays a crucial role in determining who may be punished by no means requires approval of retribution as a general justification for punishment. It is the question whether retribution can provide a moral justification for punishment—in particular, capital punishment—that we must consider.

My Brothers Stewart, Powell, and Stevens, offer the following explanation of the retributive justification for capital punishment:

"The instinct for retribution is part of the nature of man, and channeling that instinct in the administration of criminal justice serves an important purpose in promoting the stability of a society governed by law. When people begin to believe that organized society is unwilling or unable to impose upon criminal offenders the punishment they 'deserve,' then there are sown the seeds of anarchy—of self-help, vigilante justice, and lynch law."

This statement is wholly inadequate to justify the death penalty. As my Brother Brennan stated in *Furman,* "There is no evidence whatever that utilization of imprisonment rather than death encourages private blood feuds and other disorders." It simply defies belief to suggest that the death penalty is necessary to prevent the American people from taking the law into their own hands. . . . The death penalty, unnecessary to promote the goal of deterrence or to further any legitimate notion of retribution, is an excessive penalty forbidden by the Eighth and Fourteenth Amendments. I respectfully dissent from the Court's judgment upholding the sentences of death imposed upon the petitioners in these cases.

Despite the many opinions in *Gregg,* the majority of justices agreed that the Georgia law was constitutional; indeed, some members of the Court referred to it as a model death penalty scheme. Those who believed that *Furman* had signaled the end of capital punishment in the United States were clearly mistaken. *Furman* represented the rejection of a capital punishment system that allowed racial discrimination to influence sentencing, but, as *Gregg* demonstrates, *Furman* did not represent a judicial rejection of capital punishment *per se.*

In the Aftermath of Gregg

In some ways, *Gregg* settled the death penalty issue: The Court asserted that capital punishment did not violate the Constitution, a position to which it still adheres. But opponents of the death penalty have not given up. They continue to bring lawsuits, many of which are aimed at narrowing the application of capital punishment. In other words, this litigation challenges procedural practices adopted by the states, not the constitutionality of the death penalty.

Many of these challenges have not succeeded. In *McCleskey v. Kemp* (1987) the justices rejected a new attempt to strike down the death penalty because of continuing racial disparities. Furthermore, in *McCleskey v. Zant* (1991) the Court upheld limits on the right of convicts to use habeas corpus petitions to file additional legal actions to block the death penalty. In *Baze v. Rees* (2008) the justices rejected a challenge to the use of lethal injection as a method for executing those convicted of a capital offense. Writing for a deeply divided Court, Chief Justice Roberts held: "Simply because an execution method may result in pain, either by accident or as an inescapable consequence of death, does not establish the sort of 'objectively intolerable risk of harm' that qualifies as cruel and unusual."

Capital punishment opponents have, however, also scored some victories in the courts, persuading the justices to be more attentive to the fairness of death penalty trials. In *Wiggins v. Smith* (2003) the Court overturned a death sentence because the accused did not receive effective counsel; and in *Ring v. Arizona* (2002) they rejected the authority of a single judge to impose capital punish-

ment, holding that a death sentence can only be issued by a jury. Perhaps the most significant of the recent legal victories by death penalty opponents came in *Atkins v. Virginia* (2002), a case presenting the justices with an opportunity to revisit a 1989 decision that permitted the execution of mentally retarded murderers.

Atkins v. Virginia

536 U.S. 304 (2002)
http://laws.findlaw.com/US/000/00-8452.html
Oral arguments may be found at: http://www.oyez.org
Vote: 6 (Breyer, Ginsburg, Kennedy, O'Connor, Souter, Stevens)
    3 (Rehnquist, Scalia, Thomas)
Opinion of the Court: Stevens
Dissenting opinions: Rehnquist, Scalia

Close to midnight on August 16, 1996, Daryl Renard Atkins and William Jones, after a day spent drinking and smoking marijuana, walked to a convenience store to buy more beer. Upon realizing that they did not have enough money to make the purchase, Atkins and Jones decided to rob a customer. Armed with a semiautomatic handgun, they confronted Eric Nesbitt, an airman from Langley Air Force Base, as he left the store. Atkins and Jones robbed Nesbitt of the money he was carrying, seized control of his pickup truck, and drove him to an automated teller machine, where they forced him to withdraw $200. That done, they took Nesbitt to an isolated location where he was shot eight times in the "thorax, chest, abdomen, arms, and legs," resulting in his death.

Atkins and Jones were initially charged with capital murder, but prosecutors permitted Jones to plead guilty to first-degree murder in exchange for his testimony against Atkins. By pleading guilty, Jones was ineligible for the death penalty under Virginia law. At Atkins's trial, both men confirmed most of the details of the incident, with the important exception that each claimed that the other had shot Nesbitt. The jury believed Jones's account, convicting Atkins and sentencing him to death. The Virginia Supreme Court upheld the conviction, but ordered a new sentencing hearing because the trial court had used an improper verdict form. At the second hearing,

Daryl Renard Atkins glances over his shoulder in a Virginia courtroom in February 1998 before being sentenced to death for carjacking and killing an airman. Four years later the Supreme Court would use the Atkins case to strike down Virginia's law permitting the execution of mentally retarded defendants.

the jury heard testimony from a forensic psychologist, hired by the defense, that Atkins was mildly retarded, with an IQ of 59 and an impaired capacity either to understand the criminality of his conduct or to conform his behavior to the law. A psychologist for the prosecution claimed, however, that although Atkins may have had an antisocial personality disorder, he was at least of average intelligence. The jury also heard about Atkins's sixteen prior felony convictions for robbery, attempted robbery, abduction, firearms violations, and maiming. After considering the evidence, it sentenced Atkins to death.

Atkins's lawyers asked the Virginia Supreme Court to commute the sentence to life in prison on the ground that it is unconstitutional to execute an individual who is mentally retarded. The Virginia court rejected this argument, relying on the U.S. Supreme Court's ruling in *Penry v. Lynaugh* (1989). The Supreme Court accepted the case in order to reconsider the *Penry* precedent.

JUSTICE STEVENS delivered the opinion of the Court.

Those mentally retarded persons who meet the law's requirements for criminal responsibility should be tried and punished when they commit crimes. Because of their disabilities in areas of reasoning, judgment, and control of their impulses, however, they do not act with the level of moral culpability that characterizes the most serious adult criminal conduct. Moreover, their impairments can jeopardize the reliability and fairness of capital proceedings against mentally retarded defendants. Presumably for these reasons, in the 13 years since we decided *Penry v. Lynaugh* (1989), the American public, legislators, scholars, and judges have deliberated over the question whether the death penalty should ever be imposed on a mentally retarded criminal. The consensus reflected in those deliberations informs our answer to the question presented by this case: whether such executions are "cruel and unusual punishments" prohibited by the Eighth Amendment to the Federal Constitution. . . .

The Eighth Amendment succinctly prohibits "excessive" sanctions. It provides: "Excessive bail shall not be required, nor excessive fines imposed, nor cruel and unusual punishments inflicted." In *Weems v. United States* (1910), we held that a punishment of 12 years jailed in irons at hard and painful labor for the crime of falsifying records was excessive. We explained "that it is a precept of justice that punishment for crime should be graduated and proportioned to the offense." We have repeatedly applied this proportionality precept in later cases interpreting the Eighth Amendment. . . .

A claim that punishment is excessive is judged not by the standards that prevailed in 1685 when Lord Jeffreys presided over the "Bloody Assizes" or when the Bill of Rights was adopted, but rather by those that currently prevail. As Chief Justice Warren explained in his opinion in *Trop v. Dulles* (1958): "The basic concept underlying the Eighth Amendment is nothing less than the dignity of man. . . . The Amendment must draw its meaning from the evolving standards of decency that mark the progress of a maturing society."

Proportionality review under those evolving standards should be informed by "objective factors to the maximum possible extent." We have pinpointed that the "clearest and most reliable objective evidence of contemporary values is the legislation enacted by the country's legislatures." *Penry.*

Relying in part on such legislative evidence, we have held that death is an impermissibly excessive punishment for the rape of an adult woman, *Coker v. Georgia* (1977), or for a defendant who neither took life, attempted to take life, nor intended to take life, *Enmund v. Florida* (1982). . . .

We also acknowledged in *Coker* that the objective evidence, though of great importance, did not "wholly determine" the controversy, "for the Constitution contemplates that in the end our own judgment will be brought to bear on the question of the acceptability of the death penalty under the Eighth Amendment." . . .

Thus, in cases involving a consensus, our own judgment is "brought to bear," *Coker,* by asking whether there is reason to disagree with the judgment reached by the citizenry and its legislators.

Guided by our approach in these cases, we shall first review the judgment of legislatures that have addressed the suitability of imposing the death penalty on the mentally retarded and then consider reasons for agreeing or disagreeing with their judgment.

The parties have not called our attention to any state legislative consideration of the suitability of imposing the death penalty on mentally retarded offenders prior to 1986. In that year, the public reaction to the execution of a mentally retarded murderer [Jerome Bowden] in Georgia apparently led to the enactment of the first state statute prohibiting such executions. In 1988, when Congress enacted legislation reinstating the federal death penalty, it expressly provided that a "sentence of death shall not be carried out upon a person who is mentally retarded." In 1989, Maryland enacted a similar prohibition. It was in that year that we decided *Penry,* and concluded that those two state enactments, "even when added to the 14 States that have rejected capital punishment completely, do not provide sufficient evidence at present of a national consensus."

Much has changed since then. Responding to the national attention received by the Bowden execution and our decision in *Penry,* state legislatures across the country began to address the issue. In 1990 Kentucky and Tennessee enacted statutes similar to those in Georgia and Maryland, as did New Mexico in 1991, and Arkansas, Colorado, Washington, Indiana, and Kansas in 1993 and 1994. In 1995, when New York reinstated its death penalty, it emulated the Federal Government by expressly exempting the mentally retarded. Nebraska followed suit in 1998. There appear to have been no similar enactments during the next two years, but in 2000 and 2001 six more States—South Dakota, Arizona, Connecticut, Florida, Missouri, and North Carolina—joined the procession. The Texas Legislature unanimously adopted a similar bill, and bills have passed at least one house in other States, including Virginia and Nevada.

It is not so much the number of these States that is significant, but the consistency of the direction of change. Given the well-known fact that anticrime legislation is far more popular than legislation providing protections for persons guilty of violent crime, the large number of States prohibiting the execution of mentally retarded persons (and the complete absence of States passing legislation reinstating the power to conduct such executions) provides powerful evidence that today our society views mentally retarded offenders as categorically less culpable than the average criminal. The evidence carries even greater force when it is noted that the legislatures that have addressed the issue have voted overwhelmingly in favor of the prohibition. Moreover, even in those States that allow the execution of mentally retarded offenders, the practice is uncommon. Some States, for example New Hampshire and New Jersey, continue to authorize executions, but none have been carried out in decades. Thus there is little need to pursue legislation barring the execution of the mentally retarded in those States. And it appears that even among those States that regularly execute offenders and that have no prohibition with regard to the mentally retarded, only five have executed offenders possessing a known IQ [of] less than 70 since we decided *Penry.* The practice, therefore, has become truly unusual, and it is fair to say that a national consensus has developed against it.*

To the extent there is serious disagreement about the execution of mentally retarded offenders, it is in determining

*Additional evidence makes it clear that this legislative judgment reflects a much broader social and professional consensus. For example, several organizations with germane expertise have adopted official positions opposing the imposition of the death penalty upon a mentally retarded offender. See Brief for American Psychological Association et al. as *Amici Curiae;* Brief for AAMR et. al. as *Amici Curiae.* In addition, representatives of widely diverse religious communities in the United States, reflecting Christian, Jewish, Muslim, and Buddhist traditions, have filed an amicus curiae brief explaining that even though their views about the death penalty differ, they all "share a conviction that the execution of persons with mental retardation cannot be morally justified." See Brief for United States Catholic Conference et al. as *Amici Curiae* in *McCarver v. North Carolina.* Moreover, within the world community, the imposition of the death penalty for crimes committed by mentally retarded offenders is over-which offenders are in fact retarded. In this case, for instance, the Commonwealth of Virginia disputes that Atkins suffers from mental retardation. Not all people who claim to be mentally retarded will be so impaired as to fall within the range of mentally retarded offenders about whom there is a national consensus. As was our approach in *Ford v. Wainwright* [1986], with regard to insanity, "we leave to the State[s] the task of developing appropriate ways to enforce the constitutional restriction upon its execution of sentences." . . .

. . . [O]ur death penalty jurisprudence provides two reasons consistent with the legislative consensus that the mentally retarded should be categorically excluded from execution. First, there is a serious question as to whether either justification that we have recognized as a basis for the death penalty applies to mentally retarded offenders. *Gregg v. Georgia* (1976) identified "retribution and deterrence of capital crimes by prospective offenders" as the social purposes served by the death penalty. Unless the imposition of the death penalty on a mentally retarded person "measurably contributes to one or both of these goals, it 'is nothing more than the purposeless and needless imposition of pain and suffering,' and hence an unconstitutional punishment." *Enmund.*

With respect to retribution—the interest in seeing that the offender gets his "just deserts"—the severity of the appropriate punishment necessarily depends on the culpability of the offender. Since *Gregg*, our jurisprudence has consistently confined the imposition of the death penalty to a narrow category of the most serious crimes. For example, in *Godfrey v. Georgia* (1980), we set aside a death sentence because the petitioner's crimes did not reflect "a consciousness materially more 'depraved' than that of any person guilty of murder." If the culpability of the average murderer is insufficient to justify the most extreme sanction available to the State, the lesser culpability of the mentally retarded offender surely does not merit that form of retribution. Thus, pursuant to our narrowing jurisprudence, which seeks to ensure that only the most deserving of execution are put to death, an exclusion for the mentally retarded is appropriate.

With respect to deterrence—the interest in preventing capital crimes by prospective offenders—"it seems likely that 'capital punishment can serve as a deterrent only when murder is the result of premeditation and deliberation,'" *Enmund.* Exempting the mentally retarded from that punishment will not affect the "cold calculus that precedes the decision" of other potential murderers. Indeed, that sort of calculus is at the opposite end of the spectrum from behavior of mentally retarded offenders. . . . Nor will exempting the mentally retarded from execution lessen the deterrent effect of the death penalty with respect to offenders who are not mentally retarded. Such individuals are unprotected by the exemption and will continue to face the threat of execution. Thus, executing the mentally retarded will not measurably further the goal of deterrence.

The reduced capacity of mentally retarded offenders provides a second justification for a categorical rule making such offenders ineligible for the death penalty. The risk "that the death penalty will be imposed in spite of factors which may call for a less severe penalty," *Lockett v. Ohio* (1978), is enhanced, not only by the possibility of false confessions, but also by the lesser ability of mentally retarded defendants to make a persuasive showing of mitigation in the face of prosecutorial evidence of one or more aggravating factors. Mentally retarded defendants may be less able to give meaningful assistance to their counsel and are typically poor witnesses, and their demeanor may create an unwarranted impression of lack of remorse for their crimes. . . . Mentally retarded defendants in the aggregate face a special risk of wrongful execution.

Our independent evaluation of the issue reveals no reason to disagree with the judgment of "the legislatures that have recently addressed the matter" and concluded that death is not a suitable punishment for a mentally retarded criminal. We are not persuaded that the execution of mentally retarded criminals will measurably advance the deterrent or the retributive purpose of the death penalty. Construing and applying the Eighth Amendment in the light of our "evolving standards of decency," we therefore conclude that such punishment is excessive and that the Constitution

---

whelmingly disapproved. Brief for The European Union as *Amicus Curiae* in *McCarver v. North Carolina*. Finally, polling data shows a widespread consensus among Americans, even those who support the death penalty, that executing the mentally retarded is wrong. R. Bonner & S. Rimer, Executing the Mentally Retarded Even as Laws Begin to Shift, *New York Times*, Aug. 7, 2000, p. A1; App. B to Brief for AAMR as *Amicus Curiae* in *McCarver v. North Carolina*, O.T. 2001, No. 00—8727 (appending approximately 20 state and national polls on the issue). Although these factors are by no means dispositive, their consistency with the legislative evidence lends further support to our conclusion that there is a consensus among those who have addressed the issue. See *Thompson v. Oklahoma* (1988) (considering the views of "respected professional organizations, by other nations that share our Anglo-American heritage, and by the leading members of the Western European community").

"places a substantive restriction on the State's power to take the life" of a mentally retarded offender.

The judgment of the Virginia Supreme Court is reversed and the case is remanded for further proceedings not inconsistent with this opinion.

It is so ordered.

JUSTICE SCALIA, with whom THE CHIEF JUSTICE and JUSTICE THOMAS join, dissenting.

Today's decision is the pinnacle of our Eighth Amendment death-is-different jurisprudence. Not only does it, like all of that jurisprudence, find no support in the text or history of the Eighth Amendment; it does not even have support in current social attitudes regarding the conditions that render an otherwise just death penalty inappropriate. Seldom has an opinion of this Court rested so obviously upon nothing but the personal views of its members. . . .

. . . [The] petitioner's mental retardation was a *central issue* at sentencing. The jury concluded, however, that his alleged retardation was not a compelling reason to exempt him from the death penalty in light of the brutality of his crime and his long demonstrated propensity for violence. "In upsetting this particularized judgment on the basis of a constitutional absolute," the Court concludes that no one who is even slightly mentally retarded can have sufficient "moral responsibility to be subjected to capital punishment for any crime. As a sociological and moral conclusion that is implausible; and it is doubly implausible as an interpretation of the United States Constitution." *Thompson v. Oklahoma* (1988) (SCALIA, J., dissenting).

Under our Eighth Amendment jurisprudence, a punishment is "cruel and unusual" if it falls within one of two categories: "those modes or acts of punishment that had been considered cruel and unusual at the time that the Bill of Rights was adopted," *Ford v. Wainwright* (1986), and modes of punishment that are inconsistent with modern "standards of decency," as evinced by objective indicia, the most important of which is "legislation enacted by the country's legislatures," *Penry v. Lynaugh* (1989).

The Court makes no pretense that execution of the mildly mentally retarded would have been considered "cruel and unusual" in 1791. . . .

The Court is left to argue, therefore, that execution of the mildly retarded is inconsistent with the "evolving standards of decency that mark the progress of a maturing society." *Trop v. Dulles* (1958). Before today, our opinions consistently emphasized that Eighth Amendment judgments regarding the existence of social "standards" "should be informed by objective factors to the maximum possible extent" and "should not be, or appear to be, merely the subjective views of individual Justices." *Coker v. Georgia* (1977). "First" among these objective factors are the "statutes passed by society's elected representatives," *Stanford v. Kentucky* (1989), because it "will rarely if ever be the case that the Members of this Court will have a better sense of the evolution in views of the American people than do their elected representatives," *Thompson* (SCALIA, J., dissenting).

The Court pays lip service to these precedents as it miraculously extracts a "national consensus" forbidding execution of the mentally retarded from the fact that 18 States—less than *half* (47%) of the 38 States that permit capital punishment (for whom the issue exists)—have very recently enacted legislation barring execution of the mentally retarded. . . .

. . . How is it possible that agreement among 47% of the death penalty jurisdictions amounts to "consensus"? Our prior cases have generally required a much higher degree of agreement before finding a punishment cruel and unusual on "evolving standards" grounds. In *Coker*, we proscribed the death penalty for rape of an adult woman after finding that only one jurisdiction, Georgia, authorized such a punishment. In *Enmund*, we invalidated the death penalty for mere participation in a robbery in which an accomplice took a life, a punishment not permitted in 28 of the death penalty States (78%). . . . What the Court calls evidence of "consensus" in the present case (a fudged 47%) more closely resembles evidence that we found *inadequate* to establish consensus in earlier cases. . . .

Moreover, a major factor that the Court entirely disregards is that the legislation of all 18 States it relies on is still in its infancy. The oldest of the statutes is only 14 years old; five were enacted last year; over half were enacted within the past eight years. Few, if any, of the States have had sufficient experience with these laws to know whether they are sensible in the long term. It is "myopic to base sweeping constitutional principles upon the narrow experience of [a few] years."

The Court attempts to bolster its embarrassingly feeble evidence of "consensus" with the following: "It is not so much the number of these States that is significant, but the *consistency* of the direction of change." But in what *other* direction *could we possibly* see change? Given that 14 years ago *all* the death penalty statutes included the mentally retarded, *any* change (except precipitate undoing of what had just been done) was *bound to be* in the one direction the Court finds significant enough to overcome the lack of real consensus. . . . In any event, reliance upon "trends," even those of much longer duration than a mere 14 years, is a perilous basis for constitutional adjudication. . . .

But the Prize for the Court's Most Feeble Effort to fabricate "national consensus" must go to its appeal (deservedly relegated to a footnote) to the views of assorted professional and religious organizations, members of the so-called "world community," and respondents to opinion polls. I agree with the Chief Justice that the views of professional and religious organizations and the results of opinion polls are irrelevant. Equally irrelevant are the practices of the "world community," whose notions of justice are (thankfully) not always those of our people. "We must never forget that it is a Constitution for the United States of America that we are expounding. . . . [W]here there is not first a settled consensus among our own people, the views of other nations, however enlightened the Justices of this Court may think them to be, cannot be imposed upon Americans through the Constitution." *Thompson* (SCALIA, J., dissenting).

Beyond the empty talk of a "national consensus," the Court gives us a brief glimpse of what really underlies today's decision: pretension to a power confined *neither* by the moral sentiments originally enshrined in the Eighth Amendment (its original meaning) *nor even* by the current moral sentiments of the American people. " '[T]he Constitution,' " the Court says, "contemplates that in the end *our own judgment* will be brought to bear on the question of the acceptability of the death penalty under the Eighth Amendment.' " The arrogance of this assumption of power takes one's breath away. And it explains, of course, why the Court can be so cavalier about the evidence of consensus. It is just a game, after all. "[I]n the end," it is the *feelings* and *intuition* of a majority of the Justices that count—"the perceptions of decency, or of penology, or of mercy, entertained . . . by a majority of the small and unrepresentative segment of our society that sits on this Court." *Thompson* (SCALIA, J., dissenting). . . .

. . . [T]he Court gives two reasons why the death penalty is an excessive punishment for all mentally retarded offenders. First, the "diminished capacities" of the mentally retarded raise a "serious question" whether their execution contributes to the "social purposes" of the death penalty, viz., retribution and deterrence. (The Court conveniently ignores a third "social purpose" of the death penalty—"incapacitation of dangerous criminals and the consequent prevention of crimes that they may otherwise commit in the future," *Gregg v. Georgia* (1976) (joint opinion of STEWART, POWELL, and STEVENS, JJ.). But never mind; its discussion of even the other two does not bear analysis.) Retribution is not advanced, the argument goes, because the mentally retarded are *no more culpable* than the average murderer, whom we have already held lacks sufficient culpability to warrant the death penalty, see *Godfrey v. Georgia* (1980). Who says so? Is there an established correlation between mental acuity and the ability to conform one's conduct to the law in such a rudimentary matter as murder? Are the mentally retarded really more disposed (and hence more likely) to commit willfully cruel and serious crime than others? In my experience, the opposite is true: being childlike generally suggests innocence rather than brutality. . . .

. . . The fact that juries continue to sentence mentally retarded offenders to death for extreme crimes shows that society's moral outrage sometimes demands execution of retarded offenders. By what principle of law, science, or logic can the Court pronounce that this is wrong? There is none. Once the Court admits (as it does) that mental retardation does not render the offender morally *blameless*, there is no basis for saying that the death penalty is *never* appropriate retribution, no matter *how* heinous the crime. As long as a mentally retarded offender knows "the difference between right and wrong," only the sentencer can assess whether his retardation reduces his culpability enough to exempt him from the death penalty for the particular murder in question.

As for the other social purpose of the death penalty that the Court discusses, deterrence: That is not advanced, the Court tells us, because the mentally retarded are "less likely" than their non-retarded counterparts to "process the information of the possibility of execution as a penalty and . . . control their conduct based upon that information." . . . [T]he Court does not say that *all* mentally retarded individuals cannot "process the information of the possibility of execution as a penalty and . . . control their conduct based upon that information"; it merely asserts that they are "less likely" to be able to do so. But surely the deterrent effect of a penalty is adequately vindicated if it successfully deters many, but not all, of the target class. Virginia's death penalty, for example, does not fail of its deterrent effect simply because *some* criminals are unaware that Virginia *has* the death penalty . . . I am not sure that a murderer is somehow less blameworthy if (though he knew his act was wrong) he did not fully appreciate that he could die for it; but if so, we should treat a mentally retarded murderer the way we treat an offender who may be "less likely" to respond to the death penalty because he was abused as a child. We do not hold him immune from capital punishment, but require his background to be considered by the sentencer as a mitigating factor. *Eddings v. Oklahoma* (1982).

The Court throws one last factor into its grab bag of reasons why execution of the retarded is "excessive" in all cases: Mentally retarded offenders "face a special risk of wrongful execution" because they are less able "to make a persuasive showing of mitigation," "to give meaningful assistance to their counsel," and to be effective witnesses. "Special risk" is pretty flabby language (even flabbier than "less likely")—and I suppose a similar "special risk" could be said to exist for just plain stupid people, inarticulate people, even ugly people. If this unsupported claim has any substance to it (which I doubt) it might support a due process claim in all criminal prosecutions of the mentally retarded; but it is hard to see how it has anything to do with an Eighth Amendment claim that execution of the mentally retarded is cruel and unusual. . . .

I respectfully dissent.

Although the justices may agree that capital punishment is not inherently unconstitutional, they evince considerable conflict over specific applications of the death penalty relative to the constitutional ban against cruel and unusual punishments. As the opinions in *Atkins* demonstrate, the justices are often at loggerheads over the meaning of cruel and unusual punishment and how the nation's evolving standards of decency should be identified. To what should the justices look to determine changing societal standards? The actions of state legislatures? Jury verdicts? Public opinion polls? Is world opinion a relevant consideration? And how should we decide if the interests of retribution, deterrence, and incapacitation are advanced through the application of the death penalty? Undoubtedly the justices, and the nation as a whole, are a long way from arriving at final answers to these questions.

POST-TRIAL STAGES

Individuals convicted of crimes can appeal their convictions in the hope that appellate judges will find errors in the trial court's handling of the case. Under the American concept of due process, someone convicted of a criminal offense is entitled to at least one appeal. A new trial might be granted if new evidence is discovered that brings into serious question the guilt of the defendant, although such instances are rare.

An additional guarantee governing the post-trial stage is the Fifth Amendment's ban against double jeopardy: "nor shall any person be subject for the same offence to be twice put in jeopardy of life or limb." The clause reflected the framers' belief that it is essentially unfair for any person to be tried twice for the same criminal charge. The government should have one attempt, and one attempt only, to convince a jury that the accused is guilty. A person who already has been acquitted of an offense by a court of law cannot be tried a second time for that same offense. Also, the government may not prosecute a convicted person a second time in the hope of obtaining a more severe sentence. Once a trial on a given criminal charge is completed, the defendant is protected against any subsequent trial on that charge that might lead to more adverse consequences.

A great deal of the confusion surrounding the double jeopardy clause stems from the words *same offence.* If a man sets fire to an apartment building, killing five residents, has he committed one homicide or five? If a man spends an evening robbing a series of liquor stores, has he committed a single offense or several? What does the double jeopardy clause mean when it prohibits trying a person more than once for the same offense? We find a partial answer in *Ashe v. Swenson* (1970). A group of individuals playing poker one night were robbed by three or four masked men. Several months later Bob Ashe was charged with the crime. The prosecutor first placed him on trial for robbing one of the card players. The jury found him not guilty because of insufficient evidence. Then the prosecutor charged him with robbing a second poker player. Ashe objected, claiming the second trial would violate the double jeopardy clause. On appeal the Supreme Court agreed. The robbing of the poker party was a single act, and once acquitted of robbing the first poker player, Ashe could not be tried for robbing another member of the group that same evening. In Justice Stewart's words, the Fifth Amendment "surely protects a man who has been acquitted from having to 'run the gauntlet' a second time."

The double jeopardy clause does not, however, bar separate governments from prosecuting an individual for the same crime. In *Heath v. Alabama* (1985) the Court applied this dual sovereignty doctrine to Larry Gene Heath, who had arranged to have his wife, who was nine months pregnant, kidnapped and killed. The hired killers took Rebecca Heath from her home in Alabama and murdered her in Georgia. Heath was arrested in Georgia and pleaded guilty to murder charges as part of a plea bargain arrangement to avoid the death penalty. Alabama authorities, independently investigating the crime, then indicted Heath for kidnapping and murder. Heath objected on double jeopardy grounds, but the Supreme Court held that the Fifth Amendment did not prohibit prosecution by Alabama. An act that offends the criminal laws of two jurisdictions may be punished by both.

READINGS

Abramson, Jeffrey. *We, the Jury: The Jury System and the Ideal of Democracy.* New York: Basic Books, 1994.

Adler, Stephen J. *The Jury: Trial and Error in the American Courtroom.* New York: Times Books, 1994.

Baldus, David C., George G. Woodworth, and Charles A. Pulaski Jr. *Equal Justice and the Death Penalty.* Boston: Northeastern University Press, 1990.

Banner, Stuart. *The Death Penalty: An American History.* Cambridge: Harvard University Press, 2002.

Dayan, Colin. *The Story of Cruel and Unusual.* Cambridge: MIT Press, 2007.

Eisenstein, James, and Herbert Jacob. *Felony Justice.* Boston: Little, Brown, 1977.

Epstein, Lee, and Joseph F. Kobylka. *The Supreme Court and Legal Change.* Chapel Hill: University of North Carolina Press, 1992.

Gerber, Rudolph J. *Cruel and Unusual: Our Criminal Justice System.* Westport: Praeger: 1999.

Haines, Herbert H. *Against Capital Punishment: The Anti-Death Penalty Movement in America, 1972–1994.* New York: Oxford University Press, 1996.

Hastie, Reid, Steven D. Penrod, and Nancy Pennington. *Inside the Jury.* Cambridge: Harvard University Press, 1983.

Hood, Roger G. *Death Penalty: A Worldwide Perspective.* New York: Oxford University Press, 2002.

Jonakait, Randolph N. *The American Jury System.* New Haven: Yale University Press, 2003.

Kalven, Harry, Jr., and Hans Zeisel. *The American Jury.* Boston: Little, Brown, 1966.

Lewis, Anthony. *Gideon's Trumpet.* New York: Vintage Books, 1964.

Meltsner, Michael. *Cruel and Unusual: The Supreme Court and Capital Punishment.* New York: Random House, 1973.

Russell, Gregory D. *The Death Penalty and Racial Bias: Overturning Supreme Court Assumptions.* Westport, Conn.: Greenwood Press, 1994.

Sarat, Austin. *When the State Kills: Capital Punishment and the American Condition.* Princeton: Princeton University Press, 2001.

Sigler, Jay A. *Double Jeopardy: The Development of Legal and Social Policy.* Ithaca, N.Y.: Cornell University Press, 1969.

Thaler, Paul. *The Watchful Eye: American Justice in the Age of the Television Trial.* Westport, Conn.: Greenwood Press, 1994.

Thomas, George C. *Double Jeopardy: The History, the Law.* New York: Oxford University Press, 2000.

Walker, Thomas G. *Eligible for Execution: The Story of the Daryl Atkins Case.* Washington, D.C.: CQ Press, 2009.

White, Welsh. *Litigating in the Shadow of Death: Defense Attorneys in Capital Cases.* Ann Arbor: University of Michigan Press, 2006.

In marked contrast to the colonial period, when most Americans came from British roots, Americans today are from many different backgrounds. Immigration has diversified the population, and this trend is expected to continue. Americans are a people of wide-ranging religions, races, ethnic backgrounds, and levels of wealth. Given this diversity, the slogan *e pluribus unum*, or "one from many," appears to be more of a challenge than a statement of fact. In spite of the differences, the nation has pledged itself to fairness and equality. All Americans are to be free from unconstitutional discrimination, to have equal opportunity, and to participate fully in the political process.

Even so, many times people feel they have been mistreated by their government, not because of what they have done but because of who they are. They claim that discrimination has occurred because of race, creed, national origin, sex, sexual orientation, economic status, or some other characteristic that government should not use as a basis for policy. When disputes over such charges arise, the court system provides a venue for their resolution. In this part, we discuss the civil rights of Americans and how the Supreme Court has interpreted them. By civil rights we mean those legal provisions emanating from the concept of equality. Unlike civil liberties issues, which focus on personal freedoms protected by the Bill of Rights, civil rights issues involve the status of persons with shared characteristics who historically have been disadvantaged in some way. Civil rights laws attempt to guarantee full and equal citizenship for such persons and

to protect them from arbitrary and capricious treatment. Chapter 19 examines discrimination, and chapter 20 explores the rights of political participation. Before we confront those subjects, however, a review of some basic concepts of history and law might be useful.

Today we are used to hearing not only about charges of discrimination, but also about Supreme Court rulings on the proper meaning of the Constitution governing such issues. These phenomena are comparatively recent. Although "equality" in the United States was relatively advanced for that period, colonial Americans discriminated in a number of ways that people today consider abhorrent. The most significant breach of fundamental equality was the institution of slavery. In spite of the Declaration of Independence, which proclaimed all men were created equal, the enslavement of Africans brought to North America against their will was politically accepted, although not universally supported. The Constitution recognized this form of inequality, stipulating in Article I that a slave would be counted as three-fifths of a person for representation purposes; it also gave slavery a degree of protection by prohibiting any federal restrictions on the importation of slaves until 1808. Other forms of discrimination were also common. Voting qualifications, for example, were quite restrictive: Only men could vote, and in some states only men who owned property.

Guarantees of equality did not officially become part of the Constitution until after the Civil War. When the Radical Republicans took control of the legislative branch, three constitutional amendments, generally referred to as the Civil War Amendments, were proposed and ratified. They incorporated into the Constitution what had been won on the battlefield and dramatically changed the concept of civil rights in the United States. The Thirteenth Amendment, ratified in 1865, unambiguously ended the institution of slavery. Although some disputes have arisen about the involuntary servitude provision (in relation, for example, to the military draft), the slavery issue, over which the nation had been divided since the Constitutional Convention, was finally put to rest. The other two amendments, the Fourteenth and Fifteenth, have generated a great deal of litigation and many Supreme Court cases, and we discuss them in turn.

THE FOURTEENTH AMENDMENT

The Fourteenth Amendment, ratified in 1868, is unlike the other two because of its length and complexity. The first section is the most significant. It states that U.S. citizenship is superior to state citizenship, constitutionally reinforcing the Civil War outcome of national superiority over states' rights. This idea was a dramatic change from the pre–Civil War concept that national citizenship was dependent upon state citizenship. The first section also includes the due process and privileges and immunities clauses we discussed in earlier chapters, as well as the equal protection clause. Because this last clause forms the basis of constitutional protections against discrimination, we describe it in some detail. The remaining parts of the Fourteenth Amendment require the former slaves to be fully counted for representational purposes, impose (with a few exceptions) universal adult male suffrage, restrict the civil rights of certain participants in the rebellion, and guarantee the public debt resulting from the war.

An analysis of the equal protection clause helps us to understand what it covers and what its limitations are. It says: "[N]or shall any State . . . deny to any person within its jurisdiction the equal protection of the laws."

The first significant element of the clause is the word *state*. The members of Congress who drafted the Fourteenth Amendment were concerned primarily with the danger of the states (especially those in the South) imposing discriminatory laws. With the Radical Republicans, who were deeply committed to an abolition ideol-

ogy, in control of Congress, the legislators had little fear that the federal government would impose discriminatory policies. Consequently, the prohibitions of the clause apply only to the states and their political subdivisions, such as counties and cities.

Second, the amendment protects *all* persons within a state's jurisdiction, not just former slaves. In an early dispute over the amendment, the Supreme Court acknowledged its broad applicability. *Yick Wo v. Hopkins* (1886) concerned the discriminatory enforcement of fire safety regulations in San Francisco. The Court held that the equal protection clause applies to persons other than black Americans, even to noncitizens such as Yick Wo. As Justice Stanley Matthews wrote in his opinion for the Court, the provisions of the Fourteenth Amendment "are universal in their application, to all persons within the territorial jurisdiction, without regard to any differences of race, of color, or of nationality."

Finally, the clause outlaws a denial of equal protection of the laws; in other words, it prohibits discrimination. Any person within a state's jurisdiction is constitutionally entitled to be treated equitably, to be free from arbitrary and unreasonable treatment at the hands of the state government.

The wording of the equal protection clause means that before an individual can legitimately assert a claim of its violation, two important elements must be demonstrated. First, the aggrieved party must prove some form of unequal treatment or discrimination. Second, there must be state action; that is, the discrimination must have been initiated or supported by the state or its local governments. These two requirements have undergone substantial interpretation by the justices of the Supreme Court, and we need to understand what is included in each requirement.

Discrimination

Discrimination simply means to distinguish between people or things. It occurs in many forms, not all of which are prohibited by the Constitution. For example, in administering an admissions program, a state university must discriminate among its applicants. It admits some, rejects others. Decisions usually are based on an applicant's high school grades, standardized test scores, and letters of recommendation. The university admits those who, based on valid predictors of performance, have the best chance to succeed. The applicants who are rejected usually accept the decision because the university's admissions criteria appear reasonable. But the reaction would be quite different if an applicant received a letter from a state college that said, "In spite of your demonstrated potential for college studies, we cannot admit you because of our policy not to accept students of your religion." In this case, the rejected applicant would rightly feel victimized by unreasonable discrimination.

What rule of law distinguishes acceptable discrimination from that which violates the Constitution? The Supreme Court answered this question by declaring that the equal protection clause goes no further than prohibiting "invidious discrimination."[1] By invidious discrimination, the Court means discrimination that is arbitrary and capricious, unequal treatment that has no rational basis. Reasonable discrimination, in contrast, is not unconstitutional. When the state treats two individuals differently, we need to ask upon what criteria the state is distinguishing them. If two surgeons perform heart operations on patients and one is thrown in jail but the other is not, we might feel that the imprisoned person has not been treated fairly. Our opinion would change, however, if we learned that the jailed person had never been to medical school and was not licensed. Here the state would be discriminating on the basis of legitimate, reasonable criteria. The equal protection clause demands that similarly situated persons be treated equally. The two surgeons, because of their vastly different qualifications, are not similarly situated, and consequently the Constitution does not require that they be treated the same.

Almost every government action involves some form of discrimination. Most are perfectly legitimate, although those affected might not agree. For example, when a state government passes an income tax law that imposes a higher rate on the wealthy than it does on the poor, the rich may feel they are targets of unconstitutional discrimination. When individuals believe they have been denied

equal protection at the hands of the state, the courts must decide if the government's discrimination runs afoul of the Fourteenth Amendment. For taxes, the courts have ruled that progressive rate structures are not invidious, but reasonable.

To assist the judiciary in deciding such disputes, the Supreme Court has developed three basic tests of the equal protection clause. Which test is applied in any given case is determined by the alleged discrimination and the government interests at stake.

The traditional test used to decide discrimination cases is the *rational basis* test. When using this approach to the Constitution, the justices ask: Is the challenged discrimination rational? Or is it arbitrary and capricious? If a state passes a law that says a person must be at least eighteen years old to enter a legally binding contract, it is imposing age-based discrimination. Individuals under eighteen are not granted the right to consummate legal agreements; those over eighteen are. If a dispute over the validity of this law were brought to court, the judge would have to decide whether the state had acted reasonably to achieve a legitimate government objective.[2] Using the rational basis test, the Court generally defers to the state and presumes the validity of the government's action. The burden of proof rests with the party challenging the law to establish that the statute is irrational. Unless the Court has determined otherwise, discrimination claims proceed according to the rules of the rational basis test.

The second test is the *suspect class,* or *strict scrutiny,* test. This test is used when the state discriminates on the basis of a criterion that the Supreme Court has declared to be inherently suspect or when there is a claim that a fundamental right has been violated. A suspect classification is based on characteristics, such as race, assumed to be irrational. Laws that discriminate on racial grounds are given strict scrutiny by the courts. The reason for moving racial discrimination from the rational basis test to the suspect class test is that the Court has concluded that racial criteria are inherently arbitrary, that compelling state interests are rarely served by treating people differently according to race. For a law to be valid under

1. *Williamson v. Lee Optical* (1955).

2. *McGowan v. Maryland* (1961).

TABLE VII-1 Equal Protection Tests

Test	Examples of Applicability	Validity Standard
Rational basis test	Age discrimination	The law must be a *reasonable* measure designed to achieve a *legitimate* government purpose.
Intermediate ("heightened") scrutiny test	Sex discrimination	The law must be *substantially related* to the achievment of an *important* objective.
Suspect class (strict scrutiny) test	Racial discrimination; cases involving fundamental rights (e.g., voting)	The law must be the *least restrictive* means available to achieve a *compelling* state interest.

strict scrutiny, it must be found to advance a compelling state interest by the least restrictive means available. When the suspect class test is used, the Court presumes that the state action is unconstitutional, and the burden of proof is on the government to demonstrate that the law is constitutional.

Given the rules associated with these two tests, it should be obvious that it is much easier to establish that a violation of the Constitution has occurred if the suspect class test is used. Therefore, many cases before the Court have been filed by attorneys representing groups seeking that classification. The Court has ruled that suspect class status should be accorded only to those groups that constitute discrete and insular minorities that have experienced a history of unequal treatment and a lack of political power.[3] Applying such criteria is difficult and has given rise to sharp divisions of opinion among the justices.

Legal battles over what rules should apply to sex discrimination cases were particularly difficult for the Court to resolve.[4] A majority could not agree to elevate sex to suspect class status, but the rational basis test was also deemed inappropriate for dealing with sex discrimination. This conflict gave rise to a third test of the equal protection clause, the *intermediate (or heightened) scrutiny* test. This test holds that to be valid the unequal treatment must serve important government objectives and must be substantially related to the achievement of those objec-

tives.[5] As such, this test falls squarely between the rational basis test and the suspect class test *(see Table VII-1)*.

This three-tiered approach can be confusing, and the Supreme Court has been neither clear nor consistent in applying the principles. Justice Thurgood Marshall in *Dunn v. Blumstein* (1972) acknowledged that the tests do not have the "precision of mathematical formulas." Justice Byron White hinted that in reality the Court may be using a spectrum of tests rather than three separate tests. Frustration over the status of the equal protection clause tests prompted Justice John Paul Stevens to claim in his concurring opinion in *Cleburne v. Cleburne Living Center* (1985) that a continuum of standards was being used. Not persuaded of the wisdom of the Court's approach, Stevens has argued that a single test should be adopted for all equal protection claims. In spite of these criticisms, the Court has stuck to the three-tiered approach, which reflects the belief that the more historically disadvantaged and politically powerless a class of people has been, the greater justification government must provide for any state action that discriminates against the members of that class.

State Action

As noted, the equal protection clause specifically prohibits discrimination by any state. The Supreme Court has interpreted the concept to include a wide array of state actions—statutes, their enforcement and administration, and the actions of state officials. We have already

---

3. See *United States v. Carolene Products* (1938); *San Antonio Independent School District v. Rodriguez* (1973).

4. See, for example, *Frontiero v. Richardson* (1973).

5. *Craig v. Boren* (1976).

mentioned *Yick Wo v. Hopkins,* in which the Court struck down a fire safety regulation that was racially neutral as written but enforced in a discriminatory manner against Chinese laundry operators. State action includes the policies of political subdivisions such as towns, cities, counties, and special purpose agencies. The states are prohibited from engaging in invidious discrimination either directly or indirectly. A city, for example, may not run its municipal swimming pools in a racially segregated manner, nor may it donate the pools to a private organization that will restrict pool use to a particular racial group. But no matter what form the discrimination takes, some element of state action supporting it must be shown before a violation of the equal protection clause occurs.

This requirement means that discrimination by purely private individuals or organizations is not prohibited by the equal protection clause. A white apartment house owner who refuses to rent to a black family is not in violation of the Constitution; neither are a restaurant manager who will not serve Hispanics, a private club that will not admit women, nor an employer who will not hire applicants over forty years of age. In each of these cases there is ample evidence of irrational discrimination, but no state action. The discrimination is conducted by private individuals or organizations. These forms of discrimination may well violate any number of state or federal statutes, but they do not offend the equal protection clause of the Fourteenth Amendment.

Moreover, because it is restricted to the states, the equal protection clause does not prohibit the federal government from engaging in discrimination. The Supreme Court, therefore, faced a difficult situation in 1954 in the school desegregation cases. The best-known is *Brown v. Board of Education of Topeka, Kansas,* but *Brown* was only one of several cases involving the same issue. In **Bolling v. Sharpe** the Court faced the thorny problem of racial segregation in the Washington, D.C., public schools. The District of Columbia is not a state. In the 1950s Congress was the ultimate authority over Washington, as it is today. The equal protection clause was not applicable there. Given the political situation at the time, the Court had to find a way to declare *all* segregated public schools unconstitutional.

The justices found a solution in the due process clause of the Fifth Amendment, which states, "No person shall . . . be deprived of life, liberty, or property, without due process of law." This guarantee of essential fairness applies to the federal government and was used by the justices in *Bolling* as a bar to racial discrimination. Chief Justice Earl Warren explained for a unanimous Court:

The Fifth Amendment, which is applicable in the District of Columbia, does not contain an equal protection clause as does the Fourteenth Amendment which applies only to the states. But the concepts of equal protection and due process, both stemming from our American ideal of fairness, are not mutually exclusive. The "equal protection of the laws" is a more explicit safeguard of prohibited unfairness than "due process of law," and, therefore, we do not imply that the two are always interchangeable phrases. But, as this Court has recognized, discrimination may be so unjustifiable as to be violative of due process.

Although Warren cautioned that the due process clause and the equal protection clause could not be used interchangeably, the Court has consistently ruled that both provisions stand for the same general principles. In most areas of discrimination law (but not all), the justices have applied the same standards to both state and federal governments by using these two constitutional provisions. As a rule, any discriminatory action by a state found to be in violation of the equal protection clause would also be a violation of the Fifth Amendment if engaged in by the federal government. We should, however, understand which provision of the Constitution is offended when invidious discrimination is practiced by either the state governments or the federal government. If the U.S. National Park Service were to require racially segregated campgrounds at Yellowstone, it would violate the due process clause of the Fifth Amendment; if a state imposed the same restriction at a state park, it would violate the equal protection clause of the Fourteenth Amendment.

Congressional Enforcement of the Fourteenth Amendment

The civil rights of Americans are defined and protected by more than just the Constitution. Over the years Congress has passed laws designed to enforce and extend

BOX VII-1   A SAMPLE OF MAJOR CIVIL RIGHTS ACTS

SINCE THE END of the Civil War, Congress has enacted scores of civil rights statutes. In what follows we describe a few of the more prominent acts.

CIVIL RIGHTS ACTS OF 1866, 1870, 1871, AND 1875

Congress passed these laws after the Civil War to provide blacks with equal political and legal rights, but later repealed many of them, and the Supreme Court struck down others. For example, in the *Civil Rights Cases* (1883), the Court invalidated the "public accommodation" provision of the 1875 act, which guaranteed "That citizens of every race and color," regardless of whether they were slaves, "be entitled to the full and equal enjoyment of the accommodations, advantages, facilities, and privileges of inns, public conveyances on land or water, theaters, and other places of public amusement." *(See page 635 for a discussion of the 1883 decision.)*

Today, a few major provisions remain from the acts of 1866 and 1871. One makes it a federal crime for any person acting under the authority of a state law to deprive another of any rights protected by the Constitution or by laws of the United States. Another authorizes suits for civil damages against state or local officials by persons whose rights are abridged. Others permit actions against persons who conspire to deprive people of their rights.

CIVIL RIGHTS ACTS OF 1957 AND 1960

These acts were the first major civil rights laws passed since the 1875 act, and they were largely (but not exclusively) designed to secure voting rights for blacks. Many viewed them as weak and, ultimately, ineffective. The 1957 legislation did, however, create the Civil Rights Commission to investigate civil rights violations and make policy recommendations. The 1957 act also established the Civil Rights Division in the Department of Justice and empowered the attorney general to bring suit against any deprivation of voting rights.

EQUAL PAY ACT OF 1963

Passed as an amendment to the Fair Labor Standards Act, this law prohibits discrimination in wages based on sex. It mandates that men and women receive the same pay "for equal work on jobs, the performance of which requires equal skill, effort, and responsibility, and which are performed under similar working conditions." It excluded wages paid pursuant to seniority or merit systems, among other exceptions.

CIVIL RIGHTS ACTS OF 1964 AND 1968

Considered by some commentators to be among the most important civil rights law ever enacted by Congress, the 1964 law was designed to eradicate discrimination in many areas of American social, economic, and political life. Major provisions include Title I (on voting rights), which outlaws discrimination in voter registration and outlines procedures for expedited review of voting rights litigation. Title II (on public accommodations) guarantees that "all persons shall be entitled to the full and equal enjoyment of the goods, services, facilities, and privileges, advantages, and accommodations of any place of public accommodation, including hotels, restaurants, and theaters." Titles III and IV cover desegregation of public facilities and education, and empower the attor-

constitutional guarantees *(see Box VII-1)*. These laws expand prohibitions against discriminatory behavior, give the federal executive branch authority to enforce civil rights protections, and enlarge the opportunities for aggrieved parties to seek redress in the courts. The rules of evidence and procedure in some of these laws make it easier for litigants to prevail by proving a violation of a civil rights statute rather than a constitutional violation.

The authority for Congress to pass such laws can be found in several constitutional provisions. Each Civil War amendment contains a section granting Congress the power to enforce the amendment with appropriate legislation. Consequently, these amendments have had considerable impact not only because of their basic substantive content, but also because they gave Congress new legislative power. Immediately following the Civil War, Congress used this authority to pass laws intended to give teeth to the new amendments. The Civil Rights Act of 1866, passed over the veto of President Andrew Johnson, guaranteed blacks the right to purchase, lease, ney general to initiate desegregation suits. Finally, Title VII guarantees equal opportunity in the employment context by making it illegal, for example, for employers with fifteen or more employees "to fail or refuse to hire or to discharge any individual, or otherwise to discriminate against any individual with respect to his compensation, terms, conditions, or privileges of employment, because of such individual's race, color, religion, sex, or national origin."

As comprehensive as it was, the Civil Rights Act of 1964 did not cover discrimination in housing. Four years later, Congress enacted the Civil Rights Act of 1968, which prohibits discrimination over the sale, rental, advertising, and financing of housing based on race, religion, national origin, (and as later amended) sex, handicapped status, and families with children. Under the law, it is unlawful to refuse to sell a house to a buyer on any of these grounds (race, religion, and so on).

VOTING RIGHTS ACT OF 1965

Another major law, the Voting Rights Act of 1965 (and subsequent renewals) sought to eradicate racial discrimination in voting. For more on this law, see *South Carolina v. Katzenbach (pages 690–693)*, a 1966 case in which the Supreme Court upheld its constitutionality.

AGE DISCRIMINATION IN EMPLOYMENT OF 1967

This act bans employment discrimination based on age. It covers individuals who are forty and older and applies to employers with twenty or more employees.

TITLE IX OF THE EDUCATION AMENDMENTS OF 1972

This provision bars sex discrimination in federally funded education programs. It covers a range of programs, but is probably best known for prohibiting sex discrimination in college sports.

AMERICANS WITH DISABILITIES ACT OF 1990

Signed into law by President George H. W. Bush, this law (often called the ADA) sought to eliminate discrimination against the disabled in the spheres of employment and public services and accommodations. It defines "disability" as "a physical or mental impairment that substantially limits one or more of the major life activities."

CIVIL RIGHTS OF 1991

Congress enacted this law primarily to override several decisions issued by the Supreme Court during its 1988 term—all of which made it more difficult for litigants to challenge discriminatory employment practices in the employment context. Legislators thought the Court's decisions had "weakened the scope and effectiveness of Federal civil rights protections," and set out to strengthen them.

SOURCE: Jody Feder, *Federal Civil Rights Statutes: A Primer*, CRS Report for Congress, September 9, 2005; William N. Eskridge Jr., Philip P. Frickey, and Elizabeth Garrett, *Cases and Materials on Legislation* (St. Paul: West, 2001).

and use real property. The Supreme Court upheld the law, ruling that the Thirteenth Amendment's enforcement section gave Congress the power not only to outlaw slavery but also to legislate against the "badges and incidents of slavery."[6] Much of the federal regulation on fair housing is based on this authority.

Congress learned by trial and error to ground legislation in the correct Civil War amendment. In 1883 the

6. *Jones v. Alfred Mayer, Inc.* (1968).

Supreme Court handed down its decisions in the *Civil Rights Cases*, which involved challenges to the Civil Rights Act of 1875, a statute based on the Fourteenth Amendment that made discrimination in public accommodations unlawful. Because the law covered privately owned businesses, the owners of hotels, entertainment facilities, and transportation companies claimed that Congress had exceeded the authority granted to it by the amendment. The Court, with only one justice dissenting, struck down the statute, holding that any legislation based on the

Fourteenth Amendment could regulate only discrimination promoted by state action. Discrimination by private individuals was not covered by the amendment and, therefore, Congress could not prohibit it through an enforcement statute.

Congress eventually overcame the private discrimination problem by finding a different constitutional grant of power upon which to base the Civil Rights Act of 1964. The most comprehensive civil rights statute ever enacted, the law regulated discrimination in employment, education, and public accommodations. It placed restrictions on federal appropriations and programs to ensure that nondiscrimination principles were followed in any activity supported by the U.S. government. The act outlawed discrimination based not only on race but also on factors such as sex, national origin, and religion. Much of what was regulated by the statute was private behavior, including prohibitions of discrimination by restaurants, hotels, and other privately run public accommodations. Instead of the Fourteenth Amendment, Congress used the commerce clause of Article I. That clause gives the national legislature the power to regulate interstate commerce, and the provisions of the 1964 Civil Rights Act apply to all activities in interstate commerce. The Supreme Court upheld the constitutionality of the law and gave it increased effectiveness by broadly defining what is considered to be within interstate commerce.[7]

Since then, Congress has expanded the scope of federal regulation over civil rights by passing amendments to the 1964 act and by enacting additional legislation *(see Box vii-1)*. For example, the Civil Rights Act of 1968 made unlawful discrimination in the sale, rental, or financing of housing, and the Americans with Disabilities Act of 1990 extended federal protections to the disabled in employment, public services, and access to public places. As a result of such legislative actions, a large portion of federal civil rights law is based on congressional statutes rather than constitutional provisions.

Federal civil rights laws provide great opportunities for those who wish to challenge discriminatory behavior. Not only do these statutes regulate private-sector dis-

crimination, but also they frequently impose thresholds of proof that are easier to satisfy than those the Supreme Court requires for constitutional challenges. Under the civil rights laws a worker claiming employment discrimination based on race may not have to establish discriminatory intent (a requirement for a violation of the Constitution) but may instead submit statistical evidence that the employer treats racial groups differently. Because of the growth of civil rights laws, the federal courts today hear many more cases involving alleged violations of civil rights statutes than those claiming a violation of the Constitution.

THE FIFTEENTH AMENDMENT

The Fifteenth Amendment prohibits the states from denying the right to vote on the basis of race, color, or previous condition of servitude. Unlike the Thirteenth Amendment, which was almost self-executing, the policy expressed so clearly in the Fifteenth Amendment in 1870 did not become a reality until almost a century later. Stubborn resistance by the southern states denied African American citizens full participatory rights.

The long delay in implementing the principles of the Fifteenth Amendment has several explanations. Although the nation's leaders seemed unshakably committed to equality right after the Civil War, they soon turned their attention to other matters. Issues ranging from political corruption to the nation's industrialization moved to the top of the political agenda. At the same time, the white power structure of the prewar South began to reassert itself. Although forced to accept the Civil War amendments as a condition of rejoining the Union, the southern states survived Reconstruction and, once freed from the direct supervision of their victors, began to reinstitute discriminatory laws. Slavery was never again seriously considered, but, in its place, racial segregation became the official policy. For years the federal legislative and executive branches showed little interest in pursuing civil rights issues. And, even though the Supreme Court issued several important rulings, the nation did not turn its attention to freedom from discrimination and full participatory rights for all until the civil rights movement gained momentum in the 1960s.

---

7. In *Heart of Atlanta Motel v. United States* (1964).

The Fifteenth Amendment extended significant powers to the federal government to preserve fairness and equality in the political process. So too have the Nineteenth, Twenty-fourth, and Twenty-sixth Amendments, which, respectively, expanded the electorate by prohibiting the states to deny voting rights based on sex or the ability to pay a tax and by lowering the voting age to eighteen years. From the enforcement provisions of these four voting rights amendments, Congress has passed a number of statutes ensuring the integrity of the election process. The most important of these is the Voting Rights Act of 1965, which has been strengthened by amendment over the years. This statute provided the machinery for federal enforcement of voting rights and prosecution for their violations. Its provisions have been the catalyst for significant growth in voter registration rates among segments of the population where political participation historically had been depressed.

Because this volume deals with constitutional law, our discussion of the various forms of discrimination focuses on the civil rights guarantees provided in the three Civil War amendment as well as the subsequent voting rights amendments. As you read the cases and narrative to follow, however, keep in mind that in many areas Congress has passed statutes that extend those constitutional provisions to create various legal rights that go well beyond protections included in the Constitution itself.

CHAPTER 19

DISCRIMINATION

In a 1987 address, delivered amid the planning for the bicentennial celebration of the Constitution, Justice Thurgood Marshall said that the document was "defective from the start," that its first words—"We the People"—left out the majority of Americans because the phrase did not include women and blacks. He further alleged:

These omissions were intentional. . . . The record of the Framers' debates on the slave question is especially clear: The Southern states acceded to the demands of the New England states for giving Congress broad power to regulate commerce in exchange for the right to continue the slave trade. The economic interests of the regions coalesced.

One does not have to agree with Marshall to believe that discrimination has been a difficult and persistent problem for the United States since its beginnings. Although the founders were considered the vanguard of enlightened politics in that era, different treatment based on race, economic status, religious affiliation, and sex was the rule in the colonies. Since those early years of nationhood, issues of discrimination have been prominent on the country's political agenda. During the 1800s, slavery eroded national unity. Although officially settled by the Civil War and the constitutional amendments that followed, racial inequity did not disappear. Rather, it continued through the Jim Crow era and the organized civil rights struggle, and it persists today.

In recent years the national spotlight has been turned on to claims of unfair treatment based on sex, sexual orientation, economic status, and physical ability. Attempts to force government to address these claims have given rise to counterclaims by those who fear that a government overly sensitive to the needs of minorities will deprive the majority of its rights. With each new argument, the issues become more complex. In this chapter we explore the kinds of discrimination that have occurred (and continue to occur) in American society and how the Supreme Court has responded. We also consider contemporary remedies that have been offered to blunt the effects of past discrimination.

RACIAL DISCRIMINATION

The institution of slavery is a blight on the record of a nation that otherwise has led the way in protecting individual rights. From 1619, when the first slaves were brought to Jamestown, to the ratification of the Civil War Amendments 250 years later, people of African ancestry were considered an inferior race; they could be bought, sold, and used as personal property. Although some states extended various civil and political rights to emancipated slaves and their descendants, the national Constitution did not recognize black Americans as full citizens. In *Scott v. Sandford* (1857), Chief Justice Roger Taney, delivering the opinion of the Court, described the prevailing view of blacks at the time the Constitution was drafted and ratified:

They had for more than a century before been regarded as beings of an inferior order, and altogether unfit to associate with the white race, either in social or political relations; and so far inferior, that they had no rights which the white man was bound to respect; and that the negro might justly and lawfully be reduced to slavery for his benefit. He was bought and sold, and treated as an ordinary article of merchandise and traffic, whenever a profit could be made by it. This opinion was at that time fixed and universal in the civilized portion of the white race.

The Court's decision in *Scott* interpreted the Constitution in a manner consistent with this view and helped set the stage for the Civil War. The ruling, which held that a black slave could not become a full member of the political community and be entitled to all of the constitutional privileges of citizens, undermined the legitimacy of the Court and forever damaged Taney's reputation. Union victories on the battlefield eventually reunited the country, and the Constitution was amended to end slavery and confer full national citizenship on black Americans.

Congress moved with dispatch to give force to the new Civil War amendments, but the Supreme Court did not act with the same level of zeal. Although the justices supported the claims of newly emancipated African Americans in some cases, they did not construe the new amendments broadly, nor did they enthusiastically support new legislation designed to enforce them. In the **Slaughterhouse Cases** (1873), for example, the Court interpreted the Fourteenth Amendment's privileges and immunities clause quite narrowly. A broader view might have provided expanded opportunities for minorities to challenge discriminatory state policies. In *United States v. Harris* and the **Civil Rights Cases**, both decided in 1883, the justices nullified major provisions of the Ku Klux Klan Act of 1871 and the Civil Rights Act of 1875 for attempting to prevent discriminatory actions by private institutions. It was clear that the battle for legal equality of the races was far from over.

At the end of the nineteenth century, the Supreme Court still had not answered what was perhaps the most important question arising from the Fourteenth Amendment: What is equal protection? As the vitality of the Reconstruction Acts and federal efforts to enforce them gradually waned, the political forces of the old order began to reassert control in the South. From the 1880s to the 1950s, the Jim Crow era, what progress that had been made to achieve racial equality not only came to a halt—it began to run in reverse. The South, where 90 percent of the African American population lived, began to enact laws that reimposed an inferior legal status on them and commanded a strict separation of the races. Northern liberals were of little help: With the battle against slavery won, they turned their attention to other issues.

Although the Constitution made it clear that slavery was dead and the right to vote could not be denied on the basis of race, the validity of many other racially based state actions remained unresolved. With more conservative political forces gaining power in Congress, it was left to the Court to give meaning to the constitutional phrase *equal protection of the laws.*

The most important case of this period was *Plessy v. Ferguson* (1896), in which the justices were forced to confront directly the meaning of equality under the Constitution. At odds were the equal protection clause of the Fourteenth Amendment and a host of segregation statutes by then in force in the southern and border states. While reading *Plessy,* note that the Court uses the reasonableness standard (rational basis test) to interpret the equal protection clause. Ironically, Justice Henry B. Brown, a Lincoln Republican, who had grown up in New England and supported the abolitionist movement, wrote the majority opinion upholding the separation standards of the South. Justice John Marshall Harlan, an aristocratic Kentuckian whose family had owned slaves, wrote the lone dissent. Harlan's dissent is considered a classic and one of the most prophetic ever registered.

Plessy v. Ferguson

163 U.S. 537 (1896)
http://laws.findlaw.com/US/163/537.html
Vote: 7 (Brown, Field, Fuller, Gray, Peckham, Shiras, White)
    1 (Harlan)
Opinion of the Court: Brown
Dissenting opinion: Harlan
Not participating: Brewer

Following the lead of Florida, Mississippi, and Texas, Louisiana passed a statute in 1890 ordering the separation of the races on all railroads. In response, a group of New Orleans residents of black and mixed-race heritage formed the Citizens Committee to Test the Constitution-

Attorney and equal rights activist Albion Tourgée, who argued Homer Plessy's case and lost in the Supreme Court. Justice Harlan's lone dissent said that the Constitution must be color-blind, a phrase suggested by Tourgée's brief.

ality of the Separate Car Law.[1] The railroads, which found compliance with the segregation law costly, supported the group's efforts. Attempts to have the judiciary invalidate the statute were partially successful when the Louisiana Supreme Court struck down the law as applied to passengers crossing state lines because it placed an unconstitutional burden on interstate commerce. This decision, however, left unanswered the question of segregated travel wholly within the state's borders.

The Citizens Committee's New York lawyer, Albion Tourgée, continued the legal attack. Part of Tourgée's strategy was to select an individual of mixed-race background to violate the segregation statute as it applied to intrastate travel. He chose Homer Adolph Plessy, who

had been active in civil rights efforts in New Orleans for some time. Plessy described himself as being "of seven-eighths Caucasian and one-eighth African" blood. Although he had the physical characteristics of a white person, he was classified a black under Louisiana law.

On June 7, 1892, Plessy bought a first-class rail ticket from New Orleans to Covington, Louisiana. He took a seat in a car reserved for white passengers. Tourgée and the committee had enlisted the cooperation of the railroad to have Plessy arrested for violating the statute. The conductor demanded that Plessy, under pain of ejection and imprisonment, move to a car for black passengers. When he refused, he was taken off the train and held in a New Orleans jail to await trial.

Tourgée moved to block the trial on the ground that the segregation law was in violation of the U.S. Constitution. Judge John Ferguson denied the motion, and appeal was taken to the Louisiana Supreme Court. The state high court, under the leadership of Chief Justice Francis Tillou Nicholls, who, as governor two years earlier, had signed the segregation statute into law, denied Plessy's petition, and the case moved to the U.S. Supreme Court.

MR. JUSTICE BROWN delivered the opinion of the Court.

This case turns upon the constitutionality of an act of the General Assembly of the State of Louisiana, passed in 1890, providing for separate railway carriages for the white and colored races. . . .

By the Fourteenth Amendment, all persons born or naturalized in the United States, and subject to the jurisdiction thereof, are made citizens of the United States and of the State wherein they reside; and the States are forbidden from making or enforcing any law which shall abridge the privileges or immunities of citizens of the United States, or shall deprive any person of life, liberty or property without due process of law, or deny to any person within their jurisdiction the equal protection of the laws. . . .

The object of the amendment was undoubtedly to enforce the absolute equality of the two races before the law, but in the nature of things it could not have been intended to abolish distinctions based upon color, or to enforce social, as distinguished from political equality, or a commingling of the two races upon terms unsatisfactory to either. Laws permitting, and even requiring, their separation in

1. For a more complete description of the facts in this case, see Ellen Holmes Pearson, "Homer Plessy: Validation of Jim Crow," in Melvin I. Urofsky, ed. *100 Americans Making Constitutional History* (Washington, D.C.: CQ Press, 2004), 159–161.

places where they are liable to be brought into contact do not necessarily imply the inferiority of either race to the other, and have been generally, if not universally, recognized as within the competency of the state legislatures in the exercise of their police power. The most common instance of this is connected with the establishment of separate schools for white and colored children, which has been held to be a valid exercise of the legislative power even by courts of States where the political rights of the colored race have been longest and most earnestly enforced.

One of the earliest of these cases is that of *Roberts v. City of Boston*, in which the Supreme Judicial Court of Massachusetts held that the general school committee of Boston had power to make provision for the instruction of colored children in separate schools established exclusively for them, and to prohibit their attendance upon the other schools. . . .

Laws forbidding the intermarriage of the two races may be said in a technical sense to interfere with the freedom of contract, and yet have been universally recognized as within the police power of the State.

The distinction between laws interfering with the political equality of the negro and those requiring the separation of the two races in schools, theatres and railway carriages has been frequently drawn by this court. Thus in *Strauder v. West Virginia* [1880] it was held that a law of West Virginia limiting to white male persons, 21 years of age and citizens of the State, the right to sit upon juries, was a discrimination which implied a legal inferiority in civil society, which lessened the security of the right of the colored race, and was a step toward reducing them to a condition of servility. Indeed, the right of a colored man that, in the selection of jurors to pass upon his life, liberty, and property, there shall be no exclusion of his race, and no discrimination against them because of color, has been asserted in a number of cases. . . .

So far, then, as a conflict with the Fourteenth Amendment is concerned, the case reduces itself to the question whether the statute of Louisiana is a reasonable regulation, and with respect to this there must necessarily be a large discretion on the part of the legislature. In determining the question of reasonableness it is at liberty to act with reference to the established usages, customs and traditions of the people, and with a view to the promotion of their comfort, and the preservation of the public peace and good order. Gauged by this standard, we cannot say that a law which authorizes or even requires the separation of the two races in public conveyances is unreasonable, or more obnoxious to the Fourteenth Amendment than the acts of Congress requiring separate schools for colored children in the District of Columbia, the constitutionality of which does not seem to have been questioned, or the corresponding acts of state legislatures.

We consider the underlying fallacy of the plaintiff's argument to consist in the assumption that the enforced separation of the two races stamps the colored race with a badge of inferiority. If this be so, it is not by reason of anything found in the act, but solely because the colored race chooses to put that construction upon it. The argument necessarily assumes that if, as has been more than once the case, and is not unlikely to be so again, the colored race should become the dominant power in the state legislature, and should enact a law in precisely similar terms, it would thereby relegate the white race to an inferior position. We imagine that the white race, at least, would not acquiesce in this assumption. The argument also assumes that social prejudices may be overcome by legislation, and that equal rights cannot be secured to the negro except by an enforced commingling of the two races. We cannot accept this proposition. If the two races are to meet upon terms of social equality, it must be the result of natural affinities, a mutual appreciation of each other's merits and a voluntary consent of individuals. . . . Legislation is powerless to eradicate racial instincts or to abolish distinctions based upon physical differences, and the attempt to do so can only result in accentuating the difficulties of the present situation. If the civil and political rights of both races be equal one cannot be inferior to the other civilly or politically. If one race be inferior to the other socially, the Constitution of the United States cannot put them upon the same plane. . . .

The judgment of the court below is, therefore,

Affirmed.

MR. JUSTICE HARLAN dissenting.

In respect of civil rights, common to all citizens, the Constitution of the United States does not, I think, permit any public authority to know the race of those entitled to be protected in the enjoyment of such rights. Every true man has pride of race, and under appropriate circumstances when the rights of others, his equals before the law, are not to be affected, it is his privilege to express such pride and to take such action based upon it as to him seems proper. But I deny that any legislative body or judicial tribunal may have regard to the race of citizens when the civil rights of those citizens are involved. Indeed, such legislation, as that here in question, is inconsistent not only with that equality of rights which pertains to citizenship, National and State, but with the personal liberty enjoyed by every one within the United States.

The Thirteenth Amendment does not permit the withholding or the deprivation of any right necessarily inhering in freedom. It not only struck down the institution of slavery as previously existing in the United States, but it prevents the imposition of any burdens or disabilities that constitute badges of slavery or servitude. It decreed universal civil freedom in this country. This court has so adjudged. But that amendment having been found inadequate to the protection of the rights of those who had been in slavery, it was followed by the Fourteenth Amendment, which added greatly to the dignity and glory of American citizenship, and to the security of personal liberty. . . . These two amendments, if enforced according to their true intent and meaning, will protect all the civil rights that pertain to freedom and citizenship. Finally, and to the end that no citizen should be denied, on account of his race, the privilege of participating in the political control of his country, it was declared by the Fifteenth Amendment that "the right of citizens of the United States to vote shall not be denied or abridged by the United States or by any State on account of race, color or previous condition of servitude."

These notable additions to the fundamental law were welcomed by the friends of liberty throughout the world. They removed the race line from our governmental systems. They had, as this court has said, a common purpose, namely, to secure "to a race recently emancipated, a race that through many generations have been held in slavery, all the civil rights that the superior race enjoy." . . .

If a State can prescribe, as a rule of civil conduct, that whites and blacks shall not travel as passengers in the same railroad coach, why may it not so regulate the use of the streets of its cities and towns as to compel white citizens to keep on one side of a street and black citizens to keep on the other? Why may it not, upon like grounds, punish whites and blacks who ride together in street cars or in open vehicles on a public road or street? Why may it not require sheriffs to assign whites to one side of a court-room and blacks to the other? And why may it not also prohibit the commingling of the two races in the galleries of legislative halls or in public assemblages convened for the consideration of the political questions of the day? Further, if this statute of Louisiana is consistent with the personal liberty of citizens, why may not the State require the separation in railroad coaches of native and naturalized citizens of the United States, or of Protestants and Roman Catholics? . . .

The white race deems itself to be the dominant race in this country. And so it is, in prestige, in achievements, in education, in wealth and in power. So, I doubt not, it will continue to be for all time, if it remains true to its great heritage and holds fast to the principles of constitutional liberty. But in view of the Constitution, in the eye of the law, there is in this country no superior, dominant, ruling class of citizens. There is no caste here. Our Constitution is colorblind, and neither knows nor tolerates classes among citizens. In respect of civil rights, all citizens are equal before the law. The humblest is the peer of the most powerful. The law regards man as man, and takes no account of his surroundings or of his color when his civil rights as guaranteed by the supreme law of the land are involved. It is, therefore, to be regretted that this high tribunal, the final expositor of the fundamental law of the land, has reached the conclusion that it is competent for a State to regulate the enjoyment by citizens of their civil rights solely upon the basis of race.

In my opinion, the judgment this day rendered will, in time, prove to be quite as pernicious as the decision made by this tribunal in the *Dred Scott* case. . . .

I am of opinion that the statute of Louisiana is inconsistent with the personal liberty of citizens, white and black, in that State, and hostile to both the spirit and letter of the Constitution of the United States. If laws of like character should be enacted in the several States of the Union, the effect would be in the highest degree mischievous. Slavery, as an institution tolerated by law would, it is true, have disappeared from our country, but there would remain a power in the States, by sinister legislation, to interfere with the full enjoyment of the blessings of freedom; to regulate civil rights, common to all citizens, upon the basis of race; and to place in a condition of legal inferiority a large body of American citizens, now constituting a part of the political community called the People of the United States, for whom, and by whom through representatives, our government is administered. Such a system is inconsistent with the guarantee given by the Constitution to each State of a republican form of government, and may be stricken down by

Under the rule of law established in *Plessy v. Ferguson* (1896), states could require racial separation if facilities for blacks and whites were of equal quality. In public education black schools were not always equal to those reserved for whites.

Congressional action, or by the courts in the discharge of their solemn duty to maintain the supreme law of the land, anything in the constitution or laws of any State to the contrary notwithstanding.

For the reasons stated, I am constrained to withhold my assent from the opinion and judgment of the majority.

The *Plessy* decision's separate but equal doctrine ushered in full-scale segregation in the southern and border states. According to the Court, separation did not constitute inequality under the Fourteenth Amendment; if the facilities and opportunities were somewhat similar, the equal protection clause permitted the separation of the races. Encouraged by the ruling, the legislatures of the South passed a wide variety of statutes to keep blacks segregated from the white population. The segregation laws affected transportation, schools, hospitals, parks, public restrooms and water fountains, libraries, cemeteries, recreational facilities, hotels, restaurants, and almost every other public and commercial facility. These laws, coupled with segregated private lives, inevitably resulted in two separate societies.

During the first half of the twentieth century, the separate but equal doctrine dominated race relations law. The southern states continued to pass and enforce segregationist laws, largely insulated from legal attack. Over the years, however, it became clear that the "equality" part of the separate but equal doctrine was being ignored.

As the inequality of segregated public facilities grew worse, the disadvantages of the black population increased. The disparities extended to almost every area of life, but they were felt most keenly in education. Whites and blacks were given access to public schools, but the black schools, at all levels, received support and funding far inferior to that of white institutions.

These conditions spurred the growth of civil rights groups dedicated to eradicating segregation. None was more prominent than the National Association for the Advancement of Colored People (NAACP) and its affiliate, the Legal Defense and Educational Fund (commonly referred to as the Legal Defense Fund or the LDF). Thurgood Marshall, who had been associated with the NAACP since he graduated first in his class at Howard University Law School, became the head of the LDF in

BOX 19-1   THURGOOD MARSHALL (1967–1991)

Thurgood marshall was born July 2, 1908, in Baltimore, Maryland. He was the son of a primary school teacher and a club steward. In 1926 he left Baltimore to attend the all-black Lincoln University in Chester, Pennsylvania, where he developed a reputation as an outstanding debater. He graduated cum laude in 1930 and decided to study law at Howard University in Washington, D.C.

During his law school years, Marshall developed an interest in civil rights. After graduating first in his class in 1933, he began a long and historic involvement with the National Association for the Advancement of Colored People (NAACP). In 1940 he became the

head of the newly formed NAACP Legal Defense and Educational Fund, a position he held for more than twenty years.

Over those two decades, Marshall coordinated the fund's attack on segregation in voting, housing, public accommodations, and education. The culmination of his career as a civil rights attorney came in 1954 as chief counsel in a series of cases grouped under the title *Brown v. Board of Education.* In that historic case, civil rights advocates persuaded the Supreme Court to declare segregation in public schools unconstitutional.

Marshall and Vivian Burey were married on September 4, 1929. Vivian Marshall died in February 1955, and Marshall married Cecilia Suyat, December 17, 1955. They had two sons.

In 1961 President John F. Kennedy appointed Marshall to the Second Circuit Court of Appeals, but because of heated opposition from southern Democratic senators, Marshall was not confirmed for a year.

Four years after he was named to the appeals court, Marshall was chosen by President Lyndon B. Johnson to be solicitor general. Marshall was the first black to serve in that capacity. During his years as the government's chief advocate before the Supreme Court, Marshall scored impressive victories in the areas of civil and constitutional rights. He won Supreme Court approval of the 1965 Voting Rights Act, voluntarily informed the Court that the government had used eavesdropping devices in two cases, and joined a suit that successfully overturned a California constitutional amendment that prohibited open housing legislation.

On June 13, 1967, President Johnson nominated Marshall to the seat vacated by Justice Tom C. Clark, who had retired. Marshall was confirmed by the Senate, 69–11, August 30, 1967. Marshall, the first black justice of the Supreme Court, retired on October 1, 1991. He died January 24, 1993.

source: Adapted from David Savage, *Guide to the U.S. Supreme Court,* 4th ed. (Washington, D.C.: CQ Press, 2004), 1010–1011.

1940 and initiated a twenty-year campaign in the courts to win equal rights for black Americans. During those years, Marshall and his staff won substantial victories in the Supreme Court in housing, voting rights, public education, employment, and public accommodations. Marshall also served as a judge on the court of appeals and as U.S. solicitor general before being appointed in 1967 to the Supreme Court. He was the first African American to serve on the Court *(see Box 19-1).*

When Marshall took over leadership of the LDF, the rule set in *Plessy* was already on shaky ground. In 1938 the Court had handed segregationist forces a significant defeat in *Missouri ex rel. Gaines v. Canada.* Lloyd Gaines, a Missouri resident who had graduated from the all-black Lincoln University, applied for admission to the University of Missouri's law school. He was denied admission because of his race. Missouri did not have a law school for its black citizens, so the state offered to finance the education of qualified black students who would attend law school in a neighboring state that did not have segregationist policies. The Supreme Court, 7–2, concluded that the Missouri plan to provide opportunities out of state did not meet the obligations imposed by the equal protection clause.

The Supreme Court's message was reinforced in 1948 when in two cases, *Sipuel v. Board of Regents* and *Fisher v. Hurst,* the justices unanimously demanded that states provide equal facilities for blacks pursuing a legal education. Two years later the justices followed up with **Sweatt v. Painter,** in which the Court ruled that the Constitution had been violated by the University of Texas when its law school refused to admit a black applicant. The state had argued that its newly created law school for blacks met the separate but equal requirement and allowed the state to continue to run the University of Texas law school on a whites-only basis. The justices concluded that quality differences between the two schools were such that the black law school did not provide an education equal to that of the white law school. The same day the Court decided *Sweatt,* it also issued a ruling in **McLaurin v. Oklahoma State Regents** (1950), which took another step toward racial equality in higher education. Oklahoma, to comply with court orders, admitted some black students to graduate programs at the University of Oklahoma, but kept the minority students segregated in special areas of the classrooms, libraries, and dining halls. The Supreme Court unanimously found this segregated system in violation of the equal protection clause.[2]

In the early 1950s, conditions were ripe for a final assault on the separate but equal doctrine. Civil rights groups continued to marshal legal arguments and political support to eliminate segregation. Legal challenges to a wide array of discriminatory laws were filed throughout the country, and the Justice Department under President Harry S. Truman supported these efforts. The Supreme Court, through its unanimous rulings in favor of racial equality in higher education, appeared on the verge of seriously considering an end to *Plessy.* In addition, an important leadership change had occurred on the Court.

Chief Justice Fred Vinson died on September 8, 1953, and was replaced by Earl Warren, a former governor of California, who was much more comfortable with activist judicial policies than was his predecessor.

All of these factors combined to produce *Brown v. Board of Education of Topeka* (1954), considered by many to be the Supreme Court's most significant decision of the twentieth century. Unlike earlier civil rights cases that involved relatively small professional and graduate education programs, the *Brown* case challenged official racial segregation in the nation's primary and secondary public schools. The decision affected thousands of school districts, concentrated primarily in southern and border states. In addition, it was apparent to all that the precedent to be set for public education would be extended to other areas as well.

As you read Warren's opinion for a unanimous Court, note how the concept of equality has changed. No longer does the Court examine only physical facilities and tangible items such as buildings, libraries, teacher qualifications, and funding levels; instead, it emphasizes the intangible negative effect of racial segregation on children. Warren's opinion includes a footnote listing social science references as authorities for his arguments. This opinion was criticized for citing sociological and psychological studies to support the Court's conclusions rather than confining the analysis to legal arguments. Are these criticisms valid? Should the Court take social science evidence into account in arriving at constitutional decisions? Consider how similar Warren's opinion is to Justice John Harlan's lone dissent in the *Plessy* decision.

Brown v. Board of Education of Topeka

347 U.S. 483 (1954)
http://laws.findlaw.com/US/347/483.html
Vote: 9 (Black, Burton, Clark, Douglas, Frankfurter, Jackson,
*   Minton, Reed, Warren)*
        0
Opinion of the Court: Warren

Brown v. Board of Education was one of five cases involving similar issues consolidated by the Court for con-

2. For a discussion of the Supreme Court's decisions leading up to *Brown v. Board of Education,* see Richard Kluger, *Simple Justice* (New York: Random House, 1976).

Pictured on the steps of the U.S. Supreme Court are the NAACP Legal Defense Fund lawyers who argued the school segregation cases that resulted in the May 17, 1954, *Brown v. Board of Education* precedent. Left to right: Howard Jenkins, James M. Nabrit Jr., Spottswood W. Robinson III, Frank Reeves, Jack Greenberg, Special Counsel Thurgood Marshall, Louis Redding, U. Simpson Tate, and George E.C. Hayes. Missing from the photograph is Robert L. Carter, who argued the Topeka, Kansas, case.

sideration at the same time. As part of the desegregation litigation strategy orchestrated by Thurgood Marshall and funded by the NAACP, these cases challenged the segregated public schools of Delaware, South Carolina, Virginia, and the District of Columbia, in addition to Topeka, Kansas. The most prominent lawyers in the civil rights movement, Spottswood Robinson III, Louis Redding, Jack Greenberg, Constance Baker Motley, Robert Carter, and James Nabrit Jr., prepared the cases. As Marshall had expected, the suits were unsuccessful at the trial level, where the lower courts relied on *Plessy* as precedent. The lead attorney for the states was John W. Davis, a prominent constitutional lawyer and the Democratic candidate for president in 1924. Davis represented the steel mills in *Youngstown Sheet and Tube Co. v. Sawyer* (1952), the Korean War steel seizure case discussed in chapter 5.

Linda Carol Brown was an eight-year-old black girl. Her father, Oliver Brown, was an assistant pastor of a Topeka church. The Browns lived in a predominantly white neighborhood only a short distance from an elementary school. Under state law, cities with populations over fifteen thousand were permitted to administer racially segregated schools, and the Board of Education in Topeka required its elementary schools to be racially divided. The Browns did not want their daughter to be sent to the school reserved for black students. It was far from home, and they considered the trip dangerous. In addition, their neighborhood school was a good one, and the Browns wanted their daughter to attend that school. They filed suit challenging the segregated school system as violating their daughter's rights under the equal protection clause of the Fourteenth Amendment.

The *Brown* appeal was joined by those from the other four suits. The cases were originally argued in December 1952, but the following June, the Court issued an order for the cases to be reargued in December 1953, with special emphasis to be placed on a series of questions dealing with the history and meaning of the Fourteenth Amendment. This delay also allowed the newly appointed Earl Warren to participate fully in the decision. Six months later, on May 17, 1954, the Court issued its ruling.

This photograph of Linda Brown, plaintiff in *Brown v. Board of Education*, was taken in 1952 when she was nine years old.

MR. CHIEF JUSTICE WARREN delivered the opinion of the Court.

In each of the cases, minors of the Negro race, through their legal representatives, seek the aid of the courts in obtaining admission to the public schools of their community on a nonsegregated basis. In each instance, they had been denied admission to schools attended by white children under laws requiring or permitting segregation according to race. This segregation was alleged to deprive the plaintiffs of the equal protection of the laws under the Fourteenth Amendment. . . .

The plaintiffs contend that segregated public schools are not "equal" and cannot be made "equal," and that hence they are deprived of the equal protection of the laws. Because of the obvious importance of the question presented, the Court took jurisdiction. Argument was heard in the 1952 Term, and reargument was heard this Term on certain questions propounded by the Court.

Reargument was largely devoted to the circumstances surrounding the adoption of the Fourteenth Amendment in 1868. It covered exhaustively consideration of the Amendment in Congress, ratification by the states, then existing practices in racial segregation, and the views of proponents and opponents of the Amendment. This discussion and our own investigation convince us that, although these sources cast some light, it is not enough to resolve the problem with which we are faced. At best, they are inconclusive. . . .

An additional reason for the inconclusive nature of the Amendment's history, with respect to segregated schools, is the status of public education at that time. In the South, the movement toward free common schools, supported by general taxation, had not yet taken hold. Education of white children was largely in the hands of private groups. Education of Negroes was almost nonexistent, and practically all of the race were illiterate. In fact, any education of Negroes was forbidden by law in some states. Today, in contrast, many Negroes have achieved outstanding success in the arts and sciences as well as in the business and professional world. It is true that public school education at the time of the Amendment had advanced further in the North, but the effect of the Amendment on Northern States was generally ignored in the congressional debates. Even in the North, the conditions of public education did not approximate those existing today. The curriculum was usually rudimentary; ungraded schools were common in rural areas; the school term was but three months a year in many states; and compulsory school attendance was virtually unknown. As a consequence, it is not surprising that there should be so little in the history of the Fourteenth Amendment relating to its intended effect on public education.

In the first cases in this Court construing the Fourteenth Amendment, decided shortly after its adoption, the Court interpreted it as proscribing all state-imposed discriminations against the Negro race. The doctrine of "separate but equal" did not make its appearance in this Court until 1896 in the case of *Plessy v. Ferguson*, involving not education but transportation. American courts have since labored with the doctrine for over half a century. . . .

Here, unlike *Sweatt v. Painter*, there are findings below that the Negro and white schools involved have been equalized, or are being equalized, with respect to buildings, curricula, qualifications and salaries of teachers, and other "tangible" factors. Our decision, therefore, cannot turn on merely a comparison of these tangible factors in the Negro and white schools involved in each of the cases. We must look instead to the effect of segregation itself on public education.

In approaching this problem, we cannot turn the clock back to 1868 when the Amendment was adopted, or even to 1896 when *Plessy v. Ferguson* was written. We must consider public education in the light of its full development and its present place in American life throughout the Nation. Only in this way can it be determined if segregation in public schools deprives these plaintiffs of the equal protection of the laws.

Today, education is perhaps the most important function of state and local governments. Compulsory school attendance laws and the great expenditures for education both demonstrate our recognition of the importance of education to our democratic society. It is required in the performance of our most basic public responsibilities, even service in the armed forces. It is the very foundation of good citizenship. Today it is a principal instrument in awakening the child to cultural values, in preparing him for later professional training, and in helping him to adjust normally to his environment. In these days, it is doubtful that any child may reasonably be expected to succeed in life if he is denied the opportunity of an education. Such an opportunity, where the state has undertaken to provide it, is a right which must be made available to all on equal terms.

We come then to the question presented: Does segregation of children in public schools solely on the basis of race, even though the physical facilities and other "tangible" factors may be equal, deprive the children of the minority group of equal educational opportunities? We believe that it does.

In *Sweatt v. Painter*, in finding that a segregated law school of Negroes could not provide them equal educational opportunities, this Court relied in large part on "those qualities which are incapable of objective measurement but which make for greatness in a law school." In *McLaurin v. Oklahoma State Regents*, the Court, in requiring that a Negro admitted to a white graduate school be treated like all other students, again resorted to intangible considerations: ". . . his ability to study, to engage in discussions and exchange views with other students, and, in general, to learn his profession." Such considerations apply with added force to children in grade and high schools. To separate them from others of similar age and qualifications solely be-

cause of their race generates a feeling of inferiority as to their status in the community that may affect their hearts and minds in a way unlikely ever to be undone. The effect of this separation on their educational opportunities was well stated by a finding in the Kansas case by a court which nevertheless felt compelled to rule against the Negro plaintiffs:

"Segregation of white and colored children in public schools has a detrimental effect upon the colored children. The impact is greater when it has the sanction of the law; for the policy of separating the races is usually interpreted as denoting the inferiority of the negro group. A sense of inferiority affects the motivation of a child to learn. Segregation with the sanction of law, therefore, has a tendency to [retard] the educational and mental development of negro children and to deprive them of some of the benefits they would receive in a racial[ly] integrated school system."

Whatever may have been the extent of psychological knowledge at the time of *Plessy v. Ferguson*, this finding is amply supported by modern authority.* Any language in *Plessy v. Ferguson* contrary to this finding is rejected.

We conclude that in the field of public education the doctrine of "separate but equal" has no place. Separate educational facilities are inherently unequal. Therefore, we hold that the plaintiffs and others similarly situated for whom the actions have been brought are, by reason of the segregation complained of, deprived of the equal protection of the laws guaranteed by the Fourteenth Amendment. . . .

It is so ordered.

As is typical of many Supreme Court litigants, Linda Brown did not personally benefit from winning her case *(see Box 19-2)*. Implementation of the *Brown* decision faced many barriers. Of obvious importance to the Court was public acceptance of the ruling. The Court has no formal enforcement powers, and the justices expected

*K. B. Clark, *Effect of Prejudice and Discrimination on Personality Development* (Midcentury White House Conference on Children and Youth, 1950); Witmer and Kotinsky, *Personality in the Making* (1952), c. VI; Deutscher and Chein, *The Psychological Effects of Enforced Segregation: A Survey of Social Science Opinion*, 26 J. Psychol. 259 (1948); Chein, *What Are the Psychological Effects of Segregation Under Conditions of Equal Facilities?*, 3 Int. J. Opinion and Attitude Res. 229 (1949); Brameld, *Educational Costs, in Discrimination and National Welfare* (Maciver, ed., 1949), 44–48; Frazier, *The Negro in the United States* (1949), 674–681. And see generally Myrdal, *An American Dilemma* (1944).

Linda Brown Buckner, now a Head Start teacher in Topeka, Kansas, was eight years old in 1951 when her father, Oliver, included her in a lawsuit to desegregate public schools that led to the Supreme Court's landmark *Brown v. Board of Education* decision in 1954.

"I was just starting school when the local NAACP was recruiting people to join its case. Topeka had eighteen elementary schools for whites and four for African Americans. The closest school to my family was four blocks away, the Sumner School. But I went to Monroe Elementary School, which was two and a half miles across town. Often, I came home crying because it was so cold waiting for the bus.

"My father hadn't been involved with the NAACP, but he was upset with the distance I had to go. One of his childhood friends was Charles Scott, one of the attorneys for the case, and Dad agreed to try to enroll me at the Sumner School. Dad's name wasn't first alphabetically, and my sister Cheryl always suspected there was sexism involved in his name coming first in the court records: among the twelve other plaintiffs, he was the only man.

"The day the decision was handed down, my mother was home and heard it on the radio. The news was shared with the family, and there was a rally that evening at the Monroe School. But I never did go to the Sumner School. That fall I went to the junior-high school, which had been integrated in Topeka since 1879."

SOURCE: Copyright 1993 *U.S. News and World Report*, L.P. Reprinted with permission.

to argue the question of remedies. That is, once the segregationist policies were declared unconstitutional, how would the discriminatory system be dismantled? In **Brown v. Board of Education** (1955), commonly referred to as *Brown II*, the justices held that desegregation of the public schools must occur "with all deliberate speed." This rather ambiguous standard recognized that not all districts could be placed on the same timetable. The extent of segregation, the proportion of minority students, the size of the district, the district's resources, and the like were all factors that would have to be considered in developing desegregation plans. Important to note is that the justices gave primary responsibility to the federal district courts to monitor the actions taken by local school boards to implement the *Brown* mandate.

The post-*Brown* era was marked by massive resistance to desegregation, especially in the South. School board members, most of whom were elected officials, did not pursue the implementation of *Brown* gladly. Federal district judges were often called upon to demand that school officials comply with the ruling.[3] Desegregating the schools was periodically marked with violence, and the mobilization of the National Guard and federal troops was sometimes necessary to enforce *Brown* in a reluctant region.

For the remaining years of the Warren Court, the justices held steadfast in their desegregation goals. In **Cooper v. Aaron** (1958) the Court responded firmly to popular resistance in Arkansas by declaring that violence or threats of violence would not be allowed to slow the progress toward full desegregation. In **Griffin v. Prince Edward County School Board** (1964) the Court stopped a Virginia plan to close down public schools rather than integrate them. In **Green v. School Board of New Kent County** (1968) the justices struck down a "freedom of choice" plan as failing to bring about a nondiscriminatory school system. By the mid-1960s the justices had begun to lose patience. Justice Hugo Black remarked in his opinion for the Court in *Griffin* that "there has been entirely too much deliberation and not enough speed" in enforcing *Brown*'s desegregation mandate.

resistance, especially in the South. Chief Justice Warren went to great pains to obtain a unanimous vote and to unite the Court in a single opinion, written by him, demonstrating that the justices wanted to speak with all the authority they could muster in the hopes of encouraging voluntary compliance.

The justices clearly realized that setting the constitutional standard was one thing, but gaining compliance with it was quite another. After issuing its ruling in *Brown*, the Court asked the parties to return the next year

3. See J. W. Peltason, *Fifty-Eight Lonely Men* (Urbana: University of Illinois Press, 1961); J. Harvie Wilkinson III, *The Supreme Court from Brown to Bakke* (New York: Oxford University Press, 1979).

In short, the justices of the Warren Court tried to make it clear that dilatory tactics would not be tolerated.[4] Yet they continued. The freedom given to district judges to approve desegregation plans led to a wide variety of schemes, some of which were criticized by school officials for going too far, and some by civil rights advocates for not going far enough. The specific methods of integration commonly were attacked for exceeding the powers of the district courts.

Clearing up this confusion was left to the Burger Court. In *Swann v. Charlotte-Mecklenburg Board of Education* (1971) it approved a wide array of desegregation tools, including mandatory busing of students, teacher transfers, court supervision of spending and new construction, and the altering of attendance zones. *Swann* gave wide latitude to district judges to fashion desegregation programs appropriate to local conditions. But the Court made clear that such remedial actions could be imposed in a school district only if it could be proven that a violation of the Constitution had occurred there. This requirement made it difficult to impose an effective desegregation plan in metropolitan areas with multiple school districts.[5]

The discrimination decisions of the Supreme Court in the post-*Brown* era have not focused exclusively on public education. Instead, the Court has regularly confronted questions of racial discrimination over a wide array of issues. The death of the separate but equal doctrine had widespread ramifications for American society because many states and local governments had laws that mandated segregated facilities. Other rules and restrictions, while not segregating the races, discriminated directly or indirectly against African Americans. Civil rights groups launched attacks on many of these discriminatory policies, as did the Justice Department.

As such challenges were brought before the Court, the justices faithfully applied the *Brown* precedent. If a case presented intentional discrimination by the government, the justices were not reluctant to declare that the Constitution had been violated. The Court presumed that racial classifications used to discriminate against black Americans violated the equal protection clause of the Four-

teenth Amendment (state government discrimination) or the due process clause of the Fifth (federal government discrimination). Attempts to justify such actions faced a heavy burden of proof. Because race is a suspect classification, black litigants enjoyed the advantages of the strict scrutiny test. These factors made it difficult for federal, state, and local governments to withstand the attacks made against discriminatory policies and practices. One by one the legal barriers between the races fell.

Since 1954 the Court has developed constitutional doctrine in many areas related to race. Some of these, such as the civil rights protesters' freedom of expression, we have already discussed; others, such as affirmative action and voting rights, will be covered in this chapter and the next. The justices have not always agreed, especially on how to eliminate the effects of past discrimination. But throughout the Court's post-*Brown* history, the justices have said consistently that the Constitution does not permit government classifications that penalize historically disadvantaged racial minorities or that impose distinctions that imply the racial inferiority of any group.

SEX DISCRIMINATION

Before the 1970s lawsuits based on claims of sex discrimination were rare, and those that reached the Supreme Court ended in decisions that reinforced traditional views of sex roles. In *Bradwell v. Illinois* (1873), for example, the Court heard a challenge to an action by the Illinois Supreme Court denying Myra Bradwell a license to practice law solely because of her sex. The Court, with only Chief Justice Salmon P. Chase dissenting, upheld the state action. Justice Joseph P. Bradley's concurring opinion, which Justices Noah H. Swayne and Stephen J. Field joined, illustrates the attitude of the legal community toward women. Bradley said that he gave his "heartiest concurrence" to contemporary society's "multiplication of avenues for women's advancement," but he added, "The natural and proper timidity and delicacy which belongs to the female sex evidently unfits it for many of the occupations of civil life." This condition, according to Bradley, was the product of divine ordinance.

Similar decisions followed. In 1875 the Court in *Minor v. Happersett* upheld Missouri's denial of voting rights to women, a precedent in effect until ratification of the

---

4. See *Alexander v. Holmes Board of Education* (1969).
5. *Milliken v. Bradley* (1974).

Myra Bradwell studied law with her husband, a judge, and edited and published the *Chicago Legal News,* the most important legal publication in the Midwest. Although she passed the bar exam, the Illinois Supreme Court refused to admit her to the state bar because of her sex. She appealed to the U.S. Supreme Court, but lost.

Nineteenth Amendment in 1920. As late as 1948 the Court upheld the right of the state to ban women from certain occupations. In *Goesaert v. Cleary,* decided that year, the justices declared valid a Michigan law that barred women from becoming bartenders unless they belonged to the immediate family of the bar owner. In explaining the ruling, Justice Frankfurter wrote:

The fact that women may now have achieved the virtues that men have long claimed as their prerogatives and now indulge in vices that men have long practiced, does not preclude the States from drawing a sharp line between the sexes, certainly in such matters as the regulation of the liquor traffic.

During the first half of the twentieth century, the Court upheld many state laws enacted to protect women in the workplace. These laws dealt with matters such as hours, working conditions, physical demands, and compensation. At the time of their implementation these statutes were seen as a progressive response to the problems faced by the growing number of women employed outside the home. Today these protective laws are considered paternalistic, based as they are on the assumption that women are not the equals of men.

Social change in the 1950s and 1960s, and the growing strength of the women's movement, prompted major alterations in the law. Congress passed several federal statutes extending equal rights to women, among them the Equal Pay Act of 1963 and various amendments to the 1964 Civil Rights Act. Many states have passed similar laws to eliminate discriminatory conditions in the marketplace and in state legal codes.

In addition to these legislative actions, in 1972 Congress proposed an amendment to the Constitution. Known as the equal rights amendment, it declared, "Equality of rights under the law shall not be denied or abridged by the United States or by any State on account of sex." The amendment failed to gain approval from the required number of states, even though Congress extended the deadline for ratification.

In addition to working for changes in the Constitution and laws, women turned to the courts for redress of their grievances. Many in the women's movement believed that the due process and equal protection clauses held the same potential for ensuring women's rights as they had for black Americans, and they began organizing to assert their claims in court.

The Supreme Court issued its first major sex discrimination decision of the contemporary period in 1971. In *Reed v. Reed* the justices considered the validity of an Idaho inheritance statute that used sex classifications. The statute was challenged on the ground that it was in violation of the equal protection clause of the Fourteenth Amendment. It was clear from the outset that the same requirements that had developed in race relations cases would apply here; that is, the statute's challenger would have to demonstrate both invidious discrimination and state action before a violation could be found.

What was not so clear was what standard of scrutiny the justices would use. In the racial discrimination cases,

BOX 19-3   RUTH BADER GINSBURG (1993–   )

When President Bill Clinton nominated Ruth Bader Ginsburg in 1993 to fill the vacancy left by retiring justice Byron White, the president was enjoying the first such opportunity for a Democrat in more than a quarter century. Ginsburg became the second woman to sit on the Court and the first Jewish justice since the resignation of Abe Fortas in 1969. She brought to the Court a sterling record as a law professor, advocate, and federal judge. She earned a reputation as the "Thurgood Marshall of sex discrimination law" for her pioneering work in that field.

Ginsburg was born in Brooklyn, New York, in 1933 to Nathan and Celia Bader. In 1950 she began her undergraduate studies at Cornell University, where she met her future husband, Martin Ginsburg. After her graduation in 1954, the Ginsburgs lived briefly in Oklahoma, where Martin was stationed in the army and Ruth worked for the Social Security Administration. In 1956 they moved to Cambridge, Massachusetts, to attend Harvard Law School. After graduation Martin accepted a job in New York City and Ruth transferred to Columbia Law School to finish her legal training. She graduated from Columbia in 1959, tied for first in her class and having the distinction of serving on the law review staffs at both Harvard and Columbia.

In spite of her academic credentials, Ginsburg's attempts to obtain employment in a major law firm were unsuccessful. She later explained these rejections by noting: "To be a woman, a Jew and a mother to boot, that combination was a bit much." She secured a clerkship with federal district judge Edmund Palmieri, where she worked from 1959 to 1961. She then joined a Columbia University research project on civil law procedures in other countries and became an expert on the Swedish legal system. Ginsburg joined the law faculty at Rutgers University where she worked her way up the ranks from assistant professor to full professor. In 1972 she returned to Columbia University as professor of law and became the first woman to be awarded tenure at that school.

While on the faculty at Columbia, Ginsburg served as general counsel for the American Civil Liberties Union, heading the Women's Rights Project. In that capacity she was in the vanguard of sex discrimination cases of the 1970s. Her legal arguments before the Supreme Court had a profound impact on the development of sex discrimination law. Of the six cases she argued before the justices, she was successful in five. She participated in *Reed v. Reed* (1971), *Frontiero v. Richardson* (1973), *Kahn v. Shevin* (1974), *Weinberger v. Wiesenfeld* (1975), and *Craig v. Boren* (1976).

In 1980 President Jimmy Carter nominated Ginsburg for the Court of Appeals for the District of Columbia. She was later joined on that court by Clarence Thomas and Antonin Scalia, both of whom would precede her to the Supreme Court. In thirteen years as a federal appellate judge, Ginsburg developed a reputation as an intelligent, highly competent jurist with a moderate political ideology.

Ginsburg's nomination to the Supreme Court met with broad, bipartisan approval. She received the highest rating of the American Bar Association. On August 3, 1993, by a vote of 96–3 the Senate confirmed Ruth Bader Ginsburg as the Supreme Court's 107th justice.

SOURCE: "Ruth Ginsburg: Carving a Career Path Through a Male-Dominated Legal World," *Congressional Quarterly Weekly Report*, July 17, 1993, 1876–1877.

the Court had declared strict scrutiny the appropriate standard. The Court had decided that classifications based on race were presumed to be unconstitutional, and the state had a heavy burden of proof if it wished to show that a law based on race was the least restrictive means to achieve a compelling state interest. Much of the success enjoyed by civil rights groups resulted from this favorable legal status. The advocates of equal rights for women, especially American Civil Liberties Union (ACLU) attorneys such as Ruth Bader Ginsburg *(see Box 19-3),* hoped the

Court would adopt the same standard for sex discrimination claims.

Reed v. Reed

404 U.S. 71 (1971)
http://laws.findlaw.com/US/404/71.html
Oral arguments may be found at: http://www.oyez.org
Vote: 7 (Blackmun, Brennan, Burger, Douglas, Marshall,
   Stewart, White)

   0

Opinion of the Court: Burger

Richard Reed was the adopted child of Sally and Cecil Reed. He died March 29, 1967, in Ada County, Idaho, leaving no will. Richard's parents, who had separated before his death, became involved in a legal dispute over who should administer their son's estate. The estate was insignificant, consisting of a few personal items and a small savings account. The total value was less than $1,000. The probate court judge named Cecil Reed administrator of the estate, in accordance with Idaho law. Section 15-312 of the Idaho code stipulated that when a person died intestate (without a will) an administrator would be appointed according to a list of priority relationships. First priority went to a surviving spouse, second priority to children, third to parents, and so forth. Section 15-314 of the statute stated that in the case of competing petitions from otherwise qualified individuals of the same priority relationship, "males must be preferred to females."

Sally Reed challenged the law as a violation of the equal protection clause of the Fourteenth Amendment. The state district court agreed with her argument, but the Idaho Supreme Court reversed the decision. With the assistance of Ginsburg and other ACLU attorneys, Reed took her case to the U.S. Supreme Court.

MR. CHIEF JUSTICE BURGER delivered the opinion of the Court.

Having examined the record and considered the briefs and oral arguments of the parties, we have concluded that

Sally Reed, pictured with her attorney Allen Derr, challenged an Idaho law that gave preference to males over females in designating administrators of estates. *Reed v. Reed* ushered in the modern era of sex discrimination litigation.

the arbitrary preference established in favor of males by §15-314 of the Idaho Code cannot stand in the face of the Fourteenth Amendment's command that no State deny the equal protection of the laws to any person within its jurisdiction.

Idaho does not, of course, deny letters of administration to women altogether. Indeed, under §15-312, a woman whose spouse dies intestate has a preference over a son, father, brother, or any other male relative of the decedent. Moreover, we can judicially notice that in this country, presumably due to the greater longevity of women, a large proportion of estates, both intestate and under wills of decedents, are administered by surviving widows.

Section 15-314 is restricted in its operation to those situations where competing applications for letters of administration have been filed by both male and female members of the same entitlement class established by §15-312. In such situations, §15-314 provides that different treatment be accorded to the applicants on the basis of their sex; it thus establishes a classification subject to scrutiny under the Equal Protection Clause.

In applying that clause, this Court has consistently recognized that the Fourteenth Amendment does not deny to States the power to treat different classes of persons in different ways. The Equal Protection Clause of that amendment does, however, deny to States the power to legislate that different treatment be accorded to persons placed by a statute into different classes on the basis of criteria wholly unrelated to the objective of that statute. A classification "must be reasonable, not arbitrary, and must rest upon some ground of difference having a fair and substantial relation to the object of the legislation, so that all persons similarly circumstanced shall be treated alike." The question presented by this case, then, is whether a difference in the sex of competing applicants for letters of administration bears a rational relationship to a state objective that is sought to be advanced by the operation of §§15-312 and 15-314.

In upholding the latter section, the Idaho Supreme Court concluded that its objective was to eliminate one area of controversy when two or more persons, equally entitled under §15-312, seek letters of administration and thereby present the probate court "with the issue of which one should be named." The court also concluded that where such persons are not of the same sex, the elimination of females from consideration "is neither an illogical nor arbitrary method devised by the legislature to resolve an issue that would otherwise require a hearing as to the relative merits . . . of the two or more petitioning relatives. . . ."

Clearly the objective of reducing the workload on probate courts by eliminating one class of contests is not without some legitimacy. The crucial question, however, is whether §15-314 advances that objective in a manner consistent with the command of the Equal Protection Clause. We hold that it does not. To give a mandatory preference to members of either sex over members of the other, merely to accomplish the elimination of hearings on the merits, is to make the very kind of arbitrary legislative choice forbidden by the Equal Protection Clause of the Fourteenth Amendment; and whatever may be said as to the positive values of avoiding intrafamily controversy, the choice in this context may not lawfully be mandated solely on the basis of sex.

We note finally that if §15-314 is viewed merely as a modifying appendage to §15-312 and aimed at the same objec-

tive, its constitutionality is not thereby saved. The objective of §15-312 clearly is to establish degrees of entitlement of various classes of persons in accordance with their varying degrees and kinds of relationship to the intestate. Regardless of their sex, persons within any one of the enumerated classes of that section are similarly situated with respect to that objective. By providing dissimilar treatment for men and women who are thus similarly situated, the challenged section violates the Equal Protection Clause. The judgment of the Idaho Supreme Court is reversed and the case remanded for further proceedings not inconsistent with this opinion.

Reversed and remanded.

The Court's unanimous decision in *Reed* applied two important principles to sex discrimination. First, the Court refused to accept Idaho's defense of its statute. The state had contended that it was inefficient to hold full court hearings on the relative merits of competing candidates to administer estates, especially small estates. Imposing arbitrary criteria saved court time and avoided intrafamily squabbles. The Court held that administrative convenience is no justification for violating the Constitution. Second, defenders of the Idaho law argued that the arbitrary favoring of males over females made sense because, in most cases, the male will have had more education and experience in financial matters than the competing female. In rejecting this argument, the justices said that laws containing overbroad, sex-based assumptions violate the equal protection clause.

The *Reed* case also signaled that the justices were receptive to sex discrimination claims and would not hesitate to strike down state laws that imposed arbitrary sex classifications. Although *Reed* was certainly good news for women's rights advocates, the standard used in the case was not. Chief Justice Warren Burger clearly articulated the rational basis test, holding that laws based on gender classifications must be reasonable and have a rational relationship to a state objective. The Idaho law was sufficiently arbitrary to fail the rational basis test, but other laws and policies might well survive it.

Over the next several years following *Reed* many sex discrimination appeals reached the Court.[6] Although these cases dealt with differing subject matter, the most important question explicitly or implicitly presented to the justices had to do with the proper standard of scrutiny to use in sex discrimination cases. Women's rights organizations were committed to persuading the Court to elevate sex discrimination to suspect class test status. The justices were closely divided on the issue, however, and until 1976 no change occurred. In that year the Court decided *Craig v. Boren*, which was to change sex discrimination law fundamentally.

In *Craig* the justices adopted an entirely new standard of scrutiny for sex discrimination cases. This test, known as intermediate or heightened scrutiny, requires that laws that classify on the basis of sex be substantially related to an important government objective. It was originally suggested as a compromise solution by attorneys for women's rights groups, who feared that the Court majority would remain committed to rational basis. It appealed especially to justices in the center of the Court who were not happy with either the more conservative rational basis test or the liberal suspect class test. Observe how William J. Brennan Jr., writing for the Court, justifies the new test as being consistent with *Reed* and how he treats the use of social science evidence. Also, read carefully William Rehnquist's dissenting opinion rejecting the new test, especially as beneficially applied to men.

Craig v. Boren

429 U.S. 190 (1976)
http://laws.findlaw.com/US/429/190.html
Oral arguments may be found at: http://www.oyez.org
Vote: 7 (Blackmun, Brennan, Marshall, Powell, Stevens,
    Stewart, White)
    2 (Burger, Rehnquist)

Opinion of the Court: Brennan
Concurring opinions: Powell, Stevens
Opinion concurring in judgment: Stewart
Opinion concurring in part: Blackmun
Dissenting opinions: Burger, Rehnquist

6. See, for example, *Frontiero v. Richardson* (1973), *Kahn v. Shevin* (1974), *Stanton v. Stanton* (1975).

In 1972 Oklahoma passed a statute setting the age of legal majority for both males and females at eighteen. Before then, females reached legal age at eighteen and males at twenty-one. The equalization statute, however, contained one exception. Men could not purchase beer, even with the low 3.2 percent alcohol level, until they reached twenty-one; women could buy beer at eighteen. The state differentiated between the sexes in response to statistical evidence indicating a much greater tendency for men in the eighteen-to-twenty-one age bracket to be involved in alcohol-related traffic accidents, including fatalities.

Viewing the Oklahoma law as a form of sex discrimination, Mark Walker, a twenty-year-old Oklahoma State University student who wanted to buy beer, and Carolyn Whitener, the owner of the "Honk-N-Holler" convenience store, who wanted to sell it, brought suit in federal trial court challenging the law on equal protection grounds. While the case slowly progressed, Walker turned twenty-one and was no longer subject to the state restrictions on purchasing alcohol. To protect against the case being declared moot, eighteen-year-old Curtis Craig replaced his friend Walker as the lead party.

A three-judge district court ruled that the rational basis test was the appropriate standard to apply. In doing so, the judges concluded that the statistical evidence supporting differences in male and female drinking and driving behavior was sufficient to justify the state's sex-based alcohol policy. The plaintiffs appealed to the Supreme Court arguing that sex discrimination claims required a higher standard of scrutiny. Ruth Bader Ginsburg, who filed an amicus brief on behalf of the ACLU, supported this position.

MR. JUSTICE BRENNAN delivered the opinion of the Court.

Analysis may appropriately begin with the reminder that *Reed* [*v. Reed* (1971)] emphasized that statutory classifications that distinguish between males and females are "subject to scrutiny under the Equal Protection Clause." To withstand constitutional challenge, previous cases establish that classifications by gender must serve important governmental objectives and must be substantially related to achievement of those objectives. Thus, in *Reed*, the objectives of "reducing the workload on probate courts" and "avoiding

Mark Walker (left), an Oklahoma State University student, joined with beer vender Carolyn Whitener (middle), to challenge the state's drinking age law that treated males and females differently. When Walker turned twenty-one and was no longer adversely affected by the law, he persuaded freshman fraternity brother Curtis Craig (right) to join the lawsuit. Walker died in a car accident shortly before the Supreme Court decided *Craig v. Boren.*

intrafamily controversy" were deemed of insufficient importance to sustain use of an overt gender criterion in the appointment of administrators of intestate decedents' estates. Decisions following *Reed* similarly have rejected administrative ease and convenience as sufficiently important objectives to justify gender-based classifications. . . .

Reed v. Reed has also provided the underpinning for decisions that have invalidated statutes employing gender as an inaccurate proxy for other, more germane bases of classification. Hence, "archaic and overbroad" generalizations could not justify use of a gender line in determining eligibility for certain governmental entitlements. Similarly, increasingly outdated misconceptions concerning the role of females in the home rather than in the "marketplace and world of ideas" were rejected as loose-fitting characterizations incapable of supporting state statutory schemes that were premised upon their accuracy. In light of the weak congruence between gender and the characteristic or trait that gender purported to represent, it was necessary that the legislatures choose either to realign their substantive laws in a gender-neutral fashion, or to adopt procedures for identifying those instances where the sex-centered generalization actually comported with fact.

In this case, too, "*Reed,* we feel, is controlling. . . ." We turn then to the question whether, under *Reed,* the differ-ence between males and females with respect to the purchase of 3.2% beer warrants the differential in age drawn by the Oklahoma statute. We conclude that it does not.

The District Court recognized that *Reed v. Reed* was controlling. In applying the teachings of that case, the court found the requisite important governmental objective in the traffic-safety goal proffered by the Oklahoma Attorney General. It then concluded that the statistics introduced by the appellees established that the gender-based distinction was substantially related to achievement of that goal.

. . . Clearly, the protection of public health and safety represents an important function of state and local governments. However, appellees' statistics in our view cannot support the conclusion that the gender-based distinction closely serves to achieve that objective and therefore the distinction cannot under *Reed* withstand equal protection challenge.

The appellees introduced a variety of statistical surveys. First, an analysis of arrest statistics for 1973 demonstrated that 18–20-year-old male arrests for "driving under the influence" and "drunkenness" substantially exceeded female arrests for that same age period. Similarly, youths aged 17–21 were found to be overrepresented among those killed or injured in traffic accidents, with males again numerically exceeding females in this regard. Third, a random roadside survey in Oklahoma City revealed that young males were more inclined to drive and drink beer than were their female counterparts. Fourth, Federal Bureau of Investigation nationwide statistics exhibited a notable increase in arrests for "driving under the influence." Finally, statistical evidence gathered in other jurisdictions, particularly Minnesota and Michigan, was offered to corroborate Oklahoma's experience by indicating the pervasiveness of youthful participation in motor vehicle accidents following the imbibing of alcohol. . . .

Even were this statistical evidence accepted as accurate, it nevertheless offers only a weak answer to the equal protection question presented here. The most focused and relevant of the statistical surveys, arrests of 18–20-year-olds for alcohol-related driving offenses, exemplifies the ultimate unpersuasiveness of this evidentiary record. Viewed in terms of the correlation between sex and the actual activity that Oklahoma seeks to regulate—driving while under the influence of alcohol—the statistics broadly establish that .18% of females and 2% of males in that age group were arrested for that offense. While such a disparity is not trivial in a statistical sense, it hardly can form the basis for employment of a gender line as a classifying device. Certainly if maleness is to serve as a proxy for drinking and driving, a correlation of 2% must be considered an unduly tenuous "fit." Indeed, prior cases have consistently rejected the use of sex as a decisionmaking factor even though the statutes in question certainly rested on far more predictive empirical relationships than this.

Moreover, the statistics exhibit a variety of other shortcomings that seriously impugn their value to equal protection analysis. Setting aside the obvious methodological problems, the surveys do not adequately justify the salient features of Oklahoma's gender-based traffic-safety law. None purports to measure the use and dangerousness of 3.2% beer as opposed to alcohol generally, a detail that is of particular importance since, in light of its low alcohol level, Oklahoma apparently considers the 3.2% beverage to be "nonintoxicating." Moreover, many of the studies, while graphically documenting the unfortunate increase in driving while under the influence of alcohol, make no effort to relate their findings to age-sex differentials as involved here. Indeed, the only survey that explicitly centered its attention upon young drivers and their use of beer—albeit apparently

not of the diluted 3.2% variety—reached results that hardly can be viewed as impressive in justifying either a gender or age classification.

There is no reason to belabor this line of analysis. It is unrealistic to expect either members of the judiciary or state officials to be well versed in the rigors of experimental or statistical technique. But this merely illustrates that proving broad sociological propositions by statistics is a dubious business, and one that inevitably is in tension with the normative philosophy that underlies the Equal Protection Clause. Suffice to say that the showing offered by the appellees does not satisfy us that sex represents a legitimate, accurate proxy for the regulation of drinking and driving. In fact, when it is further recognized that Oklahoma's statute prohibits only the selling of 3.2% beer to young males and not their drinking the beverage once acquired (even after purchase by their 18–20-year-old female companions), the relationship between gender and traffic safety becomes far too tenuous to satisfy *Reed's* requirement that the gender-based difference be substantially related to achievement of the statutory objective.

We hold, therefore, that under *Reed,* Oklahoma's 3.2% beer statute invidiously discriminates against males 18–20 years of age.

MR. JUSTICE REHNQUIST, dissenting.

The Court's disposition of this case is objectionable on two grounds. First is its conclusion that *men* challenging a gender-based statute which treats them less favorably than women may invoke a more stringent standard of judicial review than pertains to most other types of classifications. Second is the Court's enunciation of this standard, without citation to any source, as being that "classification by gender must serve *important* governmental objectives and must be *substantially* related to achievement of those objectives." (Emphasis added.) The only redeeming feature of the Court's opinion, to my mind, is that it apparently signals a retreat by those who joined the plurality opinion in *Frontiero v. Richardson* (1973) from their view that sex is a "suspect" classification for purposes of equal protection analysis. I think the Oklahoma statute challenged here need pass only the "rational basis" equal protection analysis expounded in cases such as *McGowan v. Maryland* (1961) and *Williamson v.*

Lee Optical Co. (1955), and I believe that it is constitutional under that analysis.

In *Frontiero v. Richardson,* the opinion for the plurality sets forth the reasons of four Justices for concluding that sex should be regarded as a suspect classification for purposes of equal protection analysis. These reasons center on our Nation's "long and unfortunate history of sex discrimination," which has been reflected in a whole range of restrictions on the legal rights of women, not the least of which have concerned the ownership of property and participation in the electoral process. Noting that the pervasive and persistent nature of the discrimination experienced by women is in part the result of their ready identifiability, the plurality rested its invocation of strict scrutiny largely upon the fact that "statutory distinctions between the sexes often have the effect of invidiously relegating the entire class of females to inferior legal status without regard to the actual capabilities of its individual members."

Subsequent to *Frontiero,* the Court has declined to hold that sex is a suspect class, and no such holding is imported by the Court's resolution of this case. However, the Court's application here of an elevated or "intermediate" level scrutiny, like that invoked in cases dealing with discrimination against females, raises the question of why the statute here should be treated any differently from countless legislative classifications unrelated to sex which have been upheld under a minimum rationality standard.

Most obviously unavailable to support any kind of special scrutiny in this case, is a history or pattern of past discrimination, such as was relied on by the plurality in *Frontiero* to support its invocation of strict scrutiny. There is no suggestion in the Court's opinion that males in this age group are in any way peculiarly disadvantaged, subject to systematic discriminatory treatment, or otherwise in need of special solicitude from the courts.

The Court does not discuss the nature of the right involved, and there is no reason to believe that it sees the purchase of 3.2% beer as implicating any important interest, let alone one that is "fundamental" in the constitutional sense of invoking strict scrutiny. Indeed, the Court's accurate observation that the statute affects the selling but not the drinking of 3.2% beer further emphasizes the limited effect that it has on even those persons in the age group involved. There is, in sum, nothing about the statutory classification

involved here to suggest that it affects an interest, or works against a group, which can claim under the Equal Protection Clause that it is entitled to special judicial protection.

It is true that a number of our opinions contain broadly phrased dicta implying that the same test should be applied to all classifications based on sex, whether affecting females or males. However, before today, no decision of this Court has applied an elevated level of scrutiny to invalidate a statutory discrimination harmful to males, except where the statute impaired an important personal interest protected by the Constitution. There being no such interest here, and there being no plausible argument that this is a discrimination against females, the Court's reliance on our previous sex-discrimination cases is ill-founded. It treats gender classification as a talisman which—without regard to the rights involved or the persons affected—calls into effect a heavier burden of judicial review.

The Court's conclusion that a law which treats males less favorably than females "must serve important governmental objectives and must be substantially related to achievement of those objectives" apparently comes out of thin air. The Equal Protection Clause contains no such language, and none of our previous cases adopt that standard. I would think we have had enough difficulty with the two standards of review which our cases have recognized—the norm of "rational basis," and the "compelling state interest" required where a "suspect classification" is involved—so as to counsel weightily against the insertion of still another "standard" between those two. How is this Court to divine what objectives are important? How is it to determine whether a particular law is "substantially" related to the achievement of such objective, rather than related in some other way to its achievement? Both of the phrases used are so diaphanous and elastic as to invite subjective judicial preferences or prejudices relating to particular types of legislation, masquerading as judgments whether such legislation is directed at "important" objectives or, whether the relationship to those objectives is "substantial" enough.

I would have thought that if this Court were to leave anything to decision by the popularly elected branches of the Government, where no constitutional claim other than that of equal protection is invoked, it would be the decision as to what governmental objectives to be achieved by law are "important," and which are not. As for the second part of the Court's new test, the Judicial Branch is probably in no worse position than the Legislative or Executive Branches to determine if there is *any* rational relationship between a classification and the purpose which it might be thought to serve. But the introduction of the adverb "substantially" requires courts to make subjective judgments as to operational effects, for which neither their expertise nor their access to data fits them. And even if we manage to avoid both confusion and the mirroring of our own preferences in the development of this new doctrine, the thousands of judges in other courts who must interpret the Equal Protection Clause may not be so fortunate.

The heightened scrutiny test was adopted by a narrow margin. Although six justices joined the opinion, the concurring views of Justices Lewis F. Powell Jr. and John Paul Stevens indicated that their agreement with Brennan's new standard was qualified. Nevertheless, the elevated level of scrutiny was established and since then has been used in sex discrimination cases. The battle between strict scrutiny advocates and rational basis proponents thus ended with neither side able to claim victory. The strict scrutiny justices were forced to moderate their position just enough to capture sufficient votes to adopt an intermediate level test.

In the years following *Craig* the Court confronted many claims of unconstitutional discrimination on the basis of sex. In general, the Court continued to strike down laws and government actions that treated individuals differently on the basis of sex simply because it was administratively convenient to do so. The Court also has taken a dim view of laws that include overbroad sex-based assumptions, particularly if a presumption of female inferiority appears to be the basis for the statute. For example, in *Orr v. Orr* (1979) the justices struck down an Alabama law that permitted courts to impose alimony obligations on husbands but not on wives. The law, according to Justice Brennan, speaking for the majority, contained an outdated stereotype that women are dependent upon men. Similarly, in **Mississippi University for Women v. Hogan** (1982) the Court struck down the all-female admissions standard used by a state university on

the ground that it was based on a presumption that female students were inferior and needed an academic environment without competition from males to succeed. The justices reemphasized this position in **United States v. Virginia** (1996) when they struck down the men-only admissions policies at Virginia Military Institute, a state-supported military college. The justices held that a state institution cannot constitutionally restrict participation to one sex on the ground that the educational experiences provided are inappropriate for the other.

In other cases, however, the Court found some laws that discriminated between males and females to be valid because they recognized legitimate differences between the sexes. In **Michael M. v. Superior Court of Sonoma County** (1981) the justices, by a 5 to 4 vote, upheld a statutory rape law that applied to males only. The fact that only females can become pregnant was a significant sex difference that the majority took into account. In **Rostker v. Goldberg** (1981) the Court upheld the federal draft law that required men but not women to register for military service. Here the justices deferred to the judgment of the military and Congress that the nation required a system for quickly raising combat forces, for which men were better suited.

ECONOMIC DISCRIMINATION

As with matters of race and gender, society's views on economic status have changed. In the nation's early days, wealth was considered a reflection of individual worth. The poor were thought to be less deserving. The free enterprise philosophy that emphasized personal economic responsibility discouraged public policies designed to help the poor. An example of the period's hard-line approach to economic failure was that people could be imprisoned for failure to pay debts. James Wilson, a sitting Supreme Court justice, was imprisoned in 1796 because of a failure to satisfy his creditors. In *City of New York v. Miln* (1837) the Court supported the power of the state to take "precautionary measures against the moral pestilence of paupers."

As American society evolved, the plight of the poor became a major public policy concern. Although opinions differ widely on the proper role of government in poverty, housing, and health care, the U.S. political system has developed social programs that would have been inconceivable to leaders during the nation's formative years. Moreover, economic disadvantage is no longer seen as a justification for denying a person full political and social rights. As a consequence, the Supreme Court has reviewed many government policies challenged as discriminating on the basis of economic status. Among such cases none is more important than *San Antonio Independent School District v. Rodriguez* (1973).

The *Rodriguez* decision is important for several reasons. First, the case involved the right of children to receive a public education, the surest way for the disadvantaged to improve their prospects for economic and social advancement. Second, it attacked the constitutionality of the Texas method of funding public schools. Education is the most expensive of all state programs, and any change in the method of distributing school funds can have a tremendous effect. Third, the Texas system challenged here was similar to schemes used by most states in determining the allocation of education dollars. Whatever the Court decided, this case was going to have a strong economic and social effect.

At the heart of *Rodriguez* was the contention that the Texas system for funding schools discriminated against the poor. It was undeniable that children who lived in wealthy school districts had access to a higher quality education than children in poor districts. But does this difference violate the Constitution? In large measure, the answer to that question rests on which equal protection standard is used. Under strict scrutiny the Texas funding system almost certainly would fall. But before strict scrutiny can be applied, one of two requirements has to be met. Either the poor, like black Americans in the racial discrimination cases, would have to be declared a suspect class, or education would have to be declared a fundamental right. If the Court failed to support at least one of these two positions, the rational basis test would control, and the state plan likely would stand. As you read Justice Powell's decision, think about his reasoning and conclusions on these two points.

San Antonio Independent School District v. Rodriguez

411 U.S. 1 (1973)
http://laws.findlaw.com/US/411/1.html
Oral arguments may be found at: http://www.oyez.org
Vote: 5 (Blackmun, Burger, Powell, Rehnquist, Stewart)
    4 (Brennan, Douglas, Marshall, White)
Opinion of the Court: Powell
Concurring opinion: Stewart
Dissenting opinions: Brennan, Marshall, White

Demetrio Rodriguez and other Mexican American parents whose children attended the public schools of the Edgewood Independent School District in San Antonio, Texas, were concerned about the quality of these schools. The Edgewood district was about 90 percent Mexican American and quite poor. Efforts to improve their children's schools were unsuccessful due to insufficient funding. Because the state formula for distributing education funds resulted in low levels of financial support for economically depressed districts, the parents filed suit to declare the state funding system in violation of the equal protection clause. The funding program guaranteed each child in the state a minimum basic education by appropriating funds to local school districts through a complex formula designed to take into account economic variations across school districts. Local districts levied property taxes to meet their assigned contributions to the state program but also could use the property taxing power to obtain additional funds.

In the Edgewood district the average assessed property value per pupil was $5,960, the lowest in the San Antonio area, and the median family income of $4,686 was also the lowest. The district taxed its residents at a rate of $1.05 per $100 in assessed valuation, the area's highest rate. This local tax yielded $26 per pupil above the contributions that had to be made to the state for the 1967–1968 school year. Funds from the state added $222 per pupil, and federal programs contributed $108. These sources combined for a total of $356 per pupil for the year. In the nearby Alamo Heights district, property values

Demetrio Rodriguez and other Mexican-American parents challenged the Texas public school financing system as discriminatory on the basis of economic status, but in 1973 the Supreme Court ruled against them.

amounted to $49,000 per pupil; and property was taxed at a rate of $0.85 per $100 of assessed valuation. These property taxes yielded $333 additional available revenues per pupil. Combined with $225 from state funds and $36 from federal sources, Alamo Heights enjoyed a total funding level of $594 per pupil.

The suit filed by Rodriguez and the other parents was based on these disparities. Although the residents of Edgewood taxed themselves at a much higher rate, the yield from local taxes in Alamo Heights was almost thirteen times greater. To achieve equal property tax dollars with Alamo Heights, Edgewood would have had to raise its tax rate to $13 per $100 in assessed valuation, but state law placed a $1.50 ceiling on such taxes. There was no way for the Edgewood parents to achieve funding equality.

A three-judge federal court agreed with the Rodriguez suit, finding that the Texas funding program invidiously discriminated against children on the basis of economic status. According to the federal court, poverty was a suspect classification, and education was a fundamental right. The state appealed to the Supreme Court. Twenty-five states filed amicus curiae briefs supporting the Texas funding system. Groups such as the NAACP, the ACLU, and the American Education Association filed briefs backing Rodriguez.

MR. JUSTICE POWELL delivered the opinion of the Court.

Texas virtually concedes that its historically rooted dual system of financing education could not withstand the strict judicial scrutiny that this Court has found appropriate in reviewing legislative judgments that interfere with fundamental constitutional rights or that involve suspect classifications. If, as previous decisions have indicated, strict scrutiny means that the State's system is not entitled to the usual presumption of validity, that the State rather than the complainants must carry a "heavy burden of justification," that the State must demonstrate that its educational system has been structured with "precision," and is "tailored" narrowly to serve legitimate objectives and that it has selected the "less drastic means" for effectuating its objectives, the Texas financing system and its counterpart in virtually every other State will not pass muster. The State candidly admits that "[n]o one familiar with the Texas system would contend that it has yet achieved perfection." Apart from its concession that educational financing in Texas has "defects" and "imperfections," the State defends the system's rationality with vigor and disputes the District Court's finding that it lacks a "reasonable basis."

This, then, establishes the framework for our analysis. We must decide, first, whether the Texas system of financing public education operates to the disadvantage of some suspect class or impinges upon a fundamental right explicitly or implicitly protected by the Constitution, thereby requiring strict judicial scrutiny. If so, the judgment of the District Court should be affirmed. If not, the Texas scheme must still be examined to determine whether it rationally furthers some legitimate, articulated state purpose and therefore does not constitute an invidious discrimination in violation of the Equal Protection Clause of the Fourteenth Amendment.

The District Court's opinion does not reflect the novelty and complexity of the constitutional questions posed by appellees' challenge to Texas' system of school financing. In concluding that strict judicial scrutiny was required, that court relied on decisions dealing with the rights of indigents to equal treatment in the criminal trial and appellate processes, and on cases disapproving wealth restrictions on the right to vote. Those cases, the District Court concluded, established wealth as a suspect classification. Finding that the local property tax system discriminated on the basis of wealth, it regarded those precedents as controlling. It then reasoned, based on decisions of this Court affirming the undeniable importance of education, that there is a fundamental right to education and that, absent some compelling state justification, the Texas system could not stand.

We are unable to agree that this case, which in significant aspects is *sui generis,* may be so neatly fitted into the conventional mosaic of constitutional analysis under the Equal Protection Clause. Indeed, for the several reasons that follow, we find neither the suspect-classification nor the fundamental-interest analysis persuasive.

The wealth discrimination discovered by the District Court in this case, and by several other courts that have recently struck down school-financing laws in other States, is quite unlike any of the forms of wealth discrimination heretofore reviewed by this Court. Rather than focusing on the unique features of the alleged discrimination, the courts in these cases have virtually assumed their findings of a suspect classification through a simplistic process of analysis: since, under the traditional systems of financing public schools, some poorer people receive less expensive educations than other more affluent people, these systems discriminate on the basis of wealth. This approach largely ignores the hard threshold questions, including whether it makes a difference for purposes of consideration under the Constitution that the class of disadvantaged "poor" cannot be identified or defined in customary equal protection terms, and whether the relative—rather than absolute—nature of the asserted deprivation is of significant consequence. Before a State's laws and the justification for the classifications they create are subjected to strict judicial scrutiny, we think these threshold considerations must be analyzed more closely than they were in the court below. . . .

First, in support of their charge that the system discriminates against the "poor," appellees have made no effort to demonstrate that it operates to the peculiar disadvantage of any class fairly definable as indigent, or as composed of persons whose incomes are beneath any designated poverty level. Indeed, there is reason to believe that the poorest families are not necessarily clustered in the poorest property districts. A recent and exhaustive study of school districts in Connecticut concluded that . . . the poor were clustered around commercial and industrial areas—those same areas that provide the most attractive sources of property tax income for school districts. Whether a similar pattern would be discovered in Texas is not known, but there is no basis on the record in this case for assuming that the poorest people—defined by reference to any level of absolute impecunity—are concentrated in the poorest districts.

Second, neither appellees nor the District Court addressed the fact that, unlike each of the foregoing cases, lack of personal resources has not occasioned an absolute deprivation of the desired benefit. The argument here is not that the children in districts having relatively low assessable property values are receiving no public education; rather, it is that they are receiving a poorer quality education than that available to children in districts having more assessable wealth. Apart from the unsettled and disputed question whether the quality of education may be determined by the amount of money expended for it, a sufficient answer to appellees' argument is that, at least where wealth is involved, the Equal Protection Clause does not require absolute equality or precisely equal advantages. . . .

However described, it is clear that appellees' suit asks this Court to extend its most exacting scrutiny to review a system that allegedly discriminates against a large, diverse, and amorphous class, unified only by the common factor of residence in districts that happen to have less taxable wealth than other districts. The system of alleged discrimination and the class it defines have none of the traditional indicia of suspectness: the class is not saddled with such disabilities, or subjected to such a history of purposeful unequal treatment, or relegated to such a position of political powerlessness as to command extraordinary protection from the majoritarian political process.

We thus conclude that the Texas system does not operate to the peculiar disadvantage of any suspect class. But in recognition of the fact that this Court has never heretofore held that wealth discrimination alone provides an adequate basis for invoking strict scrutiny, appellees have not relied solely on this contention. They also assert that the State's system impermissibly interferes with the exercise of a "fundamental" right and that accordingly the prior decisions of this Court require the application of the strict standard of judicial review. It is this question—whether education is a fundamental right, in the sense that it is among the rights and liberties protected by the Constitution—which has so consumed the attention of courts and commentators in recent years.

In *Brown v. Board of Education* (1954) a unanimous Court recognized that "education is perhaps the most important function of state and local governments." . . . This theme, expressing an abiding respect for the vital role of education in a free society, may be found in numerous opinions of Justices of this Court writing both before and after *Brown* was decided.

Nothing this Court holds today in any way detracts from our historic dedication to public education. We are in complete agreement with the conclusion of the three-judge panel below that "the grave significance of education both to the individual and to our society" cannot be doubted. But the importance of a service performed by the State does not determine whether it must be regarded as fundamental for purposes of examination under the Equal Protection Clause. . . .

Education, of course, is not among the rights afforded explicit protection under our Federal Constitution. Nor do we find any basis for saying it is implicitly so protected. As we have said, the undisputed importance of education will not alone cause this Court to depart from the usual standard for reviewing a State's social and economic legislation. It is appellees' contention, however, that education is distinguishable from other services and benefits provided by the State because it bears a peculiarly close relationship to other rights and liberties accorded protection under the Constitution. Specifically, they insist that education is itself a fundamental personal right because it is essential to the effective exercise of First Amendment freedoms and to intelligent utilization of the right to vote. In asserting a nexus between speech and education, appellees urge that the right to speak is meaningless unless the speaker is capable of articulating his thoughts intelligently and persuasively. The "marketplace of ideas" is an empty forum for those lacking basic communicative tools. Likewise, they argue that the corollary right to receive information becomes little more than a hollow privilege when the recipient has not been taught to read, assimilate, and utilize available knowledge. . . .

We need not dispute any of these propositions. The Court has long afforded zealous protection against unjustifiable governmental interference with the individual's rights to speak and to vote. Yet we have never presumed to possess either the ability or the authority to guarantee to the citizenry the most *effective* speech or the most *informed* electoral choice. That these may be desirable goals of a system of freedom of expression and of a representative form of government is not to be doubted. These are indeed goals to be pursued by a people whose thoughts and beliefs are freed from governmental interference. But they are not values to be implemented by judicial intrusion into otherwise legitimate state activities. . . .

It should be clear, for the reasons stated above and in accord with the prior decisions of this Court, that this is not a case in which the challenged state action must be subjected to the searching judicial scrutiny reserved for laws that create suspect classifications or impinge upon constitutionally protected rights.

We need not rest our decision, however, solely on the inappropriateness of the strict-scrutiny test. A century of Supreme Court adjudication under the Equal Protection Clause affirmatively supports the application of the traditional standard of review, which requires only that the State's system be shown to bear some rational relationship to legitimate state purposes. This case represents far more than a challenge to the manner in which Texas provides for the education of its children. We have here nothing less than a direct attack on the way in which Texas has chosen to raise and disburse state and local tax revenues. We are asked to condemn the State's judgment in conferring on political subdivisions the power to tax local property to supply revenues for local interests. In so doing, appellees would have the Court intrude in an area in which it has traditionally deferred to state legislatures. This Court has often admonished against such interferences with the State's fiscal policies under the Equal Protection Clause. . . .

Thus, we stand on familiar grounds when we continue to acknowledge that the Justices of this Court lack both the expertise and the familiarity with local problems so necessary to the making of wise decisions with respect to the raising and disposition of public revenues. Yet, we are urged to direct the States either to alter drastically the present system or to throw out the property tax altogether in favor of some other form of taxation. No scheme of taxation, whether the tax is imposed on property, income, or purchases of goods and services, has yet been devised which is free of all discriminatory impact. In such a complex arena in which no perfect alternatives exist, the Court does well not to impose too rigorous a standard of scrutiny lest all local fiscal schemes become subjects of criticism under the Equal Protection Clause.

In addition to matters of fiscal policy, this case also involves the most persistent and difficult questions of educational policy, another area in which this Court's lack of specialized knowledge and experience counsels against premature interference with the informed judgments made at the state and local levels. Education, perhaps even more than welfare assistance, presents a myriad of "intractable economic, social, and even philosophical problems." The very complexity of the problems of financing and managing a statewide public school system suggests that "there will be more than one constitutionally permissible method of solving them," and that, within the limits of rationality, "the legislature's efforts to tackle the problems" should be entitled to respect. . . .

It must be remembered, also, that every claim arising under the Equal Protection Clause has implications for the relationship between national and state power under our federal system. Questions of federalism are always inherent in the process of determining whether a State's laws are to be accorded the traditional presumption of constitutionality, or are to be subjected instead to rigorous judicial scrutiny. While "[t]he maintenance of the principles of federalism is a foremost consideration in interpreting any of the pertinent constitutional provisions under which this Court examines state action," it would be difficult to imagine a case having a greater potential impact on our federal system than the one now before us, in which we are urged to abrogate systems of financing public education presently in existence in virtually every State.

The foregoing considerations buttress our conclusion that Texas' system of public school finance is an inappropriate candidate for strict judicial scrutiny. These same considerations are relevant to the determination whether that system, with its conceded imperfections, nevertheless bears some rational relationship to a legitimate state purpose. . . .

In sum, to the extent that the Texas system of school financing results in unequal expenditures between children who happen to reside in different districts, we cannot say that such disparities are the product of a system that is so irrational as to be invidiously discriminatory. Texas has acknowledged its shortcomings and has persistently endeavored—not without some success—to ameliorate the differences in levels of expenditures without sacrificing the benefits of local participation. The Texas plan is not the result of hurried, ill-conceived legislation. It certainly is not the product of purposeful discrimination against any group or class. On the contrary, it is rooted in decades of experience in Texas and elsewhere, and in major part is the product of responsible studies by qualified people. . . .

These practical considerations, of course, play no role in the adjudication of the constitutional issues presented here. But they serve to highlight the wisdom of the traditional limitations on this Court's function. The consideration and initiation of fundamental reforms with respect to state taxation and education are matters reserved for the legislative processes of the various States, and we do no violence to the values of federalism and separation of powers by staying our hand. We hardly need add that this Court's action today is not to be viewed as placing its judicial imprimatur on the status quo. The need is apparent for reform in tax systems which may well have relied too long and too heavily on the local property tax. And certainly innovative thinking as to public education, its methods, and its funding is necessary to assure both a higher level of quality and greater uniformity of opportunity. These matters merit the continued attention of the scholars who already have contributed much by their challenges. But the ultimate solutions must come from the lawmakers and from the democratic pressures of those who elect them.

Reversed.

MR. JUSTICE MARSHALL . . . dissenting.

The Court today decides, in effect, that a State may constitutionally vary the quality of education which it offers its children in accordance with the amount of taxable wealth located in the school districts within which they reside. The majority's decision represents an abrupt departure from the mainstream of recent state and federal court decisions concerning the unconstitutionality of state educational financing schemes dependent upon taxable local wealth. More unfortunately, though, the majority's holding can only be seen as a retreat from our historic commitment to equality of educational opportunity and as unsupportable acquiescence in a system which deprives children in their earliest years of the chance to reach their full potential as citizens. The Court does this despite the absence of any substantial justification for a scheme which arbitrarily channels educational resources in accordance with the fortuity of the amount of taxable wealth within each district.

In my judgment, the right of every American to an equal start in life, so far as the provision of a state service as important as education is concerned, is far too vital to permit state discrimination on grounds as tenuous as those presented by this record. Nor can I accept the notion that it is sufficient to remit these appellees to the vagaries of the political process which, contrary to the majority's suggestion, has proved singularly unsuited to the task of providing a remedy for this discrimination. I, for one, am unsatisfied with the hope of an ultimate "political" solution sometime in the indefinite future while, in the meantime, countless children unjustifiably receive inferior educations that "may affect their hearts and minds in a way unlikely ever to be undone." I must therefore respectfully dissent.

The decision in *Rodriguez* was a blow to civil rights advocates. It had a substantial impact on education by validating financing systems that perpetuated inequity. Many states, however, reacted by adjusting their financing schemes to reduce funding disparities, and a few state supreme courts found unequal funding systems to be in violation of state constitutional provisions.

In regard to constitutional development, the ruling introduced problems for future litigation in behalf of the poor. The Court expressly held that the poor were not a suspect class. Unlike other groups, such as black Americans and aliens, that were granted such status, the poor were neither an easily identified group nor politically powerless; as a group they did not have a history of overt discrimination. The decision not to elevate the poor to suspect class status meant that a rational basis test would be used in economic discrimination cases. The rational basis test, as we know, provides the government with an advantage in demonstrating that challenged laws are valid.

In addition, the Court in *Rodriguez* held that education was not a fundamental right under the Constitution. This holding also created potential problems for future cases. Advocates for the poor have concentrated their efforts on education because of its crucial role in human development. By not according it fundamental right status, the Court decreased the chances of successful legal actions in behalf of the economically disadvantaged.

When economic discrimination compromises a fundamental right, however, a higher standard is used, and a state finds it more difficult to justify distinguishing people on the basis of their economic status. In *Gideon v. Wainwright* (1963) we saw the Court act boldly to provide assistance to indigents when poverty affected the right to be represented by an attorney in a criminal case. In the next chapter we will see how the Court refused to allow the states to engage in economic discrimination with respect to the fundamental right to vote. Similarly, when state welfare laws had the effect of placing unreasonable burdens on the fundamental right to travel freely among the states, the Court struck down those statutes.[7]

DISCRIMINATION BASED ON SEXUAL ORIENTATION

Discrimination against gays and lesbians has been one of the more recent civil rights issues to come before the courts. Following the example set by organizations advocating civil rights for African Americans and women, gay rights groups have been active in supporting measures to protect homosexuals from discriminatory practices. In promoting their interests, gay rights groups have suffered from lower levels of public support than other civil rights groups have enjoyed. Public opinion polls over the past three decades have consistently found that a majority of Americans believe that homosexuality is wrong.[8] Perhaps

7. See, for example, *Edwards v. California* (1941), *Shapiro v. Thompson* (1969), *Saenz v. Roe* (1999). The legal challenges to the state laws in these cases involved equal protection clause and privileges and immunities clause arguments.

8. Lee Epstein, Jeffrey A. Segal, Harold J. Spaeth, and Thomas G. Walker, *The Supreme Court Compendium: Data, Decisions, and Developments*, 4th ed. (Washington, D.C.: CQ Press, 2007), Table 8-21.

because of this lack of popular support, Congress and other government agencies have not enacted many of the legislative goals of the gay rights movement. In fact, Congress has passed some laws that have been specifically aimed at blocking gay rights advances. In 1996 Congress passed the Defense of Marriage Act, which denies federal recognition of same-sex marriages and permits states to refuse to recognize same-sex marriages performed in other states. Congress also has refused to include sexual orientation as a protected category under the 1964 Civil Rights Act.

Although the Supreme Court has issued many decisions regarding race, sex, and economic classifications, it has said very little about the rights of gays and lesbians. Moreover, the few decisions it has issued have been decidedly mixed. We have already discussed **Bowers v. Hardwick** (1986), in which the Court upheld state antisodomy laws, and *Lawrence v. Texas* (2003), in which it Court reversed itself. The Court relied on the Constitution's privacy guarantees to hold that *Lawrence* protected private, consensual sexual behavior from criminal prosecution. Therefore, the decision does not directly control the Court's interpretation of the equal protection clause as it applies to general discrimination against gays and lesbians. To date the Court's most important ruling on discriminatory behavior based on sexual orientation is *Romer v. Evans* (1996). Given the justices' general reluctance to accept such disputes, Court observers were interested in how the case would be decided, and they were especially concerned about which the standard of scrutiny the Court would apply.

Romer v. Evans

517 U.S. 620 (1996)
http://laws.findlaw.com/US/517/620.html
Oral arguments may be found at: http://www.oyez.org
Vote: 6 (Breyer, Ginsburg, Kennedy, O'Connor, Souter, Stevens)
    3 (Rehnquist, Scalia, Thomas)
Opinion of the Court: Kennedy
Dissenting opinion: Scalia

This case involved a challenge to an amendment to the Colorado state constitution, which had been adopted by statewide referendum. The referendum arose in response to local laws passed by communities such as Boulder, Aspen, and Denver making sexual orientation an impermissible ground upon which to discriminate. In effect, the local laws gave sexual orientation the same status as race, sex, and other protected categories. To reverse this trend and remove the possibility of future legislation, a sufficient number of citizens signed a petition to place a proposed constitutional amendment on the ballot for the November 1992 elections. Known as Amendment 2, it passed with the support of 53.4 percent of those voting. The amendment stated:

Neither the State of Colorado, through any of its branches or departments, nor any of its agencies, political subdivisions, municipalities or school districts, shall enact, adopt or enforce any statute, regulation, ordinance or policy whereby homosexual, lesbian or bisexual orientation, conduct, practices or relationships shall constitute or otherwise be the basis of or entitle any person or class of persons to have or claim any minority status, quota preferences, protected status or claim of discrimination. This Section of the Constitution shall be in all respects self-executing.

Almost immediately Richard G. Evans, a gay employee in the office of the mayor of Denver, other citizens, and several Colorado local governments sued Gov. Roy Romer and the state of Colorado, claiming that the new amendment was in violation of the Fourteenth Amendment's equal protection clause. The Colorado Supreme Court, 6–1, struck down the amendment, and the state appealed to the U.S. Supreme Court.

JUSTICE KENNEDY delivered the opinion of the Court.

One century ago, the first Justice Harlan admonished this Court that the Constitution "neither knows nor tolerates classes among citizens." *Plessy v. Ferguson* (1896) (dissenting opinion). Unheeded then, those words now are understood to state a commitment to the law's neutrality where the rights of persons are at stake. The Equal Protection Clause enforces this principle and today requires us to hold invalid a provision of Colorado's Constitution. . . .

Soon after Amendment 2 was adopted, this litigation to declare its invalidity and enjoin its enforcement was commenced in the District Court for the City and County of Denver. . . .

Attorney Jean Dubofsky hugs Priscilla Inkpen, one of the plaintiffs who challenged Colorado's antigay rights initiative, after the Supreme Court ruled the measure unconstitutional. Richard Evans, the first named plantiff in the case, is at left.

The trial court granted a preliminary injunction to stay enforcement of Amendment 2, and an appeal was taken to the Supreme Court of Colorado. Sustaining the interim injunction and remanding the case for further proceedings, the State Supreme Court held that Amendment 2 was subject to strict scrutiny under the Fourteenth Amendment because it infringed the fundamental right of gays and lesbians to participate in the political process. . . . On remand, the State advanced various arguments in an effort to show that Amendment 2 was narrowly tailored to serve compelling interests, but the trial court found none sufficient. It enjoined enforcement of Amendment 2, and the Supreme Court of Colorado, in a second opinion, affirmed the ruling. We granted certiorari and now affirm the judgment, but on a rationale different from that adopted by the State Supreme Court.

The State's principal argument in defense of Amendment 2 is that it puts gays and lesbians in the same position as all other persons. So, the State says, the measure does no more than deny homosexuals special rights. This reading of the amendment's language is implausible. We rely not upon our own interpretation of the amendment but upon the authoritative construction of Colorado's Supreme Court. The state court, deeming it unnecessary to determine the full extent of the amendment's reach, found it invalid even on a modest reading of its implications. The critical discussion of the amendment, set out [by the Colorado Supreme Court], is as follows:

"The immediate objective of Amendment 2 is, at a minimum, to repeal existing statutes, regulations, ordinances, and policies of state and local entities that barred discrimination based on sexual orientation. . . .

"The 'ultimate effect' of Amendment 2 is to prohibit any governmental entity from adopting similar, or more protective statutes, regulations, ordinances, or policies in the future unless the state constitution is first amended to permit such measures."

Sweeping and comprehensive is the change in legal status effected by this law. So much is evident from the ordinances that the Colorado Supreme Court declared would be void by operation of Amendment 2. Homosexuals, by state decree, are put in a solitary class with respect to transactions and relations in both the private and governmental spheres. The amendment withdraws from homosexuals, but no others, specific legal protection from the injuries caused by discrimination, and it forbids reinstatement of these laws and policies.

The change that Amendment 2 works in the legal status of gays and lesbians in the private sphere is far-reaching, both on its own terms and when considered in light of the structure and operation of modern anti-discrimination laws. That structure is well illustrated by contemporary statutes and ordinances prohibiting discrimination by providers of public accommodations. . . .

Amendment 2 bars homosexuals from securing protection against the injuries that these public-accommodations laws address. That in itself is a severe consequence, but there is more. Amendment 2, in addition, nullifies specific legal protections for this targeted class in all transactions in housing, sale of real estate, insurance, health and welfare services, private education, and employment.

Not confined to the private sphere, Amendment 2 also operates to repeal and forbid all laws or policies providing specific protection for gays or lesbians from discrimination by every level of Colorado government. . . . The repeal of these measures and the prohibition against their future reenactment demonstrates that Amendment 2 has the same force and effect in Colorado's governmental sector as it does elsewhere and that it applies to policies as well as ordinary legislation.

Amendment 2's reach may not be limited to specific laws passed for the benefit of gays and lesbians. It is a fair, if not necessary, inference from the broad language of the amendment that it deprives gays and lesbians even of the protection of general laws and policies that prohibit arbitrary discrimination in governmental and private settings. . . .

. . . [W]e cannot accept the view that Amendment 2's prohibition on specific legal protections does no more than deprive homosexuals of special rights. To the contrary, the amendment imposes a special disability upon those persons alone. Homosexuals are forbidden the safeguards that others enjoy or may seek without constraint. They can obtain specific protection against discrimination only by enlisting the citizenry of Colorado to amend the state constitution or perhaps, on the State's view, by trying to pass helpful laws of general applicability. This is so no matter how local or discrete the harm, no matter how public and widespread the injury. We find nothing special in the protections Amendment 2 withholds. These are protections taken for granted by most people either because they already have them or do not need them; these are protections against exclusion from an almost limitless number of transactions and endeavors that constitute ordinary civic life in a free society.

The Fourteenth Amendment's promise that no person shall be denied the equal protection of the laws must coexist with the practical necessity that most legislation classifies for one purpose or another, with resulting disadvantage to various groups or persons. We have attempted to reconcile the principle with the reality by stating that, if a law neither burdens a fundamental right nor targets a suspect class, we will uphold the legislative classification so long as it bears a rational relation to some legitimate end. See, *e.g.*, *Heller v. Doe* (1993).

Amendment 2 fails, indeed defies, even this conventional inquiry. First, the amendment has the peculiar property of imposing a broad and undifferentiated disability on a single named group, an exceptional and, as we shall explain, invalid form of legislation. Second, its sheer breadth is so discontinuous with the reasons offered for it that the amendment seems inexplicable by anything but animus toward the class that it affects; it lacks a rational relationship to legitimate state interests.

Taking the first point, even in the ordinary equal protection case calling for the most deferential of standards, we insist on knowing the relation between the classification adopted and the object to be attained. The search for the link between classification and objective gives substance to the Equal Protection Clause; it provides guidance and discipline for the legislature, which is entitled to know what sorts of laws it can pass; and it marks the limits of our own authority. In the ordinary case, a law will be sustained if it can be said to advance a legitimate government interest, even if the law seems unwise or works to the disadvantage of a particular group, or if the rationale for it seems tenuous. . . . By requiring that the classification bear a rational relationship to an independent and legitimate legislative end, we ensure that classifications are not drawn for the purpose of disadvantaging the group burdened by the law.

Amendment 2 confounds this normal process of judicial review. It is at once too narrow and too broad. It identifies persons by a single trait and then denies them protection across the board. The resulting disqualification of a class of persons from the right to seek specific protection from the law is unprecedented in our jurisprudence. . . .

It is not within our constitutional tradition to enact laws of this sort. Central both to the idea of the rule of law and to our own Constitution's guarantee of equal protection is the principle that government and each of its parts remain open on impartial terms to all who seek its assistance. . . .

Respect for this principle explains why laws singling out a certain class of citizens for disfavored legal status or general hardships are rare. A law declaring that in general it shall be more difficult for one group of citizens than for all others to seek aid from the government is itself a denial of equal protection of the laws in the most literal sense. . . .

. . . [L]aws of the kind now before us raise the inevitable inference that the disadvantage imposed is born of animosity toward the class of persons affected. . . . Even laws enacted for broad and ambitious purposes often can be explained by reference to legitimate public policies which justify the incidental disadvantages they impose on certain persons. Amendment 2, however, in making a general announcement that gays and lesbians shall not have any particular protections from the law, inflicts on them immediate, continuing, and real injuries that outrun and belie any legitimate justifications that may be claimed for it. We conclude that, in addition to the far-reaching deficiencies of Amendment 2 that we have noted, the principles it offends, in another sense, are conventional and venerable; a law must bear a rational relationship to a legitimate governmental purpose, and Amendment 2 does not.

The primary rationale the State offers for Amendment 2 is respect for other citizens' freedom of association, and in particular the liberties of landlords or employers who have personal or religious objections to homosexuality. Colorado also cites its interest in conserving resources to fight discrimination against other groups. The breadth of the Amendment is so far removed from these particular justifications that we find it impossible to credit them. We cannot say that Amendment 2 is directed to any identifiable legitimate purpose or discrete objective. It is a status-based enactment divorced from any factual context from which we could discern a relationship to legitimate state interests; it is a classification of persons undertaken for its own sake, something the Equal Protection Clause does not permit.

We must conclude that Amendment 2 classifies homosexuals not to further a proper legislative end but to make them unequal to everyone else. This Colorado cannot do. A State cannot so deem a class of persons a stranger to its laws. Amendment 2 violates the Equal Protection Clause, and the judgment of the Supreme Court of Colorado is affirmed.

It is so ordered.

JUSTICE SCALIA, with whom the CHIEF JUSTICE and JUSTICE THOMAS join, dissenting.

The Court has mistaken a Kulturkampf for a fit of spite. The constitutional amendment before us here is not the manifestation of a " 'bare . . . desire to harm' " homosexuals, but is rather a modest attempt by seemingly tolerant Coloradans to preserve traditional sexual mores against the efforts of a politically powerful minority to revise those mores through use of the laws. That objective, and the means chosen to achieve it, are not only unimpeachable under any constitutional doctrine hitherto pronounced (hence the opinion's heavy reliance upon principles of righteousness rather than judicial holdings); they have been specifically approved by the Congress of the United States and by this Court.

In holding that homosexuality cannot be singled out for disfavorable treatment, the Court contradicts a decision, unchallenged here, pronounced only 10 years ago, see *Bowers v. Hardwick* (1986), and places the prestige of this institution behind the proposition that opposition to homosexuality is as reprehensible as racial or religious bias. Whether it is or not is *precisely* the cultural debate that gave rise to the Colorado constitutional amendment (and to the preferential laws against which the amendment was directed). Since the Constitution of the United States says nothing about this subject, it is left to be resolved by normal democratic means, including the democratic adoption of provisions in state constitutions. This Court has no business imposing upon all Americans the resolution favored by the elite class from which the Members of this institution are selected, pronouncing that "animosity" toward homosexuality is evil. I vigorously dissent.

Let me first discuss [the section of the Court's opinion that] is devoted to rejecting the State's arguments that Amendment 2 "puts gays and lesbians in the same position as all other persons," and "does no more than deny homosexuals special rights." . . .

. . . [T]he principle underlying the Court's opinion is that one who is accorded equal treatment under the laws, but cannot as readily as others obtain *preferential* treatment under the laws, has been denied equal protection of the laws. If merely stating this alleged "equal protection" violation does not suffice to refute it, our constitutional jurisprudence has achieved terminal silliness. . . .

... The Court's opinion contains grim, disapproving hints that Coloradans have been guilty of "animus" or "animosity" toward homosexuality, as though that has been established as Unamerican. Of course it is our moral heritage that one should not hate any human being or class of human beings. But I had thought that one could consider certain conduct reprehensible—murder, for example, or polygamy, or cruelty to animals—and could exhibit even "animus" toward such conduct. Surely that is the only sort of "animus" at issue here: moral disapproval of homosexual conduct, the same sort of moral disapproval that produced the centuries-old criminal laws that we held constitutional in *Bowers.* . . .

But though Coloradans are, as I say, *entitled* to be hostile toward homosexual conduct, the fact is that the degree of hostility reflected by Amendment 2 is the smallest conceivable. The Court's portrayal of Coloradans as a society fallen victim to pointless, hate-filled "gay-bashing" is so false as to be comical. Colorado not only is one of the 25 States that have repealed their antisodomy laws, but was among the first to do so. But the society that eliminates criminal punishment for homosexual acts does not necessarily abandon the view that homosexuality is morally wrong and socially harmful; often, abolition simply reflects the view that enforcement of such criminal laws involves unseemly intrusion into the intimate lives of citizens. . . .

When the Court takes sides in the culture wars, it tends to be with the knights rather than the villeins—and more specifically with the Templars, reflecting the views and values of the lawyer class from which the Court's Members are drawn. How that class feels about homosexuality will be evident to anyone who wishes to interview job applicants at virtually any of the Nation's law schools. The interviewer may refuse to offer a job because the applicant is a Republican; because he is an adulterer; because he went to the wrong prep school or belongs to the wrong country club; because he eats snails; because he is a womanizer; because she wears real-animal fur; or even because he hates the Chicago Cubs. But if the interviewer should wish not to be an associate or partner of an applicant because he disapproves of the applicant's homosexuality, *then* he will have violated the pledge which the Association of American Law Schools requires all its member-schools to exact from job interviewers: "assurance of the employer's willingness" to hire homosexuals. This law school view of what "prejudices" must be stamped out may be contrasted with the more plebeian attitudes that apparently still prevail in the United States Congress, which has been unresponsive to repeated attempts to extend to homosexuals the protections of federal civil rights laws, and which took the pains to exclude them specifically from the Americans With Disabilities Act of 1990.

Today's opinion has no foundation in American constitutional law, and barely pretends to. The people of Colorado have adopted an entirely reasonable provision which does not even disfavor homosexuals in any substantive sense, but merely denies them preferential treatment. Amendment 2 is designed to prevent piecemeal deterioration of the sexual morality favored by a majority of Coloradans, and is not only an appropriate means to that legitimate end, but a means that Americans have employed before. Striking it down is an act, not of judicial judgment, but of political will. I dissent.

The majority's opinion is a strong statement against laws that single out homosexuals for discriminatory treatment. But the ruling is also important for other reasons. The justices explicitly distanced themselves from the "strict scrutiny" approach of the Colorado Supreme Court and did not even engage in a full discussion of the relative merits of the three equal protection tests as applied to gay rights. Instead, the Court concluded that Amendment 2 offends even the lowest level of scrutiny (rational basis), leaving little necessity to engage in additional argument regarding an appropriate test. The Court struck down Amendment 2, but created no new rights or protections.

So, despite *Romer*'s importance, it will not be the Court's last word on the rights of gays and lesbians. *Romer,* along with *Lawrence v. Texas,* already has encouraged additional legal challenges of laws having a discriminatory impact based on sexual orientation.

One issue of intense political and legal controversy is same-sex marriage. Although the debate over gay marriage had been simmering for many years, the controversy became especially prominent in 2003 when the Massachusetts Supreme Judicial Court held, 4–3, in *Goodridge v. Department of Public Health* that state laws allowing only heterosexual couples to marry discriminated against gay persons in violation of the state constitution. The court directed the Massachusetts legislature to bring the state's laws into compliance with its ruling. One year later, the court held that a domestic partnership law, as had been adopted in Vermont in 2000, was an inadequate substitute for full marriage rights. Massachusetts thus became the first state to allow gay couples to marry. The same-sex marriage movement got its next big boost in 2008, when the Supreme Court of California, also by a one-vote margin, handed down a similar ruling in *In re Marriage Cases.*

Most states reacted to the prospect of legalization of same-sex marriages by enacting or reinforcing existing state laws restricting marriage to heterosexual couples. Often these laws and amendments were passed by popular referendum. The federal Defense of Marriage Act supports states that define marriage in traditional terms by allowing them to deny recognition of gay marriages legally performed in other jurisdictions. A handful of states, however, have taken a more moderate approach, enacting statues that give a degree of recognition and some benefits to same-sex couples.

The decisions striking down bans against same-sex marriage have been based on interpretations of state constitutional provisions, some of which include wording similar to that in the U.S. Constitution. It is inevitable that the Supreme Court will be asked to rule on whether state bans against same-sex couples marrying violate the equal protection clause of the Fourteenth Amendment.

REMEDYING THE EFFECTS OF DISCRIMINATION: AFFIRMATIVE ACTION

Creating appropriate standards for interpreting the equal protection principles of the Constitution and determining when governments have engaged in impermissible discrimination are, as we now know, exceedingly difficult tasks. But even when they have been accomplished, the Court's business is not finished. In addition to condemning unconstitutional discrimination, the Court confronts the problem of remedies. To do so means considering acceptable ways to eliminate the discrimination, to implement nondiscriminatory policies, and to compensate the victims of discrimination. The question of appropriate and fair remedies is often even more divisive than determining initial equal protection principles.

For some discrimination issues, remedial action is minimal. Striking down a statute is often sufficient: Nullifying Idaho's discriminatory inheritance statute in *Reed v. Reed* required no significant remedial action. The state simply had to decide future estate administration disputes without regard to sex. For other discrimination issues, however, enforcing the Court's orders can be a lengthy, complex process, such as the nation experienced with the public schools in the aftermath of *Brown v. Board of Education.*

Few issues of constitutional law have prompted as much controversy as the remedial policy known as affirmative action. Based on the notion that the principles of the equal protection clause cannot be achieved by simply terminating illegal discrimination, affirmative action programs direct government and private institutions to take positive measures to ensure that equality becomes a reality.

Affirmative action programs have their roots in presidential orders, issued as early as the 1940s, that expanded government employment opportunities for African Americans. These programs received their most significant boost in 1965 when President Lyndon Johnson issued Executive Order 11246, instructing the Labor Department to ensure that businesses contracting with the federal government were nondiscriminatory. To meet the requirements, government contractors altered their employment policies and recruited minority workers.

Over the years, these requirements were strengthened and expanded. Failure to comply with the government's principles of nondiscriminatory employment was grounds for stripping a business or institution of its federal contract or appropriated funds. Some state and local governments adopted similar programs, many aggressively establishing numerical standards for minority participation. Private businesses also began to adopt programs to increase the numbers of women and minorities, especially in positions where their numbers historically had been low. Are these programs desirable? Constitutional? Such questions have generated debates in political and legal circles.

Those supporting affirmative action marshal many arguments. Taking issue with Justice Harlan's assertion in his *Plessy v. Ferguson* dissent that the Constitution is "color-blind," supporters hold that characteristics associated with disadvantaged status must be considered and taken into account. Special programs and incentives for people from disadvantaged groups are warranted to eradicate and compensate for the effects of past discrimination.

Advocates also suggest that affirmative action plans do not benefit just one or two groups in society; rather, they benefit the entire community. These programs strengthen the country by taking advantage of the talents of all citizens, creating a stronger and more diverse political and social system.

Opponents of special programs see things very differently. Many valued goods and opportunities in society— jobs, promotions, and admission to education and training programs—are sometimes scarce. When, instead of merit alone, factors such as race and sex are used to determine who obtains these opportunities, the losers may claim they are the victims of reverse discrimination. The principles of equal protection, affirmative action opponents assert, should prohibit discrimination against whites and men just as they prohibit discrimination against blacks and women. Those who have been negatively affected by affirmative action view it as inconsistent with the nation's commitment to equal opportunity.

Opponents also note two legal obstacles to affirmative action programs: the Constitution and the Civil Rights Act of 1964. Opponents claim that the equal protection clause of the Fourteenth Amendment and the due process clause of the Fifth prohibit the government from giving special consideration to individuals because of their race, sex, or national origin. As Justice Potter Stewart once wrote, "The Fourteenth Amendment was adopted to ensure that every person must be treated equally by each State regardless of the color of his skin. The Amendment promised to carry to its necessary conclusion a fundamental principle upon which this Nation had been founded—that the law would honor no prefer-

ence based on lineage."[9] The Civil Rights Act of 1964, specifically Title VII, states, with respect to private employment, that race, color, religion, sex, and national origin cannot be used to discriminate against any employee. It further holds:

It shall be an unlawful employment practice for an employer . . . to limit, segregate, or classify his employees or applicants for employment in any way which would deprive or tend to deprive any individual of employment opportunities or otherwise adversely affect his status as an employee, because of such individual's race, color, religion, sex, or national origin.

Title VI of the same statute contains similar provisions for state and local government programs that receive federal funding. These provisions were originally intended to prohibit discrimination against members of groups that historically have been the victims of prejudice. Whether giving preference to such individuals, at the possible expense of others, also violates these constitutional or statutory provisions remained for the Supreme Court to determine.

Which side of this debate would the Court favor? This question was very much on the minds of civil rights groups, scholars, and the public when the justices agreed to hear *Regents of the University of California v. Bakke* (1978).

The stakes were high. For civil rights groups, the case represented a threat to the best way yet devised to eliminate the effects of past discrimination in education and promote minority students into professional positions. For opponents of affirmative action, it was an opportunity to overturn the growing burden of paying for the sins of the past and return to a system based on merit. Fifty-seven amicus briefs were filed by various organizations and interested parties.

Bakke was a challenge to the admissions policies of the medical school of the University of California at Davis, which began operations in 1968. During its first two years it admitted only three minority students, all Asians. To improve minority participation, the school developed two admissions programs to fill the one hundred seats in its entry class—a regular admissions program and a special

9. *Fullilove v. Klutznick* (1980).

admissions program. The regular program worked in the customary way. The school evaluated applicants on the basis of undergraduate grades, standardized test scores, letters of recommendation, extracurricular activities, and an interview. The special program was for applicants who indicated that they were economically or educationally disadvantaged, or were black, Chicano, Asian, or Native American. Such applicants could choose to go through the regular admissions process or be referred to a special admissions committee. Special admissions applicants were judged on the same characteristics as regular applicants, but they competed only against each other. The school reserved sixteen seats to be filled from the special admissions pool. Many white applicants, claiming poverty, indicated a desire to be considered by the special admissions committee, but none was admitted. Only members of the designated racial and ethnic minority groups qualified for special admittance.

Allan Bakke was a white man of Scandinavian descent. He graduated with honors in engineering from the University of Minnesota and was a veteran of the Vietnam War. He worked for the National Aeronautics and Space Administration and received his master's degree in engineering from Stanford. When he developed an interest in pursuing a medical career, Bakke took extra science courses and did volunteer work in a local hospital. At age thirty-three, he applied for admission to the 1973 entry class of the medical school at Davis. He was rejected. He applied in 1974 and was again rejected. Because applicants admitted under the special admissions program were, at least statistically, less qualified than he *(see Table 19-1)*, Bakke sued for admission, claiming that the university's dual admissions program violated the equal protection clause of the Fourteenth Amendment.

The state trial court struck down the special program, declaring that race could not be constitutionally taken into account in deciding who would be admitted, but the court refused to order Bakke's admission. Both Bakke and the university appealed. The California Supreme Court found the special admissions program unconstitutional, holding that "no applicant may be rejected because of his race, in favor of another who is less qualified, as measured by standards applied without regard to race." The state supreme court's order to admit Bakke was stayed, pending the university's appeal to the U.S. Supreme Court.

The justices were deeply divided over this case. Four gave strong support to affirmative action programs, four others had serious reservations about them, and Justice Lewis Powell found himself in the middle. Portions of his opinion announcing the judgment of the Court were supported by one set of four justices, and other parts were joined by an entirely different group of four. As the "swing" justice in this case, Powell was effectively able to determine what the Constitution means with respect to affirmative action programs.

Powell found portions of the University of California program constitutionally sound. A diverse student body, he concluded, was an important goal for an educational institution. To achieve that aim, taking race and ethnicity into account in the admissions process was permissible. Thus, students with minority backgrounds may be accorded a "plus" in the selection process.

But Powell also found that the university's special admissions program crossed the constitutional line. Although race or ethnicity may be considered in the process of assembling a diverse student body, other factors that promote diversity must also be considered. Applicants should be evaluated based on an individualized review of their credentials and may not be classified by racial characteristics alone. It therefore violates the Constitution for the university to segregate minority applicants into a special admissions tract in which they only compete among themselves. Furthermore, absent a history of significant racial discrimination, it also offends the Fourteenth Amendment for the school to reserve a number of seats exclusively for minority candidates, seats for which majority applicants may not compete.

The *Bakke* decision was decidedly mixed. Important was that the Court approved the general concept of affirmative action; but equally significant were constitutional limitations placed on such programs.

In the years immediately following *Bakke*, the Court was generally sympathetic to affirmative action programs—especially where a history of discrimination could be demonstrated. Under such circumstances the

TABLE 19-1 Admissions Data for the Entering Class of the Medical School of the University of
California at Davis, 1973 and 1974

CLASS ENTERING IN 1973

	SGPA[a]	OGPA[b]	Verbal	MCAT (Percentiles) Quantitative	Science	Gen. Infor.
Bakke	3.44	3.46	96	94	97	72
Average of regular admittees	3.51	3.49	81	76	83	69
Average of special admittees	2.62	2.88	46	24	35	33

CLASS ENTERING IN 1974

	SGPA[a]	OGPA[b]	Verbal	MCAT (Percentiles) Quantitative	Science	Gen. Infor.
Bakke	3.44	3.46	96	94	97	72
Average of regular admittees	3.36	3.29	69	67	82	72
Average of special admittees	2.42	2.62	34	30	37	18

SOURCE: *Regents of the University of California v. Bakke* (1978).
a. Science grade point average.   b. Overall grade point average.

justices were more lenient with respect to the use of racial, ethnic, or gender classifications in both the public and private sectors.[10]

Occasionally, when the situation has demanded it, the Court has even allowed the use of quotas, which it condemned in *Bakke*. In *United States v. Paradise* (1987) the Court upheld the ruling of a district court imposing a hiring and promotion quota on the Alabama Department of Public Safety. The quota was ordered because the state had not hired a single black state trooper in thirty-seven years, and less radical remedial orders had not produced the desired action from the state. The justices, in a 5–4 vote, upheld the temporary quota as a necessary response to extreme violations of the Constitution.

With the elevation of William Rehnquist to the chief justice position and the appointments of Antonin Scalia in 1986 and Anthony Kennedy in 1988, the ideological balance of the Court began to move in a more conservative direction that did not bode well for affirmative action

programs. The first indication that a major change was afoot came in *City of Richmond v. J. A. Croson Co.* (1989). This dispute centered on a variation of affirmative action called the minority set-aside program. Minority set-asides attempt to enhance the prospects of disadvantaged groups by granting them special considerations in the awarding of government contracts and benefits. The justification for such programs is the long history of discrimination against minority-owned businesses in general commercial activity and in providing goods and services for the government. Set-asides are based on the principle that just eliminating discrimination in the letting of government contracts will not result in more business for minority-owned firms. Because of past discrimination, many minority businesses lack capital, management experience, and eligibility for bonding. They cannot compete successfully with more solid, better-financed white firms. Consequently, minority set-aside programs propose for a time to reserve a percentage of government business and contracts for minority-owned enterprises.

In 1983 the Richmond City Council, consisting of five black and four white members, adopted the Minority

10. Public sector: see, for example, *Johnson v. Transportation Agency of Santa Clara County, California* (1987); private sector: *United Steelworkers of America v. Weber* (1979).

Utilization Plan, which required the city's prime contractors to award subcontracts of at least 30 percent of the dollar amount of the total contract to one or more minority business enterprises (MBEs). Minority contractors were defined as businesses at least 51 percent owned by persons who were black, Spanish-speaking, Asian, Native American, Eskimo, or Aleut. The minority business did not have to be located in Richmond.

The plan was developed to correct the effects of racial discrimination. Richmond's population was 50 percent black, but between 1978 and 1983 only 0.678 percent of the city's construction business had been awarded to minority contractors. There was no specific finding that the city had discriminated in awarding contracts to minority companies; the problem stemmed largely from a lack of minority-owned contracting businesses in the Richmond area.

Croson Company was the only bidder on a project to install plumbing fixtures at the city jail, but the company had difficulty finding a minority subcontractor to supply the materials. Once Croson located a qualified company willing to participate, the projected price was too high. Croson requested a waiver from the set-aside requirements or permission to raise the cost of the project. The city refused and elected to rebid the contract. Croson sued to have the set-aside program declared unconstitutional as a violation of the equal protection clause of the Fourteenth Amendment.

Although the Court had approved federal minority set-aside programs in *Fullilove v. Klutznick* (1980), the justices decided in favor of Croson, striking down the Richmond program. Justice O'Connor's strongly worded opinion written for the majority found numerous defects in the Richmond plan. First, there had been no finding based on evidence that the situation in the Richmond construction industry was the result of any constitutional violation that required a remedial response. Second, the program included groups for which there was no evidence whatever of discrimination in Richmond (specifically, Hispanics, Asians, Native Americans, Eskimos, and Aleuts). Third, the program allowed contracting dollars to be given to out-of-state minority firms, hardly a strategy that was tailored to remedy discrimination against Richmond firms. Fourth, there was no evidence that the

city of Richmond had considered race-neutral alternatives. Fifth, the 30 percent figure appeared to have been arbitrarily set. Sixth, the plan was not a temporary one to correct a specific constitutional violation.

The Court emphasized that state and local affirmative action polices must be evaluated according to strict scrutiny standards. The Fourteenth Amendment requires that such programs be in pursuit of a compelling state interest and formulated using the least restrictive means possible. The Court's strong condemnation of Richmond's minority set-aside program was a clear signal to other state and local governments that plans to increase business for minority-owned enterprises were going to be difficult to justify. The decision also gave encouragement to those majority-owned businesses that wanted to challenge such plans.

In the five years following the *Croson* ruling, William Brennan, Thurgood Marshall, Byron White, and Harry Blackmun retired. These four justices constituted the liberal minority that voted to approve the University of California's special admissions policy in *Bakke*. Court observers saw their departure as an opportunity for the more conservative wing of the Court to impose additional restrictions on affirmative action programs.

In *Adarand Constructors, Inc. v. Peña* (1995) the Court did just that. In another vigorous opinion by Justice O'Connor, the Court extended the strict scrutiny test to cover federal minority set-aside programs, overruling an earlier decision that permitted federal affirmative action plans to be evaluated according to intermediate scrutiny.[11] Following the *Adarand* decision, federal, state, and local affirmative action programs all had to meet strict scrutiny standards to be ruled constitutionally valid.

Decisions such as *Croson* and *Adarand* cast considerable doubt on the constitutional viability of affirmative action programs. This uncertainty was reinforced when the Court began rejecting plans that took race into account in constructing legislative districts *(see chapter 20)*. Court observers began to speculate that the justices had turned away from the principles set in Justice Powell's opinion in *Bakke* and had become skeptical of minority preference programs of all kinds.

11. *Metro Broadcasting v. FCC* (1990).

Encouraged by these events, opponents of affirmative action programs orchestrated political and legal efforts to eliminate them. In several instances they were successful: California, Florida, and Washington State enacted measures by popular initiative or legislative action that banned the use of racial preferences. In *Hopwood v. Texas* (1996) the Fifth Circuit Court of Appeals ruled that preferential admissions policies violated the Constitution, a decision binding on Louisiana, Mississippi, and Texas, the three states under its jurisdiction. Several district courts around the country came to similar conclusions.

Where they were prohibited by law or judicial order, the elimination of affirmative action programs had a demonstrable impact. In California's university system, the proportion of black and Hispanic students dropped substantially. The population of white students remained relatively constant or declined slightly at some schools. The largest beneficiaries of race-blind admissions were Asian students, whose numbers increased significantly.[12] The University of Texas at Austin experienced similar enrollment patterns, with declines in the number of black and Hispanic students and increases in Asians. The university's student body became less reflective of the state's population. In 2002, for example, black enrollment was only 3 percent of the entry class, whereas blacks constituted 11 percent of the Texas population; Hispanics represented 14 percent of the freshman class, but 32 percent of the state population. On the other hand, Asians made up only 3 percent of the state population, but 18 percent of the entry class.[13] Faced with such statistics, the colleges and universities that had been forced to abandon preference programs worked to develop race-neutral methods of improving diversity.

With states and judicial districts taking different positions on the question, it was inevitable that the U.S. Supreme Court would attempt to clarify the constitutionality of affirmative action. The showdown occurred in 2003 when the justices took up two appeals challenging affirmative action at the University of Michigan. One suit, *Gratz v. Bollinger*, attacked the university's undergraduate admissions policies, and the other, *Grutter v. Bollinger*,

challenged admissions to the university's law school. In both cases the admissions policies were adopted voluntarily rather than in response to a court order to compensate for past constitutional violations.

Speculation on the outcome of the Court's deliberations generally conceded that the votes of seven of the nine justices were all but certain. Justices Stevens, Souter, Ginsburg, and Breyer had records of consistent support for the limited use of racial preferences. On the other side, Chief Justice Rehnquist and Justices Scalia and Thomas had consistently and vigorously opposed affirmative action. Most observers believed that Justices O'Connor and Kennedy held the key to the outcome. For affirmative action to receive constitutional approval at least one of these two moderate conservatives would have to vote with the Court's more liberal bloc.

Would the Court reaffirm Justice Powell's *Bakke* decision, or would its later pattern of rejecting race-based policies prevail? Would the justices remain committed to the strict scrutiny test for deciding racial preference cases? If so, would the creation of a diverse student body qualify as a sufficiently compelling state interest to justify taking race into account?

In the material that follows, we discuss both cases and provide an excerpt of the Court's decision in *Grutter v. Bollinger*.

Grutter v. Bollinger

539 U.S. 306 (2003)
http://laws.findlaw.com/US/539/306.html
Oral arguments may be found at: http://www.oyez.org
Vote: 5 (*Breyer, Ginsburg, O'Connor, Souter, Stevens*)
4 (*Kennedy, Rehnquist, Scalia, Thomas*)
Opinion of the Court: O'Connor
Concurring opinion: Ginsburg
Dissenting opinions: Kennedy, Rehnquist
Opinions concurring in part and dissenting in part: Scalia, Thomas

Gratz v. Bollinger (2003) involved the University of Michigan's undergraduate admissions policies. White Michigan residents Jennifer Gratz and Patrick Hamacher applied for admission, Gratz in 1995 and Hamacher in

---

12. *New York Times*, February 2, 2003.
13. Ibid.

1997. Based on their academic credentials, Gratz fell into the university's "well-qualified" category and Hamacher was judged to be "qualified." The university denied them admission. Gratz and Hamacher sued the university, in the name of president Lee Bollinger, claiming that their rejections were due to the university's racial preference policies.

Committed to having a diverse student body, the university used various methods of enhancing the admissions opportunities for applicants from underrepresented groups, specifically African Americans, Hispanics, and Native Americans. When Gratz applied, the policy of the university was to add .5 to the grade point averages of applicants from the designated minority groups, to use different grade point average/test score grids for minority and nonminority students, and to protect a number slots for certain kinds of students, including minority applicants. The university later changed its policies, eliminating the protected slots and instead assigning points to applicants based on academic and nonacademic factors. Under this system there was a maximum of 150 possible points, with 100 points necessary to be admitted. In order to promote a diverse student body, 20 points were automatically given to every applicant from the designated underrepresented groups. It was this revised system on which the case focused.

In *Grutter v. Bollinger,* Barbara Grutter, a white Michigan resident, applied for admission to the University of Michigan Law School in 1996, presenting a 3.8 undergraduate grade point average and a 161 law school admissions test score. She was first placed on the school's waiting list and ultimately denied admission. She sued the university, claiming that her rejection was due to an admissions policy that awarded preferences based on race in violation of the equal protection clause.

The University of Michigan Law School, one of the nation's finest, annually received about 3,500 applications for the 350 seats in its first-year class. The school sought the most capable class of students possible, but it also wanted students with varying backgrounds and experiences. To achieve a diverse student body, the school looked beyond grade point averages and test scores. It did not confine diversity to racial and ethnic categories, nor did it limit the number of factors that might be con-

sidered in assembling a diverse student body, but it made a commitment to black, Hispanic, and Native American applicants who, without a special consideration, might be underrepresented. The law school desired a "critical mass" of minority students so that they would not be isolated or feel like spokespersons for their race. The law school argued that such a critical mass was necessary to attain the educational benefits of a diverse student body.

At trial, admissions officers testified that the "critical mass" goal did not imply any particular proportion of the entry class. No predetermined number of points was given to minority applicants, but each application was individually considered on its own merits. During the height of the admissions process, school officials kept daily watch over the number of minority students who had been admitted. Expert testimony indicated that in 2000, 35 percent of underrepresented minority candidates were admitted, but if race had not been considered only 10 percent of minority applications would have been successful.

Both *Gratz* and *Grutter* attracted significant amicus curiae participation. The position of the rejected students was supported by a collection of conservative groups with long histories opposing racial preferences, but the most important amicus brief was submitted by Solicitor General Theodore Olson, who expressed the Bush administration's opposition to the admissions policies. Supporting the university was an even larger group of interests. Among them, as expected, was an array of traditional civil rights groups, but, surprisingly, by individuals associated with the military and business interests also submitted briefs.

Decisions in both cases were handed down on June 23, 2003. In *Gratz* the Supreme Court, by a 6–3 vote, found that the university's undergraduate admissions policies violated the equal protection clause. The justices ruled that the automatic distribution of 20 points, or one-fifth of those necessary for admission, to every underrepresented minority applicant, solely because of race, was not narrowly tailored to achieve the goal of educational diversity. The system lacked the necessary individualized consideration that Justice Powell had emphasized in *Bakke* and elevated race to the point that it became a decisive factor for virtually every minimally qualified minority applicant.

Barbara Grutter, shown in her Plymouth, Michigan, home in 2003, challenged the constitutionality of the University of Michigan Law School's admissions policies. In *Grutter v. Bollinger*, the Supreme Court found that the school's affirmative action admissions program did not violate the Equal Protection Clause.

O'Connor and Kennedy, the two swing justices, voted against the university and joined the majority opinion.

Gratz was a victory for affirmative action opponents, but *Grutter*, the suit challenging the admissions policies of the university's law school, was a very different matter. Here the Court considered whether the goal of a diverse student body was a compelling governmental interest and whether an individualized preference policy passed constitutional muster.

JUSTICE O'CONNOR delivered the opinion of the Court.

We last addressed the use of race in public higher education over 25 years ago. In the landmark [*Regents of the University of California v.*] *Bakke* [1978] case, we reviewed a racial set-aside program that reserved 16 out of 100 seats in a medical school class for members of certain minority groups. The decision produced six separate opinions, none of which commanded a majority of the Court. Four Justices would have upheld the program against all attack on the ground that the government can use race to "remedy disadvantages cast on minorities by past racial prejudice." Four other Justices avoided the constitutional question altogether and struck down the program on statutory grounds. Justice Powell provided a fifth vote not only for invalidating the set-aside

program, but also for reversing the state court's injunction against any use of race whatsoever. The only holding for the Court in *Bakke* was that a "State has a substantial interest that legitimately may be served by a properly devised admissions program involving the competitive consideration of race and ethnic origin." Thus, we reversed that part of the lower court's judgment that enjoined the university "from any consideration of the race of any applicant."

Since this Court's splintered decision in *Bakke*, Justice Powell's opinion announcing the judgment of the Court has served as the touchstone for constitutional analysis of race-conscious admissions policies. Public and private universities across the Nation have modeled their own admissions programs on Justice Powell's views on permissible race-conscious policies. . . .

Justice Powell began by stating that "[t]he guarantee of equal protection cannot mean one thing when applied to one individual and something else when applied to a person of another color. If both are not accorded the same protection, then it is not equal." In Justice Powell's view, when governmental decisions "touch upon an individual's race or ethnic background, he is entitled to a judicial determination that the burden he is asked to bear on that basis is precisely tailored to serve a compelling governmental interest." Under this exacting standard, only one of the interests asserted by the university survived Justice Powell's scrutiny.

First, Justice Powell rejected an interest in " 'reducing the historic deficit of traditionally disfavored minorities in medical schools and in the medical profession' " as an unlawful interest in racial balancing. Second, Justice Powell rejected an interest in remedying societal discrimination because such measures would risk placing unnecessary burdens on innocent third parties "who bear no responsibility for whatever harm the beneficiaries of the special admissions program are thought to have suffered." Third, Justice Powell rejected an interest in "increasing the number of physicians who will practice in communities currently underserved," concluding that even if such an interest could be compelling in some circumstances the program under review was not "geared to promote that goal."

Justice Powell approved the university's use of race to further only one interest: "the attainment of a diverse student body." With the important proviso that "constitutional limitations protecting individual rights may not be disregarded," Justice Powell grounded his analysis in the academic freedom that "long has been viewed as a special concern of the First Amendment." Justice Powell emphasized that nothing less than the " 'nation's future depends upon leaders trained through wide exposure' to the ideas and mores of students as diverse as this Nation of many peoples." In seeking the "right to select those students who will contribute the most to the 'robust exchange of ideas,' " a university seeks "to achieve a goal that is of paramount importance in the fulfillment of its mission." Both "tradition and experience lend support to the view that the contribution of diversity is substantial."

Justice Powell was, however, careful to emphasize that in his view race "is only one element in a range of factors a university properly may consider in attaining the goal of a heterogeneous student body.". . . .

. . . [T]oday we endorse Justice Powell's view that student body diversity is a compelling state interest that can justify the use of race in university admissions.

The Equal Protection Clause provides that no State shall "deny to any person within its jurisdiction the equal protection of the laws." Because the Fourteenth Amendment "protect[s] persons, not groups," all "governmental action based on race—a group classification long recognized as in most circumstances irrelevant and therefore prohibited—should be subjected to detailed judicial inquiry to ensure that the personal right to equal protection of the laws has not been infringed." *Adarand Constructors, Inc. v. Peña* (1995). . . . It follows from this principle that "government may treat people differently because of their race only for the most compelling reasons." . . .

The Law School's educational judgment that such diversity is essential to its educational mission is one to which we defer. The Law School's assessment that diversity will, in fact, yield educational benefits is substantiated by respondents and their *amici*. Our scrutiny of the interest asserted by the Law School is no less strict for taking into account complex educational judgments in an area that lies primarily within the expertise of the university. Our holding today is in keeping with our tradition of giving a degree of deference to a university's academic decisions, within constitutionally prescribed limits. . . .

As part of its goal of "assembling a class that is both exceptionally academically qualified and broadly diverse," the Law School seeks to "enroll a 'critical mass' of minority students." The Law School's interest is not simply "to assure within its student body some specified percentage of a particular group merely because of its race or ethnic origin." That would amount to outright racial balancing, which is patently unconstitutional. Rather, the Law School's concept of critical mass is defined by reference to the educational benefits that diversity is designed to produce.

These benefits are substantial. As the District Court emphasized, the Law School's admissions policy promotes "cross-racial understanding," helps to break down racial stereotypes, and "enables [students] to better understand persons of different races." These benefits are "important and laudable," because "classroom discussion is livelier, more spirited, and simply more enlightening and interesting" when the students have "the greatest possible variety of backgrounds."

The Law School's claim of a compelling interest is further bolstered by its *amici*, who point to the educational benefits that flow from student body diversity. In addition to the expert studies and reports entered into evidence at trial, numerous studies show that student body diversity promotes learning outcomes, and "better prepares students for an increasingly diverse workforce and society, and better prepares them as professionals."

These benefits are not theoretical but real, as major American businesses have made clear that the skills needed in today's increasingly global marketplace can only be developed through exposure to widely diverse people, cultures, ideas, and viewpoints. What is more, high-ranking retired officers and civilian leaders of the United States military assert that, "[b]ased on [their] decades of experience," a "highly qualified, racially diverse officer corps . . . is essential to the military's ability to fulfill its principle mission to provide national security." . . .

Moreover, universities, and in particular, law schools, represent the training ground for a large number of our Nation's leaders. . . .

In order to cultivate a set of leaders with legitimacy in the eyes of the citizenry, it is necessary that the path to leadership be visibly open to talented and qualified individuals of every race and ethnicity. . . .

Even in the limited circumstance when drawing racial distinctions is permissible to further a compelling state interest, government is still "constrained in how it may pursue that end: [T]he means chosen to accomplish the [government's] asserted purpose must be specifically and narrowly framed to accomplish that purpose." *Shaw v. Hunt* (1996). . . .

To be narrowly tailored, a race-conscious admissions program cannot use a quota system—it cannot "insulat[e] each category of applicants with certain desired qualifications from competition with all other applicants." *Bakke.* Instead, a university may consider race or ethnicity only as a "'plus' in a particular applicant's file," without "insulat[ing] the individual from comparison with all other candidates for the available seats." In other words, an admissions program must be "flexible enough to consider all pertinent elements of diversity in light of the particular qualifications of each applicant, and to place them on the same footing for consideration, although not necessarily according them the same weight." . . .

We are satisfied that the Law School's admissions program, like the Harvard plan described by Justice Powell, does not operate as a quota. Properly understood, a "quota" is a program in which a certain fixed number or proportion of opportunities are "reserved exclusively for certain minority groups." Quotas "impose a fixed number or percentage which must be attained, or which cannot be exceeded," and "insulate the individual from comparison with all other candidates for the available seats." In contrast, "a permissible goal . . . require[s] only a good-faith effort . . . to come within a range demarcated by the goal itself," and permits consideration of race as a "plus" factor in any given case

while still ensuring that each candidate "compete[s] with all other qualified applicants." . . .

Here, the Law School engages in a highly individualized, holistic review of each applicant's file, giving serious consideration to all the ways an applicant might contribute to a diverse educational environment. The Law School affords this individualized consideration to applicants of all races. There is no policy, either *de jure* or *de facto,* of automatic acceptance or rejection based on any single "soft" variable. . . .

What is more, the Law School actually gives substantial weight to diversity factors besides race. The Law School frequently accepts nonminority applicants with grades and test scores lower than underrepresented minority applicants (and other nonminority applicants) who are rejected. This shows that the Law School seriously weighs many other diversity factors besides race that can make a real and dispositive difference for nonminority applicants as well. By this flexible approach, the Law School sufficiently takes into account, in practice as well as in theory, a wide variety of characteristics besides race and ethnicity that contribute to a diverse student body. . . .

Petitioner and the United States argue that the Law School's plan is not narrowly tailored because race-neutral means exist to obtain the educational benefits of student body diversity that the Law School seeks. We disagree. Narrow tailoring does not require exhaustion of every conceivable race-neutral alternative. Nor does it require a university to choose between maintaining a reputation for excellence or fulfilling a commitment to provide educational opportunities to members of all racial groups. Narrow tailoring does, however, require serious, good faith consideration of workable race-neutral alternatives that will achieve the diversity the university seeks.

We agree with the Court of Appeals that the Law School sufficiently considered workable race-neutral alternatives. . . .

We acknowledge that "there are serious problems of justice connected with the idea of preference itself." *Bakke.* Narrow tailoring, therefore, requires that a race-conscious admissions program not unduly harm members of any racial group. . . . To be narrowly tailored, a race-conscious admissions program must not "unduly burden individuals who are not members of the favored racial and ethnic groups."

We are satisfied that the Law School's admissions program does not. Because the Law School considers "all pertinent elements of diversity," it can (and does) select nonminority applicants who have greater potential to enhance student body diversity over underrepresented minority applicants. As Justice Powell recognized in *Bakke,* so long as a race-conscious admissions program uses race as a "plus" factor in the context of individualized consideration, a rejected applicant "will not have been foreclosed from all consideration for that seat simply because he was not the right color or had the wrong surname. . . . His qualifications would have been weighed fairly and competitively, and he would have no basis to complain of unequal treatment under the Fourteenth Amendment."

We agree that, in the context of its individualized inquiry into the possible diversity contributions of all applicants, the Law School's race-conscious admissions program does not unduly harm nonminority applicants.

We are mindful, however, that "[a] core purpose of the Fourteenth Amendment was to do away with all governmentally imposed discrimination based on race." *Palmore v. Sidoti* (1984). Accordingly, race-conscious admissions policies must be limited in time. . . . We see no reason to exempt race-conscious admissions programs from the requirement that all governmental use of race must have a logical end point. . . .

In the context of higher education, the durational requirement can be met by sunset provisions in race-conscious admissions policies and periodic reviews to determine whether racial preferences are still necessary to achieve student body diversity. Universities in California, Florida, and Washington State, where racial preferences in admissions are prohibited by state law, are currently engaged in experimenting with a wide variety of alternative approaches. Universities in other States can and should draw on the most promising aspects of these race-neutral alternatives as they develop. . . .

. . . It has been 25 years since Justice Powell first approved the use of race to further an interest in student body diversity in the context of public higher education. Since that time, the number of minority applicants with high grades and test scores has indeed increased. We expect that 25 years from now, the use of racial preferences will no longer be necessary to further the interest approved today.

In summary, the Equal Protection Clause does not prohibit the Law School's narrowly tailored use of race in admissions decisions to further a compelling interest in obtaining the educational benefits that flow from a diverse student body. . . . The judgment of the Court of Appeals for the Sixth Circuit, accordingly, is affirmed.

It is so ordered.

CHIEF JUSTICE REHNQUIST, with whom JUSTICE SCALIA, JUSTICE KENNEDY, and JUSTICE THOMAS join, dissenting.

I agree with the Court that, "in the limited circumstance when drawing racial distinctions is permissible," the government must ensure that its means are narrowly tailored to achieve a compelling state interest. I do not believe, however, that the University of Michigan Law School's (Law School) means are narrowly tailored to the interest it asserts. The Law School claims it must take the steps it does to achieve a "critical mass" of underrepresented minority students. But its actual program bears no relation to this asserted goal. Stripped of its "critical mass" veil, the Law School's program is revealed as a naked effort to achieve racial balancing. . . .

In practice, the Law School's program bears little or no relation to its asserted goal of achieving "critical mass." Respondents explain that the Law School seeks to accumulate a "critical mass" of *each* underrepresented minority group. But the record demonstrates that the Law School's admissions practices with respect to these groups differ dramatically and cannot be defended under any consistent use of the term "critical mass."

From 1995 through 2000, the Law School admitted between 1,130 and 1,310 students. Of those, between 13 and 19 were Native American, between 91 and 108 were African-Americans, and between 47 and 56 were Hispanic. If the Law School is admitting between 91 and 108 African-Americans in order to achieve "critical mass," thereby preventing African-American students from feeling "isolated or like spokespersons for their race," one would think that a number of the same order of magnitude would be necessary to accomplish the same purpose for Hispanics and Native Americans. Similarly, even if all of the Native American applicants admitted in a given year matriculate, which the record demonstrates is not at all the case, how can this possibly constitute a "critical mass" of Native Americans in a class of over 350 students? In order for this pattern of admission to be consistent with the Law School's explanation of "critical mass," one would have to believe that the objectives of "critical mass" offered by respondents are achieved with only half the number of Hispanics and one-sixth the number of Native Americans as compared to African-Americans. But respondents offer no race-specific reasons for such disparities. Instead, they simply emphasize the importance of achieving "critical mass," without any explanation of why that concept is applied differently among the three underrepresented minority groups.

These different numbers, moreover, come only as a result of substantially different treatment among the three underrepresented minority groups, as is apparent in an example offered by the Law School and highlighted by the Court. . . . The Law School states that "[s]ixty-nine minority applicants were rejected between 1995 and 2000 with at least a 3.5 [grade point average] and a [score of] 159 or higher on the [law school admissions test]" while a number of Caucasian and Asian-American applicants with similar or lower scores were admitted.

Review of the record reveals only 67 such individuals. Of these 67 individuals, 56 were Hispanic, while only 6 were African-American, and only 5 were Native American. This discrepancy reflects a consistent practice. For example, in 2000, 12 Hispanics who scored between a 159–160 on the LSAT and earned a GPA of 3.00 or higher applied for admission and only 2 were admitted. Meanwhile, 12 African-Americans in the same range of qualifications applied for admission and all 12 were admitted. Likewise, that same year, 16 Hispanics who scored between a 151–153 on the LSAT and earned a 3.00 or higher applied for admission and only 1 of those applicants was admitted. Twenty-three similarly qualified African-Americans applied for admission and 14 were admitted.

These statistics have a significant bearing on petitioner's case. Respondents have *never* offered any race-specific arguments explaining why significantly more individuals from one underrepresented minority group are needed in order to achieve "critical mass" or further student body diversity. They certainly have not explained why Hispanics, who they have said are among "the groups most isolated by racial barriers in our country," should have their admission capped out in this manner. True, petitioner is neither Hispanic nor Native American. But the Law School's disparate admissions practices with respect to these minority groups

demonstrate that its alleged goal of "critical mass" is simply a sham. . . .

I do not believe that the Constitution gives the Law School such free rein in the use of race. . . . [T]his is precisely the type of racial balancing that the Court itself calls "patently unconstitutional."

JUSTICE KENNEDY, dissenting.

The Law School has the burden of proving, in conformance with the standard of strict scrutiny, that it did not utilize race in an unconstitutional way. *Adarand Constructors.* . . . At the very least, the constancy of admitted minority students and the close correlation between the racial breakdown of admitted minorities and the composition of the applicant pool . . . require the Law School either to produce a convincing explanation or to show it has taken adequate steps to ensure individual assessment. The Law School does neither.

The obvious tension between the pursuit of critical mass and the requirement of individual review increased by the end of the admissions season. Most of the decisions where race may decide the outcome are made during this period. The admissions officers consulted the daily reports which indicated the composition of the incoming class along racial lines. . . .

The consultation of daily reports during the last stages in the admissions process suggests there was no further attempt at individual review save for race itself. The admissions officers could use the reports to recalibrate the plus factor given to race depending on how close they were to achieving the Law School's goal of critical mass. The bonus factor of race would then become divorced from individual review; it would be premised instead on the numerical objective set by the Law School.

The Law School made no effort to guard against this danger. It provided no guidelines to its admissions personnel on how to reconcile individual assessment with the directive to admit a critical mass of minority students. . . .

To be constitutional, a university's compelling interest in a diverse student body must be achieved by a system where individual assessment is safeguarded through the entire process. . . . The Law School failed to comply with this requirement, and by no means has it carried its burden to show otherwise by the test of strict scrutiny.

JUSTICE SCALIA, with whom JUSTICE THOMAS joins, concurring in part and dissenting in part.

Unlike a clear constitutional holding that racial preferences in state educational institutions are impermissible, or even a clear anticonstitutional holding that racial preferences in state educational institutions are OK, today's [decision] seems perversely designed to prolong the controversy and the litigation. Some future lawsuits will presumably focus on whether the discriminatory scheme in question contains enough evaluation of the applicant "as an individual," and sufficiently avoids "separate admissions tracks." . . . Some will focus on whether a university has gone beyond the bounds of a "good faith effort" and has so zealously pursued its "critical mass" as to make it an unconstitutional *de facto* quota system, rather than merely "a permissible goal." Other lawsuits may focus on whether, in the particular setting at issue, any educational benefits flow from racial diversity. Still other suits may challenge the bona fides of the institution's expressed commitment to the educational benefits of diversity that immunize the discriminatory scheme in *Grutter*. (Tempting targets, one would suppose, will be those universities that talk the talk of multiculturalism and racial diversity in the courts but walk the walk of tribalism and racial segregation on their campuses—through minority-only student organizations, separate minority housing opportunities, separate minority student centers, even separate minority-only graduation ceremonies.) And still other suits may claim that the institution's racial preferences have gone below or above the mystical *Grutter*-approved "critical mass." Finally, litigation can be expected on behalf of minority groups intentionally short changed in the institution's composition of its generic minority "critical mass." I do not look forward to any of these cases. The Constitution proscribes government discrimination on the basis of race, and state-provided education is no exception.

JUSTICE THOMAS, with whom JUSTICE SCALIA joins . . . , concurring in part and dissenting in part.

Frederick Douglass, speaking to a group of abolitionists almost 140 years ago, delivered a message lost on today's majority:

"[I]n regard to the colored people, there is always more that is benevolent, I perceive, than just, manifested towards us. What I ask for the negro is not benevolence, not pity, not sympathy, but simply justice. The American people have always been anxious to know what they shall do with us. . . . I have had but one answer from the beginning. Do nothing with us! Your doing with us has already played the mischief with us. Do nothing with us! If the apples will not remain on the tree of their own strength, if they are worm-eaten at the core, if they are early ripe and disposed to fall, let them fall! . . . And if the negro cannot stand on his own legs, let him fall also. All I ask is, give him a chance to stand on his own legs! Let him alone! . . . [Y]our interference is doing him positive injury." What the Black Man Wants: An Address Delivered in Boston, Massachusetts, on 26 January 1865.

Like Douglass, I believe blacks can achieve in every avenue of American life without the meddling of university administrators. Because I wish to see all students succeed whatever their color, I share, in some respect, the sympathies of those who sponsor the type of discrimination advanced by the University of Michigan Law School (Law School). The Constitution does not, however, tolerate institutional devotion to the status quo in admissions policies when such devotion ripens into racial discrimination. Nor does the Constitution countenance the unprecedented deference the Court gives to the Law School, an approach inconsistent with the very concept of "strict scrutiny."

No one would argue that a university could set up a lower general admission standard and then impose heightened requirements only on black applicants. Similarly, a university may not maintain a high admission standard and grant exemptions to favored races. . . .

The majority upholds the Law School's racial discrimination not by interpreting the people's Constitution, but by responding to a faddish slogan of the cognoscenti. . . . I agree with the Court's holding that racial discrimination in higher education admissions will be illegal in 25 years. I respectfully dissent from the remainder of the Court's opinion and the judgment, however, because I believe that the Law School's current use of race violates the Equal Protection Clause and that the Constitution means the same thing today as it will in 300 months. . . .

The strict scrutiny standard that the Court purports to apply in this case was first enunciated in *Korematsu v. United States* (1944). There the Court held that "[p]ressing public necessity may sometimes justify the existence of [racial discrimination]; racial antagonism never can." This standard of "pressing public necessity" has more frequently been termed "compelling governmental interest." . . .

Where the Court has accepted only national security . . . as a justification for racial discrimination, I conclude that only those measures the State must take to provide a bulwark against anarchy, or to prevent violence, will constitute a "pressing public necessity." . . .

The Constitution abhors classifications based on race, not only because those classifications can harm favored races or are based on illegitimate motives, but also because every time the government places citizens on racial registers and makes race relevant to the provision of burdens or benefits, it demeans us all. . . .

Justice Powell's opinion in *Bakke* and the Court's decision today rest on the fundamentally flawed proposition that racial discrimination can be contextualized so that a goal, such as classroom aesthetics, can be compelling in one context but not in another. This "we know it when we see it" approach to evaluating state interests is not capable of judicial application. Today, the Court insists on radically expanding the range of permissible uses of race to something as trivial (by comparison) as the assembling of a law school class. I can only presume that the majority's failure to justify its decision by reference to any principle arises from the absence of any such principle.

Under the proper standard, there is no pressing public necessity in maintaining a public law school at all and, it follows, certainly not an elite law school. Likewise, marginal improvements in legal education do not qualify as a compelling state interest. . . .

The Court bases its unprecedented deference to the Law School—a deference antithetical to strict scrutiny—on an idea of "educational autonomy" grounded in the First Amendment. In my view, there is no basis for a right of public universities to do what would otherwise violate the Equal Protection Clause. . . .

Moreover one would think, in light of the Court's decision in *United States v. Virginia* (1996), that before being given license to use racial discrimination, the Law School would be required to radically reshape its admissions process, even to the point of sacrificing some elements of its character. In *Virginia*, a majority of the Court, without a word about academic freedom, accepted the all-male Virginia Military Institute's (VMI) representation that some changes in its "adversative" method of education would be required with the admission of women, but did not defer to VMI's judgment that these changes would be too great. In-

stead, the Court concluded that they were "manageable." That case involved sex discrimination, which is subjected to intermediate, not strict, scrutiny. So in *Virginia*, where the standard of review dictated that greater flexibility be granted to VMI's educational policies than the Law School deserves here, this Court gave no deference. Apparently where the status quo being defended is that of the elite establishment—here the Law School—rather than a less fashionable Southern military institution, the Court will defer without serious inquiry and without regard to the applicable legal standard.

Virginia is also notable for the fact that the Court relied on the "experience" of formerly single-sex institutions, such as the service academies, to conclude that admission of women to VMI would be "manageable." Today, however, the majority ignores the "experience" of those institutions that have been forced to abandon explicit racial discrimination in admissions.

The sky has not fallen at Boalt Hall at the University of California, Berkeley, for example. Prior to Proposition 209's adoption of Cal. Const., Art. 1, §31(a), which bars the State from "grant[ing] preferential treatment . . . on the basis of race . . . in the operation of . . . public education," Boalt Hall enrolled 20 blacks and 28 Hispanics in its first-year class for 1996. In 2002, without deploying express racial discrimination in admissions, Boalt's entering class enrolled 14 blacks and 36 Hispanics. Total underrepresented minority student enrollment at Boalt Hall now exceeds 1996 levels. Apparently the Law School cannot be counted on to be as resourceful. The Court is willfully blind to the very real experience in California and elsewhere, which raises the inference that institutions with "reputation[s] for excellence" rivaling the Law School's have satisfied their sense of mission without resorting to prohibited racial discrimination. . . .

. . . [N]o modern law school can claim ignorance of the poor performance of blacks, relatively speaking, on the Law School Admissions Test (LSAT). Nevertheless, law schools continue to use the test and then attempt to "correct" for black underperformance by using racial discrimination in admissions so as to obtain their aesthetic student body. The Law School's continued adherence to measures it knows produce racially skewed results is not entitled to deference by this Court. . . .

Having decided to use the LSAT, the Law School must accept the constitutional burdens that come with this decision. The Law School may freely continue to employ the LSAT and other allegedly merit-based standards in whatever fashion it likes. What the Equal Protection Clause forbids, but the Court today allows, is the use of these standards hand-in-hand with racial discrimination. An infinite variety of admissions methods are available to the Law School. Considering all of the radical thinking that has historically occurred at this country's universities, the Law School's intractable approach toward admissions is striking.

The Court will not even deign to make the Law School try other methods, however, preferring instead to grant a 25-year license to violate the Constitution. And the same Court that had the courage to order the desegregation of all public schools in the South now fears, on the basis of platitudes rather than principle, to force the Law School to abandon a decidedly imperfect admissions regime that provides the basis for racial discrimination.

. . . I believe what lies beneath the Court's decision today are the benighted notions that one can tell when racial discrimination benefits (rather than hurts) minority groups, and that racial discrimination is necessary to remedy general societal ills. This Court's precedents supposedly settled both issues, but clearly the majority still cannot commit to the principle that racial classifications are *per se* harmful and that almost no amount of benefit in the eye of the beholder can justify such classifications. . . .

The silence in this case is deafening to those of us who view higher education's purpose as imparting knowledge and skills to students, rather than a communal, rubber-stamp, credentialing process. The Law School is not looking for those students who, despite a lower LSAT score or undergraduate grade point average, will succeed in the study of law. The Law School seeks only a facade—it is sufficient that the class looks right, even if it does not perform right.

The Law School tantalizes unprepared students with the promise of a University of Michigan degree and all of the opportunities that it offers. These overmatched students take the bait, only to find that they cannot succeed in the cauldron of competition. . . . While these students may graduate with law degrees, there is no evidence that they have received a qualitatively better legal education (or become better lawyers) than if they had gone to a less "elite"

law school for which they were better prepared. And the aestheticists will never address the real problems facing "underrepresented minorities," instead continuing their social experiments on other people's children.

. . . "These programs stamp minorities with a badge of inferiority and may cause them to develop dependencies or to adopt an attitude that they are 'entitled' to preferences" [*Adarand*, THOMAS, J., concurring in part and concurring in judgment].

It is uncontested that each year, the Law School admits a handful of blacks who would be admitted in the absence of racial discrimination. Who can differentiate between those who belong and those who do not? The majority of blacks are admitted to the Law School because of discrimination, and because of this policy all are tarred as undeserving. This problem of stigma does not depend on determinacy as to whether those stigmatized are actually the "beneficiaries" of racial discrimination. When blacks take positions in the highest places of government, industry, or academia, it is an open question today whether their skin color played a part in their advancement. The question itself is the stigma—because either racial discrimination did play a role, in which case the person may be deemed "otherwise unqualified," or it did not, in which case asking the question itself unfairly marks those blacks who would succeed without discrimination. . . .

For the immediate future . . . the majority has placed its *imprimatur* on a practice that can only weaken the principle of equality embodied in the Declaration of Independence and the Equal Protection Clause. "Our Constitution is color-blind, and neither knows nor tolerates classes among citizens." *Plessy v. Ferguson* (1896) (Harlan, J., dissenting). It has been nearly 140 years since Frederick Douglass asked the intellectual ancestors of the Law School to "[d]o nothing with us!" and the Nation adopted the Fourteenth Amendment. Now we must wait another 25 years to see this principle of equality vindicated. I therefore respectfully dissent from the remainder of the Court's opinion and the judgment.

Grutter was an important victory for the supporters of affirmative action, especially in the area of higher education. The Court held that educational diversity constitutes a compelling state interest and that affirmative-

BOX 19-4   SANDRA DAY O'CONNOR (1981–2006)

Sandra day's grandfather left Kansas in 1880 to take up farming in the desert Southwest, founding the 162,000-acre Lazy B ranch in Arizona. Her parents, Harry A. Day and Ada Mae Wilkey Day, later managed the ranch. Sandra Day was born in El Paso because her mother had gone there to stay with her parents, rather than give birth at the Lazy B which was far from any hospital. Day grew up dividing her time between El Paso, where she lived with her maternal grandmother and attended a private girls school, and the Lazy B, where she spent her summers.

After graduating from high school at sixteen, Day attended Stanford University, earning a degree in economics,

magna cum laude, in 1950. She stayed at Stanford for her law degree which she received in 1952. At law school she met two men who would figure largely in her adult life—John O'Connor, whom she married in 1952, and William H. Rehnquist, whom she joined as a colleague on the U.S. Supreme Court in 1981.

Her law school record was outstanding. She was an editor of the *Stanford Law Review* and a member of the Order of the Coif, a legal honor society. But she was a woman in a field where women were oddities, so it was difficult for her to find a job as an attorney. She applied, among other places, to the firm in which William French Smith was a partner, and was offered a job as a secretary. Smith, as U.S. attorney general, later played a part in her nomination to the U.S. Supreme Court.

O'Connor found a job as a deputy county attorney for San Mateo County, California. When her husband finished school, he joined the Army, and the O'Connors moved to Germany where she worked as a civilian attorney for the U.S. Army. The O'Connors returned to civilian life in 1957 and settled in Phoenix, Arizona. For eight years, O'Connor combined child rearing with volunteer work and some pri-

vate practice of law. She also became active in Republican politics.

In 1965 O'Connor became an assistant attorney general of Arizona, the first woman to hold the position. After four years she was appointed to the state Senate, and the following year she won election to that body. During her six years as a state senator, she served for two years as majority leader—the first woman in the nation to hold such a post of legislative leadership.

Having served in the executive and legislative branches of state government, O'Connor rounded out her experience by moving to the bench in 1974, elected to the superior court of Maricopa County. Five years later, Governor Bruce Babbitt—acting some said to remove a political rival—appointed her to the Arizona Court of Appeals. A year earlier Arizona Republican leaders had pushed O'Connor to make a gubernatorial bid, but she had declined. It was from that state appeals court seat that President Reagan chose her as his first nominee to the Supreme Court. Once again, Sandra Day O'Connor was "the first woman"—this time the first of her sex to sit on the U. S. Supreme Court.

On the Court, O'Connor was at first solidly in the conservative wing, voting in most cases with fellow Arizonan William H. Rehnquist. Over time she moved to the center, becoming the important swing vote on an ideologically divided Court. Her vote often determined the nation's legal policy on important issues such as privacy rights, abortion, affirmative action, and states' rights.

Justice O'Connor retired in 2006 at the age of seventy-five after almost a quarter century of service to the Supreme Court.

SOURCE: Adapted from David Savage, *Guide to the U.S. Supreme Court*, 4th ed. (Washington, D.C.: CQ Press, 2004), 1016–1017.

action programs, if properly tailored, are constitutionally acceptable means of achieving the state's goals. Contrary to its findings in *Gratz*, the majority concluded that the law school's admissions process was based on a flexible, individualized consideration of applications in which race was only one of several diversity factors taken into account. Consistent with Justice Powell's opinion in *Bakke*, race was a "plus" in the application process. Race did not automatically determine acceptance or rejection. As such it met the justices' approval. The Court's ruling provides guidelines for constitutionally valid affirmative action programs that other colleges and universities can employ where state laws do not otherwise prohibit the use of racial and ethnic preferences.

The Court, however, was far from unified. The result was largely due to Justice O'Connor's decision to vote with her more liberal colleagues, giving them a 5–4 majority. The decision reemphasized the crucial role Justice O'Connor played as the Court's swing vote on many important and controversial issues during her years on the Rehnquist Court *(see Box 19-4)*.

Court observers have speculated that amicus curiae participation may have exerted significant influence on the outcome. Seen as especially important were the positions taken by the military and major corporations such as General Motors and 3-M. These interests, not usually advocates of liberal policies, spoke with powerful voices on the value of affirmative action programs, and O'Connor repeatedly quoted their positions in her opinion for the Court. Also important was the law school community, which expressed overwhelming support for the importance of diverse student bodies in the training of the nation's lawyers.

In spite of the Court's decision, a number of questions remain unanswered: Did the Court adequately distinguish between a valid "critical mass" and an unconstitutional "quota"? Is the Court's *Grutter* rationale applicable only to the university setting, or can it be extended to minority set-aside programs as well? Is there danger that a flexible, individualized consideration of applications might unconstitutionally place excessive emphasis on race, and if so, how would we know if it occurred? Is the

---

BOX 19-5   AFFIRMATIVE ACTION/MINORITY SET-ASIDE PRINCIPLES

THE SUPREME COURT'S affirmative action and minority set-aside decisions have been criticized for failing to develop a consistent and coherent set of legal principles. The unstable majorities that have controlled these cases surely have contributed to this result. While the Court seems to have settled on strict scrutiny as the appropriate test to decide such cases, various aspects of a challenged affirmative action plan may have an important bearing on its validity. While there are no absolutes, there are certain characteristics that make minority enhancement plans more acceptable.

An affirmative action or minority set-aside program is more likely to be found constitutional if it:

1. is narrowly tailored to achieve a compelling government interest;

2. is enacted in response to clear and demonstrable acts of unconstitutional or illegal discrimination, or is intended to eliminate the continuing effects of that illegal discrimination;

3. is designed to assist only those groups who have been the victim of illegal discrimination;

4. is not based on racial, ethnic, or gender stereotypes, or presumes the inferiority of such groups;

5. avoids the use of quotas and does not absolutely bar any group from competing or participating;

6. is temporary, with clear indicators of plan termination when certain thresholds are met;

7. seeks to eliminate racial imbalance, not maintain racial balance;

8. is based on data from relevant labor pools or other appropriate statistical comparisons;

9. does not trammel the rights of the majority;

10. provides new benefits to minorities rather than taking already earned benefits away from the majority;

11. is imposed by a federal court as a remedy for demonstrated constitutional violations; and

12. is imposed where the government's interest cannot reasonably be attained through the use of alternative plans that are neutral with respect to race, sex, or ethnicity.

unusual deference given to the judgment of university officials consistent with strict scrutiny, and will such deference be extended beyond academia? Is Justice O'Connor's comment concerning a twenty-five-year constitutional limit on affirmative action programs a significant part of this ruling or just tangential speculation? These and other questions, along with the fragile nature of the *Grutter* majority and O'Connor's retirement from the Court, undoubtedly mean that legal battle over affirmative action is far from over and the appropriate legal standards are not yet permanently fixed *(see Box 19-5).*

READINGS

Anderson, Terry H. *The Pursuit of Fairness: A History of Affirmative Action.* New York: Oxford University Press, 2004.

Baer, Judith. *Equality under the Constitution.* Ithaca, N.Y.: Cornell University Press, 1983.

———. *Women in American Law: The Struggle toward Equality from the New Deal to the Present.* New York: Holmes and Meier, 1991.

Ball, Howard. *The Bakke Case: Race, Education, and Affirmative Action.* Lawrence: University Press of Kansas, 2000.

Bok, Derek, and William Bowen. *The Shape of the River: Long Term Consequences of Considering Race in College and University Admissions.* Princeton: Princeton University Press, 1998.

Cortner, Richard C. *Civil Rights and Public Accommodations: The Heart of Atlanta and McClung Cases.* Lawrence: University Press of Kansas, 2001.

DuBois, W. E. B. "Does the Negro Need Separate Schools?" *Journal of Negro Education* 4 (1935): 328–335.

Ehrlander, Mary E. *Equal Educational Opportunity: Brown's Elusive Mandate.* New York: LFB Scholarly Publishing, 2002.

Eskridge, William N, Jr. *Gaylaw: Challenging the Apartheid of the Closet.* Cambridge: Harvard University Press, 1999.

Glazer, Nathan. *Affirmative Discrimination.* New York: Basic Books, 1975.

Goldstein, Leslie Friedman. *The Constitutional Rights of Women,* 2nd ed. Madison: University of Wisconsin Press, 1988.

Graglia, Lino A. *Disaster by Decree: The Supreme Court's Decisions on Race and the Schools.* Ithaca, N.Y.: Cornell University Press, 1976.

Kellough, J. Edward. *Understanding Affirmative Action: Politics, Discrimination, and the Search for Justice.* Washington, D.C.: Georgetown University Press. 2006.

Klarman, Michael J. *From Jim Crow to Civil Rights: The Supreme Court and the Struggle for Racial Equality.* New York: Oxford University Press, 2004.

Kluger, Richard. *Simple Justice.* New York: Knopf, 1976.

Koppelman, Andrew. *Same Sex, Different States: When Same-Sex Marriages Cross State Lines.* New Haven: Yale University Press, 2006

Kull, Andrew. *The Color-Blind Constitution.* Cambridge: Harvard University Press, 1994.

Mezey, Susan Gluck. *Elusive Equality: Women's Rights, Public Policy, and the Law.* Boulder: Lynne Rienner, 2003.

———. *In Pursuit of Equality.* New York: St. Martin's Press, 1992.

Murdoch, Joyce, and Deb Price. *Courting Justice: Gay Men and Lesbians v. the Supreme Court.* New York: Basic Books, 2001.

Park, John S. W. *Elusive Citizenship: Immigration, Asian Americans, and the Paradox of Civil Rights.* New York: New York University Press, 2004.

Patterson, James T. *Brown v. Board of Education: A Civil Rights Milestone and Its Troubled Legacy.* New York: Oxford University Press, 2001.

Peltason, Jack. *Fifty-Eight Lonely Men.* Urbana: University of Illinois Press, 1971.

Perry, Michael J. *The People: The Fourteenth Amendment and the Supreme Court.* New York: Oxford University Press, 1999.

Peterson, Paul E. *Classifying by Race.* Princeton: Princeton University Press, 1996.

Pinello, Daniel R. *Gay Rights and American Law.* New York: Cambridge University Press, 2003.

Rosenberg, Gerald N. *The Hollow Hope.* Chicago: University of Chicago Press, 1991.

Schwartz, Bernard. *Swann's Way: The School Busing Case and the Supreme Court.* New York: Oxford University Press, 1986.

Sracic, Paul A. *San Antonio v. Rodriguez and the Pursuit of Equal Education: The Debate Over Discrimination and School Funding.* Lawrence: University Press of Kansas, 2006.

Strasser, Mark. *The Challenge of Same-Sex Marriage: Federalist Principles and Constitutional Protections.* Westport, Conn.: Praeger, 1999.

Strum, Philippa. *Women in the Barracks: The VMI Case and Equal Rights.* Lawrence: University Press of Kansas, 2002.

Tsesis, Alexander. *The Thirteenth Amendment and American Freedom: A Legal History.* New York: New York University Press, 2004.

———. *We Shall Overcome: A History of Civil Rights and the Law.* New Haven: Yale University Press, 2008.

Urofsky, Melvin I. *Affirmative Action on Trial: Sex Discrimination in Johnson v. Santa Clara.* Lawrence: University Press of Kansas, 1997.

Vose, Clement E. *Caucasians Only: The Supreme Court, the NAACP, and the Restrictive Covenant Cases.* Berkeley: University of California Press, 1959.

Wilkinson, J. Harvie. *From Brown to Bakke: The Supreme Court and School Integration,* 1954–1978. New York: Oxford University Press, 1979.

CHAPTER 20

VOTING AND REPRESENTATION

For any government built on a foundation of popular sovereignty, voting and representation are of critical importance. Through these mechanisms the people express their political will and ultimately control the institutions of government. Representative democracy can function properly only when the citizenry has full rights to regular and meaningful elections and when the system is structured so that public officials act on behalf of their constituents. If any segment of society is denied the right to vote or is denied legitimate representation, the ideals of a republican form of government are not completely realized. Because elections and representation are the primary links between the people and their government, it is not surprising that the history of American constitutional law is replete with disputes over rights of political participation.

VOTING RIGHTS

When the framers met at the Philadelphia Convention of 1787, the states already had election systems, with their own requirements for qualifying voters and procedures for selecting state and local officials. By European standards, the states were quite liberal in extending the right to vote.[1] But suffrage was not universal. Ballot access generally was granted only to free adult men, and in several states only to men who owned sufficient property. Women, slaves, Indians, minors, and the poor could not vote. Some states prohibited Jews and Catholics from voting as well.

With state systems in place, the framers saw no reason to create a separate set of qualifications for participating in federal elections. Because there was little uniformity from state to state and qualifications often changed, the addition of a new body of federal voting requirements could cause conflict. In addition, under the constitution drafted at Philadelphia, only one agency of the new national government, the House of Representatives, was to be elected directly by the people—further reason why the federal government need not develop its own voter rolls. In Article I, Section 2, the Constitution says with respect to House elections that "the Electors in each State shall have the Qualifications requisite for Electors of the most numerous Branch of the State Legislature." If citizens were qualified to cast ballots in their state's legislative elections, they were also qualified to vote in congressional elections. The authority of the states to set voting rights policy began to change after the Civil War when this power started to shift steadily toward the federal government.

Ratification of four constitutional amendments substantially limited the states' authority to restrict the right to vote. The first was the Fifteenth Amendment in 1870. Part of the Reconstruction package initiated by the Radical Republicans after the Civil War, the Fifteenth Amendment prohibits the denial of the right to vote on the basis of race, color, or previous condition of servitude. It bars such discrimination by either the federal government or

---

1. Melvin I. Urofsky and Paul Finkelman, *A March of Liberty*, 2nd ed. (New York: Oxford University Press, 2002), 296.

the states, but, at the time, the obvious target was the South. Most members of the Reconstructionist Congress reasoned that unless some action was taken to protect the political rights of the newly freed slaves, the white majority would reinstitute measures to deny black citizens full participation.

Fifty years later the Constitution was again amended to expand the electorate. The Nineteenth Amendment, ratified in 1920, stipulated that the right to vote could not be denied on account of sex. This amendment was the culmination of decades of effort by supporters of women's suffrage. Although some states already allowed women to vote, a change in the Constitution was necessary to extend that right uniformly across the nation.

The third voter qualification amendment went into effect in 1964. The Twenty-fourth Amendment denied the federal government and the states the power to impose a poll tax as a voter qualification for federal elections. The levying of a tax on the right to vote was a common practice in the South and was identified by Congress as one of many tactics used to keep blacks from voting, and thereby circumventing the clear intent of the Fifteenth Amendment.

In 1971 the last of the voting rights amendments, the Twenty-sixth, was ratified. It set eighteen years as the minimum voting age for all state and federal elections. Before 1971 individual states determined the minimum voting age, which ranged from eighteen to twenty-one. Earlier, Congress had attempted to impose the eighteen-year minimum through legislation. The constitutionality of that act was challenged in *Oregon v. Mitchell* (1970). In a 5 to 4 vote, the justices held that Congress had the power under Article I to set a minimum age for voting in federal elections but lacked the constitutional authority to impose an age standard on state and local elections. Rather than face the possible confusion of conflicting sets of qualifications, Congress abrogated the *Mitchell* ruling by proposing the Twenty-sixth Amendment.

Each of these four constitutional changes altered the balance of authority over the establishment of voter qualifications. The states retained the basic right to set such qualifications, but with restrictions. States may no longer abridge voting rights by denying access to the ballot on the basis of race, sex, age, or ability to pay a tax; any actions by the states affecting voting rights are also constrained by the Fourteenth Amendment's guarantee of equal protection of the laws. In addition to limiting state power, the voting rights amendments increased congressional authority. Clauses in the Fourteenth, Fifteenth, Nineteenth, Twenty-fourth, and Twenty-sixth Amendments declare: "The Congress shall have the power to enforce this article by appropriate legislation." These enforcement clauses grant Congress authority over an area that had been left entirely to the states.

Congress has not been reluctant to use its enforcement authority. Shortly after ratification of the Fourteenth and Fifteenth Amendments, it demonstrated the federal government's interest in extending the franchise to African Americans by passing the Enforcement Act of 1870. This statute made it unlawful for state election officials to discriminate against black citizens in the application of state voting regulations. It also made acts of electoral corruption, including bribery, violence, and intimidation federal crimes. The following year Congress passed the Enforcement Act of 1871, which allowed for federal supervision of congressional elections. The federal government also intervened to stem the growing incidence of private intimidation of black voters with the Ku Klux Klan Act of 1871, which gave the president broad powers to combat conspiracies against voting rights.

The Supreme Court's response to these post–Civil War enforcement statutes was mixed. In some of its decisions the justices questioned the breadth of the congressional actions that regulated state elections beyond the specific racial purposes of the Fifteenth Amendment. In *United States v. Reese* (1876) the justices declined to uphold the indictment of a Kentucky election official who refused to register a qualified black voter for a state election. The Court justified its conclusion on the ground that the Enforcement Act of 1870 was too broadly drawn. On the same day as *Reese,* and for the same reason, the Court in *United States v. Cruikshank* dismissed the federal indictments of ninety-six Louisiana whites who were charged with intimidating potential black voters by shooting them.

The Court also was reluctant to approve sanctions under the Ku Klux Klan Act when the prosecution centered on purely private behavior (*United States v. Harris*, 1883). In *Ex parte Yarbrough* (1884), however, the justices gave strong support to federal enforcement actions against even private behavior when the right to vote in national elections was abridged. Similarly, in *Ex parte Clark* (1880), *Ex parte Siebold* (1880), and *United States v. Gale* (1883) the Court approved criminal charges against state officials who compromised the integrity of federal elections.

Although these enforcement measures had an impact on the South, their influence was short-lived. By the time the nation entered the 1890s, the zeal behind the Reconstruction efforts had waned. White southerners had regained control of their home states and began passing measures to restrict black participation in state and federal elections. The Jim Crow era had begun. The Civil War amendments officially had reduced the power of the states to discriminate and had given regulatory authority to the federal government, but full voting rights were not a reality until after the struggles of the civil rights movement of the mid-twentieth century.

State Restrictions on Voting

In 1869, during the congressional debate over the Fifteenth Amendment, Sen. Waitman T. Willey, a Republican from West Virginia, proclaimed from the Senate floor: "This amendment, when adopted, will settle the question for all time of negro suffrage in the insurgent States, where it has lately been extended under the pressure of congressional legislation, and will preclude the possibility of any future denial of this privilege by any change in the constitutions of those States."

In retrospect, it would be hard to imagine a more overly optimistic prediction of the effect of the Fifteenth Amendment. Although ratification meant that the states were constitutionally prohibited from engaging in racial discrimination in extending the right to vote, the southern states, once out from under the policies of Reconstruction, acted to keep African Americans out of the voting booth.

Actions by the southern states to limit black participation in voting took many forms. They included tactics such as "white only" voting in Democratic Party primary elections, poll taxes, difficult registration requirements, literacy and understanding tests, and outright intimidation. These strategies were effective. African American participation at the ballot box in the South was negligible well into the middle of the twentieth century.

Beginning in the 1960s the federal government took measures to reduce racial discrimination in voting. All three branches were involved: Congress passed legislation to enforce voting rights and remove legal barriers to the ballot box; the executive branch brought suits against state governments and election officials who deprived blacks of their rights; and the judiciary heard legal disputes over claims of voter discrimination. In **Louisiana v. United States** (1965) the Court struck down Louisiana's "understanding test," which permitted local voting registrars to determine whether individuals attempting to register had a sufficient understanding of state and federal constitutions to be qualified to vote. The decisions of these local voting officials discriminated notoriously on the basis of race. In striking down this practice, the Court gave a stern warning that it would no longer tolerate state schemes designed to deny individuals, and particularly minorities, access to the ballot.

Racially discriminatory state practices were not the only barriers to voting that the Court struck down in the 1960s and 1970s. In **Harper v. Virginia State Board of Elections** (1966) the justices found that poll taxes imposed as a requirement to vote in state elections violated the Fourteenth Amendment. This decision, coupled with the Twenty-fourth Amendment's prohibition against poll taxes in federal elections, effectively eliminated willingness or ability to pay a tax as a voting rights requirement. In **Kramer v. Union Free School District** (1969), the Court removed ownership or rental of real property as a requirement some states had imposed for voting on certain property tax issues. Similarly, in **Dunn v. Blumstein** (1972) the Court struck down state laws that established residency requirements of up to a year as a voting prerequisite. The justices held that a thirty-day requirement would be sufficient for the state to ensure that only bona fide residents voted.

Lawsuits claiming that state policies unconstitutionally deprive individuals of their right to vote reached a peak in the 1960s and 1970s, but continue even today. In *Crawford v. Marion County Election Board* (2008) the justices heard a challenge to an Indiana statute that required voters to present government-issued photo identification at the polls. The state offered free voting identification cards to individuals who did not have a driver's license, passport, or other acceptable form of identification. Where disputes arose at the polls over the identification question, the law allowed the voter to cast a provisional ballot that would be counted if the voter within ten days provided a sworn statement establishing identity. The law did not apply to absentee ballots submitted by mail and allowed an exception for residents of nursing homes and similar institutions. Indiana justified the law as a means of combating voter fraud.

Opponents claimed that the law would depress voting participation among the poor, minorities, and the elderly who disproportionately did not have acceptable identification and found it difficult to travel to the offices that issued the free ID cards. Opponents further argued that the state had exaggerated the voter fraud problem. The controversy also had partisan overtones, with Republicans generally supporting the law and Democrats actively opposing it.

Although the Court did not reach consensus on a majority opinion, six justices voted to uphold the law. They concluded that the state had an important interest protecting the integrity and reliability of the electoral process as well as the electorate's confidence in it. Thwarting fraudulent voting was clearly related to this interest. The overall burdens of the law were seen as insufficient to invalidate it.

The Voting Rights Act of 1965

Although Supreme Court decisions did much to define the right to vote and limit the state actions that restricted the franchise, court rulings alone were insufficient to prompt major changes—particularly with respect to voting participation among minorities. Too many alternative measures, many of them informal, were available to block or delay the effective exercise of the right to vote. Registration numbers in the southern states highlight the fact that court victories did not necessarily translate into social change. According to Justice Department statistics, between 1958 and 1964 black voter registration in Alabama rose to 19.4 percent from 14.2 percent. From 1956 to 1965 Louisiana black registration increased only to 31.8 percent from 31.7 percent. And in Mississippi the ten years from 1954 to 1964 saw black registration rates rise to only 6.4 percent from 4.4 percent. In each of these states the registration rates for whites was fifty percentage points or more ahead of black rates. Figures such as these convinced Congress that its strategy of passing legislation to expand opportunities for taking civil rights claims to court had been ineffective and that a more aggressive policy was required. President Lyndon Johnson is reported to have instructed Attorney General Nicholas Katzenbach to "write the god-damnedest, toughest voting rights act that you can devise."[2] The result was the Voting Rights Act of 1965, the most comprehensive statute ever enacted by Congress to enforce the guarantees of the Fifteenth Amendment.

The provisions of the Voting Rights Act did not apply equally to all sections of the country. Instead, the act targeted certain areas. The coverage formula stipulated that the most stringent provisions of the statute would govern all states or counties that met the following criteria: (1) that a discriminatory test or device was in operation in November 1964; and (2) that less than 40 percent of the voting age population was registered to vote or voted in the 1964 presidential general election.

In 1965 the states covered were Alabama, Alaska, Georgia, Louisiana, Mississippi, South Carolina, and Virginia, as well as portions of Arizona, Hawaii, Idaho, and North Carolina. A state could be removed from the list by convincing the District Court for the District of Columbia that no discrimination had been practiced for five years. The act's most significant provision authorized the U.S. attorney general to appoint federal examiners to supervise registration and voting procedures

2. Howard Ball, "The Voting Rights Act of 1965," in *The Oxford Companion to the Supreme Court of the United States*, ed. Kermit L. Hall, James W. Ely Jr., Joel B. Grossman, and William M. Wiecek (New York: Oxford University Press, 1992), 903.

when the Justice Department determined that low black participation rates were a probable result of racial discrimination. The law prohibited literacy tests and stipulated that any changes in state election laws had to be approved by the U.S. attorney general or the District Court for the District of Columbia before they could take effect. The 1965 Voting Rights Act was Congress's most comprehensive intervention into the state's traditional powers over voter qualifications, and it was not surprising that it was almost immediately challenged as exceeding constitutional limits on federal power.

South Carolina v. Katzenbach

383 U.S. 301 (1966)

http://laws.findlaw.com/US/383/301.html

Oral arguments may be found at: http://www.oyez.org

Vote: 8 (Brennan, Clark, Douglas, Fortas, Harlan, Stewart, Warren, White)

  1 (Black)

Opinion of the Court: Warren

Opinion concurring in part and dissenting in part: Black

To gain a review of the constitutionality of the 1965 Voting Rights Act, South Carolina instituted legal action against Attorney General Katzenbach, asking that he be enjoined from enforcing the act's provisions. Because the suit was between a state and a citizen of another state, and because of the importance of the issues involved, the Supreme Court accepted the case under its original jurisdiction. The hearing before the Court involved not only South Carolina and the federal government but also other states invited by the Court to participate. Five states (all southern) appeared in support of South Carolina, and twenty-one states submitted legal arguments urging the Court to approve the act.

MR. CHIEF JUSTICE WARREN delivered the opinion of the Court.

The Voting Rights Act was designed by Congress to banish the blight of racial discrimination in voting, which has infected the electoral process in parts of our country for nearly a century. The Act creates stringent new remedies for voting discrimination where it persists on a pervasive scale, and in addition the statute strengthens existing remedies for pockets of voting discrimination elsewhere in the country. Congress assumed the power to prescribe these remedies from §2 of the Fifteenth Amendment, which authorizes the National Legislature to effectuate by "appropriate" measures the constitutional prohibition against racial discrimination in voting. We hold that the sections of the Act which are properly before us are an appropriate means for carrying out Congress' constitutional responsibilities and are consonant with all other provisions of the Constitution. We therefore deny South Carolina's request that enforcement of these sections of the Act be enjoined.

The constitutional propriety of the Voting Rights Act of 1965 must be judged with reference to the historical experience which it reflects. Before enacting the measure, Congress explored with great care the problem of racial discrimination in voting. The House and Senate Committees on the Judiciary each held hearings for nine days and received testimony from a total of 67 witnesses. More than three full days were consumed discussing the bill on the floor of the House, while the debate in the Senate covered 26 days in all. At the close of these deliberations, the verdict of both chambers was overwhelming. The House approved the bill by a vote of 328–74, and the measure passed the Senate by a margin of 79–18.

Two points emerge vividly from the voluminous legislative history of the Act contained in the committee hearings and floor debates. First: Congress felt itself confronted by an insidious and pervasive evil which had been perpetuated in certain parts of our country through unremitting and ingenious defiance of the Constitution. Second: Congress concluded that the unsuccessful remedies which it had prescribed in the past would have to be replaced by sterner and more elaborate measures in order to satisfy the clear commands of the Fifteenth Amendment. . . .

The Voting Rights Act of 1965 reflects Congress' firm intention to rid the country of racial discrimination in voting. The heart of the Act is a complex scheme of stringent remedies aimed at areas where voting discrimination has been most flagrant. Section 4(a)–(d) lays down a formula defining the States and political subdivisions to which these new remedies apply. The first of the remedies, contained in §4(a), is the suspension of literacy tests and similar voting qualifications for a period of five years from the last occurrence of substantial voting discrimination. Section 5 prescribes a second remedy, the suspension of all new voting regulations pending review by federal authorities to determine whether their use would perpetuate voting discrimination. The third remedy, covered in §§6(b), 7, 9, and 13(a), is the assignment of federal examiners on certification by the Attorney General to list qualified applicants who are thereafter entitled to vote in all elections.

Other provisions of the Act prescribe subsidiary cures for persistent voting discrimination. Section 8 authorizes the appointment of federal poll-watchers in places to which federal examiners have already been assigned. Section 10(d) excuses those made eligible to vote in sections of the country covered by §4(b) of the Act from paying accumulated past poll taxes for state and local elections. Section 12(e) provides for balloting by persons denied access to the polls in areas where federal examiners have been appointed.

The remaining remedial portions of the Act are aimed at voting discrimination in any area of the country where it may occur. Section 2 broadly prohibits the use of voting rules to abridge exercise of the franchise on racial grounds. Sections 3, 6(a), and 13(b) strengthen existing procedures for attacking voting discrimination by means of litigation. Section 4(e) excuses citizens educated in American schools conducted in a foreign language from passing English-language literacy tests. Section 10(a)–(c) facilitates constitutional litigation challenging the imposition of all poll taxes for state and local elections. Sections 11 and 12(a)–(d) authorize civil and criminal sanctions against interference with the exercise of rights guaranteed by the Act. . . .

These provisions of the Voting Rights Act of 1965 are challenged on the fundamental ground that they exceed the powers of Congress and encroach on an area reserved to the States by the Constitution. . . .

The ground rules for resolving this question are clear. The language and purpose of the Fifteenth Amendment, the prior decisions construing its several provisions, and the general doctrines of constitutional interpretation, all point to one fundamental principle. As against the reserved powers of the States, Congress may use any rational means to effectuate the constitutional prohibition of racial discrimination in voting. . . .

Section 1 of the Fifteenth Amendment declares that "[t]he right of citizens of the United States to vote shall not be denied or abridged by the United States or by any State on account of race, color, or previous condition of servitude." This declaration has always been treated as self-executing and has repeatedly been construed, without further legislative specification, to invalidate state voting qualifications or procedures which are discriminatory on their face or in practice. . . . [T]he Fifteenth Amendment expressly declares that "Congress shall have power to enforce this article by appropriate legislation." . . . Accordingly, in addition to the courts, Congress has full remedial powers to effectuate the constitutional prohibition against racial discrimination in voting.

Congress has repeatedly exercised these powers in the past, and its enactments have repeatedly been upheld. . . . On the rare occasions when the Court has found an unconstitutional exercise of these powers, in its opinion Congress had attacked evils not comprehended by the Fifteenth Amendment.

The basic test to be applied in a case involving §2 of the Fifteenth Amendment is the same as in all cases concerning the express powers of Congress with relation to the reserved powers of the States. Chief Justice Marshall laid down the classic formulation, 50 years before the Fifteenth Amendment was ratified:

"Let the end be legitimate, let it be within the scope of the constitution, and all means which are appropriate, which are plainly adapted to that end, which are not prohibited, but consist with the letter and spirit of the constitution, are constitutional." *McCulloch v. Maryland.*

The Court has subsequently echoed his language in describing each of the Civil War Amendments:

"Whatever legislation is appropriate, that is, adapted to carry out the objects the amendments have in view, whatever tends to enforce submission to the prohibitions they contain, and to secure to all persons the enjoyment of perfect equality of civil rights and the equal protection of the laws against State denial or invasion, if not prohibited, is brought within the domain of congressional power." *Ex parte Virginia.*

. . . We therefore reject South Carolina's argument that Congress may appropriately do no more than to forbid violations of the Fifteenth Amendment in general terms—that the task of fashioning specific remedies or of applying them to particular localities must necessarily be left entirely to the courts. Congress is not circumscribed by any such artificial rules under §2 of the Fifteenth Amendment. . . .

Congress exercised its authority under the Fifteenth Amendment in an inventive manner when it enacted the Voting Rights Act of 1965. First: The measure prescribes remedies for voting discrimination which go into effect without any need for prior adjudication. This was clearly a legitimate response to the problem, for which there is ample precedent under other constitutional provisions. . . . Second: The Act intentionally confines these remedies to a small number of States and political subdivisions which in most instances were familiar to Congress by name. This, too, was a permissible method of dealing with the problem. Congress had learned that substantial voting discrimination presently occurs in certain sections of the country, and it knew no way of accurately forecasting whether the evil might spread elsewhere in the future. In acceptable legislative fashion, Congress chose to limit its attention to the geographic areas where immediate action seemed necessary. . . .

After enduring nearly a century of widespread resistance to the Fifteenth Amendment, Congress has marshalled an array of potent weapons against the evil, with authority in the Attorney General to employ them effectively. Many of the areas directly affected by this development have indicated their willingness to abide by any restraints legitimately imposed upon them. We here hold that the portions of the Voting Rights Act properly before us are a valid means for carrying out the commands of the Fifteenth Amendment. Hopefully, millions of nonwhite Americans will now be able to participate for the first time on an equal basis in the government under which they live. We may finally look forward to the day when truly "[t]he right of citizens of the United States to vote shall not be denied or abridged by the United States or by any State on account of race, color, or previous condition of servitude."

The bill of complaint is dismissed.

MR. JUSTICE BLACK, concurring and dissenting.

Though . . . I agree with most of the Court's conclusions, I dissent from its holding that every part of §5 of the Act is constitutional. . . . I think this section is unconstitutional on at least two grounds.

(a) The Constitution gives federal courts jurisdiction over cases and controversies only. If it can be said that any case or controversy arises under this section which gives the District Court for the District of Columbia jurisdiction to approve or reject state laws or constitutional amendments, then the case or controversy must be between a State and the United States Government. But it is hard for me to believe that a justiciable controversy can arise in the constitutional sense from a desire by the United States Government or some of its officials to determine in advance what legislative provisions a State may enact or what constitutional amendments it may adopt. If this dispute between the Federal Government and the States amounts to a case or controversy it is a far cry from the traditional constitutional notion of a case or controversy as a dispute over the meaning of enforceable laws or the manner in which they are applied. . . .

(b) My second and more basic objection to §5 is that Congress has here exercised its power under §2 of the Fifteenth Amendment through the adoption of means that conflict with the most basic principles of the Constitution. . . . Section 5, by providing that some of the States cannot pass state laws or adopt state constitutional amendments without first being compelled to beg federal authorities to approve their policies, so distorts our constitutional structure of government as to render any distinction drawn in the Constitution between state and federal power almost meaningless. One of the most basic premises upon which our structure of government was founded was that the Federal Government was to have certain specific and limited powers and no others, and all other power was to be reserved either "to the States respectively, or to the people." Certainly if all the provisions of our Constitution which limit the power of the Federal Government and reserve other power to the States are to mean anything, they mean at least that the States have power to pass laws and amend their constitutions without first sending their officials hundreds of miles away to beg federal authorities to approve them. Moreover, it seems to me that §5 which gives federal officials power to veto state laws they do not like is in direct conflict with the clear command of our Constitution that "The United States shall guarantee to every State in this Union a Republican Form of Government." I cannot help but believe that the inevitable effect of any such law which forces any one of the States to entreat federal authorities in far-away places for approval of local laws before they can become effective is to create the impression that the State or States treated in this way are little more than conquered provinces. . . .

. . . I would hold §5 invalid for the reasons stated above with full confidence that the Attorney General has ample power to give vigorous, expeditious and effective protection to the voting rights of all citizens.

With the Court's approval of the Voting Rights Act, the federal government was free to launch a vigorous campaign to make the goals of the Fifteenth Amendment a reality. The executive branch actively enforced the law, and Congress periodically strengthened and extended its provisions. These efforts, coupled with large-scale voter registration drives conducted by civil rights organizations, have resulted in voter registration for southern African Americans almost equal to that of whites.

ELECTION CAMPAIGN REGULATION

Following the 1968 presidential election and associated Watergate controversy, the integrity of federal elections became a national issue. In 1974 Congress moved to reform presidential elections, especially with respect to the role of campaign contributions and expenditures, by amending the Federal Election Campaign Act of 1971 (FECA). The law restricted how much individuals and groups could contribute to candidates, parties, and political action committees (PACs) for use in federal elections. It also imposed record-keeping requirements and provided for federal funding of presidential election campaigns. In *Buckley v. Valeo* (1976) the Supreme Court upheld these provisions but struck down others that limited independent campaign expenditures and candidate expenditures of personal funds. The Court's decision rested on an assumption that restricting campaign expenditures was equivalent to limiting political speech. In addition, the justices balanced the need to secure the integrity of federal elections against the right to political expression. The Court concluded that reducing electoral corruption was a sufficient interest to limit campaign contributions, but not to restrict campaign expenditures.

In the years following the implementation of FECA, political strategists developed creative ways to circumvent the law. First, campaign contributors were able to exploit a loophole that distinguished money given to a

TABLE 20-1 The Growth of Soft Money (millions of dollars)

	1991–1992	1993–1994	1995–1996	1997–1998	1999–2000
Democrats					
Hard money	$155.5	$121.1	$210.0	$153.4	$269.9
Soft money	36.3	49.1	122.3	91.5	243.1
Republicans					
Hard money	266.3	223.7	407.5	273.6	447.4
Soft money	49.8	52.5	141.2	131.0	244.4
TOTAL	$507.9	$446.4	$881.0	$649.5	$1,204.8

SOURCES: Federal Election Commission; "Debating McCain-Feingold," *CQ Weekly,* March 10, 2001, 524–526.

NOTE: Although hard money contributions given directly to candidates provided the bulk of money spent on political campaigns, soft money donations to political party committees grew significantly in the years immediately preceding passage of the Bipartisan Campaign Reform Act of 2002.

candidate's political campaign from contributions made to political party organizations for "party building" activities or "get out the vote" drives. Amounts of money given to campaign organizations in support of a candidate ("hard money") were clearly regulated and limited by FECA, but general funds given to political parties ("soft money") were not. Funded by unregulated soft money, political parties were able shrewdly to develop advertising campaigns that supported the election of candidates without explicit pleas to voters to cast their ballots for specific candidates. As a consequence, the use of soft money to fund campaign activities grew exponentially and undercut the goals of FECA. (*See Table 20-1.*)

Second, interest groups and other entities launched "issue campaigns" that promoted certain public policies. These campaigns were unregulated because, at least on their face, they did not urge voters to cast their ballots for any particular candidate. In fact, as long as the advertisements avoided words such as "Vote for John Smith" or "Defeat Nancy Johnson," they were considered issue ads outside the reach of FECA regulation. Such advertisements often promoted or attacked policies or positions clearly associated with specific candidates and even praised or criticized the candidates themselves. They were often run during the heat of a political campaign.

Again, these activities tended to undermine the policy goals of FECA.

Increasing dissatisfaction with the inability of FECA to control the growing problems related to soft money contributions and issue advertising prompted Congress to pass the Bipartisan Campaign Reform Act of 2002 (BCRA). The law placed new restrictions on political contributions and expenditures. Because several provisions of the law seemed at odds with *Buckley* and many perceived them as unconstitutional restraints on political speech, it is not surprising that the law was immediately challenged.

McConnell v. Federal Election Commission

540 U.S. 93 (2003)
http://laws.findlaw.com/US/540/93.html
Oral arguments may be found at: http://www.oyez.org
Vote on primary constitutional issues:
    5 (Breyer, Ginsburg, O'Connor, Souter, Stevens)
    4 (Kennedy, Rehnquist, Scalia, Thomas)
Opinion of the Court: O'Connor and Stevens (joint) on primary constitutional issues; Breyer and Rehnquist on secondary issues.
Opinions dissenting in part: Rehnquist, Stevens
Opinions concurring in part and dissenting in part: Kennedy, Scalia, Thomas

The Bipartisan Campaign Reform Act was an attempt to plug loopholes in the Federal Election Campaign Act. Title I deals with soft money—campaign contributions not previously regulated by FECA. It prohibits the national political parties from raising or spending soft money, bars officeholders and candidates for federal office from soliciting or receiving soft money, and prevents state and local party organizations from spending soft money to promote or attack candidates for federal office. Title II prohibits labor unions and corporations, including incorporated interest groups, from using their general funds to engage in "electioneering communication," defined as advertising (primarily televised) clearly referring to a candidate for federal office that appears within sixty days of a general election or thirty days of a primary

election and targets the relevant constituency. This provision was intended to stop unions and corporations from funding candidate advertising thinly cloaked in the form of issue advocacy. The law also requires comprehensive disclosure and record keeping related to such advertising. Other sections of the act deal with a broad range of less significant issues that Congress believed were in need of reform.

To compensate political organizations for the loss of soft money contributions, the law increased the ceiling on hard money contributions and allowed the limits to be adjusted periodically for inflation. Initially, individuals were permitted give up to $2,000 per election to a candidate, $25,000 annually to a national political party, $10,000 annually to a state or local party, and $5,000 annually to a PAC. In aggregate such contributions could not exceed $95,000 per two-year election cycle (with limits of $37,500 to candidates and $57,500 to groups, such as national party organizations and political action committees). Higher limits were allowed for individual contributions to candidates running against wealthy opponents financing their own campaigns. Not changed from earlier FECA ceilings were contribution limitations for multicandidate committees ($5,000 to a candidate per election, $15,000 annually to a national party, and $5,000 annually to a political action committee) and for other political committees ($1,000 to a candidate per election, $20,000 annually to a national party, and $5,000 to a PAC).

A number of individuals and organizations challenged the BCRA in court as soon as it became effective. The challengers included groups that rarely found themselves on the same side of public policy issues: the National Rifle Association, the National Right to Life Committee, the American Civil Liberties Union, the California Democratic Party, the Republican National Committee, the Chamber of Commerce of the United States, and the AFL/CIO. All believed that the new law violated the First Amendment. Most vigorously attacked were the soft money and issue advocacy provisions.

The cases were consolidated in the district court, with the lawsuit filed by Sen. Mitch McConnell, R-Ky., designated as the lead case. In May 2003 a divided three-judge district court struck down nine of twenty challenged pro-

Sen. Mitch McConnell, R-Ky, flanked by legal counsel John Baran *(left)* and Floyd Abrams *(right)*, challenged the constitutionality of the Bipartisan Campaign Reform Act of 2002.

visions in the act. The opinion ran more than 1,600 pages. Parties on both sides of the case were dissatisfied with the ruling, and direct appeals were made to the Supreme Court. Because of the importance of the case, the Supreme Court held a special hearing in September 2003 and issued its ruling in December. The opinions approached 300 pages in length.

In addition to the primary constitutional issues that are discussed in the excerpted opinions appearing below, Chief Justice Rehnquist and Justice Breyer in separate majority opinions announced the Court's decisions on less significant BRCA provisions. Rehnquist's opinion struck down the law's ban on political contributions by individuals under eighteen years old, and Breyer's upheld the requirement that broadcasters keep comprehensive records of political advertising activity.

JUSTICE STEVENS and JUSTICE O'CONNOR delivered the opinion of the Court with respect to BCRA Titles I and II.

BCRA is the most recent federal enactment designed "to purge national politics of what was conceived to be the pernicious influence of 'big money' campaign contributions." . . .

BCRA's central provisions are designed to address Congress' concerns about the increasing use of soft money and issue advertising to influence federal elections. Title I regulates the use of soft money by political parties, officeholders, and candidates. Title II primarily prohibits corporations and labor unions from using general treasury funds for communications that are intended to, or have the effect of, influencing the outcome of federal elections. . . .

Title I is Congress' effort to plug the soft-money loophole. The cornerstone of Title I is new FECA §323(a), which prohibits national party committees and their agents from soliciting, receiving, directing, or spending any soft money. In short, §323(a) takes national parties out of the soft-money business. . . .

Our treatment of contribution restrictions reflects more than the limited burdens they impose on First Amendment freedoms. It also reflects the importance of the interests that underlie contribution limits—interests in preventing "both the actual corruption threatened by large financial contributions and the eroding of public confidence in the electoral process through the appearance of corruption." We have said that these interests directly implicate "the integrity of our electoral process, and, not less, the responsibility of the individual citizen for the successful functioning of that process." Because the electoral process is the very "means through which a free society democratically translates political speech into concrete governmental action," contribution limits, like other measures aimed at protecting the integrity of the process, tangibly benefit public participation in political debate. For that reason, when reviewing Congress' decision to enact contribution limits, "there is no place for a strong presumption against constitutionality, of the sort often thought to accompany the words 'strict scrutiny.'" The less rigorous standard of review we have applied to contribution limits (*Buckley*'s "closely drawn" scrutiny) shows proper deference to Congress' ability to weigh competing constitutional interests in an area in which it enjoys particular expertise. It also provides Congress with sufficient room to anticipate and respond to concerns about circumvention of regulations designed to protect the integrity of the political process. . . .

The question for present purposes is whether large *soft-money* contributions to national party committees have a corrupting influence or give rise to the appearance of corruption. Both common sense and the ample record in these cases confirm Congress' belief that they do. . . . [T]he FEC's allocation regime has invited widespread circumvention of FECA's limits on contributions to parties for the purpose of influencing federal elections. Under this system, corporate, union, and wealthy individual donors have been free to contribute substantial sums of soft money to the national parties, which the parties can spend for the specific purpose of influencing a particular candidate's federal election. It is not only plausible, but likely, that candidates would feel grateful for such donations and that donors would seek to exploit that gratitude.

The evidence in the record shows that candidates and donors alike have in fact exploited the soft-money loophole, the former to increase their prospects of election and the latter to create debt on the part of officeholders, with the national parties serving as willing intermediaries. Thus, despite FECA's hard-money limits on direct contributions to candidates, federal officeholders have commonly asked donors to make soft-money donations to national and state committees "solely in order to assist federal campaigns," including the officeholder's own. Parties kept tallies of the amounts of soft money raised by each officeholder, and "the amount of money a Member of Congress raise[d] for the national political committees often affect[ed] the amount the

committees g[a]ve to assist the Member's campaign." Donors often asked that their contributions be credited to particular candidates, and the parties obliged, irrespective of whether the funds were hard or soft. National party committees often teamed with individual candidates' campaign committees to create joint fundraising committees, which enabled the candidates to take advantage of the party's higher contribution limits while still allowing donors to give to their preferred candidate. Even when not participating directly in the fundraising, federal officeholders were well aware of the identities of the donors: National party committees would distribute lists of potential or actual donors, or donors themselves would report their generosity to officeholders.

For their part, lobbyists, CEOs, and wealthy individuals alike all have candidly admitted donating substantial sums of soft money to national committees not on ideological grounds, but for the express purpose of securing influence over federal officials. For example, a former lobbyist and partner at a lobbying firm in Washington, D. C., stated in his declaration:

You are doing a favor for somebody by making a large [soft-money] donation and they appreciate it. Ordinarily, people feel inclined to reciprocate favors. Do a bigger favor for someone—that is, write a larger check—and they feel even more compelled to reciprocate. In my experience, overt words are rarely exchanged about contributions, but people do have understandings.

Particularly telling is the fact that, in 1996 and 2000, more than half of the top 50 soft-money donors gave substantial sums to *both* major national parties, leaving room for no other conclusion but that these donors were seeking influence, or avoiding retaliation, rather than promoting any particular ideology. . . .

Plaintiffs argue that without concrete evidence of an instance in which a federal officeholder has actually switched a vote (or, presumably, evidence of a specific instance where the public believes a vote was switched), Congress has not shown that there exists real or apparent corruption. But the record is to the contrary. The evidence connects soft money to manipulations of the legislative calendar, leading to Congress' failure to enact, among other things, generic drug legislation, tort reform, and tobacco legislation. To claim that such actions do not change legislative outcomes surely misunderstands the legislative process.

More importantly, plaintiffs conceive of corruption too narrowly. . . .

. . . This crabbed view of corruption, and particularly of the appearance of corruption, ignores precedent, common sense, and the realities of political fundraising exposed by the record in this litigation. . . .

In sum, there is substantial evidence to support Congress' determination that large soft-money contributions to national political parties give rise to corruption and the appearance of corruption. . . .

Title II of BCRA [is] entitled "Noncandidate Campaign Expenditures." . . .

. . . [W]e must examine the degree to which BCRA burdens First Amendment expression and evaluate whether a compelling governmental interest justifies that burden. The latter question—whether the state interest is compelling—is easily answered by our prior decisions regarding campaign finance regulation, which "represent respect for the 'legislative judgment that the special characteristics of the corporate structure require particularly careful regulation.'" We have repeatedly sustained legislation aimed at "the corrosive and distorting effects of immense aggregations of wealth that are accumulated with the help of the corporate form and that have little or no correlation to the public's support for the corporation's political ideas." . . .

In light of our precedents, plaintiffs do not contest that the Government has a compelling interest in regulating advertisements that expressly advocate the election or defeat of a candidate for federal office. Nor do they contend that the speech involved in so-called issue advocacy is any more core political speech than are words of express advocacy. After all, "the constitutional guarantee has its fullest and most urgent application precisely to the conduct of campaigns for political office," *Monitor Patriot Co. v. Roy* (1971), and "[a]dvocacy of the election or defeat of candidates for federal office is no less entitled to protection under the First Amendment than the discussion of political policy generally or advocacy of the passage or defeat of legislation." *Buckley*. Rather, plaintiffs argue that the justifications that adequately support the regulation of express advocacy do not apply to significant quantities of speech encompassed by the definition of electioneering communications.

This argument fails to the extent that the issue ads broadcast during the 30- and 60-day periods preceding federal primary and general elections are the functional equivalent of express advocacy. The justifications for the regulation of express advocacy apply equally to ads aired during those periods if the ads are intended to influence the voters' decisions and have that effect. The precise percentage of issue ads that clearly identified a candidate and were aired during those relatively brief preelection time spans but had no electioneering purpose is a matter of dispute between the parties and among the judges on the District Court. Nevertheless, the vast majority of ads clearly had such a purpose. Moreover, whatever the precise percentage may have been in the past, in the future corporations and unions may finance genuine issue ads during those time frames by simply avoiding any specific reference to federal candidates, or in doubtful cases by paying for the ad from a segregated fund.

We are therefore not persuaded that plaintiffs have carried their heavy burden of proving that amended FECA §316(b)(2) is overbroad. Even if we assumed that BCRA will inhibit some constitutionally protected corporate and union speech, that assumption would not "justify prohibiting all enforcement" of the law unless its application to protected speech is substantial, "not only in an absolute sense, but also relative to the scope of the law's plainly legitimate applications." *Virginia v. Hicks* (2003). Far from establishing that BCRA's application to pure issue ads is substantial, either in an absolute sense or relative to its application to election-related advertising, the record strongly supports the contrary conclusion.

Plaintiffs also argue that FECA §316(b)(2)'s segregated-fund requirement for electioneering communications is underinclusive because it does not apply to advertising in the print media or on the Internet. The records developed in this litigation and by the Senate Committee adequately explain the reasons for this legislative choice. Congress found that corporations and unions used soft money to finance a virtual torrent of televised election-related ads during the periods immediately preceding federal elections, and that remedial legislation was needed to stanch that flow of money. As we held in *Buckley*, "reform may take one step at a time, addressing itself to the phase of the problem which seems most acute to the legislative mind." One might just as well argue that the electioneering communication definition is underinclusive because it leaves advertising 61 days in advance of an election entirely unregulated. The record amply justifies Congress' line drawing.

In addition to arguing that §316(b)(2)'s segregated-fund requirement is underinclusive, some plaintiffs contend that it unconstitutionally discriminates in favor of media companies. FECA §304(f)(3)(B)(i) excludes from the definition of electioneering communications any "communication appearing in a news story, commentary, or editorial distributed through the facilities of any broadcasting station, unless such facilities are owned or controlled by any political party, political committee, or candidate." Plaintiffs argue this provision gives free rein to media companies to engage in speech without resort to PAC money. Section 304(f)(3) (B)(i)'s effect, however, is much narrower than plaintiffs suggest. The provision excepts news items and commentary only; it does not afford *carte blanche* to media companies generally to ignore FECA's provisions. The statute's narrow exception is wholly consistent with First Amendment principles. "A valid distinction . . . exists between corporations that are part of the media industry and other corporations that are not involved in the regular business of imparting news to the public." Numerous federal statutes have drawn this distinction to ensure that the law "does not hinder or prevent the institutional press from reporting on, and publishing editorials about, newsworthy events." . . .

Many years ago we observed that "[t]o say that Congress is without power to pass appropriate legislation to safeguard . . . an election from the improper use of money to influence the result is to deny to the nation in a vital particular the power of self protection." *Burroughs v. United States.* We abide by that conviction in considering Congress' most recent effort to confine the ill effects of aggregated wealth on our political system. We are under no illusion that BCRA will be the last congressional statement on the matter. Money, like water, will always find an outlet. What problems will arise, and how Congress will respond, are concerns for another day. In the main we uphold BCRA's two principal, complementary features: the control of soft money and the regulation of electioneering communications. . . .

It is so ordered.

[*Authors' note:* In separate majority opinions, Chief Justice Rehnquist and Justice Breyer announced the Court's decisions on less significant portions of BCRA. Rehnquist's opinion dealt with miscellaneous provisions in Titles III and IV. Most importantly, his opinion struck down as unconstitutional the law's ban on political contributions by individuals under eighteen years old. Breyer wrote upholding Title V provisions requiring broadcasters to keep comprehensive records of political advertising activity.]

CHIEF JUSTICE REHNQUIST, dissenting. . . .

The issue presented by Title I is not, as the Court implies, whether Congress can permissibly regulate campaign contributions to candidates, *de facto* or otherwise, or seek to eliminate corruption in the political process. Rather, the issue is whether Congress can permissibly regulate much speech that has no plausible connection to candidate contributions or corruption to achieve those goals. Under our precedent, restrictions on political contributions implicate important First Amendment values and are constitutional only if they are "closely drawn" to reduce the corruption of federal candidates or the appearance of corruption. *Buckley v. Valeo.*

Yet, the Court glosses over the breadth of the restrictions, characterizing Title I of BCRA as "do[ing] little more that regulat[ing] the ability of wealthy individuals, corporations, and unions to contribute large sums of money to influence federal elections, federal candidates, and federal officeholders." Because, in reality, Title I is much broader than the Court allows, regulating a good deal of speech that does *not* have the potential to corrupt federal candidates and officeholders, I dissent.

The lynchpin of Title I, new FECA §323(a), prohibits national political party committees from "solicit[ing]," "receiv[ing]," "direct[ing] to another person," and "spend[ing]" *any* funds not subject to federal regulation, even if those funds are used for nonelection related activities. The Court concludes that such a restriction is justified because under FECA, "donors have been free to contribute substantial sums of soft money to the national parties, which the parties can spend for the specific purpose of influencing a particular candidate's federal election." Accordingly, "[i]t is not only plausible, but likely, that candidates would feel grateful for such donations and that donors would seek to exploit that gratitude." But the Court misses the point. Certainly "infusions of money into [candidates'] campaigns," can be regulated, but §323(a) does not regulate only donations given to influence a particular federal election; it regulates *all donations* to national political committees, no matter the use to which the funds are put.

The Court attempts to sidestep the unprecedented breadth of this regulation by stating that the "close relationship between federal officeholders and the national parties" makes all donations to the national parties "suspect." But a close association with others, especially in the realm of political speech, is not a surrogate for corruption; it is one of our most treasured First Amendment rights. The Court's willingness to impute corruption on the basis of a relationship greatly infringes associational rights and expands Congress' ability to regulate political speech. . . .

The Court fails to recognize that the national political parties are exemplars of political speech at all levels of government, in addition to effective fundraisers for federal candidates and officeholders. For sure, national political party committees exist in large part to elect federal candidates, but as a majority of the District Court found, they also promote coordinated political messages and participate in public policy debates unrelated to federal elections, promote, even in off-year elections, state and local candidates and seek to influence policy at those levels, and increase public participation in the electoral process. Indeed, some national political parties exist primarily for the purpose of expressing ideas and generating debate.

As these activities illustrate, political parties often foster speech crucial to a healthy democracy and fulfill the need for like-minded individuals to band together and promote a political philosophy. When political parties engage in pure political speech that has little or no potential to corrupt their federal candidates and officeholders, the government cannot constitutionally burden their speech any more than it could burden the speech of individuals engaging in these same activities. . . .

JUSTICE SCALIA . . . dissenting in part. . . .

This is a sad day for the freedom of speech. Who could have imagined that the same Court which, within the past four years, has sternly disapproved of restrictions upon such inconsequential forms of expression as virtual child pornography, *Ashcroft v. Free Speech Coalition* (2002), tobacco advertising, *Lorillard Tobacco Co. v. Reilly* (2001), dissemination of illegally intercepted communications, *Bartnicki v. Vopper* (2001), and sexually explicit cable programming, *United States v. Playboy Entertainment Group, Inc.* (2000), would smile with favor upon a law that cuts to the heart of what the First Amendment is meant to protect: the right to criticize the government. For that is what the most offensive provisions of this legislation are all about. We are governed by Congress, and this legislation prohibits the criticism of

Members of Congress by those entities most capable of giving such criticism loud voice: national political parties and corporations, both of the commercial and the not-for-profit sort. It forbids pre-election criticism of incumbents by corporations, even not-for-profit corporations, by use of their general funds; and forbids national-party use of "soft" money to fund "issue ads" that incumbents find so offensive.

To be sure, the legislation is evenhanded: It similarly prohibits criticism of the candidates who oppose Members of Congress in their reelection bids. But as everyone knows, this is an area in which evenhandedness is not fairness. If *all* electioneering were evenhandedly prohibited, incumbents would have an enormous advantage. Likewise, if incumbents and challengers are limited to the same quantity of electioneering, incumbents are favored. In other words, *any* restriction upon a type of campaign speech that is equally available to challengers and incumbents tends to favor incumbents.

Beyond that, however, the present legislation *targets* for prohibition certain categories of campaign speech that are particularly harmful to incumbents. Is it accidental, do you think, that incumbents raise about three times as much "hard money"—the sort of funding generally *not* restricted by this legislation—as do their challengers? Or that lobbyists (who seek the favor of incumbents) give 92 percent of their money in "hard" contributions? Is it an oversight, do you suppose, that the so-called "millionaire provisions" raise the contribution limit for a candidate running against an individual who devotes to the campaign (as challengers often do) great personal wealth, but do not raise the limit for a candidate running against an individual who devotes to the campaign (as incumbents often do) a massive election "war chest"? And is it mere happenstance, do you estimate, that national-party funding, which is severely limited by the Act, is more likely to assist cash-strapped challengers than flush-with-hard-money incumbents? . . .

. . . This litigation is about preventing criticism of the government. I cannot say for certain that many, or some, or even any, of the Members of Congress who voted for this legislation did so not to produce "fairer" campaigns, but to mute criticism of their records and facilitate reelection. Indeed, I will stipulate that all those who voted for the Act believed they were acting for the good of the country. . . . Those in power, even giving them the benefit of the greatest good will, are inclined to believe that what is good for them is good for the country. . . .

. . . The most frightening passage in the lengthy floor debates on this legislation is the following assurance given by one of the cosponsoring Senators to his colleagues:

"This is a modest step, it is a first step, it is an essential step, but it does not even begin to address, in some ways, the fundamental problems that exist with the hard money aspect of the system." ([S]tatement of Sen. Feingold).

The system indeed. The first instinct of power is the retention of power, and, under a Constitution that requires periodic elections, that is best achieved by the suppression of election-time speech. We have witnessed merely the second scene of Act I of what promises to be a lengthy tragedy. In scene 3 the Court, having abandoned most of the First Amendment weaponry that *Buckley* left intact, will be even less equipped to resist the incumbents' writing of the rules of political debate. The federal election campaign laws, which are already (as today's opinions show) so voluminous, so detailed, so complex, that no ordinary citizen dare run for office, or even contribute a significant sum, without hiring an expert advisor in the field, can be expected to grow more voluminous, more detailed, and more complex in the years to come—and always, always, with the objective of reducing the excessive amount of speech.

JUSTICE THOMAS [concurring in part and dissenting in part].

The First Amendment provides that "Congress shall make no law . . . abridging the freedom of speech." Nevertheless, the Court today upholds what can only be described as the most significant abridgment of the freedoms of speech and association since the Civil War. With breathtaking scope, the Bipartisan Campaign Reform Act of 2002 (BCRA), directly targets and constricts core political speech, the "primary object of First Amendment protection." Because "the First Amendment 'has its fullest and most urgent application' to speech uttered during a campaign for political office," our duty is to approach these restrictions "with the utmost skepticism" and subject them to the "strictest scrutiny."

In response to this assault on the free exchange of ideas and with only the slightest consideration of the appropriate standard of review or of the Court's traditional role of protecting First Amendment freedoms, the Court has placed its *imprimatur* on these unprecedented restrictions. The very "purpose of the First Amendment [is] to preserve an uninhibited marketplace of ideas in which truth will ultimately prevail." *Red Lion Broadcasting Co. v. FCC* (1969). Yet today the fundamental principle that "the best test of truth is the power of the thought to get itself accepted in the competition of the market," *Abrams v. United States* (1919) (HOLMES, J., dissenting), is cast aside in the purported service of preventing "corruption," or the mere "appearance of corruption." *Buckley v. Valeo* (1976). Apparently, the marketplace of ideas is to be fully open only to defamers, *New York Times Co. v. Sullivan* (1964); nude dancers, *Barnes v. Glen Theatre, Inc.* (1991); pornographers, *Ashcroft v. Free Speech Coalition* (2002); flag burners, *United States v. Eichman* (1990); and cross burners, *Virginia v. Black* (2003). . . .

The chilling endpoint of the Court's reasoning is not difficult to foresee: outright regulation of the press. None of the rationales offered by the defendants, and none of the reasoning employed by the Court, exempts the press. "This is so because of the difficulty, and perhaps impossibility, of distinguishing, either as a matter of fact or constitutional law, media corporations from [nonmedia] corporations." Media companies can run procandidate editorials as easily as nonmedia corporations can pay for advertisements. Candidates can be just as grateful to media companies as they can be to corporations and unions. In terms of "the corrosive and distorting effects" of wealth accumulated by corporations that has "little or no correlation to the public's support for the corporation's political ideas," there is no distinction between a media corporation and a nonmedia corporation. Media corporations are influential. There is little doubt that the editorials and commentary they run can affect elections. Nor is there any doubt that media companies often wish to influence elections. One would think that the *New York Times* fervently hopes that its endorsement of Presidential candidates will actually influence people. What is to stop a future Congress from determining that the press is "too influential," and that the "appearance of corruption" is significant when media organizations endorse candidates or run "slanted" or "biased" news stories in favor of candidates or parties? Or, even easier, what is to stop a future Congress from concluding that the availability of unregulated media corporations creates a loophole that allows for easy "circumvention" of the limitations of the current campaign finance laws? . . .

Hence, "the freedom of the press," described as "one of the greatest bulwarks of liberty," could be next on the chopping block. Although today's opinion does not expressly strip the press of First Amendment protection, there is no principle of law or logic that would prevent the application of the Court's reasoning in that setting. The press now operates at the whim of Congress.

JUSTICE KENNEDY [concurring in part and dissenting in part].

The First Amendment guarantees our citizens the right to judge for themselves the most effective means for the expression of political views and to decide for themselves which entities to trust as reliable speakers. Significant portions of Titles I and II of the Bipartisan Campaign Reform Act of 2002 (BCRA or Act) constrain that freedom. These new laws force speakers to abandon their own preference for speaking through parties and organizations. . . .

Today's decision upholding these laws purports simply to follow *Buckley v. Valeo* (1976) and to abide by *stare decisis*, but the majority, to make its decision work, must abridge free speech where *Buckley* did not. *Buckley* did not authorize Congress to decide what shapes and forms the national political dialogue is to take. To reach today's decision, the Court surpasses *Buckley*'s limits and expands Congress' regulatory power. In so doing, it replaces discrete and respected First Amendment principles with new, amorphous, and unsound rules, rules which dismantle basic protections for speech. . . .

Our precedents teach, above all, that Government cannot be trusted to moderate its own rules for suppression of speech. The dangers posed by speech regulations have led the Court to insist upon principled constitutional lines and a rigorous standard of review. The majority now abandons these distinctions and limitations. . . .

The First Amendment underwrites the freedom to experiment and to create in the realm of thought and speech. Citizens must be free to use new forms, and new forums, for the expression of ideas. The civic discourse belongs to the people and the Government may not prescribe the means used to conduct it.

The First Amendment commands that Congress "shall make no law . . . abridging the freedom of speech.". . . The Court, upholding multiple laws that suppress both sponta-

neous and concerted speech, leaves us less free than before. Today's decision breaks faith with our tradition of robust and unfettered debate. . . .

McConnell presented the Court with a conflict between two important values: the freedom of speech and the need to protect the real and perceived integrity of the electoral process. The result was a badly fractured 5–4 decision with the justices writing eight different opinions expressing their views. The unstable nature of the Court's position on campaign finance reform became even more so in 2006 when Justice Samuel Alito replaced Justice O'Connor, an author of the joint opinion for the Court in *McConnell.* Over the next two years, the Court heard two important campaign finance cases, and in both Alito voted with the majority to strike down the regulations.

Just five months after Alito took his seat, the Court in ***Randall v. Sorrell*** (2006) struck down a Vermont law that placed stringent ceilings on campaign contributions. Among its other provisions, the law limited individual donations to candidates for statewide office to $400 per two-year election cycle, with lower limits of $200 for some local offices. The law also put strict ceilings on the amount of money candidates could spend. The Court invalidated the law, saying that the Constitution is violated when contribution and spending limitations, like those imposed by the Vermont law, become so severe as to damage freedom of speech interests.

In *Davis v. Federal Election Commission* (2008) the justices declared unconstitutional the so-called millionaire's amendment to the BCRA. This provision dealt with wealthy candidates who in large part finance their campaigns with personal funds. Under the law, once those personal funds exceeded a particular threshold as determined by a complex statistical formula, supporters of the self-financing candidate's opponent were allowed to donate up to three times the regular contribution limits permitted under the BCRA. Supporters of the self-financing candidate, however, were required to abide by the normal contribution ceilings. The law was designed to reduce the advantage of wealthy candidates, but the justices found that it placed an impermissible burden on candidates' First Amendment rights to use their own money for campaign speech.

Although the *McConnell* ruling was a strong statement in support of campaign financing regulation, the follow-up cases, *Randall* and *Davis,* lead us to question how secure that ruling is. Furthermore, in spite of the seemingly comprehensive nature of the BCRA, candidates and political parties, as well as corporations and interest groups, have found various ways to avoid many of the act's restrictions. As Justices Stevens and O'Connor wrote in their *McConnell* opinion, "Money, like water, will always find an outlet."

POLITICAL REPRESENTATION

Having the right to vote and maintaining clean election campaigns does not guarantee that people share equally in political influence. The United States is not a direct democracy; consequently, few public policy decisions are made in the voting booth. In a republican form of government, most political decisions are made by officials who are elected by the people from defined geographical districts. The duty of these officials is to represent the interests of their constituencies in the policy-making process.

How well and how equitably this representational process works depends in part on how the boundary lines of political units are drawn. Because district lines determine political representation, the authority to draw those boundaries carries with it a great deal of political power. Skillful construction of political subdivisions can be used to great advantage, and politicians have never been reluctant to use this power to advance their own interests. Since 1812 the art of structuring legislative districts to ensure political success has been known as *gerrymandering.* The term refers to the political maneuverings of Gov. Elbridge Gerry of Massachusetts, who persuaded the state legislature to draw district lines so that his partisan supporters would have a high probability of reelection. Gerrymandered districts frequently are characterized by the rather strange geographical configurations necessary to achieve the desired political ends.

Establishing or modifying the district lines historically has been a political matter. Battles over drawing the

In 1812 Elkanah Tinsdale lampooned the political maneuverings of Gov. Elbridge Gerry of Massachusetts, who deftly engineered the construction of constituency boundaries to aid in the election of a member of his own party. Because the district resembled a mythological salamander in the cartoonist's illustration, the term *gerrymander* has come to mean the drawing of political district lines for partisan advantage.

boundaries of political subdivisions usually are fought within the halls of the state legislatures. Serious legal or even constitutional questions may arise when officials use inappropriate criteria for drawing boundaries, or when the process results in the discriminatory treatment of certain groups of voters. In such cases the courts may be called upon to intervene in what is otherwise a legislative duty.

The Reapportionment Controversy

In drafting Article I of the Constitution, the framers clearly intended that representation in the lower house of Congress would be based upon population. Each state was allotted at least one representative, with additional seats based upon the number of persons residing within its boundaries.

The Constitutional Convention wisely anticipated that the nation would undergo considerable growth and population shifts and consequently determined that the number of congressional seats allocated to each state would be reformulated every ten years following completion of the national census. States that grew in population would gain increased congressional representation, and those that lost population would lose representation. This process remains relatively unchanged today. The number of voting seats in the House of Representatives is fixed by federal law, currently at 435. Every ten years, when the Census Bureau completes its work, the allocation of those 435 seats among the states must be recalculated to reflect changes since the previous population count.

After the census has been taken, each state is told the number of representatives it will have for the next decade. The state legislature then geographically divides the state into separate congressional districts, each of which elects a member of Congress. This scheme is known as the single-member constituency system of representation. Political representation is equitable only if the state legislature constructs its congressional districts so that each contains approximately the same number of residents.

The process of devising the legislative districts is called apportionment. When the legislature creates equally populated districts, the system is properly apportioned. But when the districts are not in proper balance, when some districts have substantially larger populations than others, they are said to be malapportioned. A state can be malapportioned if the legislature does not draw the district lines properly or fails to adjust boundaries to keep pace with population shifts.

Representational districts are used not only for congressional seats, but for other government units as well. State legislatures generally are based on a single-member constituency system, as are many county commissions and city councils. Even special purpose commissions, such as boards of education and public utility districts, often follow the same scheme. In each case, a legislative body must create districts from which representatives will be selected. The same apportionment concepts apply to these bodies as apply to the lower house of Congress.

The constitutional issues regarding apportionment rose to the surface after World War II. Spurred by indus-trialization, two major wars, and an economic depression, major population shifts took place during the first half of the twentieth century. Large numbers of people moved from rural areas and small towns into larger urban centers. Cities grew rapidly and agricultural areas declined, but state legislatures failed to respond adequately to these migration patterns by reapportioning their congressional and state legislative districts. The more state legislatures came to be dominated by rural interests, the less incumbent legislators wished to consider redistricting. To apportion the districts properly would mean fewer legislative seats for the rural areas, and that meant abolishing some seats held by incumbents. At the midpoint of the century, many states had not reapportioned since the 1900 census.

The first major apportionment case to come before the Supreme Court was *Colegrove v. Green* (1946), a challenge to the congressional districts in Illinois, where the most populous district had almost nine times as many residents as the least populous. This imbalance was challenged on the ground that it resulted in a system that violated the Constitution's guarantee of a republican form of government. The Supreme Court refused to rule on the case, holding that reapportionment was a political issue that should be resolved at the ballot box and not in court.

The Court's admonishment presented an insurmountable problem for urban residents living in disproportionately large districts. Many states were so badly malapportioned and the dominant rural interests so opposed to change that electing enough state legislators sympathetic to reapportionment was almost impossible. But the Court maintained its position that reapportionment questions were outside the purview of judicial scrutiny. Meanwhile, the census figures for 1950 and 1960 indicated that the malapportionment problem was growing.

By 1958 only one of the four justices in the majority in *Colegrove*, Felix Frankfurter, remained on the bench. The Court, under the leadership of Earl Warren, radically changed its position on the jurisdictional issue. After a lower federal court had refused to hear a challenge to the badly malapportioned Tennessee state legislature, the justices in *Baker v. Carr* (1962) ruled that apportionment issues raise serious equal protection questions that are justiciable. In effect, the Court announced that it would welcome reapportionment challenges.

The first reapportionment dispute heard by the Supreme Court following *Baker* was **Wesberry v. Sanders** (1964), which involved a challenge to the way Georgia apportioned its congressional districts. This suit was filed by James P. Wesberry and other qualified voters of Georgia's Fifth Congressional District against Gov. Carl Sanders and other state officials. The Fifth (metropolitan Atlanta) was the largest of Georgia's ten congressional districts, with a population of 823,680. By comparison the Ninth District had only 272,154 residents, and the population of the average district was 394,312. This inequality meant that the Fifth District's legislator represented two to three times as many people as the other members of Congress from Georgia. The districting scheme had been enacted by the state legislature in 1931, and no effort to bring the districts into balance had occurred since then.

The justices held that this condition of significant malapportionment violated Article I, Section 2, of the Constitution, which says, "The House of Representatives shall be composed of Members chosen every second Year by the People of the several States." To satisfy that constitutional provision, the Court ruled, the congressional districts within a state must be as equal in population as possible. The decision required the state legislature to redraw its congressional districts to meet this standard.

Wesberry, however, did not resolve the reapportionment controversy. A more difficult and politically charged issue centered on malapportionment within the state legislatures. It was one thing to command the state legislators to alter the boundaries of congressional districts, but another to require them to reapportion their own legislative districts. Many states would regard such an action as an infringement of their sovereignty. In addition, the wholesale alteration of state legislative districts would mean that many state representatives would lose their districts or become politically vulnerable, and legislative power would shift from rural to urban interests. That the state legislatures were less than enthusiastic about such prospects is hardly surprising.

It did not take the Supreme Court long to address the dilemma of the state legislatures. Only four months after *Wesberry*, the Court announced its decision in *Reynolds v. Sims*. Although *Reynolds* shares with *Wesberry* questions of representational equality, the legal basis for the two cases is very different. Article I, Section 2, of the Constitution, upon which the *Wesberry* outcome rested, deals only with the U.S. House of Representatives. Consequently, a challenge to state representational schemes had to be based on other grounds. In addition, all state legislatures except Nebraska's are bicameral, leaving open for dispute whether both houses of the state assembly must be based on population. Notice in Chief Justice Warren's majority opinion in *Reynolds* how the Court reaches a conclusion consistent with *Wesberry* while using entirely different constitutional grounds. Also, consider the Court's holding on the issue of bicameralism. Is this ruling reasonable? Or should the states be allowed to base representation in one house of the legislature on interests other than population alone? How compelling is Justice John Harlan's dissent?

Reynolds v. Sims

377 U.S. 533 (1964)
http://laws.findlaw.com/US/377/533.html
Oral arguments may be found at: http://www.oyez.org
Vote: 8 (Black, Brennan, Clark, Douglas, Goldberg, Stewart, Warren, White)
        1 (Harlan)
Opinion of the Court: Warren
Concurring opinions: Clark, Stewart
Dissenting opinion: Harlan

Alabama's 1901 constitution authorized a state legislature of 106 House members and 35 senators. These legislators were to represent districts created generally on the basis of population. Although obliged to reapportion following each national census, the legislature had never altered the districts drawn following the 1900 census. Because of population shifts and a state constitutional requirement that each county, regardless of size, have at least one representative, Alabama had become severely malapportioned. For the state House of Representatives, the most populous legislative district had sixteen times as many people as the least populous. Conditions in the state senate were even more inequitable. The largest senatorial district had a population forty-one times the population of the smallest. As was the case in other states, rural areas enjoyed representation levels far in excess of what their populations warranted. For example, urban Jefferson County's single senator represented more than 600,000 residents, and rural Lowndes County's senator represented 15,417.

Voters in urban counties filed suit to have the Alabama system declared unconstitutional as a violation of the equal protection clause of the Fourteenth Amendment. Pressured by the threat of legal action in light of the Supreme Court's decision in *Baker v. Carr,* the state legislature offered two reapportionment plans to improve the situation. A three-judge district court declared the existing system unconstitutional and the proposed reforms inadequate. A temporary reapportionment plan was imposed by the trial court judges, and the state appealed to the Supreme Court. The *Reynolds* case was one of six state legislative reapportionment disputes the Court heard at the same time. The others came from Colorado, Delaware, Maryland, New York, and Virginia. The justices used the opinion in *Reynolds* as the primary vehicle for articulating the Court's position on the state redistricting issue.

MR. CHIEF JUSTICE WARREN delivered the opinion of the Court.

Legislators represent people, not trees or acres. Legislators are elected by voters, not farms or cities or economic interests. As long as ours is a representative form of government, and our legislatures are those instruments of government elected directly by and directly representative of the people, the right to elect legislators in a free and unimpaired fashion is a bedrock of our political system. It could hardly be gainsaid that a constitutional claim had been asserted by an allegation that certain otherwise qualified voters had been entirely prohibited from voting for members of their state legislature. And, if a State should provide that the votes of citizens in one part of the State should be given two times, or five times, or 10 times the weight of votes of citizens in another part of the State, it could hardly be contended that the right to vote of those residing in the disfavored areas had not been effectively diluted. It would appear extraordinary to suggest that a State could be constitutionally permitted to enact a law providing that certain of the State's voters could vote two, five, or 10 times for their legislative representatives, while voters living elsewhere could vote only once. And it is inconceivable that a state law to the effect that, in counting votes for legislators, the votes of citizens in one part of the State would be multiplied by two, five, or 10 while the votes of persons in another area would be counted only at face value, could be constitutionally sustainable. Of course, the effect of state legislative districting schemes which give the same number of representatives to unequal numbers of constituents is identical. Overweighting and overvaluation of the votes of those living here has the certain effect of dilution and undervaluation of the votes of those living there. The resulting discrimination against those individual voters living in disfavored areas is easily demonstrable mathematically. Their right to vote is simply not the same right to vote as that of those living in a favored part of the State. Two, five, or 10 of them must vote before the effect of their voting is equivalent to that of their favored neighbor. Weighting the votes of citizens differently, by any method or means, merely because of where they happen to reside, hardly seems justifiable. One must be ever aware that the Constitution forbids "sophisticated as well as simpleminded modes of discrimination." . . .

Logically, in a society ostensibly grounded on representative government, it would seem reasonable that a majority of the people of a State could elect a majority of that State's legislators. To conclude differently, and to sanction minority control of state legislative bodies, would appear to deny majority rights in a way that far surpasses any possible denial of minority rights that might otherwise be thought to result. Since legislatures are responsible for enacting laws by which all citizens are to be governed, they should be bodies which are collectively responsive to the popular will. And the concept of equal protection has been traditionally viewed as requiring the uniform treatment of persons standing in the same relation to the governmental action questioned or challenged. With respect to the allocation of legislative representation, all voters, as citizens of a State, stand in the same relation regardless of where they live. Any suggested criteria for the differentiation of citizens are insufficient to justify any discrimination, as to the weight of their votes, unless relevant to the permissible purposes of legislative apportionment. Since the achieving of fair and effective representation for all citizens is concededly the basic aim of legislative apportionment, we conclude that the Equal Protection Clause guarantees the opportunity for equal participation by all voters in the election of state legislators. Diluting the weight of votes because of place of residence impairs basic constitutional rights under the Fourteenth Amendment just as much as invidious discriminations based upon factors such as race or economic status. . . .

We are told that the matter of apportioning representation in a state legislature is a complex and many-faceted one. We are advised that States can rationally consider factors other than population in apportioning legislative representation. We are admonished not to restrict the power of the States to impose differing views as to political philosophy on their citizens. We are cautioned about the dangers of entering into political thickets and mathematical quagmires. Our answer is this: a denial of constitutionally protected rights demands judicial protection; our oath and our office require no less of us. . . . To the extent that a citizen's right to vote is debased, he is that much less a citizen. The fact that an individual lives here or there is not a legitimate reason for overweighting or diluting the efficacy of his vote. The complexions of societies and civilizations change, often with amazing rapidity. A nation once primarily rural in character becomes predominantly urban. Representation schemes once fair and equitable become archaic and outdated. But the basic principle of representative government remains, and must remain, unchanged—the weight of a citizen's vote cannot be made to depend on where he lives. Population is, of necessity, the starting point for consideration and the controlling criterion for judgment in legislative apportionment controversies. A citizen, a qualified voter, is no more nor no less so because he lives in the city or on the farm. This is the clear and strong command of our Constitution's Equal Protection Clause. This is an essential part of the concept of a government of laws and not men. This is at the heart of Lincoln's vision of "government of the people, by the people, [and] for the people." The Equal Protection Clause demands no less than substantially equal state legislative representation for all citizens, of all places as well as of all races.

We hold that, as a basic constitutional standard, the Equal Protection Clause requires that the seats in both houses of a bicameral state legislature must be apportioned on a population basis. Simply stated, an individual's right to vote for state legislators is unconstitutionally impaired when its weight is in a substantial fashion diluted when compared with votes of citizens living in other parts of the State. . . .

Legislative apportionment in Alabama is signally illustrative and symptomatic of the seriousness of this problem in a number of the States. At the time this litigation was commenced, there had been no reapportionment of seats in the Alabama Legislature for over 60 years. Legislative inaction, coupled with the unavailability of any political or judicial remedy, had resulted, with the passage of years, in the perpetuated scheme becoming little more than an irrational anachronism. Consistent failure by the Alabama Legislature to comply with state constitutional requirements as to the frequency of reapportionment and the bases of legislative representation resulted in a minority stranglehold on the State Legislature. Inequality of representation in one house added to the inequality in the other. . . . Since neither of the houses of the Alabama Legislature, under any of the three plans considered by the District Court, was apportioned on a population basis, we would be justified in proceeding no further. However, one of the proposed plans, that contained in the so-called 67-Senator Amendment, at least superficially resembles the scheme of legislative representation followed in the Federal Congress. Under this plan, each of Alabama's 67 counties is allotted one senator, and no counties are given more than one Senate seat. Arguably, this is analogous to the allocation of two Senate seats, in the Federal Congress, to each of the 50 States, regardless of population. Seats in the Alabama House, under the proposed constitutional amendment, are distributed by giving each of the 67 counties at least one, with the remaining 39 seats being allotted among the more populous counties on a population basis. This scheme, at least at first glance, appears to resemble that prescribed for the Federal House of Representatives, where the 435 seats are distributed among the States on a population basis, although each State, regardless of its population, is given at least one Congressman. Thus, although there are substantial differences in underlying rationale and results, the 67-Senator Amendment, as proposed by the Alabama Legislature, at least arguably presents for consideration a scheme analogous to that used for apportioning seats in Congress. . . .

We agree with the District Court, and find the federal analogy inapposite and irrelevant to state legislative districting schemes. Attempted reliance on the federal analogy appears often to be little more than an after-the-fact rationalization offered in defense of maladjusted state apportionment arrangements. The original constitutions of 36 of our States provided that representation in both houses of the state legislatures would be based completely, or predominantly, on population. And the Founding Fathers clearly had no intention of establishing a pattern or model for the apportionment of seats in state legislatures when the system of representation in the Federal Congress was adopted. . . .

The system of representation in the two Houses of the Federal Congress is one ingrained in our Constitution, as part of the law of the land. It is one conceived out of compromise and concession indispensable to the establishment of our federal republic. Arising from unique historical circumstances, it is based on the consideration that in establishing our type of federalism a group of formerly independent States bound themselves together under one national government. . . .

Political subdivisions of States—counties, cities, or whatever—never were and never have been considered as sovereign entities. Rather, they have been traditionally regarded as subordinate governmental instrumentalities created by the State to assist in the carrying out of state governmental functions. . . . The relationship of the States to the Federal Government could hardly be less analogous.

Thus, we conclude that the plan contained in the 67 Senator Amendment for apportioning seats in the Alabama Legislature cannot be sustained by recourse to the so-called federal analogy. Nor can any other inequitable state legislative apportionment scheme be justified. . . .

By holding that as a federal constitutional requisite both houses of a state legislature must be apportioned on a population basis, we mean that the Equal Protection Clause requires that a State make an honest and good faith effort to construct districts, in both houses of its legislature, as nearly of equal population as is practicable. We realize that it is a practical impossibility to arrange legislative districts so that each one has an identical number of residents, or citizens, or voters. Mathematical exactness or precision is hardly a workable constitutional requirement. . . .

A State may legitimately desire to maintain the integrity of various political subdivisions, insofar as possible, and provide for compact districts of contiguous territory in designing a legislative apportionment scheme. Valid considerations may underlie such aims. Indiscriminate districting, without any regard for political subdivision or natural or historical boundary lines, may be little more than an open invitation to partisan gerrymandering. Single-member districts may be the rule in one State, while another State might desire to achieve some flexibility by creating multimember or floterial districts. Whatever the means of accomplishment, the overriding objective must be substantial equality of population among the various districts, so that the vote of any citizen is approximately equal in weight to that of any other citizen in the State.

History indicates, however, that many States have deviated, to a greater or lesser degree, from the equal-population principle in the apportionment of seats in at least one house of their legislatures. So long as the divergences from a strict population standard are based on legitimate considerations incident to the effectuation of a rational state policy, some deviations from the equal-population principle are constitutionally permissible with respect to the apportionment of seats in either or both of the two houses of a bicameral state legislature. But neither history alone, nor economic or other sorts of group interests, are permissible factors in attempting to justify disparities from population-based representation. Citizens, not history or economic interests, cast votes. Considerations of area alone provide an insufficient justification for deviations from the equal population principle. . . .

We find, therefore, that the action taken by the District Court in this case, in ordering into effect a reapportionment of both houses of the Alabama Legislature for purposes of the 1962 primary and general elections, by using the best parts of the two proposed plans which it had found, as a whole, to be invalid, was an appropriate and well-considered exercise of judicial power. Admittedly, the lower court's ordered plan was intended only as a temporary and provisional measure and the District Court correctly indicated that the plan was invalid as a permanent apportionment. In retaining jurisdiction while deferring a hearing on the issuance of a final injunction in order to give the provisionally reapportioned legislature an opportunity to act effectively, the court below proceeded in a proper fashion. . . .

Affirmed and remanded.

MR. JUSTICE HARLAN, dissenting.

In these cases the Court holds that seats in the legislatures of six States are apportioned in ways that violate the Federal Constitution. Under the Court's ruling it is bound to follow that the legislature in all but a few of the other 44 States will meet the same fate. These decisions, with *Wesberry v. Sanders*, involving congressional districting by the States, and *Gray v. Sanders*, relating to elections for statewide office, have the effect of placing basic aspects of state political systems under the pervasive overlordship of the federal judiciary. Once again, I must register my protest.

Today's holding is that the Equal Protection Clause of the Fourteenth Amendment requires every State to structure its legislature so that all the members of each house represent substantially the same number of people; other factors may be given play only to the extent that they do not significantly encroach on this basic "population" principle. Whatever may be thought of this holding as a piece of political ideology—and even on that score the political history and practices of this country from its earliest beginnings leave wide room for debate . . . I think it demonstrable that the Fourteenth Amendment does not impose this political tenet on the States or authorize this Court to do so. . . .

Had the Court paused to probe more deeply into the matter, it would have found that the Equal Protection Clause was never intended to inhibit the States in choosing any democratic method they pleased for the apportionment of their legislatures. This is shown by the language of the Fourteenth Amendment taken as a whole, by the understanding of those who proposed and ratified it, and by the political practices of the States at the time the Amendment was adopted. It is confirmed by numerous state and congressional actions since the adoption of the Fourteenth Amendment, and by the common understanding of the Amendment as evidenced by subsequent constitutional amendments and decisions of this Court before *Baker v. Carr* made an abrupt break with the past in 1962. . . .

So far as the Federal Constitution is concerned, the complaints in these cases should all have been dismissed below for failure to state a cause of action because what has been alleged or proved shows no violation of any constitutional right.

Harlan's dissent in *Reynolds*, predicting that the legislatures of all the states would be affected by the Court's one person, one vote principle, proved to be accurate. At first, there was some disagreement with the Court's ruling. State advocates began a movement to amend the Constitution to provide states the authority to have at least one house of their legislatures based on factors other than population, but the proposal failed to garner sufficient support. As the states began the Court-imposed reapportionment process, opposition started to wane. Today, reapportionment of congressional and state legislative districts occurs each decade following the national census. In addition, the reapportionment rulings have been extended to representation systems used at the local level, expanding the influence of decisions such as *Wesberry* and *Reynolds*.

Upon his retirement, Chief Justice Warren said that, in his opinion, the reapportionment decisions were the most significant rulings rendered during his sixteen-year tenure. That statement was remarkable, considering that under his leadership the Court handed down landmark decisions on race relations, criminal justice, obscenity, libel, and school prayer.

Political Representation and Minority Rights

So long as the one person, one vote principle is observed, the Supreme Court generally has allowed the states freedom in constructing representational districts. That latitude, however, is not without limit. The Court is aware that representational schemes that satisfy standards of numerical equality may still offend basic constitutional principles. Plans that discriminate on the basis of race or ethnicity have been of particular concern. The justices have served notice that boundary lines cannot be drawn in a way that dilutes the political power of minorities.

An early example of how lines can be drawn to reduce the influence of minorities is shown in **Gomillion v. Lightfoot** (1960). Prior to 1957 the city limits of Tuskegee, Alabama, were in the shape of a square that covered the entire urban area. With the growing civil rights activism of the time and the increasing tendency of black citizens to vote, the white establishment in Tuskegee feared a loss of political control. Consequently, members of the Alabama legislature sympathetic to the city's white leaders successfully sponsored a bill that changed the boundary lines. No longer a square, the altered city limits formed, in Justice Frankfurter's words, "an uncouth twenty-eight-sided figure."

The effect of the redistricting was phenomenal. The law removed from the city all but four or five of its four hundred black voters, but no white voters. The black plaintiffs, now former residents of Tuskegee, claimed that their removal from the city denied them the right to vote on the basis of race and, therefore, violated their Fifteenth Amendment rights. The city did not deny that race was at issue but claimed that the state of Alabama had an unrestricted right to draw city boundaries as it saw fit and that the courts could not intervene to limit that authority. A unanimous Supreme Court ruled to the contrary, holding that when an otherwise lawful exercise of state power is used to circumvent a federally protected right, the courts may indeed intervene. A legislative act that removes citizens from the municipal voting rolls in a racially discriminatory fashion violates the Fifteenth Amendment.

Beginning in the 1970s the issue of race and representation took on a new twist when legislatures started to enact districting plans designed to ensure the election of minority officials. The legislatures created "majority-minority" districts, representational units in which a majority of the residents were members of a particular minority group. These districts virtually ensured the election of minority officeholders. In **United Jewish Organizations of Williamsburgh v. Carey** (1977), the Supreme Court upheld such legislative actions. For the Court Justice Byron White declared:

[T]he Constitution does not prevent a State subject to the Voting Rights Act from deliberately creating or preserving black majorities in particular districts. . . . [N]either the Fourteenth nor the Fifteenth Amendment mandates any per se rule against using racial factors in districting and apportionment. . . . The

permissible use of racial criteria is not confined to eliminating the effects of past discriminatory districting or apportionment.

The decisions in *United Jewish Organizations* and subsequent cases encouraged state legislatures to engage in racially aware districting practices. Civil rights groups and other liberal organizations had been advocating this practice as the only meaningful way to guarantee African Americans, Hispanics, and other minorities a fair share of legislative seats.

In promoting this cause, advocates of increasing the political power of minorities received significant support from the Justice Department under Presidents Ronald Reagan and George H. W. Bush. Why would a Republican administration back efforts to increase the number of African American representatives, especially when these legislators probably would be Democrats? The answer is simple. When lines are drawn to create districts with high concentrations of black voters, the other districts become more white and more Republican. In other words, by creating a few districts that are dominated by minorities, the state legislatures could also fashion other districts that are more likely to elect Republicans.

In many states the reapportionment battles that followed the 1990 census were not over one person, one vote issues; rather, they focused on drawing district boundary lines in a manner that would increase the number of minority officeholders. The successful creation of districts with heavy concentrations of racial and ethnic minorities had its intended effect. In the 1992 congressional elections, sixteen new African American representatives were elected, bringing the total membership of the Black Caucus to forty. Eight newly elected Hispanic representatives also took their seats after the 1992 elections.

To draw these new majority-minority districts, state legislatures often had to engage in very creative mapping methods. Critics contended that legislators went too far, frequently establishing districts that were highly irregular in shape and sprawled across large areas. It was one thing, they argued, to create districts that did not purposefully dilute minority voting strength, but a much different matter to base representational boundaries exclusively on race. As a consequence, lawsuits filed in

Florida, Georgia, Louisiana, North Carolina, and Texas challenged the constitutionality of many new districts.

The first appeal to reach the Supreme Court was *Shaw v. Reno* (1993), a challenge to two majority-minority congressional districts in North Carolina. The decision in that case shocked the civil rights community; the Court ruled that congressional districts created to maximize minority representation under some circumstances may be unconstitutional. At risk were district lines that created bizarrely shaped configurations explainable in racial terms only. After establishing this new standard, the justices sent the case back down to the lower courts for additional proceedings.

It was only a matter of time before the Court would receive an appeal requiring it to apply the *Shaw* principles. How much latitude would the Court give state legislatures in fashioning districts designed to enhance minority voting strength? To what extent would the *Shaw* standard allow race to be taken into account? The Court was not clear in *Shaw,* and its 5–4 vote left the districting waters muddy, but it did not take long for the Court to try again. The first appeal to reach the justices was a 1995 case challenging a majority-minority district in Georgia. As you read *Miller v. Johnson,* pay close attention to the different views expressed.

Miller v. Johnson

515 U.S. 900 (1995)
http://laws.findlaw.com/US/515/900.html
Oral arguments may be found at: http://www.oyez.org
Vote: 5 (Kennedy, O'Connor, Rehnquist, Scalia, Thomas)
    4 (Breyer, Ginsburg, Souter, Stevens)
Opinion of the Court: Kennedy
Concurring opinion: O'Connor
Dissenting opinions: Ginsburg, Stevens

Following the 1990 census Georgia needed to redraw the lines of its eleven congressional districts. The first plan, passed by the state legislature in 1991, included two districts that had a majority of black voters. Because Georgia is subject to the provisions of the 1965 Voting Rights Act, the plan was submitted to the Justice Depart-

ment for approval ("preclearance"). The Justice Department rejected the plan, holding that it did not give sufficient attention to black voting strength. The state revised its apportionment plan, but the new version also included only two majority black districts. This plan also failed to receive Justice Department approval. Finally, in 1992 the state passed, and the Justice Department approved, a new districting plan. This legislation created three majority black districts: the Second (southwest Georgia), the Fifth (Atlanta), and the Eleventh, the district challenged in this case.

The Eleventh District ran diagonally across the state from the edge of Atlanta to the Atlantic Ocean. It included portions of urban Atlanta, Savannah, and Augusta, as well as sparsely populated, but overwhelmingly black, rural areas in its central part. The Eleventh covered 6,784 square miles, splitting eight counties and five cities along the way. Numerous narrow land bridges were used to incorporate areas with significant African American populations into the district. The district was 60 percent black, and in the 1992 and 1994 elections sent Cynthia McKinney, an African American Democrat, to the House of Representatives.

In 1994 five white voters from the Eleventh District, including Davida Johnson, filed suit claiming that the legislature violated the equal protection clause of the Fourteenth Amendment by adopting a redistricting plan driven primarily by considerations of race. A three-judge federal court, applying principles articulated in *Shaw v. Reno,* struck down the district. The Constitution was violated, the judges ruled, because race was the overriding, predominant factor employed to determine the lines of the district. Gov. Zell Miller, on behalf of the state, appealed to the Supreme Court.

JUSTICE KENNEDY delivered the opinion of the Court.

The Equal Protection Clause of the Fourteenth Amendment provides that no State shall "deny to any person within its jurisdiction the equal protection of the laws." Its central mandate is racial neutrality in governmental decisionmaking. See, e.g., *Loving v. Virginia* (1967); *McLaughlin v. Florida* (1964); see also *Brown v. Board of Education* (1954). Though application of this imperative raises difficult ques-

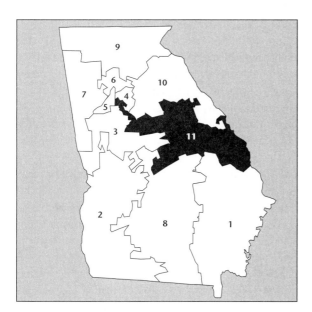

Georgia's Eleventh Congressional District was challenged in *Miller v. Johnson* (1995). Although the district is not generally irregular in shape, note the thin fingerlike extensions in the northwestern, northeastern, and western sections of the district. These were designed to incorporate high concentrations of black voters in Savannah, Augusta, and Atlanta.

tions, the basic principle is straightforward: "Racial and ethnic distinctions of any sort are inherently suspect and thus call for the most exacting judicial examination.... This perception of racial and ethnic distinctions is rooted in our Nation's constitutional and demographic history." *Regents of Univ. of California v. Bakke* (1978) (opinion of Powell, J.). This rule obtains with equal force regardless of "the race of those burdened or benefited by a particular classification." *Richmond v. J. A. Croson Co.* (1989) (plurality opinion). Laws classifying citizens on the basis of race cannot be upheld unless they are narrowly tailored to achieving a compelling state interest.

In *Shaw v. Reno* [1993] we recognized that these equal protection principles govern a State's drawing of congressional districts, though, as our cautious approach there discloses, application of these principles to electoral districting is a most delicate task. Our analysis began from the premise that "[l]aws that explicitly distinguish between individuals on racial grounds fall within the core of [the Equal Protec-

tion Clause's] prohibition." This prohibition extends not just to explicit racial classifications, but also to laws neutral on their face but " 'unexplainable on grounds other than race.' " Applying this basic Equal Protection analysis in the voting rights context, we held that "redistricting legislation that is so bizarre on its face that it is 'unexplainable on grounds other than race,' ... demands the same close scrutiny that we give other state laws that classify citizens by race."

This case requires us to apply the principles articulated in *Shaw* to the most recent congressional redistricting plan enacted by the State of Georgia. . . .

. . . Just as the State may not, absent extraordinary justification, segregate citizens on the basis of race in its public parks, buses, golf courses, beaches, and schools, so did we recognize in *Shaw* that it may not separate its citizens into different voting districts on the basis of race. The idea is a simple one: "At the heart of the Constitution's guarantee of equal protection lies the simple command that the Government must treat citizens 'as individuals, not as simply components of a racial, religious, sexual or national class.' " *Metro Broadcasting, Inc. v. FCC* (1990) (O'CONNOR, J., dissenting). When the State assigns voters on the basis of race, it engages in the offensive and demeaning assumption that voters of a particular race, because of their race, "think alike, share the same political interests, and will prefer the same candidates at the polls." *Shaw*; see *Metro Broadcasting* (KENNEDY, J., dissenting). Race-based assignments "embody stereotypes that treat individuals as the product of their race, evaluating their thoughts and efforts—their very worth as citizens—according to a criterion barred to the Government by history and the Constitution." *Metro Broadcasting* (O'CONNOR, J., dissenting). They also cause society serious harm. As we concluded in *Shaw*:

"Racial classifications with respect to voting carry particular dangers. Racial gerrymandering, even for remedial purposes, may balkanize us into competing racial factions; it threatens to carry us further from the goal of a political system in which race no longer matters—a goal that the Fourteenth and Fifteenth Amendments embody, and to which the Nation continues to aspire. It is for these reasons that race-based districting by our state legislatures demands close judicial scrutiny."

Our observation in *Shaw* of the consequences of racial stereotyping was not meant to suggest that a district must be bizarre on its face before there is a constitutional violation.

Nor was our conclusion in *Shaw* that in certain instances a district's appearance (or, to be more precise, its appearance in combination with certain demographic evidence) can give rise to an equal protection claim, a holding that bizarreness was a threshold showing, as appellants believe it to be. Our circumspect approach and narrow holding in *Shaw* did not erect an artificial rule barring accepted equal protection analysis in other redistricting cases. Shape is relevant not because bizarreness is a necessary element of the constitutional wrong or a threshold requirement of proof, but because it may be persuasive circumstantial evidence that race for its own sake, and not other districting principles, was the legislature's dominant and controlling rationale in drawing its district lines. The logical implication, as courts applying *Shaw* have recognized, is that parties may rely on evidence other than bizarreness to establish race-based districting.

Our reasoning in *Shaw* compels this conclusion. We recognized in *Shaw* that, outside the districting context, statutes are subject to strict scrutiny under the Equal Protection Clause not just when they contain express racial classifications, but also when, though race neutral on their face, they are motivated by a racial purpose or object. . . .

Shaw applied these same principles to redistricting. "In some exceptional cases, a reapportionment plan may be so highly irregular that, on its face, it rationally cannot be understood as anything other than an effort to 'segregat[e] . . . voters' on the basis of race." In other cases, where the district is not so bizarre on its face that it discloses a racial design, the proof will be more "difficul[t]." Although it was not necessary in *Shaw* to consider further the proof required in these more difficult cases, the logical import of our reasoning is that evidence other than a district's bizarre shape can be used to support the claim. . . .

In sum, we make clear that parties alleging that a State has assigned voters on the basis of race are neither confined in their proof to evidence regarding the district's geometry and makeup nor required to make a threshold showing of bizarreness. Today's case requires us further to consider the requirements of the proof necessary to sustain this equal protection challenge.

. . . Electoral districting is a most difficult subject for legislatures, and so the States must have discretion to exercise the political judgment necessary to balance competing interests. Although race-based decisionmaking is inherently suspect, until a claimant makes a showing sufficient to support that allegation the good faith of a state legislature must be presumed. The courts, in assessing the sufficiency of a challenge to a districting plan, must be sensitive to the complex interplay of forces that enter a legislature's redistricting calculus. Redistricting legislatures will, for example, almost always be aware of racial demographics; but it does not follow that race predominates in the redistricting process. The distinction between being aware of racial considerations and being motivated by them may be difficult to make. This evidentiary difficulty, together with the sensitive nature of redistricting and the presumption of good faith that must be accorded legislative enactments, requires courts to exercise extraordinary caution in adjudicating claims that a state has drawn district lines on the basis of race. The plaintiff's burden is to show, either through circumstantial evidence of a district's shape and demographics or more direct evidence going to legislative purpose, that race was the predominant factor motivating the legislature's decision to place a significant number of voters within or without a particular district. To make this showing, a plaintiff must prove that the legislature subordinated traditional race-neutral districting principles, including but not limited to compactness, contiguity, respect for political subdivisions or communities defined by actual shared interests, to racial considerations. Where these or other race-neutral considerations are the basis for redistricting legislation, and are not subordinated to race, a state can "defeat a claim that a district has been gerrymandered on racial lines." *Shaw*. These principles inform the plaintiff's burden of proof at trial. . . .

In our view, the District Court applied the correct analysis, and its finding that race was the predominant factor motivating the drawing of the Eleventh District was not clearly erroneous. The court found it was "exceedingly obvious" from the shape of the Eleventh District, together with the relevant racial demographics, that the drawing of narrow land bridges to incorporate within the District outlying appendages containing nearly 80% of the district's total black population was a deliberate attempt to bring black populations into the district. Although by comparison with other districts the geometric shape of the Eleventh District may not seem bizarre on its face, when its shape is considered in conjunction with its racial and population densities, the story of racial gerrymandering seen by the District Court becomes much clearer. Although this evidence is quite compelling, we need not determine whether it was, standing alone, sufficient to establish a *Shaw* claim that the Eleventh District is unexplainable other than by race. The District Court had before it considerable additional evidence showing that the General Assembly was motivated by a predominant, overriding desire to assign black populations to the Eleventh District and thereby permit the creation of a third majority-black district. . . .

The court found that "it became obvious," both from the Justice Department's objection letters and the three preclearance rounds in general, "that [the Justice Department] would accept nothing less than abject surrender to its maximization agenda." It further found that the General Assembly acquiesced and as a consequence was driven by its overriding desire to comply with the Department's maximization demands.

In light of its well-supported finding, the District Court was justified in rejecting the various alternative explanations offered for the District. Although a legislature's compliance with "traditional districting principles such as compactness, contiguity, and respect for political subdivisions" may well suffice to refute a claim of racial gerrymandering, *Shaw*, appellants cannot make such a refutation where, as here, those factors were subordinated to racial objectives. Georgia's Attorney General objected to the Justice Department's demand for three majority-black districts on the ground that to do so the State would have to "violate all reasonable standards of compactness and contiguity." This statement from a state official is powerful evidence that the legislature subordinated traditional districting principles to race when it ultimately enacted a plan creating three majority-black districts, and justified the District Court's finding that "every [objective districting] factor that could realistically be subordinated to racial tinkering in fact suffered that fate."

Nor can the State's districting legislation be rescued by mere recitation of purported communities of interest. The evidence was compelling "that there are no tangible 'communities of interest' spanning the hundreds of miles of the Eleventh District." A comprehensive report demonstrated the fractured political, social, and economic interests within the Eleventh District's black population. It is apparent that it was not alleged shared interests but rather the object of maximizing the District's black population and obtaining Justice Department approval that in fact explained the General Assembly's actions. A State is free to recognize commu-

nities that have a particular racial makeup, provided its action is directed toward some common thread of relevant interests. . . . But where the State assumes from a group of voters' race that they "think alike, share the same political interests, and will prefer the same candidates at the polls," it engages in racial stereotyping at odds with equal protection mandates.

Race was, as the District Court found, the predominant, overriding factor explaining the General Assembly's decision to attach to the Eleventh District various appendages containing dense majority-black populations. As a result, Georgia's congressional redistricting plan cannot be upheld unless it satisfies strict scrutiny, our most rigorous and exacting standard of constitutional review.

To satisfy strict scrutiny, the State must demonstrate that its districting legislation is narrowly tailored to achieve a compelling interest. *Shaw*. There is a "significant state interest in eradicating the effects of past racial discrimination." *Shaw*. The State does not argue, however, that it created the Eleventh District to remedy past discrimination, and with good reason: there is little doubt that the State's true interest in designing the Eleventh District was creating a third majority-black district to satisfy the Justice Department's preclearance demands. . . . Whether or not in some cases compliance with the Voting Rights Act, standing alone, can provide a compelling interest independent of any interest in remedying past discrimination, it cannot do so here. As we suggested in *Shaw*, compliance with federal antidiscrimination laws cannot justify race-based districting where the challenged district was not reasonably necessary under a constitutional reading and application of those laws. The congressional plan challenged here was not required by the Voting Rights Act under a correct reading of the statute. . . .

We do not accept the contention that the State has a compelling interest in complying with whatever preclearance mandates the Justice Department issues. When a state governmental entity seeks to justify race-based remedies to cure the effects of past discrimination, we do not accept the government's mere assertion that the remedial action is required. Rather, we insist on a strong basis in evidence of the harm being remedied. "The history of racial classifications in this country suggests that blind judicial deference to legislative or executive pronouncements of necessity has no place in equal protection analysis." *Croson*. Our presumptive skepticism of all racial classifications, prohibits us as well from accepting on its face the Justice Department's conclusion that racial districting is necessary under the Voting Rights Act. Where a State relies on the Department's determination that race-based districting is necessary to comply with the Voting Rights Act, the judiciary retains an independent obligation in adjudicating consequent equal protection challenges to ensure that the State's actions are narrowly tailored to achieve a compelling interest. See *Shaw*. Were we to accept the Justice Department's objection itself as a compelling interest adequate to insulate racial districting from constitutional review, we would be surrendering to the Executive Branch our role in enforcing the constitutional limits on race-based official action. We may not do so. . . .

The Voting Rights Act, and its grant of authority to the federal courts to uncover official efforts to abridge minorities' right to vote, has been of vital importance in eradicating invidious discrimination from the electoral process and enhancing the legitimacy of our political institutions. Only if our political system and our society cleanse themselves of that discrimination will all members of the polity share an equal opportunity to gain public office regardless of race. As a Nation we share both the obligation and the aspiration of working toward this end. The end is neither assured nor well served, however, by carving electorates into racial blocs. "If our society is to continue to progress as a multiracial democracy, it must recognize that the automatic invocation of race stereotypes retards that progress and causes continued hurt and injury." *Edmondson v. Leesville Concrete Co.* (1991). It takes a shortsighted and unauthorized view of the Voting Rights Act to invoke that statute, which has played a decisive role in redressing some of our worst forms of discrimination, to demand the very racial stereotyping the Fourteenth Amendment forbids.

The judgment of the District Court is affirmed, and the case is remanded for further proceedings consistent with this decision.

It is so ordered.

JUSTICE GINSBURG, with whom JUSTICES STEVENS, BREYER . . . and . . . SOUTER join, dissenting.

Legislative districting is highly political business. This Court has generally respected the competence of state legislatures to attend to the task. When race is the issue, however, we have recognized the need for judicial intervention to prevent dilution of minority voting strength. Generations of rank discrimination against African-Americans, as citizens and voters, account for that surveillance.

Two Terms ago, in *Shaw v. Reno* (1993), this Court took up a claim "analytically distinct" from a vote dilution claim. *Shaw* authorized judicial intervention in "extremely irregular" apportionments in which the legislature cast aside traditional districting practices to consider race alone—in the *Shaw* case, to create a district in North Carolina in which African-Americans would compose a majority of the voters.

Today the Court expands the judicial role, announcing that federal courts are to undertake searching review of any district with contours "predominantly motivated" by race: "strict scrutiny" will be triggered not only when traditional districting practices are abandoned, but also when those practices are "subordinated to"—given less weight than—race. Applying this new "race-as-predominant-factor" standard, the Court invalidates Georgia's districting plan even though Georgia's Eleventh District, the focus of today's dispute, bears the imprint of familiar districting practices. Because I do not endorse the Court's new standard and would not upset Georgia's plan, I dissent. . . .

Before *Shaw v. Reno* this Court invoked the Equal Protection Clause to justify intervention in the quintessentially political task of legislative districting in two circumstances: to enforce the one-person-one-vote requirement, see *Reynolds v. Sims* (1964); and to prevent dilution of a minority group's voting strength.

In *Shaw,* the Court recognized a third basis for an equal protection challenge to a State's apportionment plan. The Court wrote cautiously, emphasizing that judicial intervention is exceptional: "[S]trict [judicial] scrutiny" is in order, the Court declared, if a district is "so extremely irregular on its face that it rationally can be viewed only as an effort to segregate the races for purposes of voting." . . .

The problem in *Shaw* was not the plan architects' consideration of race as relevant in redistricting. Rather, in the Court's estimation, it was the virtual exclusion of other factors from the calculus. Traditional districting practices were cast aside, the Court concluded, with race alone steering placement of district lines.

The record before us does not show that race similarly overwhelmed traditional districting practices in Georgia. Although the Georgia General Assembly prominently considered race in shaping the Eleventh District, race did not crowd out all other factors, as the Court found it did in North Carolina's delineation of the *Shaw* district.

In contrast to the snake-like North Carolina district inspected in *Shaw*, Georgia's Eleventh District is hardly "bizarre," "extremely irregular," or "irrational on its face." Instead, the Eleventh District's design reflects significant consideration of "traditional districting factors (such as keeping political subdivisions intact) and the usual political process of compromise and trades for a variety of nonracial reasons." . . .

Nor does the Eleventh District disrespect the boundaries of political subdivisions. Of the 22 counties in the District, 14 are intact and 8 are divided. That puts the Eleventh District at about the state average in divided counties. . . .

Evidence at trial similarly shows that considerations other than race went into determining the Eleventh District's boundaries. For a "political reason"—to accommodate the request of an incumbent State Senator regarding the placement of the precinct in which his son lived—the DeKalb County portion of the Eleventh District was drawn to include a particular (largely white) precinct. The corridor through Effingham County was substantially narrowed at the request of a (white) State Representative. In Chatham County, the District was trimmed to exclude a heavily black community in Garden City because a State Representative wanted to keep the city intact inside the neighboring First District. The Savannah extension was configured by "the narrowest means possible" to avoid splitting the city of Port Wentworth.

Georgia's Eleventh District, in sum, is not an outlier district shaped without reference to familiar districting techniques. . . .

The Court suggests that it was not Georgia's legislature, but the U. S. Department of Justice, that effectively drew the lines, and that Department officers did so with nothing but race in mind. . . .

And although the Attorney General refused preclearance to the first two plans approved by Georgia's legislature, the State was not thereby disarmed; Georgia could have demanded relief from the Department's objections by instituting a civil action in the United States District Court for the District of Columbia, with ultimate review in this Court. Instead of pursuing that avenue, the State chose to adopt the plan here in controversy—a plan the State forcefully defends before us. We should respect Georgia's choice by taking its position on brief as genuine.

Along with attention to size, shape, and political subdivisions, the Court recognizes as an appropriate districting principle, "respect for . . . communities defined by actual shared interests." The Court finds no community here, however, because a report in the record showed "fractured political, social, and economic interests within the Eleventh District's black population."

But ethnicity itself can tie people together, as volumes of social science literature have documented—even people with divergent economic interests. For this reason, ethnicity is a significant force in political life. . . .

To accommodate the reality of ethnic bonds, legislatures have long drawn voting districts along ethnic lines. Our Nation's cities are full of districts identified by their ethnic character—Chinese, Irish, Italian, Jewish, Polish, Russian, for example. . . .

To separate permissible and impermissible use of race in legislative apportionment, the Court orders strict scrutiny for districting plans "predominantly motivated" by race. No longer can a State avoid judicial oversight by giving—as in this case—genuine and measurable consideration to traditional districting practices. Instead, a federal case can be mounted whenever plaintiffs plausibly allege that other factors carried less weight than race. This invitation to litigate against the State seems to me neither necessary nor proper.

The Court derives its test from diverse opinions on the relevance of race in contexts distinctly unlike apportionment. The controlling idea, the Court says, is " 'the simple command [at the heart of the Constitution's guarantee of equal protection] that the Government must treat citizens as individuals, not as simply components of a racial, religious, sexual or national class.' " . . .

In adopting districting plans, however, States do not treat people as individuals. Apportionment schemes, by their very nature, assemble people in groups. States do not assign voters to districts based on merit or achievement, standards States might use in hiring employees or engaging contractors. Rather, legislators classify voters in groups—by economic, geographical, political, or social characteristics—and then "reconcile the competing claims of [these] groups." *Davis v. Bandemer* (1986) (O'CONNOR, J., concurring in judgment).

That ethnicity defines some of these groups is a political reality. Until now, no constitutional infirmity has been seen in districting Irish or Italian voters together, for example, so long as the delineation does not abandon familiar apportionment practices. If Chinese-Americans and Russian-Americans may seek and secure group recognition in the delineation of voting districts, then African-Americans should not be dissimilarly treated. Otherwise, in the name of equal protection, we would shut out "the very minority group whose history in the United States gave birth to the Equal Protection Clause." See *Shaw* (STEVENS, J., dissenting). . . .

Only after litigation—under either the Voting Rights Act, the Court's new *Miller* standard, or both—will States now be assured that plans conscious of race are safe. Federal judges in large numbers may be drawn into the fray. This enlargement of the judicial role is unwarranted. The reapportionment plan that resulted from Georgia's political process merited this Court's approbation, not its condemnation. Accordingly, I dissent.

With *Miller v. Johnson* the Court continued on its path of applying strict scrutiny standards to legislative redistricting designed to create majority-minority districts. Once again the decision was the result of a 5 to 4 voting split. The more conservative justices, Kennedy, O'Connor, Rehnquist, Scalia, and Thomas, formed a solid bloc against districts with boundaries that are "unexplainable on grounds other than race" and where legislatures had "subordinated traditional race-neutral districting principles . . . to racial considerations." The same five-justice coalition constituted the majority in *Shaw v Reno* two years earlier. Liberal justices Breyer, Ginsburg, Souter, and Stevens expressed their solidarity with legislative and executive branch efforts to enhance the representation of historically disadvantaged minorities. As Box 20-1 shows, these efforts have met with a degree of success.

In spite of the consistency of direction in the Court's recent rulings, the law pertaining to majority-minority districts lacks clarity. How much attention can the legislature give to racial considerations without violating the Fourteenth Amendment? At what point do traditional race-neutral factors take a subordinate position to racial factors? Perhaps these questions will be answered as the

Court responds to the next round of challenges to state reapportionment efforts.

THE 2000 PRESIDENTIAL ELECTION

Political questions are generally considered outside the judiciary's sphere of authority. In the area of elections and voting rights, however, the political and the legal often overlap, making it difficult to mark the boundaries of judicial influence. The Court has never shied away from judging the constitutionality of laws or procedures that affect citizens' rights to express their preferences at the polls. But the Court generally has refrained from deciding cases that determine election outcomes, preferring to allow the political process to settle political questions. That, however, was not the case in 2000 when a dispute over vote count procedures in Florida led to the Supreme Court's decision in *Bush v. Gore*.

Bush v. Gore

531 U.S. 98 (2000)
http://laws.findlaw.com/US/531/98.html
Oral arguments may be found at: http://www.oyez.org
Vote: 5 (Kennedy, O'Connor, Rehnquist, Scalia, Thomas)
   4 (Breyer, Ginsburg, Souter, Stevens)
Opinion of the Court: Per curiam
Concurring opinion: Rehnquist
Dissenting opinions: Breyer, Ginsburg, Souter, Stevens

The presidential election of November 7, 2000, was one of the closest races in American history. On election night it became clear that the battle between Republican governor George W. Bush of Texas and Democratic vice president Al Gore for the 270 Electoral College votes necessary for victory would be decided by the outcome in the state of Florida.

First vote counts in Florida gave Governor Bush a lead of some 1,780 votes out of 6 million cast. This narrow margin triggered an automatic machine recount held on November 10. The results gave Bush a victory, but the margin had slipped to a scant 250 votes, with absentee overseas ballots still to be counted. By this time

---

BOX 20-1 AFTERMATH . . . *MILLER V. JOHNSON*

THE IMMEDIATE impact of *Miller v. Johnson,* which struck down Georgia's redistricting plan, was to send the map back to the state legislature for revision. Despite numerous attempts, the lawmakers were unable to develop an acceptable plan, and the task of redesigning the congressional districts fell to the federal district court. After considering several plans, the court approved a scheme that included only one majority black district. This judicially imposed redistricting plan was challenged by civil rights advocates. The Supreme Court upheld the plan in *Abrams v. Johnson* (1997), with the justices divided into the same 5–4 voting blocs that occurred in *Shaw v. Reno* and *Miller v. Johnson.*

Despite this legal setback, Georgia's black representatives held their positions in Congress. Rep. Cynthia McKinney, whose district was the primary target of the *Miller v. Johnson* litigation, found herself representing a district that was 58.4 percent white. She captured 58 percent of the vote in 1996 and 61 percent in 1998. Rep. Sanford Bishop's Second District became 59.5 percent white under the revised apportionment plan; he was reelected with 54 percent of the vote in 1996 and 57 percent in 1998. John Lewis, the lone representative of a majority black district, ran unopposed in 1996 and received 79 percent of the vote in 1998. Following the 2000 census, Georgia received an additional congressional seat, prompting the legislature to redraw the state's congressional districts. The new apportionment plan included two majority black districts. In the 2002 elections four of Georgia's thirteen congressional districts sent black representatives to Congress. In *Georgia v. Ashcroft* (2003) the justices rejected a Voting Rights Act claim that the new plan excessively retrograded black voting strength.

Data for the entire House of Representatives show that the number of African American and Hispanic representatives has doubled since 1985.

Year	Hispanic Representatives	Black Representatives
1985	11	20
1987	11	22
1989	10	23
1991	11	26
1993	17	39
1995	17	39
1997	17	37
1999	19	37
2001	19	37
2003	22	37
2005	22	40
2007	22	42

SOURCES: Norman J. Ornstein, Thomas E. Mann, and Michael J. Malbin, *Vital Statistics on Congress, 1999–2000* (Washington, D.C.: The AEI Press, 2000); Michael Barone and Grant Ujifusa, with Richard E. Cohen and Charles E. Cook Jr., *The Almanac of American Politics 2000* (Washington, D.C.: National Journal, 1999); Associated Press, January 7, 2003; and http://www.ethnicmajority.com/congress.htm.

---

charges and countercharges of voting irregularities led to lawsuits and political protests. As the various issues sorted themselves out over the ensuing days, the outcome of the election appeared to hinge on one major issue: the large numbers of undercounted ballots in a select number of traditionally Democratic counties. Undercounted ballots were those for which vote-counting machines did not register a presidential preference. In many cases such undercounting resulted from the voter's failure to perforate the computer punch card ballot. In other cases, machine malfunction may have been the cause. Gore supporters demanded a hand recount of the undercounted ballots.

Three statutory deadlines imposed obstacles for the labor-intensive and time-consuming manual recounts. First, Florida law directed the secretary of state to certify the election results by November 18. Second, federal law provided that if all controversies and contests over a state's presidential electors were resolved by December 12, the state's slate would be considered conclusive and beyond challenge (the so-called safe harbor provision). And third, federal law set December 18 as the date the electors would cast their ballots.

As the manual recounts proceeded, it became clear that the process would not be completed prior to the November 18 deadline for certification. Florida's Republican secretary of state, Katherine Harris, announced her intention to certify the vote on November 18, regardless of the ongoing recounts. Gore forces went to court to block Harris from doing so. A unanimous Florida Supreme Court, emphasizing that every cast vote should be counted, ruled that the recounts should continue and extended the certification date to November 26. Believing the Florida court had exceeded its authority, Bush's lawyers appealed this decision to the U.S. Supreme Court. On December 4 the justices set aside the Florida court's certification extension and asked the court to explain the reasoning behind its decision (*Bush v. Palm Beach Canvassing Board*, 2000). In the meantime, on November 26 Secretary Harris certified that Bush had won the state by 537 votes.

Four days after the U.S. Supreme Court's decision, the Florida high court, in response to an appeal by Vice President Gore, ordered a new statewide manual recount of all undervotes to begin immediately. The recounts were to be conducted by local officials guided only by the instruction to determine voter intent on each ballot. Governor Bush appealed this decision to the U.S. Supreme Court. On December 9 the justices scheduled the case for oral argument and ordered the recounts to stop pending a final decision.

Two major issues dominated the case. First, did the Florida Supreme Court violate federal law by altering the election procedures in place prior to the election? Second, did it violate the equal protection clause of the Fourteenth Amendment when it ordered a recount to take place without setting a single uniform standard for determining voter intent?

A badly divided Supreme Court issued its ruling on December 12. The majority opinion focuses on the equal protection claim. The concurring and dissenting opinions include a wide range of views on the issues presented and debate what remedies should be imposed for any constitutional or statutory violations found.

PER CURIAM.

The closeness of this election, and the multitude of legal challenges which have followed in its wake, have brought into sharp focus a common, if heretofore unnoticed, phenomenon. Nationwide statistics reveal that an estimated 2%

Theresa LePore, Palm Beach County election supervisor, examines a ballot during the manual recount following the disputed 2000 presidential election in Florida.

of ballots cast do not register a vote for President for whatever reason, including deliberately choosing no candidate at all or some voter error, such as voting for two candidates or insufficiently marking a ballot. In certifying election results, the votes eligible for inclusion in the certification are the votes meeting the properly established legal requirements.

This case has shown that punch card balloting machines can produce an unfortunate number of ballots which are not punched in a clean, complete way by the voter. After the current counting, it is likely legislative bodies nationwide will examine ways to improve the mechanisms and machinery for voting.

The individual citizen has no federal constitutional right to vote for electors for the President of the United States unless and until the state legislature chooses a statewide election as the means to implement its power to appoint members of the Electoral College. U.S. Const., Art. II, §1. This is the source for the statement in *McPherson v. Blacker* (1892) that the State legislature's power to select the manner for appointing electors is plenary; it may, if it so chooses, select the electors itself, which indeed was the manner used by State legislatures in several States for many years after the Framing of our Constitution. History has now favored the voter, and in each of the several States the citizens themselves vote for Presidential electors. When the state legislature vests the right to vote for President in its people, the right to vote as the legislature has prescribed is fundamental; and one source of its fundamental nature lies in the equal weight accorded to each vote and the equal dignity owed to each voter. The State, of course, after granting the franchise in the special context of Article II, can take back the power to appoint electors.

The right to vote is protected in more than the initial allocation of the franchise. Equal protection applies as well to the manner of its exercise. Having once granted the right to vote on equal terms, the State may not, by later arbitrary and disparate treatment, value one person's vote over that of another. . . .

There is no difference between the two sides of the present controversy on these basic propositions. Respondents say that the very purpose of vindicating the right to vote justifies the recount procedures now at issue. The question before us, however, is whether the recount procedures the Florida Supreme Court has adopted are consistent with its obligation to avoid arbitrary and disparate treatment of the members of its electorate.

Much of the controversy seems to revolve around ballot cards designed to be perforated by a stylus but which, either through error or deliberate omission, have not been perforated with sufficient precision for a machine to count them. In some cases a piece of the card—a chad—is hanging, say by two corners. In other cases there is no separation at all, just an indentation.

The Florida Supreme Court has ordered that the intent of the voter be discerned from such ballots. For purposes of resolving the equal protection challenge, it is not necessary to decide whether the Florida Supreme Court had the authority under the legislative scheme for resolving election disputes to define what a legal vote is and to mandate a manual recount implementing that definition. The recount mechanisms implemented in response to the decisions of the Florida Supreme Court do not satisfy the minimum requirement for non-arbitrary treatment of voters necessary to secure the fundamental right. Florida's basic command for the count of legally cast votes is to consider the "intent of the voter." This is unobjectionable as an abstract proposition and a starting principle. The problem inheres in the absence of specific standards to ensure its equal application. The formulation of uniform rules to determine intent based on these recurring circumstances is practicable and, we conclude, necessary.

The law does not refrain from searching for the intent of the actor in a multitude of circumstances; and in some cases the general command to ascertain intent is not susceptible to much further refinement. In this instance, however, the question is . . . how to interpret the marks or holes or scratches on an inanimate object, a piece of cardboard or paper which, it is said, might not have registered as a vote during the machine count. The factfinder confronts a thing, not a person. The search for intent can be confined by specific rules designed to ensure uniform treatment.

The want of those rules here has led to unequal evaluation of ballots in various respects. As seems to have been acknowledged at oral argument, the standards for accepting or rejecting contested ballots might vary not only from county to county but indeed within a single county from one recount team to another.

The record provides some examples. A monitor in Miami-Dade County testified at trial that he observed that three members of the county canvassing board applied different standards in defining a legal vote. And testimony at trial also revealed that at least one county changed its evaluative standards during the counting process. Palm Beach County, for example, began the process with a 1990 guideline which precluded counting completely attached chads, switched to a rule that considered a vote to be legal if any light could be seen through a chad, changed back to the 1990 rule, and then abandoned any pretense of a *per se* rule, only to have a court order that the county consider dimpled chads legal. This is not a process with sufficient guarantees of equal treatment. . . .

The State Supreme Court ratified this uneven treatment. It mandated that the recount totals from two counties, Miami-Dade and Palm Beach, be included in the certified total. The court also appeared to hold *sub silentio* that the recount totals from Broward County, which were not completed until after the original November 14 certification by the Secretary of State, were to be considered part of the new certified vote totals even though the county certification was not contested by Vice President Gore. Yet each of the counties used varying standards to determine what was a legal vote. Broward County used a more forgiving standard than Palm Beach County, and uncovered almost three times as many new votes, a result markedly disproportionate to the difference in population between the counties.

In addition, the recounts in these three counties were not limited to so-called undervotes but extended to all of the ballots. The distinction has real consequences. A manual recount of all ballots identifies not only those ballots which show no vote but also those which contain more than one, the so-called overvotes. Neither category will be counted by the machine. This is not a trivial concern. At oral argument, respondents estimated there are as many as 110,000 overvotes statewide. As a result, the citizen whose ballot was not read by a machine because he failed to vote for a candidate in a way readable by a machine may still have his vote counted in a manual recount; on the other hand, the citizen who marks two candidates in a way discernable by the machine will not have the same opportunity to have his vote count, even if a manual examination of the ballot would reveal the requisite indicia of intent. Furthermore, the citizen who marks two candidates, only one of which is discernable by the machine, will have his vote counted even though it should have been read as an invalid ballot. The State Supreme Court's inclusion of vote counts based on these variant standards exemplifies concerns with the remedial processes that were under way.

That brings the analysis to yet a further equal protection problem. The votes certified by the court included a partial total from one county, Miami-Dade. The Florida Supreme Court's decision thus gives no assurance that the recounts included in a final certification must be complete. Indeed, it is respondent's submission that it would be consistent with the rules of the recount procedures to include whatever partial counts are done by the time of final certification, and we interpret the Florida Supreme Court's decision to permit this. This accommodation no doubt results from the truncated contest period established by the Florida Supreme Court in *Bush I*, at respondents' own urging. The press of

time does not diminish the constitutional concern. A desire for speed is not a general excuse for ignoring equal protection guarantees.

In addition to these difficulties the actual process by which the votes were to be counted under the Florida Supreme Court's decision raises further concerns. That order did not specify who would recount the ballots. The county canvassing boards were forced to pull together ad hoc teams comprised of judges from various Circuits who had no previous training in handling and interpreting ballots. Furthermore, while others were permitted to observe, they were prohibited from objecting during the recount.

The recount process, in its features here described, is inconsistent with the minimum procedures necessary to protect the fundamental right of each voter in the special instance of a statewide recount under the authority of a single state judicial officer. Our consideration is limited to the present circumstances, for the problem of equal protection in election processes generally presents many complexities.

The question before the Court is not whether local entities, in the exercise of their expertise, may develop different systems for implementing elections. Instead, we are presented with a situation where a state court with the power to assure uniformity has ordered a statewide recount with minimal procedural safeguards. When a court orders a statewide remedy, there must be at least some assurance that the rudimentary requirements of equal treatment and fundamental fairness are satisfied.

Given the Court's assessment that the recount process underway was probably being conducted in an unconstitutional manner, the Court stayed the order directing the recount so it could hear this case and render an expedited decision. The contest provision, as it was mandated by the State Supreme Court, is not well calculated to sustain the confidence that all citizens must have in the outcome of elections. The State has not shown that its procedures include the necessary safeguards. The problem, for instance, of the estimated 110,000 overvotes has not been addressed. . . .

Upon due consideration of the difficulties identified to this point, it is obvious that the recount cannot be conducted in compliance with the requirements of equal protection and due process without substantial additional work. It would require not only the adoption (after opportunity for argument) of adequate statewide standards for determining what is a legal vote, and practicable procedures to implement them, but also orderly judicial review of any disputed matters that might arise. In addition, the Secretary of State has advised that the recount of only a portion of the ballots requires that the vote tabulation equipment be used to screen out undervotes, a function for which the machines were not designed. If a recount of overvotes were also required, perhaps even a second screening would be necessary. Use of the equipment for this purpose, and any new software developed for it, would have to be evaluated for accuracy by the Secretary of State, as required by [Florida law].

The Supreme Court of Florida has said that the legislature intended the State's electors to "participat[e] fully in the federal electoral process," as provided in 3 U.S.C. §5. That statute, in turn, requires that any controversy or contest that is designed to lead to a conclusive selection of electors be completed by December 12. That date is upon us, and there is no recount procedure in place under the State Supreme Court's order that comports with minimal constitutional standards. Because it is evident that any recount seeking to meet the December 12 date will be unconstitutional for the reasons we have discussed, we reverse the judgment of the Supreme Court of Florida ordering a recount to proceed.

Seven Justices of the Court agree that there are constitutional problems with the recount ordered by the Florida Supreme Court that demand a remedy. The only disagreement is as to the remedy. Because the Florida Supreme Court has said that the Florida Legislature intended to obtain the safe-harbor benefits of 3 U.S.C. §5, JUSTICE BREYER'S proposed remedy—remanding to the Florida Supreme Court for its ordering of a constitutionally proper contest until December 18—contemplates action in violation of the Florida election code, and hence could not be part of an "appropriate" order authorized by [Florida law].

None are more conscious of the vital limits on judicial authority than are the members of this Court, and none stand more in admiration of the Constitution's design to leave the selection of the President to the people, through their legislatures, and to the political sphere. When contending parties invoke the process of the courts, however, it becomes our unsought responsibility to resolve the federal and constitutional issues the judicial system has been forced to confront.

The judgment of the Supreme Court of Florida is reversed, and the case is remanded for further proceedings not inconsistent with this opinion. . . .

CHIEF JUSTICE REHNQUIST, with whom JUSTICE SCALIA and JUSTICE THOMAS join, concurring.

We join the *per curiam* opinion. . . .

We deal here not with an ordinary election, but with an election for the President of the United States. . . .

In most cases, comity and respect for federalism compel us to defer to the decisions of state courts on issues of state law. . . . But there are a few exceptional cases in which the Constitution imposes a duty or confers a power on a particular branch of a State's government. This is one of them. Article II, §1, cl. 2, provides that "[e]ach State shall appoint, in such Manner as the *Legislature* thereof may direct," electors for President and Vice President. (Emphasis added.) Thus, the text of the election law itself, and not just its interpretation by the courts of the States, takes on independent significance.

In *McPherson v. Blacker* (1892), we explained that Art. II, §1, cl. 2, "convey[s] the broadest power of determination" and "leaves it to the legislature exclusively to define the method" of appointment. A significant departure from the legislative scheme for appointing Presidential electors presents a federal constitutional question. . . .

In Florida, the legislature has chosen to hold statewide elections to appoint the State's 25 electors. Importantly, the legislature has delegated the authority to run the elections and to oversee election disputes to the Secretary of State (Secretary) and to state circuit courts. Isolated sections of the code may well admit of more than one interpretation, but the general coherence of the legislative scheme may not be altered by judicial interpretation so as to wholly change the statutorily provided apportionment of responsibility among these various bodies. In any election but a Presidential election, the Florida Supreme Court can give as little or as much deference to Florida's executives as it chooses, so far as Article II is concerned, and this Court will have no cause to question the court's actions. But, with respect to a Presidential election, the court must be both mindful of the legislature's role under Article II in choosing the manner of appointing electors and deferential to those bodies expressly empowered by the legislature to carry out its constitutional mandate. . . .

This inquiry does not imply a disrespect for state *courts* but rather a respect for the constitutionally prescribed role of state *legislatures.* To attach definitive weight to the pronouncement of a state court, when the very question at issue is whether the court has actually departed from the statutory meaning, would be to abdicate our responsibility to enforce the explicit requirements of Article II.

JUSTICE STEVENS, with whom JUSTICE GINSBURG and JUSTICE BREYER join, dissenting.

Even assuming that aspects of the remedial scheme might ultimately be found to violate the Equal Protection Clause, I could not subscribe to the majority's disposition of the case. As the majority explicitly holds, once a state legislature determines to select electors through a popular vote, the right to have one's vote counted is of constitutional stature. As the majority further acknowledges, Florida law holds that all ballots that reveal the intent of the voter constitute valid votes. Recognizing these principles, the majority nonetheless orders the termination of the contest proceeding before all such votes have been tabulated. Under their own reasoning, the appropriate course of action would be to remand to allow more specific procedures for implementing the legislature's uniform general standard to be established.

In the interest of finality, however, the majority effectively orders the disenfranchisement of an unknown number of voters whose ballots reveal their intent—and are therefore legal votes under state law—but were for some reason rejected by ballot-counting machines. It does so on the basis of the deadlines set forth in Title 3 of the United States Code. But . . . those provisions merely provide rules of decision for Congress to follow when selecting among conflicting slates of electors. They do not prohibit a State from counting what the majority concedes to be legal votes until a bona fide winner is determined. . . . Thus, nothing prevents the majority, even if it properly found an equal protection violation, from ordering relief appropriate to remedy that violation without depriving Florida voters of their right to have their votes counted. As the majority notes, "[a] desire for speed is not a general excuse for ignoring equal protection guarantees." . . .

What must underlie petitioners' entire federal assault on the Florida election procedures is an unstated lack of confidence in the impartiality and capacity of the state judges who would make the critical decisions if the vote count were to proceed. Otherwise, their position is wholly without merit. The endorsement of that position by the majority of this Court can only lend credence to the most cynical appraisal of the work of judges throughout the land. It is confidence in the men and women who administer the judicial system that is the true backbone of the rule of law. Time will one day heal the wound to that confidence that will be inflicted by today's decision. One thing, however, is certain. Although we may never know with complete certainty the identity of the winner of this year's Presidential election, the identity of the loser is perfectly clear. It is the Nation's confidence in the judge as an impartial guardian of the rule of law.

I respectfully dissent.

JUSTICE SOUTER, with whom JUSTICE BREYER joins and with whom JUSTICE STEVENS and JUSTICE GINSBURG join with regard to all but [the paragraphs dealing with the equal protection issue], dissenting.

The Court should not have reviewed either *Bush v. Palm Beach County Canvassing Bd.* or this case, and should not have stopped Florida's attempt to recount all undervote ballots by issuing a stay of the Florida Supreme Court's orders during the period of this review. If this Court had allowed the State to follow the course indicated by the opinions of its own Supreme Court, it is entirely possible that there would ultimately have been no issue requiring our review, and political tension could have worked itself out in the Congress. . . . The case being before us, however, its resolution by the majority is another erroneous decision. . . .

[Only the issue of whether the manner of interpreting markings on disputed ballots violates equal protection presents] a meritorious argument for relief, as this Court's *Per Curiam* opinion recognizes. It is an issue that might well have been dealt with adequately by the Florida courts if the state proceedings had not been interrupted, and if not disposed of at the state level it could have been considered by the Congress in any electoral vote dispute. But because the course of state proceedings has been interrupted, time is short, and the issue is before us, I think it sensible for the Court to address it.

Petitioners have raised an equal protection claim, in the charge that unjustifiably disparate standards are applied in different electoral jurisdictions to otherwise identical facts. It is true that the Equal Protection Clause does not forbid the use of a variety of voting mechanisms within a jurisdiction, even though different mechanisms will have different levels of effectiveness in recording voters' intentions; local variety can be justified by concerns about cost, the potential value of innovation, and so on. But evidence in the record here suggests that a different order of disparity obtains under rules for determining a voter's intent that have been applied (and could continue to be applied) to identical types of ballots used in identical brands of machines and exhibiting identical physical characteristics (such as "hanging" or "dimpled" chads). I can conceive of no legitimate state interest served by these differing treatments of the expressions of voters' fundamental rights. The differences appear wholly arbitrary.

In deciding what to do about this, we should take account of the fact that electoral votes are due to be cast in six days. I would therefore remand the case to the courts of Florida with instructions to establish uniform standards for evaluating the several types of ballots that have prompted differing treatments, to be applied within and among counties when passing on such identical ballots in any further recounting (or successive recounting) that the courts might order.

Unlike the majority, I see no warrant for this Court to assume that Florida could not possibly comply with this requirement before the date set for the meeting of electors, December 18. . . . To recount these [disputed votes] manually would be a tall order, but before this Court stayed the effort to do that the courts of Florida were ready to do their best to get that job done. There is no justification for denying the State the opportunity to try to count all disputed ballots now.

I respectfully dissent.

JUSTICE GINSBURG, with whom JUSTICE STEVENS joins, and with whom JUSTICE SOUTER and JUSTICE BREYER join [except as to the portion of the opinion dealing with the equal protection claim], dissenting.

The extraordinary setting of this case has obscured the ordinary principle that dictates its proper resolution: Federal courts defer to state high courts' interpretations of their state's own law. This principle reflects the core of federalism, on which all agree. "The Framers split the atom of sovereignty. It was the genius of their idea that our citizens would have two political capacities, one state and one federal, each protected from incursion by the other." . . . Were the other members of this Court as mindful as they generally are of our system of dual sovereignty, they would affirm the judgment of the Florida Supreme Court.

I agree with JUSTICE STEVENS that petitioners have not presented a substantial equal protection claim. Ideally, perfection would be the appropriate standard for judging the recount. But we live in an imperfect world, one in which thousands of votes have not been counted. I cannot agree that the recount adopted by the Florida court, flawed as it may be, would yield a result any less fair or precise than the certification that preceded that recount.

Even if there were an equal protection violation, I would agree with JUSTICE STEVENS, JUSTICE SOUTER, and JUSTICE BREYER that the Court's concern about "the December 12 deadline," is misplaced. . . .

The Court assumes that time will not permit "orderly judicial review of any disputed matters that might arise." But no one has doubted the good faith and diligence with which Florida election officials, attorneys for all sides of this controversy, and the courts of law have performed their duties. Notably, the Florida Supreme Court has produced two substantial opinions within 29 hours of oral argument. In sum, the Court's conclusion that a constitutionally adequate recount is impractical is a prophecy the Court's own judgment will not allow to be tested. Such an untested prophecy should not decide the Presidency of the United States.

I dissent.

JUSTICE BREYER, with whom JUSTICE STEVENS and JUSTICE GINSBURG join except as [to paragraph 3 below], and with whom JUSTICE SOUTER joins . . . , dissenting.

The Court was wrong to take this case. It was wrong to grant a stay. It should now vacate that stay and permit the Florida Supreme Court to decide whether the recount should resume.

BOX 20-2   AFTERMATH . . . . *BUSH V. GORE*

Bush v. Gore (2000) effectively ended the 2000 presidential election controversy. On December 13, 2000, the day after the justices ruled, Vice President Al Gore announced that he was ending his campaign: "I accept the finality of this outcome. . . . And tonight, for the sake of our unity as a people and the strength of our democracy, I offer my concession."

Florida's twenty-five electoral votes gave Goerge W. Bush a total of 271, just one more than needed to become the forty-third president of the United States. He became only the fourth president in U.S. history to win the Electoral College while losing the popular vote to his chief opponent. Vice President Gore captured 48.39 percent of the popular vote to Governor Bush's 47.88 percent. Before Bush only John Quincy Adams in 1824, Rutherford B. Hayes in 1876, and Benjamin Harrison in 1888 had been elected president without leading in the popular vote count.

Because of the voting controversies in Florida, many states revised election laws and upgraded vote-counting equipment to avoid similar problems in future elections. The two Florida officials at the center of the controversy, Gov. Jeb Bush and Secretary of State Katherine Harris, continued their political careers. Jeb Bush was reelected governor of Florida in 2002 and Harris won a congressional seat that same year. Theodore Olson, the lawyer who successfully argued George Bush's case before the Supreme Court, was appointed solicitor general of the United States by the new president.

George Bush was reelected to the presidency in 2004. Gore seriously considered a rematch against him, but in late 2002 he announced that he would not be a candidate. Gore instead focused his activities on environmental policy. *An Inconvenient Truth*, a film on global warming that Gore wrote and narrated, won a 2006 Academy Award for Best Documentary. In 2007 he received the Nobel Peace Prize for his efforts to combat global climate change.

Public opinion polls taken after the Court's ruling showed that a large majority of Americans accepted Bush as the legitimate president; and, contrary to many predictions, the polls failed to find any appreciable decline in public support for the Supreme Court due to its incursion into the 2000 presidential election.

The political implications of this case for the country are momentous. But the federal legal questions presented, with one exception, are insubstantial. . . .

. . . The majority concludes that the Equal Protection Clause requires that a manual recount be governed not only by the uniform general standard of the "clear intent of the voter," but also by uniform subsidiary standards (for example, a uniform determination whether indented, but not perforated, "undervotes" should count). The opinion points out that the Florida Supreme Court ordered the inclusion of Broward County's undercounted "legal votes" even though those votes included ballots that were not perforated but simply "dimpled," while newly recounted ballots from other counties will likely include only votes determined to be "legal" on the basis of a stricter standard. In light of our previous remand, the Florida Supreme Court may have been reluctant to adopt a more specific standard than that provided for by the legislature for fear of exceeding its authority under Article II. However, since the use of different stan-

dards could favor one or the other of the candidates, since time was, and is, too short to permit the lower courts to iron out significant differences through ordinary judicial review, and since the relevant distinction was embodied in the order of the State's highest court, I agree that, in these very special circumstances, basic principles of fairness may well have counseled the adoption of a uniform standard to address the problem. In light of the majority's disposition, I need not decide whether, or the extent to which, as a remedial matter, the Constitution would place limits upon the content of the uniform standard.

Nonetheless, there is no justification for the majority's remedy, which is simply to reverse the lower court and halt the recount entirely. An appropriate remedy would be, instead, to remand this case with instructions that, even at this late date, would permit the Florida Supreme Court to require recounting *all* undercounted votes in Florida, including those from Broward, Volusia, Palm Beach, and Miami-Dade Counties, whether or not previously recounted prior to the end of the protest period, and to do so in accordance with a single-uniform substandard. . . .

I respectfully dissent.

The Court's decision in *Bush v. Gore* became the final chapter in the presidential election controversy of 2000 *(see Box 20-2)*. Although the extraordinary circumstances that gave birth to the case may limit the decision's applicability as a precedent, there is no doubt that it had important historical consequences. By stopping the Florida recount, the Court removed Vice President Gore's last hope of capturing the state's twenty-five electoral votes and guaranteed that Governor Bush would become the next president. Much of the nation was happy to see the election finally resolved, but the Court's action caused intense debate in political and academic circles. Not only was there a question of whether the Supreme Court should have heard the case in the first place, but also many believed that the justices' votes were excessively influenced by their own political preferences. The five-justice majority ruling in favor of Bush (Rehnquist, Kennedy, O'Connor, Scalia, and Thomas) was composed only of Republicans, and the Court's sole Democrats (Ginsburg and Breyer) favored Gore's position.

READINGS

Clayton, Dewey M. *African Americans and the Politics of Congressional Redistricting.* New York: Garland, 2000.

Cortner, Richard C. *The Apportionment Cases.* Knoxville: University of Tennessee Press, 1970.

Davidson, Chandler, and Bernard Grofman, eds. *Quiet Revolution in the South: The Impact of the Voting Rights Act, 1965–1990.* Princeton: Princeton University Press, 1994.

Dershowitz, Alan M. *Supreme Injustice: How the High Court Hijacked Election 2000.* New York: Oxford University Press, 2001.

Gillman, Howard. *The Votes that Counted: How the Court Decided the 2000 Presidential Election.* Chicago: University of Chicago Press, 2001.

Greene, Abner. *Understanding the 2000 Election: A Guide to the Legal Battles that Decided the Presidency.* New York: New York University Press, 2001.

Grofman, Bernard. *Political Gerrymandering and the Courts.* New York: Agathon Press, 1990.

Hasen, Richard L. *The Supreme Court and Election Law: Judging Equality from Baker v. Carr to Bush v. Gore.* New York: New York University Press, 2003.

Hudson, David Michael. *Along Racial Lines: Consequences of the 1965 Voting Rights Act.* New York: Peter Lang, 1998.

Keyssar, Alexander. *The Right to Vote: The Contested History of Democracy in the United States.* New York: Basic Books, 2000.

Maveety, Nancy. *Representation Rights and the Burger Court Years.* Ann Arbor: University of Michigan Press, 1991.

McCool, Daniel, Susan M. Olson, and Jennifer L. Robinson. *Native Vote: American Indians, the Voting Rights Act, and the Right to Vote.* New York: Cambridge University Press, 2007.

Norell, Robert J. *Reaping the Whirlwind: The Civil Rights Movement in Tuskegee.* Chapel Hill: University of North Carolina Press, 1998.

Pinaire, Brian K. *The Constitution of Electoral Speech Law.* Stanford: Stanford University Press, 2008.

Posner, Richard A. *Breaking the Deadlock: The 2000 Election, the Constitution, and the Courts.* Princeton: Princeton University Press, 2001.

Ryden, David K., ed. *The U.S. Supreme Court and the Electoral Process.* Washington, D.C.: Georgetown University Press, 2000.

Scher, Richard K., Jon L. Mills, and John J. Hotaling. *Voting Rights and Democracy: The Law and Politics of Districting.* Chicago: Nelson-Hall Publishers, 1997.

Stephenson, Donald Greer, Jr. *The Right to Vote: Rights and Liberties under the Law.* Santa Barbara, Calif.: ABC-CLIO, 2004.

Sunstein, Cass R., and Richard A. Epstein, eds. *The Vote: Bush, Gore, and the Supreme Court.* Chicago: University of Chicago Press, 2001.

Taper, Bernard. *Gomillion v. Lightfoot: Apartheid in Alabama.* New York: McGraw-Hill, 1967.

Thernston, Abigail. *Whose Votes Count?* Cambridge: Harvard University Press, 1987.

Thompson, Dianne T. *Congressional Districting in North Carolina: Reconsidering Traditional Criteria.* New York: FB Scholarly Publishing, 2002.

Valelly, Richard M. *Two Reconstructions: The Struggle for Black Enfranchisement.* Chicago: University of Chicago Press, 2004.

Yarbrough, Tinsley E. *Race and Redistricting: The Shaw-Cromartie Cases.* Lawrence: University Press of Kansas, 2002.

Zelden, Charles L. *The Battle for the Black Ballot: Smith v. Allwright and the Defeat of the Texas All-White Primary.* Lawrence: University Press of Kansas, 204.

REFERENCE MATERIAL

CONSTITUTION OF THE UNITED STATES

We the People of the United States, in Order to form a more perfect Union, establish Justice, insure domestic Tranquility, provide for the common defence, promote the general Welfare, and secure the Blessings of Liberty to ourselves and our Posterity, do ordain and establish this Constitution for the United States of America.

ARTICLE I

Section 1. All legislative Powers herein granted shall be vested in a Congress of the United States, which shall consist of a Senate and House of Representatives.

Section 2. The House of Representatives shall be composed of Members chosen every second Year by the People of the several States, and the Electors in each State shall have the Qualifications requisite for Electors of the most numerous Branch of the State Legislature.

No Person shall be a Representative who shall not have attained to the age of twenty five Years, and been seven Years a Citizen of the United States, and who shall not, when elected, be an Inhabitant of that State in which he shall be chosen.

[Representatives and direct Taxes shall be apportioned among the several States which may be included within this Union, according to their respective Numbers, which shall be determined by adding to the whole Number of free Persons, including those bound to Service for a Term of Years, and excluding Indians not taxed, three fifths of all other Persons.][1] The actual Enumeration shall be made within three Years after the first Meeting of the Congress of the United States, and within every subsequent Term of ten Years, in such Manner as they shall by Law direct. The Number of Representatives shall not exceed one for every thirty Thousand, but each State shall have at Least one Representative; and until such enumeration shall be made, the State of New Hampshire shall be entitled to chuse three, Massachusetts eight,

Rhode-Island and Providence Plantations one, Connecticut five, New-York six, New Jersey four, Pennsylvania eight, Delaware one, Maryland six, Virginia ten, North Carolina five, South Carolina five, and Georgia three.

When vacancies happen in the Representation from any State, the Executive Authority thereof shall issue Writs of Election to fill such Vacancies.

The House of Representatives shall chuse their Speaker and other Officers; and shall have the sole Power of Impeachment.

Section 3. The Senate of the United States shall be composed of two Senators from each State, [chosen by the Legislature thereof,][2] for six Years; and each Senator shall have one Vote.

Immediately after they shall be assembled in Consequence of the first Election, they shall be divided as equally as may be into three Classes. The Seats of the Senators of the first Class shall be vacated at the Expiration of the second Year, of the second Class at the Expiration of the fourth Year, and of the third Class at the Expiration of the sixth Year, so that one third may be chosen every second Year; [and if Vacancies happen by Resignation, or otherwise, during the Recess of the Legislature of any State, the Executive thereof may make temporary Appointments until the next Meeting of the Legislature, which shall then fill such Vacancies.][3]

No Person shall be a Senator who shall not have attained to the Age of thirty Years, and been nine Years a Citizen of the United States, and who shall not, when elected, be an Inhabitant of that State for which he shall be chosen.

The Vice President of the United States shall be President of the Senate, but shall have no Vote, unless they be equally divided.

The Senate shall chuse their other Officers, and also a President pro tempore, in the Absence of the Vice President, or when he shall exercise the Office of President of the United States.

1. The part in brackets was changed by section 2 of the Fourteenth Amendment.

2. The part in brackets was changed by the first paragraph of the Seventeenth Amendment.
3. The part in brackets was changed by the second paragraph of the Seventeenth Amendment.

The Senate shall have the sole Power to try all Impeachments. When sitting for that Purpose, they shall be on Oath or Affirmation. When the President of the United States is tried, the Chief Justice shall preside: And no Person shall be convicted without the Concurrence of two thirds of the Members present.

Judgment in Cases of Impeachment shall not extend further than to removal from Office, and disqualification to hold and enjoy any Office of honor, Trust or Profit under the United States: but the Party convicted shall nevertheless be liable and subject to Indictment, Trial, Judgment and Punishment, according to Law.

Section 4. The Times, Places and Manner of holding Elections for Senators and Representatives, shall be prescribed in each State by the Legislature thereof; but the Congress may at any time by Law make or alter such Regulations, except as to the Places of chusing Senators.

The Congress shall assemble at least once in every Year, and such Meeting shall [be on the first Monday in December],[4] unless they shall by Law appoint a different Day.

Section 5. Each House shall be the Judge of the Elections, Returns and Qualifications of its own Members, and a Majority of each shall constitute a Quorum to do Business; but a smaller Number may adjourn from day to day, and may be authorized to compel the Attendance of absent Members, in such Manner, and under such Penalties as each House may provide.

Each House may determine the Rules of its Proceedings, punish its Members for disorderly Behaviour, and, with the Concurrence of two thirds, expel a Member.

Each House shall keep a Journal of its Proceedings, and from time to time publish the same, excepting such Parts as may in their Judgment require Secrecy; and the Yeas and Nays of the Members of either House on any question shall, at the Desire of one fifth of those Present, be entered on the Journal.

Neither House, during the Session of Congress, shall, without the Consent of the other, adjourn for more than three days, nor to any other Place than that in which the two Houses shall be sitting.

Section 6. The Senators and Representatives shall receive a Compensation for their Services, to be ascertained by Law, and paid out of the Treasury of the United States. They shall in all Cases, except Treason, Felony and Breach of the Peace, be privileged from Arrest during their Attendance at the Session of their respective Houses, and in going to and returning from the same; and for any Speech or Debate in either House, they shall not be questioned in any other Place.

No Senator or Representative shall, during the Time for which he was elected, be appointed to any civil Office under the Authority of the United States, which shall have been created, or the Emoluments whereof shall have been encreased during such time;

4. The part in brackets was changed by section 2 of the Twentieth Amendment.

and no Person holding any Office under the United States, shall be a Member of either House during his Continuance in Office.

Section 7. All Bills for raising Revenue shall originate in the House of Representatives; but the Senate may propose or concur with Amendments as on other Bills.

Every Bill which shall have passed the House of Representatives and the Senate, shall, before it become a Law, be presented to the President of the United States; If he approve he shall sign it, but if not he shall return it, with his Objections to that House in which it shall have originated, who shall enter the Objections at large on their Journal, and proceed to reconsider it. If after such Reconsideration two thirds of that House shall agree to pass the Bill, it shall be sent, together with the Objections, to the other House, by which it shall likewise be reconsidered, and if approved by two thirds of that House, it shall become a Law. But in all such Cases the Votes of both Houses shall be determined by yeas and Nays, and the Names of the Persons voting for and against the Bill shall be entered on the Journal of each House respectively. If any Bill shall not be returned by the President within ten Days (Sundays excepted) after it shall have been presented to him, the Same shall be a Law, in like Manner as if he had signed it, unless the Congress by their Adjournment prevent its Return, in which Case it shall not be a Law.

Every Order, Resolution, or Vote to which the Concurrence of the Senate and House of Representatives may be necessary (except on a question of Adjournment) shall be presented to the President of the United States; and before the Same shall take Effect, shall be approved by him, or being disapproved by him, shall be repassed by two thirds of the Senate and House of Representatives, according to the Rules and Limitations prescribed in the Case of a Bill.

Section 8. The Congress shall have Power To lay and collect Taxes, Duties, Imposts and Excises, to pay the Debts and provide for the common Defence and general Welfare of the United States; but all Duties, Imposts and Excises shall be uniform throughout the United States;

To borrow Money on the credit of the United States;

To regulate Commerce with foreign Nations, and among the several States, and with the Indian Tribes;

To establish an uniform Rule of Naturalization, and uniform Laws on the subject of Bankruptcies throughout the United States;

To coin Money, regulate the Value thereof, and of foreign Coin, and fix the Standard of Weights and Measures;

To provide for the Punishment of counterfeiting the Securities and current Coin of the United States;

To establish Post Offices and post Roads;

To promote the Progress of Science and useful Arts, by securing for limited Times to Authors and Inventors the exclusive Right to their respective Writings and Discoveries;

To constitute Tribunals inferior to the supreme Court;

To define and punish Piracies and Felonies committed on the high Seas, and Offences against the Law of Nations;

To declare War, grant Letters of Marque and Reprisal, and make Rules concerning Captures on Land and Water;

To raise and support Armies, but no Appropriation of Money to that Use shall be for a longer Term than two Years;

To provide and maintain a Navy;

To make Rules for the Government and Regulation of the land and naval Forces;

To provide for calling forth the Militia to execute the Laws of the Union, suppress Insurrections and repel Invasions;

To provide for organizing, arming, and disciplining, the Militia, and for governing such Part of them as may be employed in the Service of the United States, reserving to the States respectively, the Appointment of the Officers, and the Authority of training the Militia according to the discipline prescribed by Congress;

To exercise exclusive Legislation in all Cases whatsoever, over such District (not exceeding ten Miles square) as may, by Cession of particular States, and the Acceptance of Congress, become the Seat of the Government of the United States, and to exercise like Authority over all Places purchased by the Consent of the Legislature of the State in which the Same shall be, for the Erection of Forts, Magazines, Arsenals, dock-Yards, and other needful Buildings;—And

To make all Laws which shall be necessary and proper for carrying into Execution the foregoing Powers, and all other Powers vested by this Constitution in the Government of the United States, or in any Department or Officer thereof.

Section 9. The Migration or Importation of such Persons as any of the States now existing shall think proper to admit, shall not be prohibited by the Congress prior to the Year one thousand eight hundred and eight, but a Tax or duty may be imposed on such Importation, not exceeding ten dollars for each Person.

The Privilege of the Writ of Habeas Corpus shall not be suspended, unless when in Cases of Rebellion or Invasion the public Safety may require it.

No Bill of Attainder or ex post facto Law shall be passed.

No Capitation, or other direct, Tax shall be laid, unless in Proportion to the Census or Enumeration herein before directed to be taken.[5]

No Tax or Duty shall be laid on Articles exported from any State.

No Preference shall be given by any Regulation of Commerce or Revenue to the Ports of one State over those of another; nor shall Vessels bound to, or from, one State, be obliged to enter, clear, or pay Duties in another.

No Money shall be drawn from the Treasury, but in Consequence of Appropriations made by Law; and a regular Statement

5. The Sixteenth Amendment gave Congress the power to tax incomes.

and Account of the Receipts and Expenditures of all public Money shall be published from time to time.

No Title of Nobility shall be granted by the United States: And no Person holding any Office of Profit or Trust under them, shall, without the Consent of the Congress, accept of any present, Emolument, Office, or Title, of any kind whatever, from any King, Prince, or foreign State.

Section 10. No State shall enter into any Treaty, Alliance, or Confederation; grant Letters of Marque and Reprisal; coin Money; emit Bills of Credit; make any Thing but gold and silver Coin a Tender in Payment of Debts; pass any Bill of Attainder, ex post facto Law, or Law impairing the Obligation of Contracts, or grant any Title of Nobility.

No State shall, without the Consent of the Congress, lay any Imposts or Duties on Imports or Exports, except what may be absolutely necessary for executing it's inspection Laws: and the net Produce of all Duties and Imposts, laid by any State on Imports or Exports, shall be for the Use of the Treasury of the United States; and all such Laws shall be subject to the Revision and Controul of the Congress.

No State shall, without the Consent of Congress, lay any Duty of Tonnage, keep Troops, or Ships of War in time of Peace, enter into any Agreement or Compact with another State, or with a foreign Power, or engage in War, unless actually invaded, or in such imminent Danger as will not admit of delay.

ARTICLE II

Section 1. The executive Power shall be vested in a President of the United States of America. He shall hold his Office during the Term of four Years, and, together with the Vice President, chosen for the same Term, be elected, as follows

Each State shall appoint, in such Manner as the Legislature thereof may direct, a Number of Electors, equal to the whole Number of Senators and Representatives to which the State may be entitled in the Congress: but no Senator or Representative, or Person holding an Office of Trust or Profit under the United States, shall be appointed an Elector.

[The Electors shall meet in their respective States, and vote by Ballot for two Persons, of whom one at least shall not be an Inhabitant of the same State with themselves. And they shall make a List of all the Persons voted for, and of the Number of Votes for each; which List they shall sign and certify, and transmit sealed to the Seat of the Government of the United States, directed to the President of the Senate. The President of the Senate shall, in the Presence of the Senate and House of Representatives, open all the Certificates, and the Votes shall then be counted. The Person having the greatest Number of Votes shall be the President, if such Number be a Majority of the whole Number of Electors appointed; and if there be more than one who have such Majority, and have an equal Number of Votes, then the House of Representatives shall immediately chuse by Ballot one of them for President; and if no Person have a Majority, then from the five highest on the list the said House shall in like Manner chuse the President. But in chusing the President, the Votes shall be taken by States, the Representation from each State having one Vote; A quorum for this Purpose shall consist of a Member or Members from two thirds of the States, and a Majority of all the States shall be necessary to a Choice. In every Case, after the Choice of the President, the Person having the greatest Number of Votes of the Electors shall be the Vice President. But if there should remain two or more who have equal Votes, the Senate shall chuse from them by Ballot the Vice President.] [6]

The Congress may determine the Time of chusing the Electors, and the Day on which they shall give their Votes; which Day shall be the same throughout the United States.

No Person except a natural born Citizen, or a Citizen of the United States, at the time of the Adoption of this Constitution, shall be eligible to the Office of President; neither shall any Person be eligible to that Office who shall not have attained to the Age of thirty five Years, and been fourteen Years a Resident within the United States.

In Case of the Removal of the President from Office, or of his Death, Resignation, or Inability to discharge the Powers and Duties of the said Office,[7] the Same shall devolve on the Vice President, and the Congress may by Law provide for the Case of Removal, Death, Resignation or Inability, both of the President and Vice President, declaring what Officer shall then act as President, and such Officer shall act accordingly, until the Disability be removed, or a President shall be elected.

The President shall, at stated Times, receive for his Services, a Compensation, which shall neither be encreased nor diminished during the Period for which he shall have been elected, and he shall not receive within that Period any other Emolument from the United States, or any of them.

Before he enter on the Execution of his Office, he shall take the following Oath or Affirmation:—"I do solemnly swear (or affirm) that I will faithfully execute the Office of President of the United States, and will to the best of my Ability, preserve, protect and defend the Constitution of the United States."

Section 2. The President shall be Commander in Chief of the Army and Navy of the United States, and of the Militia of the several States, when called into the actual Service of the United States; he may require the Opinion, in writing, of the principal Officer in each of the executive Departments, upon any Subject relating to the Duties of their respective Offices, and he shall have Power to grant Reprieves and Pardons for Offences against the United States, except in Cases of Impeachment.

He shall have Power, by and with the Advice and Consent of the Senate, to make Treaties, provided two thirds of the Senators present concur; and he shall nominate, and by and with the Advice and Consent of the Senate, shall appoint Ambassadors, other public Ministers and Consuls, Judges of the supreme Court, and all other Officers of the United States, whose Appointments are not herein otherwise provided for, and which shall be established by Law: but the Congress may by Law vest the Appointment of such inferior Officers, as they think proper, in the President alone, in the Courts of Law, or in the Heads of Departments.

The President shall have Power to fill up all Vacancies that may happen during the Recess of the Senate, by granting Commissions which shall expire at the End of their next Session.

Section 3. He shall from time to time give to the Congress Information of the State of the Union, and recommend to their Consideration such Measures as he shall judge necessary and expedient; he may, on extraordinary Occasions, convene both Houses, or either of them, and in Case of Disagreement between them, with Respect to the Time of Adjournment, he may adjourn them to such Time as he shall think proper; he shall receive Ambassadors and other public Ministers; he shall take Care that the Laws be faithfully executed, and shall Commission all the Officers of the United States.

Section 4. The President, Vice President and all civil Officers of the United States, shall be removed from Office on Impeachment for, and Conviction of, Treason, Bribery, or other high Crimes and Misdemeanors.

ARTICLE III

Section 1. The judicial Power of the United States, shall be vested in one supreme Court, and in such inferior Courts as the Congress may from time to time ordain and establish. The Judges, both of the supreme and inferior Courts, shall hold their Offices during good Behaviour, and shall, at stated Times, receive for their Services, a Compensation, which shall not be diminished during their Continuance in Office.

Section 2. The judicial Power shall extend to all Cases, in Law and Equity, arising under this Constitution, the Laws of the United States, and Treaties made, or which shall be made, under their Authority;—to all Cases affecting Ambassadors, other public Ministers and Consuls;—to all Cases of admiralty and maritime Jurisdiction;—to Controversies to which the United States shall be a Party;—to Controversies between two or more States;—between a State and Citizens of another State;[8]—between Citizens of different States;—between Citizens of the same State claiming Lands under Grants of different States, and between a State, or the Citizens thereof, and foreign States, Citizens or Subjects.[8]

In all Cases affecting Ambassadors, other public Ministers and

---

6. The material in brackets has been superseded by the Twelfth Amendment.

7. This provision has been affected by the Twenty-fifth Amendment.

8. These clauses were affected by the Eleventh Amendment.

Consuls, and those in which a State shall be Party, the supreme Court shall have original Jurisdiction. In all the other Cases before mentioned, the supreme Court shall have appellate Jurisdiction, both as to Law and Fact, with such Exceptions, and under such Regulations as the Congress shall make.

The Trial of all Crimes, except in Cases of Impeachment, shall be by Jury; and such Trial shall be held in the State where the said Crimes shall have been committed; but when not committed within any State, the Trial shall be at such Place or Places as the Congress may by Law have directed.

Section 3. Treason against the United States, shall consist only in levying War against them, or in adhering to their Enemies, giving them Aid and Comfort. No Person shall be convicted of Treason unless on the Testimony of two Witnesses to the same overt Act, or on Confession in open Court.

The Congress shall have Power to declare the Punishment of Treason, but no Attainder of Treason shall work Corruption of Blood, or Forfeiture except during the Life of the Person attainted.

ARTICLE IV

Section 1. Full Faith and Credit shall be given in each State to the public Acts, Records, and judicial Proceedings of every other State. And the Congress may by general Laws prescribe the Manner in which such Acts, Records and Proceedings shall be proved, and the Effect thereof.

Section 2. The Citizens of each State shall be entitled to all Privileges and Immunities of Citizens in the several States.

A Person charged in any State with Treason, Felony, or other Crime, who shall flee from Justice, and be found in another State, shall on Demand of the executive Authority of the State from which he fled, be delivered up, to be removed to the State having Jurisdiction of the Crime.

[No Person held to Service or Labour in one State, under the Laws thereof, escaping into another, shall, in Consequence of any Law or Regulation therein, be discharged from such Service or Labour, but shall be delivered up on Claim of the Party to whom such Service or Labour may be due.][9]

Section 3. New States may be admitted by the Congress into this Union; but no new State shall be formed or erected within the Jurisdiction of any other State; nor any State be formed by the Junction of two or more States, or Parts of States, without the Consent of the Legislatures of the States concerned as well as of the Congress.

The Congress shall have Power to dispose of and make all needful Rules and Regulations respecting the Territory or other Property belonging to the United States; and nothing in this Constitution shall be so construed as to Prejudice any Claims of the United States, or of any particular State.

Section 4. The United States shall guarantee to every State in this Union a Republican Form of Government, and shall protect each of them against Invasion; and on Application of the Legislature, or of the Executive (when the Legislature cannot be convened) against domestic Violence.

ARTICLE V

The Congress, whenever two thirds of both Houses shall deem it necessary, shall propose Amendments to this Constitution, or, on the Application of the Legislatures of two thirds of the several States, shall call a Convention for proposing Amendments, which, in either Case, shall be valid to all Intents and Purposes, as Part of this Constitution, when ratified by the Legislatures of three fourths of the several States, or by Conventions in three fourths thereof, as the one or the other Mode of Ratification may be proposed by the Congress; Provided [that no Amendment which may be made prior to the Year One thousand eight hundred and eight shall in any Manner affect the first and fourth Clauses in the Ninth Section of the first Article; and][10] that no State, without its Consent, shall be deprived of its equal Suffrage in the Senate.

ARTICLE VI

All Debts contracted and Engagements entered into, before the Adoption of this Constitution, shall be as valid against the United States under this Constitution, as under the Confederation.

This Constitution, and the Laws of the United States which shall be made in Pursuance thereof; and all Treaties made, or which shall be made, under the Authority of the United States, shall be the supreme Law of the Land; and the Judges in every State shall be bound thereby, any Thing in the Constitution or Laws of any State to the Contrary notwithstanding.

The Senators and Representatives before mentioned, and the Members of the several State Legislatures, and all executive and judicial Officers, both of the United States and of the several States, shall be bound by Oath or Affirmation, to support this Constitution; but no religious Test shall ever be required as a Qualification to any Office or public Trust under the United States.

ARTICLE VII

The Ratification of the Conventions of nine States, shall be sufficient for the Establishment of this Constitution between the States so ratifying the Same. Done in Convention by the Unanimous Consent of the States present the Seventeenth Day of September in the Year of our Lord one thousand seven hundred and Eighty seven and of the Independence of the United States of America the Twelfth. IN WITNESS whereof We have hereunto subscribed our Names,

George Washington,
President and deputy from Virginia.

9. This paragraph has been superseded by the Thirteenth Amendment.

10. Obsolete.

New Hampshire:	John Langdon,
	Nicholas Gilman.
Massachusetts:	Nathaniel Gorham,
	Rufus King.
Connecticut:	William Samuel Johnson,
	Roger Sherman.
New York:	Alexander Hamilton.
New Jersey:	William Livingston,
	David Brearley,
	William Paterson,
	Jonathan Dayton.
Pennsylvania:	Benjamin Franklin,
	Thomas Mifflin,
	Robert Morris,
	George Clymer,
	Thomas FitzSimons,
	Jared Ingersoll,
	James Wilson,
	Gouverneur Morris.
Delaware:	George Read,
	Gunning Bedford Jr.,
	John Dickinson,
	Richard Bassett,
	Jacob Broom.
Maryland:	James McHenry,
	Daniel of St. Thomas Jenifer,
	Daniel Carroll.
Virginia:	John Blair,
	James Madison Jr.
North Carolina:	William Blount,
	Richard Dobbs Spaight,
	Hugh Williamson.
South Carolina:	John Rutledge,
	Charles Cotesworth Pinckney,
	Charles Pinckney,
	Pierce Butler.
Georgia:	William Few,
	Abraham Baldwin.

[The language of the original Constitution, not including the Amendments, was adopted by a convention of the states on September 17, 1787, and was subsequently ratified by the states on the following dates: Delaware, December 7, 1787; Pennsylvania, December 12, 1787; New Jersey, December 18, 1787; Georgia, January 2, 1788; Connecticut, January 9, 1788; Massachusetts, February 6, 1788; Maryland, April 28, 1788; South Carolina, May 23, 1788; New Hampshire, June 21, 1788.

Ratification was completed on June 21, 1788.

The Constitution subsequently was ratified by Virginia, June 25, 1788; New York, July 26, 1788; North Carolina, November 21, 1789; Rhode Island, May 29, 1790; and Vermont, January 10, 1791.]

AMENDMENTS

Amendment I

(First ten amendments ratified December 15, 1791.)

Congress shall make no law respecting an establishment of religion, or prohibiting the free exercise thereof; or abridging the freedom of speech, or of the press; or the right of the people peaceably to assemble, and to petition the Government for a redress of grievances.

Amendment II

A well regulated Militia, being necessary to the security of a free State, the right of the people to keep and bear Arms, shall not be infringed.

Amendment III

No Soldier shall, in time of peace be quartered in any house, without the consent of the Owner, nor in time of war, but in a manner to be prescribed by law.

Amendment IV

The right of the people to be secure in their persons, houses, papers, and effects, against unreasonable searches and seizures, shall not be violated, and no Warrants shall issue, but upon probable cause, supported by Oath or affirmation, and particularly describing the place to be searched, and the persons or things to be seized.

Amendment V

No person shall be held to answer for a capital, or otherwise infamous crime, unless on a presentment or indictment of a Grand Jury, except in cases arising in the land or naval forces, or in the Militia, when in actual service in time of War or public danger; nor shall any person be subject for the same offence to be twice put in jeopardy of life or limb; nor shall be compelled in any criminal case to be a witness against himself, nor be deprived of life, liberty, or property, without due process of law; nor shall private property be taken for public use, without just compensation.

Amendment VI

In all criminal prosecutions, the accused shall enjoy the right to a speedy and public trial, by an impartial jury of the State and district wherein the crime shall have been committed, which district shall have been previously ascertained by law, and to be informed of the nature and cause of the accusation; to be confronted with the witnesses against him; to have compulsory process for obtaining witnesses in his favor, and to have the Assistance of Counsel for his defence.

Amendment VII

In Suits at common law, where the value in controversy shall exceed twenty dollars, the right of trial by jury shall be preserved, and no fact tried by a jury, shall be otherwise re-examined in any Court of the United States, than according to the rules of the common law.

Amendment VIII

Excessive bail shall not be required, nor excessive fines imposed, nor cruel and unusual punishments inflicted.

Amendment IX

The enumeration in the Constitution, of certain rights, shall not be construed to deny or disparage others retained by the people.

Amendment X

The powers not delegated to the United States by the Constitution, nor prohibited by it to the States, are reserved to the States respectively, or to the people.

Amendment XI

(Ratified February 7, 1795)

The Judicial power of the United States shall not be construed to extend to any suit in law or equity, commenced or prosecuted against one of the United States by Citizens of another State, or by Citizens or Subjects of any Foreign State.

Amendment XII

(Ratified June 15, 1804)

The Electors shall meet in their respective states and vote by ballot for President and Vice-President, one of whom, at least, shall not be an inhabitant of the same state with themselves; they shall name in their ballots the person voted for as President, and in distinct ballots the person voted for as Vice-President, and they shall make distinct lists of all persons voted for as President, and of all persons voted for as Vice-President, and of the number of votes for each, which lists they shall sign and certify, and transmit sealed to the seat of the government of the United States, directed to the President of the Senate;—The President of the Senate shall, in the presence of the Senate and House of Representatives, open all the certificates and the votes shall then be counted;—The person having the greatest number of votes for President, shall be the President, if such number be a majority of the whole number of Electors appointed; and if no person have such majority, then from the persons having the highest numbers not exceeding three on the list of those voted for as President, the House of Representatives shall choose immediately, by ballot, the President. But in choosing the President, the votes shall be taken by states, the representation from each state having one vote; a quorum for this purpose shall consist of a member or members from two-thirds of the states, and a majority of all the states shall be necessary to a choice. [And if the House of Representatives shall not choose a President whenever the right of choice shall devolve upon them, before the fourth day of March next following, then the Vice-President shall act as President, as in the case of the death or other constitutional disability of the President.][11] The person having the

11. The part in brackets has been superseded by section 3 of the Twentieth Amendment.

greatest number of votes as Vice-President, shall be the Vice-President, if such number be a majority of the whole number of Electors appointed, and if no person have a majority, then from the two highest numbers on the list, the Senate shall choose the Vice-President; a quorum for the purpose shall consist of two-thirds of the whole number of Senators, and a majority of the whole number shall be necessary to a choice. But no person constitutionally ineligible to the office of President shall be eligible to that of Vice-President of the United States.

Amendment XIII

(Ratified December 6, 1865)

Section 1. Neither slavery nor involuntary servitude, except as a punishment for crime whereof the party shall have been duly convicted, shall exist within the United States, or any place subject to their jurisdiction.

Section 2. Congress shall have power to enforce this article by appropriate legislation.

Amendment XIV

(Ratified July 9, 1868)

Section 1. All persons born or naturalized in the United States, and subject to the jurisdiction thereof, are citizens of the United States and of the State wherein they reside. No State shall make or enforce any law which shall abridge the privileges or immunities of citizens of the United States; nor shall any State deprive any person of life, liberty, or property, without due process of law; nor deny to any person within its jurisdiction the equal protection of the laws.

Section 2. Representatives shall be apportioned among the several States according to their respective numbers, counting the whole number of persons in each State, excluding Indians not taxed. But when the right to vote at any election for the choice of electors for President and Vice President of the United States, Representatives in Congress, the Executive and Judicial officers of a State, or the members of the Legislature thereof, is denied to any of the male inhabitants of such State, being twenty-one years of age,[12] and citizens of the United States, or in any way abridged, except for participation in rebellion, or other crime, the basis of representation therein shall be reduced in the proportion which the number of such male citizens shall bear to the whole number of male citizens twenty-one years of age in such State.

Section 3. No person shall be a Senator or Representative in Congress, or elector of President and Vice President, or hold any office, civil or military, under the United States, or under any State, who, having previously taken an oath, as a member of Congress, or as an officer of the United States, or as a member of any State legislature, or as an executive or judicial officer of any State, to support the Constitution of the United States, shall have engaged in insurrection or rebellion against the same, or given aid

12. See the Nineteenth and Twenty-sixth Amendments.

or comfort to the enemies thereof. But Congress may by a vote of two-thirds of each House, remove such disability.

Section 4. The validity of the public debt of the United States, authorized by law, including debts incurred for payment of pensions and bounties for services in suppressing insurrection or rebellion, shall not be questioned. But neither the United States nor any State shall assume or pay any debt or obligation incurred in aid of insurrection or rebellion against the United States, or any claim for the loss or emancipation of any slave; but all such debts, obligations and claims shall be held illegal and void.

Section 5. The Congress shall have power to enforce, by appropriate legislation, the provisions of this article.

Amendment XV

(Ratified February 3, 1870)

Section 1. The right of citizens of the United States to vote shall not be denied or abridged by the United States or by any State on account of race, color, or previous condition of servitude.

Section 2. The Congress shall have power to enforce this article by appropriate legislation.

Amendment XVI

(Ratified February 3, 1913)

The Congress shall have power to lay and collect taxes on incomes, from whatever source derived, without apportionment among the several States, and without regard to any census or enumeration.

Amendment XVII

(Ratified April 8, 1913)

The Senate of the United States shall be composed of two Senators from each State, elected by the people thereof, for six years; and each Senator shall have one vote. The electors in each State shall have the qualifications requisite for electors of the most numerous branch of the State legislatures.

When vacancies happen in the representation of any State in the Senate, the executive authority of such State shall issue writs of election to fill such vacancies: *Provided,* That the legislature of any State may empower the executive thereof to make temporary appointments until the people fill the vacancies by election as the legislature may direct.

This amendment shall not be so construed as to affect the election or term of any Senator chosen before it becomes valid as part of the Constitution.

Amendment XVIII

(Ratified January 16, 1919)

Section 1. After one year from the ratification of this article the manufacture, sale, or transportation of intoxicating liquors within, the importation thereof into, or the exportation thereof from the United States and all territory subject to the jurisdiction thereof for beverage purposes is hereby prohibited.

Section 2. The Congress and the several States shall have concurrent power to enforce this article by appropriate legislation.

Section 3. This article shall be inoperative unless it shall have been ratified as an amendment to the Constitution by the legislatures of the several States, as provided in the Constitution, within seven years from the date of the submission hereof to the States by the Congress.][13]

Amendment XIX

(Ratified August 18, 1920)

The right of citizens of the United States to vote shall not be denied or abridged by the United States or by any State on account of sex.

Congress shall have power to enforce this article by appropriate legislation.

Amendment XX

(Ratified January 23, 1933)

Section 1. The terms of the President and Vice President shall end at noon on the 20th day of January, and the terms of Senators and Representatives at noon on the 3d day of January, of the years in which such terms would have ended if this article had not been ratified; and the terms of their successors shall then begin.

Section 2. The Congress shall assemble at least once in every year, and such meeting shall begin at noon on the 3d day of January, unless they shall by law appoint a different day.

Section 3.[14] If, at the time fixed for the beginning of the term of the President, the President elect shall have died, the Vice President elect shall become President. If a President shall not have been chosen before the time fixed for the beginning of his term, or if the President elect shall have failed to qualify, then the Vice President elect shall act as President until a President shall have qualified; and the Congress may by law provide for the case wherein neither a President elect nor a Vice President elect shall have qualified, declaring who shall then act as President, or the manner in which one who is to act shall be selected, and such person shall act accordingly until a President or Vice President shall have qualified.

Section 4. The Congress may by law provide for the case of the death of any of the persons from whom the House of Representatives may choose a President whenever the right of choice shall have devolved upon them, and for the case of the death of any of the persons from whom the Senate may choose a Vice President whenever the right of choice shall have devolved upon them.

Section 5. Sections 1 and 2 shall take effect on the 15th day of October following the ratification of this article.

Section 6. This article shall be inoperative unless it shall have been ratified as an amendment to the Constitution by the legisla-

13. This Amendment was repealed by section 1 of the Twenty-first Amendment.

14. See the Twenty-fifth Amendment.

tures of three-fourths of the several States within seven years from the date of its submission.

Amendment XXI

(Ratified December 5, 1933)

Section 1. The eighteenth article of amendment to the Constitution of the United States is hereby repealed.

Section 2. The transportation or importation into any State, Territory, or possession of the United States for delivery or use therein of intoxicating liquors, in violation of the laws thereof, is hereby prohibited.

Section 3. This article shall be inoperative unless it shall have been ratified as an amendment to the Constitution by conventions in the several States, as provided in the Constitution, within seven years from the date of the submission hereof to the States by the Congress.

Amendment XXII

(Ratified February 27, 1951)

Section 1. No person shall be elected to the office of the President more than twice, and no person who has held the office of President, or acted as President, for more than two years of a term to which some other person was elected President shall be elected to the office of the President more than once. But this Article shall not apply to any person holding the office of President when this Article was proposed by the Congress, and shall not prevent any person who may be holding the office of President, or acting as President, during the term within which this Article become operative from holding the office of President or acting as President during the remainder of such term.

Section 2. This article shall be inoperative unless it shall have been ratified as an amendment to the Constitution by the legislatures of three-fourths of the several States within seven years from the date of its submission to the States by the Congress.

Amendment XXIII

(Ratified March 29, 1961)

Section 1. The District constituting the seat of Government of the United States shall appoint in such manner as the Congress may direct:

A number of electors of President and Vice President equal to the whole number of Senators and Representatives in Congress to which the District would be entitled if it were a State, but in no event more than the least populous State; they shall be in addition to those appointed by the States, but they shall be considered, for the purposes of the election of President and Vice President, to be electors appointed by a State; and they shall meet in the District and perform such duties as provided by the twelfth article of amendment.

Section 2. The Congress shall have power to enforce this article by appropriate legislation.

Amendment XXIV

(Ratified January 23, 1964)

Section 1. The right of citizens of the United States to vote in any primary or other election for President or Vice President, for electors for President or Vice President, or for Senator or Representative in Congress, shall not be denied or abridged by the United States or any State by reason of failure to pay any poll tax or other tax.

Section 2. The Congress shall have power to enforce this article by appropriate legislation.

Amendment XXV

(Ratified February 10, 1967)

Section 1. In case of the removal of the President from office or of his death or resignation, the Vice President shall become President.

Section 2. Whenever there is a vacancy in the office of the Vice President, the President shall nominate a Vice President who shall take office upon confirmation by a majority vote of both Houses of Congress.

Section 3. Whenever the President transmits to the President pro tempore of the Senate and the Speaker of the House of Representatives his written declaration that he is unable to discharge the powers and duties of his office, and until he transmits to them a written declaration to the contrary, such powers and duties shall be discharged by the Vice President as Acting President.

Section 4. Whenever the Vice President and a majority of either the principal officers of the executive departments or of such other body as Congress may by law provide, transmit to the President pro tempore of the Senate and the Speaker of the House of Representatives their written declaration that the President is unable to discharge the powers and duties of his office, the Vice President shall immediately assume the powers and duties of the office as Acting President.

Thereafter, when the President transmits to the President pro tempore of the Senate and the Speaker of the House of Representatives his written declaration that no inability exists, he shall resume the powers and duties of his office unless the Vice President and a majority of either the principal officers of the executive department or of such other body as Congress may by law provide, transmit within four days to the President pro tempore of the Senate and the Speaker of the House of Representatives their written declaration that the President is unable to discharge the powers and duties of his office. Thereupon Congress shall decide the issue, assembling within forty-eight hours for that purpose if not in session. If the Congress, within twenty-one days after receipt of the latter written declaration, or, if Congress is not in session, within twenty-one days after Congress is required to assemble, determines by two-thirds vote of both Houses that the President is unable to discharge the powers and duties of his office, the Vice

President shall continue to discharge the same as Acting President; otherwise, the President shall resume the powers and duties of his office.

Amendment XXVI

(Ratified July 1, 1971)

Section 1. The right of citizens of the United States, who are eighteen years of age or older, to vote shall not be denied or abridged by the United States or by any State on account of age.

Section 2. The Congress shall have power to enforce this article by appropriate legislation.

Amendment XXVII

(Ratified May 7, 1992)

No law varying the compensation for the services of the Senators and Representatives shall take effect, until an election of Representatives shall have intervened.

SOURCE: *United States Government Manual, 1993–94* (Washington, D.C.: Government Printing Office, 1993), 5–20.

APPENDIX 2
FEDERALIST PAPER, NO. 78

A VIEW OF THE CONSTITUTION OF THE JUDICIAL DEPARTMENT IN RELATION TO THE TENURE OF GOOD BEHAVIOUR

We proceed now to an examination of the judiciary department of the proposed government.

In unfolding the defects of the existing Confederation, the utility and necessity of a federal judicature have been clearly pointed out. It is the less necessary to recapitulate the considerations there urged as the propriety of the institution in the abstract is not disputed; the only questions which have been raised being relative to the manner of constituting it, and to its extent. To these points, therefore, our observations shall be confined.

The manner of constituting it seems to embrace these several objects: 1st. The mode of appointing the judges. 2nd. The tenure by which they are to hold their places. 3rd. The partition of the judiciary authority between different courts and their relations to each other.

First. As to the mode of appointing the judges: this is the same with that of appointing the officers of the Union in general and has been so fully discussed in the two last numbers that nothing can be said here which would not be useless repetition.

Second. As to the tenure by which the judges are to hold their places: this chiefly concerns their duration in office, the provisions for their support, the precautions for their responsibility.

According to the plan of the convention, all judges who may be appointed by the United States are to hold their offices *during good behavior;* which is conformable to the most approved of the State constitutions, and among the rest, to that of the State. Its propriety having been drawn into question by the adversaries of that plan is no light symptom of the rage for objection which disorders their imaginations and judgments. The standard of good behavior for the continuance in office of the judicial magistracy is certainly one of the most valuable of the modern improvements in the practice of government. In a monarchy it is an excellent barrier to the despotism of the prince; in a republic it is a no less excellent barrier to the encroachments and oppressions of the representative body. And it is the best expedient which can be devised in any government to secure a steady, upright, and impartial administration of the laws.

Whoever attentively considers the different departments of power must perceive that, in a government in which they are separated from each other, the judiciary, from the nature of its functions, will always be the least dangerous to the political rights of the Constitution; because it will be least in a capacity to annoy or injure them. The executive not only dispenses the honors but holds the sword of the community. The legislature not only commands the purse but prescribes the rules by which the duties and rights of every citizen are to be regulated. The judiciary, on the contrary, has no influence over either the sword or the purse; no direction either of the strength or of the wealth of the society, and can take no active resolution whatever. It may truly be said to have neither FORCE nor WILL but merely judgment; and must ultimately depend upon the aid of the executive arm even for the efficacy of its judgments.

This simple view of the matter suggests several important consequences. It proves incontestably that the judiciary is beyond comparison the weakest of the three departments of power; that it can never attack with success either of the other two; and that all possible care is requisite to enable it to defend itself against their attacks. It equally proves that though individual oppression may now and then proceed from the courts of justice, the general liberty of the people can never be endangered from that quarter; I mean so long as the judiciary remains truly distinct from both the legislature and the executive. For I agree that "there is no liberty if the power of judging be not separated from the legislative and executive powers." And it proves, in the last place, that as liberty can have nothing to fear from the judiciary alone, but would have everything to fear from its union with either of the other departments; that as all the effects of such a union must ensue from a dependence of the former on the latter, notwithstanding a nominal and apparent separation; that as, from the natural feebleness of the judiciary, it is in continual jeopardy of being overpowered, awed, or influenced by its co-ordinate branches; and that as nothing can contribute so much to its firmness and independence as permanency in office, this quality may therefore be justly regarded as an indispensable ingredient in its constitution, and, in a great measure, as the citadel of the public justice and the public security.

The complete independence of the courts of justice is peculiarly essential in a limited Constitution. By a limited Constitution, I understand one which contains certain specified exceptions to the legislative authority; such, for instance, as that it shall pass no bills of attainder, no *ex post facto* laws, and the like. Limitations of this kind can be preserved in practice no other way than through the medium of courts of justice, whose duty it must be to declare all acts contrary to the manifest tenor of the Constitution void. Without this, all the reservations of particular rights or privileges would amount to nothing.

Some perplexity respecting the rights of the courts to pronounce legislative acts void, because contrary to the Constitution, has arisen from an imagination that the doctrine would imply a superiority of the judiciary to the legislative power. It is urged that the authority which can declare the acts of another void must necessarily be superior to the one whose acts may be declared void. As this doctrine is of great importance in all the American constitutions, a brief discussion of the grounds on which it rests cannot be unacceptable.

There is no position which depends on clearer principles than that every act of a delegated authority, contrary to the tenor of the commission under which it is exercised, is void. No legislative act, therefore, contrary to the Constitution, can be valid. To deny this would be to affirm that the deputy is greater than his principal; that the servant is above his master; that the representatives of the people are superior to the people themselves; that men acting by virtue of powers may do not only what their powers do not authorize, but what they forbid.

If it be said that the legislative body are themselves the constitutional judges of their own powers and that the construction they put upon them is conclusive upon the other departments it may be answered that this cannot be the natural presumption where it is not to be collected from any particular provisions in the Constitution. It is not otherwise to be supposed that the Constitution could intend to enable the representatives of the people to substitute their *will* to that of their constituents. It is far more rational to suppose that the courts were designed to be an intermediate body between the people and the legislature in order, among other things, to keep the latter within the limits assigned to their authority. The interpretation of the laws is the proper and peculiar province of the courts. A constitution is, in fact, and must be regarded by the judges as, a fundamental law. It therefore belongs to them to ascertain its meaning as well as the meaning of any particular act proceeding from the legislative body. If there should happen to be an irreconcilable variance between the two, that which has the superior obligation and validity ought, of course, to be preferred: or, in other words, the Constitution ought to be preferred to the statute, the intention of the people to the intention of their agents.

Nor does this conclusion by any means suppose a superiority of the judicial to the legislative power. It only supposes that the power of the people is superior to both, and that where the will of the legislature, declared in its statutes, stands in opposition to that of the people, declared in the Constitution, the judges ought to be governed by the latter rather than the former. They ought to regulate their decisions by the fundamental laws rather than by those which are not fundamental.

This exercise of judicial discretion in determining between two contradictory laws is exemplified in a familiar instance. It not uncommonly happens that there are two statutes existing at one time, clashing in whole or in part with each other and neither of them containing any repealing clause or expression. In such a case, it is the province of the courts to liquidate and fix their meaning and operation. So far as they can, by fair construction, be reconciled to each other, reason and law conspire to dictate that this should be done; where this is impracticable, it becomes a matter of necessity to give effect to one in exclusion of the other. The rule which has obtained in the courts for determining their relative validity is that the last in order of time shall be preferred to the first. But this is a mere rule of construction, not derived from any positive law but from the nature and reason of the thing. It is a rule not enjoined upon the courts by legislative provision but adopted by themselves, as consonant to truth and propriety, for the direction of their conduct as interpreters of the law. They thought it reasonable that between the interfering acts of an *equal* authority that which was the last indication of its will should have the preference.

But in regard to the interfering acts of a superior and subordinate authority of an original and derivative power, the nature and reason of the thing indicate the converse of that rule as proper to be followed. They teach us that the prior act of a superior ought to be preferred to the subsequent act of an inferior and subordinate authority; and that accordingly, whenever a particular statute contravenes the Constitution, it will be the duty of the judicial tribunals to adhere to the latter and disregard the former.

It can be of no weight to say that the courts, on the pretense of a repugnancy, may substitute their own pleasure to the constitutional intentions of the legislature. This might as well happen in the case of two contradictory statutes; or it might as well happen in every adjudication upon any single statute. The courts must declare the sense of the law; and if they should be disposed to exercise WILL instead of JUDGMENT, the consequence would equally be the substitution of their pleasure for that of the legislative body. The observation, if it proved anything, would prove that there ought to be no judges distinct from that body.

If, then, the courts of justice are to be considered as the bulwarks of a limited Constitution against legislative encroachments, this consideration will afford a strong argument for the permanent tenure of judicial offices, since nothing will contribute so much as this to that independent spirit in the judges which must be essential to the faithful performance of so arduous a duty.

This independence of the judges is equally requisite to guard the Constitution and the rights of individuals from the effects of those ill humors which the arts of designing men, or the influence of particular conjunctures, sometimes disseminate among the people themselves, and which, though they speedily give place to better information, and more deliberate reflection, have a tendency, in the meantime, to occasion dangerous innovations in the government, and serious oppressions of the minor party in the community. Though I trust the friends of the proposed Constitution will never concur with its enemies in questioning that fundamental principle of republican government which admits the right of the people to alter or abolish the established Constitution whenever they find it inconsistent with their happiness; yet it is not to be inferred from this principle that the representatives of the people, whenever a momentary inclination happens to lay hold of a majority of their constituents incompatible with the provisions in the existing Constitution, would, on that account, be justifiable in a violation of those provisions; or that the courts would be under a greater obligation to connive at infractions in this shape than when they had proceeded wholly from the cabals of the representative body. Until the people have, by some solemn and authoritative act, annulled or changed the established form, it is binding upon themselves collectively, as well as individually; and no presumption, or even knowledge, of their sentiment can warrant their representatives in a departure from it prior to such an act. But it is easy to see that it would require an uncommon portion of fortitude in the judges to do their duty as faithful guardians of the Constitution, where legislative invasions of it had been instigated by the major voice of the community.

But it is not with a view to infractions of the Constitution only that the independence of the judges may be an essential safeguard against the effects of occasional ill humors in the society. These sometimes extend no farther than to the injury of the private rights of particular classes of citizens, by unjust and partial laws. Here also the firmness of the judicial magistracy is of vast importance in mitigating the severity and confining the operation of such laws. It not only serves to moderate the immediate mischiefs of those which may have been passed but it operates as a check upon the legislative body in passing them; who, perceiving that obstacles to the success of an iniquitous intention are to be expected from the scruples of the courts, are in a manner compelled, by the very motives of the injustice they meditate, to qualify their attempts. This is a circumstance calculated to have more influence upon the character of our governments than but few may be aware of. The benefits of the integrity and moderation of the judi-

ciary have already been felt in more States than one; and though they may have displeased those whose sinister expectations they may have disappointed, they must have commanded the esteem and applause of all the virtuous and disinterested. Considerate men of every description ought to prize whatever will tend to beget or fortify that temper in the courts; as no man can be sure that he may not be tomorrow the victim of a spirit of injustice, by which he may be a gainer today. And every man must now feel that the inevitable tendency of such a spirit is to sap the foundations of public and private confidence and to introduce in its stead universal distrust and distress.

That inflexible and uniform adherence to the rights of the Constitution, and of individuals, which we perceive to be indispensable in the courts of justice, can certainly not be expected from judges who hold their offices by a temporary commission. Periodical appointments, however regulated, or by whomsoever made, would, in some way or other, be fatal to their necessary independence. If the power of making them was committed either to the executive or legislature there would be danger of an improper complaisance to the branch which possessed it; if to both, there would be an unwillingness to hazard the displeasure of either; if to the people, or to persons chosen by them for the special purpose, there would be too great a disposition to consult popularity to justify a reliance that nothing would be consulted but the Constitution and the laws.

There is yet a further and weighty reason for the permanency of the judicial offices which is deducible from the nature of the qualifications they require. It has been frequently remarked with great propriety that a voluminous code of laws is one of the inconveniences necessarily connected with the advantages of a free government. To avoid an arbitrary discretion in the courts, it is indispensable that they should be bound down by strict rules and precedents which serve to define and point out their duty in every particular case that comes before them; and it will readily be conceived from the variety of controversies which grow out of the folly and wickedness of mankind that the records of those precedents must unavoidably swell to a very considerable bulk and must demand long and laborious study to acquire a competent knowledge of them. Hence it is that there can be but few men in the society who will have sufficient skill in the laws to qualify them for the stations of judges. And making the proper deductions for the ordinary depravity of human nature, the number must be still smaller of those who unite the requisite integrity with the requisite knowledge. These considerations apprise us that the government can have no great option between fit characters; and that a temporary duration in office which would naturally discourage such characters from quitting a lucrative line of practice to accept a seat on the bench would have a tendency to throw the administration of justice into hands less able and less well qualified to conduct it with utility and dignity. In the present circumstances of this country and in those in which it is likely to be for a long time to come, the disadvantages on this score would be greater than they may at first sight appear; but it must be confessed that they are far inferior to those which present themselves under the other aspects of the subject.

Upon the whole, there can be no room to doubt that the convention acted wisely in copying from the models of those constitutions which have established *good behavior* as the tenure of their judicial offices, in the point of duration; and that so far from being blamable on this account, their plan would have been inexcusably defective if it had wanted this important feature of good government. The experience of Great Britain affords an illustrious comment on the excellence of the institution.

PUBLIUS [Hamilton]

U.S. PRESIDENTS

President	Political Party	Term of Service
George Washington	Federalist	April 30, 1789–March 4, 1793
George Washington	Federalist	March 4, 1793–March 4, 1797
John Adams	Federalist	March 4, 1797–March 4, 1801
Thomas Jefferson	Democratic Republican	March 4, 1801–March 4, 1805
Thomas Jefferson	Democratic Republican	March 4, 1805–March 4, 1809
James Madison	Democratic Republican	March 4, 1809–March 4, 1813
James Madison	Democratic Republican	March 4, 1813–March 4, 1817
James Monroe	Democratic Republican	March 4, 1817–March 4, 1821
James Monroe	Democratic Republican	March 4, 1821–March 4, 1825
John Q. Adams	Democratic Republican	March 4, 1825–March 4, 1829
Andrew Jackson	Democrat	March 4, 1829–March 4, 1833
Andrew Jackson	Democrat	March 4, 1833–March 4, 1837
Martin Van Buren	Democrat	March 4, 1837–March 4, 1841
W. H. Harrison	Whig	March 4, 1841–April 4, 1841
John Tyler	Whig	April 6, 1841–March 4, 1845
James K. Polk	Democrat	March 4, 1845–March 4, 1849
Zachary Taylor	Whig	March 4, 1849–July 9, 1850
Millard Fillmore	Whig	July 10, 1850–March 4, 1853
Franklin Pierce	Democrat	March 4, 1853–March 4, 1857
James Buchanan	Democrat	March 4, 1857–March 4, 1861
Abraham Lincoln	Republican	March 4, 1861–March 4, 1865
Abraham Lincoln	Republican	March 4, 1865–April 15, 1865
Andrew Johnson	Republican	April 15, 1865–March 4, 1869
Ulysses S. Grant	Republican	March 4, 1869–March 4, 1873
Ulysses S. Grant	Republican	March 4, 1873–March 4, 1877
Rutherford B. Hayes	Republican	March 4, 1877–March 4, 1881
James A. Garfield	Republican	March 4, 1881–Sept. 19, 1881
Chester A. Arthur	Republican	Sept. 20, 1881–March 4, 1885
Grover Cleveland	Democrat	March 4, 1885–March 4, 1889

President	Political Party	Term of Service
Benjamin Harrison	Republican	March 4, 1889–March 4, 1893
Grover Cleveland	Democrat	March 4, 1893–March 4, 1897
William McKinley	Republican	March 4, 1897–March 4, 1901
William McKinley	Republican	March 4, 1901–Sept. 14, 1901
Theodore Roosevelt	Republican	Sept. 14, 1901–March 4, 1905
Theodore Roosevelt	Republican	March 4, 1905–March 4, 1909
William H. Taft	Republican	March 4, 1909–March 4, 1913
Woodrow Wilson	Democrat	March 4, 1913–March 4, 1917
Woodrow Wilson	Democrat	March 4, 1917–March 4, 1921
Warren G. Harding	Republican	March 4, 1921–Aug. 2, 1923
Calvin Coolidge	Republican	Aug. 3, 1923–March 4, 1925
Calvin Coolidge	Republican	March 4, 1925–March 4, 1929
Herbert Hoover	Republican	March 4, 1929–March 4, 1933
Franklin D. Roosevelt	Democrat	March 4, 1933–Jan. 20, 1937
Franklin D. Roosevelt	Democrat	Jan. 20, 1937–Jan. 20, 1941
Franklin D. Roosevelt	Democrat	Jan. 20, 1941–Jan. 20, 1945
Franklin D. Roosevelt	Democrat	Jan. 20, 1945–April 12, 1945
Harry S. Truman	Democrat	April 12, 1945–Jan. 20, 1949
Harry S. Truman	Democrat	Jan. 20, 1949–Jan. 20, 1953
Dwight D. Eisenhower	Republican	Jan. 20, 1953–Jan. 20, 1957
Dwight D. Eisenhower	Republican	Jan. 20, 1957–Jan. 20, 1961
John F. Kennedy	Democrat	Jan. 20, 1961–Nov. 22, 1963
Lyndon B. Johnson	Democrat	Nov. 22, 1963–Jan. 20, 1965
Lyndon B. Johnson	Democrat	Jan. 20, 1965–Jan. 20, 1969
Richard Nixon	Republican	Jan. 20, 1969–Jan. 20, 1973
Richard Nixon	Republican	Jan. 20, 1973–Aug. 9, 1974
Gerald R. Ford	Republican	Aug. 9, 1974–Jan. 20, 1977
Jimmy Carter	Democrat	Jan. 20, 1977–Jan. 20, 1981
Ronald Reagan	Republican	Jan. 20, 1981–Jan. 20, 1985
Ronald Reagan	Republican	Jan. 20, 1985–Jan. 20, 1989
George H.W. Bush	Republican	Jan. 20, 1989–Jan. 20, 1993
William J. Clinton	Democrat	Jan. 20, 1993–Jan. 20, 1997
William J. Clinton	Democrat	Jan. 20, 1997–Jan. 20, 2001
George W. Bush	Republican	Jan. 20, 2001–Jan. 20, 2005
George W. Bush	Republican	Jan. 20, 2005–

THUMBNAIL SKETCH OF THE SUPREME COURT'S HISTORY

Court Era	Chief Justices	Defining Characteristics	Major Court Cases
Developmental Period (1789–1800)	John Jay (1789–1795) John Rutledge (1795) Oliver Ellsworth (1796–1800)	Low prestige: spotty attendance by justices, resignations for more "prestigious positions," hears about fifty cases Business of the Court: largely admiralty and maritime disputes Use of seriatim opinion practice	*Chisholm v. Georgia* (1793) *Ware v. Hylton* (1796) *Hylton v. United States* (1796)
The Marshall Court (1801–1835)	John Marshall (1801–1835)	Establishment of Court's role in governmental process Strong Court support for national powers (especially commerce) over states' rights Use of "Opinions of the Court," rather than seriatim practice Beginning of systematic reporting of Court opinions Despite the importance of its opinions interpreting the Constitution, the business of the Court continues to involve private law issues (maritime, property, contracts)	*Marbury v. Madison* (1803) *Fletcher v. Peck* (1810) *Dartmouth College v. Woodward* (1819) *McCulloch v. Maryland* (1819) *Cohens v. Virginia* (1821) *Gibbons v. Ogden* (1824)
Taney and Civil War Courts (1836–1888)	Roger Taney (1836–1864) Salmon Chase (1864–1873) Morrison Waite (1874–1888)	Continued assertion of federal power over states (with some accommodation for state police powers) Growing North-South splits on the Court Court showdowns with Congress at the onset and conclusion of the Civil War Growth of Court's caseload, with the majority of post–Civil War cases involving private law issues and war litigation Congress fixes Court size at nine	*Charles River Bridge v. Warren Bridge* (1837) *New York v. Miln* (1837) *Luther v. Borden* (1849) *Scott v. Sandford* (1857) *Ex parte Milligan* (1866) *Ex parte McCardle* (1869) *Civil Rights Cases* (1883)
Conservative Court Eras (1889–1937)	Melville Fuller (1888–1910) Edward White (1910–1921) William Howard Taft (1921–1930) Charles Evans Hughes (1930–1937)	Except for a brief period reflecting progressivism, the Courts of this era tended to protect business interests over government police powers Court sets "civil rights" policy of "separate but equal" Congress relieves justices of circuit-riding duty	*United States v. E. C. Knight* (1895) *Pollock v. Farmers' Loan* (1895) *Plessy v. Ferguson* (1896) *Allgeyer v. Louisiana* (1897) *Lochner v. New York* (1905) *Hammer v. Dagenhart* (1918)

Court Era	Chief Justices	Defining Characteristics	Major Court Cases
Conservative Court Eras (1889–1937)	Melville Fuller (1888–1910) Edward White (1910–1921) William Howard Taft (1921–1930) Charles Evans Hughes (1930–1937)	Congress, in 1925 Judiciary Act, gives Court greater discretion over its docket Despite Judiciary Act, Court's docket continues to grow, with many cases reflecting economic issues (e.g., congressional power under the commerce clause) Some important construction of Bill of Rights guarantees (protection of rights increases after WW I) Showdown with FDR over New Deal legislation: Court continues to strike down New Deal leading the president to propose a Court-packing plan	*Schenck v. United States* (1919) *Adkins v. Children's Hospital* (1923) *Near v. Minnesota* (1931) *Powell v. Alabama* (1932) *Schechter Poultry v. United States* (1935)
The Roosevelt and World War II Court Eras (1937–1953)	Charles Evans Hughes (1937–1941) Harlan Fiske Stone (1941–1946) Fred Vinson (1946–1953)	With the "switch in time that saved nine" the Court begins to uphold federal regulations under the commerce clause, as well as state use of police powers Expansion of rights and liberties, until WW II and ensuing cold war Increases in nonconsensual behavior (dissents and concurrences) among the justices	*NLRB v. Jones & Laughlin Steel* (1937) *United States v. Carolene Products* (1938) *Korematsu v. United States* (1944) *Dennis v. United States* (1951) *Youngstown Sheet & Tube v. Sawyer* (1952)
The Warren Court Era (1953–1969)	Earl Warren (1953–1969)	Expansion of rights, liberties, and criminal justice Establishment of the right to privacy Emergence of Court as national policy maker Continued increase in Court's docket, with steady growth in the number of *in forma pauperis* petitions Growth in the percentage of constitutional cases on Court's plenary docket First African American (Marshall) appointed to the Court	*Brown v. Board of Education* (1954) *Roth v. United States* (1957) *Mapp v. Ohio* (1961) *Baker v. Carr* (1962) *Abington School District v. Schempp* (1963) *Gideon v. Wainwright* (1963) *Heart of Atlanta Motel v. United States* (1964) *New York Times v. Sullivan* (1964) *Griswold v. Connecticut* (1965) *Miranda v. Arizona* (1966)
Republican Court Eras (1969–)	Warren Burger (1969–1986) William Rehnquist (1986–2005) John G. Roberts Jr. (2005–)	Attempts in some areas (e.g., criminal law) to limit or rescind Warren Court rulings Expansion of women's rights, including right to abortion Some attempt to increase state power Legitimation of affirmative action issues Increased importance of separation of powers disputes Appointment of first woman (O'Connor, 1981) to the Court Rejection of race-based legislative districting Increased recognition of gay rights Intervention in the 2000 presidential election Court scrutiny of government's antiterrorism policies Approved campaign finance reforms Controversy over takings clause powers Emergence of war on terror disputes Reinterpretation of Second Amendment	*Reed v. Reed* (1971) *Miller v. California* (1973) *Roe v. Wade* (1973) *United States v. Nixon* (1974) *Gregg v. Georgia* (1976) *Regents of the University of California v. Bakke* (1978) *Garcia v. SAMTA* (1985) *Planned Parenthood of Southeastern Pennsylvania v. Casey* (1992) *Clinton v. Jones* (1997) *Alden v. Maine* (1999) *Boy Scouts of America v. Dale* (2000) *Bush v. Gore* (2000) *Zelman v. Simmons-Harris* (2000) *Grutter v. Bollinger* (2003) *Lawrence v. Texas* (2003) *Hamdi v. Rumsfeld* (2004) *Kelo v. City of New London* (2005) *Hamdan v. Rumsfeld* (2006) *Boumediene v. Bush* (2008) *District of Columbia v. Heller* (2008)

APPENDIX 5
THE JUSTICES

The justices of the Supreme Court are listed below in alphabetical order, with their birth and death years, state from which they were appointed, political party affiliation at time of appointment, educational institutions attended, appointing president, confirmation date and vote, date of service termination, and significant preappointment offices and activities.

Alito, Samuel A., Jr. (1950–). New Jersey. Republican. Princeton, Yale. Nominated associate justice by George W. Bush; confirmed 2006 by 58–42 vote. Federal appeals court judge.

Baldwin, Henry (1780–1844). Pennsylvania. Democrat. Yale. Nominated associate justice by Andrew Jackson; confirmed 1830 by 41–2 vote; died in office 1844. U.S. representative.

Barbour, Philip Pendleton (1783–1841). Virginia. Democrat. College of William and Mary. Nominated associate justice by Andrew Jackson; confirmed 1836 by 30–11 vote; died in office 1841. Virginia state legislator, U.S. representative, U.S. Speaker of the House, state court judge, federal district court judge.

Black, Hugo Lafayette (1886–1971). Alabama. Democrat. Birmingham Medical College, University of Alabama. Nominated associate justice by Franklin Roosevelt; confirmed 1937 by 63–16 vote; retired 1971. Alabama police court judge, county solicitor, U.S. senator.

Blackmun, Harry Andrew (1908–1999). Minnesota. Republican. Harvard. Nominated associate justice by Richard Nixon; confirmed 1970 by 94–0 vote; retired 1994. Federal appeals court judge.

Blair, John, Jr. (1732–1800). Virginia. Federalist. College of William and Mary; Middle Temple (England). Nominated associate justice by George Washington; confirmed 1789 by voice vote; resigned 1796. Virginia legislator, state court judge, delegate to Constitutional Convention.

Blatchford, Samuel (1820–1893). New York. Republican. Columbia. Nominated associate justice by Chester A. Arthur; confirmed 1882 by voice vote; died in office 1893. Federal district court judge, federal circuit court judge.

Bradley, Joseph P. (1813–1892). New Jersey. Republican. Rutgers. Nominated associate justice by Ulysses S. Grant; confirmed 1870 by 46–9 vote; died in office 1892. Private practice.

Brandeis, Louis Dembitz (1856–1941). Massachusetts. Republican. Harvard. Nominated associate justice by Woodrow Wilson; confirmed 1916 by 47–22 vote; retired 1939. Private practice.

Brennan, William Joseph, Jr. (1906–1997). New Jersey. Democrat. University of Pennsylvania, Harvard. Received recess appointment from Dwight Eisenhower to be associate justice 1956; confirmed 1957 by voice vote; retired 1990. New Jersey Supreme Court.

Brewer, David Josiah (1837–1910). Kansas. Republican. Wesleyan, Yale, Albany Law School. Nominated associate justice by Benjamin Harrison; confirmed 1889 by 53–11 vote; died in office 1910. Kansas state court judge, federal circuit court judge.

Breyer, Stephen G. (1938–). Massachusetts. Democrat. Stanford, Oxford, Harvard. Nominated associate justice by William Clinton; confirmed 1994 by 87–9 vote. Law professor; chief counsel, Senate Judiciary Committee; federal appeals court judge.

Brown, Henry B. (1836–1913). Michigan. Republican. Yale, Harvard. Nominated associate justice by Benjamin Harrison; confirmed 1890 by voice vote; retired 1906. Michigan state court judge, federal district court judge.

Burger, Warren Earl (1907–1995). Virginia. Republican. University of Minnesota, St. Paul College of Law. Nominated chief justice by Richard Nixon; confirmed 1969 by 74–3 vote; retired 1986. Assistant U.S. attorney general, federal appeals court judge.

Burton, Harold Hitz (1888–1964). Ohio. Republican. Bowdoin College, Harvard. Nominated associate justice by Harry Truman; confirmed 1945 by voice vote; retired 1958. Ohio state legislator, mayor of Cleveland, U.S. senator.

Butler, Pierce (1866–1939). Minnesota. Republican. Carleton College. Nominated associate justice by Warren G. Harding; confirmed 1922 by 61–8 vote; died in office 1939. Minnesota county attorney, private practice.

Byrnes, James Francis (1879–1972). South Carolina. Democrat. Privately educated. Nominated associate justice by Franklin Roosevelt; confirmed 1941 by voice vote; resigned 1942. South Carolina local solicitor, U.S. representative, U.S. senator.

Campbell, John Archibald (1811–1889). Alabama. Democrat. Franklin College (University of Georgia), U.S. Military Academy. Nominated associate justice by Franklin Pierce; confirmed 1853 by voice vote; resigned 1861. Alabama state legislator.

Cardozo, Benjamin Nathan (1870–1938). New York. Democrat. Columbia. Nominated associate justice by Herbert Hoover; confirmed 1932 by voice vote; died in office 1938. State court judge.

Catron, John (1786–1865). Tennessee. Democrat. Self-educated. Nominated associate justice by Andrew Jackson; confirmed 1837 by 28–15 vote; died in office 1865. Tennessee state court judge, state chief justice.

Chase, Salmon Portland (1808–1873). Ohio. Republican. Dartmouth. Nominated chief justice by Abraham Lincoln; confirmed 1864 by voice vote; died in office 1873. U.S. senator, Ohio governor, U.S. secretary of the Treasury.

Chase, Samuel (1741–1811). Maryland. Federalist. Privately educated. Nominated associate justice by George Washington; confirmed 1796 by voice vote; died in office 1811. Maryland state legislator, delegate to Continental Congress, state court judge.

Clark, Tom Campbell (1899–1977). Texas. Democrat. University of Texas. Nominated associate justice by Harry Truman; confirmed 1949 by 73–8 vote; retired 1967. Texas local district attorney, U.S. attorney general.

Clarke, John Hessin (1857–1945). Ohio. Democrat. Western Reserve University. Nominated associate justice by Woodrow Wilson; confirmed 1916 by voice vote; resigned 1922. Federal district judge.

Clifford, Nathan (1803–1881). Maine. Democrat. Privately educated. Nominated associate justice by James Buchanan; confirmed 1858 by 26–23 vote; died in office 1881. Maine state legislator, state attorney general, U.S. representative, U.S. attorney general, minister to Mexico.

Curtis, Benjamin Robbins (1809–1874). Massachusetts. Whig. Harvard. Nominated associate justice by Millard Fill-more; confirmed 1851 by voice vote; resigned 1857. Massachusetts state legislator.

Cushing, William (1732–1810). Massachusetts. Federalist. Harvard. Nominated associate justice by George Washington; confirmed 1789 by voice vote; died in office 1810. Massachusetts state court judge, electoral college delegate.

Daniel, Peter Vivian (1784–1860). Virginia. Democrat. Princeton. Nominated associate justice by Martin Van Buren; confirmed 1841 by 22–5 vote; died in office 1860. Virginia state legislator, state Privy Council, federal district court judge.

Davis, David (1815–1886). Illinois. Republican. Kenyon College, Yale. Nominated associate justice by Abraham Lincoln; confirmed 1862 by voice vote; resigned 1877. Illinois state legislator, state court judge.

Day, William Rufus (1849–1923). Ohio. Republican. University of Michigan. Nominated associate justice by Theodore Roosevelt; confirmed 1903 by voice vote; resigned 1922. Ohio state court judge, U.S. secretary of state, federal court of appeals judge.

Douglas, William Orville (1898–1980). Connecticut. Democrat. Whitman College, Columbia. Nominated associate justice by Franklin Roosevelt; confirmed 1939 by 62–4 vote; retired 1975. Law professor, Securities and Exchange Commission.

Duvall, Gabriel (1752–1844). Maryland. Democratic/Republican. Privately educated. Nominated associate justice by James Madison; confirmed 1811 by voice vote; resigned 1835. Maryland state legislator, U.S. representative, state court judge, presidential elector, comptroller of the U.S. Treasury.

Ellsworth, Oliver (1745–1807). Connecticut. Federalist. Princeton. Nominated chief justice by George Washington; confirmed 1796 by 21–1 vote; resigned 1800. Connecticut state legislator, delegate to Continental Congress and Constitutional Convention, state court judge, U.S. senator.

Field, Stephen J. (1816–1899). California. Democrat. Williams College. Nominated associate justice by Abraham Lincoln; confirmed 1863 by voice vote; retired 1897. California state legislator, California Supreme Court.

Fortas, Abe (1910–1982). Tennessee. Democrat. Southwestern College, Yale. Nominated associate justice by Lyndon Johnson; confirmed 1965 by voice vote; resigned 1969. Counsel for numerous federal agencies, private practice.

Frankfurter, Felix (1882–1965). Massachusetts. Independent. College of the City of New York, Harvard. Nominated associate justice by Franklin Roosevelt; confirmed 1939 by voice vote; retired 1962. Law professor, War Department law officer, assistant to secretary of war, assistant to secretary of labor, War Labor Policies Board chairman.

Fuller, Melville Weston (1833–1910). Illinois. Democrat. Bowdoin College, Harvard. Nominated chief justice by Grover

Cleveland; confirmed 1888 by 41–20 vote; died in office 1910. Illinois state legislator.

Ginsburg, Ruth Bader (1933–). New York. Democrat. Columbia. Nominated associate justice by William Clinton; confirmed 1993 by 96–3 vote. Professor, federal court of appeals judge.

Goldberg, Arthur J. (1908–1990). Illinois. Democrat. Northwestern. Nominated associate justice by John Kennedy; confirmed 1962 by voice vote; resigned 1965. Secretary of labor.

Gray, Horace (1828–1902). Massachusetts. Republican. Harvard. Nominated associate justice by Chester A. Arthur; confirmed 1881 by 51–5 vote; died in office 1902. Massachusetts Supreme Court.

Grier, Robert Cooper (1794–1870). Pennsylvania. Democrat. Dickinson College. Nominated associate justice by James Polk; confirmed 1846 by voice vote; retired 1870. Pennsylvania state court judge.

Harlan, John Marshall (1833–1911). Kentucky. Republican. Centre College, Transylvania University. Nominated associate justice by Rutherford B. Hayes; confirmed 1877 by voice vote; died in office 1911. Kentucky attorney general.

Harlan, John Marshall (1899–1971). New York. Republican. Princeton, Oxford, New York Law School. Nominated associate justice by Dwight Eisenhower; confirmed 1955 by 71–11 vote; retired 1971. Chief counsel for New York State Crime Commission, federal court of appeals.

Holmes, Oliver Wendell, Jr. (1841–1935). Massachusetts. Republican. Harvard. Nominated associate justice by Theodore Roosevelt; confirmed 1902 by voice vote; retired 1932. Law professor; justice, Supreme Judicial Court of Massachusetts.

Hughes, Charles Evans (1862–1948). New York. Republican. Colgate, Brown, Columbia. Nominated associate justice by William Howard Taft; confirmed 1910 by voice vote; resigned 1916; nominated chief justice by Herbert Hoover; confirmed 1930 by 52–26 vote; retired 1941. New York governor, U.S. secretary of state, Court of International Justice judge.

Hunt, Ward (1810–1886). New York. Republican. Union College. Nominated associate justice by Ulysses S. Grant; confirmed 1872 by voice vote; retired 1882. New York state legislator, mayor of Utica, state court judge.

Iredell, James (1751–1799). North Carolina. Federalist. English schools. Nominated associate justice by George Washington; confirmed 1790 by voice vote; died in office 1799. Customs official, state court judge, state attorney general.

Jackson, Howell Edmunds (1832–1895). Tennessee. Democrat. West Tennessee College, University of Virginia, Cumberland University. Nominated associate justice by Benjamin Harrison; confirmed 1893 by voice vote; died in office 1895. Tennessee state legislator, U.S. senator, federal circuit court judge, federal court of appeals judge.

Jackson, Robert Houghwout (1892–1954). New York. Democrat. Albany Law School. Nominated associate justice by Franklin Roosevelt; confirmed 1941 by voice vote; died in office 1954. Counsel for Internal Revenue Bureau and Securities and Exchange Commission, U.S. solicitor general, U.S. attorney general.

Jay, John (1745–1829). New York. Federalist. King's College (Columbia University). Nominated chief justice by George Washington; confirmed 1789 by voice vote; resigned 1795. Delegate to Continental Congress, chief justice of New York, minister to Spain and Great Britain, secretary of foreign affairs.

Johnson, Thomas (1732–1819). Maryland. Federalist. Privately educated. Nominated associate justice by George Washington; confirmed 1791 by voice vote; resigned 1793. Delegate to Annapolis Convention and Continental Congress, governor, state legislator, state court judge.

Johnson, William (1771–1834). South Carolina. Democratic/Republican. Princeton. Nominated associate justice by Thomas Jefferson; confirmed 1804 by voice vote; died in office 1834. South Carolina state legislator, state court judge.

Kennedy, Anthony McLeod (1936–). California. Republican. Stanford, London School of Economics, Harvard. Nominated associate justice by Ronald Reagan; confirmed 1988 by 97–0 vote. Federal appeals court judge.

Lamar, Joseph Rucker (1857–1916). Georgia. Democrat. University of Georgia, Bethany College, Washington and Lee. Nominated associate justice by William Howard Taft; confirmed 1910 by voice vote; died in office 1916. Georgia state legislator, Georgia Supreme Court.

Lamar, Lucius Quintus Cincinnatus (1825–1893). Mississippi. Democrat. Emory College. Nominated associate justice by Grover Cleveland; confirmed 1888 by 32–28 vote; died in office 1893. Georgia state legislator, U.S. representative, U.S. senator, U.S. secretary of the interior.

Livingston, Henry Brockholst (1757–1823). New York. Democratic/Republican. Princeton. Nominated associate justice by Thomas Jefferson; confirmed 1806 by voice vote; died in office 1823. New York state legislator, state court judge.

Lurton, Horace Harmon (1844–1914). Tennessee. Democrat. University of Chicago, Cumberland. Nominated associate justice by William Howard Taft; confirmed 1909 by voice vote; died in office 1914. Tennessee Supreme Court, federal court of appeals judge.

McKenna, Joseph (1843–1926). California. Republican. Benicia Collegiate Institute. Nominated associate justice by William McKinley; confirmed 1898 by voice vote; retired 1925. California state legislator, U.S. representative, federal court of appeals judge, U.S. attorney general.

McKinley, John (1780–1852). Alabama. Democrat. Self educated. Nominated associate justice by Martin Van Buren;

confirmed 1837 by voice vote; died in office 1852.   Alabama state legislator, U.S. senator, U.S. representative.

McLean, John (1785–1861).   Ohio.   Democrat.   Privately educated.   Nominated associate justice by Andrew Jackson; confirmed 1829 by voice vote; died in office 1861.   U.S. representative, Ohio Supreme Court, commissioner of U.S. General Land Office, U.S. postmaster general.

McReynolds, James Clark (1862–1946).   Tennessee. Democrat.   Vanderbilt, University of Virginia.   Nominated associate justice by Woodrow Wilson; confirmed 1914 by 44–6 vote; retired 1941.   U.S. attorney general.

Marshall, John (1755–1835).   Virginia.   Federalist.   Privately educated, College of William and Mary.   Nominated chief justice by John Adams; confirmed 1801 by voice vote; died in office 1835.   Virginia state legislator, minister to France, U.S. representative, U.S. secretary of state.

Marshall, Thurgood (1908–1993).   New York.   Democrat. Lincoln University, Howard University.   Nominated associate justice by Lyndon Johnson; confirmed 1967 by 69–11 vote; retired 1991.   NAACP Legal Defense Fund, federal court of appeals judge, U.S. solicitor general.

Matthews, Stanley (1824–1889).   Ohio.   Republican. Kenyon College.   Nominated associate justice by Rutherford B. Hayes; no Senate action on nomination; renominated associate justice by James A. Garfield; confirmed 1881 by 24–23 vote; died in office 1889.   Ohio state legislator, state court judge, U.S. attorney for southern Ohio, U.S. senator.

Miller, Samuel Freeman (1816–1890).   Iowa.   Republican. Transylvania University.   Nominated associate justice by Abraham Lincoln; confirmed 1862 by voice vote; died in office 1890. Medical doctor, private law practice, justice of the peace.

Minton, Sherman (1890–1965).   Indiana.   Democrat. Indiana University, Yale.   Nominated associate justice by Harry Truman; confirmed 1949 by 48–16 vote; retired 1956.   U.S. senator, federal court of appeals judge.

Moody, William Henry (1853–1917).   Massachusetts.   Republican.   Harvard.   Nominated associate justice by Theodore Roosevelt; confirmed 1906 by voice vote; retired 1910.   Massachusetts local district attorney, U.S. representative, secretary of the navy, U.S. attorney general.

Moore, Alfred (1755–1810).   North Carolina.   Federalist. Privately educated.   Nominated associate justice by John Adams; confirmed 1799 by voice vote; resigned 1804. North Carolina legislator, state attorney general, state court judge.

Murphy, Francis William (1880–1949).   Michigan.   Democrat.   University of Michigan, London's Inn (England), Trinity College (Ireland).   Nominated associate justice by Franklin Roosevelt; confirmed 1940 by voice vote; died in office 1949. Michigan state court judge, mayor of Detroit, governor of the Philippines, governor of Michigan, U.S. attorney general.

Nelson, Samuel (1792–1873).   New York.   Democrat. Middlebury College.   Nominated associate justice by John Tyler; confirmed 1845 by voice vote; retired 1872.   Presidential elector, state court judge, New York Supreme Court chief justice.

O'Connor, Sandra Day (1930–   ).   Arizona.   Republican. Stanford.   Nominated associate justice by Ronald Reagan; confirmed 1981 by 99–0 vote; retired 2006.   Arizona state legislator, state court judge.

Paterson, William (1745–1806).   New Jersey.   Federalist. Princeton.   Nominated associate justice by George Washington; confirmed 1793 by voice vote; died in office 1806.   New Jersey attorney general, delegate to Constitutional Convention, U.S. senator, governor.

Peckham, Rufus Wheeler (1838–1909).   New York.   Democrat.   Albany Boys' Academy.   Nominated associate justice by Grover Cleveland; confirmed 1895 by voice vote; died in office 1909.   New York local district attorney, city attorney, state court judge.

Pitney, Mahlon (1858–1924).   New Jersey.   Republican. Princeton.   Nominated associate justice by William Howard Taft; confirmed 1912 by 50–26 vote; retired 1922.   U.S. representative, New Jersey state legislator, New Jersey Supreme Court, Chancellor of New Jersey.

Powell, Lewis Franklin, Jr. (1907–1998).   Virginia.   Democrat.   Washington and Lee, Harvard.   Nominated associate justice by Richard Nixon; confirmed 1971 by 89–1 vote; retired 1987.   Private practice, Virginia State Board of Education, American Bar Association president, American College of Trial Lawyers president.

Reed, Stanley Forman (1884–1980).   Kentucky.   Democrat.   Kentucky Wesleyan, Yale, Virginia, Columbia, University of Paris.   Nominated associate justice by Franklin Roosevelt; confirmed 1938 by voice vote; retired 1957.   Federal Farm Board general counsel, Reconstruction Finance Corporation general counsel, U.S. solicitor general.

Rehnquist, William Hubbs (1924–2005).   Arizona. Republican.   Stanford, Harvard.   Nominated associate justice by Richard Nixon; confirmed 1971 by 68–26 vote; nominated chief justice by Ronald Reagan; confirmed 1986 by 65–33 vote; died in office 2005.   Private practice, assistant U.S. attorney general.

Roberts, John G., Jr. (1955–   ).   Maryland.   Republican. Harvard.   Nominated associate justice by George W. Bush 2005; nomination withdrawn; nominated chief justice by George W. Bush; confirmed 2005 by 78–22 vote.   Federal appeals court judge.

Roberts, Owen Josephus (1875–1955).   Pennsylvania. Republican.   University of Pennsylvania.   Nominated associate justice by Herbert Hoover; confirmed 1930 by voice vote; resigned 1945.   Private practice, Pennsylvania local prosecutor, special U.S. attorney.

Rutledge, John (1739–1800). South Carolina. Federalist. Middle Temple (England). Nominated associate justice by George Washington; confirmed 1789 by voice vote; resigned 1791. Nominated chief justice by George Washington August 1795 and served as recess appointment; confirmation denied and service terminated December 1795. South Carolina legislator, state attorney general, governor, chief justice of South Carolina, delegate to Continental Congress and Constitutional Convention.

Rutledge, Wiley Blount (1894–1949). Iowa. Democrat. Maryville College, University of Wisconsin, University of Colorado. Nominated associate justice by Franklin Roosevelt; confirmed 1943 by voice vote; died in office 1949. Law professor, federal court of appeals judge.

Sanford, Edward Terry (1865–1930). Tennessee. Republican. University of Tennessee, Harvard. Nominated associate justice by Warren G. Harding; confirmed 1923 by voice vote; died in office 1930. Assistant U.S. attorney general, federal district court judge.

Scalia, Antonin (1936–). Virginia. Republican. Georgetown, Harvard. Nominated associate justice by Ronald Reagan; confirmed 1986 by 98–0 vote. Assistant U.S. attorney general, federal court of appeals judge.

Shiras, George, Jr. (1832–1924). Pennsylvania. Republican. Ohio University, Yale. Nominated associate justice by Benjamin Harrison; confirmed 1892 by voice vote; retired 1903. Private practice.

Souter, David Hackett (1939–). New Hampshire. Republican. Harvard, Oxford. Nominated associate justice by George H.W. Bush; confirmed 1990 by 90–9 vote. New Hampshire attorney general, state court judge, federal appeals court judge.

Stevens, John Paul (1920–). Illinois. Republican. Chicago, Northwestern. Nominated associate justice by Gerald Ford; confirmed 1975 by 98–0 vote. Federal court of appeals judge.

Stewart, Potter (1915–1985). Ohio. Republican. Yale, Cambridge. Received recess appointment from Dwight Eisenhower to be associate justice in 1958; confirmed 1959 by 70–17 vote; retired 1981. Cincinnati city council, federal court of appeals judge.

Stone, Harlan Fiske (1872–1946). New York. Republican. Amherst College, Columbia. Nominated associate justice by Calvin Coolidge; confirmed 1925 by 71–6 vote; nominated chief justice by Franklin Roosevelt; confirmed 1941 by voice vote; died in office 1946. Law professor, U.S. attorney general.

Story, Joseph (1779–1845). Massachusetts. Democratic/Republican. Harvard. Nominated associate justice by James Madison; confirmed 1811 by voice vote; died in office 1845. Massachusetts state legislator, U.S. representative.

Strong, William (1808–1895). Pennsylvania. Republican. Yale. Nominated associate justice by Ulysses S. Grant; con-firmed 1870 by voice vote; retired 1880. U.S. representative, Pennsylvania Supreme Court.

Sutherland, George (1862–1942). Utah. Republican. Brigham Young, University of Michigan. Nominated associate justice by Warren G. Harding; confirmed 1922 by voice vote; retired 1938. Utah state legislator, U.S. representative, U.S. senator.

Swayne, Noah Haynes (1804–1884). Ohio. Republican. Privately educated. Nominated associate justice by Abraham Lincoln; confirmed 1862 by 38–1 vote; retired 1881. Ohio state legislator, local prosecutor, U.S. attorney for Ohio, Columbus city council.

Taft, William Howard (1857–1930). Connecticut. Republican. Yale, Cincinnati. Nominated chief justice by Warren G. Harding; confirmed 1921 by voice vote; retired 1930. Ohio local prosecutor, state court judge, U.S. solicitor general, federal court of appeals judge, governor of the Philippines, secretary of war, U.S. president.

Taney, Roger Brooke (1777–1864). Maryland. Democrat. Dickinson College. Nominated associate justice by Andrew Jackson; nomination not confirmed 1835; nominated chief justice by Andrew Jackson; confirmed 1836 by 29–15 vote; died in office 1864. Maryland state legislator, state attorney general, acting secretary of war, secretary of the Treasury (nomination later rejected by Senate).

Thomas, Clarence (1948–). Georgia. Republican. Holy Cross, Yale. Nominated associate justice by George H.W. Bush; confirmed 1991 by 52–48 vote. Department of Education, Equal Employment Opportunity Commission, federal appeals court judge.

Thompson, Smith (1768–1843). New York. Democratic/Republican. Princeton. Nominated associate justice by James Monroe; confirmed 1823 by voice vote; died in office 1843. New York state legislator, state court judge, secretary of the navy.

Todd, Thomas (1765–1826). Kentucky. Democratic/Republican. Liberty Hall (Washington and Lee). Nominated associate justice by Thomas Jefferson; confirmed 1807 by voice vote; died in office 1826. Kentucky state court judge, state chief justice.

Trimble, Robert (1776–1828). Kentucky. Democratic/Republican. Kentucky Academy. Nominated associate justice by John Quincy Adams; confirmed 1826 by 27–5 vote; died in office 1828. Kentucky state legislator, state court judge, U.S. attorney, federal district court judge.

Van Devanter, Willis (1859–1941). Wyoming. Republican. Indiana Asbury University, University of Cincinnati. Nominated associate justice by William Howard Taft; confirmed 1910 by voice vote; retired 1937. Cheyenne city attorney, Wyoming territorial legislature, Wyoming Supreme Court, assistant U.S. attorney general, federal court of appeals judge.

Vinson, Frederick Moore (1890–1953). Kentucky. Democrat. Centre College. Nominated chief justice by Harry Truman; confirmed 1946 by voice vote; died in office 1953.   U.S. representative, federal appeals court judge, director of Office of Economic Stabilization, secretary of the Treasury.

Waite, Morrison Remick (1816–1888).   Ohio.   Republican.   Yale.   Nominated chief justice by Ulysses S. Grant; confirmed 1874 by 63–0 vote; died in office 1888.   Private practice, Ohio state legislator.

Warren, Earl (1891–1974).   California.   Republican.   University of California.   Recess appointment as chief justice by Dwight Eisenhower 1953; confirmed 1954 by voice vote; retired 1969.   California local district attorney, state attorney general, governor.

Washington, Bushrod (1762–1829).   Virginia.   Federalist.   College of William and Mary.   Nominated associate justice by John Adams; confirmed 1798 by voice vote; died in office 1829.   Virginia state legislator.

Wayne, James Moore (1790–1867).   Georgia.   Democrat.   Princeton.   Nominated associate justice by Andrew Jackson; confirmed 1835 by voice vote; died in office 1867.   Georgia state legislator, mayor of Savannah, state court judge, U.S. representative.

White, Byron Raymond (1917–2000).   Colorado.   Democrat.   University of Colorado, Oxford, Yale.   Nominated associate justice by John Kennedy; confirmed 1962 by voice vote; retired 1993.   Deputy U.S. attorney general.

White, Edward Douglass (1845–1921).   Louisiana.   Democrat.   Mount St. Mary's College, Georgetown.   Nominated associate justice by Grover Cleveland; confirmed 1894 by voice vote; nominated chief justice by William Howard Taft; confirmed 1910 by voice vote; died in office 1921.   Louisiana state legislator, Louisiana Supreme Court, U.S. senator.

Whittaker, Charles Evans (1901–1973).   Missouri.   Republican.   University of Kansas City.   Nominated associate justice by Dwight Eisenhower; confirmed 1957 by voice vote; retired 1962.   Federal district court judge, federal appeals court judge.

Wilson, James (1742–1798).   Pennsylvania.   Federalist.   University of St. Andrews (Scotland).   Nominated associate justice by George Washington; confirmed 1789 by voice vote; died in office 1798.   Delegate to Continental Congress and Constitutional Convention.

Woodbury, Levi (1789–1851).   New Hampshire.   Democrat.   Dartmouth, Tapping Reeve Law School.   Nominated associate justice by James Polk; confirmed 1846 by voice vote; died in office 1851.   New Hampshire state legislator, state court judge, governor, U.S. senator, secretary of the navy, secretary of the Treasury.

Woods, William B. (1824–1887).   Georgia.   Republican.   Western Reserve College, Yale.   Nominated associate justice by Rutherford B. Hayes; confirmed 1880 by 39–8 vote; died in office 1887.   Ohio state legislator, Alabama chancellor, federal circuit court judge.

NATURAL COURTS

Natural Court[a]	Justices[b]	Dates	U.S. Reports[c]
Jay 1	Jay (*o* October 19, 1789), J. Rutledge (*o* February 15, 1790), Cushing (*o* February 2, 1790), Wilson (*o* October 5, 1789), Blair (*o* February 2, 1790)	October 5, 1789– May 12, 1790	2
Jay 2	Jay, Rutledge (*r* March 5, 1791), Cushing, Wilson, Blair, Iredell (*o* May 12, 1790)	May 12, 1790– August 6, 1792	2
Jay 3	Jay, Cushing, Wilson, Blair, Iredell, T. Johnson (*o* August 6, 1792; *r* January 16, 1793)	August 6, 1792– March 11, 1793	2
Jay 4	Jay (*r* June 29, 1795), Cushing, Wilson, Blair, Iredell, Paterson (*o* March 11, 1793)	March 11, 1793– August 12, 1795	2–3
Rutledge 1	J. Rutledge (*o* August 12, 1795; *rj* December 15, 1795), Cushing, Wilson, Blair (*r* January 27, 1796), Iredell, Paterson	August 12, 1795– February 4, 1796	3
No chief justice	Cushing, Wilson, Iredell, Paterson, S. Chase (*o* February 4, 1796)	February 4, 1796– March 8, 1796	3
Ellsworth 1	Ellsworth (*o* March 8, 1796), Cushing, Wilson (*d* August 21, 1798), Iredell, Paterson, S. Chase	March 8, 1796– November 9, 1798	3
Ellsworth 2	Ellsworth, Cushing, Iredell (*d* October 20, 1799), Paterson, S. Chase, Washington (*o* November 9, 1798)	November 9, 1798– April 21, 1800	3–4
Ellsworth 3	Ellsworth (*r* December 15, 1800), Cushing, Paterson, S. Chase, Washington, Moore (*o* April 21, 1800)	April 21, 1800– February 4, 1801	4
Marshall 1	Marshall (*o* February 4, 1801), Cushing, Paterson, S. Chase, Washington, Moore (*r* January 26, 1804)	February 4, 1801– May 7, 1804	5–6
Marshall 2	Marshall, Cushing, Paterson (*d* September 9, 1806), S. Chase, Washington, W. Johnson (*o* May 7, 1804)	May 7, 1804– January 20, 1807	6–7
Marshall 3	Marshall, Cushing, S. Chase, Washington, W. Johnson, Livingston (*o* January 20, 1807)	January 20, 1807– May 4, 1807	8
Marshall 4	Marshall, Cushing (*d* September 13, 1810), S. Chase (*d* June 19, 1811), Washington, W. Johnson, Livingston, Todd (*o* May 4, 1807)	May 4, 1807– November 23, 1811	8–10

Natural Court[a]	Justices[b]	Dates	U.S. Reports[c]
Marshall 5	Marshall, Washington, W. Johnson, Livingston, Todd, Duvall (*o* November 23, 1811)	November 23, 1811– February 3, 1812	11
Marshall 6	Marshall, Washington, W. Johnson, Livingston (*d* March 18, 1823), Todd, Duvall, Story (*o* February 3, 1812)	February 3, 1812– September 1, 1823	11–21
Marshall 7	Marshall, Washington, W. Johnson, Todd (*d* February 7, 1826), Duvall, Story, Thompson (*o* September 1, 1823)	September 1, 1823– June 16, 1826	22–24
Marshall 8	Marshall, Washington (*d* November 26, 1829), W. Johnson, Duvall, Story, Thompson, Trimble (*o* June 16, 1826; *d* August 25, 1828)	June 16, 1826– January 11, 1830	25–27
Marshall 9	Marshall, W. Johnson (*d* August 4, 1834), Duvall (*r* January 14, 1835), Story, Thompson, McLean (*o* January 11, 1830), Baldwin (*o* January 18, 1830)	January 11, 1830– January 14, 1835	28–33
Marshall 10	Marshall (*d* July 6, 1835), Story, Thompson, McLean, Baldwin, Wayne (*o* January 14, 1835)	January 14, 1835– March 28, 1836	34–35
Taney 1	Taney (*o* March 28, 1836), Story, Thompson, McLean, Baldwin, Wayne	March 28, 1836– May 12, 1836	35
Taney 2	Taney, Story, Thompson, McLean, Baldwin, Wayne, Barbour (*o* May 12, 1836)	May 12, 1836– May 1, 1837	35–36
Taney 3	Taney, Story, Thompson, McLean, Baldwin, Wayne, Barbour, Catron (*o* May 1, 1837)	May 1, 1837– January 9, 1838	36
Taney 4	Taney, Story, Thompson, McLean, Baldwin, Wayne, Barbour (*d* February 25, 1841), Catron, McKinley (*o* January 9, 1838)	January 9, 1838– January 10, 1842	37–40
Taney 5	Taney, Story, Thompson (*d* December 18, 1843), McLean, Baldwin (*d* April 21, 1844), Wayne, Catron, McKinley, Daniel (*o* January 10, 1842)	January 10, 1842– February 27, 1845	40–44
Taney 6	Taney, Story (*d* September 10, 1845), McLean, Wayne, Catron, McKinley, Daniel, Nelson (*o* February 27, 1845)	February 27, 1845– September 23, 1845	44
Taney 7	Taney, McLean, Wayne, Catron, McKinley, Daniel, Nelson, Woodbury (*o* September 23, 1845)	September 23, 1845– August 10, 1846	44–45
Taney 8	Taney, McLean, Wayne, Catron, McKinley, Daniel, Nelson, Woodbury (*d* September 4, 1851), Grier (*o* August 10, 1846)	August 10, 1846– October 10, 1851	46–52
Taney 9	Taney, McLean, Wayne, Catron, McKinley (*d* July 19, 1852), Daniel, Nelson, Grier, Curtis (*o* October 10, 1851)	October 10, 1851– April 11, 1853	53–55
Taney 10	Taney, McLean, Wayne, Catron, Daniel, Nelson, Grier, Curtis (*r* September 30, 1857), Campbell (*o* April 11, 1853)	April 11, 1853– January 21, 1858	56–61
Taney 11	Taney, McLean (*d* April 4, 1861), Wayne, Catron, Daniel (*d* May 31, 1860), Nelson, Grier, Campbell (*r* April 30, 1861), Clifford (*o* January 21, 1858)	January 21, 1858– January 27, 1862	61–66
Taney 12	Taney, Wayne, Catron, Nelson, Grier, Clifford, Swayne (*o* January 27, 1862)	January 27, 1862– July 21, 1862	66
Taney 13	Taney, Wayne, Catron, Nelson, Grier, Clifford, Swayne, Miller (*o* July 21, 1862)	July 21, 1862– December 10, 1862	67

Natural Court[a]	Justices[b]	Dates	U.S. Reports[c]
Taney 14	Taney, Wayne, Catron, Nelson, Grier, Clifford, Swayne, Miller, Davis (o December 10, 1862)	December 10, 1862–May 20, 1863	67
Taney 15	Taney (d October 12, 1864), Wayne, Catron, Nelson, Grier, Clifford, Swayne, Miller, Davis, Field (o May 20, 1863)	May 20, 1863–December 15, 1864	67–68
Chase 1	S. P. Chase (o December 15, 1864), Wayne (d July 5, 1867), Catron (d May 30, 1865), Nelson, Grier (r January 31, 1870), Clifford, Swayne, Miller, Davis, Field	December 15, 1864–March 14, 1870	69–76
Chase 2	S. P. Chase, Nelson (r November 28, 1872), Clifford, Swayne, Miller, Davis, Field, Strong (o March 14, 1870), Bradley (o March 23, 1870)	March 14, 1870–January 9, 1873	76–82
Chase 3	S. P. Chase (d May 7, 1873), Clifford, Swayne, Miller, Davis, Field, Strong, Bradley, Hunt (o January 9, 1873)	January 9, 1873–March 4, 1874	82–86
Waite 1	Waite (o March 4, 1874), Clifford, Swayne, Miller, Davis (r March 4, 1877), Field, Strong, Bradley, Hunt	March 4, 1874–December 10, 1877	86–95
Waite 2	Waite, Clifford, Swayne, Miller, Field, Strong (r December 14, 1880), Bradley, Hunt, Harlan I (o December 10, 1877)	December 10, 1877–January 5, 1881	95–103
Waite 3	Waite, Clifford, Swayne (r January 24, 1881), Miller, Field, Bradley, Hunt, Harlan I, Woods (o January 5, 1881)	January 5, 1881–May 17, 1881	103
Waite 4	Waite, Clifford (d July 25, 1881), Miller, Field, Bradley, Hunt, Harlan I, Woods, Matthews (o May 17, 1881)	May 17, 1881–January 9, 1882	103–104
Waite 5	Waite, Miller, Field, Bradley, Hunt (r January 27, 1882), Harlan I, Woods, Matthews, Gray (o January 9, 1882)	January 9, 1882–April 3, 1882	104–105
Waite 6	Waite, Miller, Field, Bradley, Harlan I, Woods (d May 14, 1887), Matthews, Gray, Blatchford (o April 3, 1882)	April 3, 1882–January 18, 1888	105–124
Waite 7	Waite (d March 23, 1888), Miller, Field, Bradley, Harlan I, Matthews, Gray, Blatchford, L. Lamar (o January 18, 1888)	January 18, 1888–October 8, 1888	124–127
Fuller 1	Fuller (o October 8, 1888), Miller, Field, Bradley, Harlan I, Matthews (d March 22, 1889), Gray, Blatchford, L. Lamar	October 8, 1888–January 6, 1890	128–132
Fuller 2	Fuller, Miller (d October 13, 1890), Field, Bradley, Harlan I, Gray, Blatchford, L. Lamar, Brewer (o January 6, 1890)	January 6, 1890–January 5, 1891	132–137
Fuller 3	Fuller, Field, Bradley (d January 22, 1892), Harlan I, Gray, Blatchford, L. Lamar, Brewer, Brown (o January 5, 1891)	January 5, 1891–October 10, 1892	137–145
Fuller 4	Fuller, Field, Harlan I, Gray, Blatchford, L. Lamar (d January 23, 1893), Brewer, Brown, Shiras (o October 10, 1892)	October 10, 1892–March 4, 1893	146–148
Fuller 5	Fuller, Field, Harlan I, Gray, Blatchford (d July 7, 1893), Brewer, Brown, Shiras, H. Jackson (o March 4, 1893)	March 4, 1893–March 12, 1894	148–151
Fuller 6	Fuller, Field, Harlan I, Gray, Brewer, Brown, Shiras, H. Jackson (d August 8, 1895), E. White (o March 12, 1894)	March 12, 1894–January 6, 1896	152–160

Natural Court[a]	Justices[b]	Dates	U.S. Reports[c]
Fuller 7	Fuller, Field (r December 1, 1897), Harlan I, Gray, Brewer, Brown, Shiras, E. White, Peckham (o January 6, 1896)	January 6, 1896–January 26, 1898	160–169
Fuller 8	Fuller, Harlan I, Gray (d September 15, 1902), Brewer, Brown, Shiras, E. White, Peckham, McKenna (o January 26, 1898)	January 26, 1898–December 8, 1902	169–187
Fuller 9	Fuller, Harlan I, Brewer, Brown, Shiras (r February 23, 1903), E. White, Peckham, McKenna, Holmes (o December 8, 1902)	December 8, 1902–March 2, 1903	187–188
Fuller 10	Fuller, Harlan I, Brewer, Brown (r May 28, 1906), E. White, Peckham, McKenna, Holmes, Day (o March 2, 1903)	March 2, 1903–December 17, 1906	188–203
Fuller 11	Fuller, Harlan I, Brewer, E. White, Peckham (d October 24, 1909), McKenna, Holmes, Day, Moody (o December 17, 1906)	December 17, 1906–January 3, 1910	203–215
Fuller 12	Fuller (d July 4, 1910), Harlan I, Brewer (d March 28, 1910), E. White, McKenna, Holmes, Day, Moody, Lurton (o January 3, 1910)	January 3, 1910–October 10, 1910	215–217
No chief justice	Harlan I, E. White (p December 18, 1910), McKenna, Holmes, Day, Moody (r November 20, 1910), Lurton, Hughes (o October 10, 1910)	October 10, 1910–December 19, 1910	218
White 1	E. White (o December 19, 1910), Harlan I (d October 14, 1911), McKenna, Holmes, Day, Lurton, Hughes, Van Devanter (o January 3, 1911), J. Lamar (o January 3, 1911)	December 19, 1910–March 18, 1912	218–223
White 2	E. White, McKenna, Holmes, Day, Lurton (d July 12, 1914), Hughes, Van Devanter, J. Lamar, Pitney (o March 18, 1912)	March 18, 1912–October 12, 1914	223–234
White 3	E. White, McKenna, Holmes, Day, Hughes, Van Devanter, J. Lamar (d January 2, 1916), Pitney, McReynolds (o October 12, 1914)	October 12, 1914–June 5, 1916	235–241
White 4	E. White, McKenna, Holmes, Day, Hughes (r June 10, 1916), Van Devanter, Pitney, McReynolds, Brandeis (o June 5, 1916)	June 5, 1916–October 9, 1916	241
White 5	E. White (d May 19, 1921), McKenna, Holmes, Day, Van Devanter, Pitney, McReynolds, Brandeis, Clarke (o October 9, 1916)	October 9, 1916–July 11, 1921	242–256
Taft 1	Taft (o July 11, 1921), McKenna, Holmes, Day, Van Devanter, Pitney, McReynolds, Brandeis, Clarke (r September 18, 1922)	July 11, 1921–October 2, 1922	257–259
Taft 2	Taft, McKenna, Holmes, Day (r November 13, 1922), Van Devanter, Pitney (r December 31, 1922), McReynolds, Brandeis, Sutherland (o October 2, 1922)	October 2, 1922–January 2, 1923	260
Taft 3	Taft, McKenna, Holmes, Van Devanter, McReynolds, Brandeis, Sutherland, Butler (o January 2, 1923)	January 2, 1923–February 19, 1923	260
Taft 4	Taft, McKenna (r January 5, 1925), Holmes, Van Devanter, McReynolds, Brandeis, Sutherland, Butler, Sanford (o February 19, 1923)	February 19, 1923–March 2, 1925	260–267
Taft 5	Taft (r February 3, 1930), Holmes, Van Devanter, McReynolds, Brandeis, Sutherland, Butler, Sanford, Stone (o March 2, 1925)	March 2, 1925–February 24, 1930	267–280
Hughes 1	Hughes (o February 24, 1930), Holmes, Van Devanter, McReynolds, Brandeis, Sutherland, Butler, Sanford (d March 8, 1930), Stone	February 24, 1930–June 2, 1930	280–281
Hughes 2	Hughes, Holmes (r January 12, 1932), Van Devanter, McReynolds, Brandeis, Sutherland, Butler, Stone, Roberts (o June 2, 1930)	June 2, 1930–March 14, 1932	281–285

Natural Court[a]	Justices[b]	Dates	U.S. Reports[c]
Hughes 3	Hughes, Van Devanter (r June 2, 1937), McReynolds, Brandeis, Sutherland, Butler, Stone, Roberts, Cardozo (o March 14, 1932)	March 14, 1932– August 19, 1937	285–301
Hughes 4	Hughes, McReynolds, Brandeis, Sutherland (r January 17, 1938), Butler, Stone, Roberts, Cardozo, Black (o August 19, 1937)	August 19, 1937– January 31, 1938	302–303
Hughes 5	Hughes, McReynolds, Brandeis, Butler, Stone, Roberts, Cardozo (d July 9, 1938), Black, Reed (o January 31, 1938)	January 31, 1938– January 30, 1939	303–305
Hughes 6	Hughes, McReynolds, Brandeis (r February 13, 1939), Butler, Stone, Roberts, Black, Reed, Frankfurter (o January 30, 1939)	January 30, 1939– April 17, 1939	306
Hughes 7	Hughes, McReynolds, Butler (d November 16, 1939), Stone, Roberts, Black, Reed, Frankfurter, Douglas (o April 17, 1939)	April 17, 1939– February 5, 1940	306–308
Hughes 8	Hughes (r July 1, 1941), McReynolds (r January 31, 1941), Stone (p July 2, 1941), Roberts, Black, Reed, Frankfurter, Douglas, Murphy (o February 5, 1940)	February 5, 1940– July 3, 1941	308–313
Stone 1	Stone (o July 3, 1941), Roberts, Black, Reed, Frankfurter, Douglas, Murphy, Byrnes (o July 8, 1941; r October 3, 1942), R. Jackson (o July 11, 1941)	July 3, 1941– February 15, 1943	314–318
Stone 2	Stone, Roberts (r July 31, 1945), Black, Reed, Frankfurter, Douglas, Murphy, R. Jackson, W. Rutledge (o February 15, 1943)	February 15, 1943– October 1, 1945	318–326
Stone 3	Stone (d April 22, 1946), Black, Reed, Frankfurter, Douglas, Murphy, R. Jackson, W. Rutledge, Burton (o October 1, 1945)	October 1, 1945– June 24, 1946	326–328
Vinson 1	Vinson (o June 24, 1946), Black, Reed, Frankfurter, Douglas, Murphy (d July 19, 1949), R. Jackson, W. Rutledge, Burton	June 24, 1946– August 24, 1949	329–338
Vinson 2	Vinson, Black, Reed, Frankfurter, Douglas, R. Jackson, W. Rutledge (d September 10, 1949), Burton, Clark (o August 24, 1949)	August 24, 1949– October 12, 1949	338
Vinson 3	Vinson (d September 8, 1953), Black, Reed, Frankfurter, Douglas, R. Jackson, Burton, Clark, Minton (o October 12, 1949)	October 12, 1949– October 5, 1953	338–346
Warren 1	Warren (o October 5, 1953), Black, Reed, Frankfurter, Douglas, R. Jackson (d October 9, 1954), Burton, Clark, Minton	October 5, 1953– March 28, 1955	346–348
Warren 2	Warren, Black, Reed, Frankfurter, Douglas, Burton, Clark, Minton (r October 15, 1956), Harlan II (o March 28, 1955)	March 28, 1955– October 16, 1956	348–352
Warren 3	Warren, Black, Reed (r February 25, 1957), Frankfurter, Douglas, Burton, Clark, Harlan II, Brennan (o October 16, 1956)	October 16, 1956– March 25, 1957	352
Warren 4	Warren, Black, Frankfurter, Douglas, Burton (r October 13, 1958), Clark, Harlan II, Brennan, Whittaker (o March 25, 1957)	March 25, 1957– October 14, 1958	352–358
Warren 5	Warren, Black, Frankfurter, Douglas, Clark, Harlan II, Brennan, Whittaker (r March 31, 1962), Stewart (o October 14, 1958)	October 14, 1958– April 16, 1962	358–369
Warren 6	Warren, Black, Frankfurter (r August 28, 1962), Douglas, Clark, Harlan II, Brennan, Stewart, B. White (o April 16, 1962)	April 16, 1962– October 1, 1962	369–370
Warren 7	Warren, Black, Douglas, Clark, Harlan II, Brennan, Stewart, B. White, Goldberg (o October 1, 1962; r July 25, 1965)	October 1, 1962– October 4, 1965	371–381

Natural Court[a]	Justices[b]	Dates	U.S. Reports[c]
Warren 8	Warren, Black, Douglas, Clark (*r* June 12, 1967), Harlan II, Brennan, Stewart, B. White, Fortas (*o* October 4, 1965)	October 4, 1965–October 2, 1967	382–388
Warren 9	Warren (*r* June 23, 1969), Black, Douglas, Harlan II, Brennan, Stewart, B. White, Fortas (*r* May 14, 1969), T. Marshall (*o* October 2, 1967)	October 2, 1967–June 23, 1969	389–395
Burger 1	Burger (*o* June 23, 1969), Black, Douglas, Harlan II, Brennan, Stewart, B. White, T. Marshall	June 23, 1969–June 9, 1970	395–397
Burger 2	Burger, Black (*r* September 17, 1971), Douglas, Harlan II (*r* September 23, 1971), Brennan, Stewart, B. White, T. Marshall, Blackmun (*o* June 9, 1970)	June 9, 1970–January 7, 1972	397–404
Burger 3	Burger, Douglas (*r* November 12, 1975), Brennan, Stewart, B. White, T. Marshall, Blackmun, Powell (*o* January 7, 1972), Rehnquist (*o* January 7, 1972)	January 7, 1972–December 19, 1975	404–423
Burger 4	Burger, Brennan, Stewart (*r* July 3, 1981), B. White, T. Marshall, Blackmun, Powell, Rehnquist, Stevens (*o* December 19, 1975)	December 19, 1975–September 25, 1981	423–453
Burger 5	Burger (*r* September 26, 1986), Brennan, B. White, T. Marshall, Blackmun, Powell, Rehnquist (*p* September 26, 1986), Stevens, O'Connor (*o* September 25, 1981)	September 25, 1981–September 26, 1986	453–478
Rehnquist 1	Rehnquist (*o* September 26, 1986), Brennan, B. White, T. Marshall, Blackmun, Powell (*r* June 26, 1987), Stevens, O'Connor, Scalia (*o* September 26, 1986)	September 26, 1986–February 18, 1988	478–484
Rehnquist 2	Rehnquist, Brennan (*r* July 20, 1990), B. White, T. Marshall, Blackmun, Stevens, O'Connor, Scalia, Kennedy (*o* February 18, 1988)	February 18, 1988–October 9, 1990	484–498
Rehnquist 3	Rehnquist, B. White, T. Marshall (*r* October 1, 1991), Blackmun, Stevens, O'Connor, Scalia, Kennedy, Souter (*o* October 9, 1990)	October 9, 1990–October 23, 1991	498–501
Rehnquist 4	Rehnquist, B. White (*r* June 28, 1993), Blackmun, Stevens, O'Connor, Scalia, Kennedy, Souter, Thomas (*o* October 23, 1991)	October 23, 1991–August 10, 1993	502–509
Rehnquist 5	Rehnquist, Blackmun (*r* August 3, 1994), Stevens, O'Connor, Scalia, Kennedy, Souter, Thomas, Ginsburg (*o* August 10, 1993)	August 10, 1993–August 3, 1994	510–512
Rehnquist 6	Rehnquist (*d* September 3, 2005), Stevens, O'Connor, Scalia, Kennedy, Souter, Thomas, Ginsburg, Breyer (*o* August 3, 1994)	August 3, 1994–September 29, 2005	513–545
Roberts 1	J. Roberts (*o* September 29, 2005), Stevens, O'Connor (*r* January 31, 2006), Scalia, Kennedy, Souter, Thomas, Ginsburg, Breyer	September 29, 2005–January 31, 2006	546
Roberts 2	J. Roberts, Stevens, Scalia, Kennedy, Souter, Thomas, Ginsburg, Breyer, Alito (*o* January 31, 2006)	January 31, 2006–	546–

SOURCE: Lee Epstein, Jeffrey A. Segal, Harold J. Spaeth, and Thomas G. Walker, *The Supreme Court Compendium: Data, Decisions, and Developments,* 4th ed. (Washington, D.C.: CQ Press, 2007), Table 5-2.

NOTE: The term *natural court* refers to a period of time during which the membership of the Court remains stable. There are a number of ways to determine the beginning and end of a natural court. Here a natural court begins when a new justice takes the oath of office and continues until the next new justice takes the oath. When two or more justices join the Court within a period of fifteen or fewer days, we treat it as the beginning of a single natural court (for example, Marshall 9, Chase 2, White 1, and Stone 1).

a. Numbered sequentially within the tenure of each chief justice.

b. The name of the chief justice appears first, with associate justices fol-lowing in order of descending seniority. In addition, the date a justice left the Court, creating a vacancy for the next justice to be appointed, is given, as well as the date the new justice took the oath of office. *o* = oath of office taken, *d* = died, *r* = resigned or retired, *rj* = recess appointment rejected by Senate, *p* = promoted from associate justice to chief justice.

c. Volumes of *United States Reports* in which the actions of each natural court generally may be found. Because of the way decisions were published prior to the twentieth century, these volume numbers may not contain all of the decisions of a given natural court. They do, however, provide a general guide to the location of each natural court's published decisions. Natural courts of short duration may have little business published in the reports.

APPENDIX 7
SUPREME COURT CALENDAR

Activity	Time
Start of Term	First Monday in October
Oral Argument Cycle	October–April: Mondays, Tuesdays, Wednesdays in seven two-week sessions
Recess Cycle	October–April: two or more consecutive weeks after two weeks of oral argument; additional days of recess during holiday periods
Conferences	October–April: conferences are held on the Friday before each two-week oral argument cycle and on the two Fridays during each oral argument cycle; May–June: conferences are held each Thursday
Majority Opinion Assignment	Within two weeks following oral arguments/conferences
Opinion Announcement	Throughout term with bulk coming in spring/early summer
Summer Recess	Late June/early July until first Monday in October
Initial Conference	Late September (resolve old business, consider certiorari petitions from the summer)

SOURCE: Information based on the Court's published calendar for the October 2007 term.

BRIEFING SUPREME COURT CASES

1. **What is the name of the case?**

   The name is important because it *generally* reveals which party is asking the Court to review the case. The name appearing first is usually (but not always) the appellant/petitioner, the party that lost in the court below.

2. **In what year did the Supreme Court decide the case?**

   The year is important because it will help to put the case into a legal and historical context. See Thumbnail Sketch of Supreme Court History for more detail.

3. **What circumstances triggered the dispute?**

4. **What statute or action triggered the dispute?**

5. **What provision of the Constitution is at issue?**

6. **What is the basic legal question(s) the Court is being asked to address?**

7. **What was the outcome of the dispute?**

8. **How did the majority reach its decision? What was its legal reasoning?**

9. **What legal doctrine, standards, or policy did the majority announce?**

10. **What other views (dissents, concurrences) were expressed?**

AN EXAMPLE: *Texas v. Johnson* (1989)

1. Case Name. *Texas v. Johnson*
2. Year Case Decided by Supreme Court. 1989
3. Facts that Triggered the Dispute. While the Republican National Convention was meeting in Dallas, Texas, in 1984, Gregory Johnson took part in a demonstration protesting policies of the Reagan administration. During the demonstration, Johnson burned an American flag, and Dallas police arrested him.
4. Statute. Johnson was arrested and subsequently convicted under a Texas law that made it a criminal activity to desecrate a "venerable" object, including a state or a national flag.
5. Provision of the Constitution. Johnson alleged that his conviction, under the Texas state law, violated First Amendment guarantees of freedom of expression.
6. Legal Question. Is flag burning, in the context of this dispute, an activity protected by the First Amendment?
7. Outcome. In a 5–4 ruling, the Court held for Johnson.
8. Legal Reasoning of the Majority. In delivering the opinion of the Court, Justice William J. Brennan Jr. held that:

   a. Johnson's action constituted expressive conduct, allowing him to raise a First Amendment claim.

   b. Although governments have a "freer hand" in restricting "conduct" (as opposed to pure speech or writing), they still must demonstrate a sufficiently important governmental interest in regulating the activity in question.

   c. Texas' stated interests—preventing breaches of the peace and preserving the flag as a symbol of national unity—are insufficient to prohibit Johnson's expressive conduct.

9. Legal Doctrine. The majority:

   a. set policy in an area of the law that was previously murky. States may not "foster" their own view "of the flag by prohibiting expressive conduct relating to it."

   b. reaffirmed past precedents, suggesting that in such cases the Court will not only consider the nature of the expression (whether it is verbal or nonverbal), but the governmental interest at stake.

   c. reaffirmed a general commitment to the fundamental nature of the First Amendment: "If there is a bedrock principle underlying the First Amendment, it is that the Government may not prohibit the expression of an idea simply because society finds that idea itself offensive or disagreeable."

10. Other Points of View.

   a. Justice Kennedy concurred: While the flag "holds a lonely place of honor," the Constitution mandates the outcome expressed by the majority. In short, sometimes justices "make decisions" they do not "like." But they make them "because they are right."

   b. Chief Justice Rehnquist (joined by White and O'Connor) dissented: Freedom of expression is not absolute: conduct may be prohibited in light of legitimate governmental interests. Here, those interests outweigh the expression.

   i. Johnson's conduct had the tendency to incite a breach of the peace.

   ii. the American flag is a "visible symbol embodying our Nation"; it does not represent a political idea or philosophy, nor is it just "another symbol."

   c. Justice Stevens dissented: The question of flag desecration is unique. Cases involving other forms of symbolic expression are not dispositive of it. Our nation's flag symbolizes those values—liberty and equality—that "are worth fighting for." As such it cannot be "true that the flag . . . is not itself worthy of protection from unnecessary desecration."

GLOSSARY

Abstention A doctrine or policy of the federal courts to refrain from deciding a case so that the issues involved may first be definitively resolved by state courts.

Acquittal A decision by a court that a person charged with a crime is not guilty.

Advisory opinion An opinion issued by a court indicating how it would rule on a question of law should such a question come before it in an actual case. Federal courts do not hand down advisory opinions, but some state courts do.

Affidavit A written statement of facts voluntarily made under oath or affirmation.

Affirm To uphold a decision of a lower court.

A fortiori With greater force or reason.

Aggravating circumstances Conditions that increase the seriousness of a crime but are not a part of its legal definition.

Amicus curiae "Friend of the court." A person (or group), not a party to a case, who submits views (usually in the form of written briefs) on how the case should be decided.

Ante Prior to.

Appeal The procedure by which a case is taken to a superior court for a review of the lower court's decision.

Appellant The party dissatisfied with a lower court ruling who appeals the case to a superior court for review.

Appellate jurisdiction The legal authority of a superior court to review and render judgment on a decision by a lower court.

Appellee The party usually satisfied with a lower court ruling against whom an appeal is taken.

Arbitrary Unreasonable; capricious; not done in accordance with established principles.

Arguendo In the course of argument.

Arraignment A formal stage of the criminal process in which the defendants are brought before a judge, confronted with the charges against them, and they enter a plea to those charges.

Arrest Physically taking into custody or otherwise depriving freedom of a person suspected of violating the law.

Attainder, Bill of A legislative act declaring a person or easily identified group of people guilty of a crime and imposing punishments without the benefit of a trial. Such legislative acts are prohibited by the United States Constitution.

Attest To swear to; to be a witness.

Bail A security deposit, usually in the form of cash or bond, which allows those accused of crimes to be released from jail and guarantees their appearance at trial.

Balancing test A process of judicial decision making in which the court weighs the relative merits of the rights of the individual against the interests of the government.

Bench trial A trial, without a jury, conducted before a judge.

Bicameral A legislature, such as the U.S. Congress, with two houses.

Bona fide Good faith.

Brandeis brief A legal argument that stresses economic and sociological evidence along with traditional legal authorities. Named after Louis Brandeis, who pioneered its use.

Brief A written argument of law and fact submitted to the court by an attorney representing a party having an interest in a lawsuit.

Case A legal dispute or controversy brought to a court for resolution.

Case-in-chief The primary evidence offered by a party in a court case.

Case law Law that has evolved from past court decisions, as opposed to law created by legislative acts.

Case or controversy rule The constitutional requirement that courts may only hear real disputes brought by adverse parties.

Casus faederis In international law, the case of a treaty. The particular event contemplated by the treaty or stipulated for, or which comes within the treaty's terms.

Certification A procedure whereby a lower court requests that a superior court rule on specified legal questions so that the lower court may correctly apply the law.

Certiorari, Writ of An order of an appellate court to an inferior court to send up the records of a case that the appellate court has elected to review. The primary method by which the U.S. Supreme Court exercises its discretionary jurisdiction to accept appeals for a full hearing.

Civil law Law that deals with the private rights of individuals (e.g., property, contracts, negligence), as contrasted with criminal law.

Class action A lawsuit brought by one or more persons who represent themselves and all others similarly situated.

Collateral estoppel A rule of law that prohibits an already settled issue from being relitigated in another form.

Comity The principle by which the courts of one jurisdiction give respect and deference to the laws and legal decisions of another jurisdiction.

Common law Law that has evolved from usage and custom as reflected in the decisions of courts.

Compensatory damages A monetary award, equivalent to the loss sustained, to be paid to the injured party by the party at fault.

Concurrent powers Authority that may be exercised by both the state and federal governments.

Concurring opinion An opinion that agrees with the result reached by the majority, but disagrees as to the appropriate rationale for reaching that result.

Confrontation The right of a criminal defendant to see the testimony of prosecution witnesses and subject such witnesses to cross examination.

Consent decree A court-ratified agreement voluntarily reached by parties to settle a lawsuit.

Constitutional court A court created under authority of Article III of the Constitution. Judges serve for terms of good behavior and are protected against having their salaries reduced by the legislature.

Contempt A purposeful failure to carry out an order of a court (civil contempt) or a willful display of disrespect for the court (criminal contempt).

Contraband Articles that are illegal to possess.

Courts of appeals (federal) The intermediate level appellate courts in the federal system having jurisdiction over a particular region known as a circuit.

Criminal law Law governing the relationship between individuals and society. Deals with the enforcement of laws and the punishment of those who, by breaking laws, commit crimes.

Curtilage The land and outbuildings immediately adjacent to a home and regularly used by its occupants.

Declaratory judgment A court ruling determining a legal right or interpretation of the law, but not imposing any relief or remedy.

De facto In fact, actual.

Defendant A party at the trial level being sued in a civil case or charged with a crime in a criminal case.

De jure As a result of law or official government action.

De minimis Small or unimportant. A de minimis issue is considered one too trivial for a court to consider.

Demurrer A motion to dismiss a lawsuit in which the defendant admits to the facts alleged by the plaintiff but contends that those facts are insufficient to justify a legal cause of action.

De novo New, from the beginning.

Deposition Sworn testimony taken out of court.

Dicta; Obiter dicta Those portions of a judge's opinion that are not essential to deciding the case.

Directed verdict An action by a judge ordering a jury to return a specified verdict.

Discovery A pretrial procedure whereby one party to a lawsuit gains access to information or evidence held by the opposing party.

Dissenting opinion A formal written expression by a judge who disagrees with the result reached by the majority.

Distinguish A court's explanation of why a particular precedent is inapplicable to the case under consideration.

District courts The trial courts of general jurisdiction in the federal system.

Diversity jurisdiction The authority of federal courts to hear cases in which a party from one state is suing a party from another state.

Docket The schedule of cases to be heard by a court.

Double jeopardy The trying of a defendant a second time for the same offense. Prohibited by the Fifth Amendment to the Constitution.

Due process Government procedures that follow principles of essential fairness.

Eminent domain The authority of the government to take private property for public purpose.

En banc An appellate court hearing with all the judges of the court participating.

Enjoin An order from a court requiring a party to do or refrain from doing certain acts.

Entrapment Law enforcement officials inducing an otherwise innocent person into the commision of a criminal act.

Equity Law based on principles of fairness rather than strictly applied statutes.

Error, Writ of An order issued by an appeals court commanding a lower court to send up the full record of a case for review.

Exclusionary rule A principle of law that illegally gathered evidence may not be admitted in court.

Exclusive powers Powers reserved for either the federal government or the state governments, but not exercised by both.

Ex parte A hearing in which only one party to a dispute is present.

Ex post facto law A criminal law passed by the legislature and made applicable to acts committed prior to passage of the law. Prohibited by the U.S. Constitution.

Ex rel Upon information from. Used to designate a court case instituted by the government but instigated by a private party.

Ex vi termini From the force or very meaning of the term or expression.

Federal question A legal issue based on the U.S. Constitution, laws, or treaties.

Felony A serious criminal offense, usually punishable by incarceration of one year or more.

Gerrymander To construct political boundaries for the purpose of giving advantage to a particular political party or interest.

Grand jury A panel of twelve to twenty-three citizens who review prosecutorial evidence to determine if there are sufficient grounds to issue an indictment binding an individual over for trial on criminal charges.

Guilty A determination that a person accused of a criminal offense is legally responsible as charged.

Habeas corpus "You have the body." A writ issued to determine if a person held in custody is being unlawfully detained or imprisoned.

Harmless error An error occurring in a court proceeding that is insufficient in magnitude to justify the overturning of the court's final determination.

Hearsay Testimony not based on the personal knowledge of the witness, but a repetition of what the witness has heard others say.

Immunity An exemption from prosecution granted in exchange for testimony.

In camera A legal hearing held in the judge's chambers or otherwise in private.

Incorporation The process whereby provisions of the Bill of Rights are declared to be included in the due process guarantee of the

Fourteenth Amendment and made applicable to state and local governments.

Indictment A document issued by a grand jury officially charging an individual with criminal violations and binding the accused over for trial.

In forma pauperis "In the form of a pauper." A special status granted to indigents that allows them to proceed without payment of court fees and to be exempt from certain procedural requirements.

Information A document, serving the same purpose as an indictment, but issued directly by the prosecutor.

Infra Below.

Injunction A writ prohibiting the person to whom it is directed from committing certain specified acts.

In re "In the matter of." The designation used in a judicial proceeding in which there are no formal adversaries.

In rem An act directed against a thing and not against a person.

Inter alia Among other things.

Interlocutory decree A provisional action that temporarily settles a legal question pending the final determination of a dispute.

Ipse dixit A statement that depends for its persuasiveness on the authority of the one who said it.

Judgment of the court The final ruling of a court, independent of the legal reasoning supporting it.

Judicial activism A philosophy that courts should not be reluctant to review and if necessary strike down legislative and executive actions.

Judicial notice The recognition by a court of the truth of certain facts without requiring one of the parties to put them into evidence.

Judicial restraint A philosophy that courts should defer to the legislative and executive branches whenever possible.

Judicial review The authority of a court to determine the constitutionality of acts committed by the legislative and executive branches and to strike down acts judged to be in violation of the Constitution.

Jurisdiction The authority of a court to hear and decide legal disputes and to enforce its rulings.

Justiciable Capable of being heard and decided by a court.

Legislative court A court created by Congress under authority of Article I of the Constitution to assist in carrying out the powers of the legislature.

Litigant A party to a lawsuit.

Magistrate A low level judge with limited authority.

Mandamus "We command." A writ issued by a court commanding a public official to carry out a particular act or duty.

Mandatory jurisdiction A case that a court is required to hear.

Marque and reprisal An order from the government of one country requesting and legitimizing the seizure of persons and property of another country. Prohibited by the Constitution.

Merits The central issues of a case.

Misdemeanor A less serious criminal act, usually punishable by less than one year of incarceration.

Mistrial A trial that is prematurely ended by a judge because of procedural irregularities.

Mitigating circumstances Conditions that lower the moral blame of a criminal act, but do not justify or excuse it.

Moot Unsettled or undecided. A question presented in a lawsuit that cannot be answered by a court either because the issue has resolved itself or conditions have so changed that the court is unable to grant the requested relief.

Motion A request made to a court for a certain ruling or action.

Natural law Laws considered applicable to all persons in all nations because they are thought to be basic to human nature.

Nolle prosequi The decision of a prosecutor to drop criminal charges against an accused.

Nolo contendere No contest. A plea entered by a criminal defendant in which the accused does not admit guilt but submits to sentencing and punishment as if guilty.

Opinion of the court An opinion announcing the judgment and reasoning of a court endorsed by a majority of the judges participating.

Order A written command issued by a judge.

Original jurisdiction The authority of a court to try a case and to decide it, as opposed to appellate jurisdiction.

Per curiam An unsigned or collectively written opinion issued by a court.

Peremptory challenge Excusing a prospective juror without explaining the reasons for doing so.

Per se In and of itself.

Petitioner A party seeking relief in court.

Petit jury A trial court jury to decide criminal or civil cases.

Plaintiff The party who brings a legal action to court for resolution or remedy.

Plea bargain An arrangement in a criminal case in which the defendant agrees to plead guilty in return for the prosecutor reducing the criminal charges or recommending a lenient sentence.

Plurality opinion An opinion announcing the judgment of a court with supporting reasoning that is not endorsed by a majority of the justices participating.

Police powers The power of the state to regulate for the health, safety, morals, and general welfare of its citizens.

Political question An issue more appropriate for determination by the legislative or executive branch than the judiciary.

Precedent A previously decided case that serves as a guide for deciding a current case.

Preemption A doctrine under which an area of authority previously left to the states is, by act of Congress, brought into the exclusive jurisdiction of the federal government.

Prima facie "At first sight." A case that is sufficient to prevail unless effectively countered by the opposing side.

Pro bono publico "For the public good." Usually refers to legal representation done without fee for some charitable or public purpose.

Pro se A person who appears in court without an attorney.

Punitive damages A monetary award (separate from compensatory damages) imposed by a court for punishment purposes to be paid by the party at fault to the injured party.

Quash To annul, vacate, or totally do away with.

Ratio decidendi A court's primary reasoning for deciding a case the way it did.

Recuse The action of a judge not to participate in a case because of conflict of interest or other disqualifying condition.

Remand To send a case back to an inferior court for additional action.

Res judicata A legal issue that has been finally settled by a court judgment.

Respondent The party against whom a legal action is filed.

Reverse An action by an appellate court setting aside or changing a decision of a lower court.

Ripeness A condition in which a legal dispute has evolved to the point where the issues it presents can be effectively resolved by a court.

Selective incorporation The policy of the Supreme Court to decide incorporation issues on a case-by-case, right-by-right basis.

Show cause A judicial order commanding a party to appear in court and explain why the court should not take a proposed action.

Solicitor general Justice Department official whose office represents the federal government in all litigation before the U.S. Supreme Court.

Standing; standing to sue The right of parties to bring legal actions because they are directly affected by the legal issues raised.

Stare decisis "Let the decision stand." The doctrine that once a legal issue has been settled it should be followed as precedent in future cases presenting the same question.

State action An action taken by an agency or official of a state or local government.

Stay To stop or suspend.

Strict construction Narrow interpretation of the provisions of laws.

Subpoena ad testificandum An order compelling a person to testify before a court, legislative hearing, or grand jury.

Subpoena duces tecum An order compelling a person to produce a document or other piece of physical evidence that is relevant to issues pending before a court, legislative hearing, or grand jury.

Sub silentio "Under silence." A court action taken without explicit notice or indication.

Summary judgment A decision by a court made without a full hearing or without receiving briefs or oral arguments.

Supra Above.

Temporary restraining order A judicial order prohibiting certain challenged actions from being taken prior to a full hearing on the question.

Test A criterion or set of criteria used by courts to determine if certain legal thresholds have been met or constitutional provisions violated.

Three-judge court A special federal court made up of appellate and trial court judges created to expedite the processing of certain issues made eligible for such priority treatment by congressional statute.

Ultra vires Actions taken that exceed the legal authority of the person or agency performing them.

Usus loquendi The common usage of ordinary language.

Vacate To void or rescind.

Vel non "Or not."

Venireman A juror.

Venue The geographical jurisdiction in which a case is heard.

Voir dire "To speak the truth." The stage of a trial in which potential jurors are questioned to determine their competence to sit in judgment of a case.

Warrant A judicial order authorizing an arrest or search and seizure.

Writ A written order of a court commanding the recipient to perform or not to perform certain specified acts.

ONLINE CASE ARCHIVE

Space limitations prevent us from including in this volume excerpts of every important Supreme Court decision dealing with the constitutional powers of government and the rights of the people. To make a larger number of decisions available to instructors and students, we have created an online archive of additional case excerpts *(see list below)*. In the text, boldface case names indicate that they are in the archive. As the Court hands down new rulings of significance, we will add them to the archive to ensure that the materials available to our readers will always be current. Access the archive at: www.cqpress.com/college/clca.htm.

CASE INDEX

Boldface indicates excerpted case.

SUBJECT INDEX

IMAGE CREDITS